ORTHODOX SEMINARY
W9-BVC-367

A History of Russia:
Peoples, Legends, Events, Forces

A History of Russia: Peoples, Legends, Events, Forces

CATHERINE EVTUHOV
Georgetown University

DAVID GOLDFRANK
Georgetown University

LINDSEY HUGHES
University College, London

RICHARD STITES
Georgetown University

HOUGHTON MIFFLIN COMPANY
Boston New York

To our colleagues and students from whom we continue to learn.

Editor-in-Chief: Jean Woy
Sponsoring Editor: Nancy Blaine
Development Editor: Jan Fitter
Editorial Associate: Annette Fantasia
Production Editorial Assistant: Kendra Johnson
Senior Production/Design Coordinator: Jodi O'Rourke
Senior Manufacturing Manager: Florence Cadran
Senior Marketing Manager: Sandra McGuire

Cover: Anatoly Sapronenkov/SuperStock.
View of Senate Square and Sadovaya Street in Nevsky Avenue Direction; Jean Baptiste Arnout.

Photograph on p. 518 from the personal archives of Professor Temira Pachmuss.

Printed in the U.S.A.

Library of Congress Control Number: 2001133352

ISBN: 0-395-66072-6

5 6 7 8 9 10 DOC 11 10 09

CONTENTS

MAPS

PREFACE

The French medievalist historian Marc Bloch, in *In Defense of History*, tells the story of his visit to Stockholm where, to the surprise of his hosts, he insisted on seeing the newest and most modern sights and buildings and avoiding the museums. Dramatic and exciting contemporary events inevitably inspire the imagination of historians, providing them with new angles and prisms through which to re-examine the past. The Eastern European Revolutions of 1989-1991 have had profound—and still not fully realized—resonance for the writing and understanding of the history of Russia and neighboring lands. More broadly, they have restored our sense of the vitality and importance of history itself, after a time when—it now seems, naively—it had become fashionable to speak of "history's end." The present textbook was conceived in the moment immediately following the collapse of the Soviet Union. We were fascinated by the possibilities offered by new sources, new perspectives, and new cooperation between Russian and Western scholars. We wished to construct a narrative of the history of Russia that, while maintaining a clear and balanced chronology of basic events, incorporated those aspects of history that have most captured the imagination of recent students and historians.

Our book addresses the concerns of the present generation by balancing political narrative and economic history with explorations of everyday life, social roles and identities, cultural dynamics, and gender issues. Religious experience—including devotional life, ecclesiastical organization, reform currents, and antireligious movements—played a vital role throughout Russian history and is here given its proper attention. We have also given considerable space to the frequently neglected non-Russian (and non-Slavic) nationalities and their role in Russian history. In several chapters and sub-chapters, we have paused to offer a cross section of the Russian Empire and the Soviet Union, in order to examine the major nationalities—their inner life, their relations with the center, and the shifts that have taken place over the centuries. In this manner, we hope to clarify for readers some of the issues on nationality history that helped bring down the Soviet Union in 1991.

One interesting feature of the book is that it has evolved in step with the burgeoning historiography of the 1990s. In keeping with our own research interests, we have sought to write the history of culture into the mainstream of history, and to pay more than the usual attention to a sense of place—that is, to regions and provinces. It has been a satisfying experiment to see what happens when subjects of recent path-breaking research are integrated into a synthetic narrative. For example, we cast the origin of Russia in keeping with modern archaeological findings rather than old written sources of doubtful accuracy and standard narratives of medieval chroniclers. Readers will also find the ceremony and pageantry of the Russian monarchy playing a significant role in our presentation of the workings of Muscovy and the Russian empire. New books and articles on the emergence and development of civil society, the importance of entrepreneurship in the economy, state power and possibilities of reform, and church and religion as social forces have created a rich and varied picture of Russia from the seventeenth century onward. Current interest in world history provides broad comparative contexts: sometimes it is as appropriate to compare Russian developments with the Mongol khanates, the Ottoman Empire, or even China or Brazil, as with Poland-Lithuania, the Hapsburg Empire, France, Germany, and the United States.

Another novel feature that we would like our readers to notice is the invocation of cultural legend and historical memory. Every period of history has a multiple identity: the primary one is based on what happened at the time—as far as we can reconstruct it. The others are the resonances of that history—filtered through ancestral recollection, nostalgic dreams, folk traditions, and formal historiography. Events such as the exploits of the earliest princes, the wars with the Mongols, the schism in the Orthodox church, the reforms of Peter the Great, the Decembrist uprising of 1825, the conquest of the Caucasus in the 1850s, or the siege of Leningrad in 1941 have generated a richness of popular mythology and historical interpretation. Our work attempts to embrace not only the history of people but—in a modest way—the history of their imagination. We wish to cast our net more broadly, to get a sense not just of what went wrong, but also of what worked well; to be sympathetic without being rosily optimistic; and to do our best to look at what Russia was rather than what it was not.

David Goldfrank wrote chapters 1-8; Lindsey Hughes, chapters 9-15; Catherine Evtuhov wrote chapters 16-18, 21-28, and 43; and Richard Stites wrote chapters 19-20 and 29-42.

We wish to thank the following people who have read portions of the book or have helped in other ways for their valuable suggestions: Harley Balzer, Roger Bartlett, Chris Chulos, Debra Coulter, James Cutshall, Simon Dixon, Boris Gasparov, Abbott Gleason, Charles Halperin, Benjamin Lapp, Eric Lohr, Gary Marker, Joan Neuberger, Thomas Noonan(†), Daniel Orlovsky, Donald Ostrowski, Argyrios Pisiotis, Marc Raeff, Donald Raleigh, Johannes Remy, Gabor Rittersporn, Aviel Roshwald, Anatol Shmelev, Jeremy Smith, Carol Tarlow, Timo Vihavainen, Mark Von Hagen, Chris Ward, Theodore Weeks, and David Wolff. Anna Salnykova provided useful current data. We thank Donald Raleigh and the Southern Conference on Slavic Studies for the opportunity of presenting our ideas in a panel on Writing a Textbook for the New Generation. We are also grateful to the following outside readers who have reviewed our manuscript at various stages:

Girish Bhat, SUNY Cortland
Aaron Cohen, California State University, Sacramento
Andrew Drozd, University of Alabama
Ronald Jensen, George Mason University
Michael Khodarkovsky, Loyola University Chicago
Nadieszda Kizenko, SUNY Albany
Thomas C. Owen, Louisiana State University
Jeff Plaks, University of Central Oklahoma
Alexis Pogorelskin, University of Minnesota, Duluth
Daniel Rowland, University of Kentucky
Robert W. Thurston, Miami University
Edward Vajda, Western Washington University
Paul Werth, University of Nevada, Las Vegas

We also wish to thank the staff at Houghton Mifflin: Jean Woy, Nancy Blaine, Jan Fitter, Florence Kilgo, Linda Sykes, Annette Fantasia, and Kendra Johnson.

A Note on Dates and Transliteration

In 1582, Catholic countries adopted the Gregorian calendar (named for Pope Gregory XIII). Russia retained the older Julian calendar until 1918. In the seventeenth century the Russian calendar was ten days behind the Western one and fell a further day behind at the start of the next three centuries. This book uses dates in the old Russian calendar (Old Style) until February 1918, when the new Soviet government switched to the Western calendar (New Style).

The Russian language uses the Cyrillic alphabet. In transliterating Russian words into English, we have made a compromise between the various literal systems and the forms that are more familiar to English-speaking readers. Thus we use established transliteration for certain well-known names: Tolstoy for Tolstoi, Witte for Vitte, Tchaikovsky for Chaikovskii; and we keep to the accepted English version of first names for certain members of the royal family—Catherine for Ekaterina, Nicholas for Nikolai, etc., but Ivan (not John) and Vasily (not Basil) for the princes and early tsars of Moscow.

PART I

From Frontier to Tsardom: The Foundations of Russia, 750–1613

This account of Russia's history begins in the period 750–850 C.E., when Slavic agriculturalists, Finnic forest dwellers, and Scandinavian warrior-merchants created the skeletal state of Rus in the historic Novgorod region. In the 900s Kiev became their chief center, and in 988 Eastern Orthodox Christianity the official religion. By the mid-1110s, a new Slavic Christian civilization was flourishing in a dozen Rus principalities. Novgorod became an aristocratic-mercantile republic, and the town of Vladimir emerged as the northern capital—each with a distinct architectural style.

The devastating Mongol conquest of 1237–1240 ended an epoch of Rus history. The new Mongol Qipchak khanate protected the Orthodox Church and cooperative Rus subjects, but the western and southern Rus lands eventually came under Lithuanian and Polish rule, and separate Belarusian and Ukrainian nationalities formed. In the 1330s the princes of Moscow, as Mongol vassals, established their supremacy in the Rus north and east. The Qipchak khanate, however, was weakened by bubonic plague and civil and foreign wars, and by 1455 it had fragmented. Meanwhile northern Rus—or Russia—experienced a revived, more spiritualized Orthodox culture, with artistic genius and the spread of rural monasteries.

Grand Prince Ivan III (r. 1462–1505) ruthlessly unified Russia, establishing a system of military service landholding. He also commissioned Italian builders to redesign and enlarge the Moscow Kremlin walls and major churches. Simultaneously, the Church authorities suppressed dissidence. Under the first crowned tsar, Ivan IV (r. 1533–1584), Russia overran the khanates of Kazan and Astrakhan, initiated the conquest of Siberia, and developed a solid central administration and the ideological and ceremonial trappings of a holy empire. Ivan's irrational terror and continuous aggressive wars, though, weakened the country and hastened the development of serfdom. The original Moscow dynasty died out in 1598, and a nearly fatal civil war ensued. At its end, in 1613, Russia united, prevailed over foreign intervention, and established a new ruling dynasty, the Romanovs.

CHAPTER 1

The Origin of Rus, 750–1000

In the year 859, Varangians from across the Baltic Sea collected tribute from the Chudians, Slovenians, Merians, Vesians, and Krivichians, while the Khazars took a squirrel skin from each household of the Polyanians, Severians, and Vyatichans.

—*Primary Chronicle*

From the start, several major threads have run through the history of Russia in a story of conquest and, later, tragic abuse of nature by people struggling to enrich themselves or just survive. The story reveals the mingling of peoples and the formation and transformation of a major nation—Slavic and Orthodox Christian—and of a multiethnic realm. The story takes in institutional development, kinship and ecclesiastical, as well as local, regional, and central state structures. And the story sets several major political and cultural revolutions against the rhythms of regional and global history.

This history begins around 750 in northern, boggy, primeval forests. At that time, the huge expanse of Eurasia that today makes up Russia had little agriculture, few people, and no urban centers. It was still relatively underpopulated two hundred and fifty years later, but its western 10 percent, taking in the Volkhov-Neva and Upper Volga River watersheds, was part of the recognized, if loosely governed, realm of Rus. In the intervening period, Slavic agriculturalists migrated eastward, especially into the central Dnieper River basin, which is now part of Ukraine, where Turkic Khazars established loose dominion. At the same time, Vikings, known as Varangians or Rus, took over the northern watersheds, developed the fur-trading operations of the local Finno-Ugrian and Baltic peoples, and built several towns. Then the Rus moved down the Dnieper and established Kiev as their chief center. The culmination of these developments came in 988 or 989, when the Rus leader Vladimir returned to Kiev from a successful military expedition to the Byzantine outpost of Cherson on the Tauride (now Crimean) Peninsula. Bringing back priests, holy vessels and relics, and an imperial bride, he reoriented and solidified Rus as a Christian polity.

THE NATURAL SETTING

Geography, a major determinant of human conditions, offers up a variety of images of historic Russia. We see a land covering one-sixth of the world's surface, with a dazzling underground storehouse of minerals, immense rivers with human mules dragging flatboat cargoes, and vast northern forests with endless supplies of timber and furs. In regions with rich soil, thousands of wooden villages and fields of grain fill the landscape. On the steppe—miles and miles of grassland prairie—nomads pasture their flocks. We also see a huge and forbidding Arctic zone and everywhere the reality of bitter-cold winters—the scourge of more than one invading army.

Indeed Russia today, despite the breakup of the Soviet Union in 1991, remains the world's largest country. It stretches as much as five thousand miles eastward from its borders at Finland, the Baltic Sea, and Belarus to the Pacific Ocean, and fifteen hundred to eighteen hundred miles southward from the Arctic Ocean to its borders at Ukraine, the Black and Caspian Seas, Kazakhstan, Mongolia, China, and Korea. Around the year 1000, however, Rus, the common ancestor of Russia, Ukraine, and Belarus, comprised an area of about five hundred by eight hundred fifty miles, more than twice the size of France and covering much of contemporary Ukraine and almost all of Belarus, but only a slice of western Russia.

Climate and Resources

Russia, like Canada, lies roughly between the 42nd and 82nd parallels of latitude. Russia's capital, Moscow, stands slightly farther north than Edmonton, while Kiev, the center of Rus around 940–1240 and now the capital of Ukraine, is more on a plane with Calgary or Winnipeg. Not surprisingly, some climatic conditions of most of Russia are close to those of west-central Canada and North Dakota. Russia experiences very cold winters, warm-to-hot summers, and, except for its southern regions, relatively short growing seasons. However, Russia barely has sufficient rainfall in most agricultural regions—just sixteen to twenty-four inches of annual precipitation—much less than in the United States or Canada, not to mention France or England. Polar winds are known to bring early summer frosts about every fifteen years; two such occurrences or major droughts in a row can cause catastrophic famine. Tundra covers the northernmost parts of Russia, a treeless plain with frozen subsoil, where the only vegetation is a dense growth of dwarf-size herb plants. This forbidding landform makes human habitation extremely sparse.

With good reason, Russians excel in woodworking skills. To the south of the tundra lie three forest belts: the coniferous (evergreen) taiga with poor, sandy soil; mixed coniferous and deciduous (leafy) woodlands, more suitable for crops; and the chiefly deciduous wooded steppe. All of Russia's forest lands used to support a multitude of fur-bearing animals—the further north, the thicker and richer the pelts.

The southern parts of Russia and Ukraine are pure steppe, an unforested prairie, similar to parts of Montana and Saskatchewan. Actually stretching from Romania across Eurasia to Mongolia, and rich with grasses suitable for livestock, the steppe

Siberian Taiga: The natural setting of coniferous forests and large rivers, typical of uncleared, wooded, northern Rus in the initial centuries. *Hutchinson Publishing Ltd., London, England.*

from time to time experienced massive westward migrations of warlike herdsmen, who looted, weakened, or overran whoever was in their path or nearby. Until about 1700, steppe migrations, military campaigns, and raids for slaves and other booty played a major role in Russia and other lands within or bordering this prairie.

Like North America, some 300 million years ago, Russia and the neighboring lands experienced a much hotter climate and a dense cover of trees and bushes, the residue of which has formed huge deposits of fossil fuels—coal, oil, and natural gas. This residue also helped to create a large belt of extremely fertile and moist soil—the so-called black earth, or *chernozëm,* found in the wooded steppe and steppe zones, from Romania through Ukraine (just south of Kiev) to southwestern Siberia. At times deadly competition grew up for this, the best farmland in Russia and Ukraine, with the settled agriculturalists seeking the relative safety of the forest zones to avoid warrior herdsmen. Fortunately, several more northern mixed forest regions are endowed with relatively rich gray soils.

Modern Russia's majestic mountains—the Caucasus between the Black and Caspian Seas and the Altai region where Siberia, Kazakhstan, China, and Mongolia meet—harbor rich deposits of industrial and precious minerals. The more restricted East Slavic lands around 900, however, were not so well endowed, though ample iron ore in the bogs of the forest and wooded steppe zones met the simple industrial needs of the time. The chief export commodities then were forest and steppe products—furs, beeswax, honey, hides, grain—and also, owing to demand in the Middle East, slaves.

Waterways

The anonymous authors of the Rus *Primary Chronicle*—Russia's first written history, compiled during the mid eleventh to the early twelfth centuries—noted that in the Valday uplands the headwaters of four major river systems can be connected by overland portage: the Volkhov-Lake Ladoga-Neva system and the Dvina, which flow into the Baltic Sea; the Volga, which empties into the Caspian Sea; and the Dnieper, which runs to the Black Sea. The chroniclers thereby identified one of the basic facts of early Rus life, namely, the importance of waterways for trade and communication. For Rus arose as a conquest realm of Baltic traders in the basin of the Volkhov River and then fanned out eastward to the Upper Volga and southward to the Dnieper. The Volga, we should note, is the largest river of Russia (and all of Europe, too). Its westernmost reach and tributaries commence in the historic heart of Russia—within two hundred miles of Moscow. About five hundred miles to the east, the Volga picks up its northeastern feeder and link to Siberia, the Kama River, and then curls southward to the Caspian Sea—a gateway to the Caucasus region, Central Asia, and Persia. The Dnieper, whose system drains much of present Ukraine into the Black Sea, has seven impassable cataracts (rapids) over a forty-mile stretch at its southern bend. In earlier times, these obstacles required portaging under protection from raiders for a ready maritime connection with the rich and strategic city of Constantinople (now Istanbul)—the leading emporium of Black Sea commerce and for many centuries the center of a flourishing Byzantine (Eastern Roman) Empire, as well as the Greek Orthodox Church. The Don River, well east of the Dnieper and flowing into the Sea of Azov, provided an alternative route to the Black Sea.

THE EASTERN SLAVS

Today we speak of three East Slavic peoples—Russians, Ukrainians, and Belarusians. For the centuries before about 1350, however, it is more accurate to refer to their common linguistic ancestors, who developed one literary language, which prevailed over all of Rus for several centuries. The mixing of local dialects to create three distinct languages and nationalities took a long time. In addition, Russia ruled over eastern Ukraine from 1667 to 1795 and over most of Ukraine and Belarus from 1795 to 1991. This fact, along with the relatively weak development of a specific Belarus culture, caused the cultural and identity boundaries among these nationalities to become somewhat fluid.

Origins and Diffusion

Linguistically the eastern Slavs belonged to the Indo-European megafamily of languages that includes the Baltic, Germanic, Romance, Hellenic, Armenian, Iranian, and Indic families. The original Indo-European tongue arose by 2700 B.C.E. in eastern Europe or Central Asia among crop-raising herdsmen. Slavic was the last of the Indo-European language divisions to crystallize as a distinct dialect, which occurred as early as 750–500 B.C.E. or as late as 500 C.E. Present-day practice divides Slavic-speakers into three subgroups—western (Polish, Czech, Slovak) and southern (Slovenian, Serbo-Croatian, Bulgarian, Macedonian), as well as eastern (Ukrainian, Belarusian, and Russian). This division is the result of migrations and linguistic and political developments that occurred after 500 C.E.

Most recent scholarship places the Slavs' beginnings somewhere in the territory stretching from the northern Carpathian Mountains to the Dnieper River. Several attempts have been made to identify as Slavs the mysterious "Scythians of the plow," recorded around 450 B.C.E. by the Ancient Greek historian Herodotus as residing in the lower Dnieper region. Solid evidence is lacking, but linguistic data indicate that the Iranian-speaking Scythians or Sarmatians, who dominated the Black Sea steppe and its hinterlands from around 700 B.C.E. to 200 C.E., influenced the forebears of the Slavs, as did Germanic-speaking peoples. Supporting this notion is the common Iranian and Old Slavic vocabulary for such religious terms as *god, evil,* and *repent* and some related Old Slavic and Germanic words. Indisputably, Slavic people first appear in extant writings only in the 500s. How and when the Slavic-speakers emerged from obscurity are still matters of learned conjecture. No map, table, or diagram can be considered the final word.

The diffusion of Slavic-speakers derived from the successive migrations of Goths from the Baltic region and Huns and Avars from inner Asia into eastern Europe from about 190 C.E. onward. Contingents of reportedly fierce and clever Slavic warriors fought alongside the Huns and other so-called barbarian invaders of the late Roman Empire. A people or succession of peoples, known from a few third- to seventh-century writings as the Antae (Antes), resided north of the Black Sea. Some specialists consider them to have been the predecessors of the east Slavs. However, it was the partially Slavic, Danube-centered realm of the Turkic Avars (ca. 550–800) that provided the conditions for the explosion of Slavic settlements, first from the Balkans to the Baltic Sea, and eventually to the Dnieper River and points further east. Not all Slavs benefited from this diffuse process of migration. By the eighth century so many captive or otherwise victimized Slavs appeared for sale in European markets that the word *slav* in its late Latin form *sclavus* became a standard term for slave, and in various forms remains so in most Western languages.

Early Civilization

Most east Slavs at this time and for centuries afterward lived near the margins of survival. The typical Slavic dwelling was a fifteen-by-twelve-foot hut, half submerged into the ground, often with an adjoining structure to house livestock during the long winters. The people mainly hunted, herded, farmed, fished, and gathered wild honey found in tree cavities. They chiefly used wooden farming implements, though archaeologists have uncovered some iron plowshares and hoes. In most forest zones farmers would slash a ring in the bark in the trees to kill them, cut them down, and burn them when they were dry to prepare seedbeds rich with ash. Tilling with hoes or simple scratch plows until the soils were exhausted, farmers would then relocate, usually within a restricted area, and allow nature to restore fertility. Plenty of live stumps survived the process to sprout new growth. In the wooded steppe, agriculturalists worked the soil and moved from farmland to farmland without slashing and burning. In the black earth zones, they sometimes employed a simple two-field system, leaving a fallow field for grazing to be fertilized by manure. Barley, oats, rye, millet, and occasionally wheat constituted the basic food grains; the standard vegetables were legumes such as peas and beans. Swine abounded as the most common livestock, but some Slavs kept sheep, goats, cattle, and horses, as well as fowl. Honey provided mead, the staple alcoholic drink.

The Slavs usually wore tunics, trousers, and long frocks or chemises made from crude linen that they spun from cultivated flax fibers, but they sometimes wore hides and pelts. For footwear they used hides, bast (wood fiber), or tree bark. Women did the spinning and weaving, as well as a great deal of the agriculture and food production, and they wore special head and chest ornaments for protection against evil forces. Finer garments and jewelry from abroad were available for the few who could afford it. Marriage customs included bride abduction and polygamy. Some scholars have argued that the extended family under a powerful patriarch served as the typical social organization accompanying slash-and-burn agriculture. In the forest zones families often lived in small groups, but in the more dangerous wooded steppe where nomadic herdsmen might roam, larger villages of up to eight households built wooden stockades and earthworks. Where possible, these agriculturalists, like everybody else in the region, trapped and traded furs. Graves assumed by archaeologists to be Slavic reveal a rather egalitarian social structure up to the 800s.

Later Rus written sources concerning the mid-800s list a dozen or so East Slavic tribes—that is, lineage-based sociopolitical formations. These included the Dulebians of western Ukraine, the earliest known; the Polyanians around Kiev; the Severians and Vyatichans east of the Dnieper; and the Krivichians and Slovenians farther north. The origin of these tribes, perhaps caused by population growth or the imposition from the outside of tributary or commercial networks, remains obscure, as does the extent of tribal cohesion and power. No material evidence has survived of any early East Slavic castle towns or a stratum of specialized warriors.

Nature, its manifestations and imagined spirits, pervaded early Slavic religious life. People named the months for characteristic occurrences, such as *listopad* (leaf-falling) for October or November. Major festivals welcomed the seasons. In later years, when Russia became officially Christian, churchmen would rail against the revival or persistence of pagan celebrations that masqueraded as Christian festivals—for example mixed-gender nude swimming on the eve of the summer solstice, which happened to be the feast of John the Baptist. No elaborate Slavic mythology survives, and only three presumed, but not proven, common Slavic deities are known: Perun, a god of thunder; Svarog or Dazhbog, a sun god; and Veles or Volos, a cattle god. East Slavs also observed cults of the wind god Stribog and of the female Mokosh, whom some scholars link to rain, fertility, and a Great Goddess type venerated over the centuries by all sorts of peoples. Evidence suggests

Slavic worship of Mother Earth in some form or other. Slavs also believed in virgin forest and water nymphs, potent household gods who had to be fed and appeased, and a host of other sprites and spirits.

Slavs, Balts, and Finno-Ugrians

Within the early East Slavic zone, the future Russian core lands in the Volkhov and Upper Volga regions followed their own rhythms. Place names indicate that before the coming of the Slavs, Balts inhabited a slice of Russia as far east as Moscow, as well as present northern Ukraine, all of Belarus, and Latvia, Lithuania, and northern Poland. To the north and east dwelled the linguistically distinct Finno-Ugrian peoples, such as the Chudians, Merians, and Vesians, who gathered furs for the suppliers of foreign markets well before and after the formation of the Rus realm. The very slow immigration of Slavs, starting in the 700s, does not seem to have been disruptive. Rather, Slavs, Balts, and Finno-Ugrians coexisted rather peacefully, being quite similar to each other and sharing related Germanic-origin words for *prince, iron, plow,* and *bread,* among others. What distinguished Slavs was their greater attention to agriculture, a focus reflected in the relative scarcity of animal

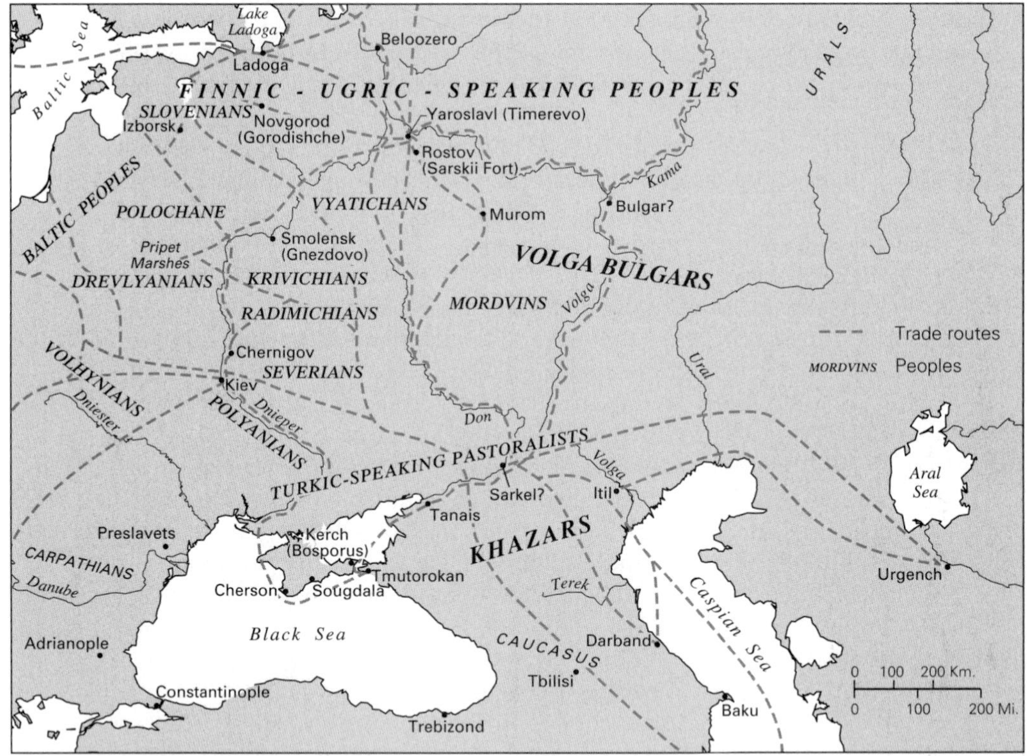

Early Rus: Tribes and Trade, ca. 930.

motifs in their burial artifacts as compared with the graves of the other local folk. As has often happened with neighboring and mingling peoples, the various forms of paganism, nature worship, and magic were compatible or virtually identical. Daily life in the future Russian north also had its peculiarities. Aboveground homes were common, in contrast to the partially underground huts farther south. So was the characteristic Russian heated bathhouse (*banya*), where people beat each other with leafy birch branches, which astounded some southern Rus.

New dialects and languages eventually developed as a result of the eastward and northeastward Slavic migrations, with a Finno-Ugrian impact on Russian vocabulary and syntax and a Baltic influence on Belarusian word forms. The Baltic and Finno-Ugrians continued to play a role in Rus and Russian history. Finnish, Estonian, now spoken outside of Russia, and the languages of a dozen small peoples still part of Russia (as well as Magyar or Hungarian) descend from ancient Finnic tongues. Lithuanian and Latvian, also now spoken outside of Russia, are the only direct linguistic survivals of the ancient Baltic languages.

THE KHAZAR *QAGANATE*

The establishment of the Khazar realm in the Lower Volga in the mid-600s was a catalyst for the migration of Slavs eastward and the rise of Rus. The Turkic-speaking Khazars inherited a western portion of the immense Turkic *qaganate,* or confederated empire, which around 550–650 stretched from the northeast Chinese borderlands to the Danube. With core lands in the Volga delta and the north Caucasus region, the Khazar *qaganate* at its peak (around 800–920) extended to eastern Crimea, central Ukraine, and the borders of the flourishing Muslim emirate of Khwarazm (Khorezm, Choresm) near the Aral Sea. In the 800s Slavic agriculturalists lived as far east as the Don River under Khazar protection, some in stockaded settlements interspersed among Turkic- and Iranian-speaking cavalry-herdsmen. By the early 900s, the historic East Slavic tribes of the Dnieper region were functioning as tributaries to the Khazars. Kiev, the future Rus capital, served as a regional Khazar outpost.

Although the scanty sources tell us little about the governance of the multiethnic Khazar realm, we know it antedated the formation of the first Rus state by almost two centuries and most likely influenced its political structure. As later among the Rus, the succession practices of the ruling lineages—both lateral (by brother, nephew, or cousin) and filial (by son)—often involved bloody conflicts. Junior princes might rule over subordinate territories while they awaited a hoped-for turn in the highest office. The authorities taxed local merchandise, transit trade passing through the realm, and, apparently, all households in tribute-bearing provinces. The broad masses of taxable commoners—as opposed to the tax-exempt nobles and officials—were called *black people.* The Rus later used this term for rural commoners. To control the movements of other steppe peoples in the region, the Khazars maintained the town of Sarkel, a huge moated bastion built with Byzantine aid on the Don River, and several other smaller stone fortresses.

The Khazar *qaganate* possessed some unique, cosmopolitan features. Its capital, Itil, a planned construction located on the western side of the Volga delta, had a Khazar side, a mercantile side, and an island fortress in the middle. The city had seven official judges, two each for Muslims, Christians, and Jews, and one for pagans. Despite strong Muslim influence, part of the Khazar elite adhered to Judaism by the 860s—some scholars believe as early as the 770s. How Judaism came to the Khazars is a mystery. Jews, as well as Muslims and Christians, were involved in long-distance trade and disseminated their expertise in the region. The Khazar elite probably saw in Judaism, which had no political base at the time, a way of acquiring the fruits of literate civilization without having to choose between the Islam of the caliphate and the Christianity of Byzantium. A few surviving Hebrew language documents attest to a Jewish presence in Kiev as well as Itil in the early 900s. One of the original portals of Kiev was the Jewish Gates, indicating a significant Jewish community and role in commerce there.

The Khazar hinterland in the Middle Volga included by about 800, if not earlier, a subordinate Turkic Bulgar tribal confederation ruled by its own *qagan,* with urban centers to control the tributary Finno-Ugrian peoples. The Bulgars also used some iron plowshares, in the 900s minted coins similar to the Central Asian dirhams of the time, and occasionally supplied the Rus with grain. This northeastern branch of the Bulgars forged a huge fur-trading network linking the Caspian Sea, Central Asia, the Middle East, the Baltic, and other parts of Europe. Thus Bulgar on the Volga became the first organized, tribute-collecting, commerce-promoting, and partially agricultural state to be established so far to the north in what is now European Russia. As such it may well have provided a model for the northern Rus. (This Bulgar should not be confused with Bulgaria in the Balkans—a fusion of western Bulgars and southern Slavs).

The Khazar realm owed its success in part to an economic upturn that the Baghdad-centered Muslim caliphate, the Byzantine Empire, and more distant western Europe enjoyed as of the mid-700s. In the early 900s, however, Turkic nomads known as Pechenegs crossed the Volga from the east, destroyed a string of Khazar strongholds, and compelled many of the Don basin Slavs to move further north. At this point Khazar power began to weaken, and the Bulgars, enriched by silver coming directly overland from Khwarazm, became more autonomous—which explains their adoption of Islam in the 920s. The weakening of the Khazars also set the scene for a dramatic southward movement along the Dnieper. The people who took this opportunity had by about 830 organized the fur gathering in the Volkhov and Upper Volga regions. These were Scandinavian Vikings who called themselves Varangians or *Rus.*

THE RUS

Stories of the origins of peoples and kingdoms are invariably wrapped in myths, and this certainly holds for the Rus, whose *Primary Chronicle* established the basic narrative still followed today. On the one hand, the basic elements of this narrative ring true—geographic and economic underpinnings, the intermingling of Slavs and Finno-Ugrians in the north, the Khazar overlordship over Slavic immigrants in the south, the Varangian-led conquest of power, and the eventual orientation to Byzantium. On the other hand, the *Primary Chronicle* contains legends, errors, and biased accounts favoring the dynasts in power at the time of writing and the outlook of the churchmen who did the writing. All the same, if archaeology and non-Rus sources enable us to correct and augment the chronicle account, they also show that enterprising Scandinavians did spearhead the formation of Rus.

In Search of Riches

During the economic upswing of the eighth to the tenth centuries, the relatively undeveloped lands of eastern Europe beckoned merchant-adventurers to exploit their resources for the expanding markets of the Middle East and Mediterranean sea coasts. Scandinavians, known as Vikings or Norsemen in western Europe, were well positioned to move in and establish needed rudimentary political structures for this purpose. Improvements in their iron and steel production resulted in superior armor, swords, and battle-axes. The perfection of their ships, reinforced with metal riveting and powered by oars and sails, allowed them by 800 to seize control of Europe's northern sea lanes from Ireland to Estonia. So while Khazars and then Bulgars initiated the organized hunt over most of the Volga and Kama basins for furs and other goods, Swedish Varangians proceeded to master the river and land routes of the north as far as the Upper Volga. As for the mainly Finno-Ugrian indigenous residents, some of them, especially young women, ended up in slave markets; others got off more easily, portaging and hauling for the Varangians and delivering tributary furs and food. Still others enriched themselves by trading and may well have developed their local settlements to profit from the growing commerce. Some of the Slavic and Finno-Ugrian tribes noted in the *Primary Chronicle* likely rose to prominence simultaneously with the expansion of Khazar, Bulgar, and Varangian mercantile and tributary activities in eastern Europe.

Archaeology has established that the permanent presence of Varangians in northern Russia commenced in Staraya Ladoga on the lower Volkhov as early as the 750s, the same time they built up a few other Baltic outposts. Greek, German, Arabic, Persian, and Scandinavian sources show that as early as the 830s Swedes who called themselves *Rhos* or *Rus* were drawn southward, not only to the Black Sea and Byzantium, but also to the Caspian, Khwarazm, and the caliphate. In the early or mid 800s these adventurers founded Gorodishche near the future Novgorod (*Novgorod* means "new city" in Russian), and they mounted a major, destructive expedition against Constantinople in 860. As of 900, however, Bulgar may have been the Varangians' single most important overseas marketplace. The Varangians also came under Khazar or Bulgar political influence, as they claimed in the early 800s to have their own reigning *qagan*.

In general the Varangians combined coercion with commerce and seem to have coopted like-minded Slavs, Balts, and Finno-Ugrians. We might envision some of their expeditions as one-shot affairs to open up markets and trade, as well as to pillage, levy tribute, or fulfill political obligations to launch an attack. Anyone who took part—Varangian chiefs acting as Rus territorial princes, professional warriors and merchants, or enterprising locals—obtained a share of the profits. For the period 904–944, the Rus and their Slavic and Finno-Ugrian confederates mounted seven recorded military campaigns in search of trade and booty against Constantinople, across the Black Sea, and into the Caspian and Caucasus regions. Undoubtedly there were more. In one case, reports the *Primary Chronicle,* they "hung their shields upon the gates [of Constantinople] as a sign of victory." Most of their profits, though, ended up back home. For several centuries Scandinavians considered the territory of Rus to be a Swedish hinterland.

The rise of Kiev occurred as the Varangians increased their use of the Dnieper. Ideally located on a plateau near a favorable Dnieper crossing slightly north of the wooded steppe, Kiev began to be significant only around 900, when it functioned as a Khazar administrative and commercial outpost and as the chief town of the local Slavs. The permanent move of some Varangians to Kiev by 930 under the leadership of the prince, or *qagan,* Igor (*Ingvar* in Swedish, d. 944?) and, perhaps, his confederate Oleg, was a major breakthrough. They established an equally important center in Chernigov, located on an eastern tributary of the Dnieper with excellent connections to the Don and Volga. Here, in the central Dnieper region, with its rich agricultural resources and more numerous Slavs than in the north, a more stratified society developed, dominated by Rus warriors. This created a growing base—the first non-nomadic state ever in the region—from which the Rus could regularly trade with Byzantium as well as points west and east. Rus treaties with Byzantium recorded in the *Primary Chronicle* under the years 907, 911, and 944 regulated this trade. Attempting to get the best terms for Rus merchants, Igor's widow Olga (d. 969?) visited Constantinople and there converted to Christianity.

From a vivid description written by the Byzantine emperor Constantine VII in 950 we learn of annual southbound river expeditions organized out of Kiev to transport for sale the forest products collected as tribute. The Rus used hundreds of hastily constructed oak dugouts equipped with oars, sails, and a forty-man crew, not the superb Viking craft that braved the northern seas. With Pechenegs and other steppe peoples poised to raid, portaging the Dnieper cataracts involved great danger.

The culmination of bold and risky Varangian-Rus moves arrived in 962–972 under Igor's son Svyatoslav (d. 972), the first Rus prince to have a Slavic name. The *Primary Chronicle* and Byzantine sources depict him as a warrior's warrior who shared the Spartan life of his troops and wore a gold earring. On his bald head, he had a single lock of hair, in the style of the steppe warriors of his time—and which was adopted by some Ukrainian Cossacks seven hundred years later. Svyatoslav aimed to dominate the Volga River, its Caspian Sea commerce, and the entire northern Black Sea. From the mouth of the Danube River, he would tax the international trade of its hinterland—in the words of the chronicler: from Bohemia and Hungary, "silver and horses"; from Rus, "furs, wax, honey and slaves"; from Byzantium, "gold, expensive cloths, wines, and fruits of many kinds." To these ends he subdued the easternmost Slavs, smashed the Bulgars and Khazars, and sacked their capitals. From the Khazars he seized the Don River stronghold of Sarkel and Tmutorokan at the strategic Straits of Kerch (between the Azov and Black Seas). He ventured well into the north Caucasus region and attacked Byzantium's clients in the Crimea. Penetrating and devastating Balkan Bulgaria as well, Svyatoslav impaled resisters and established a new capital on the lower Danube, concentrating so many forces there that he exposed Kiev to a Pecheneg siege. In the end, despite having recruited more warriors from the steppe, Svyatoslav overreached himself and was expelled from the Balkans by the Byzantines. On his way home with his loot, some Pechenegs ambushed and killed him. The Volga Bulgars recovered from his attack, but the Khazar state never revived.

Lasting Legends

The story of the Varangians in Rus provided material for legend, epic, and modern literature. These accounts start in the *Primary Chronicle* in 862 when Novgorodian Slavs (before Novgorod existed, according to archaeology) and the local Finnic tribes resolved "to seek a prince . . . who might rule by law." They summoned the Rus leader Ryurik, and his two brothers, and, as if justifying elective monarchy, pleaded to him: "Our land is great and rich, but there is no order in it. Come reign and rule over us." The chronicle also contains the myth of Kiev's foundation by the ferryman Ky and his two brothers. The account goes on to bolster the dynasty of Rus princes, who claimed Ryurik as their common ancestor. Accordingly, in Ryurik's time, two of his countrymen, Askold and Dir, took over Kiev and led an expedition against Constantinople. But before Ryurik died in 879, he entrusted his infant son Igor to their kinsman Oleg, who around 880–882 seized Kiev in Igor's name, killed Askold and Dir for ruling without being princes of the blood, and proclaimed Kiev the "Rus metropolis (mother-city)"—in other words, the capital.

Other chronicle tales with folklorish motifs follow, starting with a shaman's fatal prophecy that Oleg, himself considered by his followers to be a seer, would be killed by his favorite horse. The mythic history reports that even though he put that steed out to pasture, many years later he was fatally bitten by a poisonous snake that crawled out from the dead horse's skull. Igor, on the other hand, died from greed—he and his men were killed attempting to exact a double tribute from Slavs living to the west of Kiev. The Slavs' leader, Prince Mal, then had the temerity to ask for the hand of Igor's clever widow, Olga. She in turn proceeded to trick Mal's men four times: she buried one embassy alive, immolated a second in a bathhouse, massacred their drunken soldiers after a pseudo-funeral feast for Igor, and set their wooden strongholds afire with incendiary homing pigeons. Her son Svyatoslav also died from avarice, according to the chronicle, disregarding the advice to drop his booty and quickly return from the Danube to Kiev by horse. After the Pechenegs slew him, they followed regional tradition and fashioned a gilded drinking goblet from his skull. Twenty years later the Rus obtained revenge, when an unnamed youth, who with his bare hands could rip the hide off a raging bull, strangled a Pecheneg Goliath in single combat. The early princes also had a place in the Icelandic sagas that sang of the feats and misfortunes of Viking heroes in Rus. Centuries later Russia's greatest poet, Alexander Pushkin (1799–1837), created an ironic little masterpiece directly from the *Primary Chronicle:* "The Tale of Oleg the Seer."

Princess (and Saint) Olga, depicted here as a nun, tricks the Drevlyanian embassy in 945 or 946 and buries the envoys alive. Illustrated Radzivill Chronicle of 15th c. *Academy of Science, St. Petersburg, Russia/Erich Lessing/Art Resource, NY.*

THE KIEVAN MONARCHY

The chronicle legends make for interesting reading, and they are part of the traditional presentation of Russian (and Ukrainian) history, but they merely supplement archaeology and more reliable written data. Behind these tales and the solid evidence of Rus piratical raids and the stuffing of Swedish coffers with Middle Eastern and Central Asian silver, a new east European realm began to take shape where none had existed before. This was just a start, and hardly a state, as understood today. In the modern state, public authority on local, regional, and national levels stands largely separated from private institutions, such as family units, businesses, churches, and other elements of civil society. In premodern societies, public authority was almost completely enmeshed in the private interests of those who exercised it. Public institutions were also private sources of power and income, so far as officials were concerned. Central authority, to be effective over time, required social and economic ties with provinces—something that was lacking or weak in Rus for centuries. In this regard Rus was not so different from neighboring lands.

Elements of Order

After about 960, the Scandinavian element weakened, as Slavic became the language of the original Varangians' descendants. Real towns with an artisan and commercial sector developed in Kiev, Chernigov, Novgorod, and Smolensk. The *Primary Chronicle* relates that Princess Olga created tax districts. This may have occurred later, but a series of strongholds tied to the reigning dynasty began to dot the land and displace those of the tribes. At the same time, a few other elite Varangian strongmen established ruling centers. As in other parts of Europe, this royalty lived together with their personal retinues in special palaces (Kiev's were made of stone) similar to what the English called halls. A leader's personal treasury served as the focal point of a regular exchange of gifts between him and his chief followers, as well as a source of prestige and insurance for them all against bad times.

The survival in altered form of several Rus-Byzantine treaties furnishes a glimpse into the notions of public and private law among the Rus in the 900s. Designated agents of the Rus princes and magnates negotiated with the Byzantine emperors. The two officially friendly realms were expected to help and protect each other's ships in distress, to extradite each other's felons, and to allow the ransoming and return of each other's enslaved subjects. Rus merchants bearing goods, whom the Byzantines considered to be rendering a service, could expect to be well supplied as guests while in Constantinople and provided with the necessary equipment for the return sail. In matters of personal crimes as well as simple torts and damages, Rus law adhered then, as it would for several more centuries, to principles of retaliation and recompense. Thieves had to pay their victims a double or triple restitution for stolen goods, not suffer mutilation or execution, as in the more developed public law of the Byzantine codes. Similarly, murderers were placed under the rules of family vengeance (killing the killer) or material compensation to the victim's family, not execution by state authorities. Assault with a weapon also carried a punitive payment to the victim. In the absence of witnesses, an individual's sworn testimony was sufficient to establish ownership of goods, including slaves. These stipulations resembled later Rus law and treaty provisions with Baltic Germans and Scandinavians. The pre-Christian Rus of the 900s were thus capable of placing commercial and judicial life and external relations on a legal and rational basis according to the general standards of the times.

Starting no later than Svyatoslav's reign (962–972), the prince of Kiev placed his sons as subordinate rulers in some of the other towns. In the case of Novgorod, the ethnically mixed local elite demanded as their prince Svyatoslav's son Vladimir (?–1015). His mother was Olga's local lady in waiting, and her brother Dobrynya thereby became Vladimir's chief adviser. The growth of such towns with their own princes and power structures weakened the lineage-based political structures of the surrounding peoples, but it also fostered armed political rivalries and bloody successions within the newly established Rus dynasty. Thus Svyatoslav's death was followed by carnage among his three sons, Yaropolk (r. 972–980), Oleg (d. 976/977), and Vladimir (r. 980–1015). The winner and sole survivor, Vladimir, owed his success in 980 to recruiting fresh Varangians in Sweden, defeating his rivals in the north, and then allying with one contingent of the Kievans against Yaropolk, who had earlier killed Oleg. In the process Vladimir caused some other Kievans to flee to the Pechenegs, who renewed their attacks on Rus, now with some Rus allies. This was the first of recurring occasions when a warring Rus faction would ally with outsiders.

Vladimir's Revolution

In this new situation, with a growing productive population and a dangerous steppe next door, Vladimir and his advisers concentrated less than his ancestors had on expeditions for plunder and trade and more on building up Kiev's southern defenses and on rounding out his realm by extending his rule to the borders of Hungary and Poland. The only foothold on the Black Sea that he controlled was strategic Tmutorokan, the gateway to the north Caucasus from the straits at the mouth of the Sea of Azov. As a polygamist, Vladimir had many sons and appointed about ten of them to be subordinate rulers of provincial towns, but he also assigned military governors and troops on the wooded steppe frontier.

Vladimir commenced his reign as a dedicated pagan, and, according to the hostile Christian account in the *Primary Chronicle,* erected a central shrine in Kiev to six different gods. Within ten years, however, he arranged an official conversion to Christianity. This gave Rus a network of bishoprics with their staffs, a literate stratum of clerics, a unifying ideology justifying monarchy, and a more symbolically prestigious palace complex in Kiev. An episode in the chronicle similar to a Khazar story tells us that Vladimir and his elite were courted by missionaries—Bulgar Muslims, rival Greek Orthodox and German Roman Catholic Christians, and even Khazar Jews. He in turn sent inquiring emissaries to the Bulgars, Germans, and Byzantine Greeks, since religion was indeed a matter of high state policy. Evidence indicates that Kiev already had some Jewish and Moslem residents, but Christianity gained the upper hand in this contest from the start. Some Varangian Rus and Scandinavians were already Christians, as were the neighboring Danube Bulgarian, Polish, and Hungarian realms and Vladimir's westernmost Slavic subjects, and a Slavic liturgy was available. Moreover, despite the Muslim Volga Bulgar emporium, Rus commerce on the whole was directed toward the Christian world more than the Islamic. Finally, the Byzantine Empire at this time was the most prestigious state within the diplomatic orbit of Rus, and Vladimir was able to make an arrangement with its emperor, Basil II. Varangian mercenaries would aid Basil in a civil war, and Rus would convert to Christianity. In return Basil's sister Anna would become Vladimir's sole legitimate wife—a tremendous diplomatic coup, which virtually placed the prince of Kiev on a par with Europe's greatest rulers. Politically, as well as culturally and religiously, Vladimir's conversion of the Rus elite to Orthodox Christianity constituted a revolution from above.

Approaching the year 1000, then, Rus had developed as a multiethnic realm in a sparsely populated wooded expanse, at a time when other states were crystallizing in eastern and northern Europe. The Khazars and Bulgars played a role in this process, but a greater Scandinavian influence over Rus personal names, administrative and legal terminology, weaponry, and literature is indisputable. By the year 1000 or so, however, *Rus* was beginning to signify the predominantly Slavic Rus state and especially the region around Kiev. Meanwhile, the reigning Prince Vladimir and his advisers had set aside paganism and selected Greek Orthodoxy as the state religion—a move that forever tied Rus and its successors to Europe, while giving them a particular identity of their own. A new Christian civilization thus came into being in eastern Europe, from the wooded steppe frontier in the Dnieper basin to the marshy forests east of the Baltic, and as far west as the upper reaches of the Dniester and Vistula Rivers.

CHAPTER 2

Kievan Rus: Structures and Events, 988–1240

"My sons, I am about to quit this world. Love one another, since you are brothers by one father and mother. If you abide in love towards each other, God will be among you, and you shall reduce your enemies to subjection, and you shall live in peace. But if you live in hatred and quarrel among yourselves, then you will perish and destroy the land of your fathers and grandfathers, which they acquired with immense labors."
—Primary Chronicle, *attributed to Grand Prince Yaroslav the Wise, 1054*

In the year 988, according to the *Primary Chronicle,* Prince Vladimir returned to Kiev from a successful military expedition to the Byzantine outpost of Cherson on the Crimean Peninsula. Bringing back priests, vessels, relics, and, most important, an imperial Byzantine bride, he ordered a mass baptism of the Kievans in the Dnieper River and reoriented his domains as a Christian polity.

Vladimir's policies initiated what some Russians and Ukrainians have considered a golden age, when their land took its place as the largest, richest, and most prestigious of the new Christian realms of eastern and northern Europe. During this period, which lasted until the Mongols overran the country in 1237–1240, the population, economy, towns, regional principalities, and a distinct Rus civilization developed apace.

Indeed, the steady demographic growth, in the absence of effective instruments of central rule, ensured the triumph of regionalism. In the northern zones of Rus—the future Russia—this regionalism took three different forms. Commercial Novgorod, oriented toward the Baltic Sea, showcased a noteworthy evolution of both a city-state and junior towns, with a mild tribute-collecting system over the numerous Finno-Urgian peoples in vast forest domains. Ryazan, which faced the wooded steppe of the upper Don basin, nurtured a fearsome cavalry. Between the two, the lands of Rostov and Suzdal emerged as powerful rivals to Kiev by the 1160s, with elements of strong monarchism balanced by kinship units and other social and political forces.

This epoch also appeared to later generations as a heroic time, whose saints enlightened a largely illiterate population with the faith, and whose semimythical champions lived on for generations in oral poetry cycles. It was both a constructive and a swashbuckling age, full of internecine strife and battles with steppe nomads

Leading Rus Princes, ca. 900–1240s

I) From Oleg through Yaroslav I (ca. 900–1054) Chiefly monarchy under the strongest kinsman or son

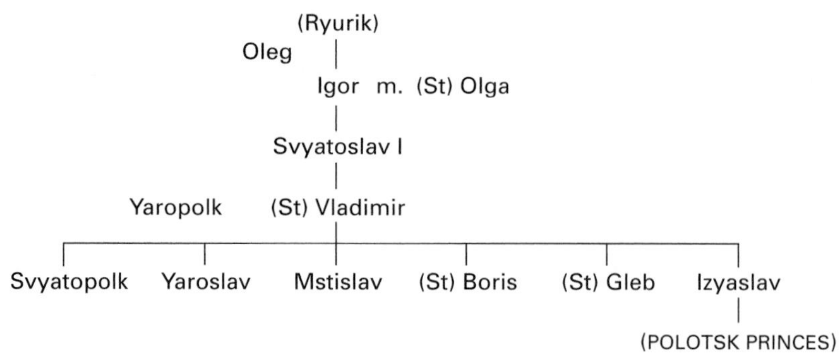

II) From the "Triumvirate" to Vladimir Monomakh's Dynasty (1054–1139)

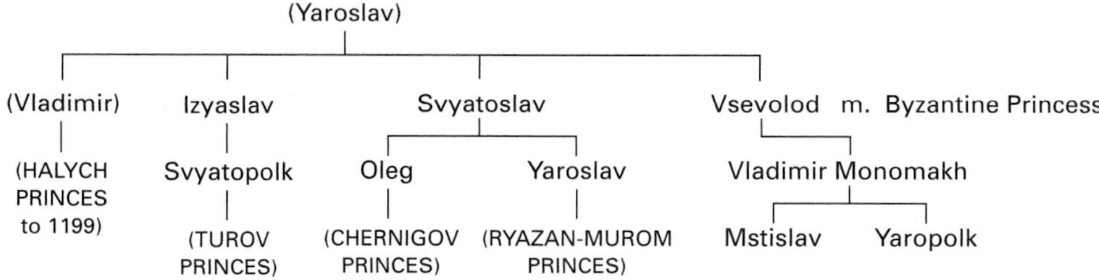

III) Yuri Dolgoruky's and Andrei Bogolyubsky's attempts to obtain or dominate Kiev (1139–1175); Kiev princes from various lines

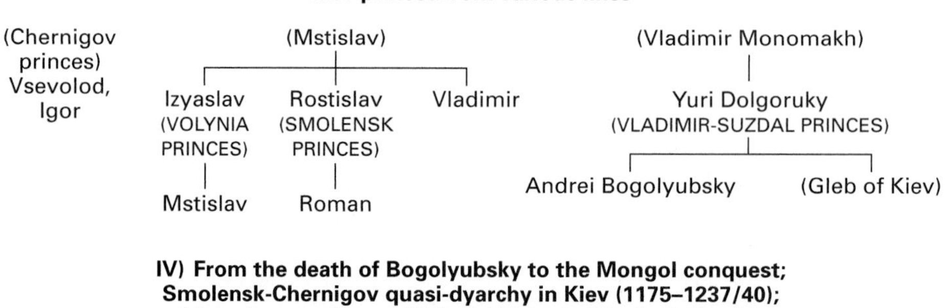

IV) From the death of Bogolyubsky to the Mongol conquest; Smolensk-Chernigov quasi-dyarchy in Kiev (1175–1237/40); Virtual separation of (Halych-) Volynia, Vladimir-Suzdal

and forest peoples, yet free from the heavy hand of a centralized state. At the same time, for the majority, it was first and foremost a period of migration and struggles merely to survive.

AN EXPANDING ECONOMY

Throughout the Kievan period, what strikes us most is the sheer increase of settlements and people. With them came parallel growth in production and internal commerce. If written sources, such as the chronicles and law codes, attest to the variety of activities and products, archaeology is our surest indicator of these quantitative leaps.

Town and Country

Historical demographers estimate for Rus an average population rise during 988–1237 of 1.3 percent per year, or a doubling every fifty-five years and a total increase by a factor of eleven. According to these very rough estimates, an entire population of just 1 million in 988 would have increased to 10 million to 12 million on the eve of the Mongol conquest.

Cultivation methods in established settlements progressed from slash-and-burn to natural fallow (leaving prepared cropland unseeded for a season or more) techniques. In some places the Rus started to structure two-field systems with the regular, alternating planting of grains one year on one field and special, soil-enriching crops on the other field, and then reversing them the following year. The black-earth wooded steppe and the fine gray-soil mixed forest belts remained the most productive. People steadily migrated inland from settlements along rivers and moved also into northern and eastern regions. By the early 1200s, the resulting profusion of Slavic communities formed the basis for a dozen major Rus principalities and many minor ones.

A few estates where slaves or otherwise bound dependents cultivated individual small plots or land the owner controlled for his own private use began to appear around 1000. Princes, who earlier had only taxed the farming population, started to employ slave labor to grow crops on court lands, supplementing their hunting grounds, herds, and stables. By the late eleventh century a few major churches and monasteries owned villages with slaves. By the mid twelfth century, an estate of the Chernigov princes had seven hundred slaves and hundreds of horses and other livestock. Some of the elite also possessed agricultural lands with barns, threshing floors, and beehives. These were all worked by slave, indentured, or free labor.

The towns of Rus, home to at most 4 or 5 percent of the population, served as centers of tribute-collecting, administration, production, trade, culture, and military organization. Most major cities were located at river junctures or high points that could control movements of people and trade. Rostov and Suzdal, however, arose in the best Upper Volga gray-soil areas, and Halych (Galicia) emerged on a

Dniester River trade route near saltworks. Princes founded strategically important new cities, including Yaroslav I's Yurev (1030, now Tartu) in eastern Estonia, Vladimir Monomakh's Vladimir (ca. 1100) near Suzdal, and Yuri II's Nizhny Novgorod (1223) facing former Bulgar-dominated territory at the all-important confluence of the Oka and Volga Rivers. Townsmen produced the iron weapons needed to dominate the countryside and manned the local armies.

Kiev, the urban jewel of Rus in this period, from the tenth century onward had an unprotected lower region near the river and was settled with artisans. Its walls were extended at least four times, so that by 1150–1200 about 1.25 square miles were enclosed. Within were located two huge churches, several monasteries, the prince's major palace—all of stone and brick—and the wooden villas of the elite along with many workshops. The fortifications combined reinforced earthen walls, upper wooden towers, and masonry work gateposts. By the late 1100s, Kiev, with at least fifty thousand inhabitants, had become one of Europe's larger cities, rivaling Paris or Venice. Eleven Rus towns ranged from eight thousand to twenty thousand in the early 1200s, and another eighty ranged from fifteen hundred to five thousand. To deal with the mud from spring thaws, Novgorod, the leading northern city, and some other towns constructed wooden streets—layers of joined log crossbeams—on top of earlier ones that had sunk in mire. This renewal device lasted for centuries.

Producing for Markets

Rus was self-sufficient in basic commodities. The 95 percent of the population living in rural areas worked with wood, hides, fur, sackcloth, bog iron, and simple potter's wheels to supply their needs. Some country folk also produced metal for the market, fashioning jewelry or slate whorls (the perforated disks needed for spindles). Major cities produced bricks, candles, and other basic supplies for construction and church services, as well as weapons and some luxury goods. Until its fall in 1240, Kiev was the most sophisticated productive center in Rus, and by 1200 had a thousand or more workshops. Under Byzantine influence, the Kievans manufactured all sorts of colored glass bracelets, bronze pieces with enamels, decorative and religious items from precious metals, and iron objects, thereby reducing the demand for imports. Novgorod's mail armor, knives, agricultural implements, and carved ivory from White Sea walrus tusks supplied an all-Rus market. Some of this work required forging at extremely high temperatures and other such technological ingenuity.

Commerce spread widely across Rus, despite such a shortage of coin—because the great supply of Middle Eastern silver coins had dried up around the year 1000, and nothing replaced it—that prices were sometimes reckoned in marten or squirrel hides. Although much of the trade was thus a sophisticated form of barter, foreign merchants came to Rus from all directions. Princes continued to traffic in the furs, honey, beeswax, and slaves obtained as tribute, but Rus merchants maintained bases in Constantinople and on the island of Gotland off Sweden. Imports included Flemish cloth, German iron products, and Western church items; Byzantine silks, wine, oil, nuts and dried fruits; horses, sheep, and cattle from the steppe; and a variety of goods from the Caucasus, the Middle East, and Central Asia. Diplomacy played its role, as cooperation with Bulgar and the steppe nomads was essential for the overland trade to the east and south. As for the Rus interior, surviving letters and writs on birch bark (the cheapest available paper) indicate the presence of a horde of petty traders and widespread lending in the Rus north.

STRATIFIED SOCIETY

Rus society, like its medieval counterparts, allowed some social mobility, but otherwise was sharply differentiated—horizontally, vertically, and by gender. For their own security, individuals needed to be part of a group. The alternative was to be a social outcast (*izgoi*), dependent upon the Church for protection. Kinship as well as community units therefore played an important role for everybody. A sharp consciousness of status and honor found expression in the material compensation paid to families or individuals in cases of murder, physical injury, rape, and other outrages and abuses. The Church organizations, personnel, and dependent people intertwined with the rest of society.

The two basic law codes of Rus, *Rus Justice* (*Pravda ruska*) and *Yaroslav's Charter* to the Church, mostly compiled over time in the eleventh and twelfth centuries, provide the best sources for information on medieval Rus society. Written mainly in a readily accessible judicial shorthand, the codes set norms for restitution for damages, sometimes with a steep sliding scale. For example, the compensation for

Rus People from Pre-Mongol Era: composite modern drawings of soldier, prince, chief prelate, townsman, peasant, and princess, based on remains of clothing and equipment, as well as book miniatures and church frescos. *Tolochko,* Kiev I Kievskaia zemlia v epokhu feodalnoi razdroblennosti XII–XIII vekov, *1980, pg. 94–95, 101, 216.*

abducting or raping the daughter of a "great boyar" was a prohibitive five gold grivnas (2.2–2.8 pounds of gold); of a "lesser boyar," one gold grivna; of a "solid" citizen, two silver grivnas; and of a commoner, twelve fur grivnas.

Ethnicity and the Social Ladder

Not only Slavs, but other peoples lived within the loosely defined and porous boundaries of Rus, where, as everywhere, religion, language, and real or imagined origins constituted prime features of people's identity. The conversion of the east Slavs to Christianity proceeded slowly, and pockets of pagans long survived, some retaining their tribal identity and burial customs into the 1100s, as did the Baltic-speaking population in present Belarus. The Finno-Ugrian peoples, inhabiting a huge arc of territory stretching from Estonia to Mordvinia and points north, remained for the most part pagan, often under their own princes, except where they assimilated to the Rus. The Mordvinians to the east were usually allied with Muslim Bulgar, while the Ingrians and Karelians to the northwest of Novgorod became over time loyal constituents of that regional principality. An analogous situation held in the south. As of the late eleventh century, small numbers of settled Turkic tribesmen of various origins, later known as the "Black Hats," served as guards along the tributaries of the Dnieper near the steppe frontier and, though pagan, were standing members of the regional Kievan polity.

Germans, Scandinavians, Greeks, Armenians, Jews, Ossetians, and others, at times whole colonies, could be found in a variety of towns as merchants, artists, architects, and physicians. Roman Catholics built their own churches for Latin liturgies, and Jews had their own rabbinical leadership. In 1113, the rich Jews of Kiev, among other residents of the city, became targets of mass plunder, but it is not clear why. It was more likely because of their presumed involvement in usury, the hated salt monopoly, and other princely fiscal operations, than due to their Judaism.

At the summit of Rus society stood the charismatic clan of princes, whose members were recognized as having the exclusive right to reign in Kiev and other towns and as being equal only to similar clans ruling other peoples. Thus the Ryurikids—the purported descendants of the semimythical Ryurik—almost always married a distant cousin or foreign royalty. The most prestigious match was with a Byzantine imperial house. After about 1100, the princes' most common foreign brides were Qipchak princesses from the steppe.

Beneath the princes stood the boyars, or leading warrior nobles, members of the senior retinue (*druzhina*) of a given prince or of the chief families of a major city. The boyars, having access to the highest positions, formed a hereditary but not closed elite, since princes could recruit and elevate new people from home or abroad. Nobility—that is, the privileges of the "well-born"—itself developed over time. In fact the initial statute of the earliest version of *Rus Justice* envisioned no differences among free men. Around 1000, a prince's retainers usually lived at his court; two centuries later, many of them had their own landed estates with full property rights. However, boyars, the Rus equivalent of European aristocrats down through the seventeenth century, tended to live in the cities like many of their Italian and Byzantine counterparts, not on country estates, like English, French, and German nobles.

The city of Kiev, with the chief palace and churches and the leading cloister of the realm, was the center of southern and central Rus society and had an elite of mixed origins and interests. As of about 1100, other Kiev monasteries served as the headquarters of several nearby regional princely families with periodic claims to the primary throne of Rus. In Novgorod and similar fur-trading cities, the ruling boyar elite possessed urban villas, as well as the largest stock of goods for commerce. In northeastern Vladimir-Suzdal, some leading families had distant estates but served at court. Halych in the extreme west supported the most developed landed nobility with residences away from the towns.

Middle-level service people, the equivalent of the Western knight or vassal and similarly called "boys" (*detski*), occupied the next rung down the social ladder. Collectively they might make up the prince's personal army or junior retinue and double as his administrators. A different sort of middle-level type, related in name to the Anglo-Saxon and Scottish *thane,* was the *tiun*—a prince's or boyar's agent, who carried out a variety of private and public duties. Legally often a slave, sometimes even a eunuch, he enjoyed whatever authority and status his lord delegated to him and might well abuse it under protection from above. The Kiev chronicle noted two hated *tiuns,* Ratsha and Tudor, who extorted local residents under Prince Vsevolod Olgovich (r. 1139–1146; the *-(v)ich* ending means *son of,* the *-ovna/evna* ending means *daughter of*). The non-noble mercantile elite represented another upper-middle stratum with some independent authority. In Novgorod, for example, the wax merchants at their Church of St. John controlled the city's official commercial weights.

Urban commoners seem to have been of two sorts: those attached to households of the more powerful people and those who were independent. Free artisans sometimes clustered by craft. Constituting a core element of town militias, they could join with the urban elites to form an assembly of freemen called the *veche.* This type of conclave, which may have sprung from an ancient tribal assembly, seems to have convened in times of emergency or extraordinary decision making.

The vast majority of Rus lived in the countryside as free peasants and forest dwellers known as *smerdy*—a term deriving from either an Iranian word for *man* or the Slavic word for *stink*. The collective subjects of the princes or towns, *smerdy* were generally liable for taxes or tribute, labor services, and horses for military campaigns. As in England in the eleventh century, such people had their own customary law, which was not recorded; but they were subject to the law of the realm when they dealt with the outer world and were collectively responsible for unsolved crimes committed in their communities.

Indentured servants, who had contracted to be virtual slaves for a limited term and were liable to corporal punishment at the hands of their lords, occupied an intermediate status. Lacking the full rights of freemen, they could only serve as witnesses in judicial proceedings when no one else was available, and they could be reduced to full slavery for certain offenses. Yet they could litigate regarding their indentures and win freedom if their lord abused them.

On the lowest rung of the social ladder stood slaves. Those who originated as captives or were born into servitude could be bought and sold and had virtually no legal rights to property or anything else. In other words, Rus slaves, like most of their counterparts elsewhere and at other times, were "socially dead." They normally could not testify in court or even pay restitution for their offenses, their owners instead being liable. One exception in Rus was rape by a nonowner, where the compensation for the shaming might go to the woman herself rather than her owner. A slave who struck a freeman could be killed on the spot or flogged by the victim. A free person wishing to marry a slave needed the owner's dispensation to avoid enslavement, too. The ex-debtor slaves, whose status originated in self-sale, however, could not be bought or sold and were thus more like indentured servants.

Men and Women

Males almost always occupied the highest and physically most powerful positions in early Rus society. They hunted, fought, pursued the most prestigious public professions, and dominated political and religious life, wielding sword, scepter, and cross. Alongside men, women engaged in numerous agricultural, forest, and artisanal tasks, such as harvesting and weaving, and joined in the desperate defense of cities. On their own they might be professional spinners and weavers or run businesses, lend and borrow money, make contracts, and work as midwives. Early Rus law valued free women less than men, the compensation for their injuries being half that for men, but the reproductive capacity of slave girls rendered their value one-fifth higher than that of enslaved men.

Marriage customs entailed some remnants of pagan abduction and an initial rape, but unions were usually practical and arranged affairs, and this became the rule where Christian values prevailed. Family coercion of daughters was punishable by law if it resulted in injury or suicide. Women took dowries into their marriages and had the right, sometimes challenged by the husband, to control their personal property. For example, a surviving birch bark letter from the 1100s shows a certain Anna, who had lent her own money at interest, asking her son to defend her from her furious husband. Women could expect some emotional fulfillment not from husbands, but from children, especially sons, who were more likely than daughters to remain in the household or nearby after marriage.

Sons normally inherited family property. Daughters received dowries to bring into their marriages. If both parents died before this happened, surviving brothers were expected to marry off their orphaned sisters and provide dowries. Elite families without sons could leave estates to daughters. We are not sure about the lower orders.

Quite a few princes maintained concubines, including slave girls acquired as tribute, and wedded princesses sometimes fled back to their original families. Desertion and bigamy occurred among commoners. Wives were expected to have sex with their husbands upon demand, except, in keeping with the boundaries of Orthodox Christian notions of cleanliness, around the time of menstruation or up to forty days after childbirth. Matrimony trapped women more than men, since only the latter could obtain legal separation on the grounds of adultery. But women could divorce when physically abused to the extreme. In practice some people acted as they pleased. The Church codes and other writings reflected clerical fears of rampant, freewheeling sexuality on the part of both genders, as well as abuse of power over wives, stepchildren, full offspring, and even parents. In practice the Church overlooked bachelor indulgence with slave girls and prostitutes, and it treated the sexual license of powerful men as part of the normal social order.

Still, women had several avenues to power and influence commensurate with their family situation and wealth. Widows often controlled their children and the family property, purchased land, and donated some of it and other goods to churches or monasteries as soul-saving charity. The mother of the most celebrated Rus monk, Feodosy, physically prevented him for several years from abandoning the normal military training of youths of his social class. Elite single women or widows established or entered urban convents, where they lived as nuns in honorable retirement or exercised power as abbesses. In Novgorod, at least around 1200, the heads of the leading female convents were significant personages in their own right.

After Igor's widow Olga relinquished power around 962, Rus had no prominent governing or regent princess at all until the 1400s, but women sometimes mediated among squabbling princes. In 1097, at the behest of the Kievans, the widow of the late prince of Kiev Vsevolod Yaroslavich (1030–1093), helped make peace between his nephew and successor Svyatopolk (II) Izyaslavich (1050–1113) and the latter's cousin Vladimir (II) Vsevolodovich Monomakh (1053–1125). Foreign-born princesses also served as diplomats connecting Rus to their native land. Several Rus princesses, for example, Anna Yaroslavona (1024–post-1075), wife of King Henry I of France, married European or Byzantine royalty and enjoyed splendid political or cultural careers in their new countries.

Finally, the presence of mothers and women warriors as both enablers and obstacles in the cycle of heroic Rus poetry reveals a widespread perception of female power over individual male lives. And this should not be a surprise, especially since the death of warriors left many of their offspring without fathers. The heroes of this poetry, to be discussed in the next chapter, often had to be empowered by their magic-bearing mothers or brides to perform their feats. On the negative side, women ran the risk of being blamed for natural disasters and killed as witches, as happened during a famine in the Rostov district in 1071, though such tragedies rarely occurred.

TRIBUTARY POLITICS AND INSTITUTIONS

The Rus political order originated to organize tribute collection, military expeditions, and commerce; distribute the spoils of battle and conquest; and mediate or judge domestic disputes. As Rus became a territorial and Christian entity, the rulers

High clergy, led by a bishop, reconciles rival princes by acting as go-betweens in negotiations in 1201. *Academy of Science, St. Petersburg, Russia.*

necessarily added to these tasks, devising means to hold their realm together and to protect it and the Church against internal and external foes. Essentially, politics consisted of an endless series of verbal and armed negotiations over the distribution and redistribution of lucrative offices and assets. All the same, public law also came into play, for example, to fix wages for urban public works, limit interest on loans, collect taxes, guide the judicial process, and requisition soldiers, horses, and labor when needed.

In Rus, as in many other premodern societies, physical coercion or its threat enforced the collection of tribute, requisition of labor, and social differentiation. Force operated as well in the commercial and artisanal spheres, which were usually monopolized and restricted to select groups and individuals. Prevailing warrior values placed a rather high premium on defense of one's honor and a low premium on human life, while the small number of public officials forced individuals and families to fend for themselves.

The fundamental Rus political unit, the territorial principality, operated as rule under a prince and his senior retinue, whose informal joint council came to be known in later periods as the *duma*. At certain points down to the middle of the eleventh century, the prince (or grand prince) of Kiev was able to treat almost all of Rus as one megaprincipality, but this did not last. Individual princes strove to possess domains with their own courts and armies; towns aimed for greater autonomy and their own local or regional ascendancy; and internal development continuously led to new towns and new subprincipalities. Rus as a whole lacked the economic or administrative glue to fight these centrifugal tendencies.

High officials analogous to those of the kingdoms of other parts of Europe, such as swordbearer, palatine or steward, master of the horse or marshal, and chancellor or keeper of the seal, staffed the courts of the major princes. These people shared prestige with the princes' personal retinues, military commanders, urban mayors, and militia heads. Beneath them served a host of knights, *tiuns,* fine collectors, and other subalterns, all eager for a share of the spoils of power.

When the system within a given principality functioned properly, junior princes—some hoping to advance up the ladder to better posts, others founding local dynasties—deferred to the senior prince, who doubled as family patriarch and assigned them various towns. The ideal was set, according to the *Primary Chronicle,* by the political testament of Yaroslav I (978–1054) to his sons, cited at the head of this chapter. It reads further:

> Therefore remain in peace, brother heeding brother. The throne of Kiev I bequeath to my eldest son, your brother Izyaslav. Heed him as you have heeded me. . . . To Svyatoslav I give Chernigov, to Vesvolod Pereyaslavl, to Igor the city of Vladimir [in Volynia], and to Vyacheslav Smolensk.

Two modes of princely succession operated, the simplest being armed struggle among the strongest princes within a kinship circle. Besides this, a *rota* (extended oath) system took shape with the working out of Yaroslav's testament. Each surviving son obtained a throne, the eldest living brother always having the right to Kiev, and the others moving up a fluid ladder. Then the next generation would acquire the senior throne in a rational order among brothers and cousins. Sometimes it worked, and sometimes it did not. Quite often brothers, half-brothers, uncles, nephews, and cousins resorted to armed conflict, with the crucial participation of both the Kievans themselves and outsiders. The same uneasy operation of *rota* and armed struggle also functioned in most regional principalities, with frequent overlaps of family and political alliances across international borders with Qipchaks, Poles, Hungarians, and others. At times everyone else stood aside, as small princely retinues battled each other for a throne—the outcome, like a medieval judicial duel, seen as God's will.

Alongside the princes and their personal dependents stood the nearly sovereign city-state structures of the major towns under their mayors, militia commanders, and citizen assemblies. Owing to the mixed picture in the Rus chronicles, historians still disagree regarding who had the upper hand, the princes or the major towns and their boyars. A few historians have used the Classical Greek categories, arguing that in this epoch Rus government was a mixed polity with monarchial (princely), aristocratic (boyar), and democratic (urban-assembly) elements.

Kiev was acknowledged as the "Rus Metropolis," or mother city. As a token of subordination, Novgorod owed a substantial traditional tribute to Kiev, and later, when Rus had competing capitals, half of it to Kiev and half to northern Vladimir. Major cities looked upon the smaller or newer towns in their regions as suburbs with limited rights. Both Kiev and Novgorod had several substantial suburbs and sometimes invited their representatives to important deliberations. Haughty elites of older towns could be fiercely jealous of successful new ones and their common-origin leadership. "Our slave stone-cutters" is what the Rostov, Suzdal, and Murom boyars called the men of northern Vladimir and Pereyaslavl in 1175.

In the course of the 1100s only Novgorod freed itself fully from the domination of a single line of long-reigning princes. After a citizen uprising in 1136 to secure exclusive urban sovereignty over the tributary rural people, most princes lasted only a year or two there. Elsewhere leading townsmen were sometimes involved in questions of war, peace, relations with the steppe, commerce, and princely succession.

Halych and Vladimir-Suzdal had the equivalent of general assemblies at several junctures in the late twelfth and early thirteenth centuries. Urban and local power notwithstanding, the princes, with their allies, personal armies, and administrators, could make life miserable for the townsmen in various ways: by imposing a salt monopoly or massive fines, by massacring or mutilating political opponents, or by pillaging the insubordinate. Kiev itself was sacked twice by fellow Rus, in 1169 and 1204. Reciprocally, irate townsmen might expel, imprison, or even murder their prince. In 1211 the Halychans hanged three princes, who had massacred local nobles. Townsmen also used succession struggles to settle accounts with tyrannical officials and exact sworn promises from new princes to govern justly.

Starting as early as 1054, princes held infrequent congresses to determine policy and mediate disputes. "Why do we ruin the land of Rus by our continued strife against one another?," the *Primary Chronicle* reports the princes saying at a meeting at the Dnieper town of Lyubech in 1097. Bishops, abbots, senior princesses, and elder statesmen, as well as leading townsmen, tried to resolve interprincely conflicts, but this was not easy. Some princes preferred to trust their arms or guile and were loath to submit to what they considered to be the judgment of commoners. In 1217 two Ryazan princes invited their brother and five cousins to a conclave and murdered them all.

A POLITICAL CHRONICLE, 1015–1240

Behind the limited chronicle record of wars and rebellions, diplomacy and statesmanship, marriages and successions, perfidy and murder, a pattern of development emerges. The supreme prince personified in the early Vladimir I (r. 982–1015) is an adventurous, polygamous collector of personal allies and clients. He transforms into a Christian monarch with institutional legitimacy and territorial responsibilities. Boyars and townsmen acquire at least a share of real power. By concerted action the Rus usually attain the upper hand over the steppe nomads, but regional principalities and dynasties become a permanent fixture in the 1100s. Northern Vladimir emerges as a second capital, while Novgorod enjoys singular success as a city-state. And through all of this Rus survives as a quasi-confederated realm into the 1230s. A brief examination of the careers of some major princes after Vladimir I provides us with illustrations of these developments as well as the nearly chronic internecine strife.

Under the Ascendancy of Kiev

The resoundingly successful life and reign of Vladimir ended in 1015, at the time of an unexplained Novgorodian revolt under his own son Yaroslav, later known as "the Wise" (d. 1054). A new bout of fratricide ensued, as Yaroslav's half-brother Svyatoslav "the Accursed" (ca. 978–1019) killed three other half-brothers and seized Kiev. Despite Polish help, however, Svyatoslav lost out to Yaroslav, who took the Kievan throne in 1019. He in turn faced Mstislav of Tmutorokan and Chernigov (d. 1036), who, according to the *Primary Chronicle,* slew a Circassian local prince following an epic, winner-take-all wrestling bout. Mstislav then aimed for supreme power, using Khazars, Circassians, and Severian Slavs to fill his ranks. He was checked in 1024, however, in a bloody, indecisive encounter by Yaroslav with his Novgorodians and fresh Varangian mercenaries. But by matching these Vikings on the battlefield, the Severians showed that Slavic Rus had come into its own, militarily speaking.

Relative domestic peace prevailed from 1026 to 1054. First came a ten-year dyarchy (two-man rule), when Mstislav converted Chernigov into a competitive rival of Yaroslav's Kiev. After Mstislav's death, Yaroslav, as sole senior ruler, restored Kiev's preeminence. In 1043 he launched the last great Rus expedition against Constantinople. But Yaroslav is less known for his military adventures than for his building projects; his patronage of learning; the marriages with French, Byzantine, and other royalty he contracted for his children; and his attempt to stabilize the succession. The initiation of Rus written law, both the earliest version of *Rus Justice* and the first detailed church code, to be discussed in the next chapter, "Kievan Rus: Christian Civilization, 988–1240," are associated with his name. And his solemn instructions to his younger sons to obey the eldest set the ideal model for princes, which was, unfortunately, frequently violated.

Yaroslav's three eldest surviving sons—Izyaslav (1024–1078), Svyatoslav (1027–1076), and Vsevolod (1030–1093)—tried to maintain a princely triumvirate from the southern cluster of Kiev, Chernigov, and Pereyaslavl, respectively. For fourteen years they barely fended off relatives excluded from these and other prizes, and they did even less well against the steppe nomads. At one point the enraged Kievans even placed the imprisoned Prince Vseslav of Polotsk (d. 1101) on their throne to lead them against the Qipchaks. (Vseslav had been jailed for looting Novgorod to build up his dynastic principality in present Belarus.) Finally in 1073 the three princes fell out among themselves. At that point Svyatoslav seized Kiev and ruled until he died in 1076. Izyaslav returned but was killed two years later fighting Svyatoslav's sons. Genuine unity among the descendants of Yaroslav the Wise never returned, though some leading princes still respected the *rota* system.

Chief among the redoubtable losers in contests for major thrones stands Svyatoslav's son Oleg (d. 1115), a constant thorn in the side of the surviving triumvir Vsevolod and his renowned son Vladimir Monomakh. Oleg's career reveals the dangers and possibilities that awaited ambitious middle-level Rus princes as more sublineages were established. Repeatedly excluded from his father's Chernigov, in 1078–1079 Oleg used Tmutorokan as a launching pad against fellow Rus and enlisted treacherous Qipchak allies. Captured by Khazars and shipped to the Byzantines, who exiled him further to the Isle of Rhodes, he married a Greek, returned in 1083 to Tmutorokan as its Byzantine governor, and slaughtered his Khazar enemies. Ten years later he again employed Qipchak troops in a bid to gain Chernigov but settled for control of that region's pagan Slavs. Subsequently maligned as "Son of Infamy" for being the first Rus prince to employ Qipchaks in a civil war, he was posthumously successful. His more politic brother Davyd (d. 1123) reestablished

Chernigov as the family patrimony and mighty regional principality and was locally canonized as an ideal ruler and saint. Oleg's direct line included five princes of Kiev and, later on, several eminent Russian families.

Vladimir II Monomakh (ca. 1060–1125), the son of the third triumvir Vsevolod and a Byzantine princess, revealed statesmanlike qualities and the results of sound political leadership in his era. A self-advertised indefatigable warrior-diplomat, hunter, family man, and model Christian, he respected the seniority of his older cousin Svyatopolk Izyaslavich (1050–1113). In dealing with the Qipchaks, Monomakh was a ruthless master of coalition warfare and diplomacy and was as responsible as anyone else for pacifying them by the year 1111. Intervening effectively during the Kiev uprising of 1113 (which followed Svyatopolk's death), Monomakh instituted a limitation on interest payments and easily occupied the Kievan throne for the remainder of his life. He was succeeded by his two oldest surviving sons: first Mstislav the Great (1076–1132), also a grandson of the last Anglo-Saxon King of England, and then Yaropolk (1082–1139). Mstislav's sons founded the powerful regional dynasties of Vladimir-in-Volynia (Volhynia) and Smolensk, but during Yaropolk's reign in Kiev, Novgorod secured more control over its princes—a sure sign of the permanent eclipse of Kiev's earlier authority.

A Century of Regional Balance

Starting in 1139, the possession of the Kievan throne rotated among several regional dynasties—mainly those of Smolensk (almost half of the time until 1240) in the center and Chernigov to the east. Meanwhile, Monomakh's aspiring junior son Yuri Dolgoruky ("Long-Arm") of Rostov and Suzdal expanded his ring of fortress towns, including Moscow, first mentioned in a chronicle under the year 1147. His lasting legacy was the growth of the Suzdal land and the dynasty he founded there, rather than his short, hated reign in Kiev (1155–1157). He died there, perhaps from poisoning, after a banquet hosted by a tax collector, and the Kievans quickly massacred his Suzdalian troops and officials and pillaged his two armed camps outside the city.

By this time his brilliant eldest surviving son, Andrei Bogolyubsky (1111?–1175), a half-Qipchak energetic warrior and builder who was sensitive to the dislike of northerners in the Rus south, abandoned his father and returned home. Bypassing the senior towns Rostov and Suzdal, he built up northern Vladimir to be a rival capital to Kiev and converted the nearby village of Bogolyubovo into a private palace complex—hence his sobriquet. While lavishly supporting the local church, Andrei broke all precedent by expelling his younger half-brothers from his entire principality and simultaneously "attempting to be the monarch of all Rus" from the north. To chase away a Volynian rival, Andrei sent the coalition army that sacked Kiev in 1169 and had his younger brother Gleb (d. 1172) enthroned there. Subsequently, however, Andrei overreached himself, dispatching further expeditions against Novgorod, the Volga Bulgars, and Kiev again, of which only the second succeeded. Finally his senior retinue and court officials, fearing for their own lives at his hand, surprised him in his sleep and butchered this quasi-precursor, in style and

0 100 200 Km.
0 100 200 Mi.
White Sea
DEPENDENCIES OF NOVGOROD
FINNS
Beloozero
Ladoga
Neva
NOVGOROD
Novgorod
Revel
Yurev/ Dorpat
Pskov
Izborsk
Volkhov
Torzhok
VLADIMIR - SUZDAL
VOLGA BULGARS
Yaroslavl
Rostov
Pereyaslavl
Suzdal
Nizhny Novgorod
Volga
Bulgar
Vladimir
Bogolyubovo
Murom
Moscow
Toropets
Riga
Dvina
Baltic Sea
Polotsk
SMOLENSK
LITHUANIANS
Vitebsk
Smolensk
Oka
Ryazan
MUROM-RYAZAN
Kovno
POLOTSK
Minsk
Grodno
CHERNIGOV
Novgorod-Seversk
Kursk
Vistula
TUROV
Pinsk
Turov
POLAND
Lyubech
Chernigov
VOLYNIA
Ovruch
KIEV
Vladimir
Lutsk
Kiev
Belgorod
PEREYASLAVL
Pereyaslavl
Cracow
Kanev
Dnieper
QIPCHAKS (CUMANS OR POLOVTSY)
Peremyshl
HALYCH (GALICIA)
Halych/Galich
Don
Dniester
QIPCHAKS (CUMANS OR POLOVTSY)
CARPATHIANS
HUNGARY
Sudak
Black Sea
BYZANTINE EMPIRE
Constantinople

Rus ca. 1225.

Prince Andrei Bogolyubsky and the post-assassination popular uprising and pillaging of the Bogolyubovo Palace Elite, 1175. On the left is a modern reconstruction by the Soviet-era forensic sculptor M.M. Gerasimov of the half-Qipchak Andrei Bogolyubsky from his skull. (Left) Istorii a SSSR s drevneishikh vermen d. nashikh dnei, *Ser 1, vol. 1, Moscow, 1996. Academy of Science, St. Petersburg, Russia/Erich Lessing/Art Resource, NY.*

policy, of some Muscovite autocrats. The chronicles of the time treated him as a semitragic figure, an object lesson against unreasoned ambition.

A thousand miles to the southwest of Bogolyubovo, and much closer to Constantinople, lay Halych, the Dniester River seat of another bright warrior who overreached himself—Andrei's brother-in-law Yaroslav (r. 1153–1187). Likewise the son of an enterprising regional potentate, Yaroslav, "who knew many languages," similarly expanded and adorned his capital, excluded relatives and other competitors from any share of his principality, and influenced the succession in Kiev. His personal life, however, outraged the local boyars, who brazenly burned his commoner concubine as a witch and later poisoned his son by her in favor of the legitimate successor. Accordingly, the Halych grandees acquired a collective reputation for treacherous willfulness.

The immediate political prize in the Rus west fell to Roman of Volynia (d. 1205). Wickedly immortalized in a proverb for "enslaving [captive] Lithuanians to plow his fields," he illustrated the instabilities of the Rus political system and the precariousness of political marriages. This restless great-grandson of Monomakh seized the vacant throne of neighboring Halych in 1199, liquidated his major opponents there, and in 1204 forced both his wife and her father, Prince Ryurik of Kiev, to enter cloisters. Immediately taking over Kiev as well, Roman intervened forcefully in Poland, where he was finally ambushed and killed. The upshot was the return of Ryurik (d. 1212) to the Kievan throne but prolonged instability in Halych.

Meanwhile Vladimir-Suzdal was enjoying a period of relative peace under Andrei Bogolyubsky's younger half-brother Vsevolod, called "Big Nest" (due to his many children, 1154–1212), who had earlier been in exile in Byzantium. Following Andrei's murder in 1174 and a vicious class and civil war, Vsevolod took over Andrei's domains and exercised a looser seniority over the rest of Rus than the latter had done. Avoiding any adventurous meddling in the south, Vsevolod strengthened Vladimir's position as a separate grand principality in the north—westward into Novgorod, southward into Ryazan, and eastward toward Bulgar—thus foreshadowing the thrust of Moscow's power under his descendants a century and a half later. At the time of his death, however, Novgorod had slipped from his orbit, and his two chief cities, Vladimir and Rostov, were at loggerheads. A war of succession erupted among his sons in 1214–1216. Vladimir remained the senior city, but the principle of territorial division took firm root in this core region of the future Russia and would last for three centuries.

We can end this narrative of political history with Mstislav the Daring of Toropets (d. 1228), whose very junior position within the Smolensk dynasty precluded him from obtaining a major throne by normal means. Early in his career he served as invited prince of Novgorod, protecting its position on the Baltic and bolstering its autonomy. Around 1219, however, he abandoned Novgorod for faraway Halych and ruled there for about eight years, despite a turbulent relationship with the local boyars, who feared a treacherous massacre at the hands of his Qipchak auxiliaries. In 1223 he joined the uncoordinated coalition that advanced against the first Mongol expeditionary force to approach Rus, but for reasons unknown he was late for the disastrous decisive battle and returned unharmed. On the eve of his death, he tried to cede Halych to the neighboring king of Hungary in return for some southern border districts, but the Halychans themselves expelled the Hungarian governor.

Mstislav's intrepid career and pathetic personal finale symbolize the passing of what has been considered by many specialists the Kievan order. Almost all of the eminent Rus princes of the 1230s either perished at the hands of the Mongols during 1237–1245 or ended up as their subordinates. Thus ended the freewheeling, heroic era of Rus domestic politics.

THE OUTSIDE WORLD

The old adage that foreign policy is an extension of domestic politics into the international arena certainly held true for Rus and the neighboring realms, themselves also being conglomerates of smaller sovereignties. In this world of competing tributary networks, multiple loyalties, and fluid borders, rulers made individual or family alliances with foreign counterparts. A striking anomaly is that while the population and production of Rus grew dramatically, simultaneous developments in Europe and Central Asia meant that by 1200 Rus was more vulnerable to encroachments from the West and then invasion from the East than in 1000.

Byzantium

The religious connection, to be discussed in more detail in the next chapter, made relations with Byzantium unique, since the other Christian neighbors of Rus were Roman Catholic. Some time between 988 and 1037 the territories of Rus became a metropolitan archdiocese of the Orthodox patriarchate of Constantinople. Consequently, the Rus princes and cities were bound by canon law and custom to accept ecclesiastical subordination, pray for the emperor and the patriarch, and make fiscal contributions to the Byzantine (Greek) Church—itself a virtual branch of the Byzantine state. The Rus respected this arrangement and called Constantinople *Tsargrad* ("The Emperor's City"). Only two Rus clerics during the Kievan period became metropolitan (senior archbishop) of their church, and neither for very long. All the others were Greeks. Nevertheless, and probably due to services performed by the Greeks and the prestige Rus obtained from joining the Christian world, little ecclesiastical friction ensued. In the sphere of practical relations, both sides seem to have ignored the implications of Byzantium's claim to universal empire, especially with regard to Orthodox Christians. Rus did vie with Byzantium for Tmutorokan and its strategic hinterland until the Qipchaks secured control there in the late eleventh century. Subsequently Rus and Byzantium became peaceful neighbors in the lower Dniester and Danube regions on Halych's steppe frontier. In the 1100s, refugee Rus princes manned some of Byzantium's lower Danubian fortresses, while Halych served as a place of honorable exile for disgraced Byzantine royalty.

As of 1204 a new situation held in the Black Sea. Venetians seized control of Constantinople from their Byzantine debtors during the Fourth Crusade and opened the Black Sea to Italian commerce. As a result, the Byzantine authorities (relocated further east in Nicea during 1204–1261) had to maintain Rus as a source of financial and political support for regaining their sacred capital city. Meanwhile Muslim Seljuk Turks, who possessed much of present Turkey, attempted to spread their influence northward across the water to the Qipchak-controlled northern coast of the Black Sea.

Sedentary Neighbors

One can go counterclockwise around a semicircle from northeast to southwest and chart the competition between the Rus principalities and the neighboring states. To the northeast, starting in the 1160s, Vladimir-Suzdal contended with Bulgar for control of the pagan eastern Finno-Ugrian peoples. These campaigns thus had an anti-Muslim crusading flavor and climaxed with the foundation of Nizhny Novgorod in 1223. Nevertheless, Rus trade with Bulgar was lively. In addition, the Suzdalians forged dynastic connections across the Qipchak-controlled steppe with states in the Caucasus region.

To the northwest a commercially dynamic Novgorod vied with Sweden. A devastating Novgorodian-Karelian raid on Sweden's old capital of Sigtuna in 1187 could not prevent the Swedish takeover of southern Finland. As a defensive measure, the Novgorodians baptized the Karelian Finnish elite into the Orthodox Church. The present Russian-Finnish border is close to the lines established by Novgorod and Sweden in the late twelfth century.

By this time, along the eastern Baltic coast (present-day Estonia and Latvia), Novgorod, its dependency Pskov, and Polotsk faced the Swedes, the Danes, German merchants and armed Roman Catholic missionaries, and eventually the crusading German monks known as Teutonic Knights. The establishment of the city of

Riga by German merchants and missionaries near the mouth of the western Dvina in 1202, however, signaled increased commercial opportunities for the Rus, as well as the onset of the German presence in this region, which would last in several forms until 1945. Powerful pagan Lithuanian tribes also emerged in the late 1100s, raiding Rus and other neighboring territories.

To the far west, Poles and Rus fought, intermarried, and intervened in each other's domestic affairs and borderlands. A little farther south, Halych and Hungary competed for control of the eastern Carpathian Mountains, where the population would eventually become mainly Rus. In the late 1100s and early 1200s, however, while Volynia more or less held its own against Poland, Hungary made a serious if unsuccessful bid to annex Halych. These struggles did not have much of a national character at the time, but their outcome helped determine Poland's present borders with Belarus and Ukraine.

Across the Porous Steppe Frontier

Relations with the neighboring steppe peoples followed certain patterns and became generally the most important of all for the Rus once the Kievan realm was established and absorbed some steppe elements. The nomadic herders' way of life fostered ruthless competition for grazing lands and water resources, both among steppe peoples themselves and against the agriculturalists of the wooded steppe. Political fragmentation on both sides fostered partial alliances across frontiers, so that groups of Rus and nomads often combined as allies in their respective domestic struggles. In addition, various individuals or groups of nomadic origin always lived among the Rus, just as numbers of Rus dwelled among the nomads. It was recorded that a polygamous Qipchak who had guarded a captive Rus monk later had his entire family baptized and became a monk himself. Only rarely do the chronicles indicate sharp battle lines between the Rus and one of the steppe peoples. Both Rus and nomads, moreover, had goods to trade with the other, and all participants benefited from open trade routes. Nevertheless, a standing temptation for all armed groups was to raid someone else in search of horses, cattle, other booty, and marketable captives.

Some of the most important milestones of Rus history are connected with steppe politics. As noted earlier, the Varangians established themselves in Kiev around the time the Pechenegs first broke through the Khazar defenses and menaced trade routes. As Kiev developed, Pechenegs became a major threat until Vladimir established the defensive line in the south. Around 1040, as a result of demographic and military upheavals in Central Asia, Oghuz or Torks took over much of the Black Sea steppe but do not seem to have caused Rus any harm. An unexplained, devastating attack on them in 1060 by the Rus triumvirs (Izyaslav and his brothers Svyatoslav and Vsevolod), however, had unforeseen consequences, since the more formidable Qipchaks followed the Torks into the Black Sea steppe.

The first Qipchak invasion of Rus in 1055, though contained and settled by negotiation, turned out to be the advent of a new era of Rus-steppe relations, for the loosely interconnected grid of Qipchak clans survived as the dominant steppe peoples from the Aral Sea to the lower Danube and from the Lower Volga to the north Caucasus until the Mongol conquest. A certain mystery surrounds these nomads, since the combined Rus, European, Byzantine, and Muslim sources show the Qipchaks east of the Volga and those called Polovtsy or Cumans to the west as the same family of peoples, yet we have little evidence of direct political connections between the two branches. In any case, the principalities of Ryazan, Chernigov, (southern) Pereyaslavl, Kiev, and Halych all had Qipchak frontiers, which together stretched about a thousand miles.

Our picture of Rus-Qipchak connections is incomplete—we do not know the specific causes and goals of the various wars—but the Rus chronicles give us the following highlights. The first and most serious period of Qipchak invasions and raids peaked in the 1080s and 1090s. It was then that a chronicler created a lasting, one-sided, barbaric, apocalyptic literary image of them, as "unclean peoples," descendants of Ishmael, "who shall come forth at the end of the world." At the same time, the Chernigov princes proved singularly adept in forging alliances with their Qipchak counterparts. Eventually Vladimir Monomakh's coalition attacked their home base in the upper Donets and so ferociously cowed them into making peace that Qipchak mothers reportedly later used his name to frighten their children. Meanwhile the Rus agreed that the string of southern fortress districts the Kiev princes had established would be held by members of the major princely subdynasties to protect the capital and the Dnieper trade.

Qipchak raiding resumed in the 1150s and became a serious menace in the 1170s and 1180s, possibly connected to the brutal sharpening of Central Asian rivalries then and resultant instability on the steppe. Among other things, in 1184 a Muslim engineer provided the attacking Qipchaks, under the renowned ("godless and thrice-cursed," according to the Rus) prince Konchak, with an incendiary artillery machine having the pull force of fifty or so archers. But the Qipchaks did not gain the upper hand. Rather, interpenetration of Rus and Qipchak prevailed. The next year Konchak overwhelmed the retaliatory expeditionary force of Igor of Novgorod-Seversk (part of Chernigov), but then let him escape without a ransom and in a few years forged a marriage alliance with his son. Konchak also named one of his sons Yuri—a sign of strong ties to Rus. For a while other Rus and their Turkic Black Hat border confederates went on the attack, raiding and looting Qipchaks, but the southern Rus then resumed fighting each other instead.

The early 1200s witnessed rather amicable Rus-Qipchak relations. Around 1221 or 1226 a joint army under Rus leadership came to the relief of the Qipchak-protected Black Sea port of Sudak against a Seljuk Turk seaborne expedition. In 1223, when the Mongols appeared on the Black Sea steppe and defeated Yuri Konchakovich's contingent of Qipchaks, the senior Qipchak prince Basty accepted baptism, as he sounded the alarm leading to a general Rus mobilization.

Seventeen years later, the Kievan period of Rus history would come to a decisive end at the hands of these very same Mongols. Some scholars have credited the fall of Kiev to what are fanciful and unprovable catastrophic economic consequences of

Qipchak control of the Black Sea steppe. Others have contended that the normal interprincely rivalries made Rus too vulnerable to outside invasion. But neither of these explanations takes into account the simple fact that the thirteenth-century Mongols overpowered and defeated everyone in their way. Before we turn to this problem, however, we shall examine the culture that developed in the Kievan period and enabled the Rus to preserve and strengthen their identity under Mongol domination.

CHAPTER 3

Kievan Rus: Christian Civilization, 988–1240

The grace of faith has spread all over the earth, and it has reached our nation, Rus.
—Ilarion of Kiev, *Sermon on Law and Grace*, ca. 1047–1049

Russia has experienced three traumatic cultural revolutions in its history. The first of these began with the conversion of the Rus elite and townsmen and then gradually much of the realm to Orthodox Christianity. Tsar Peter the Great initiated the second in 1698 with his radical reforms, and Lenin and the Bolshevik Revolution the third in 1917 by introducing the Soviet experiment. A fourth has been occurring since about 1985 with the breakdown of the Soviet system. In this chapter, we consider the nature and effects of the first of these great transformations.

When Vladimir I, his comrades, counselors, and supporters converted to Eastern Orthodox Christianity, they made one of those rare, fateful choices that determines the cultural direction of a large society for centuries. By adopting Christianity, the Rus accepted and then adapted in their own way a foreign, yet cosmopolitan intellectual and ethical framework that had developed over several millennia and sank deep roots in diverse societies. The following discussion of the Christian civilization of Kievan Rus—its religion, art, architecture, and literature—as they flourished within a larger Byzantine framework, is therefore also an introduction to a cornerstone of Russian, Ukrainian, and Belarusian identity, which unites them. Despite the important differences from Catholics or Protestants, the eastern Slavic nations see themselves today as European not only because of language and race, but also because of their Christian heritage. Of course Rus culture after the conversion entailed more than religion. Human society is too complex and variegated not to allow for that, but the Slavic form of Orthodox Christianity affected popular life and created the original high culture of Rus.

SLAVIC ORTHODOXY

The new religion of Rus, one of the Slavic branches of Eastern (Greek) Orthodoxy, fell under the authority of the Byzantine Church. By becoming Orthodox, Rus also joined the larger family of competitive and divided monotheistic religions: Judaism, Islam, and Christianity. Together they were entrenched by the year 900 from Ireland in Europe's far west all the way to eastern Persia, and they shared a common Greco-Roman-Middle Eastern intellectual heritage. However, the Eastern Orthodox and Roman Catholics were slowly separating from each other over major jurisdictional and minor theological issues.

Foundations of Medieval Christianity

Taken literally, Christianity, like Islam and Judaism, holds that the one almighty God created the world and humanity less than eight thousand years ago, that God predetermines and foresees everything, but that humans nonetheless have free will to believe and behave correctly. Accordingly, God has given human beings a succession of ritual, ethical, and social commandments, and he desires repentance with self-correction—including charity, respect for public order, and a weekly day of rest with special prayer services. These positive actions allow God to act within the faithful believer. At the end of the world, as conceived by these monotheisms, a final judgment of all the living and the dead shall occur, with paradise as the reward for those deemed righteous and hell for the others.

Christianity, like Islam, is indifferent to ethnicity but diverges from both the other monotheisms in several crucial ways. The central figure of Jesus *Christ* ("Messiah" or "Anointed") differs from the superprophets and lawgivers Moses and Mohammed. Christ is the eternal God himself and his Word, yet incarnated as his human son, and born in discrete time to the Virgin Mary—she herself having been physically impregnated by God's spirit. From this belief derives the doctrine of the Trinity, that God has three *persons* (or faces), Father, Son/Word, and Spirit, the Son possessing two equal natures—divine and human. Despite controversy over the nature of the Trinity and Christ, these doctrines became enshrined in liturgies (church services) and creeds (statements of faith), as stipulated by the seven ecumenical councils held from 325 to 787 C.E., and they defined Orthodoxy. From earliest times, using the Psalms of the Old Testament, Christians individually and collectively prayed directly to the ancient God of Israel and simultaneously invoked him as a Holy Trinity and as the God-man Christ, who had established the New Testament.

Both the Eastern and Western (Latin-liturgy, Roman) Churches have sacraments. Baptism cleanses the newborn of the "original sin" of the first man and the newly converted of their previous transgressions. Periodic confession, combined with penance, expiates sins. At communion, following confession, the faithful partake of consecrated bread and wine—held to be at that moment Christ's body and blood, as recorded in the New Testament at the Last Supper on the eve of his universally redemptive crucifixion.

To administer the sacraments, the Eastern and Western Churches maintain orders of consecrated priests, and, to supervise the priests and their parishes, a hierarchical network of bishops, archbishops, and metropolitans leading up to a patriarch, pope, or analogous senior prelate. Alongside this secular clergy, who serve laypeople, functions a regular (rule-bound) clergy—communities of monks

Section of the lamentation of the Virgin over the Crucified Christ, fresco from the Pskov Mirozhsky Monastery Cathedral of the Transfiguration, 12th century. The style is very close to contemporary Byzantine and pre-Early Renaissance European painting. *Yamshchikov, Pskov.* Art Treasures and Archaeological Monuments 12–17th c., *Leningrad, 1978 pl. 20.*

and nuns who take vows of poverty, chastity, and obedience. Early on, spokesmen for monasticism claimed that their lifestyle was "angelic," the highest form of spirituality and of discipleship to Christ.

The medieval Christian churches possessed two other striking features: saints' cults (female and male) and widespread use of holy objects and iconography (depictions of the sacred). These still play an important role among numerous believers, who hold that saints can intercede with God on humanity's behalf. From about 750 to 850 the Byzantine Church withstood and prevailed over a vicious, internal challenge from iconoclasts—opponents of specific images or any veneration of them. The victorious mainstream Orthodox held that prayers directed toward icons and other hallowed things, such as crucifixes, actually went through them to God or a saint. By around the year 1000, the Virgin Mary, termed Mother of God (in Slavic, *Bogoroditsa*), had become the most venerated saint. Some analysts see here a return or continuation in Christian form of ancient Great Goddess cults.

From the start Christianity shared certain features with pagan religions. The favorite patron saints of health, crops, herds, crafts, and travel functionally replaced popular goddesses and gods. Christian festivals, like their Jewish predecessors, were rooted in natural cycles and celebrations of fertility. Churchmen reckoned liturgical time, that is, the scheduling of services, on the basis of seasonal daylight variants, not the regularity of the mechanical clock. In virtually everybody's mind, until the rise of modern science, the heavens were close and their interaction with Earth constant. Nature appeared as a formidable mystery. Despite clerical hostility, many people believed that alchemists, magicians, and sorcerers could influence nature, and astrologers and folk seers could gaze into the future.

The Bulgarian Achievement

Credit for the creation of Slavic Orthodoxy rests mainly with two Greek missionaries and a Bulgarian translation enterprise of the 860s–960s, a time of competitive missionary activity in east-central and southeastern Europe. In 862–863, two brothers from the Greek port of Thessaloniki—Cyril (Constantine the Philosopher) and Methodius—introduced a Slavic liturgy in Czech Moravia. A few years later the Bulgarian khan or tsar Boris I (r. 852–888) converted his realm under the Byzantine Church. Roman Catholic German authorities from the revived empire in the West (often termed Holy Roman Empire) soon closed down the Moravian mission and forced the Czechs to remain within the Latin-liturgy orbit. However, under Tsar Boris and his son Symeon the Wise (r. 893–927), Bulgaria turned into a dynamic and productive center of Slavic Orthodox Christian culture. The Greek-based *Cyrillic* alphabet eventually eclipsed the alternative, Syrian-based *Glagolitic* script (which one Cyril actually devised remains uncertain) and became the standard for the new Slavic Orthodoxy. As "Apostles to the Slavs," Sts. Cyril and Methodius became cultural heroes.

It is difficult to exaggerate the importance of the work performed by a rather small number of Bulgarian and other scholars, when they put the basic body of Greek Orthodox literature into an artificially designed literary dialect accessible to all Slavs. These translations included all the genres needed by a complex and busy church. Scriptural texts provided an authentic foundation—not quite the complete anthology that we call the Bible, but all of the New Testament and most of the Old, including the all-important Psalms, which many pious souls committed to memory. The collections of saints' lives and prayers were read daily in the monasteries and major churches. Bishops, abbots, monks, and father-confessors needed other handbooks: legal digests, cloister rules, spiritual guides, and penitentials (manuals for the expiation of sins). To compose or deliver sermons they required the models provided by or attributed to earlier Christian rhetoricians and poets. For intellectual leadership and fending off competitors and dissidents, the clergy needed authoritative theological tracts.

Most crucial of all, liturgical books contained and coordinated the various types of services (a normal day could have six or more) and three different calendar cycles. This was no mean feat. Each day of the week had its precise requirements. The fixed, solar-calendar holidays such as Christmas had specific sets of rituals, as did the movable, lunar-calendar festivals from the onset of Lent through Whitsunday (Pentecost).*

The translators did their job well. By the time the Rus leadership decided to convert, Bulgaria's Slavic Orthodoxy presented a ready-made package in a written language sufficiently flexible to be used as such or modified to suit local dialects. It

*These calculations were based on the original replacement of the lunar-calculated Jewish Passover by Easter, even as the Christians were using the (pagan) Roman solar calendar to calculate birth and death dates for the other holidays. In the 300s C.E., the Jewish and Christian lunar calendars diverged, so that the Easter and Passover seasons no longer coincided. The later divergence of festive days among Eastern and Western Christians is due to calendar reforms initiated by Roman Catholics in the late 1500s.

became the basis of a religious and alphabetic civilization zone, eventually stretching from the Serb lands across Bulgaria and (before modern times) non-Slavic Romania, to present Ukraine, up to Belarus and European Russia, and finally across Siberia.

CONVERSION AND CONSOLIDATION

In the late 980s, the *Primary Chronicle* relates, Vladimir ordered the mass baptism of his Kiev subjects in the Dnieper River, demonstrably destroyed the pagan idols he had established a decade earlier, and warned that all who refused conversion would be his personal enemies. Mass baptisms and destruction of idols soon followed in Novgorod and, we assume, other major towns. Actually the conversion process may have started as early as the 860s, and, after Vladimir's baptism, still took several centuries to effect. It also abetted the subduing and undermining of the Slavic tribes by princely and urban authorities in the eleventh and twelfth centuries. From the start, except for the lingering of pagan customs, resistance to the new religion was limited chiefly to the intense rivalry of some Finno-Ugrian shamans in the north. Still, many questions concerning the conversion of Rus and the consolidation of Orthodoxy remain unanswerable.

Decisive Moves

The first Byzantine attempts to proselytize the Rus took place in the Black Sea region in the 860s, and Rus sources indicate that by 944 Christian Varangians had their own church in Kiev. Then came the conversion of Princess Olga some time during 946–957, her acceptance of a Byzantine rank, and her parallel diplomatic-religious flirtations with the German emperor in the 960s. Her baptismal name Helena, the revered mother of the first Christian Roman emperor Constantine I (288?–337), signaled an interest in converting more subjects. Her grandson Yaropolk (r. 972–980) took a Bulgarian Christian wife and also sent an embassy to

Finnic pagan shamans in Yaroslavl killing women accused of hoarding food during a famine; recorded under the year 1071. These women were likely accused of evil witchcraft according to community notions of the time. *Academy of Science, St. Petersburg, Russia.*

the Germans. So the initial pro-pagan policies of his murderer and successor Vladimir I may have been a counter to Christianity's rising appeal.

Our first chapter touched on the political and economic circumstances of the conversion to Orthodoxy. But there is more to this story. The *Primary Chronicle* offers a colorful description of the reported competitive religious missions to Kiev and Vladimir's subsequent dispatch of envoys to check out Islam in Volga Bulgar, Catholicism in Germany, and Eastern Orthodoxy in Constantinople. The practical reasons given for his choice of Orthodoxy included a drive for prestige, Orthodoxy's full acceptance of the drinking customs of northern, forest peoples, and appreciation of beauty in its fullest sensual scope. Judaism's humiliating diaspora (lack of a homeland) and Islam's prohibition of alcohol rendered both odious to Vladimir's triumphant Varangians and Slavs. "Drinking is the joy of the Rus," the chronicler has Vladimir exclaim. As for Christianity, at this time when East and West had not yet formally split, the Latin liturgy paled in comparison to what the Rus envoys experienced at that "heaven on earth," the magnificent St. Sophia Cathedral in Constantinople. Nevertheless, a few German sources and the murky record of Rus Church history before 1037 suggest that, starting in 859, Catholic missionaries, envoys, and allies played a larger religious role in early Rus than the Orthodox-inspired Rus chronicles recorded.

Recently some scholars have attempted to pinpoint the mass baptism in Kiev, placed by the chronicler on August 1, 988, as occurring a year or two later. But the first years of official Rus Christianity, including its leadership, the advent of the Slavic liturgy, and the spread of the new religion outside of Kiev, remain clouded in mystery. Among the established facts are that Vladimir dispatched a recorded six thousand Varangians to help the Byzantine emperor Basil II in his civil war and obtained in return his imperial bride. It is also documented that Vladimir successfully besieged the Byzantine outpost of Cherson in the Tauride (Crimea) before his conversion and then brought back a Greek collaborator, the archpriest Anastasios, and some of the items needed for Kiev's lavish Tithe Church of the Mother-of-God, founded in 996. By 1015 bishoprics existed in at least Novgorod and two towns near Kiev, and probably also Kiev itself, where the head of the Rus Church likely resided.

Taking Root

Yaroslav I's eighteen years as sole senior prince (1036–1054) represented a new beginning for the Church of Kiev, if not for Rus Christianity. The Rus metropolitanate was firmly established in that city, the local St. Sophia Cathedral built, and the Slavic liturgy set firmly in place. Native monasticism also acquired prestige. The *Primary Chronicle* asserts that Yaroslav promoted translations, though no hard evidence exists of such work being done in Rus, and that he set up schools (for men only), which appears more likely, since Rus needed clerics and scribes. The earliest surviving Rus manuscript, the *Ostromir Gospel*, a 1056–1057 copy of an existing Slavic integration of the four gospels, stems from Yaroslav's original city, Novgorod. It reveals accomplished orthography and craftsmanship. Recent finds of

Novgorodian wooden tablets with several psalms indicate local Slavic literacy as early as the 1020s.

Rus Christianity took another giant stride forward with the reorganization of Kiev's Monastery of the Caves (*Pechersky*) under Yaroslav's son Izyaslav I (r. 1054–1068, 1069–1073, 1076–1078). Once more Byzantium provided the models, chiefly the well-ordered Studion Monastery inside Constantinople and the newer *Laura* (literally, "cave") of St. Athanasios at Mount Athos on the Greek coast. The latter combined the traditional, austere ascetic individualism of some of the early Christian monks, who lived as desert and cave hermits in Egypt and Judea (Palestine), with the settled monastery's equally traditional communalism, and with the liturgical order of Byzantium's great cathedrals.

Pechersky originated before 1051 as the locus of individual cave hermits outside of Kiev. Their future leader Antony (d. after 1069) chose the monastic name of the most famous early Egyptian desert recluse (Anthony the Great, d. 356). He visited Mount Athos in 1051, became a monk there, and soon returned to Kiev. Among his followers appeared a runaway youth from a military family, who defied his widowed mother and society's norms by refusing to train as a soldier. Joining Antony, the young man took the name Feodosy for the founder of the first communal monastery in Palestine (Theodosius the Coenobiarch, d. 529). Chosen by Antony's disciples to be their second formal superior, Feodosy relocated the community outside of the caves in 1062, constructed the necessary buildings, and adopted a version of the Studion Rule. But individualistic principles soon prevailed over communal ones, as the cloister became renowned for its heroically eccentric ascetics. Following the ancient monks' attempt to imitate Christ's self-sacrifice, several brothers relentlessly mortified their flesh. Isaaky, for example, a disciple of Antony, lived in a tiny cave for seven years without leaving it, wore a hair shirt covered with a dried goatskin, consumed a minimum of bread and water, and slept sitting up.

At the same time Pechersky served as a scriptorium and, informally, a writers' workshop, painting studio, liturgical music conservatory, and elite seminary matriculating qualified monks to be bishops and abbots throughout the land. As well as being the religious and cultural hub of Kievan Rus, the monastery operated a healing clinic and a soup kitchen. Antony and Feodosy became the first Rus clerics of any stamp to be sainted. Perhaps in an even more extreme form than in other European societies of the time, the monastic spirit of service and self-denial coexisted with the fusion of Christian, warrior, and mercantile values prevailing among laypeople.

Christianity's presence in Rus strengthened by the late eleventh and twelfth centuries, and every town of note possessed at least one major cathedral where the all-important liturgies were performed every day. In this manner God was properly honored daily throughout the land. (Both the Greek *orthodoksia* and the Slavic equivalent *pravoslavie* mean "correct glorification.") The originally wooden cathedrals soon gave way to stone edifices. Inside, the worshipers, amid mosaics, frescoes, icons, candles, and incense, engaged in prostrations, signs of the cross, supplications, and chanting—sometimes in Greek as well as Slavic. All of this created an aura of holiness, even heavenliness, unknown outside the church walls. As a chronicler wrote about Andrei Bogolyubsky's Dormition Cathedral in Vladimir, "All who saw it were unable to describe its extraordinary beauty, with gold, enamel, and every sort of gem." In the towns the senior clergy directed public ceremonies to welcome and honor political and religious dignitaries and try to ward off natural disasters or military defeat. "When the men of Vladimir [in 1176] saw their prince coming, they proceeded out with crosses and joy and honor." Earlier, claimed a local report, the Novgorodians had defeated the Suzdalians "with the power of the cross and the Holy Mother of God and the prayers of the pious bishop Ilya."

The Church blossomed into a powerful institution reaching well into communities, families, and individual life. The bishops' courts held jurisdiction over sex, marriage, family life, beliefs, rituals, and pure pagan holdovers. The Church code ascribed to Vladimir I specifically outlawed bride abduction, abortions, infanticide, and praying in oak groves. The handbooks of father-confessors instructed them to probe the most intimate details of their charges' personal lives, including dreams. Clerics ran the occasional welfare institutions that existed and, by law more than practice, supervised the medical profession. Accordingly, the Pechersky monastery healers were jealous of non-Orthodox physicians, such as Armenians, and represented them as perhaps skillful, but unable to obtain essential divine help. The bishops also had exclusive authority over the clergy and their families—Orthodox priests, unlike their Catholic counterparts as of 1075, being able, even required, to marry, but before their formal ordination. Orthodox bishops, though, were by custom celibate and always monks first. Episcopal authority extended as well to the other clerical employees and dependents and to all sorts of marginal people—wanderers, widows and orphans, the lame and the blind, and outcasts.

Signs of the power of Orthodoxy within Rus abounded by the twelfth century. Pilgrims visited the Holy Land, and distinct social groups had their own churches. Clerics accompanied armies deep into the steppe, performed services along the way, and treated campaigns against pagans as a holy enterprise. Responsible father-confessors pondered the application of canon law to Rus conditions and sought advice concerning the minutiae of daily living, especially the bodily functions. Accordingly, while avoiding the major sins such as murder, libel, hardheartedness, and blasphemy, the faithful also had to be sure not to take communion too soon after permitted sexual intercourse within marriage, not to have such relations too soon after menstruation ended, and so forth. Both priests and their wives were expected to live exemplary lives.

Pious people normally wished to be remembered in the fullest sense of the word—publicly memorialized on earth by the clergy and thus remembered to God on behalf of their souls. For this purpose those with the means founded and endowed churches and monasteries or set up special funds for requiems and prayer services. The secular law envisioned that if a man died without making a will, a portion of his estate would be set aside for such commemorations.

Memory of death was supposed to guide the living along the straight and narrow path to heaven, but here as in other domains everyday Orthodoxy sometimes fused with popular practices. At baptism a baby obtained a saint's name, a reminder of an ideal Christian life-script for a person to follow, while one's given name contained rich secular imagery. For example, Mstislav means "vengeful glory," and one so named might relate to the image of several earlier renowned Mstislavs. However, Prince Mstislav Davydovich of Smolensk (1193–1230) also bore the Christian name Fëdor (Theodore), for one of the most popular Roman soldier-martyrs, Theodore Stratelates. People established icon corners or shrines inside their homes to replace the old clan cults, while they continued to fear household spirits. On the productive level, they had priests bless fields before the sowing and also bless horses once a year.

Holy festivals and popular religious songs created fresh combinations of Christian saints and veneration of nature. "Take me, Moist Mother earth, take me to you," laments Mary as she mourns over Christ in an undated lament. On the canonical level, some transgressors paid a fine to their bishop in addition to undergoing spiritual penance, as if a sin were also a concrete offense against him or the heavenly lord. A dying person was expected to forgive wrongs suffered and ask for reciprocal forgiveness, but the culture assumed that one could pursue personal litigation at the last judgment. People also invoked divine powers to protect their contracts and wills. Sometimes brutal rituals accompanied warfare. The celebrated prince Vladimir Monomakh (1053–1125), advertised as a model Christian, bragged of killing captive Qipchak (Polovtsy) princes and casting them into the river at the battle site—as if making a victory sacrifice. The blessing of fields and the popular religious songs and agricultural festivals lasted down to modern times. The icon corner still persists among many faithful.

INTELLECTUAL CULTURE

The conversion of Rus conveyed a book culture. Along with it came a comprehensive view of the world that begged questions from the curious and a stimulus for literary creativity within the framework of established genres, as well as a need for practical writers. Like other such peoples undergoing conversion, the Rus not only borrowed from another culture selectively to meet their own interests and inclinations but also were restricted by it. The culture of *Slavia Orthodoxa,* as a ready-made whole from the confined world of the provincial Byzantine monastery, discouraged the dialogue among competing schools of thought found occasionally in the courts and academic centers of other lands. Such a narrow worldview suited Rus clerics for many generations. Imitation of high Christian rhetoric might be valued at Kiev's court and high pulpit, and the chance surviving letter of Metropolitan Klim (r. 1147–1155) shows a sharp-witted cleric venturing to show off his acumen and erudition in detailed scriptural exegesis (commentary). But he knew that he walked a thin line between permissible Classical literary allusions and outlawed pre-Christian philosophical speculation, which might have led to charges of heresy against him. The Novgorodian monk-choirmaster Kirik's 1134 brief and practical arithmetic tract on calendrical calculations represents the furthest any Rus at this time went in the realm of explicit scientific thinking. The early Rus writers, so far as we know, were sensitive to style, curious about geography, and historically imaginative. But in the philosophical, scientific, and related speculative spheres they remained intellectually silent.

Writer and Audience

For the Kievan period, the few very fine pieces among the small number of extant Rus works tantalize specialists. Metropolitans Ilarion (r. 1050–1054) and Klim, the only Rus clerics to head their church in the Kievan period, wrote skillfully—an indication that mastery of ecclesiastical rhetoric did carry weight in the Rus Church. In fact, Christian Rus provided a fair environment for native literary talent by the time of Yaroslav I (r. 1019–1054). Abundant livestock supplied membranes for parchment, the high-class paper of the time. Living traditions of oral poetry and folklore nurtured imaginations. Monasteries soon provided instruction and discipleship. Church Slavic conveyed biblical and Classical literary devices and thereby created a community of letters among those who "feasted to fulfillment on the sweetness of books," to quote Ilarion. As prevailing Byzantine literary doctrine dictated emulation of the proven masters, gifted Rus writers could acquire their craft simply from careful study of the abundant translations. But what were they to write?

The educated Christian Rus, as practical people, exercised their talents as needed. The obvious location for the able pen had to be the church and monastery, since extraordinary events called for special sermons and prayers. The Byzantine-style Easter Cycle sermons of Bishop Kirill of Turov (r. 1160s–1180s) show that audiences could appreciate a new crystallization of standard themes. The metaphor of a cyclical universal transfiguration, occasioned by Christ's self-sacrifice, soars when Kirill speaks of Easter: "Last Sunday earth became heaven, purified by God of demonic stain." Though rare in Rus, the process of establishing saints' cults, such as Feodosy Pechersky's or that of Boris and Gleb (Yaroslav I's murdered brothers), required a skilled wordsmith. For a saint's life served as an uplifting sermon, meant to be read in public as well as private. City-states and dynasties also profited from salutary histories and thus commissioned chronicles, which, though modeled in places on Byzantine originals, combine elaborate story telling and briefer entries of events in the manner of contemporary European annals. Thus arose the comprehensive *Primary Chronicle* (or *Tale of Bygone Years*), its colorful Kievan, Halych-Volhynian, and Vladimir-Suzdal continuations, and a separate, locally focused *Chronicle of Novgorod.* Accounts of pilgrimages, such as that by Abbot Daniil of Chernigov who visited the Holy Land in 1106–1107, enabled readers and listeners to participate vicariously in the perilous voyage. For "nobody can restrain his tears, when he gazes yearningly upon this land and these holy places where Christ walked for our deliverance."

Rus, like all literate societies, had some ambitious individuals served by self-promotion. This could take several forms: autobiography, for example, Prince Vladimir Monomakh's *Testament*; public dispute, as in Metropolitan Klim's theological exegesis; or cynical aphorisms. "Don't place your village near the prince's, for his steward is like a fire on a hornet's nest and his vassals are like sparks," states the semibitter *Supplication* of the shadowy Daniil the Exile, who served in Vladimir-Suzdal in the early 1200s. The lay poet, however, operated chiefly within the framework of the oral culture.

Forging Identity

Some of Kiev's best minds and writers turned to political sermon, hagiography (saints' lives), and history and in so doing created a lasting consciousness for the Rus and their Russian and Ukrainian descendants. The earliest and one of the best extant examples of Rus literature of any genre is Ilarion's three-part *Sermon on Law and Grace* (ca. 1047–1049), written when he was Yaroslav I's court preacher. Filled with well-crafted, sequenced contrasts, the sermon glorifies the enlightenment of Rus as the realization of the Hebrew prophets' universal vision. Ilarion continues with a panegyric (eulogy or honorific oration) to Vladimir I—"the likeness of the Great Constantine"—and concludes with a long prayer for the entire country. This piece constituted part of a larger Rus body of rhetoric devoted to the conversion of Rus and to its regal champions: Olga the initiator, Vladimir I the chief agent, Boris and Gleb the martyr-witnesses, and Yaroslav I the perfecter. In Ilarion's own words, "Now we are called Christians, no longer idolaters . . . in this land of Rus, which is known and renowned to the ends of the earth."

Following Ilarion came the Pechersky monk Nestor (ca. 1056–1113), a versatile historiographer. He initiated Rus formal hagiography with his *Lesson on the Life and Murder of the Blessed Passion-Sufferers Boris and Gleb* (ca. 1074–1077), whose violent, seemingly unprovoked deaths at the hands of their older half-brother Sviatopolk in 1015 led to the most important native cult in early Rus. Masonry churches to their honor went up in a dozen towns or so, and even the Rus community in Constantinople built one. The theme of royal martyrdom for the cause of the Christian principle of nonresistance to violence—partially inspired by the Slavic life of the Czech prince Vaclav (or Wenceslaus, d. 935)—became a favorite among devout Russians, for whom suffering in and of itself was considered a road to salvation. Some scholars use the Greek term *kenosis* (adj. *kenotic*)—emptying of oneself—to characterize this humble way of imitating Christ.

Nestor also composed the original *Life of Our Venerable Father Feodosy, Superior of Pechersky Monastery* (ca. 1083–1088) and helped to initiate the miracle-filled *Pechersky Monastery Paterikon* (or *Book of the Fathers*, 1073–1257), both based on Greek prototypes. According to tradition Nestor also figured as one of the authors of the multilayered *Primary Chronicle*, produced in stages in Pechersky Monastery from about 1073 to 1113. Together these works of Ilarion, Nestor, and their colleagues created a sacred history of Rus—its dynasty, church, holy men and women, and Christian citizens—in which the Greek metropolitans hardly figure.

In the *Primary Chronicle*, the mythical past of Rus commences with the biblical origins of nations and the rise of Christianity and follows with a fanciful legend about the Apostle Andrew visiting the site of Kiev, predicting its glory and planting a cross there. "See ye these hills?" he says to his disciples. "On these hills the grace of God shall shine, and there shall be a great city, where God will build many churches." After moving on to Novgorod and marveling at the local heated bathhouses, Andrew passes through Varangian territory—all as if to legitimize Rus as an ancient home of the true faith. An account of one of Vladimir Monomakh's campaigns has defeated Qipchaks attesting to angels aiding the Rus—a motif hearkening back to the pagan substrata of the Old Testament. Down to today, the standard grand narratives of both Russian and Ukrainian history have derived their notions of origin and destiny from the *Primary Chronicle*, which also served as the basis of medieval Rus's regional chronicles.

Popular Genres and Outlooks

The chronicle tales do not exhaust the storehouse of imaginative Rus letters. The Rus produced their own poetic and dramatic versions of motifs from the Apocrypha—the supplementary or alternative biblical books. Favorite subjects included the imprisonment of the righteous in hell prior to Christ's descent and their release, and the Mother of God lightening the gruesome tortures of the sinful Christian souls in hell. Popular oral traditions also exhibited a fresh willingness to combine epic and hagiographic motifs. In one such work, Boris and Gleb became partially responsible for their own deaths by failing to heed their mother's warning to avoid their brother Svyatopolk. But some of these stories may be later creations on earlier themes.

History, literature, and legend also meet in the *bylyny* or *staryny*, the Russian cycles of oral poetry about historical and semimythical figures, recorded in the nineteenth century and of uncertain date. Originating perhaps as a form of court entertainment, the *bylyny* survived only in popular form. The favorite heroes include Vladimir I's Novgorodian uncle Dobrynya, the priest's son Alyosha Popovich from the time of Vladimir Monomakh, and Ilya of Murom of peasant stock. Their lives and adventures fit the general patterns of heroic folklore, with perilous journeys, magical rivers, ambiguous riddles, menacing portents, potent witches, supernatural birds, deadly dragons, and other forces of nature and mythic beasts looming very large. "I am not afraid of the clashing mountains/I am not afraid of the pecking birds," exclaims a young knight in one version, as he sets off for Kiev with his mother's blessing. The traditional notion "pride goeth before a fall" is a common thread. In a very famous, but probably later, story from Novgorod, the arrogant merchant-adventurer Sadko is saved from punishment at the hands of water sprites and the *Sea Tsar* only by his supplications and the intercession of St. Nicholas. Paganism and Christianity cohabit the world of the *bylyny* with scant conflict.

The most impressive literary creation attributed to the Kievan period is a brief, anti-Qipchak, patriotic epic of about five hundred lines—*The Lay of the Host of Igor.* It concerns the failed campaign of 1185 against Khan Konchak and subsequent opportune escape of Igor of Novgorod-Seversk (see the previous chapter, p. 30). The sophistication of its poetics and imagery place it on a par with some of Russia's best eighteenth-century poetry and nothing earlier. Its authenticity, however, is questionable, because it contains words unexplainable for the time of medieval Rus, it was unknown until the early 1800s, and the lone, alleged manuscript disappeared in the great 1812 Moscow fire. So until this issue is cleared up, cautious historians should view the core of the Igor story as a more or less reliable Kievan-era, southern Rus chronicle report. Nevertheless, its poetic version (dated variously from the late twelfth to the early nineteenth century) and Alexander Borodin's derivative opera *Prince Igor* (1869–1889) have made it a part of modern Russia's creative tradition and Russia's and Ukraine's imagined Rus past.

IMAGE AND EDIFICE

In 1997 New York's Metropolitan Museum of Art mounted a crowd-packing exhibition entitled "The Glory of Byzantium," covering the period 843–1261. It included Christian art and artifacts from the Middle East, Transcaucasia, and Catholic Europe (where Byzantine influences also abounded), as well as the Slavic Orthodox lands. A striking feature of many of the religious objects on display was their apparent lack of national traits. Indeed, in many ways Byzantium, the Balkans, Rus, and Georgia constituted a distinct religious-aesthetic world in the eleventh and twelfth centuries. Still, national styles and regional differences did emerge. In art and architecture, as well as literature, Christian Rus actively participated in what has been termed the "Byzantine Commonwealth," but not merely as blind imitators of the Greeks.

Houses of Worship

Churches constituted by far the most important buildings and public spaces in Rus, outside as well as inside—the more churches in a given city or country, the more protection by divine powers. Inside churches people communed with God and each other. City assemblies convened in the plazas outside of the major cathedrals. Hemispherical church cupolas (not onion domes at this time), often capped with gilded copper and invariably with crosses atop, defined a city's silhouette and image, and the city in turn stood for society and the state. Following the example of Constantinople, the Rus protected major entrances, such as Kiev's Golden Gate and the Pechersky Monastery portal, by placing small churches above them.

Builders designed churches to meet the needs of services, which consisted chiefly of chanting, but also of sermons and rituals, most importantly communion. The standard Rus church floor plan, adopted from Byzantium, was an inscribed cross within a nearly square rectangle, which had one or three decorated semicircular apses (vaulted recesses) appended to the east end (the top of the cross) behind the altar. Everyone stood, and, in major churches, everywhere worshipers looked—up, down, straight ahead, and all around—they could gaze upon representations of the divinity, saints, prophets, or patriarchs within geometrically perfect enclosures. Upon the four piers (squared columns) at the corners of the inner square formed by the cross stood a raised, cylindrical drum with a cupola (dome) on top representing heaven. This flexible design invited all sorts of modifications according to needs,

St Dmitry Cathedral in (Northern) Vladimir, 1193–97, commissioned by Vsevolod Big Nest with external sculpture and other Romanesque features, including symbols of his prowess and authority: David, Solomon, Hercules, Alexander the Great, Christ, and the warrior martyr-saints; made of sandstone, and originally surrounded by an external gallery.
© *William Brumfield.*

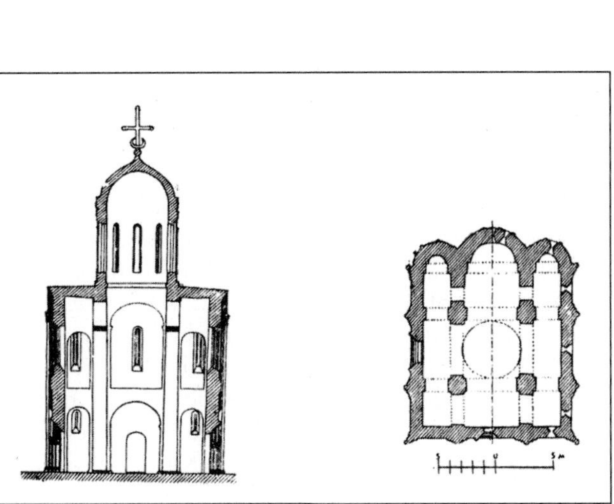

A. Rukhliadev © William Brumfield.

tastes, building materials, and climatic conditions. Structures could be expanded for greater capacity, with more piers replacing the original walls and supporting additional drums and domes, the drum windows providing natural light for the interior. The central dome of a major church could rise a hundred feet or so and be surrounded by four smaller cupolas, themselves forming a heavenly square. Builders frequently added a second-story choir on the west (entrance) end and, less often, upper galleries with chapels along the inner sides, allowing the prince's family to have its own special space. They might also attach practical outer structures or decorative miniature churches and towers at the west corners. And they employed arches for portals, windows, arcades, interior supports, and ornamental false arcades of the semicircular Roman type common then in the West as well. This basic layout remains the norm for Russian Orthodox churches.

The principal cathedrals had specific practical and symbolic significance. Vladimir I erected Kiev's Tithe Church (988–996) in his original citadel near wrecked pagan altars and adorned it with marble columns and objects looted from Cherson. With its dedication he placed Kiev and Rus under the protection of the Mother of God. In 1034, his son Mstislav started the second major Rus cathedral—the oldest still standing—in Chernigov. Finished in the 1070s, it was consecrated to the Transfiguration of Christ, a symbol both of the revolution wrought by conversion and of local ambitions. Yaroslav the Wise's masterpiece, Kiev's St. Sophia (1037–1060s), modeled on a Byzantine palace church, contained five aisles and apses, instead of three, and also five cupolas. Eventually it would have an apostolic twelve cupolas ascending to the center. Unique frescoes of Yaroslav's family devotions and of Constantinople's emperor, palaces, and hippodrome entertainment adorned the upper gallery. Their imagery expressed the harmony of church and state (a key Byzantine principle adopted by the Rus), of sacred and profane, of Rus and Byzantium. Now Rus could proclaim that it, like Byzantium with its extraordinary sixth-century St. Sophia Cathedral, enjoyed the shield and guidance of God's Holy Wisdom (*sophia* means wisdom). Novgorod's less elaborate, smaller, yet seemingly more vertical St. Sophia (erected 1045–1052) served for over four hundred years as a declaration of that city's separate status as a capital and city-state, likewise protected by Divine Wisdom and the Mother of God. Byzantine architects and master craftsmen, we believe, directed the construction and adornment of all of these edifices.

A simpler, but truly national stage of church architecture began to emerge with the building, paradoxically also under a team of Greeks, of the Kiev Pechersky Monastery Dormition Cathedral (*Uspensky Sobor*, 1073–1077). It was consecrated to what Catholics call the Assumption of the Virgin and the Orthodox the Dormition, that is, the falling asleep into heaven of the Mother of God. With three aisles and apses, just one dome, and no interior frills, this structure emphasized height for visibility above the monastery walls. It also had a useful extra narthex (vestibule) at the west end, where monks could congregate for brief prayer services. Over the next century dozens of adaptations of this edifice went up all over Rus, many of them also consecrated to the Dormition, creating visual unity even as Kiev's political ascendance waned.

Small but prosperous congregations adapted a popular modification of the Byzantine style—the three-aisle, one-apse, one-dome church, with a corner height about the same as the width to create a cubic block effect. Standing examples survive in many towns with a variety of symmetrical roof designs, from simple slants to the ascending arches typical of later Russian developments. Some regions developed distinct styles. As early as the 1060s, Novgorod adapted the European church bell, but with a separate wall-like tower, and experimented with just one or two extra domes of different sizes, as in the large, cuboid Yurev Monastery church (1119–1130). Halych (now a ruin) became a center of Western imports and innovations for Rus in the 1150s, with such Classical and Romanesque features as elongated interiors useful for sermons, columns with capital scrolls and foliage, and exterior sculpture.

Vladimir-Suzdal took another path. Starting in the 1150s and 1160s, local builders skillfully adopted squared stone masonry and utilized sandstone to great effect. Romanesque exterior sculpture, false arcades, receding portals, and other designs introduced in the 1160s became a regional specialty. Aiming to rival or displace Kiev, Andrei Bogolyubsky (r. 1155–1174) freely employed Western master builders and adorned Vladimir and its environs with an elaborate Golden Gate, a new Dormition Cathedral, and an imposing suburban palace complex at Bogolyubovo with a richly endowed portal church. To these he added a small, cuboid architectural jewel along the Nerl River dedicated to his designated patroness for Vladimir-Suzdal—the Virgin's Protective Veil (*Pokrov*)—for bringing him victory over the Bulgars in 1164. Vsevolod Big Nest (r. 1176–1212) expanded Vladimir's Dormition Cathedral to have five aisles and apses, matching Kiev's St. Sophia. He also built a smaller palace church with elaborate exterior sculpture in Vladimir, dedicated to his patron warrior-saint, Dmitry of Salonica (Demetrios of Thessaloniki), a protector against pagans. This edifice expressed his pretension as a Christian monarch and his family's special status. Over the next three centuries the regional fashion of Vladimir-Suzdal developed into Russia's national style. Similarly, the regional festival on First October was instituted in honor of the Virgin's Veil, possibly by Andrei Bogolyubsky himself. It was the first of its kind in northeastern Rus and is still celebrated by the Russian Church.

Iconography

To separate architecture and painting would have seemed strange to Byzantines or Rus, who could not conceive a major church without the illustrations on all available wall and column space. A major cathedral thus presented a visual textbook of the faith. Master builders had to envision the placement of the required picture sequences, which themselves mirrored and partook of the living web of theology, sacred history, and liturgy.

The most important iconography in a church appeared visible from just outside the enclosure of its liturgical heart, the sacramental altar. For example, in Kiev's St. Sophia, the worshiper can see symbolic depictions of the great drama of redemption. The columns in front portray the Archangel Gabriel and the Mother of God, representing his Annunciation to her of the Incarnation of the Word of God within her womb. Farther behind in the upper apse she appears standing with arms stretched upward, the classical praying pose, interceding for humanity, while, below, Christ administers communion to the Twelve Apostles. Directly above, on the ceiling of the central cupola, Christ Almighty, the universal judge, gazes down, with archangels below him, Old Testament prophets on the drum, and the four evangelists—Matthew, Mark, Luke, and John—on its supports. Other depictions inside any substantial church included the Church fathers, that is, the great bishops and theologians of the past, as well as famous martyrs, favorite saints, and the events marked by the cycle of major church holidays celebrating the lives of the Savior and the Mother of God. Two crucial standard items were the paired intercessions for the faithful by the Mother of God and John the Baptist above the entrance to the altar, and the Last Judgment at the west end—a reminder when one exited of the bliss or torments to come.

The Byzantine masters who decorated the first Rus cathedrals used their native media, methods, models, and even written language and script. On the higher levels, accessible to the natural light of the drum windows, glittered mosaic pictures composed of thousands of pieces of colored glass. The other walls, columns, and ceilings contained simpler painted frescoes. Icons at this time hung near the altar enclosure. Floors too were sometimes covered with mosaics or painted tiles.

Rus artistic style developed from the Byzantine, which in the eleventh century still favored the correct bodily proportions and frontal views when depicting humans. Several surviving icons that specialists have attributed to Rus masters from the eleventh and twelfth centuries display a classical harmony of composition and a calm composure—for example, the *Archangel with the Golden Hair* and *St. George the Warrior*, the very popular and probably mythical patron of soldiers. According to recent Russian art historians, a pair of icons from around 1200 of St. Nicholas, the highly revered benefactor of those in distress, reveals psychological sensitivity—here also foreshadowing later Russian developments. The most influential icon to survive from this epoch, however, stems from a twelfth-century Byzantine workshop, the *Vladimir Mother of God.* By tradition, Andrei Bogolyubsky brought the piece north in 1155. Of the Virgin-of-Tenderness type, with the child's face against the mother's, it became a standard model for private devotions in the Rus northeast and then Russia and has been venerated for centuries as a miracle-working icon.

In retrospect, we might note that Rus culture during the first few Christian centuries possessed some of the characteristics of other newly converted European lands at that time or earlier. An imported international civilization developed some national characteristics and regional variations. Educated immigrants worked alongside natives in developing the national culture. The Christian religion, which from the start had incorporated some elements of eastern Mediterranean and Middle Eastern popular religion, underwent in Rus a new infusion of pagan motifs and nature worship without, however, losing its theological and liturgical core. As in the case of the German peoples from about 375 to 750, the warrior ethic and worldly folk values flourished alongside the world-rejecting, salvation orientation of early

Christianity. But unlike the Germans, or even the Anglo-Saxons who developed a native language version of their Christian civilization, the Rus remained confined by their specific literacy in the world of *Slavia orthodoxa*. The Anglo-Saxons used Latin as well as their own language, while Rus familiarity with other languages stayed practical, amateurish, and chiefly oral. All the same, the Rus of the Kievan period had a vibrant and creative, if not highly erudite, Christian culture, which borrowed from central Europe as well as Byzantium, and on the popular level, from steppe neighbors as well. Mongol expansion would put the Rus people and their evolving culture to a very severe test.

CHAPTER 4

The First Mongol Century: Hardship and Adaptations, 1237–1341

Because of our sins God has brought wild beasts out of the desert to eat the flesh of the strong and drink the blood of the boyars.

—*Chronicle of Novgorod* (for year 1259)

In the year 1238, as told in a northern Rus chronicle, "aliens called Mongols attacked the Ryazan land in countless numbers, like locusts . . . and sent as envoys to the Ryazan princes a sorceress and two men, demanding a full tenth from the princes and the people—a tenth of their horses and everything." This event, reported with literary flourish, typifies the initial stage of the Mongol conquest of Rus. For between 1237 and 1240 Mongol armies under Chingis Khan's grandson Batu and his confederates overran most of Rus, causing widespread death and destruction and initiating an epoch often termed the *Mongol Yoke.* Archaeology and written records attest to material and cultural devastation and to the hardships the Rus population endured at the hands of their new masters. The Mongol conquest and pillage represent only part of a much more complicated story. The economy recovered, though with a different regional look than before. Orthodox Christianity, its culture, and its influence over popular life, far from weakening, waxed stronger. Mongol suzerainty over Rus lasted in various forms more than two hundred years, during which Moscow in the east and Lithuania in the west emerged as the leading states with Rus populations and became more imposing political entities than any of the pre-Mongol Rus regional principalities had been.

The historian must ask some basic questions about the overall effects of Mongol domination. Did it have little impact, or did it alter Rus political structures and the relationship between governing and governed in a fundamental way? Did it even create the conditions for solving the problem of weak central rule? In the cultural arena, outside of religion, did Mongol domination open new vistas and possibilities for interaction with other peoples of Eurasia, thereby promoting the development of a distinctly Russian civilization? Did Mongol domination at the same time cut Russia off from Europe or in any other way retard Russian development, causing lags that are visible today? We visit these questions and others over the next three chapters as we examine the facts and changing aspects of the Mongol period in Russian history.

STORM OUT OF THE EAST, 1190–1242

Chingis Khan of Mongolia (1162–1227), one of the greatest conquerors in history, employed terrifying force, as he and his progeny established the largest empire ever seen on Earth. The Rus—like everybody else, united or disunited, who faced the Mongol armies—lacked the means to stop their determined efforts.

The Rise of the Mongols

A common misperception that the barbarian Mongols appeared out of nowhere to invade Rus stands in need of correction. Actually, about the same time Kievan Rus took shape, Mongolian peoples led by the Chitan nation also joined the orbit of literate civilization. Among other achievements, they established a steppe-based conquest empire over northern China and developed an alphabet. Organizing kinship networks into a command hierarchy, the Chitan mobilized some of the most effective armies seen by then in the Chinese borderlands and caused a military revolution in Central Asia. After another conquest state replaced the Chitan in northern China, some of the Mongolian peoples reunited under an upstart named Kabul and his band of loyal warriors. It was his grandson Temujin who created the renowned Mongol Empire, beginning around 1190. Proclaimed *Chingis Khan* (Universal Emperor) by the Mongol elite in 1206, he attacked similarly ambitious rivals in the Chinese borderlands and Central Asia. The north Chinese capital of Beijing fell in 1215, as did Khwarazm and the rest of Central Asia by 1221. Mongols then advanced in all directions for half a century, subduing Transcaucasia, Bulgar, the Qipchak steppe, Rus, Persia, Afghanistan, Mesopotamia, Korea, and all of China.

How did the Mongols conquer so many lands? Chingis Khan led the way, as his charismatic genius attracted followers who subordinated their kinship ties to their personal loyalty to him. The Mongols mastered the old Chinese practice of absorbing neighboring steppe and forest "barbarians" and employing some of them to fight others. Like all steppe empire builders, the Mongols wooed some of their potential rivals with offers of a share of conquests and booty. Forces of light and heavy cavalry and arsenals of iron arrowheads and siege engines covered all military needs. Advancing the commercial interests of some of their subjects, the Mongols employed caravan merchants as spies. They also used deceitful as well as honest peace proposals to separate enemies or to induce surrender. And they did not shrink from wholesale massacre or placing the captives of one town or fortress at the head of the army attacking the next stronghold along their route. All Mongol males trained in horsemanship and archery from youth, and Mongol women also possessed equestrian and shooting skills.

This "nation of archers," as an Armenian historian called them around 1300, believed that God granted them the entire world as their dominion. To remain at peace with the Mongols meant to give up when their envoys arrived to demand submission. Then the new subjects might have to surrender a tenth of their goods, flocks, and people—including the most skilled craftsmen—and to furnish laborers

The Dynasty and Rulers of Northern Rus and Muscovy, 1157–1613

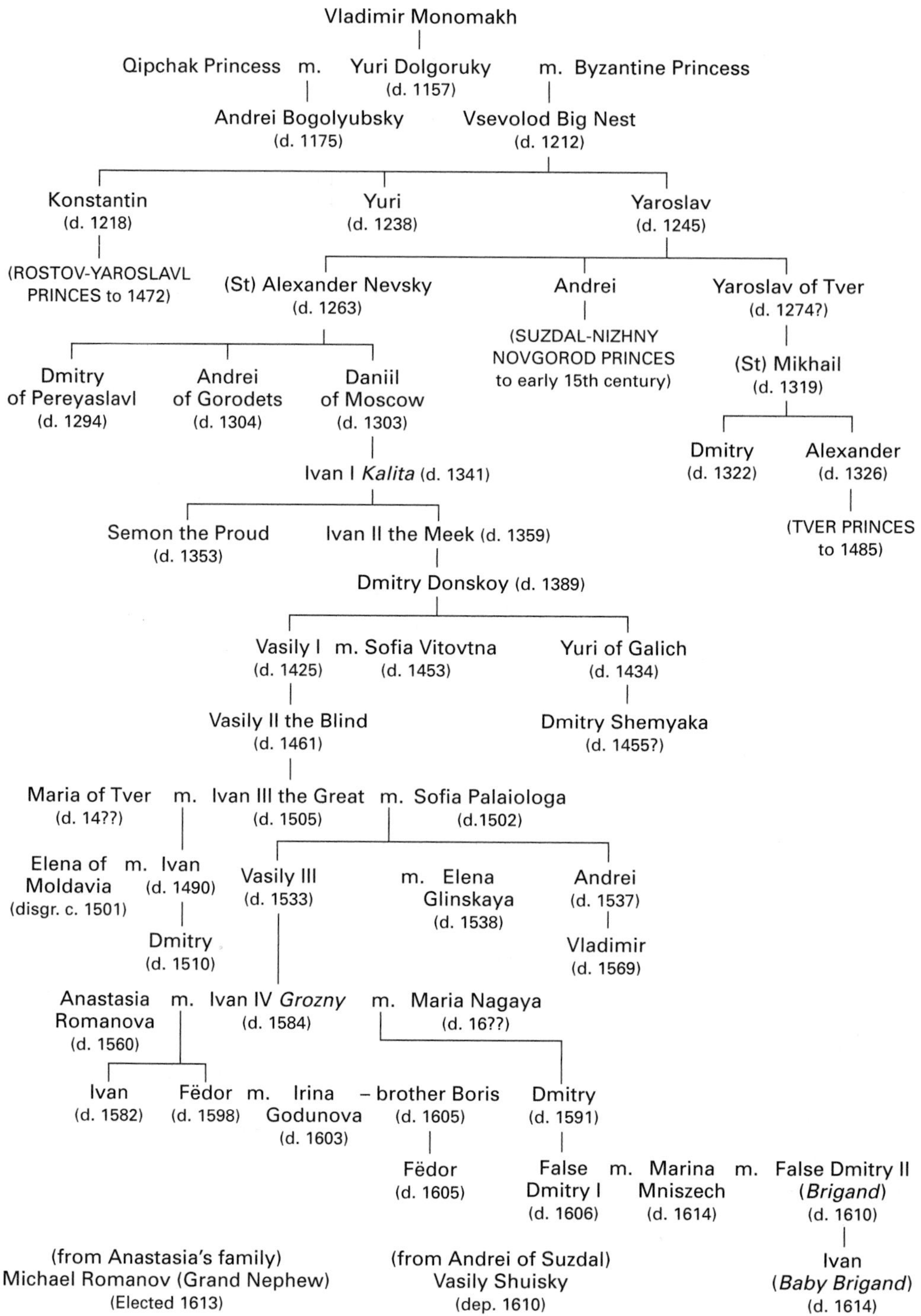

and soldiers upon demand. Since most peoples would not accept tributary status without putting up a fight, the initial Mongol offer of peace became a declaration of war.

The Conquest of Rus

The Mongol move into Rus commenced as if accidentally from the subjugation of Khwarazm and proceeded in stages. It began in 1220 with a thrust into northern Persia and Transcaucasia, where the Mongols eventually defeated the Christian Georgians and sacked Muslim Shirvan (present Azerbaijan). In 1223 this force crossed the mountains into the north Caucasus and defeated an Ossetian and two Qipchak armies, the second near present Crimea.

At this point Khan Kotian of the westernmost Qipchaks appealed to his son-in-law, Mstislav the Daring of Halych, who mobilized all of southern and central Rus. Fearing Mongol control of the nearby steppe, the Rus audaciously killed the first Mongol envoys who demanded submission and went on the offensive. But in late May 1223 at the Battle of the Kalka near the Sea of Azov, the normally successful, if loose, Rus coalition forces proved no match for their hardened and better organized enemy. The Mongols massacred the Rus who surrendered (three captured princes were crushed to death under the platform holding the victory banquet), pursued those who fled, and butchered the peaceful civilians greeting them with crosses outside Novgorod-Seversk. They then withdrew to Central Asia across the steppe.

The Volga Bulgars, who viewed the Mongols as enemies, inflicted damage on them on their way home in 1223 but could not prevent their return. Around 1230 fresh Mongol armies seized the mouth of the Volga. The Rus, Bulgars, and Qipchaks did not even attempt a unified resistance. Instead, just as the Mongols finalized their invasion plans, the Rus south fell into civil war, and the northern Rus failed to unite. The Mongols, for their part, did not aim to occupy Rus so much as to force it to accept tributary status and use its resources for other conquests.

In 1236, Batu (in Rus, Baty) Khan (1208?–1255), the designated heir to the Mongols' western domains and conquests, led a ravaging army into Bulgar, while a second army attacked the western Qipchaks. The next year Batu crossed into Ryazan, defeated every force sent against him, massacred the local princes, and devastated the cities. Fourteen Suzdalian fortress towns—that is, virtually all of them—fell in the winter of 1238. Grand Prince Yuri (1189–1236) and his sons perished in the decisive Battle on the Sitka well north of Vladimir. The Mongols also sacked Torzhok just inside Novgorodian territory and advanced further westward, but, stalled by the spring thaws, they did not proceed up to Novgorod itself. Rather, they fought their way through hostile Chernigov domains back to the steppe. For seven weeks the minor town of Kozelsk resisted to the last man with such savagery that the Mongols called it "the evil city" and "dared not utter its name."

Enriched with prisoners and booty, Batu established new headquarters in the Lower Volga, which became the center of Mongol power in eastern Europe for the next two centuries. Resuming his offensive into southern Rus in 1239 or early

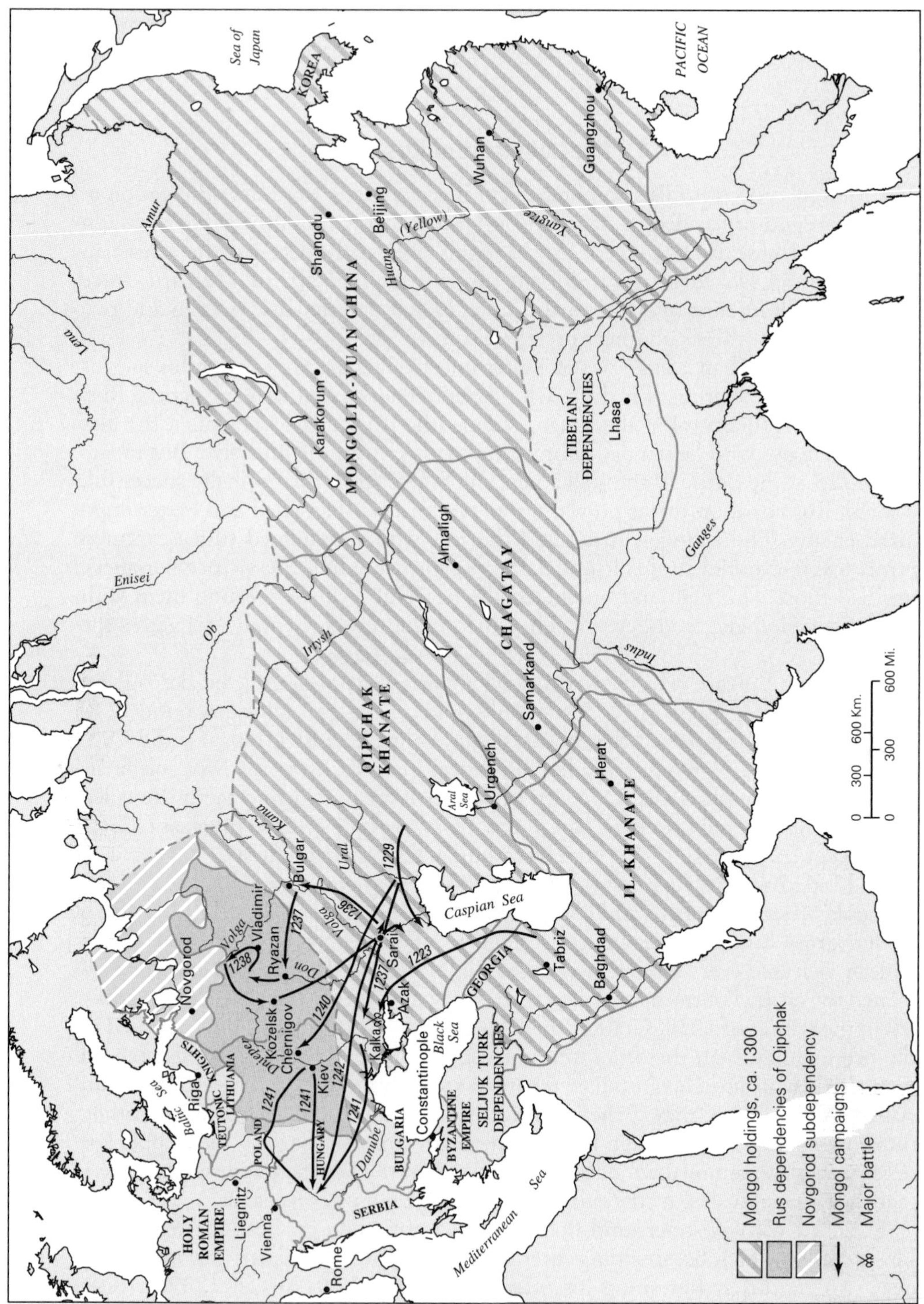

The Mongol Empire and the Conquest of Rus, 1220s–1320s.

1240, he captured the key regional towns east of the Dnieper: southern Pereyaslavl and Chernigov. Late in 1240 he stormed Kiev and pillaged it with immense carnage. Vladimir I's Tithe Church served as the final stronghold and crumbled at last, never to rise again. Dmytro, the captured wounded commander there, joined the Mongols and got them to spare some of the western Rus towns as they proceeded westward.

The next year, Batu launched a three-pronged invasion from Halych and Volynia through Moldavia and Poland into Hungary, planning to use its Great Plain as a forward base. The invaders plundered the land but suffered huge losses and could not take all of its Adriatic fortresses. Then in 1242, when Batu returned to Mongolia to take part in succession politics, his army retreated to the Volga with their captives and plunder. As for Rus, the new northern grand prince Yaroslav (1190?–1246) was now one of the major vassals of the Great Khan in Mongolia. Owing to the enhanced vulnerability of southern Rus from the steppe, the grand principality of Kiev, once the greatest European realm east of Germany, existed in theory only.

In retrospect, it is hard to imagine how even a united Rus in the late 1230s could have stopped the Mongols for very long. For the Mongols held the strategic initiative in choosing their offensive targets and routes, and their steppe empire possessed greater reserves of warriors. Central and southern China, with at least five times the population of Rus, an advanced economy, and a central command structure, resisted longer, but also eventually fell.

EMPIRE OF THE STEPPE

As of 1241, Rus found itself subject to the largest empire the world had ever seen, one in which nomadic clan heads, long-distance merchants, expert equestrian archers, and professional administrators all played crucial roles. The structure and policies of this empire and its successor states determined several key contours of Rus history for the next two centuries and even beyond. Notably, the Mongols found ways to combine central authority and regional autonomy over vast expanses of territory—something that had earlier eluded the Rus.

The Mongol Empire

The enormous realm of Chingis Khan and his descendants—the Chingisids—was already multiethnic and split into subunits by the time it included Rus. The founder divided his territories into four domains (*uluses*), which underwent further division and recombination as time went on. By the 1280s these units, each with its own subdynasty, covered present China and Mongolia (under the Great Khan), most of Central Asia and Afghanistan (called Chagatai), Persia and Mesopotamia (the Ilkhanate), and the entire former Qipchak steppe with its new dependencies, Bulgar and Rus. Despite division and civil wars, the ideal of imperial unity remained alive. In theory sometimes more than practice, the Great Khan of Mongolia (as of 1279 also the Yuan dynasty emperor of China) could command all subjects and redistribute *uluses* among the ruling clan. The Rus numbered among the indirect subjects of the Great Khan.

Such unity, though imperfect, promoted caravan and seaborne long-distance international commerce on a scale never seen before, which in turn generated a large part of Mongol state income. Indeed, some scholars have argued that the empire was essentially a trading realm, perhaps even promoted and financed by inner and Central Asian merchants. In any event, Mongol commercial policies opened up possibilities for the Rus and others who survived the initial invasions and made their peace with the conquerors.

Mongol kinship patterns and mode of conquest conditioned the structure of the empire and its successor states. In the steppe zones, following Chitan precedent, Mongol overlords organized clans and tribes hierarchically into myriads (ten thousands), thousands, hundreds, and tens—with an assignment of herds, pasture, and service requirements according to rank; the higher one's rank, the greater one's wealth and the more soldiers one brought to the field. Intermarriage expedited the integration of conquered peoples and elites into this order. Elsewhere local dynasties, such as the surviving Rus princes, retained autonomous power, but Mongol administrators and census takers used the decimal system to calculate Rus obligations. These regions experienced a form of dual power, with native rulers and Mongol supervisors wielding authority simultaneously.

Mongol governance from above was more developed than anything Rus had previously experienced, though nothing like a modern administration with permanent employees down to the local level. Mongol officials in the provinces enjoyed full powers: the *daruga,* or military-administrative commander in chief; and the *basqaq,* or head tax collector. Early on, the Mongols employed existing Chinese and inner and Central Asian protobureaucratic structures, postal roads, mints, and commercial networks. The goal of some traditionally educated Islamic and Chinese officials was to keep civil administration and taxation out of the hands of military men and rapacious tax farmers (private tax collectors who purchased their office). But such principles often did not hold, and sporadic popular revolts erupted against abusive officials and policies in various domains, including Rus.

The Mongols, like other steppe imperialists, faced the contradictions between agrarian and industrial production on the one hand and the herding and looting practices of nomadic warriors on the other. Prestige among polygamous steppe elites was based on the size of a man's flocks and the number of households in his personal camp. So wherever grazing was possible, it expanded, thus diminishing the land under cultivation by settled, subject agriculturalists. Southern Rus certainly suffered from this extension of pasture. The extraordinary requisitions needed to support the Mongol war machine created a further problem for settled and pastoral peoples alike, both conquerors and conquered, and a potential drain on the economy as a whole. Thus the northern Rus, who benefited from lack of good grazing lands, still had to supply taxes and soldiers for Mongol wars.

Like the Khazars, the Mongols governed from their own cities part of the time.

To serve in these imperial centers, they conscripted skilled craftsmen and other laborers from all over the empire. Some of the captives from Batu's Rus and Hungarian campaigns populated his new capital, Saray, on the Lower Volga. Other prisoners ended up along with Chinese in Karakorum, the new imperial capital in western Mongolia. Medieval Kiev never recovered from the loss of its artisans and luxury production in 1240.

The Qipchak Khanate

For the first forty years or so of Mongol rule, the Rus had to satisfy occasional extraordinary taxation and conscription demands. The Rus princes also had to travel to the Mongol regional headquarters on the Lower Volga to pay homage and receive directives. This was the center of what Muslim sources called the Qipchak khanate or just Qipchak, as the local Mongols' fused with the Qipchaks and adopted their language. The Russians much later called it the Golden Horde—*orda* meaning movable camp or headquarters in Mongolian, "golden" for the gilded throne of the supreme ruler. The longest lasting of Chingis's original four *uluses*, Qipchak stretched two thousand miles from the lower Dniester to the upper Ob River in Siberia, with extensive steppe and forest lands and Caspian and Black Sea ports.

Like other Mongol realms, the Qipchak khanate derived its income from herds, sales taxes and transit tolls, tribute, and war booty. Commerce and political ties connected the khanate to places as far-flung as China, Mesopotamia, Byzantium, Egypt, and the German Baltic towns. A state-run hunting enterprise provided meat for the khan's court and furs and hides for export. His trappers, huntsmen, and falconers enjoyed special rights within Rus and other northern domains. The Volga River resumed the central role it enjoyed in Khazar times, and the Don acquired new importance alongside the Dnieper as a route to the Black Sea. The Black Sea ports attracted Italian traders from Genoa and Venice, as well as local merchants; the Caspian Sea ports brought in Muslims. Bulgar was the khanate's chief center of trade and taxation in the forest zone and minted coins for the Mongols as early as the 1250s. Hides, furs, wax, honey, and slaves remained among the region's chief exports, as did horses from the steppe. Slave soldiers, mainly ethnic Qipchaks, became prize exports to the Middle East. Due to the absence of treasury and customs records, we have a murky picture of khanate and Rus trade at this time. Some scholars have claimed the silver from Europe acquired by Novgorod in exchange for furs was crucial for the khanate's money economy, insofar as it had one. Recent research, though, indicates that the Rus role in generating wealth for the khanate's economy was secondary.

Khan Uzbek (Özbeg, r. 1313–1341) made Islam, the faith of his Bulgar and Central Asian subjects, the state religion of Qipchak. Here following in the wake of the neighboring Chagatai and Ilkhanate rulers, Uzbek thereby cemented an essential barrier from Rus. Already by the 1270s Muslims had provided Qipchak with officials and diplomats. Now a regular Muslim administration crystallized, with a *begliarbeg* (commander in chief) running the army, a *vizier* (minister) managing

Khan Uzbek's Silver *Paitsze:* a token of his authority for his officials to use in his name, written in Arabic script, early 14th c. Muslims formed the backbone of the Qipchak Khanate's administration well before Uzbek adopted Islam as the state religion. *State Historical Museum, Moscow, Russia.*

civilian affairs, and *kadis* (Islamic judges) in charge of law and jurisprudence. This system survived in the Qipchak khanate and its Islamic successors down to the late 1700s.

The khan's court maintained age-old nomadic traditions by making summer migrations with livestock, but in the 1300s urban life expanded along with Islam in the steppe. The chief cities stood along the Volga—the capital, Saray, and, as of the 1330s, New Saray farther up river. The original Saray grew to be as large and productive as Kiev once had been, with quarters and markets for Mongols, ethnic Qipchaks, Caucasus peoples, Greeks, and Rus.

The learned Moroccan traveler Ibn Batuta (1304–1378) visited Qipchak in the early 1330s and found a familiarly flourishing, multiethnic Islamic society, with mosques, schools, and other charitable foundations. Qipchak khanate Islam, being of the moderate Hanafi school, allowed consumption of fermented alcoholic beverages, such as honey mead (also a Rus favorite). Mongol grandees possessed hundreds of slaves. Women, remarkably in Ibn Batuta's eyes, bore great esteem and did not wear the veil in public, as was common among other Muslims. Court ceremony and precedence demanded minute attention and included the intermingling and some intermarriage of royal relatives and the top military governors—a phenomenon we shall see among the Russians, too.

The khanate's durability required workable balances between the administrative-commercial center and the provinces with their clans of herdsmen and reserves of soldiers. Appropriate functions fell to subject elites, whether Genoese Black Sea merchants, Khwarazmian tax farmers, or Rus boyars representing their princes. The khan's court became somewhat of an international center where Rus, Caucasus, and other non-Mongol royalty spent parts of their youth in the shadow of high politics and judicial proceedings. In one recorded case this multinational contingent witnessed the humiliating execution of a Rus prince for taking the law into his own hands in a conflict with a rival. Thus at the khan's court, the Rus quarter in Saray, and on military campaigns, a significant number of the Rus had ample opportunities for interaction with the Mongols of Qipchak and their other subjects.

RUS AND THE NEW ORDER, 1237–1300

Deep controversy, sometimes tinged with chauvinistic prejudice and racism, characterizes opinions concerning the nature and effects of Mongol rule in Rus. One widespread view holds that the Mongols' chief effect on Rus was to retard economic and cultural development. The issue is complex and must remain moot, since we have few useful statistics or measures. Some specialists now see the degree of initial destruction as exaggerated. For example, the chronicle report that "they killed . . . all the abbots, and monks, and nuns, and priests and deacons . . . or led them away barefoot and naked to their camp" is followed by depictions of normal church life for the next year. The century-old "Eurasian School" of Russian historiography holds that the Mongols brought the Rus into a cosmopolitan world with new opportunities for contacts and commerce.

The invasions caused demographic shifts and political regrouping, but little transformation of Rus social structures or institutions during the first century of Mongol domination. Some urban self-government persisted along with princely rule. However, in many places the relative importance of productive townsmen underwent a slow but steady decline in favor of professional soldiers, landholders, and whoever was collecting taxes.

Rus and Mongol

From the conquerors' standpoint, the first century of Mongol power over Rus breaks down roughly into three periods: invasion and the establishment of the Qipchak khanate (Golden Horde) within the larger Mongol Empire, 1237–1270; a time of two competing centers of khanate power, 1270–1300; and reunification and Islamization, 1300–1341. As for Rus, the Mongols displayed no inclination to interfere with the political and social structure, which they manipulated for their own purposes by mediating local disputes while leaving the tasks of governance to the Rus themselves. In so acting, the Qipchak khanate proved rather successful in solving at minimum expense the perennial problem of relations between the center and peripheral regions.

Essentially the Mongols required the Rus to accept their subordinate status, pay tribute, and through their princes make tokens of this submission upon demand. Like other lands conquered by the Mongols, Rus underwent partial occupation by *basqaqs* and *darugas,* who arrived with military contingents to supervise recruitment, taxation, and the establishment of postal roads. In the first century of Mongol rule virtually every Rus town of note experienced more than one visitation of Mongol envoys, sometimes in the company of Rus princes, and rarely without some sort of extraordinary payment of tribute or taxes. Nevertheless, the Rus principalities retained wide autonomy as border states in forest zones, unsuitable for settlement and direct rule by Mongol herdsmen. By protecting local trade routes and other sources of income, the Rus authorities served useful functions for the Mongols. So did the defensive military stances of Halych-Volynia, Vladimir-

Suzdal, and Great Novgorod toward western neighbors. Princes who cooperated with the Mongols obtained rewards, returning from visits to Saray "with honor," that is, lavish gifts signifying their high status and favor in the eyes of the khans.

The Rus Church also benefited from the Mongol custom of lenience toward the religion and clergies of subject peoples and from Byzantine-Mongol accommodation in the interests of the Black Sea-Mediterranean trade. By the 1260s, if not earlier, Mongol charters (*yarlyk*) freed the Church from most taxes. The Rus clergy in turn had to pray for the health of the Mongol *tsar*, as they called the khan, and treat him as the legitimate earthly ruler, toward whom Christians must obey the biblical injunction: "Render unto Caesar what is Caesar's, and to God what is God's." Around 1261 the Mongols welcomed the relocation of the Orthodox bishopric of southern Pereyaslavl to Saray. If anything, the Rus Church became stronger, not weaker, under the Mongols.

Owing to the nature of the pastoral economy and security needs, however, the Mongols proved to be less generous to the agriculturalists of southern Rus. The conquerors allowed a forest barrier to develop between their own grazing fields in the steppe and the Slavic farmlands farther north. Therefore the wooded steppe borderlands and Kiev atrophied as productive centers, and Smolensk lost its central position in Rus trade. Large numbers of Rus moved from the southern regions to the lands of Vladimir-Suzdal, helping to create population growth there despite Mongol exactions. The influx of these newcomers also meant that leaders of warrior bands among them, undistracted by local ties, could enter a political fray and tip a balance here or there in favor of a given prince.

The fate of Prince Michael of Chernigov (1179–1246) characterizes the rapid decline of southern Rus after the Mongol conquest. He had almost brought Chernigov, Kiev, and Halych-Volynia together before 1240, but his attempt to exercise seniority rule from postinvasion Kiev was futile. Equally unsuccessful in a bid for Halych, Michael was summoned to Batu's court in 1246, where he accepted execution—in Rus eyes, a martyr's crown—rather than pass between two fires, a required ritual symbolizing political submission. By the mid-1240s Rus had only three major territorial principalities: Vladimir-Suzdal, Novgorod, and Halych-Volhynia.

Challenges from West and East

The ambitions of neighbors to the west and the Catholic Church, as well as the rhythms of Mongol developments, influenced Rus politics. Rome hoped to use Rus vulnerability to spread papal power eastward; the Catholic Teutonic Knights and Swedes attempted to expand their holdings into Novgorod's borderlands; and pagan Lithuanians planned their own invasions of the domains of Polotsk and Smolensk. Because of these threats at the time the Qipchak khanate was starting to take shape, some Rus found it worthwhile to oblige Mongol demands rather than resist them. At the same time the Rus princes and cities continued their rivalries, simply taking into account the Mongols as a crucial political factor.

After the Mongols retreated from northern Rus in 1238, Vsevolod Big Nest's third son Yaroslav (1190?–1246) occupied Vladimir and asserted its and his seniority with a redistribution of districts to his younger brothers. He and the clergy then organized a lavish state and family funeral for his older brother Yuri, who had perished fighting the Mongols. Outside of Vladimir-Suzdal, Yaroslav expelled the invading Lithuanians from Smolensk's territory and reestablished the political order there, but he also looted one of Michael of Chernigov's fortresses—this at a time when the southern Rus were trying to organize against the impending Mongol attacks.

Meanwhile Novgorod needed the services of Yaroslav's eldest son, Alexander (1220–1263). In 1240, Swedes with Norwegian and Finnish allies launched a seaborne expedition that occupied the mouth of the Neva. Summoned by loyal Ingrian subjects, a Novgorodian army under Alexander surprised the invaders and drove them off, earning their leader the name "Nevsky." A year later the Teutonic Knights seized Pskov, leading to the Battle on the Ice (of nearby Lake Peipus) in 1242, which entered Russian legend and later was the basis for a masterful film. There Alexander's Novgorodian militia and the allied Suzdalian troops sent by Yaroslav absorbed the charge of the armored German-Estonian "pig" or phalanx and gained another resounding victory. The Novgorodians followed up this victory with successful counterattacks against the Lithuanians.

Such was the situation for the northern Rus when the Mongols began to reorganize their territories in 1243. Yaroslav, followed by the Rostov princes, visited Batu in the Lower Volga, returning "with honor"—in other words, signs of recognized authority in their domains. This became a pattern whereby the Mongols would confirm the autonomy or independence of the greater and lesser Rus princes. Yaroslav also sent a younger son all the way to the Great Khan in Mongolia and then went there himself in 1245, where, as "King of Rus," he was treated as a major figure. But he died soon afterward, either from poisoning at the hands of a Mongol faction, or en route home from natural causes, as conflicting chronicles report.

Alexander and his brother Andrei (d. 1264) quickly bypassed normal succession rules by visiting Batu and proceeding to Mongolia, where the Great Khan agreed to a novel arrangement. Upon returning in 1249, Andrei became the grand prince of Vladimir, while Alexander became titular grand prince of Kiev and all Rus, though residing mainly in Novgorod. Three years later Alexander obtained the Vladimir throne from the Mongols and with it full seniority within his family, while "Andrei and his boyars resolved to flee, rather than serve the khans." This produced in turn a devastating Mongol punitive raid against Andrei's local allies, followed by his return and establishment of a subdynasty in Suzdal.

More successful up to a point in pursuing independent policies was Andrei's brother-in-law Danilo (1202–1264), the senior prince of Halych-Volynia, who made the proper submission to Batu in 1245. For the next dozen years the Halych-Volynians fought and looted rivals in all directions, including Mongols and other Rus. In 1255, on the urging of some Polish allies and his mother, Danilo ventured to accept the nominal overlordship of the Roman Catholic pope in return for a royal crown with the title *Rex Russiae* (King of Rus). Since the additional promise of Catholic military aid against the Mongols did not materialize, neither did the local Orthodox Church union with Rome.

In fact, nothing at this time could stop the Mongols' determination to have their way in Rus. Rather, in the late 1250s they increased taxation and conducted a general census throughout the entire empire in preparation for further fighting in China and the Middle East. In 1259 overwhelming Mongol forces invaded Halych-Volynia and compelled the western Rus to dismantle their fortresses and support fresh campaigns into Poland and Hungary. In a parallel move a few years later, the Mongols broke up the coalition of Volynians and friendly Lithuanian princes, some of whom had become Orthodox and reigned in Polotsk and the nearby Rus towns.

The Mongol census carried out in the Rus north by Muslim tax farmers resulted in renewed exactions, and it provoked general opposition, but to little avail. In 1257 and 1259 Grand Prince Alexander, backed by Mongol officials, faced down Novgorod's resistance to the Mongol taxes and household registration. He even had one anti-Mongol band of soldiers mutilated by blinding or nose-slitting. In 1262 popular uprisings erupted in several northern towns against the census and tax farmers. Moneylenders, including one Rus townsman who turned Muslim himself, incurred vindictive popular wrath, because high-interest loans to cover Mongol taxes often resulted in debt slavery for the borrower. To intercede for his countrymen, Alexander went again to the Lower Volga, where he was retained for a year by Batu's successor, Berke. Falling ill there, Alexander died en route home. "Relief . . . from Muslim oppression," to use the chronicler's words, came only after Berke died in 1266.

Meanwhile, without much Mongol interference, Vladimir-Suzdal remained nominally under the senior rule of Alexander's brothers until the last one died in 1276. Like Kiev earlier, it also subdivided further into rival principalities with their own subdynasties. Rostov became a prosperous fur emporium, attracting even Mongol immigrants. Tver and Kostroma on the Upper Volga and Ustyug on a tributary of the northern Dvina River flourished as transit points for Mongol tribute and centers of the fur trade.

The revolts may have caused an eventual change in Mongol policy, however, for by the end of the century, the Rus princes themselves collected most of the Mongol tribute. Still the Mongols continued to dispatch envoys to collect arrears, and they arrived accompanied by troops and moneylenders—the instruments of extortion, debt servitude, and outright seizure of goods and people. At the same time, the second competing Qipchak center during 1270–1300 enabled Alexander's competing sons and grandsons to turn to rival Mongol patrons for three decades. In 1281–1282 and again in 1293, northeast Rus suffered mightily from Mongol armies aiding one side or the other. Nevertheless, conclaves of northern princes and the influence of leading churchmen maintained some Rus cohesiveness. Metropolitan Maksim (r. 1283–1305) formally recognized the preponderance of the north within Rus and bolstered the role of the Church there. In 1299 he shifted his main residence from Kiev to Vladimir on the grounds of "too much Mongol violence." So as Vladimir declined as a political center in its own right, it grew in ecclesiastical stature.

THE ADVENT OF MOSCOW, 1301–1341

Northern Rus politics in the early 1300s featured a struggle for seniority between the territorial princes of Tver and their Moscow rivals. At the same time, the Rus princes' added role as tax collectors for the Mongols spawned fiscal intrigues. A number of these princes from various domains faced execution in Saray for disloyalty—sometimes on specific charges of withholding portions of tax revenues. Yet by acting as conduits for Mongol revenue and trade, the most successful princes also enriched their towns.

Tver and Moscow each had special advantages in the competition for primacy in the north. Though relative upstarts as towns, they possessed favorable border locations in western parts of Vladimir-Suzdal. Tver lay on the uppermost Volga on the direct route connecting the Baltic to the heartland of northern Rus and the Qipchak khanate. Moscow, sitting on a tributary of the Oka River in the middle of the Upper Volga watershed, had ideal links as well with the Don and eastern Dnieper river systems. Tver enjoyed the best site within Vladimir-Suzdal for pressuring Novgorod economically and militarily, and the better one for obtaining pelts, but Moscow had one of the very best locations for communicating with all of Rus and the better one for attracting refugees from the south. Tver's princes had stronger legitimacy of descent, but Moscow's competed in this regard and proved less tradition-bound.

Such was evident in the very early 1300s, when Moscow's prince Daniil (1261–1303—a son of Alexander Nevsky), and his son Yuri (d. 1325) encroached on the border regions of Ryazan and Smolensk and seized three towns. This gave Moscow, like Tver, a two-hundred-mile stretch of territory—the size of Belgium and, if sufficiently populated, quite adequate for the core land of a competitive medieval state. Moscow now possessed iron deposits, apiaries, and some good acreage.

Tver's Brief Ascendancy

With the death of the last son of Alexander Nevsky in 1304, his grandson Yuri Daniilovich of Moscow contested the more legitimate grandson Michael Yaroslavich of Tver (d. 1318). The leading grand principality boyars sided with Michael, whom the Mongols designated grand prince, while two key northern towns, Pereyaslavl and Kostroma, joined by newcomers from the south, backed Yuri.

Church politics and Novgorod also aided Yuri in this wider contest for regional supremacy. When Metropolitan Maksim died in 1305, both Michael and the "King of Rus" Yuri of Halych-Volhynia sent candidates for metropolitan to Constantinople. The Byzantines selected the Halychan Peter (r. 1309–1326), whom Moscow profitably backed, while he subverted Tver's ecclesiastical autonomy. The Novgorodians tended to favor Yuri over Michael, a more talented warrior and leader. Tverian tradition treated him as the model Christian prince, but he also extorted heavy tribute from Novgorod. In this struggle, each prince also brought armed Mongol envoys and tax collectors back from Saray, who exploited the local Rus.

As the contest between the two princes reached a showdown, Michael of Tver won on the military battlefield but fell to bad luck and political intrigue. In 1317 Yuri returned from Saray married to Khan Uzbek's sister and designated grand prince. In Vladimir-Suzdal, if not Rus history, this was the first breach of the principle that for a prince to acquire an established major throne, his father must have once occupied it. However, the Mongol khan's approval or even appointment had become a new source of political legitimacy. Michael then lost by winning after he routed the Moscow-Mongol army advancing on Tver and captured Yuri's Mongol wife, for she died in captivity. Uzbek then executed Michael on the charge of planning to flee "to the Germans" with Mongol taxes and confirmed Yuri as grand prince.

For unexplained reasons, in 1322 Uzbek replaced Yuri as grand prince of Vladimir with Michael's son Dmitry of Tver. But four years later Dmitry rashly and fatally overplayed his hand by murdering Yuri near the khan's court. Still banking on Tver after executing Dmitry, Uzbek appointed Dmitry's brother Alexander (r. 1326–1327), but also sent a high-ranking envoy to Tver to oversee tax collection. The Tverian commoners responded with a massive uprising in 1327, killing all the Mongols they could find.

Donor's Icon of (St/Prince) Mikhail of Tver (d. 1319) and wife Ksenia for the Transfiguration Cathedral, which tradition holds they founded. He was martyred by the Mongol and she became a nun-benefactress of churches. The icon is from the 17th century, but the Tver looks somewhat as it did in the 15th century. The enthroned Christ looks down from above, as if radiating and protecting the city from close by. The cruel fate of Mikhail and his two sons, not to say the city itself, from 1319 through 1327 is nowhere in sight. Quite a few other Rus towns developed cults of saintly native princes, among them, Pskov, Suzdal, Murom, and Chernigov. *Ruble Museum of Early Art, Moscow, Russia.*

Ivan (I) Kalita

The rebellion in Tver proved a godsend to the late Yuri's brother and successor in Moscow, Ivan (?–1341), who became known as *Kalita,* or Moneybag, for his combination of ruthless fiscal ingenuity and calculated generosity. Ivan had just achieved a symbolic political coup by inducing Metropolitan Peter to designate Moscow's Dormition Cathedral, then under construction, as the site of his own tomb. Now Ivan led a combined Mongol-Rus force that crushed the Tver insurgents and burned the city.

Moscow did not squander this second chance. Sharing supreme power with a Suzdal prince for a few years before becoming sole grand prince (1331–3141), Ivan continued the useful cooperation with the Church under the next metropolitan, the Byzantine Greek Feognost (or Theognostos, r. 1328–1353). Ivan also forged a new policy of overseeing tribute collections for the khanate from some of the territories outside of Moscow's control, and he readily employed Mongol auxiliaries to this end. Using stick and carrot methods, he induced people to move to his underpopulated lands, for example, by flogging fiscal contributions out of rich neighboring elites and then granting tax breaks to those who migrated to his domains.

By 1341, the pre-Mongol order in Rus had vanished. Owing to Mongol encroachments from the south, the old Dnieper River core regions of Kiev, Chernigov, and Smolensk had become secondary factors in regional politics. In the Rus far west in the early 1300s, the powerful Halych-Volynian princes tried to establish their own separate Orthodox metropolitanate and sometimes succeeded temporarily. But by the 1320s or 1330s the local male line of princes there had died out, and Polish princes reigned, foreshadowing the future conversion of Halych into a full Polish crown land in 1349. Slightly to the east and north, Lithuania, tempered by chronic wars with the Teutonic Knights and Novgorod, became stronger. Under Grand Prince Gedimin (Lith. Gediminas, r. 1313–1341) this last stronghold of paganism in Europe completed the absorption of the future Belarusian lands. Lithuania thus became a major competing Rus power, with Orthodox princes and Rus law in its Rus territory. Farther east and north Novgorod had reacquired full autonomy in the later 1200s, but Pskov had become a city-state in its own right under the military leadership of the converted, refugee Lithuanian prince Dovmont (r. ca. 1264–1299). And in the Rus northeast, Vladimir had lost its preeminence first to Tver and then to Moscow.

At this time Moscow's territory, though no larger than it had been thirty-five years earlier, had become wealthier and stronger. Tver, in contrast, had risen under Michael, but far from being a serious rival to Moscow in 1341, hardly recovered in the fourteen years after the 1327 uprising and its senior princes remained fatally suspect in the eyes of the khanate. Rather, starting around 1327 and for more than two centuries, internal Rus high politics flowed around Lithuania in the west and Moscow in the east.

SPIRITUAL SURVIVAL

"The Mongols brought us neither Aristotle nor algebra," lamented Russia's greatest poet, Pushkin (1799–1837), referring to the rich Arabic legacy in Sicily and Spain that fueled western Europe's university culture of the 1200s and beyond. However, the Mongols did not prevent other subject peoples, like the Persians or Armenians, from maintaining their high civilizations. As for the Rus, the invasions, migrations, and political changes did have a few creative effects in the realm of literature. Still, as earlier, wherever impoverishment persisted, it permanently reduced the patronage of the arts. In some places only the standard activities connected with everyday religious and secular life continued as before.

Cultural Reorientation

On the most basic level, that of language, the Mongols' western conquests resulted in some new Rus vocabulary connected with taxation and administration. Examples are *yam* (postal road), *tamga* (stamp, then meaning commercial stamp tax), *yarlyk* (stamp, label—originally charter), *tarkhanii* (immune, as in free from taxes), *chelobitie* (petition, a purely Russian word deriving ultimately from the Chinese *ko-to*—kowtow), and both *doroga* (road) and *dorogoy* (expensive), from *daruga* (resident proconsul).

Despite the khanate's turn to Islam, the Mongols fully tolerated Rus Christianity. But only the handful of individual Mongols who migrated to Rus converted to Orthodoxy. Among them appeared a member of the ruling clan, *Tsarevich* ("the khan's son") Peter, who settled in Rostov in the late 1200s, protected it from fellow Mongols, and became locally revered as a saint. A small stream of Mongol settlers continued. Later, more than one Russian noble family would trace its origin to a Mongol immigrant.

Mongol hostage policy broadened Rus horizons. Princes, chieftains, and nobles, sent from all subject peoples as pledges of good behavior to the khan's court, joined special guards units, where they constituted a supraethnic imperial nobility. Rus princes and their retainers who had spent time with the Mongols acquired the knowledge to frame policy with an eye to political realities. This upper crust, only a thin layer of the population, stood in contrast to the masses remaining outside of the larger world of the khanate.

The self-contained, closed sphere of Rus Christianity, which persisted for centuries, enabled some of the Orthodox writers to treat the Mongol overlordship as a secondary matter, allowing life to go on as in the past as much as possible. In fact, church law in Rus became stronger under the Mongols, who saw in the clergy a prop for the khan's power. Christianity continued to make converts among the northern Finnic peoples who lived near the Slavs. Bolstered by their fiscal privileges, the Orthodox hierarchy held several synods or councils to iron out local problems and try to enforce moral standards.

High Culture in a Time of Adversity

Archaeology and surviving buildings indicate that the Mongol invasions and the first century of rule devastated the Rus south, impoverished the southwest and northeast, and damaged Novgorod's profits from commerce. The major building efforts went toward restoration and upkeep. Masonry churches did go up in such new centers of power and commerce as Tver, Ustyug, and Moscow, but nothing yet matched in scale or innovation the pre-Mongol architectural complexes of Kiev, Novgorod, and Vladimir. For the Mongols' part, archaeological studies and travelers' reports show fourteenth-century Saray and New Saray as, typically for Islam, well-planned capital cities with lavish urban villas, irrigated gardens, and big squares. The Rus who visited these places surely knew how far their towns lagged behind the khanate materially.

Rus literature and historiography exhibited the greatest Mongol impact. The simplest written expression of political self-consciousness—chronicle writing—dried up in Kiev and, after a final flourish, withered in Halych-Volynia, but it continued in the major northern towns. In all genres, standard biblical and heroic themes and native myth-making prevailed among Rus writers, who castigated the rapaciousness of Mongols and the Rus who fought under their orders. The expertly crafted sermons of the Kievan monk and abbot Serapion, who became bishop of Vladimir at the end of his life (1273–1275), blamed the Rus and their persistent sinfulness, especially social injustice, for angering God and bringing misery upon themselves. On the positive side, the *Life of Alexander Nevsky* (ca. 1270–1280s) depicts the Heavenly Host of warrior angels assisting Novgorod under this "invincible" prince with his "incomparable beauty" and "voice like a trumpet among the people" against the Swedes. The semifolkloric *Deeds of St. Merkury of Smolensk* (written down around 1500) tells of a pious youth who saves his city from the Mongols by following the instructions of the Mother of God, single-handedly defeating Batu's army, and then allowing his head to be severed, before returning miraculously to die and be buried in her church. As if setting the stage for future attitudes toward the past, the anonymous poetic *Sermon on the Ruination of the Rus' Land* (originally ca. 1238–1246) idealizes a glorious and prosperous pre-Mongol Rus, "shining light and beautifully adorned," while collecting tribute from all of its neighbors.

One of the finest original Rus works dealing with the Mongol invasion, the heroic chronicle *Tale of the Destruction of Ryazan* (? 1270s), interweaves the story of princely and mass martyrdom. Only this piece, among the above-mentioned works, can be proven to have been written down during the first century of Mongol rule, but the themes and legends of all of them belong to this period. Also directly related to this era are the *bylyna* (folkloric poetry) episodes, where the heroes of the Kievan epoch brazenly, and hence fatally, take on the equally magical and much larger horde of invading Mongols, only to be defeated and turned to stone.

Paradoxically, the nature of warrior literature required the enemy at times be a recognizably gallant foe, residing in the same moral universe as the protagonist.

Otherwise, for example, Batu could not recognize the valor of Dmytro, Alexander Nevsky, and other Rus heroes. Folklore sometimes even sang praises to Rus soldiers who fought alongside the Mongols against other enemies.

Isolation from Europe?

The widespread claim by many scholars, publicists, and journalists that the Mongols cut Rus or Russia off from Europe does not stand up to scrutiny. Mongol trans-Eurasian commercial policy permitted Italians to trade in the Black Sea ports and Germans to enter Novgorod's hinterlands, and it did nothing to interrupt that city's links to Livonia, Scandinavia, and the Rus interior. The Germans in Novgorod had a Catholic church. Soon after 1240 a Rus imposter calling himself Archbishop Peter settled as a monk in western Europe and provided his new hosts with a well-informed, if embellished version of the origin and conquests of the Mongols. Another emigrant became bishop of Cracow in the 1290s. A host of other contacts existed between western Rus and Poland after the Mongol conquest, even some sharing of chronicle information. The chancery of the Lithuanian grand princes churned out documents in both Latin and Rus.

The Mongol conquest, by favoring the Orthodox clergy, bolstered traditional Christian values among the eastern Rus, but the Mongols did not require any hostile exclusion of Western culture. Principled antagonism toward the West hardly figured in the Rus writings of the first Mongol century, even in depicting the conflicts with the Teutonic Knights. Rather, the Rus churchmen and their Byzantine mentors wished chiefly to shore up and spread the positive Christian outlook among the people. The Rus bookmen themselves continued to make the choice to avoid immersion in any of the available high cultures to the west or south. Such Orthodox-centeredness would only intensify in the following century among the northern and eastern Rus—the future Russians.

CHAPTER 5

Shifting Fortunes, 1341–1456

In the year 1395, . . . 13 years after the Mongol attack and capture of Moscow, . . . the Emperor Tamerlane came from the East . . . and waged a great war, causing many upheavals in the khanate and in Rus.

—Moscow Chronicle

In 1380, a half century after Ivan I faithfully collected tribute for the Mongols and established Moscow's primacy in northern Rus, his more independent-minded grandson Dmitry advanced to Rus's southeastern frontier and gained a striking victory over an upstart Mongol general. Was Mongol rule over Rus finished? Hardly. Two years later the Qipchak khan Tokhtamish sacked Moscow and forced Dmitry back into submission and tribute payments.

In 1445 the displaced former khan Ulug Mehmed captured Dmitry's grandson Grand Prince Vasily II during a skirmish outside of Suzdal, but he chose simply to extract a large ransom and even allowed Vasily to return home and collect it himself as a sovereign prince. What befell the khanate in the interim? Since 1390 it had suffered several major reversals and split into smaller units, while Moscow, despite the setback in 1382, continued to grow within northeastern Rus.

At the same time, however, Lithuania had become Moscow's biggest rival. By the 1360s Lithuania's grand prince dominated almost all of western and southern Rus and appeared to be the political successor of Kiev's early rulers. Meanwhile the city-states of Novgorod and its daughter republic Pskov flourished and balanced between Lithuania and Moscow.

Horrendous natural calamities struck but did not prevent this century from being one of overall growth for Rus. Despite the appearance of bubonic plague in the 1350s and its recurrence for a hundred years, Rus enjoyed relative prosperity. Cultural self-confidence returned. Monasticism revived and spread into the forested countryside. Spirituality, literature, architecture, iconography, and jurisprudence all developed in new directions.

THE FRAGMENTATION OF QIPCHAK

All of the great Mongol khanates weakened in the 1300s owing to internal rivalries and the contradictions between nomadic herding and settled life. In the 1330s the Ilkhanate (Persia and Mesopotamia) and Chagatai (Central Asia) split permanently into smaller units. A bigger blow came in 1368, when rebels overthrew the Mongol Yuan dynasty and expelled the Mongols from the Chinese heartland forever. Soon thereafter Tamerlane (Timur, 1336–1405)—a brilliant and ruthless Chagatai warlord—attempted to reunite and extend the empire as a purely Islamic realm. But his short-lived conquests hastened the fragmentation of the Qipchak khanate and the emancipation of Rus from the Mongols.

Qipchak's troubles commenced in 1346 with the onset of the plague, which disrupted trade. Civil war followed in 1357, leading to the loss of territories west of the Dnieper to Lithuania and reduced Mongol influence over Rus. Struggles among a succession of rival strongmen—the emir (general) Mamai (d. 1381), Khan Tokhtamish (d. 1406?), and another emir, Edigei (d. 1419)—further weakened the khanate. Most devastating were invasions by Tokhtamish's erstwhile patron Tamerlane in 1391 and 1395. During the second, Tamerlane captured a Rus border town on the Don but returned to the steppe, where he sacked the chief cities of the khanate. A legend preserved in Russian chronicles claims that a dream dissuaded him from continuing on to Moscow. The effects of these power struggles were momentous. The khanate's urban and cultural life, agriculture, and transit trade never fully recovered, while the ensuing political fragmentation of Qipchak over the next half century created several new historic peoples.

East of the Volga, two steppe hordes coalesced: the Nogais and Uzbeks. The Uzbeks would later migrate southward into Central Asia, assume power, and adopt the Chagatai Turkic dialect—but keep their name and become the modern Uzbek nation. The horse-breeding Nogais, ancestors of the modern Kazakhs, remained on the steppe east of the Volga. To the north and east, the khanate of Sibir (Siberia) coalesced east of the Urals in a vast, fur-rich region stretching from the wooded steppe almost to the Arctic Ocean. In the Lower Volga, the nomadic Great Horde claimed legitimacy as the senior khanate. Several grandees in its capital still carried the title *daruga* and oversaw relations with various Rus principalities, but numerous Qipchak Mongols, or Tatars, as Russians called them, entered the service of Lithuania and Moscow.

Separate khanates with important urban centers also arose in the 1420s in Crimea and by 1445 in Kazan. Located to the northwest of the Volga-Kama confluence and supported by black soil agriculture, Kazan represented a new extension of Qipchak Mongol colonization into the forest zones of European Russia. The fusion of the newcomers and the Bulgars created the Kazan Tatars, who remained formidable opponents of Moscow for a century. Crimea, situated next door to the rising power of the Ottoman Turks, became the latter's client state in 1475. A major slave-raiding and military power in its own right, the Crimean khanate controlled most of the Don and Kuban steppe and became the most successful

Shifting Fortunes: Lithuania, Moscow, Qipchak Khanate. 1300–1456.

claimant to the entire inheritance of the Qipchak khanate, including tribute from the old Rus lands. Well into the eighteenth century the old Qipchak steppe remained a nemesis for Russians and Ukrainians. Qipchak itself disappeared, but the Kazan and Crimean Tatars have survived as recognized nationalities.

THE CHALLENGE OF LITHUANIA

Histories of Russia usually concentrate on the Rus northeast and Novgorod after the Kievan period because the Russian nation and state developed there, while the Belarusian and Ukrainian nations developed in the Rus west and south. Still, as these two regions diverged from Russia, all three remained intimately linked by religion and culture and influenced one another. The Lithuanian grand prince, moreover, at times stood out as the most powerful figure in Rus.

Halych as Prelude

The annexation of Halych around 1349 by Poland proved a harbinger of things to come in western Rus, where the Mongol presence all but disappeared. The Polish authorities respected many of the Rus laws and traditions, but sometimes obtained for Halych its own Orthodox metropolitanate and permitted the founding of Catholic bishoprics and abbeys there. Germans, Jews, Poles, and Armenians settled in the Rus towns. Starting as early as 1339, the German townsmen of Halych began to obtain Magdeburg Law, one of several forms of strong urban autonomy that prevailed wherever Germans settled in central and east-central Europe. This constitutional arrangement soon benefited non-German city dwellers as well.

In the countryside, Polish and other European warriors acquired lands and the special rights that nobles possessed in most of Catholic Europe: to occupy the highest state offices, dominate provincial governance, enjoy protection from arbitrary state power, and have ready access to courts of law. By 1431 the indigenous Rus boyars of Halych had procured these rights, too, but the peasants' status deteriorated. In 1435 Halych copied the new Polish practice of limiting internal peasant migrations to a short period around Christmas after the repayment of debts. This measure represented the first general legal step toward peasant serfdom in Rus—a process that throughout east-central and eastern Europe occurred much later than in western Europe and commenced with restrictions on peasants' traditional right to migrate in search of better lands and leasing conditions.

The old Halych thus disappeared as a serious factor in Rus politics. Its substantial resources now strengthened the Polish crown, and Halych's artists decorated in Rus style some Polish churches and castles in Cracow and Lublin, thus contributing to the richness and diversity of late medieval Polish life. But Halych itself still remained primarily Rus in its population and religion. The symbiosis between western Rus and Polish culture, then just beginning to take shape in Halych, would make a significant contribution to the future of Ukraine and Russia.

Lithuania and the Polish Marriage

Paradoxically, the Polish annexation of Halych also signified a shift in the center of gravity of western Rus to Lithuania under Grand Prince Gedimin's three mighty successors: his son Olgerd (Lith. Algirdas, r. 1345–1377), and grandsons Jagailo (Lith. Jogaila, Pol. Jagiello, r. in Lithuania 1377–1392, in Poland, 1386–1434) and Vitovt (Lith. Vytautas, Pol. Witold, r. 1392–1430). Olgerd and Vitovt vastly expanded Lithuania's territory in western and southern Rus, and they exerted influence eastward as well. Styling themselves "Grand Prince of Lithuania, Samogitia (a northern, ethnic Lithuanian territory), and Rus," they used a local Rus dialect as their chief chancery language, introduced Rus law and official terms into their ethnic Lithuanian provinces, and several times convinced the patriarch of Constantinople to appoint a separate metropolitan for western Rus.

Olgerd, the last of the Lithuanian sovereigns to remain ostensibly a pagan all of his life, cut a striking figure in his time. Later Russian chroniclers singled him out as a model ruler for his intelligence and sobriety—"he hated intoxication"—and the extent of his conquests. A master of the surprise attack, he annexed the Kievan and Volynian lands on the right (western) bank of the Dnieper to his other Rus domains and became the overlord of some left bank Rus princes as well. His smashing victory over the Mongols in 1363 expelled them from the steppe west of the Dnieper and added the rest of southern Rus to his realm. Assaulting Moscow twice, Olgerd once left his spear in the city walls to symbolize his ability to attack at will. But he also walked a thin line, as he tried to balance the religions of his subjects. Both his wives were Orthodox, and he may have secretly been, too. But he bowed to pagan pressure and raised his second set of sons as traditional Lithuanians, having installed the first set as Orthodox princes of his western Rus provinces. Several of these Orthodox offspring and their towns were quite independent-minded, and so the immense Lithuanian realm faced the same challenge of cohesiveness that had bedeviled pre-Mongol Rus.

Olgerd's eldest pagan son, Jagailo, succeeded to a shaky throne in 1377, but he shored up his position against his cousin Vitovt and the western Rus princes by marrying the Polish royal heiress Jadwiga in 1386 and becoming king of Poland. Negotiated in the Rus border town of Krevo in 1385, the arrangement suited both sides. The Polish elite avoided rival Austrian and Czech suitors, likely to favor their countrymen. The pagan Lithuanian elite, who also accepted Catholicism as part of the deal, avoided the danger of being overwhelmed in their own realm by the majority Orthodox Rus. The Poles and Lithuanians, moreover, had a common enemy—the Teutonic Order, which blocked them both from direct access to the Baltic Sea.

In 1386–1387, Jagailo, now also King Wladislaw II of Poland, initiated the Westernization of Lithuania by conceding to landed warriors full hereditary rights over their property and the freedom to make marriage alliances without interference from above. In return, they recognized their traditional obligations to provide the state with personal military service and the labor of their dependents. Jagailo also granted the Lithuanian capital, Vilnius, a modified form of Magdeburg Law—

a policy soon extended to some Rus towns. In 1388 he followed yet another Polish example by legalizing the autonomous Jewish community in Brest-Litovsk. Polish policy since the 1340s had been to attract Jews with such privileges in the interest of economic development and strengthening the state's tax base.

Jagailo ultimately could not satisfy both halves of his realm, and in 1392 recognized his redoubtable cousin Vitovt as the lifetime, though not hereditary, grand prince of Lithuania. This son of a pagan priestess soon made himself the most powerful man in eastern Europe. His daughter Sofia (ca. 1371–1453) married Vasily I of Moscow and gained some influence there. She in turn served as a go-between for the two grand princes, as Vitovt extended his power into the Smolensk lands and competed with Moscow for suzerainty over Pskov and Novgorod. His bold attempt in 1399 to move into the southeastern steppe, though, suffered a crushing defeat at the hands of Edigei. The victorious Tatars then crossed the Dnieper and looted the Kievan lands, which had enjoyed forty years of relative peace.

Despite this setback, Vitovt kept control over the Kiev region and held the Tatars farther south at bay. Moreover, in 1410 he helped the Poles crush the Teutonic Knights in a battle of epic proportions at Tannenberg—pitting as many as fifty thousand Poles, Lithuanians, Rus, allied Tatars, and Czech mercenaries against twenty-five thousand Germans. By the later 1420s, Vitovt brought all of Rus and part of the steppe into his personal orbit of influence, and he reached even higher. In 1429, at the age of seventy-nine, Vitovt held a major congress in Volynia of east and east-central European sovereigns and their representatives and almost succeeded in making himself king of Lithuania, on a technical par with the ruler of Poland and other European kings.

Vitovt's death in 1430, however, plunged Lithuania into a ten-year civil war before stability returned. The Orthodox Rus elite had a standing complaint, since a Polish-Lithuanian assembly held in 1413 stipulated that only Lithuania's Catholic nobility would have the same rights as Poland's and a voice in royal successions. In 1435, in an attempt to cow one Orthodox faction, the beleaguered grand prince Svidrigailo of Lithuania (r. 1430–1435) burnt at the stake the new all-Rus (Orthodox) metropolitan Gerasim on grounds of "treason." Grand Prince Casimir (r. 1440–1492) was more politic, and when he became king of Poland as well in 1447, he confirmed the legal equality of the Catholic and Orthodox nobles. By then, however, Lithuanian power had peaked, and in 1449 Casimir abandoned any pretensions to be supreme in Rus and agreed to legal parity with the grand prince of Moscow, whose realm had also just experienced civil strife.

THE ASCENT OF MOSCOW

Historians do not consider the reunification and expansion of northeastern Rus at the end of Europe's medieval epoch to have been a unique event. The same occurred elsewhere. The more pertinent question concerns Moscow. How did its subdynasty retain its initial dominant position after the death of Ivan I in 1341, couple its interests with those of the many other Russians, and acquire hereditary legitimacy?

People and Power

Luck and the effects of the plague played their part. Ivan I had no surviving brothers or nephews and could leave all his family domains and influence in the northern fur territories to his three sons and his widow. The eldest son, Semeon the Proud (r. 1341–1353), easily obtained from the khanate the prestigious title to the grand principality of Vladimir with its two key attached towns—Pereyaslavl and Kostroma. The heirless Semeon and his brothers, Ivan II the Meek (r. 1353–1359) and Andrei (d. 1359), continued to maintain the unity of their domains and passed them on to Ivan I's three grandsons, led by the nine-year-old Dmitry Ivanovich (1350–1389). The succession of Ivan II set a Moscow precedent whereby most or all of the appanage (hereditary domain) of a prince lacking a son passed to the senior member of the line, thereby strengthening the center. For a few years, the Suzdal princes challenged Dmitry's claim to the grand principality, but they quickly gave up. By the middle of Dmitry's reign, Moscow proved to be the most successful northern capital since pre-Mongol Vladimir.

Surviving fourteenth-century documents, the earliest we have for any principality of this type in Rus, indicate that the twin nerve centers of Moscow's domains were the dynasty and the city itself. The senior prince and the head of the church (due to Ivan I's earlier courting of Metropolitan Peter) had their chief residences in Moscow. All the grand prince's boyars resided there at least part of the year. The central stables, the most important financiers and merchants, and several major monasteries were located there as well. Operating in a semiautonomous fashion under the highest-ranking boyar, the city controlled several productive enterprises. And in 1367–1368, Moscow's *kremlin* (citadel) became Rus's sole interior stronghold with stone walls.

The Moscow princes adhered for over a century to the cooperative family principles first enunciated by Yaroslav the Wise in 1054 (see the chapter "Kievan Rus: Structures and Events, 988–1240"), and they generally resisted the temptation to seek external support for internal squabbles. Via expansion of territory and income, Moscow gained useful supporters and additional princes of the blood. A reigning grand prince's mother commanded great respect, as did, for example, Grand Prince Dmitry's widow, Evdokia of Suzdal (d. 1407). Surviving her husband by eighteen years, she oversaw family patronage of churches and monasteries and settled disputes among her sons. Strategic marriages also helped bolster support and family prestige. In addition to the marriage of Vasily I (r. 1389–1425) and Vitovt's daughter Sofia, Vasily's sister wed the reigning Byzantine emperor. Moreover, according to family law enshrined in formal wills, the grand and lesser princes ruled jointly—"as one man"—over the city of Moscow, the central stables, service registry rolls, and the people technically designated as khanate personnel. This evidence points to rudimentary state institutions, independent of the staffs or whims of individual princes.

The Moscow boyars appear in the sources as a special group, beloved by their princes: "To me you are not boyars, but princes of my land," said Grand Prince Dmitry, according to a later report. A number of historians have argued that the leading boyar families, with a variety of kinship ties within elite society, ruled or coruled behind the facade of an increasingly strong monarchy through the seventeenth century. The scanty sources indicate that the Moscow boyars of the mid fourteenth century were often relative newcomers, sometimes immigrants of obscure origins, who joined the dynasty and the city in the interest of territorial expansion and revenue. A few had come earlier with their own armed retinues numbering more than a thousand and were seeking a new land—a sign of the dislocations of the times. Under the leadership of one of their own family members, Metropolitan Aleksy (r. 1354–1378), the Moscow boyars managed the principality very well during the minority of Dmitry. The chief assets of this largely illiterate, incipient aristocracy were movable goods and extended households of men-at-arms and tax-exempt slaves.

Boyar rights included access to the prince's council and the most lucrative offices, such as the rotating district governorships. The eldest son or senior member of established boyar families automatically acquired boyar status. By enshrined custom, the entire upper stratum of warriors, officials, and voluntary retainers possessed a right of free departure. They could serve any prince without risking confiscation of property or physical punishment, unless they were blatantly disloyal to the center, for which eminent heads could and did roll. Specialists have also discerned a phenomenon of very infrequent, defensive purging, whereby a given boyar who attempted to amass too much power might be driven into exile or even murdered.

A mixture of people with diverse loyalties comprised the middle and lower orders. Slavery, often the result of debt or poverty, existed in virtually every profession outside of the clergy. The majority of commoners were free and mobile, so rival princes and landowners had to compete with each other in offering favorable leasing terms to attract residents. Consequently, a variety of peasants, beekeepers, fishermen, trappers, craftsmen, and their families lived under generous conditions in settlements owned by the grand prince, his relatives and servitors, and bishoprics and monasteries. As part of the social exchange for basic protection, all free laymen, urban and rural, were liable for public service, such as portage, foraging, upkeep, fortification work, or combat. Warriors could contract to serve the prince of their choice, but in times of emergency they fought under the local territorial commander where they resided.

During the Mongol period, the state in northeastern Rus and elsewhere further developed its profitable mediating role in judicial life, as people litigated over what counted most for them—their honor (social status and reputation) and their property—according to the principles encoded earlier in Rus law. As a whole the Moscow principality functioned very well with a combination of coercion and consensus, and it revealed vast potential for internal as well as external expansion. By 1450, despite a century of plague, Moscow's central regions were well populated.

Trials by Combat

Moscow's leaders faced two inevitable questions: How much growth would the Qipchak khanate tolerate and how should Moscow respond to the increasing might of Lithuania? These issues came to a head under Dmitry. As of 1327, when Tver was sacked, the dual policy of the khanate had been to allow a strong Moscow as a counterweight to Lithuania but also to bolster the other major dynastic principalities of eastern Rus: Tver, Ryazan, and Suzdal. With the onset of civil war in the khanate in 1357, Moscow virtually ignored the Mongols and smashed a threatening alliance between Lithuania and Tver. By 1377 Moscow exercised a tenuous suzerainty over all of eastern Rus and over Bulgar as well, which kept the northern trade routes free from brigands, such as adventurous Novgorodian freebooters.

At this point Russians and Mamai's Mongols were clashing along several frontiers and heading for a showdown. The first climax occurred in 1380 at Kulikovo on the upper Don River, where, according to Russian sources, Dmitry's Moscow

Dmitry Donskoy in His Field Chapel at Kulikovo: 16th c. Chronicle Miniature. The icons on the top row are a modified, simple *Deesis* (intercession of the saints for humanity) with Metropolitan Peter of Moscow (r. 1309–26) instead of John Baptist on the viewer's right of Christ, and the Virgin on the viewer's left in her usual place. Lower row: Boris and Gleb, the all-Rus prince-martyrs from the 11th c. Since Peter was not yet officially canonized in 1380, it is likely this drawing reflects more the ruler's field chapel of the 16th c., but it shows how the Battle of Kulikovo became a sacred, inspiring legend for Russians. The Tale of the Battle on the Kulikovo Field *by Likhachev, 1980 pg. 98.*

and grand principality armies, aided by some Lithuanian-Rus princes, routed Mamai. The terrain, not being open steppe, worked against the Mongols and their favorite cavalry tactics of encirclement. Russian literary treatments of this event from the 1400s have created estimates of over one hundred thousand on each side—stretching over a front as long as seven miles and making Kulikovo a clash of truly epic proportions for the time. Other calculations based on economic and demographic estimates have placed the numbers on both sides below ten thousand. The later myth-filled, crusading and patriotic military tales—one has angels aiding Dmitry—speak of an opening and mutually fatal joust between a Mongol prince and a Russian knight-turned-monk. They sing of the heroism of Dmitry and of his allied Lithuanian-Rus contingents. They single out the crucial role of the concealed reserve led by his cousin Prince Vladimir Andreevich. And they speak of tremendous losses on both sides. No Russian source, however, reports—as does a German chronicle—that Mamai's Lithuanian ally, Grand Prince Jagailo, cut up Dmitry's forces on their way home.

The real winner of this round turned out to be the Mongol khan Tokhtamish, who mounted a surprise raid on Moscow in 1382 after he had overcome Mamai. Dmitry withdrew his depleted armies from the city to protect the deeper interior, and the inhabitants of Moscow, chiefly commoners, improvised their own defense. The Mongols agreed to negotiate, but they treacherously sacked the city. To contemporaries, then, this warrior-prince later known as Dmitry Donskoy from his 1380 victory, could not have been a simple hero. Nor could his success at Kulikovo have been seen as the starting point of liberation from the Mongols, as depicted in later literary treatments and historiography. Rather, Dmitry's ability to endure Tokhtamish's invasion led to a new pattern of tenuous, submissive relations with the khanate, which recognized the permanence of Moscow's primacy in northern and eastern Rus.

As soon as Tokhtamish retreated with his booty, Dmitry resumed tribute payments, sent his oldest son, Vasily, to Saray as a hostage, and even treated Tver and Ryazan as formal equals. But his territory, henceforth to be called Muscovy, now included the lands attached to the grand principality of Vladimir, as well as several large fur districts north of the Volga. Tver's clash with the Mongols in 1327 had been much more devastating. Muscovy weathered its invasion and pillage and continued to grow.

Dmitry's eldest son, Grand Prince Vasily I (r. 1389–1425), pursued a more cautious and subtle policy toward the Lithuanians and the Mongols. He also reversed his father's and Metropolitan Aleksy's narrow, Moscow-first policy toward the church, which could remain united only as an all-Rus institution. Rather, the talented Bulgarian-born metropolitan Kiprian (r. 1381–1382, 1389–1408 in all Rus) and Vasily's wife, Sofia, helped smooth relations with Vitovt and Lithuania. Meanwhile, soon after Tamerlane first defeated Tokhtamish in 1391, Vasily obtained from him title to several eastern Rus towns, including Nizhny Novgorod, Russia's gateway to the east on the Volga artery. After Tamerlane's second rout of Tokhtamish in 1395, Vasily prepared a defense of Moscow. When Tamerlane left Rus alone and despoiled the khanate instead, Vasily suspended tribute payments.

Then when Edigei besieged Moscow in 1408, the defenses held, and Vasily agreed to renew tribute, more as a nuisance payment than a genuine recognition of the Mongol sovereignty of former times. Edigei's power quickly collapsed in another khanate civil war.

When Vasily I died in 1425, he had also acquired the strategic fur center of Ustyug on the Northern Dvina River network and, like his father, left a larger and stronger Muscovy than he had inherited. But Muscovy had its own internal problems. For example, in 1410 two of the ousted Nizhny Novgorod princes sent an army of Russians, Mongols, Bulgars, and Mordvinians (a local Finnic people) to sack Vladimir. The heavy hand of Moscow's authority elicited criticism even from its supporters, such as the writer Epifany the Wise (d. 1420), who placed these words in the mouth of a Finnic shaman:

> Can any good come to us from Moscow? Do we not already obtain burdens, heavy tributes, oppression, stewards, informers, and bailiffs from there?

Dynastic War

In 1431 Moscow's first uncle-nephew conflict erupted and soon led to bloodshed. The young Vasily II (1415–1462) had four paternal uncles. By customary Rus family law, the eldest uncle, Yuri, possessed the stronger claim to the senior throne. But Vasily I selected his son as successor, in part because the Moscow boyars and their entire patronage network did not wish to share their posts and profits with Yuri's followers. Vasily II's maternal grandfather, Vitovt, also had a stake in the boy's succession, as did the able Greek-born metropolitan Foty (Photius, r. 1410–1431), who desired amity with Lithuania and a united Rus Church.

A complex war, punctuated by intrigues, skirmishes, battles, atrocities, alliances across borders, and roving bands of displaced Tatars, dragged on with intervals of peace for over twenty years. Yuri and Moscow's senior boyar Ivan Vsevolozhsky argued the dispute in front of Khan Ulug Mehmed (r. 1419–1437) of the diminished Qipchak khanate, who decided in Vasily's favor. But then Yuri's army of commoners defeated Vasily's regulars in repeated encounters. The struggle turned vicious, when Yuri's sons murdered his conciliatory leading boyar, and Vasily's men captured and blinded Vsevolozhsky, who had defected over a family quarrel. Yuri briefly occupied Moscow twice in 1433–1434 but died before he could consolidate power. His eldest son, Vasily *Kosoy* ("Squint-eye," d. 1444), then flouted legitimacy and took up the challenge. But lacking most of his father's supporters, he fell captive in 1436 to Vasily II's men, who blinded him.

Next ensued a very cold peace between Vasily II and Kosoy's brother Dmitry Shemyaka (d. 1453), and Moscow's security attentions turned to the incursions of Tatars. In one encounter in 1445 outside Suzdal, Vasily became the prisoner of his former backer, Ulug Mehmed, who had lost his throne, moved north, and now demanded a huge ransom. Shemyaka called for resistance, and Moscow prepared for yet another siege, but then suffered a major fire followed by an uprising of irate commoners opposed to the payment and the Tatars who accompanied Vasily home. A goodly number of eminent monks as well as boyars and rich merchants also supported Shemyaka. With this support, he seized power and treacherously captured and blinded Vasily II while he was making a pilgrimage to a monastery.

Dmitry Shemyaka now became grand prince of Moscow and had the backing of Novgorod, while Vasily, reduced to an appanage prince, obtained the armed support of Ulug Mehmed's younger sons. In this dangerous situation, many powerful Russians gravitated toward Vasily, with his assurance, backed by the church, that once he made peace, he would relocate his Tatar troops. Bolstered by a new family ally, Grand Prince Boris of Tver (r. 1425–1461), and some freshly obtained cannon, Vasily's troops regained Moscow in 1447 and occupied Shemyaka's main town three years later. Finally in 1452, Shemyaka fled to Novgorod, where he soon died. Vasily solved the problem of his Tatar auxiliaries by establishing a useful vassal khanate under Ulug Mehmed's son Kasim in an eastern Oka town, later renamed Kasimov.

Vasily II's resurgence after 1445 indicates that, despite the popular anger over his ransom, both the Muscovite elites and the new military men preferred the legitimate dynastic ruler to a provincial supported by common folk. Lay and clerical landholders had used the disarray at the top since 1430 to appropriate formerly free peasant lands and sought to stabilize the new social and economic situation. Typical for the time, Moscow's two most potent Russian rivals, Novgorod and Tver, often fought each other and never tried to reorganize Russia in their own parochial interests.

Mongol Influences?

Scholars have long pondered without any consensus whether Moscow specifically borrowed any institutions, besides a few types of taxes, from the Mongols. Moscow did adopt a Mongol cavalry formation—deploying a chief regiment in the center and four more on the compass points to avoid ambushes from any direction in an open field—but we do not know when or how this first occurred. It might have come after Moscow became independent. We also cannot discover a direct line from the Mongol to the later Muscovite postal road system, other than the name. A recent attempt to envision Moscow's central military and civil institutions as clearly separate from each other on the model of the Qipchak khanate has run up against stiff denials that such prevailed in either place. Tempting but unprovable linguistic evidence suggests that Mongol officials or other Turkic-speakers developed Moscow's chancery language.

On the other hand, the early Moscow princes were, in a sense, tax farmers, who had to conform to khanate fiscal practices. Grand Prince Dmitry also acted like a khan when he gained temporary control over Bulgar and placed his own proconsul and tax officials there. But no one has been able to specify with certainty a Mongol or khanate institution that the Moscow princes used to rule Russian territory during or after the period under consideration. Only some aspects of public life, such as the use of the Chinese term *kowtow* in greeting equals or superiors, or foot-sole-beating as a form of corporal punishment, appear to have been due to Mongol influence.

Quite a few observers believe that at the end of the Mongol period Russians were more subservient and the Muscovite ruling elite more imperious and arbitrary than the Rus people and elites had been before 1237. In this interpretation the main change due to the Mongols was the solution of the old problem of weak central government by taking as a ready model the powerful Mongol sovereign and his instruments of power. A later Russian chronicle reveals such an understanding of the khan's authority, imputing to Vasily II's spokesmen in Saray the following words:

> Prince Yuri . . . wishes to seize the grand principality according to the dead writ of his father and not by your grant, that of a sovereign tsar. But you have full authority in your domain.

THE APOGEE OF NOVGOROD

Novgorod and its daughter republic Pskov—today Russia's greatest repositories of medieval churches—represent the apex of Rus urban-republican developments, analogous in structure and significance to medieval western Europe's leading city-states, such as Venice and Genoa. Of course medieval republics were not like modern, democratic ones. Distinct social groups had special rights, and families and official religions had immense authority. Churches possessed wealth and power over individuals that would be unimaginable today.

The Setting

From the 1150s to the end of its autonomy in 1478, Novgorod operated with two or three outside political systems claiming authority over its affairs, and it continued to pay out as well as receive tribute. Paradoxically, after the Mongol conquest Novgorod could appeal to a sovereign force above any of the Rus princes. From the 1330s onward Lithuania's princes served as counterweights to Moscow, giving Novgorod's leaders some room to maneuver. Still, the grand princes of Vladimir and later Moscow never relinquished the claim that Novgorod constituted part of their realm.

On paper Novgorod governed or collected tribute from a hinterland larger than the Canadian province of Ontario and double that of present-day Ukraine. The Volkhov River enabled Novgorod to dominate the easternmost Baltic shores, connect with other river systems, and exploit the sparsely inhabited northernmost parts of European Russia up to the White Sea and east to the Urals—here with competition from Rostov, Ustyug, and, later, Moscow. Novgorod's beeswax and furs, mainly gray squirrel, were mainstays of northern Europe's seaborne commerce. Other exports included timber, walrus ivory, and flax. Novgorod's coast, though, lacked a good natural harbor, and its people lacked the resources to initiate a competitive shipbuilding industry or to improve the available outlets to the Baltic. Rather, by the 1300s, Novgorod's own seaborne external commerce mostly disappeared, displaced by new German ships with deeper hulls for carrying large cargoes. In fact, to a great extent Novgorod subordinated its westward commercial policies to the north German cities and their Hanseatic League, which crystallized around 1350 and dominated Baltic and north European trade. In contrast, Novgorod strictly limited German participation in domestic economic life and restricted the German colony in the city to one enclosed settlement.

Novgorodians (and Pskovians)—skilled in defensive engineering, such as flooding invasion routes and building forts and palisades—could usually raise armies sufficient for defense. A citizen army of traders and artisans also enabled Novgorod to maintain a vast commercial and tribute-exacting realm. However, because of relatively poor soil, Novgorod could not support a large native professional military class and normally required an outside prince with his retinue for defense against major Rus rivals or foreign enemies.

Social and Political Life

Novgorod, like many cities, straddled a river. The main palace and St. Sophia Cathedral were on the western Sophia Side of the Volkhov, while economic life concentrated on the eastern Mercantile Side, which included wharves and Peterhof, the German settlement. The Church of St. Nicholas served as the nerve center of the Mercantile Side and during civil strife might be the site of a rival assembly to the one that normally convened outside St. Sophia. Some of Novgorod's streets were lined with boyar villas having artisan and servants' quarters; others had homes of merchants, petty traders, and craftsmen. Each of the five boroughs had its own assembly, mayor, and chief abbot. The streets also had autonomous organizations. The boyar-dominated Prussian Street spanned two of the three boroughs on Sophia Side, and its inhabitants dominated the city for several centuries. Each borough seems to have been associated with the governance of a "fifth" of the hinterlands.

The boyars and "people of substance," despite their rampant factionalism, constituted a ruling class who outlawed court testimony against themselves from slaves and indentured servants. In the 1400s, with the decline in the European market for Novgorod's abundant squirrel furs, this elite seized lands both near the city and in distant domains and bound to themselves many chronically indebted peasants and foresters. By the 1450s Novgorod's elites were major proprietors. Some families controlled up to two hundred square miles and expanded their activities to flax cultivation and salt processing for the market. Among the churches commissioned by this class stands the Transfiguration on Elijah Street, built in 1374, decorated in a new style by Theophanes the Greek (active in Russia, 1378–early 1440s), and containing the city's protective Icon of the Virgin of the Sign. The self-serving *Praying Novgorodians* icon from 1467 was arranged with six finely dressed men and one woman set below the enthroned Christ, who was flanked by six intercessors—as if to suggest that this elite enjoyed divine protection.

Local and German sources reveal that Novgorod's governing institutions of the 1300s and 1400s combined the monarchic, aristocratic, and democratic elements typical of many city-states. The permanent Council of Lords—fifty or sixty boyars

Icon of Praying Novgorodian Elite, ca. 1467. Above is Christ Enthroned with the *Deesis* of the Virgin and John the Baptist, two chief Archangels, and the Apostles Peter and Paul. Gender helps affirm the earthly-heavenly symmetry, as each tier has one female and six male figures. The Novgorodian clothing style is unique. *Novgorod Museum of Art, Novgorod, Russia.*

and former mayors and militia commanders led by the archbishop—was balanced by the free citizens' assembly, whose bell symbolized the city's sovereignty. The assembly approved major laws and chose the three candidates for archbishop, from whom one was selected by lot and confirmed by the metropolitan.

Executive and judicial power remained divided among the chief mayor, the militia commander, the prince, and the archbishop. The chief mayor, who presided over a supreme court staffed by a boyar and a commoner from each borough, had to be a boyar. He served for only a year after 1354 and six months after 1416. By then this office no longer belonged to two or three leading families. The commander, as of the 1300s also a boyar, headed the merchants' court. Over time the power of the merchants declined, and their seal disappeared from court decisions in the 1400s. The prince's court handled normal civil cases.

The archbishop, who in theory enjoyed life tenure, could often be the most powerful political figure. He controlled up to a third of the republic's resources, contributed a third to all public expenses, and exercised the standard episcopal supervision of clerical and lay "church people" and the family, sexual, and spiritual life of the entire population (see the chapter "Kievan Rus: Christian Civilization, 988–1240"). The archimandrite (a high ranking abbot) of the local Yurev Monastery, as ceremonial doyen of the city's monastic clergy, balanced the archbishop to a degree. The names of at least 160 churches in Novgorod and its immediate suburbs survive. This means that at least ten thousand to twenty thousand people could have attended services simultaneously.

By the early 1400s Novgorod's monasteries ranged from the large, older, landowning establishments, to medium-sized abbeys, a few of which also served as boyar granaries, to small cloisters that perhaps served as old-age homes. As in the rest of northern Rus, Novgorod's monastic colonization movement was just beginning. Vaalamo in ethnically Finnish Karelia and Solovetsky on the White Sea stand out among the new foundations. The latter eventually became a major fishing and saltworks center and fortified Russian outpost.

Novgorod's hinterlands continued to enjoy wide autonomy, but they were not always loyal. Pskov received its formal independence from Novgorod in 1348. Far to the north, in the Northern Dvina basin, the local Rus often clashed with the metropolis. Twice during 1397–1401 Moscow wrested the Dvina land from Novgorod to give the Upper Volga region a direct link to the White Sea. In its first known charter to any province, Moscow left the local Dvina "boyars" in charge and granted them trading rights in the main towns down to the Volga. The second time the Novgorod authorities returned, they executed some of the locals and forced others into monasteries.

Pskov

The city-state of Pskov prospered from trade, fishing, and agriculture and appeared small only in contrast to Novgorod. Running along the eastern borders of Estonia and Livonia, Pskov's territory measured roughly the size of today's Netherlands. In contrast to Novgorod, neither large-scale landholding nor cripplingly severe social gaps developed. Independent small farmers and townsmen formed the backbone of society. Pskov lacked a militia commander but had two chief mayors, along with the Council of Lords and the assembly. The hired prince exercised police and judicial powers.

Pskov had no bishop of its own, only the archbishop of Novgorod's vicar. As the city and its boroughs expanded, new ecclesiastical districts were forged around central cathedrals. The city may have added a new cathedral for each new contingent of one hundred or so priests and their parishes, in part to facilitate the religious processions, so essential to medieval urban life. Between 1357 and 1471 Pskov built five more cathedrals. The original one, Holy Trinity, remained the symbol of the city, keeper of its archive, and seat of the vicar. One of Pskov's older urban monasteries became a hotbed of dissidence in the 1410s and 1420s, while an important new cloister produced Russia's first original monastic rule in the 1460s or 1470s.

The evolution from an oral to a written legal culture in Rus also commenced in Pskov, whose law, evincing some German influence, appears to have been the most developed in northern Rus. The local Code (*Sudebnik*) of 1397–1467 ranged over a variety of procedural, economic, and social issues, such as the separation of public office from private interest, equitable police and grand jury investigations, and due compensation. "If a lessee of a fishery misses the spring catch," reads one provision, "he shall pay the landlord according to the yield . . . from his other fisheries." Another reads: "If a son leaves his home and fails to feed his father and mother until their death, he has no portion of their estate." Pskov also had Rus's first known general provisions for the execution of thieves—in this case after the third offense, as well as for horse theft and for crimes against the state or society. Yet Pskovian law corresponded to premodern notions of evidence and recompense. Simple murder still carried compensation and a fine. Judicial duels were often mandated to determine the truth as if God determined the outcome, with only selective hiring of substitutes permitted. As for a suit between women, "A duel may be ordered . . . , but neither may hire a substitute."

Tensions and Visions

Both Novgorod and Pskov experienced the typical medieval urban woes resulting from the climate, low crop yields, poor sanitation, and flammable wooden structures—all of which caused natural population decline within Europe's towns. From 1347 to 1448 Novgorod suffered at least twenty-three major fires, six devastating storms, six visitations of plague, five serious popular uprisings, and three sets of political executions—for heresy, to be discussed shortly, arson, and currency debasement. An unexplained witch craze erupted in Pskov in 1411, according to its chronicle: "In that year the Pskovians burned twelve sorceresses." Hunger ensued whenever warring neighbors disrupted food imports, and usury could prove ruinous. The growing money economy—Novgorod's mint opened in 1420, Pskov's in 1424—contributed to mounting debt bondage (quasi-serfdom) in the countryside but helped the cities. Urban revolts were rarer after 1420.

Such problems notwithstanding, Novgorod and Pskov became, for Rus, rather lively centers of culture. An expanded version of the *Novgorod Chronicle*, running through 1445, represents history told by elite churchmen. It depicted urban strife "instigated by the devil" and showed an archbishop "shedding tears" and using a ceremonious procession and moral suasion to stop the fighting. The accounts of Alexander Nevsky sing of boyar and warrior heroism, while the *Tale of Shchil the Mayor*, who could not be properly buried until the victims of his usury were compensated, uses dramatic narrative to teach morality. The poetic tale of *Sadko* (see the chapter "Kievan Rus: Christian Civilization, 988–1240") reflects Novgorod's mercantile adventurism. The fantastic and the pious blend together in the story of three Novgorodians who visited the original Paradise and in another about the twelfth-century bishop Ioann, whom a demon attempted to corrupt. And a Novgorodian liturgical book from the time mixes the sacred and profane by depicting popular minstrels and their instruments in the margins.

Like some towns of northern Italy in the same period, Novgorod and Pskov developed distinctive styles of painting and architecture. According to one specialist,

> Unlike the ringing color range of Novgorod, the predominant [Pskovian] tones are earthy and green . . . the color comes from somewhere in the depth of the panel, . . . begins to burn, to glow, expressing the inner fires of the spirit, and

> corresponds to the . . . intent expression in the faces of the Pskov saints. In the Novgorod icons the bright colors burn in the clear light of day.

A patriotic Novgorodian icon from the 1400s depicts the victory over the Suzdalians in 1170, with angels, Boris and Gleb, and the protective Virgin of the Sign icon aiding the city in accord with tradition. In 1433 Archbishop Evfimy employed a European architect to supervise local masters and workers to build his new palace, the first Gothic structure in northern Rus. On the practical plane, merchants used the basements of churches they financed for storage.

The appearance of Rus's first authenticated heretics, the *strigolniki*, around 1370–1430, presents another Novgorodian and Pskovian similarity to west European urban experiences. We can conclude from the spotty sources that they, like other such medieval urban groups, protested the worldliness of the church. Arguing specifically that the entire hierarchy was soiled by simony, the requirement of ordination fees from priests and bishops, the *strigolniki* rejected the church taxes and official clergy. Novgorod executed three of them in 1375, and if such dissidence still persisted in the region for half a century, it never developed into mass violence, as did some similar movements in western Europe.

The mounting might of Moscow by the mid fifteenth century proved to be the ultimate political problem facing Novgorod and perhaps the central historical fact of late medieval Russia. In retrospect, we can compare late medieval Novgorod to the contemporary aristocratic Polish, Czech, and Hungarian kingdoms to the west. Had Novgorod's model, with its separation and devolution of power, rather than the undivided Moscow monarchy, united northern and eastern Rus, Russia might have developed a more Western legal and institutional configuration. As it was, Novgorod's boyars had no concept of confederation with other Rus entities or of the ingredients of a successful, multiclass polity, even within their own city. They never transcended the narrow city-state mentality—the Achilles' heel of Classical Greek democracy and many medieval and Renaissance European towns with educational opportunities far superior to Novgorod's. As Vasily II consolidated power following the dynastic war, he forced Novgorod to limit its external sovereignty. Full incorporation into Muscovy would come next.

SPIRITUAL RENEWAL

The Rus found the period of Mongol decline both difficult and creative. As material exactions receded, bubonic plague took its toll, and the insecurity of medieval life persisted. The basic attitudes of the church hardly changed from pre-Mongol times. Staunch adherence to established dogma and monastic ideals, a penchant for ceremony, and a realistic acceptance of prevailing behavior remained the norms. The majority—those who failed to be charitable; to believe, behave, and worship correctly; or to repent in time—were to suffer eternal torments. The popular *Emerald*, a fourteenth-century collection of translated and adapted admonitions from Greek originals, expressed these attitudes in the strongest possible terms. For example,

> A dancing woman is called Satan's bride, the devil's mistress, a demon's wife. Not only will she be cast to the bottom of hell, but also those who look at her with love and burn with love.

Continued recovery, however, marked this period of Russian history. The return of relative prosperity meant that masonry churches went up more frequently than before 1240, and iconographers were needed. Novgorod, Pskov, and Moscow experimented with new types of church roofs: Novgorod with a clover façade on the upper sides, Pskov with a separate upper roof at the center, and Moscow with pointed arches. Moscow obtained its first mechanical clock in 1404, and Russians, in addition to using cannon, copied their Western neighbors in designing some frontier fortifications. Clothing styles intermingled, with Moscow's fashion looking more toward the Turko-Islamic world of its Tatar neighbors than to Europe.

Monasticism and the Fruits of Late Byzantium

In its last centuries, a weakened Byzantium, though under political pressure from Catholic Europe and physically attacked by Muslim Turks, enjoyed a cultural renaissance. This included a secular revival, which had little effect on Rus, and a religious resurgence, which most certainly did. The mainstream Orthodox, ill at ease with the systematic use of formal (Aristotelian) logic by Catholics to explain theology and their fractious attempts to reconcile secular and religious thinking, refurbished and fortified Byzantium's traditional, liturgy-based spirituality. This consciously anti-Western project, radiating from Mount Athos and Constantinople, involved a multinational coterie of Orthodox churchmen, among them some Bulgarians and Serbs proficient in Greek as well as Slavic. For Rus bookmen at this time, the equivalent to joining the community of scholars of the European university was to spend time in a monastery in Constantinople or Mount Athos.

Another aspect of this movement was *hesychasm*—a Greek word denoting tranquility but here signifying the monk's striving for inner illumination via concentrated silence. Greeks and Balkan Slavs composed, translated, retranslated, and circulated a host of monastic spiritual writings, and their icons and frescoes became more expressive of spirituality and emotions. A more spiritualized liturgy and the new iconography were brought into line with each other. At the same time an elaborate writing style known as *word-weaving* came into vogue. The spiritual and the ornate thus balanced each other. Scholars have called the overall effects of these cultural impulses upon Russia the Second South Slavic or Byzantine influence. Two outstanding metropolitans, the Bulgarian Kiprian and then the Greek Foty, reigned over the Rus Church from Moscow during 1389–1431 and helped solidify the transmission and domestication of these impulses.

A novel factor in the patronage of high culture in northern Rus was the rise of the rural monastery, which balanced the practical and the spiritual and housed sages, whom others sought out for advice, including conflict resolution. It was said of the Tverian recluse Varsonofy:

> Many came to him from all parts, monks and noble laymen, some for a profitable word, others seeking an explanation of the Divine Writings.

From modest beginnings, when the founders and their disciples lived in extreme poverty and built everything by hand, the abbeys became rich landowners, controlling scores of peasants, operating commercial ventures over hundreds of miles, and carefully protecting and increasing their wealth. However, these monks also copied hundreds of books devoted to ethical themes and spirituality and painted sensitive, idealistic frescoes, icons, and manuscript illuminations, demonstrating a sincere deepening of religiosity. The cloisters were also charity-dispensing communities of venerators, linking a group of the living and the dead, laity and clergy alike, around the cults of each abbey's founder and the institution's patron saint. Donors to cloisters expected both the monks and the recipients of charity from the donations to pray for designated souls.

This peculiarly medieval combination of opportunism, pious tradition, and miracle cult characterized northern Rus monasticism from about 1350 well into the seventeenth century. Enterprising abbots fought tooth and nail in court to acquire or retain a useful plot of land for their cloisters. But they also commissioned their calligraphers to copy the classical Orthodox mystics and urged other literate monks to combine physical labor, a share in administration, active and attentive participation in the lengthy liturgical chants, and solitary contemplation and spiritual exercises in their daily activities.

Sergy of Radonezh (ca. 1314–1392) stands out as the key figure for this movement. The son of a Rostovian who migrated under pressure from Ivan I's tax collectors to serve in Moscow, Sergy shone as an outstanding, charismatic example of personal poverty and nonresistance to evil. His network of friends and disciples founded dozens of monasteries. His Trinity (*Troitsa*) Monastery, located about forty-five miles northeast of Moscow, became Russia's leading shrine and one of the country's greatest landowners and granaries. Kirill of Beloozero (d.1427), an orphan related to a leading Moscow boyar family, founded his monastery along a huge lake about four hundred miles north of Moscow. It later patronized a plethora of hermitages with hesychastic monks. Both of these abbeys became great book repositories as well.

The well-crafted *Lives* of Sergy and Kirill by Epifany the Wise and Pakhomy the Serb (active in Russia, ca. 1438–1484) stand out among the most important original Russian writings of the period. Commencing as follows, Epifany's *Life* of Sergy introduced repetitive word-weaving to Rus hagiography and established the model for such a depiction:

> Glory to God for everything and on account of everything, for which is glorified His great and thrice-holy name, which is eternally glorified. . . . The Lord knows

> how those glorifying him glorify and how those eulogize him eulogize—Who eternally glorifies His saints, who glorify Him with a pure, God-pleasing and virtuous life.

Pakhomy's reworking of this piece and his *Life* of Kirill brought more rhetorical balance to this style. The mixture of biography, idealization, and reported miracles in these works created models for the pious to emulate for several centuries.

The career of the missionary bishop Stefan of Perm (ca. 1340–1396), who "prophesized prophetic prophesies," according to Epifany, provided another gifted and ambitious subject for the new hagiography. A priest's son from Ustyug on the Slavo-Finnic linguistic frontier of the Russian north, Stefan learned Greek in a Rostov monastery, created a writing system for his Finnic neighbors, and translated liturgical books and other works into their language. At a time when the vast majority of Rus, including princes, were illiterate, Stefan's new alphabet served as a secret script for a few initiates. Epifany's *Life* of Stefan contains a fictionalized debate between the bishop and the local shaman Pam, whose complaint against Moscow officials is cited earlier in this chapter. Stefan's polemical refutation of Novgorod's dissident *strigolniki* and their opposition to any ecclesiastical authority was Russia's first such original theological work. More would follow in subsequent centuries, when book culture developed among laypeople.

Copying of monastic cell literature peaked around 1370–1430, concurrent with an outburst of masonry church construction and artistic genius in northern Rus. Simultaneously the iconostasis or icon screen in front of the altar became higher, as it stands today, adding mystery to the elements of communion, which were prepared behind the closed "royal doors." Worshipers inside churches now directly faced large representations of the patriarchs, prophets, apostles, major saints, and chief festive occasions, with a focus on the redemptive aspect of the Incarnation and the intercession of the Virgin and John the Baptist for the faithful. Facing the path to salvation, they participated in this sacred history, which, some of the theologians argue, also exists outside of time.

The accomplished Greek iconographer Theophanes, who decorated Novgorod's new Transfiguration Church, played a crucial role in the new iconography. Seen by contemporaries as "a renowned sage and most artful philosopher," he had an uncanny ability to improvise, judge color and distance, and express emotion, character, and pessimism. Andrei Rublëv (1360s–ca. 1430), widely hailed as premodern Russia's greatest native artist, may have worked with Theophanes. Using his unique sense of color, Rublëv tried to combine the outer beauty of classical traditions and the inner beauty of perfected souls and Christian divinity. His graceful, serene, and geometrically perfect Old Testament Trinity—the hospitality of Abraham and Sarah to three men or angels—exemplifies this combination (see the photo of the Trinity icon in the next chapter). Rublëv's psychological imagination burst forth in the wonder on the faces of the apostles on his Last Judgment frescoes in Vladimir's Dormition Cathedral. The iconography of Theophanes and Rublëv set the aspirations for Russians for more than a century, as one monk under hesychastic influence argued around 1505–1515:

> to elevate mind and thought to the immaterial and divine light . . . and paint images from material pigments of the Lord Christ, his Immaculate Mother, and all the saints.

Historical Vistas

Historical writing also revived in northern Rus during the period of Mongol decline. Pskov joined Novgorod in producing a locally oriented chronicle, in this case starting with the onset of independence in the late 1200s. Tver's annals, while reporting and respecting Moscow's successes, evince local pride in their own grand princes, such as Michael Alexandrovich (1334–1399). His thirty-four-year reign brought peace, prosperity, and a flourishing church life to the "sons of Tver." Smolensk's mid-fifteenth-century chronicle reveals that central city's ties to both Lithuania and Vladimir-Moscow.

Moscow's chronicles reflect the conciliating and unifying efforts of Metropolitans Kiprian and Foty. Just as the *Primary Chronicle* still informs and slants our vision of the origin of Rus and the rise of Kiev, so these works have had an inordinate influence on our views of Moscow's rise. In their perspective, which crystallized by about 1450, the role of Moscow as the northern political and religious center came to the fore, bolstered by literary legends depicting Dmitry Donskoy as a self-sacrificing warrior-saint. Sometime in the 1400s an entire cycle of Kulikovo tales were written, epitomizing the theme of devout Russians opposing barbaric Mongols and cloaking counteraggression and expansion in religious ideology—motifs that continued as Russia expanded eastward in later centuries and still ring today in patriotic Russian images of the past. The touching, stereotyped depiction of the departure from Moscow in 1380 for the Don could be valid for any major campaign:

> The Grand Princess Evdokia, Vladimir's princess Maria, and the princesses of the other Orthodox princes, and many generals' wives, Moscow boyarinas, and the serving mens' wives accompanied with tears and wailing of the heart, unable to utter a word, as they gave their final kiss. . . . The grand prince himself could barely restrain his tears, but did not cry on account of the people, yet in his heart was crying profusely. He comforted his princess, saying: "My wife, if God is for us, who can stand against us!"

THE END OF BYZANTIUM

If the Qipchak khanate, Muscovy, and Lithuania all experienced civil wars in the 1430s and 1440s, so in a sense did the Orthodox Church. Harried by Ottoman Turkish incursions, the Byzantine civil authorities tried to conciliate the Catholic world in the 1430s in exchange for military aid. A major church council took place in Italy in 1438–1439, first in Ferrara and then at Florence. There the papacy persuaded, bribed, and extorted Orthodox adherence to a union with the Catholic

Church and recognition of Rome's supremacy and offered a compromise on outstanding theological differences. Isidore, the recently appointed and, as it turned out, last Greek metropolitan of Kiev and all Rus (r. 1436–1458), whom the Byzantines selected over Moscow's candidate, endorsed this agreement. The delegates from the provincial dioceses in Moscow's orbit, however, soon pulled back. They later noted sarcastically that three languages were spoken at the council: Greek, Latin, and "Philosophy," that is, the alien reasoning of Catholic theologians. Due to Poland's quarrels with Rome on other issues, neither the Catholic nor the Orthodox clergies of western Rus sent delegates.

Isidore scandalized Moscow by returning in 1441 with a Catholic cardinal's hat and by mentioning the pope in public prayers. Soon Vasily II imprisoned him but then avoided a diplomatic complication by letting him escape to Lithuania. After seven years of indecision, the Muscovites replaced him with their old candidate, Bishop Iona of Ryazan (metropolitan, 1448–1461), without seeking Byzantine approval. Also confronted by powerful opposition at home, the Byzantine authorities themselves could not enforce the union with Rome, which in strict Orthodox eyes was uncanonical simply due to the lack of participation by the other Eastern patriarchates (Alexandria, Antioch, and Jerusalem). Before the Greeks and Russians could reconcile their differences, Constantinople fell to a Turkish onslaught in 1453, the great city itself unable to withstand cannonade. The Russians took this event and their own possession of the world's only sovereign Orthodox Christian realm as signs of God's wrath toward the Greeks and favorable judgment toward themselves. At this very moment Vasily II was completing the reunification of his Muscovite domains. A new era for Russia was about to begin.

CHAPTER 6

Russia's New Monarchy, 1456–1533

O Rus. May God preserve it! There is no country in the world like it, even if its princes . . . are inequitable. May Rus be well-governed and know justice!
—Afanasii Nikitin of Tver, *Travels Beyond Three Seas*, 1468–1475

The church pastor must pray for his reigning lord; the lord must defend the pastor and the wealth of the church; and the peasant must labor and feed them both.
—*Brief Discourse*, written for Archbishop Gennady of Novgorod, 1497

The European artillery that breached the walls of Constantinople for the Ottoman Turks in 1453 symbolized the new era in which Western technology and culture would have a global impact. Gunpowder simplified the consolidation and growth of older empires and newer monarchies, among them Muscovy, which expanded in all directions, and Poland-Lithuania, which consolidated both its royal and its aristocratic structures. To the south the Crimean khanate carried on after 1475 as a client of the imposing Ottoman Empire and became the most powerful successor of the shattered Qipchak khanate. Overseas expeditions, booty and trade, and the abatement of the plague stimulated a century of demographic and economic growth all over Europe and Asia. Renaissance culture and eventually the Protestant Reformation rocked Europe and began to have a profound impact upon Rus, especially in its western parts under Catholic rule.

Historians generally treat the period of Russian history from about 1456 to 1533 in a positive light. The combination of relative prosperity, expansion, consolidation, a national law code, new cultural attainments, and the reconstruction of the capital city recalls the achievements and glory of eleventh-century Kiev. According to a contemporary source, this was an epoch of renovation and rejuvenation. Three centuries later the conservative writer-historian Nikolai Karamzin, who was promoting a Russian national narrative, argued that the Russian monarchy functioned best at this time of mutual understanding between rulers and free subjects. Life, of course, is never so rosy. The losers in the unification process and many commoners suffered during this era. Nevertheless, more than one observer has echoed Karamzin's admiration for the reigns of Ivan III "the Great" of Moscow (r. 1462–1505) and his son Vasily III (r. 1505–1533).

FOUNDATIONS: POLITICAL AND ECONOMIC

The grand principality of Muscovy was far more potent at the close of its dynastic civil war in 1455 than it had ever been, and it shared several underpinnings with western Europe's "new" monarchies of the late 1400s and the 1500s. Europe's monarchs developed a solid and sufficient tax base, most commonly through war contributions levied during emergencies and augmented by taxing commerce. Cannon, which only central governments could afford in bulk, made them much stronger than earlier. Military victories in external and civil wars augmented royal prestige. Crowns continued to harmonize their interests with the prevailing social structures. At one and the same time monarchs presented themselves as protectors of churches, leaders among fellow nobles, sponsors of merchants, patrons of scholars and artists, and model family patriarchs for the traditional peasantry. The official churches continued to serve as a bedrock of the crown; the king was God's representative on Earth, bound by Christian law, always to be obeyed so long as he followed it, and sometimes when he did not.

At the hub of power in Moscow in 1456 stood the blind grand prince, Vasily II (r. 1425–1462), whose direct rule and patronage network extended over the Rus east and north. His eldest son, Ivan, the heir-presumptive and ceremonial coruler, was already affianced to the daughter of the grand prince of Tver. In 1456 Vasily II pledged one of his own daughters to Ryazan's young grand prince, brought him to Moscow, and sent governors to rule in his stead. Because Novgorod had harbored the rebel Dmitry Shemyaka and flirted with Lithuania, in 1456 Moscow organized attacks all over the republic's vast territory. Tver, Pskov, and vassal Tatars sent contingents to help Moscow. Soon Novgorod agreed to recognize Vasily's suzerainty, pay a high tribute, coordinate foreign policies, and shun the Lithuanian princes. Only Muscovy was fully sovereign in Russia, as we now call eastern Rus.

If the ruler's court and person served as the nerve center of this powerhouse, the authority of the leading women there depended on their ability as well as their domestic position. Ivan III's mother, Maria Yaroslavna (d. 1485), remained a powerful figure and, even after she became a nun, helped soothe family disputes. His second wife, the Italian-raised, refugee Byzantine princess Sofia Palaiologa (d. 1502), was an important cultural and diplomatic figure, and she aided her son Vasily III in gaining the throne, as we shall see in the discussion of succession late in this chapter. And, before Vasily died, he designated his wife Elena Glinskaya regent.

As Moscow annexed other principalities and grew, so did the grand prince's palace lands. At the head of the administration stood a small number of magnates with the official court rank (as opposed to general designation) of boyar, who functioned as state counselors. A small number of literate secretaries provided the necessary administrative glue. In the absence of a centralized military levy, the system of autonomous appanages ruled by the senior prince's closest relatives survived, but precariously. Both Ivan III (1440–1505) and Vasily III (1479–1533) began their reigns by dealing with four brothers who ruled over their own appanages with miniature courts and armies. Overt opposition to the center proved dangerous;

conspirators who tried to free an imprisoned appanage prince in 1462 were publicly tortured and executed.

Short-term lieutenants or district chiefs, appointed by the ruling princes, supervised provincial towns and the state or "black" lands—those neither subject to a prince's palace administration nor lying within the jurisdiction of bishops, monasteries, or boyars. Since these officials received traditional contributions or taxes (called "feeding") from their charges, this arrangement served a double purpose: maintaining political and judicial control, and rewarding members of the elite well beyond the narrow circle of official boyars. At times brutal and corrupt, the institution of "feeding" also functioned as a form of ritualized exchange between the ruling class and the governed, who, while owing taxes and service to the state, expected protection and justice from the representatives of the sovereign. As Muscovy expanded, so did the reserve of "black" lands and available income for both state and ruling class. But taxes at this time did not prove overly burdensome, and Muscovy's underadministered mosaic of jurisdictions, with most authority heading upward to the grand prince, functioned quite well for the eighty relatively prosperous years after Vasily II's dynastic war.

Russia's productive base remained small-scale agriculture and forest enterprises. Even within the growing number of large and middle-sized estates, individually farmed plots predominated, and the peasants provided the estate owners with part of the produce, not direct labor services. Further land clearing and drainage and the spread of western Europe's standard three-field system (how much it was used is a matter of debate) represented the major agrarian changes. Increased food production and the concomitant rise of the population and commerce gave Russia some advantage over the neighboring Tatars, once the Qipchak khanate broke apart. In the early 1500s the city of Moscow by one probably exaggerated count had more than forty thousand households (i.e., 120,000–160,000 people), making it much larger than any other Rus city had ever been.

Foreigners marveled at the richness of Russia's northern lakes and forests, with their "fish, game, and hides of all kinds of abundant beasts," and also at the variety of foods, furs, cloth, and jewelry in Moscow's busy markets. Several monasteries, such as Trinity and Kirillov, played a special economic role, with their far-flung holdings, depots in many towns, and moneylending, thereby joining the richest urban merchants as Russia's commercial elite. Muscovy's external commerce remained essential for the acquisition of certain things. The Nogay Tatars supplied up to twenty thousand horses per year to the Russians in return for Russian metal and leather goods. Exports also proved essential to generate money, since Russia lacked good sources of silver or gold until the 1700s and needed a trade surplus to acquire these precious metals. Consequently Russians often paid for foreign commodities with other commodities such as bundles of furs. Paper money was unknown, and Russia had few if any private bankers—none with international connections. As during the Mongol period, foreigners carried most of Russia's seaborne external trade, with local authorities controlling commerce inside Russia's borders. Russian merchants, however, continued to venture overland into Lithuania and the former territories of the Qipchak khanate, profiting from connections forged in bygone years.

UNIFICATION DRAMAS, 1463–1521

Moscow's acquisition of Rus territories proceeded apace, taking several forms: confiscation, inheritance, purchase, enticement, intimidation, and outright conquest. Starting with Vasily II, the grand princes confiscated the appanages of rebellious, suspect, or superfluous relatives—a process one scholar called "pruning the family

Moscow's Unification Acquisitions, 1456–1523. *From Allen F. Chew,* An Atlas of Russian History. *Published by Yale University Press. Copyright © 1967. Reprinted by permission of Yale University Press.*

tree." As a matter of state policy, Ivan III and Vasily III inherited the appanages of their loyal relatives who lacked sons—Vasily going one step further in forbidding his four younger brothers to marry until he himself produced an heir. Acting rather civilly, Ivan III purchased the remnants of the domains of the princes of Yaroslavl and Rostov in 1463 and 1474 and converted their rulers into service princes. Using more brutal means, he defeated Novgorod's armies and then bullied its citizens into submission in the years 1471–1478. With demonstrative shows of force in 1485 and 1489 he compelled his ineffectual brother-in-law, the grand prince of Tver, to flee, and the distant, northeastern, semibrigand republic of Vyatka to relinquish its autonomy. In addition, in the course of 1493–1500, Ivan enticed and coerced the territorial princes along the upper Oka River to switch allegiance from Lithuania to Moscow and then fought Lithuania for the next three years to secure them. Vasily III simply assumed control of the republic of Pskov in 1510 following local opposition to his representative's behavior there. He seized Smolensk from Lithuania in 1514 and took over the domains of his cousin, the grand prince of Ryazan, and some Upper Oka princes in 1518–1523. So, in brief, went the story of unification and expansion—the "gathering of Rus lands"—under Russia's "new" monarchy. The actual interplay of domestic and foreign policy in these events was more complex.

Novgorod's Tragedy

Novgorod, with its wealth, huge hinterland, cultural resources, and international connections, proved to be by far the most important of Moscow's annexations. Muscovite propaganda treated the issue as a defense of Orthodoxy against Catholicism. Later chronicles blamed a "wily, . . . accursed" woman, the boyar widow Marfa Boretskaya, for bribing Novgorod's assembly to turn to the Catholic king and grand prince Casimir of Poland-Lithuania for protection—the story found in most histories of Russia. Close examination of the sources, however, shows that in 1470 Novgorod, rather, was divided over which Orthodox metropolitan would install its new archbishop, Moscow's locally chosen Filip or the Lithuanian-backed Grigory of Kiev. So in 1471, to prevent the return of any Lithuanian influence in Novgorod, Moscow orchestrated several simultaneous invasions of Novgorodian territory. In the key battle at the Shelon River outside of Novgorod, Moscow won an easy victory, since many Novgorodians refused to fight. After the capitulation, Ivan III executed or imprisoned a few pro-Lithuania leaders and made peace with the rest of the city on terms of reduced autonomy.

That was the beginning of the end for the venerable republic. During the 1470s, the Muscovites, reinforced by the armies of Tver, Pskov, and service Tatars, treated Novgorod as a rich cow to be milked. In 1475–1476 Ivan III's Muscovite troops were back in Novgorod, and he came in person to investigate reports of disloyalty, encourage denunciations, and extort lavish gifts and displays of loyalty. He returned again with a large troop in late 1477–1478 to demand recognition of his unlimited authority there and confiscate a goodly amount of church property. This time he formally abrogated Novgorod's sovereignty and republican structure and removed its assembly bell to Moscow. He also broke his earlier promise and confiscated the lands of the local boyars in the years 1484–1489. By 1500 at least one thousand and possibly as many as eight thousand Novgorodian families, merchants as well as nobles, had lost their property.

The Southern and Western Borderlands

The fall of Novgorod sent shock waves throughout the region and upset two of Ivan III's brothers, the Lithuanians, and the Tatar Great Horde, which mounted an invasion to bring him to heel. "Great panic" ensued in Moscow, "especially among the avaricious and pot-bellied rich," so reported a chronicle. But the grand prince's rivals could not mount a coordinated assault. Rather, in 1480 his armies faced down the Tatars on the Ugra River well to the south, and they fled to avoid the winter. Moscow emerged from the crisis stronger than ever. At this point, the ruling dynasty, with support from the church, considered itself released from its traditional oath of allegiance to Saray—a move that historians have traditionally seen as "the end of the Mongol yoke." In fact the old steppe policy of requiring gifts and tribute hardly ceased. The Crimean Tatars continued to be very successful practitioners of such extortion and to mount slave raids against both Russia and Poland-Lithuania for two more centuries.

At the same time, Russia's unification process shifted to the broader international arena. Onto this diplomatic chessboard, with its balance of power politics, stepped the acknowledgedly skillful Ivan III and his state secretaries, who deftly applied divide-and-conquer tactics. So long as the Great Horde lasted—until about 1502—Crimea was Moscow's natural ally. Ivan III understood this very well, and in the early 1480s he reduced Kazan to a client, sometimes with a Crimean prince on the throne. In 1483 he invited the Crimeans to invade Poland-Lithuania and profited strategically and fiscally as they sacked Kiev mercilessly and gave him some of the booty.

Ivan III seized another great opportunity for gain when Casimir of Poland-Lithuania died in 1492. The following year some of Lithuania's upper Oka border princes shifted their allegiance and their lands to Moscow, and Russia mobilized. Lacking Polish military support at the time, the Lithuanians had to make peace. Their new grand prince, Alexander, agreed to marry Ivan III's daughter Elena, and the treaty expressly permitted the princess to remain Orthodox. This provided the type of semi-legal grounds—defense of Orthodoxy—that Russian diplomats would use time and again against Lithuania and Poland for three centuries until that state disappeared from the map.

Under the pretext of Orthodoxy endangered, Ivan III renewed hostilities against Lithuania in 1500. The Crimeans attacked from the south. Soon more border princes defected, and Moscow acquired most of the old Chernigovian domains. The desperate Lithuanians convened a special parliament in 1502 to secure military service from all landholders. But only when he had to deal as well with a Livonian incursion into Pskov's territory did Ivan III call off his western offensive and make a truce with Lithuania in 1503.

Peace did not hold for long under the new grand prince, Vasily III. Strengthened by the defection of Mikhail Glinsky, a talented Lithuanian with a Mongol pedigree and a European university education, the Muscovites reopened hostilities in 1513 and used cannon to capture Smolensk in 1514. Moscow retained this crucial town, even after the Poles helped the Lithuanian-Rus army achieve a stunning victory over the Russians at Orsha farther west.

By this time the Crimeans were supporting Lithuania, and with puppets often ruling both Kazan and Astrakhan, virtually re-created the Qipchak khanate west of the Volga. Moscow responded to this new alignment in the years 1514–1521 by constructing stone walls around Tula, about 105 miles south of Moscow and 40 miles south of the Oka. The fortification proved a sound investment in an iron-rich area on the edge of the wooded steppe. Nevertheless, a brutal Crimean raid on the southern frontier in 1521 induced Moscow to make another truce with Lithuania on the basis of the status quo.

Overall, from the 1490s through 1521 Moscow's larger population and appeal to the Orthodox outweighed Lithuania's aristocratic allures and greater liberties in the competition between these two Rus realms. Still, for the next two decades Russia's further expansion would be blocked by the combination of Lithuania, Crimea, and Kazan.

INSTRUMENTS OF POWER

The more territories Muscovy acquired, the more it needed to devise means to govern them and mobilize their resources, lest they fall away again—a recurrent problem for the pre-Mongol Rus princes. Personal ties between the grand prince and various semisovereign princes and towns had proven shaky in the past. But how to replace them? As in the development of many other monarchies in world history, the existing palace and palace-land administration provided the core around which the sovereigns and their closest associates built up the state.

Crown and Magnates

With every annexation, the Muscovite rulers had to decide what to do with the leading families of the new territories. Vanquished rulers, their closest kin, and manifest or suspected opponents of Moscow were normally driven into exile, confined in remote towns or monasteries, or simply killed. Other princes, usually distant relatives of the sovereign, were allowed to serve alongside Moscow's nontitled boyars, that is, those who did not descend from Rus or neighboring royalty. Princes from the new southwestern periphery remained petty sovereigns at home but did not join the boyar ranks. Lesser princes from the interior, as well as some eminent Lithuanian and Rus immigrants and their progeny, worked their way into the small select circle of magnates enjoying the highest official ranks. Forging marriage ties within the elite, including the ruling family, attained utmost importance in this political jockeying.

As concerning pre-Mongol times, historians of Muscovy at this time are divided over the existence of a formal *Boyar Duma,* or Council, rather than an ad hoc privy council. But scholars do agree that in Muscovy a select number of hereditary aristocrats and elite servitors held *duma,* or council, ranks. According to the most recent findings, the number in this select group fluctuated between twelve and fifteen during the reign of Ivan III and twelve and twenty-four under Vasily III. Under Ivan III the number of ranking boyars decreased, but beneath them developed the council rank of *okolnichii* (attendant), whose holders tended to work in the court, state administration, or diplomatic missions, rather than military service. Gradually, princes eclipsed the nontitled boyars in the highest levels. Under Ivan the highest-ranking boyar was the senior lieutenant or governor of Moscow, a position held by his cousin Prince Ivan Patrikeev until his fall in 1499 during a succession crisis. Subsequently the position or title of equerry or marshal (master of the horse) became the most prestigious. Boyars with council ranks usually held governorships of such key border towns as Novgorod, Pskov, and (as of 1514) Smolensk.

A clear analogy with medieval and early modern western and east-central Europe is found in the high judicial functions of boyars and *okolnichii.* Together they formed a quasi court of law, which helped the sovereign legislate, combining innovation and the sanctioning of established practices, such as writs of manumission masters gave to slaves.

In several ways, however, Muscovy was not at all like the European states to the west. Moscow's boyars and *okolnichii,* were, as judges, simple extensions of the sovereign's person and power and lacked any formal, corporate, or legal means of checking him, unlike their Western counterparts. Moreover, if the loyalty of a high-ranking person were suspect, he and a huge circle of connected people from magnates down to full slaves could be compelled to sign a guarantee of his loyalty and to pledge immense sums of money to the sovereign in case of any treachery.

The problem of integrating highborn immigrants, service princes, and members of Moscow's old boyar families led to the development of a unique system of rank-ordering known as *mestnichestvo*—a code of precedence. According to its principles, which favored the established boyar clans over most new princes, families possessed relative ranking, and individuals, according to their place within these families, possessed an operational standing relative to individuals within other families. If boyar A had held a higher command in a campaign than boyar B, then the eldest son of A had the right not to serve on a campaign in a lower rank than any of B's sons. But how about A's other sons? Did they, too, have an automatic right not to serve under B's eldest son? If by serving under him, would they, in keeping with Old Russian values, disgrace their family? Such was the fear, and consequently the code of precedence eventually led to numerous disputes among the elite—more after the able reigns of Ivan III and Vasily III than before 1533. But this unwritten code did accomplish two things. It provided a means of incorporating people of diverse origin into a national officer corps with some sense of hereditary ranking, and it helped prevent the fractious elite from coalescing into a European type of aristocracy with a corporate identity and political rights independent of the crown. Rather, to some degree or other—in the absence of memoirs or council minutes, we really do not know precisely how—the boyars ruled Muscovy together with the sovereign.

Interpretations continue to differ in this regard. Some specialists use *autocracy* to describe a Muscovite state without anything approaching the legal, corporate autonomy of Europe's nobilities and towns. Others use *despotism* or *tyranny* to characterize the ruler's or the ruling elite's power over subjects' lives, labor, and property. Still others consider Muscovy essentially to have been a boyar *oligarchy* (rule of the few) operating under the mediating and sometimes decisive leadership of the sovereign, but with an impressive ceremonial *façade of autocracy*. Whatever the truth behind these concepts, the strong rulers, such as Ivan III, clearly held immense power and might order an execution on their own authority. According to disgruntled Muscovites, the sovereigns consulted only with a favorite state secretary and "completely heeded him," or they decided matters in their private chamber with two advisers by taking one of their suggestions. Starting in the 1490s, most observers from other parts of Europe found the elite Muscovites to be servile toward their ruler and even proud of it. "All confess themselves to be slaves . . . of the prince," states the famous account of Vasily III's Russia by the German ambassador Sigismund von Herberstein (1486–1566). A recent attempt to reconcile the power and the vulnerability of Russia's elites sees them as "enfranchised subjects."

Paradoxically, the decades that rendered the foreign-born grand princesses Sofia Palaiologa and Elena Glinskaya so powerful also witnessed the developing seclusion of elite Russian women from male society outside of their families. This practice may have protected female chastity, but it also set Russia apart from other Christian lands, including western Rus. Even secluded women, however, often remained key brokers of family politics and alliances.

Landholding and Peasants

Moscow's ruler faced the monumental task of creating a genuine national army to replace the traditional mix of diverse territorial levies. Between 1484 and 1505, Ivan III's government systematically confiscated all the holdings of Novgorod's elite and some of the local church lands—about six thousand square miles in all—settling there about twenty-three hundred warriors on ample estates (*pomestie*) of eight hundred to twenty-four hundred acres. In return, they (and their heirs) provided military service, with needy surviving widows obtaining a small portion of these lands. About 60 percent of these new estate-holders (*pomeshchiks*) were rank-and-file servicemen, 20 percent were from distinguished service families, and 5 percent were elite servitors who acquired supplementary estates. The remaining three hundred-odd were former military slaves or servants, chiefly of exiled Novgorodian families.

Thus was born the *pomestie* system, combining aspects of several antecedents: conditional land grants from princes to their lowly palace servitors and slaves; the rural "feeding," whereby peasants living on state lands gave traditional amounts of support to temporary lords; recent restrictions on the disposal of hereditary lands; and the general obligation of free people to serve that had existed under the Mongols, if not also earlier.

The Novgorodian pattern was repeated to some extent in Pskov and Smolensk after Moscow annexed them in the early 1500s. The *pomestie* system spread as well to the central districts, since incursions and slave raids from Kazan and Crimea forced Vasily III's regime to establish a continuous watch on the southern and southeastern frontiers. As military needs increased and the service land system developed, the state increasingly treated the fully heritable lands as *pomestie* in exacting service from their owners.

An estate is useless without labor, and so it is logical that Muscovy's first general restriction on free peasant movement was enacted as the *pomestie* system was taking hold. On the request of specific landholders, the state had earlier in the 1400s bound certain peasants, termed *old dwellers,* to their domiciles. According to a new statute, placed in the 1497 national law code (*sudebnik*) and operative for nearly a century, peasants, once they had paid all debts, were free to move only during two weeks in November (around St. George's festival). Such regularity benefited not only *pomestie* holders, but other landowners, merchants, and the central treasury to boot—a welcome effect, for the state faced the rising costs of Europe's new military technology. Muscovy had hired foreign artillery experts as early as the 1470s and employed German and Czech mercenaries in the Smolensk campaign of 1513–1514. Moscow's restrictions on peasant movements were similar to measures enacted around this time or earlier in Poland and western Rus.

Moscow's Administration

Integrating diverse territories, forging a national army, and conducting the foreign policy of an expanded and fully sovereign realm required some full-time officials and institutional regularity. Accordingly, Russia's continuous record of diplomatic instructions, reports, and correspondence originates in the 1470s, and Russia's first national law code in 1497. The key functionaries were the state secretary (*dyak*—from *diakon* or deacon, like the English *clerk* from *cleric*—as literate clergy provided the first clerks in both England and Russia) and the undersecretary. In the Mongol period these scribes may have been slaves, but by the 1470s the state secretaries were a crucial if minuscule group, some coming from middle-level service families. Accompanying missions abroad, sometimes leading them, and playing a special role in the unification process, state secretaries made and kept the land, tax, and military records and assisted the major provincial governors and highest courts.

The 1497 code endowed the state with greater control over criminal justice than before. Murderers, brigands, arsonists, kidnappers, church robbers, conspiring slaves, and "other known evil people" were to be executed, possibly upon the character testimony of the leading servicemen or peasants of a district. A simple thief was flogged for the first offense and executed for the second, the felony against the state now having precedence over the loss to the victim who might wish to enslave the perpetrator in order to recoup losses. As per the code, the state also registered enslavement (from birth, marriage, sale, indebtedness, inheritance, or contract), manumission, and horse sales.

By the late 1400s Moscow's armies used the Mongol-inspired five-regiment system, allowing the main army and commander in chief in the center always to be protected from any direction by a vanguard, a rearguard, a left wing and a right. Eventually relying on service estates for recruits, but facing disputes over rank-ordering, the army itself needed records. The earliest known muster lists for a campaign, with the distribution of troops among various regiments, stems from the period 1475–1486.

As literate officials, state secretaries also oversaw some fortification work and directed the new system of postal and military roads. Notwithstanding the appropriation of the Mongol term *yam*, this regional communication system appears to have been more developed than anything the Mongols operated in Russia. With postal stations for supplies and remounts at intervals of about twenty-five miles, messengers could cover the two hundred and seventy-odd miles between Moscow and Novgorod in three days.

By 1533 several offices headed by state secretaries had virtually separated from the treasury. Most adult males and heads of families were registered on communal or district tax registers, land surveys, or muster rolls. But the officialdom was far from satisfactory in people's eyes. If the 1497 code guaranteed access to courts, around 1530 a monk in Novgorod complained to Moscow's head bureaucrat there:

> Many people say you arrive late to the palace, and until you do, no work gets done there. . . . As you won't resolve cases, plaintiffs waste their resources on red tape and don't attend to their businesses, and their crafts lay idle.

IDEALS IN CONFLICT

Unification, expansion, complete independence, novel technologies, and other direct contacts with late medieval and early Renaissance Europe combined to make the era of Ivan III and Vasily III both innovative and stressful for Russia. Ivan III's second marriage in 1472 to Sofia Palaiologa helped to strengthen Russia's growing connections with Europe. Latin now displaced Greek as the principal source of new translations, and a variety of European practical works, such as calendars and herbals (medical guides), started to appear in Russian versions. Russian leaders, both lay and clerical, needed fresh self-definitions and visions of their society and its place in a changing world.

The best and most innovative Russian iconography of this time reflected the deep Orthodox consensus among most churchmen and specific, current concerns. Medieval Russia's last great painter Dionisy (d. post–1502) and his circle portrayed the victory of Orthodoxy over heresy and immorality, the spirituality of the individual monk, and overall gratitude to the Mother of God for her role in the scheme of salvation. Russian artists for the first time depicted the apocalypse and conflated the immediate judgment of the soul after death with the Last Judgment. Trying to counter the appeal of astrology, they triumphally represented Divine Wisdom and Providence controlling human destiny.

New Vistas

Nowhere were the changes of the time so evident as in the simple effects of travel both to and from Russia. About 1468–1474, the Tver merchant Afanasy Nikitin journeyed via the Volga, the Caspian, and Persia to India. There he feigned conversion to Islam to save his life and somehow survived to compose a spicy account of his travails that reflected the biculturalism of his later life and contains Arabic incantations such as *Allah akbar* (God is great). The powerful state secretary Fëdor Kuritsyn (d. ca. 1502) returned from a mission to Hungary and Moldavia in the 1480s and, apparently, composed or transmitted three eye-opening works. His brief ode on the "sovereignty" of the studious believer's soul betrays a Jewish origin or influence. An introduction to the formal study of grammar and literature (the basis of premodern, Christian higher education) contains an enthusiasm for letters as God's redemptive gift to humankind, rare for Russia at the time. And the chilling tale of the historic Dracula—the brutal Wallachian prince, Vlad the Impaler (d. 1476)—served equally as a diplomatic report about the more successful powerful rulers on the Hungarian and Moldavian thrones. Another leading diplomat, Dmitry Gerasimov (ca. 1465–1530s/40), translated an ancient grammar text from Latin and apprised the papacy of a possible northern maritime passage to China, which could be beneficial for international commerce. Still another diplomat, Fëdor Karpov (d. 1540), defended astrology and quoted from Ovid, Cicero, and Aristotle in support of Classical and Western notions of law, property, and dignity, which were hardly known in Muscovy. Russia's first few Westernizers stemmed from the time of Ivan III and Vasily III.

The Italian influence became especially marked in the rebuilding and enlarging of the Moscow Kremlin structures during 1475–1508, after Russians had proven unequal to the task of enclosing the sovereign's residence within high-rising symbols of the holy. The first of a half dozen or so Italian architects and master builders to arrive, the experienced Aristotle Fioravanti (ca. 1418–1486), amazed the Russians with his various skills. To emphasize the definitive advent of Moscow as an ecclesiastical capital, he reconstructed Moscow's modest Dormition Cathedral with decorative motifs taken from Vladimir's. Using lighter materials, iron tie rods, and external pilasters (rectangular columns), he obtained higher vaulting and a greater sense of interior space than Rus had ever known. As the seat of the head of the Russian Church into the early 1700s, Moscow's Dormition Cathedral became the model for many provincial churches and the site of coronations from that of Ivan III's first presumed heir, Dmitry, in 1498 to Russia's last one in 1896.

Italians also reconstructed Moscow's Kremlin walls on the model of one of their ducal fortresses and built the crown's Faceted Palace. The latter had interior Gothic vaulting and Italian external ornamentation and hosted a more elaborate court ritual

Moscow's Dormition Cathedral (Uspensky Sobor), built by the Italian Aristotle Fioravanti, 1475–79, with some decorations typical of Vladimir's Dormition Cathedral (upper left) and other great 12th-century churches, but using Western construction techniques to create height, mass, and interior space. © *William Brumfield.*

than earlier, which is usually credited to the influence of Sofia Palaiologa. The reconstructed Archangel Cathedral, which became the mausoleum for the male members of the dynasty, only looks Russian from the outside because of the cupolas; otherwise it is Renaissance Italian. In addition, Italians constructed the then 197-feet-high, Italian-style "Ivan the Great" Bell Tower (about the same height as Pisa's Leaning Tower in Italy, and named for a seventh-century Sinai monk, not Ivan III, as is commonly assumed). Next to it, in the early 1530s, an Italian-built Church of the Resurrection went up to symbolize Moscow's claim to be a New Jerusalem.

Of course, Russia's Byzantine heritage and strict piety precluded the wholesale adaptation of the Classical Greco-Roman legacy that characterized Renaissance Italy. The interior floor space and iconography of the new churches remained thoroughly Orthodox. Still, paradoxically, the ensemble of Moscow's Kremlin structures, which today is one of the emblems of Russia, was to an extent a creation of Italy's late *quattrocento* (1400s) and made Moscow appear more outwardly European than otherwise would have been the case. It stands as testimony to the degree of Russian openness during the rise of the new Muscovite monarchy—when, we should add, most European courts were also dazzled by the Italians, as was the Ottoman. Even the Crimean Tatars employed an Italian master builder.

At what point Russians acquired the skill to apply the new European devices to produce original hybrids is not certain. The 190-feet-high Church of the Ascension at Vasily III's suburban retreat of Kolomenskoe presents a good example of such an edifice, which Italians also may have designed. Started in 1529 as an offering for the heir Vasily sought, this structure has a central octagonal drum with triple-tiered, pointed gable arches. It peaks into an octagonal cone—a unique, geometrically intricate style, which reappeared in some later Russian churches and used mathematical perfection and a wisdom symbol to express earthly piety.

Orthodoxy and Dissent

The dramatic events and new vistas and images of this epoch affected Russia's leading religious minds. This in turn led to bitter controversies over ritual, doctrine,

Andrei Rublev's "Hospitality of Abraham" or Old Testament Trinity Icon (1410s), one of Russia's most famous paintings. Iosif Volotsky's attack on the "Novgorod Heretics" (or "Judaizers") included a defense of this standard theme, based on the classical Christian interpretation that the mysterious visit of three men or angels to Abraham and Sarah (Genesis 18.1–16) was, in fact, God appearing as the Trinity. *Tretyakov Gallery Moscow, Russia/Scala/Art Resource, NY.*

cultural norms, ultimate authority, and the role of the church in society. The problem first appeared in conquered Novgorod, whose residents did not take readily to their new masters, while the first Moscow-appointed prelates showed insufficient respect for local practices and mentalities. Then in 1487, Archbishop Gennady (r. 1485–1503) claimed to have discovered among the better educated local clergy some "Jewish-thinking" heretics, who feigned Orthodoxy but attacked icons, the clergy, and even basic Christian dogmas. They are commonly called by the very misleading term *Judaizers.* Dissident thinking spread to Moscow around 1478, when Ivan III placed two Novgorodian priests in his Moscow cathedrals. They later formed an intellectual circle that included the influential diplomat and purported adept in astrology, Fëdor Kuritsyn, and Moscow's leading scribe-historiographer, Ivan Chërny. Great anxiety, moreover, stemmed from a calendrical accident. The year 1492 in our modern reckoning was the year 7000 according to Orthodox Christian calculations, and it was seen by some writers as an apocalyptic date. Thus the fear that the reign of the Antichrist was about to commence compounded the dread among church authorities opposing this unmasked, but probably exaggerated heresy within their midst.

To meet this challenge, Gennady enlisted the aide of a few foreign Catholics and Russia's most learned monks. The Catholics helped him procure and translate theological works, issue a report of execution and dispossession of convicted heretics by the Spanish Inquisition, compose a defense of church property, and, in 1499, compile the first complete Slavic Bible. Gennady's own persuasive efforts resulted in a few prison terms meted out to the accused at a Moscow synod in 1490. Then the monks, led by the founder-abbot of the Volokolamsk Monastery, Joseph Volotsky (1439/40–1515), took over the active fight and drove from office Metropolitan Zosima (r. 1490–1494), who was friendly to Kuritsyn. Over the period 1493–1515 or so Joseph and like-minded ascetics produced Russia's first comprehensive original theological-didactic work, known as the *Enlightener*, with an entire section devoted to the repression of heresy. Their crowning victory came in 1504, when the ailing Ivan III gave the required state authorization for another Moscow synod. This one condemned to death Kuritsyn's surviving brother (a state secretary, diplomat, and legal expert) and a few-other "evil-thinking . . . godless heretics" as "Satan's instruments"—to use Joseph's words—which he clearly believed to be true. Others were imprisoned in what was more of a preemptive strike against dissidence than a genuine, permanent inquisition à la Spain.

Soon after these punishments a fissure within Russian monasticism erupted between Joseph's faction and monks residing north of the Volga, mainly in the rich Kirillov Monastery in Beloozero or in hermitages attached to it. Both parties came out of the monastic movement associated with the late Byzantine spiritual flowering. The Trans-Volgans (the self-styled "Non-Possessors") were disciples of Russia's greatest premodern spiritual theorist, Nil Sorsky (ca. 1433–1508). They emphasized a more individualistic monasticism—rigorous contemplation, crafts for self-support, and avoidance of the worldly and any superfluous wealth, as outlined in Nil's *Tradition* and *Rule*. Nil had also helped produce Joseph's antiheretical *Enlightener*, but the Trans-Volgans as a whole considered execution of heretics to be un-Orthodox.

The Josephites (pejoratively called "Possessors") emphasized communally oriented liturgical prayer, labor, discipline, and practical administration, as mandated by Joseph's *Rule*. With their ritualistic rigor and active scriptorium, they turned their monastery into a quasi academy for prelates and helpmates of the monarchy. Placing a critical mass of trainees and allies on Russia's episcopal thrones under Vasily III and his successor, this cloister served as Russia's guardian of strict Orthodoxy for seventy years or so.

Joseph's systematization of the very popular commemorative prayers for the dead, which centered on the miracle cult of a given cloister's founder, proved to be a cornerstone of his monastery's success and of others as well. Individuals seeking their own or a loved one's salvation financed these rituals with gifts of money, land, icons, and books. Then the profits from these services supported needed charitable works in this underserviced society and thereby justified the wealth acquired by Joseph's and other big monasteries.

Later tradition claimed that Nil and Joseph themselves debated at a Moscow synod in 1503 whether monasteries should possess entire villages. It seems now that this dispute started after both died and really concerned whether the state should limit monastic acquisition of land and perhaps even administer church estates. These issues were complicated after 1518, due to the arrival of the Italian-educated Greek monk Maximos (Michael) Trivolis (ca. 1475–1556), known in Russia as Maxim the Greek. He had been invited to translate the standard Greek *Interpreted Psalter*, that is, the biblical *Psalms* with the commentary of the leading church fathers, and to help resolve theological questions. Almost immediately he was embroiled in Russia's disputes. A strict Orthodox Christian, he opposed Vasily III's German physician, who was promoting a strange mix of astrology and church union with Rome. At the same time, Maxim's use of his classical literary training, his concurrence with the Trans-Volgans on monastic poverty, and his canonical objection to Vasily III's divorce of his childless wife threatened the highest church and state authorities.

Joseph's successor as abbot, Daniel, who was Metropolitan of Moscow during 1522–1539, ensured that the standing justifications of all church property remained sacrosanct. In 1525, presenting no more hard evidence than some translation errors, Daniel confined Maxim on trumped-up heresy charges. Six years later Daniel did the same to the influential disciple of Nil Sorsky, the prince-monk Vassian Patrikeev—a mercilessly caustic critic of Joseph Volotsky and his followers. By having the two leading critics of monastic villages imprisoned as heretics, the church constrained not only a mighty political opponent, but also, in Maxim, a formidable mind, who was trying to introduce some new approaches to education in Russia while protecting Orthodoxy. But people knew that Maxim had something to teach the faithful, and after 1531 his condition became house arrest, which afforded him some scope for literary work.

The contrast between Russian narrowness and western Rus relative openness at this time is striking. While Catholic activity in Muscovy was circumscribed and Jews were generally prohibited from even entering the realm, literary, philosophical, and religious works were translated from Czech, Polish, Latin, and even Hebrew into a Belarusian dialect in western Rus. Print culture there commenced with a German who published a few service manuals in 1491. A bit later Frantsisk Skoryna of Polotsk, who had studied at the Universities of Padua and Prague, printed parts of the Bible and a little almanac in Prague (1517–1519) and then Vilnius (1525). Printing remained unknown in Muscovy until the 1560s. Residing in the multicultural environment of Poland-Lithuania, the Orthodox of western Rus remained generally more receptive than Russians to European influences for almost two centuries.

THE SOVEREIGN'S MAJESTY

With the fall of Novgorod and the other republics, elite Russian political thought became thoroughly monarchical. The most basic principle that the sovereign not only was, but had to be, *gosudar*—that is, the master—made that term a favorite one, used along with *tsar* and, later, emperor from the time of Ivan III until the end

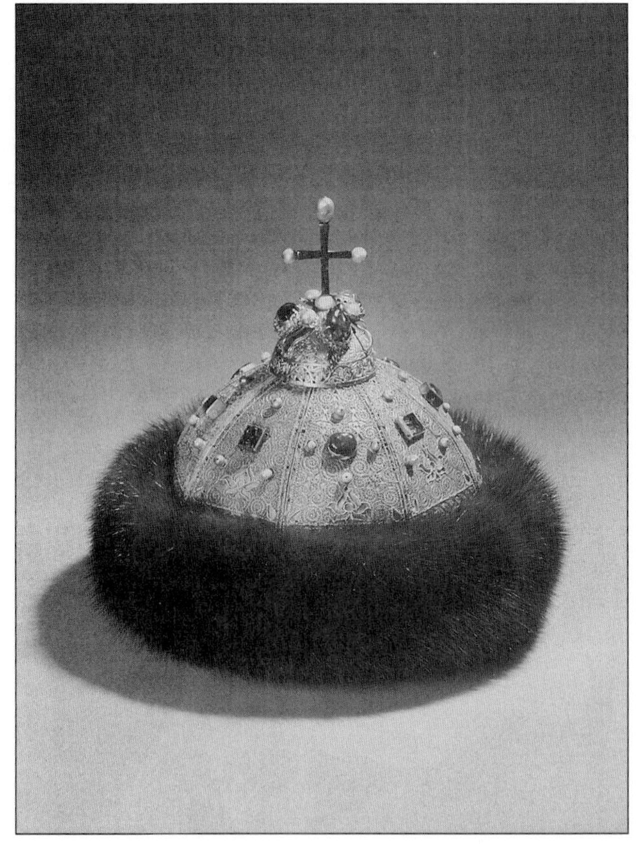

The Crown of Monomakh of the Grand Princes of Vladimir and Moscow. Originally from the 14th c., it was golden, jeweled, and fur-ringed. Moscow's political ideologists created the historical mythology that it was an imperial Byzantine gift to Vladimir Monomakh, thus granting special authority to him and his reigning descendants. *Armory of the Kremlin, Moscow, Russia/Scala/Art Resource, NY.*

of the Russian Empire in 1917. Alongside of this was the widely held belief that certain families or clans were inherently special and privileged. Accordingly their leaders had the right to be consulted in major state decisions, even if the sovereign, whose clan was supposed to be the most eminent, held life and death power over them.

For both domestic and international purposes, the secular authorities promoted the antiquity and venerability of the reigning dynasty and their sovereigns' equality with the German emperor, the Ottoman sultan, and other great rulers. Thus Moscow responded haughtily in 1489 to an imperial German envoy who offered a royal crown to Ivan III, were he to accept church union with Rome: "It is by God's grace that we have been sovereigns in our own lands since the beginning, since our early ancestors. Our authority comes from God." Accordingly, Moscow's diplomats aimed to know if the head of another state was fully sovereign and hence the equal of their sovereign, or constrained by ties of vassalage or loyalty to another ruler, and hence below the Russian *gosudar* in dignity. Around this time Moscow followed the imperial German adoptation of the Byzantine double-head eagle (signifying the later Roman Empire with two capitals) as the state seal. In the chronic bickering between Moscow and Lithuania, Ivan III proclaimed in the 1490s that he was "Sovereign of all Rus." By the 1520s Moscow was asserting that its dynasty had descended from the ancient Roman emperors, while the Polish-Lithuanian ruling house stemmed from a stableboy.

In keeping with the Byzantine heritage, Russia's churchmen argued that the sovereign's authority came from God, and he was to be honored and served. And they went so far as to repeat the sixth-century formula, "The king (*tsar*) by nature is like unto all men, but by authority is like unto God." However, in keeping with this heritage, they balanced the extreme elevation of monarchial majesty with the primacy of Orthodox Christianity, as in this passage from Joseph Volotsky's *Enlightener*:

> It is pleasing to God to be submissive and obedient to authorities, since they must care and provide for us. . . . The king (*tsar*) is God's servant, with the authority to grace and punish men. But if the king ruling over men is himself ruled by passions and sin, avarice and wrath, evil and injustice, pride and fury, and, worst of all, unbelief and blasphemy, such a king is not God's servant, but the devil's, and not a king but a tyrant. . . . Do not obey such a king or prince who leads you to impiety and evil, even if he tortures or threatens you with death.

Joseph and his followers further elaborated a doctrine of theocratic monarchy for Russia as the world's only remaining independent Orthodox realm. Accordingly, all the other Orthodox kingdoms had fallen on account of heresy, so Russia's "Orthodox tsar" was duty bound to follow canon law and protect the purity of the faith. In a similar vein, in the 1520s the learned Pskovian monk Filofey, from another strict cloister, argued apocalyptically that "two Romes [Rome and Constantinople] have fallen, the third [Moscow or Russia] stands, and there shall be no fourth." This notion was no program for imperialism, as some people have contended, but defensive and inward looking, written in the interests of the Russian Church, and rarely put to use by churchmen or the state. Venturing further afield, one of Joseph's nephews compiled a patriotic fusion of universal and Rus history, the *Russian Chronograph*. Metropolitan Daniel, as abbot, produced what is known as the *Nikon Chronicle,* which has influenced views of Russia's past down to today. It doctored the earlier history to make Moscow the undisputed heir to Kiev and evoke a five-century legacy of a pious realm ruled by Orthodox autocrats.

The monarchy needed other means besides the writings of churchmen to reach the populace, publicize its legitimacy, and obtain assent. As was traditional, church services regularly included prayers for the ruler and his family. Following the lead of Vasily II and Sofia Palaiologa, Vasily III made grandiose pilgrimages to the great Trinity Monastery, which became a spiritual patron of his rule and dynasty. Around 1520–1525, he also authorized an elaborate annual ceremony on Epiphany (January 6, commemorating both the arrival of the Magi and Christ's baptism), which continued into the 1690s. The ruler would lead the court to the frozen Moscow River, where the head of the church would consecrate the water through a hole in the ice and sprinkle the bare heads of the sovereign and leading courtiers. After this the people of Moscow and even their animals could be blessed and the ailing dipped for curative purposes. Accompanying this official manifestation of popular monarchism, people with "devilish" masks reflecting underlying pagan rites engaged in carnivalesque festivities without hindrance from the authorities. Such ceremonies linked solemn monarchism and popular culture.

The development of monarchical principles and rituals, however, did not resolve the thorny issue of succession. The eldest among brothers had precedence within his family, but Russia lacked any strict succession rule. Most successions from 1425 to 1825 entailed some violence and murder. After Ivan III outlived his four brothers, one of whom he imprisoned and possibly killed, he still had to choose between his eldest son, Vasily, by Sofia Palaiologa and his grandson Dmitry, who stemmed from his first marriage. Historians have long pondered what combination of maternal intrigues, boyar alliances, church politics, and foreign policy interests led to the initial choice of Dmitry in 1498, and then to his imprisonment in 1502 in favor of Vasily III. Among other factors in Vasily's favor, Sofia's Italian education, Byzantine imperial origin, and diplomatic functions prepared her to wield religious symbols and curry favor with the church. Dmitry's mother, Elena, though raised more strictly Orthodox in Moldavia, was tainted by her association with accused heretics.

Once on the throne, Vasily confined Dmitry until his early death in 1510 and, as noted earlier, forbade his four brothers to marry until he had produced a direct heir. When Vasily's first marriage to Solomonya Saburova from a modest boyar family proved barren, he favored as his second-in-command his sister's husband, the baptized Tatar prince or *tsarevich* Peter (d. 1523). Had Peter produced an acceptable heir for Vasily, they could have joined the Byzantine, Russian, and Mongol crown dynasties in one person. Finally, when Vasily, like Henry VIII of England a few years later, sought a new wife, Solomonya resisted. Russian society split over the propriety of a divorce, which Orthodox canon law generally restricted to major offenses on the part of the wife. Nevertheless, in a calculated political move, Metropolitan Daniel permitted it, and in 1526 Vasily married the much younger Elena Glinskaya, a niece of the unscrupulously ambitious Mikhail Glinsky. In 1530, when Vasily was already fifty-one, Elena gave birth to the future Ivan IV, which elevated her stature in Russia immensely. Three years later Vasily was dead.

How would the system created by strong monarchs, with immense discretionary power bolstered by a sacred ideology, operate under a regency tainted by a questionable divorce and with such an interloper as Glinsky in the boyar council? What kind of training would they give Ivan, the three-year-old autocrat-in-waiting? These were the crucial political questions at the summit of the Russian state in 1533.

CHAPTER 7

Ivan IV and the Birth Pangs of Tsardom, 1533–1584

Lord, our God, Tsar of tsars and Lord of lords, who through the Prophet Samuel selected His servant David and anointed him tsar over His people Israel. Hear Thou now the prayer of us the unworthy, and gaze now from Thy holy dwelling upon Thy pious servant, Grand Prince Ivan Vasilevich, whom Thou hast favored to elevate as tsar of Thy people, which Thou hast acquired with the venerable blood of Thy only begotten Son.

—Coronation words attributed to Metropolitan Makary, 1547

The death of Vasily III in 1533 ended eighty years of nearly unbroken Muscovite stability as well as growth. For the next half century Russia was nominally and then actually ruled by the strange, problematic, and elusive sovereign, Ivan IV, or, as the Russians called him, Ivan *Grozny* (1530–1584; Grand Prince from 1533, Tsar and Grand Prince from 1547). Traditionally rendered in English as *the Terrible*, *Grozny* might be translated more positively as *Majestic* or *Awesome.*

Ivan IV's troubled, uneven, and contradictory career mirrored the drama and pathos of his era. Orphaned at age seven, he became at sixteen the first Russian ruler formally crowned *tsar*. He presided over the spectacular if costly expansion of his realm down the Volga to the Caspian Sea, and he took Russia's first steps across the Urals into Siberia. He started a promising war in Livonia, but with shortsighted diplomacy wasted his victories. He welcomed Europeans into his service but defended Orthodoxy from Catholicism and Protestantism. While raging at times against Russia's aristocrats, he left them with their own autonomous judicial system and promoted state-strengthening domestic reforms. He also instituted a seven-year bloody reign of terror, at the height of which his minions massacred several thousand innocent subjects, but then he later financed memorial services for their souls. He wrote or had written in his name a number of sarcastic and invective letters and perhaps composed some liturgical music under the humble pseudonym Parfeny (Innocent) the Fool. But in the end, with his paranoia and brutality, he destroyed his family's three-hundred-year-old dynasty.

One of the biggest problems for the historian of this reign is that the key sources for Ivan's childhood and personality are dubious thriller stories issued by hostile

Ivan IV Waiting in Aleksandrovskaya Sloboda for the Petitioning Moscow Crowd, winter 1565, as he prepares to institute the *oprichnina.* The vampire-like presentation of him is the creation of the Soviet cinematographer genius, Sergei Eisenstein for *Ivan the Terrible,* Part II (1945). The notion of powerful, dynamic interplay for good and evil between a super-human ruler and the mass of people has modern overtones. *Photofest.*

foreigners and a history attributed to Ivan's political enemy, the renegade Prince Andrei Kurbsky (1528–1583), whose authorship and reliability have been questioned. Similarly suspect is the famous alleged exchange of abusive letters in which Kurbsky set forth an ideal image of monarchy limited by Christian morality and divinely provided advisers, and in response to which Ivan advanced the notion of an equally divinely installed monarch possessing unquestioned punitive authority over slavish subordinates. One scholar, certain that both Kurbsky and Ivan IV were illiterate, has argued from a close textual reading that these writings stem from the 1600s. Yet other evidence indicates that letters written in Kurbsky's name existed in the 1590s; most interested scholars have favored at least some authorship for him and Ivan. As for the tsar, a reliable document indicates that he once borrowed a theological tract, but he might have had it read to him. Reports of court debates with Europeans over theology in 1570 and 1582 also show that the tsar could memorize a few lines from the Bible, but they reveal none of the vast knowledge of Holy Scripture and Greek church fathers found in a treatise issued under his name. We shall probably never know for sure if either Ivan or Kurbsky ever composed anything credited to them then or later, so we do best using other, more reliable sources.

Aside from the person of the ruler, this reign proved to be transitional in several ways. It ended half a millennium in which the northern Rus/Russians were confined to the original lands of Novgorod, Vladimir-Suzdal, and Ryazan and opened an era of steady expansion southward and eastward. It initiated Russia's direct commercial and political ties to England and western Europe via the secure northern maritime route. It engendered Russia's first national assembly of any kind, and it ended with functioning central and provincial institutions of a military-fiscal state. It also witnessed the climax and sudden end of the monastic-based literary movements, while the central church authorities and the royal court emerged as the arbiters of Russian culture—a situation that held until the 1690s.

BOYAR INTERLUDE, 1533–1547

The suspect account of Ivan IV depicts his childhood as replete with continuous treachery, murder, theft, and disrespect of his own person by a coterie of worthless aristocrats. The Kurbsky history treats his princess-regent mother Elena Glinskaya (d. 1538) as a morally derelict murderess and the young Ivan as a sadistic lad. And until recently historians tended to believe the worst about everybody. Doubtless some boyars may have been vicious, but the period 1533–1547 was also notable for its constructive domestic measures.

Under Ivan III and Vasily III, Moscow's elites had usually harmonized their interests with each other and with the crown. After Vasily's unexpected demise in 1533, however, various cliques vied to govern in Ivan IV's name and initiated a new level of political murder. For the next fourteen years at least seven real or would-be leadership teams came and went, violent death being the fate of the chief losers. These victims included Vasily's two surviving brothers, Ivan's great uncle Michael Glinsky, and several illustrious service princes—one of whom, Andrei Shuisky, the young Ivan IV's huntsmen killed in 1543, when Ivan, in the official chronicle's words, "could no longer endure boyar disorder."

Early in 1547, Ivan's other Glinsky uncles tried to secure ascendancy by combining with the church leadership to elevate Ivan's title to tsar, but a Moscow mob enraged by an outbreak of destructive fires killed one of them. Following the fire, which the young tsar publicly treated as divine punishment for his own sins, domestic politics stabilized. The leading place at court devolved upon an old Moscow boyar family, the Yurev-Zakharins, who provided Ivan's bride Anastasia Romanova (d. 1560) soon after the coronation ceremony.

Paradoxically during Ivan IV's minority, the fractious boyars implemented and consolidated a set of reforms that strengthened the state and its ties to the country. In 1535, to combat counterfeiting and debasing of the silver content of coins, the regency established a lighter 2.4-ounce silver ruble as Russia's only lawful standard monetary unit. Provincial officials took over some of the tax collection, and Moscow set up a few antibrigandage districts with landowners and free peasants handling routine policing and criminal justice. As a result, the duties of the rotating city lieutenants and district chiefs decreased and hence so did the amount of "feeding" contributions exacted by them. With the unification of the realm and the rise of the service gentry, such reforms were overdue.

The boyar government also expanded the system of border fortifications, especially on the southern frontier. Moscow concurrently distributed more central lands as service estates and further integrated the holders of these *pomesties* and of hereditary estates into a single military service class. Middle-level servicemen were specifically forbidden to donate lands to monasteries. The court (*dvor*) of the sovereign, in whose name these measures had been enacted, now came to mean the elite strata of aristocrats, service cavalry, and chancery officials, as well as the palace and lands under his personal control.

VISIONS OF PIETY, 1542–1570

The political jockeying behind the scenes in the 1540s also involved the leading churchmen, who positioned themselves to shepherd the adolescent Ivan as he began to shoulder some of his responsibilities. Ecclesiastical writings constituted whatever education he had with books, and he was continuously involved in court and religious ceremonial activities. The disarray at the top begged for intervention on behalf of social peace, and the new metropolitan, Makary (1482?–1563), installed in 1542 after sixteen fruitful years as archbishop of Novgorod, was up to the task. The senior prelate assumed the role of spiritual guide to an outwardly repentant young ruler eager to lead his realm along a godly path.

Rituals and Symbols

Makary's most dramatic act was to preside over Ivan IV's coronation as tsar and grand prince early in 1547. In assuming the *tsarstvo* or supreme authority as God's anointed, Ivan obtained the dignity due him as a successor to the biblical kings David and Solomon, as a follower of the first and "apostlelike" Christian Roman emperor, Constantine the Great, and as a descendant of the half-Byzantine Vladimir Monomakh (see p. 21 in the chapter "Kievan Rus: Structures and Events, 988–1240"), whose purported crown Moscow's sovereign wore. The ceremony stressed the tsar's responsibility as Orthodox Christian sovereign without granting him any new substantial authority, but it added a symbolic aura and mystique to his office. It increased his stature by bestowing upon him the same title used for the Byzantine emperors and Tatar khans, which in Russian eyes stood higher than that of the neighboring Polish-Lithuanian or Swedish kings.

Church and court coupled Ivan's coronation with his marriage to Anastasia Romanovna, Russia's first official *tsaritsa,* who some historians believe calmed him during his most fruitful years on the throne. Pioneering the ceremonial role of this office, which included hearing petitions from subjects, she sometimes acted with the metropolitan as a special intercessor with God for the realm. The public image of Muscovy's royal consort, which had developed over two centuries, made her a model of virtue and possessed of a "blessed womb" capable of bearing future tsars. Ivan respected his wife's memory after she died in 1560, but we have no solid evidence about her inner character or influence over him. The actual wedding ritual included the typical Russian mixture of Christian and traditional pagan elements, such as the bride's elaborate headdress, and hence connected the monarchy to the life of the people.

During the year of the coronation and wedding, 1547, Makary also presided over the canonization of about a dozen Russian saints from different locales and walks of life. This act capped the century-old policy of recognizing independent Russia's "new wonder-workers." Around 1548 he introduced a novel public ritual in Moscow, which owed something to his long tenure in Novgorod and to Roman

Catholic influences. In the procession on Palm Sunday (initiating Passion Week before Easter), the tsar himself led the donkey carrying the chief prelate who represented Jesus of Nazareth. This symbolized the sovereign's and Russia's submission to the spiritual authority of the church. Church and court supported their new pretensions and rituals with visual imagery. Following the 1547 fire, new palace frescoes in the public reception space likened Russia's ruling dynasty, guided by Divine Wisdom, to the Old Testament kings.

Earlier, as archbishop of Novgorod, Makary had used his access to Russia's richest library to initiate *The Great Menaia*—daily readings placed in twelve volumes covering the months. Enlarged from the standard Orthodox annual cycle of prayers and of saints' lives, this massive collection added theological works, sermons, and some original Russian writings, such as saints' lives, monastic rules, and defenses of the faith to create an authoritative Russian Orthodox corpus. In Moscow Makary expanded the *Menaia* and commissioned more Russian saints' lives and the recasting of native history. The resultant *Ascending Album (or Book of Degrees) of the Tsar's Ancestry*, commencing with the dynasty's sainted matriarch Olga (see the chapter "The Origin of Rus, 750–1000"), created a tableau of a holy ruling family and exemplary churchmen, designating princes who fell fighting the Mongols as martyrs. This became the most popular history of Russia down to the 1700s.

Makary's protégé Silvester (d. 1566), an enterprising, well-connected Novgorod iconographer and priest, compiled or wrote the widely copied *Household Economy* (*Domostroy*). This was a practical handbook for the large household, with daily life ordered under the keen eye of the family patriarch and his obedient wife. It covered activities such as securing and preparing victuals, and supervising and chastising servants. In the properly managed household children were to be reared, adolescents married off (age twelve for girls, fifteen for boys), gossip suppressed, dice and chess banned, and strict piety observed. But, unlike analogous Western works, *Household Economy* omitted genuine education. And the work only scratches the surface of the brutal side of women's strict subordination to husbands empowered to administer physical punishments. Later copies appended simple predictive or divination tables, based on days of the week or random combinations of the numbers one through six. Though heretical, these constituted another link between piety and popular culture.

Contradictions and Dissent

Reality rarely matches ideals, and in mid-sixteenth-century Russia the dissonance between the two was clearly expressed in the *Hundred Chapters* (*Stoglav*)—the report of a church synod in 1551. Guided by Makary, the young tsar put before the church leadership a set of problems, ranging from the fashionable divination devices, pagan rites, popular healing cults beyond the control of the church, and inconsistent liturgical practices to illiteracy, unruliness, and drunkenness among the clergy. A different kind of issue, the unchecked expansion of monastic estates, gobbling up land needed to support military service, threatened state security. Had all of the recommendations and rules of the synod been followed, Russia would have emerged in the late 1500s with a thorough network of church schools, a model clergy, and a generally sober, chaste, and devout populace. Society, however, lacked the resources or will to actualize the synod's directives, though the bishops did take a few initial steps to enhance their authority over the parishes within their immense and unwieldy dioceses. The synod's official response resolutely defended church lands, but the tsar soon issued a decree prohibiting any further acquisition by monasteries without his permission. Still wishing to use land to pay for commemorations and to shelter it from taxes, people often evaded this decree, and it had to be repeated several times.

The church allowed Pskovian painters to introduce some novel, Western-inspired symbolism in Moscow, but otherwise remained a bulwark of tradition, especially against dissidence, which resurfaced in the 1550s. Matvey Bashkin, a rising serviceman from Tver, considered slavery incompatible with the Gospels. The escaped slave Feodosy Kosoy attracted disciples also around simple evangelical principles, which potentially threatened the authority of the church. And the strictly Orthodox Artemy of Pskov—"Writings are numerous, but not all are divine," he wrote, repeating Nil Sorsky—tried to reform the great Trinity Monastery and thought that the church made unfair accusations of heresy. Fearing both the moderate and radical wings of the Protestant Reformation, which had already gained a foothold in Poland, Lithuania, and Livonia, the church subjected the three would-be reformers to typically slanted heresy trials. Imprisoned in monasteries, Feodosy and Artemy escaped and fled to Lithuania, where one became a Protestant preacher, while the other defended Orthodoxy. Russian dissidence may have had a purely secular side as well. For in 1570, to protect the church against philosophical as well as religious radicalism, the moralizing Novgorodian monk Zinovy Otensky issued a lengthy *Demonstration of the Truth*, commencing with the divine creation of the universe.

STATE CONSOLIDATION, 1547–1562

The state reforms, relative stability, and successful foreign policies of the years 1547–1562 have caused historians to speak of Ivan IV's "good period." Yet in these fifteen years, the century-long economic upswing ended, and a crisis ensued in the 1550s or early 1560s due to military outlays outpacing growth and revenues. How these economic realities affected the reforms, however, is not clear.

Ideas and Policies

Proposals to overhaul the state, army, and ethics of public life accompanied the midcentury calls to overhaul the church and religion. The summons for reform ranged over a variety of topics. Around 1547, as if echoing a standard Western criticism of Russia that still holds today, the venerable Greek monk Maxim, under house arrest in Tver since 1531, advised the young tsar to adopt just laws and uphold them. About this time the Pskovian priest and advocate of social peace Ermolay devised a simplification of land grants and urged that military servicemen live in towns and receive fixed upkeep from assigned peasants, rather than be their personal lords. A tract attributed to the soldier-of-fortune Ivan Peresvetov—the earliest surviving copies are from the 1630s—invoked the Ottoman Empire as a model, berated Russian anarchy and tyranny, and pressed for more support of Russia's warrior class. It also urged the young tsar to use his awesome majesty to establish justice by executing unruly boyars, corrupt judges, crooked merchants, and cowardly troops. These notions are indicative of what some people were counseling the Russian government around 1547–1550.

Tsar Ivan's initial privy council included his Romanov in-laws, several members of the old princely and Moscow boyar elites, and two outstanding figures of more modest origin: Alexei Adashev (d. 1561), son of a diplomat, and the outspoken state secretary Ivan Viskovaty (d. 1571). As treasurer, Adashev was Ivan's chief minister (if one can use such a term) until the end of the 1550s, while Viskovaty ran the foreign chancery and controlled day-to-day diplomacy. How much power the boyar clan chiefs or the sovereign himself wielded in these years is uncertain.

A conclave of tsar and boyars in 1549, followed by an address by Ivan to the leading gentry (higher-ranking servicemen), launched the reforms. The tsar freed provincial military servitors from the judicial power of lieutenants and district chiefs in all but felony offenses. This measure went into the Law Code of 1550, which revised and expanded its 1497 predecessor. A decree of 1555 on the antibrigandage districts, which had proliferated in the north after 1539, mandated that the local elites staff them. Later in the decade Moscow replaced many lieutenants with land boards (*zemstvo*) elected by local servicemen and assigned urban officials to manage provincial tax collection on behalf of the central treasury. These measures further strengthened overall governance and restricted the scope of "feedings" collected by high provincial officials, but as a way of provincial life, "feeding" of the powerful never disappeared.

Several reform measures touched on problems raised in the works of Maxim, Ermolay, and Peresvetov. In a futile attempt to end corruption, the new code provided for litigation against officials and prescribed flogging with the knout (a whip with leather thongs) for malfeasance. Another decree of 1549 outlawed disruptive precedence disputes when the army was arraying for battle. Then in 1550 Moscow established the first permanent, regular companies of state-supported infantry harquebusiers or musketeers (*streltsy*)—infantry who doubled as garrison troops and police in peacetime. Also that year, to deal with the rapid natural increase of military families, the regime earmarked service estates in the vicinity of Moscow for a "select thousand" servicemen, mainly the junior members of established, high-ranking families and provincial elites. Following this came a new, systematic land survey with differentiated categories of soil usage to help equalize tax burdens within the social orders, although boyar and church estates obtained the lowest assessment rates. The Service Statute of 1556 fixed the number of soldiers each unit of land was to provide and thereby even further diminished the distinction between hereditary and service lands. Finally, a decree of 1562 limited the right of most princes to dispose freely of their land and empowered the treasury to enforce the 1556 statute and confiscate illegal acquisitions dating back to the beginning of Ivan's reign (1533). A more rationalized statewide system of landholding, service requirements, and taxation resulted from these laws.

The 1550 code confirmed the earlier limitation of peasant movement to two weeks in November and intruded more deeply into the realm of everyday life. A new law restricted contract slavery, a form of indentured servitude that could easily become permanent and thus deprive the state of soldiers and taxpayers. To limit the damage to society from civil suits, another law set a sliding scale of maximum awards, based on ability to pay. But in keeping with the prevailing social hierarchy and attitudes toward marriage, the code established another sliding scale of amends for insults and other outrages against honor based on the status of the offended party—wives of all classes gaining a double sum for slights against their virtue. A constitutional provision appeared as well: if a new type of case came before the courts, the tsar and boyars together could amend the code.

All of these measures contributed to the ongoing development of distinct administrative bodies to complement the preeminent ambassadors' (i.e., foreign) office. The Department of Service Estates, the Department of Military Assignments, the Brigandage Department, and the Great Treasury Department, which coordinated provincial tax collection, were among the most important new ones. Such bureaus oversaw the musketeers, registered slaves, and ran the postal road system. Secretaries supported by staffs of scribes managed these offices and became *de facto* judges, often called by that name, as they resolved disputes brought to their attention. As elsewhere in the world at this time, military requirements remained the underlying catalyst for most reform measures.

The Steppe Frontier and the Cossacks

As Russia expanded, the steppe frontier—where for centuries Slavic, Turkic, and other peoples had eked out a living mostly free from state control—became an administrative as well as a defensive issue. Steppe dwellers, if cleverly subsidized and recruited, made excellent soldiers, but they also could turn into parasitic marauders. The word *Cossack* (Ukr. *kozak*, Rus. *kazak*) itself probably derives from a Turkic word meaning *free man* or *freebooter*. The basic Cossack structure of bands or camps under elected *atamans* (also a Turkic word) was not so different from that of pirates—reflecting a common military way of life, the crucial role of booty, and the semianarchy of the fringes of organized society. Some people became Cossacks simply to escape the confines of normal life.

Cossacks had served a Rus state as early as 1444 during a Ryazan-Tatar skirmish. The khans of Kazan had their own Cossack palace guard. The Christian element among the free Cossack communities came to predominate over Tatars and Muslims by the late fifteenth century, when many Ukrainian and Russian peasants, who doubled as frontier soldiers, ran away from their lords or the state to join Cossack settlements. These then became the real buffer between the Crimean khanate and both Russia and Poland-Lithuania.

Starting in the 1520s, Ukrainian lords and officials on Poland-Lithuania's southern border employed Cossacks against Tatars. Later, in the 1550s, Prince Dmytro Vyshnevetsky, technically a subject of Lithuania, but for the moment strategically cooperating with Moscow, too, fortified a Cossack-held Dnieper island below the rapids near the Crimean frontier. Thus was born the first Zaporozhian Cossack camp (*sich/sech*). As Russia's reach extended into the Middle and Lower Volga and Don Rivers in the 1550s, Moscow also began to employ and control local Cossacks. Later in the sixteenth century, detachments of them manned garrisons and fought in various Russian campaigns.

EASTWARD HO!, 1545–1559

In 1552 Ivan IV rode in splendor into the conquered city of Kazan to establish his rule there. The anonymous Russian author of *The History of Kazan*, dated by specialists between the 1560s and early 1600s, understood that the incorporation of this khanate transformed Muscovy from an Orthodox Russian realm with a host of small tributary peoples into a multinational empire. The author thus rightly saw the campaign of 1552 as a central event in Russian history, preparing the way for expansion down to the Caspian Sea and across the Urals.

Kazan and Astrakhan

Viewed with hindsight, Muslim Kazan in the 1540s stood in a position somewhat similar to Novgorod in the 1460s—its waterways, fur supplies, and other assets attractive to outsiders, its core too weak to defend immense hinterlands, and its autonomy dependent on a regional balance of power. The Crimeans forced the Kazan issue by launching another assault on Russia in 1541. After stopping them at the Oka, the Russians decided that the only way to avoid the threat of a huge new Tatar confederation was to reduce Kazan to vassalage and take over the entire Volga, even though this would require the mobilization of tens of thousands of men. Starting in 1545, the Russians forced some of the local Chuvash and Cheremis peoples to switch allegiance from Kazan to Moscow. Then in 1551, by means of prefabricated wooden walls, a technique they used for building homes, the Russians quickly erected the new fortress of Sviyazhsk on the hilly right bank of the Volga, just twenty-five miles upstream from Kazan. Russian promises of moderate tributes enticed further defections of non-Tatar subject peoples from the khanate.

The Kazan Tatars now had to resist by arms or recognize Moscow's supremacy and free thousands of enslaved Russians in return for an uncertain autonomy. Goaded by the Crimeans, the Kazan elite resisted. In 1552 Moscow launched a powerful, two-pronged campaign against Kazan. One army corps moved along a southern route to deflect a Crimean diversionary force bolstered by Ottoman troops and artillery. With the aid of women and children, the Russians repulsed these invaders at Tula. Within the main Russian army, sappers, engineers, and gun-

Wars and Expansion: 1545–1598.

ners led by a foreigner and a state secretary, not a typically illiterate boyar, made the final difference. Fully investing Kazan with a ring of towers and stockades, the Russians blocked the city's underground water conduit and blew a breach in the walls. A general slaughter of defenders followed—"it was impossible to quench the warriors' fury," states the *History of Kazan*—before Tsar Ivan entered the city. By 1555–1556 the Russians had expelled the surviving Kazanians to an autonomous suburb and converted the main mosque into an Orthodox cathedral. The khan's crown domains passed directly to the tsar and formed a nucleus of lands distributed to Russian servicemen.

The pacification of all of Kazan's 180,000-odd square miles—roughly the size of Spain or Sweden—drained Russian manpower and was never completed in the sixteenth century. But Kazan's former structure was compatible with Russia's. The majority of Udmurt, Cheremis, Chuvash, and Mordvinian forest dwellers paid tribute directly to the state. Provincial Tatar and Bashkir princes and nobles, themselves supported by peasants and herdsmen, rendered valuable military service. Some Tatars eventually migrated into Russia as far as Novgorod, where they cultivated abandoned lands and served in the army. Under Russian occupation, agriculture grew apace in the former khanate.

Once Kazan's core lands were subdued, securing full control of the khanate of Astrakhan on the Lower Volga became Russia's next logical step. In 1556, after a client khan there proved unreliable, the Russians sent a flotilla with artillery down the Volga to occupy the city, which readily surrendered. However, the Nogays and other nomads on the steppe lands to the east, which were nominally subject to Astrakhan, remained free from Muscovite control for almost two centuries. Russian Cossacks, meanwhile, expanded their settlements along the rivers Don, Volga, Yaik, and, in the north Caucasus, Terek.

The conquest of Kazan and Astrakhan had other consequences for Russia. The khanate of Sibir formally, if insincerely, acknowledged the tsar's supremacy. The Kabardians (western Circassians of the north Caucasus) appealed to Moscow for protection and thereby produced a contest with the Turks and Crimeans for influence in the region. Russia launched probing attacks on Crimea itself in 1556 and 1559, but then desisted for over a century.

The Significance of the Volga Conquest

Russian commerce benefited as Moscow's domination of the Volga opened up direct routes from the Baltic and White Seas to the Caspian and its Persian and Central Asian shores at an opportune time. In 1553 the Englishman Richard Chancellor (d. 1556), in search of an Arctic route to China, landed at the mouth of the northern Dvina and was invited to Moscow. He returned to Russia in 1555 as agent of England's newly chartered Muscovy or Russia Company, to which the tsar granted free trade and access to special courts. In 1557 Osip Nepaya, Russia's first official envoy to England, brought back a physician, an apothecary, and other specialists. With them came the Company's agent Anthony Jenkinson (1530–1611), who obtained permission to initiate ties with Persia and Central Asia via Astrakhan.

Even though nothing much resulted from Jenkinson's endeavor, Anglo-Russian relations profited both sides. The English supplied Russia with military equipment and organized rope production for their ships in the far north. Kazan, Nizhny Novgorod, Yaroslavl, Vologda, and Kholmogory (in the northern Dvina land) prospered as the principal entrepôt along the Caspian to White Sea route. Astrakhan became Russia's direct window to Persia and points east, while Arkhangelsk, founded at the mouth of the northern Dvina in 1583, gave Russia a direct link to England and the Netherlands. Pskov and Novgorod, meanwhile, remained the key centers for the export of honey, wax, flax, and hemp, and Russia also furnished its eastern and southern neighbors with metal goods.

Beyond Russia's political, diplomatic, and economic life, the conquest of Kazan, like other great victories, produced major repercussions in the realm of symbolism as well. A new icon, placed in Moscow's Dormition Cathedral, depicted the Heavenly Host, Ivan IV's most illustrious ancestors, and the tsar himself leading a procession of troops home toward Heavenly Jerusalem or Moscow as Jerusalem—all to signify the ideal harmony of church and state in defense of Orthodoxy. Outside Moscow's Kremlin walls, Ivan commemorated his victory by erecting the elaborate Church of the Intercession of the Virgin, because the storming of Kazan was prepared on the very day when the Intercession is celebrated. The entrance chapel, consecrated to Christ's entrance into Jerusalem, underscored the growing identification of Russia with ancient Israel. The main edifice, designed and built by the Russians Barma and Postnik Iakovlev with an Italian-influenced octagonal geometric interior, eventually boasted unique, intricate, exterior decorations and an onion dome, as did the eight unique exterior chapels. Not completed until the end of the century, it was (and is) known unofficially by the name of a locally revered prophet and holy fool, who died the year of the campaign, Vasily (Basil) the Blessed (1469–1552)—yet another tie between acceptable popular piety and the official religion. This edifice has been one of the enduring symbols of Russia for several centuries.

The Icon "Blessed Be the Host of the Celestial King" mid-late 1550s, commemorating the victorious return from Kazan in 1552. In this depiction, Ivan IV's troups, those of his direct and typological ancestors, and the heavenly forces are riding toward a fusion of Moscow and eternal Jerusalem, where the departed saints dwell. *Erich Lessing/Tretyakov Gallery, Moscow/Art Resource, NY.*

THE LIVONIAN WAR, 1558–1583

Ivan IV would not be so fortunate in his next war and his drive for the major eastern Baltic ports. Ever since the Swedish conquest of Finland in the twelfth century, Russia's Baltic coast was limited to a stretch from the present Russian-Estonian border to a point northwest of where St. Petersburg now stands. As the region developed, Russia had nothing comparable to the chief Estonian and Livonian seaports, Reval (Tallin) and especially Riga at the mouth of the western Dvina. So after Moscow annexed Novgorod, it was tempting to try to redress this situation. Ivan III had started by building the fortress of Ivangorod opposite Narva and curtailing the privileges of the Hanseatic League. The uncontrollable Ivan IV aimed much higher, and Russia paid heavily for his lack of circumspection.

The Lure of the Baltic

By the 1550s an independent Livonia (including Estonia) was a fractured anomaly in northeastern Europe. Having been ruled by the crusading Catholic Teutonic Knights for several centuries, Livonia remained loyal to them and separated from Prussia in 1525, when the Reformation spread there. Nevertheless, the Livonian towns, nobility, and enserfed peasants embraced Lutheranism under the noses of their direct overlords, the Catholic bishoprics and monasteries. With the power of all four Baltic monarchies—Denmark, Sweden, Poland-Lithuania, and Muscovy—rising, Livonia was ripe for the picking.

The Russians, however, were divided on policy. Adashev's faction wished to avoid complications to the northwest, preferring to extend the recent gains in the southeast toward Crimea, even at the risk of a vigorous Ottoman response. The opposing party, which Ivan favored, wished to secure more of the Baltic coast and a good harbor. Accordingly, in 1558, even before the forays into Crimean territory ceased, Moscow revived old Rus claims of suzerainty over eastern Estonia and demanded tribute with arrears, prompting the Livonians to seek an alliance with Lithuania. Moscow responded by dispatching an army augmented by Tatars, Cheremis, and Kabardians, which overran Dorpat and Narva. Offering generous terms to the vanquished, Moscow set up a commercial zone encompassing Novgorod, Pskov, and eastern Estonia, with Narva as the chief outlet. The tsar also accepted Germans directly into Russian service, transferred some Russians to new estates in Estonia, and started to build a fleet.

A partition of Livonian lands soon began. The Danes occupied Oesel (Saaremaa) Island, and the Lithuanians took most of present southwestern Latvia. Smashing a futile Livonian counterattack in 1560, the Russians took central Estonia as well. The next year the Swedes quickly occupied western Estonia, including Reval. The Livonians then ceded Riga and most of present Latvia to Lithuania but retained Courland (Kurland) in the northwest as a vassal duchy under the Polish crown.

Lithuania, Crimea, and the First Assembly of the Land

Adashev, meanwhile, had fallen from favor. Ivan IV and his new set of advisers, refusing to settle for just eastern Estonia, made a truce with Sweden and set out to capture Riga and its hinterland from Lithuania. In 1563 the tsar personally led another multiethnic army against Polotsk, then a key Lithuanian provincial town on the western Dvina, about 220 miles upstream from Riga. Russian artillery took only three weeks to breach Polotsk's walls and force a surrender. Once there, Ivan confiscated all sorts of riches and secured Russian power by refortifying the citadel and removing all native laypeople from it. He otherwise left the traditional institutions of the Orthodox majority in place. However, animated by the same intolerant and murderous crusading spirit that west European knights had displayed four centuries earlier, the tsar, who had no Jews in his own realm, drowned the Polotsk Jews who refused to convert, possibly three hundred of them. The following year the Lithuanians crushed the Russians as they advanced further westward, and the Crimeans raided the weakly defended southern part of Ryazan.

The fighting persisted until 1566, when the Lithuanians offered to let Russia keep Polotsk in return for assured possession of Riga. Ivan refused, and to generate and display support for Russia's claim to Riga, he convened Russia's first genuine Assembly of the Land, called by the generic term *zemsky sobor*. More assemblies would meet over the course of the next one hundred years. In coming chapters we shall encounter them electing tsars, levying emergency taxes, approving laws, and advising on foreign policy. This first one included over three hundred fifty high clergy, boyars, upper-level servicemen, state secretaries, and merchants. The experienced foreign chancery head Ivan Viskovaty stood out as the only cautious and negative voice. The tsar then designated the Danish duke Magnus as Russia's vassal king of Livonia, betrothed him to a very high ranking Russian princess, and, in 1570, sent him to besiege Swedish-held Reval.

The tsar, however, could not spare enough troops for Magnus to succeed because of a serious threat from the south. The year before, 1569, an Ottoman-led force of Turks, Crimeans, Nogays, and Circassians tried to expel Russia from Astrakhan. This daring venture collapsed when the invaders were unable to dig a forty-mile canal through hilly terrain between the Don and Volga Rivers to transport their heavy artillery. Undaunted, the Crimean Tatars invaded the Russian heartland in 1571, burned much of Moscow and its suburbs, and retreated with tens of thousands of captives. The next year the Crimeans invaded again, but the beefed up Russian defense force at the Oka River destroyed most of their army. All the same, Crimean and Nogay slave raids on Russia continued for another twenty years.

This continuous warfare notwithstanding, the Russians returned to Estonia in 1573 and took several fortresses from the Swedes. Polish royal elections in 1574 and 1576 gave Moscow another opening to intrigue for influence or more territory in the borderlands. This policy collapsed in 1576 when the Poles and Lithuanians, whose joint realm had been strengthened in 1569 by the formal Union of Lublin, to be discussed in the next chapter, enthroned Prince Stefan Bathory of Transylvania, a veteran commander determined to push back the Russians. Although the tsar's troops overran all of Estonia and Livonia except for Reval and Riga in 1577, he now faced two serious enemies to the west, Poland and Sweden, who would soon reverse Russia's fortunes. In his own mind, moreover, he had also been facing domestic enemies for years, and still was.

TERROR AT HOME, 1563–1576

The greatest mystery of Ivan IV's reign concerns why he divided his realm into two separate parts in 1565, introduced a period of terror, and got away with it. Explanations for the terror range far and wide. Ivan possessed, perhaps from his childhood, a sadistic and paranoiac character, compounded by the side effects of a degenerative bone disease and the immense pain he endured in his later years (as his remains indicate). He still resented the boyars as a class for their treatment of him as a youth and for their alleged political intrigues when he was gravely ill in 1553 and wished to secure the throne for his infant son. By 1565 the two purported restraining forces on Ivan's life had died, his first wife, Anastasia, in 1560 and Metropolitan Makary in 1563. The Cherkassky family, his new in-laws from the Caucasus, counseled him in political savagery. He was fed up with real instances of treason, corruption, and rot within the regular government. A declining economy and competition among a growing number of land-hungry military servitors helped unleash ferocious power struggles and false denunciations of treason. Ambitious new people simply seized the opportunity to rise at the expense of established aristocrats and chancery secretaries. Mongol legacies of domestic repression, the popular culture and political mores of the period, a sense that one was living in apocalyptic times, and the lack of any conceivable alternative to a legitimate monarch's personal autocracy rendered effective opposition to the tsar unthinkable. All of these explanations may contain a kernel of truth. None of them stand as the verifiably most significant factor.

The problem of treason—a legal ground for execution—was exacerbated by the divergent path at this time of western Rus, where the great nobles enjoyed independent wealth and autonomous power far beyond their Muscovite counterparts. Polish-Lithuanian oral communications and written propaganda during the Livonian War emphasized the contrast between the two realms and urged elite Russians to defect.

The *Oprichnina* and Its Aftermath

The tsar's inner circle underwent a fundamental change in the early 1560s after the death of Anastasia. Adashev was disgraced and soon died, and the new head of the treasury, Nikita Funikov, along with Ivan Viskovaty dominated the regular administration for a decade. Alexei Basmanov of an old Moscow boyar clan came to the fore, replacing Anastasia's kinsmen. Ivan also married his second wife, Maria (d. 1569), three months after Anastasia's death, since state ceremony required a *tsaritsa.*

His new in-laws from the Caucasus did come as foreign royalty, but also bearing a tradition of deadly internecine strife.

A fresh set of repressions began in 1561–1562—the first since 1546—with the execution of Adashev's relatives. Next, when the 1562–1563 campaign against Polotsk began, real or feared defections to Lithuania provoked a round of denunciations, inquests, confiscations, forced monastic vows, executions, and, perhaps as later reported, the murder of two generals while they were praying. Protests by high clergy and increasing desertions encouraged by Poland-Lithuania deepened Ivan IV's suspicions. In April 1564 Prince Andrei Kurbsky, one of Ivan's trusted generals, fled westward and led the Lithuanian counterattack, while the Crimeans invaded the province of Ryazan.

The tsar then made a dramatic move. In late 1564–early 1565, he stunned Moscow by relocating along with a select guard, their families, and much treasure to his Aleksandrovskaya palace, about sixty miles northeast of Moscow. Sending back heralds to proclaim his displeasure with the clergy, boyars, and officials, he underscored his benevolence toward the commoners. Fearful of this threatened alliance of crown and mob, the elite hastened to pledge loyalty to the tsar and invite him to return to Moscow on his own majestic (we might say "despotic") terms: the right to punish "traitors" without interference; the establishment of a personal domain—the *oprichnina* (from *oprich*—separate)—by reorganizing and expanding the palace administration with other lands as he chose; and his absolute control over the regular state (often called the *zemshchina*, from *zemlya*—land), which would continue to function under the nominal direction of the boyars. In this high-handed manner, Ivan achieved a coup d'état within the state structure he had inherited.

Had the *oprichnina* merely been an augmented and economically profitable network of palace lands and towns, it would hardly command much attention. At this time it was not unusual for states in Asia or Europe—such as Persia, Bukhara, or Poland—to have such institutions. Accordingly, Ivan did include in his *oprichnina* several central agricultural districts and the wealthy Stroganov family's extensive commercial empire in the east, as well as the salt-producing towns of the north, Vologda, the English Russia Company, part of Moscow, and, eventually, the mercantile side of Novgorod.

The *oprichnina*, however, *was* more than an extension of crown domains. Having freed the court from its more powerful outgrowth, the regular state administration or *zemshchina*, Ivan created his own ministate with a few trusted boyars and secretaries, a service hierarchy, and ten thousand to twenty thousand rank-and-file serving men. Some of these happened to be middle- and lower-ranking inhabitants of *oprichnina* domains. Clothed in black garb with emblems of dogs and brooms symbolizing their cleansing of the realm, *oprichniki* were required to shun the generally better pedigreed *zemshchina* men. But these arrangements appear to have been improvised with some blurred jurisdictional boundaries between *oprichnina* and *zemshchina*.

The specific *oprichnina* repression began in 1565 with the execution of four boyars—including a sixteen-year-old prince. It also entailed the forced removal from

Suzdal to Kazan's hinterland of about 180 families, many of which held prominent positions at court. The following year the tsar allowed them to return, but they had already lost much of their wealth and social power. When delegates to the 1566 assembly objected to such procedures, Ivan had three protesters executed and fifty publicly beaten. Facing more remonstrances from the highest circles, the tsar fortified the *oprichnina*'s Arbat quarter in Moscow. At this point he sensed such strong opposition that he sounded out England's Queen Elizabeth about political asylum in her country. Like a corrupt, modern dictator he made contingency plans to abscond with his treasury but remained in command of his cruel operation.

Indeed, the terror intensified. In 1568, claiming Lithuanian intrigues and challenges to the throne, Ivan had his *oprichniki* conduct security investigations. These led to the execution of the senior boyar—the equerry I. P. Fëdorov-Chelyadin—three more council members, another 150 serving men and chancery officials, and some of their families and servants; a recorded 369 people were killed in one day on the Chelyadin estates. Metropolitan Filip Kolychev (r. 1566–1568), a relative of some of the victims and an opponent of the outrages, was murdered in cold blood. During 1568–1569, the web of terror engulfed the tsar's first cousin and only potential adult replacement, Prince Vladimir Andreevich of Staritsa (1535–1569), who was forced to take poison. Likewise executed were Vladimir's mother, the abbess Evfrosinya, whose nunnery produced Russia's finest embroidery; his second wife and younger daughter; and at least one hundred others implicated as his supporters.

In 1570 the terror peaked, climaxed by a major purge in personnel in both the *oprichnina* and the state. Fearing treason in his western domains, and rumored to hold a special grudge against Novgorod, Ivan himself conducted the *oprichniki* to that city, as well as Tver, Torzhok, and Pskov. At least twenty-five hundred to three thousand people of all classes, including five hundred service cavalry, were killed, mostly in Novgorod. Entire families, including the very young and very old, were slain: "Peter Blekloy, his wife, daughter, and grandson," reads one official list. Major and minor chancery officials, clergy, and silversmiths figured heavily among the known victims, but some rich merchants and leading abbots also perished. The *oprichniki* plundered Novgorod's churches and monasteries and led the archbishop, his underlings, and the elite of Novgorod's service cavalry back to Moscow, where the inquests recommenced. The alleged plot now implicated but did not harm Ivan's oldest son, the sixteen-year-old heir Ivan Ivanovich (1554–1582). Doomed to a torturous death, however, stood most of Moscow's senior chancery officials, headed by Viskovaty and Funikov, as well as several ranking state and *oprichnina* boyars, among them Basmanov, some of the heir's in-laws, the tsar's chief cook, and a hundred other people.

The Crimean Tatar invasions of 1571–1572 hastened the end of the *oprichnina*. The burning of Moscow in 1571 served as the pretext for the execution of most of the remaining top *oprichniki*, including Prince Mikhail Cherkassky, brother of the tsar's recently deceased second wife. Pressing reconstruction costs precluded the planned expansion of *oprichnina* fortresses. And mounting anarchy, including common thugs and marauders posing as *oprichniki*, prompted Ivan to abolish this special corps, restore most lands to the regular government, and be satisfied with an enlarged personal court.

The liquidation of the *oprichnina* did not, however, terminate the bifurcation at the top or the executions. The rising star during 1569–1573 was a brutal ex-*oprichnik* of modest origins, Malyuta Skuratov (the strangler of Metropolitan Filip). After Skuratov died fighting in Livonia in 1573, his colleagues as a group lasted about two years. During this time the tsar's security net entrapped and beheaded the commander who defeated the Crimeans in 1572. Then another coup of sorts took place in Ivan's court in 1575—a year of plague and famine, which took far more lives than did the terror. A faction comprising Ivan's future Nagoy in-laws, Skuratov's son-in-law Bogdan Belsky (d. 1611), and the allied Godunovs—none of them aristocrats—took charge and survived a bloody purge of the other leading ex-*oprichniki* and council boyars. Once more real or imagined plots in Novgorod and threats to Ivan's person served as pretexts. He expanded his court lands again in 1575–1576 during a charade abdication, when he carried the simple title prince of Moscow, having named his recently baptized in-law, the former vassal khan ("tsar") of Kasimov, Semën Bekbulatovich (1545?–1616), grand prince of all Russia. Soon Ivan was back on his throne with enhanced security forces to protect him.

The Culture of Terror

Did this wave of domestic political violence, extraordinary even for a medieval society, spawn its own culture? The letters attributed to Ivan IV, regardless of actual authorship, offer insights into a mentality in which God has placed the tsar on his throne far, far above his subjects. Anyone who questions the tsar's authority or demands a share in governance is implicitly a heretic or traitor. The innocent need not fear wrongful death, for this renders them saintly martyrs who obtain immediate salvation. And Ivan's later financing of memorial services for his victims provided an acceptable means for him to expiate his sins. It also indicates an urge for reconciliation and avoidance of torments in the afterlife. Ivan's promotion of elaborately illustrated official chronicles and ecclesiastical culture at his private court shows that the terror operated alongside of a religious mindset. His son Ivan, a brute in some eyes, a promising heir in others, reportedly wrote a saint's life.

The tsar's skewing of the standard, premodern Christian doctrines of divine-right monarchy had a carnivalesque side. He sought and obtained public support and acclaim for rooting out treason. Many beastly executions, such as quartering or boiling, were carried out in public. The privileged *oprichnina* troops, with their fearsome insignia and their license to kill, were a base parody of a European knightly order. Ivan's courts featured bawdy entertainments and torture chambers—he personally participated in both—as well as his own quasi-monastic rule, which he likewise enforced. The liquidation of entire families was a mark of pre-Christian notions of vengeance and retribution. Popular ballads sang of his wrathful killing with his staff of an unruly servitor—just as an angry abbot might bludgeon a monk with an iron rod—and of his lamenting that no one interceded when he raged against his son.

In principle the terror was also compatible with military and technical modernization. The *oprichnina* army accepted European mercenaries, and Tsar Ivan himself employed an English physician. In 1564, after Makary died, his former protégé, Russia's first master printer Ivan Fëdorov, left Moscow for western Rus, where he did his greatest work, for example, printing Archbishop Gennady's 1499 Bible in 1580–1581. But the tsar had the press moved to Aleksandrovskaya, where it issued a few more religious books in the 1570s. Still Muscovy's culture at this time stood in stark contrast to western Rus, where, due to the influence of Europe's Reformation and Counter Reformation, the Orthodox established some genuine schools and academies. Studies there included Greek and Latin, as well as Slavonic, augmented at times with introductions to the liberal arts of Catholic education: literature, rhetoric, philosophy-theology, mathematics, music, and physical science as then conceived.

In contrast, education still hardly existed in Russia. Moreover, the creative, autonomous, reform movements within the Muscovite Church, which were associated with monasticism, virtually disappeared as the terror set in. Although the pilgrimages and memorial services remained as potent as ever in the great landholding cloisters such as Trinity, Kirillov, and Iosifov, the monks' spiritual and intellectual independence eventually migrated to a distant island on the White Sea. There, at the Solovetsky Monastery, with its prosperous saltworks and fisheries and expanding library, the organic ties with an earlier, freer time were strong, as they were in much of the Russian far north.

THE FINAL YEARS, 1576–1584

The conclusion of Ivan IV's reign in some ways resembled the final act of a bloody tragedy, well beyond any individual's control. On the positive side for Russia, the conquest of Sibir—a logical next step following the annexation of Kazan—commenced in 1582, and state institutions continued to develop. But the wartorn economy of the central and western regions had deteriorated. In some districts peasant population was down 90 percent. In addition, Moscow had to accept losses in the west in order to escape from the Livonian War, and Ivan's reign ended under a personal cloud.

Siberia

Russia's equivalent to Europe's dramatic and profitable colonial and mercantilistic expansion in the 1500s and 1600s was the conquest of Siberia. Typically for such ventures at that time, Russia's initial expansion east of the Urals was spearheaded by state-supported entrepreneurs, in this case the Stroganovs, a family whose salt- and ironworks supported a countrywide commercial network. Based near the Kama River, the Stroganovs were ideally situated to penetrate Kazan's eastern hinterlands, where they clashed with the westward expansionist thrust of the Tatar khan Kuchum of Sibir (r. ca. 1563–1598) and his forest-dwelling vassals.

This conflict came to a head in 1582 when nine hundred Stroganov soldiers and Don and Volga Cossacks under the *ataman* and former brigand Ermak ventured up the Irtysh River and sacked Kuchum's capital. Ermak was soon killed in battle, but Moscow sent enough men and arms to crush Kuchum in 1598. Meanwhile, the Russians erected a string of river strongholds in Sibir. By 1604, with the construction of Tomsk further east, most of the Ob-Irtysh basin north of the steppe was under Moscow's control. Tobolsk, built in 1587 at the juncture of the Tobol and the Irtysh Rivers in western Sibir, became the regional capital.

Domestic and especially international demand for furs—the same catalyst for the ventures of the French trappers across North America—served as the stimulus for this eastward expansion and absorption of more peoples into the empire. The generally colder weather of the so-called Little Ice Age, 1550–1700, helped fuel this profitable demand. In Siberia, the Moscow state treasury obtained from the natives the traditional tribute in furs paid to overlords. Russian traders and trappers had to turn over at least 10 percent of their profits to the state, which depended heavily on these revenues. Russia's eastward expansion proved onerous for some indigenous peoples, but it was accompanied by little of the genocide that Old World diseases like influenza and measles caused in the New World after the European arrival in 1492.

Provisioning and manning the Siberian forts remained difficult, even after the Russians started to raise crops in their vicinity. The state forcibly settled criminals, prisoners of war, and simple Russian townsmen there. A shortage of Russian women led to the taking of indigenous wives. Eventually Siberia acquired a distinctive character, with a new breed of hardy, rustic Russian-speakers, who never experienced personal serfdom.

The Paradoxical End

Stefan Bathory's election to the Polish throne in 1576 initiated the turning point in Moscow's military fortunes to the west. In 1577 Poland-Lithuania, bolstered by Hungarian and German infantry and artillery and superior organization and tactics, recaptured Polotsk and besieged Pskov—"like an ominous and great serpent wriggling from its cave." The epic, six-month resistance of Pskov, with womenfolk once more fighting alongside men, induced Bathory to settle in 1582 merely for Livonia and the recovery of Polotsk. Simultaneously, the Swedes drove the tsar's armies not only from Estonia, but also from all of Pskov's and Novgorod's historic coast. The exhausted Russians, facing additional chronic problems from some of their new subjects in the south and east, accepted another armistice with Sweden in 1583. Thus a quarter century of mostly aggressive fighting and a string of victories on western fronts were followed in the end by a net loss of territory and expulsion from the Baltic shores.

Meanwhile continued domestic insecurity characterized the tsar's last eight years, as he remained mostly in his Moscow and suburban palaces, isolated from society.

All the same, his regime proceeded here and there with constructive policies. A church synod in 1580 repeated the earlier state prohibition against new donations of land to monasteries. Two new judicial courts made their appearance: the Vladimir Department for boyars and the Moscow Department for lesser nobles and servicemen. Large taxation districts, which had first appeared in the *oprichnina*, continued to function under the regular state. These fiscal units complemented the five large border provinces and former khanates—Novgorod, Pskov, Smolensk, Kazan, and Astrakhan—operating with cohesive administrations under military governors and state secretaries. Thus, despite the terror, a stronger state requiring services and/or taxes from all free subjects emerged by the end of the reign of Russia's first tsar. It was also a society in which elites possessed legalized privileges and many others enjoyed supervised autonomy. The *oprichnina* and terror neither caused nor blocked Russia's development of a class- and clan-based, resource-mobilizing, military-fiscal state. Mighty swords required pens, and by the end of the century over forty respectable service gentry families had switched from military careers to the powerful chanceries.

Ivan IV's ultimate spectacular act of violence came in 1581, when, for personal or political reasons—we shall never know—he struck his pregnant daughter-in-law so hard that she miscarried and then inflicted a mortal blow upon her husband, the heir apparent Ivan Ivanovich. Soon afterward the tsar had his court scribes collect the available lists of victims of his repressions going back to 1565, so that he could distribute money to churches and monasteries to commemorate them.

Meanwhile, after the four aborted marriages that had followed the death of his second wife in 1569, Ivan had made a seventh and uncanonical union with Maria of the Nagoy clan and sired a son, Dmitry, in 1582. (The Orthodox Church considered only the first three marriages proper, but more than six was an open breach of canon law.) The tsar's only other son and now heir, Fëdor (1557–1598), was weak of body and mind. Thus, when after a horrible affliction of the stomach, its first tsar died on March 19, 1584, Russia once more faced the rule of magnates without any clear institutional boundaries or rule of law to prevent further anarchy and tyranny. And the prospects for the ruling dynasty were much shakier than at the start of Ivan's reign.

CHAPTER 8

Boris Godunov and the Time of Troubles, 1584–1613

And now let every age group ponder and everyone lend an ear to hear how, on account of our sins, our Lord God set loose his righteous punishment over all of Russia, from border to border; and how the entire Slavic nation rebelled; and how every place in Russia was devoured by fire and sword.

—Avraamy Palytsin of Trinity Monastery,
A History of the Previous Generation, 1620

After Ivan IV died, Russians confronted his legacy of war and tyranny, including a population crisis, later compounded by unusually cold weather and a horrendous famine in the years 1601–1603. Russia also faced several serious challenges from abroad, among them, the adoption of improved European military training and tactics by Sweden and Poland-Lithuania and the chronic slave raids of the Ottoman-supported Crimeans. Russia in turn continued to develop a variant of early modern Europe's military-fiscal state, which taxed and recruited the population to the limit to expand armies, navies, and fortifications. Accordingly, the period 1584–1613 brought the establishment of serfdom and the beginning of two centuries of tension between a state geared primarily for war and its Cossacks, who periodically mounted major rebellions. This process proved especially problematic at the turn of the century. Both the death of Tsar Fëdor Ivanovich in 1598, causing the end of Moscow's dynasty of three centuries, and the famine created instability. The common term *Time of Troubles* (*Smutnoe vremia*) refers specifically to Russia's affliction during the years 1598–1613, by hunger, disorientation, popular uprisings, civil war, and foreign intervention of the years. Yet the events of this period also revealed the utility of Russia's deep hinterland and the resilience of the social structures and values that had developed over the preceding century and a half.

SOCIAL FISSURES

Successive late summer frosts in 1601 and 1602 destroyed much of the Russian crop and drastically reduced the store of seed grains for 1603, when milder weather returned. Bereft of food supplies, employers and owners released thousands of hirelings and bondsmen, including military retainers and slaves, who now joined the thousands of other starving Russians in search of food. The famine thereby intensified popular discontent, which had been festering for several decades among townsmen, Cossacks, slaves, and poor service cavalry. A deeper problem, the rise of serfdom, constituted the greatest of the social issues in Russia and would continue to do so for centuries.

Enserfed Peasants

We can best understand the development of Russian serfdom within a regional context. Between 1450 and 1600 the majority of eastern and east-central European peasants lost their traditional freedom to relocate once they had paid off their debts, and they did not regain full liberty for several centuries. States and elites alike needed to secure peasant produce and labor for consumption, exports, armies, navies, and fortifications. The spread of the three-field system, which maximized production while restoring fertility, often led landlords to take up acreage with serf labor for their own personal use. Unlike New World slavery, which originated around the same time, east European serfdom did not result from international demand for a commodity such as sugar. But serfdom later proved ideal for export-driven grain production, which in turn helped fuel the expansion of this form of compulsory labor.

As elsewhere in eastern Europe, Russian serfdom developed gradually. Going back to the Mongol period, some peasants known as old dwellers were already bound to their lands, and chronically indebted peasants also lost their right to move. During the sixteenth century, holders of service and other estates forcibly required labor from resident peasants—a practice that intensified within the *oprichnina*. Thus commenced *barshchina*, the labor obligations of agricultural serfs, which over time grew to rival *obrok*, payments by serfs in cash or kind to their lords.

The population crisis in western and central Russia caused a labor shortage for landed service cavalry and tax shortfalls for the government. With some villages virtually depopulated, by 1580 peasants were ignoring the law restricting movement to November and relocating whenever they chose, often with the complicity of landlords offering more favorable conditions. Russia's traditions of obligatory service pointed to a simple solution in the 1590s. Heads of households everywhere were forced to stay put or find substitutes for themselves. Such policies caused more illegal flight and outright popular opposition in southern frontier districts, but a typically vicious, preemptive state inquest crushed the protesters in 1592. According to a Russian chronicle, "A multitude of people died from torture; others they executed or had their tongues cut out; and others died in prison." Despite such repression, scattered disturbances became a regular feature of the Russian countryside for centuries and constituted an essential element in the civil war following the famine.

No single Russian law fixing domiciles, even temporarily, is extant from the sixteenth century, and the first such rulings may have been local. Exceptional decrees allowing some movement during the famine years of 1601 and 1602 show that state officials had already issued renewable, annual suspensions of peasant relocation. The first such general or regional "forbidden" or "decree year" may have come as early as 1585 or even 1581, and certainly before 1592. For in 1597, the state mandated a five-year limit on searches for runaways from taxed domiciles. However, authorities readily ignored many cases, since fugitives proved useful as frontiersmen, soldiers, Cossacks, or new settlers on old estates.

It was probably no accident that the virtual abolition of legal peasant movement in Russia at this time coincided with a labor-intensive expansion of the movable, wooden fortified lines in the south and southeast against the Tatars and the bastions in the west against Poland-Lithuania. Smolensk's four-odd miles of new walls, built between 1595 and 1602, required over 150 million bricks and a mammoth levy of the realm's stonecutters, brick-workers, and even potters, as well as other workers. This project may have been the most massive fortress anywhere at that time.

By the early 1600s, Russia was in the throes of a four-way struggle. Peasants demanded a full restoration of the right to move. Officials on the southern frontiers were willing to enroll fugitives as garrison soldiers. Large landowners generally favored a compromise five-year limitation on recovery suits. And middle- and lower-ranking servicemen called for an unlimited recovery period for runaway peasants. Requiring secure peasant labor support and sometimes having as few as one peasant household on their lands, these servicemen urged the permanent abolition of free movement and thereby contributed to peasant discontent.

Restless Troops

The economic crisis also affected the motley collection of fighters comprising the Russian army: service cavalry; free contract soldiers, such as Cossacks, garrison troops, and gunners; and military slaves, some of whom were former service cavalry. The basic problem of the middle and lower servicemen was impoverishment and insecurity of status. Starting with the 1556 statute that increased service requirements, some destitute cavalrymen illegally sold themselves to richer colleagues and became their combat slaves. Many fled to the southern frontiers, some joining the Cossacks, others enrolling as garrison troops. At the same time state authorities were inclined to enlist as servicemen willing and able Cossacks, military slaves, or other commoners if they possessed horses. Established service cavalry, however, protested that such promotions dishonored service gentry status, especially when newcomers obtained estates.

In another drastic measure of 1597 (possibly tried earlier) the state made all contract slavery permanent, which seems to have deterred such self-sale (see the chapter "Ivan IV and the Birth Pangs of Tsardom, 1533–1584"). All the same, around 1600, Russia's roughly twenty-five thousand service cavalry, many of them dirt poor, owned an aggregate eight thousand fighting slaves and another sixteen thousand slaves of various origin, who provided logistical support on campaigns. In normal times they were perfectly loyal, but when hungry or oppressed, they and poor servicemen could become destabilizing elements.

This was even truer of Cossacks and garrison troops. The state wished to mobilize Cossacks in an orderly fashion. Accordingly, the authorities tried to control Cossacks with the carrot of subsidies and the stick of new fortresses near Cossack territory and periodic bans from border towns and their markets. When Volga Cossacks in 1588 attacked a friendly Persian embassy caravan in south Russia, state reprisals were severe. Still, numerous poor Cossacks enrolled as garrison troops, some of them even constructing new strongholds. Most garrison troops, though, originated as free contract soldiers, those along the southern frontiers obtaining land to grow food. But at the end of the century the contracts disappeared, and the state treated garrison soldiers as permanently domiciled townsmen.

With disgruntled peasants, soldiers, service gentry, and also subject nationalities, such as Tatars and Chuvash, chafing over onerous burdens and the loss of status, conditions were ripe for massive, violent protests against Russia's state and its ways of mobilizing resources.

THE NEW STRONG MAN, 1584–1605

The material catalyst for Russia's social crisis in the early seventeenth century was the devastating famine in 1601–1603, which some historians estimate carried off a fourth of the population. The human catalyst for massive discontent and eventual outbreak of civil war was one of the most able and controversial figures in Russian history, Boris Godunov (1552?–1605). By a combination of luck and skill, he became the dominant figure in the reign of his feeble brother-in-law Fëdor (1557–1598) and succeeded him as tsar in 1598. Due to suspicious circumstances surrounding the death of Fëdor's young half-brother Dmitry in 1591, some people suspected Boris of murder—a tradition enshrined in Romanov dynasty propaganda after 1613, in modern comparisons of Boris to Shakespeare's guilt-ridden in Macbeth, and in Modest Mussorgsky's opera classic *Boris Godunov* (1874). Specialists, however, credit the real Boris with normalizing Russia's government and restoring its position abroad, albeit at the expense of one of the most basic of human freedoms—the right to move.

Power Politics

Ivan IV's death early in March 1584 and the split between court and state threatened Russia with another round of the bloody semianarchy that had attended his childhood. For outside of personal piety and exemplary devotion to his wife, the sluggish and mentally impaired heir Fëdor (r. 1584–1598) proved almost totally unfit to rule. He spent hours in churches, rang the bells, and enjoyed both court jesters and mortal combats between a huntsman and a bear.

The regency council Ivan had set up for his afflicted son was an unworkable foursome of three senior boyars and the most recent favorite, Bogdan Belsky (d. 1611), an ex-*oprichnik* and natural leader. But behind the scenes stood the masterful state secretary Andrei Shchelkalov (d. ca. 1597) and Tsar Fëdor's astute brother-in-law and favorite, Boris Godunov, whose kinsmen controlled the court chancery and treasury. A pious man and a brilliant orator, Boris obtained the authoritative title of boyar-equerry at the time of Fëdor's coronation in May 1584. The regency quickly sent Fëdor's five-year-old half-brother, Dmitry, to live in Uglich in the north, scattered Dmitry's maternal relatives, and deployed Belsky in the provinces.

Fëdor's frail health and the many miscarriages of his wife, the *tsaritsa* Irina Godunova, inspired further intrigue. Boris hired a physician and a midwife from England to shepherd one pregnancy but was compelled by his xenophobic compatriots to repudiate these foreigners as heretics, unsuitable for such a sacred task. All the same, the support of the palace troops and Fëdor's refusal to divorce Irina enabled her brother Boris to prevail over his boyar competitors. By 1587 he held effective power in alliance with Shchelkalov and a new metropolitan, Yov (r. 1587–1605). That year Boris exiled dozens of nobles and had six leading Moscow merchants beheaded for supporting his chief competitor for power, Prince Ivan Shuisky, but he later made peace with the kinsmen of his fallen rivals. Enjoying overall policy successes as well as personal influence, Boris became the near ceremonial equal of Fëdor—"By grace of God . . . his [Tsar Fëdor's] Noble and Wise Brother-in-Law, Ruler, Right-Hand Man, Boyar-Equerry, Court Commander, and Lord of the Khanates of Kazan and Astrakhan."

The strange death of Fëdor's epileptic half-brother, Dmitry, in Uglich in 1591 compromised but did not derail Boris. Assuming foul play, incensed locals rioted and killed Moscow's resident agent. But the official investigatory commission, headed by the new senior Shuisky prince, Vasily (1552–1612), concluded from eyewitnesses that Dmitry had fallen and cut his own throat while playing a form of mumblety-peg with a large knife. The authorities then executed several Uglich townsmen for sedition and exiled others to Siberia. Godunov weathered this storm in the short term, but rumors abounded that he had ordered the boy murdered. Modern authorities, however, agree that in 1591 Boris would have had no reason to assassinate the *tsarevich*, especially since Irina was still fertile. Indeed in 1592 she gave birth to a daughter, Feodosia. Boris immediately approached the Austrian Hapsburgs for an adolescent prince to train for the role of tsar-consort. But the child's death two years later weakened hopes for a direct heir and the survival of the old Moscow dynasty.

Effective Governance

If Boris's political ruthlessness has sullied his reputation, his administrative skills, statesmanship, and plans for Russia have rescued him as a man of his epoch in the eyes of historians. It was Boris who directed the repressive and partially stabilizing policies that tied all taxpayers to their domiciles and slaves to their masters. But these measures are only part of the story of the "second Adashev," as some contemporaries called Boris, recalling Ivan IV's treasurer of the 1550s.

The restoration of state finances headed the agenda when Fëdor ascended the throne. His regime immediately curtailed the fiscal immunities of the monasteries and conducted a general census over the course of three years. With the mounting impoverishment of servicemen in the early 1590s, the state freed from taxes all acreage cultivated directly by or for them. The regency also needed to reintegrate the tsar's expanded court of 1565–1584 into the regular state mechanism and to ensure support for the elite cavalry. Accordingly, Boris and Shchelkalov revisited the reforms of the 1550s and 1560s and allocated central lands to about eleven hundred servicemen in a way that favored older families over Ivan IV's newer people. The state also rationalized the military muster further. A descending ladder of council, court, and Moscow ranks headed the service hierarchy, followed by a new status of provincial city selectmen for the local service elite, seated well above servicemen with meager or even no allotments of lands and peasants. By the end of the century the greatest families of the realm accepted that they were also servitors. This integration of aristocrats into the ruling apparatus would last until 1762.

Boris achieved a personal coup with the elevation of Russia's chief prelate in 1589. Eagerly aided by Tsar Fëdor's lone foray into statesmanship, Boris persuaded a visiting patriarch of Constantinople to ordain Metropolitan Yov patriarch of Moscow. Boris also financed the required assent by the other high prelates, all of whom lived under Ottoman sovereignty and gave the sultan a share of their "alms"—in this case, outright bribe money. Having a patriarch, the highest rank for an Orthodox prelate, gave Russia greater prestige in the Orthodox world and also made the head of Russia's church a more authoritative figure at home.

In the international arena, Russia remained vulnerable on three fronts in 1584. The Swedes held Novgorod's former Baltic coast; King Stefan Bathory dreamed of taking Pskov and regaining Smolensk and other borderlands for Poland-Lithuania; and the Crimean Tatars could still raid deep into Russia from the south. So with relative calm on the western fronts, the Russians established a Department of Masonry Work, started a massive extension of Moscow's walls, and fortified Solovetsky Monastery in the far north with stone and artillery. Over the period 1585–1590, they expanded the southern defenses with a masonry citadel at Astrakhan (1588), and new forts at other key river points, including Tsaritsyn, named for Irina, on the Lower Volga.

Bathory's death in 1586 created the opening for a crown union and state alliance of Russia and Poland-Lithuania under Tsar Fëdor. Earlier, in 1569, at a joint *seym,* or parliament, in Lublin, the Poles had used their superior assets and Lithuania's vulnerability to convert the loose Polish-Lithuanian dynastic tie into a state union. By this arrangement, Lithuania's Rus lands in present-day Ukraine were also transferred to the Polish part of the realm. Now the confident Poles pursued a state union with Russia as well, and, failing at that, took a Swedish prince as their King Sigismund III (r. 1587–1632). Fortunately for Russia, although he was briefly king of Sweden, too (1592–1599), neither a Swedish-Polish state union nor a firm alliance materialized. Boris, rather, gambling that he could defeat Sweden, opened hostilities in 1590. A costly storming of Narva failed, hindered by Godunov's amateurish military leadership, but by 1595 Russia had regained most of the seacoast ceded to Sweden in 1583. Russia's lack of a fleet, however, meant that foreigners still almost completely controlled Russia's Baltic trade.

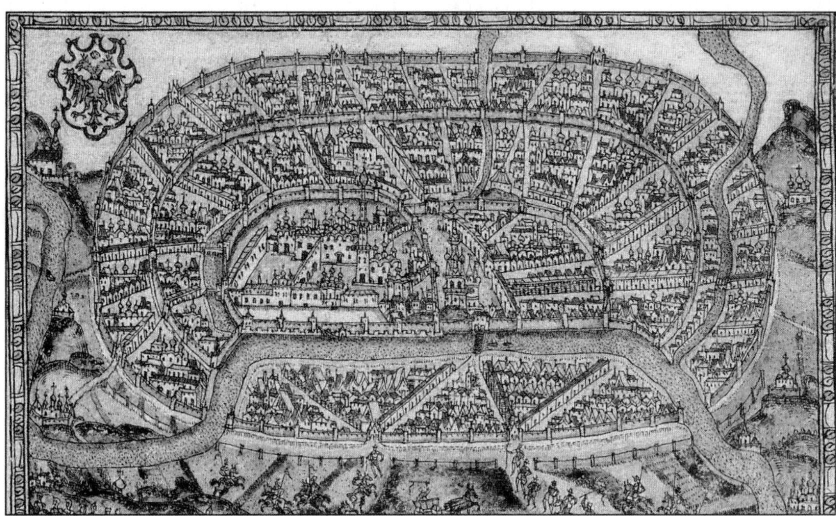

Moscow and its Planned Sections and Rings of Fortifications, 1606–07, as depicted by the resident Dutchman, Isaac Massa. The Kremlin is in the left center, and the second oldest walled section, Kitay Gorod, is in the right center, with St. Basil's Cathedral just outside the Kremlin wall. *Koninklijke Bibliotheek, The Hague, National Library of the Netherlands.*

Russia's fresh involvement in a Swedish war triggered another Turkish-backed Crimean raid on Moscow in 1591. But, with Tsar Fëdor's prayerful and prophetic encouragement—"Fear not," he reportedly said from his palace overlooking the encampments; "this night the pagans will flee"—Boris and Russia's artillery outside the city walls repelled the invasion. On the site of his camp outside Moscow in 1591, Boris founded the Donskoy Monastery—named for Our Lady of the Don to recall the 1380 victory over the Mongols, which was credited in part to the Virgin. Meanwhile, feverish construction and reconstruction of strongholds in the southern steppe districts ensued, including Belgorod on the Donets (1593), which became a nodal point of defense.

Boris Enthroned

Tsar Fëdor's death in January 1598 gave Boris an opportunity to display his political savvy in a situation where some type of electoral conclave was the only means of legitimizing a successor. Fëdor's widow, Irina, having earlier been proclaimed Great Sovereign in her own right, accepted a general oath of allegiance and amnestied prisoners. She had already done a splendid job of presiding over the further development of female court ceremonial and public processions, receiving petitions, and making her office, which represented a softer, somewhat maternal side of royal power, an essential element of governance. Paintings rendered at this time in the court women's Terem Palace used legend to emphasize the independence, authority, and also manly valor of the ideal queen. But after nine days of reigning in her own name, Irina retired to the fortified and prestigious Novodevichy (New Maidens) Convent outside Moscow and promoted her brother's candidacy.

Boris stayed with his sister and from Novodevichy contrived to summon an Assembly of the Land to have himself elected tsar. The divided boyar council rejected him but could not agree on any other candidate, such as the late tsar's popular cousin, Fëdor Nikitich Romanov (1553?–1633). Support from Patriarch Yov, Bogdan Belsky, servicemen, and merchants proved crucial to Boris. Late in 1598, after eight tense months of politicking, he became Russia's first elected tsar and moved back to Moscow's Kremlin.

As ruler in his own right, Boris attempted a grand reconciliation with the aristocracy. Yet intrigues at court proliferated, marked by charges not only of disloyalty, but also of political witchcraft—that is, the use of potions and spells to influence court politics and dynastic affairs. Avoiding public execution of magnates, if not their hastened death in exile, Boris dealt severely with two major rivals and a potential competitor. He temporarily disgraced Vasily Shuisky, forced Fëdor Romanov to become a monk, and had Belsky's beard pulled out.

The disputed succession led to a new Polish-Lithuanian diplomatic offensive. In 1600, on the eve of the Russian famine, the Lithuanian chancellor Lev Sapieha came to Moscow to propose a confederation, yet demanded the return of the borderlands that Ivan III and Vasily III had taken a century earlier—as if Russia were a crippled entity. This offer was especially brazen, since Poland's Catholic king and high clergy had recently browbeaten six of their realm's eight Orthodox bishops to recognize papal supremacy—formalized at a synod in Brest-Litovsk in 1596. The majority of the Orthodox in Poland-Lithuania resisted this regional church union, leaving their church hierarchy without many believers and most believers without a hierarchy. As a result, the cohesion of Poland-Lithuania, which, like Russia, also had discontented Cossacks and enserfed peasants, was more fragile than its leaders chose to imagine.

A confident Boris might have capitalized on Polish vulnerability, since Russia generally supported Orthodoxy abroad with money, books, and even iconographers. But he acted defensively, refusing of course to cede territory with Orthodox subjects to a Catholic state. He also concentrated on bolstering Russia's official image at home as the New Israel. As his centerpiece, he planned a huge new cathedral modeled on the Church of the Resurrection in Jerusalem and situated next to the Ivan the Great Bell Tower, which he had extended to its present height of 266 feet.

At the same time, Russia's overall relations with western and central Europeans under Tsar Boris became more open. From his adolescent days during the *oprichnina*, he was accustomed to foreigners with their education, weapons, gadgets, medical training, productive techniques, and commercial ways, and he desired some of this for Russia. He sent at least nine young Russians to England and Germany—possibly some to France as well—for language and other formal study (none who survived ever chose to return), and it was rumored that he hoped to found a genuine university. Boris also granted European residents an enclave in Moscow, the precursor of the German or European settlement that would later become a stimulus for Westernization. European-style decoration became more common on buildings, and Russians began to compose polyphonic music, a medieval Western invention, which broke with ancient church traditions. Simultaneously, Russia's innovative onion domes, combining the spherical and conical and providing a novel national flavor to churches, made their first appearance.

Boris's declining health and the famine of 1601–1603, seen by some at that time as divine judgment on him, weakened his authority. As hunger descended, the sheer number of starving people overwhelmed his price fixing and heroic attempts at relief, as well as the humane efforts of individuals, such as the pious widow Yuliana Osorina, to feed their slaves and peasants. Many people, in desperation, turned to brigandage. The ailing tsar placed his hopes for the future in medicinal sorcery, as well as his educated cartographer son and junior coruler, Fëdor (1589–1605), and his daughter Ksenya (1582–post-1621), who was betrothed to the Danish Archduke Hans—a possible tsar-consort. Boris also tried to secure his dynasty by means of his grandiose building projects in Moscow and policies designed to satisfy all the elites. But several factors combined to ruin his dreams. Archduke Hans fell fatally ill in 1602, and widespread banditry progressed to pitched battles with regular troops. In September 1603 about five hundred former military slaves ambushed and almost wiped out about a hundred musketeers west of Moscow. Soon a larger troop led by service cavalry crushed this riffraff. Meanwhile Boris's physical deterioration accelerated. Finally, the year 1604 brought invasion by an armed pretender claiming to be *tsarevich* Dmitry.

THE TROUBLES I: IMPOSTORS AND ADVENTURERS, 1605–1610

Boris Godunov died, possibly poisoned, in 1605. After seven weeks of nominal rule by his son Fëdor, an intrigue-filled eleven months proceeded with the pretender Dmitry as tsar. Next came four years of the nominal rule of Vasily Shuisky, marked by large-scale rebellions and new pretenders. A council of seven boyars then tried to govern in the name of the Polish crown prince but had to contend with a Swedish occupation of Novgorod, more pretenders and rebellion, and finally a national movement against all foreign intervention. No wonder Russian contemporaries and later scholars called this disorienting period of civil strife the Time of Troubles, some dating it back to the death of Tsar Fëdor in 1598. Throughout these years, however, Russia's fundamental social and administrative order held. Most free people, from beekeepers to boyars, Cossacks to commanders, scribes to state secretaries, and priests to prelates, were seeking a return to political normality under an authoritative, but legitimate and hopefully benevolent tsar.

"Tsar" Dmitry and Marina Mniszech as engraved by Europeans in 1605–06. They were Russia's first royalty and the only ones before Peter the Great in the late 1690s to make themselves appear Western. The Latin inscription defining Dmitry reads, "Dmitry son of Ivan, by Grace of God, Tsar and Grand Duke of all Russia and Lord and King of the Muscovite Monarchy." The adventurous Polish Marina was the wife of two Russian pretenders and the mother of a third. *Rovinskii, D. A.,* Materialy dlia russkoi ikonografii, pt. 2. *St. Petersburg, 1884.*

"Tsar Dmitry"

The majority of specialists, following skeptical contemporaries, have identified the first pretender Dmitry as Grigory Otrepev (1582?–1606), a talented runaway monk and former patriarchal clerk who had fled to Poland. This man convinced himself and some ambitious Poles that he either was or could readily pass for the dead *tsarevich* Dmitry. Secretly and superficially converting to Catholicism to gain Polish and Jesuit backing, Otrepev attached himself to an indebted Polish magnate, Jerzy Mniszech, and became betrothed to his daughter Marina (d. 1614). Then in October 1604, with much fanfare and propaganda, but against the wishes of the Polish king, this Dmitry crossed into southern Russia with an army of only four thousand Poles, Ukrainians, and Don Cossacks.

Civil war followed. A large number of servicemen and other residents of the southern districts flocked to the pretender's banner in hopes of obtaining better conditions or riches, as did some Zaporozhian Cossacks from Polish Ukraine. Boris's army had the advantage in numbers, but not in food, motivation, tactical skills, or even common sense. For example, Vasily Shuisky's punitive force, sent to pacify the rich upper Oka peasant district of Komaritsk, was notably savage. According to a German in Russian service, "many thousands of peasants, with their wives and children, were suspended by one leg from trees and shot through with bullets." Dmitry, in contrast, restrained his troops from looting and won over more of the population. Almost all of the garrisons of the new southern fortresses went over to him.

The opposing armies were stalemated when Boris died in April 1605. The new boy-tsar Fëdor Godunov and his relatives could not keep the elite in line. Commanders and regular military units defected, and rebel troops approached the capital. Then Bogdan Belsky, whom the frightened Godunovs had recalled to Moscow, directed a popular, bloodless coup in the name of Dmitry. The pretender's agents proceeded to strangle Fëdor and his mother and confiscate the property of their relatives and two allied boyar clans. Negotiations with the other leading boyars followed, and Dmitry amnestied the victims of Boris Godunov's repressions. Patriarch Yov had to resign, the tonsured Fëdor Romanov reemerged as Metropolitan Filaret of Rostov, and the man known in Russian history as False Dmitry stood at the head of the realm as tsar.

Only Vasily Shuisky objected, claiming the throne as the senior descendant of the historic Vladimir princes. Dmitry quickly made an example of Shuisky by indicting and condemning him for treason at a show trial in front of an assembly of notables. But as the executioner's axe was about to fall, Dmitry commuted Shuisky's sentence to exile (his two leading supporters were not so fortunate). The real Dmitry's mother, Maria, and her relatives hastened to recognize the pretender as genuine and obtained ample rewards for cooperating.

History and mythology have left contrasting images of Tsar Dmitry. In one version, he was an unprincipled butcher of any who might unmask him, a satyr who ravished nuns, and a practitioner of witchcraft. In the other, his deeds reveal a relatively open-minded and courageous Westernizer put in an impossible position. He had to contend with Russia's weak finances and narrow cultural horizons. Elite opinion always considered him a fake, and his Polish backers unrealistically expected lavish rewards of money and estates.

Dmitry's outward-looking military, foreign, cultural, and ceremonial policies anticipated Russia's eighteenth century. To shore up the social structure, he favored exclusive privileges for the gentry servicemen, who were the equivalent of Poland's nobles, but he also tried to modernize the artillery and introduce new infantry tactics, which would necessarily promote commoners. Although unwilling to restore borderlands to Poland-Lithuania or replace Orthodoxy with Catholicism, as some Poles demanded, he was ready to join with them against Sweden—the port of Narva again being Russia's goal. He also prepared operations against Crimean Tatars as part of a Russo-Polish anti-Ottoman crusade. Open to petitioners, tolerant in religious matters, and lax regarding the tedious and elaborate court rituals, Dmitry, like Boris, reputedly hoped to establish a university in Russia.

Tsar Dmitry's relations with the Poles who came to Moscow in his wake finally ruined him. Muscovites resented his Polish advisers, his unruly Polish guardsmen and mercenaries, and the first Catholic churches ever built in the capital. After bloody riots in Moscow, Dmitry had to expel some of the Polish soldiers with only a fraction of their promised pay. His impending marriage to Marina Mniszech, who refused to convert to Orthodoxy, caused a storm. Dmitry threw caution to the wind, despite the discovery of several plots against him. Soon after the wedding ceremony, two hundred-odd servicemen and merchants from Novgorod, Pskov, and Smolensk, organized by the recently pardoned Vasily Shuisky, broke into the palace and slaughtered Dmitry as he tried to escape. His naked corpse was dragged by the genitals through Moscow and burned, and his ashes fired from a cannon back toward Poland, as he was proclaimed a satanic sorcerer—the complete opposite of a legitimate, divinely sanctioned tsar.

Conflicting accounts by resident foreigners leave us in a fog regarding general opinion of Tsar Dmitry. The German mercenary Konrad Bussow claimed that Muscovites gladly joined in the kill. In contrast, the Dutch agent Isaac Massa reported that they supported Dmitry, but boyar conspirators shrewdly turned the crowd against the Polish wedding guests by imputing to them plans to murder the tsar. At any rate, a general massacre of foreigners ensued with anywhere from five hundred to thirty-five hundred killed on both sides.

Shuisky and Bolotnikov

After the death of Tsar Dmitry, the leading boyars were divided, but Vasily Shuisky and his supporters staged his acclamation as tsar. The boyars then balanced Shuisky with one of their own by naming Filaret (Fëdor) Romanov as patriarch. In a naive scheme to discredit the former regime, the new tsar tried to fabricate a wonder-working saint out of a phony corpse of the original Dmitry, but it soon decayed, which saints' bodies are not supposed to do. In a more straightforward move, Shuisky replaced Filaret as patriarch with Metropolitan Germogen of Kazan (d. 1612)—a resolute and unblemished frontier missionary prelate and a tireless spokesman for the new regime. Shuisky also had the backing of the true Dmitry's relatives and Bogdan Belsky, who reversed course and agreed that the pretender had been an imposter.

Controlling Moscow was the least of Shuisky's problems. No sooner had Tsar Dmitry been murdered than rumors surfaced that he had escaped. The same diverse group of southerners who had supported the first pretender raised a new banner of revolt, thereby reopening the civil war. Widespread fear of a boyar-tsar, memories of Shuisky's punitive expedition in 1604, and lingering popular hopes for a resurrected tsar-savior fanned the flames against Shuisky. The rebels found two excellent leaders in the local serviceman Istoma Pashkov and the huge, imposing figure of Ivan Bolotnikov (d. 1608). Bolotnikov had been an impoverished serviceman, a military contract slave, a runaway turned Don Cossack, and a captive Turkish galley oarsman, before he escaped and went to Poland. From there, at the behest of several of Shuisky's Russian opponents and the Polish Mniszechs, Bolotnikov moved into Russia and assumed nominal command of the revolt in Tsar Dmitry's name.

The rebels at first enjoyed spectacular success, repulsing Shuisky's advance units, driving right on to Moscow, picking up scores of defectors along the way, and garnering support in the central Volga region among Russians and minority peoples—Chermis, Chuvash, Mordvinians, and some Tatars. By late autumn 1606, Bolotnikov and Pashkov, bolstered by the Ryazan gentry cavalry and other regular troops, had about fifty thousand men besieging the capital. In opposition, however, a line stretching from Smolensk to Kazan through Moscow and Nizhny Novgorod, including almost all the major commercial centers of the realm, stood by Shuisky. The tsar also had some excellent commanders, such as his nephew Mikhail Skopin-Shuisky (1587–1610). In bold and deft moves, Shuisky armed Moscow's townsmen and induced the Ryazan cavalrymen to defect. Meanwhile, Bolotnikov quarreled with Pashkov, who betrayed the rebels and helped defeat them in early December. Thousands of Bolotnikov's men died on the battlefield, and thousands of captives were stunned like cattle with blows to the head and then drowned.

Bolotnikov retreated southward to Tula and obtained fresh aid from Cossacks fighting under the banner of a new pretender, Pëtr Fëdorovich—a fictitious grandson of Ivan IV. This former cook and tradesman turned Terek Cossack and bandit established a pseudocourt and dealt vindictively with government supporters by reviving Ivan's practice of crowd-pleasing public executions. In a frightful war of attrition, Shuisky's armies gained the upper hand in October 1607 by damming Tula's river and flooding the city. By the terms of surrender, Shuisky freed all the rebels, except a handful of leaders. Despite promises to the contrary, he had pseudo-Pëtr hanged in Moscow and Bolotnikov drowned in exile.

Moscow and Tushino

By now it was clear that the civil war was not only a story of battles and sieges but also an intensive struggle to attract soldiers and political support, which entailed inducements, pressure, propaganda, and disinformation. In March 1607 Shuisky had made a bid for both gentry and common soldier support with two laws, one extending the search period for runaway peasants to fifteen years, the other reversing one of Godunov's 1597 decrees and freeing service contract slaves from permanent bondage. But neither these measures nor the collapse of Bolotnikov and pseudo-Pëtr could stop the groundswell of support for yet another pretender and false Dmitry—a mysterious Russian or western Rus, perhaps a priest's son, who led a mixed force of several thousand from Poland into Russia that summer. This "Thief" or "Brigand" benefited greatly from his pseudonym. Attracting most of the former rebel forces to his side, he also, like the first imposter, was a law-and-order candidate, not a revolutionary or anarchist. Shuisky competed by offering freedom to any slave or peasant who enrolled in his armies, but by June 1608 pseudo-Dmitry had established a base and a quasi government in the Moscow suburb of Tushino.

A rather strange spectacle unfolded, with two tsars and two heads of the church. Over to the Tushino court came several leading Moscow families, headed by the Romanovs under Filaret, who became pseudo-Dmitry's patriarch-designate. Shuisky in turn freed all his Polish captives in hopes of inducing King Sigismund III to order home those of his subjects who were serving pseudo-Dmitry. Then the first Dmitry's widow, Marina, appeared in Tushino and claimed to recognize the second Dmitry as her real husband. At first he did quite well in gaining the allegiance of Pskov, Vladimir, Kostroma, and Yaroslavl and some other important towns, but the great cloisters and such crucial cities as Novgorod, Nizhny Novgorod, and Kazan stood by Shuisky. When pseudo-Dmitry's mercenaries and Cossacks extorted too much from their own territory, they too faced widespread popular rebellion, in this case led by prosperous merchants. Lithunian Chancellor Lev Saphieha's kinsman Jan-Piotr added to the near anarchy of the time by joining pseudo-Dmitry with several thousand cavalry and subjecting Trinity Monastery to a sixteen-month siege in 1608–1609. Shuisky's armies could do nothing to help, but the cloister's garrison held out, supported by the local population.

Little by little Shuisky's authority weakened. To conciliate the boyars he rescinded the freeing of service contract slaves, but boyars and other elite continued to shift allegiances. A few hatched assassination plots against him and paid with their lives. Desperate for foreign aid to counter pseudo-Dmitry's Poles, Shuisky again ceded the mouth of the Neva to Sweden. His nephew Skopin then beat the bankrupt Tushinites so badly that their regime collapsed by the end of 1609. But Shuisky now faced Sigismund III of Poland, who entered the fray, claiming and besieging Smolensk.

A free-for-all ensued. Shuisky even employed Crimean Tatar raiders against pseudo-Dmitry, who had retreated southward to new headquarters in the town of Kaluga. The former Tushino elite, led by Filaret, negotiated with Sigismund to enthrone his son Wladyslaw (1595–1648) in Moscow with strict conditions. He was to convert to Orthodoxy, consult with the boyars and patriarch on important matters, support servicemen with modest estates, retain serfdom, and ban slaves from the army. Such an alliance of crown, church, and nobility represented the ideal of most of Russia's elite at the time. Pseudo-Dmitry, meanwhile, smashed Shuisky's Crimean allies and revived as a major force, despite facing treachery within his own ranks and the massacre of several thousand of his Cossacks. As for Shuisky, his popular young nephew Skopin, having secured the area around Moscow, suddenly died. Many suspected—and legend recounts—his poisoning at the hands of his presumably envious uncle. Shuisky soon lost most of his remaining support.

Finally, following a botched Russian attempt to clear the road to Smolensk, Shuisky's Swedish mercenaries abandoned him in June 1610. The boyars quickly forced the tsar to become a monk. Then a compromise Council of Seven, which included several Tushinites, took over. In November 1610, prodded by the Polish commander Stanislaw Zolkiewski, the Council sent an embassy in to Sigismund III to secure his son Wladyslaw on the terms Filaret had offered. The king, however, desired the throne for himself and arrested the delegation leaders, including the ex-patriarch Filaret and ex-tsar Shuisky. At the same time, taking advantage of the boyars' appeals for help, Zolkiewski sent a detachment of troops into the Moscow Kremlin without a firm commitment to any conditions. Patriarch Germogen, a firm opponent of foreigners, was placed under arrest. Real power in the capital passed from the boyars to the Polish garrison commander, Gosiewski. To complicate matters further, that December, pseudo-Dmitry became murderously paranoiac and was slain by the chief of his bodyguard.

THE TROUBLES II: NATIONAL REVIVAL, 1611–1613

As the year 1611 dawned, Russia had no tsar, no pretender with popular support, no clear candidate for the throne, and no boyar leadership to fill in the gap—only a stubborn patriarch under house arrest. An array of forces in the capital and the countryside faced each other, and the mutually hostile Polish and Swedish kings angled for large parcels of Russian border territory and the crown to boot. At the same time, Polish and Swedish involvement in Russia brought the issue of national survival into question, and some of the provinces in the deep hinterhand took up the challenge. Within two years, despite more dissension, the Russians expelled the Poles from Moscow and chose a new tsar whose line would last three centuries. Significantly, in the very process of liberation and reconstitution, Russians of all free classes re-created their own peculiar, legitimate form of autocracy, bureaucracy, and precedence and shored up domestic serfdom and slavery.

Cossacks and Gentry

After the death of the second pseudo-Dmitry, his Cossack forces split into two major groups. One contingent stayed in Kaluga with the aspiring commander, Prince Dmitry Trubetskoy (d. 1625?), who eyed the crown for himself. The other followed the adventuristic Ukrainian Ivan Zarutsky (d. 1614) and the widowed tsarina Marina Mniszech. They marched under the banner of her newborn baby, the imposter-*tsarevich* Ivan (1610–1614), known to their enemies as the Little Thief. Provincial leaders who opposed the Poles, including Prokofy Lyapunov (d. 1611), the ambitious head of the Ryazan gentry militia, joined Trubetskoy and Zarutsky in a loose coalition. Together they occupied Moscow's suburbs and set off an uprising in the city. The Polish garrison saved itself and the Council of Seven by burning most of Moscow outside the Kremlin but could not reoccupy the suburbs and thus faced isolation. Encouraged by the smuggled appeals of the confined and dying patriarch Germogen, town after town declared against the Council. Kazan patriots dispatched the redoubtable Bogdan Belsky, their pro-Council military governor, by hurling him from the city ramparts. Novgorodians impaled their governor in retaliation for his butchering anti-Council Cossack prisoners.

Bolstered by the defection of chancery officials from Moscow to the besiegers, Lyapunov convened an Assembly of the Land to re-create the key government offices, coordinate the national movement, distribute service estates and salaries, and elect a new tsar. But since he also needed foreign support, he adopted Shuisky's risky policy, made a new agreement with the Swedes, and secretly negotiated the admittance of a Swedish force into Novgorod. This policy backfired when the Swedes, far from helping Russia against Poland, occupied all of Russia's Baltic coast by early 1612 and proceeded to attack Russia's White Sea outlets and besiege Pskov. The depleted Smolensk garrison, meanwhile, surrendered to the Poles in June 1611.

Also in June 1611, aiming to satisfy both the poor landed servicemen and the Cossacks, Lyapunov's Assembly of the Land issued a compromise decree,

Civil War and Foreign Intervention, 1605–1613.

demanding the return of all runaway serfs, except for those who had become soldiers. Then dissension between the Ryazan leadership and some thieving soldiers led to Lyapunov's assassination at a heated Cossack assembly. All the same, servicemen and Cossacks continued to cooperate in the siege of Moscow throughout 1611 under Zarutsky's military leadership and blocked a Lithuanian relief force. But after Zarutsky's attempts to storm the capital failed, he isolated himself from the other leading patriots by promoting Marina's baby Ivan as tsar. Most gentry departed for their estates as winter set in and their supplies ran out.

Minin and Pozharsky

The movement that finally liberated Moscow and reestablished the central government is associated primarily with two names, Kuzma Minin (d. 1616) and Dmitry Pozharsky (1578?–1642), and with two mercantile cities on the Volga—Nizhny Novgorod and Yaroslavl. A gifted provincial commander, Pozharsky sought

Kuzma Minin appeals to the Nizhny Novgorodians in 1611 to bolster and finance the regular army and expel the Poles, as painted by Vladimir. A. Makovsky in 1896 in the Populist style, emphasizing the role of the masses of Russian people in their history. Bol'shaia sovetskaia entsiklopediia, *2nd ed. Moscow, 1954, v 27, p. 526.*

compromise among all free classes of Russians. Minin, a successful meat merchant from Nizhny Novgorod, proved to be a superb organizer. Their drive began in August 1611, when the leading service gentry and townsmen of Nizhny Novgorod and Kazan agreed to oppose both foreigners and Zarutsky's Cossacks and accept only a nationally selected tsar. Nizhny Novgorod gave extraordinary powers to Minin, who set an example by exacting hefty contributions from monasteries and the free population, and demanding active service from estate-holders on pain of confiscation for noncompliance. This region, benefiting from relative tranquility during the civil war, from an eastward migration of Russians since the 1550s, and from uninterrupted, Volga-based trade, was well placed to provide logistical and also political leadership. Nizhny Novgorod could pay its troops. Minin selected Pozharsky as commander in chief, and his military council acted like an Assembly of the Land, with legislative and electoral authority.

By the end of 1611, Russia had three competing national governments demanding revenues: the discredited Council of Seven in Moscow, the Assembly of the Land outside of Moscow, and the war council in Nizhny Novgorod. In addition a third pseudo-Dmitry, this time a Russian commoner, took over Pskov in December and lasted there as a petty tyrant into the spring. The essential political contest soon centered on Yaroslavl, the key city on the Volga between the White Sea ports and both Moscow and Nizhny Novgorod. In a race to see whose army would oversee the course of events, Pozharsky beat Zarutsky to Yaroslavl in February 1612. This enabled Minin to create a functioning government there, which consulted and coopted representatives of tax-paying commoners. When the Cossacks outside Moscow declared for the latest Dmitry in March 1612, many servicemen and officials abandoned the Assembly of the Land there and moved to Yaroslavl. Mounting numbers of gentry and aristocrats followed, including defectors from the Council of Seven eager to secure a place for themselves in what seemed to be a new, emerging government.

At this point the old families and veteran bureaucrats, as if effecting a semi-hostile takeover of amateurs, pushed the new leaders into lesser positions. Still, in August 1612 it was Pozharsky and Minin who led ten thousand or so Russians to block another Lithuanian relief force from reaching Moscow. Then in September, to liberate what was left of the city, Trubetskoy and his Cossacks went over to Pozharsky. Zarutsky, Marina, little Ivan, and their Cossacks headed south. The stranded and starving Polish garrison troops, who had already looted the tsarist treasury and resorted to cannibalism, finally surrendered in late October. Meanwhile Pozharsky rejected Cossack demands for confiscation of the property of the Council of Seven and their clients and reconciled the entire Russian elite. The time had come to select a new tsar.

The Election of Mikhail Romanov

The Assembly of the Land that convened in Moscow in late 1612 proved to be one of the largest and most representative ever held and included commoners and Tatar military servitors. Among the possible candidates were the Polish prince Wladyslaw the Swedish prince Karl Philipp, several vassal Tatar princes, three Russian princes with old dynastic connections, the war heroes Trubetskoy and Pozharsky, and the two-year-old pretender Ivan. Electoral politics revealed the same north-south and elite-commoner divides that had bedeviled Russia even before the first false Dmitry challenged Boris Godunov. As armed men representing social groups, the regular army units, provincial servicemen, urban militias, and loyal Cossacks all held a veto power. The most popular candidate turned out to be sixteen-year-old Michael Romanov (1596–1645). A cousin of Tsar Fëdor I, Moscow's last dynastic ruler, Michael was also the son of the ex-patriarch and Tushino magnate Filaret, who now languished in a Polish prison.

Explicit threats by the numerically preponderant Cossacks, representing the Tushino wing of the patriots, compelled the boyars to accept Michael in early 1613. The eight hundred-odd delegates then "unanimously" elected him. But this was a last hurrah for some of the armed runaways. Many Cossacks were forced back into serfdom or slavery by the relentless pressure of former masters, while others were made to serve in the regular army. In a few places, skirmishing between Cossacks and state forces continued for several years.

Bringing all of the little pretender Ivan's supporters to heel proved difficult, but a combination of generosity and threats toward Don Cossacks and other southern bands induced them to recognize Tsar Michael. In 1614 they handed over Zarutsky, who was impaled; the four-year-old Ivan, who was hanged; and Marina, who soon died in prison. Agreements with Sweden (1617) and Poland (1619) cost Russia the loss of contested borderlands but secured recognition of the new dynasty.

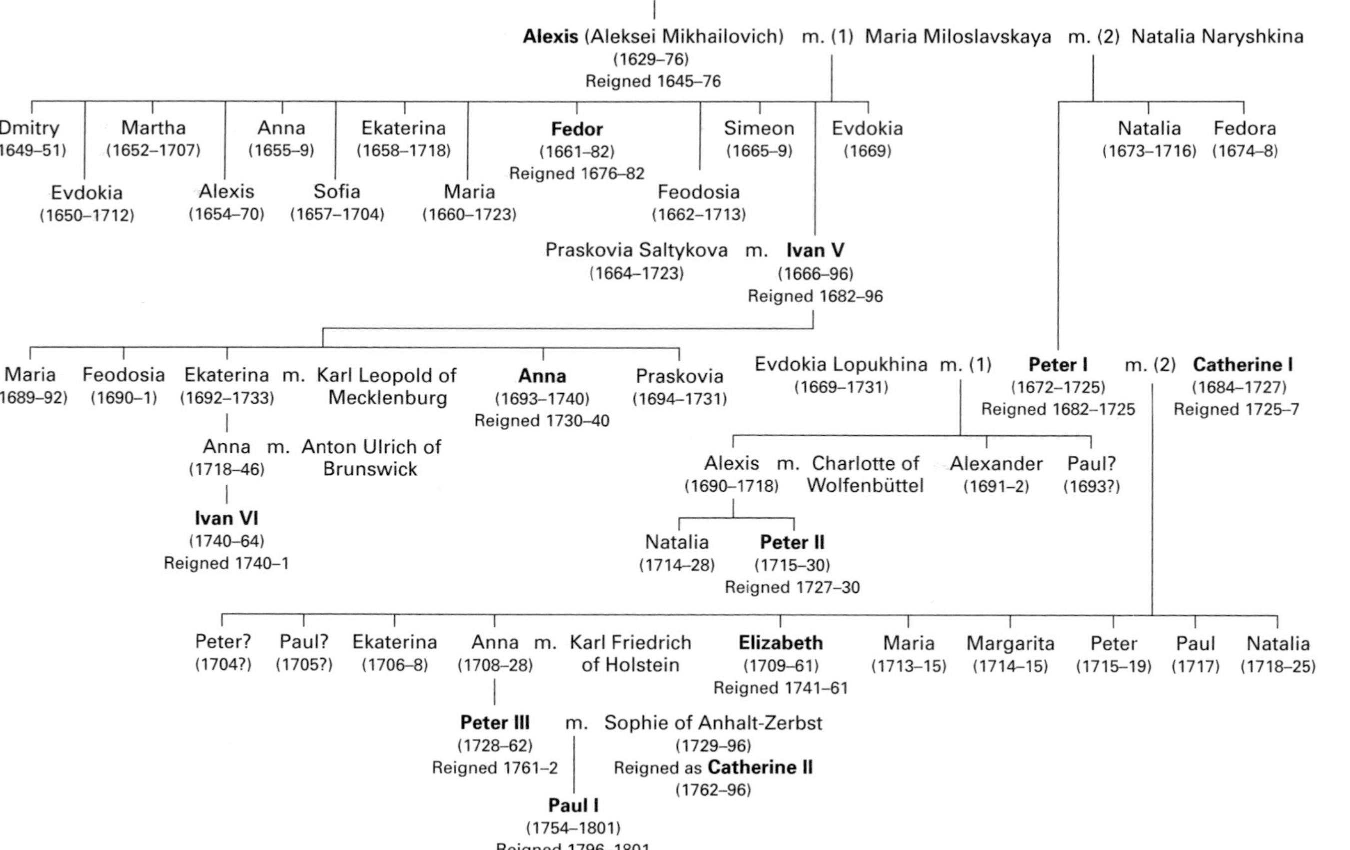

Romanov family tree: 17th–18th centuries. *From Lindsey Hughes,* Peter the Great: A Biography. *Published by Yale University Press. Copyright © 2002. Reprinted by permission of Yale University Press.*

PART II

The Growth of Empire: Russia Looks West, 1613–1796

In 1613 Muscovy was exhausted by civil war and foreign invasion. By 1796 the Russian Empire, as it renamed itself in 1721, was a leading player in world affairs and ruled from the new capital of St. Petersburg. Success in war and diplomacy led to spectacular expansion to the south and west, creating a multiethnic empire of Russians, Ukrainians, Belarusians, Poles, Finns, Tatars, Latvians, Jews, Lithuanians, and Estonians and numerous smaller groups. To the east the pursuit of economic goals drew Russia farther into Asia.

Imperial successes owed much to the state's ability to harness Russia's human resources and to combine modernization with old social and political institutions. In 1649 serfdom became law. Some 90 percent of the tsars' subjects were peasants, mostly engaged in subsistence agriculture. Towns remained relatively underdeveloped. Yet the population was fed, and in the later eighteenth century Russia experienced vigorous economic growth.

The installation in 1613 of a new ruling dynasty—the Romanovs—did not change Russia's political system. The monarch's power remained unlimited. Some of Russia's autocratic rulers—notably Alexis (1645–1676), Peter the Great (1682–1725), and Catherine the Great (1762–1796)—energetically implemented their own agendas, while others were mere figureheads. In 1762 the Russian nobility gained exemption from compulsory service, but without gaining any political rights.

In the seventeenth century the Russian Orthodox Church was split by opposition to reforms. In the eighteenth it lost much of its power and resources, and its grip on upper-class culture declined as Western influences grew. Innovations in the arts and literature, dress, and manners affected the lives of thousands of men and women, but the mass of the people retained their traditional piety and way of life. To Western observers Russia remained a tantalizing mix of Europe and Asia.

CHAPTER 9

Muscovy Expands, 1613–1676

Not only the boyars and the state servitors but the common folk as well and even children, all cried out with a loud voice that they wished Michael Fedorovich Romanov to rule the Muscovite state. And in Moscow that day there was great rejoicing.
—Chronicle account of the Assembly of the Land of February 21, 1613

The election of Michael Romanov to the vacant throne was a momentous event. It was widely believed that the new tsar was chosen by God and that his election as Russia's unlimited ruler would promote reconciliation and renewal after the devastating Troubles. Sixteen-year-old Michael's appeal had little to do with his personal abilities or popularity, however. His youth and his mild disposition attracted certain powerful boyars who favored a malleable figurehead. The relative lowliness of his family in the current hierarchy averted possible feuds among more powerful rivals, but at the same time the fact that Ivan IV's first wife, Anastasia, was Michael's great-aunt provided credentials for establishing his authority, a vital consideration for those who believed that the extinction of the legitimate line unleashed the Troubles in the first place. In July Michael was duly crowned in the Kremlin Dormition Cathedral.

Old customs and institutions survived the Troubles and were revived. The ruler's absolute power was undiminished. Serfdom was finally enshrined in law. At the same time, the need for recovery prompted an intensification of the policy of borrowing military technology and hiring skilled men from the West. This chapter and the next look at continuity and change in an "age of transition," as Russia's seventeenth century is sometimes called. We consider the conflicts that arose during the reigns of the first Romanovs between attachment to tradition and the need for innovation against a background of territorial expansion, reform of state and church, and economic and social unrest.

RECONSTRUCTION

Tsar Michael (r. 1613–1645) is generally dismissed as a mediocrity, a token "autocrat" who ruled through others. Some people doubt whether he was even literate.

But Michael's supposed weakness may owe as much to the faintness of his image as to reality, for his reign remains one of the least studied periods of Russian history. We are not even sure what he looked like, as no authentic portraits survive from this period when secular art was still very rare in Russia. Whether or not to adopt Western cultural practices was just one of many issues that faced the new tsar and his advisers in their struggle to recover from the near collapse of the Time of Troubles.

Michael and Filaret

In 1613–1619 the Assembly of the Land was in constant session. Boyars set its agenda, but decrees were issued by the tsar "with the ratification of all the land." Then in 1619 Michael's father, Filaret (ca. 1554–1633), returned from imprisonment in Poland, and his appointment as patriarch was ratified. Thereafter the Assembly faded into the background, and historians speak of a dual power, or dyarchy: "Their royal majesty is indivisible," as a contemporary wrote. In fact, Filaret was by far the more authoritative of the two men. He adopted the title Great Sovereign, hitherto reserved for the tsar, and received foreign delegations alongside his son. As well as wielding power in national politics, Filaret built up a personal base in the Patriarch's Department, which had some thirty thousand peasants and several thousand armed retainers under its control. His authority was rooted in his relationship with the tsar, which he emphasized by dealing firmly with potential rivals and operating through kinship and patron networks to elevate men close to him.

Filaret's reputation rests chiefly on his activities in secular government, but he did preside over a program of correcting and printing church books. He also banned books published in Lithuania to combat the "Latin" (i.e., Catholic) influences, which had proliferated with the Polish presence during the Time of Troubles, as well as to fight Lutheran (Protestant) propaganda from Sweden. "O most immaculate Mother of our Lord God Christ," Minin and Pozharsky allegedly declared after the liberation of Moscow in 1612. "If you had not shown mercy on us sinners, who would have freed this city from the possession of the Lutherans and the Latins?" It was, of course, vital for Filaret to demonstrate his own Orthodox credentials, having been subjected to "contaminating" influences during his eight years of captivity in Poland.

Links with the past were important for legitimizing the new regime's authority, especially by reviving the notion of Moscow as the center of true Christianity and heir to Constantinople under God's protection. The violation of the sacred Kremlin by Poles in 1610–1612 was interpreted as punishment for sins; chaos and horrors fueled a belief in the need for repentance. In 1625 Muscovites celebrated the arrival of a gift from the shah of Persia, a wonder-working fragment of a robe said to have been worn by Jesus Christ, which was interpreted as a sign of God's renewed favor for Russia. The authorities instituted a building program to boost the new dynasty's image. A Scottish engineer added the ornate upper portions to the Savior Tower, the main entrance to the Kremlin, and installed a clock. Inside the Kremlin, the tsar's new Terem Palace contained a set of richly decorated vaulted apartments, and in 1637 the Cathedral of Our Lady of Kazan on Red Square was consecrated to commemorate the national resistance of 1612. The "upstart" Romanovs thus presented themselves as the impressive heirs to the holy princes and tsars of Muscovite and Kievan Rus.

It was also vital for the dynasty to assure its future by producing sons. After his first wife died childless, in 1626 Michael married a provincial nobleman's daughter, Evdokia Streshneva (?–1645), who had three sons and three daughters. When two boys died in infancy, the nightmare vision of another extinct dynasty prompted a group at court to devise a plan to marry Michael's daughter Irina to Prince Valdemar of Denmark and to make the prince and his heirs candidates for the throne, but the plan foundered on religious differences. Meanwhile, another group actively cultivated the surviving son, Alexis (born 1629), as successor.

Poles and Swedes

Michael's reign was a crucial time for Russia's relations with the West. Russia needed allies, in the first instance to help deal with the aftermath of the Swedish and Polish occupation. With this in mind, in June 1613 a delegation set out for distant England to inform King James I (r. 1603–1625) of the accession of the new tsar, to ask for money and military supplies, and to brief themselves on the international situation. The ambassador's instructions stressed the legality of Michael's position, mentioning the "great injustices" committed by the Poles in aiding the second False Dmitry, and relating how they and the Swedes desecrated churches and spilled innocent blood.

King James did not provide any material aid, but he did agree to mediate in Russia's peace negotiations with Sweden. In 1617 the two sides signed the Treaty of Stolbovo, under the terms of which Sweden returned Novgorod and recognized the new tsar and his titles, while Russia paid Sweden compensation and ceded part of Karelia and Ingria. It proved more difficult to agree to terms with Poland. Although historians often talk of the inevitable "decline" of Poland and the "rise" of Russia in the seventeenth century, to Michael and Filaret Poland-Lithuania looked like a formidable enemy. Disappointed by the failure to install King Wladyslaw as tsar, the Poles attacked Russia again. The ensuing Peace of Deulino (January 1619) established a fourteen-and-a-half-year armistice. Moscow suspended, but did not renounce, its claim to Smolensk and parts of Ukraine. Likewise, King Wladyslaw did not renounce his claims to the Muscovite throne.

Both Sweden and Poland were affected by the outbreak in 1618 of what came to be known as the Thirty Years War, during which Protestant and Catholic rulers fought for control of the German-speaking lands of central and northern Europe. As a result of supporting Sweden with supplies, Moscow made big profits from grain sales and in 1632 felt ready to declare its own war on Poland in the hope of regaining Smolensk. In 1634 this war ended in stalemate. Lack of resources precluded adventures in the south. In 1637 Don Cossacks captured the Ottoman-held port of Azov at the mouth of the river Don and invited the tsar to accept it, but in 1642 they were forced to return it on the advice of an Assembly of the Land, which feared provoking a war with the Ottoman Empire.

Raising Revenues and Armies

It was a defining fact of Michael's reign that he came to power a decade after devastating famine had drastically reduced the population of Muscovy and driven people to cannibalism. As stated in the instructions issued to the 1613 mission to England: "It is not possible to give a salary quickly to the soldiers of the Muscovite state . . . there is nowhere for soldiers or their horses to find food and nothing to give them." The "military-fiscal" state needed to find ways of remobilizing its resources.

The bulk of incomes had to come from the peasants and from the paltry 2 percent or so of people registered as taxpaying town dwellers. But many people had fled their home villages and towns during the Troubles, making the old tax registers redundant. The government also had to resolve the competing demands of the landowners and the state on the paying power of the peasants and to ensure that money reached Moscow rather than ending up in the pockets of local officials. Initially Michael's government made special tax collections—seven between 1613 and 1618—and increased the duty on alcohol. An Assembly of the Land launched a survey to produce new registers of taxpayers, but it was done inconsistently and without much coordination, and in 1626 most of the records were destroyed in a fire. A system of sorts did emerge based on counting taxpaying households.

A related issue was service landholding. Land was up for grabs after the Troubles, and many servicemen complained that their peasants were fleeing to larger estates, leaving their land untilled. The government responded by attempting to curb peasant movement, not only to pin down peasant taxpayers but also to assure the livelihood and hence the fighting capacity of the gentry servitors. It responded to petitions submitted in 1637 and 1641 by members of that class by extending the time limit on the recovery of fugitive peasants from five to nine, then fifteen years. At the same time landowners increasingly came to regard their service lands as the equivalent of hereditary estates, which could be bequeathed and sold. Urban communities also longed for stability. In view of their collective tax responsibilities, they tried to prevent fellow townspeople from leaving the urban estates to pledge themselves to landlord protectors, and they resented competition from outsiders, particularly from resident foreign merchants with tax-free status and other privileges.

The regime attempted to short-circuit its difficulties by calling on outside help to swell its fighting forces. From the 1630s onward it formed "new model" infantry regiments, totaling some sixty-six thousand men staffed by about twenty-five hundred foreign officers. Colonel Alexander Leslie, one of many Scots who settled in Russia, was sent on several missions to Western countries to hire mercenaries and buy muskets. Weapon makers, iron founders, and experts on fortification and explosives were also hired abroad. Trade with the West resumed, mainly through the port of Archangel, with the British and the Dutch competing fiercely for Russian business.

The Michael-Filaret regime has been dismissed as "undistinguished." But we should not underestimate its achievements. Muscovy did not fall into dependency on Sweden or Poland, as could easily have happened in the wake of the Troubles, and it did not succumb to mass revolt and famine. On the contrary, national independence was preserved, population levels began to recover, and basic institutions and social norms survived. In particular, the regime took a pragmatic approach to foreigners, attempting to balance its policies of hiring experts and encouraging trade by maintaining the ideology of Muscovite religious superiority. Preserving this balance remained a burning issue for the rest of the century.

ALEXIS COMES TO POWER, 1645

Tsar Alexis (Aleksei Mikhailovich; 1629–1676) succeeded to the throne upon his father's death in July 1645. Alexis was only sixteen when he became tsar and just forty-seven when he died, but his reign was a crucial one in his country's history. His empire expanded. He issued a new law code, best remembered for its clauses instituting serfdom. He opened Russia's first court theater and employed foreign craftsmen to satisfy his taste for Western fashions. Not least, Alexis presided over a series of crises in the Orthodox church, which led to a decisive shift in the balance between the church and the state in favor of the latter. He also survived several major revolts.

The Quiet Tsar?

In contemporary documents Alexis was often described as "the quietest" and "the most pious." Nineteenth-century Slavophile (nationalist) historians regarded him as the ideal ruler, whose cautious approach to government was inspired by religion and respect for tradition. Those who admired him less regarded him as a weak monarch who ruled through others. The most often reproduced portraits of Alexis tend to confirm the image of a static, crowned figure in heavy robes, carrying symbols of office, as though about to set forth to attend a church service. But we should bear in mind that contemporary writings and pictures echoed current ideology by using set formulae. A Muscovite tsar's fervent adherence to Orthodox Christianity was his most essential attribute, without which, it was believed, neither he nor his realm could prosper. Official records thus cultivated the image of the devout tsar, paying detailed attention to the religious ceremonies in which he participated.

Alexis's own letters and foreigners' accounts reveal a man who was genuinely devout. But the "quietest one" also had a violent temper, revealed, for example, when he dragged his father-in-law from a room by the beard. The catalog of horrors perpetrated in Alexis's reign includes the retribution meted out to some rebels in Astrakhan by quartering, burning, and burying them alive and ripping out their tongues; the execution of the pretender "Tsarevich Simeon" on Red Square in 1674 (limbs cut off and trunk impaled); and the starving to death of female religious dissidents in an underground cell. Muscovy under Alexis was no more barbaric than many of its European neighbors, but Alexis's regime was not noticeably milder than those that preceded and followed it.

Portrait of Tsar Alexis (r. 1645–1676), by an anonymous artist. Mid-17th century. *Courtesy Professor Lindsey Hughes.*

Inner Circle

At the beginning of his reign the young Alexis was under the thumb of his former tutor Boris Morozov (1590–1661). Morozov's path to power followed a familiar pattern: proximity to Alexis as tsarevich won him promotion to the Boyar Duma and proximity to Alexis as tsar gave him a personal power base in government departments, most profitably in the Great Treasury. Morozov accumulated a substantial fortune based on income from peasant households and business enterprises and consolidated his position by marrying the sister of Maria Miloslavskaya (1625–1669), Alexis's first wife, and by installing his relatives and their clients in key posts.

Some of the tsar's blood relatives and many wealthy landowners also enjoyed prominence at court, but men from lowlier backgrounds established themselves, too. The astute Afanasy Ordin-Nashchokin (ca. 1605–1680), from a service gentry family, became Alexis's chief adviser on foreign affairs, while a later Foreign Office director, Artamon Matveev (1625–1682), also a member of the lesser gentry, owed his good fortune to being Alexis's companion in his youth and introducing him to his second wife, Natalia Naryshkina (1651–1694). Another influential friend was Fëdor Rtishchev (1626–1673), famed for his charitable works, who became tutor to Alexis's eldest son. In turn, Rtishchev's kinsmen acquired posts in government departments. As modern scholars stress, the key to understanding power in Muscovite Russia lies in investigating persons and their links with each other rather than in studying the history of institutions.

In theory, top appointments continued to be regulated by the code of precedence (*mestnichestvo*, see the chapter "Russia's New Monarchy, 1456–1533"), but the code was often suspended during military campaigns and was to be abolished entirely in 1682. Even so, the family honor system was deeply embedded in the consciousness of the boyar elite and honor disputes would occur long after the code's disappearance. The tsar of Muscovy was not unique among European rulers in needing to balance advancement. On the one hand, he had to ensure the loyalties of those born to privilege; on the other, to allow himself the freedom to appoint some men on grounds of merit or friendship, and to adjust the pecking order when an event such as a royal marriage created new candidates for favor. Alexis's task was made easier not only by the lack of any formal institutions that could shelter an opposition, but also by the fact that top men had nowhere to run if they fell out of favor, except to exile abroad. When it came down to it, the best place to be was by the tsar's side. Alexis, who has been described as a good "manager of men," generally commanded the loyalty of those around him, ruling by consensus without ever conceding any of his powers as autocrat.

The 1649 Law Code

Alexis inherited a budget deficit that Boris Morozov took steps to reduce, initially with such cost-cutting measures as withholding the allowances of officials and musketeers. He also tried to raise money from duties on the sale of tobacco, officially outlawed by the Orthodox Church, and by increasing certain indirect taxes, notably the salt tax, which rose four times in 1646. The tax was repealed in 1647, but by then the government was being bombarded not only with complaints about high taxes, but also with appeals from servicemen on the southern borders against richer landowners stealing their peasants and from townsmen denouncing nontaxpayers and the "blood-sucking" officials who fleeced them. In 1648 there were riots in Moscow and the unrest spread to other towns. (See later in this chapter) Alarmed, Alexis summoned an Assembly of the Land. At the same time, he appointed a commission to collect and collate the laws, an enormous and daunting task.

The outcome was the Law Code of the Assembly of the Land, published on January 29, 1649. The code was a systematic attempt, set out in 967 articles arranged in twenty-five chapters, to compile and make accessible existing laws and edicts, not only Russian but also Byzantine and Lithuanian statutes. The first two chapter headings—"On Blasphemers and Church Troublemakers" and "The Sovereign's Honor"—indicated its traditional priorities. Chapter 11 ratified serfdom, which effectively already existed as a result of the imposition of "forbidden years" prohibiting peasant relocation, the first dating back to the 1580s. Serfs—peasants belonging to the boyars and service gentry—with all their dependents and descendants were now bound to the land "in perpetuity." The boyar owners of the large estates to which serfs often fled in search of better conditions faced stiff penalties if they harbored fugitives.

The Law Code's chapters 16 and 17 (on service and hereditary estates) tended to equalize the status of the two categories of landholding, hastening the emergence of an undifferentiated land- and serf-owning class—the nobility—in the eighteenth century. At the same time, nothing in the code specifically diminished the power of the boyar elite, which, as we have seen, rested on closeness to the tsar and custom rather than on laws or institutions. The church, on the other hand, lost ground. Chapter 12 allowed those who failed to get justice in the patriarch's court to appeal to the secular courts. Chapter 13 created the Monastery Department, whose secular officials could try any priest below the rank of patriarch in civil suits, while chapter 17 limited the expansion of church lands. Some of the church's properties also lost their tax-exempt status, part of an ongoing erosion of the church's economic power.

The preface to the Law Code spoke of equality of justice, but this was a reference to the administration of justice—which must not be impeded by nepotism, bribes, red tape, whim or general "wickedness"—not to the laws themselves. The tsar's subjects were judged according to the particular law and in the particular court appropriate to their social status. In other words, the new code observed the old social hierarchies. In general, lawbreakers could expect harsh punishments, including beatings with the knout, whip, or sticks; slitting nostrils; cutting off hands and feet; burying alive; and death by fire and drinking molten metal. Women who killed their husbands were buried in the ground up to their necks and left to die.

This was the first Russian law code to be printed. One of the problems in getting justice before 1649 was that officials frequently could not even locate copies of relevant statutes. From now on the printed volume was made available in all government offices. Even so, with no independent judiciary and with officials still apt to supplement their inadequate allowances by demanding bribes and requisitions, going before the law remained a hazardous process. Torture of both defendants and witnesses continued to be the approved method of taking evidence. And serfs had no recourse to the laws as set out in the code. They continued to settle their disputes or to be tried either through their communes or by their landlords. The 1649 code remained Russia's basic legal statute until the 1830s.

Tsar and Patriarch

From an early age Alexis was made aware of his special responsibilities toward the Orthodox Church at home and abroad. In 1649, for example, the patriarch of Jerusalem urged him to "liberate pious Orthodox Christians from the clutch of the infidels." Alexis seems to have taken such ideas seriously, even though they were part of a well-established rhetoric and it was impractical to implement them. He was also influenced by a group of parish priests known as the Zealots of Piety, who wished to restore "pure" practices to make the Russian church conform with the wider Orthodox world, to the leadership of which it aspired. The Zealots aimed to improve public morals by targeting drunkenness and sexual immorality and banning strolling players who sang "unseemly" songs and other manifestations of "pagan" folk culture that challenged Orthodox authority. Their influence was reflected in a royal edict of December 1648 denouncing "diabolical" music and mass bathing, and in orders to close shops and taverns on Sundays. The new puritanical atmosphere even infiltrated the wedding feast of Alexis and Maria Miloslavskaya in 1648, at which they cut down on strong liquor and replaced the usual dancing and singing with choral music. There were no restrictions on eating, however. The banquet featured swan, suckling pig, goose, pies, pancakes, and various confections.

Joseph (?–1652), who became patriarch of Moscow in 1642, broadly supported the Zealots and adopted their program for replacing the old church hierarchy with more reform-minded churchmen. One of these "new men" was Nikon (1605–1681), who in 1649 was installed as metropolitan of Novgorod. Nikon proved useful in a number of ways, for example by identifying and bringing to Moscow the remains of selected saints, whose relics were believed to cure the sick.

In April 1652 Patriarch Joseph died, and in July Nikon succeeded him as patriarch, with the tsar's approval. Nikon, it should be emphasized, was also committed to a Zealot program, but he alienated most of his former associates with his overbearing manner and violent temper. Paisios Ligarides, the metropolitan of Gaza, left a striking description of Nikon as a "monster" of a man, with a thick neck and a huge head covered with black hair, an "expression of madness," and a "gaping, and unbridled and unshuttable mouth." Other sources, including Nikon's own writings, confirm that he was an emotional and forceful personality. Nikon was one of the first Russian churchmen to be painted from life, and surviving portraits show a tall, powerfully built man. As was the custom, Alexis duly promised to obey him as his spiritual father, but before long it became clear that Nikon regarded the tsar's pledge of obedience as more than mere rhetoric.

"ALL GREAT, LITTLE AND WHITE RUSSIA"

Alexis was raised to regard foreign policy, conducted in the Orthodox context, as a sovereign's chief concern. He was better informed about his country's contours than any of his predecessors, but his interest did not stop at the borders of his realm or the Polish and Swedish terrain over which he and his ancestors waged their wars. He also owned a map of "the whole world" and collected globes, as if to indicate his concern with Russian's place in the world, which was soon to undergo a radical shift.

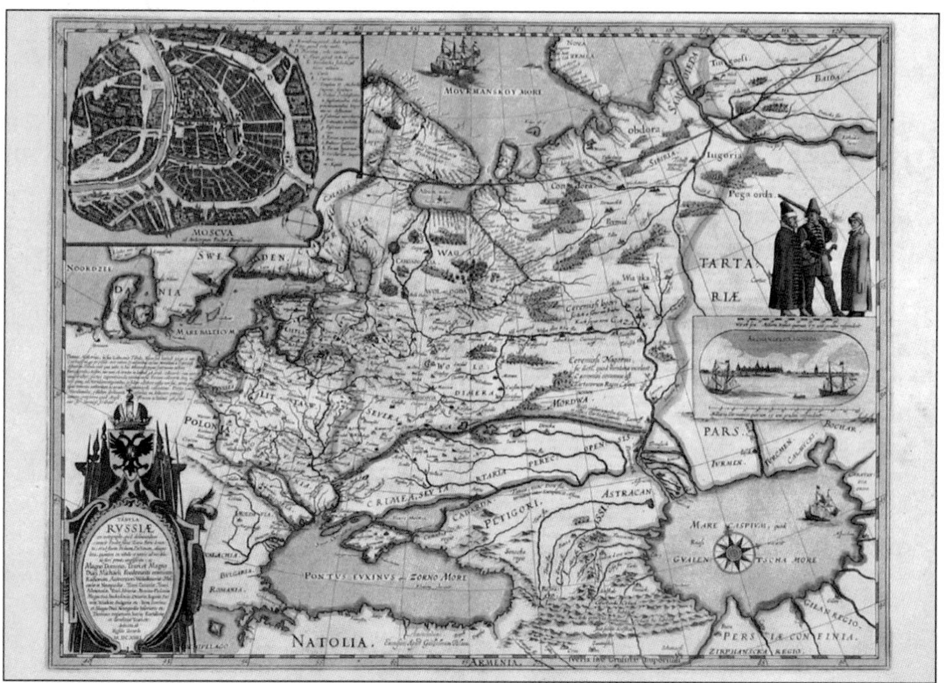

Hessel Gerritsz's map of Muscovy, with a large inset of the city of Moscow. Map maker: Willem Blaeu, Amsterdam, 1630. *Barry Ruderman Antique Maps (www.raremaps.com).*

If we examine mid-seventeenth-century maps of Muscovy—all the work of foreign cartographers—we see a country of vast size intersected by many river systems but with no warm water ports, with enormously long and, in some cases, ill-defined land borders. To the north of the Oka River lies the Russian forested heartland of old appanage principalities, with Moscow at its center. The ancient lands of Novgorod lie farther north, and to the north of them the White Sea, with Archangel, Russia's lone major port, cut off by ice for more than half the year but offering the only point of entry for foreign ships.

To the west on the map, the elusive foothold on the Baltic is still just out of Moscow's reach. The farthest major Muscovite outpost is Pskov, beyond which lie the Swedish-held Baltic territories—Ingria (Ingermanland), Livonia, and Estonia—with the prosperous seaports of Riga and Reval. To the south of them is the Grand Duchy of Lithuania, forming part of the Polish-Lithuanian Commonwealth, which includes the lands of present-day Belarus, with the much fought-over city of Smolensk. In the Grand Duchy the peasant population was mainly Orthodox Christians, while many of the nobles were Catholics. In the major cities there were substantial communities of Jews, who were banned from entering Muscovy.

In the southeast the map suggests more unfinished business on borderlands. Moscow's foothold on the Don River fizzles out below the Cossack settlements at

Cherkassk, below which lies the Turkish-held port of Azov. Farther east, the full course of the Volga had been in Russian hands since the 1550s, terminating at the cosmopolitan port of Astrakhan, but the shores of the Caspian Sea below Astrakhan were held by Persia. The Christian peoples of the Caucasus, stuck between Persia and the Ottoman Empire, intermittently appealed for the tsar's help, but Moscow's resources did not stretch much beyond occasionally entertaining visiting Georgian princes.

Muscovy was consolidating its position on the southern steppes, which offered the attraction of fertile agricultural land but were far from the major centers of population and suffered from the constant threat of raids by Tatars and other nomads, hence the area's designation in some sources as the "wild field." From the 1630s on Moscow constructed the so-called Belgorod defense line, a series of garrisons to protect colonists. If we are looking at a map drawn before the late 1660s, Ukraine or "Little Russia"—the old southern princedoms of Kievan Rus, with largely Orthodox peasant populations but with Catholic or Uniate landowners and sizable Jewish communities in the cities—remains in the Kingdom of Poland. After 1667, as we shall see, the Dnieper River was to provide a new border of sorts between Russian and Polish Ukraine, but if we trace the river southward through the stronghold of the Zaporozhian Cossacks in the Sech and to the Dnieper delta on the Black Sea, we reach an area with no established authority. The Poles and Turks claimed it, but Cossacks and Tatars rode back and forth across it with impunity. Farther west along the shores of the Black Sea toward the delta of the Danube lived the Ottoman sultan's Orthodox Christian subjects, the Moldavians and Wallachians, who appealed intermittently for the tsar's protection.

To the east on the map the picture is different. Beyond the Ural Mountains Siberia lies open without any sovereign powers to impede expansion until the Amur River and the borders of China. During the 1630s–1640s Russian fur traders, soldiers, and Arctic seafarers extended the reach of Moscow twenty-five hundred miles eastward to the Pacific Ocean and contested the rising Manchu dynasty in China for control of the territories north of the Amur. The resistance of local tribes created only sporadic annoyance, and most were either wiped out or forced to pay tribute in furs. Pioneer settlers established forts, which in turn attracted other Russian settlers and grew into towns. In later Tsarist and Soviet times Siberia was associated with prison camps. In the early modern period, however, the connotation was more of freedom and escape, albeit to a tough life. There was no serfdom in Siberia because there were no serf owners settled there. Not only were there minerals and furs for the taking but also pockets of agricultural land. In the wake of the independent or semi-independent Cossack units who conquered Siberia, thousands of state peasants moved there voluntarily to till the land and harvest forest products in return for paying taxes to the state.

The map explains why no seventeenth-century Russian ruler was likely to regard his realm as complete and neatly confined within well-marked borders, and also why it was so difficult to rule it effectively. The authorities constantly had to push back nomads, follow up the initiatives of colonists and Cossacks, and respond to appeals for aid from coreligionist populations ruled by non-Orthodox neighbors.

Muscovy in the Seventeenth Century. *From Allen F. Chew,* An Atlas of Russian History. *Published by Yale University Press. Copyright © 1967. Reprinted by permission of Yale University Press.*

There were also economic objectives to be pursued, such as outlets to the sea through warm water ports and access to fertile lands and other resources, as well as the historical imperative of reclaiming "patrimonial" lands. All required an active foreign policy, tempered chiefly by financial constraints.

The Thirteen Years War, 1654–1667

Tsar Alexis's first foreign adventures were in the south. In 1648 Bohdan Khmelnytsky (ca. 1595–1657), hetman of the Zaporozhian Cossack Host in Polish Ukraine, led a rebellion against Poland. The Cossacks' grievances centered on the erosion of self-government, deteriorating terms of service to the Polish crown, and religious persecution. In 1648–1649, with local peasant and Tatar support, they won several victories against the Poles, at the same time slaughtering tens of thousands of Jews, who inspired hatred as "outsiders" and profiteers. But Khmelnytsky did not accomplish his aims against Poland. What he sought was autonomy, and he calculated (or rather, miscalculated) that the Orthodox tsar in Moscow might help him to get it, so he appealed to Alexis to take the Cossacks under the protection of his "lofty hand."

In Moscow Alexis and his advisers had mixed feelings about Khemlnytsky's request. On the one hand, they did not feel ready for another war with Poland. On the other hand, there was deep dissatisfaction with the settlement of the stalemated conflict of the 1630s. Moscow routinely complained to Warsaw about the ill-treatment of Orthodox Christians living under Polish rule and maintained its claim to Smolensk and other "Russian" lands, while insisting on proper use of the tsar's complicated titles. Expanding the empire into the rich grain belt of Ukraine was a tempting prospect, especially when accompanied by the rhetoric of "a great crusade of liberation." The decision to accede to Cossack requests and to prepare for war was ratified by no less than three Assemblies of the Land in 1653.

In January 1654 Khmelnytsky signed an agreement with Moscow at the border town of Pereyaslav. The hetman understood this document as an alliance between equals against Poland, with guarantees of autonomy for Cossacks, who saw their pledge of "eternal loyalty" as mere words, since the terms of the treaty suggested self-rule. Ukrainian nobles and cities retained their rights and the Cossack Host kept its own laws and command structure. In fact, Alexis now regarded Khmelnytsky as his "subject."

In late October 1654 Poland reacted by declaring war. Russia responded by capturing a number of key towns in the Grand Duchy of Lithuania, including Smolensk. Fighting in Vilna was particularly bloody, with Cossacks massacring Jews and Catholics. In the summer of 1655, however, the Swedes invaded Poland-Lithuania with the aim of halting a Russian advance that could threaten their territory. In 1656 Moscow made a truce with Poland and went to war with Sweden, in what is called the First Northern War (1656–1661). In December 1658 Russia and Sweden declared an armistice and in 1661 signed the Peace of Kardis, which left the 1617 borders unchanged. In 1659 the war between Russia and Poland resumed, and the Russian armies found themselves driven back from territories occupied in the earlier campaigns. Just when Muscovite fortunes were at a low ebb, civil war broke out in Poland over attempted constitutional reforms and the Polish-appointed hetman of west Ukraine, Peter Doroshenko (1627–1698), defected to the Turks. At this point the Poles decided to sue for peace.

In 1667 the Truce of Andrusovo, set for a term of thirteen and a half years, confirmed Moscow's possession of Smolensk, part of Belarus, and Left Bank Ukraine (the lands east of the Dnieper River). Kiev on the right bank was leased to Russia for a two-year period. Alexis now styled himself sovereign of all Great and Little and White Russia, even though possession of most of Ukraine and all Belarus would be achieved only at the end of the eighteenth century. As for the Cossack leaders, they never fully accepted Russian authority. In 1657 Bohdan Khmelnytsky's successor as hetman, Ivan Vyhovsky (?–1664), had rejected Moscow and accepted Tatar aid. In 1663 Alexis appointed a "reliable" hetman, Ivan Briukhovetsky (?–1668), but in 1668 Briukhhovetsky too teamed up with the Tatars and attacked Muscovite garrisons, then in his turn was ousted by a rival. Ukraine entered a period of invasions and internal strife known as the "Ruin."

A weakened Poland brought new problems for Alexis. In May 1672 the Ottoman sultan attacked Poland and forced the king to accept Ottoman rule over western Ukraine. As it turned out, this proved no more permanent than previous divisions of the Ukrainian cake. Periodically there were proposals for ending the conflict in the region by uniting the crowns of Muscovy and Poland; for example, in 1668 when Jan II Casimir, king since 1648, abdicated and again in 1673 following the death of King Michael of Poland (r.1669–1673), when the Poles asked for the tsar's eldest son as a candidate, on the condition that he become a Catholic. In 1674 Jan III Sobieski (d. 1696) was elected, the last king of Poland not to be dependent on Russian influence.

The War Machine

In addition to looking abroad for weapons and expertise, Alexis extended the use of the "new model" troops established by his father, which by the end of his reign constituted 80 percent of the army. In 1646 dragoon regiments of mounted infantrymen were formed, the word *dragun* itself one of many foreign loan words that entered the Russian language. Despite these innovations, one should beware of exaggerating the extent of change. The bulk of the Russian army, even when organized into new-style regiments, was still recruited from among the Russian peasantry, on the basis of so many men from so many households. In 1654, for example, the draft took one man from every twenty households. In addition, auxiliaries were called up from non-Russian tribesmen; whole divisions of Kalmyks, for example. The musketeers (*streltsy*) continued to provide a substantial section of the armed forces, but after riots in Moscow in 1648, when some musketeers proved unreliable, six elite regiments of a thousand handpicked men each were formed as escorts for the royal family.

The received wisdom is that the old gentry cavalry was outdated and that infantry was superior. But Russian armies had to fight in a variety of circumstances and what was effective in Western-style pitched battles was not necessarily so against the Tatars. The logistics of moving armies around thinly populated, flat, barren terrain were also very different from what was needed in, say, the heavily settled Netherlands. Alexis employed new military knowledge—for example, in 1647 the Moscow press published *The Art of Infantry*, translated from a German original—but religious armament also continued to be regarded as vital. As Alexis told his troops before the start of the 1654 campaign against Poland: "If you obey Christ's commandment and renew yourselves with blessed repentance the Angel of the Lord will take up arms about your regiment . . . But if through your negligence even one man should fail to renew himself through confession, then you will answer for it at Christ's terrible day of judgement." In war, as in all areas of human endeavor, seventeenth-century Russians believed that God's will was the deciding factor.

Economy and Finance

Alexis's wars put a terrible strain on the population, which was additionally devastated by a major outbreak of plague in 1654. The tsar's English doctor Samuel Collins, writing in 1670, believed that "This Empire is impoverish'd, depopulated and spoil'd so much in ten years, as it will not recover its pristine prosperity in forty." Peasants suffered grain requisitions for the military and conscription on top of direct taxation. Townspeople faced special tax levies, and the introduction of debased copper coins for domestic use caused inflation.

Employing foreign officers and importing weapons was expensive, too. More generally, the proliferation of foreign merchants operating inside Russia provoked complaints from locals of unfair competition. In 1667 a new trade statute placed limitations on foreign traders. Heavy import duties and a ban on the export of precious metals were imposed. Another approach was to encourage domestic manufacturing, although here, too, foreigners played a key role. Ironworks were established under foreign management in the Tula-Kashira region in the 1630s–1660s. In many northern towns a homegrown merchant-manufacturing elite consolidated itself, which some historians have seen as the beginnings of a Russian bourgeoisie. The most successful were the Stroganovs, who initially accumulated their fortune through the fur trade.

Large-scale merchant enterprise was the exception rather than the rule. By 1700 there were only about thirty factories in Russia. More common was commercial activity on large serf estates. The tsar's favorite, Boris Morozov, produced potash for export and iron and grain for sale, doing on a smaller scale what the crown domains belonging to the royal family did on an even larger one, for the tsar himself was the single largest trader, exporter, and manufacturer in the realm. Alexis signed silk deals with Persia and dispatched embassies to Bukhara and India for trade talks. In 1667 he ordered the construction of a fleet of four vessels, built by Dutch shipwrights and manned by a Dutch crew, for sailing the Caspian. Alexis also experimented with some quite radical schemes, involving thousands of peasant households on crown domains, trying out new crops such as vines, mulberries, and pears and using crop rotation, irrigation, and water and wind power. This modern program relied on autocratic methods: lands and resources that the tsar required were sometimes just confiscated, and, of course, he used forced peasant labor. Ultimately, both the war and the economy that supported it were run from the center, while self-sufficient agriculture remained the basis of the preindustrial economy of the country at large.

PEOPLE OF ALL RANKS

There may have been between 9 and 10 million people in Russia by 1678, when a survey of taxpaying households was carried out. Censuses that assessed tax liabilities are the main source of population statistics for early modern Russia, but they focused on households, not individuals; counted only males; and omitted nontaxable persons such as nobles and priests. The "orders" of Russian society were by no means clear-cut, either. Historians once took a fairly rigid view of social classification, picturing the Muscovite "service state" in the seventeenth century as a pyramid with the all-powerful tsar at the top supported by a narrow layer of the elite (boyars and service gentry, top merchants and churchmen) and a small group of townspeople, all standing on a great base made up of the peasantry. Everyone was regarded as more or less fixed in his or her station, women's status being determined by that of their fathers or husbands. Indeed, defining the population in terms of the duties they performed or the taxes they paid collectively suited the authorities, who sought to harness the capacity of the whole population. Moral and spiritual welfare was handled by the church, which preached a message of punishment of sins, obedience to higher authority, and contentment with one's lot, however wretched.

Modern scholars take a less rigid view, seeing Russian society as more porous and social status as often changeable. People in apparently well-defined categories could confound expectations. Many peasants lived in towns and ran businesses, for example; provincial servicemen without serfs worked their own land; so-called single householders (*odnodvortsy*) had the right to own serfs and the obligation to pay taxes; free people fallen on hard times voluntarily became slaves by taking out a contract of bondage. The government constantly battled to extract either service or taxes or both from fringe groups of evaders: fugitives, shirkers, dissidents, and vagrants.

Servitors and Townspeople

The Moscow-based upper echelons of Russia's servicemen, roughly the equivalent of the Western aristocracy, were known collectively, as we have seen (see the chapter "Shifting Fortunes, 1341–1456"), as the boyars. The very top rung of the boyar ladder was the so-called Boyar Duma (council), which in the seventeenth century varied in number from 28 to 153 members. Membership rested chiefly on hereditary right, but royal favor would provide fast-track entry. Large powerful clans such as the Golitsyns and the Dolgorukys had men in the Duma throughout the seventeenth century and remained prominent in the eighteenth. Others, like the Miloslavskys, who owed their rise to Tsar Alexis's first marriage, enjoyed a fairly brief time at the top. In Alexis's reign the rank of boyar became more ceremonial and less regularly linked with high office, with lower-ranking servicemen just as likely as boyars to preside over government departments. Secretaries and clerks from non-noble families could also rise in the administrative hierarchy. But men from old families still dominated military commands and some top civil posts.

Historians have called the boyars "abased" or "supine," wondering why the elite did not rebel against its dependency or impose conditions on the crown. Various explanations have been offered, for example, that the boyars needed state support to keep and exploit their peasants and genuinely believed that to challenge God's representative was a sin. The horrors of the "tsarless" Time of Troubles remained a vivid memory, which the authorities readily evoked when dissension threatened. "Anarchic" Poland, with its weak monarch and empowered nobility, also served as a warning. The best explanation may be that the relationship between crown and elite suited the latter as much as it did the former. With access to the court and a range of other privileges, the seventeenth century was not a bad time to be a boyar.

The elite of the provincial towns and countryside—the men of the "middle service class" or service gentry—continued to perform policing duties and formed the backbone of the army in wartime. These men were inferior to the Moscow-based nobles in that they were not, literally, close to the tsar, but they still shared the privilege of exemption from tax and labor burdens and the right to hold land and serfs. Their *pomestie* lands (see the chapter "Russia's New Monarchy, 1456–1533"), initially granted and held on condition of service, increasingly passed on from generation to generation.

The registered non-noble population of Russia's towns continued to be bound to their communities by collective tax obligations. Including merchants and ordinary traders and craftsmen, the total male registered urban population in the 1670s has been estimated at just 185,000, but town populations were swelled by servicemen such as musketeers, artillery men, and postal drivers; by priests; and by peasants who lived either temporarily or permanently in towns but paid their taxes through their village communes. Even if one adds in such residents, however, most seventeenth-century Russian towns were sparsely populated and possessed few, if any, civic amenities. Even in vast Moscow the streets were unpaved and most buildings were made of wood. The capital lacked the sort of professional people—bankers, scholars and scientists, doctors, school teachers, lawyers, actors and so on—that could be found in most sizable western European towns. All the same, from the provinces the capital with its royal court and countless churches must have seemed sophisticated. Even Russian provincial nobles lacked the manorial tradition and "gentility" associated with noble status elsewhere in Europe, and the general picture of noble life in the provinces was one of coarseness, drunkenness, and violence.

The Ploughing Peasantry

In seventeenth-century Muscovy, peasants accounted for about 90 percent of the population, a proportion that would diminish only slightly over the next two centuries. The 1678 land survey recorded 906,101 peasant households, of which just under half—435, 924—belonged to boyars and service gentry (the serfs), the rest to churches and monasteries (church peasants), the royal family (court or crown peasants), and the state (state peasants.) The last category did not strictly speaking "belong" to anyone, but they were obliged collectively to pay taxes and perform labor obligations to the state through their communes. The 1649 Law Code, as we saw, fixed serfdom as a hereditary status in perpetuity, and the state put great effort into establishing the administrative apparatus to enforce the measure. For example, it empowered the Search Department to root out fugitives and imposed harsh penalties on people who lured or harbored runaway serfs. Even so, throughout the seventeenth century peasant flight remained a fact of life. In some cases, for example on the thinly populated southern borders, it suited the authorities to turn a blind eye and allow runaways to enlist in garrisons in exchange for small land grants. Certain peasants who succeeded in getting registered in towns were also allowed to remain there and pay their taxes to the urban communities, which had come to rely on their contributions.

Soviet historians were bound to a class analysis of serfdom in Russia, presenting it in terms of struggle, oppression, and exploitation. Many Western historians took a similar approach. Recent studies, however, have shifted away from explanations based on coercion, acknowledging that to a large extent serfdom met the needs of the peasants themselves by allowing them access to land, for being tied to the land implied entitlement to work the land. Peasants, it is argued, were not simply "victims," but generally retained some control over their own lives, not in terms of abstract liberties, but of feeding themselves and their families in an economy of marginal sufficiency. The main reason why the system endured for so long was its ability to adapt and change, with the help, admittedly, of the safety valve of flight.

This is not to say that serfdom was good in itself, that there were not poor peasants, or that peasants enthusiastically embraced it. But the stock picture of the cruel landlord making his peasants' lives a misery was the exception rather than the rule. In the seventeenth century serfs, unless they were household servants, often had minimal contact with their owners, especially if the latter were boyars living far off in Moscow. Work was organized by various combinations of stewards and peasant self-regulation through the village commune. Documents record individual cases of village elders cooperating with bailiffs and local officials to regulate work patterns or select army recruits, as well as evidence of client networks among peasants, with richer peasants "protecting" poorer ones in return for favors. Most important, many village communes regulated repartitions of land to take account of changing household composition. This was one of the many mechanisms that perpetuated serfdom by making it tolerable. Throughout central and eastern Europe serfdom remained the norm. Russia was by no means unique, even if Russian serfdom, which would be abolished in 1861, played a special role in the further development of the Russian economy and society.

REBELLIOUS RUSSIA

Soviet historians referred to the seventeenth century as the "rebellious" century. Indeed, the notion of struggle was built into their analysis of Russian history, to the extent of detecting an embryonic revolutionary movement in the early modern period, destined to culminate in the overthrow of tsarism in 1917. The emphasis was upon conflict, unrest, and change rather than cooperation, stability, and continuity. Divisions in the Orthodox Church, too, were presented in terms of popular grassroots rebellion against the church hierarchy. More recent studies, however, have argued that the century was marked as much by consensus as by conflict and that society had mechanisms for suppressing differences. Seventeenth-century rebellions look less like systematic opposition movements with well-considered ideologies than like a series of unrelated revolts sparked off by immediate circumstances and often cloaked in what historians have called "naive monarchism," which hinged on the notion that wicked officials created a barrier between the common people and the "little father" tsar.

Urban Unrest

The Moscow revolt of 1648 demonstrated some of the features just described. In June of that year discontent about high taxes and food prices prompted a mob to complain directly to the tsar against corrupt officials, centering on Leonty Pleshcheev, a crony of Boris Morozov. Possible reconciliation was undermined by the intervention of representatives of those same corrupt "evil-doers," who attacked the crowd and made arrests. Rumors spread through defamatory leaflets: "The sovereign is a young fool and looks on everything through the eyes of the boyars Morozov and Miloslavsky. The Devil has robbed him of his mind." In response to a second attempt by crowds to get the tsar's attention, the authorities called out the musketeers, who then complicated matters by making a distinction between the person of the tsar, whom they were ready to protect, and "traitors" and "blood-suckers," whom they were not. The mob's anger then settled on Morozov himself. Rioters ransacked his house in the sort of destructive frenzy that was a common feature of these urban revolts, as was the brutal murder and mutilation of the corpses of selected victims. The fury only began to abate after Pleshcheev and another hated official were lynched and their corpses abused. Alexis banished Morozov temporarily to an out-of-town estate and the troubles in Moscow died down. As we saw earlier, this rebellion was a catalyst for codifying the laws.

In 1650 disorders broke out in Novgorod and Pskov, and there were revolts among some of the tsar's non-Russian subjects, but the next major disturbances were again focused in Moscow, where in 1662 protests erupted over the inflation created by the introduction of copper coinage. During the "Copper Coin rebellion" popular anger was vented first on "counterfeiters" and speculators, then on wicked advisers, including Ilia Miloslavsky (?–1688), the tsar's father-in-law. A tax levy on townspeople sparked further protests. In July 1662 crowds marched on the tsar's summer residence at Kolomenskoe and demanded to see Alexis, handing him a list of names of "traitorous boyars" and their "foreign accomplices," some of whom were men close to the tsar. This time Alexis, confronted by a mob nine thousand-strong, was nearly killed, but the musketeers came to the rescue at the last minute. Hundreds of people were slaughtered or injured on the spot and others were executed or mutilated, branded and exiled.

The Razin Revolt

None of these outbreaks quite prepared Alexis for the major civil disturbance of his reign. This was the rebellion led in 1670–1671 by the Don Cossack Stepan Razin (ca. 1630–1671), one of several revolts to flare up on the semilawless Cossack periphery in the seventeenth and eighteenth centuries. The Cossacks jealously guarded their liberties and traditional way of life, and their territories remained a sort of no man's land for government officials, who had to negotiate with them using diplomatic skills usually reserved for foreign courts. Their semiautonomy attracted fugitives, who made a precarious living in the vicinity of Cossack settlements. In the 1660s severe food shortages triggered disturbances among these newcomers, the so-called naked and hungry ones.

The leader who took up their cause, Stepan (Stenka) Razin, was a member of the Cossack establishment, a man of magnetic personality, who probably acted out of a spirit of adventure as much as sympathy for the downtrodden. In the late 1660s Razin led some daring pirate raids along the Volga and in Persian towns on the Caspian. This was annoying for Moscow but could be accommodated, especially when in 1669 Razin swore loyalty to the tsar. In 1670, however, he provoked Moscow by having Alexis's envoy murdered. Gathering supporters, Razin took Tsaritsyn on the Volga, then Astrakhan, where the population included many dissident elements. The rebels tossed the governor from a belfry, hanged his son on a pendulum, and tortured officials to death amid an orgy of looting. This set the violent tone for what followed.

Turning in the direction of Moscow, Razin's motley army picked up various malcontents along the way—religious dissidents, peasants, lesser servitors, non-Russian tribespeople—but he got most of his support from the urban poor, who were responsive to appeals to establish "the Cossack way of life" and regarded Razin as a redeemer. In October 1670 Razin was defeated outside Simbirsk by superior government forces with artillery. Mass executions followed, but Razin himself escaped. The tsar's armies pursued rebels elsewhere along the Don and Volga, where an English witness recorded scenes of carnage, reminiscent of "the suburbs of hell," with gallows loaded with forty or fifty men apiece. Eventually Razin was captured by Cossacks loyal to the tsar, who took him to Moscow where he was tortured with hot irons and subjected to other torments, then executed by quartering in June 1671 "for evil and loathsome acts against God." His severed limbs were displayed on stakes and his torso was fed to dogs.

Razin's program was not antitsarist. As he stated, he intended to remove "the sovereign's enemies . . . the treacherous boyars and the men of the council and the governors and the officials in the towns" and to give freedom to the "common people." Razin never pretended to be royal, but his entourage included a pretender, "Tsarevich Alexis" (Tsar Alexis's eldest son, Alexis, had died in 1670), and a "patriarch of Moscow." As in other similar rebellions, the rebels targeted boyars and officials, in the belief that the key to a better life lay in changing the personnel at the top. The rebels were doomed to failure by their marginal location and lack of coordination, their vastly inferior military skills and weaponry, and the tendency of such outbreaks to burn themselves out once the participants had vented their frustrations in pillaging and bloodletting. But Razin's exploits endured in folk tales and songs.

Autocracy reappraised.

The rebellions of the seventeenth century did little to diminish the power of the "true sovereign." On the contrary, the trend was toward fewer central checks on royal power. The boyars' participation in decision making was still indicated by the formula: "the tsar has decreed and the boyars have affirmed." But the lack of a clear institutional framework made it hard for the boyars to wield independent power, even if they had wished to. Alexis consulted with them as a body less and less and increasingly suspended the code of precedence, which nominally governed the monarch's choice of appointees to high commands. Alexis deployed and relied on trusted individuals, for example in his Office of Secret Affairs and in his Falconry Department, where the rules for "the sovereign's beautiful bird hunt" provided a sort of veiled philosophy of autocracy that underlined the importance of measure and proportion, with everything in its place. Personal rule included granting or withholding favors, anything from major land grants to a slice of nameday cake.

On the face of it, then, the ruler was set above ordinary beings and could do what he liked to whom he liked, even though a good tsar was expected to heed good advice and dispense justice. The authority of even the weakest tsar was bolstered by grandiose dynastic claims going back to Ryurik and through him to the Roman emperor Augustus Caesar. Royal power was demonstrated in impressive court ceremonial. Yet the idea that Russia was an "autocratic and absolutist" state, where everyone trembled under the thumb of a despotic monarch, was in part a convenient construct for maintaining stability. All Russia's seventeenth-century rulers were underaged or incapacitated on their accession to the throne, so older, more experienced people ruled on their behalf. And when the tsars came into their own power, as Alexis did in the 1650s, elite networks cooperated through consensus rather than conflict, making it superfluous for the tsar to behave "tyrannically." Observing the rhetoric of unlimited royal power, even the grandest members of the tsar's entourage underwent ritual forms of abasement, referring to themselves as the tsar's "slaves" and prostrating themselves in the royal presence. People of lower social status often called themselves "orphans" to emphasize their need of assistance and compassion from the man who was everyone's father. It is clear from the use of such language well into the eighteenth century that people continued to view the ruler in this light.

Still, the tsar's safety could not be taken for granted, as the violent revolts just described indicate. Following Alexis's narrow escape from petitioners in 1648, an article in the new Law Code of 1649 forbade the petitioning of the tsar in person. "Word and deed" court cases involving verbal abuse or intended harm against the tsar's health or honor increased greatly after 1662. The culprits sometimes tried to justify their crimes by arguing that the tsar was not the "true" sovereign. The shift away from direct, personal contact between the tsar and people may also be seen in the disappearance of the Assembly of the Land. After 1653 the authorities no longer saw the need to call the assemblies and were not obliged to do so.

The tsar's government may have been unhampered by independent agencies, but we should not exaggerate the extent to which it was able to or desired to control all activities. In the provinces an unspoken moral contract existed between communities of service gentry and Moscow officialdom, linking the gentry with the center for purposes of military service and other duties, while allowing them scope for autonomous local action. There is a growing consensus among historians that while Muscovite autocracy in theory claimed a monopoly of power, in practice geography, scant resources, and poor communications inhibited the state from exercising that power universally. The central government understood its own limitations. To conserve its hard-pressed resources for national defense and the maintenance of order, the state fostered local participation in such areas as self-government, tax collection, and combating brigandage.

Least of all was the state in a position to interfere in the routine everyday lives of the mass of the population, which was governed by the church calendar, custom, and communes. The state stepped in to curb those who willfully escaped obligations or caused major disruption, but with only limited success. All sorts of separatist communities formed. For example, monks and nuns set up unofficial settlements in remote localities; runaways joined Cossack communities; and whole districts of Russia were more or less run by brigands and regarded as out of bounds to both state and church officials, while various "wandering people," "fools in Christ" and the like slipped through the net of obligations. Muscovite government was not *totalitarian*, a term that is an anachronism in reference even to the growth of its absolute monarchy. State power was at its most awe-inspiring at the center where the civil and religious authorities acted out their divinely ordained mission in ceremonials against impressive architectural settings. But, as we shall see, some cracks were appearing in the edifice of church and state.

CHAPTER 10

Religion and Culture at the Crossroads, 1645–1689

Last year, in 7186 [1678], on the tenth day of July, on the feast of the Deposition of the Robe of our Lord God and Saviour Jesus Christ, the great sovereign tsar and great prince Fëdor Alekseevich, autocrat of all Great and Little and White Russia, deigned to attend the divine service in the [Kremlin] cathedral and apostolic church of the Dormition of the most Holy Mother of God. Behind the great sovereign went the boyars and lords-in-waiting and gentlemen of the council and privy councillors and table attendants and crown agents and Moscow nobles and secretaries and palace attendants and military and chancellery servitors of all ranks in fresh ceremonial robes of gold and silver thread.

—Entry in the Kremlin Palace Book of Ceremonies

Throughout the seventeenth century, palace officials kept a meticulous record of the tsars' participation in a relentless round of religious ceremonies. Religion was not just an optional embellishment; Russians continued to believe that divine providence played a decisive role in human affairs and that Russia was the guardian of true Christianity. Indeed, it is impossible to understand Muscovy without appreciating the key role played by the church in everything from foreign policy to publishing. At the same time, the abstract notion of Moscow as the "Third Rome" was tempered by real politics and expressed more through images and rituals than through theological or political writings.

In this chapter, we preface our examination of late Muscovite culture by looking at the challenges that confronted the Orthodox Church. Although the church calendar continued to govern life at the tsar's court, and large sums were spent on commissioning churches and religious art, as we shall see, new ideas were reaching Russia from the West. Church leaders may have paid lip service to the wickedness of Catholics and Protestants, but foreigners were hired in ever greater numbers to provide much needed skills as Orthodoxy struggled to find its place in a changing world. These trends in cultural assimilation accelerated in the short reign of Alexis's son Fëdor (1676–1682) and in the regency of Sofia Alekseevna (1682–1689).

REFORMING THE CHURCH

Religious life in Muscovy was complex. Attendance at church was formally required only once a year for confession, usually at Easter, but most people worshiped more regularly, making additional visits to popular shrines or to pray for the souls of departed relatives. Others did not attend at all, practicing their religion outside official places of prayer. Charters issued in the 1640s–1650s complained: "Many Christians die without repentance and do not feel in the least obliged to confess their sins, or to receive the Body and Blood of the Lord Jesus Christ." Evidence exists, in Russia as elsewhere, of the persistence of pagan and folk practices, which were sometimes integrated into the cycle of the church calendar and farming year. The church generally turned a blind eye, but at times it declared war. In 1658 Patriarch Nikon established a new bishopric in Vyatka, where there were "many remnants of pagan customs and idol worship has survived as well." In the forefront of the church's campaigns against deviation were its regular "troops," the parish clergy.

Black and White Clergy

There were about ten thousand five hundred churches and cathedrals in Russia in 1650 and an estimated figure of between fifty thousand and sixty thousand married clergymen, known as "white" priests. These married parish priests and deacons tended to replenish their own ranks. Some 50 percent of recruits to the priesthood in the seventeenth century were closely related to priests, most often priests' sons. Priests' wives played a vital role in their local communities and were an essential asset to their husbands in more ways than one, for second marriages were forbidden and widowed priests were generally obliged to take monastic vows.

There are no precise figures for the number of "black" or monastic clergy and monks who inhabited Russia's twelve hundred monasteries by the end of the century. The prelates of the church—patriarch, metropolitans, bishops, and abbots of monasteries—were drawn from this celibate priesthood. Women could also make a career as nuns. The abbesses in charge of some of the larger convents enjoyed considerable power and wealth. For the majority of nuns, however, convents offered little more than food and shelter and some security in old age. They were also convenient places to send unwanted wives.

The church enjoyed many privileges, even after the Law Code of 1649 reduced some of them. In particular, the 1678 census showed that the patriarch, prelates, monasteries, and cathedrals owned lands inhabited by 148,997 peasant households, which made up about a fifth of all peasants in the realm. Leading churchmen lived well, entertaining lavishly and building impressive churches and palaces, but the rural and provincial town clergy, both white and black, like the lesser rural gentry, were often barely better off than the peasants.

In the seventeenth century the parish clergy came under considerable pressure to reform, especially during the six disruptive years of Nikon's patriarchate (1652–1658). In 1654 it was stated that a candidate for the priesthood must be "literate and humble," as well as versed in the rules of the church, and should not be a drunkard, gambler, thief, robber, or murderer. In 1681, however, a church council complained that priests "do not live according to the rules, they drink excessively and are so impertinent that they celebrate the mass and other services while intoxicated . . . paying no attention to the Holy Scriptures." In other words, priests were often no better behaved than their parishioners.

Priests suffered the effects of famine, war, and unrest like everyone else. The plague of 1654 may have killed as many as 70–90 percent of the parish and cathedral clergy in Moscow and other central regions. Many parish priests working in the areas affected by the Razin revolt sided with the rebels, helping Razin to produce his propaganda leaflets and in some cases persuading their parishioners to support the rebels. It is a misconception that the church was uniformly the mouthpiece of the autocracy and its priests the agents of the state.

Ecclesiastical Power Struggles

In a society where access to powerful positions at court was determined largely by hereditary right or family ties, the church offered an alternative path to power and riches for individuals outside the court-based hierarchy. When Nikon became patriarch in 1652 and launched a program of reform, there was an amicable division of power. When Alexis went off to war in 1654, he left Nikon to look after the tsaritsa and their children, whose lives he probably saved by getting them out of Moscow when plague erupted. Like Patriarch Filaret, Nikon used the title Great Sovereign, and he emphasized his authority further by publishing a new edition of the church's canon law book to parallel Alexis's Law Code of 1649 and by commissioning a splendid new palace and cathedral in the heart of the Kremlin. In three new monasteries he created symbolic landscapes full of references to the Holy Land, to emphasize that Russia was the center of true holiness. For example, the Cathedral of the Resurrection at "New Jerusalem" near Moscow was closely based on the church of the Holy Sepulcher of Christ in Jerusalem.

Alexis approved of such symbolism, but he was less happy about the expansion of Nikon's personal power base. Nikon attached lands to his monasteries and filched other people's peasants, including those of a bishop who had opposed his candidature as patriarch in 1652. He sacked other bishops and replaced the heads of all major monasteries. Backbiting and power struggles had long been a staple feature of church politics, but many people felt that Nikon went too far by adopting a "papal" style. Alexis and Nikon also had public clashes, for example, when Nikon refused Alexis's request for a special blessing for a repentant priest. In 1657 the metropolitan of Kiev died and Nikon was instructed to appoint a successor but failed to do so, a particular annoyance for Alexis when Moscow was trying to consolidate its hold over Ukraine.

Matters came to a head in mid July 1658 when a boyar struck one of Nikon's officials but Alexis refused to instigate an inquiry. He also forbade Nikon to use the title Great Sovereign. Shortly afterward Nikon conducted mass in the Kremlin Dormition Cathedral as usual, then denounced Alexis and left Moscow, later wishing damnation on the stand-in whom Alexis appointed in his absence. Because Nikon did not formally abdicate, even experts on canon law were unable to agree whether he was still patriarch. Finally, in December 1666 Nikon was tried and deposed on the grounds that "out of his own caprice, of his own will . . . he quit the ecumenical and apostolic church and abandoned the patriarchate," leaving the church "widowed and without a shepherd." It was concluded that the tsar had dominion over the church and guarded its "good order." Nikon was exiled to a distant monastery as a simple monk and died in 1681, shortly after being granted permission to return to Moscow.

Religious Revolt

A Byzantine law states: "Whoever troubles the emperor and disturbs his empire has no defense." The trouble Nikon caused Alexis led to the prelate's own downfall, but Nikon's reforms survived and had wide repercussions. As we have seen, in the 1640s the Zealots of Piety spearheaded a campaign for church reform that Nikon continued. One aspect of the program was to correct and revise the church service books, to which end learned monks were invited from Greece, the Holy Land, and Ukraine. It has been argued that for Alexis the motivation for reform was political rather than a spiritual quest to return to the original "pure" texts. Conforming to Greek and other Orthodox practices would promote Russian leadership of Orthodoxy by silencing accusations that the Russian church had deviated from the norm. Accordingly, the correctors worked from seventeenth-century Greek and Ukrainian texts, not ancient ones. In 1653–1654 Nikon issued a rule about making the sign of cross not with two fingers, as was usual in Russia, but with three fingers after the Greek practice. He also introduced Greek-style vestments for priests and revised various details of the liturgy to be followed during worship. In 1655–1658 corrected service books and commentaries on the liturgy were published.

The master narrative has generally been that a group later known as Old Believers, led by the Zealot archpriest Avvakum (1620–1682), protested against these reforms, on the grounds that "until the time of Nikon the Apostate the Orthodox faith in Russia was pure and undefiled." Traditionalists regarded worship using the new books as mortal danger to the soul, for, some argued, the correctors were "Catholics, trained by the Jesuits." It was better to die than to submit, for accepting the new books and the new sign of the cross implied that not only you but also your ancestors had been worshiping incorrectly and had damned their souls by accepting heresy. Orthodox religious practice was a mesh of gesture, movement, symbol, image, and spoken and sung word, hence the vital importance of crossing oneself, which Orthodox believers did repeatedly during their everyday lives.

Later admirers of the Old Believers saw them as the representatives of the popular masses and defenders of Russian national identity, while detractors condemned them as unthinking fundamentalists. Soviet historians integrated religious revolt into the framework of class warfare. Protests prompted by deep conservatism could be dubbed "progressive" because they defied the status quo as represented by the church, which was an arm of the tsarist government representing the interests of the ruling class. Archpriest Avvakum, a sort of folk hero, also had the distinction of writing the first Russian autobiography, using colorful, pithy language. He was burned at the stake in 1682, thus becoming a martyr for his faith. Some historians now question whether Avvakum was widely acknowledged as a leader during his own lifetime. The writings of Avvakum and his supporters became more accessible only in the early eighteenth century, when the history of the Old Believers and its leaders was written and handed down by Old Believers themselves.

Many early protesters against Nikon's reforms, including Avvakum, were motivated by personal hostility to Nikon, caught up in a web of church politics, intrigue, and personality clashes. A few, highly literate dissenters consciously wished to preserve the prereform forms of worship and conducted a coherent counterargument to the reforms from the start, but ordinary, illiterate Russians were probably unaware of the technicalities of new practices until the authorities started to impose them. This phase came when the church council of 1666–1667 condemned as schismatics not only anyone who opposed Nikon's reforms but also those who defied the authority of the church. This declaration sparked off major outbreaks, such as a revolt by monks at Solovki on the White Sea, who held out against government troops for seven years. Elsewhere protests were directed not just against innovations in books and worship but against church authority in general.

Many women became dissenters. The biography of the highborn Feodosia Morozova (?–1675), the widow of a relative of Boris Morozov, recounts that when she learned about Nikon's reforms, "she became very fervent for Orthodoxy and filled with revulsion and disgust for all innovations." She renounced her wealth and court connections to live like a nun and dispensed charity to the poor. Under interrogation she crossed herself with two fingers, and all attempts to make her adopt the three-fingered sign failed. She and her sister stubbornly refused to recant under all sorts of tortures and were thrown into an underground cell, where they died of starvation in 1675. Communities of men, women, and children burnt themselves to death rather than accept "Nikonian" practices on the grounds that it was better to burn in purifying fire on earth than in hell. Protests were rooted in popular belief and fears, which, for example, interpreted the terrible plague of 1654 as the scourge of God. They were fueled by paganism, ignorance, and apocalyptic visions, which continued throughout the imperial period.

AT THE TSAR'S COURT

The religious turmoil in the country rarely disturbed the orderly ritual of the tsar's court, which represented the heart of the realm. Here scenarios of royal power could be acted out and idealized hierarchies expressed through ritual. This was true of other European courts, but the Muscovite version, as we shall see, had a number of unusual features, not least in the role of women.

In the Kremlin

In the seventeenth century the life of the court and the church hierarchy remained inextricably linked, centered on the Kremlin cathedrals built by Ivan III in the late fifteenth century (see the chapter "Russia's New Monarchy, 1456–1533") and the royal family's private apartments in the palace. The palace was the Kremlin's inner sanctum, often referred to in documents simply as "up above." The general public was not admitted even to the palace courtyard, and the building itself contained no public rooms like the ones usually found in Western royal residences. Even high officials had to dismount from their horses at a specified distance from the entrance and proceed toward it on foot. Palace chaplains and boyars attended the tsar in the antechamber, which adjoined the Golden Throne Room, adorned with frescoes depicting the exploits of the kings of Israel and scenes from the lives of the princes of Rus. Beyond was the royal study, which only selected boyars were allowed to enter, and beyond that the tsar's bedchamber. Most of the rooms were quite sparsely furnished, but richly decorated with frescoes on religious subjects and colorful floral motifs.

The Kremlin and its immediate vicinity provided the setting for events in the court calendar, which revolved around the Orthodox liturgical year, the anniversaries of living and dead members of the royal family, and rites of passage such as baptisms and funerals. Also on the calendar were selected saints' days and special

The Krestovaya Chamber of the tsars' residence in the Moscow Kremlin. 17th century. *Archivo Iconografico, S. A./ Corbis.*

anniversaries of national events, many linked with the feasts of miracle-working icons. Court life was conducted within a closely defined historical context that was reflected in ritual, rhetoric, and art. Each year on Palm Sunday, for example, a week before Easter, the tsar took the reins of a horse on which the patriarch was mounted and walked in a procession that acted out Christ's entry into Jerusalem. Among the most impressive events of Alexis's reign was the presentation of his heir Fëdor (born 1661) in September 1674 to "all ranks of people in the Muscovite state." The carefully orchestrated procession of leading churchmen and boyars bearing precious icons progressed along a route lined with musketeers onto Red Square, where there was a specially devised religious ceremony and speeches.

Tsar Alexis loved to go on pilgrimages. In 1650 he prayed at Uglich, where Prince Dmitry was murdered in 1591 (see the chapter "Boris Godunov and the Time of Troubles, 1584–1613"), and at Kashin at the shrine of Princess Anna of Tver, who saved the city from the Poles during the Time of Troubles. Among his favorite places was the Monastery of St. Sabbas, who he believed had saved him from a bear. Such visitations extended the royal presence beyond Moscow, linking outlying towns to the center through reference to their part in national history. In the capital, courtly display reinforced both the bonds and the distance between autocrat and the elite. In peacetime a major proportion of the Moscow elite's time was spent in ceremonial activities, while their independent cultural life outside the royal household was extremely restricted. There were no schools or universities, no public theaters, no secular press. Travel abroad required the permission of the tsar and the patriarch. Even boyars did not compose or play music or take a scholarly interest in the arts and sciences. There were exceptions. The Foreign Office director Artamon Matveev (1625–1682), who had a Scottish wife, staged home theatricals, and Prince Vasily Golitsyn (1643–1714), one of the few Russians to know Latin, owned musical instruments. But by and large in their accomplishments and culture Muscovite nobles were closer to ordinary Russians than to their counterparts elsewhere in Europe.

Royal Recreations

In summer the tsar's family and its entourage often traveled to out-of-town estates that were equipped for entertainments. At Izmailovo Alexis had a zoo with lions and tigers, model gardens and orchards. There were displays of bearbaiting and Alexis's favorite sport of falconry. In October 1672 he sat down in a house on another royal estate to watch a company of German amateur actors directed by a Lutheran pastor perform a play, the first such event in Russian history. Court theatrical performances continued until Alexis's death in 1676, after which they were stopped under pressure from the conservative Patriarch Joachim (in office 1674–1690). The repertoire included the "comedies" of Bacchus, the Greek and Roman god of wine, featuring drunkards, maidens and performing bears, and military tales, with lively battle scenes and explosive effects. All the plays performed, even comedies, were strongly moralizing and most were based on biblical subjects.

The new theater opened the doors to Western-style instrumental music. Russian sacred unaccompanied vocal music had already been influenced by Western compositional techniques via Ukraine, but the development of secular instrumental music was hampered by the disapproval of the church. An edict of 1645 stated: "Take great care that nowhere should there be . . . wandering minstrels with tambourines and flutes either in the towns or the villages." The objection here was not so much to the instruments themselves as to their use for "pagan" entertainments, since seemly musical offerings at court functions and diplomatic receptions were tolerated. For example, Alexis had organs, pipes, and drums played at his wedding in 1671. Even so, the tsar was at first hesitant about instrumental music for his new theater, until the players persuaded him otherwise. For decades to come, foreigners dominated court musical life.

A Woman's Place

Perhaps the feature that most distinguished the Muscovite court from its European counterparts was the segregation of men and women. Historians have generally agreed that Muscovite royal women lived in a separate women's quarters known as the *terem,* an arrangement that was replicated in boyar households. Foreigners reported that Russians kept their women "locked up like slaves" and that "no man is allowed to look them in the face." Women's clothes were layered and loose-fitting, revealing only their hands and neck, and married women always covered their hair. However, non-Orthodox foreigners exaggerated the helplessness of Muscovite women, with whom they had little contact. Upper-class women enjoyed more freedom than outsiders realized, wielding power behind the scenes, arranging marriages, and petitioning and gathering information on behalf of male relatives. They were entitled to own property, to manage their own estates, and to sue and make contracts in their own name, although such activities were the exception rather than the rule. The tsars' wives and daughters in particular had an important public role, dispensing charity, receiving petitions, and standing in when men were absent. Their prayers on behalf of the Muscovite realm were regarded as particularly powerful. The royal terem had a large domestic staff and considerable resources. Even so, for formal public purposes segregation of the sexes was practiced, with elite women using curtained recesses in church and closed carriages for outings. At theatrical performances, even Tsaritsa Natalia watched through chinks in a specially boarded-off royal box.

Women's role in Muscovite power networks, as elsewhere, focused on their usefulness as marriage partners. Their main task was to bear children, a risky business even in the relative affluence of the palace. Mortality among both mothers and infants was high. Alexis's first wife, Tsaritsa Maria, did well in giving birth in twenty-one years of marriage to thirteen live children, of whom only four died in infancy, but in 1669, when she was forty-three, the birth of the thirteenth, a girl who died two days later, killed her. In the case of the tsars' daughters, the *tsarevny,* however, a lack of foreign Orthodox suitors of suitably high status led to a policy, nowhere officially articulated, of keeping them unmarried. This practice also reduced the complications of accommodating Russian sons-in-law in the hierarchy.

In the Kremlin the sense of exclusiveness and mystery cultivated by the tsar himself naturally extended to the women, whose quarters were out-of-bounds to all except close family members, ladies in waiting, and priests. The Golden Hall of the Tsaritsy provided a space for female receptions. All-female parties visited churches and convents, but there was no place for women in the tsar's formal receptions and processions. Balls, masques, and other such mixed-sex entertainments were out of the question. In a period when few portraits existed even of Russian men, female portraits were scarcely permissible at all outside the religious context, in sharp contrast to western Europe where the female portrait was an established genre. Visual celebrations of female beauty and sexuality, not to mention nudity, were as yet unknown in Russia and remained so for some time. Outside the Kremlin, custom eased restrictions somewhat. The tsaritsa and her attendants often joined hunting parties. During the brief period of Alexis's marriage to Natalia Naryshkina, royal women were seen more often in public. Even so, semiseclusion survived until the very end of the seventeenth century.

There was no seclusion for ordinary townswomen, who presided over their family's domestic arrangements and contributed to household incomes with skills such as spinning and embroidery and the preservation and preparation of foodstuffs. But they, too, were bound by traditional requirements in dress and behavior and had their marriages arranged by their parents. Models for correct female behavior continued to resemble those in the sixteenth-century *Book of Household Management* (*Domostroi*), which praised the virtues of piety, modesty, abstemiousness, hard work, and thrift. In the countryside, peasant women worked alongside their menfolk, although in rural communities, too, there was a division of male and female labor, sometimes based on ancient lore; for example, men sowed and women reaped, men worked with wood, women with textiles, and so on. Life was hard, life expectancy low, but women of all classes found relaxation in gatherings where they met to gossip, tell stories, and sing songs and in special occasions such as wedding feasts and Shrovetide and Yuletide celebrations.

ARTS IN TRANSITION

The royal family took the lead in commissioning architecture and art objects, from gem-encrusted icons to illuminated manuscripts. Boyars, leading churchmen, and rich merchants, too, spent considerable sums on embellishing churches and residences, and even peasants bought icons and crosses. Traditional genres and styles prevailed, especially in the provinces, but the seventeenth century was a time of considerable innovation.

Icons, Frescoes, and Portraits

The royal residences and churches were adorned with items produced in the workshops of the Kremlin Armory, where in 1683 a studio for nonreligious art was created under the direction of the icon painter Simon Ushakov (1629–1686). Sometimes presented as a pioneer of realism in art, Ushakov in fact looked back as much as forward. His icon "The Tree of the Muscovite Realm" (1668), for example, ignores real time and space, bringing together Heaven and Earth, architecture of different periods, and holy men of different epochs, all presided over by an image of the Vladimir Mother of God (see the chapter "Kievan Rus: Christian Civilization, 988–1240"), who blesses Ivan I and Metropolitan Peter, the "founders" of Muscovy in the fourteenth century. Tsar Alexis, Tsaritsa Maria, and their sons Alexis and Fëdor stand in poses of supplication and gratitude, indicating the continuity of God's blessing on the Muscovite realm. At the same time, the precisely delineated representations of the Kremlin walls show that Ushakov also worked from direct observation.

"The Tree of the Muscovite Realm" (1668), icon by Simon Ushakov. *Tretyakov Gallery, Moscow, Russia/Scala/Art Resource, NY.*

Outside Moscow, in towns such as Yaroslavl, Vologda, and Solvychegodsk, where the workshops of the Stroganov merchant-manufacturers were located, merchant patrons commissioned churches, icons, frescoes, and artifacts from skilled artists working in the Orthodox idiom, often adding stylized ornamentalism and jewel-like details alongside more naturalistic elements. The intricate decorativeness and bright colors that are a hallmark of much seventeenth-century Russian art and crafts appear to owe as much to Oriental as to Western influences, although one might equally trace some of the characteristics to native folk art. Sources of Western influence include illustrations from the Dutch "Piscator" Bible, which served as models for frescoes in Yaroslavl churches, but they were adapted to Orthodox conventions and local tastes.

Direct cultural influences came to Moscow during Alexis's reign with hired artists such as the German Peter Engels, "master of perspective," who painted scenery for the tsar's theater. The majority of the non-Russian craftsmen working in the Armory in the 1660s–1670s were Belarusians and Ukrainians, who were able to paint portraits, historical subjects, and "perspective" studies in the Polish Renaissance and Baroque styles of the sixteenth and seventeenth centuries. Not enough authenticated work by these artists survives to assess their talents, but they undoubtedly transmitted skills and ideas to their Russian colleagues at a time when the tastes of the Russian elite were undergoing changes.

In some quarters, imported pictures, prints, maps, and illustrated books were acquired, for example by the Foreign Office. Painters like Ushakov borrowed architectural and other motifs from such printed sources, while a handful of Russians picked up artistic ideas abroad. An embassy to Italy in the 1650s sent back reports of marvelous palaces, fountains, statues, gardens, and theaters. Tsar Alexis's own observation of foreign architecture while on campaign in Lithuania and the Baltic in the 1650s inspired him to furnish some of his own residences in Western style.

Perhaps the most "modern" art form to emerge from these various influences were the secular portraits known as *parsuny.* Russian portraiture had its roots in Byzantine religious art, in which saintly images could be joined by those of noncanonized and even living people in attitudes of prayer and supplication. Realistic likenesses of persons detached from a religious context and painted from life, part of the development of a secular vision in the Renaissance in the West, are extremely rare in Russia before the early eighteenth century. In the 1670s–1680s a few Russian boyars began to commission portraits painted on canvas in oils, and some even had portrait galleries in their homes, but few examples survive. Images of common folk are even rarer. As usual, Alexis led the fashion by being painted from life several times, but he favored a conservative approach. The best-known surviving portrait is anonymous and undated, stiff and stylized, with much attention devoted to conveying details of costly fabrics. It recalls similarly static and decorative portraits on panels painted in England more than a century earlier. (See the portrait of Alexis in the previous chapter.)

Moscow Baroque

Architecture in this period displayed similar transitional features to painting. Traditional brick-built churches, capped by one or five onion-domed cupolas, began to display elements of Western styles in their exterior decoration; for example, recessed half-columns and classically profiled pediments. New architectural ideas were assimilated mainly through foreign illustrated books and engravings. Alexis, for example, owned a book illustrating "the stone buildings of all German states" and works by theoreticians of the Renaissance and Baroque eras. The fusion of tradition and innovation may be seen in his palace at Kolomenskoe. Begun in 1667 and described by a Russian poet as "the eighth wonder of the world," it was built of timber, which was regarded in Russia as a healthier material than stone. With its turrets capped with double-headed eagles and its two hundred rooms, the palace was fantastic looking to contemporary Western eyes. But it also had twisting columns derived from Western sources, a pair of sculptures of lions, and signs of the zodiac painted on its ceilings.

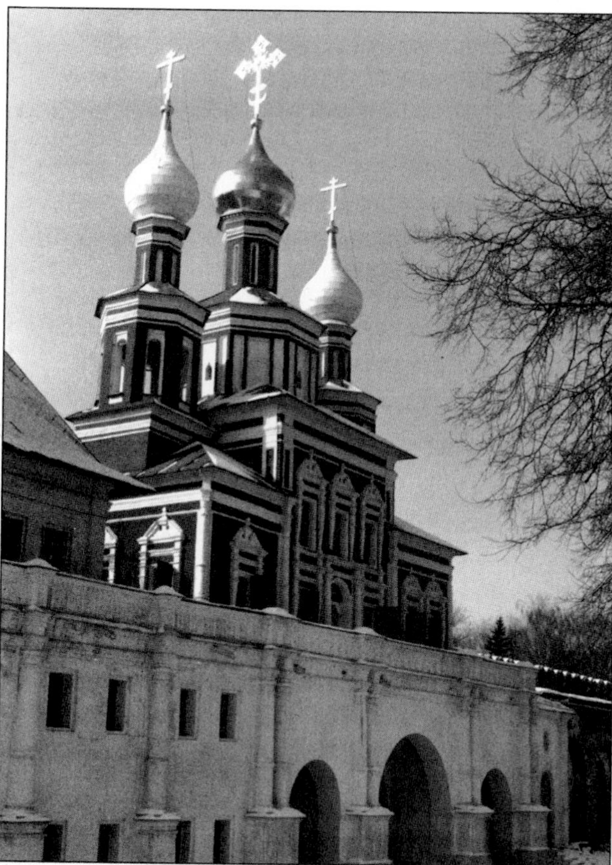

"Moscow Baroque" Church of the Intercession (1680s), Novodevichy Convent, Moscow. Architects unknown. © *William Brumfield.*

The culmination of these diverse yet undirected influences came around 1680 with the arrival of the so-called Moscow Baroque style. Although the structures and building materials were often traditional, Old Russian devices were replaced entirely by Western details, such as window surrounds with broken pediments. The tower church at Fili (1690–1694), with its tiers of receding octagons, owes something to distant prototypes in Russian wooden architecture, but the new sense of harmony in design and planning harks back to the era of the Renaissance. Yet there is scant evidence of foreign architects working in Russia during the 1680s–1690s, and no Moscow Baroque building, with the exception of some Ukrainian designs, can be traced back to foreign prototypes. For the interiors of their residences, also often in the new style, richer boyars began to acquire items from the West such as mirrors, carved furniture, clocks, prints, maps, and fabric hangings. These trends hint at cautiously expanding cultural horizons.

Book Culture and Learning

Statistics on Muscovite printing and publishing are unimpressive. In the whole of the seventeenth century the single, church-run press in Moscow published fewer than ten books that were not wholly religious in content, including the 1649 Law Code and a manual for training infantry regiments. Even liturgical and devotional works amounted to only a few hundred titles and were mostly heavy tomes for use in church. The Books of Psalms was a bestseller. There were no journals or almanacs, no plays, poetry, or philosophy, in print. The biggest print runs were for alphabet primers for teaching basic literacy. Some foreign books reached Moscow, but they were mainly of curiosity value as almost no Russians were capable of reading foreign languages, apart from a little Polish, which spread among the elite in the second half of the century.

It is perhaps not surprising, therefore, that historians who view Russia from a Western viewpoint regard low achievements in learning and "book culture" as clear indicators of the wide gap between Muscovy and western Europe. The idea that Russia lagged behind in this respect runs like a refrain, along with denunciations of despotism, drunkenness, and wife beating, through accounts written by Western travelers from the sixteenth century onward. Russians did not send their children abroad to study, foreigners claimed, because they feared that the superior customs and the "blessed freedoms" of foreign lands would lure them into heresy.

Straight comparisons make bleak reading. The absence of Russian names among the luminaries of the so-called Scientific Revolution is hardly surprising when we consider that not only did Muscovy have no universities or academies but also lacked even elementary schools. The impression that Russians were "ignorant" was deepened by the active celebration of ignorance by certain Orthodox churchmen, who equated foreign learning with "guile" and "deception." At the same time, we should beware of exaggerating the differences. Russia's European neighbors did not enjoy universal literacy or schooling. For the mass of people all over Europe the world was explained by divine providence, not the laws of science. Everywhere book learning was for the few—it is just that in Russia, where urban culture remained underdeveloped, it was for fewer.

Russia was a latecomer to print culture (see the chapter "Ivan IV and the Birth Pangs of Tsardom, 1533–1584"), but the limited output of printing presses was supplemented by literature that circulated in handwritten manuscripts and a flourishing oral tradition. Adventure tales were popular, including stories translated from the Polish. Nobles and townspeople read or listened to courtly romances and picaresque tales and enjoyed irreverent works of parody like "Liturgy to the Ale House," alongside the ever-popular lives of saints and miracle tales of the Virgin Mary.

Education, too, was expanding, if mainly in the palace. The young tsar Alexis's early lessons were from primers and biblical texts, but later he read cosmography, astronomy, and mechanics, ancient history and travel accounts. In the early 1660s the learned monk Simeon Polotsky (1629–1680) from Belarus came to Moscow as tutor to Alexis's son Alexis, who in 1667 was able to deliver a speech in Latin and Polish to a Polish delegation. Polotsky pioneered the writing in Russian of verses on the Polish model, composing plays and sermons as well.

Secularization Revisited

As this chapter has shown, traditional, religious culture remained strong and Western, secular trends were the exception rather than the rule, even at court. Both Soviet and Western historians have identified "realistic" tendencies, even a delayed "Renaissance" in seventeenth-century Muscovy, but this does not alter the fact that the typical Russian nobleman and his wife still owned icons and books of psalms rather than portraits and poetry, lived in a traditional timber house, and spoke only Russian. They knew nothing of science or philosophy and wrote nothing apart from occasional appeals to the tsar and formulaic letters to relatives. "We are all well, by God's grace, and henceforth according to the will of our Lord and Creator," wrote Prince Vasily Golitsyn's daughter Irina in 1678. "Your daughter begs your blessing and pays you her most humble respects." Members of the elite employed scribes to write their correspondence.

Tsar Alexis conducted experiments in horticulture using foreign experts, but he also had holy water sprinkled in the sign of the cross on fields to improve crop yields, sought advice on witchcraft remedies when his son fell ill in 1670, and carried around a tooth of St. Sabbas to cure toothache. The issue of secular culture in Russia's "age of transition" needs to be examined in the context of the extent and limits of secularization in the West, too, where most people also still adhered to a religious worldview.

RUSSIA AND THE WEST

Defining Russia's relationship with the West and the West's with Russia is a recurring theme in Russian history, literature, and thought. The Time of Troubles sharpened hostility toward foreigners—"The Latins are the most impure and ferocious of all heretics," wrote Patriarch Filaret in 1620, "like unto dogs, known to be enemies of God"—but Russia's collapse exposed technical and economic deficiencies that could be remedied in the short term only by increasing contacts with the outside world. From the 1620s, as we have seen, foreign mercenaries reformed the Russian army. Overseas trade resumed. Foreign craftsmen made clocks and painted portraits. Such contacts brought conflicts.

Contacts and Clashes

In the seventeenth century Russia's sense of being low in the hierarchy of European states intensified. The English poet John Milton may have described Muscovy as "the most northerly Region of Europe reputed civil" (1647), but in the West its envoys were regarded as not much different from the Muslim "infidels"; their appearance and negotiating style set them apart. Westerners regarded Muscovites as not quite full members of Christendom, and Muscovites, for their part, struggled to improve their image abroad, while still being saddled with the notion of their own superiority. This called for a new approach to publicity and diplomacy. After suffering a series of defeats by the Poles in 1659–1660, for example, Alexis commissioned counterpublicity against a Swedish campaign to "belittle the Muscovite state." Foreign news reports were now regularly monitored and digested in the Foreign Office, which had knowledgeable personnel on its payroll, including translators and interpreters. Alexis and his successors maintained resident envoys in several capitals, including Warsaw, but elsewhere diplomatic business was carried on by special missions, such as a 1662 embassy to Prussia, Denmark, Holland, England, and Venice, which was briefed to make clear that Alexis was "qualified to rule not only his own state but many other lands as well." In 1672, when the Turks threatened western Ukraine, Muscovite envoys were dispatched all over Europe, including England and France, to appeal for aid. They were unsuccessful, but Russian diplomacy made its presence felt as never before.

Traffic in the opposite direction was even busier, with regular missions to Moscow from Western countries and growing foreign communities in Moscow and other towns, mostly merchants and mercenaries. Russians had special terms for referring to outsiders. The most common word for North Europeans was *nemtsy*, now the modern Russian word for Germans, but meaning literally someone who cannot speak. There were Swedish *nemtsy*, English *nemtsy*, and so on. Roman Catholics were *latyny* and Protestants *liuterany* and *kalvinisty*. In the early 1640s, following appeals from local residents, Tsar Michael ordered the demolition of foreign churches in central Moscow and their removal beyond the city walls. A few years later Alexis devised a more radical solution.

The German Quarter

The young Alexis, as we have seen, was much influenced by the Zealots of Piety, whose campaign to purify Orthodoxy was tinged with xenophobia. Regulations barred foreigners from hiring Russian servants and banned the sale of "devilish" tobacco, along with icons "depicted after the manner of the Latin and German deceivers" that displayed "human lusts." Antiforeign sentiment was accompanied by a largely unsuccessful campaign to persuade foreigners to convert to Orthodoxy. This reached a climax in 1652, when the Scottish colonel Alexander Leslie was charged with taking potshots at the crosses on a church, and his wife was accused of forcing her Russian servants to eat dog meat during fasts. Both agreed to convert. Patriarch Nikon himself was apparently outraged when he inadvertently administered a blessing to some "Germans" in a crowd, which prompted a law prohibiting foreigners to wear Russian dress to stop them entering churches undetected.

Tsar Alexis and his advisers also heeded Russian merchants, who resented the exemptions and privileges enjoyed by some foreign traders. In 1649 the authorities actually expelled English merchants from Moscow, on the pretext that their fellow countrymen had "murdered their rightful king," Charles I. The Law Code of 1649 repeated prohibitions on "Germans" employing Russians and buying land and property in the city. Foreign churches were to be located "distant from the [true] churches of God." These measures were the prelude to an edict of October 1652 that removed west Europeans to their own self-contained district on the northeastern outskirts of Moscow, a walled enclave known as the "New German Quarter." The Quarter acquired its own stone-built Protestant churches. Its streets were lined with the solid houses and gardens of soldiers, merchants, doctors, artists, and craftsmen, as well as with shops and coffeehouses. For Muscovites it must have been both terrifying and alluring.

"Latins and Lutherans"

Confining the foreigners to their own district did little to calm deep-seated fears of contamination by "Latins and Lutherans." When Archpriest Avvakum exclaimed "Poor Russia, what do you want with German ways and customs?," shaving was probably one of the things he had in mind, for the Orthodox believed that God made man in his own bearded image and to be clean-shaven was to be damned. In the latter half of the seventeenth century being moustached or clean-shaven became the fashion throughout the urban classes in most Western countries, strengthening the beard as a symbol of Orthodox Russians' separateness from foreigners. "Look often at the icon of the Second Coming of Christ," a tract warned, "and observe the righteous standing at the right side of Christ, all with beards. At the left stand the Muslims and heretics, Lutherans and Poles and other shavers of their ilk, with just whiskers, such as cats and dogs have. Take heed whom to imitate and which side you will be on."

In the later seventeenth century a few elite Russians began to adopt Western fashions, too. Tsar Alexis protested: "Courtiers are forbidden to adopt foreign and German and other customs, to cut the hair on their heads and to wear robes, caftans and hats of foreign design." All the same, Alexis was fascinated by foreign "novelties." As a child he had suits of Western clothing made for him, but these were regarded as a sort of fancy dress for wearing in the privacy of the palace, never on public occasions. He and his immediate successors had the patriarch at their shoulder to remind them of the perils of too much contact with "heretics." Patriarch Joachim was particularly alarmed by such developments. In his Testament

(1690) he denounced the policy of hiring foreigners "in the pious tsarist realm." He appealed to the tsars to ban the churches of "heretic dissenters" and not to allow "any new Latin and alien customs, nor to introduce the wearing of foreign dress." His successor Adrian (in office 1690–1700) held similar views.

Retaining separateness from foreigners was a matter of life and death for some Russians. The Orthodox understanding of Russia's place in the world continued to be rooted in the idea of a cosmic plan according to which Orthodox Russians were God's chosen people. Catholic and Protestant Christians, not to mention Muslims and other "infidels," would be excluded from the paradise in which the history of humankind would culminate. At the same time, Russia had to find its place in the real, modern world on an immediate and practical level, which meant accommodation with foreigners. National policy had to supplement the protecting powers of ancient miracle-working icons and the relics of national saints by importing "novelties" from that dangerous world.

FËDOR AND SOFIA, 1676–1689

In January 1676 Tsar Alexis died, aged forty-seven, possibly from kidney failure. He was survived by two sons, Fëdor (b. 1661) and Ivan (b. 1666) from his first marriage to Maria Miloslavskaya, and one, Peter (b. 1672), by Natalia Naryshkina, his second wife. Fourteen-year-old Fëdor, intelligent but ailing, succeeded to the throne. Stories of attempts to make three-year-old Peter tsar instead of him are probably unfounded, but the very existence of such rumors reflected the rivalries at court. The Miloslavskys and their clients had been pushed into the background when their kinswoman Tsaritsa Maria died and Alexis remarried in 1671. With Fëdor's accession, Miloslavsky fortunes rose again and the Narsyhkins' declined. There is no reason to believe that Fëdor bore any personal grudges against his young half-brother, but leading members of Tsaritsa Natalia's clan were exiled as a result of denunciations from the Miloslavsky camp.

Fëdor

Historians seem unable to decide whether Fëdor was a sickly nonentity manipulated by unscrupulous favorites or whether he showed promise of being a strong ruler. The central factor of Fëdor's reign was an unsuccessful war against the Ottoman Empire and Crimea (1676–1681), during which Turks and Tatars invaded Ukraine, and Russia was forced to abandon several forts on the Dnieper. War determined economic policy. In 1678 a major land survey was carried out to reassess the population's tax obligations, providing the only reliable, if incomplete, population figures for the whole seventeenth century. In September 1679 the household, rather than land, uniformly became the basis for taxation, a measure that initially increased revenues but stored up new problems by encouraging households to join together illegally to reduce their tax liability.

The major reform to affect the elite was the abolition in 1681–1682 of the code of precedence, following the recommendation of a committee headed by Prince Vasily Golitsyn. The registers of appointments were burned with the pronouncement that the code "hateful to God, creating enmity, hateful to brotherhood and destructive of love" should "nevermore be recalled for all time." Improving military efficiency by making promotions on merit was not the paramount reason for this measure, but rather the need to readjust the balance of power at court, as old clan networks gave way to new configurations who found their progress barred by historically determined precedence. A general perception existed that clan honor disputes were disruptive and the obligation to be ever alert for breaches of the code was wearisome for all concerned. An associated scheme would have separated civil and military offices and created permanent top posts, but it was shelved, allegedly after the patriarch warned of the independent power that such high officials might accumulate.

One of Fëdor's last acts before his death in 1682 was to approve a charter of privileges for an academy in Moscow to teach subjects including grammar, poetics, rhetoric, philosophy, and the "free sciences." The model was the academy in Kiev, founded in the 1630s, but the plan was not implemented until several years after Fëdor's death. Fëdor is said to have studied Latin with Simeon Polotsky, but surviving evidence is silent on this point, indicating rather that Fëdor's education was fairly traditional and that he had bad handwriting. He loved church singing and encouraged the introduction of part-singing from Kiev. Following his first marriage to a woman of Polish descent, Polish fashions became popular at court, from poetry to daring women's hats that showed a glimpse of hair, but, as we have seen, traditionalists regarded "Latin" novelties with suspicion and foreign fashions remained officially outlawed. Patriarch Joachim even had Tsar Alexis's theater closed down.

Miloslavsky Versus Naryshkin

On April 27, 1682, Fëdor died. His first wife and her newborn son had died in July 1681, and rumors that his second wife, Martha Apraksina (1667–1714), whom he married just two months before his death, might be pregnant proved unfounded. Custom dictated that his younger brother, sixteen-year-old Ivan, succeed him, but on the day of Fëdor's death a group at court declared Peter, aged nine, as tsar on the grounds that Ivan was "weak-minded." Matters might have rested there. Ivan's afflictions, which included serious visual impairment and a speech impediment, evidently precluded him from playing an active role in government. Russia had no written law of succession to prevent a younger brother from succeeding to the throne, and Peter had the support of Patriarch Joachim.

But the politics of kinship proved stronger than pragmatism. The Naryshkins had not reckoned on a combination of unrest among the musketeers and the fury of the Miloslavskys and their clients, who found a spokeswoman in Tsarevich Ivan's twenty-five-year-old sister Sofia, that "ambitious and power-hungry princess," as a contemporary described her. Sofia (1657–1704) had been raised in the semiseclusion typical for Russian princesses, but she enjoyed the authority and religious charisma that came with royal birth and had probably developed her own network of acquaintances during Fëdor's reign. To get Tsarevich Ivan on the throne, Sofia's party needed to find support beyond boyar circles, where loyalties were fairly evenly balanced. At the time of Fëdor's death the musketeers, as a result of ongoing disputes over management, pay, and conditions, were ultrasensitive to rumors of abuses and injustice in high places. After two weeks of negotiations between the musketeers and the new government, in late May a rumor that "traitors" had strangled Tsarevich Ivan and were preparing to massacre the musketeers brought mutinous regiments to the Kremlin. Here the musketeers, possibly prompted by Sofia or her associates, butchered some of their own commanding officers and unpopular government officials and also singled out members of the Naryshkin clan and their associates as the chief "traitors." Some forty persons fell victim to axe and pike, some of them hacked to pieces in front of Peter and his mother.

Regent Sofia

Once the musketeers had retreated from the Kremlin, a compromise was found in a joint tsardom, justified by Byzantine precedents, with Ivan as senior tsar and Peter as junior. No official records survive of the formal appointment of Sofia as regent, but from about 1686 on she began not only to add her name to those of her brothers in royal edicts but also to use the title *samoderzhitsa,* the feminine form of *samoderzhets* (autocrat). She also appeared in portraits—the first female images of their kind in Russia—wearing something similar to the tsar's regalia and was a major patron of architecture in the new Moscow Baroque style. But titles and buildings could not disguise the basic dilemma that Sofia would have to step aside when Peter came of age.

Neither Peter nor Ivan played any direct role in formulating the domestic and foreign policy of Sofia's regency, even though their names headed all official documents. In general, Sofia's government continued the policies of Tsars Alexis and Fëdor in areas such as the founding in 1687 of the Moscow (Slavonic-Greek-Latin) Academy and granting concessions to foreign merchants and industrialists. Efforts continued to stem the flood of runaway serfs and to persecute religious dissidents. The regime was particularly active in foreign affairs. In 1686 Russia signed a treaty of "eternal peace" with Poland, which ratified the 1667 Truce of Andrusovo (see the chapter "Muscovy Expands, 1613–1676"). In return Russia agreed to break its 1681 truce with Ottoman Turkey and Crimea in support of a Holy League against the Ottomans, which was initiated by Poland, Austria, and the Venetian Republic and sponsored by the pope. In 1689 Russia signed commercial treaties with Prussia, and in the same year, following hostilities with China, the Treaty of Nerchinsk established a border between the two countries in the Amur valley.

The brain behind most of these measures was Prince Vasily Golitsyn, probably the most able man of his generation. Sofia depended on Golitsyn for all areas of policy, but her overreliance on his skills as a military commander was to hasten her own downfall as well as his. Some historians believe that she was blinded by love, but evidence of the couple's intimacy rests mainly on hearsay and rumor. Despite

Engraved portrait of Tsarevna Sofia Alekseevna (1689). Made by Abraham Blooteling in Amsterdam from a painting on canvas. *Courtesy Professor Lindsey Hughes.*

his being a cultured man, who enjoyed conversing with foreigners in Latin, Golitsyn was poor at handling court politics, which in the period 1682–1689 were unusually complicated and tense.

To fulfill Russia's commitments to the Holy League, in 1687 Golitsyn led a huge army south toward the Crimea, but he was forced to turn back by food shortages and sickness among the troops. Official reports later claimed that the khan and his Tatars "were seized with fear and terror . . . and plunged into the depths of despair" by the approach of the Russian army. Thus a campaign that allowed little scope for military exploits acquired an exaggeratedly heroic coloring. On a second campaign in 1689, Golitsyn reached the Crimea and had several engagements with the enemy. But once again, logistical problems forced the Russian armies to retreat with even greater losses than before. Golitsyn seems to have acted honorably and conscientiously in a difficult situation, but his opponents seized the opportunity to undermine both him and Sofia, whose "unseemly" appearances in public Tsar Peter had begun to criticize. In August 1689 unfounded rumors that Sofia was sending the musketeers to kill him forced Peter to flee to the Trinity-St. Sergius Monastery, where he summoned troops. Deserted by the military, Sofia had to capitulate and was locked up in the Novodevichy Convent, where she remained until her death in 1704. Golitsyn was exiled to the north of Russia, where he died unforgiven in 1714.

For the rest of his life Peter associated Sofia with the dark forces of opposition. He recognized her intelligence, but in his view it was overshadowed by malice and cunning. In a letter to Tsar Ivan written in mid September 1689, Peter declared: "And now, brother sovereign, the time has come for us to rule the realm entrusted to us by God." The stage was set for one of the most dramatic and crucial reigns in Russian history.

CHAPTER 11

Peter the Great: From Tsar to Emperor, 1689–1725

This monarch brought our fatherland to a level with others; he taught us to recognize that we are people too; in a word, whatever you look at in Russia, all has its beginnings with him and whatever is done henceforth will also derive its source from that beginning.

—Ivan Nepliuev (1693–1773), former naval student, on Peter the Great

The reign of Peter the Great (Peter I; r. 1682–1725) marked a watershed in Russian history, which writers still often divide into the "pre-Petrine" and "post-Petrine" eras. Almost everything Peter did provoked controversy. His military campaigns won territory on the Baltic and raised Russia's profile in world affairs, but they also aroused fears abroad of Russian expansionism. He founded a new capital, St. Petersburg, his "Window on the West," and created a fleet, but these and other major projects were unpopular and imposed huge burdens on all his subjects, from the richest to the poorest. His many reforms aimed to make Russia more modern and efficient, but, like his military program, they relied on the old institutions of autocracy and serfdom. His experiments in social and cultural engineering offended religious sensibilities and sharply divided the elite from the mass of the population. To his admirers, like Ivan Nepliuev, Peter was godlike; to his most extreme opponents he was the devil or Antichrist.

A PORTRAIT OF PETER

Six foot seven inches tall, Peter towered above his contemporaries, literally forcing them to run to catch up as he rushed on ahead with long strides. He was always in a hurry. As he once wrote to some officials: "You have to work even harder and have everything prepared ahead of time, because wasted time, like death, cannot be reversed." He was careless about his appearance, often wearing a workman's apron to indulge in one of his practical hobbies, which included shipbuilding, woodturning, dentistry, performing autopsies, and making fireworks. "The tsar sets no store by rich garments, fine furniture, carriages and residences," wrote a foreign envoy. At

Peter I (r. 1682–1725) at the battle of Poltava in 1709. Oil painting by Peter's German court artist Johann Gottfried Tannauer (c. 1710). *The Russian State Museum/Corbis.*

the same time, the tsar-carpenter, as he was sometimes called, left no one in any doubt about who was in charge. Many of his interests and attitudes can be traced back to the peculiar circumstances of his childhood.

The Making of a Reformer

Born in Moscow in May 1672, Peter was raised in the mildly Westernized atmosphere of first Tsar Alexis's, then Fëdor's household. His early upbringing was similar to his father's and included games with toy soldiers and cannon, but generally Peter received indifferent tutoring. He apparently never had instruction in Polish or Latin, and his handwriting and spelling were atrocious. Peter grew up to be a doer rather than a thinker or a writer, the author of short instructions and regulations with practical aims rather than of learned treatises. His practical side was developed further by informal contacts with foreigner experts in Moscow's German Quarter. Experienced soldiers such as the Scot Patrick Gordon (1635–1699) and the Swiss Franz Lefort (ca. 1655–1699) became close friends and advisers. Both had come to Russia during his father's reign. One thing is certain: in his own future reforms Peter would build on foundations laid by his predecessors, even if he articulated and implemented his Westernizing program much more explicitly and forcefully than they had.

During the musketeers' rampage of May 1682 Peter witnessed several brutal murders and the frenzy of a mob out of control. Even though the rioters' fury was not directed at Peter himself, but at "traitors," the experience must have been psychologically damaging. This musketeer revolt and subsequent demonstrations of popular resistance inculcated in Peter a basically pessimistic notion of human nature. He concluded that barbarism can only be overcome by barbarism, to allow the rule of reason to flourish for the common good.

Kept out of the public eye by his half-sister Sofia, who was happy that Peter's handicapped co-ruler Tsar Ivan (r. 1682–1696) performed most of the ceremonial duties, during the 1680s Peter had time and space to develop personal interests. The official history of the Russian fleet began when he discovered a dilapidated English sailing boat in a shed and had a Dutch shipwright repair it. This small boat became known as the "grandfather" of the future Russian fleet. For Peter sailing and equipping ships and deploying them in a fleet was to serve as a model for running an orderly state and a metaphor for humankind's ability to subdue the elements. He also began to sign up young nobles and others to play military games in two "play" regiments, which later became the elite Preobrazhensky and Semenovsky guards. Several of Peter's companions from this time became his close friends and major figures in his regime, most notably Alexander Menshikov (1673–1729), a commoner whose father was said to be a pie seller. (See the chapter "Peter the Great: Carving Out the New Russia, 1703–1725.)"

The trainee Russian guardsmen were forced to serve in the lower ranks or as noncommissioned officers under foreign commanders, to emphasize that only the fully qualified could aspire to high office. During training Peter himself assumed the identity of an ordinary bombardier, while royal ceremonial functions were performed by a mock tsar known as Prince Caesar, the boyar Fëdor Romodanovsky (ca. 1640–1717), whom Peter addressed in letters as "Sire." By forcing someone else to take on the ceremonial role of tsar (especially after his brother Ivan died in 1696), Peter seemed to emphasize that his own authentic right to the royal throne required none of the usual trappings of kingship. Peter played out this and other roles for the rest of his life, thus adding to the sense of disorientation that many Russians experienced during his "transforming" reign.

The Grand Embassy

In 1695 Peter reopened hostilities against the Turks in an attack on the fort of Azov at the mouth of the Don River. The campaign was a failure, partly because the Turks were able to replenish their supplies from the sea. Peter therefore ordered the construction of galleys at Voronezh on the Don, forcing leading churchmen and merchants to supply the cash and peasant laborers to hack boats from green wood. In 1696 Russian troops accompanied by Austrian engineers again laid siege to Azov, which surrendered in July after Peter's new flotilla took to the sea and cut off the Turks' access to reinforcements.

This victory encouraged Peter to try to revive the Holy League, which had been inactive since the early 1690s. In March 1697 he set off on a tour to seek financial and military aid for further campaigns against the Turks, visiting the Baltic states, Prussia, the Netherlands, England, Austria, Saxony, and Poland. This so-called Grand Embassy was also a personal voyage of discovery for Peter, whose seal bore the inscription: "I am a student and I require teachers." That a Muscovite monarch should come to the West to be educated was regarded as remarkable.

Equally remarkable to foreign observers was the fact that Peter traveled incognito as "Peter Mikhailov," one of thirty-five young Russians bound for the Dutch Republic to study shipbuilding. Peter's disguise has usually been attributed to his loathing of diplomatic protocol and his desire to retain the freedom to work and observe, but, as we have seen, role-playing was already well established as an element in his style of rulership. Few people were fooled by tall "Mikhailov," and the disguise even got him into trouble. Visiting Riga in Swedish Livonia in March 1697, "Mikhailov" tried to sketch a plan of the fortifications, thus arousing the suspicions of the town's governor, who ordered sentries to move him along. Peter left in a rage. The "insult" at Riga later served as a pretext for declaring war on Sweden, although for the time being relations remained officially cordial. In December 1697 Peter congratulated sixteen-year-old King Charles XII (r. 1697–1718) on his accession to the Swedish throne.

In Amsterdam in the Dutch Republic the East India Company agreed to admit "the distinguished personage living incognito," together with ten of his companions, to work in its shipyards. There Peter met the Dutch ruler William of Orange (1650–1702), since 1689 also king of England, and attended naval regattas and fireworks displays and inspected windmills, gardens, and collections of curiosities and rarities. He took away the impression of a well-ordered state, with clean, well-planned towns, thriving commerce and crafts, and a people in control of their environment.

In January 1698 Peter sailed to England, where he stayed for more than three months, hoping to learn more about designing ships. Peter appreciated Britain first and foremost as a seafaring nation. In the words of a British engineer: "He thinks it a much happier Life to be an Admiral in England, than Czar in Russia." In addition to working in the Royal Naval Dockyards at Deptford, where he and his friends memorably vandalized the house and garden where they stayed, he sailed on the Thames and reviewed the fleet. He met many people, from merchants to mathematicians, and visited such major sights as the Royal Observatory and the Tower of London. Peter also visited Parliament. But he was adamant that "English freedom is not appropriate in Russia. . . . You have to know your people to know how to govern them." Later in 1698 he traveled to Vienna in Austria, where reports reached him that the musketeers had mutinied again. He decided to cancel the next stage of his journey, to Venice, renowned for its galley fleet, and returned to Moscow.

The Grand Embassy did not revive the Holy League, which was on the verge of making peace with the Ottomans, but it was crucial for crystallizing Peter's image of west Europeans. On the day after his return to Moscow in August 1698, with visions of clean-shaven men in Western garments fresh in his mind, Peter amazed and horrified the boyars who flocked to greet him by cutting off the beards of selected victims with his own hands. At the start of 1700 Peter imposed the Western custom of starting the year on January 1 instead of September 1 and numbering years from the birth of Jesus Christ rather then the notional beginning of the world. In both instances, Peter was offending religious sentiments, for, as a foreign observer wrote, "the holy Men of old had worn their Beards according to the Model of the Picture of their Saints" and traditionalists believed that God created the world in autumn. Other decrees forced townspeople to wear Western dress. Peter even dispatched his "old-fashioned" wife, the Russian noblewoman Evdokia Lopukhina (1669–1731), whom he had married in January 1689, to a convent and considered himself divorced from her. So as the new century dawned, Peter embarked on a campaign against tradition, which he waged just as energetically as he waged war.

THE GREAT NORTHERN WAR, 1700–1721

On August 18, 1700, Peter celebrated the signing of a thirty-year truce with the Ottomans, and the following day he declared war on Sweden on the grounds of the Swedish crown's failure to give satisfaction for the "insult" at Riga and its "illegal" occupation of the Baltic provinces of Ingria and Karelia, "which belonged to our ancestors for many centuries." In 1699 Russia had formally joined anti-Swedish coalitions with Denmark and with Augustus II (1670–1733), elector of Saxony and king of Poland (r. 1697–1704, 1709–1733), who hoped to take Livonia. Peter was encouraged by the accession of Charles XII, a mere boy, to the Swedish throne and by the aspirations of nobles in Livonia to break free of Swedish rule. The time seemed ripe for Russia to reestablish a foothold on the Baltic. It would take twenty-one years for this aim to be accomplished and ratified in what came to be known as the Great Northern War.

War with Sweden Begins

At first it seemed that Peter had miscalculated. His Danish allies were quickly knocked out of the war, and in November 1700 Charles XII, who turned out to be a precocious and talented military commander, defeated the Russians at the Baltic port of Narva. Thousands of Russian troops, already in bad shape after a month-long siege, were killed or captured. Luckily for Peter, he did not have to meet Charles's main army in pitched battle before he had raised more troops and replaced lost guns. The ease of the Swedish victory at Narva may have persuaded Charles that Russia was finished and influenced him to move against King Augustus, whom he defeated first in Poland, then in Saxony. The outbreak of the long anticipated War of the Spanish Succession (1701–1714), which involved Austria, Britain, the Netherlands, Portugal, and Denmark against France, Spain, and Bavaria, lessened the likelihood of intervention by other powers. Russian troops advanced against poorly defended Swedish-held towns in the Baltic area and in the fall of 1702 captured the fortress of Nöteborg (Schlüsselburg) on Lake Ladoga.

In May 1703 the Russians captured a Swedish fort on the Neva River, creating the site for Peter's future capital city, St. Petersburg, named for the tsar's patron saint. At about this time Peter met his future wife, Martha Skavronskaya (ca. 1684–1727), a Livonian peasant who later took the name Catherine. (See the chapter "Peter the Great: Carving Out the New Russia, 1703–1725.") Russian successes in the Baltic continued, but King Augustus was deposed by Charles in 1704, formally renounced the Polish crown, and broke his alliance with Russia, while the Swedes installed their own candidate, Stanislaw Leszczynski (r. 1704–1709, 1733–1736), on the Polish throne. At the end of 1707 Peter learned that a Swedish army forty-five thousand strong was marching through Poland toward the Russian border.

Just as he prepared to meet the Swedes, Peter had to tackle a major revolt led by the Don Cossack Kondraty Bulavin (ca. 1660–1708). Trouble flared up in the fall of 1707, when Bulavin's men massacred Russian troops sent to implement an edict on the return to their owners of runaway serfs and other deserters living on the Don. This new clash between the encroaching center, anxious to mobilize its resources, and the periphery, desperate to maintain its liberties, recalled the Razin revolt of 1670–1671. In addition, Cossacks were alarmed by rumors that the authorities intended to cut off their beards, a special affront to Cossack dignity. Bulavin escaped from the fresh troops sent by Peter to capture him and issued a declaration that "we cannot be silent about the evil deeds of wicked men . . . cannot forgive them for diverting people away from the true Christian faith with their signs and cunning tricks." He made common cause with shipyard workers, with the Kalmyk and Tatar nomads of the region, and with peasants and Old Believers, thereby provoking separate outbreaks of protest all over the Don area and beyond. It took more than thirty thousand government troops to "quench the fire of rebellion" and dispose of Bulavin, who was killed in July 1708.

Peter anticipated that Charles would head for Moscow or even St. Petersburg, where a city was being constructed. (See the chapter "Peter the Great: Carving Out the New Russia, 1703–1725.") But in mid September 1708 the main Swedish army turned south toward Ukraine, which Charles believed to be a rich country "flowing with milk and honey" where he could obtain urgently needed supplies. To this end Charles had made a secret agreement with Ivan Mazepa (1644–1709), hetman since 1687 of Left Bank Ukraine. But in November Peter's right-hand man, Alexander Menshikov, now a general, learned of the deal and stormed Mazepa's headquarters, killing, according to one estimate, some six thousand persons "without distinction of age or sex." Mazepa, who escaped to join Charles and died in exile the following year, was denounced as a "new Judas" and excommunicated from the Orthodox Church. Mazepa, however, did not regard himself as Peter's subject, believing that the tsar had reneged on his duties toward Ukraine. He remains a controversial figure in modern-day Ukraine and has inspired many works of art, literature, and music.

Russia at War (1700–1725). Atlas of Russian History *by Martin Gilbert (New Edition published by Routledge in 2002) 0415281199 PB & 0415281180 HB. Please visit our website for further details on the new edition: www.taylorandfrancis.com.*

Victory at Poltava

The winter of 1708–1709 was one of the most severe in living memory in eastern Europe. Hundreds of Swedish soldiers on campaign froze to death, and survivors were exhausted after several years on the move in alien terrain. Charles tried but failed to enlist the support of the Crimean khan. When auxiliaries and supplies from the north and aid from the Zaporozhian Cossacks also failed to materialize, the Swedes holed up near the small Ukrainian town of Poltava, where the Russians struck on June 27, 1709, with numerically superior forces. For the first time Peter found himself in command of troops in a major pitched battle with the enemy's main force. Charles, immobilized by a wounded foot, decided not to deploy his artillery, anticipating a quick breakthrough with cavalry, only to witness guns from the Russian camp laying his men low, "as grass before a scythe." The tattered remnants of the Swedish army, hitherto thought invincible, surrendered to Menshikov. Charles escaped into Turkish territory. Ultimately, vast distances, harsh climate, sparse population, poor villages, and a social structure based on serfdom that allowed unlimited recruitment were the formidable weapons that destroyed Charles's army.

Many foreign observers viewed the Russian victory at Poltava with foreboding. The German philosopher Gottfried Leibniz (1646–1716) wrote to the Russian en-

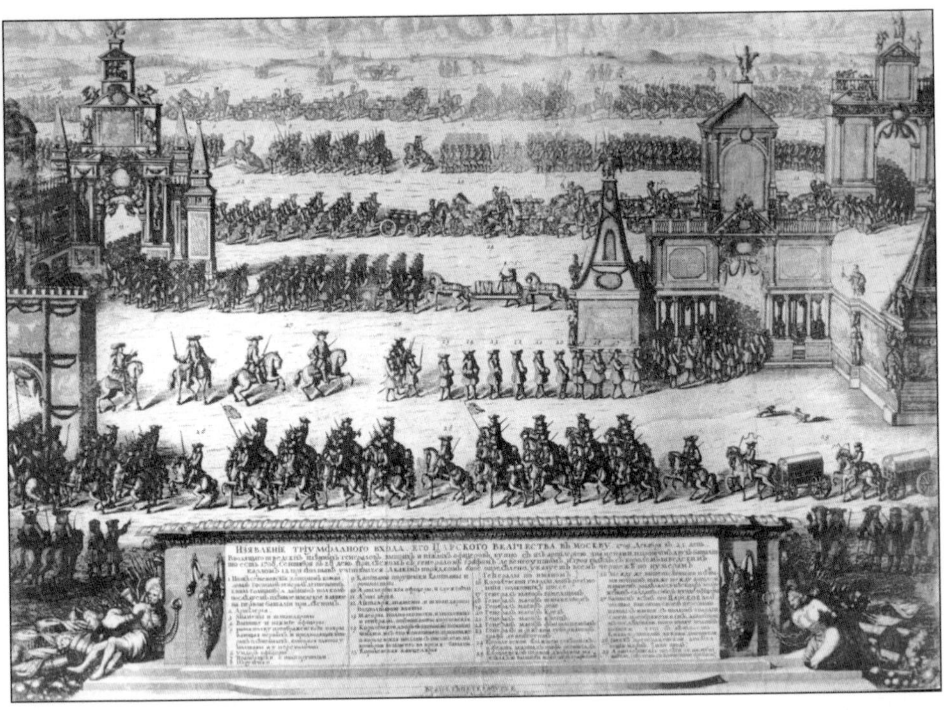

Engraving of the Poltava victory parade in Moscow (1709), by A. Zubov. *Courtesy of Prof. E. Mozgovaia, St. Petersburg, Russia.*

voy in Vienna: "You can imagine how the great revolution in the north has astounded people. It is being said that the tsar will be formidable to the whole of Europe, that he will be a sort of Turk of the North." In the summer and autumn of 1710 Russia made further gains along the Baltic coast, including the major ports of Riga and Reval (Tallinn). It consolidated its occupation by maintaining or restoring local privileges and laws and offering incentives for Baltic German experts of various kinds to work in Russia. The Russian authorities combined concessions with watchfulness, not hesitating to interfere in local affairs. Thus the eastern Baltic region fell under Russian control and would remain so until 1918.

Defeat on the Pruth

In December 1710 Peter received the unwelcome news that the Turks had broken the truce of 1700 and declared war. Ottoman Turkish and Crimean affairs were important factors throughout the Great Northern War. The Turks stopped short of intervention at the time of Poltava, but now Charles's escape to their territory and his efforts to get the Turks to attack Russia tipped the scales. The anti-Russian Crimean khan offered Tatar troops to escort Charles back north and succeeded in winning the sultan's ear. Peter made routine peace proposals to the Swedes, in the hope of avoiding war on two fronts, but Charles refused to relinquish even one province to buy a "shameful peace."

Russia's subsequent campaign against the Ottomans was a near disaster. Attempts to inject a crusading element foundered when the Christian rulers of Ottoman-ruled Moldavia and Wallachia failed to give promised support and the Russian army under Peter's command ran short of supplies. In July 1711, thirty-eight thousand Russian troops faced a Turkish-Tatar force of a hundred and thirty thousand men on the Pruth River in Moldavia. The battle was inconclusive, but the Russians lacked the resources to fight on. Only the moderateness of Turkish demands averted a catastrophe.

Peter agreed to surrender Azov and its district to Turkey, to destroy his southern fleet and raze forts on the lower Dnieper. Peter was devastated by the loss of Azov, which he had planned to develop as a major port, and his slowness in evacuating it provoked further declarations of war by the Turks. A settlement was reached only in June 1713 in the Treaty of Adrianople, few clauses of which had any lasting effect, however. The Russo-Turkish border remained fluid; and Cossacks and Tatars paid little heed to agreements between the tsar in St. Petersburg and the sultan in Constantinople. But peace allowed Peter once again to concentrate his efforts in the north.

Peace at Nystad

In the 1710s the Great Northern War became bogged down in continental politics, which centered on Prussian and Danish claims to Sweden's remaining territories along the German Baltic coast. In 1714 the War of the Spanish Succession ended, allowing France, Sweden's traditional ally, and Britain, which feared Russia's growing naval power, more leisure to interfere in northern affairs. Peter became further involved in Europe by engaging in the politics of dynastic marriage. In 1710 he married his niece Anna to the duke of Courland, whose strategically useful territory on the Baltic had been under Polish protection. The duke died from alcoholic poisoning shortly after the wedding, but Anna stayed on in Courland. In 1711 Peter's eldest son by his first marriage, Alexis (1690–1718), wed the German princess Charlotte of Wolfenbüttel, who was related to the king of Prussia and the emperor of Austria, and in 1716 his niece Ekaterina married the duke of Mecklenburg, another German Baltic link that extended Russia's commercial and strategic influence. In 1724 Peter betrothed his daughter Anna (b. 1708) to the duke of Holstein, a claimant to the Swedish throne. These marriages laid the foundations for Russia's close dynastic links with European Protestant courts for the next two centuries.

In 1713 the Russians launched a campaign in Swedish-ruled Finland, in the first year taking Helsingfors (Helsinki) and Abo (Turku) and in 1714 winning a naval battle against the Swedes off Cape Hangö. Still the war dragged on. In February 1716 Peter set off on another major tour of western Europe, which took him back to the Netherlands and to Denmark (allied to Russia again since 1710) and, in summer 1717, to France, with which Peter unsuccessfully sought a friendship treaty. The highlight of the French visit was a stay in Paris, the fashion capital of Europe, where Peter toured the major sights. The king's magnificent out-of-town palace at Versailles made an especially deep impression on Peter and influenced some of his own building projects.

In December 1718 Charles XII was killed by a stray bullet while on campaign in Norway. His successors continued the war. In 1719–1720 Russia scored several victories at sea and bombarded the Swedish coast, which prompted the British, fearful of further disruption to the trade in naval supplies, to send a token naval force into the Baltic to curb Russian operations. But Britain's attempts to form an anti-Russian coalition failed, and it withdrew its squadron. A peace treaty was finally signed at Nystad in Finland on August 30, 1721. Twenty-four clauses established "eternal peace" on land and sea. Sweden ceded Livonia, Estonia, Ingria, and part of Karelia to Russia, and Russia agreed to evacuate Finland and to pay Sweden cash compensation.

Compared with the conquests of Ivan the Terrible or later in the century under Catherine II, Peter's territorial acquisitions were modest in size, but of enormous significance. In 1721 Peter accepted the title of emperor. Russia, already a multinational empire in fact, became an empire in name also. Peter's reign consolidated or initiated policies that were to bring Russia into conflict with powers beyond its own borders and gave birth to the image of the aggressive Russian "bear." In beating Sweden, Russia also gained further ascendancy over Poland-Lithuania, which was exhausted by decades of war in its territories and divided by internal disputes about war aims. In contrast, Russia's heartland was barely touched by enemy troops and Peter retained the support, if not always the enthusiasm, of the Russian elite. Livonia, which was to have been Poland's prize, went to Russia, which thereby gained a valuable strategic and economic asset. Courland, previously within Poland's sphere of influence, came under Russian protection. Having restored a grateful Augustus to the Polish throne after Poltava in 1709, Russia retained a major voice in the election of subsequent kings of Poland and the right to send troops into Poland if events there seemed to threaten Russia's security.

Russia's new world role was summed up in a paper by one of the officials of King George I of England: "Germany and the entire North have never been in such grave peril as now, because the Russians should be feared more than the Turks . . . and are gradually advancing closer and closer to our lives." Peter never formulated any plans for world domination and remained convinced that the northern territories that he conquered were all Russian and therefore his by right. But he set a tough agenda for his successors, who were obliged to maintain Russia's expanded land and sea forces and to keep a high profile in foreign affairs if Russia was not to revert to being a second- or third-rate power.

SOLDIERS AND SAILORS OF THE TSAR

War rather than domestic needs shaped the course of Peter's reign, determining the order, pace, and methods of reform. Indeed, Peter regarded military order as a model for his other reforms. A passage in the Spiritual Regulation of 1721 (see the chapter "Peter the Great: Carving Out the New Russia, 1703–1725") reads: "It is known to all the world how inadequate and weak was the Russian army when it did not have proper training and how incomparably its numbers increased and how it became great and formidable beyond expectation when Our Most Powerful Monarch, His Tsarist Majesty, Peter I, instructed it with most excellent regulations." Despite the obvious importance of Peter's personal input, debate continues about the nature of his military reforms and the extent to which they broke with the past.

"The Sovereign's Land and Sea Forces"

The troops Peter inherited from seventeenth-century Muscovy have sometimes been dismissed as poorly equipped, virtually untrained, and ill-disciplined, an "Asiatic" horde or "uncouth mob." In this view Peter so transformed the military that when he died in 1725 the empire could deploy some two hundred thousand men, efficiently armed and provisioned and commanded by officers trained in the contemporary Western manner. The balance had shifted emphatically from old-fashioned cavalry to modern infantry. Land forces had naval support. Army administration was centralized. A new military ethos had developed, inspired by Peter himself.

In fact, as we have seen, the shift to regular infantry and dragoon regiments and the employment of foreign officers was well under way by the mid seventeenth century. The numbers that Peter managed to mobilize at any one time were not exceptional—Ivan IV could muster one hundred fifty thousand men against Kazan—although the period during which Peter's men were under arms was unusually protracted. It took ingenuity to obtain the thousands of new recruits needed each year to fill the gaps created as much by disease and desertion as by battle casualties. Appeals for volunteers were supplemented by conscription drives. In 1705 there was an attempt to systematize call-up, enlisting men between the ages of fifteen and twenty on the basis of taking one recruit from every twenty peasant households, but this rule was not uniformly applied. Nontraditional recruits were also signed up, for example, selected sons of secretaries in the Moscow chancelleries, "excess" clerks and scribes, and some sons of priests and deacons. In creating his army Peter combined old methods of mass recruitment with novel elements.

Training these men was bound to be inadequate because the time between call-up and deployment was short. Recent studies have questioned whether proficiency was universal in Peter's army, indeed, whether Peter succeeded in creating a regular Russian army at all. The guards regiments, the new army's elite core, were the exception. Marksmanship among the rank and file must have been poor, but this did not prove crucial: the Russian army experienced relatively few set-piece battles requiring precision volleys, and infantry maneuvers in linear formation were the exception, not the rule. Officers and technical specialists received better training, combined with attempts to provide a general education for young nobles, sometimes abroad. The literate received rules of conduct and command in military manuals and instructions. In 1705 General George Ogilvie, one of many British officers in Peter's army, complained of "general disobedience and absence of any discipline" among the troops under his command. He admired the guards but was less enthusiastic about the newer infantry.

Peter aimed to end dependency on foreigners. If initially modern muskets and flintlocks were imported, by the 1710s home industries supplied most guns, as well as bayonets, grenades, powder, bullets, and shells. The artillery was much improved, using Russian-produced siege guns and field artillery. General Ogilvie "never saw any Nation go better to work with their cannon and mortars." But the role of modern firearms should not be exaggerated. The Russian army continued to use pikes and swords suitable for steppe warfare, as well as spades and axes.

One of the most visible marks of Peter's army was the use of color-coordinated uniforms, the style and cut of which followed the Western fashion—knee breeches, shirt, vest, and cloth tunic worn with a three-cornered hat. Fitting out annual contingents of new recruits required bulk orders on a grand scale, wherever possible from Russian cloth. Logistical factors were as crucial as tactical ones. The time and effort spent in actual combat were minimal compared with that expended on moving around, feeding, and quartering troops. In Russian conditions, army self-sufficiency was not a virtue but a necessity; there was no other way of supplying armies in regions with few towns and little surplus food for sale or requisition.

Peter rarely composed ideological statements. The clearest written expression of the ethos of the Petrine armed services appeared in the *Military Statute* of 1716, based on Swedish and Austrian codes. The first two chapters underline the religious basis of military success: soldiers must respect and heed God in the service of their sovereign. Although Peter was not keen on parade drill, he expected obedience to rules and regulations and strict adherence to hierarchy at all levels. In the oath of allegiance men pledged to be "honorable, loyal, obedient, brave and determined." The supreme military commander was, of course, the tsar himself, who had a personal hand in virtually every aspect of military organization, including direct command. In 1718 most military departments were subsumed in the College of War (see next section), the first president of which was Alexander Menshikov.

Peter's army was the product of trial and error, adaptation and resourcefulness. Georg Grund, a Danish commercial agent who lived in Russia for several years, was impressed that Peter managed to replenish his armies, "in spite of the fact that in Russia they have not yet learnt to value a man, but often treat him worse than a horse." He found the simple soldier "capable of accomplishing the longest marches, whatever is demanded of him." A huge army could be maintained precisely because Russia did not "value a man." Autocracy and serfdom were the keys.

In the 1700s Peter began to build a fleet on the Baltic, based at the island base of Kronstadt in the Finnish gulf just to the west of St. Petersburg. Ships were built at home or purchased abroad, often through British agents, hence names like *Britannia, London,* and *Devonshire*. By 1725 the Baltic fleet consisted of 36 warships, 16 frigates, 70 galleys, and 280 other vessels, supported by a complex of shipyards, ports and wharves, rope and canvas factories, metalworks, and training establishments under the supervision of the Admiralty.

Peter adored ships, devoting much time to studying every aspect of navigation and construction, but few Russians shared his enthusiasm and the new navy was manned overwhelmingly by foreign commanders. "The Russian nation has little inclination for naval affairs but rather regards it all as an unnecessary expense," wrote one foreign observer. Some historians, too, have used the fleet to demonstrate the "wastefulness" of Peter's reforms in general, arguing that its military usefulness did not justify the time and expense invested in it. The very existence of the fleet may have tempted Peter to overreach himself, it is argued, to extend and maintain an empire that could only survive by condemning the mass of the Russian population to servitude and high taxation. The counterargument is that the fleet made a valuable contribution to the war against Sweden, particularly in the latter stages when it supported raids on the Swedish mainland. It was a vital bargaining counter in negotiations. That it fell into disuse after Peter's death was attributed to his successors' restricted vision and lack of personal commitment, rather than any failing on Peter's part.

The Table of Ranks

A major outcome of the protracted war was the systematization of military and naval commands. From the 1690s on, the old Muscovite ranks were increasingly superseded by new ones based on foreign originals, which clearly differentiated military, civil, and court posts. Edicts made plain that even nobles must earn their promotions. Toward the end of the war, Peter proceeded to impose a rational framework on a jumble of terms and measures governing rank, consulting Prussian and Swedish statutes and other foreign ranking systems. The Table of Ranks, issued on January 24, 1722, divided the services into three columns: military, civil, and

TABLE 1 **Peter the Great's Table of Ranks**
24 January, 1722

Military		**Civil Service**
Navy	**Army**	
I. Admiral General	Field Marshal	Chancellor
II. Admiral	Artillery General Cavalry General Infantry General	Right Privy Councilor
III. Vice-Admiral	Lieutenant General	Privy Councilor
IV. Rear Admiral	Major General	Active State Councilor
V. Captain Commodore	Brigadier	State Councilor
VI. First Captain	Colonel	College Councilor
VII. Second Captain	Lieutenant Colonel	Court Councilor
VIII. Lieutenant Captain of Fleet, Third Captain of Artillery	Major	College Assessor
IX. Lieutenant of the Fleet	Captain or Calvary Captain	Titular Councilor
X. Lieutenant Captain of Artillery	Staff Captain or Staff Calvary Captain	College Secretary
XI. Purser		Secretary of the Senate
XII. Midshipman	Lieutenant	Provincial Secretary
XIII. Artillery Constable	Sublieutenant	Registrar of Senate
XIV.	Ensign	College Registrar

This is a simplified table. There was an additional list for courtiers and many different posts within each of the fourteen grades, especially in the civil service. The Table was modified many times over the next two centuries.

court, accompanied by nineteen explanatory points. The layout (see table 1) made plain that one of the purposes of the Table was to correlate status and identify seniority across the different branches of the services. Its very design satisfied Peter's passion for orderly, regulated legislation.

The provisions of the Table of Ranks applied only to the service elite—army and navy officers, government and court officials. No post was supposed to be allocated to any candidate who was unqualified for the duties involved, however illustrious his origins. Even nobles of ancient lineage would not be awarded any rank until they had served the emperor and their country. No one could inherit or buy a grade or post and people demanding deference or a post higher than their position in the Table were punished. Elite women's place in society depended on the ranks of their fathers or their husbands. They could not enter the military or civil service themselves, although a few noblewomen served at court as ladies in waiting, who had their own ranking system.

Birth and marriage into the elite continued to confer privilege, however. There was "free access" at court to sons of princes, counts, barons, and the aristocracy "before others of lowly office." The Table of Ranks did not promote such modern concepts as equality of opportunity. It was intended to encourage the existing nobility to perform more efficiently than hitherto, and it endorsed the concept of nobles as natural leaders of society by granting noble status to any commoner who attained military grade 14 or civil grade 8, including the right to pass his nobility to his children, daughters included. As a contemporary observed, "What [Peter] had in mind was not the abasement of the noble estate. On the contrary, it all tended toward instilling in the nobility a desire to distinguish themselves from common folk by merit as well as by birth." The Table of Ranks would remain a cornerstone of Russia's social hierarchy until the fall of tsarism in 1917.

GOVERNING RUSSIA

In the seventeenth century persons more than institutions provide the key to how Russia was ruled. This was true also of Peter's Russia, where kinship networks and clan politics continued to be influential and the tsar's favor could make or break a man, despite the creation of rational systems such as the Table of Ranks. Even so, Peter himself enjoyed inventing institutions and was attracted to modern theories of state building, notably that the "common good" could be served best by a state mechanism created and run along rational lines, like a machine. To this end he phased out the Boyar Duma and the old Muscovite system of overlapping chancelleries, replacing them with bodies based wholly or partly on foreign models. An interlocking system of central government emerged, but finding a framework for governing the provinces proved troublesome.

Senate and Colleges

In February 1711 Peter created the Senate as the highest organ of state, in response to the impending conflict with Turkey "for reason of our continual absences in these wars." Peter expected much of his ten new senators, who were asked to perform a multiplicity of tasks, including acting as judges, raising revenues, recruiting officers, and promoting trade. Of the first senators, at least one was probably illiterate, and two were punished in 1714 for corruption. Peter constantly chided them for procrastination, laziness, and generally for acting "in the old stupid manner," although by the end of his reign the institution was working fairly efficiently and issuing its own edicts. It would survive to 1917.

In December 1717 Peter announced the establishment of new government departments known as Colleges (*kollegii*), based on the Swedish system. The dozens of old Muscovite offices with overlapping functions and regional designations, many of which had already disappeared or been renamed, were consolidated under the centralized Colleges of Foreign Affairs, War, Admiralty, State Revenues, State Expenses, State Accounting, Justice, Commerce, and Mines and Manufacture. The principle behind the Colleges was that decisions were reached by a collegiate board of voting members: a president and vice president and eight or nine councilors and assessors. Professional officials supported the boards and in turn were serviced by a team of lower-level clerical and domestic assistants. This system survived until the early nineteenth century.

In 1718 the presidents of the Colleges joined the Senate. But Peter still felt the need for someone to "guard the guardians." In April 1722 he formulated the duties of a procurator-general to act as the "tsar's eye," ensuring that the Senate did its duty "truthfully, diligently and correctly, without wasting time and in accordance with the regulations and edicts." The first procurator-general, Pavel Yaguzhinsky (1683-1736), the son of an organist in the Lutheran Church in Moscow, had served in the guards and was a personal favorite of Peter's. In 1724 the procurator-general's oversight was extended to Colleges, where underprocurators were also appointed. Everybody was watching or being watched by someone.

The nuts and bolts of the new central system, from the hierarchy of the officials to the names of the Colleges, were mainly borrowed from Sweden, but Peter warned against slavish imitation. A systematic explanation of the functions and duties of College staff was set out in a General Regulation of 1720. One of the principles behind the new institutions was the notion that the system should work without any need for the intervention of its inventor. An edict of 1718 reminded petitioners how many there were of them, "whereas it is one person [the tsar] they petition, and he is surrounded by so much military business and other burdensome work, . . . how would it be possible for one man to look after so many?"

In fact, Peter himself did too little to shift responsibilities onto institutions. The proportion of legislation issued as the tsar's personal decree, sometimes handwritten, increased rather than diminished. Much business was handled by Peter's private secretariat, the Cabinet, which was run with rule-book efficiency by his personal assistant Aleksei Makarov (1674/5?–1750), who came from a family of chancellery clerks. The Cabinet also supervised such business as Russians studying abroad and the royal aviaries and menagerie, dealt with Peter's petty expenditures, and kept his appointment diaries and records.

Policing the Provinces

If central government at least corresponded on paper to the well-oiled machine of Peter's dreams, provincial government was his nightmare. In Muscovy the tsars' main representatives in the provinces were the military governors (*voevody*), whose central tasks were army recruitment and collecting direct taxes. To the ambitious, a governorship offered rich pickings. The government mistrusted the system, as numerous investigations of abuses indicate, but failed to pay proper salaries and was too far off to exercise much control. Taxes disappearing into local officials' pockets not only put a strain on the local population but also depleted government revenues.

In 1699 Peter attempted to replace governors by a new collective body called the Chamber of Burgomasters, with officials elected by local taxpayers to collect duties and taxes. The advance of Charles XII's army prompted a more radical provincial reform. A decree of December 1708 announced the formation of eight provinces (*gubernii*), each to be administered by a powerful governor (*gubernator*), who would take over the functions of the burgomasters and other local officials, especially with reference to revenues and accounts. The new provinces were to support designated military units. Posts with German-sounding titles were created to support the governors. In 1712–1715 new provincial subunits and new categories of provincial councilors were introduced, followed by yet another attempt at reorganization in 1718–1719 and yet more designations of officials.

Many of these new posts were never filled and were abolished after Peter's death, although the idea of dividing Russia into *gubernii* was retained. By and large, the provinces were undergoverned rather than overgoverned, with too few rather than too many officials to cope with the work. The average provincial nobleman had little desire to deal with paperwork and procedures, which were associated with low status. In 1714 a Law of Single Inheritance forced landowners to leave their estates to just one heir instead of dividing them among all their children as had been the custom. The aim was to avoid "wasteful" division of land and to encourage those who did not inherit to devote themselves to service. But attempts to force nobles into provincial government met with little success. In fact, in the provinces nobles already had much of the law in their own hands, for landowners had legal jurisdiction over their serfs and often disregarded laws on property and inheritance.

In 1721 Peter created the Chief Magistracy to "facilitate laws and justice and nurture good order and morality" in towns and to increase commerce and manufacture. Magistrates were appointed and registered urban dwellers were assigned to two guilds. Still, outside Moscow and St. Petersburg urban life remained underdeveloped, and most towns were not much more than villages, with agriculture constituting by far the major occupation. As for peasants, for most purposes their communes governed them. Peasant life was unregulated from above by the state, in sharp contrast to the plethora of Peter's rules and regulations applying to nobles and increasingly to town dwellers. The bulk of state legislation affecting peasants had to do with counting them, taxing them, recruiting them, and recovering them if they ran away. There was little attempt to meddle in their dress, customs, or lifestyle. Betrothals, weddings, and funerals combined Orthodox ritual with folk customs, often with regional variations. Peasant dress, produced for the most part by peasant women, was not required to follow Western fashions. Peasants were required to shave their beards only if they went to town, where most never ventured. As the saying went, the tsar was far off.

Law and Order

A 1722 decree declared: "The sovereign is concerned for his subjects to ensure that each [court] case will always receive fair and swift judgement and that cases are resolved as His Majesty's edicts command, justly and in the stipulated time and that no-one should be oppressed by unfair judges and red tape." Above the right of individuals to get justice, however, the sovereign was concerned with good order, which he believed proceeded from good statutes. Law must be unambiguous and there must be plenty of it, for wickedness was all-pervasive, and some people would always try to undermine the "fortress" of the law. Peter's reign is remarkable not only for the sheer number of edicts issued, far exceeding anything in Muscovite Russia, but also for the quest for "superlaws" to bring about general happiness.

Peter was concerned, too, that those who administered the laws should be honest and just, but attempts to separate the judicial powers from the administrative on the model of Swedish courts failed. Likewise, a program to recodify the laws dragged on for years to little effect. The Law Code of 1649 remained the only printed lawbook, although for certain criminal offenses the 1716 *Military Statute* became the authority. There was some reform of the courts system, for example, to reduce the chaotic number of jurisdictions by concentrating criminal and civil cases in the Justice College (1717), which incorporated all departments with judicial functions except for the Estates College (1721), which handled landed property, and the Preobrazhensky Office. The latter originated in the headquarters of Peter's own guard's regiment and dealt with treason cases. In 1718–1719 Peter set up new courts at various levels in the provinces, "in order that true justice and protection be available for every person." They were quickly subverted by local officials and later closed.

A decree of 1722 tried to reduce the routine use of torture for obtaining evidence, "because even in minor cases torture is used and on people who are only suspected." At the same time, penalties remained harsh. For failing to keep clean the area in front of their houses, for example, homeowners were sentenced to beating with canes; for a second offense, beating plus a five-ruble fine; and for a third, the knout and a ten-ruble fine. Cutting down an oak of any size whatsoever was punishable by death, for hardwood suitable for shipbuilding was scarce. Permutations of punishment by flogging, mutilation, and hard labor were used for many offenses. For treason and rebellion, cruel capital punishment was employed, including breaking on the wheel, quartering, and impalement. Cases are recorded of condemned men being supplied with fur coats in winter to keep them alive and suffering for as long as possible while sentence was being carried out.

Despite the harsh penalties, a state of near lawlessness prevailed in many provincial towns, where the strong continued to exploit the weak with impunity, "like wolves attacking sheep." The peasant entrepreneur Ivan Pososhkov (1652–1726) summed it up: "Whatever laws His Imperial Majesty promulgates are all set at naught and everyone continues in the bad old ways. Until the rule of law is established in Russia and firmly and universally takes root among us measures applied to remedy abuses as in other countries will have no effect."

Ultimately, all roads led back to the sovereign. Any decree issued by him had the force of law. As the *Military Statute* stated, he was "not answerable to anyone in the world in his affairs, but holds the power and authority to rule his realms and his lands as a Christian monarch by his own will and good opinion." There was no question of Peter sharing his powers with representative bodies. His preferred brand of absolutism was customized for him by churchmen, such as the Ukrainian Feofan Prokopovich (1681–1736), later archbishop of Pskov, one of several leading Ukrainians who played a prominent role in promoting Peter's reforms. In his *Primer for Youths* (1720), for example, Prokopovich set out the basic principles of governmental hierarchy within a natural patriarchal order; people's first duty was to "the supreme authorities instituted by God to rule the people, of whom the highest authority is the tsar." Peter consciously played down divine associations in the way he presented himself, adopting plain dress and an informality of behavior calculated to make him seem more like an "ordinary" person than a divine emperor. At the same time, he drew parallels between himself and the emperors of ancient Rome by introducing a new Roman imperial image on coins and medals and organizing Roman-style victory parades. Byzantine motifs disappeared.

FINANCES: "THE ARTERY OF WAR"

No area of government policy was so driven by war as fiscal affairs, for, as Peter himself said on several occasions, "Money is the artery of war." Sample budget figures for 1704 indicate a division of revenues that did not change much in the course of the war. Military expenditure swallowed up 40.9 percent; the state apparatus (which included the departments of military and naval affairs), 37.6 percent; whereas education, medicine, and postal services were allocated a meager 0.5 percent. Raising sufficient revenues to meet military commitments was a major concern.

Taxing the Population

Direct taxation, based on assessment by household, produced the bulk of revenues. However, in 1710 a review of spending on the army and fleet revealed a shortfall of income against expenditure, while a census of rural and urban taxpayers indicated, contrary to expectations, an almost 20 percent decrease in population (as households) since the last survey in 1678, a figure attributed among other things to landlords concealing peasants and households joining together. At the same time, all sorts of complicated petty taxes had proliferated. These problems prompted the introduction of a poll or "soul" tax, imposed on each tax-liable male. Several censuses eventually identified some 5.5 million male souls liable to pay the tax, which was collected for the first time in 1724 at a rate of seventy-four kopecks per head per annum for serfs, with crown and state peasants paying an additional forty kopecks and urban taxpayers one ruble twenty kopecks. At these levels it was reckoned that it took forty-seven serfs to maintain one infantryman and fifty-seven to maintain one cavalryman and horse for a year; in other words, the rationale for the tax was to support the army.

Historians fail to agree on whether the poll tax increased the burden on taxpayers. A growth in revenues collected from direct taxes suggests this to be the case. Individual levies were fixed regardless of ability to work or pay, with boy babies and old men registered as taxpayers, which must have caused hardship to those who had to pay on their behalf. Still, it has also been argued that, by and large, the poll tax reduced the individual's burden, and healthier revenues were generated by more taxpayers being included on the registers. A period of harsh winters and associated famine in parts of Russia in 1721–1724 may have increased the perception of hardship.

Peter also added to a long list of existing duties on goods and services, everything from livestock, cheeses, and tubs to cups, spoons, cabbages, cucumbers, and brand marks on hats and boots. Among Peter's innovations were a stamp duty on official "eagle crest" paper for contracts and taxes on private bathhouses, graded according to the owner's status, and on oak coffins and foreign playing cards. Some taxes were symbolic rather than profitable, for example, an infamous tax on beards (1705) and fines for wearing traditional Russian clothing in towns. Liquor licenses and sales duty on tobacco and salt, however, were a lucrative source of revenue. In addition, as his father, Alexis, had done with copper coins, Peter debased the currency, but with more success. Reducing both the silver and bronze content of redesigned coins produced massive profits for the treasury.

Industry and Enterprise

It is often argued that the state played a disproportionate role in Russian economic life, acting as number one producer and number one customer, suffocating the Russian entrepreneurial class and discouraging private initiative and the accumulation of wealth by honest means. Under Peter the state sector grew to service the war effort. In St. Petersburg its enterprises included the Admiralty wharf, sawmills, and rope-making works, and artillery, sailcloth, textile, leather, and gunpowder factories. Metals represented by far the greatest achievement of Peter's industrial drive. By 1725 Russia was the major producer in Europe of iron, of which 60 percent came from newly worked mines in the Ural mountains. Peter's reign laid the foundations for Russia's future economic activity, including its infrastructure of roads and canals.

Despite the relative strength of the state sector, as judged by the standards of a preindustrial age, Peter was still eager to encourage private enterprise. The charter of the College of Mining (1719), for example, complained that the large quantities of useful metals and minerals in Russia were not being exploited because the tsar's subjects were unwilling to risk investing money and labor. But at the same time as it appealed to individuals "whatever their rank or dignity" to excavate and refine metals, the charter emphasized that such enterprise was for the good of the state. Business and industry could contribute to national "glory." Within a framework of "manufacturing the manufacturers" there were successes, notably increased numbers of applications for manufacturing charters of "privileges" in the 1720s, which entitled the holders variously to loans and subsidies, shares of lands and forest, and exemption from taxes and the army draft. Success stories included that of Nikita Demidov (1656–1725), who started out as a smith in the ironworks at Tula, established foundries in the Urals, and was ennobled in 1720. Other companies quickly folded, despite being offered such concessions as bans on exports of needed raw materials, interest-free loans, and state orders at fixed prices. The state guaranteed that it would not confiscate factories that were in "good order," but it took over failing enterprises, many of which foundered because of the problem of finding a workforce.

Workers and Peasants

State enterprises were mostly operated by so-called ascribed state peasants, who were uprooted from their home villages to live and work in factories and mines. The state also set convicted criminals and debtors to hard labor; vagrants, beggars, and "loose women" were rounded up to do unskilled work. Peter believed that free labor was more productive than the forced labor of serfs and ascribed peasants, but the Russian population's limited social mobility meant there were too few workers legally and permanently for hire to private individuals. This impeded the growth of a free factory-owning class or bourgeoisie. In 1721 Peter granted merchant entrepreneurs the right to buy serfs to staff their enterprises, but this decree did not lead to a boom in serf sales by non-nobles, perhaps because the purchase of "souls" required major capital outlay and owners often preferred to hire peasant workers during quiet periods in the agricultural year. Serf owners, especially those with less fertile agricultural land, sanctioned the latter arrangement as they could benefit from their serfs' seasonal earnings by increasing their dues. This arrangement was not ideal for the entrepreneurs, however. As one linen factory director complained: "In the winter they work, but in summer they go off to their villages to their own work and as a result there is a great stoppage in our business." The government sometimes sanctioned the use of illegal workers. Decrees of 1722–1723 stated that peasant workers with obligations elsewhere must not be sent away from factories "in order not to abandon those works and thereby stop the enterprise," but that they should pay their taxes to the state and legal owners as before. This applied also to peasant laborers working in shipbuilding.

Finding skilled men was even more of a problem. The Admiralty, for example, was forever reporting "considerable delays in shipbuilding works for a lack of carpenters and other workers." In 1719 a search was ordered in the Petrozavodsk district for three hundred literate young men to be apprenticed in weapons making, but only two "church people" and sixty peasants were found, of whom nine ran away.

Shipbuilding, industry, mining, construction, transport, and services associated with the Northern War created a bottomless pit that swallowed up countless Russians, a vast number of whom perished. Conditions were harsh, especially in the new capital, St. Petersburg, which was more or less a building site for much of Peter's reign. (See the next chapter.) Even so, workers' social welfare was not entirely neglected. The Admiralty Regulation (1722), for example, made provisions for hospital care, while admonishing supervisors to ensure "that the workers are working honestly and not just having a good time, and to beat the lazy ones with clubs."

As for agriculture, Peter paid it little attention, except in areas related to industry and equipment, as, for instance, in decrees on improving scythes by copying the implements used by Baltic peasants (1721) and on sheep rearing for wool production in Ukraine (1724). In general, peasants were left to use customary techniques, which ensured survival from one generation to the next and in good years produced a little bit extra. The internal market for Russian grain increased, as did flax and hemp production for export, but most peasants practiced subsistence farming. Peter saw no need to interfere in age-old practices that fed the population, except in crisis years. In this respect, he was of one mind with other contemporary rulers who left peasants and agriculture to take care of themselves.

Managing Backwardness

It was the war, not theories, that created the momentum of the Petrine economy, autocracy and serfdom that allowed Peter to cope with its demands. He and his advisers borrowed little directly from Western economic theories, although some historians argue that Peter was a mercantilist. Thus he aimed through protectionist policies to make Russian goods more attractive than imports and to create a favorable monetary or commercial trade balance to endow Russia with an autonomous, prosperous economy. The state established standard weights and measures, abolished tolls on roads, improved communications, and reformed the currency.

On paper Peter's financial administration looked more efficient than that of his predecessors. Seventeenth-century Muscovy had no central fiscal administration, whereas Peter dedicated three of his nine Colleges to fiscal affairs, and the Colleges of Commerce and Mines and Manufacture were concerned with promoting national wealth. In reality, however, the fundamentals of the Russian economy involved marshaling resources to fund military ventures, which boiled down to making the most of Russia's "backwardness" by applying absolute power to extract service, labor, and taxes from all parts of the population, with the bulk coming from the peasants.

Peter may have promoted industry and technology, trade and fiscal departments, but underneath was a subsistence economy that generated just enough surplus for the state to take its share without utterly ruining the population. Accounting methods were rough and ready. If the money ran out, crude emergency measures were applied. But the economy worked, insofar as it allowed Russia to be at war for nearly all of Peter's reign. We are not talking about high levels of prosperity or public services, but keeping a war economy running and the population out of the breadline, with some surplus for show projects such as the new capital, St. Petersburg. This Peter managed to achieve without borrowing money abroad or plunging the country into chaos. By and large, peasants and townspeople survived in an economy that produced marginal sufficiency. Only the elite could aspire to something more, to educational and cultural attainments and to a Westernized lifestyle, as we shall see in the next chapter.

CHAPTER 12

Peter the Great: Carving Out the New Russia, 1703–1725

"All Russia is your statue, transformed by you with skilful craftsmanship."
—Archbishop Feofan Prokopovich on Peter I, in a sermon of 1726

Writers and artists employed many metaphors for Peter's radical brand of rulership from above. One set of motifs characterized Peter as the "skipper" or "navigator" of the ship of the Russian state. Another set related to sculpting and carving. A plaque on the side of a bronze bust of Peter made by the Italian artist Carlo Rastrelli in 1723 shows the emperor as a sculptor putting the finishing touches with his chisel to a figure of a young woman clad in armor. Commentators interpreted the raw block of stone from which she emerges as barbaric Old Russia, the resultant beautiful statue, still incomplete, as New Russia, which was being created by Peter's "genius." As we shall see in this chapter, Peter tried to transform real people, too, to make them into "decent, beardless European" in the setting of his new model city, St. Petersburg, forcing them to go to school, to read books, to adopt Western manners. To assist in the task of dragging people into Peter's version of the modern world, the Orthodox Church, too, had to be reformed. This radical program of social and cultural engineering remains one of the most controversial aspects of Peter's work.

PETER'S PARADISE

Perhaps the most ambitious of all Peter's projects was the creation of the city of St. Petersburg on the Finnish Gulf. The city began modestly in 1703 as an earthwork fort on a small island in the Neva River, but it soon expanded and acquired a whole set of symbolic and mythological associations, linking it to the founding of Byzantium and the legendary travels of the apostle St. Andrew in the vicinity of Peter's new city. The notion that St. Petersburg was built on "empty" land contributed to an additional myth that Peter created his city "from nothing," although there were actually a number of Swedish settlements in the area.

Constructing St. Petersburg

Peter attached special personal significance to Sankt-Piter-burkh (its original Russian name). It was his "Paradise." After the victory at Poltava in 1709 secured Russia's position on the Baltic, he wrote to Alexander Menshikov: "If only you could be here to see the beauty of this Paradise as a reward for our joint labors, . . . for this place really is thriving, like a fine infant." In the 1710s St. Petersburg became the seat of government, although no official declaration was issued and the shift from Moscow proceeded in stages. The Senate transferred there in 1713.

In Russia's battle for international recognition, St. Petersburg was more than a naval base and port, more even than "a great window recently opened in the north through which Russia looks on Europe," as the Italian traveler Francesco Algarotti described it in 1739. It was a sort of clean sheet on which Peter could create a blueprint for his new Russia. The Western designs and decoration of the buildings, the foreign-sounding names of institutions, the European fashions that inhabitants

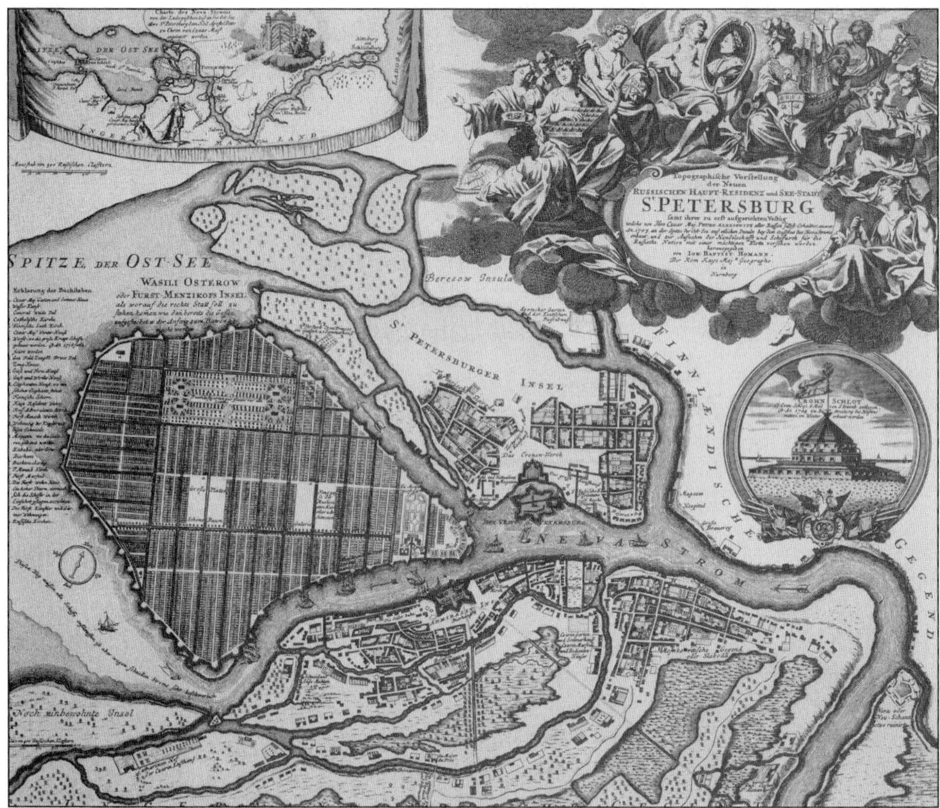

Plan of St. Petersburg from the Atlas of Johann Baptiste Homann, Nuremberg, 1725. The regular grid plan on Vasilevsky island was never completed. *AKG, London.*

were forced to wear—all were calculated to make foreigners feel that they were in Europe rather than in Asia. Peter felt at home there, too. If Moscow represented Russia's old, Orthodox, "barbaric," bearded face, then St. Petersburg was its clean-shaven, civilized Western image. Unlike chaotic Moscow, the city's layout was planned, its spirit was rational.

The reality was not so civilized. Construction was carried out by teams of state peasants drafted for the summer building season, fifteen or twenty thousand at a time, accompanied by armed guards to prevent them escaping. Casualties were high, both during transfer and on the sites. Canals and harbors had to be excavated, bogs drained, embankments constructed, wooden piles driven deep into the marshy ground to support the foundations of houses. Skilled craftsmen from all over the country joined the laborers. In 1714 a thousand noble families were ordered to move permanently to St. Petersburg, and others followed thereafter. Senate archives are full of their petitions. One nobleman reported that he was living in St. Petersburg "in great hardship" and begged leave to visit his Moscow estates to try to reclaim runaway peasants and get food supplies. Like hundreds of other applicants, he was given only a short leave of absence. There was no escape from Paradise.

Despite the protests, Peter was determined to create a model city. In 1718 he established a "police" administration, in the eighteenth-century sense of provision for civic order, cleanliness and welfare, as well as crime prevention. Public hygiene and safety measures involved regular refuse collections and a fire service, reducing the pollution of waterways, and clearing beggars off the streets. Better-off districts were provided with street lighting, drainage pipes, and paving. Other decrees aimed to beautify the city, for example, by ordering residents to plant trees outside their homes. Exhortation was supplemented by penalties. A decree of 1720 ordered owners of horses to supply a cartload of manure for each horse they possessed to enrich the soil of parks and gardens, but "if people fail to carry out this order they will be fined the sum of one ruble for each [undelivered] cartload. Let this be announced in St. Petersburg to the beat of drums."

Peter's critics have seen St. Petersburg as another illustration of the high cost of personal indulgence "from above," as well as a symbol of the fundamental error of discarding tradition. "How many people perished, how much money and labor was expended to carry out this intent? Truly, Petersburg is founded on tears and corpses," wrote the historian Nicholas Karamzin in 1810. Dislike of the new "artificial" capital was an important element in later critiques of Peter's reforms. But Peter never acknowledged the dark side of St. Petersburg. For him it remained "Paradise," even if the reality was short, hot, mosquito-infested summers and long, cold, sunless winters, polluted water, frequent floods, half-finished buildings, and expensive food and drink, for nearly everything had to be imported.

Architects and Painters

After 1709 Peter increased the pace of construction, taking an interest in the smallest details. The tsar's Summer and Winter Palaces were begun in 1710, as were the mansions of Menshikov and other magnates and the monastery of St. Alexander

Nevsky. In 1711 a straight central avenue, later named Nevsky Prospect, was laid. The city was intersected by canals and streets according to a plan, in contrast to Moscow's haphazard maze of streets. The buildings had a uniform roofline. Outside the city on the Finnish Gulf Peter built grand palaces at Peterhof and Strelna, both sometimes referred to as his "Versailles," with extensive gardens, terraces, fountains, and statues. The chief architect of many of these projects was the Swiss-Italian Domenico Trezzini (1670–1734), who came to Russia in 1703 and died there without ever returning home. All the major architects of early St. Petersburg were west European, working in the latest styles and passing on their skills to Russian apprentices.

Peter's court artists also came from the West, mainly to paint portraits. All were expected to teach painting to Russian pupils, who usually had some experience as icon painters. Still, Russian painters fully trained in modern techniques, like architects, remained in short supply during Peter's lifetime, and information about them is often fragmentary. Ivan Nikitin (ca. 1680–after 1742), whom Peter sent to study in Italy, is known as the founder of Russian portraiture, but a full list of his works remains to be established. Engraving was more quickly assimilated, with Russian etchers producing prints of St. Petersburg, battle and naval scenes, firework displays, and processions, all for wide distribution.

Sculpture in stone and metal, still stigmatized by the church as the art of graven images, was slower to develop, despite Peter's sponsorship. The best-known sculptor to work for him was Carlo Bartolomeo Rastrelli (1675?–1744), whose equestrian statue of the tsar now stands in front of the Michael Castle in St. Petersburg. The bulk of the statues and pictures that adorned St. Petersburg residences were imported from abroad. Peter's taste was for marine and battle pictures, but he also purchased the work of old masters for his galleries.

The buildings lining St. Petersburg's embankments were mostly constructed of brick, plastered in bright colors, and decorated on the exterior with bands of flat white columns and window surrounds. The city's grandest building was Menshikov's palace on Vasilevsky Island, Italian in its decoration and topped with a steep Dutch roofline. Behind was a formal garden with hothouses and fountains. Inside the palace Dutch influence was even more evident in the blue and white Delft tiles that lined many walls. The Grand Hall was decorated with mirrors, classical statues alluding to military victories, and columns topped with coronets and Menshikov's knightly orders.

Peter's fourteen-room Summer Palace was more modest. His second wife Catherine's apartments, stylishly decorated with painted ceilings and Chinese silks and tapestries, were on the second floor. Peter's more austere quarters were on the ground floor, with an exit directly to the river so that he could leap into his boat. The palace was set in formal gardens, which provided a venue for the couple's summer parties, when the vodka flowed and armed guards prevented exhausted guests from leaving early. Across the river the boldest point on the skyline was Trezzini's Cathedral of Saints Peter and Paul (1712–1733) with its bell tower topped with a tall golden spire. The design departed radically from Muscovite traditions.

But it should not be forgotten that all over Russia, including the back streets of

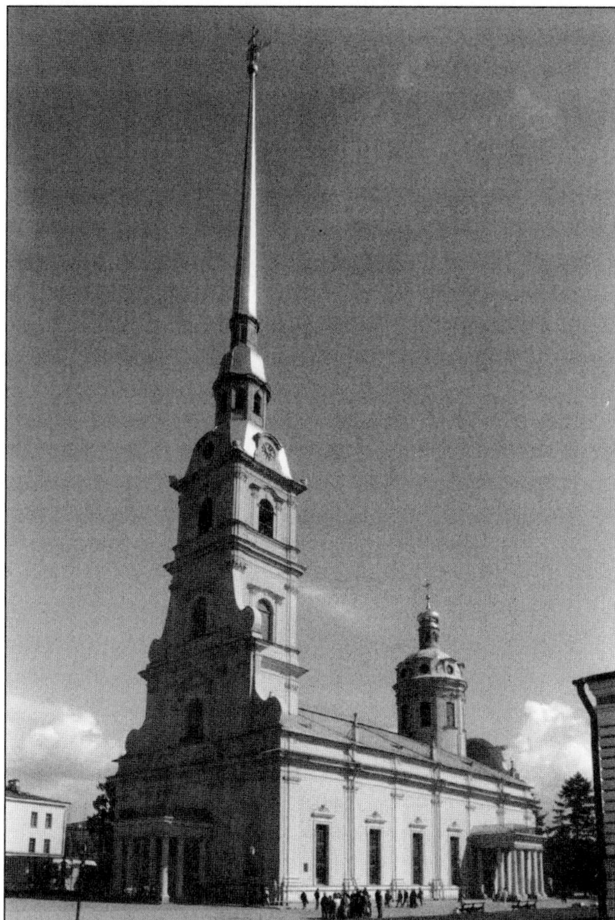

Cathedral of Saints Peter and Paul, St. Petersburg (1712–33), by Domenico Trezzini. © *William Brumfield.*

St. Petersburg, wood remained the standard building material, and icons continued to be produced in far greater numbers than secular portraits. With leading nobles more or less permanently absent from their estates doing military service, it was several decades before the impact of the Petrine "revolution" in art and architecture was felt in the countryside, where the Moscow baroque style of the 1680s remained popular for decades and many wooden churches also continued to be built.

Playing Games

One of the most radical consequences of the creation of a new capital was the transfer there of Peter's court. The Table of Ranks contained a column of court posts, but these were implemented only in Tsaritsa Catherine's household. Peter's household centered on his intimate circle of perhaps no more than a few dozen men and

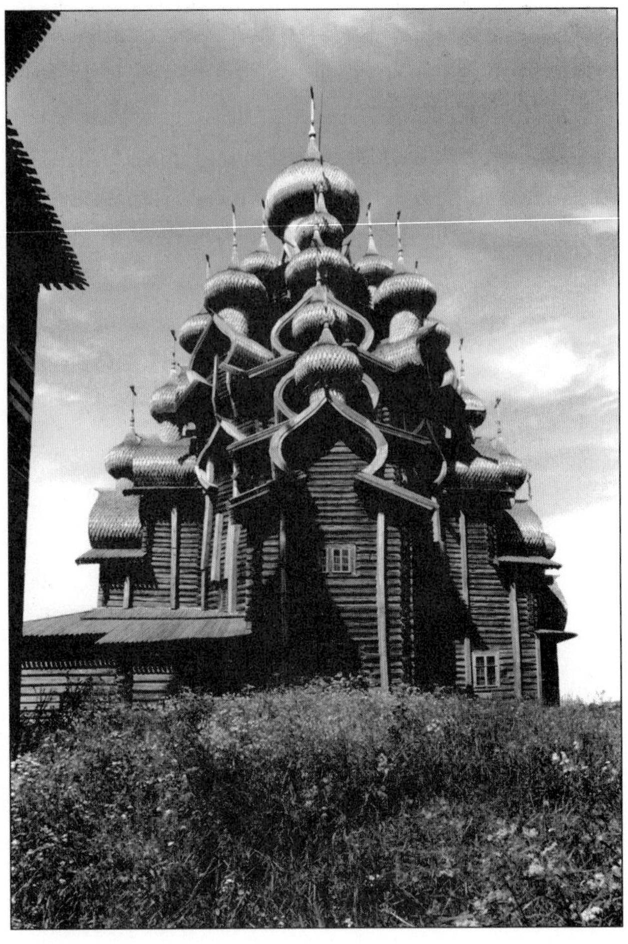

Wooden church of the Transfiguration at Kizhi (1714). Builders unknown. © *William Brumfield.*

possessed no readily discernible hierarchy, although a number of its members held high ranks in the army, navy, and administration. It included his Dutch cook and an assortment of jesters, foreign shipwrights, and other outsiders. Royal household accounts for 1721 listed 115 service personnel, including architects and painters, librarians, cooks, tutors, bird keepers, orderlies, oarsmen, dwarfs, stable lads, lackeys, and an unidentified "old woman."

In St. Petersburg the Muscovite closed model of the tsar's residence—a walled citadel (the Kremlin) containing the main churches and state edifices in a restricted space—was replaced by a more open plan, with separate buildings and public spaces located along the banks of the river Neva and adjoining waterways. In these settings Peter's motley courtiers and officials were often required to assist in games, masquerades, and role-play as members of the All-Jesting, All-Drunken Assembly, which Peter founded in the 1690s. Participants, willingly or otherwise, engaged in burlesque religious ceremonies, presided over by a Russian playing the role of "Prince-Pope" with a retinue of "cardinals" and "archdeacons." (The tsar often appeared in the latter role.) For the wedding in 1715 of the eighty-year-old Prince-Pope Nikita Zotov, stammerers delivered the invitations, and the priest was allegedly almost a hundred years old. Peter dressed as a sailor, and guests played whistles and rattled plates. After the wedding of Zotov's successor in September 1721, the bride and groom slept in an improvised bedchamber inside a wooden pyramid with holes drilled in the walls for spectators. On the next day Prince-Pope and his "cardinals" crossed the river in wooden beer barrels.

Some historians explain the Assembly's antics as a method of poking fun at or even undermining religion, but its target was not Orthodoxy as such, which remained central to Petrine ideology, but rather old attitudes and conventions that hampered the introduction of new ideas. The Drunken Assembly harnessed members of Peter's immediate circle to an unconventional form of service, in which they had to cast aside deference for old institutions along with their inhibitions and demonstrate their willingness to do whatever Peter ordered, however humiliating.

These and other events, such as regattas and carnivals, the latter held twice a year in the 1720s, were stage-managed by Peter, who took special pleasure in organizing them. A good example of how regular and mock occasions mingled was the wedding in October 1710 of Peter's niece, seventeen-year-old Anna to Frederick William, duke of Courland. Two weeks later Anna and Frederick were guests at the wedding of the chief royal dwarf and his dwarf bride. The tall tsar loved dwarfs, who were liable to surprise guests by leaping naked from pies, dancing on tables, or trotting in on miniature ponies. At the wedding dwarfs sat at small tables in the center of the room or danced, while full-sized guests watched them from tables at the sides of the room. The juxtaposition with the wedding of Anna and the duke suggested that the full-sized guests were watching caricatures of themselves, miniature lords and ladies clad, like them, in still unfamiliar Western dress. Peter's courtiers, like his new city, still had a long way to go before they were "fully grown" Europeans.

Life must have been uncomfortable for Peter's associates. At a carnival in 1724, for example, senators had to wear their masquerade costumes during the morning session of the Senate, which one observer thought "most unbecoming to elderly men, judges and councillors." Thus Peter set his inimitable stamp on St. Petersburg, where people enjoyed themselves by decree.

TEACHERS AND PUPILS

Peter alternated the roles of teacher and pupil. He himself studied shipbuilding, woodturning, and other crafts, but he was ever ready to play the strict schoolmaster. His travels abroad confirmed in his own mind the existence of the "learning gap" that separated Muscovy from many of its Western neighbors. Despite his own inadequate schooling, he grasped that education was a key to unlock Russia's potential and that there was no room for wounded national pride that equated foreign learning with "cunning" and "deception." His program was to include not only founding schools and academies on Western lines, but also encouraging publishing and printing.

Educating Russians

As the Spiritual Regulation of 1721 declared: "Learning is beneficial and basic for the good of both the Fatherland and the Church, just like the root and the seed and the foundation." Peter's own approach to education was fundamentally practical and concrete. Among his new institutions were the Guards and Artillery Schools, the Moscow School of Engineering, and the St. Petersburg Medical School. The best-known and most successful of the new technical schools was the Moscow School of Mathematics and Navigation (1701), which was modeled on the Royal Mathematical School at Christ's Hospital in London and run by British teachers whom Peter hired in 1698. In 1715 the school's higher classes moved to St. Petersburg to form the Naval Academy, which produced the first generation of Russian explorers, surveyors, cartographers, and astronomers. The Academy's graduates were later dispatched to teach in the elementary "cipher" or arithmetic schools, first mentioned in decrees of 1714.

The cipher schools were not a success. Richer nobles preferred to educate their sons at home, the poorer ones to send them to the village priest, despite the fact that nobles were not supposed to marry until they had graduated from elementary school. In 1721 merchants petitioned for their sons to be exempted on the grounds that taking them away from the business would damage the community's ability to pay its taxes. In 1721–1722 sons of clergy, too, were removed from the school rolls and transferred to church schools, which by and large were much more successful than the new state schools. In Russia, as elsewhere, children in rural communities, where child labor was vital to the economy, remained uneducated. There were no measures for extending education to the peasantry or to girls.

Some Russians went abroad for specialist training. In 1697 Peter sent sixty noble youths to Italy and the Netherlands to study navigation and seamanship. There are also records of Russians abroad studying metalwork, copper work, and joinery; Turkish, Arabic, and Persian; commerce; and painting and architecture. These trips were a mixed blessing. Many students complained of hardship and ill-treatment or succumbed to alcohol and lust in the "pursuit of Bacchus and Venus," or to gambling and brawling. One student ran off to Greece to become a monk, another went mad in Spain, no doubt confirming conservatives in their view that foreign travel was a dangerous thing.

The Academy of Sciences is generally regarded as the major achievement of Peter's education program, although it did not open until shortly after his death in 1725. In founding it Peter was strongly influenced by foreign scholars' advice on the need to "civilize" Russia in the eyes of the world and by discussions with academics during his visit to Paris in 1717. The notion of the glory of scientific endeavor is found in a speech in which Peter imagined the "transmigration of sciences" from ancient Greece to England, France, and Germany, thence to Russia, which had the potential to "put other civilized nations to the blush, and to carry the glory of the Russian name to the highest pitch."

Petrine education was a compromise, with native and foreign, religious and secular, elements. It was closely supervised and usually selectively elitist. The state imposed education for the interests of the state, not the enlightenment of the individual, and it was underfunded. This was not so very different from the situation in many other countries, but in Russia, which had no tradition of schooling outside the home or the village church and where all classes of the population thought themselves overburdened by other obligations, apathy and hostility often frustrated the government's best efforts.

Books and Readers

Peter's reign has been associated with a printing "revolution" in secular literature. In the period 1700–1725 one hundred times more publications were produced in Russia than the Moscow press printed in the whole of the seventeenth century. During his travels abroad Peter grew to appreciate the usefulness of printed words and images. In 1700 he issued a charter to a Dutchman to print material "about land and naval troops, mathematics, arithmetic, architecture and town building and other crafts . . . for the glory of the great sovereign and his tsardom [and] for the general usefulness and profit of the nation." In 1701 the Moscow Printing House, which had been run by the church, was placed under civil control. One of its new products was Russia's first newspaper, *Moscow News,* created in 1702 to report "military and other affairs which need to be made known to the people of the Russian realm and neighbouring states." This paper mirrored official concerns rather than popular ones; its target audience were government officials and army and naval officers. St. Petersburg got its own press in 1711, and others were set up in the Senate and other institutions.

In 1707–1710 Peter commissioned and implemented a new simplified Russian typeface for nonreligious works, the so-called civil script, based on modern designs for Latin letters. Topics printed in the new script ranged from the etiquette of letter-writing to siege warfare, from geography to descriptions of triumphal gates. Civil script did not replace the more ornate church script, but supplemented it. Large numbers of liturgical and devotional works continued to be published.

Publishing policy was firmly shaped by the tsar's priorities, which prompted translations of books on such topics as shipbuilding, architecture and fortification, contemporary national history ("for His Majesty's eternal praise for posterity"), and Russian military victories. There was no private publishing as existed in some Western countries and no outlet for individual authors outside the state publishing establishment, except in handwritten manuscripts. Records show that few private individuals bought books, and probably even fewer read them. The first public library in Russia, which formed the basis of the Academy of Sciences library, had almost twelve thousand volumes by 1725; but in 1724 only five readers borrowed books. Most technical books were published in very small print runs, while the biggest demand was for calendars and alphabet primers. In 1700–1725 laws, regulations, and official notices accounted for 58.6 percent of titles published but literature a mere 0.2 percent. Still, a few Russian nobles built up quite impressive private collections, including foreign books, and some leading churchmen also owned books in foreign languages and secular works. It is, of course, misleading to make a sharp distinction between the secular printed word and the sacred. In Peter's view, religious literature and writers also served the state, and religious topics still accounted for over 40 percent of books published. Sermons and prayers of thanksgiving for victories and royal namedays provided the essential theological underpinnings of autocracy, as did the best-selling primers, which inculcated faith, piety and obedience in young minds.

To concentrate on printed books gives a distorted picture of what early-eighteenth-century Russians wrote and read. Tales popular in the seventeenth century continued to circulate in manuscripts, as did chronicles, saints' lives, and other religious works with strong narratives. The two best-known examples of secular tales believed to have originated in Peter's reign are the "History of the Russian Sailor Vasily Koriotsky" and the "History of the Valiant Russian Cavalier Alexander," which fuse travelers' tales, love stories, and exotic detail with contemporary references, such as young men being sent to Holland to study. Celebratory verse was the dominant poetic genre of the Petrine era—poetry harnessed to the service of the common good. Writers such as Feofan Prokopovich used the Polish verse forms pioneered at the courts of Tsar Alexis and Fëdor to praise the Petrine state.

So, although Peter's reign undoubtedly represented a new chapter in Russian secular publishing, it is premature to speak of publishing or readership on a Western scale. Books signified new priorities and values; they were symbols of modernity. This is why someone like Menshikov, who probably could not even read, required a large library. Books on technology and science had a cultural value, like Western dress and buildings. Whether people actually read them is not always the point.

The *Kunstkamera* and Other Curiosities

In February 1718 Peter issued a decree on "monsters" or "freaks, which are collected in all countries as objects of wonder." Some people might regard such freaks as works of the devil out of ignorance, the decree explained, whereas in fact they were products of nature. Examples were to be delivered to officials in towns for a scale of rewards. The impulse behind this decree was. broadly speaking "scientific," to dismiss superstitious fear of "natural" freaks and to boast that the Russian Empire could yield up specimens just as curious as those that Western collectors traveled to the ends of the earth to find. The idea was to establish a public museum that people would visit to look and learn, tempted inside by free coffee or vodka. "Monsters" handed in, both real and faked, included an eight-legged lamb, a three-legged baby, a two-headed baby, Siamese twins joined at the chest, a baby with a fish's tail, and "two dogs born to a sixty-year-old virgin." In 1718 Peter ordered a new building for his "Kunstkamera" (from the Dutch or German for a chamber of curiosities), which opened in St. Petersburg in 1719.

The Kunstkamera Museum was just one example of Peter's efforts to introduce his subjects to a wider world, not just of "freaks" but of curious objects gathered from all over the globe. Indeed, the tower of the new museum building housed the famous giant globe of Gotthorp, a gift to Peter from the duke of Holstein. Scientific curiosity—knowledge for its own sake—was not entirely overshadowed by practical aims, and Peter's admirers abroad were inspired not so much by his rather modest achievements in establishing schools, as by his aspirations to civilize a "savage" nation. The idea is captured in a well-known engraving in which the tsar presents two globes, scientific books, and mathematical instruments to a maiden representing Russia.

In an age of shifting borders and expanding horizons, Peter's new Russians were encouraged to take a broader view. The section on seminaries in the Spiritual Regulation, for example, recommended that teachers should use a map or a globe, to which students would be asked to point in response to the questions: "Where is Asia? Where is Africa? In what direction does America lie?" In Russia Peter encouraged mapmaking and surveying and sponsored the successful expeditions of the German Daniel Messerschmidt (1685–1735) to Siberia and the Dane Vitus Bering (1681–1741), the first European to see Alaska. He also encouraged exploration of the human body through the science of anatomy. He himself enjoyed conducting autopsies and observing surgical operations, but few Russians shared his interest. Notwithstanding attempts to turn him into a thinker and inventor, in matters scientific as in most things Peter was an enthusiastic amateur. Petrine science and learning, like Petrine art and architecture, were a public, propagandistic exercise, which sowed the seeds of a future native "intelligentsia" but failed to bear much fruit in Peter's lifetime.

THE SERVICE CHURCH

In the seventeenth century the Orthodox Church had conceded ground to the state. Following the fall of Patriarch Nikon, no other patriarch would henceforth call himself "Great Sovereign." But the notion of the parallelism or "symphony" of church and state was not officially revoked in the late 1600s. The patriarch still enjoyed a place of honor at ceremonies and lived in a palace next to the tsar's in the Kremlin. The church remained a substantial landed proprietor that, by and large, served the state rather than opposing it. Priests in Muscovy were expected to report persistent absentees from church, to ensure that people coming to be married were not deserters or fugitive peasants, to publicize decrees, and so on. Demands on the church's assistance were to intensify under Peter, as its structure was overhauled and some of its traditions were discarded.

"Of Priests and Monks"

Peter's first clashes with the church were mostly over money. During the expensive Azov campaigns (1695–1696), he forbade "superfluous" church building and expenditure. Churches and monasteries were forced to contribute to building the fleet and to supply recruits from their lands for the army. Then in October 1700 Patriarch Adrian died, and Peter declined to install a new patriarch but appointed a temporary stand-in, the Ukrainian metropolitan Stefan Yavorsky (1658–1722). In 1701 Peter revived the secular Monastery Department to supervise church courts and run church lands. Part of monastery income was now to go straight into state coffers for the upkeep of poorhouses. Peter had no compunction about exacting taxes from the clergy and allocating church income to the state. He insisted that only monks and nuns were to live in monasteries, to deter "shirkers" from finding refuge there, and set the minimum age for a woman to become a nun at forty, which was later raised to fifty. Peter did not want women of childbearing age to avoid what he regarded as their prime duty. He hated monasteries not only because they provided a refuge from obligations—he liked to cite the example of fifteenth-century Constantinople, where great numbers of men taking monastic vows undermined army recruitment—but also because he suspected them of harboring opposition.

Peter tried to rationalize the parish clergy, too. "You know yourselves what neglect of God's glory there is in superfluous churches and a multitude of priests," he declared in July 1721. Many sons of priests, who in the past expected to follow in their fathers' footsteps, found themselves recruited into the army or civil service. New churches could be constructed only with special permission. In Peter's view, priests of a new type were just as necessary as "new" nobles. For both, education was the key. Generally, parish priests required only the rudiments of literacy to conduct services but some lacked even those basic skills. Priests were expected to improve their preaching, including practicing effective speaking and body language. Approved topics for sermons included respect for the authorities, especially the supreme authority of the tsar. By the end of Peter's reign, a system for training priests in episcopal schools was established, but by and large, education for priests, like that for laypersons, only made modest strides.

Priests took an oath of allegiance modeled on the one for civil servants, in which they swore to be obedient servants of the emperor and not to spare their lives in service and usefulness to state and church. They were to act as disseminators of public information, such as treaties and edicts on taxes, and to keep registers of births, deaths, and marriages. People who failed to attend church on Sundays and feast days were denounced on the grounds that they not only failed to hear the word of God, but also missed the monarch's commands. In 1722 Peter added a new task to the clergy's policing duties: they must report evil intentions against the sovereign, his family, or the state revealed by parishioners during confession, which according to canon law was supposed to be strictly confidential. There is little evidence, however, that priests complied with this ruling. Rural parish clergy, in particular, continued to function in their communities much as they had always done. Neither the church nor the state had the resources to monitor all priests' activities.

The Holy Synod

In February 1721 Peter attended the first meeting of the so-called Spiritual College, which immediately changed its name to the Most Holy Governing Synod. The rationale for its creation and its functions were set out in the Spiritual Regulation. The new Synod board was modeled on the Colleges, made up of eleven churchmen, plus a twelfth man: "an honest, right-thinking person of secular rank." The Regulation made clear that the Synod was interlocked with the state apparatus and, like it, subjugated to the tsar himself. Gone were the days when a Russian patriarch could assert, as Nikon had, that "the tsar must be lower than the prelate and obedient to him." Peter had the major voice in appointing bishops and constantly interfered in the Synod's business. In 1722 he created the post of overprocurator of the Holy Synod, who, like the procurator-general of government departments, was to act as the "tsar's eye." The Spiritual Regulation and a supplement published in 1722 also addressed the issue of monks again. There were now so many restrictions on taking monastic vows that it became almost impossible for a young, fit person to enter a monastery or a nunnery. Between 1724 and 1738 the numbers of monks and nuns in Russia almost halved.

Peter devised several methods for dealing with religious dissidents, although none was particularly successful in returning them to the official church. He abandoned

A German barber shaves the Old Believer, early 18th c. "lubok" wood print. *Bettmann/Corbis.*

violent persecution as "wasteful," in 1705 making concessions to the Old Believers at Vyg in Karelia in return for contributing to the development of local ironworks as employees of the Admiralty. In 1716 he imposed a double tax on Old Believers, who had to wear distinguishing clothing and medallions as receipts for paying the tax for keeping their beards. The state left in peace Old Believers who desisted from public criticism of the tsar and his government, did not set themselves up as teachers or operate as priests, refrained from luring or harboring fugitives, paid their taxes, and did useful work. Their numbers continued to grow.

Religion and Empire

Orthodoxy remained on the agenda of foreign policy, be it protesting against abuses of Orthodox Christians in Poland and Sweden or giving moral support to fellow Orthodox rulers. But it was not a priority. Peter championed Orthodox unity when it suited him, as in relations with Ukraine. Active intervention beyond Russia's borders—for example, against the forced conversion to Catholicism of Orthodox believers in south Hungary—was another matter. The crusading element was subordinated to more immediate practical concerns in relations with Turkey and Crimea, where eliminating border raids, slave-taking, and tribute payments were deemed more important than fighting for Orthodoxy. Guarantees on freedom of worship and religion for the Orthodox in the Ottoman Empire, although raised in negotiations, were not included in Russia's 1700 treaty with Turkey. In 1711 Peter appealed, unsuccessfully, to Orthodox Christians in the Balkans to rise against their Muslim oppressors to aid his campaign against the Turks. In spring 1722 Russia announced a war against Persia and the declaration mentioned "saving Christians from Muslim domination." In general, though, the idea of Russian leadership of the Orthodox world remained more a religious abstraction than an active policy.

Efforts to convert the tsar's "heathen" subjects were sporadic, although generous cash payments and tax incentives would induce many non-Russians tribespeople to convert in the next few decades. Sometimes more violent measures were employed. In 1714 the metropolitan of Tobolsk in Siberia received orders to seek out and burn the "seductive false gods and idols" of local tribes, to destroy their "heathen temples" and build churches instead. For west Europeans working in Russia, however, free exercise of their faith was guaranteed in a manifesto of 1702, which readily allowed "each Christian to work for his own salvation at his own risk." Major denominations built their own churches in St. Petersburg. Freedom of worship for Peter's new Christian subjects in the Baltic states was also guaranteed. In addition, Peter authorized mixed marriages between Orthodox subjects and other Christians.

Peter's approach to religion combined political, ideological, and practical goals, aimed not at destroying the Orthodox Church but at improving it and putting it in its place. Peter was suspicious of monks and nuns, but he was equally suspicious of the godless. For Peter, like his fellow European monarchs, life without religion was inconceivable. He himself attended church assiduously and never doubted that divine providence played a part in determining human fate. As he said after the Battle of Poltava: "To God alone belong the glory and honor, for this is a divine deed; he raises up the humble and subdues the mighty."

Like his predecessors, Peter accepted that the church had power over people's spiritual lives and, like them, he wanted the church to minister to its flock more effectively. What he would not accept was the church's claims to wield power outside the sphere of worship and morality, for, in so claiming, the church challenged the state's need for a free hand in deploying its resources. Under Peter the state appropriated authority over matters previously regarded as in the religious sphere, such as personal appearance and dress. It challenged many of the church's taboos. For example, a story about the negotiation of tobacco contracts in London in 1698 relates how Peter declared that the patriarch would do well not to interfere. "He is only the guardian of the faith, not a customs inspector." Even so, Peter did not secularize Russia. It is true that he harnessed the church more firmly to the state, but the core of its activity—services, texts, ritual—survived more or less unchanged to the present day, while in church art and architecture ancient traditions lived on alongside Westernized forms. Orthodoxy proved remarkably resilient, not least in the everyday lives of the common people. Rather, he harnessed a slimmed-down priesthood even more firmly to the tsardom than his predecessors had succeeded in doing. The tsar no longer saw his main function as primarily to aid the salvation of his subjects' souls and to prepare for Jesus Christ's second coming by maintaining a pious earthly realm, but actively to pursue the "common good" through worldly achievements.

NEW MEN AND WOMEN

Of all the tasks facing Peter, the hardest was reforming people. He started at the top, subjecting the nobles and other privileged individuals, along with their wives and daughters, to a program for the "transformation of savage manners." In the longer term, this created a Westernized elite who, in time, produced both the loyal imperial service elite, who ran the empire, and the Russian intelligentsia, who were to question the political system. For practical reasons the mass of the population—the peasantry—was excluded from this process, exempt from requirements on Western dress, shaving, manners, habitations, and education. Thus Peter created the notorious "divide" between the elite and the masses, which was to survive well into the twentieth century.

Etiquette and Assemblies

Regardless of their origins, Peter's associates were expected to adopt certain cultural standards, the most fundamental of which was shaving and wearing Western dress. Peter worked hard to inculcate Western manners in those around him, although the hard-drinking, often boorish tsar, who paid scant attention to dress or etiquette, was not the best of role models. Trips abroad aided the transformation of a select few, while those at home could study behavior books such as *The Honorable Mirror of Youth,* translated into Russian from various foreign sources and first published in 1717. The etiquette section included advice to young men on how to behave at table and make polite conversation, and the second half was devoted to advice to young ladies. Chapters on "Maidenly Honor and Virtue" and "Maidenly Humility" made clear that women were expected to combine Muscovite bashfulness and decorum with the new social graces of the French drawing room.

New manners had to be rehearsed. In 1702 Peter arranged the wedding of one of his jesters. For two days the guests celebrated in old Russian style, men and women in separate rooms. On the third day they were commanded to appear in "German" dress, and both sexes sat down at table together. This ceremony typified Peter's practice of providing explicit examples of the new culture, often through acting out an "old and new" scenario. In 1718 he issued a Decree on Assemblies in an attempt to extend polite society beyond the court into the homes of the nobility and richer merchants. Access to social gatherings in private houses was to be open to any decently dressed persons, male or female, except servants and peasants. Peter used a characteristic degree of compulsion both in the manner of the introduction of assemblies and their subsequent supervision. Hosts' homes were visited by the police to check that everything was in order, and the authorities sometimes demanded lists of those who had attended.

Peter's assemblies, feasts, balls, and regattas were mixed-sex gatherings. Ladies, now referred to by the foreign word *damy,* were required to abandon seclusion, discard their traditional loose-fitting garments for revealing Paris fashions, and show off their hair dressed in the latest style. Attendance at public gatherings required wigs, fans, and other accessories virtually unknown in Muscovite times. New consumer items such as coffee services appeared in the setting of palaces furnished in Western style containing paintings and sculptures. The young German noble Frederick Bergholz enthusiastically declared: "The Russian woman, until recently coarse and uneducated, has changed for the better to such a degree that now she concedes little to German or French ladies in subtlety of manners and good breeding and in some respects is even superior to them."

Although people complied with the new requirements, Western manners aroused hostility in many. Russians who spent time abroad often found themselves subject to private ridicule and suspicion when they returned. Once in retirement and out of the public eye, nobles often reverted to comfortable old Muscovite lifestyles. For example, Count Gavrila Golovkin (1660–1734), head of the Foreign Office and state chancellor, who traced his boyar ancestors back to the early sixteenth century, liked to wear an old-fashioned brown caftan and hated wearing a wig. He wished to end his days in a monastery, but Peter refused permission. In Moscow, a foreigner observed, "Ladies of Quality are dressed after the German Fashion, which indeed they prefer to their old . . . Dress; but as to their Courtesies, still the old Custom prevails of bowing with the Head to the Ground." There was ample room for religious culture, which maintained a firm grip on everyday life and behavior at all levels of society throughout Peter's reign and beyond. Peter's sister

Natalia (1673–1716) wore the latest fashions, including newfangled corsets, and decorated her home with portraits, but she also owned a large collection of icons and religious books.

For people living in Peter's immediate vicinity, life must have been an uncomfortable and sometimes confusing experience. At the same time as they were required to adopt the externals of Western culture, they had to put up with Peter's hobby of exploding experimental fireworks or with being forced to drink themselves unconscious from the Great Eagle Cup, a huge tankard that Peter used to punish those who arrived late or misbehaved in some other minor way. Compulsory sailing lessons and regattas added to the torments. There was little time to devote to private cultural and leisure pursuits. "My God and Creator," wrote General Boris Sheremetev in 1711, "Deliver us from this and allow us a little peace to live on this earth, just to live a little." After Peter's death, under the influence of foreign travel and books, a select few began to think about the deeper implications of becoming more like an Englishman or a Frenchman and to demand that Russian nobles be treated more like their peers in other Western countries in terms of political rights and freedom from service.

Menshikov and Catherine

Two outstanding examples of Peter's new men and women were his friend Alexander Menshikov and Peter's second wife, Catherine. Both not only enthusiastically adopted the new culture but were also both "rags to riches" stories. Menshikov was versatile, energetic, and loyal. His impressive record in the army in the early stages of the Great Northern War earned him the governorship of St. Petersburg. In 1707 he was created prince of Russia and Ingria, the first example of the hitherto hereditary title of prince being bestowed on a commoner. In 1718 he became director of the War College. He also remained to all intents and purposes illiterate. In other respects, Menshikov was everything Peter wanted his reformed nobles to be. He built splendid palaces, dressed fashionably, collected pictures, and owned an impressive library of books and maps. His was one of the most musical Russian households of its day, with musicians and singers on the permanent staff. But Menshikov was corrupt. Much of his vast fortune of cash, real estate, lands in Lithuania and Ukraine, and more than three hundred thousand serfs was acquired illegally. On several occasions, he managed to evade serious charges of embezzlement brought by his many enemies, relying on his closeness to the tsar to save him.

Peter fashioned his own creation as a role model for women. Catherine (Ekaterina) was born Martha Skavronskaya into a peasant family in Livonia in about 1684. Having met Peter after she was captured by Russian soldiers in 1702, she was soon an established fixture in the royal entourage, accompanying Peter on campaign. She bore him probably ten children in all, but only two survived into adulthood, Anna (1708–1728) and the future empress Elizabeth (1709–1761).There are rumors that Peter and Catherine married secretly in 1707, but their public wedding took place only in February 1712 in St. Petersburg. Certain members of the elite and many ordinary folk deplored Peter's unconventional choice: Catherine was a commoner and a foreigner, and Peter's first wife, Tsaritsa Evdokia, was still alive.

In character and tastes Catherine was a match for Peter, physically strong and sharing his fondness for practical jokes and drink. She rarely seems to have been intimidated by him, even when he was in a rage. In 1714 he introduced the Order of St. Catherine for distinguished women and made her the first recipient, in recognition of her personal courage at the Battle of Pruth, where she behaved "in a manner more male than female" when the Russian army was surrounded by the Turks. In May 1724 in a lavish ceremony in the Kremlin he crowned Catherine as his consort, thus posing a challenge to anyone who continued to mutter about her humble origins. Not only did she succeed, with Peter's help, in inventing her own identity as an emperor's wife, but shortly she was to be empress in her own right.

"FATHER OF THE FATHERLAND"

On October 22, 1721, St. Petersburg formally celebrated the Peace of Nystad, and Peter accepted the titles Father of the Fatherland, Emperor of All Russia, Peter the Great, "after the manner of the ancients, especially the Roman and Greek people." Peter, a senator declared in a speech, had rescued Russia from "nonexistence" and raised it as from the dead. In his own speech, Peter acknowledged God's help in obtaining peace and encouraged Russians to strive for the common good.

Peter's new titles were intended primarily as a reminder to foreign powers of Russia's imperial status. But since his last surviving son had died in 1719, who would inherit the titles? In February 1722 Peter published a Manifesto on the Succession to the Throne, which stated that the ruling monarch could appoint "whom he wishes" to the succession or remove the one he has appointed in the case of unseemly behavior. Accidents of birth and custom were firmly subordinated to reason and the common good, but the choice of heir remained the monarch's. There was no thought of entrusting it to popular acclaim or to the elite. These ideas were more fully expressed in Feofan Prokopovich's book *The Justice of the Monarch's Right to Appoint the Heir to the Throne* (1722), which stressed the divine basis of monarchical power but also used a Western frame of reference to underline affinities with European natural law theory. The author argued that succession by the firstborn (primogeniture) was a mere custom that could be set aside for a higher purpose.

The Affair of Tsarevich Alexis

The new law of succession was rooted in Peter's personal tragedy: the condemnation to death of his eldest son, Alexis. Alexis had been separated from his banished mother, Evdokia, in 1698 and educated by German tutors whom he hated. Peter dragged him off to sieges and battle sites to toughen him up, entrusted him with supervising army provisions, fortification, and recruitment and in 1711 married him to Princess Charlotte of Wollfenbüttel. Nothing Alexis did was quite good enough for Peter. He was unenthusiastic about Peter's pet projects, especially the fleet and St. Petersburg; he mixed with the wrong sort of friends; and he preferred devotional books to works about shipbuilding. He neglected his German wife and took a peasant mistress. In 1715 Peter wrote Alexis several letters in which he expressed his fears for Russia's future if Alexis were to survive him. "I have not spared and do not spare my own life for my country and my people, so why should I spare you who are so unworthy? Better a worthy stranger [on the throne] than my own unworthy son."

In October 1715, after both Catherine and Charlotte gave birth to sons, both named Peter, Alexis expressed his desire to relinquish the throne. Nothing was resolved. Early in 1716 Peter departed for his extended European tour, and in August he summoned Alexis to join him in Denmark. Instead, Alexis fled with his mistress to Vienna to seek asylum with his wife's brother-in-law, the Habsburg emperor Charles VI (r. 1711–1740). In 1717 Peter wrote to inform Alexis that although he had acted "like a traitor," he was ready to forgive him if he returned to Russia. Alexis agreed, but upon his return found himself under pressure to name the "accomplices" who had helped him to flee Russia and allegedly plotted against Peter's life. In 1718 Peter issued a manifesto removing Alexis from the succession and naming three-year-old Peter Petrovich as the new heir: "We could not keep an heir who would lose that which with God's help his father had obtained and who would overturn the glory and honour of the Russian people, for which I spent my health, in some cases not even sparing my life."

An investigation followed that turned into a witch-hunt. A number of Alexis's close friends were tortured and executed. Even his mother was interrogated and banished to a more distant convent for allegedly communicating with her son. Testimonies revealed that Alexis enjoyed the sympathy of many members of the ruling elite, who were weary of the unrelieved burdens of Peter's reign and were hostile to Alexander Menshikov. There is no evidence of a strong desire among leading servitors to restore Muscovite traditions, but they may well have wished to extend the process of Westernization to the political sphere in some form or other. In this scenario, Alexis begins to look like a suitable candidate as a constitutional monarch.

Alexis was accused of moral and physical failings, indifference to the common good, and attempting to escape the succession. But the crucial charge was that he had sought Austrian aid to overthrow and assassinate Peter. Scant evidence exists for these last allegations (the Austrians had been reluctant to get involved), but Alexis confessed under interrogation by torture. On June 26 the senators and civil officials of the tribunal in St. Petersburg delivered a guilty verdict and a sentence of death, but the torture continued, for Peter was desperate to extract more information. By that same evening Alexis was dead, allegedly of a seizure or "apoplectic fit," although there were rumors that Peter strangled his son with his bare hands or had him suffocated. The most likely cause of death is that Alexis, already weakened by imprisonment and illness, succumbed to torture. Peter was first and foremost a monarch, "father of the fatherland," a private father only second. He could not separate Alexis's fate from the fate of Russia. Just how much this cost him personally is impossible to tell. People attending Alexis's funeral reported that the tsar was "bathed in tears."

"Leave everything to . . ."

In the last four years of his life Peter did not slacken the pace. He waged a successful campaign against Persia on the Caspian Sea in 1722–1723 and issued much of the major legislation examined earlier. In the winter of 1723 a disease came to light that finally killed him—inflammation of the urinary tract and bladder, which may have been linked with venereal disease. In the summer of 1724 his doctors performed an operation, and by the fall he was on the move again, inspecting work on a new canal. Around this time legend has it that Peter saved the lives of a boatload of soldiers and sailors from a shipwreck on the Finnish Gulf. There is little trace of this incident in contemporary documents, but the moral point is clear: Peter refused to spare himself and ultimately sacrificed his life for the good of Russia.

On January 17, 1725, the keeper of the court journal recorded: "His Imperial Majesty was ill and did not deign to go anywhere." After days of agony caused by a recurrence of his old illness, Peter died on the morning of January 28. Shortly before losing consciousness, he is said to have summoned his eldest daughter, Anna, and scrawled an unfinished note: "Leave everything to . . .", an incident cited by many later writers. In fact, the story appears in only one contemporary source, the memoir of a retainer of the duke of Holstein, whose aim may have been to persuade readers that Anna, the duke's fiancée, was Peter's intended heir. The fact remains that Peter did not implement his new Law of Succession by naming his successor, perhaps because he had not seriously contemplated the possibility of dying so soon.

In the end it suited a group of powerful men at court, led by Menshikov, to have Catherine as empress. The widely held belief that Peter had signaled his wish for her to succeed him by crowning her as his consort in 1724 helped to secure the crucial backing of the guards regiments. Peter's funeral was orchestrated to smooth the succession. His corpse went on show in the Winter Palace until mid March in an unprecedented lying-in-state organized "after the manner of other European countries," then his coffin was taken to the Peter-Paul Cathedral in a lavish procession. Archbishop Feofan Prokopovich's funeral oration proclaimed that not only did Peter "give birth" to Russia, he also "created" Catherine, "mother of all Russians" and the embodiment of her husband's spirit.

Peter's Legacy

Officially, Peter's reputation was untarnished, but in reality, Russia's condition gave cause for grave concern. The early 1720s had seen a number of crises resulting from the accumulated costs of decades of relentless war and mobilization. Poor harvests triggered famine. Salaries were reduced or left unpaid. In 1724 the poll tax was collected for the first time, bringing protests. So many peasants were fleeing across the borders that the authorities set up pickets. Crime and corruption were endemic. In 1723 Wilhelm Henning, inspector of mines in Siberia, sent Peter his own analysis of why even "good men" turned to crime:

> Terrible deeds are in evidence here; the poor peasants suffer ruin at the hands of officials, and in the towns much oppression is caused by the local officials sent from the finance office and the merchantry has been so badly damaged that an artisan with any capital is scarcely to be found.

The weak, like their counterparts in much of Europe, were as vulnerable as ever, despite the attempts at overhauling the provincial administration and stamping out corruption.

In 1726 a group of Peter's close associates gave a similarly frank assessment of Russia's condition in a memorandum to the new empress, admitting that "nearly all affairs—both spiritual and temporal—are in disarray and require speedy correction." But the memorandum contained no word of criticism against Peter himself. Petrine principles—devotion to duty, concern for the common good, pride in Russia, determination to maintain and expand the empire—were to remain the models for Russia's rulers in the coming centuries. A number of Peter's institutions would survive, albeit with some amendments, until 1917. These included the Table of Ranks, the Holy Synod, the Senate, and the Academy of Sciences. St. Petersburg remained the capital until 1918. The Russian navy honored Peter as its founder and the army celebrated Petrine traditions. Cultural trends were never reversed among the elite, even if excessive borrowing of "alien" cultures was later criticized.

However, it is worth bearing in mind the darker side of Peter's legacy when examining the record of his immediate successors. Frustrated by his subjects' reluctance to "leap forward" on their own initiative, Peter imposed unendurable burdens. He summed up the problem laconically in November 1723 in a manifesto on the encouragement of industry: "Our people are like children who, out of ignorance, will never get down to learning their alphabet unless the master forces them to do so." The cane that Peter sometimes used to chastise members of his inner circle could not reach every one of his subjects, but nobles and peasants alike variously felt the painful blows of conscription and forced labor, heavy taxes and intrusive legislation.

Ironically, Peter's very successes added to the burden of his descendants—the maintenance of empire required a standing army, which demanded peasant conscripts and reliable revenues. The high level of diplomatic activity demanded the upkeep of a splendid court, which in turn put pressures on the nobles to maintain their own expensive households, based on serf labor, in a new city where prices were high. Outside St. Petersburg, Moscow, and a few towns, in the vast Russian countryside life continued much as it had always done. Extending "civilization" to those parts of Russia that Peter had failed to reach was the unenviable task of his successors.

CHAPTER 13

"Between Two Greats," 1725–1762

O Mother of your people!
Nature has created you
To complete the tasks of Peter.
—The poet Aleksei Sumarokov, on the accession to the throne of Empress Elizabeth in 1741

The period between the death of Peter I and the accession of Catherine II has acquired several more or less pejorative titles, such as the "era of palace revolutions" and the "Doldrums." Historians have often treated it as a thin and unappetizing filling sandwiched between the reigns of two Great rulers, sometimes allocating just enough space to dismiss the imperial "mediocrities" and their hangers-on. Of the three women who ruled Russia between 1725 and 1761, Catherine I is remembered as an illiterate peasant who died of drink, Anna had a reputation for cruelty and a liking for dwarfs, and Elizabeth is renowned for the fifteen thousand dresses discovered in her closets after her death. The three male rulers were even less prepossessing and had no time to prove themselves before they departed the scene. Peter II was just fourteen when he died from smallpox; the unfortunate Ivan VI was deposed at the age of eighteen months; and Peter III reigned for a mere six months before he was overthrown by his wife, who ruled as Catherine II.

Viewed more positively, the period 1725–1762 could be seen as a time of consolidation, when Russia managed to maintain its hard-won position in the world and to build on Peter I's innovations in the arts, science, and education. This is a fascinating time for anyone interested in the dynamics of dynastic politics and "autocratic" government, in the balance between official scenarios of power and powers behind the throne. In this chapter we look at how Russian autocracy or absolutism—no term was consistently in use at the time to describe the system of government—operated and survived under "weak" rulers.

WHO RULES RUSSIA?

Some writers speak of the "problem" of female rule in eighteenth-century Russia, but at the time the novelty of female rulers apparently failed to spark controversy in

Russia itself. Peter I paved the way for empresses not only by his 1722 Law of Succession, but also by making women more visible in elite society and providing his wife Catherine with her own court. A woman on the throne was hardly a shocking idea: there were many precedents in both western Europe and Byzantium. In ancient Rus and Muscovy a woman representing her absent, dead, underaged, or incapacitated male relative was also well accepted and underpinned by religious rhetoric. The question was not so much how a woman stayed in power—all four Russian empresses died in office of natural causes—as how she behaved in order to rule effectively and how much she relied on advisers. None of the empresses had husband consorts; three were widows and one was unmarried. So they needed escorts, preferably men who would not compete for political power or antagonize loyal members of the established elite. The latter accepted an empress's need for male company as long as the chosen companion did not threaten their power bases. The Russian nobility, with the exception of a few renegades, supported the rhetoric of a feminine "scenario of power" and vied among themselves to get a part in it. If an empress was criticized, it was generally not with reference to her gender. Problems arose for other reasons.

From Catherine I to Peter II, 1725–1730

Immediately following Peter's death, Catherine (b. ca. 1684) was presented to the public as both the great man's grieving widow and his worthy successor. Her short reign, which lasted from January 1725 to May 1727, provides a good illustration of how autocracy continued to operate successfully under an unassertive ruler who had little talent for government. In fact, Catherine's feminine "weakness" proved to be an advantage rather than a handicap. Her qualifications were strengthened by the claim that not only would she rule in Peter's spirit, but had actually been "created" by him. A woman on the throne promised a respite, too, for the last thing the men close to the throne actually wanted was another Peter, with all the implications of exhausting work schedules and the danger of being abused or humiliated. Add the rhetoric that Catherine was an all-loving mother, caring for orphaned Russia as she cared for her orphaned daughters, and make some stock comparisons with Classical rulers and goddesses, and the illiterate peasant woman was transformed into Empress of All Russia.

In view of Catherine's poor health, the question of the succession arose almost as soon as she was crowned. Menshikov pulled off what looked like a brilliant move, outsmarting the supporters of Peter I's grandson Peter (1715–1730) by taking the boy under his wing and betrothing him to his daughter Maria. In 1727 he succeeded in banishing some of his main rivals. By persuading Catherine to name Peter as her successor under a regency council headed by himself, Menshikov probably hoped to rob the "old" nobility of its base while gaining popularity by restoring the male line. On the day of Catherine's death, eleven-year-old Peter was proclaimed emperor, and a few weeks later it was announced that he would soon wed Maria Menshikova.

For the rest of Peter's short life it was a question of who could manipulate him before he developed a mind of his own. At first Menshikov kept the emperor under his wing, but when Menshikov fell sick and was absent from court in summer 1727, his enemies turned Peter against him. The arrival at court of the new emperor's grandmother, Peter I's ex-wife Evdokia (1669–1731), who loathed Menshikov, added to the latter's troubles. In September 1727 Andrei (Heinrich) Osterman (1686–1747), a German who had entered Peter I's service in 1703 and whose influence had grown dramatically during Catherine I's reign, joined forces with several members of the powerful Dolgoruky clan. They had Menshikov arrested on a charge of "tyranny" and banished to Siberia, where he died in wretched circumstances in November 1729. "This colossus of a pygmy, raised almost to royal status" was how Feofan Prokopovich, a member of the successful clique, described him. Menshikov, one of the most talented and probably most corrupt figures of his era, still awaits a proper biography in English.

Peter II went to Moscow to be crowned in February 1728. His chief adviser was now Prince Alexis Dolgoruky (?–1734), but the power behind the throne was Osterman. Both were members of the six-man Supreme Privy Council, created by Menshikov in 1726. Its members controlled the Colleges of War and Foreign Affairs and the Admiralty as well as the finance departments. After his coronation Peter II stayed in Moscow, where he devoted much of his time to hunting. Portraits show a handsome boy, clad in the latest Western fashion. Despite rumors that he would transfer the capital back to Moscow, there is no evidence that he or his circle planned to return to the "old ways," even if many magnates welcomed the opportunity to spend more time on their Moscow estates. In November 1729 Peter was betrothed to Prince Alexis Dolgoruky's daughter Catherine, but the wedding never took place. In late January 1730 he died, apparently from smallpox, and was buried in the Archangel Cathedral in Moscow.

Peter II died without naming a successor. At the sickbed Alexis Dolgoruky urged the boy to nominate his fiancée Catherine, but Peter was too sick to sign a testament. There were voices in favor of ex-Tsaritsa Evdokia or Peter I's twenty-one-year-old daughter, Elizabeth; but Dolgoruky and his allies, chief among them Prince Dmitry Golitsyn (1665–1737), decided to install a ruler whom they expected to give them little trouble, Peter's niece Anna, duchess of Courland. Now aged thirty-six, she had been forced to take up residence in Courland to maintain a Russian presence there after her husband's premature death in 1710.

In an attempt to limit the ruler's powers, Dmitry Golitsyn drew up conditions for Anna's rule. She was to agree not to marry or to designate a successor; she must maintain the Supreme Privy Council, without the consent of which she must not start a war or make peace, raise new taxes, deploy the guards, or spend state revenues. Nor could she on her own promote or discipline members of the nobility. Leading men outside the Golitsyn-Dolgoruky circle were alarmed by this "conspiracy of privy councillors," and many came up with schemes of their own. Counter-petitions begged Anna to rule with the same powers as her predecessors, pleading "better one autocrat then multiple tyranny by Dolgorukys and Golitsyns" or "ten despotic and powerful families." Anna took heed and tore up the conditions. The Dolgoruky and Golitsyn "conspirators" were tried and banished.

If implemented, the limitation on autocracy would have been incomplete—the choice of the membership of the council, for example, remained the sovereign's—but it would have made Russia a constitutional monarchy where the ruler shared power. Instead, yet another reshuffling of the ruling elite followed. Influence passed from the banished privy councilors to Osterman, now in charge of foreign affairs, and to Count Burchard Christopher Münnich (1683–1767), head of the War College, who were joined by Anna's chancellor from Courland, Ernst Johann Biron (Bühren) (1690–1772), and Rheinhold Gustav von Löwenwolde (?–1735), grand marshal of her court. Anna settled down for a ten-year reign.

"Germans Rule": From Anna to Ivan VI

It is difficult to form a fair impression of Empress Anna Ivanovna. Her contemporaries disagreed about whether she was ugly or attractive, intelligent or stupid, but mostly negative judgments predominate. Historians often refer to her dour, morose personality, dismissing her for being virtually a German and cut off from things Russian, although, in fact, during the 1710s–1720a she spent long periods in St. Petersburg. Her reputation is not enhanced today by the best-known image of her—the rather threatening bulky mass of Carlo Rastrelli's bronze statue, cast in 1739, made even less acceptable to modern eyes by the addition of a black servant holding a globe. To eighteenth-century viewers its very weightiness, the opulence of the jewel-studded robes and the signs of imperial power in the regalia, conveyed an image of powerful rule, and the servant symbolized the loyalty appropriate to all subjects. Poets praised the empress's "masculine" virtues, imagining "brave Anna" wielding a sword. Anna, of course, never went near a battlefield and seems to have been governed by common sense and instinct rather than bravery or intellect. She enjoyed active pastimes such as tobogganing and hunting and also picked up some habits from her uncle Peter, enjoying his weddings for dwarfs and his collections of "monsters" and exotic beasts and sharing his passion for jesters and masquerades.

Anna's reign was once associated with the term *Bironovshchina,* which refers to the "bad rule" of her favorite, Biron. From 1730 on he served as her senior chamberlain, and in 1737 he was made duke of Courland. He held no posts in the government or military establishment; his was a personal power grounded in strong emotional ties with Anna, although whether their relationship was sexual remains a matter of conjecture. Modern historians reject the inflated estimates of Biron's wickedness, without denying that Anna's reign witnessed many cruel episodes. Notorious trials conducted by her Secret Chancellery, which handled treason cases, included those of the disgraced Dolgorukys and Prince Dmitry Golitsyn and, most disturbing to contemporaries, of cabinet minister Artemy Volynsky, who unwisely made unflattering remarks about the empress in a letter. In 1740 Volynsky's tongue was cut out, and he and some fellow "conspirators" were beheaded. Many others were knouted and banished. There was nothing new in the Secret Chancellery's procedures. For example, the interrogation of both accuser and denouncer under torture was a Muscovite practice that survived under Peter the Great. The culture of denunciation was deeply rooted.

Anna's reign has been associated not only with cruelty, but also with foreign or "German" domination, which, it is argued, Biron encouraged. In fact, contemporaries

Bronze statue of Empress Anna (r. 1730–1740) and her black servant, cast in 1739 by Bartolomeo Carlo Rastrelli. *The State Russian Museum, St. Petersburg, Russia/Corbis.*

were largely unconcerned about "Germans" in government. It is true that a number of foreigners held prominent posts, but at least two of them—Münnich and Osterman—were promoted by Peter I, while Count von Löwenwolde came from Russian Livonia and was one of many successful Baltic Germans to work in the Russian government. An analysis of the origins of men in the Table of Ranks during Anna's reign fails to demonstrate a preponderance of non-Russians.

Anna was keen to keep the succession on her own side of the family by nominating as her heir the son, Ivan, born in 1740 to her niece Anna Leopoldovna and the duke of Brunswick. A couple of months later the empress was dead, having nominated Biron as regent. Münnich soon had Biron, who had fallen out with Anna Leopoldovna and her husband, arrested and imprisoned. Münnich installed the baby's mother as regent and announced a cabinet equally composed of Russians and Germans.

With the prospect of more than a decade under a regency, the infant Ivan VI's regime fell quickly, more as a result of its vulnerability to rivals than any mismanagement or abuse. The twenty-two-year-old regent became the target of gossip and scandal. In turn, rumors circulated of a conspiracy in favor of Tsarevna Elizabeth, the fifth child of Peter and Catherine, who seized her chance in late November 1741. She personally accompanied guardsmen to arrest Anna Leopoldovna and deposed the infant Ivan VI. Osterman and Münnich were sentenced to death, but they were reprieved and banished to Siberia at the last minute. As for the deposed imperial family, they ended up in the Russian Far North. Anna gave birth to two daughters and two sons before her death in 1746. The ex-emperor Ivan was to die in Schlüsselburg fortress in 1764, the victim of an ill-conceived plot to release him and restore him to the throne.

Elizabeth: Daughter of Peter the Great

Elizabeth (Elizaveta Petrovna) was born in December 1709. Officially she never married or had children, although rumors abound of secret husbands and offspring. Her trump card was undoubtedly that she was Peter I's last surviving child, an especially potent advantage when supporters contrasted her rule with that of the non-Petrine line, which they presented for political purposes as "dark" German forces. Elizabeth's accession was publicized as an act of salvation, carried out by a woman who had the right to rule not only by descent but also by acclaim, for the guards begged her to govern in the name of her subjects. The "oppression" she had suffered since her father's death was exaggerated for rhetorical effect so as to seem like an insult to Peter himself. "Saving Peter's heritage from the hands of foreigners" became a leading motif, and her supporters lost no opportunity to express patriotic indignation about times past.

Proving herself worthy to be Peter's daughter was a tall order for a woman who, although intelligent, regarded reading as injurious to health and banned conversations on scientific matters in her presence. If anything, she inherited some of Peter's worst characteristics, including impatience, unpredictability, and difficulty staying for long in one place. She was an instinctive ruler with a sense of self-preservation, made cautious by her years on the fringes of power. But her actual abilities were less important than the way she and her supporters presented and packaged her. Elizabeth laid claim to honorary male virtues. She could never lead her armies into battle or command warships as her father had done, but she could assume the symbols of military leadership. For example, she sometimes wore a female version of the uniform of Peter's own Preobrazhensky guards. She preceded her crowning in Moscow in April 1742 with a triumphal entry parade, mimicking those organized by Peter after military victories. The ruler's piety remained important, too, and Elizabeth's schedule included visits to monasteries and convents, starting with the Trinity Monastery, which had strong associations with her father.

Elizabeth is perhaps best known for her love of pleasure. The conservative social critic Prince Michael Shcherbatov (1733–1790) later complained in his exposé of the corruption of morals in Russia that ladies might spend ten thousand rubles or more on their outfits in order to participate in Elizabeth's court spectacles, thus contributing to the impoverishment of the nobility. From another angle, Soviet historians denounced the empress's spendthrift frivolity and "time-wasting" as incongruous and insensitive when the mass of the population lived in poverty. It is true that Elizabeth devoted little time to government business, in part, perhaps, because she rarely got up before noon and stayed awake all night. She was uninterested in anything to do with state finances, trade, or domestic legislation. But records show that she took a keen interest in foreign affairs, for diplomacy and dynastic matters were natural extensions of court life. Modern historians have argued that even by enjoying herself, she was doing her duty by keeping up appearances and encouraging optimism.

It is doubtful whether Elizabeth's court was a pleasanter or safer place than Anna's. Elizabeth abolished the death penalty, but the Secret Chancellery continued to operate much as before. A group of courtiers alleged to have made "unflattering" remarks about the empress, for example, were knouted, had their tongues shortened, and were banished to Siberia. Elizabeth's deep attachment to Orthodoxy also had its negative side. She persecuted Old Believers and expelled Jews from Russia. She also had Muslim mosques demolished, albeit in the context of a highly successful campaign for voluntary conversions to Orthodoxy in the Volga region. Unpleasant

Portrait of Empress Elizabeth (r. 1741–1761), after Aleksei Antropov (1741). *Hillwood Museum and Gardens, Washington, DC.*

stories about the empress's vindictiveness survive, such as the one about the jester who brought a hedgehog to show Elizabeth, which she mistook for a mouse and took such fright that dinner was canceled and the jester was dragged off to the torture chamber. The fate of both jester and hedgehog are unknown.

Favorites and Institutions

Unlike Anna, who consulted Biron on almost everything, Elizabeth was unwilling to entrust policymaking to any one person. She ruled through a number of advisers, including Michael Vorontsov (1714–1767), her vice chancellor, whom she regarded as a trusted friend until he alienated her with his pro-Prussian sympathies in 1745. From 1731 her personal favorite was the Ukrainian Alexis Razumovsky (1709–1771), a singer in the court choir whom she may have married secretly in 1742. Elizabeth heaped honors and gifts on him, but he had no political ambitions and held no government posts. His brother Kirill (1728–1803), educated abroad at the empress's expense, became president of the Academy of Sciences and in 1750, at the age of twenty-two, hetman of the Ukrainian Cossacks, by now an honorary post. A key feature of Elizabeth's household was that it included the junior court of her nominated heir, her nephew, Peter (1728–1762), son of her late sister, Anna. In 1745 she married him off to Princess Sophia Auguste Frederike of Anhalt-Zerbst (1729–1796), the daughter of Prince Christian August of the minor north German principality of Anhalt-Zerbst and his wife Johanna Elisabeth of Holstein-Gotthorp. Sophia took the name Catherine when she converted to Orthodoxy. In time husband and wife drifted apart, establishing their own separate alliances and households.

The complexities of favoritism are illustrated by the career of Peter Shuvalov (1710–1762), who married Elizabeth's maid of honor in 1742 and rose to dominate domestic affairs, without being intimate with the empress. He made a vast personal fortune, at the same time as he helped fill state coffers by means of financial reforms. Shuvalov had his own favorite, to whom other nobles deferred, and he also operated through his cousin Ivan Shuvalov (1727–1797), whom he promoted at court. In September 1749 Ivan became gentleman of the bedchamber and in 1751 chamberlain, which was interpreted as a sign that he was now Elizabeth's lover; but he always refused high political or military office. Instead, he made his mark in cultural affairs as cofounder and curator of Moscow University and first president of the Academy of Fine Arts.

Power bases and coalitions overlapped with institutional bodies. Officially it was the Senate that chose Catherine I in 1725, but it was then pushed into the background after Menshikov set up the Supreme Privy Council. Anna abolished the Council in 1730, restored the Senate, and in 1731 established Her Imperial Majesty's Cabinet. Elizabeth replaced that with her Special Chancellery, enhancing the power of the Senate. In general, though, she preferred to operate through "conferences" of advisers, as first informal but from 1756 more regular, although never defined in law. These bodies initiated a number of schemes, notably a commission established in 1755 to recodify the laws. In turn, in January 1762 Peter III would abolish Elizabeth's conference in favor of a military council, reducing the power of the Senate again. None of these changes altered the fact that throughout the period 1730–1761 Russia was governed not by institutions but by men operating within the framework of autocracy. All decisions continued to be cloaked in the rhetoric of autocratic power, according to which no one intervened between rulers and their people or between them and God.

RUSSIA AND THE WORLD

In March 1730 a writer in *The British Journal* expressed fears that "unless the Empire of Russia rouses itself from under the lethargic slumber, which it is now fallen into, their furred Gowns and long Petticoats will return upon them; and all the sordid affectation of a singularity from all the world, which made them so truly contemptible before, will do the like again." But Russia's slumber was an illusion and both the writer's predictions—about reversion to Muscovite traditions and withdrawal from the world stage—proved false. In the period 1725–1762 territorial expansion was slight, but Russia maintained the embassies Peter I had established all over Europe—twelve on his death, as compared with just one when he came to the throne—and had a voice in all the major disputes on the continent of Europe and some beyond.

The Costs and Benefits of Empire

Luckily for Peter I's successors, the late 1720s saw no major conflicts, allowing them to make savings by disbanding some army units. But territorial expansion had posed additional problems of defense. Throughout the eighteenth century Russia needed to maintain not just European-style infantry and cavalry together with siege and field artillery, but also lighter units to fight steppe nomads. The fleet, too, was kept up as a useful bargaining chip and a symbol of national pride, even though parts of it fell into disrepair. At the same time, the eighteenth-century wars in which Russia engaged scarcely touched Russian home territory. The population suffered from the inexorable demands of conscription and taxation and from war casualties on a grand scale—one hundred thousand dead in the Russo-Turkish war of 1735–1739, for example—but not from occupation by enemy troops.

In one important respect the empire building of the rest of the century differed from Peter I's variant: none of his successors was involved personally in armed combat, although Peter III and Paul I would have liked to be. Russia's rulers, like their foreign counterparts, had substitutes fight their battles, while they themselves could safely either be wreathed in the imagery of victory or, in the case of defeat, distanced from the mess the generals had created. Military success and limiting the impact of war on the home front were major factors in maintaining autocracy intact.

Historians have asked whether the growth of the Russian Empire was driven by the need to overcome backwardness by acquiring ports, grain-rich areas, and additional human and material resources. Or did expansion actually delay Russia's modernization by concentrating human and natural resources on sustaining an ultimately unsustainable empire? It has been argued that in the process of becoming a multiethnic state, Russia failed to become a nation, severely restricting the development of either a civic or an ethnic consciousness vital to nationhood. The burdens of an empire ruled from St. Petersburg required the preservation of autocracy and serfdom and the categorization of the population in terms of service or tax liabilities rather than rights and privileges.

One of the costs of empire was the notorious rift between the "two Russias"—the elite and the masses—which widened as maintaining great power status required completion of the cultural Westernization of the upper classes to achieve parity with elites elsewhere in Europe. By 1762 a generation of nobles had grown up who felt at ease in Western clothes, could converse in French, and were closer to a German or English counterpart than to a Russian peasant. By and large, in the period 1725–1762 this dilemma was not debated or even recognized in Russia itself. It fell to a later generation to acknowledge the price that Russia may have paid for becoming a world power.

War and Diplomacy

The international tasks facing Russia arose from Peter I's successes in the Baltic against Sweden, his failure in the south against Turkey, and the advantage that he consolidated against Poland. Peter's dynastic marriage politics also set the tone for some areas of diplomacy. European powers were reluctant to recognize the imperial titles claimed by Peter after the Treaty of Nystad: Austria and Britain did so only in 1742, France and Spain in 1745. But they were anxious to maintain a presence in St. Petersburg, where the international community continued to grow.

Russia sometimes did not have to do much at all to benefit from the shifting balance of power in Europe, which included the decline of France—the traditional friend of Russia's enemies Sweden, Poland, and Turkey—and enmity between Prussia and Austria. The latter's Catholic rulers, the Habsburg dynasty, still regarded themselves as rulers of the Holy Roman Empire, to which many German princes retained at least nominal allegiance. A treaty Russia made with Austria in 1726 confirmed the two countries' shared interests in Poland and Turkey, underpinning Russian alliances for much of the eighteenth century. Austria reckoned that this pact, renewed in 1746, would limit Russian interference with Orthodox populations within the Habsburg Empire, while allowing Russia a freer hand in Orthodox lands ruled by Poland and Turkey. The pact helped to decide the War of the Polish Succession (1733–1736), in which Russia and Austria clashed with France and Spain to head off the election of a French candidate, ex-king Stanislaw Leszczynski, to the Polish throne. Empress Anna dispatched Russian troops to dispute the "illegal" election, allowing an opposition Polish confederation to elect Austria's favored candidate, Augustus III (r. 1733–1763), son of Augustus II.

The 1730s brought renewed conflict with Ottoman Turkey. The brain behind Russia's foreign policy in the 1720s–1730s, Andrei Osterman, had plans for partitioning the Ottoman Empire, and in 1735 Russia, with Austrian support, went to war. Russia achieved major victories in the Crimea and Moldavia, but at high cost—three hundred thousand to four hundred thousand men mobilized in four years and one hundred thousand lost, mainly to disease. The Turkish war of 1735–1739 secured the restoration of Azov to Russia and some lands between Azov and the Dniester. Access to the Black Sea continued to be barred. But Turkey was clearly in trouble and would soon lose its French backing as France's influence in eastern Europe declined.

Hoping to recover some of its lost territories, Sweden attacked Russia in 1741 and was repelled. Elizabeth countered by occupying Finland. By the Treaty of Abo in 1743 Russia extended its occupation of the Viborg area to the north of St. Petersburg. In 1744 the former Swedish provinces there were joined to form Viborg Province, which in the early nineteenth century would become known as "Old Finland."

The nearly simultaneous succession in 1740 of Frederick II (the Great, 1712–1786) to the Prussian throne and Maria Theresa (1717–1780) to the hereditary Habsburg lands (although not to the Holy Roman Empire, which women were barred from ruling) set off a chain of events that would influence Elizabeth's entire reign. The ambitious Frederick promptly seized most of the duchy of Silesia from Maria Theresa, then part of her Bohemian crown lands, thereby sparking the War of Austrian Succession (1740–1748), which pitted France, Prussia, and Bavaria against Austria, Britain, and Holland. At the beginning of Elizabeth's reign there was a pro-Prussian party at court headed by Michael Vorontsov, which in 1743 secured a mutual aid alliance with France, Prussia's friend. But Elizabeth was hostile to Frederick II, and in 1745 the anti-Prussian Alexis Bestuzhev-Ryumin (1693–1766) seized the initiative. His "system" envisaged alliances with Britain and Netherlands, Saxony, and Austria. The appearance on the Rhine of a Russian expeditionary force hastened the conclusion of peace (1748), which left Silesia under Prussia but granted the title Holy Roman Emperor to Maria Theresa's husband Francis I, rather than to a French client.

For the next six years Bestuzhev-Ryumin worked to obtain British subsidies to contain Prussia. He succeeded only in 1755, when a new Anglo-French colonial war was on the horizon. However, his Austrian counterpart Count Kaunitz (1711–1794) worked at cross-purposes by wooing France as a counterweight to Prussia. The result was the "Diplomatic Revolution" of 1756, whereby Britain and Prussia formed one alliance and France, Austria, and Russia another, with a proviso for the restoration of Silesia to Austria. Frederick II quickly went on the offensive, occupying Saxony and invading Bohemia.

The ensuing conflict, known as the Seven Years' War in Europe and the French and Indian War in British North America, was global in scope. Patriotic Russians point with pride to their successes against the highly regarded Prussians. Russia's armies won several battles, and in 1760 even temporarily occupied Berlin. Frederick evacuated Saxony. But the large Russian expeditionary forces lacked supplies for sustained initiatives and proved incapable of pursuing Frederick's mauled and much smaller, but still well supplied army. A chief reason that Russia did not exploit the military possibilities of the Seven Years' War was the internal misgivings over war aims, which led to indecisive leadership. Some people were reluctant to destroy Prussia, which had often been a valuable partner to Russia in Swedish and Polish affairs. One area of general agreement was that few among the Russian elite wished to strengthen France at the expense of Britain. Indeed Russian diplomacy successfully stayed out of the Anglo-French part of the war, while the French helped keep Russo-Turkish relations quiet.

As it turned out, mounting financial problems and desertion rates by unpaid troops in 1761 and then Elizabeth's death in December that year led Russia to withdraw from the war, at the initiative of the new emperor Peter III (see the section "The Emancipation of the Nobility" in this chapter), who was a great admirer of Frederick II. He restored captured lands to Frederick and even allied with him in 1762. Within a year the other belligerents made their own peace. Prussia retained Silesia, but Russia was clearly the dominant power in northeastern Europe and growing in strength relative to Turkey.

Far less public attention was devoted to developments in the East. In 1727 the Treaty of Kiakhta with China settled the border previously hazily defined in the Treaty of Nerchinsk (1689) and regularized trade between the two empires for the next 131 years. In 1737–1752 the Russians constructed about two thousand miles of new fortified lines from the mouth of the Yaik River (at the Caspian Sea) to the upper reaches of the Irtysh in Siberia. But the territories won by Peter I on the southern shores of the Caspian proved too costly to maintain, and in 1732 Russia withdrew from the region. During the war against Turkey, Russia gave up Baku and Derbent also. Expeditions eastward through Siberia established Russia in the New World. In 1728 the Dane Vitus Bering, whom Peter I had commissioned, sailed northeastward about fifteen hundred miles through the Arctic Ocean and discovered the strait between Asia and Alaska that bears his name. Thirteen years later, he and the Russian A. I. Chirikov discovered the southern coasts of Alaska and on their return voyage, the Aleutian Islands.

Economic Perspectives

Territorial expansion should, in theory, bring blessings. "Will not each feel the common good which, flowing from region to region of the empire's borders, overflows, feeding the inhabitants so abundantly that it is beyond expectation?" wrote Peter Shuvalov in 1754. Empire building stimulated the economy in various ways. It ensured, for example, that Peter's industrialization drive was not allowed to slacken and that attempts to put enterprises in private hands continued. Metal refining flourished in Anna's reign, with Russia becoming the world's top producer of cast iron by 1740. Russia's manufacturing work force grew from about eighteen thousand to sixty–eighty thousand during 1725–1770. But the dilemma of staffing factories in a serf economy remained. Merchants were offered the chance to become pseudonobles by a repeat (1744) of Peter's 1721 decree on the purchase of serfs for factories.

Methods of boosting state revenues included minting currency and increasing indirect taxation. In 1745 Peter Shuvalov started to promote new schemes for taxes on salt and spirits. Trade was not the great incentive for Russia that it was in the expansion of overseas empires, but it was not unimportant. In 1753 internal customs dues were abolished and import duties increased under a new protectionist policy. A huge duty-free market unmatched in Europe was created. But the bulk of state revenues still had to come from the more than 90 percent of the population who paid direct taxes. In 1726 Catherine I's advisers had warned that the peasants were "in dire need and being reduced to final and utter ruin by heavy taxes." In 1730 and 1735 the government granted concessions on poll tax arrears and appealed to landlords to provide their serfs with seed for planting. Elizabeth granted a tax amnesty backdated to 1725 and made several more temporary poll tax reductions in the course of her reign. But a new census in 1744—the first since 1722–1723—revealed a one-sixth increase in taxable males and allowed a corresponding new assessment of communities. None of these measures was sufficient in time of war, when Russia had to resort to raising foreign loans and debasing the currency. It is difficult not to conclude that had resources and lives spent on Anna's and Elizabeth's Turkish and Prussian wars been devoted to domestic economic and cultural development, Russia would have been even stronger in 1762, just as secure, and certainly more prosperous.

ARTS AND SCIENCES

Peter I's immediate successors built on foundations that he had laid in the visual arts and architecture, education and publishing, and also sponsored areas that he had neglected, such as theater and music. All such developments continued to focus on St. Petersburg. Moscow, the old capital, was used for coronations, underlining dynastic continuity, but after her own coronation, Anna formally confirmed the return of the court to St. Petersburg, where it would remain, along with practically all major institutions, until its demise in 1917. None of the men behind the throne, themselves nearly all well educated by Russian standards, advocated a return to Muscovite beards and boyars.

Court Life and Courtiers

Peter I set little store by the conventional trappings of a European-style household, and Catherine I and Peter II had little time to embellish theirs. A more or less regular court establishment emerged only in the reign of Anna. As one foreign observer remarked, she loved magnificence in her household and encouraged luxury and outward display until they "rivalled that of the court of France." But if some writers regarded Anna's as the first Russian court with any claim to refinement, in the view of others, the sumptuousness was both vulgar and bizarre. Anna relegated several nobles to the role of jester, most memorably Prince Michael Golitsyn, who had to pretend to be a chicken and sit on eggs in a large basket. In 1740 Anna married him off to a woman from the Kalmyk tribe of nomads. The newly wedded pair were transported on an elephant, with attendants in carriages drawn by camels, goats, and pigs, to a palace on the ice of the Neva River, where they had to lie naked on an ice bed wearing ice nightcaps and slippers. Playing the fool may have been regarded as just another form of Russian state service, but such events tended to confirm in Western eyes that the Russian nobility did not enjoy the respect and dignity due its rank.

Not all Anna's court functions were quite so bizarre. On January 4, 1740, the *St. Petersburg News* reported: "On New Year's Day, Her Imperial Majesty was pleased to receive the most humble season's greetings from all the foreign ministers attached to the court and other distinguished persons of both sexes." In the evening from four till eight there was a ball and after the ball a magnificent firework display on the Neva River in front of the imperial palace. Such displays were probably unmatched in splendor in Europe.

Elizabeth was famed for even more lavish entertainments in which her own attractive person took center stage. The future Russian playwright Denis Fonvizin (1744?–1792) observed: "I confess sincerely that I was amazed by the splendour of the court of our empress. . . . The palace seemed to me the habitation of a being higher than mortal." It has been said that Elizabeth's pageants, parades, and festivals celebrated a monarch who promoted the welfare of her fortunate subjects. That Elizabeth was regarded as a beauty and had a graceful and majestic bearing was vital to the success of this particular scenario, as was her love of dancing and dressing up. She really did own thousands of costly outfits, most worn only once. Her rules on court dress and accessories also included restrictions to ensure that her own costumes and hairstyle were not duplicated. All eyes had to be on the empress. She particularly loved transvestite masquerades. The sheer expense of court life could ruin even influential men like Peter Shuvalov, who died leaving enormous debts.

Music and dance were important at both Anna's and Elizabeth's courts. Elizabeth herself enjoyed singing Italian and Russian folk songs. A 1749 decree declared: "Henceforth at court each week after noon there will be music: on Mondays dance music, on Wednesdays Italian music and on Tuesdays and Fridays comedies." Foreign masters wrote new works for the court orchestra, made up mainly of Italian and French musicians, and directed operatic and ballet spectacles involving lavish and intricate scenery, lighting effects, and costumes. Theatricals and the "real" life of the court intermingled.

Paintings and Palaces

Court life required new architectural designs and spaces; for example, linked series of rooms for promenading in mixed company and grand halls with high ceilings for balls and concerts. The new palaces reserved private space for rulers and their favorites and always had a chapel, but usually just one, rather than the dozen or so in the Kremlin. Maintaining winter and summer palaces, reflecting the radically different weather in the two seasons, went back to earlier times, as did stopover palaces for the royal party. By Elizabeth's time there were twenty-five such palaces on the Moscow to St. Petersburg road alone.

Little of Anna's program for extending and embellishing the court's architectural setting survives today. She did, however, launch the career of mid-eighteenth-century Russia's most influential architect, Bartolomeo Francesco Rastrelli (1700–1771), the son of the eminent sculptor. The younger Rastrelli became famous as the master of "Elizabethan baroque." His blue-and-white Smolny Convent with its splendid five-domed cathedral was commissioned by Elizabeth as a possible retreat in her old age. In the 1740s–1750s he replaced a small palace built for Catherine I at Tsarskoe Selo outside St. Petersburg with the grand Catherine Palace, an amazing confection of vast length, with turquoise blue walls set off by white stone and gilded ornamentation and ornate plaster work. Inside guests were ushered into a seemingly endless series of rooms, all decorated in gilt and with painted ceilings and full of rare furniture and porcelain. The mirrors and chandeliers of the great hall created a magical setting for balls. The equally vast Winter Palace in central St. Petersburg, completed in 1762, was, in Rastrelli's words, created "for the glory of Russia."

Pictures were now required by the square meter, often covering whole walls without any gaps in between. Foreign artists made numerous copies of Russian royal portraits, aided by their Russian pupils, such as Ivan Vishniakov (1699–1761) and Aleksei Antropov (1716–1795). Andrei Matveev (1701?–1739), who trained abroad, is credited with the first Russian easel painting on an allegorical subject, *Al-*

The Winter Palace in St. Petersburg (completed 1762), by Bartolomeo Rastrelli. Façade facing the Neva river. © *William Brumfield.*

legory of Painting (1725), but it took time to assimilate the full repertoire of Western genres. In particular, Peter's efforts to train Russian sculptors failed almost entirely and statues continued to be imported from abroad. The founding of the St. Petersburg Academy of Fine Arts on the initiative of Ivan Shuvalov in 1757 was an attempt to provide not only training but also a career path for Russian artists, with the aim of bringing more "glory" to the empire. It initially relied on foreign teachers, but Russians of any social class, occasionally even serfs, could gain access. The talents of Academy-trained artists such as the sculptor Fëdor Shubin (1740–1805), the architect Vasily Bazhenov (1737?–1799), and the painter Anton Losenko (1737–1773) would flourish in Catherine II's reign.

Learning and Literature

Peter's immediate successors, none of whom was well educated or attached to scholarly pursuits, inherited distinctly patchy educational provision, even by eighteenth-century European standards. Peter I's piecemeal experiments were undermined by lack of funding and popular indifference or even hostility. The Russian nobility generally accepted institutional education only when it was directly linked to service, for example, the Cadet Corps school (founded 1731), which allowed quick promotion to first officer grade (Table of Ranks grade 14). The best schools were run by the church, offering programs that provided a good modern education for young men of non-noble status. After Peter's death some seventeen ecclesiastical academies were created, which, along with older religious establishments such as the Moscow Academy, not only educated top churchmen but also prepared most of the staff and students for secular higher schools.

The Academy of Sciences opened in St. Petersburg in August 1725, with an all-foreign, mostly German faculty. The Academy was supposed to combine scientific research with teaching in a university, although the latter did not materialize. In the eighteenth century only a quarter of full members of the Academy were Russian born, of whom the most illustrious was Mikhail Lomonosov (1711–1765), son of a White Sea peasant, who after training in the Moscow Academy was sent to study in Germany. In 1741 he became the first Russian full academician and went on to distinguish himself as a chemist, linguist, poet, historian, and maker of mosaics. Soviet historians extolled Lomonosov as a thoroughly "new" man, a great genius and patriot. Only in recent times has it become possible to reach a more impartial assessment of a man who. although multitalented, made no original scientific discoveries and retained a degree of traditional Orthodox piety.

In 1754 Ivan Shuvalov and Lomonosov corresponded about founding a university, "for the true good and glory of our country." Lomonosov initially doubted the feasibility of a national university when there was such a scarcity of "men of learning" in Russia. He proposed founding two grammar schools—one for nobles, one for non-nobles—but making no distinctions of social category in the university itself. And "since learning does not tolerate coercion and is rightly included among the noblest institutions of humankind," no serfs would be admitted; if nobles wished to educate talented serfs, they must first emancipate them. Moscow University opened in a building on Red Square in June 1755 under Shuvalov's direction. Denis Fonvizin, one of the first students enrolled, recorded "learning without order," drunken and negligent teachers, and poorly prepared classes. It took many decades for the university to become Russia's leading institution of higher education. Fonvizin's bad experience as a student did not prevent him becoming one of Russia's first prominent men of letters.

In general, nobles outside court circles were slow to cultivate the arts or to develop a taste for books. Peter I's publishing operation was all but dismantled, with only about twenty books published each year in the late 1720s. Literary life picked up in the reigns of Anna and Elizabeth, but even then original work by Russian writers represented an insignificant proportion of what was published. Some writers now famous remained unpublished in their lifetimes; for example, Antiokh Kantemir (1708–1744), whose nine satires in verse heaped scorn upon detractors of learning. Other authors of the post-Petrine generation, such as Vasily Trediakovsky (1703–1769) and Lomonosov, specialized in celebratory verses to the crown, such as Lomonosov's "Ode on the Victory over the Turks and Tatars and the Capture of Khotin" (1739). Both men were interested in theories of literature, pioneering and writing about the use of verse based on English and German models.

Russians began to write seriously for the theater. Classical drama was in vogue, especially tragedy, with its aim of inculcating virtue and warning against vice. In 1756 Elizabeth appointed A. P. Sumarokov (1717–1777) as the first director of the Russian theater. His play *Khorev* (1747) was the first Russian classical tragedy, with allusions to the relationship between the monarch and the nobles and warnings against tyranny, excessive favoritism, and arbitrary disgrace. It played alongside Shakespeare's *Hamlet* (1748) in Sumarokov's translation.

The crucial issue hanging over Russian art, learning, and literature at this time concerned national identity. The phenomenon of a major power acquiring contemporary culture more or less from scratch was unprecedented in Europe. Driving the process was the idea that learning was essential in a civilized country and that European cultural values, based on ancient Classical models, were universal. In Russia in the first half of the eighteenth century, however, the achievements were limited; knowledge was pursued primarily for the good of the state, not the development of the individual. Only in the second half of the century did art and culture spread more widely from the court to a wider public and a few people begin to react against the excessive adulation of all things French ("Gallomania") and other examples of blindly imitating foreigners.

PETER III AND THE NOBLES

Apart from the imperial family and its immediate circle, the chief consumers and beneficiaries of new cultural opportunities were nobles. But in the decades after Peter I's death the Russian nobility remained a service elite rather than a cultural elite Gradually they succeeded in whittling away the service requirement, until in the short reign of Peter III (1761–1762) they were freed from compulsory service altogether. This concession did not save Peter from a violent end, as we shall see.

Serving the State

Membership of the Table of Ranks (see the chapter "Peter the Great: Birth of an Empire, 1689–1725") provides a snapshot of the men actively engaged in military, civil, or court service, ranging from the select few generals, admirals, and ministers of state in ranks 1–4 down to the numerous junior ensigns, midshipmen, and college registrars in rank 14. Some lesser nobles never even reached rank 14 but served in the lower, noncommissioned grades for years, while the better-off registered their sons in guards regiments as children to ensure that they became officers at a very early age. Performing some form of state service was the chief factor that still united the nobles as a class, for outside public service there were virtually no acceptable paid outlets for a nobleman's talents. Russian nobles did not, with rare exceptions, become priests, and Russia lacked the legal profession and parliament that kept many members of the British nobility occupied, for example. The visual arts, poetry, and playwriting were pursued in one's spare time only.

The principle that nobles served may not have changed much since Muscovite times, but a new noble consciousness did begin to emerge, as expressed, for example, during the attempts to limit Anna's powers in the "constitutional" crisis of 1730, when both eminent and lesser nobles engaged with the government on such issues as the period and terms of service, access to promotion, and inheritance legislation. Peter I's unpopular Law of Single Inheritance was repealed in 1731. In particular, nobles challenged the norm of lifelong service. In 1736 the requirement was reduced from life to twenty-five years, and one son was allowed to stay home to look after the estate. This development suited the state as much as it suited the nobles, for paying salaries was an expensive business. But nobles still complained about lack of personal property rights, the threat of arbitrary exile or confiscation, and the absence of representative noble institutions.

Some historians have spoken of the emergence of the Russian nobility as a "unified estate," where distinctions were of wealth and prestige rather than of rights and status. In other words, the nobles themselves opposed the awarding of special privileges and special access to political power to an elite group from within their midst, as was attempted in 1730. At the same time, existing nobles resented infiltration by outsiders via the Table of Ranks, where reaching rank 14 (military) or rank 8 (civil service) conferred hereditary nobility. In practice the Table became more a closed shop, and achieving noble status through service became harder. Peter I's "democratic" assemblies in private homes, which any decently dressed nonpeasant could attend, met a similar fate. For purposes of socializing and entertaining, the nobles became more exclusive.

The economic status of nobles varied enormously. A mere 1 percent owned more than a thousand male serfs (only males were counted in censuses), while over 50 percent owned fewer than twenty and some owned none at all. Those with the most serfs often took the least personal interest in agriculture because in general the greater a man's wealth and number of "souls," the greater the imperative to chase the power and status of high office, which usually meant living in St. Petersburg. Most richer nobles owned not one single, consolidated estate, but many packages of land that had been acquired separately over generations and could just as easily be further fragmented by the practice of owners bequeathing their estates to all their children. Some nobles were able to take advantage of state incentives, for example, taking out loans from the State Loan Bank, founded in 1754, although borrowing often led to the mortgaging of serfs as collateral. After 1755 nobles enjoyed a monopoly on the distillation of alcohol.

Nobles tried to retain as large a share as possible of their peasants' labor at the state's expense and also to gain a freer hand in disposing of their human property. In 1742 serfs were forbidden from enlisting voluntarily in the army, and in 1747 landlords gained the right to sell off serfs as recruits to fellow nobles who could not meet their recruit quota. Sales of individual serfs without accompanying land, discouraged by Peter I, also became widespread. A 1760 decree allowed owners, as part of their recruit quota, to exile troublesome but able-bodied serfs to Siberia, where they would become state peasants. Then in 1762 a measure that allowed the nobles to gain more control over their own lives was passed by an unlikely initiator.

The Emancipation of the Nobility

The future emperor Peter III was born in Germany in February 1728 and raised as a Lutheran in the court of his father, Duke Karl of Holstein. His mother, Peter I's daughter Anna, died when he was an infant. On his father's side he was related to the Swedish royal family (his grandmother was a sister of Charles XII) and had a strong claim to the Swedish throne. After his aunt Elizabeth brought him to Russia to be groomed as her heir, he received instruction in the Russian language and the Orthodox religion, to which he converted. His main interests were military, particularly drill and fortifications. In 1745, as we saw, he was married off to a fifteen-year-old German bride, who would later become known as Catherine the Great.

Catherine's memoirs (started in 1771) painted a bleak picture of this teenage marriage. Incidents that stick in the mind are Peter court-martialing rats, bringing hunting dogs to the marriage bed, and peeping through a hole in the wall at Empress Elizabeth and her lover. Catherine suggested that Peter was mentally retarded. Moreover, she hinted strongly that their marriage was never consummated and that her first child, the future emperor Paul (b. 1754), was in fact the son of the Russian nobleman Sergei Saltykov, who was thrust upon her when she had failed to produce an heir after almost ten years of marriage. Peter was an "absurd husband," in fact, not a husband at all, and his own acquisition of a long-term mistress was something of a relief for his wife. Catherine, of course, had good reason to blacken the reputation of the husband whose throne she later snatched. Even so, witnesses corroborate the essence, if not all the details, of Catherine's portrait of Peter, who generally failed to win people's respect. He seems to have been immature to the point of childishness, impulsive, and unpredictable. He loved dolls and puppets and enjoyed practical jokes and drinking. A favorite hobby was playing the violin, in imitation of Frederick II of Prussia, whom he regarded as one of "the greatest heroes in the world." Surviving portraits tend to confirm his rather weedy, unprepossessing appearance, in sharp contrast to his giant grandfather Peter I, some of whose character traits he nevertheless shared.

Being "absurd" and childlike were not sufficient reasons for a Russian ruler to forfeit his rightful throne. On the contrary, powerful courtiers could easily accommodate such monarchs; they were less happy with unpredictable rulers with minds of their own, who acted contrary to consensus. In Russia such a ruler would be even more vulnerable if he alienated the guards regiments, who over four decades had gained the confidence that they influenced who ruled Russia. In this respect, Peter's greatest mistake was not the peace that he made with Prussia in May 1762, acting "out of compassion for suffering humanity and from personal friendship for the King of Prussia," but a new personally motivated campaign to take Schleswig, formerly the possession of his Holstein ancestors, from Denmark. There was no support for this scheme among the Russian military, who were further alarmed by rumors that Peter intended to replace existing Russian guards with men from Holstein.

The impending peace with Prussia probably triggered the most significant piece of legislation of Peter's short reign, the manifesto releasing the Russian nobility from compulsory state service, issued on February 18, 1762. The manifesto flattered the nobles: "Coarseness in those who neglect the general good has been eradicated, ignorance has been transformed into healthy reason, useful knowledge and assiduity in service have increased the number of skilful and brave generals in military affairs, and have put informed and suitable people in civil and political affairs." The decree was not an invitation to wholesale retirement, however. There was no release from service immediately prior to and during military campaigns; men serving abroad were expected to rally to serve their country if the monarch summoned them; nobles' sons must present themselves at the age of twelve to prove they were educated; and nobles now in the lower ranks could not retire until they had completed twelve years of service. The document concluded by scorning "all those people who have never served anywhere, but spend all their time in sloth and idleness, . . . for they are negligent of the common good; and they will not be allowed to appear at Our Court, or at public meetings or celebrations."

The emancipation of the nobility has been attributed to pressure both from above—the state ridding itself of superfluous servitors—and from below—nobles demanding more rights. In the case of noble demands, it was the culmination of trends since the death of Peter I toward reducing the period of service. From the state's viewpoint, the timing of the end of the Seven Years' War, which necessitated demobilization, was crucial. With the prospect of many officers returning from active service came a chance to save salaries and redeploy the released nobles to the management of their estates and local affairs. At the same time, the manifesto recognized that state service was becoming more professional and no longer need depend on "forced labor." Nevertheless, as we shall see, most nobles continued to serve for the sake of salaries, perks, and honors.

The emancipation act, together with several other measures regarded as just and humane, later made Peter III a popular subject for impersonation by pretenders to the throne. During his six-month reign, in consultation with advisers, he implemented a reduction in the tax on salt, a temporary ban on the purchase of serfs for factories, and the lifting of some sanctions on Old Believers. One of his most remarkable measures was the transfer of about 2 million peasants on monastery estates from the church to the jurisdiction of the state-run College of Economy, a measure that continued trends over the past century to reduce the church's wealth and power. This did not constitute liberation but was regarded as an improvement in status by the peasants themselves. In conjunction with the emancipation of the nobility, the measure increased speculation that Peter might have been planning to emancipate the nobles' serfs.

None of this saved Peter III, who further sealed his fate by his apparent contempt for Orthodox ritual and icons. It was rumored that he neglected fasts and that he intended to convert Russia to the Lutheranism in which he was raised. Such accusations were stock ones against Russian rulers who came from outside, such as the first False Dmitry during the Time of Troubles. True or not, they served the purposes of Peter's many opponents. On June 28, 1762, his wife Grand Duchess Catherine seized power with the support of guards regiments, headed by her lover Grigory Orlov. "All unanimously agree that Grand Duke Peter Fedorovich is incompetent and Russia has nothing to expect but calamity," she declared in her accession manifesto. After vain efforts to rally support, Peter abdicated and was placed under house arrest. In July he died, officially of " haemorrhoidal colic." Rumors hinted at murder by poison, strangulation, suffocation, beating, or shooting. The head of the ex-emperor's escort reported an unfortunate scuffle. No one was charged, but even if Peter was not killed on Catherine's explicit orders, his death did not arouse her regret.

CHAPTER 14

Catherine the Great: In Pursuit of Enlightenment and Empire, 1762–1796

Posterity judges, and will judge, Catherine with all human prejudice. The new philosophy, by which she was unfortunately influenced and which was the mainspring of her failings, covered as with a thick veil her great and fine qualities. But it seems only just to dwell for a moment on the period of her splendid dawn, before condemning and wiping out the memory of her glory and her unspeakable goodness.

—From the memoirs of Countess V. N. Golovina, born 1766

Few rulers have provoked such controversy as Catherine II (1729–1796), known as the "Great." During her thirty-four-year reign the Russian Empire expanded and the economy grew. Nobles and townspeople received charters. Provincial government was reformed. Public education developed. Literature and the arts flourished. This was, a contemporary concluded, "the happiest of all the known epochs in Russian history." At the same time, fundamental institutions—autocracy and serfdom—survived intact, leading many writers to conclude that Russia remained a "backward" country. One of the most savage rebellions in Russian history, led by the Cossack Emelian Pugachev, was brutally suppressed. Some elite rebels, too, found themselves banished. Many historians judged Catherine harshly, condemning her for providing the veneer of reform without the substance. In this chapter and the next we examine major developments in the latter half of the eighteenth century, returning constantly to the tension between the enlightened theories that guided Catherine and her advisers and the stark practicalities of governing a vast, multiethnic empire.

A PORTRAIT OF CATHERINE

That we know more about Catherine II than any of her female predecessors on the Russian throne is largely thanks to her own voluminous writings. She left a memoir of her early years in Russia, corresponded with people in Russia and abroad, and wrote plays and stories as well as decrees and charters. And writers all over Europe, those who had met her and those who had not, penned impressions of her. She was, quite simply, the most famous woman of her era.

Apprenticeship

Catherine found life at Elizabeth's court irksome. Elizabeth, in Catherine's view, was a real "battle-axe," often drunk, jealous, and suspicious. Kept at arm's length by the empress and neglected by her unsatisfactory husband Grand Duke Peter, Catherine devoured books and dabbled in court intrigues. Toward the end of Elizabeth's reign these intrigues began to focus on Catherine supplanting her husband as empress in her own right or as regent to her son Paul. That she chose the former arrangement was further to sour relations with the son who was taken away from her when he was an infant and whom she apparently never much liked.

The manifesto on Catherine's accession to the throne that she presented in June 1762 condemned Peter III for being contemptuous of Russia and Orthodoxy. It was coauthored by Count Nikita Panin (1718–1783), who served as her foreign minister for the next nineteen years. The aim was to distract attention from Catherine's own "outsider" credentials and lack of formal entitlement to Peter's throne. The manifesto contrasted her concern for Russia with his lack of it. "All the respected traditions of our fatherland are being trampled underfoot. So we, being conscious that it is the honest desire of all our loyal subjects, and having God and justice on our side, have ascended the throne as Catherine II, autocrat of all Russia." Catherine really did intend to rule in the best interests of her adopted people and to make Russia more civilized and enlightened according to the understanding of the time.

The first few years of Catherine's reign were devoted mainly to clearing up her predecessors' unfinished business, including ratifying cordial relations with Prussia, reviewing the terms of the emancipation of the nobility from service, and revising the decree on the transfer of church peasants to the state, which was completed in 1764. She also continued the restructuring of central and provincial government, for example, by reducing the legislative powers of the Senate and extending the powers of governors. But she rejected Panin's project for an imperial council, which might have limited her power. In July 1764 a minor nobleman tried to free ex-emperor Ivan VI from the Schlüsselburg fortress. His guards followed the set procedures for dealing with an escape bid and killed Ivan. In the eyes of some foreign observers, Catherine's reputation never recovered from suspicions of double regicide. Certainly the awkward fact that two former emperors had met death within two years provided Catherine with another motive for exercising caution. She was inexperienced and vulnerable, dependent upon the loyalty of a close group of friends and officials. These men and a few women provided crucial political support for a widowed female ruler who refused to be a mere figurehead.

Lovers and Friends

The issue of Catherine's lovers presents a challenge to historians: if they ignore it, they risk the accusation of suppressing historical evidence; if they explore it, they risk the charge of pandering to the prurient. But the topic cannot be avoided, for the "institutionalization" of favoritism was an essential element in Catherine's style of rulership and had an impact on relations at court and beyond. It is therefore just as well to clear up the basic facts from the outset.

Catherine had just twelve lovers who enjoyed official or semiofficial status as her consorts, all men, consecutively over a period of forty-four years, nine of them after she was widowed. While still grand duchess, Catherine had semiclandestine affairs with the Russian nobleman Sergei Saltykov, with the future king of Poland Count Stanislaw Poniatowski (1732–1798; r. 1764–1795) and the Russian war hero Grigory Orlov (1734–1783), who fathered her son Alexis Bobrinskoy (b. 1762). When Orlov's successor, the young guards officer Alexander Vasilchikov, moved into the palace in 1772, Orlov departed with a hundred fifty thousand rubles, a further one hundred thousand rubles "relocation expenses," a palace, ten thousand peasants, fine porcelain, and other gifts. This set the tone for future "retirement" packages. Being the empress's lover could set a man up for life.

The flamboyant guards officer Grigory Potemkin (1739–1791) occupied the post of official lover for just over two years in 1774–1776, but he remained Catherine's virtual coruler, a major figure in foreign and military affairs until his death. They probably married secretly, although documentary evidence is lacking. Their passionate affair settled into domesticity and friendship in an odd extended household, which included Potemkin's own mistresses and Catherine's favorite of the moment. In 1776 the Ukrainian Peter Zavadovsky (1739–1812) became the favorite but was dismissed the following year. He was succeeded by Simon Zorich (aged thirty-two to Catherine's forty-eight), who made way in 1778 for Ivan Rimsky-Korsakov (aged twenty-four). Catherine was devastated when his successor, Alexander Lanskoy, died at the age of twenty-six in 1784. Both Lanskoy and thirty-year-old Alexander Ermolov were aides-de-camp to Potemkin, which aroused rumors that Potemkin "procured" the empress's young lovers. But it would be fairer to say that the circle from which Catherine selected her lovers was of necessity a very restricted one. Alexander Dmitriev-Mamonov, aged twenty-six, took over as favorite in 1786 but soon betrayed Catherine with a younger mistress and was replaced in 1789 by the even younger Platon Zubov (1767–1822), who remained in post until Catherine's death.

Catherine's lovers from Orlov onward shared certain common features. All but one were guardsmen; they tended to come from minor noble clans (possibly to reduce jealousies among top families); they were all younger than she was, the age gap increasing as she grew older. Good looks and charm generally provided the initial attraction. Mostly they shared her interests in literature and culture, while she saw herself as "educating" the younger ones, a metaphor, perhaps, for enlightening Russia. After they were banished from the bedroom, they were neither disgraced nor humiliated, even if they had done wrong. Redeployed harmlessly with generous allowances, they were disinclined to stir up trouble. Only Potemkin, Zavadovsky, and Zubov had prominent careers in public service thereafter.

The foreign press equated the empress's appetite for sexual conquests with her appetite for territorial expansion, to be discussed later. In fact, the tone of Catherine's private circle was of domesticity rather than decadence, and Catherine herself was prudish even about bad language. An avowed workaholic, she rarely allowed love to disrupt her orderly timetable. Everything was in its place. The everyday routine of the palace was low-key—private parties, card playing, and conversation, with the occasional masked ball or visit to the theater to liven things up—and became more so as Catherine grew older.

All this was accompanied by an element of showmanship. Catherine cultivated "simplicity," but she appreciated that a monarch must dress for the occasion and that both subjects and foreigners had certain expectations of the imperial personage. If the situation demanded, she would wear the orders, stars, and ribbons of Saints Andrew, George, Alexander Nevsky, Catherine, and Vladimir all at once. Her favorite portraits of herself showed her in sumptuous gowns surrounded by symbols of power.

Empress Catherine II (r. 1762–1796) in the Temple of Justice (1783), by Dmitry Levitsky. *Tretyakov Gallery, Moscow, Russia/Art Resource, NY.*

ENLIGHTENED ABSOLUTISM

The ideological underpinnings of Catherine's policies developed from her readings of the leading writers of the European Enlightenment. The "Enlightenment" originated in seventeenth-century Europe and reached its height in the middle of the eighteenth century, when it spread to North America, too. The term embodies the notion of the light of reason banishing the darkness of ignorance, intolerance, and cruelty. The leading thinkers of the Enlightenment, often referred to by the French terms *philosophes* or *lumières* (luminaries), all agreed that society could be perfected by applying rational concepts and banishing unthinking tradition. In their view, all people were in their nature rational and good and must in time enjoy freedom and equality before the law. The key to allowing all people to enjoy their full potential lay in education. To this end, one of the philosophes' major collaborative ventures was compiling the *Encyclopaedia* of "all human knowledge," which eventually reached completion in seventeen volumes in 1772. Although the philosophes believed that national and religious differences were temporary, they agreed that different countries were at different stages on the path toward perfection. In big, poor countries like Russia improvement would come from above, driven by rulers who accepted Enlightened principles and deployed their unlimited powers for the common good, hence the terms *Enlightened absolutism* or *Enlightened despotism*.

The Great Instruction

In 1767 Catherine published her Enlightenment-driven vision for Russia in the document known as the "Great Instruction," a statement of general principles listed under 526 articles for the guidance of a Legislative Commission, summoned that year to discuss the recodification of the laws. This took up a process that had been initiated under Elizabeth.

Defining the nature and purpose of the "Instruction" has been central to historians' assessment of Catherine and her regime. Its main theme was the improvement of law-based monarchy. It started from the premise that laws must conform to the historical nature of the people for whom they are intended, and sovereigns must rule in harmony with them and regard them as binding. Chapter 1, Article 6 stated confidently that "Russia is a European state," for which the right form of government was monarchy, not the despotism that some writers thought inherent to vast non-European empires. At the same time, the monarch must be absolute, "for there is no other authority except that which centers on his single person that can act with a vigor proportionate to the extent of such a vast dominion" (Chapter 1, Article 10).

Catherine approached the composition of the "Instruction" as a piece of "philosophical" writing and an exercise in literary style. In eighteenth-century literature no clear separation existed between works of the imagination and works of a discursive and factual kind. Nor was there today's emphasis on originality or disapproval of "plagiarism." Skill in imitation of literary genre was highly prized. Thus some 294 of the "Instruction's" 526 articles were borrowed from the work *On the Spirit of the Laws* (1748) by the political thinker Charles Louis de Secondat Montesquieu (1689–1755) and adapted accordingly. Catherine accepted the French writer's advocacy of the separation of legislative, executive, and judicial powers and the need for fundamental laws, but she would not concede independent powers for the nobility. Freedom from oppression and encroachment as guaranteed by law did not mean license to do anything you liked. As Article 38 stated: "Liberty is the right to do everything which the laws permit." Likewise, equality implied subjugation to the same laws that were appropriate to other members of one's class or estate, not having the same laws for princes and peasants.

Another 108 articles came from the treatise *On Crime and Punishment* by the Italian thinker Cesare Beccaria (1738–1794), who advocated that punishments must be humane to induce repentance in offenders. Capital punishment was only for criminals who threatened the state, while cruel punishments and torture during investigation were condemned. Other sections of the "Instruction" drew on modern European writings on social welfare, trade, and prosperity. The document contained many concepts that were radical for Russia; for example, that a person was innocent until proven guilty. In Russian practice, defendants had to prove their innocence.

The initial audience for the "Instruction," the Legislative Commission, was itself suggested by Catherine's reading of the French *Encyclopaedia.* The Commission was convened in Moscow on July 30, 1767, and met 204 times, moving to St. Petersburg early in 1768. Attendance fluctuated between 518 and 580 delegates, of whom nobles and merchants comprised some 60 percent, with homesteaders, state peasants, Cossacks, industrialists, non-Russian tribesmen, and some miscellaneous categories. Neither the serfs nor the clergy were represented. At the third session, delegates offered Catherine the titles "Great" and "All-wise Mother of the Fatherland," which she rejected. The final session took place in December 1768, after which many deputies left to serve in a war against Turkey that had just broken out (see next section).

The "Great Instruction" and the Legislative Commission have sometimes been dismissed as exercises in publicity and power building, in which promises were not matched by concrete measures. The "Instruction" has even been mistakenly described as a draft law code or, equally unjustly, as a piece of propaganda to get easy publicity abroad but not widely distributed in Russia. In fact, it went on sale in Russian bookshops, and members of the Commission were expected to reread it every month. The Commission is best seen as an attempt at national dialogue in preparation for recodifying the laws. It was not a political forum in the modern sense, still less a forerunner to a parliament, but resembled a traditional gathering to seek advice, like the old Assemblies of the Land, or a giant salon, where the debate was the thing. Catherine was disappointed. Even the noble delegates were ill-prepared to debate national issues. If they grasped the principles in the "Instruction" at all, they found them too radical. Nobles wanted the protection of their rights over their land and serfs and clarification of their status. Townspeople wanted some of the same privileges as nobles, especially the right to buy peasants.

Catherine may well have concluded that the overwhelming majority of her subjects were deeply conservative and that radical reform was therefore impossible. Even so, the "Instruction" and the Commission set the agenda for the rest of her reign. The Commission failed to recodify the laws, it is true, but far from being all window-dressing, it formed the basis of a whole package of measures in the 1770s–1780s carried out by subcommittees.

Catherine and the Philosophes

Both the "Instruction" and much of Catherine's later thinking owed a great deal to her relationship with the philosophes. The most notable was the eminent French thinker Voltaire (pen name of François-Marie Arouet, 1694–1778), who had been imprisoned and exiled for his political writings, especially his criticism of the Catholic Church. Catherine's correspondence with Voltaire was launched after he published his *History of Peter the Great* (1760–1762) and continued to his death. They shared a number of pet hates, which included the Turks, fanaticism, and superstition. In 1765 Catherine bought the library of another French thinker, Denis Diderot (1713–1784), which he had been forced to sell to meet debts, then allowed him to use it in his lifetime. Diderot, one of the editors of the *Encyclopaedia,* visited Russia in 1773–1774, and several times each week conducted informal conversations with Catherine. She, however, found his schemes for reform unrealistic. "You only work on paper, which will put up with anything," she complained, "whereas I, poor empress, work on human skin, which is notoriously irritable and ticklish." Diderot clung to the idea that "unformed" Russia was a blank sheet that would be easier to improve than Western countries, but Catherine knew better. Catherine's closest confidant was the German thinker Friedrich Melchior Grimm (1723–1807), to whose journal she subscribed and with whom she corresponded on all sorts of subjects, public and private, right up to her death.

Catherine has been accused of flattering the philosophes and fooling them into thinking that she was reforming Russia according to their principles, but this fails to take account of the limitations of the philosophes themselves. Voltaire, for example, was a monarchist, who opposed the idea of immediate freedom for serfs and thought it natural that rulers and their courts should be the driving force for improvement. He also approved of the first partition of Poland (discussed later in this chapter). Catherine did indeed implement some of his principles, such as secularizing church lands, establishing schools, practicing religious toleration, and outlawing torture.

The language of the philosophes was not the language of twenty-first-century political discourse. Their writings were not blueprints for reform but were, to a great extent, philosophy for philosophy's sake. Catherine herself thought and wrote in their language and adopted their terms of reference. Thus, in speaking of her "republican soul," Catherine was not advocating the overthrow of rulers. As Article 19 of the "Instruction" stated: "The sovereign is the source of all political and civil power." She adhered to the general view that republican regimes (in the strict sense of nonmonarchies) were suitable for small countries, such as Holland, Switzerland,

and Italian city-states, but not for large ones, especially those with many nationalities. Even so, she believed that big countries could still apply some of the good features of republican government by fostering commerce and manufacture, tolerating different beliefs, and so on. "Republican" also implied disapproval of arbitrary despotism, in both theory and practice.

Catherine's love of debate found expression in the Free Economic Society for the Encouragement of Agriculture and Good Husbandry, which was founded under her protection in 1765. In 1766 the Society launched an essay competition with a prize sponsored by Catherine on the topic: "Which is more beneficial to society, that the peasant should own land as property or only moveable property, and how far should his rights to this or that property be widened?" The contest attracted 160 entries from home and abroad. The winner argued that the happiest peasants were peasants with their own land. Other entries were more radical, condemning the "insult, torment and oppression" that many serfs suffered, but conceding that only abuses of the system, not the system itself, should be abolished. Agriculture was the basis of the Russian economy and a rush to cities would be a bad thing. Peasants, like children, it was believed, benefited from kind but firm guidance.

In sum, Catherine's thinking leaned heavily on her dealings with the philosophes, as well as on her wider reading of German and British as well as French writers, her appreciation of Russian precedents, and her perception of the Russian people as "childlike" and in need of direction. All pushed her to favor the model of a *Polizeistaat*—a "policed" state in the eighteenth-century sense of strong central concern for the common good on the basis of regulations implemented by officials to foster good order. The socialized person must replace the uncivilized person. "Policing" did not have to mean repression. In areas where it was deemed unnecessary, for example, allowing freedom of written expression, Catherine relaxed supervision, although this was to change toward the end of her reign.

"A New Type of Person"

Catherine's reading strongly influenced her attitude toward education, which she believed had the power to overcome superstition and prejudice. "Each citizen must be taught to recognize his obligation toward the Supreme Being, toward himself, and toward society," she wrote, "and one must teach that citizen certain skills, without which he will barely get along in everyday life." In the words of the "Instruction": "The rules of education are the first principles which prepare us to be citizens."

Catherine admitted that it was impractical to educate everyone, but she was aware that in 1762 almost no one in Russia was educated. Initially, she had ambitious plans: schools would create "a new type of person," who would help to expand the civilized populations of the new towns that she wished to create. Her early ideas were summed up in the "General Plan for the Education of Persons of Both Sexes" (1764), which concluded that a rational, well-ordered program with a stress on such matters as personal hygiene, suitable clothing, and exercise was the best way to produce perfect citizens. Children were best isolated from "pernicious" parental influences. Catherine later applied these principles to the upbringing of her two eldest grandsons, Alexander and Constantine (born 1777 and 1779, respectively), who were raised away from their parents in a Spartan atmosphere of healthy pursuits and a plain diet.

Among her public institutions, the Moscow orphanage and foundling homes (1763–1764) were intended to turn orphans and outcasts into anything the state wanted. Sadly, high mortality rates in these and other homes, which were poorly funded, often prevented the children from living long enough to turn into anything. More successful was the Smolny Institute for Noble Girls (1764), which provided a finishing school for generations of young women. Two separate schools founded in 1764–1765 for boys and girls from non-noble backgrounds had only indifferent success.

Provisions for schools under the terms of the 1775 Provincial Statute, to be discussed shortly, were variable. Finally, in August 1786 the Statute on National [Public] Schools initiated Catherine's most ambitious educational project, which adopted the methods of the Prussian educationalist Johann Felbiger, who had reformed Catholic schools in Silesia for Frederick the Great and introduced his system into the Habsburg Empire. The idea of a uniform curriculum and uniform methods throughout an empire seemed appropriate in the Russian context.

The 1786 Statute provided for a two-tier system of coeducational high schools and primary schools in provincial and district towns. The teaching method was based on the use of tables and wall charts. Teachers used oral interrogation and endless repetition of passages read aloud. The curriculum included genuinely mind-expanding subjects like geography, natural history, physics, and architecture, but at the same time prescribed textbooks, such as *On the Duties of Man and Citizen,* stressed obedience to the authorities, fulfillment of social obligations, and contentment with one's lot: "In each rank it is possible to be happy. People often think that tsars, princes, nobles and aristocrats alone have a happy life, but this is incorrect. God's goodness does not exclude anyone from contentment." Tuition was to be free of charge. Corporal punishment such as beating with a cane was outlawed. The schools were secular, staffed by teachers trained at a new pedagogical institute, founded in 1783.

The new schools suffered from inadequate state funding, teacher shortages, and local indifference or hostility. Only 176,000 pupils were recorded in attendance in the years 1786–1796, of which 92 percent were male. Overall, by the end of Catherine's reign only about sixty-two thousand children were being educated in 549 state institutions of various types, although they were supplemented by private and church schools. Even so, in the Russian context, where there was still no state provision for rural schools, the schools may be regarded as an achievement on the grounds that all attempts at "civilization" had to begin from above.

EXPANDING THE EMPIRE

As Sir George Macartney, the British minister to St. Petersburg, remarked in 1768, Russia was "a great planet that has obtruded itself into our system, whose place is yet undetermined, but whose motions most powerfully affect those of every other orb." From the start of her reign, Catherine neither felt tied to one particular orbit, nor had any doubts about the powerful role that Russia must continue to play in world affairs.

The First Turkish War (1768–1774) and the First Partition of Poland (1772)

In 1762 hostilities against Prussia were not resumed, on the grounds that a strong Prussia was not such a bad thing if it meant a weaker Poland and Austria. In April 1764 Russia signed a treaty with Prussia, which, to counteract French and Habsburg moves to elect a Saxon candidate to the Polish throne, sanctioned joint intervention to make Catherine's ex-lover Stanislaw Poniatowski king of Poland. All this represented a first step in the "Northern System," as envisaged by Nikita Panin, which included an alliance with Prussia and a protectorate over Poland, backed by Britain, Denmark, and Sweden, as a counterweight to France, Austria, and Spain.

An ex-lover on the throne did not guarantee a compliant Poland. Catherine's attempts to champion the rights of so-called dissidents (disenfranchised Orthodox and Protestants) in mainly Catholic Poland and to promote representation for all religions in the Polish government met with stiff opposition. King Stanislaw, who understood the power of the Catholic Church in Poland much better than Catherine did, pushed through a program of his own for constitutional reform and played down the dissident issue. Russia responded with armed intervention, which provoked the formation in 1768 of a popular anti-Russian, Catholic armed Confederation. At the same time, an uprising of pro-Russian Orthodox Cossacks and peasants against local Catholics, Uniates, Jews, and landowners broke out in Polish Ukraine. When Cossack rebels pursued Poles across the border into a dependency of the Crimean khan, the latter's Turkish masters, with French backing, demanded that Russian troops immediately evacuate Poland. The result was a war that lasted six years.

On paper the Ottoman Turks had the larger army and the advantage of fighting closer to bases suppliable by sea. The Russians, however, stole the march in 1769 to take the Turkish fort at Khotin on the Dniester River and occupy parts of Moldavia and Wallachia. In 1770 Russia defeated three larger Turko-Tatar armies in Moldavia and captured all Turkey's strongholds there. Meanwhile, with Britain's cooperation and some British officers on her ships, Catherine dispatched the Baltic fleet to the Mediterranean. In 1770 the Russian squadron won a resounding naval victory over the Turks at Chesme in the Aegean Sea. In 1771 a Russian army occupied Crimea, which in late 1772 accepted the Russian offer of nominal independence in return for allowing Russia use of most of the Crimean ports. In light of the financial exhaustion of both sides and the toll from disease, the Russians and Turks en-

The Expansion of the Russian Empire (1762–1796). Atlas of Russian History *by Martin Gilbert (New Edition published by Routledge in 2002) 0415281199 PB & 0415281180 HB. Please visit our website for further details on the new edition: www.taylorandfrancis.com.*

tered negotiations, in which Crimea proved the biggest stumbling block. Russia's need to stem the Pugachev rebellion at home (discussed in the next section) hastened a resolution. In the Treaty of Kuchuk Kainarji (July 10, 1774) the Turks ceded to Russia lands on the Black Sea coast between the mouths of the Dnieper and Bug Rivers and several fortresses, including the port of Kerch, situated on the channel linking the Black Sea to the Sea of Azov. Russia also won the freedom for its merchant vessels to navigate the Straits between the Black Sea and the Mediterranean. Crimea's independence was confirmed.

Russia's military and naval successes now appeared as a greater threat than ever to Europe's major powers. The Austrians, adamant on keeping Moldavia and Wallachia under the Ottomans, in 1772 had offered them diplomatic help in return for the cession of Bukovina (northern Moldavia), an area that was partially Ukrainian in ethnic makeup. More important, the Prussians and Austrians made a temporary pact at Poland's expense and offered Russia a share of Poland, in compensation for Moldavia and Wallachia. Thus was born the First Partition of Poland (1772), of which Austria got the lion's share, taking former Polish territories inhabited by about 2,700,000 people, including the towns of Lwow and port of Cracow. Prussia took most of northern Poland to the west of East Prussia. Russia's share was "ancestral" lands in eastern Belarus and southeastern Latvia, bringing about 1,800,000 new subjects into the empire.

The Second Turkish War (1787–1792)

In the aftermath of the conflicts with Poland and Turkey, it was fortunate for Russia that certain major powers were otherwise engaged; for example, in 1775–1783 France, Spain, and Britain were embroiled in the American War of Independence. Early in the war the British, convinced that Russia was their "natural ally," tried to secure Russian aid against the colonists. None was forthcoming, but American patriots feared for several years that as many as twenty thousand Russian troops could arrive at any moment. In fact, Catherine aided rather than impeded the cause of the fledgling United States. In 1780 she forged a League of Armed Neutrality of states not involved in the American conflict, which pressed the rights of neutral states to trade in all but military goods with both sides in the war to protect neutral countries' trade in naval stores against confiscation by the British.

In the early 1780s Russia discarded Nikita Panin's Prussia-oriented Northern System under the influence of the anti-Turkish Greek Project, the brainchild of Grigory Potemkin. The ambitious goal was to create a new Russian Greek Empire at Constantinople, with Catherine's second grandson, appropriately named Constantine, on the throne. Within this scheme Potemkin dreamed of a Kingdom of Dacia created out of Moldavia and Wallachia. In 1780 Catherine and Emperor Joseph II of Austria (r. 1765–1790), who sought Russian aid to expand southward into the Balkans, made a secret alliance. Secured by this alliance, in 1783 Potemkin engineered the outright annexation of independent Crimea. As he reassured Catherine: 'There is no power in Europe that has not taken part in carving up Asia, Africa and America." An adverse reaction to the Russo-Austrian combination was not long in coming, as Prussia forged a league of German princes in 1785 that included Britain's dependency Hanover. Undaunted, Catherine made a tour of her new territories in the company of Joseph II, visiting Crimea and Russia's new naval base at Sebastopol early in 1787, an act regarded as particularly provocative by the Turks. This tour also generated the myth of the fake "Potemkin villages," allegedly created by Potemkin along Catherine's route to impress her. In fact, the preparations were the routine ones of cleaning up, hanging decorations, and ensuring that crowds turned out to greet the royal party.

By August that year, England and Prussia were allies and willing to support the Turks in order to limit Austrian-Russian expansion. In September the Turks were prodded by Britain to declare war on Russia.

The second war proved more difficult for Russia than the first. Initially, Russia aimed to detach Moldavia and Wallachia from Turkey, while the Turks aimed to recover Crimea. Neither side initially made much progress, but in 1788 a Russian combined sea and land operation captured the strongly defended fortress city of Ochakov that controlled part of the Dnieper estuary. This provoked Britain into declaring war on Russia, then to back down. In 1789 Russians and Austrians were able to occupy the Dniester region down to the Black Sea. The Austrians also took Belgrade in Turkish-ruled Serbia.

In 1788 Sweden had taken the opportunity to declare war on Russia with the aim of regaining territory lost in earlier conflicts. There were victories on both sides; but the conflict ended in stalemate, and in 1790 a treaty confirmed the status quo. In 1790 Austria's Joseph II died, and his successor Leopold II (r. 1790–1792) pulled out of the war in the south. The young Turkish sultan Selim III (r. 1789–1807) had no intention of capitulating to Russia and declared a Holy War. Nevertheless, the Russian Black Sea fleet and armies pressed on, taking Ottoman fortresses on the lower Danube. The most famous Russian hero of the war was the almost legendary field commander Alexander Suvorov (ca. 1729–1800), a man of humble origins who started his career as a corporal during the Seven Years' War (1756–1763) and never lost a battle. Eventually Prussian diplomacy induced Catherine to reduce Russia's territorial demands. After Russian armies crossed the Danube into eastern Bulgaria and the Russian fleet defeated the Turks on the open sea, the Ottomans accepted Russia's reduced terms. The Treaty of Jassy (January 1792) confirmed the 1774 treaty of Kuchuk Kainarji and Russia's possession of Crimea, Ochakov, and an extension of its Black Sea coast.

Poland Vanishes

While Russia was otherwise engaged, patriotic and reform-minded Poles took the opportunity to press for more independence. Catherine's policy had been to maintain King Stanislaw and keep Russian troops in Poland. In 1788 the Warsaw seym (parliament), which was in session for the next four years, encouraged by a defensive treaty with Prussia, began to work toward reforming the monarchy. The Constitution of May 1791 planned, with the king's backing, to replace Poland's elective monarchy with a hereditary one. It proposed, among other things, the disenfranchisement of landless nobles, the reduction of the privileges of the Catholic Church, legal protection for peasants, and the abolition of the liberum veto, by which a single noble could block any measure in the seym. This latter measure threatened to limit the opportunities for Russia and other states to interfere in Polish affairs on the pretext of restoring order. The specter of a revived Poland with a real army, allied to Prussia, evoked implacable hostility in Russia. Catherine argued that the Poles had breached their agreements with Russia and constituted a threat to Russia's security. In 1792 Catherine engineered a confederation among dissident Polish magnates and dispatched almost one hundred thousand Russian troops, who quickly overwhelmed the weaker Polish reformist forces. The Russians and Prussians then double-crossed their respective Polish allies and announced a new partition, whereby Russia obtained central Belarus and the eastern three fifths of what had been Polish Ukraine, while Prussia got the western sections of ethnic Poland. Now independent Poland comprised only the eastern part of ethnic Poland and parts of Ukraine, Belarus and Lithuania.

Heartened by events in revolutionary France (see the next chapter), in 1794 patriotic Poles staged an uprising under the military leadership of Tadeusz Kosciuszko (1746–1817), who had fought under George Washington against the British. The Polish insurgents succeeded in neutralizing the first Russian forces that appeared, but a force under Suvorov quickly beat Kosciuszko's troops and ended resistance in Warsaw in October 1794 by massacring as many as twenty thousand civilians in the suburbs. A third partition followed and independent Poland disappeared. Prussia and Austria shared the remainder of ethnic Poland, and Russia obtained Lithuania, Courland, and what remained of Belarus and Ukraine.

Catherine saw the elimination of Poland as a blow against the "disease" and "madness" of the French revolution, which had spread rebellion around Europe. As she wrote, "Now a number of unworthy Poles, the enemies of their fatherland, imitating the atheistic, frenzied and corrupt rabble of French insurgents, are trying to scatter and spread a pernicious new doctrine throughout Poland and thereby destroy both its own peace and the peace of its neighbours forever." Elsewhere things were seen somewhat differently. In Britain, for example, caricatures appeared in the press featuring macabre images of slaughtered Polish women and children, with Catherine herself as a bloody-handed butcher.

Austria, Prussia, and Russia vowed not to use the word *Poland* again. They were convinced that an independent Poland was incapable of establishing a stable government and declared that partition was necessary "for preserving the peace and happiness of their citizens." Russia would have preferred to keep independent Poland as a client; in the future Russian Poland would prove one of the most troublesome parts of the empire. But Prussia promoted the partitions in its drive to obtain Polish provinces as a counter to Russian and Austrian southward expansion. Poland had vanished from the map of Europe.

The Partitions of Poland (1772–1795). Atlas of Russian History *by Martin Gilbert (New Edition published by Routledge in 2002) 0415281199 PB & 0415281180 HB. Please visit our website for further details on the new edition: www.taylorandfrancis.com.*

MANY NATIONS

Imperial expansion was, it seems, the resounding success story of Catherine's reign, as Russia continued to push its borders from its own heartland to the west, south, and southeast. In 1719 the empire's population was estimated at 15.5 million; in 1762, 23.2 million; in 1782, 28.4 million; and by 1795, 37.2 million (41 million including the Polish provinces.) Looked at another way, between 1750 and 1791 Russia acquired 8.6 million square miles of land.

Russians and Non-Russians

Imperial success brought fresh permutations of the old challenge of how to cope with newly annexed populations of different races and faiths, in some cases hostile to their new masters. The new masters too cherished some deep-seated prejudices. In Catherine's reign Russia did penetrate farther west, as though to underline the claim that Russia was a European state. But at least half the empire lay outside Europe, and the European sections were not all Russian. By the mid-1780s the proportion of ethnic Russians in the empire was less than 50 percent, a figure that would not change much until the fall of the Soviet Union in the 1990s. Figures for the 1780s estimate about 18 million Russians, 7 million Ukrainians, 5 million Belarusians, 2 million Poles, half a million or more of Finns, Tatars, Latvians, Jews, Lithuanians, and Estonians, and smaller numbers of Chuvash, Moldavians, Germans, Swedes, Bashkirs, and others. These were mainly settled peoples, but the empire also acquired nomads, who in some cases then migrated again; for example, Tatars into the Ottoman Empire and Kalmyks to China. Faiths apart from Orthodoxy included other Christians (Old Believers and other dissidents, Uniates, Catholics, and Protestants of various denominations), Muslims, Jews, Buddhists, and pagans. With the exception of some Ukrainians in the Austrian Empire, to all intents and purposes the old princedoms of Kievan Rus, as well as most of the territories once held by the Golden Horde and a good deal more, were now part of the Russian Empire. Indeed, Russian imperial protection of regions that were allegedly "former Russian property" had provided a pretext for annexing them.

Expansion did not solve Russia's perennial problem of possessing lots of land and resources but not enough people to exploit them. Population density was low, with as few as one to five inhabitants per square kilometer in, for example, Novgorod and Viborg Provinces and nowhere much more than thirty. One of the solutions, inspired by Potemkin, was to invite foreign colonists to settle lands, especially in New Russia (to the north of the Black Sea), Crimea, and north Caucasus, with offers of generous subsidies and religious freedom. Successful colonists included Germans who settled on the Volga. Catherine also encouraged the further immigration of Ottoman Christians of all nationalities. She was indulgent toward Old Believers who had fled from Russia, lifted the double tax that Peter the Great had laid on them, and urged them to return. Many Old Believers established successful businesses and were to make a significant contribution to Russia's industrialization in the nineteenth century.

Catherine got to know her empire as best she could. She often made visits to the Moscow region, visited the Baltic in 1764, the Middle Volga in 1767, the post-Partition western provinces in 1780, Ukraine and Crimea in 1787. In 1767 she wrote to Voltaire from Kazan: "Here I am in Asia. I wanted to see it for myself. There are in this city twenty different peoples, who bear absolutely no resemblance to each other. However, I have to make them a suit which will fit them all. It is not hard to find general principles, but what about the details?" Catherine appreciated the problems of governing people with different faiths, languages, and ethnic backgrounds, but she favored, as far as possible, treating the multinational empire uniformly by applying rational laws. In a secret directive issued in 1764, she stated that to treat parts of the empire such as Ukraine, Livonia, and Finland like foreign countries would be "truly stupid." Local privileges could not be abolished at once, but they should "by the gentlest means be brought to the point where they Russify."

This process started with Ukraine, which received a governor-general instead of a hetman and lost separate territorial divisions and local freedoms. Even so, Russification on a major scale was not to occur until the end of the nineteenth century. Local languages were used in schools, and some local law codes remained in force—Swedish in Old Finland, Islamic law among Bashkirs, and so on. In the many Jewish communities acquired by Russia during the Partitions (Russia now ruled up to a half of the world's Jews), their councils known as kahals continued to operate and Jews could also elect members to new local bodies. But despite official recognition in 1786 that Jews enjoyed privileges "appropriate to their status and occupation," Jews continued to encounter local opposition. In 1791, for example, appeals from Moscow merchants against "unfair" competition inspired a ban on Jews settling in the capitals. The confinement of Russia's Jews to the so-called Pale of Settlement in Poland, Ukraine, and New Russia would be formalized only in 1804, however.

The Fruits of Empire

Historians generally agree that Russia experienced real economic growth in the eighteenth century. In particular, the fertile black earth lands of New Russia, which gave much better crop yields than those in Russia proper, offered potential for exports through new ports such as Odessa in Crimea, founded in 1795. There were pockets of famine, but by and large the empire fed itself. But the cost of expansion was high. In the course of the eighteenth century, for example, some six hundred eighty thousand men died in battle, not counting recruits who died of disease and other causes before they reached their units.

Catherine's foreign ventures, along with administrative reforms, required huge budget increases. They could not be met by simple tax increases, which barely kept up with inflation. Catherine thus became the first Russian ruler to borrow extensively on the international money market, which she was able to do at low interest rates. A Turkish war indemnity in compensation for the First Turkish War allowed her to repay some of the first loan and borrow more money to fund the second war. During the first war, the state also issued paper money (so-called assignations) that went out of control, prompting more foreign borrowing and a decline in the value of the ruble. Administrative changes also affected finances. In 1780 the finance colleges combined under a new Senate Bureau of State Income, which enabled the procurator general Alexander Viazemsky (1723–1793) to generate Russia's first true budget.

The development of mining and metal refining in Karelia and the Urals continued and spread into Siberia, where rich gold and silver deposits were exploited. Total iron output increased from about a hundred thousand metric tons in 1760 to two hundred sixty thousand in 1800. The textile industry in the central regions grew dramatically. The new town of Ivanovo northeast of Moscow developed on the basis of handicraft businesses run by serf entrepreneurs, whose masters took a share of the profits through quitrent paid in lieu of labor services. Such arrangements were especially popular in regions where agricultural yields were low. During the period 1760–1800, the number of freely hired workers increased from one hundred thousand to two hundred forty thousand, and the contingent of state peasants assigned to work in factories and mines grew from one hundred fifty thousand to more than three hundred thousand. Overall Russia's industrial expansion was more quantitative than qualitative, however. Methods remained primitive, with Russia missing out on the technological development of the early Industrial Revolution, spearheaded by Britain in the later eighteenth century. The material and personal status of those who worked for state enterprises improved somewhat, but the same cannot be said for those who labored in the private sphere.

Local trade fairs proliferated in the Russian Empire. Several older provincial towns such as Tver and Nizhny Novgorod enjoyed a renaissance as centers of regional markets. St. Petersburg remained the leading port; Moscow, the preeminent internal commercial and industrial center. The volume of international trade also increased, though it is hard to measure, because of the inflation of the ruble and the extensive smuggling into Russia across the Russian-Polish border, which some scholars believe wiped out Russia's officially recorded trade surpluses. The state fostered the growth of a native merchant marine, which expanded from seventeen ships in 1775 to more than four hundred in 1794, although foreigners still dominated merchant shipping. Despite some diplomatic tensions, Britain continued to be Russia's chief foreign supplier and to purchase the lion's share of Russian exports, notably naval stores.

Internally, the greatest potential for economic prosperity remained with those who owned labor. It has been argued that the price revolution of the eighteenth century (high prices for grain, flax, hemp, textiles) induced noble landlords to exploit their land by transferring their serfs from cash or kind payments (*obrok* or quitrent) to demesne economy (*barshchina* or corvée) where serfs worked the landlord's land. There was a shift from a 10 percent majority of serfs paying quitrent in the 1710s to a 10 percent majority doing corvée after 1790. This was a chance for landowners with large enough estates to get rich by producing for the market, and a few did. But many top aristocrats and officials, supporting lavish lifestyles, took out loans backed by serf collateral that could not be repaid. By 1796 at least 1 million serfs were mortgaged to banks.

Thus the Russian economy continued to develop in the second half of the eighteenth century, but "development" must be understood in terms of fulfilling the potential of a barely urbanized, serf-based economy. Growth rates were similar to those in Britain, but from a different starting point. So, for example, despite the well-publicized foundation of new towns during Catherine's reign, the expansion of empire did not favor urbanization. It gave no incentive to weaken serfdom, and hence to convert peasants into town dwellers; profits remained in agriculture rather than elsewhere. Exports, as before, centered on raw materials: furs, timber, tallow, rye, hemp. At the same time, we should beware of making easy assumptions about Russia's "backwardness." Levels of prosperity across the regions varied greatly. The Russian playwright Denis Fonvizin wrote from abroad in the 1760s: "In these places everything is generally worse than in our country; the people, the horses, the land, supplies of basic foodstuffs, in short everything is better in our country, and we are a greater people than the Germans." These remarks are, of course, subjective and anecdotal but are not untypical of educated Russian travelers' perception that their country, despite all its problems, had pockets of prosperity and did not lag uniformly behind its Western neighbors.

POLICING THE PROVINCES

Military success abroad depended on maintaining a steady stream of recruits, tax revenues, equipment, and provisions from the home front. But the pressures that induced peasants to flee were usually at their strongest in wartime. Catherine's government had to face crises several times during her reign. At the same time, the empress was eager to apply Enlightened principles to solve the age-old problem of governing the provinces.

Rural Revolt

Acts of violence were a fact of life in the Russian countryside, as they were in other countries in eighteenth-century Europe. A Soviet study of Moscow Province estimated 112 murders and 49 attempted murders of nobles by serfs in 1751–1773 and some 216 "revolts" involving more than ten serfs in the same period. But class warfare, which Soviet historians were obliged to emphasize for ideological reasons, was not the whole story. Serfs killed each other more often than they killed their masters or mistresses. Conflict also occurred between state peasants and government agents, between homesteaders and nobles, between rich nobles and poorer ones. Recorded peasant revolts usually involved refusal to fulfill, or attempts to reduce, obligations, rather than outright attacks on the status quo. These sporadic and unrelated crimes, it has been argued, did not threaten the fabric of society or add up to a peasant "movement." Flight remained the preferred method of defying the system. In 1782–1789, for example, thirty-five thousand serfs fled from Chernigov and Kiev Provinces alone.

Starting in 1768, the war with Turkey, with associated conscription and taxation, fueled discontent, as did bubonic plague, probably brought from the front, which killed an estimated one hundred thousand people in the Moscow region in 1770–1772. One incident vividly underlines the real-life problems of applying rational government to a country where even most town dwellers were uneducated peasants. When the commandant of Moscow and Archbishop Ambrosy realized that the infection was being spread by people kissing a wonder-working icon, they tried to remove the offending image. This provoked a riot. Angry crowds broke into the Kremlin, looted the Miracles Monastery, and eventually tracked Ambrosy down in another monastery, where they ripped him to pieces. The four ringleaders were hanged and some two hundred rioters were flogged.

Recent studies of peasant culture in Russia attempt to go beyond issues of class warfare or anthropologists' focus on arcane rituals to try to understand peasant mentality, especially regarding attitudes toward continuity and change. They reveal tensions between the peasants' respect for tradition and their willingness to risk the unknown. The former could bind peasants to fulfilling obligations to landlords on the grounds that their ancestors had done so before them or attach them to locations close to ancestors' graves, which they were unwilling to abandon. The latter could move them to migrate in response to stories about some promised land of plenty. Peasants were not totally cut off from the political scene. Their oral literature reflected current or recent events through rumor. For example, historical songs and stories sometimes coincided with peasant tales of imprisonment, escape, and wandering, such as the tales of the deposed tsars Ivan VI and Peter III. Songs lamented the hardships of the peasant's lot with reference to army recruitment or celebrated the exploits of popular heroes like Stepan Razin (see the chapter "Muscovy Expands, 1613–1676"). Brightly colored woodblock prints known as *lubki* often told tales of the "world turned upside down"; for example, the ox who didn't want to be an ox and slaughtered the butcher, or wily servants tricking their masters.

The Pugachev Revolt

The rebellion led in 1773–1774 by the Don Cossack Emelian Pugachev (ca. 1740–1775) did threaten to turn the world upside down. Soviet historians presented it as a "peasant war" and analyzed it in terms of class warfare. This oversimplifies one of the most violent and complex episodes in Russian history, in which class divisions were just one of several components. The rebellion was one of several outbreaks that Russia periodically experienced in the seventeenth and eighteenth centuries when tensions between the center and the periphery overloaded as the result of an actual or perceived increase in state demands. In the case of the Pugachev revolt, the overload resulted from high levels of mobilization, heavy taxation, and sharp price rises during the Seven Years' and First Turkish wars. The breaking point was the plight of Cossacks settled on the Yaik River, which flows into the Caspian Sea to the east of the Volga, who were experiencing loss of privileges, increased service requirements, and tensions between their elders and the rank and file. Protests against the government's recent crushing of a mutiny in Yaik resurfaced in 1773, bringing further reprisals on the Cossacks.

The catalyst that legitimized rebellion in the eyes of the participants was the arrival on the Yaik of Pugachev, who claimed to be the true tsar Peter III in search of his rightful inheritance, of which he had allegedly been robbed by the "wicked advisers" now in power in St. Petersburg. Peter III was an ideal candidate as a subject for impersonation. He had been the legitimate male ruler and his short reign had shown popular promise—freeing church peasants, making concessions for Old Believers—but his God-ordained rule was cut short under circumstances that remain suspicious to this day. The 1762 emancipation of nobles seemed to undermine the traditional order of duty, unless one believed, as many did, that it was the first stage of a general emancipation package. In this scenario representatives of the landowners had attempted to abort emancipation by trying to assassinate the would-be liberator. Pugachev told a story about how he, "Peter," had escaped abroad, which would have seemed perfectly plausible to uneducated people. His story also provided a useful legitimizing mechanism for those who found it convenient to pretend to believe it.

As in earlier rebellions, disgruntled Cossacks had no trouble in finding equally disgruntled but less well focused or well armed supporters. Pugachev's first edict in the name of Peter III (September 1773) was addressed to the "army of the Yaik" and set a pattern for later manifestos. In return for slavelike loyalty, it assured the Cossacks of imperial favor, confirmed their status in perpetuity, and promised material rewards, in this case "the river [Yaik] from the source to the mouth, land, meadows, money payments, lead, powder and grain supplies." "Peter III" issued customized decrees to Old Believers, nomadic tribespeople, factory workers, and peasants in the region. The texts contained dire threats of retribution for anyone who refused to serve to the last drop of his blood. Worries about "German" female rule played a fairly minor role in raising rebellion in areas where most people probably had the haziest of notions of what the court in St. Petersburg actually consisted of.

In October 1773 Pugachev besieged the town of Orenburg on the River Yaik, spreading revolt into the lands of the nomadic Bashkirs farther east. Other forces under rebel commanders attacked ironworks in the Urals. Pugachev established his own "College of War" and some of his officials adopted the names of courtiers in St. Petersburg, although "Peter," supposedly still married to Catherine, compromised his assumed identity by marrying the daughter of a Yaik Cossack. At first Catherine underestimated the seriousness of the situation, only sending a regular force to the area toward the end of 1773. Government troops ended the siege of Orenburg and an investigation was launched, but Pugachev escaped and disturbances broke out around the region. Gathering more support, in July 1774 he looted and burned the ancient city of Kazan on the Volga. Government troops relieved the town, but Pugachev again escaped, turning south.

At this point the Pugachev revolt did come to resemble the "peasant war" described in Soviet history books, as the rebels entered territory with a mainly Russian peasant population, mostly living on small estates and working under the corvée system on the landlords' fields. To them Pugachev addressed a number of manifestos. To the peasants of Penza Province, for example, he granted their "ancient cross and prayers, heads and beards, liberty and freedom and to live forever as

Cossacks, with no demands for recruit levies, poll tax and other money taxes, with rent-free possession of lands, forests, hay fields and fisheries and salt lakes." He liberated them from all the taxes and burdens imposed by "the wicked landlords and bribe-taking judges in the towns."

Pugachev's message boiled down to cutting out (literally) the middlemen: the manifesto commanded peasants to capture and execute the landowners. Peasants and other common folk would become "the loyal slaves of our own crown," but at the same time enjoy the fruits of their lands in a sort of utopia that would have robbed autocracy of the means to sustain itself. The rebels butchered 1,572 nobles (including 474 women and 302 children), 1,037 officials, and 237 priests. They plundered estates and stole livestock. Everywhere, anyone to whom the rebels took a dislike, they tortured and massacred. One victim was a German astronomer, cut to pieces on Pugachev's orders. Eliminating beardless "Germans" was one of his promises, echoing earlier revolts.

Doomed by the end of the Turkish war in 1774, which allowed the redeployment of government troops, Pugachev was declared an enemy of God. His support began to melt away. Most seriously, the Don Cossacks failed to respond to his appeals. Encroaching famine in the Volga region also sapped the rebels' enthusiasm. Pugachev was repelled at Tsaritsyn in August 1774 and fled down the Volga pursued by government troops. In September disillusioned former supporters handed Pugachev over to the authorities. He was brought to Moscow in a cage, where he was sentenced to the prescribed punishment for treason, which was quartering (severing the limbs from the live prisoner), followed by hanging. Catherine, however, wishing to temper retribution with mercy, ordered the executioner to hang him first, thus denying spectators the most gruesome part of the spectacle. The decision to avoid "cruel punishment," very much in the spirit of the Enlightenment, went against the advice of many top nobles.

The Provincial Reform of 1775

The major outcome of the Pugachev rebellion was the Statute on Provincial Administration (November 1775), Catherine's biggest and most complex decree. The Statute recognized that Russia's problem was not so much an overarching, all-powerful state as underadministration, which hampered both the government's ability to control the population, and also the people's access to redress and protection. For example, in 1763 Russia had a total of sixteen thousand five hundred paid officials in contrast to fourteen thousand in Prussia, which was just 1 percent of Russia's size. "There is," the act stated, "both an insufficiency of administration and a shortage of people capable of administering." The shortage was mitigated by the tradition in which landowners dealt with serfs, while peasant communes decided much of their own business by customary law. The Pugachev revolt revealed what could happen when the traditional arrangements broke down. One of the aims of the Provincial reform was to activate the nobles into serving their local communities, something that Catherine had already been thinking about when studying the role of local government in Britain and Russia's Baltic provinces.

The Provincial reform divided Russia into thirty-eight provinces or *gubernii,* each consisting of between three hundred thousand and four hundred thousand inhabitants, and further subdivided into districts (*uezdy*) of twenty thousand to thirty thousand persons. In 1796 the number of provinces was expanded to fifty. Each province had a capital with a governor (grade 4 on the Table of Ranks), directly appointed from St. Petersburg, together with a commander in chief, deputy governor, and chief of police. Financial matters were in the hands of appointed officials under the deputy governor.

Article 395 of the Statute (on the establishment of a conscience court in every province) gives a flavor of the impulse behind the reform: "Since the personal security of every loyal subject is precious to the monarch's philanthropic heart," the empress wished "to extend help to those who might be suffering more from misadventure or from oppressive circumstances." The Statute established a complex system of courts and an appeals mechanism, on the basis of separate lower courts for nobles, townspeople, and state peasants, and corresponding higher courts of appeal. Serfs remained outside the system. The reform established posts into which nobles would be elected by other nobles, for example, as assessors and judges in courts, on the grounds that the nobles should fulfill a public role above and beyond policing their own serfs. Boards of Public Welfare, with elected representation from the free estates, were set up in each province to found and run schools, hospitals, foundling homes, almshouses, mental asylums, homes for incurables, workhouses, and houses of correction.

The Provincial reform was later backed up by the 1782 Police Statute, which contained more detailed legislation for running towns. The Police Statute regulated not only law and order, but also the maintenance of streets and buildings, waste disposal, lighting, firefighting, beggars, and religious dissidents. It was also concerned with public decorum, especially good behavior in church. We still know comparatively little about how these various reforms worked in practice as opposed to the intentions expressed on paper.

Both the Police and the Provincial statutes reflected a trend toward decentralization. After 1775 some of the duties of the Senate, the supreme judiciary, were transferred to lower courts. The Colleges of Foreign Affairs, War, and the Admiralty maintained central control, but others lost their powers to local courts and boards. The latter, though, were always under the supervision of the governor, who was responsible directly to the empress. In many ways, both pieces of legislation were too advanced for Russia. Many of the district "towns" where courts and boards were supposed to sit were just villages. A good governor could accomplish a great deal, but he had to struggle with entrenched vices such as bribe-taking, evasion of tax and duties, lack of respect for individuals, and excessive deference for rank. For noble officials, no educational qualifications were required apart from a period of military service and ownership of property. Even so, both the number and quality of officials improved, and in some places, especially St. Petersburg and Moscow, local boards did good work in establishing hospitals and welfare organizations. The basic structures would remain until 1864.

CHAPTER 15

Catherine the Great: The Golden Age of the Nobility, 1776–1796

"This magnanimous act filled the whole nobility with indescribable joy. Our satisfaction was universal and most sincere."

—Andrei Bolotov (1738–1833) on the nobility's "emancipation" from service in 1762

"The Russian nobility has only the freedom not to serve, and that is all, but it possesses neither the resources nor the power to do anything else."

—The nobles of Pskov Province, local "Instruction" to the Legislative Commission, 1767

In this chapter we consider the position of the nobility and the other "estates" of the Russian realm in the latter half of the eighteenth century. We explore the cultural life of the elite in its interaction with popular culture, against the background of the government's attempts to expand towns and bring a measure of "civilization" to the provinces. In Catherine's final years the bloody events of the French Revolution would give stark warnings to both monarch and nobles of how thin was the veneer of civilization even in the Enlightened heart of the so-called civilized world.

FREEDOM AND LIBERTY

Many historians consider that the "golden age" of the Russian nobility reached its pinnacle in Catherine's reign, a fact they regard with varying degrees of condemnation or approval. All Soviet and many Western historians have constantly stressed that the nobles lived at the expense of the serfs. But they concede that this "exploitative" land-owning environment laid the foundations of Russia's world-renowned nineteenth-century literary and artistic culture. In contrast, in post-Soviet Russia the culture and manners of the eighteenth-century nobility have come to be viewed with a hint of nostalgia for a lost age of elegance and refinement.

Such topics as elite fashions and dining habits, even the lap dogs popular among highborn women have been the subject of scholarly investigation.

The Charter to the Nobility

As we saw in the preceding chapter, Catherine sought to encourage the nobles' public-spiritedness by redeploying them in the provinces, which, as the Pugachev revolt underlined, were in need of firmer control. The Statute on Provincial Administration of 1775 did persuade some nobles to take on a new role, but it did not clarify their legal status in an integrated way. In 1785 Catherine rectified this in her Charter to the Nobility, which confirmed that the Russian nobility "shall enjoy freedom and liberty in future generations for all time in perpetuity." It reiterated their exemption from compulsory service, taxes, and corporal punishment. Nobles must not suffer deprivation of their titles or property without trial by their fellow nobles. The Charter guaranteed their right to purchase villages and to exploit their lands through the sale of products, mining, and industry, but it said nothing explicit about their powers over their serfs. Importantly, it recognized the nobles' inalienable right to their property. Even if a man was convicted of a serious crime, his estate passed to his heirs. Although all nobles enjoyed equal rights, the Charter divided them into six categories based on when and where their clan was ennobled in order to maintain a historical sense of genealogical hierarchy.

The old historiography regarded the Charter as yet more perks for the already privileged (the "haves") and a further slap in the face for the peasants (the "have-nots"), but many historians now see it as a first step toward civil rights, a modernizing rather than a conservative measure. The Charter was essentially a codification of existing laws and manifestoes, part of an overall vision of a well-regulated society in which each category knew its place. It was handed down from on high, not negotiated by the nobles themselves. It still defined the nobility with reference to "service, fidelity, zeal and industry." Nobles could enter the service of friendly foreign powers, but in time of crisis they must respond to the government's summons, "sparing neither effort nor life itself in service of the State." Nobles who had never served were barred from holding office or voting in local elections. All other nobles had a duty to participate in noble assemblies to discuss local issues at the province and district level and also to elect their representatives to local courts and boards, as already laid down in the Provincial reform. But there was no hint of an institutional presence in central government or any share of political power except for favored individuals. The nobles still had no national assembly, no equivalent, for example, of the British House of Lords.

The post-1762 emancipated Russian nobility has been described as a privileged "leisure" class. No doubt some nobles irresponsibly frittered away their time in rustic self-indulgence. However, according to figures for 1797, 83.8 percent of the nobility owned fewer than a hundred serfs, which meant that few could rely on serfs alone for a comfortable standard of living. A sizable minority owned no serfs at all and scraped a livelihood by working their own land. For the vast majority, salaried military service followed by a provincial post became the norm. A civil service career, once spurned, was regarded more favorably than it had been. Retiring to their estates after they had done their duty for a decade or so allowed nobles to reclaim space away from the state with a clear conscience.

For the privileged few among the nobles the manor house became the scene of literary pursuits, musical evenings, gardening projects, and art collections. The more enterprising developed the commercial potential of their estates, and a few even tried to improve the lot of their serfs. The developments of the 1760s–1780s were important for the Russian nobles' self-image and self-confidence. If the first half of the eighteenth century was about painfully reinventing themselves as "decent beardless Europeans" following orders from above, the second half saw them asserting some sort of personal and national identity rather than just aping Western ways and being cogs in the wheels of state.

"A Third Sort of Person": The Charter to the Towns

Catherine once boasted that she created two hundred new towns in the first twenty-three years of her reign. But the insignificant size of the urban population as a percentage of the whole—still no more than 4 percent by the 1790s—continued to set Russia apart from other major European countries. Moreover, most Russian towns were extensions of the countryside. Real town dwellers wholly detached from the land were fairly rare. It could be argued that Russia did not yet have a civil society grounded in the urban middle classes and in this sense lacked "civilization."

The challenge was to expand towns and to create corporate pride and a prosperous entrepreneur class from the limited available human resources. In 1775 Catherine had attempted to restructure the urban community rationally by changing the property requirements for membership of the three guilds of higher-, middle-, and lower-ranking merchants to ten thousand rubles for the first guild, five thousand for the second, and one thousand for the third. An 88 percent drop in the number of registered merchants showed these figures to be too ambitious. In 1785 she made a further attempt with her Charter to the Towns, published on the same day as the nobles' Charter and modeled on it. The Town Charter too listed six grades, in this case based on a hierarchy of occupation and wealth, from so-called real town dwellers owning substantial property down to men with no registered skill. The thinking behind the Charter was hierarchical—it recognized different grades of privilege according to social category—but at the same time it treated urban dwellers as part of one estate.

The Charter set up town councils (*dumy*) made up of representatives of each of the six categories, who in turn elected a six-man executive and a mayor. Levels of activity varied. A study based on St. Petersburg and its district reveals quite a busy program, the executive meeting more than a hundred times per year; other towns, however, failed even to elect an executive because of a lack of suitable candidates. Townsmen continued to be excluded from buying landed estates, which meant that the wealthiest aspired to join the nobility and in some cases succeeded. Others suffered from "downward mobility," for example, merchants dropping out of guilds for failing to meet property qualifications. Restrictions on movement between towns meant that townspeople continued to be "attached" to their towns rather as the peasants were attached to their communes. Inconsistencies in the legislation, governors behaving badly, unrealistic provisions (for example, many smaller town did not have six different categories of inhabitant) limited the effectiveness of the Charter to the Towns.

The Peasant Question

In no area has Catherine been so condemned as in her apparent failure to solve the peasant question. "The peasants in Russia are in a state of abject slavery, and are reckoned the property of the nobles to whom they belong, as much as their horses or dogs," wrote the Englishman William Richardson in 1784, echoing many Western travelers. "We sell our fellow-men like pieces of wood and pity our cattle more than our people," wrote an entrant in the Free Economic Society essay competition of 1766.

Catherine herself believed that serfdom must and would disappear. Her notes contain a reference to a "convenient" way to initiate the process by freeing serfs whenever land was sold. She wrote in her memoirs that "the great motivater of agriculture is freedom and private property. When each peasant is assured that what belongs to him does not also belong to someone else, he will improve it." But this did not mean that peasants were ready for freedom now or that their owners were economically or psychologically prepared for such a measure. Catherine was forced to acknowledge the impossibility of ending serfdom by some drastic act. The politically expedient decision to safeguard the land-owning rights of the nobles made it impossible to free serfs with land unless the masters voluntarily gave some up. Creating landless laborers was not on the agenda.

On the peasant question Catherine was ahead of Russian educated opinion, a fact brought home when she was preparing her "Instruction." Counselors advised her to tone down pronouncements on limiting servitude, with the result that the published document contained no chapters on the peasantry at all, just a few hints that governments should refrain from "reducing people to a state of slavery." The Legislative Commission devoted little time to discussing serfdom. Catherine sought to tackle the problem by mitigating it rather than changing the system. For example, she enacted bans on the enserfment of orphans and illegitimate children in state homes, of prisoners of war, and of state peasants ascribed to factories. A law of 1775 forbade the reenserfment of freed serfs. However, a proposal to emancipate children born to serfs after 1785 was far too radical to be implemented.

Some historians have accused Catherine of reducing more than eight hundred thousand state peasants (those who were not the personal property of individual lords or of the imperial family) to the status of serfs. In fact, most of her grants of inhabited land as rewards to favorites and other beneficiaries came from lands belonging to the imperial family or from lands that serfs farmed in partitioned Poland as part of a policy of settling Russian landlords in the new empire. State peasants were not turned over to landlords; in fact, in 1764 their numbers expanded when former church peasants were recategorized to pay all their obligations directly to the state. Catherine did, it is true, consolidate serfdom as an institution in Ukraine, as a result of extending the same laws all over the empire; in other words, in Ukraine preexisting serfdom was finally fixed in law.

A draft survives of a Charter to the State Peasants, which registered village lands under six headings and defined status and rights using the Charter to the Towns as a template. If implemented, it would have allowed the peasants to take an oath of loyalty, like other free citizens, and form representative bodies. No evidence survives to explain why this plan was shelved. Probably it was deemed too radical for public (i.e., educated) opinion, which thought anarchy a greater evil than lack of freedom and feared that such a Charter might raise expectations of liberties among the serfs. In the end, legislation on peasant self-government was implemented only in a regulation for Ekaterinoslav in New Russia (1787).

For their part, peasants continued to believe that they could obtain justice by circumventing "middlemen" and appealing directly to the monarch in person. When Catherine traveled along the Volga in 1767, for example, she received some six hundred petitions. Edicts issued in the 1760s warning subjects of all classes to desist from "thrusting petitions into her majesty's own hands" repeated, more or less word for word, a law first issued in the reign of Tsar Alexis (1645–1676) and reiterated many times. Penalties for "not using the proper channels" were harsh: the 1767 version of the decree specified flogging with the knout and exile to hard labor.

Ironically, it was probably the success of Catherine's reign, when Russia experienced rapid territorial expansion, increased authority in world affairs, relative political stability and economic prosperity, that prevented her from doing more for the peasants. Agriculture was the source of Russia's wealth. Peasant life was hard, as it was in most countries, but the population managed to feed itself and renew itself. There was no demographic crisis, and the Pugachev revolt was to be the last great popular outbreak until 1905. In short, the serf economy was producing the goods, meager though they often were. Why mend what was not broken for the sake of principles, especially when the nobles were just beginning to enjoy the fruits of their emancipation, to refine their corporate identity, and raise their cultural levels? One may as well ask why Catherine did not put expansionist foreign policy on hold and concentrate instead on improving the lives of individuals. Successful eighteenth-century monarchs did not make such choices. Serfdom would end only when it began to hamper Russia's status in world affairs.

CULTURE: TOWN AND COUNTRY

Taking their ideas and models from the West, the ruler and her court continued to set the fashion in all areas of culture, from architecture to painting, poetry to music. But the late eighteenth century saw the extension of elite culture beyond St. Petersburg and Moscow into the provinces and the beginnings of a Russian artistic consciousness.

Restructuring the Architectural Environment

Catherine's attempts to inculcate civic pride in her subjects were not only limited to reforming the organs of local government and issuing charters but also involved improving the built environment. Catherine loved architecture. "The passion for building is a devilish thing," she wrote. "It eats up money and the more one builds the more one wants to build. It is intoxicating." Long after her system of courts and assemblies had disappeared, her town squares and civic buildings survived and still form the heart of many Russian provincial towns. Plans issued by the Commission of Masonry Construction often incorporated columned trading arcades around a central square with a radiating street plan. From the 1770s each town designated as a provincial or a district capital must provide an imposing house for its governor or chief official and, depending on size, premises for noble assemblies, theaters, and so on. Thus St. Petersburg stamped a more or less uniform blueprint all over the empire, giving emphatic visual expression to notions of harmony and order.

Rastrelli's baroque, immortalized in the Catherine and Winter Palaces, was already outmoded before Elizabeth's death. Catherine preferred neoclassicism (in Russia, usually referred to simply as classicism), the style favored by fellow monarchs farther west. From London to Berlin, architects based their designs on the conscious imitation of ancient Greek and Roman originals, which were believed to contain the essence of true art. Space and proportion, not ornament, were the watchwords. Writers declared that the virtues of antiquity were the virtues of the present day. A characteristic Russian example of neoclassical taste is the Tauride Palace, built in 1783–1789 by the architect Ivan Starov (1745–1808) for Grigory Potemkin on a scale suitable for a conquering hero. Inside there was a magnificent ballroom and winter gardens, but the facade was modestly plain, demonstrating "antique elegance." One of Catherine's favorite architects was the Scot Charles Cameron (1746–1812). Cameron's gallery addition to the Catherine Palace at Tsarskoe Selo used the shape of a Greek temple for the display of a collection of antique busts. He set Pavlovsk, a summer residence built in 1782–1786 for Catherine's son Grand Duke Paul and his wife, in a picturesquely landscaped park dotted with Greek temples and rotundas.

Nobles began to change the face of the Russian provincial landscape. In the early eighteenth century the typical country manor house, which the owner rarely visited, was often just a larger version of a peasant cottage, perhaps decorated with some crude columns. From the mid eighteenth century more gracious dwellings sprang up, still often built of wood, but of a more regular neoclassical design, typically a square house with two wings fronted by a columned portico. Inside, a procession of rooms created spaces for entertaining. Even if Russian nobles could not emulate western Europe's ancient stately homes or castles packed with ancestral portraits and heirlooms accumulated over centuries, they could still mimic the foreign aristocracy in some respects. Landscaped parks in the "natural" English style were the height of fashion. Artificial lakes and waterfalls became popular, as did garden pavilions—temples to Friendship, the Muses, and so on—and other ornaments

Pavlovsk palace and private garden (1782–1786), by the Scottish architect Charles Cameron. © *William Brumfield.*

to suggest historical, allegorical, and philosophical themes for strollers to enjoy, perhaps with a book in hand.

So in the later eighteenth century Russian nobles were influenced by and contributed to a cult of refined rusticity that raised the "natural" country above the "artificial" town. The grander noble estates could, of course, function only thanks to armies of serfs. In some cases the serfs' owners organized them into choirs, theatrical troupes, or horn bands, in which each instrument produced a single note. Good examples of such estates survive at Kuskovo and Ostankino outside Moscow, both built by members of the Sheremetev clan, the wealthiest in eighteenth-century Russia.

The Academy of Arts and Russian Painting

The center and arbiter of artistic output in Russia was the Imperial Academy of the Three Fine Arts (architecture, sculpture, and painting) in St. Petersburg, which Catherine placed directly under her own patronage in 1764. In the same year, a grand new neoclassical building, which still houses the Academy today, began to rise up by the city's Neva River. Students followed a course that included the study of history and mythology and drawing from classical sculpture and life models. The culmination of an art student's training was producing a narrative history painting, usually on a subject from the Bible, ancient history, or mythology. Successful graduates were sent abroad for further study. Few nobles contemplated a career in painting or sculpture, which continued to be regarded as high-grade trades; most academy students came from the "middling" class.

The first Russian professor of history painting was Anton Losenko (1737–1773). His *Hector Taking Leave of Andromache* (1773), a subject from the history of the ancient Greek Trojan wars, emphasizes civic duty and moral heroism, with emotion expressed by the central figures' stylized poses and the gestured commentary of the crowd. The aim of such paintings was to improve the viewer through emotional catharsis. Russia's most successful artist of the period was the Ukrainian Dmitry Levitsky (1735–1822), who painted all the leading figures of his time, including several portraits of the empress herself. Perhaps his most famous works are seven canvases (1770s) depicting students of the Smolny Institute for Noble Girls, commissioned by Catherine to celebrate her own ideal of young womanhood. Portraits by another successful artist, Vladimir Borovikovsky (1735–1825), feature young women with soulful eyes, set against outdoor greenery and clad in the flimsy garments fashionable all over Europe at the time. While patronizing native artists, Catherine also made wholesale purchases of Western old masters and applied art from abroad, making her one of the greatest collectors of her era.

"Unknown Woman in Russian Dress" (1784), by Ivan Argunov, a serf artist. *Tretyakov Gallery, Moscow, Russia/ Archivo Iconografico, S. A./Corbis.*

In the provinces local artists painted icons in the traditional manner and portraits in a naive style reminiscent of North American country portraits. Wealthier nobles trained their own serf painters and architects, sometimes whole dynasties such as the Argunovs, serfs of the Sheremetevs. *Unknown Woman in Russian Dress* (1784) by Ivan Argunov (1729–1802) suggests ambiguities of identity: it is unclear whether his subject is a peasant in her Sunday outfit or a young noblewoman wearing traditional dress.

Only a few paintings of real peasants have survived from this period. Genre subjects—scenes from humdrum everyday life—were not popular with buyers, who generally preferred Italian and classical landscapes to views of the ordinary Russian countryside. In other words, just as elsewhere in Europe and North America, in Catherine's Russia the style and content of elite art and architecture were filtered through the prism of neoclassicism, which put down deep roots and produced some remarkable works of art.

Literary and Musical Russia

As the historian Nikolai Karamzin noted with pleasure in 1802, twenty-five years earlier there had been just two bookshops in Moscow, but now there were twenty and they had spread to provincial towns, where not only men but also women were customers. Even so, Russian readers still represented a tiny fraction of the population. An estimate puts male literacy in the 1790s at between 3 and 7 percent (compared with France, 47 percent; Britain, 68 percent; Prussia, 80 percent), although literacy rates in the Baltic states and Ukraine were much higher. Practically all the printed literature in Russian at the disposal of these readers was borrowed from foreign sources, with translations from the French accounting for one in four of all books published in Russia in the second half of the eighteenth century. Literary genres—solemn odes, epics, sonnets, ballads, tragedies, and comedies—were imported and adapted with varying degrees of skill and inventiveness.

Journals provided an important vehicle for literature and literary and philosophical debate. Five hundred or so existed in the 1780s, subscribed to overwhelmingly by nobles. In 1769 the first issue of *About This and That* appeared, containing anonymous articles by Catherine herself. It sparked a debate about the nature of satire, whether it should be aimed at human vices in general, as Catherine believed, or against named individuals. One of the participants was the writer Nikolai Novikov (1743–1820), whose own journals such as *The Painter* and *The Drone* carried the debate further. For much of Catherine's reign there was a remarkably free press, with prohibitions mainly on heresy, blasphemy, and pornography; and from 1783 private individuals were allowed to run printing presses for the first time. It was possible for the *Moscow Gazette* to praise George Washington as "the founder of a republic" and for French revolutionary pamphlets to be sold in the capitals.

Eighteenth-century Russia's finest poet was Gavrila Derzhavin (1743–1816), who first won favor with "Felitsa" (1782), a playful ode in praise of Catherine. A champion of the idea that a poet's status in society was equal to that of a soldier,

Derzhavin was at the heart of an extended literary circle that included most of the leading figures of his day. Among them was Anna Bunina (1774–1829), Russia's first professional woman writer. There was a steady rise in literacy rates among noblewomen, reaching an estimated 90 percent by the end of the century. Another woman influential in literary and academic circles was the empress's friend Princess Catherine Dashkova (1744–1810), who became president of the Academy for the Russian Language, which produced the first scholarly Russian dictionary. Her memoirs are a valuable source for the period.

The major playwright of Catherine's Russia was Denis Fonvizin (1744?–1792), whose comedies of manners *The Brigadier* (first performed in 1769) and *The Adolescent* (1783) poked fun at pomposity and hypocrisy and such trends as "Gallomania"—excessive adulation of French fashions. Translations of novels by British writers were popular and provided models for the first Russian novelists. Russia's most successful man of letters was Nikolai Karamzin (1766–1826), whose story "Poor Liza" (1792), about a peasant girl who drowns herself after being abandoned by her noble suitor, spawned a spate of copycat suicides. His *History of the Russian State,* (1810s–1820s) also enjoyed a huge success.

The use of foreign models did not preclude Russian rural subjects. The play *Misfortune Over a Carriage* (1779) by Yakov Kniazhnin (1742?–1791) lampoons cruel and thoughtless serf owners who subvert the marriage plans of their serfs, while the plot of a popular comic opera *The Miller Who Was Wizard, Cheat and Matchmaker* (1779) by Alexander Ablesimov (1742–1783) focuses on a choice of husband for a Russian peasant girl. The scores of this and other Russian operas were based on well-known Russian folk songs orchestrated in a Western classical style.

Catherine sponsored the Imperial Theater Department, which staged a wide repertoire of foreign and Russian plays, including Catherine's own dramatic works such as *O Time!* (1772), a satire about meanness, gossip, and superstition. In 1785 the public Bolshoi Theater opened in St. Petersburg. There was plenty of music at court, despite Catherine's claim that she was tone deaf. Italian and French light operas were especially popular. As before, foreign composers and musicians predominated, but native composers like Dmitry Bortniansky (1751–1825) laid the foundations of the great Russian classical music traditions that would develop in the nineteenth century.

Popular Culture

The literary and cultural activities described in the last subsection were for a small elite, but it would be wrong to conclude that the mass of the population lived in a cultural vacuum. In town and country, traditional crafts such as woodwork, brass- and ironware, embroidery, and lace making flourished. Designs followed tradition, but folk art was sometimes influenced by high art, for example, figures in Western dress and foreign scenes appeared in popular woodprints (*lubki*), and neoclassical ornaments were incorporated with traditional motifs on carved and painted wooden objects. Not until the later nineteenth century, however, would peasant artifacts become fashionable among the elite.

People of all classes had access to handwritten literature, often on topics or genres on which Westernization had made little impact, such as lives of saints and other devotional works, popular tales, riddles, and songs. All these subjects were also transmitted through the thriving oral tradition of story-telling and singing. Cheap prints with lurid illustrations and minimal texts could be shared by readers and nonreaders alike. Topics included not only local subjects like "The Thief Has Come into the Yard," in which a man carrying a stolen chicken under his arm escapes from a woman lunging at him with a sharp hoe, but also more exotic, foreign themes like "The Cat-Man of Barcelona" (a half-man, half-cat said to have been discovered in Spain) and "The Mighty Elephant Beast." Religious subjects and icons were also reproduced on cheap paper prints.

It is a misconception that Westernization eliminated popular culture from the lives of the elite, for as long as Russian nobles were raised by peasant nannies and visited or resided in their country estates, they could hardly avoid the "other Russia." Catherine herself had no roots in Russian folk culture, but even she took an interest in literary adaptations of folk tales, such as her own "Tale About Prince Khlor" (1781), written for her grandsons, and the first work of Russian literature to be published in English as a separate book (1793). Adaptations of Russian folk songs were part of the musical repertoire. For example, Nikolai Lvov and Ivan Prach's collection of folk songs (1790) became popular at musical evenings on

"O send for the guard, there's a thief in my shed." 18th c. "lubok" wood print. *State Historical Museum, Moscow, Russia.*

country estates and in townhouses. The Russian tradition of choral music, closely linked to church singing, flourished. Noblewomen and merchants' wives alike enjoyed books on fortunetelling and the interpretation of dreams, which derived from both Russian and Western sources. The folk remedies and spells that peasants applied to anything from toothache to infertility were familiar also in upper-class households, where serfs did all the household chores, including nursing the sick, and qualified doctors were still a rarity. Peasants and masters were not so separate as has sometimes been suggested, but events in revolutionary France were to strengthen the conviction of most nobles that paternalism and firm guidance and correction from above must continue to govern the relationship between the "two Russias."

THE FRENCH MADNESS

In 1789 revolution broke out in France, where a new National Assembly formed from the "third estate" of commoners limited the powers of the king and abolished the privileges of the aristocracy and the church. In September 1792 France became a republic, and in January 1793 King Louis XVI was executed by guillotining. Disputes between rival political groups unleashed a bloody reign of terror, which was checked only in 1794. The unfolding of events in France was followed with varying degrees of dismay all over monarchist Europe, from London to St. Petersburg.

Catherine and the French Revolution

Catherine may initially have regarded the events of 1789 as a sort of palace coup that simply limited the power of the French monarchy. French literature, language, and fashions had become so well assimilated among the Russian elite that it was inconvenient to admit that France was undergoing radical changes that threatened the status quo in Europe. The revolutionary treatise "Declaration of the Rights of Man" even went on sale in St. Petersburg. For a while the Russian reading public continued to regard such works from a literary rather than a practical point of view.

In 1792 Catherine was still speaking in fairly mild terms of "the frivolous and flighty spirit and the inborn recklessness of the French nation." She was forced to wake up to the full implications when Louis XVI was executed. Catherine at once broke off relations with France, denouncing the "savages" who had "used the power illegally appropriated by them in such evil deeds that they have raised their hands to the killing of the sovereign anointed by God." She rescinded a Russo-French trade agreement of 1786, forbade French ships to enter Russia or Russian nationals to take goods to French ports, and banned French newspapers and periodicals. French diplomatic personnel were expelled, together with French nationals who recognized the new regime. Any French person wishing to remain had to renounce the "seditious principles" on oath. In the event, large numbers of French exiles were to seek sanctuary in Russia.

The French Revolution went against the whole ethos of Catherine's approach to government, in which the monarch's subjects operated within social categories or estates defined by law as set out in her charters. They served and communicated with the state through the corporate bodies of those estates. This system allowed no place for democracy, not to mention anarchy. There was no question of Catherine borrowing ideas from the French revolutionary leaders as once she had borrowed from the French philosophes. In fact, Catherine attached some of the blame for the Revolution to the latter. She wrote to her German friend Friedrich Grimm in February 1794: "And so you were right for never expressing the wish to be included among the luminaries, the illuminés, and the philosophes, since experience proves that all this leads to destruction," adding: "The world will never cease to need an authority." Still, a story about her throwing a marble bust of Voltaire out of the Winter Palace is probably a legend. Voltaire was, after all, a monarchist and Catherine was not given to petty vindictiveness. And she actually had little reason to fear the spread of revolutionary ideas into Russia beyond the narrowest of circles. As we saw earlier, Catherine blamed the "French disease" for the turmoil in Poland. At home in Russia, she had to expend comparatively little time and effort to nip the infection in the bud. It was to lie dormant until more than a quarter century after her death.

Radical and Conservative Opposition

Soviet historians, faced with the task of charting the rise of the Russian intelligentsia, which in their ideological scheme would culminate in the overthrow of tsarism in 1917, traced the birth of opposition to the eighteenth century, when former servants of the state, nobles "emancipated" in 1762, turned into its critics. According to this scenario, greater distance from the establishment, more leisure to read and perhaps to travel abroad, then events in France and Poland raised doubts and bred discontent among this group. The nobleman and civil servant Alexander Radishchev (1749–1802), whose book *A Journey from St. Petersburg to Moscow* was published privately in 1790, was declared the most radical of Russia's aristocratic rebels. Barely known at the time—only thirty copies reached readers before the print run of six hundred was confiscated—in Soviet Russia the *Journey* became the most famous single work of eighteenth-century Russian literature.

Radishchev's reputation as a radical was based on his stance on the serfs, whose terrible plight his fictional traveler describes during his journey through Russia. Most educated nobles took a paternalistic approach to peasants, believing that the key to improving their lot lay in humane treatment, application of scientific methods, and guidance from above. But Radishchev advocated emancipation and revolution. On reading the *Journey* Catherine wrote: "The purpose of this book is clear on every page: its author, infected with the French madness, is trying in every possible way to break down respect for authority, to stir up the people's indignation against their superiors and against the government." As she wrote of Radishchev in the margin of her copy: "He is a worse rebel than Pugachev."

Although she sympathized with the idea of emancipation in theory, Catherine did not believe that Russian peasants were economically destitute or dehumanized. Where Radishchev's traveler saw exploitation and injustice—"Have not the fields on which the bread grew been enriched by sweat, tears, and groans?"—Catherine saw her subjects becoming more rather than less prosperous and benefiting from Russia's relative stability and expansion into fertile agricultural terrain. Of course, Catherine had no direct experience of peasant life, but neither was Radishchev's work an original piece of socioeconomic research, but rather a literary work very much of its time, an imaginary journey based on literary models. A court sentenced Radishchev to death, which Catherine commuted to exile to Siberia. Broken by the experience, he later committed suicide.

Radishchev attracted few sympathizers at the time. By and large, the small literate public shared a belief in a combination of autocracy and serfdom "without cruelty," adorned with Westernization. It had no time for alternative systems or values, not to mention revolutionary overthrows, but rather favored rational improvement of the status quo. Opposition, when it occurred, came mainly from those who believed that Westernization had gone too far. Hence the conservative thinker Prince Mikhail Shcherbatov's outcry about the corruption of morals, Denis Fonvizin's attack in his plays on Gallomania, or Nikolai Novikov's denunciation of "cosmopolitan slavishness" to fashions.

Such men regarded themselves as true "sons of the fatherland," but even their reaction against certain rational Enlightenment ideas was expressed in borrowed Western forms. Many of the leading men of Catherine's reign took up Freemasonry, an international movement to promote high ideals whose members engaged in arcane rituals and mysticism. Catherine, who as a woman was barred from membership, disapproved. She feared that "the temptations dreamed up as teachings outside our borders by all sorts of Masonic lodges and other mystical heresies" might threaten Orthodoxy, with their misguided belief in "imaginary and unattainable equality" (1780). In particular, Novikov's Masonic publishing ventures annoyed the empress. Initially winning her approval by printing extracts from early Russian chronicles and memoirs, Novikov survived an investigation in 1785 of a Masonic circle around Grand Duke Paul, who was increasingly alienated from his mother and fearful that she could nominate a different heir to the throne. When in 1790 a search of the publisher's premises revealed forbidden works, Novikov—a "fanatic," in Catherine's view—was imprisoned in the Schlüsselburg fortress.

It is worth remembering that Catherine had no experience of the sort of public political life that existed in Britain and France. Russia did not have political cartoons with rude captions portraying monarchs in undignified or obscene poses, no "pamphlet wars," no electoral hustings. It suffered not so much from censorship, of which there was little before 1792, as from low levels of urbanization and literacy and an absence of independent institutions and professions. With this came overreliance on initiative from on high in everything from the first satirical journals to translations. In principle, Catherine encouraged public participation; in practice, she found it hard to handle independent initiatives.

"They Are Burying Russia"

A portrait painted by the artist Borovikovsky in 1794 shows Catherine walking in the garden at Tsarskoe Selo. The empress wears an informal coatdress done up to the neck and a prim hat. One of her favorite dogs gazes up at its mistress in a cliché of canine devotion. Clearly, this painting was intended to inspire feelings of loyalty and admiration in Catherine's human subjects. This ordinary-looking woman was the empress who brought conquests and glory to Russia, as the column commemorating the sea battle of Chesme (1770) in the background reminds us. Her great achievement was to be both a mother figure and a conquering leader of world stature. In fact, Catherine disliked the portrait, which made her look stout and homely. She much preferred the more flattering, youthful images painted in the grand manner by Levitsky and others.

In the end, Catherine did not enjoy the restful and dignified old age that Borovikovsky's painting evokes. Her final years were tinged with loss and regret, to which the disturbing events in France and Poland provided an appropriate background. In 1791 the death while on military campaign of Potemkin, her virtual coruler and closest friend, left her devastated and, in the view of some, deprived her of sound advice and support. Many other trusted advisers died before her. The self-interested new blood at court was epitomized by Catherine's last lover, Platon Zubov (1767–1822). Ambitious and unscrupulous, Zubov profoundly influenced court politics and alienated people. Hovering in the background was her unloved son Paul, who disapproved of almost everything she did, especially in the sphere of foreign policy. It must have been a great disappointment that her adored grandsons Alexander and Constantine seemed to enjoy the crude parade-ground atmosphere at their father's residence at Gatchina outside St. Petersburg more than the cultured ambience of her own court.

Catherine still worked hard, but age, illness, and excess weight slowed her down. On November 2, 1796, a maid found her collapsed in her water closet following a massive stroke. She proved too heavy to lift into bed and died thirty-six hours later still on a mattress on the floor, surrounded by weeping attendants. In a room next door Grand Duke Paul was preparing his accession manifesto. Catherine was buried in the Peter-Paul Cathedral, not far from Peter I, Catherine I, Anna, and Elizabeth. "They are burying Russia," an English diplomat declared. On Paul's orders, the remains of Peter III were transferred from their resting place in the Alexander Nevsky Monastery and placed beside her in the grave. Paul made Alexis Orlov, the last living participant of the coup by which Catherine seized the throne and disposed of her husband, walk behind the late emperor's coffin. As Paul was to remark sarcastically, in 1762 his mother had been "too busy" to arrange a proper funeral for her husband.

RECONSIDERING CATHERINE

Following Catherine's death all sorts of people leapt into print, especially abroad, with a torrent of scandalous but unfounded revelations of prodigious and perverse sexual activity. Subsequent writers were much influenced by Jean-Henri Castéra's *Life of Catherine II* (Paris, 1797), which alleged that she "contrived to blend the most daring ambition, that ever distinguished the male character, with the grossest sensuality that ever dishonored the vilest of her sex." Even today such views coexist with more balanced assessments.

Traditional and Revisionist Views

Many older studies portrayed Catherine as a "hypocrite" who won applause by dishonest means. They dismissed her cultural activities as the trappings of vanity or blatant wastefulness, while her correspondence with leading philosophes was denounced as a subterfuge for persuading them that Russia was a happy country. In particular, she was chastised for "pretending" to pity the peasants but actually enslaving them even more. That she lived with a series of lovers evoked the spectacle of empress and escorts cavorting above while the masses suffered below. In foreign policy, Catherine's contribution to the dismemberment of Poland aroused moral indignation.

This was very much the approach in Soviet Russia, where Catherine's personal history was virtually ignored for seventy years. Since the late 1980s, however, the veil has been lifted on her life. Russian intellectuals eager to demonstrate that their country once enjoyed civil rights and freedom of speech in the context of "liberal conservatism" cite Catherine's reign to challenge skeptics who assert that such things never existed in Russia and are unlikely ever to exist. As a pioneering Russian historian wrote in the early 1990s, "Catherine's image has been monstrously distorted, and this in turn has distorted our understanding of the whole epoch." She was perhaps "the most successful Russian reformer—in creating a civil society with an estate structure based on law without force or violence."

Post-Soviet treatments of Catherine's reign have been influenced by the work of modern Western scholars, who point to the beginnings of civil rights in Russia in a climate of toleration under a more humane brand of "monarchy without despotism." This did not make Catherine a democrat, for she regarded autocracy as the only viable system for such a vast country as Russia. Power-sharing and political liberties were never on her agenda. Consultation was, but only on proposals that fell within her own terms of reference; independent formulation of alternative systems could not be considered. Catherine's plan was to regulate Russian society, opening up opportunities for action for well-defined social groups, while maintaining supervision from above. Good laws were central to her scheme, and freedom was knowing what they allowed. In this her thinking coincided with many of her contemporary rulers.

As for foreign policy, revisionist historians argue, Catherine was a woman of her time in her understanding that military victories and territorial acquisitions brought glory both to a country and to its ruler. Refusing to play the imperial game was not an option. But Catherine's successes proved double-edged, for Russian expansion aroused fears in Europe of a "monstrous empire." The Western press, most graphically in cartoons and caricatures, equated Catherine's desire to take over whole countries with her allegedly excessive sexual appetite. The appeal of the diplomat Sir John Sinclair (in St. Petersburg in the 1780s) for Europe to unite "to check the ambition of a sovereign who makes one conquest only as a step to the acquisition of another" might as well have alluded to her lovers. At home in Russia Catherine's conquests were generally a source of national pride. Even the comment of Catherine's critic Prince Mikhail Shcherbatov that "the whole reign of this monarch has been marked by events relating to her love of glory" could be read as a compliment in the eighteenth-century context, for adding to his or her country's prestige was regarded as a sovereign's true calling. But the high costs of Catherine's foreign policy provoked some antiexpansionist sentiments at court. Her successor Paul abandoned a campaign on the Caspian that Catherine launched just before her death. It would be revived by his successors in the nineteenth century, when imperial rivals would play the "Great Game" to win or maintain power and influence in Transcaucasia and Central Asia.

Readers in both Russia and the West now have the chance to form a more balanced view of the late eighteenth century, in which Catherine is restored to her rightful place. Catherine was no angel and life in her Russia was no bed of roses, but modern readers who know well the key role of image and public relations and of striking a balance between private morality and public achievement are well placed to study the eighteenth-century equivalents. There is no doubt that Catherine was concerned about her image; but, like Peter I, she regarded herself as Russia's servant and rarely promoted her own fame separately from that of Russia. In both foreign and domestic policy, Peter was Catherine's inspiration. She liked to present herself as Peter's spiritual daughter, cultivating such Petrine virtues as getting up early, working hard, and not wasting time. Unlike Peter, however, she never resorted to physical violence or crude practical jokes. Prince Shcherbatov commented that "generally speaking women are more prone to despotism than men, and as far as Catherine is concerned, it can justly be averred that she is in this particular a woman among women." But this picture is simply not borne out by the testimony of people who worked closely with her. This does not mean that she was not usually deeply convinced that she was in the right and insistent on getting her own way, but her approach was to get people to do things by thinking it was their own idea: "I select the circumstances, I get advice, I explore the ideas of the educated part of the public, and conclude from this what impact my decree will have."

Russia in Comparative Perspective

It is vital to approach eighteenth-century Russia as a variation on a theme rather than uniquely bad or uniquely backward. Before the French Revolution of 1789 all European societies were hierarchical, and most were ruled by monarchs with absolute or extensive powers. The British Parliament was exceptional, but even it was elected on a very limited franchise. When Catherine died in 1796, Britain was still more than a century away from universal suffrage, as was the new United States. All over Europe there was more emphasis on obligations than on rights, which tended to be attached to groups rather than individuals. Even though there were discordant voices, slavery was accepted everywhere, including the United States, where independence was accompanied by its extension. So-called second serfdom was the norm over most of central and eastern Europe and survived in pockets farther west also. Cruel capital and corporal punishment, often also torture, were in use everywhere. The mass of people were rural and uneducated.

Russia's rulers had to deal with problems similar to those their fellow monarchs faced, but with some additional ones, such as Russia's vast size, its many nationalities and religions, its difficult climate, and the sheer extent (rather than the mere fact) of serfdom. Ruling such an empire was a daunting task, as Catherine discovered. Things could have been worse. The second half of the eighteenth century may be seen as a period of relative stability for Russia. The Pugachev revolt was horrific, but it was contained. At the top, there was a comparatively rapid turnover of favorites, but their arrivals and departures were handled in a sensible manner, and many of Catherine's senior officials and advisers stayed in their posts for decades, like Alexander Viazemsky, procurator general for thirty years. For central government Catherine relied on persons rather than institutions, a fact underlined by the

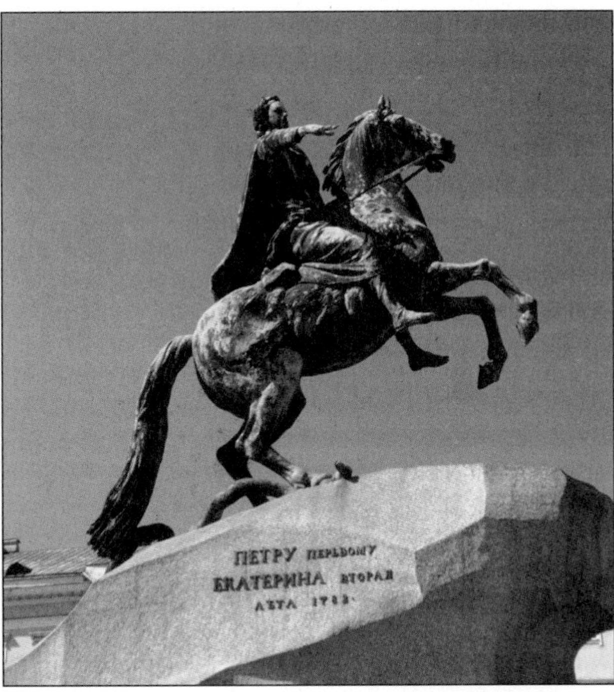

Equestrian statue of Peter I (1782) on Senate (now Decembrists') Square, St. Petersburg, by the French sculptor Etienne Falconet. *Gregor Schmid/ Corbis.*

only monument to her in St. Petersburg, a statue unveiled on Nevsky Prospect in 1873. Catherine stands proudly erect while from the base ministers, advisers, generals, and one woman—Princess Dashkova—gaze loyally at their sovereign.

Catherine rejected all projects to erect statues to her. The only public monument unveiled in her lifetime was the equestrian statue of Peter I on St. Petersburg's Senate Square, known as the "Bronze Horseman." It bears inscriptions in Russian and Latin "To Peter I from Catherine II (1782)." In contrast to the reign of Peter I, Catherine's saw no great cultural upheavals. The elite agreed that Russia was a European state, and their lifestyle reflected this. A couple of generations after Peter's reforms, the Russians depicted in portraits by Levitsky or Borovikovsky were Europeans not just on the surface but also in their language and attitudes. Meanwhile, peasant culture jogged along its traditional path without much intrusion from on high. Religious culture settled into a hybrid mode of Orthodox artistic conventions treated in the Western manner in major towns, while in the provinces much older traditions of icon painting and wooden and brick church architecture survived.

The problem of freedom in Russia was that the guarantee of liberty for Russian citizens depended on the character and intentions of the monarch and the wisdom of her or his advisers. Catherine was confident that Russians could prosper and enjoy a degree of liberty under an autocratic regime because she had confidence in her own ability to blend "republican" virtues with firm rule from above, implemented with "a good heart and good intentions" and a lot of hard work. The short reign of her successor Paul was to show how few guarantees actually existed.

PART III

Russia's European Century, 1796–1914

The nineteenth century was, for Russia, the "European century," when its culture, foreign relations, administration, and politics became a part of that continent's powerful civilization. Russia's "long nineteenth century" opens with the French Revolution and its aftermath—the Napoleonic Wars. The history of Russia in this period developed along two axes: increasing control over imperial territories, and increasing claims to inclusion by progressively broader strata of the population.

The Great Reforms of the 1860s, following Russia's defeat in the Crimean War, form a divide across the entire century. In the ages of Alexander I (r. 1801–1825) and Nicholas I (r. 1825–1855), Russia reached the height of its prestige in Europe. Yet Russia's transformation into a "modern empire" begins with the reforms, which emancipated the serfs through a remarkable feat of social engineering, and sought to introduce a greater measure of local participation into the process of governance. The reforms and the social ferment that followed were accompanied by a flowering of literature, art and music, as well as history and science. The machinery of empire, and the capacity to impose order on lands that included a rich variety of cultures, ethnicities, and religions, reached new levels between 1881 and 1905.

If reform, initiated from above, was a major driving force in Russia's evolution in the 1860s, at the turn of the century reform was replaced by revolution. Social discontent, economic change, and the desire for political representation erupted in violence in 1905. The Revolution of 1904–1907 was the culmination of the changes and uncertainties of the postreform period. It also signaled a new beginning, as religious toleration, national representation, agrarian reform, and steady economic growth became features of Russian life. Russia's European century came to an abrupt end with the outbreak of the Great War in 1914.

CHAPTER 16

Russia in the Age of Napoleon: Paul I and Alexander I, 1796–1815

Napoleon! whose corpse is not yet cold and whose colossal spirit is still so near us that we may behold its presence. Boundlessly great is that man who began our nineteenth century . . . that man who by his despotism helped the revolution fly around half the world, who was the idol of the people he had enchained, who planted his shield on the walls of the Kremlin and on the Pyramids of Egypt, and who finished out his life like those same Pyramids—on a lonely cliff he lived, the mausoleum of his fame, erected in another world, from which he ruled over a limitless steppe of waves.

—*Alexander Herzen*

Russia," proclaimed Empress Catherine II (r. 1762–1796) in her 1767 *Instruction,* "is a European state." It was not long before her firm pronouncement acquired an ironic twist. Catherine's own reign witnessed the entrenchment of serfdom—an institution that was steadily becoming less prevalent throughout the European continent. A wave of blood and violence—the mass multi-ethnic uprising led by the Cossack Emelian Pugachëv—swept the empire from the Ural mountains to Moscow in 1773–1774. Soon after Catherine uttered these words, moreover, Europe itself became unrecognizable: the French Revolution opened a new era throughout the continent, making a travesty of the administrative order that Catherine had particularly admired. As the nineteenth century began, however, Russia did, indeed, take its place in Europe—albeit neither the perfectly ordered Russian Empire nor the aristocratic Enlightenment Europe envisioned by Catherine.

Catherine's successors—her intensely disliked son Paul I (r. 1796–1801) and beloved grandson Alexander I (r. 1801–1825)—came to power as the armies of Napoleon Bonaparte began their rampage through the European continent. For contemporaries, the Napoleonic Wars, with their brilliantly clad regiments and devastating military campaigns, were terrifying, exciting, and all-absorbing. They defined an epoch in much the same way that the gray trench warfare of World War I defined the European world a century later. For two decades, until peace was signed and Napoleon exiled in 1815, Russia's foreign policy was fully determined by relations with France: bloody battles alternated with pacts of friendship. The reach of war extended to domestic politics and life: Napoleon's armies brought with them a model of government that eventually had a profound influence even on his most stalwart enemies. Thus it is not surprising that the first quarter of the nineteenth century in Russia is best understood against the backdrop of war and politics in Europe.

From Alexander I's accession in 1801, the style of the new century differed sharply from that of the eighteenth. A new law of succession, stipulating simply that the throne should pass to the ruler's eldest son, emancipated the monarch from court politics, with its powerful factions, alliances, and intrigues, and the insistent uncertainty about who would be the next ruler. The locus of government shifted from the court itself to newly established ministries and the individuals who occupied them. No longer exclusively bound by the strict rules and etiquette of the court, the Russian gentry established their own salons and drawing rooms, where careers and reputations could be made and broken amidst social chatter, song recitals, and French wines.

EUROPE IN 1800: THE NAPOLEONIC WARS

At the moment when Alexander I acceded to the Russian throne in 1801, the shadow of the French Revolution and the twenty years of war that followed it dominated the entire continent. Napoleon Bonaparte (1769–1821) had made his reputation in the campaigns of the Revolutionary Wars of the mid-1790s: in Italy (1796), where he defeated Austria, and in his subsequent invasion of Ottoman Egypt—which, though ultimately thwarted by the British, earned him the renown of a brilliant general. In 1799, Bonaparte returned to Paris, deserting his army in Egypt. One month later, on November 9 (18 Brumaire by the revolutionary calendar), Bonaparte, arranging a coalition within the reigning government of the Directory, proclaimed himself consul of the republic. Troops loyal to him dispersed the opposition, and soon he became essentially dictator in the newly established Consulate government. The Revolution ended with the replacement of the old monarchy by a powerful new dictatorship.

In the course of the subsequent fifteen years, Bonaparte succeeded in creating—through a virtually uninterrupted chain of wars—a system of satellite states that stretched from Spain and Italy to Warsaw. In 1804, Bonaparte proclaimed himself emperor of France and was crowned in the Cathedral of Notre Dame with the cooperation of Pope Pius VII. Eventually Napoleon was able to cement his gains by a system of uneasy alliances with the three great empires to the east—Austrian, Ottoman, and Russian. Napoleon's imperial inspiration came, unquestionably, from the conquests of ancient Rome. The evidence was everywhere: Roman-style temples dominated Parisian architecture of the period, imperial eagles adorned his banners, ladies dressed in high-bodiced gowns evocative of Roman fashion, and drawing rooms were decorated with innumerable Roman vases and various other Roman objects. More significantly, the scale of Napoleon's conquests was fully

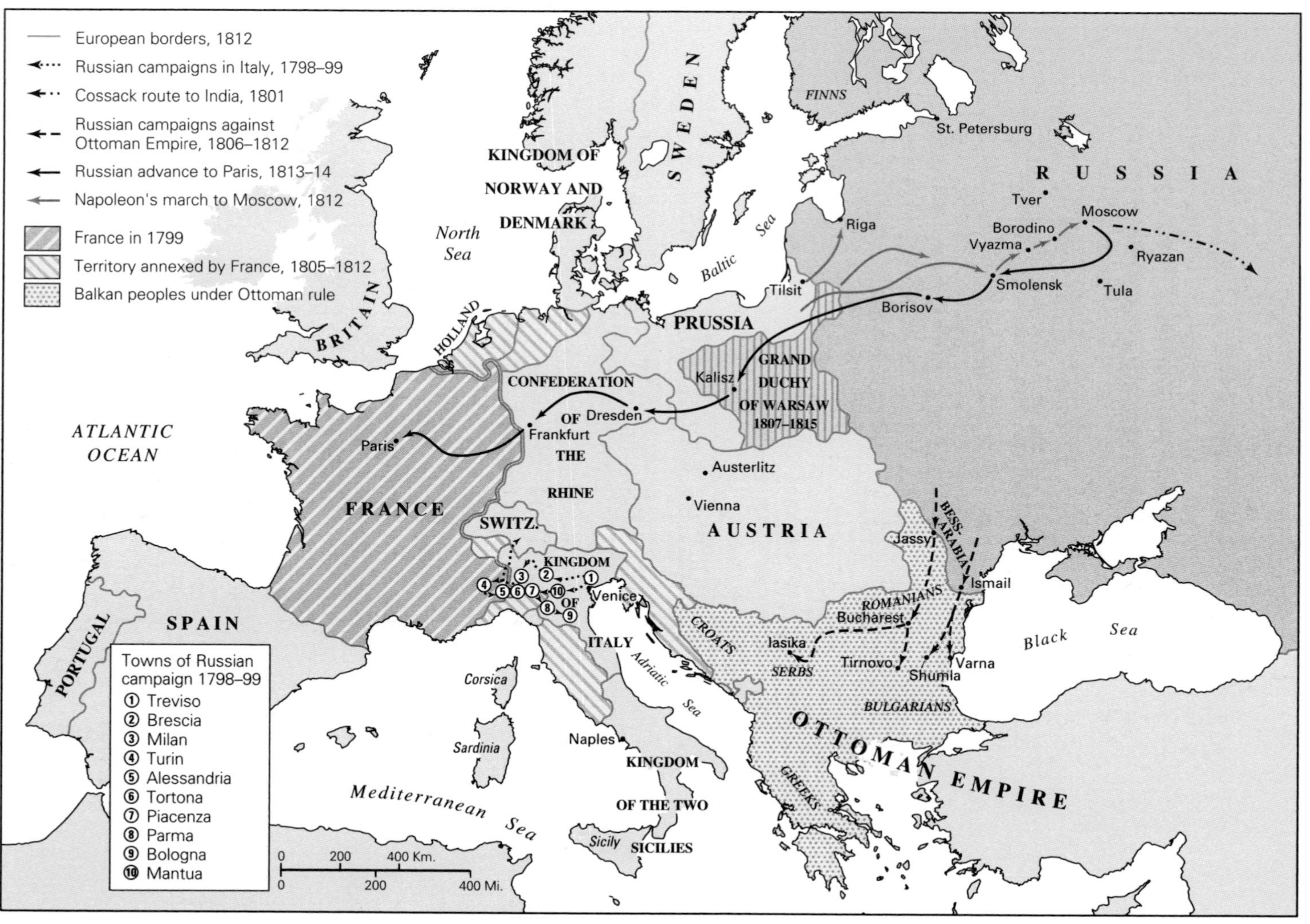
European borders, 1812
Russian campaigns in Italy, 1798–99
Cossack route to India, 1801
Russian campaigns against Ottoman Empire, 1806–1812
Russian advance to Paris, 1813–14
Napoleon's march to Moscow, 1812
France in 1799
Territory annexed by France, 1805–1812
Balkan peoples under Ottoman rule
Towns of Russian campaign 1798–99
① Treviso
② Brescia
③ Milan
④ Turin
⑤ Alessandria
⑥ Tortona
⑦ Piacenza
⑧ Parma
⑨ Bologna
⑩ Mantua
ATLANTIC OCEAN
PORTUGAL
SPAIN
FRANCE
Paris
BRITAIN
North Sea
HOLLAND
KINGDOM OF NORWAY AND DENMARK
SWEDEN
Baltic Sea
FINNS
St. Petersburg
Riga
Tilsit
PRUSSIA
CONFEDERATION OF THE RHINE
Frankfurt
Dresden
SWITZ.
KINGDOM OF ITALY
Venice
Adriatic Sea
KINGDOM OF THE TWO SICILIES
Naples
Sicily
Corsica
Sardinia
Mediterranean Sea
GRAND DUCHY OF WARSAW 1807–1815
Kalisz
Austerlitz
Vienna
AUSTRIA
CROATS
SERBS
Iasika
ROMANIANS
Bucharest
Tirnovo
BULGARIANS
Shumla
Varna
GREEKS
OTTOMAN EMPIRE
Jassy
BESSARABIA
Ismail
Black Sea
RUSSIA
Borisov
Smolensk
Vyazma
Borodino
Moscow
Tver
Tula
Ryazan
0 200 400 Km.
0 200 400 Mi.

The Revolutionary and Napoleonic Wars, 1792–1814.

Roman: the restoration of the ancient empire—this time with France at its center—was an undoubted goal of the self-proclaimed emperor.

How did an upstart officer from Corsica achieve the extraordinary feat of unifying and maintaining—if briefly—a European empire? The obvious answer, of course, is military success. Napoleon's army was well trained and well equipped, and he made good use of local troops, whom he coopted into his own forces. But behind the military façade lay another crucial element: like the ancient Roman emperors, Napoleon understood the importance of administrative machinery in maintaining vast territories. The Napoleonic empire rested on a remarkable organization that came to be known as the Napoleonic system and that, exported to the various conquered areas, eventually became the foundation of nineteenth-century administrative bureaucracy in many countries. In fact, some people in lands that were never conquered by Napoleon's armies—for example, Russia and the Ottoman Empire—were captivated by the extraordinary efficiency of the French emperor's highly centralized bureaucracy and sought, with varying degrees of success, to apply its principles to their own governments.

The core of the Napoleonic system was centralization. In this respect the new imperial administration recapitulated, though on its own terms, some of the strengths of the old French monarchy—so much so that the social thinker and statesman Alexis de Tocqueville (1805–1859) was prompted to argue that the new regime simply continued the old. At the top of Napoleon's government was a governing Council of State with the power to draw up laws and supervise local administration. The local representatives of the bureaucracy—the prefects—had an even greater allegiance to the center than their old-regime equivalents—the intendants—and even wore the same uniforms. Their functions included the regulation of local economic matters (in disarray following the Revolution), the gathering of votes for local plebiscites, and the conscription of recruits for Napoleon's unceasing wars. Napoleon centralized finances, creating a national bank, and solidified his position by signing a Concordat with the papacy (1801) and making the Catholic Church's participation a cornerstone of his rule.

The most important product of his reign, however—for France, Russia, and the rest of Europe—was the Napoleonic Code: the unified, systematized code of law that brought over two thousand articles together in one volume and articulated the major gains of the Revolution. Above all, the code advanced the principle of law itself as an independent quantity from administration: it encoded equality before the law, religious toleration, and abolition of privileges, and it made provisions for property rights and inheritance. (The greatest losers from the law were women, whose property rights were curtailed; marriage and divorce laws were also tightened.) The Code Napoléon was imposed throughout the conquered territories—in Prussia, the Kingdom of Italy, and Spain it became the basis for future legislation—and elements were adopted by regimes outside the empire. In fact, probably the only country that remained completely immune to Napoleonic notions of government and legislation was France's consistent enemy, Great Britain.

Times of war and upheaval can sometimes also be times of intense creativity and cultural flowering. Although art and literature in France itself became rather turgid and official—as can be seen in the paintings of Jacques-Louis David and the sculptures of Antonio Canova—the years of the Revolutionary Wars and especially the late 1790s proved extraordinarily productive for some of France's enemies. In England and the German states, particularly, the turn of the nineteenth century signaled the emergence of a new aesthetic and philosophical movement—Romanticism, whose early stages are associated with such poets and writers as Wordsworth, Coleridge, and Goethe. If thinkers of the Enlightenment had made man the center of their universe and were fascinated by the immense potential of human rationality, the Romantics shifted their emphasis away from the thinking subject to the surrounding world. Nature with its uncontrollable forces—forests, streams, snow-capped mountains, love—and a sense of striving for mystical unity with the universe: such was the stuff of the Romantic imagination. It was precisely the irrational factors in human existence, the forces beyond human control, and how we might coexist with them, that drew the attention of Romantic poets and writers. The earliest representative of this orientation in France itself was François-Auguste de Chateaubriand, whose 1802 *The Genius of Christianity* coincided with the revival of religion in the Napoleonic era.

PALACE AND PARADE GROUND: PAUL I, 1796–1801

The dominant sentiments animating Catherine II's son and successor, Paul I (1754–1801) seem to have been hatred, fear, and mistrust. These emotions are not difficult to understand. Taken away from his mother at birth by Empress Elizabeth (r. 1741–1761), Paul had been raised to dislike Catherine and was in turn disliked by her. He spent her reign in anxious seclusion at the palace of Gatchina, consumed by a not unjustified fear of exile or assassination. Indeed, Catherine tried to arrange that the succession pass not to him but to her grandson, Alexander, but the disapproval of her counselors prevented her from executing the plan before her death. Paul idolized the man he thought was his father, Peter III (1728–1762), but in all likelihood Paul was actually the son of Count Saltykov, Catherine's first lover. Paul's inspirations were the two eighteenth-century male monarchs, Peter the Great (Peter I) (r. 1682–1725) and Peter III (r. 1762). The first Peter's fondness for military games in his youth, and Peter III's admiration for the Prussian ruler Frederick the Great (r. 1740–1786) had become legendary. Paul spent his days at Gatchina training and reviewing his own troops, dressing them in Prussian regalia and reiterating Peter III's dreams of Frederick the Great's military successes. Apparently, when messengers reached him with the news of Catherine's death from a stroke and his consequent succession to the throne, Paul at first hid from them, thinking they had at long last come to lock him up.

Paul and the Gentry

The fundamental emotion of hatred goes a long way toward explaining aspects of Paul's reign. Paul's hatred had two major objects in particular. The first was, of course, Catherine herself. Witnesses reported that, within the first hour of his reign, Paul transformed the elaborate, glittering court of Elizabeth's and Catherine's times into military barracks where soldiers stomped hither and fro on urgent business while the old favorites among the nobility stood uselessly to the side. One of Paul's main motivations in making policy was simply to spite his no longer living mother. Thus his most important decree established male primogeniture as the principle of succession to the throne. The consequences were far reaching: Paul's rule of primogeniture amounted to the first stable system of succession since the beginning of the Romanov dynasty in 1613 and indeed assured a relatively unhampered transition from one ruler to another throughout the nineteenth century.

The second major object of Paul's hatred was related to the first: he detested everything French and, as time went on, particularly anything related to the French Revolution. Francophobia was rather a difficult sentiment to espouse in the Russian capital at a time when St. Petersburg was a colorful mélange of French people of various political persuasions, and the Russian nobility used the French language in preference to Russian. In the wake of the Revolution, Russia—as a reliable monarchy—was flooded with émigrés who most frequently took up posts as tutors or governesses in Russian families. (By the time of the poet Alexander Pushkin [1799–1837] many Russian young ladies would know French better than their own native language.) French fashion, and salons in the Parisian spirit, were the rage—as they were throughout Europe and even in some circles of Turkish society. Paul's measures for counteracting the infatuation with everything French were unambiguous: he simply legislated a new dress code that eliminated anything vaguely French and drew up an entire list of French words (including *pantalon* and *gilet*) that had entered the Russian vocabulary and whose use was now forbidden. He proceeded to close the Russian borders, permitting no books or even sheet music to enter from abroad and no Russians to leave their country. Thus he brought observers to remark on Russia's sudden reversion from the European Enlightenment to "Asiatic despotism" or "Turkish methods of rule."

These negative aspects of Paul's personality have often led to a caricatural depiction of him, and hence a dismissal of his reign as unimportant—a brief hiatus between the brilliant regimes of Catherine and Alexander. Actually, his negative disposition contributed to some quite significant changes that occurred during his rule. The deepest structural change occurred in the status of the gentry. Paul's relations with the nobility were terrible; the hatred and fear he felt toward them were fully reciprocated. He was inspired, moreover, by Peter I's ideal of universal service: he wished to reassert the nobility's obligation to the state, which a major decree issued by Peter III emancipating the nobility from service (1762) had effectively negated. His treatment of the nobility, therefore, was arbitrary and unpredictable. Anyone in state service might, from one moment to the next, be transferred, dismissed, exiled, or even imprisoned, while others, for no apparent reason, gained lucrative appointments or made stellar careers. People trembled as they went to Paul's balls and military parades (attendance at the latter, every morning, was mandatory), never knowing whether misfortune might strike at this particular occasion.

Peter I had succeeded in pressing a resentful nobility into unavoidable state service, but Paul's reassertions of his ideal in new conditions a century later had a curious result. The gentry simply deserted the service (no longer legally binding) in droves and fled either to their country estates or—an increasingly popular response—to Moscow, where they remained at a distance from the arm of government. Once they were out of state service, there was nothing the tsar could do to them. This massive flight from service had interesting repercussions for the structure of politics. By 1800, the Moscow (or Petersburg) drawing room had replaced the sparkling and uncomfortable imperial court as the main locus of political intrigue, social advancement, and cultural life as the nobility constructed their own sphere in counterposition to the unwelcoming court world.

The gentry drawing room, which was to come into its own in the succeeding reigns of Alexander I and Nicholas I, soon developed a set of rules or codes governing the behavior of its occupants. It was a world of balls, dinners, conversations about politics or literature, poetry readings, and musical recitals. If the sensibilities of the Catherinian elite were offended by the newly martial, masculine atmosphere of Paul's court, it was women who continued to define the tone of social intercourse in the new drawing room culture. Poets, thinkers, and composers—from Nikolai Karamzin (1766–1826) and Konstantin Batyushkov (1787–1856) at the turn of the century to Pëtr Chaadaev (1794–1856) in the mid-1820s—had a feminine audience in mind. Indeed, one of the most talked-about rules of the day defined a poet as one "who writes as he speaks, and who is read by ladies." The intimate domestic atmosphere actually gave birth to a number of artistic genres peculiar to Russia in this period: the "album"—the proud possession of every lady, in which her admirers inscribed verses dedicated to her; the "romance"—a sentimental art song, frequently taking love and the gentle beauties of nature as its theme; and the intimate "instructional letter" to an earnest young woman, thirsting for knowledge. All were oriented to the feminine sex. In general, the creators of this intimate literature and music retained a foothold in the masculine world of state service: officers in uniforms of the Guards regiments were a fixture of social gatherings, and duels were as much a part of the social code as the intimate letters or incautious glances that might cause them.

The antagonism between Paul's world and that of the gentry had some consequences for social legislation as well. Originating in pure spitefulness, a decree issued by Paul in a show of piety on the day of his coronation stipulated that peasants should not work more than three days a week for their landlord and should not work at all on Sundays. The decree, however benign it may have sounded, was directed against the detested nobility rather than toward the peasants; in any case, it was construed as a suggestion rather than as a law and had almost no practical consequences. Since the eighteenth century, Russian peasants had been divided into two categories—the state peasants, paying dues directly to the state, and those responsible to a landlord and working his lands. A second, well-intentioned, decree transferred significant numbers of state peasants into private ownership, following Paul's mistaken notion that they would be better off in private hands. Nonetheless, Paul has the distinction of introducing the first legislation directed in any way toward improving the lot of the peasantry—an important precedent that would be expanded by his successors.

Russia in the Revolutionary Wars

Paul's love for military spectacle continued unabated throughout his reign, perhaps augmented by the excitement of dealing with "real" troops instead of the Gatchina regiments of his youth. In quieter fashion, the eighteenth-century empresses Anna (r. 1730–1740), Elizabeth (r. 1741–1761), and Catherine had made of the Russian fighting forces one of the most redoubtable armies in Europe. Indeed they claimed victory over Frederick the Great of Prussia until Peter III reversed the course of the war owing to his respect for Frederick, and consistently drove the less technologically and structurally sophisticated Turkish armies into retreat.

Paul's military enthusiasm did not, apparently, go along with any particular talent for strategy or for foreign policy. Initially, his foreign policy decisions reflected the same motivations as his domestic measures: he withdrew from the coalition against France into which Catherine had brought Russia and immediately went about taking Russia out of the Persian war Catherine had begun. It was not long, however, before necessity brought Paul back in against France, which gradually took the Netherlands, Switzerland, and, under Napoleon's direction, almost all of Italy; Napoleon also began an invasion of Ireland and Poland. Everywhere they went, the French instituted a republican order, so distasteful to the Russian ruler. In 1798, following the Treaty of Campoformio (which produced temporary peace between Austria and France), Russia joined England, Austria, the Kingdom of Naples, and Turkey in a Second Coalition against France. In the Mediterranean, Admiral Fëdor Ushakov took the Ionian Islands (off the western coast of Greece) from France, and in 1798–1799 Russian armies landed on the coast of Naples. General Alexander Suvorov's army was sent to help Austria in the battle against Napoleon, in the hope of liberating occupied Italy.

Suvorov's Italian campaign—one of the great heroic tales of Russian military mythology—took place in 1799. Suvorov wished to take northern Italy from France and then move into France itself, meeting up with the Austrians along the Alps. Suvorov's army took Milan and Turin, consistently fending off French attacks from the side. The attacks, however, delayed the Russian army long enough to permit French forces to defeat the Austrians in the north. Suvorov found himself pressed up against the Alps by General André Masséna's army. His much sung heroic exploit, essentially, was to make the best of defeat by marching the Russian army across the Alps (evoking images of the Carthaginian general Hannibal's campaign against ancient Rome), thus avoiding complete humiliation and saving the army from destruction.

The Italian campaign marked a temporary end to Russian participation in the

Revolutionary Wars. In 1800 Paul broke the alliance with Austria, which he held responsible for Suvorov's defeat, and also with Britain. In the meantime he launched a far-fetched plan for a Russian march into India. At the same time he began a rapprochement with France. As France and Austria signed the peace of Lunéville in 1801, Russia found itself not yet allied with France, almost at war with Britain, and having no diplomatic relations with Austria.

In any case, Paul's foreign policy schemes were brought to an end in a rather abrupt fashion. Paul's insistence on subjugating the gentry and making them dance to his military tune did not mix well with the actual status and power they had acquired by the end of the eighteenth century. His fear, distrust, and hatred of the nobility, indeed, was a recipe for disaster and a self-fulfilling prophecy: the more he mistreated them, the more likely became their feared and anticipated revolt. Indeed, in March 1801 Paul was murdered by a group of drunken conspirators, who strangled him with a guardsman's sash. The coup was managed by his adviser, Count P. A. Pahlen (1745–1826), and the act (if not the specific means) had the clear if tacit consent of gentry society in general. Paul's assassination was much more than the standard palace coup, for it demonstrated, in the beginning new century, the impossibility of rule without the active consent of an increasingly powerful and independent nobility.

ALEXANDER COMES TO POWER: PEACE AND WAR, 1801–1807

To all appearances, the coup against Paul that brought his eldest son, the twenty-four-year-old Alexander I (1777–1825) to the throne replicated the eighteenth-century pattern of succession by violence: Anna, Elizabeth, and Catherine had all been installed by palace revolutions instigated by officers of the Guards. Count Pahlen had reason to believe that his faction would now become dominant at court, following the pattern of, for example, the Orlovs or the Panin party. He thought that the tender young sovereign would become his creature, as the eighteenth-century empresses had been creatures of their favorites—if only briefly—before they managed to construct their own power bases at court. The terms of the game, however, had changed with the inception of the new century.

The New Monarchy

In addition to profound changes in the structure of court politics, the turn of the nineteenth century witnessed, even more deeply, changes in the myth and image of the Russian monarchy itself. The ideas of the French Revolution—advocating liberty, equality, and fraternity, and exported rapidly throughout Europe—forced a redefinition of the traditional notion of monarchical rule. Defenders of the principle of monarchy now had to show that, no longer the only conceivable means of rule, monarchy was actually better in some way than republican government. Two main defenses were possible: monarchy could be shown to be a more efficient and orderly means of government; even more significantly, older arguments asserting the divine right of kings could be revived with the claim that monarchy possessed a divine sanction utterly inaccessible to republican forms.

Other changes had taken place in the years between the 1762 coup that put Catherine II on the throne and the one that installed Alexander I in 1801. Among them were Paul's crystal-clear law of succession and subtle differences in relations between ruler and favorites now that the ruler was male. Least tangible, but most important, was the emergence of an independent and highly sophisticated society—the nobility's drawing room culture—shaped by political, philosophical, and literary ideas independent of a mere factional struggle for power in the domain of palace politics. The emancipation of the nobility of 1762 had finally come to fruition.

The persona of Alexander I as monarch emerged at the intersection of all these new currents. To the gentry society that made him as it had broken Paul, Alexander was, to their good fortune and his, ideal material for the new kind of monarch. Drawing rooms in the capitals buzzed with ill-concealed joy at the news of Paul's demise. Alexander, from childhood, had possessed the image of a sunny, good-humored, kind, and reasonable person—the opposite of his father's dark and chaotic unpredictability—and was, presumably, a young person fit to resume the enlightened spirit of his grandmother's reign.

Alexander's "myth" was invested, from the first, with the proper elements. He was, as befitted a sovereign after the French Revolution, human. His reign, while displaying all the advantages of orderly centralized rule, carried an image of softness and humanity toward his subjects. Much was made of his constantly expressed reluctance to rule. He spoke of his desire to grant his subjects a constitution and then withdraw to a quiet, forested place for the rest of his days. In another image, the poet Vasily Zhukovsky portrayed him as a martyr, bearing on his slight shoulders the burdens of the empire. At the same time, the sacrality of his role carried equal weight. Alexander, in these early days, was seen as an "angel" on the throne—a perfect creature sent from the heavens to oversee earthly life. A Christlike element completed the amalgam: the amateur historian Mikhail Bogdanovich, writing in 1870, describes a remarkable incident in which—on Alexander's inaugural travels through the Baltics after his assumption of power—the young monarch practically resurrected a drowned peasant from the dead, restoring him to life (as did Christ with Lazarus) after the doctors had given up hope.

Perhaps the most remarkable aspect of Alexander's persona, however, was the degree to which—his sacrality apart—he was like the gentry society in which he lived. All were, figuratively speaking, Catherine's children. Alexander's contemporaries had been educated by French-speaking tutors and brought up on the Enlightenment ideas Catherine so strongly encouraged. Their monarch, as well, had been taken from his parents and educated according to Catherine's personal instructions, redolent with the spirit of the Enlightenment philosopher Jean-Jacques Rousseau (1712–1778). Like them, too, Alexander had had a Swiss tutor, César de

La Harpe (1754–1838), who had taught him republican and constitutional ideas along with the French language. When he came to the throne, Alexander was filled with Enlightenment and constitutional dreams that matched precisely those of his contemporaries. The monarch and the gentry officers, in short, understood each other perfectly—perhaps too well. Historians of ideas and culture have not failed to note the remarkable degree to which Alexander existed in harmony with the cultural and intellectual currents of his age. His evolution was subject precisely to the same vagaries as that of the poets and thinkers in the surrounding society.

Early Reforms

Alexander's mode of governance in the early years coincided exactly with the intimate domestic tone of social life. He quickly liquidated Paul's foreign policy mistakes by making an immediate peace with England while maintaining good relations with France and Spain as well. Alexander surrounded himself with a circle of friends, quietly but effectively removing Pahlen and his supporters from the court. Friendship thus became the means of government as it was the form of social intercourse in gentry society. Specifically, Alexander's "friends" were Count V. P. Kochubei, N. N. Novosiltsev, the Polish prince Adam Czartoryski, and Count P. A. Stroganov. Together, the foursome formed Alexander's "Unofficial Committee," jokingly referred to as his "Committee of Public Safety" (in reference to the committee that had spearheaded Robespierre's reign of terror in France in 1793–1794). They were responsible for the formulation of Alexander's early legislation, which, indeed, quickly turned in the direction of reform in keeping with Enlightenment principles. Several of them eventually held important posts in the government.

On the day of his accession to the throne, Alexander made clear, to a joyfully celebrating society, his intention of continuing the fundamental direction of his grandmother's reign. The announcement was followed by a number of concrete measures. Russia's borders were reopened, military uniforms reverted to the old style, the Secret Expedition (secret police) was abolished, and some of Paul's political prisoners were released. Catherine II's Charter to the Nobility and Charter to the Towns were reaffirmed. Reform, it was clear to everyone, would be the spirit of the new tsardom.

Indeed, in the first three years of his rule, Alexander, in consultation with his Unofficial Committee, set about implementing significant changes. He renewed his grandmother's abortive dream at last—to create an up-to-date and coherent law code to replace the still active law code of 1649. His advisers began immediately to work out details. In other spheres, however, the reforming monarchy could move more quickly. In keeping with its projected image of order and efficiency, the structure of administration was brought into conformity with the latest notions. In a near-mimicry of Napoleon's bureaucratic organization, Alexander's government in 1802 restored the Senate to its previous powerful position (analogously with that of the first consul's State Council) and replaced Peter's twelve colleges with ministries—eight initially, eventually expanded to nine. The function of the Senate was to mediate between the ministers and the sovereign, monitoring whether the ministers' actions remained in conformity with the desired direction of policy and communicating their decisions to the tsar. The Senate also served as the highest judicial organ. As in France, the eight original ministries dealt with the army, the navy, foreign affairs, internal affairs, justice, finance, commerce, and education. Effectively, this reorganization granted quite significant powers to the ministers: having no need to answer before a representative body of any sort, they were responsible only to the tsar, who had appointed them himself, with the approval of the Senate. The restructuring of government set up a system for the entire nineteenth century in which those ministers who had a strong character were able to play an extremely influential role in government. By the end of the century, it was often specific ministers who were responsible for important policies and indeed set the tone of a reign more than the tsar himself.

The second major sphere of reform was social policy. The inhabitants of Imperial Russia were officially organized into five *soslovie* categories ("estates," or status groups). These were the gentry (or nobility), clergy, merchants, *meshchanstvo* (a difficult-to-translate term referring roughly to townsmen and artisans, or the petty bourgeoisie), and peasants. Like his contemporaries, Alexander paid lip service to the idea of emancipating the serfs. Although the project in its full dimensions was daunting and did not even seem terribly pressing, Alexander's administration made use of Count Sergei Rumyantsev's emancipation proposals to implement an intermediate measure—the "law on free agriculturists" of February 20, 1803. This law provided for individual agreements between serfs and landowners, by means of which the peasants could be freed and granted a piece of land. They would thus become free farmers. The significance of this measure was not so much in any concrete changes that might affect large numbers of the peasantry—only a handful of landlords and peasants took advantage of the possibility—as in the fact that it broke the heretofore indestructible link between the activity of agricultural labor and the condition of serfdom. In this respect, the law on free agriculturists, admitting the possibility of an independent peasant proprietor, fit into a pattern of social legislation in Alexander's early years: An 1801 law made it possible for merchants, *meshchanstvo*, and state peasants to buy land. In 1802, landlords were allowed to engage in foreign trade (formerly the province only of proper merchants); in 1812, peasants, too, were allowed to engage in trade. Together, these laws signified the beginning of the breakdown of the rigid *soslovie* system—the matching of a person to a single activity—and introduced the greater flux in social categories that eventually was to characterize nineteenth-century society.

Alexander's third set of early reforms complemented the second. In 1800, Russia had only one university—Moscow University, established by Enlightenment writer and scholar Mikhail Lomonosov (1711–1765) in 1755. A commission set up in 1802 to oversee education passed a law in 1804 establishing provincial universities in Kazan, Kharkov, Vilna, and Dorpat (the latter two were revivals of venerable universities that had been established in the sixteenth and seventeenth centuries). Universities in St. Petersburg (1819) and later Kiev (1833) followed. Universities are institutions where one goes to become someone else, intellectually and socially. The provincial Russian universities, initially staffed by German professors, were part of the larger vision, in Alexander's reign, of bringing knowledge and opportunity to nongentry members of Russian society. The universities were the culmination of an educational support system that included the establishment of new parish and local schools at all levels, technical institutes and pedagogical institutes, and a revitalized Academy of Sciences in St. Petersburg.

War: Europe and the Caucasus

The flurry of domestic reform, however, was brought to a halt by 1805 because of the renewed claims of the Napoleonic Wars on the Russian government's attention. Napoleon's gains in Italy and along France's eastern borders had been ratified in the Treaty of Lunéville with Austria (1801) and the Peace of Amiens with Britain (1802). These agreements recognized the extension of the French boundary to the Rhine and acknowledged the imperial client Cisalpine and Ligurian republics in northern Italy, the Helvetic Republic in Switzerland, and the Batavian Republic of the Dutch. The primary goal of Napoleon's empire, it has been said, always remained war, and he was now free to turn his attention—and that of his Grande Armée—to the German states. Ever precariously poised on the brink of war since Alexander had reversed the pro-French policy of Paul's last days, in 1805 Russia entered, with Britain and Austria, the Third Coalition against France.

Although British naval forces won a decisive victory over the French at Trafalgar in the summer of 1805, the fate of the Austrian and Russian armies in this phase of the Napoleonic Wars was nothing short of disastrous. Napoleon wiped out an Austrian force of forty thousand men at Ulm on October 19, 1805, before they were able to meet up with an equally large contingent led by General Mikhail Kutuzov (1745–1813). An even more dramatic and humiliating victory over a combined Austrian-Russian force followed at Austerlitz on December 2. The Russians, commanded by Alexander himself (the first tsar personally to lead an army since Peter I), and their Austrian allies lost nearly half of their sixty thousand men. As a result of their defeat, the Austrians withdrew from the coalition in the Treaty of Pressburg (December 26, 1805), with major territorial losses in northern Italy. The Holy Roman Empire—a loose association of German states dating back to medieval times—was officially dissolved a month later. The supposedly invincible Prussia suffered a double defeat at Jena and at Auerstädt in 1806, thus breaking the last barrier to the formation of Napoleon's Confederation of the Rhine. Soon afterward, a Napoleonic Grand Duchy of Warsaw, constructed from the Prussian part of Poland, was formed along the border of the Russian Empire. To seal an already quite thorough defeat, Russo-Prussian forces were vanquished once again at Friedland on June 14, 1807.

In the meantime, the Russian army was also engaged in war on another front. The Caucasus nations of Georgia and Armenia had to maneuver among three empires: Ottoman, Persian, and Russian. Georgia allied itself with Russia in Catherine II's war against Turkey. When Persia sought to recapture its ancient Georgian territories, massacring the population of the capital, Tbilisi, in 1795, Georgia's rulers unequivocally opted for Russian protection. Paul finally acceded to Georgian demands for annexation by Russia (in part justified by a common adherence to Orthodox Christianity), confirmed in a manifesto by Alexander in 1801. Russian domination in the Caucasus was thereby established. Many parts of Georgia itself, however, were less accepting of Russian rule than the Georgians: thus Imeretia and Abkhazia were won by war in the first years of Alexander's reign. Russia's southward expansion, of course, prompted unease on the part of its primary eighteenth-century adversary—the Ottoman Empire. In 1806 Russia found itself once again at war with Turkey over the Romanian principalities of Moldavia and Wallachia. Heated at first, the war cooled down as Russian forces were needed in Europe and the Turkish sultan became occupied by his own internal problems.

Like most of the treaties of the Napoleonic Wars, the Treaty of Tilsit, dramatically concluded between Alexander and the French emperor on a raft in the middle of the River Niemen on July 27, 1807, was a matter of necessity for Alexander and a matter of temporary advantage for Napoleon. Tilsit was presented as an alliance of two great empires rather than as a Russian capitulation; nonetheless, the new imperial "friendship," reaffirmed in a second meeting at Erfurt in 1808, was sealed between two clearly unequal partners. Concretely, Russia gained Bialystok (part of Prussian Poland) and lost the Adriatic port of Cattaro and the Ionian Islands off the western coast of Greece. Alexander also recognized Napoleon as emperor, as well as the kings Napoleon had installed as puppets in Holland and Sicily. He promised to mediate between France and England, while France was to mediate between Russia and the Ottoman Empire.

The less specific implications of Tilsit, however, were more significant: Napoleon subtly directed Alexander's attention to Finland as a distraction from Central Europe, while the treaty marked only a brief hiatus in Russia's hostilities with Turkey. Indeed, in the years following Tilsit, Russia found itself engaged in three simultaneous wars: with Sweden, from which Finland was acquired in 1809; with Turkey, which finally yielded Bessarabia in 1812; and in Georgia, where an 1813 treaty codified Russian gains up to that point. Thus, without the explicit imperial aims of a ruler like Catherine II or Peter I, Alexander found his empire expanding with extraordinary rapidity.

ALLIANCE WITH NAPOLEON AND SPERANSKY'S VISION, 1807–1812

On the raft at Tilsit, the two great European emperors had divided Europe between them. A period of personal friendship and rapprochement between the two powers followed. The subsequent course of domestic reform in Russia took the shape of an unabashed admiration for the French imperial order and an effort to restructure Russian law and government on the Napoleonic model. In 1806, Alexander was fortunate to find, among the members of his bureaucracy, a man whose tastes and visions fit his own conception of his monarchy with remarkable precision. Like Napoleon himself, Mikhail Speransky (1772–1839) was a new type of person, a man of humble origin (he was of the clerical estate) who could not have aspired to

The Imperial Embrace. Alexander I and Napoleon on the raft in the River Niemen at Tilsit (1807). Contemporary British cartoon. *British Museum.*

political power in the closed world of the eighteenth-century ruling nobility. By the time Alexander discovered him, Speransky had already made his mark on Russian institutions: he had been responsible for a major reform of seminary schools; had played a role in the establishment of the secular high school, or Lyceum, at Tsarskoe Selo; and, as a bureaucrat in the Ministry of the Interior, had participated in Alexander's social reforms.

Speransky's moment of glory began with his resolution of the gravest problem that faced the empire at the conclusion of peace in 1807. This was a severe deficit in the imperial budget, accumulated not only through expensive military campaigns but, more profoundly, through an irresponsible policy, followed since Catherine's time, of covering expenditures by printing paper money (assignats). By 1809, the budget showed 127.5 million rubles of revenue and 278.5 million in expenditures; the value of the paper ruble had fallen to a third of a silver ruble. (This irresponsible printing of money, incidentally, had been implemented by Tsar Alexei Mikhailovich in the seventeenth century and became a favorite tactic of the Soviet and post-Soviet governments in the late 1980s and early 1990s.) Speransky's achievement was to halt the printing of assignats, which were by definition not backed by hard currency, and to institute an extensive system of taxation to fill the government's coffers.

Speransky was inspired by a larger vision as well. Like other defenders of monarchy following the French Revolution, he was gripped by the notion of monarchy's efficiency and orderliness. Thus many of his measures were aimed at tightening up the ministerial system instituted at the outset of Alexander's reign. Two new ministries were added, and ministerial duties were more clearly defined. To this end, as well, Speransky advocated the creation of a State Council in addition to the Senate to oversee the central administration. Speransky also suggested new administrative divisions in the empire, establishing *dumas* (councils), courts, and administrative boards at the local, district, and provincial levels, culminating with the State Council, the Senate as highest judicial organ, the ministries, and the central executive power.

Much of the four years in which Speransky wielded power was taken up by the major project of instituting a uniform code of law—a project he inherited from the unsuccessful earlier commission of 1801. Speransky's project, which he completed by 1812, was clearly and explicitly modeled on the Napoleonic Code Civil, although Russian laws were painstakingly unearthed to fit each article. The Code Civil by then already formed the basis of the Prussian and Austrian legal systems as well as that of the French. By borrowing from it and relying on general principle, Speransky avoided the messy and difficult task of making order of the vast chaos of decrees and legislation that had, in haphazard fashion, formed the basis for legal decisions since the 1649 law code. Speransky's detractors, Nikolai Karamzin foremost among them, accused him rather exaggeratedly of literally copying the French code. Eventually, he himself acknowledged that his task could not be completed without making sense of the chaos of existing Russian laws. The code thus remained an abstract, if attractive, idea, which, in an unusual and fortunate twist of fate, Speransky himself was able to implement in more practical form in the succeeding tsardom. In any case, when Napoleon's forces began their invasion of Russia in 1812, the project's unambiguous French origins led to the shelving not only of the code itself but of its creator as well: Speransky was exiled to Nizhny Novgorod and then Perm to wait out the rest of Alexander's reign.

Speransky had, as well, a scheme for the transformation of Russian society at large that found resonance in Alexander's conception of his monarchy. In what amounted to a formalization of Alexander's rather unsystematic early measures divorcing status from its immediate link with type of work, Speransky proposed the abolition of the five *soslovie* categories and the substitution of three categories of Russian people. These would be the gentry (with the right to own populated lands and freedom from obligatory service); the "working people" (peasants, artisans, and servants); and the most interesting category, the "people of middle status"—a rubric that grouped together merchants, *meshchanstvo,* and peasantless landholders. The social categories would correspond with three kinds of rights: general civil rights (basically what we would today call human rights), special civil rights (with a service exemption), and political rights (or the right to participate in government). The gentry would have all three, the middle would have civil and political, and working people only civil. Although it is difficult to see what it would mean to apply such an abstract plan in practice, the conception itself indicates how important the question of a "middle estate"—continuing early social measures and advances in education—had become for policymakers in the Alexandrine period.

THE HORNED BEAST: INVASION AND TRIUMPH, 1812–1815

Cracks in the imperial friendship of Napoleon and Alexander began to appear just two years after the 1808 meeting at Erfurt. Napoleon had taken advantage of the peace to consolidate his gains, converting the heretofore independent kingdoms of Spain and Holland into integrated parts of the French Empire, while Russia fought Sweden over Finland and engaged in war with Turkey over Bessarabia. In the course of his appropriations, Napoleon seized the property of the Duke of Oldenburg, who happened to be married to Alexander's sister. Russia's protest came on top of already souring relations caused by unsuccessful negotiations to have Napoleon marry a Russian princess (his first wife, Josephine, had proved infertile, and Napoleon managed to obtain a papal annulment ending the marriage); both sides stalled, and in the end Napoleon married the Austrian princess Marie Louise. The real reason, however, for the growing rift was economic: Russia had reluctantly agreed to participate in the continental blockade against British trade as a condition of the Treaty of Tilsit. A boycott of British shipping, however, made no economic sense whatsoever for Russia, since Britain was its main trading partner. It was not long before Russia reneged on its promise and instead instituted a heavy tariff on French imports (1810), thus antagonizing Napoleon: economic warfare was a crucial aspect of his imperial system.

In the meantime, Russia had provided only lukewarm, indeed even feigned, support in a new French engagement with Austria in 1809. Once Russia had concluded peace with both Sweden and Turkey, Napoleon had exhausted his tactic of occupying Russia with other wars; he, in turn, concluded alliances with Prussia and Austria as he prepared for confrontation with Russia. By 1811 he was amassing large numbers of troops in the Grand Duchy of Warsaw, along Russia's border. At this point, the European continent was effectively divided up between the two great empires. Any further expansion on Napoleon's part was bound to intrude on Russian interests.

The Campaign of 1812

On June 24, 1812, news reached Alexander—who was at that moment attending a Vilna ball—that Napoleon's troops had entered Russian territory, moving between Kovno and Grodno in the direction of Moscow. Napoleon's forces eventually counted 600,000—a colorful army with men from all parts of his empire, from Spain to Poland. Russian forces—which in any case numbered a mere 200,000—were split into two armies under the respective direction of Field Marshal Prince Mikhail Barclay de Tolly (1761–1818) and General Prince Peter Bagration (1765–1812). Napoleon took advantage of this strategic mistake to cut right through to Vilna. Throughout the summer, the Russian armies were in retreat. Though Barclay engaged the French army near Vitebsk and Bagration did so near Mogilëv, the first real battle occurred at Smolensk, where the two Russian forces were able to meet up following a conscious and intelligent retreat by Barclay, who realized that Napoleon's army would encircle his if he advanced. After two unsuccessful efforts, Napoleon took Smolensk and continued toward Moscow, the Russian armies retreating before him.

In the meantime, Barclay, whose tactic of retreat, however successful, was unprestigious and unpopular, was replaced by the hero of the Turkish wars, General Kutuzov. Kutuzov immediately decided to engage Napoleon at Borodino. What followed, on August 26, 1812, was, until the massacres of the twentieth century managed to eclipse all previous military horrors, one of the bloodiest battles in history. At Borodino, in the course of a single day, 100,000 men were killed or wounded out of 110,000 Russian and 130,000 French troops. French attacks followed, wave upon wave, throughout the entire day. At its conclusion the French retired to their camp while the remaining Russians stayed on the field, as Cossack regiments continued to stage raids on the enemy army. The results of the massive and intensive bloodshed were moot: both sides thought they had won, and Kutuzov intended to attack once again, until he realized that half of his army had been destroyed. The Russians, having inflicted severe damage on the French army, moved back toward Moscow, pursued by the French.

The campaign of 1812 was an anomaly in contemporary military history. The formal, civilized style of the eighteenth century relied on orderly regiments confronting each other. One or two battles, fought exclusively by professional soldiers, often determined the fate of an entire nation. The battles of 1812, in contrast, looked forward to the ambiguous wars of the twentieth century, or backward to the massacres of the seventeenth century (such as the Thirty Years' War), in which outcomes were unclear and civilians as prone to injury or death as combatants. Throughout their advance, Napoleon's armies were met by an unexpected patriotic outburst from the Russian people at large, who not only volunteered to fight in the army but actually engaged in their own partisan attacks against the French. Such sentiments echoed in the St. Petersburg and Moscow press, which equated Napoleon with the Antichrist: Gavrila Derzhavin's poems described his seven heads and ten horns, and the calculations of a Dorpat professor concluded that the numerical coefficients of the letters in "l'Empereur Napoléon" added up to 666.

The French in Moscow

The war's oddest (in military terms), and at the same time most terrifying, episode followed the retreat from Borodino. The Russian army, instead of stopping at Moscow, kept going east—thus effectively leaving the city to Napoleon's forces. The citizens were evacuated (Moscow salons now transferred to the wilds of Nizhny Novgorod), and fires were intentionally started throughout the city. What should have been a clear French victory became a surreal experience for the French army. Kutuzov's army, in retreat on the road to Ryazan, swung around and won two battles at Tarutino and Maloyaroslavsk. Soon the French were locked in a pocket in Moscow, with Kutuzov's forces, stationed immediately to the south, abundantly

The glare of the Moscow fire. Painting by Vasily Vereshchagin. *Anne S. K. Brown Military Collection, Brown University Library.*

supplied by the fertile black-earth region. Petersburg, too, was well defended. By mid-October the uncertainty of the situation—loss of discipline among the French troops, a continuing and successful partisan war, and the daunting prospect of the oncoming Russian winter—prompted a French decision to leave Moscow. In the end, territory and cold vanquished the imperial army: French soldiers died in droves as they moved back, pursued by Russian forces on all sides, toward the west. Although the Russians never actually encircled the fleeing Grande Armée, by the time the French ignominiously crossed the Berezina River, their army was in complete disarray and reduced to some 15,000 to 20,000 of the original 600,000 troops. Leaving his army (as he once had in Egypt), Napoleon fled to Paris in time to circumvent a coup being planned against him in the French capital.

Kutuzov, at this point, was ready to rest on his laurels and declare victory. Alexander, however, for whom the entire campaign of 1812 had been a mystical experience, would not stop until the French had been chased all the way back to Paris. Thus on January 1, 1813, Russian forces crossed the boundary of the empire and entered Prussia, which had promised neutrality. The war continued through 1813 and 1814 with varying degrees of success. A joint Russian and Prussian force met defeat at Lützen and Bautzen on, respectively, April 20 and May 9, 1813. They were joined by the Austrians in the summer of 1813. Napoleon's military fate was sealed at Leipzig in October in the immense Battle of Nations—billed as a collective revolt against Napoleon's tyranny. Thereafter victory was assured as the allied armies pursued the French army onto French territory. The Russian army entered Paris, in triumph, on March 18, 1814.

CHAPTER 17

The Age of Restoration: Russia in Europe, 1815–1830

Sonnez clairons! Polonais, à ton rang	*Sound the trumpets! Poles, to your ranks!*
Suis sous le feu ton aigle qui s'élance.	*Follow your eagles through the fire as you advance.*
La Liberté bat la charge en courant,	*Liberty sounds the charge at the double,*
Et la victoire est au bout de ta lance.	*And Victory stands at the point of your lance.*
	—Casimir Delavigne, "La Varsovienne," 1830.

Napoleon's fate was sealed, and the outlines of a new European order instituted, at the Congress of Vienna in 1815. The victors, determined to replicate old-regime Europe as closely as possible, installed what became known as the congress system: an international solidarity of monarchs grouped to prevent subversion by future Napoleons. The feared subversion, however, was not long in coming, if from another quarter. Premised on the notion of restoration and order, the congress system was challenged almost immediately by movements that took either nationalism or another innovative concept, "liberalism," as their slogans. Rebellions in Greece, Spain, and the Kingdom of Naples in the early 1820s were echoed in St. Petersburg in the December uprising of 1825. The string of uprisings culminated in 1830, when a revolution in France once again dethroned the Bourbons and provoked revolutions in other countries as well. The final challenge to the notion of restoration came from Poland, where revolution ended the fleeting friendship Alexander I had begun with the Congress Kingdom. Russia responded by incorporating Poland more rigidly into the Russian Empire.

Although there was no distinct break in Alexander I's reign in 1815, the passing years witnessed a gradual change in the character and quality of his rule. Alexander's grandmother, Catherine II, had thought of him and his brother Constantine as the rulers of a great European empire that was heir to a Byzantine and Orthodox tradition and the equal of Roman Christendom; their very names attested to such ambitions. Alexander himself, however, conceived the vastness of the Russian Empire, now augmented by territories won in the Caucasus and Central Europe and even North America, as a heavy burden as much as an honor. The symptoms of this sense of burden became steadily more apparent, acquiring a bizarre twist in the last years of his rule: not only his mood but his policies became imbued with a religious mysticism that European rulers and statesmen found alternately amusing and annoying. Domestically, his mysticism produced repressive policies and provoked severe disappointment among the fellow travelers of his youth, for whom the outset of his reign had been the focus of high hopes and constitutional dreams.

THE CONGRESS OF VIENNA AND THE HOLY ALLIANCE, 1815

A motley assortment of royal personages and their retinues converged on the Hofburg Palace in Vienna in September 1814. Over the succeeding six months, under the firm guidance of the brilliant and reactionary Prince Clemens von Metternich (1773–1859), the Austrian foreign minister, the victors in the final stage of the Napoleonic Wars set about refashioning the map of Europe. The victorious powers—Russia, Prussia, Austria, and Great Britain—were eventually joined, through adroit maneuvering, by France's representative, Charles Maurice de Talleyrand (1754–1838). The Congress of Vienna intended to return as closely as possible to the prerevolutionary European order, while conserving advantageous changes. It was a monumental task. On the ashes of the Napoleonic kingdoms and duchies, the powers set up several new states and installed, correspondingly, new political

The Congress of Vienna, 1815, as portrayed by Jean-Baptiste Isabey. Metternich is standing toward the left in white breeches, and Talleyrand has his arm on the table at the right. *Réunion des Musées Nationaux/Art Resource, NY.*

regimes. The key concept underlying the Vienna Congress as a whole was legitimacy: boundaries were to be redrawn, and political systems reinstituted, that were legal and proper after the terror and usurpation that had marked the Revolutionary and Napoleonic wars.

The Powers at Vienna

The main territorial changes, naturally, were implemented in the center of Europe, where Napoleon's conquests had caused the greatest adjustment of boundaries. The congress created a new, loosely defined German Confederation, which included an enlarged Prussia, an Austria that had absorbed Venetia and Lombardy, and the numerous smaller German states. The United Netherlands were created from the Napoleonic kingdoms of Holland and Belgium, and Switzerland was set up as an independent republic. The Italian states remained fragmented and, with the exception of Piedmont-Sardinia and the papacy, under Austrian control. The congress confirmed the Russian acquisition of Finland, while Sweden gained Norway. A new Polish state, constructed on the ashes of the Grand Duchy of Warsaw, came under primarily Russian control, with very little of former Prussian Poland remaining.

Even where territorial changes were minor, the Napoleonic political regimes themselves were replaced. This was the case in France itself, where the Peace of Paris (1814) restored the Bourbon monarchy, in the person of Louis XVIII, to power. Well aware of the dangers of a seizure of power by the old-regime aristocracy, the powers at Paris and Vienna, including Alexander I, were careful to prevent any effort at mere reversion to the old status quo. The new Bourbon regime was a constitutional monarchy; the Napoleonic Code Civil was retained, as was the Concordat with the papacy. In Spain, as well, Ferdinand VII (1784–1833, r. 1814–1833), whom Napoleon had kept away from the throne in 1808, assumed power and promised to govern in accordance with a constitution adopted in 1812. No limitations were imposed on the Austrian emperor, Francis I (r. 1804–1835), or the Prussian king, Frederick William III (r. 1797–1840).

The negotiations were dramatically interrupted in March 1815, when Napoleon, escaping from exile on the island of Elba off the Corsican coast, made his way back to Paris, where Louis XVIII quietly withdrew from harm's way. Napoleon retook control of his army, but his ensuing campaign, the "Hundred Days," ended with his spectacular defeat at Waterloo and a final exile to the island of St. Helena, from which escape was impossible. For the future conduct of diplomacy and to avoid subversion resembling Napoleon's, the Vienna Congress established a Quadruple Alliance of Prussia, Austria, Great Britain, and Russia. The same powers were to act together as a Concert of Europe, prepared at any moment to regulate conflicts that might arise.

Alexander's Holy Alliance

One of the greatest believers in the notion of legitimacy, Alexander I was not fully satisfied with these extensive and complicated arrangements. Practical measures aside, he also had a *vision* of the future European order. In July 1814, following the

Russian army's triumphant entry into Paris, the Russian Senate, the Holy Synod, and the State Council had offered Alexander the title *blagoslovennyi* ("blessed"). Though he modestly declined, the word became inextricably associated with his image. In the meantime, Alexander himself, following the near-apocalyptic experience of 1812, had become imbued with religious feeling and a sense of his own mission of Christian leadership. It was in this spirit that he proposed to the powers an alliance over and above the Concert of Europe. The "Holy Alliance," bringing together the three Christian emperors of Austria, Prussia, and Russia, was to preserve "Christian precepts of justice, charity, and peace" in international life and unite monarchs "by the bonds of true and unbreakable fraternity." Alexander seemed to have in mind the institution of Christian constitutional monarchy as a universal guarantee of domestic and international peace and justice.

Alexander had some trouble getting his prospective partners to sign the document, which had met the approval of his spiritual adviser, the Baroness Julie de Krüdener (1764–1824). Metternich, in particular, thought the alliance was sentimental nonsense. But he saw its potential advantages as a weapon against liberal and national movements. Once certain suspicious phrases mentioning the participation of the "people" had been removed, he agreed to Austrian participation. Curiously, Alexander seems originally to have meant the alliance to unite all of Europe and even the United States. On September 26,1815, the Austrian and Prussian emperors agreed to the alliance as a guarantee of future European stability and governance in accordance with Christian principles.

So far as the Russian Empire was concerned, the most important arrangements made at Vienna were those regarding Poland. A process of compromise and negotiation among the powers finally resulted in Prussia's retention of a slice of the Duchy of Warsaw, Austria's gain of Tarnopol and loss of West Galicia, and Cracow's establishment as a free city. Russia added a small piece of the duchy near Bialystok to its Polish possessions; more significantly, written into the agreement was the establishment of an independent Kingdom of Poland under Russian suzerainty. The new Polish kingdom, which came to be known as Congress Poland, reflected Alexander's feelings of enlightened friendship toward the Poles, as well as the ideas of his Polish adviser, Prince Adam Czartoryski (1770–1861). Poland had a unique status within the empire, with its own political system and right to self-governance. The powerful symbol of this independence was the Polish constitution. Alexander was a great admirer of constitutional government, however hesitant to implement it within Russia itself, and was only too happy to guarantee it. The constitution granted the Poles their own administration, judiciary, national assembly (Sejm), civil service, and, importantly, army. In addition, the Napoleonic legal code, freedom of the press, religious toleration, personal liberty, and universal rights to property ownership were guaranteed. Alexander himself, with a good deal of flourish, addressed the Polish Sejm when it first opened in 1818. Poland, and the Polish constitution, became for him the symbol of just government, a beacon of hope for the Russian Empire as a whole.

If we cast a glance at the Russian Empire as it emerged from the Vienna Con-

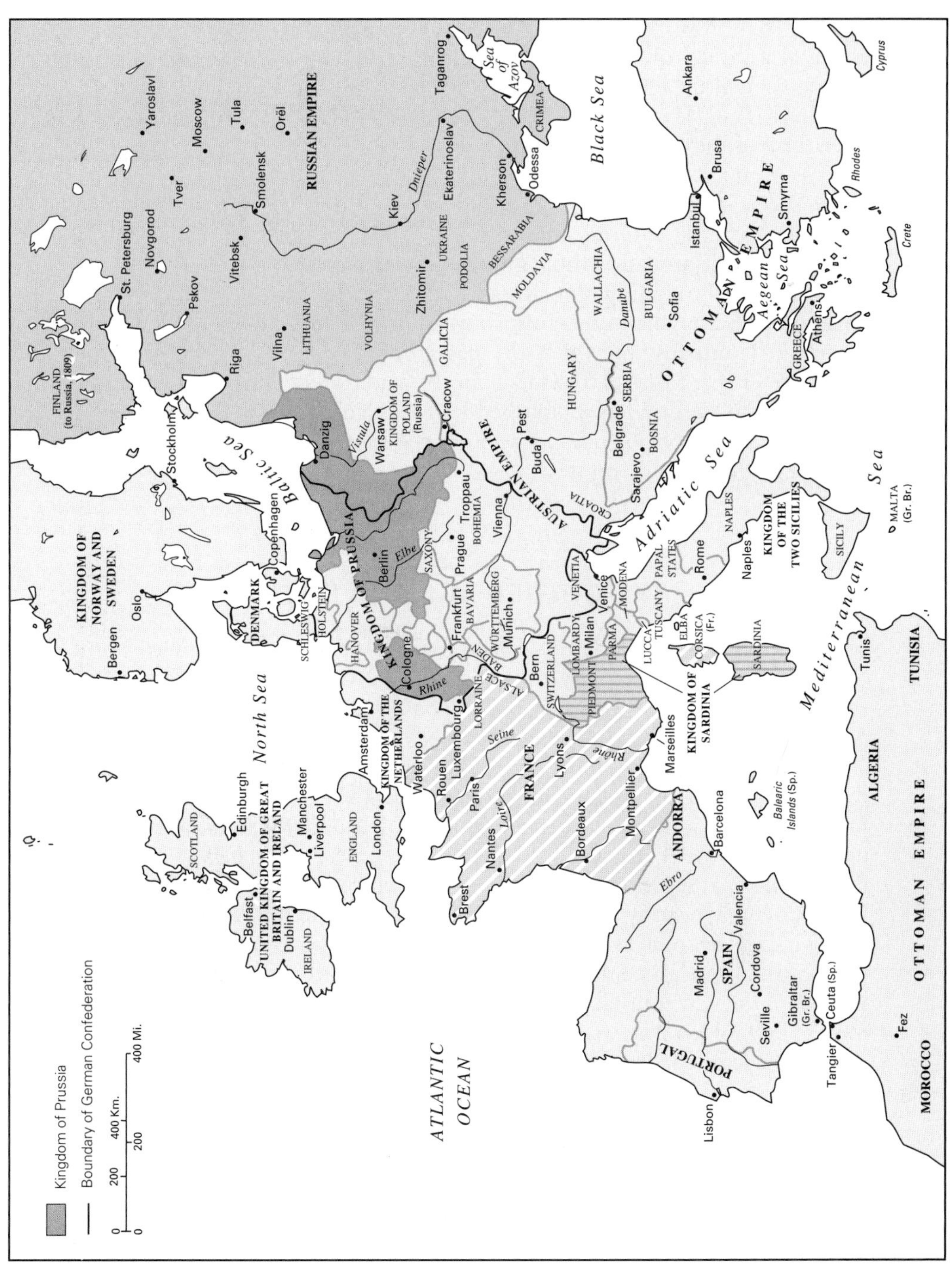

Europe in 1815.

gress in 1815, it becomes clear that Poland's special status was merely the most extreme of a variety of individual arrangements in a vast and complicated imperial structure. As if by accident, without the clearly outlined imperial dreams of Peter the Great (Peter I) (1682–1725) or Catherine II (1762–1796), Alexander had, in the course of the Napoleonic Wars, augmented Russian territories even more than his two great predecessors. Finland, annexed in 1809, provided precedent for the Polish special arrangements: it, too, had its own independent government and constitution. Georgia, entering the empire in 1801, brought an ancient civilization, separate institutions, and ethnic groups unrelated to the Finnic, Turkic, and Slavic peoples of the Eurasian plains. Russia had put its foot in the Balkans with the annexation of Bessarabia in the Turkish wars of 1806 and 1809–1812. The Russian-American Company, to which the government, otherwise occupied, paid little attention, claimed Alaska for Russia, in the tradition of the Muscovite exploration of Siberia; Russian traders established Fort Ross in northern California in 1812, at the height of the Napoleonic invasion of the motherland. Russia was at its zenith one of the great world empires.

THE GOLDEN AGE AND PUSHKIN

The tense years of the Napoleonic Wars, in Russia as elsewhere, proved a time of extraordinary cultural creativity and artistic innovation. Indeed, the early decades of the nineteenth century (roughly 1810–1830) have become known as the Golden Age of Russian culture. In the salons of St. Petersburg and Moscow, poets, musicians, and intellectuals—most of whom were also officers in the imperial army—debated questions of literary form, translated the latest of English and German romantic verse, and reflected on problems of Russian history, all with unprecedented intensity. By the second decade of the century, an entirely new forum had developed for discussions of this type: following the solitary example of Nikolai Karamzin's *Messenger of Europe,* founded in 1802, a plethora of journals emerged in the two capitals, each with its own personality and literary direction. Unlike the press of the late eighteenth century, which was subject to Catherine's personal supervision, the new journals really represented different literary and ideological currents. The Golden Age was the crucible of the rich tradition of Russian literature that has become the world's inheritance.

Language and Poetry

The innovations and ferment of the Golden Age were concentrated primarily in three fields—language, poetry, and religion. Although language has, in many countries, been the object of regulation, reform, and codification, rarely have such heated and conscious polemics surrounded the shaping of language itself as when the nineteenth century opened in Russia. Nikolai Karamzin fired the first sally in an 1802 essay: "Why can't Russia Produce any Literary Talent?" His answer referred to the nature of the Russian language itself: while other people, he said, "write as they speak," Russians, when they sit down to write, put on paper words they would never use in everyday speech, and write in a stilted, uncomfortable style unconducive to the clear expression of thoughts or emotions. Karamzin was answered, a year later, by Admiral Alexander Shishkov (1753–1841) in his "Reflections on New and Old Language." Shishkov defended the tradition that based writing on Church Slavonic—the language of the Orthodox liturgy, which is comprehensible but difficult for a Russian-speaker, and viewed the literary language as an extension of liturgical texts. Soon the two sides had crystallized into two opposing positions. The "innovators," following Karamzin, stood for the use of everyday speech in writing in as natural a manner as possible. Most importantly, the "innovators" were open to French influence in vocabulary and syntax. They argued that the development of the Russian literary language was subject to the same norms operative in France or indeed anywhere. The "archaists" objected that literary language was the "language of the gods," and should therefore be removed from everyday speech. They glorified the use of special bookish forms with a heavy element of Church Slavonic. They opposed all borrowings from the French and argued that Russian and Church Slavonic were simpler, more direct, and more appropriate. In arguing about language, of course, the two parties were also polemicizing about the shape of Russian culture and even politics: the cosmopolitan, Enlightenment, French-oriented salon culture of the innovators confronted a new awareness, on the part of the archaists, of the value of the homegrown, Slavonic, and Muscovite roots of Russian culture.

The linguistic debates of the century's first decade ultimately found their resolution through literature itself. The 1810s and 1820s were, above all, the golden age of poetry, from which the modern Russian language emerged. Vasily Zhukovsky (1783–1852), building on Karamzin's language reform, was the first to create a new poetic language: though he translated more than he composed, Zhukovsky's poetry marks a distinct break with the stiff, rugged style of eighteenth-century poets like Gavrila Derzhavin. He initiated what commentators have called "absolutely unheard-of purity, sweetness, and melodiousness of verse and diction." By the early 1810s a "Pleiad" of very young poets had taken shape, largely concentrated around the classical high school, the Lyceum, established by Alexander I at Tsarskoe Selo. These young men, united by intimate friendship and constant interaction, wrote verse as a way of life; they formed the core of a vital literary society founded soon after the War of 1812. Called Arzamas (after a provincial town), the society was conceived as a parody of the solemn meetings of Admiral Shishkov's conservative literary circle, and "cultivated poetical friendship, literary small talk, and the lighter forms of verse."

At the center of the poets' circles, both at the Lyceum and afterward, stood Alexander Sergeevich Pushkin (1799–1837). Born in Moscow, Pushkin was of African as well as Russian ancestry: his father was of venerable noble lineage; his mother was the granddaughter of Peter I's Abyssinian engineer general, Abraham Hannibal. Like most gentry parents of the Alexandrine age, Pushkin's paid little attention to their children, who were left to the care of servants while the parents fulfilled their social engagements at balls and dinners. Again typically, more French was spoken than Russian in the household. At age twelve, Pushkin was sent to the Lyceum, where he found friends and a sense of home. By 1814 his verses were published in the *Messenger of Europe,* he had joined Arzamas, and he was seen as a rival by the older poets Zhukovsky and Batyushkov.

Life after graduation proved turbulent: Pushkin was neither reverent nor chaste, and his outspoken poetry, indiscreet friendships, and incessant love affairs kept him constantly on the brink of trouble with the authorities and with women. Pushkin took a sinecure in 1817 as a clerk in the Foreign Office, and in 1820 his first major publication, *Ruslan and Lyudmila,* met with resounding success. But in the same year he found himself exiled to Kishinëv for writing revolutionary epigrams that reached the attention of Alexander I. Pushkin spent the remaining part of Alexander's reign in constant movement, in the Caucasus and Bessarabia, ending in exile at his parents' estate, Mikhailovskoe (in Pskov Province), in 1824 after the authorities had intercepted a letter in which he commented that "pure atheism" seemed "the most probable" of philosophies. During this period he wrote two long narrative poems on Oriental themes, *The Captive of the Caucasus* (1821) and *The Fountain of Bakhchisarai* (1822), and began work on his most famous composition: the Byronic novel in verse, *Evgeny Onegin* (1831).

Only Alexander's death and the new emperor's accession brought Pushkin back to Moscow in 1826. The last decade of his life was tinged with tragedy: His closest friends were involved in the Decembrist conspiracy (see later in this chapter) and were exiled to Siberia. Although *Evgeny Onegin* was completed in 1830, the new generation of poets and writers was alien to him and saw him as a venerable relic of an earlier age. Finally, his marriage, in 1830, to the beautiful and frivolous Nathalie Goncharova, soon became a source of unhappiness. In 1837 Pushkin challenged his wife's admirer, Baron Georges D'Anthès (a French royalist in the Russian service) to a duel and was fatally wounded.

Pushkin's other most important works are the historical drama *Boris Godunov* (1825/1831); a series of fairy tales; short stories; the short novel *The Captain's Daughter* (1836); and the long epic poems *The Stone Guest* (1836/1840) and *The Bronze Horseman* (1833/1841). In his writing, Pushkin placed the Russian literary language on a new level, setting a standard for nineteenth-century literature. The importance of *Evgeny Onegin,* in addition, lay in its poetic creation of characters who were to become prototypes for the novels of Lermontov, Goncharov, and Turgenev. But Pushkin's significance transcends his work: like Dante for Italy, Shakespeare for England, or Goethe for Germany, Pushkin became a national myth—a single figure around whom Russia's cultural self-definition eventually crystallized. The cult of Pushkin, originating in the late nineteenth century, has lasted through the Soviet period and beyond: his poetry has been memorized by every educated Russian and continues to form a touchstone for literature, ideas, and political views.

Religious and Mystical Currents

The flowering of poetry and the Russian language coincided with a third powerful current of the Golden Age: a renewed fascination with religious ideas, and particularly their mystical aspect. The first Masonic lodges had been founded in Russia in Elizabeth's reign and had burgeoned under Nikolai Novikov's leadership at the end of the eighteenth century. The secular religion of Freemasonry experienced a new wave of popularity in the 1810s. The Masonic lodges, with their secretive hierarchy and vague but spiritual ideals, provided a milieu for everything from social gatherings to political conspiracy. Mystical writers such as the German mystic Jakob Boehme (1575–1624) and the Swedish visionary Immanuel Swedenborg (1688–1722) were translated into Russian at a furious pace and read in the salons of the capital cities, while their major translator, Alexander Labzin (1766–1825), founded the mystical journal *Messenger of Zion.* He was said to have written all twenty-five issues himself. Labzin also founded his own lodge, with the oxymoronic title *The Dying Sphinx.* No one was immune to mystical interests: even Speransky, in the years immediately preceding his grand reform plans, read Boehme and Swedenborg under the guidance of the mystic and Freemason Ivan Lopukhin (1756–1816). In the meantime, Ekaterina Tatarinova (1783–1856) held forth in her sectarian "ship" in St. Petersburg: her salon, frequented by members of Petersburg high society, was a haven for the sects of *khlysty* and *skoptsy.* The former took their name from their central ritual of self-flagellation, while the latter castrated themselves, "physically and spiritually." Both held spiritual gatherings in which they whirled, danced, and recited verses in white clothes, replicating the traditions of these same sects in popular culture.

One of the brightest manifestations of the new religious concerns, this time with the sanction of the official church, was the Russian Bible Society (an extension of the British society, established in 1804). The society was opened in 1813, with Prince Alexander Golitsyn (1773–1884), who also happened to be over-procurator of the Holy Synod, at its head. Founded with the original intention of disseminating the Word among foreigners and non-Christians, the Bible Society soon encountered the controversial question of translating the Bible into Russian as well (from Church Slavonic), so that it could be more broadly read. Although the translation was completed by 1820 (along with translations into twenty-five non-Russian languages of the empire), it met with fiery opposition from the fanatical monk Photius—a man with a powerful influence over Alexander. Existing copies of the new Bible were dramatically burned; a Russian edition of the Bible would not appear in print until the 1860s.

In a sense, the official symbol of the mystical and religious ferment of the period was the projected Church of Christ the Savior—a monumental structure, conceived by the architect Alexander Witberg (1787–1855), to be erected in Moscow to commemorate the apocalyptic victory over Napoleon. The church, completed only many years later, embodied a theme that characterizes the age of Alexander I—the construction of a temple, a sacred structure to the greater glory of God. (No less symbolically, it was demolished in Stalin's antireligious campaign of the 1930s, to be replaced by an immense swimming pool, then rebuilt in the 1990s.)

Two general observations come to mind with respect to the cultural Golden Age as a whole. First, the turn of the nineteenth century was a time of national self-definition for Russia, when the identity crisis of the century since Peter I began to crystallize into a sense of Russia's place in the world: the place, clearly, was in Europe. The debates on language, the experience of the Napoleonic invasion of 1812 and the expulsion of the "Antichrist," and the publication of Karamzin's massive *History of Russia* in 1816 (the first national history)—all contributed to the burgeoning of national consciousness in the 1800s. Second, the culture of the Golden Age itself was remarkable in its originality, yet it incorporated elements of cultural movements in France, Germany, and England. The poets, musicians, thinkers of the Golden Age fused the lightness and elegance of French Enlightenment salon culture with the mystical revelations of German romanticism and the religious apocalypticism of seventeenth-century Russian Orthodoxy. The result, of which Pushkin's writing is the ultimate emblem, was an original, syncretic culture with tremendous creative potential for those who would follow in its path throughout the nineteenth century.

THE BLESSED EMPEROR, 1815–1825

It is impossible to understand either Alexander's domestic or his foreign policy without seeing his rootedness in the Golden Age culture of his day. Contemporaries and historians alike have called Alexander enigmatic. Yet he becomes less puzzling once we see that he experienced a synthesis of Enlightenment ideas with the Romantic and religious sentiment that followed the Napoleonic invasions in 1812. His spiritual evolution, in other words, followed the same pattern as that of the officers who accompanied him to Paris. These officers were both the creators of literary culture and, eventually, Alexander's political opponents. His participation in the mystical fashions of the time has already been noted, including his attachment to the Baroness Krüdener and the archimandrite Photius. Alexander read the same mystical authors that were fashionable in high society; the campaign of 1812 augmented an already delicate religious sensibility, and attendance at liturgy was always a touching experience for him. What is interesting is the face that these ideas acquired when they became fused with political power, as they did in the person of the autocratic ruler.

Domestic Reaction

In 1817, Golitsyn was appointed head of a new Ministry of Spiritual Affairs and Education, which united all departments dealing with religious matters with the Ministry of Education. The new ministry, which introduced a remarkable fusion of secular and sacred into the government, was supposed to reflect the principle that

"Christian morality must always be the basis of true enlightenment." Interestingly, according to the ministry's statute, all religions were declared equal; concretely, this meant that special committees to deal with the affairs of Old Believers, Muslims, and Jews were established under the ministry's auspices. In addition, the Bible Society became virtually an official arm of the government, and Alexander exercised direct patronage over the many Bible translations during the seven years of the ministry's existence. Religious instruction was strengthened in the schools. At the same time, the so-called Lancaster schools, originating, like the Bible Society, in England, were introduced into Russia. Their system of "mutual instruction," in which teachers gave lessons to older students, who in turn passed the lessons on to others, was supposed to aid religious knowledge and remedy general widespread illiteracy. Alexander's sense of the importance of education, essential to the university and school reforms of his early days in power, acquired this new form in the 1810s.

The liberal-spirited reforms of Alexander's early reign, meanwhile, acquired a sinister twist in another aspect of administration. In the course of the 1812 war, Alexander's advisers had changed: Speransky was replaced by Tsar Paul's old adviser, the Count Alexei Arakcheev (1769–1834). Contemporaries, whom Arakcheev reminded of the much-despised favorites of the age of Empress Anna (r. 1730–1740) and her henchman Biron, complained that it was impossible to gain access to Alexander without Arakcheev's mediation. Alexander, despite his enlightened ideas, was as great an admirer of parades and military spectacle as his father. Apparently inspired by the benign intention of keeping soldiers—whose term of service in the army was twenty-five years—together with their families, Alexander in 1816 accepted Arakcheev's idea of "military colonies." In this military utopia, soldiers and state peasants lived together in farming communities. The idea was that the soldiers would help the peasants in agricultural labor in peacetime, while the peasants would support the soldiers' families when they were away at war. Theoretically, the project should have removed some burden from the military budget, heavily swollen from the Napoleonic Wars. Eventually, almost three-quarters of a million people were involved. Observers, including Alexander himself, commented on the order and neatness that prevailed in the colonies—an orderliness for which Alexander, like both his father and grandmother, had a tremendous nostalgia. It was the objects of the experiment—the state peasants themselves—who made known their displeasure by revolting in 1819. In the construction of the colonies, families had been removed forcibly from their homes and whole villages razed; peasants were subjected to a military regimentation and forced to shave their beards and perform drill, and their children had to marry within the colony. The entire order of village life, in other words, was disrupted. By the end of his reign, only Alexander himself remained a believer in this utopian experiment; it was terminated at the accession of Nicholas I in 1825.

The bizarre experiment of the colonies went hand in hand with continued efforts to implement at least a limited emancipation of the serfs. Following in the tracks of the 1803 law on free agriculturalists, peasants were emancipated in the Baltic provinces of Estonia (1816), Courland (1817), and Livonia (1819)—but without land. In 1818 Alexander secretly asked Arakcheev to draw up a plan for emancipation in Russia itself. Doing so without impinging on the property of the nobility, however, remained daunting, and the plan seems to have been abandoned by about 1820.

The Congress System

European politics remained fairly tranquil—particularly in contrast to the turbulence of the Napoleonic era—in the first few years following the Congress of Vienna. But challenges to the "Christian order" of the Holy Alliance appeared by 1820. Indeed, the decade of the 1820s saw a chain of revolutionary disturbances that threatened the regimes whose legitimacy had been a source of great pride to the powers at Vienna. In Spain, where the Bourbon monarchy had been restored, a group of military officers organized a conspiracy and in March 1820 forced Ferdinand VII to govern in accordance with the 1812 constitution, as he had promised at Vienna. A few months later, revolt broke out in Naples as well. The powers held a series of congresses in the ensuing months (Troppau, Laibach, Verona), in which they discussed the right, indeed the necessity, of intervention in other countries to suppress revolt. The provisions of the Congress of Vienna and the Holy Alliance were vague and indeterminate; they did not prescribe specific conduct to uphold the European order. Largely under pressure from Metternich, they were given concrete content—corresponding to Metternich's particular interpretation—at the 1820 congresses. The Protocol of Troppau actually established the right of the allies (Austria, Russia, and Prussia) to intervene in cases of an "illegal" change in government in any state.

This new interpretation of the Holy Alliance met its first test less than a year after Troppau, in a manner that touched Russia's interests directly. In March 1821, Alexander Ypsilantis (1783–1828), a Greek officer in the Russian service, marched across Ottoman-held Moldavia and Wallachia in an effort to occupy these long-contested principalities. Before long, his challenge to Ottoman authority, which had no official sanction from Russia, grew into a full-scale revolt by Greece. The Christian Greeks immediately had the sympathy of Russian public opinion: the revolt seemed an opportunity not only to come to the aid of an oppressed Orthodox people, but also eventually to realize long-standing dreams of restoring Constantinople to the Christian world. Ypsilantis, in addition, had many supporters within the Russian army. Alexander I, however, was persuaded that the Greek rebellion was the result of a European-wide revolutionary conspiracy. After some vacillation and, apparently, some lobbying by Metternich, he gave his support instead to the Ottoman regime—although its defense had certainly not been one of the terms of the Vienna Congress. Domestically, this decision to support the status quo at all costs, even against a fellow Orthodox nation, cost Alexander his remaining popularity. The year 1821 was a decisive turning point: Alexander succeeded in alienating everyone and parted ways with the contemporaries whose Enlightenment ideals he initially shared. Even the Baroness Krüdener lost faith in him: her despair was supposedly such that she began to expose herself to extremes of temperature and eventually became ill and died.

The Last Years

The last two or three years of Alexander's reign constitute a distinct, and very bleak, period. They are best understood in terms of three men who flanked the emperor at this time. First was the monk Photius, whose influence over Alexander grew in the early 1820s. Appointed head of the Yuriev Monastery in Novgorod, Photius was responsible for closing all Masonic lodges in 1822. In the same year, the Ministry of Spiritual Affairs and Education was closed, the Bible Society liquidated, and all existing copies of the Russian Bible burned. Photius's tendencies, reminiscent of the late medieval Catholic Inquisition, were echoed by a second prominent and awe-inspiring figure of these years, Mikhail Magnitsky (1778–1855). Appointed educational inspector for the Kazan District in 1819, Magnitsky thundered against the University of Kazan as a diabolical, anti-Christian stronghold and proposed, by way of reform, to "raze the university [which Alexander's own decree had established less than twenty years earlier] to the ground." Although such extreme measures were not taken, Magnitsky managed to close several departments (most notably philosophy), expel "unreliable" professors, burn questionable books, and generally lower the level of education at Kazan for a full half century. The third figure in this rather daunting trinity was Admiral Shishkov, who in 1824 replaced Golitsyn as minister of education. Shishkov's idea was that Russian literature and morality were in decline for want of adequate governmental supervision; he set about instituting measures of control, particularly over the press.

Alexander himself, in the meantime, grew more and more despondent, as every project he undertook turned to disaster in his hands. Apparently, he spoke more and more of abdication. In 1825 he accompanied his wife to Taganrog, in the south, for a cure. There he caught cold and died unexpectedly on December 1, at the age of forty-eight. Alexander's death became the object of a plethora of popular rumors: he was said to have given up the throne and fulfilled his old dream of retreat from power. An elderly man named Fëdor Kuzmich turned up in Siberia years later, claiming to be the Emperor Alexander. Such stories, while no more than rumors, fit perfectly the persona Alexander acquired at the end of his reign: they characterize the many disappointments of a man who once dreamed of constitutions and freedom for Russia, yet was unable to achieve them, and on whom autocratic rule weighed as heavily as on many of his subjects.

SECRET SOCIETIES AND THE DECEMBER UPRISING

In 1821, concurrently with the eruption of troubles in Greece, Alexander received a note from Adjutant General Benckendorff (1783–1854), then chief of staff in the Guards regiment. The note contained a remarkably full description of a group of conspiratorial societies—with detailed and quite accurate sketches of all their members—that had arisen among the officers of the tsar's army. Inspired by the Enlightenment ideas of their own childhood education, compounded by the impressions of their sojourn in Paris in 1814 (during which a number of officers had joined Masonic lodges), these officers had formed a vaguely humanitarian, Masonic-like organization called the Union of Welfare. The union had its own set of rules, contained in a guidebook known as the Green Book, and had grown out of an earlier organization formed in 1816, immediately after the Napoleonic wars, known as the Union of Salvation. Not explicitly political in nature, the society's proclaimed goals included love of humanity, dissemination of moral principles, education, and justice. However, the organization provided a milieu in which ideas of reform—including the abolition of serfdom—and the introduction of a constitution were avidly discussed.

Some time after its formation, the group split into two distinct societies—the Northern and the Southern. The Northern Society's projects included a plan, drafted by Nikita Muraviëv, for a constitutional monarchy and a federal organization of the empire. The Southern, under the leadership of Colonel Pavel Pestel (1799–1826), was more radical and more articulate. Pestel composed a document called the *Russian Justice* (echoing the law code of Kievan Rus), in which he elaborated the principles of an authoritarian government for Russia—including relations between government and people, social classes, and distribution of land. After a while, Pestel's organization joined forces with a third group, the Society of United Slavs. A more heterogeneous organization of officers, less elite and having ties with revolutionary movements in Poland, the United Slavs professed the aim of uniting revolutionary groups of all the Slavic peoples. The appearance of a relatively well structured oppositional organization, with increasingly clear revolutionary aims and political ideology, should have been cause for at least alarm and, more consistently, repression on the part of the government. An autocratic government, after all, is by its nature intolerant of challenges to its divinely sanctioned authority. Alexander, instead, turned a blind eye to the conspirators, whose activities were suspiciously reminiscent of the *carbonari* in Italy, or the liberals in Spain. He limited his response to a mild harassment of some members and sympathizers—Pushkin's numerous exiles were a part of this policy. As he told another of his adjutant generals, "My dear Wassiltschikoff! You who have served me since the beginning of my reign, you know that I shared and encouraged these illusions and errors." The societies stood as a reproach to Alexander, a reminder of the ideals of his own early reign; fully aware of their activities, he nevertheless did nothing to stop them, even as his own depression increased and he implemented reactionary measures in other spheres.

Thus when Alexander died in December 1825, the conspiratorial organizations were in place to stage their revolt. The opportunity arose because of a lack of clarity concerning the succession: Alexander's brother Grand Duke Constantine (1779–1831), commander-in-chief in Warsaw, had formally renounced the throne in favor of his younger brother, Nicholas, two years before. However, the renunciation had been kept a secret, with the result that, upon Alexander's death, many, including the armed forces, were ready to declare allegiance to Constantine. In the interregnum, which lasted over a week, the Northern Society seized the advantage to foment rebellion among the troops: by December 14, 1825, when the troops were gathered on Senate Square to declare their allegiance to Nicholas, some three thousand of them had been persuaded to refuse to do so (another nine thousand remained loyal). The circumstances of the whole affair were foggy and confused from the start: no one was sure who the rightful successor was, and many of the "rebellious" soldiers thought they were protecting Constantine from the usurper, Nicholas. The uprising, which lasted the course of one day, was a disaster on all fronts. Inspired and determined on the level of ideas, the men who would henceforth be known as the Decembrists proved uncertain, vacillating, and vague when it came to action. The man who was supposed to be declared "dictator" according to their plan, Prince Sergei Trubetskoy, lost faith in the enterprise at the last minute and spent the day wandering through Petersburg instead of directing "his" troops.

In a striking contrast to the palace coups (staged, incidentally, by the same nobility from which the Decembrists all came) that had so effectively installed Anna, Elizabeth, Catherine, and Alexander in power, this ideologically inspired rebellion was a complete failure: the conspirators, trying to take advantage of an unexpected opportunity, did not in the end themselves know what they wanted. The disaster was aggravated by a series of mishaps. One of their members, Pëtr Kakhovsky, fired on and killed General Mikhail Miloradovich, the Petersburg governor general and a hero of the War of 1812, as the latter tried to convince the rebellious soldiers to disperse. From this moment the new emperor, horrified by the bloodshed and heretofore hesitant to take action against his own subjects, gave in to the argument that he must act in the interests of the empire he now ruled. Loyal troops fired on the rebels, and the disturbance was put down. As a result of the long and dramatic court proceedings that followed, in which Nicholas himself played the role of grand inquisitor, the uprising's five leaders—Pestel, Konrad Ryleev, Nikolai Bestuzhev-Ryumin, Sergei Muraviëv-Apostol, Kakhovsky—were hanged; the other participants were exiled to Siberia.

The December uprising was, in itself, a relatively minor event: it involved a handful of gentry officers, lasted only a day, and was easily subdued, as much from its own lack of direction as by government brutality. Its symbolic significance, however, both for contemporaries and later generations, was immense. Contemporary gentry society was horrified by the execution and exile of the flower of its youth, expecting until the last minute a commutation of the sentences. For Nicholas himself, the Decembrists became an ever-present nightmare and a grim subtext to his entire reign: While proceeding with their execution as a matter of state, he is said to have kept their plans for reform (revealed to him during the trial) always on his desk. He referred to them sarcastically as "my friends of 14 December" and seems to have been significantly influenced by their ideas in his own reform agenda. Alexander Herzen did most to create a powerful myth of the Decembrists as heroic fighters for freedom; in contrast, he portrayed Nicholas, who suppressed them, as a completely black figure, tainted with the blood of the brave rebels. Half a century later, the civic poet Nikolai Nekrasov's "Russian Women" (1872) glorified the self-sacrificing wives of the Decembrists, who followed their husbands into exile. In the twentieth century, Soviet mythology exalted the Decembrists—actually, it would seem, a group quite antipathetic to working-class ideology because of their elite, gentry background—as "the first Russian revolutionaries," initiators of a continuous, century-long struggle against "tsarist oppression." Recent scholars, too, have found appeal in the Decembrists: the semiotician Yuri Lotman attributed the failure of a full-scale literary Romanticism to take root in Russia to the death or exile of its potential practitioners.

THE POLISH UPRISING, 1830

From its inception, the Congress system was challenged by a series of revolts: Naples and Madrid in 1820, Greece in 1821, St. Petersburg in 1825. The chain of rebellions culminated in revolution in 1830: crowds in Paris took to the streets against the restoration regime, successfully installing a new constitutional government, to be known as the July Monarchy (1830–1848), with the Duke of Orléans, Louis Philippe, as king. Revolution in Paris inspired revolts in Brussels, in some of the German states, and—most critically for the Russian Empire—in Warsaw.

The idyllic-sounding constitution of Congress Poland was already provoking some dissatisfaction among the nobility (*szlachta*) in the early 1820s. The reason for this was twofold. First, the small size of the Polish kingdom was a disappointment and a frustration for patriots who dreamed of a restoration of the old Polish-Lithuanian Commonwealth, victim of the late-eighteenth-century partitions by Russia, Prussia, and Austria. Second and more important, the actual practice of independent governance proved rather less satisfying than the constitution promised. While officially independent, Poland remained subject to the tsar, who, an autocrat in Russia, turned into a constitutional monarch in the Polish kingdom. In addition, the most important potential arm of independence, the Polish army, was under the command of the Grand Duke Constantine, Alexander's brother. Constantine, who had a good reputation in Russia—in part because of a mistaken perception that he held liberal views—was quite unpopular in Poland. Some historians have perceived an inherent contradiction in the phenomenon of a constitutional state incorporated into an autocratic empire.

Although, in many fields—in particular, education and the constitutional system of government—Congress Poland functioned with relative success, political discontent began to crystallize in the 1820s. This disillusionment took the same form as in Russia itself: secret societies, modeled on Freemasonry, began to flourish among the gentry. These included the League of Free Poles, a society called All Together, the radical National Patriotic Society, and the above-mentioned Society of United Slavs. Nicholas I's accession to the throne in 1825, and his determination to prevent a Decembrist-style uprising in Poland, led to active repression of these societies, including the trial and prosecution of leaders of the Patriotic Society in 1828. Resentful of Nicholas's style of rule, which made a travesty of Polish independence, a handful of officers—headed by a military instructor, Piotr Wysocki (1794–1857) and a young colonel, Jozef Zaliwski (1797–1855)—in 1830 plotted a full-scale rebellion, which was to include the assassination of Grand Duke Constantine.

The Poles at the Battle of Grochow, 1831. One of the battles of the November uprising: the Poles won a victory over the Russian army at this village outside Warsaw. French lithograph. *Anne S. K. Brown Military Collection/Brown University Library.*

The "November uprising" was to last nearly a year; it was put down only through a full-scale war of Russia against Poland. On November 29, a group of men broke into the Belweder Palace with the mission of killing Constantine; they succeeded only in mistakenly assassinating several Polish generals who happened in their way, while the grand duke escaped unharmed. The conspiracy of gentry officers, however, in contrast to the Decembrist uprising, triggered a popular revolution: a provisional government was established by December. Tsar Nicholas greeted this development with a December 17 manifesto condemning the revolution and amounting to an ultimatum to the Poles. In Poland, a national government was elected at the end of January 1831, with Alexander I's former adviser, Prince Adam Czartoryski, as president of the Ruling Council. Russian forces, led by General Ivan von Diebitsch, invaded in early February, meeting active resistance as they made their way toward Warsaw. In the meantime, political troubles gripped the Polish capital: in June, the moderate National Government was replaced by the dictatorship of General Jan Krukowiecki (1770–1850), governor of Warsaw. The Russian army, now under the leadership of General I. F. Paskevich (1782–1856)—Diebitsch fell victim to a great cholera epidemic in that year—entered Warsaw in September. The city capitulated at midnight of September 7–8.

The military defeat of Poland was of immense importance for vanquished and conqueror alike. Congress Poland, with its constitutional charter and special status, was essentially destroyed: the charter was rescinded, the national assembly

(Sejm) closed, the Polish military eliminated, and Warsaw University shut down. In 1832 the Constitutional Charter was replaced by an "Organic Statute," signifying essentially the tighter integration of Poland into the empire. The nation was to be governed by a viceroy (Paskevich was appointed), and all matters were to be decided by an appointed council. Russians were appointed to all important positions in the government, Russian became the language used in schools and in public activities, and Russians received grants of land on Polish territory. Thus, from the emblem of constitutional dreams for the empire as whole, Poland became a symbol of a new form of imperial administration, which Nicholas I was to bring into action over his long thirty-year reign. The Russian Empire that emerged from the Russo-Polish War of 1830–1831 would be characterized by greater uniformity, tighter control, and a more conscious imperial policy.

CHAPTER 18

Nicholas I: Monarchy, Society, and Empire, 1825–1855

Russia's past is admirable; her present more than magnificent; as to her future, it is beyond the grasp of the most daring imagination.

—*Count Benckendorff*

It is oppressive and vile to live in Russia. That is the truth.

—*Alexander Herzen*

Nicholas I makes his first appearance on the pages of Alexander Herzen's *My Past and Thoughts* as "a shorn and balding jellyfish with whiskers." For Herzen (1812–1870), who did much to create a powerful image of Nicholas's reign as a time of blind political reaction, the condition of Nicholas's hairline was symbolic: his bald temples were the result not of inheritance but of the constant wear and tear of military headgear, donned daily for the parades that he, like his father, Paul, adored. Herzen went on to draw a parallel between Nicholas's facial features and those of the "military" Roman emperors, "in whom everything civilian and human has died out, and only the passion for power remains." Nicholas, from the moment he assumed power amidst the Decembrist uprising, stood for what many of his contemporaries most feared and dreaded: the "spirit of Gatchina"—the youthful reincarnation of Paul's military-mindedness and narrow, repressive, and arbitrary rule over his subjects.

In the thirty years of Nicholas's reign (1825–1855), Russia reached an apogee of power and influence on the European continent. Historians have been consistently impressed by the essential continuity of Nicholas's reign. In sharp contrast to Paul, whose grip on the throne proved weak, Nicholas was able to create a system of government that molded Russian institutions and administration in accordance with his vision. The ideology of "official nationality" proclaimed a Russia that, unlike its European neighbors, would remain firmly grounded on the principles of Orthodoxy, autocracy, and nationality. Nicholas's regime systematized the Russian bureaucracy and extended its reach deep into the provinces, by the same token reducing the influence of the gentry in government. Alexander I's adviser, Speransky, emerged from exile to draft the first code of laws since 1649, thus setting up a legal system that would remain in place until 1917. Not all of Nicholas's efforts were successful: A secret committee examined the institution of serfdom but took no decisive measures to abolish it. Instead, it fell to Russian educated society to raise the issue aloud, as "realism" in literature turned readers' attention to peasants and life in the countryside. Nicholas and the Russian army defended the "Russian path" against revolution and subversion by active intervention in an 1849 uprising in Hungary, only to be defeated, in turn, in an overly ambitious war with the Ottoman Empire. This Crimean War (1854–1856) finally closed the era in international politics that had begun with the Vienna Congress in 1815.

In an age of liberal and revolutionary currents in Europe, Russian intellectuals like Herzen felt particularly oppressed and alienated from the stream of history. After 1848 especially, Nicholas's reign earned the label of the "Nicholaevan night." Yet, however great his desire for control and order, the country he ruled—ranging from the institution of the monarchy itself, to a varied and colorful society, to an immense and ultimately ungovernable empire—had a life of its own. It was vastly more complicated and less amenable to control than the intellectuals' rigid image implies. What lay behind the image of blind reaction? How did the monarchy, the society, and the empire work in the thirty years of Russia's emergence as a modern European power?

NICHOLAS COMES TO POWER, 1825–1830

Nicholas I's accession to the throne in 1825, in contrast to the seizure of power by his recent predecessors, took the new monarch himself by surprise. A shroud of mystery surrounded the secret protocol by which his older brother Alexander had circumvented the next in line, Constantine; technically, the maneuver was illegal because Paul's law of succession denied the reigning tsar the right to designate the next ruler. In any case, the ambiguity was sufficient to make Nicholas, who had known about the secret protocol since 1819, doubt his own right to the throne: like the rebellious officers of December 14, he initially swore his allegiance to his older brother Constantine, until he learned with certainty of the latter's abdication.

Preceded by two much older brothers whose upbringing Catherine had carefully supervised, Nicholas was never intended for the Russian throne; only Alexander's childlessness, and Constantine's abdication, made him the successor. In keeping with Nicholas's image as a true son of Paul I, contemporaries and historians alike have referred to his early education as that of a "drill sergeant." His mother, Maria Fëdorovna (1759–1828), had given the directives for his education, which included early lessons with English governesses and later subjection to the methods of Count M. I. Lamsdorff, who was supposed to have slammed his charges' heads against the wall when they particularly disappointed him. Nicholas, apparently, showed little interest in or aptitude for any subject, with the single exception of military matters, which fascinated him. If relatively careless, his education was consistent: Enlightenment ideas did not interfere with military discipline.

The Crowning of Nicholas I. By Victor Adam (artist) and Louis Courtin (lithographer), 1828. *Library of Congress, courtesy Richard Wortman.*

A New Style of Rule

Nicholas's first day in power—when, at age twenty-nine, he acceded to the throne at the price of his subjects' blood—was a personal trauma that remained with him throughout his reign. His coronation took place in the dismal atmosphere that surrounded the execution of the five leaders of the Decembrist conspiracy and the exile of the others. Elements of the officers' ideas are visible in some of Nicholas's own policies. At the same time, the experience of the uprising made Nicholas extremely distrustful of the gentry, and he took care to set up his government in a manner that would circumvent their influence.

Once on the throne, Nicholas exhibited a firmness, forthrightness, and consistency that came as a relief after the dark and unpredictable vagaries of Alexander's last years. The ominous personalities of the early 1820s—Alexei Arakcheev, Mikhail Magnitsky, Alexander Shishkov, and the archimandrite Photius—were removed from power in short order, to be replaced by a circle of ministers and advisers of an energetic, bureaucratic, and practical type. Among them were Nicholas's older brother Grand Duke Constantine, the commander-in-chief in Poland; the highly influential minister of education, Count Sergei Uvarov (appointed in 1833); and Count Alexander Benckendorff, chief of police, soon to acquire an ominous reputation of his own. Count K. V. Nesselrode (1780–1861) remained at his post as minister of foreign affairs, and E. F. Kankrin continued as minister of finance. Alexander I's influential adviser, Mikhail Speransky (see the chapter "Russia in the Age of Napoleon: Paul I and Alexander I, 1796–1815") made a dramatic comeback, overcoming Nicholas's initial suspicions of his earlier constitutional sympathies to be appointed head of a commission overseeing and systematizing a code of law for the empire—the final fruition of Speransky's labors before the War of 1812.

Nicholas's relation to his advisers and ministers did not replicate the tone of an intimate circle of friends that had characterized Alexander's Unofficial Committee. The emblem of Nicholas's style, instead, became His Majesty's Own Chancellery, which, perhaps because it was most amenable to Nicholas's personal control, began to play a dominant role in government. The chancellery was divided into sections—the First Section was responsible for personal affairs of the tsar, the Second Section for legislation, the fourth for welfare and charity. It was the Third Section that, before long, became infamous. Officially, its function was to enforce observance of the law and to police the country. It had the high-sounding aim of "ensuring that the well-being and rights of citizens cannot be disturbed by anyone's personal power, or the supremacy of the strong, or misdirection by evil-thinking people." In practice, under Benckendorff's firm guidance, the Third Section covered the country with a network of spies and investigators who felt free to interfere in everything from literature to family life. Like most police regimes, the rule of the Third Section was also inefficient: there were many false accusations, and the wrong people were followed. The result was a nasty, oppressive atmosphere of general mistrust and suspicion.

The strengthening of the Third Section was supplemented by a series of measures to increase control over religion, the press, and education. The Bible Society, associated with the mystical, Masonic, and cosmopolitan religious currents of the age of Alexander, was closed in 1826. It became the norm for anyone who had an original thought to spend some portion of his life in prison; censorship was heavy, and dangerous subjects like philosophy were removed from university curricula. Schools, as well, were subject to close regulation, and an effort was made to prevent the mixing of different social strata in the same institutions. This effort to control the country's life in all its aspects linked Nicholas's regime with those of monarchs like Paul and the eighteenth-century ruler Anna (whose favorite, Biron, had imposed a police state).

In apparent contradiction to this generally repressive tone—which gave intellectuals like Herzen ample reason to detest its perpetrator—Nicholas also set up an informal group known as the Committee of 6 December, after the date of its inception in 1826. The committee was charged with reviewing Russian governance and society in all their aspects. It scrutinized issues ranging from the ministries and their relation to the Senate and State Council, to local government, to the institution of serfdom, to proposed plans for reform. The committee's work continued until 1832; its proposals remained unpublicized while it was in session.

Consolidating Imperial Power

The first five or six years after Nicholas's assumption of power were almost entirely taken up by pressing problems of imperial policy. War in the Caucasus had been continuous since the beginning of the century and led in 1826 to conflict with Persia, as Russian expansion threatened Persian boundaries. In July 1826, Persian troops entered Russian territory, occupying Lenkoran and Karabakh in Russian Armenia. Nicholas, who distrusted the maverick commander of the Caucasus forces, A. P. Ermolov, answered the latter's call for reinforcements by appointing General I. F. Paskevich head of the Caucasian army. As Paskevich defeated the Persians at Elizavetpol (September 13, 1826) and led his victorious troops into the Persian stronghold of Erevan (April 1827), Ermolov was removed from power and replaced by Paskevich. When a chain of victories at Tabriz and beyond opened a straight path to Teheran for the Russian army, the Persian shah agreed to negotiations. Peace was signed at Turkmanchai on February 10, 1828; Russian power in Transcaucasia was consolidated with the gain of the Erevan and Nakhichevan khanates and part of the Caspian shore. Other gains included the payment of damages by the Persians and the protection of Russian merchants in Persia. The dramatist Alexander Griboedov, author of *Woe from Wit* (1823) and also Russian ambassador to Persia, was perhaps the most spectacular loss of the Persian war: he was killed in 1829 by a mob that ransacked the Russian Embassy in Teheran.

It was the Ottoman Empire, however, that presented Nicholas with the greatest foreign policy challenge. Sultan Mahmud II (1808–1839) had launched an ambitious and sometimes bloody campaign to reform Turkish government and modernize the Turkish army. Part of his inspiration came from the reforms of Peter the Great (Peter I) (1682–1725) in Russia a century earlier. In 1826, in an effort to undermine the extremely powerful but technologically outmoded elite fighting force, the janissaries—which resembled Peter I's rout of their Muscovite equivalent, the *streltsy*—the sultan's forces locked them in the Topkapi Palace and slaughtered them en masse. French and Russian advisers took part in the reconstruction of the army, which the violence of the reform efforts threw into temporary disarray.

It was, at least in part, fear of a revitalized Ottoman Empire that prompted the conservative Nicholas to tread where Alexander would not and support the revolt of the Greeks—the first of a series of independence movements by Christians in the Balkans that would shape much of international politics up to World War I. Once Russia was assured of support by England, and eventually France, Nicholas felt confident in putting more pressure on Turkey. The Convention of Akkerman, signed on September 25, 1826, assured Russian rights of passage through the Black Sea straits, preserved autonomy for the principalities of Moldavia and Wallachia and stipulated certain rights of internal self-government for Serbia (including freedom of religion). The sultan appealed to his vassal, Mehmet Ali of Egypt, for support, and together they engaged an Anglo-French fleet at Navarino in October 1826. The Turkish and Egyptian fleets were completely devastated in the battle. Two years later, as Russia's Persian war was drawing to an end, the Turks protested Russian interference in Turkish internal affairs—most particularly, continued Russian insistence on its rights over Christian subjects of the Ottoman Empire. Nicholas responded by declaring war.

The Russo-Turkish War of 1828–1829 was fought on two fronts, European and Caucasian. A Russian army moved into Moldavia and Wallachia as the Caucasus corps advanced to Anapa on the east coast of the Black Sea. The campaign of 1828 in Moldavia was disastrous. The commanding general, Diebitsch, here made a tactical error, dividing his forces among three Turkish fortresses and failing to take any one of them (until Varna finally fell in October). On the Caucasian front, the Russian armies fared better, taking several cities, among them Kars, in Armenia, as well as the ports of Poti and Sukhumi on the Black Sea. Turkish victories on the European front continued into 1829, until Diebitsch's forces effected a decisive turnaround at Kulevcha on May 30. In the meantime, diplomatic efforts by Austria, Prussia, England, and France (a conference in London on the Greeks was concurrently in session) helped put pressure on both Turks and Russians to conclude peace. Thus a not-so-clear Russian victory resulted in the Peace of Adrianople (Edirne) in 1829. Its most important consequence was the affirmation of special status for Moldavia, Wallachia, and Serbia within the Ottoman Empire; Greece was granted independence. The Russo-Turkish boundary was also adjusted, Turkey was forced to acknowledge Russian gains from Persia; freedom of passage on the Danube was assured for both sides, the rights of Russians in Turkey were affirmed, and the rights of Muslims in Moldavia and Wallachia were curtailed. Adrianople paved the way for a remarkable pact four years later, the Treaty of Hünkâr Iskelesi, which marked a potential beginning of cooperation between the two eastern empires: in 1833, Turkey agreed to close the Dardanelles to any enemy of Russia if the latter became involved in a war.

This string of crises and wars that Nicholas was forced to confront in his early years in power culminated in the Polish uprising of 1830. The military occupation that followed set the tone for the decidedly more harsh and rigid notion of empire with which Nicholas replaced Alexander's constitutional dreams. Finally, in 1831, a massive cholera epidemic struck St. Petersburg, Moscow, and other cities, bringing death on an enormous scale. The sense of the burden of empire, which fairly crushed Alexander in his last years, haunted Nicholas literally from his first day in office, when he suppressed the Decembrist uprising despite his personal hesitance. It became an inseparable part of his personality as a result of the continuous challenges of the first five years.

ORTHODOXY, AUTOCRACY, NATIONALITY

Nicholas has come to epitomize autocracy: many have noted his nostalgia for order above all else. Unlike his older brother Alexander, he never seems to have entertained daydreams of peaceful retirement. Poorly prepared for his imperial role, Nicholas took his responsibilities extremely seriously and remained firm in his sense of the mission of autocracy. This vague sense of moral superiority began to take on concrete shape by the early 1830s, finally crystallizing into an ideology of rule formulated by Count Sergei Uvarov (1786–1855) and known as Official Nationality. The doctrine of Official Nationality itself took shape in the course of a dialogue between the monarch and some members of the steadily growing educated society. Some of the main contributors were conservative publicists and historians: Faddei Bulgarin, Mikhail Pogodin, Nikolai Grech, and Sergei Shevyrëv; the discussion played itself out on the pages of the publications *The Muscovite* and *The Northern Bee,* as well as in government ministries. This ideology guided Nicholas and, projected at home and abroad, contributed to the much remarked consistency of his long reign.

Uvarov became minister of education in 1832; the maxim he coined was "Orthodoxy, Autocracy, Nationality." Intended as an answer to liberal and revolutionary currents that seemed, understandably in the 1830s, about to overwhelm the European continent, Uvarov's formulation explicitly elaborated what Alexander's Holy Alliance of 1815 had merely implied. Here was a theory, an explanation of why monarchy was a superior form of government to the disorderly and pernicious republican ideas so popular in Europe (including Poland!).

"Orthodoxy" was an explicit rejection of secular notions of the French Revolution and, at the same time, a restatement in modern terms of the Byzantine conception of symphony (elaborated by Emperor Justinian in the seventh century) between secular and sacred. For both Uvarov and Nicholas, a sound government could function exclusively in accordance with religious, Christian principles. State and church complemented each other, working together though in separate spheres. "Orthodoxy," in addition, was meant as a rejection of the mystical cosmopolitanism of Alexander's last years. "Autocracy" left no room for ambiguity in politics. As Uvarov put it, "*Autocracy* constitutes the main condition of the political existence of Russia. The Russian giant stands on it as on the cornerstone of his greatness. . . . The saving conviction that Russia lives and is protected by the spirit of a strong, humane, and enlightened autocracy must permeate popular education and must develop with it." The third principle in Uvarov's maxim, *narodnost,* is the most difficult to translate: *narodnost* meant roughly the spirit of the people, the expression of their essence (*Volkstum* in German). The English term *nationality,* while close, has implications of ethnic solidarity absent in Russian. Russian governance, in short, found its ideal expression in the notion of a Christian, popular monarchy.

Official Nationality was part of a broader reconceptualization of the Russian monarchy. Nicholas initiated a number of changes in the manner in which the Romanov dynasty presented itself within Russia and abroad, essentially creating a new image and ideology of the institution for the nineteenth century. One of the novel elements in Nicholas's "dynastic scenario," evident at his coronation, in his travels through Russia, and in the incessant military pageants he adored, was his inclusion of the entire imperial family. The Empress Alexandra Fëdorovna was as much a part of the imperial imagery as the autocrat himself. In contrast to the hatred of imperial fathers or mothers for their sons in the eighteenth century, Nicholas's love for his son, Alexander, was emphasized by including the young heir in the ceremonies. Nicholas projected an image of family harmony, stability, and uprightness to his subjects. He carefully cultivated his son for future leadership, making him part of the process of rule. Historians have also commented on the innovative tendency, echoed in post-Napoleonic restoration regimes throughout Europe, to include "the people" in ceremony, in a show of unity between rulers and ruled. Official descriptions of parades and pageantry emphasized the support of the people for their tsar, in a direct refutation of the French Revolution's claims to popular sentiment. More guests were invited, and every effort was made to make the crowds an active part of ceremony.

The national theme, too, became increasingly important, as festivals of commemoration multiplied. A national hymn was composed in Nicholas's reign, as was Mikhail Glinka's national opera, *A Life for the Tsar* (1836). Nicholas self-consciously erected a column to commemorate Alexander's military victories; in 1851, toward the end of his reign, he triumphantly revealed a monument to his father, Paul I. St. Isaac's Cathedral, never finished under Alexander, was completed and became the symbol, at once, of Nicholas's heavy, cumbersome reign and of the heavy, cumbersome empire he ruled.

In general, the age of Nicholas represents an era of powerful reinvention and reaffirmation of the principle of monarchy itself. In the age of romanticism, the notion that each nation had its own special, unique path of historical development began to replace Enlightenment universalism. Nicholas himself, and many of his advisers and followers, grew to believe that Russia's "special path"—what made it distinct from its European contemporaries—was embodied in the principle of monarchy. Republicanism and liberalism might serve very well in France or England; Russia, however, had its own historical mission—indeed, a superior one—

St. Isaac's Cathedral, St. Petersburg's main cathedral. Construction was begun in 1768, the consecration ceremonies took place in May 1858. *Brian Vikander/Corbis.*

that found its expression in the monarchy. Russia's new role in Europe was the defense not only of monarchy itself but of the religiously, morally, politically superior, and more venerable system that monarchy represented.

LAW AND ADMINISTRATION, 1830–1840

The German thinker and sociologist Max Weber (1834–1920), writing as the nineteenth century came to a close, considered the formation of a "rationalized," legalistic bureaucracy to be the distinguishing feature of a modern state. Although historians have disputed the applicability of this formula to Russia, it is helpful in isolating some key features of Russian governance in the age of Nicholas I. On one hand, Nicholas's reign was Paul's writ large: Nicholas's was the last—and, ultimately, quixotic—effort to implement the ideal of universal gentry service held by Peter the Great (Peter I). Nicholas's government tried, as well, to limit the rapidly swelling ranks of the gentry, constantly raising the requirements for admission to gentry status. On the other hand, the second quarter of the nineteenth century witnessed the system of civil administration's growth and conversion into a pervasive, empirewide machine: government officials had a role to play at every level of political and civil life.

Speransky and the Code of Law, 1833

Nicholas's government placed its imprint on Russian institutions in a series of measures adopted in the 1830s. The resulting structure, distinguished by greater regulation and control, and the penetration of government into the deepest recesses of Russian life, has come to be known as the Nicholas system. The single greatest achievement of Nicholas's administration was the compilation, at long last, of a Code of Law, begun in 1826 and promulgated seven years later. The code, building on the immense background work Speransky had done in the previous reign, rested on a compilation of laws in use over the preceding two centuries; simultaneously a *Digest* was published, which included those provisions most frequently needed. The forty-eight volumes of the complete code included three categories of legislation: laws dealing with government and social structure (estates, etc.); civil law; and criminal and moral law. The code, instituted in the interests of uniformity and order, had the additional advantage of allowing people to know what the law was—previously a matter of dim speculation.

The most interesting aspects of the work of Speransky and his colleagues were those that shared the fate of Catherine II's Legislative Commission (convened in 1767 to codify Russian laws) and remained unrealized. A special code, compiling local customary law and precedent of native peoples, was instituted for Siberia in 1848 as the Code of Steppe Laws of the Nomad Peoples *(inorodtsy)* of Eastern Siberia. But a similar effort for the western provinces of the empire met with severe resistance from their centrally appointed governor. The paradoxical result was, instead of the codification in law of special western practice, the abrogation of the

Lithuanian statute in the whole region. Roughly the same happened in the newly integrated regions of Transcaucasia: proposals simply to include existing compilations of Georgian law in the imperial code were rejected, and in the end very few local regulations were enshrined in legislation. Efforts to codify church law fared equally badly, and a "Complete Collection of Spiritual Regulations from the Institution of the Holy Synod," begun in 1836, was soon shelved. Three volumes of special laws for the Baltic states, in contrast, were actually published by the 1850s; a similar compilation for Finland was near completion at the end of Nicholas's reign.

Bureaucracy and Local Administration

Although the system of civil administration in mid-nineteenth-century Russia remained within the framework of the merit-based Table of Ranks established by Peter I and the ministerial structure instituted by Alexander I, several major changes in the structure of the bureaucracy took place in the first half of the nineteenth century. The first was a sheer expansion in size: from some 38,000 officials in 1800, the number grew to 113,990 by 1856. Historians have estimated that this means roughly 1 official for every 500 members of the population, in contrast to every 1,000 in 1800. The proportion of nonserf population per official was of course much smaller, possibly less than the ratio in France or Germany.

The nature of the civil service changed, as well: while eighteenth-century bureaucracy usually employed officials who doubled in military service, by the second quarter of the nineteenth century civil service was a full-time career. Officials' status, moreover, was acquired through specialized training and education, not just social background and standing. At the higher levels, this meant passing an examination demonstrating university-level education—an impossible requirement before Alexander's university reforms made higher education more accessible. Technical education underwent a broad expansion in Nicholas's reign: a technological institute was opened in St. Petersburg in 1828, a law school in 1835, an engineering school in 1842; in Moscow, a drafting school (1826), a technical school (1830), a surveying school (1844); and in Dorpat, a technical school (1834) and veterinary institute (1848). These schools were of course all male, and one could argue that this type of education produced a rift between men and women. Given the new criterion of education, service rank came to be taken very seriously: noble officials who had left the service in Alexander's time with the expectation of being granted an "appropriate" status upon return found themselves locked into the position they last held. Equally importantly, the reaches of the civil service expanded downward: progressively lower ranks were included in the bureaucracy, and by midcentury low-level officials had responsibility for matters of inspection and administration, not just in the capital cities but throughout the provinces. The petty bureaucrat *(chinovnik)* became a character all members of the population had eventually to encounter.

Residents of Nicholas's Russia were entwined in a mesh of bureaucracy and paperwork extending from the Senate, State Council, and ministries in St. Petersburg to the local postmaster. The highest level of the administrative machine was, of course, the ministries, which were restructured for greater efficiency on the recommendation of the informal Committee of 6 December, set up in 1826 to propose reform. The ministers themselves acquired considerable power; each ministry employed numbers of officials. The empire as a whole was subdivided into provinces, each with its governor, who was generally sent from the center. These high-level officials could serve in a variety of places, from Ukraine to Siberia, in the course of a single career. Within the provinces, a whole network of lower offices followed: government at the district and local levels required a local official (these generally remained in the same province for the course of their career), with a host of inspectors, tax collectors, and post office workers.

A reform of local government was instituted in 1837. A thorough network of local administration, which Catherine II had unsuccessfully tried to create, was well in place a half century later. Considerable power was granted to the governors, who held moral and physical responsibility for residents of their province as well as the right of legal decisions and regulations. The provincial board became merely an executive rather than a consultative body, and the local police were strengthened. One of the driving considerations in propping up local administration was fiscal: the problem of how to collect taxes from Russia's huge territories and make the funds work for local needs prompted the transfer of greater responsibility onto the local level. Parallel reforms affected the cities: an effort was made to grant city *dumas* (councils) more powers, and the definition of the city "society"—that is, those with rights to participate in meetings and *duma* elections—was broadened to include almost all residents. A further symptom of the bureaucratization of the provinces, and the extension of the government's reach, was the establishment, in 1838, of a network of local *Provincial Messengers* in all the main provincial centers. This government-sponsored publication was the beginning of a local press.

The pattern for the empire was diverse: while much the same structure obtained in Siberia as in European Russia, the Caucasus, for example, remained subject to military administration. In the Baltics, Armenia, and Georgia, the government employed a strategy (as it had tried to do since the conquest of Kazan in 1552) of varying degrees of cooperation with local elites. Finland retained self-government, with Russian officials performing only limited functions. Poland's Organic Statute, imposed following the 1830 uprising, was symbolic for the empire as a whole: it signified the defeat of hopes for eventual constitutional government and integrated the once independent nation into Russian administration. One consequence was increased interaction between Polish nobility and Russian bureaucracy.

The writer Nikolai Gogol (see later in this chapter), working in an idiom similar to that of his contemporaries the English novelist Charles Dickens and the French caricaturist Honoré Daumier, painted a derogatory and sarcastic picture of the obtuseness and venality of Russian officials; perhaps the most famous depiction is in his play *The Inspector-General* (1836). Although corruption, bribery, and inefficiency were undoubtedly characteristic of both the central and provincial bureaucracies, historians have recently pointed out another side to the picture by focusing attention on the people in the civil service themselves. Many of them were liberal in their outlook; members of the liberal bureaucracy of Nicholas's reign in fact paved the way for the great reforms that would come in the 1860s and 1870s.

Alongside the administrative bureaucracy—which dealt with such matters as taxes, mail delivery, and local governance—a sophisticated organizational structure for science and exploration emerged in the age of Nicholas. As in England's Victorian period, scientific societies were founded under the auspices of the imperial government. Supplementing the Free Economic Society, which had existed since Catherine II's time and was primarily agricultural in its concerns, an Imperial Geographic Society, an Ethnographic Society, and two new Academies of Science were now established. Not limited to the exploration of Russia's farthest reaches, the Geographic Society, paralleling Darwin's *Voyage of the Beagle* (instrumental in constructing the theory of evolution) sent expeditions as far as the South Pole. The frigate *Pallada* circled the globe in the 1830s. Created under the emperor's aegis, the learned societies gradually became a center for independent discussion, as well as for rapid advances in fields like statistics and ethnography. Ethnographers reached new levels of understanding of the depths of Russian life, as geographers, scientists, and journalists investigated the variety of ethnic and religious groups and subcultures of the empire. The growth of scientific knowledge was instrumental for Russian self-awareness; political issues that never could have been openly discussed became subtexts of ethnographic and statistical investigations conducted by the learned societies.

Tariffs and Borders

At a time when the European economic system experienced the advantages of open trade and the lowering of tariffs and customs duties (perhaps the most visible examples were the German Customs Union of 1834 and the repeal of the British Corn Laws in 1846), Russia's economic and financial policies remained starkly conservative. E. F. Kankrin, appointed minister of finance under Alexander I in 1823, pursued a mercantilist (protectionist) line. Tariffs were one of the key issues of conflict with Poland, which, despite being part of the Russian Empire, was cut off from the latter by a customs barrier; Poland competed with Russia in textile and metallurgical manufacturing. After the uprising of 1830, duties on Polish goods entering Russia were raised to 12½ percent. Russian borders in the time of Nicholas became infamous: they were strictly policed and uncomfortable to cross, not only for Russians but for foreigners as well. Kankrin's protectionist policies seriously impeded Russian industrialization at a critical moment, as industry in England, France, and Germany took off. His mercantilism became untenable by the mid-1840s, and he resigned in 1844.

Russian policy toward railroads was also relatively conservative at this time, perhaps with better reason: while the first railroad connecting St. Petersburg and Pavlovsk was triumphantly opened in 1837, and Moscow–St. Petersburg and Warsaw–St. Petersburg lines followed in the 1840s, the expense gave officials and industrialists pause. Covering Russia's broad expanses with an efficient railway network was a goal that could be reasonably pursued only a half century later. In the meantime, the continued enserfment of the vast proportion of Russia's population placed insuperable barriers on the institution of a rationalized system of taxation, an amelioration of agriculture, or an expansion of industry on a large scale.

Serfdom

Nicholas liked to rely on secret committees to accomplish the business of government. The most important of these was a committee set up in 1835 to deal with the question of the reform, or even abolition, of serfdom. The committee, which included P. D. Kiselëv (1788–1872), author of a note advocating abolition, drew up a plan that would return peasants to being attached to the land only, rather than to its owner, and gradually bring about landless emancipation. The committee's conclusions were never implemented; instead, a second such committee was set up in 1839, which advocated a "middle path" between landless emancipation and taking land away from the gentry to give it to the peasants. Nicholas responded that serfdom was an evil, yet that abolition, too, was impossible. Ultimately, the result was an 1842 law that created a new type of "obligated" peasant. The peasant would have "personal" freedom and would be granted a piece of land by the landlord but would owe the landlord dues in return. Enforcement of the obligations would be overseen by the government. Even this very limited type of "emancipation" was considered voluntary; only three large landholders took advantage of the 1842 law. In the end, Nicholas remained true to his own sense that his job was to lay the groundwork for emancipation, leaving its execution to his heir.

Eventually, Nicholas confined his positive measures concerning serfdom to the state peasants, who were under his direct control. The important reform initiated by Kiselëv in the 1830s granted the state peasants a significant degree of self-government: the peasants were organized into councils, each of which had a head, elders, and its own courts. When emancipation was finally implemented in 1861, this organization served as a model for self-government for the entire peasantry. One of the most interesting episodes of Nicholas's reign concerned the state peasants. Following the poor harvests of 1839 and 1840, the government decided to urge the peasants to plant potatoes instead of grain. Though Catherine II had introduced potatoes on a massive scale, the hardy vegetable had met widespread resistance from the peasants. When Nicholas's government tried again in 1842, the peasant councils became convinced, by a circulating rumor, that the village scribes had sold their communes, behind the revered tsar's back, to a "minister," who was now insisting that they plant the unwanted crop. The rumor led to the Potato Uprising, the biggest and bloodiest peasant revolt of Nicholas's reign, in which dozens of scribes, priests, and petty officials were beaten and killed by the angry peasants. Equally bloody reprisals on the part of the government followed, in which peasants were more or less arbitrarily chosen to be whipped, sometimes to death. But potatoes became a staple of the Russian diet.

THE "MARVELOUS DECADE"

The banishment of many of Russia's most talented young writers and poets following the Decembrist uprising, and the heavy hand of censorship and repression that marked Nicholas's reign, triggered a mood of collective depression in educated society. Pëtr Chaadaev (1794–1856), a relatively minor Decembrist and a participant in golden age culture, gave voice to this feeling of destruction and abandonment in 1836. By now heavily steeped in the romantic historical consciousness of the second quarter of the nineteenth century, Chaadaev published his *First Philosophical Letter* on the pages of the Moscow journal *The Telescope,* to the accompaniment of a great scandal. The *Letter,* written in French, contained the following statement about Russia's history and destiny: Russia, he said, caught between East and West, had been placed outside of time, untouched by the universal education of the human race.

> We are alone in the world, we have given nothing to the world, we have taught it nothing. We have not added a single idea to the sum total of human ideas; we have not contributed to the progress of the human spirit, and what we have borrowed of this progress we have distorted. From the outset of our existence as a society, we have produced nothing for the common benefit of all mankind; not one useful thought has sprung from the arid soil of our fatherland; not one great truth has emerged from our midst; we have not taken the trouble to invent anything ourselves and, of the inventions of others, we have borrowed only empty conceits and useless luxuries.

Russia, in Chaadaev's Romantic vision, had somehow fallen out of the process of historical development, had failed to follow the path of Western Christianity, and remained abandoned and unproductive on the margins of culture.

Chaadaev's letter, published between the Golden Age of Russian poetry and the flowering of philosophy that would occur in the 1840s, produced no little astonishment and dismay. Yet it captured the sense of a hiatus in Russia's rich cultural life in the first decade of Nicholas's reign. Chaadaev's voice was the harbinger of a new epoch in Russian culture, entirely different in tone and content from the aristocratic poetry and romances of Alexander's time, yet if anything more intense, excited, and exalted: this was the period, roughly 1838–1848, which the brilliant memoirist P. V. Annenkov (1812–1887) christened the "Marvelous Decade."

Philosophy and Ideology

Philosophy was the vortex of Russian cultural and intellectual life in the 1830s and 1840s. The ideas of Kant, Schelling, Hegel, and Fichte had been mostly confined, in the early years of the nineteenth century in Russia, to seminaries and theological academies. The entry of German idealism and Romanticism on the broader stage of Russian public life began in the 1820s but reached its apogee only in the next two decades. Once it had arrived, German philosophy was there to stay: the enthusiasm and energy of its reception was tremendous, and the ideas of the German thinkers would continue to form a substratum of Russian thought over the entire ensuing century.

Two German thinkers in particular deserve our attention here. Friedrich Wilhelm Schelling (1775–1854) exercised a particularly powerful attraction for Russian thinkers: his *System of Transcendental Idealism* (1800) and his *Natural Philosophy* (1797) fascinated readers with ideas of organic wholeness, the union of man with the universe, and the creation of art through the interaction of the thinking subject with objective matter. George Wilhelm Friedrich Hegel (1770–1831) introduced a series of methods and problems that were equally productive for Russian thought. Hegel's notion that the Absolute Spirit realized itself in history through a dialectical process became the theme for many intense nighttime discussions for young Russian thinkers in the 1830s and 1840s and formed the basis for some of their philosophical compositions. Russian reception of these thinkers, however, occurred late enough that their ideas sometimes came in strange combinations: most notably, the same people who were fascinated by Hegel were also taken by contemporary French utopian socialists and writers such as Saint-Simon (1760–1825) and Charles Fourier (1772–1837), or the woman writer Georges Sand (1804–1876). Thus a curious syncretism of German idealism with French utopian socialism was characteristic for Russian thought in the age of Nicholas I.

This "philosophical awakening" occurred simultaneously with the effective removal of philosophy from the university curriculum as a dangerous subject. The vehicle for its transmission was informal: circles, in which a group of friends gathered to discuss the nature of the Absolute or debate the course of Russian historical development. Philosophizing had an intoxicating effect, and sessions often lasted well into the night. The intensity of discussions sometimes obviated the necessity of actually reading the works at hand: for example, the literary critic Vissarion Belinsky, at one point, was Hegel's staunchest champion without having read a word. The process had its dangers as well: friendships were made and broken over the niceties of the dialectical process, for the very nature of the philosophical friendship demanded unity of perspective.

A forerunner to the circles of the 1830s and 1840s was the Lovers of Wisdom (from the Greek-based word *philosophers* translated into Russian), based around the young poet Dmitry Venevitinov in the 1820s. The Wisdom Lovers were Schellingians; their most illustrious member, Vladimir Odoevsky, wrote the collection of sketches *Russian Nights* (1844). The "Marvelous Decade" itself opened with the circle around Nikolai Stankevich in Moscow, of which the young Mikhail Bakunin was a primary member. The Stankevich circle "discovered" Romanticism in earnest, plunging into Schelling in the 1830s; later, Hegel became for them the vehicle of a rather crude philosophical "reconciliation with reality." This particular circle was an education or apprenticeship for many budding philosophers; in the early 1840s its members included Vissarion Belinsky, the future anarchist Bakunin, the future Slavophile Konstantin Aksakov, the merchant and philosophical dabbler Vasily Botkin, and Timofei Granovsky, lecturer and then professor at Moscow

University. Granovsky, in turn, became arguably the most influential transmitter of Hegel to Russian students: his lectures were enormously popular, and he made his listeners recognize their own and Russia's fate as he spoke about medieval European history. Alexander Herzen, with his close boyhood friend Nicholas Ogarëv, formed a countercircle to Stankevich's in their university years.

A special role on the philosophical scene belonged not only to the circles but also to literary criticism. In a world of severe censorship, literature remained an area in which relatively free expression of philosophical and indeed quasi-political ideas was possible. Here Belinsky occupied center stage: his critical articles and overviews of recent Russian literature created a new genre of journalistic expression. Himself of humble origins, he represented a social group that was to become increasingly vocal into the 1850s and 1860s: the so-called *raznochintsy*—those of diverse and nongentry background.

By the 1840s it is possible to speak of a some relatively clear ideological positions that crystallized out of the endless philosophical discussions. One such position emerged in dialogue with the philosophically based doctrine of Official Nationality. The group of Moscow land-owning gentry who came to be known as the Slavophiles included Ivan Kireevsky, Alexei Khomyakov, Konstantin and Ivan Aksakov, and Yuri Samarin. These five thinkers and writers were the most brilliant of what eventually became a much broader ideological direction, based on German Romantic philosophy, that proposed, as it were, an "unofficial" theory of Russian nationality and religion. In a Romantic vein, they affirmed the specificity and, presumably, superiority of Russian life and culture over Western European models, though on a different basis from the theorists of "official" nationality. Basing their arguments on a vaguely Hegelian sense of dialectic, and a vaguely Schellingian penchant for organic unity and wholeness, Slavophile thinkers posited an essential dichotomy between Russia and the West, as well as between "old" and "new" Russia. Russia, in their vision (and particularly before Peter I), represented organic, holistic, religious, and emotional values and a focus on the inner, spiritual life; whereas the West stood for constant political struggle and conflict, excess rationality, and the spirit of cold calculation and materialism.

The key emblems of Russian nationality, to the Slavophiles, were such institutions as the family, the church, and the village commune. The commune, or *mir,* in particular, represented a uniquely Russian form of social organization in which peasants, instead of struggling against each other in individualistic competition as in "the West," lived in harmony and cooperation and accomplished their agricultural tasks as a single collectivity. In a vision a practical observer of Russian village life would be hard put to recognize, Konstantin Aksakov, in particular, spoke of the commune as a "moral choir," "an association of people who have renounced their personal egoism, their individuality, and express common accord," and in which "the individual is not lost but merely renounces his exclusivity in the name of general accord and finds himself on a higher and purer level, in mutual harmony with other individuals"—a "harmonious coexistence of rational beings" that constituted "the triumph of the human spirit." The ultimate social ideal, for the Slavophiles, was the important political concept of *sobornost*—the functioning of society as a collective, organic, integral whole in which individuals, as in the peasant commune, worked together instead of at cross-purposes.

The Slavophiles were opposed by a broad spectrum of thinkers and journalists of varied convictions who saw in their ideas an unrealistic idealization of Russia and a pandering to official ideology (though the government itself viewed the Slavophiles with considerable suspicion) and who found much to criticize in the "Russian path" and the Russian social order. Alexander Herzen, for example, had followed a complicated spiritual path from a youthful cult of the Decembrists and German poet and playwright Friedrich Schiller (1759–1805) through the usual Schelling and Hegel and thence to an infatuation with socialism. Having spent parts of his youth in Siberian exile, Herzen eventually emigrated to London. From there his highly influential radical journal, *The Bell,* pointed out the injustices of Russian life—most notably, the institution of serfdom—and brought the world of European socialism closer to Russian readers. From a completely different perspective, Vissarion Belinsky argued against a romanticization of the Russian peasants and their exalted community and religiosity. In his famous *Letter to Gogol* (1847) (actually as much an argument with Slavophile Ivan Kireevsky as with Gogol), Belinsky argued that peasants were simply ritualistic and not really religious, that the *muzhik* "prayed to God while scratching his backside."

Herzen, Belinsky, Granovsky, and some more minor figures became known at the time, and afterward, as Westernizers, as opposed to Slavophiles. Both terms were originally somewhat pejorative; both should be used with caution. Herzen was indeed a "European," who ultimately, through his natural aristocratism, found great pleasure in his life abroad and was able to communicate with European writers and politicians. But his attitude toward "the West" was in fact quite mixed: disillusionment with Western "comfort" and "bourgeois lifestyle," compounded by his disappointment with the revolutions that swept Europe in 1848 (see next section), led him, too, to look to the Russian commune as the source of future socialism. Belinsky, in contrast, knew no European languages at all. When he finally arrived in Germany to treat the tuberculosis that was soon to end his life, he was, by Annenkov's account, fairly oblivious to and quite ignorant of the life and culture around him. Many Slavophiles, in the meantime, had studied and lived abroad and were well versed in European ideas: actually, German Romanticism, with its emphasis on the folk and on national history, was the philosophical foundation of their exaltation of the Russian people.

From Romanticism to "Realism"

The world of literature proper occasionally intersected the philosophical and ideological currents of the age, but it also had its own internal development. Mikhail Lermontov (1814–1841) was a Romantic poet who, in his nostalgia for the golden age of poetry, lamented that he had been born too late. His poetry and prose painted a mysterious, ineffable nature—mostly the craggy mountains and ravines and swift-flowing rivers of the Caucasus. *A Hero of Our Time* (1840) tells the tale of a Russian officer stationed in the Caucasus and, among other things, his tragic love for the lovely, wild, and dark-eyed Chechen girl, Bela. Nikolai Gogol (1809–1852) belongs in a category of his own. Alternating lyricism with satire, his stories, novels, and dramas drew on the folk tales and legends of his native Malorossiya (Ukraine) to create a magical world of witches on broomsticks, dumplings that fly into mouths of their own volition, and deeply mysterious waters holding the secret of once-drowned beautiful maidens. The peaceful Dnieper River and the gentle wheatfields of the Ukrainian landscape form the backdrop. Gogol's *Dead Souls* (1842), composed in a more satirical vein, revolves around an enterprising man's scheme to make money off landowners who are still officially listed as owning serfs who have actually died; the tale is a series of biting portraits of different provincial characters. A collection of Gogol's essays, *Arabesques* (1835), was entirely Romantic in mode, discussing such subjects as the interrelation of the arts. Gogol became increasingly drawn to religion with time and was particularly fascinated by Catholicism (he lived for a long time in Italy and was close to some Polish circles). Religiosity became fanaticism in his last years; his behavior became increasingly erratic and peremptory, and his unceasing dissatisfaction with his own work made him burn the final manuscript of the second half of *Dead Souls*.

The 1840s initiated a new movement in Russian literature. Called the natural school by Belinsky, the short stories and novels that began to appear in these years bore the traits of what was soon to become known as realism. On one hand, this meant an attention to the details of nature and the countryside; on the other, it meant a deepening of the subject matter of literature to include "ordinary folk." D. V. Grigorovich's *The Village* (1846) and *Anton Goremyka* (1847) introduced the novel idea that a peasant's daily life could be described in a manner comprehensible and sympathetic to any human being. Ivan Turgenev's *A Hunter's Sketches* (which began to appear in serial form in 1847) caused a furor with its portrayal of peasants in a naturalistic setting. The young novelist Fëdor Dostoevsky's *Poor Folk* (1846) brought Belinsky running in the middle of the night to hail the birth of a great writer. Yet it was serfdom in particular that captured the attention of the public in the 1840s. Stories similar to the American abolitionist writer Harriet Beecher Stowe's *Uncle Tom's Cabin* (subtitled *or, Life Among the Lowly*) began to appear regularly on the pages of the illustrated journals (Herzen's "Thieving Magpie," for example, described the tribulations of a serf actress). It became an increasingly accepted commonplace among educated society that serfdom was an inappropriate and harmful institution.

Art and Culture in the Capitals

If literature and philosophy developed largely in opposition to the orientation of Nicholas's reign, painting, architecture, theater, and ballet found a welcoming sponsorship from the state. The Academy of Arts flourished under the generous sponsorship of the Ministry of the Court, to which it was transferred in 1829. The Imperial Hermitage became a national museum and expanded its collections. Art history and architectural journals were published by organizations like the Imperial Russian Archaeological Society and the Odessa Society for History and Antiquities. The age was rich in architectural innovation: much of the massive St. Isaac's Cathedral in St. Petersburg and also the ambitious Church of Christ the Savior in Moscow were constructed in Nicholas's reign. In the early 1830s, the imposing buildings of the Senate and Synod, symbolically joined by an arch, went up on the banks of the Neva. The most cohesive architectural ensemble of Nicholas's age is in Helsinki, Finland, where the German architect Karl-Ludwig Engel (1778–1840) created his characteristically columned yellow buildings to house the Diet, the palace of the governor general, the Senate, the Imperial Palace, the university, observatories, and libraries.

EUROPEAN REVOLUTION AND OTTOMAN WAR, 1848–1856

The congress system—which had, despite constant challenges, provided the general framework for European politics since 1815—finally collapsed in 1848. In Paris, liberals gathered at a series of banquets—a way of circumventing a government ban on political meetings. Revolution broke out after a banquet to celebrate George Washington's birthday (February 22). When soldiers, called in to maintain order, fired on protesting crowds the next day, killing fifty-two people, barricades went up in streets around the place de la Bastille—former site of the infamous prison. Two days later, King Louis Philippe gave up power and escaped to England. The short-lived republic that emerged was replaced four years later (1852) by the dictatorship of the man who had been elected its president, Louis Napoleon (Bonaparte's nephew). The Parisian disorders triggered some fifty other revolts throughout the continent. In Vienna, revolution resulted in the granting of a constitution, the abolition of serfdom, and the symbolic dismissal of Metternich. In the German states, the revolution was intimately tied up with the issue of national unification, and a parliament met at Frankfurt to draft a constitution and offer the throne of a united Germany to Frederick William IV of Prussia. In Italy, an effort to throw off Austrian rule and unite the Italian states under Piedmont's leadership failed thoroughly, although Piedmont itself gained a new constitution. Closest to home for Russians, both Austria and Prussia put down gentry rebellions in their parts of Poland.

Russia and the 1848 Revolutions

To Nicholas, the revolutions of 1848 were not only destructive of the existing order in Europe but a threat to the very bases of life in society. On March 14 he issued a manifesto lamenting the "destructive flow" of disorder from Paris to Germany and Austria and exhorting Russians to defend the "ancient principles" of faith, tsar, and fatherland against the revolutionary plague. When revolution reached Russian borders in the summer of 1848 with uprisings in Moldavia and Wallachia in the Ottoman Empire, rhetoric passed into action, and Russian troops entered the principalities. This military intervention in part reflected Russian nervousness at the Turks' own efforts to suppress the uprisings, which brought Ottoman forces directly to the imperial border. In April 1849, a Russo-Turkish declaration signed at Balta Liman dictated the internal order of Moldavia and Wallachia, depriving them of the right to elect their rulers and limiting representation to a noble and clerical elite.

Nicholas took his personal responsibility to defend against revolution very seriously; thus, for example, Russian aid helped Austria retain Lombardy. But Russia played its most crucial role in the European revolutions in 1849, when rebels in Hungary declared the Habsburg Empire deposed and elected the nationalist Louis Kossuth (1802–1894) ruler. Seeing in the rebellion the symptoms of a "general plot against all that is sacred," Nicholas readily agreed to the Austrian emperor's request for military aid: Russian troops, already conveniently stationed on the border (and some actually across it, in Transylvania), entered Hungary in June, and in less than two months the Hungarian army under Arthur Görgey surrendered to them. The suppression of the Hungarian rebellion seemed to vindicate Russia's status as defender of the "legitimate order," including the principle of monarchy, and marked the high point of Russian military status in Europe.

Nicholas's response to revolution was projected onto internal policy as well, and 1848 became a crucial turning point in his reign. To forestall the spread of subversive ideas inside Russia, the Ministry of Education was instructed to tighten censorship, and a special committee that included the chief of police, General L. V. Dubelt, was created to supervise the censors themselves. A long list of topics regarding virtually any aspect of public life was removed from print during 1848–1854. The second target of repression became the universities: the number of students was cut, and all lectures had to be lithographed and submitted to the Public Library; a government-sponsored article in an 1849 issue of *The Contemporary* pronounced that instruction in the sciences must be based on "religious truths in connection with theology." Starting in the fall semester of 1849, instruction in law was eliminated from the Moscow University curriculum, followed by philosophy in 1850; such dubious subjects as psychology were entrusted to professors of theology. This approach to culture extended to social questions as well: in 1851 a decree required a return to universal gentry service in the western provinces, while Kiselëv was heard to comment that the reform of serfdom had become a dead letter. The price of a foreign passport went from 50 to 250 rubles.

The post-1848 reaction went on public display with the trial of the Petrashevtsy—a group of intellectuals that had been meeting on Fridays in St. Petersburg since 1846 to discuss religion, philosophy, and literature. Apparently the group's attention to the issue of serfdom first alerted the authorities. In April 1849, agents of the Petersburg police and the Third Section arrested Mikhail Petrashevsky himself and several others. Twenty-one members, including the novelist Dostoevsky, were condemned to be executed for subversion. The young men, in their white execution shirts, were already in place on Semënovsky Square to be shot when a last-minute reprieve from Nicholas dramatically snatched them from their deaths (replacing the sentence with exile or imprisonment).

The Crimean War

In the eighty years since the Treaty of Küçük Kaynarca, which concluded the 1773–1774 Russo-Turkish war to Russian advantage, Russian power in the Black Sea region had grown significantly. The Black Sea fleet begun by Catherine II's favorite, Grigory Potëmkin, had expanded to three 120-cannon and twelve 84-cannon ships, eight frigates, and some sixty smaller vessels. The naval base established at Sevastopol in 1783 was designated the Black Sea fleet's primary port in 1804; a powerful fortress with eight bastions was constructed there in the 1820s and 1830s (but not quite finished), and the population of the city itself grew to forty-six thousand. Russian forces were constantly in and out of the principalities of Moldavia and Wallachia, occupying them between 1829 and 1834 and again in 1849–1851. Even when troops were not physically present, Russia was the dominant protector and commercial beneficiary of the principalities, with Ottoman rights limited to the collection of tribute and a voice in the choice of princes. In the Turkish wars of Alexander I and Nicholas I, Russia had carved the region of Bessarabia from Moldavian territory, acquired a strip of the Black Sea's eastern coast and the mouth of the Danube, and gained the right for its merchant ships to pass through the Black Sea straits. Russia's growing Black Sea power made everyone, from the Turkish sultan to British diplomats, nervous. War was narrowly averted in 1849 when Nicholas tried to force Sultan Abdulmecid I (1823–1861) to extradite refugees—

The Crimean War, 1854–56. *From Geoffrey Barraclough,* Times Atlas of World History. *Reprinted by permission of HarperCollins U.K.*

some of them Hungarian and Polish revolutionaries—who had fled to the Ottoman Empire when Russian troops moved in to suppress the uprisings in Hungary and Wallachia.

When the conflict we have come to know as the Crimean War did break out a few years later (1854), at issue was not so much any particular territorial question but the general problem—of primary concern to nineteenth-century European statesmen—of maintaining the balance of power. The "Eastern War" (the nineteenth-century Russian term) might be seen as a textbook case of Prussian general and military theorist Carl von Clausewitz's famous dictum "that war is only a branch of political activity; that it is in no sense autonomous." The European powers, primarily Britain and France, but with the tacit support of Austria and Prussia and the inevitable participation of Turkey, confronted the Russian Empire militarily in all the regions of its expansion since 1700—namely, the Baltic and the Black Seas and the Caucasus.

The specific transition from diplomacy to war was a result of Russian (specifically, Nicholas's) hubris; it happened on religious grounds. In 1850, the French ruler Louis Napoleon sought to reassert Roman Catholic privileges in the holy places in Jerusalem (on Ottoman territory), annoying Nicholas I, who had restored two monasteries there and encouraged Orthodox pilgrimages throughout the 1840s. Mistaking British silence for support of his position, Nicholas in 1853 sent the ill-chosen Prince Alexander Menshikov on a mission to the Turkish sultan to negotiate the delicate matter of Russia's jurisdiction over Orthodox subjects of the Ottoman Empire, including the Balkan Christians—an issue that had first been raised in the Küçük Kaynarca treaty. The mission was a disaster: Menshikov's insistence on a Russian protectorate over Ottoman Christians was rejected by Turkey, with Britain's encouragement. In response, Nicholas sent Russian troops into Moldavia and Wallachia, prompting the British and the French to send a fleet to the Dardanelles. An international conference was convened at Vienna, resulting in the Vienna Note, which reconfirmed earlier treaty provisions (Küçük Kaynarca and Adrianople [Edirne]) concerning the Christians. Although Nicholas accepted the Note, Abdulmecid did not: it did not affirm his jurisdiction over his Christian subjects clearly enough. By the end of October, Ottoman troops crossed the Danube to force Russia out of the principalities, and Russia and Turkey were at war. At the same time, the Turkish provincial army in eastern Anatolia moved into the southern Caucasus to confront Russian troops already facing a Muslim uprising led by the Avar sheikh, Shamyl (see the chapter "Around the Russian Empire, 1801–1861").

The Russian-Ottoman conflict became a full-scale European war when a Russian squadron blew up the Turkish fleet at Sinope on November 30, 1853, provoking a storm of outrage in the English and French press. Russian failure to respond to a British ultimatum led to a declaration of war by Britain and France on March 28, 1854. The first military action in the Crimean War was actually in the Baltic, where an allied fleet bombarded Hangö in the Gulf of Finland and attacked a Russian garrison in the Åland Islands. While not much more happened there, the effect was to keep some 200,000 Russian troops tied up in the Baltic region. In the meantime, the Russian-Turkish encounter in the Caucasus continued. In July the

Russian army forced the Turks back all along the front, and on August 5 General V. O. Bebutov defeated the main Turkish army at Kurudere. In August there was even action on the Arctic coast, at Kola and in Kamchatka, but by September the Russian defense had driven the allied squadron away.

Diplomatic maneuvers among the powers continued through the summer: the Russian ambassador to Vienna, Alexander Gorchakov, agreed to an Austrian demand (to Nicholas, an appalling betrayal by the empire he had just saved from revolution) to withdraw from Moldavia and Wallachia, and in August Russian troops there were replaced by an Austrian (and in Wallachia also Turkish) occupation force. In an effort to produce a peace settlement, France and Austria presented Russia with Four Points: (1) replacement of the Russian protectorate of Moldavia and Wallachia with a European guarantee; (2) freedom of navigation in the Danube; (3) rights of Orthodox subjects of the Ottoman Empire to be guaranteed by the sultan (not the tsar); and (4) revision of the Straits Convention to uphold the European balance of power. But objections to the last point led the Russian government to reject the proposal on August 26.

After some deliberation as to where to stage a response (the Caucasus was one possibility), the British and French governments decided to attack the center of Russian Black Sea naval power at Sevastopol. An allied army of sixty thousand landed at Eupatoria on September 14 and engaged a Russian force of thirty-five thousand under Menshikov's command in the Battle of the Alma on September 20. The Russian army was thoroughly defeated, with intense fighting and heavy casualties (six thousand on the Russian side), opening Sevastopol to the invading armies. But a series of strategic errors on the allied side allowed the Russians time to fortify Sevastopol. At the end of October, the allied forces met a Russian attack on their position at Balaklava with the catastrophic "Charge of the Light Brigade," restoring the Russian advantage. Ten days later, a second Russian attack failed because the Russian commanders did not mobilize reserve troops that would have given them an absolute advantage: the chaotic Battle of Inkerman resulted in eleven thousand Russian and four thousand allied casualties. Three weeks later Russia accepted the Four Points.

Sevastopol, however, still held, and the ensuing eleven months saw the drama of a prolonged siege, with the Russian defense led by Admiral Pavel Nakhimov, punctuated by diplomatic maneuverings. Continuous press coverage—the first major war to be fully reported—kept the English and French public informed of the cholera, poor supplies, and unsanitary conditions that plagued the besieging allied army. At the same time, the siege of Sevastopol was a landmark in the history of military medical organization: Florence Nightingale on one side, and the surgeon N. I. Pirogov and Grand Duchess Elena Pavlovna on the other, transformed the art of nursing and field hospitals. As the powers were preparing to meet at Vienna, Nicholas caught a nasty cold that turned serious from neglect; on March 2, 1855, he died. The Vienna Conference (March 15–June 4) ended in failure essentially because, while Sevastopol held, the Russians would not agree to the destruction of their naval power in the Black Sea. Meanwhile, the port of Novorossiisk fell to the allies with Circassian aid, while a British squadron bombarded Sveaborg (Suomenlinna) off the Finnish coast in the Baltic. Sevastopol finally fell to the allies on September 8–10, with twenty-four thousand total casualties on those days. Despite a solid Russian victory on the Caucasus front, at Kars, on November 26, the fall of Sevastopol—which meant the nearly complete destruction of the Russian navy—led the Russian government to respond to a new Austrian ultimatum in December by agreeing to peace negotiations.

The European powers convened at Paris on 25 February 1856, much as they had met at Vienna forty years earlier, to outline the post-war order. Instead of an assortment of emperors and Napoleonic puppets, the negotiators were now professional diplomats representing England, France, Austria, Russia, Turkey, Piedmont, and Prussia. The Peace of Paris, signed on 29 March, dealt exclusively with the Black Sea region, though it was couched in language of perpetual peace. All sides evacuated territory they had occupied—Crimea for the allies, eastern Anatolia for Russia. The treaty's central thrust was to neutralize, or demilitarize, the Black Sea: it was to remain open only to merchant ships; no foreign (i.e. non-Turkish) warships were to be allowed in the Straits. Moldavia and Wallachia were removed from their Russian protectorate and given autonomy under a joint European guarantee. Moldavia at the same time recovered Bessarabia from Russia (Russia's only territorial loss). Russia lost its claim to a protectorate over Ottoman Christians, but Turkey did not gain it: instead the European powers reasserted their perceived rights of intervention in Ottoman affairs by establishing an unwieldy six-power guarantee of the status of Christian subjects; in addition they required a presentation of reform plans from the Turkish sultan.

So far as Russia was concerned, the Paris treaty was a humiliation in the sense that it articulated the loss of Russia's status as the greatest power in Europe—a status based on the memory of the march to Paris in 1815, the immensity of the Russian army, and the suppression of revolution in 1849. It also really did achieve, in keeping with Clausewitz, the limitation on Russian expansion in the Black Sea region that had been the allies' political goal; recovering Bessarabia and reestablishing Black Sea naval power became the central aims of Russian foreign policy for the ensuing twenty years. Yet the Paris conference was as important for what it didn't do as for what it did. It failed to reassert the European Concert established in 1815, which had exerted at least some measure of control over internal developments in the European states. By limiting concrete discussion to a particular region, the conference left states and their increasingly independent foreign ministers plenty of room for inventive policies, thus leaving any real definition of postwar order aside. Europe after 1856 was full of surprises: if Russia lost in the Black Sea and Baltic, it won in Asia, and the 1860s saw the final subjugation of the Caucasus and the conquest of Central Asia. All eyes in the meantime turned to Piedmont and to Prussia, as the nationalist Camillo Cavour and the "iron chancellor" Otto von Bismarck totally recrafted any existing balance of power by constructing the nation-states of Italy and Germany in the very middle of Europe.

CHAPTER 19

Russian Society and Daily Life in the Twilight of Serfdom, 1800–1861

Petersburg is a dot on the map of Russia; the fashionable world is a dot on the map of Petersburg.

—*Vladimir Sollogub, 1845*

St. Petersburg and Moscow—the new and the old capitals—seemed indeed like two dots compared to the vastness of provincial Russia to which the above-cited writer took his readers in a popular novel of 1845, *The Coach.* To begin to understand Russia, one must examine both its capitals and its immense hinterland. From 1796 to 1851 the population rose from about 36 to 67 million, with peasants about 84 percent of the total. Peasant serfs, soldiers, and other lower-class people engaged in cholera riots, mutinies in the military colonies, manorial unrest, a potato rebellion, disorders during the Crimean War, and vodka riots after the war. But in the normal course of life in an agrarian economy, rural society hummed with a variety of economic activities and peasants expanded their mobility and their involvement in peaceful pursuits. Although urban growth was not spectacular, towns stirred with commerce, and conditions were emerging for a wide social and cultural transformation after the freeing of the serfs in 1861. Amid all this, the privileged estate of aristocrats and rural landowners continued to reap the benefits of the unfree labor—serfdom—on which their existence reposed.

ON THE LAND: NESTS OF GENTRY

For the gentry, the early nineteenth century was the twilight of a golden age of manorial life and culture. Although the wealthiest lords almost always wintered in the cities, the country seat was their source of income; for most landowners, the manor house was home and a site of identity. Here they lived largely off the labor of their serf peasants.

Who Were the Gentry?

The gentry—landowners, serf owners, officers, and higher state officials—though legally a single estate, were greatly divided by wealth and rank. In the 1850s, they numbered about 886,000—1.5 percent of the population and about 5 percent of those inhabiting the capitals. Of the roughly 100,000 landowners, 40 percent owned only twenty-one souls (male serfs) or fewer and were held to be "poor" in gentry terms. A wealthy 3,000 nobles possessed five hundred or more souls. Great families like the Sheremetevs, Yusupovs, and Stroganovs owned thousands of serfs, vast tracts of land, multiple estates, and palaces in Moscow or St. Petersburg. Rank, wealth, and court connections counted toward status more than pedigree or such titles as count(ess) or prince(ss), which were legion. High military and civil ranks carried great prestige and were marked by codes of grooming, costume, language, and by various amenities—down to the number of horses one's carriage could command at post stations. Courtiers and most top officials had to speak French and Russian.

The gentry were too divided ethnically and in other ways to transform themselves into a political force as in other parts of Europe. Also, landowners experienced an economic decline after the Napoleonic onslaught, from which some never recovered. About a third of the estates were mortgaged to the state. Even so, it is accurate to speak of an "aristocratic century" from the 1760s to the 1850s, a period that witnessed a magnificent flowering of gentry culture. Nobles, free to retire to their estates, held a near-monopoly of serf owning, and the wealthy ones created their own peculiar cultural worlds.

Life as a Landowner

Certain features of estate life were fairly common: winter in the capitals and summer on the estate, mutual visits, and home entertainment often featuring the legendary Russian hospitality. Winter rides by troika (a three-horse sleigh), the autumn hunt, and town balls dotted the seasons. Gentry manors formed an archipelago of culture—the piano and the library being emblems of European civilization in the wilderness of steppe and woods. In novels of the time, young folks often spun dreams—elaborate ideologies or pictures of personal fulfillment. Rural mansions nursed some of the intelligentsia's earliest aspirations and discontents. Students returned from Russian or German universities, their heads swimming with romantic philosophies to argue with their elders about values and the meaning of life. The all-night discussions of student rooms were transferred to the countryside. Here also were ignited the early stirrings of gentry girls, entranced by reading or by the ethereal talk of the young men. Some gentry wives, especially those in a loveless bond, wondered if they could take a larger place in the world. Women's letters, diaries, and novels of the time breathe the spirit of disillusionment and hope, a vague striving for something to create more meaning in their lives.

In the manorial economy, serfs either worked the lords' land as *barshchina* (unpaid labor) or paid them a fee called *obrok* (quitrent) in cash, kind, or both. The estate was run by stewards, who could be serfs, ex-serfs, ex-soldiers, or foreigners. Great magnates had agents in the capitals who oversaw far-flung properties. Operating between the lord's demands and peasant abilities to pay, the steward collected dues, oversaw field hands, and sometimes intervened in village life to curb drunkenness and foster early marriage in order to increase the estate's serf population. Inefficient and dishonest stewards could bring ruin to absentee landowners.

Many landowners brought the ruin on themselves. Afflicted by lavish spending habits, they fell into debt and mortgaged their lands. A contemporary spoke of their "luxurious tastes and excessive prodigality." Literature and drama constantly satirized the gentry's passion for expensive foreign goods. Gambling—vividly described by Pushkin and Dostoevsky—was a social diversion for many nobles that could lead them to wager away serfs or to bring their own families to financial disaster. Low productivity in some areas allowed small estates to be bought out by bigger ones—or by outsiders. Growth of the market and nongentry land owning as well as a slow rise in factory production furthered the erosion of the old agrarian order.

A few enterprising gentry, called improving landlords, eagerly devoured European agricultural journals and tried to emulate Western methods. The Free Economic Society promoted chemical fertilizer and machinery. With branches in scores of provincial towns by the 1840s, it sponsored fairs attended by landlords in search of magical or rational paths to fiscal salvation. Successful innovators became rich, or at least retained their ancestral seats, as they marketed their grain southward to Odessa for export. But most fell victim to their own helplessness and naiveté, their stewards' swindles, or the resistance of the peasants to newfangled devices. The haplessness of such experiments was captured in the writer Lev Tolstoy's 1856 semiautobiographical story "Morning of a Landowner"—an account of how his efforts to modernize the estate and improve peasant welfare met opposition from the very people he wished to help. Peasants feared machines and often destroyed them, by design or by careless handling. The innovating noble's reverence for science and technology was not always matched by understanding either of the technology or of the peasant mentality. Such lords were mercilessly mocked in fiction and on the stage.

Great cultural riches could be found in luxurious rural manor houses where, amid parks and formal gardens, residents spoke foreign languages and were served by a legion of house serfs dressed in livery. Some estates were seats of literary culture, monuments of architectural and landscape wizardry, and centers of artistic, musical, and theatrical creativity. Trained serf artists, actors, singers, musicians, and architects added to the grandeur. Great lords maintained serf theaters for their own and their guests' diversion. Serf musicians played the staples of classical chamber and dance music from Germany and Italy. Some unfree performers suffered the agony of exposure to a world of refined tastes combined with the shackling of their talent. On a whim, their owner could return an actor or violinist to the plow or the pantry. Too many lords wielded untrammeled power over their human charges in ostentatiously gargantuan entertainments where, for the amusement of guests, costumed serfs were forced to stand for hours like statues in the estate park—or where young serf ballerinas stripped before the audience in a serf theater. On the other hand, a number of serf artists won their freedom and went on to eminent careers. Landowners often seduced female house serfs, and a few even kept harems. Since legal redress against abuse was weak, peasants sometimes acted on their own and murdered their master.

Luxury and abuse were not the norm. Numerous landowners lived modest lives in the countryside, mixed little with their betters, and retained a thin cultural façade—a scatter of books and journals and fluency in French. Some middle and poor nobles, obsessed by the honor of class, pathetically imitated the grand mansions by nailing up four Doric columns and a classical pediment to their unsightly wooden cabins. Memoirs, paintings, and novels have left touching portraits of simple gentry wives fussing with the servants, older unmarried women playing solitaire and making prophecies, and inert lords sitting out a languid existence at the window. Members of the lowest level of the gentry were almost undistinguishable from their peasants. A few converted their houses into drunken dens or brothels and squandered their patrimony in a life of debauchery, often with a flourish of grandiose generosity. Young army retirees in particular offered their wine cellars for the brutish pleasure of comrades. Some hosts, so dissolute that they could attract no guests, would kidnap travelers and force them to share their festivities and drunken orgies.

ON THE LAND: LIVE SOULS

Nikolai Gogol in his novel *Dead Souls* used the term for male serfs ("souls") as it was used in law—as units of sale, taxation, and even collateral on loans around which his story turns. But the title has often been used to picture serfdom as a land of the living dead, of people so exploited that they no longer functioned in mind or spirit. Some serf owners and other nonpeasants did look at serfs as less than human, just as others romanticized them. But peasant life—in or out of serfdom—possessed great diversity and vitality even in the midst of its servitude and poverty.

Serfdom

The enserfment of once-free peasants had taken place gradually in the sixteenth and seventeenth centuries. In the eighteenth century, Empress Catherine II had granted large tracts of crown, monastic, and state lands and their populations to noble families, thus transforming many more peasants into serfs. The main features of serfdom persisted: unfree labor and a network of obligations and relationships to state, lord, other villagers, and family members. The state seldom impinged directly on the village except to take military recruits, enforce a law, or collect taxes when needed. "God is in heaven and the tsar is far away," the peasant saying went. Peasants distrusted the state and its agents but nourished a firm belief in the benevolence of the monarch. No general uprising occurred between the Pugachëv Rebellion of

1773–1774 and 1905. And yet it was precisely the state and the tsar that kept peasants enserfed: Tsar Nicholas abhorred landowners' abuse of serfs, but he also denied them education and social mobility. The state also exercised one of the cruelest measures in peasant life, military recruitment into the standing army—normally for a twenty-five year term—an event that effectively terminated village and family existence for the young draftee. Recruitment evoked as much sorrow and lamentation as a funeral.

Peasants addressed their masters deferentially as *barin* (lord) and *barynya* (lady). Owners had little contact with peasants: business was conducted through the steward. Punishment and abuse have captured much attention—and rightly so: the lord could routinely have peasants of either sex publicly flogged, assigned unpleasant labor, exiled, or—if male—drafted. An especially shaming punishment was shaving off the beard—held sacred by Orthodox peasant men. Abusively but not illegally, peasants could be squeezed for excessive quitrent or labor. The three-day suggested limit on *barshchina* (unpaid labor) from Tsar Paul's time was not enforced. Largely immune from prosecution also were those lords who forced serf marriages or who advertised, rented, sold, auctioned, and gambled their serfs away. Sale of serfs without land, and breaking up families with such sales, were practiced up to 1861. In the rare instances of torture and murder, local authorities intervened and punished the culprits.

Not all master-peasant relations were marked by mistreatment and resistance. Statistical studies suggest that, in terms of diet and relative autonomy in their work, Russian serfs actually lived better than some industrial workers elsewhere in Europe—and certainly better than New World plantation slaves, except for mortality rates. Quitrent was preferable to unpaid labor, and state peasant life was for the most part preferable to serfdom. Serf artisans, seasonal workers, and entrepreneurs, though technically bonded, possessed much effective freedom and mobility. Some conducted regular businesses, and a few even became millionaires while continuing to pay quitrent from their fortunes.

Nevertheless, serfs resisted their lot at many levels. Flight was one, but it was hazardous because police were alert to strangers to their locales, and it was severely punished. Revolt was more serious and took many forms: collective disobedience, arson, murder of the lord, or invasion of gentry property. Under Alexander I (r. 1801–1825), some 281 disorders were reported; under Nicholas I (r. 1825–1855), 556, some of them rather minor and local, motivated by vengeance, increased obligations, or rumors of emancipation. Everyday resistance was more common: small-scale theft, poaching, rent strikes, timber cutting, sabotage, and self-mutilation by recruits who would render themselves unfit for service by chopping off a toe. Peasants routinely availed themselves of the less obvious "weapons of the weak": slowdown, absenteeism, malingering. These forms of resistance were hardest to deal with, and peasants often used them in full measure, to the distress of steward and landowner. Alternating with extreme deference and "silent obedience," peasant resistance was not heroic in scale or motivated by ideas but rather rooted in survival.

The *mir,* or commune, the formal arena of interaction for both serfs and state peasants, met usually on Sundays in open-air meetings where heads of households elected an elder for three years. This gathering of largely old and middle-aged men and a few widow householders impressed outsiders in different ways: as embryonic democracy and socialism; as drunken anarchy; or as collective tyranny. Of friction, noise, and dissension there was much; but in the end a consensus was accepted by the community (if sometimes achieved by threats or bribes). The *mir* held the village together in the face of the outer world. Periodically, it divided plowland according to roughly equitable portions, reflecting a conviction that all must live and all must share the impositions of lord and state. "A thread from the *mir* becomes a shirt for the naked" went a Russian proverb. Though subject to wide variations in size and format, the peasant commune was the preeminent institution of the agrarian population in Russia beyond the family.

Village Life

The focus of community life was the church. Though Orthodoxy prevailed among Russians, much discord arose between popular devotion and the institutional church, whose hierarchy waged an unending struggle against unapproved religious practices, icons and saints, and "superstitions" such as charms and enchantments—in other words against constantly evolving "folk religion" containing vestiges of pagan faith. The church fought against worldly behavior such as nonobservance of the sacraments, unsanctified marriage, and excessive drink and rowdiness—including fights and the hysterical outbursts of females, known as shrieking, inside the church. Secular crimes—theft, murder, flight, and draft evasion—were taken to the landowner or the courts. But peasants also practiced village justice. Outsiders who violated customary laws were often treated with great ferocity: in some locales, horse thieves were roasted alive.

An extended patriarchal family, the nucleus of peasant life, dwelt in a cabin wreathed in smoke and the pungent odors of resident livestock, with poor light, abundant roaches, and minimal furniture—a bench lining the wall, a table, a stove atop which the grandmother would usually sleep for warmth, the icon corner—and very little privacy. As boss of the labor and sexual activity of this household, the eldest male assigned tasks, granted seasonal leave to work in town or mill, and approved marriages. He could enforce discipline with shouts and the fist. Field strips at planting and harvest were assigned to husband-and-wife teams (thus the choice of a wife was based on the unromantic principle of hardiness and potential fertility). Women saw to the livestock and performed routine household chores and child rearing. In the "suffering season" of July and August in central Russia, everyone toiled at the harvest from dawn to dusk. Family tensions were mostly generational and gender based: father-son arguments over work; petty persecution by the mother of the daughter-in-law; and the father's flirtation with—or, in rare cases, seduction of—a daughter-in-law. This practice could arise when a young married son was taken to the army, leaving his teenaged bride without a mate in the household.

In the peasant world, the *muzhik,* or peasant man, was seen as dignified and empowered, the *baba,* or woman, as unreliable, sharp tongued, and hysterical. Witchcraft and village arson were associated with women in peasant perception (burning the lord's property was more often a male activity). Peasant women were often mishandled by their husbands and suffered through multiple childbearing in the absence of modern medicine. Victimized women sometimes personalized the problem by accusing an enemy of witchery, burning a house down, or committing murder. The vast majority of peasant women lived orderly lives and served as the emotional centers of the household. They also stood beside or in front of their husbands in moments of peasant resistance against the raising of quitrent or other abuses by steward, state, or lord.

Repression, backbreaking labor, and mutual antagonism did not make up all of village life under serfdom. Baptisms and wedding feasts bathed in religious liturgy and adorned by ancient folk practices regularly brightened the peasant world. The wedding was preceded by weeks of matchmaking, the binding of the bride's hair, and customary laments about the loss of youth and freedom. A grand feast attended the ceremony. In some regions a bloodstained sheet was waved from the nuptial room as proof of the bride's premarital virginity. In wedding and other celebrations, abundant food, alcohol, song, and dance extended the conviviality for

Idyllic scene, idealized peasant. *Tretyakov Gallery, Moscow, Russia/Art Resource, NY.*

days. The culture of folk tale, drama, dance, and song flourished across the land, as did particular building styles and folk crafts and art. Although the values embedded in folklore—honesty, thrift, hospitality, sobriety, and hard work—were not always reflected in peasant practices, they remained as permanent ideals, as did family and village survival.

Serfs regularly cheated the lord and sometimes each other, drank to excess, and lost work time. Exploitation was embedded in the system. Life in some villages was, to quote a modern scholar, "hostile, violent, vengeful, quarrelsome, fearful, and vituperative." Serfs were in a sense colonial subjects in their own land, surrounded by lord, state, property laws, and church canons, ruled over by those who often spoke and acted in foreign ways. But peasants were also skilled and wily people, able to perform titanic labors, organize complex and elaborate festivities, and deliver rich and pungent conversational narratives in the popular language. Until the 1850s, playwrights generally presented peasants as comic figures, and painters sentimentalized them in pastoral paintings. From the 1840s onward, conservatives and Slavophiles often romanticized them as a happy, godly, and loyal folk; radicals saw them as embryonic socialists (see the chapter "Nicolas I: Monarchy, Society, Empire, 1825–1855").

Other Rural Dwellers

Household serfs—about 6 percent of the total in 1857—ranged from scullery maids, butlers, valets, and coachmen to trained musicians, actors, and painters. Their treatment depended greatly on the family who owned them: in big manors with numerous servants, house serfs, though seldom overworked, were nevertheless at the beck and call of lord and mistress. State peasants generally inhabited poorer lands, especially in the north, southwest, and Siberia. In the relative absence of landowners, the state taxed and recruited state peasants into the army directly and assigned some to specialized services: forestry, shipbuilding, and postal roads. Differentiated also in status and lifestyle, state peasants numbered in 1854 about 27 million, as opposed to 23 million serfs. State peasants were free from the oppression of landowners. Although the reforms of the 1830s (see the chapter "Nicolas I: Monarchy, Society, Empire, 1825–1855") made some improvement in local administration, much of the everyday life, family affairs, and village relations of state peasants resembled those of the serfs.

A key element of the rural scene was the white clergy, or parish priests. In the seminaries run by the monastic black clergy, future pastors received a rather impractical and unimaginative training in a socially unhealthy atmosphere replete with physical punishment. Some of the more bookish, idealistic, rebellious, or ambitious priests' sons turned to other professions or became prominent radicals in the 1860s. The peculiar and bumpy life of Russian Orthodox village priests—all married—put them in close touch with everyday peasant existence. The average priest ministered to fourteen hundred parishioners. But as a rule, the rural clergy did not enjoy the veneration or deference that it did in some other societies. As a reform-minded Russian priest despairingly put it in 1858, "Everywhere, from the most resplendent drawing rooms to smoky peasant huts, people disparage the clergy with the most vicious mockery, with words of the most profound scorn and infinite disgust." Scorned by landowners and merchants, priests were also subject to periodic harassment from the hierarchy that was dominated by the black clergy. Nor did the *batyushka,* as parishioners called their priest, rank high with them. Receiving no salary, the village priest had to live by cultivating the land, supplemented by irregular fees for ecclesiastical services. He resembled the peasant in all but the priestly function and the ability to read, and he was regularly depicted in folklore as a greedy, drunken, rowdy, and lusty figure.

The Old Believers, schismatics who had broken away from the official church in the seventeenth century and been subject to brutal persecution and isolation, had partly come to terms with the state by the nineteenth century, though they were periodically harassed and were not legally tolerated until 1905. Grouped in communities in the far north, the Volga provinces, Moscow, Tver, Kostroma, the Urals, the north Caucasus, and Siberia, they were overwhelmingly peasants, with an important element of merchants, townsfolk, and the frontier-based cavalry troops known as Cossacks. Estimates of their numbers run as high as 40 percent of the Russian peasant population. The "priestless" Old Believers were enmeshed in dilemmas about clergy, sacraments, marriage, celibacy, and sex. Those who splintered into groups such as the Wanderers and the Sighers rejected the state as the Antichrist and withdrew from society. About 2 million Sectarians—not schismatics but totally outside the Orthodox fold—provoked the state to anger with their radical ways. Dukhobors, or Strugglers with the Spirit, served in the tsar's army but would not fight. Milk Drinkers and their offshoots adopted some Jewish dietary habits, beliefs, and rituals. Most pernicious of all in the eyes of church and government were the Flagellants, known for wild dancing of religious ecstasy, and the Self-Castrators, who strove for celibacy and achieved it by means of the practice described in their name.

The peacetime army of recruited peasants was a variant of serfdom in uniform, but much harsher. Bivouacked in summer and billeted in peasant homes in winter, soldiers hated the peacetime routine of drill and inspection more than campaigning. Discipline was severe: physical punishment included running the gauntlet—walking slowly between ranks of soldiers delivering hundreds of blows with sticks. The relationship between soldier and officer was one of extreme submission, and commanders also frequently pocketed funds meant for provisions. Such things were common elsewhere in that age, but in Russia the habits of serfdom reinforced them. Aside from the hazards of combat, soldiers were subject to death by communicable disease on a massive scale that carried off as many as half the combatants in some wars. The mortality rate in the Russian army was twice that of the rest of Europe, owing to cholera and other afflictions and a serious lack of medical facilities. Between 1825 and 1850, the Russian army suffered 30,000 battlefield deaths and 300,000 from disease.

THE BIG CITY: RICH FOLK, POOR FOLK

Moscow and St. Petersburg were called the two capitals, though the older city had long ceded the title to the City of Peter. The dual character of St. Petersburg—its breathtaking magnificence and its forbidding monumentality—was immortalized in Pushkin's great poem *The Bronze Horseman* (1833). Moscow, on the other hand was a sprawling huddle of tradition, once described by Gogol as a beard. Both contained Russian and European facets, people of all classes, wealthy aristocrats, and fetid slums. But St. Petersburg remained the symbol of planned magnificence and European aristocratic culture.

The Beau Monde

High life in this glorious capital revolved around the highly theatricalized military review, court ceremony, and aristocratic social whirl. The emperors' obsession with geometric formations peaked under Nicholas I. Parades, changing of the guards, and mounted escorts did indeed give the capital the appearance of an encampment. An officer's career could turn on the execution of a review parade. Flamboyant uniforms, metallic helmets, and lances glistened in the sun as horse patrols trotted along the ruler-straight prospects. A French visitor dubbed St. Petersburg a "military camp converted to a town" and the Russian poet Apollon Grigorev called it a "splendid city of slaves / Of barracks, bordellos, and palaces." The rigid hierarchy, the color, and the iron protocols of military life were mirrored in the orchestrated court balls held in the enormous eleven-hundred-room Winter Palace. Hundreds of courtiers, officers, diplomats, and high officials and their ladies mingled with the princes of Georgia, Tatar khans, and Finnish and German aides-de-camp. All bowed low to the emperor on his appearance and whirled to a strictly organized dance series of polonaises, mazurkas, and waltzes.

High society followed suit. Prominent Petersburgers knew each other's "place" with unerring accuracy. In salons, wits and gossips held forth in nimble conversation—usually in French. Society balls emulated the court style, and some grandees could almost match the tsar in sheer opulence: halls decked with fresh flowers from the Crimea, oysters and champagne from France, and serf orchestras. Gala affairs in Moscow, Odessa, Warsaw, Kiev, Helsinki, and other centers were local variants of the St. Petersburg style. In these venues, women were valued for their beauty, charm, clever conversation, and skills in social intercourse. The ball functioned as a brokerage of ambition, politics, flirtation, and matchmaking. Russian dandies successfully imitated those of London and Paris, whose intricate costumes, lisping speech, and balletic movements underlined their utter alienation from work of any kind. In a bitter verse of 1840, the poet Lermontov wrote: "Midst music and amusement's tension / Midst empty phrases learn'd by heart / Men's heartless faces gleam and dart / Those masks contorted by convention."

Portrait of Aristocratic woman. *Tretyakov Gallery, Moscow/Dagli Orti/The Art Archive.*

Kingdoms of Darkness and Light

Moscow, with a very different visage, revealed antiquity at every corner of its twisted streets, at the Kremlin, and in the gleaming gold and azure domes of its hundreds of Orthodox churches. Moscow reeked of piety, tradition, and commerce in a way that its younger sibling did not. An 1833 guidebook spoke of its "rustic simplicity and pleasantness," where there is "fresher air, cleaner and healthier than in other European cities." In this city of about a third of a million people in 1840, the marketplace, not the parade ground, defined street life. At midcentury, thousands of businessmen and women plied their trade as vendors in outdoor bazaars, in trade rows—covered stalls and galleries—and in about forty triweekly open-air markets, in addition to temporary fairs. There was even a Thieves' Market, where one could purchase stolen goods. The petty bazaar retailers were especially notorious for sharp practices that darkened the image of the entire estate of merchants among the rest of the population. Peasants in particular saw merchants as stingy and dishonest. In addition to these traditional sites, where quick sales prevailed, foreigners ran shops and arcades with permanent clienteles. The big Russian merchants traded over a broad terrain, buying on notes, insuring, and shipping goods from one end of Russia to another and to Asia. Some rich merchants aspired to gentry status, and lucky ones like the Stroganov family had gained very high social status because of their wealth. But trade was risky, and fortunes waxed and waned rapidly, especially after 1812, partly because of competition from other classes. To fall out of the merchant guild was to become liable for military service and other obligations. With the increase of machinery production in Russia in the early nineteenth century, merchants turned to manufacturing as well.

A striking feature of the merchant estate was its large proportion of Old Believers, numbering in the 1840s about sixty thousand in Moscow and another sixty thousand in its province. As with Calvinists and Jews in certain epochs, Old Believers combined piety with entrepreneurial spirit, communal solidarity, and social isolation—though the last was eroding. Almost half the textile industry came into Old Believer hands. Their religious fellowship was reflected in charity and mutual aid. Piety in no way interfered with business; they hired cheap labor, offered each other low-interest loans, and mainly kept their fortunes intact. As a whole, the Old Believer merchantry was known for sobriety, neatness, thrift, punctuality, discipline in life and work, and basic literacy.

Rich merchants, arranged in guilds according to wealth, made up 4 to5 percent of the urban population in 1840. Merchant homes reflected a traditional Russian way of life—dark and cluttered with icons and furniture—though the more expensive ones were adorned with touches of European art. Husbands wore dark double-breasted suits, with beard, hair, and boots in a peasant style. Socially ambitious wives wore modest and heavy but expensive clothes. Family despotism, though rarely physical violence, prevailed; the nonworking wife lorded it over her servants, and the daughters were secluded. Russian merchants and businessmen made little effort to mimic gentry in everyday life, but they did invite their social betters to banquets at the Moscow Merchant Club. The gesture was rarely returned. Merchant couples, usually lacking foreign languages and gentry social skills, did not always fit well at an upper-class evening. Many merchants traveled far and wide; but at home the merchantry remained a partially closed world of family, shop, and business associates, generally wary of broad learning, and still enwrapped in patriarchal, authoritarian, religious, and even clannish mentalities.

Because of the merchantry's style of life and set of values that seemed so traditional to "modern" and European-thinking elements, a negative image had long hovered around Moscow merchants. The debate about this image crystallized in the 1850s in response to a series of plays on merchant life written by Alexander Ostrovsky and staged in Moscow. These dramas highlighted the negative qualities of merchants as cheats, tyrannical bosses and fathers, and narrow-minded philistines. This treatment—though revised in Ostrovsky's later plays—helped reinforce the intelligentsia's hostility to capitalism, business, and lowbrow values. It was canonized in a famous 1859 review of the plays by a radical publicist, Nikolai Dobrolyubov, in which he characterized the world of the merchantry as "a kingdom of darkness" whose inhabitants "become stupefied, lose their power to think and even the will and ability to feel . . . and they vegetate in imbecile impotence." But the dark image was ceding to light via the patronage by Moscow merchants of great works of art and culture. Merchant barons imbibed culture on their expensive trips to Europe. In the 1850s, the merchant P. M. Tretyakov (1832–1898) purchased European and Russian masterpieces; his collections later formed the basis of the world-famous Tretyakov Gallery in Moscow.

Urbanites: Townspeople and Workers

No less maligned by the intelligentsia were the ordinary townspeople who did not belong to the higher estates. Townspeople were taxable but lacked the merchants' privilege or income. They included petty tradesmen, artisans, children of priests, lowly government clerks, and those who fit nowhere else in the juridical order. Together with serfs, they far outnumbered all other town residents and often lived in dingy rooms. If we are to believe the fiction of the period—including Dostoevsky's early works—those who were flung into lower-middle-class destitution because of ill fortune felt its pangs more wrenchingly than those born into it, and they struggled for a sense of identity. Legions of minor clerks were portrayed in literature as impoverished and despised. However, most townspeople suffered no such ambivalence in their lives as porters, dredgers, coachmen, salesclerks, shop assistants, hired servitors of every variety, hawkers and vendors, and petty tradesfolk. It was to this colorful assortment that intellectuals liked to attribute the vice of vulgar taste and behavior.

Russian factory workers were almost all classified as peasants or serfs. Russia was not yet an industrial country: in 1860 the United States had twice the urban population of Russia, produced more than twice as much iron, and had thirty times more railway mileage. The chief Russian industrial centers were the Urals, Moscow, St. Petersburg, and the Baltic. Still, the textile industry grew rapidly, and steam power was being applied. Foreigners, Russian merchants, and even serf entrepreneurs entered the ranks of industry. The number of factories—a loose term—rose from only 1,200 or more to about 3,000 in the years 1800–1860. A " factory" was an enterprise with sixteen or more workers; only 110 could be found in St. Petersburg. Even in the big cities, serfdom, by tying people to the land, kept the factory population low. The industrial labor force—also ill defined—rose from 100,000–200,000 to 500,000–900,000. Factory categories included the manorial factory of the landowner with serfs on unpaid labor; the possessional factory with nonmovable serfs, owned by the state but rented to an industrialist; state enterprises using state peasants; and private establishments hiring "free" labor—that is, freely hired and not ascribed, though in fact the laborers were someone's serfs paying quitrent. Child and female labor was common even on night shifts, and labor legislation was virtually nonexistent.

Factory workers held no property, attended no schools, and lived in substandard housing with little access to medical care or other amenities. Most males had no family life at all, but they mingled with the other lower classes—women at the markets, men in the taverns, and all at the fairs. The government, ambivalent about industrial growth in any case, was anxious about the rise of a permanent proletariat—that is, factory workers—concentrated in the cities, for fear of labor unrest like that afflicting British and French factory towns. State authorities wanted workers to keep their seasonal ties with the village so that Russia would avoid the specter of a huge, poorly paid, and strike-prone working class. Yet the city remained a magnet, and future industrial growth would inevitably foster just such a class.

The Lowest Depths: Poverty, Crime, and Prostitution

Big Russian cities were infested with an "underlife," a shadowy world of slums, pauperdom, and beggary. On streets and church steps, even in affluent districts, one could see the lame and the blind and the hopeless and homeless, figures branded by poverty from birth, temporary lost souls, alcoholics unfit for regular work, orphans, and disabled war veterans. "At Christmastime," complained an alarmed observer in 1831, "you can see more than four hundred male and female beggars every day at both the Kazan Cathedral and the Haymarket Church. The streets of the Vladimir and Coachmen's Districts swarm with women and children." Slums were dense huddles of ramshackle housing, clustered taverns, and festering centers of vice and shabby concourse. Petersburg's Ligovsky Prospect and the sprawling Haymarket, notorious centers of slum life, are described in all their squalor in the grimly realistic novel by Vsevolod Krestovsky, *Petersburg Slums* (1864), and more famously by Dostoevsky in *Crime and Punishment* (1866)—both set in this period. In Moscow's Khitrova Market—a vast hollow of brothels, flophouses, and cellars—the lowest classes victimized mostly each other since they were largely sealed off from the rest of society. Urban crime ranged from "white collar" corruption to brutal murders among all the classes. More common was "hooliganism"—raucous or rowdy behavior in public, barroom brawls, and street fights. Vodka, the natural fuel of disorderly behavior, was available at state-licensed taverns and unofficial bars.

Prostitution stood at the crossroads of alcohol, poverty, and crime. Younger women worked in high-class establishments catering to men with money; the older or less sexually attractive walked the streets—from fancy boulevards to those entwining the haunts of the poor and desperate. About 90 percent of the prostitutes were peasant or lower-class women, including soldiers' wives, servants, and shop girls. Most prostitutes were motivated by economic concerns. Some serf women in the towns used earnings to pay quitrent to their master. Very few shelters existed to take women off the streets and "reclaim" them. State policy until the 1840s ranged from tolerance of red-light zones to periodic bans and deportation—of the prostitutes and their procurers, not the clients. Unofficial practices included blackmail and harassment by the police. In the 1840s, Tsar Nicholas I created a police-managed system of regular medical examinations. The state now licensed brothels and locked women into prostitution with the so-called yellow ticket as an identity document.

THE SMALL TOWN: PROVINCIAL RUSSIA

Old-time Russian provincial life was not limited to gentry estates and peasant villages. Much of it comprised a network—social, economic, and cultural—embracing the urban populace of thousands of small and medium-size towns: geographical and demographic sites of encounter and exchange linked together by rivers and roads. Though often maligned by travelers from the capitals and satirized by writers such as Nikolai Gogol, provincial towns possessed a vibrant life of their own.

Small-Town Life

Russian provincial towns varied immensely: from the ancient fortresses of Smolensk, Novgorod, and Pskov and bustling fair centers like Nizhny Novgorod on the Volga, to the little corners at the back of beyond that hardly differed from villages. Most towns were under fifty thousand, and many were mere administrative centers or garrison towns with undeveloped institutions. In a midsize town, wooden one-storied residences, taverns, and small shops alternated with a few stone structures to house government buildings on the central square, a police station, several churches, a covered market house, and sometimes a hotel. Cows were a common sight, and winter frosts and summer languor lent a tone of inertia. No streetlights guided the footsteps of nocturnal pedestrians. A town could contain officials and quartered troops, gentry landowners, merchants and ordinary townspeople, servants and serfs, priests, clerks, tavern keepers, and perhaps even a lonely political exile sent out from Moscow or Petersburg by the government to rot in provincial wretchedness. Males were visibly divided into the clean-shaven (gentry, officials, and foreigners) and the bearded. Most entertainment was largely segregated by class, and people of similar stations tended to flock together.

Larger provincial centers boasted a theater in which touring companies would perform translations or adaptations of foreign tragedies and comedies—including Shakespeare—melodramas, ballets, operas, and vaudevilles. Under Tsar Nicholas, Russian works became more prominent. Merchants and townspeople dominated the audience and expected to see Russian themes and to hear actors talk in plain language, not in the declamatory accents of the neoclassical stage. Realism in Russian culture to some extent was shaped by the towns and the provinces: training grounds for actors and sites of everyday life as reflected in the emerging naturalist styles of painting, theater, and fiction. At the Noble Assembly or gentry club—a center of local politics, entertainment, and upper class sociability—one could seek invitations, advantageous appointments, and available marriage partners. The ball loomed large in the life of the local gentry. It was preceded by the flutter of choosing gowns, primping, and speculation about dance partners. Once there, the young people danced modestly as their elders talked or played cards after a few rounds on the floor. Festivities, lasting well into the next morning in this public space between home life and official service, dissolved the ranks slightly and afforded women a greater range of social intercourse. Governors and marshals of nobility were hubs of provincial society, their wives often rivaling each other to preside over the more glittering balls or charity benefits. The gentry officers of the garrison, bored stiff on peacetime duty, turned to hunting, cards, billiards, drink, duels, and the provincial ball.

What kind of public life did the other social classes have in a provincial town? The lower and middle classes peopled the streets and squares, market stalls, taverns, and bathhouses (for the regular weekly bath). The market served as a recreational area as well as a commercial zone, a place where crowds of mostly women bargained and gossiped. In taverns, male adults sought tea or alcoholic beverages, conversation, sociability, and escape from work and family. Taverns were also staging areas for drunk and disorderly conduct. The church was the main gathering point for families of all classes. Since everyone usually stood throughout the three-hour service, there were no special pews. Yet social and gender differences existed in placement, costume, and even modes of devotion: the common people bowed to the ground; others showed more reserve. The church was the physical symbol of the official state view that all Orthodox people shared a spiritual unity. Yet beliefs and practices were by no means uniform. Although the religious skepticism fashionable among the upper classes before 1812 had declined markedly, it could be still be found in educated circles; the lower and middle classes tended to be more devout and also more prone to folk belief.

Another space where townspeople could mix was the great outdoors—churchyards, streets, and squares. Garrison units in gaudy uniforms turned the parade ground into an open-air theater with highly choreographed drills. The calendar of public life revolved around church seasons and holidays—Advent, Lent, and feast days. Townspeople marched in the frequent church processions through the town or around the walls. Elaborate folk festivals at holiday time featured minstrels and puppet shows, cavorting on swings, dancing and singing, eating and drinking, and wall-to-wall fist fighting. On bright winter feast days resounding with church bells, when gentry families arrived in sleighs and the town poured out of doors, social mixing reached a high—though temporary—level. There could be no regularized social intercourse of all classes, not only because of serfdom, but because the whole society was built on deference and hierarchy reinforced by vastly diverging cultural levels. People were divided not only by rank, income, housing, and attire but by language, diction, and speech patterns. In public, lower classes tended to be garrulous, colorful, humorous, and more emotionally expressive than their masters, who were sometimes constrained by the conventions of polite society.

On the Road

In this era, the common way to travel was by road and river. Winter journeying on troikas was fast but often perilous, and spring mud hindered wheel traffic. In the 1820s, it took ten days for the mail coach to get from St. Petersburg to Kiev. By the 1830s, a regular passenger stagecoach service connected the large cities of European Russia. In spite of Nicholas I's hard-surface road-building campaigns using convict labor, during the Crimean War of 1854–1856 it took months for supply convoys to reach the front by road from Moscow. "The road [is] to the Russian, in many respects, what the sea is to the Englishman," wrote an English traveler at midcentury. Over the immensity of Russia people moved continuously: regiments, couriers, officials, merchants, theater troupes, religious pilgrims, and peasants off to trade or find work. Gentry families with entourage and baggage moved seasonally, often with bedding and food. All manner of winter sledges and two- and four-wheeled vehicles—some called bone breakers and soul shakers—hauled people over huge distances. One could recognize people's identity by the vehicle they traveled in: the posted officer on a military stage coach, the Ukrainian grain hauler on an oxcart, or a caravan of elite carriages with footmen in livery. Songs, stories, and conversations lightened the tedium of the journeys, which themselves inspired "road tales" and coachmen songs.

Rivers allowed navigation over a large stretch of European Russia, and in 1815 the first steamship sailed the Neva River. When steam traffic on the Volga—Europe's longest river—began in the 1820s, its role as a major artery of Russian commerce increased dramatically, although the famous barge haulers continued their back-breaking labors and caught the fancy of songwriters and painters. The annual fair at Nizhny Novgorod on the Volga—the largest of thousands—drew a constant flow of people in pursuit of profit or temporary work: shipping cotton to China; unloading tea from Asia; and selling Tula housewares, Tatar sheepskins, and a wide array of other goods. European, Russian, Tatar, Armenian, and Persian merchants jostled one another in Nizhny Novgorod's huge squares and bazaars, their business enlivened by nearby restaurants and taverns. Elsewhere, road and waterway combined to move grain from the fertile Ukraine by cart and barge to Odessa and hence on ships across the Black Sea through the Straits to world markets. The telegraph and the railway arrived slowly, the first not until 1856. The first passenger railway from the capital to nearby Tsarskoe Selo and Pavlovsk opened in 1837. The St. Petersburg–Moscow line was completed in 1851. By then only three thousand miles of track had been laid—none to the Black Sea, a major factor in the Crimean disaster.

A familiar feature of Russian provincial life were the "wanderers on the Russian land"—beggars, peddlers, bandits, gypsies, vagabond monks, sectarians, and holy men and women. Certain shrines could pull in tens of thousands of pilgrims of all classes each year. "Holy fools" enjoyed a long tradition of veneration. Piously renouncing the world, they displayed elements of insanity, wisdom, eccentric behavior, selflessness, and a gift of prophecy—thus reflecting and replicating popular notions of religiosity and helping spread piety and folk culture. Along with certain monks of repute, holy men and women were revered by peasants and upper classes alike. Bandits had to be rounded up and arrested; but the other wanderers were also bothersome to the state and added to the fear, in some quarters, of the huge population that would be set loose if serfs were emancipated without land. Saddest of all among the many sights of itinerants tramping toward distant horizons was the nameless columns of convicts making the long trek to Siberia. Social rank counted even in prison convoys: nobles rode, and others walked, from one holding prison to another, making their way in all seasons across the vastness of Russia to the ends of the earth—many of them never to return again to their villages, provinces, hometowns, or university classrooms.

Russian society, though still based on serfdom with all its inequalities and abuses, its stultifying distinctions, and its psychologically harmful practices—to say nothing of its braking effect on economic modernization—was a complex organism in this era. But the Russian Empire was much more than Russia—it was a colossal patchwork embracing a multitude of other nationalities.

CHAPTER 20

Around the Russian Empire, 1801–1861

The ninth part of the inhabited earth, almost the ninth part of all mankind! . . . Yet the size of the land, the numbers of people, are not the only conditions of strength. Russia is a country that contains all kinds of soil, all climates, from the hottest to the coldest, from the scorched land around Erivan [in Armenia] to icy Lapland.
— *Mikhail Pogodin, "Letter on Russian History," 1837*

Within the Russian Empire—inhabited in its corners by Lutheran Finns, Orthodox Jews, Muslim mountaineers, and animist Siberians—lived well over a hundred other ethnic groups in a state encompassing more land than any in the world. Stretching from the Black and Baltic Seas to the Pacific Ocean, the empire was not just a collection of peoples and regions with discrete languages and cultures all bound together in a geopolitical knot. Nor was it a system of far-flung overseas colonies. In some places, such as Central Asia, it did indeed resemble certain colonial empires with their forts and mounted troops in pursuit of tribesmen. But in the western parts of the Romanov territories stood opera houses, synagogues, and well-established universities. Towns, villages, and marketplaces in the borderlands buzzed in a half-dozen tongues. Russia was a multinational empire dominated by Russians, who used other ethnic groups in conquest and governance. The tsarist army, officialdom, and privileged orders were replete with names of Russian, Tatar, Baltic German, Ukrainian, Georgian, and other nobles. Relations between the power center in St. Petersburg and the outer lands ranged from peaceful and mutually beneficial intercourse—as in Finland—to periodic upheavals—as in Poland—to near permanent warfare—as in the Caucasus Mountains. Despite Nicholas I's obsession with uniformity, the empire remained a patchwork of territories of varying stages of development, strategic importance, cultural and religious affiliations, and distance from the capital. That they were joined to the Russian Empire at different moments of its and their own history helps explain the striking differences from region to region.

ARCTIC OCEAN
Kara Sea
Novaya Zemlya Is.
Novo Sibirsk Is. 1770–1806
Wrangel Is.
ALASKA
Port Alexander
CHUKCHI
Bering Sea
Aleutian Islands
KAMCHATKA
Petroplavlovsk Kamchatsky
PACIFIC OCEAN
Kurile Islands
Sea of Okhotsk
Sakhalin 1853
Okhotsk
YAKUTS
Yakutsk
Lena
TUNGUSES
Enisei
Ob
Irtysh
Verkhoyansk
Lake Baikal
Irkutsk
Krasnoyarsk
Shushenskoe
Tomsk
Omsk
Nikolaevsk
AMUR 1858
Amur
Khabarovsk
USSURI 1860
Vladivostok
Sea of Japan
JAPAN
KOREA
Port Arthur
Harbin
Beijing
MONGOLIA
CHINA
TIBET
BRITISH INDIA
AFGHANISTAN
TAJIKS
KIRGIZ (KAZAKHS)
Lake Balkhash
KAZAKH KHANATES 1734–1854
Kazalinsk
Aral Sea
UZBEKS
TURKMENS
Ashkhabad
Bukhara
Tashkent
Merv
Samarkand
PERSIA
Caspian Sea
Ural
Astrakhan
GEORGIA 1801
OTTOMAN EMPIRE
Black Sea
CRIMEA
Istanbul
Sevastopol
Rostov
Volga
Samara
Ekaterinburg
Nizhny Novgorod
Ekaterinoslav
Odessa
Nikolaev
Kiev
BESSARABIA 1812
Don
Dnieper
Moscow
Arkhangelsk
St. Petersburg
Riga
Minsk
Warsaw
POLAND 1815
HAPSBURG EMPIRE (AUSTRIA)
THE GERMAN STATES
SWEDEN
FINLAND 1809
OTTOMAN EMPIRE
Mediterranean Sea
0 300 600 Km.
0 300 600 Mi.
International boundaries, 1860
Russian territory, 1800
Acquisitions, by 1860
Jewish Pale of Settlement
Russian campaign, 1853
Anglo-French campaign, 1854
Railroad

The Russian Empire, 1801–1860.

EUROPEAN BORDERLANDS

Finns, Baltic peoples, Poles, Belorussians, Ukrainians, and Jews—though differing greatly in religion and culture—shared a relative proximity to Western Europe. Poland had been an ancient and culturally advanced state, Ukraine a more short-lived one. Both the Finns and the Baltic peoples, though ruled by others, had received certain cultural advantages from those rulers.

Finland

The Finnish-speaking majority of the Grand Duchy of Finland lived for centuries under Sweden's rule and still felt the weight of its cultural and economic dominance. After Finland joined the Russian Empire in 1809 (see the chapter "Russia in the Age of Napoleon: Paul I and Alexander I, 1796–1815"), the Finland Swedes, a small elite whose language and church were officially established, held most of the important positions in Finnish life. Swedish rule had built up a high literacy rate under Lutheran influence, which encouraged Bible reading. The population was mostly engaged in farming and forestry, with very few towns of any size. The new capital, Helsinki (Helsingfors in Swedish), with a population of about sixteen thousand in 1841, emerged as one of the jewels of imperial urban architecture, built around the Senate Square, the cathedral, and the university. In Finland, one of the best-run parts of the Russian Empire, the Swedish-speaking elite ruled largely unchallenged by Russian interference or local discontent. Although the Finnish Diet, or parliament, did not meet until the reign of Alexander II (r. 1855–1881), Finland's law code of 1734—its family rule book and one of the keys to its identity—allowed the Finns extensive autonomy, and the alliance of Finnish elites and Russian officials was a fruitful one.

In this era, the Finns experienced the sweet "discovery" of a national identity through romantic folklore in a movement led by a few intellectuals. Elias Lönnrot (1802–1884) collected Finnish and Karelian folk epics and ballads and wove them into a narrative entitled *The Kalevala* (1835–1849), a landmark in cultural identity and a well of inspiration ever since. J. L. Runeberg (1804–1877) wrote poetry exalting the Finnish land and people. His poem "Our Land," written in Swedish in 1848, became the national anthem. J. V. Snellman (1806–1881) drew on intellectual currents of the time, especially the Grimm brothers, German folk tale collectors who stressed the vital role of folk culture as the vessel of national consciousness. Tsar Nicholas I occasionally evinced displeasure with the Finns: in the 1850s, he cracked down on newspapers and university life, paralleling the repression in Russia after 1848 (see the chapter "Nicholas I: Monarchy, Society, Empire, 1825–1855"). But for the most part, the Finns were left to live their own lives.

The Baltic Lands

It is common to speak of modern Estonia, Latvia, and Lithuania as the Baltic countries. But Catholic Lithuania (though its language is related to Latvian) had its own history of greatness and a long association with Poland and differed greatly from the other two in religion and social structure. What are roughly now Estonia and Latvia were then the provinces of Estland, Courland, and Livonia, with a governor general at Riga. Of their combined population of about 1.5 million, 125,000 were Germans, including the land-owning class and the richer townspeople. Each province possessed ancient rights and a local diet dominated by the Lutheran and German-speaking land-owning barons. Their power was entrenched at home and often enhanced by their frequent service in the tsarist army and administration. The region also possessed a distinguished German University at Dorpat (today Tartu in Estonia). German rule over the Estonian and Latvian peasants was not particularly enlightened—even for those times. The serfs were emancipated but landless and constituted an agrarian proletariat living at the mercy of their former owners. Nevertheless, the establishment of schools and some limited self-government for the general population enabled the two indigenous languages, Estonian and Latvian, to be used in public life for the first time. As in Finland, literacy was relatively high, and Estonian and Latvian teachers and Lutheran pastors founded cultural societies to foster the study of native folklore and historical epics.

The Polish Lands

The historic conglomerate of "Polish" lands in the Russian Empire had two parts: Congress Poland, ethnically compact but with significant urban minorities of Germans and Jews; and the vast area of Lithuania, Belorussia, and western Ukraine, called the western provinces by the Russians and the "occupied lands" by Polish patriots. Having been for centuries part of the Polish-Lithuanian kingdom, but taken by Russia in the partitions of the eighteenth century, they remained arenas of contention. Since during the 1830 revolt (see the chapter "The Age of Restoration: Russia in Europe, 1815–1830") resistance had been vigorous in this region, the Russian government abrogated old rights in the 1830s and 1840s, closed Vilna University and other educational institutions, and set out to impose Russian language and personnel in courts and schools. The Uniate Church—Catholic in allegiance, Orthodox in ritual—had been created with Polish support in the sixteenth century as a way of winning Orthodox Ukrainians to the papacy. In 1839 it was abolished by the Russian state, and troops entered villages to close churches.

Poland proper remained a problem of great magnitude after the Russian army suppressed the 1830 revolution. The Polish constitution of 1815, the diet, and the army were abolished, and the insurgents were dispossessed of land and exiled or drafted into the Russian army. Thousands fled abroad, many of them to Paris, where they nurtured memories of Poland's greatness and visions of its martyrdom and messianic destiny. Patriotic concerts of the Polish-French composer Frédéric

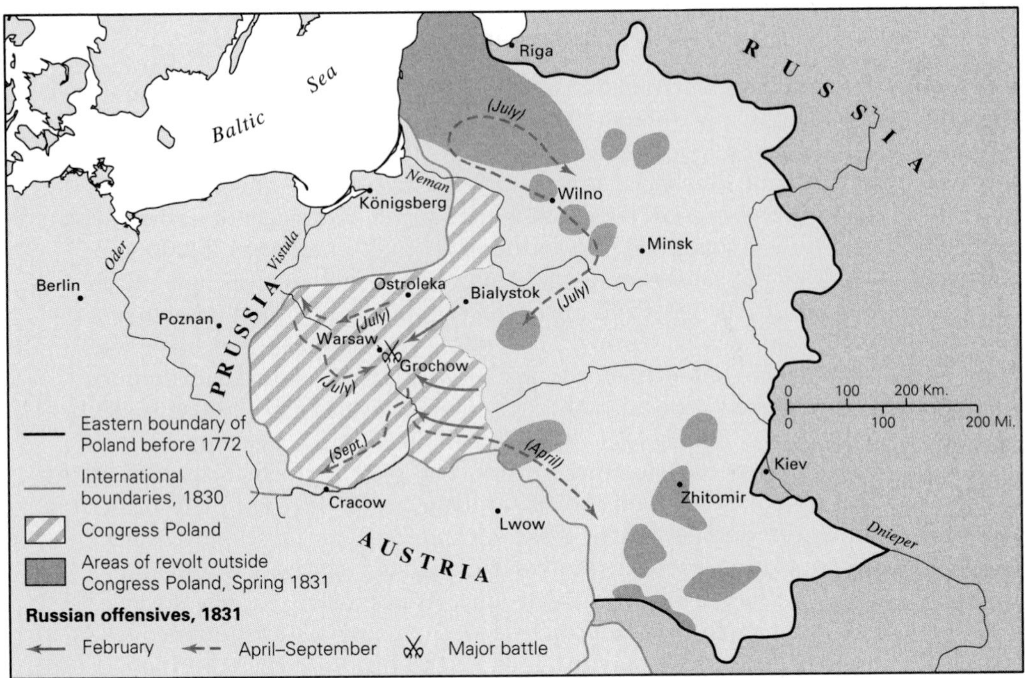

Poland. *From Arthur E. Adams, Ian M. Matley, and William O. McCagg,* Atlas of Russian and East European History. *Reprinted with permission.*

Chopin helped keep alive the Polish cause and win sympathy in Europe, as did the lectures of Poland's greatest poet, Adam Mickiewicz, whose forbidden works were smuggled into Poland for generations. Within Poland, national memory, especially among the upper classes, remained as strong as ever in the decades following 1830. When Warsaw linked up by rail to Vienna in 1848, Poland became host to the latest French and German styles. Poles continued to see themselves as culturally superior to Russians. Conversely, most Orthodox Russians distrusted and even detested the Catholic Poles on religious grounds. Even some intellectuals who were opposed to autocracy at home spoke out against Polish independence.

Ukraine

Ukraine—acquired by Russia in stages in the seventeenth and eighteenth centuries—was a site of peasant disorders, embryonic Polish and Ukrainian nationalism, and Jewish intellectual renaissance. In western, or right-bank, Ukraine (on the right bank of the Dnieper River), relations were strained between Catholic Polish landowners and Orthodox Ukrainian serfs, who unleashed about three hundred cases of disobedience or riot. The movement was one of economic grievances and not a national uprising, either in scope or meaning. The peasants had little or no national consciousness. They spoke only Ukrainian but did not know their language or themselves by that word: they called themselves Orthodox and were known to Russians as Little Russians.

In the multiethnic city of Kiev, the Poles, about 10 percent of the population, eclipsed other nationalities in public life. The upper classes dwelt largely in ethnically self-contained circles. Yet businesses were run jointly by Ukrainians, Russians, Poles, and even Jews, and there was much fluidity among the lower classes. Until 1835, historic rights of autonomy allowed a city militia, local magistrates, and powerful merchant guilds, all celebrated by flags, uniforms, and parades featuring national costumes. In the wake of the Polish rebellion, however, these were curtailed. In 1834, St. Vladimir University was founded, with instruction in Russian, though most of the students—and for a while professors also—were Polish. Polish national unrest was sustained by urban intellectuals. A Polish officer, Symon Konarski (1808–1839), organized local gentry and some students in Kiev and Vilna in the late 1830s in an attempt to spread Polish nationalism. When the authorities discovered the plot, they executed Konarski, closed the university in Kiev for a year, and dismissed suspected students and faculty. The reopened university was further Russianized.

Ukrainian national consciousness was influenced by Polish nationalism. The best-known Ukrainian group, the Cyril and Methodius Society, named for ninth-century missionaries to the Slavs, sought the emancipation of the serfs and the creation of a Pan-Slav federation of free and equal Slavic nations, with Kiev as its capital and Ukraine as a separate state. The society's leaders preached cultural revival and focused on the history of a once independent Ukraine. The best-known figure of the nationalist movement was Taras Shevchenko (1814–1861), born a serf and freed in 1838. He became a painter, poet, folklorist, and musician. His hatred of serfdom and passionate love of the common people was inscribed in poetry that was imbued with a "romantic," nostalgic nationalism inspired by the Ukrainian past. His work became a landmark in the history of Ukrainian self-consciousness.

Shevchenko's group was broken up by the police in 1847, and he spent most of the next decade in prison or exile. But Ukrainian nationalism did not perish with his arrest. His release in 1855 and his funeral in 1861 were major occasions for the display of Ukrainian identity, and Shevchenko was sainted as the national poet. Fear of a Ukrainian revival later led authorities to issue the notorious 1863 ban on publishing textbooks and nonfiction works in Ukrainian, which, because of its closeness to Russian, was declared a dialect rather than a language. But repression only underlined the difference between Ukrainians and Russians for the emerging nationalists.

The Jews

The Jewish people had dwelt amidst their neighbors in Poland, Lithuania, Belorussia, and Ukraine for centuries. After the partitions of Poland in the eighteenth century, most of them ended up in the Russian Empire, where they were confined to the Jewish Pale, an ethnic fence created in the eighteenth century to keep them out of Russia proper. Most Jews lived in shtetls—market towns—surrounded by a web of Russian officials, Polish landowners, and Orthodox, Catholic, and Uniate peasants. The Jews spoke Yiddish, studied Hebrew, and used Slavic tongues with their neighbors. Depending on how and where the laws were enforced, Jewish economic activity embraced the ownership of textile mills, tavern keeping, trade, crafts, smuggling, peddling, and some limited farming. Though the bulk of Jewry lived in abject poverty and their economic life declined under Nicholas I, the success of some Jewish merchants fed envy and hatred among their competitors. Many officials saw Jewish economic activity as "unproductive." Tsar Nicholas I despised Jewish separatism and sought to assimilate their children by a punitive method: seventy thousand Jewish boys were drafted into the army under harsh conditions, including forced conversion and physical mistreatment that caused many deaths. Jewish elders in their local self-governing body, the Kahal, were required to make the recruit selection, a special moral agony for the community.

Prejudice against Jews was rife among peasants as well. The old religious teachings about Jews as killers of Christ at worst and enemies of Christianity at best continued to plague the Jews right up the end of the tsarist empire. Jews also sounded and looked different—with their Yiddish tongue and their caftans, skullcaps, and earlocks—and tended to seal themselves off to avoid corrosion of their faith and culture. Anti-Semitism was also fed by popular anti-intellectualism and gender images. Judaic devotional life was sustained mostly by male scholars, rabbis, teachers,

Jews in Odessa, around 1800. *Hulton Archive/Getty Images.*

and laymen who ran the synagogues and pored over the holy books. To Slavic peasants, where everyday piety was associated with women, the learned men of the Jewish congregations seemed less than masculine, a view reinforced by the tendency among Jews not to partake of liquor publicly. Jews were often owners of taverns but rarely part of their conviviality.

Within the Jewish community a schism arose between tradition and enlightenment. Originating in Germany, the Haskalah (enlightenment)—an intellectual current for modernizing Jewish life—promoted secular study and productive labor, challenged some accepted religious practices, and advocated greater acculturation into the gentile world, but without loss of faith. By midcentury, the Haskalah was being spread through schools, correspondence, and travel in a network that linked Jewish centers like Vilna and Odessa with coreligionists in Berlin and Vienna. Some young radicals took Haskalah beyond speaking Russian or German in public to wearing *goyisch* (gentile) dress, and eating nonkosher foods, drinking vodka, smoking, playing the piano, and studying European science. Conservative rabbis and the pious masses feared the inroads of "European" learning and customs preached by the Haskalah. Hasidic Tsaddiks—mystical teachers and miracle men—distrusted secular learning and also stood to lose influence over their disciples. Some of the Orthodox elders believed that the enlighteners were either working for the tsar or—with more reason—felt they were too optimistic about collaboration with the regime. But the steady rise of enlightenment, and even assimilation, could not be stopped. Entire Jewish families were converting to Russian Orthodox Christianity in order to avoid unfair taxes and the dreadful experience of Jewish boys recruited into the Russian army.

IN AND BEYOND THE CAUCASUS

The word *Caucasus* refers to the spectacular mountain range that runs from the Black Sea to the Caspian Sea, long seen by Russians as the southern divider between Europe and Asia. In Transcaucasia, to the south, lay the Georgian, Armenian, and Azerbaijani lands. The mountains themselves were home to scores of different peoples and languages, and Western terminology for them is notoriously inexact. In the late eighteenth and early nineteenth centuries, the Russians made a remarkable addition to an already diverse empire by annexing Transcaucasia at the cost of several wars with Persia and Turkey. But their conquest of the mountain peoples required a decades-long colonial conflict of epic proportions.

Transcaucasia

Removing Transcaucasia from Persian and Turkish control entailed frightful massacres on both sides. It helped the cause that the Georgians and Armenians, as Christians, preferred Russian rule to the constant menace of their Muslim neighbors. Although Georgian officials served in secondary administrative positions

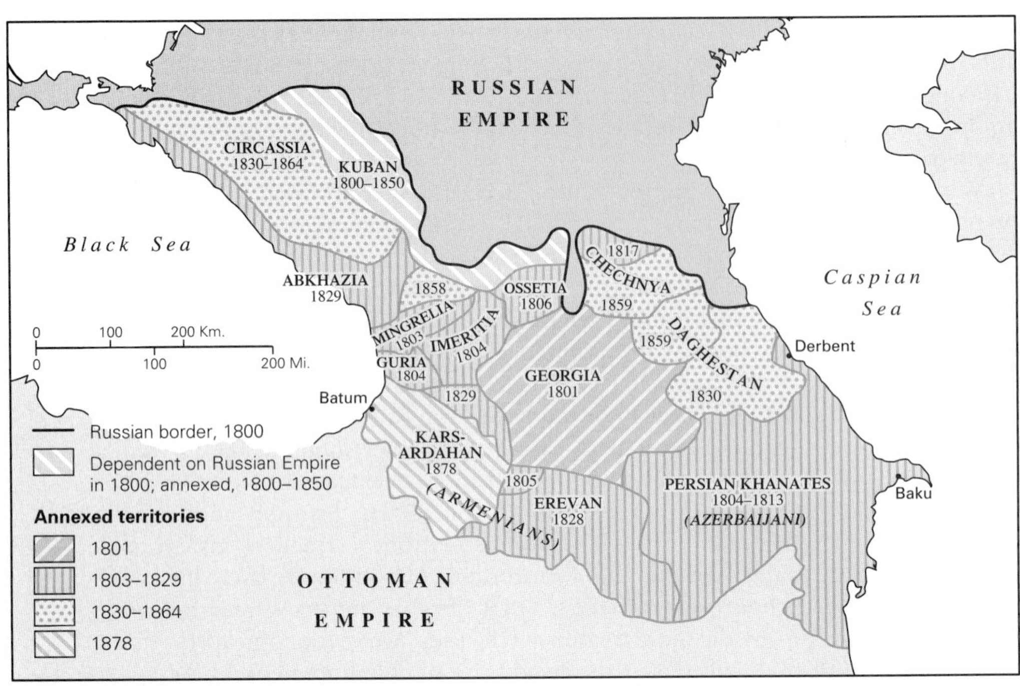

The Caucasus. *From Arthur E. Adams, Ian M. Matley, and William O. McCagg.* Atlas of Russian and East European History. *Reprinted with permission.*

under the new order, power was in Russian hands and was not always wisely used. Certain traditional modes of Georgian corruption were eliminated, but lower-level Russian officials brought in their own brand. As the years proceeded, Russians took a greater share of the administration but did not fulfill Nicholas I's desire to make Georgians and other Caucasians think, talk, and feel Russian. The Georgian Orthodox Church was joined to the Russian Orthodox Church but retained its head, the Catholicos. Georgia was feudal in the true sense of the word—with degrees of bondage and an intricate structure of rights, obligations, and privileges for all classes. By the midcentury, only some of the exceptionally numerous Georgian nobles were confirmed in the right to own land and serfs and to join the Russian gentry as equals. The rest lost their noble status. At various stages of Russian rule, princely revolts, restoration attempts, and peasant uprisings rocked the land and were repressed by force of arms. One of the most famous, in 1832, was a Decembrist-type plot involving members of prominent families.

And yet the two peoples found accommodation. Russian nobles admired those of Georgia, steeped in ancient legends filled with mountain imagery, banditry, and resistance, and with memories of the national poet Shota Rustaveli (twelfth century) and Queen Thamar (1184–1213). The proud Georgian gentry appealed to Russian occupiers with its knightly codes of honor and vengeance, brilliant horsemanship, contempt for trade, and manner of drinking, toasting, and extravagant hospitality. Many Georgians achieved the highest status in Russian society. The Georgian capital Tiflis (Tbilisi) came to resemble a Middle Eastern emporium, with its various native and foreign quarters and its economic life in the hands of the Armenians, who formed three quarters of the urban population of Georgia. Tiflis was also an incubator for Georgian intellectuals and novelists like Daniel Chonkadze, whose *Suram Fortress,* an indictment of serfdom, was later a favorite book of the young Stalin—and later, still, the subject of one of the greatest of all Soviet films, of the same title, by Sergei Parajanov.

In Armenia, the tsarist regime, while insisting on absolutist rule, launched no assault on customs, faith, or language. Armenians reciprocated the relatively benign attitude, since most Armenians saw Russia as a guarantor of peace and security against Islam. An 1836 statute confirmed the autonomy of the Armenian Gregorian Church, the oldest Christian state church. But in a primarily peasant land where the nobility had long disappeared, the merchants were the leading class, and Russian officials and gentry had little admiration for their way of life. Armenian merchants dominated Caucasus trade and urban commercial life. Like Jews and Old Believers, Armenians tended to be sober and hard working. Following a pattern of many small peoples in the European orbit, and more so than other Caucasian peoples, Armenian teachers, merchants, travelers, priests, journalists, and petty officials disseminated national consciousness. Books, schools, and secular teaching were supported by wealthy Tiflis merchants and by diaspora Armenians in distant Odessa, Astrakhan, and elsewhere. "Western" learning infiltrated church schools in spite of the Gregorian Church's efforts to suppress it. In the 1840s, the first newspaper in modern Armenian appeared. Novelists, translators, and anticlerical pamphleteers tried to erode the power of tradition. Thus, as with many other peoples in the empire and on its fringes, a secular generation of intelligentsia was already in place by midcentury.

The northern khanates of the Muslim Azerbaijan Turks were gathered into the Russian Empire in the Persian wars. Russian military governors ruled them as provinces, replacing the local rulers. In 1840, a civil government was established with Baku as the capital. Some Azerbaijani lands were transferred to Georgian and Armenian jurisdictions. As in other Muslim parts of the empire, the Russian code and the Muslim code, or shariat, shared legal precedence. The Azeris—erroneously called Tatars well into the twentieth century—were Turkic-speaking Shiite Muslims. Related to the Ottoman Turks by language and to the Persians by faith, the Azeris did not share the sense of security the new conquest brought to Armenians and Georgians. Nor were their elite families welcomed into the Russian gentry class as had some other Muslim elites.

War in the Mountains

A Russian hostility to Islam, fed by the eternal warring with Turks and Persians, came to a head in the mountain wars. Subduing the Caucasian mountaineers occupied Russian forces from the 1810s to 1860. The best known of the of mountain nationalities were the Circassians (properly Adyge), Abkhazians, Kabardians, Ossetians, Ingush, Chechens, and Avars. The mountain peoples lived in auls—vertical villages perched on cliffs—and made a living by crafts, livestock, some farming, and trade, punctuated by raids and wars with the Russians. Most mountaineers had been converted to Islam centuries earlier. The two great flashpoints in tsarist expansion were Circassia (a corruption of Cherkess) in the west and Dagestan in the east. The Circassians had close ties with the Ottoman Turks, who employed the men as mercenary troops and the women as harem slaves. The Russian campaign in Circassia alarmed British Russophobes, constantly on the alert against Russian expansion eastward or southward toward India, and volunteer British agents offered aid to the Circassians. Russian forces were unable to subdue the Circassians until the 1860s. After that, thousands of them, fleeing under cruel conditions, emigrated to the Ottoman Empire.

The struggle in Dagestan was more ferocious owing to the presence of charismatic religious resistance leaders. A puritan sect, called Muridism by the Russians, was a branch of the mystical Sufi movement within Islam. Driven by an intense faith—which enemies called fanaticism—and the willingness to die for the glory of Allah, its leaders temporarily united the Muslims of Dagestan—Chechens, Avars, and others—in a jihad, or holy war, against the infidel Russians. The mountaineers' attack began in the late 1820s and intensified in 1834 under the command of an Avar named Shamyl (Samuel, the All Embracing, 1797–1871). This austere and charismatic leader derived legendary stature from his piety, military prowess, and penchant for spectacular deeds and miraculous escapes. Shamyl's forces resisted seven major Russian offensives up to the end of the 1850s by means of the guerilla tactics natural to people defending their own land against outsiders: hit-and-run, ambush, night raids, sniping, and mercilessness toward prisoners and collaborators. The courage and discipline of the warriors was shared by their women, who sometimes would hurl themselves and their children into the steep gorges rather than face capture. The tsar's troops pursued a relentless drive to "pacify" the mountains. They established forts; ravaged lands, crops, and herds; and returned from raids with bags of enemy heads. The Russians also pitted tribes against each other and finally ground down the resistance. In spite of the bitterness of this war, when in 1859 Shamyl was captured, he was taken to St. Petersburg, and honored as a heroic enemy chieftain. The mountains now remained under Russian sway until the revolution of 1917.

The occupiers created their own world along the Caucasus ranges during the long wars that ended in 1860. Frontier towns bore poetic names such as Vladikavkaz (Lord of the Caucasus), Pyatigorsk (Five Mountains), and Kislovodsk (Curative Waters). The region offered a kind of freedom to some Russians, a chance to unleash brutality for others. Literature highlighted those officers who landed in the Caucasus out of failed love affairs, misbehavior, or politics and who affected a Byronic pose of despair and indifference to life. The aura of scandal, dueling, flirtation, and luxury in the face of danger had its own appeal. So did the awesome grandeur of the land with its sharp defiles, lofty peaks, and raging torrents. But the "romance of the Caucasus" was an indulgence of the few—most of them writers and readers in faraway St. Petersburg. The majority of those who served time there found their posting to be a murderous military operation. At the same time, everyday life saw a considerable volume of "frontier exchange"—the intermixing of peoples, goods, and values that occurs in most frontier societies. Some mountain people came down to convert and settle with the occupying forces as traders, scouts, translators, or agents. Cossacks, the backbone of the Russian border forces, became hardened by frontier settlement and organized army life into a compact military community with an identity of its own. They often intermarried with locals, worked the land, adopted the elaborate equestrian maneuvers—the *jigitovka*—of the mountain people, and proudly donned their sabers, bandoliers, tunics, and high fur hats. Frontier life was more than battlefield encounter and less than mutual assimilation. Collaboration, adaptation, linguistic borrowing, and exchange were practical modes of survival and adjustment in this danger zone of empire.

Across the Black Sea

Although the Muslim Crimean Tatars do not belong to the history of the Caucasus, their fate in some ways resembled that of their mountain coreligionists. The Tatar khanate of Crimea, vanquished and occupied during the reign of Catherine II (r. 1762–1796) (see the chapter "Nicholas I: Monarchy, Society, Empire, 1825–1855"), evoked for her visions of *The Arabian Nights,* and Pushkin immortalized the old Tatar capital with its famous Fountain of Tears in a beautiful poem, "The Fountain of Bakhchisarai." But during and after the Russian conquest, Crimea was subjected to a physical assault by invading Russian troops, who vandalized ancient Genoese towers and Islamic mosques. The Tatars felt the sting of the invaders, who dispossessed local landowners and enserfed the once free peasants on new Russian holdings. The old social structure of khans and lords, free peasants, and urban artisans was drastically reordered. Some Tatar princes were accepted into the Russian gentry class, and many served loyally as officers. Others lost lands and status in the conquest. Russian colonization policies rapidly filled the cities of the peninsula with Slavs, Greeks, and Armenians and made those cities non-Muslim islands in a sea of Tatars. Crimea eventually became a paradise of seaside towns, palatial buildings, and resorts for the tsar and his subjects. Bakhchisarai lost its ancient splendors and was replaced as the Crimean capital by Simferopol. Sevastopol and Balaklava became naval bases. New Russian cities of the Black Sea, such as Odessa, drained away some of the trade from Crimean ports. For these and other reasons, several major waves of emigration of Crimean Tatars to the Ottoman Empire took place, one of them when the Tatars were falsely accused of collaboration with the enemy during the Crimean War (1853–1856). The Muslim Tatars who remained could live according to the shariat under a tax-exempt clergy.

THE STEPPES OF CENTRAL ASIA

The great Eurasian steppe, a prairie grassland stretching from the Carpathian Mountains in Central Europe to distant Asian borders, was a major frontier site of the Russian Empire. Russian military units were deployed along the northern edge of the sector lying between the north shore of the Caspian Sea and the Chinese border—about nineteen hundred miles. The principal guardians of the line, the Orenburg and Siberian Cossacks, lived in a frontier colony created by the state. Their mission was to defend and extend the uncertain boundaries of southern Siberia and protect trade with the east. By midcentury, a huge quantity of goods moved through Central Asia. Russian caravans crawled back and forth across its long dangerous steppe and desert routes to trade in tea, cotton, printed cloth, silk, and rugs, with the fair at Nizhny Novgorod the major emporium at the western end. As late as 1850, the journey from Orenburg to Bukhara in Central Asia took seventy-five to eighty days. Facing the Russian Cossacks on the broad expanse of steppe called Turkistan were the nomadic Kazakhs—indiscriminately named Kirgiz by the Russians and other outsiders.* Kazakhs, like other nomads of inner Asia, followed a seasonal cycle, moving their horses, sheep, and goats—more rarely cattle—in wide arcs. Their frequent clashes with each other over territory and herds sometimes escalated into war. Their religion was a form of Sunni Islam, and they used familiar leadership designations such as khan, sultan, and bey.

The basic local unit of organization was the clan of about fifteen families. The largest unit was the *orda,* or horde; the main divisions were known as the Greater, Middle, and Lesser Hordes, each of about half a million. The Kazakhs came under Russian control in the nineteenth century. Through the first half of the century, Russian forces pushed their fortified lines relentlessly into the steppe and sent out punitive raids. The Kazakhs were pressed between this steady advance and frequent attacks by the Islamic city-states to the south. Russian forces interfered in succession disputes and curbed the sovereignty of the Kazakh leaders. A Russian attempt to regularize its rule over the nomads, the 1822 Steppe Charter, recognized Muslim religious autonomy and customary law *(ada)* for minor offenses and put major theft, murder, and treason under Russian law. But that law sometimes conflicted with the nomadic practice of *barymta*—retaliating for insult or wrongdoing by rustling cattle under a special code of honor and revenge, a custom celebrated in folk songs and legends. *Barymta* was not considered theft in local usage but was so defined by Russian administrators. The Steppe Charter also hindered the wide-ranging cattle-grazing itinerary of the hordes by creating artificial boundaries between them. Harsher still, the Russians tried to end nomadism itself by settling the Kazakhs and turning them into farmers—an occupation alien to them.

The greatest of the many uprisings against tsarist rule was that of Kenisary Qasi-

*The people now known as Kirgiz then lived at the southeast corner of the steppe and were known by Russians as the Kara-Kirgiz or Black Kirgiz. Kirghiz was an alternate spelling. The more accurate Kazak (for Kazakh) is now in use.

mov in the Middle Horde (1837–1846). Later called the first Kazakh nationalist—a gross exaggeration—he achieved some clan unity, popular support, and status as a folk hero. The *akyns,* or folk poets, sang of him for decades after his death, even up into our time. But Qasimov's was a classic anticolonial revolt and not a modern nationalist liberation movement, since there was hardly a shred of "national" consciousness in it. Qasimov was assisted by Polish patriots exiled to the steppe and some local Muslim rulers. After Qasimov was killed in battle, none of the subsequent smaller revolts succeeded in throwing off the Russian yoke. Subduing the Kazakh hordes was a prelude to a dramatic and extended campaign of conquest of Central Asia that would come later in the century.

SIBERIA: THE WILD EAST

Siberia has long captured the imagination of readers and travelers because of its size, its frigid climate, and its reputation as a penal colony. Siberia is indeed a huge land, covered by wild reaches of taiga and tundra, with towns strung along the southern zone—Tobolsk, Omsk, Tomsk, Krasnoyarsk, and Irkutsk—and a sparse population of dozens of native peoples devoted mostly to hunting, trapping, herding, and fishing. By the time of Nicholas I, Russians far outnumbered the natives.

Because of its immensity and distance from the capital, Siberia offers yet another pattern of rule in the Russian Empire. Early Russian governors at Tobolsk, Tomsk, and Irkutsk had established a tradition of rapacity, corruption, and harsh treatment of the natives. During the reign of Alexander I, new ones surpassed even this tradition. Though active in settling nomads and encouraging agriculture, the governors had imposed a grand illegal network of extortion, graft, and tyrannical abuse. Their subordinates at the local level ruled by force with the help of mounted Cossacks who terrorized villages. Russian merchants, the dominant economic class in a land without gentry landlords or serfs, added their voices to the chorus of complaint against the governor and his cohorts, which led the tsar to appoint as a reforming governor Mikhail Speransky, recently demoted from his high office during the Napoleonic wars (see the chapter "Russia in the Age of Napoleon: Paul I and Alexander I, 1796–1815"). Speransky's rule from 1819 to 1822 showed the limitations of even enlightened conservatism. He established indirect rule and religious tolerance and tried to replace personal rule with legal norms. Despite these useful and temporarily effective measures, local forces asserted themselves, and the abuses soon revived in full force. The next reforming governor general of eastern Siberia, Nikolai Muravëv (1809–1881), had to begin his tenure (1847–1861) by firing corrupt officials.

The discovery of gold in eastern Siberia in the 1830s turned this land of frost and forest into a potential El Dorado. The state, unable to manage or control gold mining on a large scale, allowed tens of thousands of independent gold miners and prospectors to make Siberia into one of the world's greatest producers of the precious metal. After 1849, people called it another California. The boom brought anxiety about the weak defenses of eastern Siberia. To strengthen Russia's position, Governor Muraviëv took the initiative in exploring the Amur and Ussuri Rivers and adjacent regions. In 1858 and 1860, at a moment of weakness in the Chinese Empire, Russia signed treaties assigning those enormous lands to the tsarist empire. Thus the Russian "Far East," crowned by a new naval base called Vladivostok (Lord of the East), extended the landmass down to warmer Pacific waters.

Another notable development in Siberian life was the growth of the convict population. The dreaded sentence of "hard labor and exile" was imposed on several thousand persons a year: murderers, bandits, political criminals, runaway serfs, deserters, religious offenders, and other assorted outcasts. About a million all told were sent to Siberian detention in the tsarist period, a scandalous number to Europeans of the time. Numbers swelled from two to three thousand a year under Alexander I to seventeen to eighteen thousand at midcentury. Marked by half-shaven heads and the ace of diamonds sewn on their backs, the prisoners were convoyed to holding stations at Tobolsk or Omsk and then shuttled farther on to factories, salt works, silver mines, goldfields, or labor battalions. The political prisoners included the Decembrist rebels of 1825, the Polish revolutionaries of 1830, and the Petrashevsky Circle members of 1849 (see the chapter "Nicholas I: Monarchy, Society, Empire, 1825–1855"). The hundred or so Decembrists were joined by two dozen wives—remarkable upper-class women who gave up home, children, freedom, and social position to live out their lives in bleak exile with their men. Far more numerous were the Polish exiles, who languished for decades if they did not escape to join some local anticolonial movement. Punitive exile varied widely, according to the severity of the crime—from murderous hard labor in the mines or woodlands, to prison compounds or confinement in settlements, to billeting in a village with free peasants.

The "politicals," mostly from the educated classes, suffered the dual penalty of imprisonment and physical contact with the most ruthless elements of society—murderers, thieves, rapists, and arsonists. The prison compound in Siberia—usually log barracks around an open area—was a world apart, a twisted miniature of normal society in which a Polish nobleman or a Russian student rubbed shoulders in a work gang with a cut-throat and a highwayman. The noise, dirt, stink, crudity, and danger of the rural and urban underworld were compressed into the tight space of incarceration. The violence of the guards was often outdone by that of the inmates toward each other. Yet even here in the depths, inmates welded friendships, shared food, and sustained a rough etiquette of "thieves' honor." Sufferers lowered class and ethnic barriers and forged solidarities in the search for vodka and other contraband. The writer Fëdor Dostoevsky, who served a Siberian sentence in the 1850s, called his place of exile "the house of the dead" and yet populated the book of that name with vivid human characters.

Among the hardened criminals though, little enough human compassion was evident. Every spring, tens of thousands of escapees—joined by vagrants, semi-criminal settlers, and bandits—fanned out over Siberia to raid, plunder, rape, and murder. Known popularly as General Cuckoo's Army because of their regular seasonal appearance, they terrorized the population. Temporary escape was fairly easy. Peasants often wept at the sight of prisoner convoys but feared the criminal settlers in their midst. The outlaws would ride into town with lassoes and hooks to capture, beat, or kill townspeople, sometimes inflicting frightful atrocities on men, women, and children. Since guards and lawmen were too few in number to apprehend them, the state hired bounty hunters to bring them in dead or alive. Peasants who turned in escaped convicts had their villages burned out. And yet, as with bandits in many societies, desperadoes were often mythologized as folk heroes for their great physical strength, immunity to pain, and alleged sympathy for the poor.

Siberia generated myths of all kinds. Its tremendous expanse and its free and floating population led romantics to construe it as a land of freedom peopled by simple, innocent natives—the familiar noble savage—and by Russians who were somehow more authentically "Russian" than those in the European heartland. In its distant reaches nested hidden communities of runaway serfs and sectarians and convicts—abiding in the forest right up into Soviet times. Though lacking certain features of the American "Wild West," such as its mountainous topography and the warlike culture of some Native Americans, Siberia has been likened to it for obvious similarities. Some of these—boom towns and a transcontinental railroad—emerged later. Before 1861, Siberia was still a relatively neglected multiethnic space, a loose and scattered collection of natives, Russian peasants, miners, prisoners, administrators, merchants, and priests. In later decades, Siberia would inspire Russian visions of systematic settlement, economic development, and a power base of Eurasian geopolitics.

FRONTIERS OF THE IMAGINATION

Educated opinion, literary imagination, and even popular mentalities engaged in "thinking about empire" at various levels. Racism, romanticism, science, religion, and visions of development jogged each other in the imaginative geography of empire. Some warriors, travelers, and writers confronted border peoples on the road to conquest with a fundamentally racist view. To such minds, native peoples, especially the resisting nomads and mountain peoples, were savage and beastly—deserving, at the very least, conquest, if not utter extermination. This colonial war mentality—hardly unique to Russia—never disappeared, but it was paralleled with other strains and visions. Poets and novelists created what one student has called "a large gallery of literary exhibits of foreign peoples on the empire's periphery." The imagination was especially excited by the struggle in the Caucasus. Part of the attraction was the extraordinary landscape, untamed wilderness being a major force in the topography of romantic literature and painting. In Pushkin's celebrated poem *The Captive of the Caucasus* (1821), his countrymen found in his delineation of the "Circassian" mountaineers a hint of their own "Asianness"—an unsullied inner freedom distinct from the European character. The "hero" of Mikhail Lermontov's *A Hero of Our Time* (1840)—who seduces, betrays, and kidnaps women and provokes duels from the Black Sea coast to Chechnya—became a literary idol. Even more popular at the time were the steamy and violent thriller tales of Alexander Bestuzhev, an exiled Decembrist who wrote under the name Marlinsky. His novel *Ammalat-Bek* (1832) was among the most popular books of the age, not only for its unexpected plot twists but for its evocation of breathtaking scenery, ethnographic detail, and the excitement of mountain adventure.

The "romance of empire" was steeped in orientalism: the attribution of barbarism, cruelty, overheated sexuality, and martial valor to Asian—especially Muslim—peoples. But in its ungrudging admiration of the enemy's heroism, it was more complicated than mere racism, and it fed into an emerging romantic nationalism based on the idea of "the common people" as potential vessels of freedom, primitive nobility, and honest simplicity. Border fiction also prompted a wave of tourism and enlistment in the Caucasus and served as guidebooks and manuals of behavior for new arrivals.

A more objective "mapping" of the realm by scientists and explorers promoted data gathering. The Imperial Geographical Society was founded in 1845 to study all the tsar's lands and peoples in order to promote a "science of empire." Various ministries sponsored studies of economic and social conditions in city and country. Statisticians, geographers, military topographers, and naval hydrographers added their data to the growing picture. This activity was a major step in the development of a more sophisticated—if not always wise or accurate—consciousness about the empire and its inhabitants. The Geographical Society and the Naval Ministry sent out expeditions led by scientists, journalists, novelists, portrait painters, and even a few pioneer photographers—people with a keen eye for detail. Steeped in a spirit of independent and objective inquiry, some served as ethnographers, an earlier term for anthropologists. But their opinions and descriptions of non-Russian peoples ran the gamut from sympathetic objectivity to extreme distaste.

Rebel of the Caucasus, Shamyl.

Imperialism was a popular theme of print culture. Alexandra Ishimova's best-selling *History of Russia in Stories for Children* (1837–1840) frankly promoted Russian conquest in the name of recovering lost territory, moving to natural boundaries, gathering in fellow Russians, gaining security, and offering civilization to the blighted and barbaric peoples of the Arctic and desert wastes. Converting native people to Orthodoxy was one route to this goal. Studies of non-Russian nationalities have shown that missionary work was superficial. Natives often converted in return for material gain—money, clothing, and trinkets. Popular Orthodoxy here and elsewhere required outward observance of the church rites and hoped for a transformation of the inner spiritual life.

The more subtle approach of "culturalism" aspired to turn colonials into something like Russian citizens in tastes and values. The Russian language, schooling, arts, manners, and civic consciousness would replace the crudeness of local traditions. This approach obviously reflected a sense of European identity, a belief that Europe was the center of civilization and that Russia's "civilizing mission" made it an extension of Europe. This notion both collided and coexisted with Slavophile consciousness in the complex and multilayered Russian psychology of the time. The experiences fashioned by war, adventure, travel, fiction, governance, trade, frontier exchange, and the mythologies of empire created for the Russians an entire set of identities—ranging from a sense of a special Slavic "soul" in contrast to the West to one of superior "Western" civilization to which Russia and its East should aspire.

CHAPTER 21

Alexander II and the Era of the Great Reforms, 1855–1870

At the stage of civilization in which we are, the success of armies, however brilliant they may be, is only transitory. In reality it is public opinion which wins the last victory.
—French Emperor Napoleon III (at the conclusion of the Crimean War, 1856)

The Revolutions of 1848 failed to install revolutionary regimes in France, Prussia, Austria, and Italy. But the new cycle of "restorations" that followed could more accurately be described as the creation of new kinds of monarchy throughout the European continent. The Second Empire in France and the Bismarckian Reich in Germany were founded on the experience of revolution and on the acknowledgment that liberalism, nationalism, and popular sentiment were forces to be respected, if not encouraged. The new regimes found powerful symbolic expression in the studied physical transformation of Europe's capitals. Baron Haussmann carved broad boulevards through the dark corners and alleyways of old Paris; Berlin, Vienna, and Rome acquired expansive central avenues and encircling ring roads.

In Russia, it was the humiliating defeat in the Crimean War (1856) that ushered in a new era. In some ways, Russia in the second half of the nineteenth century replicated a general European pattern. All three monarchs that followed Nicholas I's thirty-year reign held fast to the principle of absolute monarchy. Yet the reign of Nicholas's immediate successor, Alexander II, initiated limited popular participation on a local level, bringing new kinds of people into the political process. Most dramatically, Alexander II's reign witnessed the end of the institution—serfdom—that had definitively set Russia apart from other European states. Visually, Moscow's wide, tree-lined Garden Ring (which replaced the old city ramparts in Nicholas I's reign), the expanses of the Neva River, and the straight lines of St. Petersburg's Nevsky Prospect inscribed both Russian capitals comfortably in the new European urban design.

The "Great Reforms" of the 1860s were presented by the government in a spirit of continuity with the reign of Nicholas I: the son was to finish what the father had begun. The result, however, was a deep structural change in Russian economy and society. In a world where industrial progress was increasingly becoming a determining criterion of international power, the end of serfdom removed a crucial obstacle to Russia's economic growth. The reforms created a variety of new centers of power, as local and municipal institutions took over decisions that had once depended exclusively on the prerogatives of the central government. The reform era was tumultuous and filled with tension, as the government sought to involve segments of the population in the reform process and in local administration while maintaining the inviolability of absolute monarchy. The reforms did not trigger a much feared "revolution from below," in part because of the virtuosity with which this remarkable feat of social engineering was executed. Nonetheless, the reforms were punctuated by revolt and rebellion: a powerful, socialist-inspired radical movement took root in these years, and a full-scale rebellion in Poland challenged the reform process soon after its inception.

MONARCHY AND GENTRY AFTER CRIMEA

Alexander II's ceremonial role had begun long before his accession to the throne. Educated and brought up since childhood with the expectation of ruling the Russian Empire, he had, at his father's initiative, made a ceremonial journey through Russia when he was nineteen, symbolizing with his person the linkage between tsar and people. Everywhere, the heir was greeted with expressions of love and rejoicing, and he captivated his audiences with his beauty and charm. Thirty-six years old at the time he came to power, Alexander II was a product of the Golden Age of Russian culture: his personality had been shaped by the efforts of his tutor, the romantic poet Vasily Zhukovsky, as well as by conversations with the reformer and lawmaker Mikhail Speransky; he had traveled not only in Russia and western Siberia but throughout Europe. As importantly, Nicholas had consciously groomed him for rulership, introducing him to affairs of state as apprentice to the tsar over the course of some ten years. Nicholas, who died peacefully, if disappointed, at the height of the Crimean War, left his son the following apologetic and perceptive message: "I wished, taking upon myself all that was difficult and weighty, to leave you a peaceful, orderly, and happy kingdom. . . . Providence judged otherwise."

Two apparently contradictory tendencies merged in Alexander II's image as monarch. On one hand, Alexander consistently represented himself as continuing his father's reign and, more broadly, the tradition of his forefathers; even the most dramatic of his reforms—the end of serfdom—was presented as a task begun by Nicholas but left unfinished. On the other hand, in the wake of the 1848 revolutions in Europe, the concept of monarchy had, once again, undergone a transformation, yielding a variety of monarchical regimes that included some element of popular participation. Paradoxically, the new ruler of the state that had so triumphantly defended absolute monarchy by invading Hungary in 1849 now borrowed the images and metaphors of popular monarchy: the absolute monarch, his authority unchallenged, would act selflessly for the good of all the people, bestowing upon them freedom and dignity and winning their love and admiration.

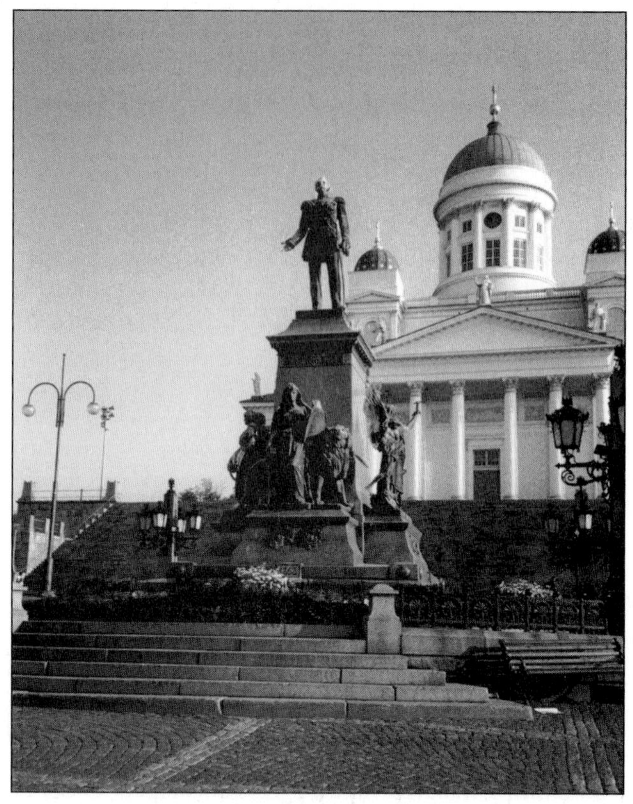

Statue of Alexander II in Helsinki, Finland (Walter Runeberg, 1894).
Photo courtesy Natalia Baschmakoff.

The first indication of the direction of Alexander's reign came in an address he delivered to the assembled Moscow nobility in March 1856. Rumors that the new tsar intended to abolish serfdom had abounded in the preceding months; now he reassured the gentry, rather unreassuringly, that he had no intention of doing so at that particular moment. However, "You yourselves know that the existing order of ruling over living souls cannot remain unchanged. It is better to abolish serfdom from above than to await the day when it will begin to abolish itself from below." Alexander, wishing to create a spirit of unanimity, proceeded to ask the gentry to reflect on how these aims might best be accomplished. The nobles were accustomed to hearing talk of abolition—every tsar since Catherine II (r. 1762–1796) had professed intentions to this effect. To them, it was not immediately clear whether the project was intended as an urgent task or as merely a vague aspiration. In fact, the question of emancipation became the central focus both of public debate and of government policy in the ensuing decade. Among the debaters were those nobles who professed liberal principles so long as they knew their rights to own land and souls were protected. To their dismay, this time the intention was serious indeed, and it was not long before they had to translate their talk into concrete action.

Free and Unfree Labor

Why did emancipation finally become more than a vague good intention? On the broadest level, the end of serfdom coincided with an era of liberation worldwide: slaves were freed in the American South, in the Caribbean, and in parts of Latin America. Generally, historians propose two reasons why societies based on unfree labor suddenly underwent dramatic transformation in the nineteenth century. The first is economic: agrarian structures were being replaced by industrial economies in which workers who could not move about freely in search of employment ceased to be efficient or even productive at all; this put slaveholding societies at a disadvantage. A no less weighty reason was moral: as ideas of liberty, equality, and fraternity gathered strength throughout the European world, the notion of a class of people born to servitude, and the abuses which frequently accompanied this condition, became increasingly unacceptable to society as a whole. Within Russia itself, most historians attribute a significant role to the Crimean defeat, which pointed to the need for reform of the Russian economy. From the military perspective, one historian has argued that Russia's huge peacetime standing army, based on the recruitment of serfs for a term of twenty-five years, was inefficient and inflexible: the abolition of serfdom might be seen as part of the streamlining of the military through the creation of a small standing army and a larger reserve force, as in most European countries.

The ultimate liberation of the serfs represented a convergence of several powerful impulses. One of them was the intellectual movement, from the Enlightenment thinker Alexander Radishchev to the Slavophiles and Alexander Herzen, who had insistently and repeatedly pointed out the evils of bondage for over half a century. Increasingly over the first half of the nineteenth century, the issue of serfdom became a magnetic focus for social criticism by writers, thinkers, and even liberal representatives of the gentry and enlightened members of the government bureaucracy. The moral indictment of serfdom reached its apogee in the 1840s; Ivan Turgenev's *A Hunter's Sketches* produced a furor with its apparently novel observation that peasants were people, too. In a tremendous outburst, Russian society greeted the 1856 Treaty of Paris with an explosion of newspaper articles, heated discussions, and works of fiction detailing the abuses of serfdom and echoing Turgenev's depiction.

A second impulse came from within the monarchy and bureaucracy. The idea of liberating the serfs had hovered over the monarchy ever since Catherine II half-seriously raised the issue in the Free Economic Society. Liberation had been a real, if frightening, aspiration for Alexander I; and Nicholas I had actually convened a secret committee to work out a plan of emancipation. These aspirations had resulted in two essential pieces of legislation: the 1803 law on "free agriculturalists" (permitting individual contracts between landlords and peasants) and Nicholas's 1842 law on "obligated peasants" (see the chapters "Russia in the Age of Napoleon: Paul I and Alexander I, 1796–1815" and "Nicholas I: Monarchy, Society, and Empire, 1825–1855"). Thus much of the groundwork for the actual terms of the emancipation had been laid. No less significant—though timeless—was the constant distress of the peasants themselves, who, as the institution of serfdom tightened its grip from the fifteenth to the eighteenth century and as physical escape became more difficult, periodically expressed their discontent in uprisings, rebellions, and the burning of landlord estates.

The Path to Reform

Alexander's Moscow speech was followed by the creation of a Secret Committee on Peasant Affairs in January 1857, on the recommendation of Sergei Lanskoi, minister of the interior. How far matters would go was not, at first, clear: after all, a similar committee had been formed by Nicholas I, and, in the new committee, a majority of members actually opposed full-scale reform. In November, however, the government issued a directive to the governor general of the Lithuanian provinces, V. I. Nazimov, providing for the creation of provincial committees among the gentry to draw up plans for emancipation of their peasants. In a rather theatrical display, coordinated by the Ministry of the Interior, the Lithuanian nobility sent to the tsar asking his approval of their desire to emancipate their serfs. This good example was broadly publicized throughout the empire, and soon other regions began to follow suit. The first to respond were the nobility of Nizhny Novgorod, who prided themselves on their progressive impulse. Then, region by region, the spirit and letter of emancipation spread through Russia.

The "Nazimov Rescript" established a pattern for the emancipation process: gently but firmly guided by centrally issued conditions, gentry committees were formed throughout the empire and instructed to work out the local details of reform; they were overseen from St. Petersburg by a Main Committee (the Secret Committee, rechristened). The gentry committees generated a wide variety of possible programs; initially, they felt that they had considerable control over the outcome of the emancipation. The programs varied, depending on regional economic conditions: in general, committees in the fertile black-soil provinces, where *barshchina* (work for the landlord) was more common, were more worried about the loss of land, whereas non-black-soil landowners were more interested in preserving their level of income. In many cases, liberal principles were as important as economic considerations. The program of the Tver gentry, for example, became known for its liberal proposals: they included the recommendation to abolish *barshchina* completely and to make the shortest possible transition from serfdom to complete emancipation. Sometimes a good amount of arm twisting was needed. Even in the case of Nizhny Novgorod, the first Russian province to give its approval to the idea of emancipation, the provincial governor, A. N. Muraviëv, did some badgering at the Provincial Assembly of the Nobility to create unanimity in favor of the autocrat's will. Having done so, he ensured success by dispatching a messenger to Moscow at 3:00 A.M., before the nobles had a chance to change their minds. Similar pressure was often applied by the local marshals of the nobility (the elected leaders of the provincial gentry).

In the early stages, a lively and incessant stream of journalistic commentary and criticism accompanied the reform process. Alexander II's reign had begun with a relaxation of censorship. Journalists and censors, moreover, cooperated in a tacit acknowledgment that the emancipation question, particularly, was subject to *glasnost*. This term, which literally means "giving voice," made its first appearance in the reform era in reference to a particular style of making government policy: instead of relying on the secret committees of Nicholas I's time, Alexander II's reforms were to be carried out in full public view. The emancipation itself had the broad and enthusiastic support of the press. The debate in the journals focused mainly on the form of peasant social organization following the reforms: one journal argued for the breakup of the peasant commune on the model of contemporary Western peasant villages; all the others supported the preservation of the commune. The radical journalist Nikolai Chernyshevsky (1828–1889) made his first public appearance in these years with a string of articles in *The Contemporary*. Inspired by the socialist vision of the French utopian Charles Fourier (1772–1837) as well as by the utilitarian philosophy of John Stuart Mill (1806–1873), Chernyshevsky urged the retention of the commune as a basis for future socialism. The right-wing journal *The Russian Messenger*, published by Mikhail Katkov (1818–1887), in the meantime supported the commune as a "traditional" Russian form of social organization. The press campaign was toned down in 1858 when the government, horrified by an article that had openly advised freeing the peasants and simply giving them all the land they currently worked on, tightened restrictions on the press.

Also in 1858, Alexander undertook another journey through the Russian provinces to nudge ahead the crafting of the reform proposals, praising here, cajoling there, and occasionally reproving the local committees for insufficient zeal. In the same year the government, anxious to retain control over the emancipation process and to limit the autonomy of the gentry committees, created guidelines—the "April Program," followed by a more rigid series of measures in October—that brought the many regional proposals into closer accord. Wishing to limit the range of discussion, the government introduced the concept of "temporary obligation," considered mandatory for all projects. Under this provision the land would, for a given term, remain fully the property of the landlords, while the peasants retained the right to work on that property; during this time, they would negotiate terms under which they could actually buy the land for themselves. Gradually, the initiative in the discussions began to drift out of the hands of the gentry and into those of the bureaucracy: well before the legislation was actually implemented, the most liberal of the landowners felt that their efforts had been coopted and that their concerns to preserve as much of their privilege as possible had been thwarted.

The emancipation process entered its final stages in 1859 when an Editing Commission, headed by Yakov Rostovstsev (1803–1860) and responsible directly to the tsar, took over the task of consolidating the input from the provinces. Gentry delegates to Petersburg complained that they were given an insufficient voice in the proceedings and, blaming "bureaucratization," began to demand changes in local administration. Provincial gentry assemblies, meeting in 1859–1860, expressed their opposition to specifics of the government program. Nonetheless, by January 1861 the proposed legislation had passed from the Editing Commission to the Main Committee and thence to the State Council (the permanent body of experts that advised the monarch); on February 19 it was ready for the emperor's signature. The concrete drafting of the complicated decree had taken only two years, thanks to the long preparatory work in the bureaucracy of the previous reign.

In 1861 the monarch and the intelligentsia reached a rare pinnacle of agreement, and even Herzen congratulated Alexander with the effusive exclamation "Thou hast conquered, Galilean!" In the American South, it took a brutal and bloody civil war finally to force landowners to relinquish their slaves. Russian emancipation, in contrast, reflected a remarkable, very carefully engineered social consensus. Like the reforms of Peter the Great (Peter I; r. 1682–1725)—affecting everything from the military to social structure—the emancipation of the Russian serfs was initiated from above. Unlike Peter's reforms, however, Alexander II's program involved an "engineering of assent," in which the pressure of public opinion and the manipulations of government officials at various levels convinced the landholding gentry that their fondest dreams would be realized with the liquidation of their power over the serfs. A government initiative transformed firm defenders of serfdom overnight into supporters of emancipation, or even into liberal enthusiasts and pillars of the new order. By 1861 there was virtually no opposition to the reforms from the gentry: their main concern was that they lose as little as possible from the precise manner in which the reforms were to be implemented.

THE GREAT REFORMS: EMANCIPATION

The opening pages of the Emancipation Manifesto of February 19, 1861, were drafted by Metropolitan Filaret of Moscow in Alexander II's name. Celebrating the love and care of the tsar for all his subjects, from aristocrat to laborer, the manifesto regretted the decline of patriarchal relations between landlords and peasants and declared the intention of "changing the situation of the serfs for the better." To this end, given the gentry's "voluntary renunciation" of their rights over the serfs as persons, the serfs were to be transformed into "free rural denizens," eventually with all the rights that this status might entail. The general guidelines for how this was to transpire followed. All the land remained the property of the landlords; peasants retained the right to permanent use of the piece of it on which they lived, plus an additional amount for cultivation. For a period of time, the peasants, now known as "temporarily obligated," continued to owe the landlord dues; however, they could then arrange, by agreement with the landlord, to purchase the land, at which point they would become "free peasant proprietors." Those serfs who were household servants would enter into a transitional state for two years, after which they would be completely free. The reform was to be implemented through a network of government-appointed mediators who would help negotiate the individual contracts between landlords and peasant communes.

These rather vague general parameters were supplemented by over three hundred pages of more specific legislation. Some outlined the peasants' new rights, such as the right to marry without the landlord's permission, to enter into independent contracts, to engage in trade, and to own property. Others dealt with new duties—taxes owed to the central and local government and the commune and subjection to the military draft. They dealt, as well, with peasant social organization: the peasants were to be organized in communes governed by a village council and a head or main elder; communes in a particular region were grouped together in a district *(volost)* with its own council, main elder, governing board, and court. The legislation set up local committees to oversee the implementation of the reform and outlined procedures for electing mediators and working out redemption payments. Specifics of land allotments varied from region to region—Great Russia, Ukraine, Belorussia, and Lithuania, with special arrangements in Siberia, Bessarabia, and the Cossack lands. In addition, industrial workers who were serfs were freed under terms similar to those governing the peasant emancipation.

The manifesto of February 19 definitively terminated the old landlord-serf relation, in which peasants were obligated to work the landlord's property or pay quitrent regardless of recompense, while the landlord was encouraged to provide for their economic and moral well-being. Responsibility for adjudicating quarrels, distributing punishment, making decisions about farming and allocating tasks, providing for orphaned children, and so on, passed from the landlord—who had been the serfs' sole recourse, with no appeals or complaints permitted—to institutions such as the peasant district court, the village council, or the peasant commune itself. This meant that peasants could no longer be bought and sold; could bring complaints against anyone, including the landlord; and were no longer subject to corporal punishment by the landlord. The peasants, in other words, were granted their personal liberty.

Emancipation: Key Issues

The manifesto that emancipated the Russian serfs belongs among the most debated, and alternately exalted and reviled, acts of legislation in history. Although it was greeted with a wave of enthusiasm and rare consensus in its first days, the half century that followed its promulgation produced prodigious amounts of criticism from both right and left. The great poet Afanasy Fet (1820–1892), also a landowner, complained in 1882 that both landlords and peasants had suffered from the loss of their benign patriarchal interdependence. From the opposite perspective, radicals in the 1890s were still complaining that the emancipation act had left a job half done by leaving all the land to the gentry and by keeping the peasantry in an inferior status. The future leader of the 1917 Bolshevik Revolution, Vladimir Lenin, echoed by three generations of Soviet historians, declared that 1861 marked the end of the feudal stage of production and the transition to capitalism in Russia. Some historians, leaping over sixty years of history, have even seen in the terms of the emancipation the direct cause of the revolution of 1917.

Through the tumult of voices judging or interpreting the emancipation, it is nonetheless possible to make a few observations concerning its substance. In comparison with other places, the scale of Russian emancipation was enormous: it affected 20 million serfs—those who had belonged to private landowners. If one adds the state peasants to this number, the total is 50 million, or some 80 percent of the population. This fact alone accounts, on one hand, for the difficulty of emancipation and, on the other, for its vast consequences. Emancipation in Prussia, begun in 1807, ended the condition of servitude for perhaps 600,000 peasants; 4 million slaves were freed in the United States in 1865; 700,000 in Brazil in 1888.

The key problem of emancipation was the question of the peasant and the land. Wherever serfs or slaves have been liberated, the question has arisen: How are they to live afterward? Should they be given land to farm for themselves? If so, where should it come from? If not, how can society cope with this new army of the free but dispossessed? It was around this issue that crucial divisions emerged that in the end defined the real status of the peasant in postemancipation society. The drafting of the reform legislation had been guided by the constant concern of avoiding excessive damage to the landlords while at the same time preventing the emergence of a vast agrarian proletariat. The multitudes involved in Russia made this game particularly dangerous, which helps explain the apprehensions that made Russia's rulers put off emancipation as long as possible. Experiments in some western regions of the empire in the two preceding reigns provided a negative example. Under Alexander I, peasants had been emancipated in the Baltic provinces with no landholding arrangements at all; the result had been large numbers of dispossessed peasants. Similar efforts in Poland had led to an actual decline in the status of the peasantry.

In Russia, the decision reached as a result of long and delicate negotiations and efforts to balance social forces was to free the peasants, not actually with land outright but with the right eventually to purchase the pieces of land they farmed at present. The term of the "temporary obligation" status was fixed at nine years. For the first two, peasants were to continue the traditional payment of dues in the form of *barshchina* (corvée) and *obrok* (quitrent) payments. For seven more years, they had to remain on their allotments while a deal for redemption of the land was worked out to the mutual satisfaction of peasant and landlord. These agreements, crafted with the help of the mediators, were the only way out of "temporarily obligated" status. After that, the peasant, in effect, took the land he needed for his livelihood out on a forty-nine-year loan; at the end of this period he was expected to have paid the price of the land (with the interest that had accrued), which then became his. (If he wished, he could, instead, accept a "pauper's allotment," granted outright but only one-fourth the size of the official norm.) While this arrangement sounded fair on paper—better, certainly, than the sharecropping and tenant farming arrangements of the American South, which frankly and openly proletarianized the former slaves—the politics of class were quite evident here. The banks charged higher interest rates to the peasants than those paid by gentry landholders; former serfs had to pay more than their gentry counterparts for the same goods and had few means of earning the necessary money. Peasants remained a different species of landowner than the gentry.

A second crucial and remarkable peculiarity of Russian emancipation was that land was granted not to individual peasants but to the commune as a whole. The campaign in the press, as well as the power of Slavophile ideas—their idealization of the commune and their energetic participation in constructing the emancipation legislation—were at least in part responsible for this aspect of the reform. The commune was an institution of peasant self-government, with a head and a council of elders. It was, at the same time, an institution to which one belonged by necessity and not choice, and it had considerable powers of coercion over individual members. The peasant commune retained the right of repartition of the land—that is, the commune could at any moment decide to shift farming of a particular strip from one peasant family to another. The commune became the basic unit of taxation, so that all members were responsible for the contribution of the others. It was therefore against the interests of the commune for any one member to leave, for the rest would then have to compensate for his share. The commune also remained the basic juridical unit. The peasants, in other words, gained their liberty not as individuals but as members of a larger collectivity to which they remained fully responsible and from which exit was difficult.

Implementation

Timed to coincide with the seven-week Great Lent that precedes Easter, the manifesto was read during March and April in gentry assemblies and peasant communes all over Russia. Frequently, its terms generated a good deal of confusion. Rumors of liberation had been circulating freely, but the peasants did not hear a clear statement

Sermon in the Village, by Vasily Perov (1861). *Tretyakov Gallery, Moscow, Russia/Scala/Art Resource, NY.*

of it in the manifesto. One common interpretation was that they had to wait two more years for *slushnyi chas*—the moment when the tsar would bestow an ill-defined great favor upon them. In some villages, the much feared uprisings occurred, despite a heavy network of police that fanned out through the countryside. The most dramatic was in the village of Bezdna (Kazan Province), where the peasant Anton Petrov preached his own interpretation of the reform: peasants were immediately fully free and owed the landlords nothing at all. The institutions of peasant self-government and mediation created by the emancipation legislation, however, proved successful in mitigating unrest: as these measures came into play over the succeeding months, the countryside subsided into the difficult work of distributing land parcels and arranging redemption payments.

The emancipation was extended to the imperial peasants (those belonging directly to the imperial family, 1.75 million in number) in 1863: the land they worked on was given to them directly, without a transitional "obligated" status; they had the same forty-nine years to complete redemption payments. The 30 million state peasants, whose status had already been affected by the Kiselëv reform of Nicholas I's reign (see the chapter "Nicholas I: Monarchy, Society, Empire, 1825–1855"), followed in 1866: to buy out their land, the state peasants had to pay a sum equivalent to their *obrok* (quitrent) in interest from government bonds. This complicated requirement generated a good deal of confusion and made execution almost impossible in practice. Separate legislation was drafted to extend the reform to other parts of the empire: land reform was instituted, after much trouble, in Poland in 1864 (discussed later in this chapter) and in Transcaucasia (Armenia and Georgia) from 1864 to 1870. In the latter case, the major distinction from the 1861 reform was in peasant social organization: the communes and elders were the same, but they were not grouped into larger districts with their own institutions. An unsuccessful effort was made to extend similar land organization to the nomadic peoples of the Kazakh steppes, and land reform constituted part of the program of the governor general of the newly created region of Turkistan (discussed in the next chapter).

Because of the many ambiguities in the reform legislation—primarily the land issue and the role of the commune—the legislative act that had resulted from the collective effort of monarchy, gentry, and bureaucracy left in the end a bitter taste. Nonetheless, the fundamental break had been made: serfdom was no longer the crucial defining mechanism of the Russian economy and Russian society.

CREATING A NEW SOCIETY? THE ZEMSTVO AND LEGAL REFORMS

The end of serfdom was the cornerstone of a reform program that eventually changed and reorganized the status of every layer of Russian society. The reforms of Alexander II's era departed from the traditional reliance on central administration, delving into the depths of Russian life to create a network of new institutions.

Local Government: The Zemstvo

Local government had been the bane of Russian monarchs since Peter I's half-hearted and entirely unsuccessful attempts to create institutions at the local level. The reforms of Catherine II in the late eighteenth century and those of Speransky and Nicholas I in the nineteenth had succeeded in extending the reach of the central administration deep into the Russian provinces. The reform of local government under Alexander II—the result of legislation crafted by Nikolai Milyutin and, following his dismissal, by the minister of internal affairs, Pëtr Valuev—differed fundamentally from these earlier efforts. The institution called the *zemstvo* was created in 1864 as an organ not of the central administration, but of local self-government, responsible for local needs and elected by local residents. It was also—and this was an important consideration for its creators—a much more efficient tax-collecting mechanism than a centralized machinery could ever be.

The very term *zemstvo* had a deep resonance for contemporaries. The word comes from *zemlia* (land). More importantly, *zemstvo* had an archaic sound, and it evoked images of sixteenth- and seventeenth-century Muscovite political structure, in which representatives from the land had gathered periodically in a *zemsky sobor* (council of the land) that advised the tsar. The creation of the zemstvo raised hopes that a national representative institution of some kind would soon follow.

Apart from maintaining their own properties and handling their own taxes, the zemstvos, set up in thirty-four provinces of European Russia, were supposed to oversee the distribution of goods and food reserves in case of poor harvest; maintain roads and bridges; manage social welfare, insurance, and church construction; provide for health and education; engage in animal husbandry and agronomy; regulate the postal service and the military draft; manage finances coming from the central government and from the local population; and serve as a channel of communication between local society and the center. The most important of these functions, especially at the beginning, proved to be education and medicine. An entire network of zemstvo-run schools was created under the jurisdiction of the Ministry of National Enlightenment, whose function was to teach the children of the new free peasants basic literacy. The zemstvos established what was virtually a socialized health care system, with the character of the rural physician becoming a major new figure in the postemancipation countryside—and in literature as well.

The zemstvo reform established an assembly at the district level and another assembly for the entire province. These bodies met once a year, with a district and a provincial zemstvo board responsible for keeping things going when the entire assembly was not in session. Elections were indirect and based on a curial system: each of three groups—gentry, peasantry, and all others—had a right to a specified number of delegates. Two things about this arrangement are worth noting: first, although a property qualification meant that landlords, merchants, and industrialists comprised the bulk of electors, peasant representation hovered somewhere around 40 percent. In the first elections to the Nizhny Novgorod zemstvo, for example, there were 189 delegates from the landlords and 175 from the peasant communes (city delegates numbered 38). Second, this was the first institution in modern

The provinces of European Russia. *Copyright © 1967 Oxford University Press. Reprinted from* The Russian Empire, *1801–1917 by Hugh Seton-Watson, by permission of Oxford University Press.*

Russia that brought the different classes together, instead of segregating them in separate estate *(soslovie)* organizations like the gentry assembly (dating to the era of Catherine II). Whatever the limitations on suffrage—and they were standard for the European world in the second half of the nineteenth century—Russia's population over the course of the four decades between 1864 and the establishment of a national representative government in 1905 grew accustomed to the process of going to the polls and making a choice of political representation.

The creation of the zemstvos was supplemented in 1870 by similar institutions in the cities: municipal self-government functioned by means of an electoral assembly, a city *duma* (legislative assembly), and a permanent city board. These organs had power over virtually all aspects of the life of the cities, from salaries of municipal employees to hospices to roads and sanitation.

Courts and Juries: The Legal Reform

Speransky's codification of Russian law in the 1830s had instituted uniformity in the laws themselves, but it had not touched the sprawling, disorderly, and largely customary network of the presumed instruments of their implementation—the Russian courts. The 1864 judicial reform opened the courts to the public; separated the judicial power from the administrative; limited the number of trials for the same offense; created a system of appeals; and instituted a jury system based on representation from all estate groups. The reform was a crucial step toward eliminating the venality that had previously characterized Russian law. It created a sophisticated network of legal institutions that covered the Russian countryside. Courts on the district level made initial decisions; these could then be appealed through a pyramidal structure of district courts, then a judicial chamber that was responsible for a group of several provinces; final appeals proceeded to the highest state institution, the national Senate. Most dramatic was the establishment of a jury system, in which peers—instead of the earlier government official—sat in judgment on the accused. Curiously, the institution of trial by jury provoked much anxiety and apprehension among the population: above all, they feared that jurors would be corruptible or politically influenced and that the jury system, far from ensuring fair trial, would actually perpetuate class prejudices and divisions.

The most successful aspect of the judicial reform was the newly created civil judge or, literally, "communal judge" (sometimes translated as justice of the peace). This was an elected position, held by people who were not professional lawyers. The civil judge's duty was to regulate "minor" matters arising in civic life—disputes that involved small sums and noncriminal offenses. In practice, this meant the bulk of problems of daily life. Whereas the district court system was not accessible to peasants, who remained confined to the separate juridical world of the exclusively peasant *volost* courts (see p. 105), the civil judge could be appealed to by all, without fear: soon he became one of the most influential figures in the Russian countryside.

Education, Censorship, and the Military

The "spirit of reform" affected government policy in matters of education and regulation of the by now extremely vocal and vociferous press. A revised university statute in 1863 granted the universities considerable rights of self-regulation, with deans and rectors playing a major role. Laws in 1864 and 1871 divided high schools into classical gymnasia based on a Greek and Latin curriculum and practical "real schools" based on the German model. Most importantly, a law of 1864 administered by the Ministry of National Enlightenment opened elementary schools to the public—meaning, in practice, children of the peasantry. In 1870, gymnasia for women were given legal sanction.

In the interests of crafting reform legislation, the government had relaxed censorship laws at the outset of Alexander II's reign. The looser regulation of the press was formalized in 1865 by "Temporary Rules" that exempted publications less than a certain length from censorship altogether and transferred responsibility for supervision to a department of the Ministry of Internal Affairs.

The cycle of reforms was rounded out by a series of legislative measures that arguably changed the lives of the peasantry more, in the short run, than had emancipation. Previously, the twenty-five-year term of military service had meant that recruits virtually vanished from the community, spelling economic devastation for their households, to say nothing of personal and family tragedy. At the very beginning of his reign, Alexander II cut the term to fifteen years, abolished corporal punishment in the army, and made provisions to raise the general level of education in the army. In 1864 military administration was regularized, and in 1874 a law instituting universal military conscription was instituted. The entire male population was now subject to the same requirements for military service: six years of active duty, nine on leave, and reserve duty up to the age of forty.

LIFE IN THE REFORM ERA

Acts of government legislation, particularly such momentous ones as emancipation, the zemstvo, and legal reforms, never work out in practice precisely as they appear on paper. People respond to policy in ways that make sense in the context of their personal lives; the results may sometimes be far indeed from the intentions of the lawmakers. The nine years that followed the initiation of the reforms—the term, in fact, specified for the "temporary obligation" of the peasants—were a period of transition.

Peasants and Landlords

By 1863 much of the allocation of land allotments was complete. Contracts concluded between the landlord and the commune specified the size and distributions of land parcels; they varied widely over the territories. In one district in the non-black-soil Novgorod region, for example, an individual peasant's plot ranged from 1.5 to 4 *desyatins* (about 4 to 11 acres); in some parts of Ukraine, family plots were as large as 25 *desyatins* (67 acres). In general, though, the plots were not small; most Russian peasants farmed larger plots than their counterparts in Europe. Most of the contracts were signed by the peasants. The process of land distribution, however, left much room for dispute: the quality of land even on an individual landowner's estate could of course vary widely. Sometimes peasants refused to sign the contracts because they felt that their assigned plot was too small or too scattered or because it included sandy or otherwise useless soil. In the meantime, the burden of continuing dues lay heavy on the "temporarily obligated" peasants: often, they now had to extract payments from land parcels smaller than the ones they had farmed before emancipation.

Up to 1870, peasants were to make arrangements to acquire the land they farmed as their property; in practice, the process continued into the 1880s. Again, conditions depended greatly on the individual communities involved. Landlords who could afford generosity sometimes gave peasants extra land without extracting payments; more often, they tried to set the price of land redemption as high as possible. In the black-soil provinces, most of the redemption agreements were voluntary, on both sides, because peasants were anxious to acquire the good land they farmed. Again, the regular payment of the high price on the land, together with interest of 5 or 6 percent, was a heavy and difficult obligation for many peasants.

It is safe to say that life changed for the peasants after emancipation—but not all that much. "Temporary obligation" represented a new relation to the landlord; but, in a very real sense, peasants remained tied to the land, as they had been of old. Peasant life unfolded in a world apart: peasants were not judged in the same courts with the other estates, they could not borrow money on the same terms, and their commune posed almost insurmountable barriers to entry into another class or profession. They found themselves encircled in a net of debts and obligations and lacking the necessary capital to consolidate and invest in agricultural business; they had few resources, and insufficient knowledge, to improve land that was often dry and barren and still carved into awkward strips. Lack of technical sophistication (irrigation, etc.) left peasant lands entirely vulnerable to the vicissitudes of rural life—famine, fire, and poor rainfall.

The palliative terms of the reform—the immediate retention of property by the landlords—did little to hide its long-term implications for the status of the gentry, for whom loss of land was an inevitable consequence of reform. Indeed, already in the first decade, gentry lands, in total, decreased by some 10 percent. Here, again, generalizations are difficult, primarily because of the vast variations in wealth and property among the gentry. In addition, farming was the full-time occupation of very few gentry: government service and, increasingly, business, industry, and culture were equally their domain. It remains fair to say that emancipation accelerated the influx of gentry into professional life, whether in the cities or by setting up factories on the territory of their estates. The landlords had to learn a new economics, farming their land using free labor. As landlord-peasant relations became redefined and different spheres of authority and mutual dependence took shape, the gentry found its survival predicated on the ability to function in new conditions. As an unintended consequence of the reform process, the gentry themselves acquired a new taste for politics: their engagement in the local committees, and later in the life of the zemstvo, made them reluctant to relinquish final decisions to the central government.

The Zemstvo: First Steps

The zemstvo institutions got off to a slow start; the years 1865–1867 were spent just putting them in place. In many provinces, gentry and peasants alike showed little interest in the new organs of self-government: many landlords saw no need to replace the gentry assembly, while peasants, at first, viewed having to attend zemstvo meetings as yet another obligation to be discharged. Before long, however, peasants began to bring matters before the zemstvo assemblies and boards to be resolved. Remarkably, cases of divisions along class lines within the assemblies were extremely rare; almost immediately decisions began to be reached by mutual consent. The zemstvos' first successes involved improvement of medical facilities, virtually nonexistent before the 1860s: the Arzamas and Balakhna Districts of Nizhny Novgorod Province, for example, voted to spend the bulk of their funds on physicians and free medical care in 1865 and 1866. The other major early sphere of action for the zemstvo was education: funds were immediately allocated for zemstvo-supervised secular schools that taught basic literacy as well as practical matters related to agricultural work.

The reforms created a variety of new roles in the Russian cities and countryside, from government-appointed mediators of the landlord-peasant contract to justices of the peace, from zemstvo-affiliated physicians and teachers to lawyers and judges connected with the new court system.

Tales of the "New People": The Radical Intelligentsia

As the first of the reforms went into effect, the city of St. Petersburg erupted in flames: block by block, the poorer areas of the city were consumed by a spate of fires that spread over the course of the spring and summer of 1862. At the same time, students at Moscow and St. Petersburg Universities had shown their restlessness beginning in the late 1850s by a chain of strikes and demonstrations. According to one story, the writer Fëdor Dostoevsky made his careful way through the flaming city to the house of the radical journalist Chernyshevsky to plead with him to stop the fires.

Chernyshevsky, of course, was not guilty of arson. Yet the story is symptomatic of the atmosphere of the early 1860s. Following in Vissarion Belinsky's footsteps, a new generation of literary critics—Chernyshevsky, Nikolai Dobrolyubov (1836–1861), and Dmitry Pisarev (1840–1868)—wielded acid and prolific pens to criticize the process of reform and to raise a series of "accursed questions" about Russian life more generally. Chernyshevsky was arrested and imprisoned in 1862; he lived in prison or in exile until 1889. Yet it was he who had the last word. His 1863 novel *What Is to Be Done?*, written in the Peter and Paul Fortress, became a cult phenomenon for a generation of young people. The novel, subtitled *Tales About the New People,* expressed Chernyshevsky's utopian socialist vision by recounting the story of a "new type" of person—young women and men who constructed their lives according to principles of "rational egoism." Social transformation, for Chernyshevsky, would come about through the transformation of personal relations, and specifically through the liberation of women. Thus in the novel, Lopukhov marries Vera Pavlovna to take her away from a miserable family existence; they have no sexual relations and are free to part ways when she falls in love with another. The perfect society of the future is foreshadowed in a sewing workshop run by Vera Pavlovna: starting from a small collective that pools its resources, the women in the workshop gradually expand in their powers until they are ultimately able to provide not only medical care and other essentials but eventually even opera tickets for their members.

The "people of the sixties" were anxious to replicate Chernyshevsky's model in real life. Thus "fictitious marriages" became popular—a means for young women, wishing to further their education, to escape from the norms of bourgeois society, discarding the prospect of a "proper" marriage together with their crinolines and crimped hairstyles. Some young people formed "communes" in Chernyshevsky's style, living together in large groups and sharing household tasks. The fashion touched many in Moscow and St. Petersburg: the composers Modest Mussorgsky (1839–1881) and Nikolai Rimsky-Korsakov (1844–1908) lived together "communally" for a while, both trying to compose operas in the confines of a small apartment.

Positivists and Nihilists

Chernyshevsky's dream of rationally ordering society resonated among his contemporaries in yet another sense. The mid-nineteenth century—in France, Germany, and England as much as in Russia—was mesmerized by the continually unfolding capacities of science. Astounding theoretical breakthroughs like Darwin's theory of evolution, which challenged the very bases of prevailing worldviews, and constant dramatic changes in technology—railways, steamships, factories, and machines—amazed and overwhelmed contemporaries. This fascination with the powers of science led, naturally, to new ways of thinking. Many began to believe that science not only could hold a key to the solution of strictly scientific and technological problems but might also have transformative potential for society and for the realm of metaphysics. This belief was expressed most powerfully by the French philosopher Auguste Comte, whose religion of science—complete with cathedrals dedicated to knowledge—strongly influenced many Russian thinkers, including Chernyshevsky. This general attitude to science, and Comte's philosophy in particular, is known as *positivism.* The Crystal Palace of the London World Exhibition of 1851 loomed as the symbol of the new belief. Its adherents not only worshipped science but believed firmly in progress and dismissed moral and metaphysical questions as trivial.

Another powerful literary prototype for the new generation was provided by the character Bazarov in Turgenev's novel *Fathers and Children*. Bazarov represented a type that came to be known as nihilists—iconoclastic, long-haired young men—or plainly dressed, short-haired young women—who despised the moral and philosophical concerns of their fathers. Turgenev's character Bazarov, on a visit from university to his friend's parents' country estate, was constantly dissecting frogs and trying to convince his disgruntled hosts—representing the idealist generation of the 1840s—that understanding human beings was no more complicated than understanding the physiology of a frog. Bazarov was painted rather negatively by Turgenev; yet Pisarev turned him into a positive hero. Bazarov, he wrote, stood for the powers of science and represented the goals that the present generation should make their own.

CHALLENGE FROM POLAND: THE 1863 REBELLION

Although the ideas of the radical intelligentsia of the 1860s swept through Russian universities and urban centers, they had no immediate consequences of real social unrest. Instead, the first true political challenge to the regime of Alexander II came from the borderlands—specifically, from Poland. The Polish nation had never accepted its partition and had manifested its discontent continuously since the late eighteenth century, culminating in revolution in 1830. The Poles actually sent three military formations to fight against Russia in the Crimean War. Alexander II's accession to the throne was greeted in Poland, as elsewhere, with high hopes and enthusiasm—to which the tsar nervously responded, on his visit there in 1856: "Pas de rêveries, messieurs!" ("No daydreams, gentlemen!") Symbolic measures—such as an amnesty to Poles sent to Siberia in 1831 and the reopening of the Polish Medical Academy—went over well. The implementation of emancipation, however, which Alexander actually hoped to begin in Poland and the western provinces, proved thornier, and the imperial government found the vocal, politically sophisticated, and anti-Muscovite Polish gentry more difficult to manipulate than the relatively pliable landlords of European Russia. Resistance to reform from above, moreover, combined with an instantaneous flowering of nationalism as soon as the reins were loosened. Alexander then tried to curb these impulses by sending Count Alexander Wielopolski (1803–1877) to Poland in 1861 and, a year later, making him head of the civil administration. Wielopolski's plans for Poland included the full implementation of the 1832 Organic Statute limiting Polish autonomy, integration of Polish officials into the civil bureaucracy, and commissions on land reform and Jewish emancipation—in short, a closer integration of Poland into the empire.

Efforts to limit Polish autonomy, however, only exacerbated tensions. After two years of near-crisis, a full-scale rebellion finally erupted in January of 1863. The immediate cause was Wielopolski's effort to draft thirty thousand young men into military service; but the insurrection that followed brought into play a sophisticated and highly organized, if poorly armed, revolutionary machine that had been in the making for the preceding thirty years. Wielopolski had, in 1861, disbanded the Agricultural Society, formed in 1858 for the ostensible purpose of implementing land reform (and, presumably, modeled on the Free Economic Society in Russia) but actually functioning as a sort of quasi-parliament for the Polish nobility. Conspiratorial activity, however, continued in various circles, some of which dated from 1830: the main camps were the "Reds," headed by a National Central Committee (KCN) in Warsaw, and the "Whites." The KCN organized a mass departure of young men from the city in early January, so that only fourteen hundred actually remained subject to the draft. This amounted to a declaration of open rebellion and was followed by the formation of an underground state and a real campaign of guerilla warfare. The uprising was led by Romuald Traugutt (1825–1864) and spread, eventually, into Lithuania and, less successfully, into Ukraine (where it met with peasant resistance). The rebellion resembled a full-scale war; there were over a thousand military engagements over its sixteen months. It ended with the capture of its leaders in the spring of 1864.

Any semblance of self-government and independence for the Kingdom of Poland came to an end with the suppression of the 1863 uprising, as Poland became systematically transformed into a Russian province. It even acquired a new name—the "Vistula lands"—and came completely under centralized Russian administration. Imperial policy in Poland foreshadowed far-reaching Russification policies that would come under Alexander III. A Russian University replaced the Polish "Main School," the Education Commission was shut down, and district towns lost their municipal rights. The use of the Napoleonic Code in civil courts, however, was retained. The most curious aspect of the rebellion, however, was the emergence of the imperial state as the defender of the Polish peasants: the major goal of the state, after putting down the uprising, became to push through the agrarian reform by whatever means necessary. The Polish reform, enacted in 1864, became, ironically, the most far reaching of any agrarian legislation in the empire: as an answer to the rebellious gentry, who felt that their property rights were infringed on by forced emancipation, it gave the Polish peasants more favorable terms than elsewhere.

The Polish rebellion divided the Russian intelligentsia. In Europe, public opinion was outraged by its suppression, and educated society throughout the continent lived the fate of the Polish rebels. The year 1863 also marked the end of the "Russian European" Herzen's fleeting romance with the Russian state: Herzen deplored the government's action and found in it new fuel for revolutionary sentiments. Others, however—particularly on the wave of self-righteousness that followed emancipation, for which the gentry were now willing to take full credit—saw in the Polish nobility's rebellion a selfish resistance to reform. In Russia itself, therefore, the rebellion provoked much less sympathy than in European countries and, indeed, revealed a certain Russian patriotism.

The first real revolutionary organizations within Russia emerged in opposition to the reforms. The short-lived Land and Freedom (not to be confused with a later organization bearing the same name) was a loose collection of groups in Petersburg, Moscow, and the provinces. They hoped that the expected turmoil of emancipation would bring about what Alexander II feared most—a revolution from below. A group called Young Russia issued a manifesto in 1862 calling for a "bloody and pitiless" peasant revolution that would utterly destroy the foundations of the existing order, reforms included. But it was a radical group called simply the Organization that made its mark on the political scene. Formed by students who had rejected their studies to dedicate themselves to the cause of the people's liberation, the Organization had a core circle known as Hell, led by the student Nikolai Ishutin (1840–1879), that was unparalleled in its extremism and dedication to the revolutionary cause.

Acting on his own initiative, a member of the Organization, Dmitry Karakozov, on April 4, 1866, fired his gun at the tsar. The assassination attempt failed, in part, as legend has it, because a peasant bystander saw what was happening and pushed Karakozov's elbow, redirecting the shot into the air. But Karakozov's shot, and the highly publicized trial that followed, signaled an end to the spirit of cooperation that had marked the early period of the reforms; the strains and open tensions of the turbulent 1870s soon followed.

CHAPTER 22

The Turbulent Seventies

The great chain is broken,
It's broken and has struck
The master with one end,
And the muzhik with the other.
—*Nikolai Nekrasov, "Who Lives Well in Russia?" (1873–76)*

Initially, the great reforms generated a good deal of confusion: the peculiar nine-year "temporary obligation" placed peasants and landlords in an ambiguous status, the zemstvo was at first viewed with suspicion, and the effectiveness and fairness of jury trials was questioned. By the 1870s, however, the effects of the reforms were in full force—if often in unexpected ways. The most dramatic effect was felt in Russia's provinces: remote provincial towns came alive, and the countryside went into motion as the end of serfdom and the establishment of local institutions removed barriers to commercial and cultural development. The immensity of the emancipation, which, after all, affected 50 million peasants, soon captured the imagination of Russian educated society. "The people" became nothing short of an obsession, and the ideal of "serving the people" became the bottom line of cultural life in the 1870s. A relatively loose approach to imperial administration permitted different mores, administrative structures, and even laws to operate in different parts of the empire, with only occasional central intervention.

At the same time, Karakozov's shot had initiated a harsh, confrontational period in Russian politics and ideology. Alexander II's government, in its effort to maintain a delicate balance between reform and control, definitely leaned toward the latter after 1866, and hopes of a constitutional monarchy or a national representative assembly faded quickly. Some elements in Russian society responded, in turn, by a progressive radicalization: revolutionaries, both men and women—dedicated, violent, and intransigent—made their appearance in town and countryside. Extreme ideologies of the left were matched by equally vociferous ideologies of the right. The ideology of pan-Slavism became one factor in a new war with the Ottoman Empire over the Balkans in 1877–1878—the first time that public opinion played a role in foreign policy.

AFTER THE REFORMS, 1866–1881

Perhaps the deepest consequence of the reforms of the 1860s was the diffusion of power, a shift of political activity from the exclusive domain of the central administration to a plurality of new focal points—institutions such as the commune, the local government and courts, the local press, and so on. These institutions, and the way of life that evolved around them, took root over the ensuing half century.

Old and New Identities

Emancipation meant, in practice, that the bulk of responsibility for managing the material aspects of peasant life was transferred to the commune; the commune, in other words, moved to the forefront in the countryside, replacing the authority of the landlord. The typical commune was made up of from four to eighty peasant households—about twenty to five hundred individuals; its territorial boundaries generally coincided with those of the village. It was the peasant commune that regulated land distribution; collected taxes for the state, zemstvo, and the commune itself; and organized peasant labor for tasks like road maintenance. The commune managed some matters of civil law; maintained public order; took charge of mutual aid and assistance and poor relief; organized public holidays; maintained local churches; and served as a channel of communication between peasants and other government institutions.

Within the commune itself, economic stratification and differentiation were considerable. One recent study of Voronezh Province has shown that, according to peasant definitions, 75 to 80 percent of households were considered to be "average" or "doing tolerably well"—that is, balancing consumption, production, and available labor and land. Economic success depended largely on family and commune support: childless or nuclear families tended to do worse than the traditional extended peasant family, while illness or drunkenness could also be causes of poverty. In general, recent studies have argued that the commune distributed resources with reasonable efficiency and that innovations and improvements did take place within the structure of communal agriculture.

A major trend in the postemancipation peasant economy was labor migration. The number of passports issued to peasants in the central industrial region, for example, went up from 510 in 1860–1870 to 1,282 in the next decade. Although many peasants had always supplemented agricultural labor with handicrafts and trade, they now left the villages, often seasonally, to work in factories. Communes, whose consent was necessary for permanent exit, fought successfully (sometimes in coalition with state or families) to maintain control over departing members and their earnings: the result was that most "peasant-workers" maintained close ties to their villages, often supporting families there and returning frequently. Whether they stayed in the village or migrated to the city, peasants and "peasant-workers" retained a strong religious sense.

The "hyphenated peasant" soon became an important character in the urban landscape as well. Russia's workers have been counted at some 800,000 by 1870—a significant increase resulting from the spurt in industrialization. No social legislation regarding workers (limiting work hours, setting a minimum wage, etc.) existed at all. In the 1870s, they were just beginning to use strikes to force employers to attend to their needs; workers struck at St. Petersburg in 1870, demanding a higher wage, and similar strikes followed in the countryside. In all, some 225 such actions took place over the course of the decade.

Peasant-workers were not the only new social group that emerged in the wake of the reforms. The "new people" of the 1860s and 1870s—to borrow Nikolai Chernyshevsky's phrase—were provincial priests, doctors, teachers, agronomists, statisticians, lawyers, veterinarians. With tremendous energy, this stratum of provincial intelligentsia took on the many tasks involved in making land distribution, local government, and peasant farming work. Agronomists and statisticians launched a campaign to improve the quality of agricultural land and peasant farming, while the zemstvo's responsibility for medicine and education gave physicians and teachers a sense of mission. Russia's priests began a much more active relationship with their parishes—giving more sermons (these had been rare in the pre-emancipation period); holding "conversations" with peasants outside the official church service; and founding, formally or informally, parish schools. They also began communicating with each other through a network of diocesan journals that sprang up all over Russia in response to the Holy Synod's request. Priests also joined zemstvo activities, becoming the most useful and avid on-the-spot collectors of agricultural and meteorological statistics.

The Provincial Landscape

If peasant life did not change as dramatically as one might expect after emancipation, the great reforms altered Russia's social fabric profoundly and irrevocably in a manner that the legislators had not planned. The 1860s and 1870s saw a sudden explosion of provincial culture and burgeoning of regional centers, as towns that had been mere administrative centers acquired genuine meaning as foci for local political, legal, and cultural life.

By the 1870s, the scarcely populated, muddy, culturally isolated provincial Russia of Nicholas I's day had come alive. The population of many regional centers and small towns doubled in the two decades that followed the reforms. Railroads began slowly to bridge the vast distances of European Russia with the construction of a line from St. Petersburg to Warsaw and from Moscow to Nizhny Novgorod. Factories sprouted on the outskirts of towns and on ambitious landowners' estates: industry flourished in the central industrial region, textiles in Ivanovo; mining and metallurgy, for which Russia had been famous in the eighteenth century, underwent a revival. The drab provincial town of Livny, south of Moscow, for example, which produced primarily agricultural products before the reforms, boasted eighteen major factories by the 1890s; the population of the district was increasing at the rate of some four thousand a year. A serious effort was made to improve sanitary conditions in the towns and villages as pipelines and sewage systems were installed and roads paved. The atmosphere of the towns and estates changed, as well, as energetic young scientists, priests, teachers, and physicians working in the countryside animated provincial living rooms and zemstvo meetings.

The zemstvo became the cornerstone of a distinctive and original political culture that sets the period 1860–1917 off both from the autocratic tradition of imperial Russia and the heavily centralized Soviet regime that followed it. The zemstvo gave people the experience of politics and was a mediating force between the gentry and the peasants. Its progressive functions, which were many, were at the same time constrained by its limited right to tax: the need to request funds from the central government kept the zemstvo more dependent on the latter than its members would have wished. The zemstvo's construction of an entire infrastructure of political participation made it the defining institution of the dynamic, active era that followed the great reforms.

A legal culture emerged around the court system: trials became an object of fascination, and local newspapers—which sprang up like mushrooms in the 1870s—reported not only weather conditions and agricultural advice but also the latest local legal sensations. In the 1870s and 1880s, Fëdor Dostoevsky picked up this theme of provincial life and turned it into fiction. The demand for lawyers increased dramatically with the reconfiguration of social relations following emancipation: inevitably, questions involving the distribution of the land, regulation of zemstvo activities, and other matters required legal solution. As novelist Mikhail Saltykov-Shchedrin's character Pavel Golovlëv commented in *The Golovlëv Family,* "Lawyers are everywhere nowadays."

Perhaps the brightest symptom of the new vitality was the press. The official government *Courier* was augmented by a spate of local newspapers and journals in the 1870s, bringing with them active local journalists and public activists. National journals multiplied and increased in circulation: most households subscribed to two or three illustrated weeklies, so that by the 1880s Russians had a shared reading culture. The most popular journal, *Niva (Plowlands),* already had a circulation of twenty thousand in 1870. Two national journals were founded specifically with a focus on Russian history and documents from Russian archives, while local historians investigated the history of their towns and launched an initiative for the preservation and publication of local materials. The programs of theaters and concert halls expanded; architects were in demand as cities grew. Museums were founded in the provincial centers, displaying not so much art as local history, ethnography, the natural environment. Instead of the gentry assembly alone, provincial residents could now take part in a variety of voluntary organizations, from the official zemstvo to clubs of science lovers, poetry reading groups, the All-Estate Club, and others. Not the least of such activities were charitable organizations: benefit recitals and charity balls were a staple of provincial life as citizens sought to take responsibility for the welfare of local society. Hostels were established where homeless people could find a cot and tea for the night. In Livny, for example, by 1890 there were six schools (three of them connected to the parish), several charitable societies, two banks, pharmacies, two hotels, bookstores, photography shops, and a sanatorium.

A special place in this wealth of activity belonged to education. Many people saw literacy as the key to ultimately integrating 20 million former serfs into society. Both the church and private initiative played a major role in a growing literacy campaign: parish and private schools were founded in large numbers in the countryside. At this time, both religious and secular schools were the product of a grassroots movement: some schools started in a peasant hut with one or two students and grew to full-fledged institutions. Peasant children were taught basic orthography, arithmetic, and, in the parish schools, the Bible. Less successful efforts by the government, in the meantime, were directed by the Ministry of National Enlightenment, which created a network of peasant schools affiliated with the zemstvo. Literacy rates went up considerably but, despite all efforts, remained deplorably low thirty years after the reforms: about 21 percent in 1897. Many teachers sought to shape the reading tastes and cultural habits of their students as well and disapproved of the popular boulevard literature that began to flourish as the reading public increased.

It is not surprising that residents of provincial Russia began to think of themselves in new ways as their environment changed. Increasingly, they began to have a sense of local identity and pride: each town had a number of local activists—for example, journalists, teachers, or prominent zemstvo members—who asserted the value of the particular cultural life of their town. They organized celebrations of events in local history and began to resent the snobbish attitude of intelligentsia in the capitals, who anachronistically continued to see all provincial towns as backwaters. Equally important, the relatively clearly defined status and set of obligations that had characterized each *soslovie* group up to the reforms were beginning to blur significantly. Landlords who ran factories, ex-serfs who opened shops, and members of the *meshchanstvo* (petty bourgeoisie) who wrote philosophical treatises could not simply and clearly be labeled in terms of their *soslovie* origins; many of them read the same journals and newspapers and attended the same meetings. Gradually, *soslovie* acquired a corporative meaning as an association that could be of use in one's professional life—rather than a stamp that carried with it a whole series of statements about the bearer's work, habits, income, and way of life.

Subcultures and Borderlands

The nature of the empire as a whole changed, too, in the second half of the century: the thirty-four provinces of European Russia, which had local institutions while others did not, began to resemble a "metropole" like England or France, clearly distinct from the "colonial" periphery. Alexander II's reign was the last gasp of the characteristic Russian imperial pattern of governing through local elites and preserving local language and institutions, soon to be replaced by the classic European-style imperialist policies of Alexander III and Nicholas II.

This less stringent attitude was reflected in the lives of some imperial subjects: one example is the Jews, whose possibilities definitely increased in these twenty years. In the reign of Alexander II, though the longed-for "Jewish Emancipation" never took place, changes were mostly reflected in greater possibilities of movement.

Many Jews who had professional training or higher education were no longer bound to the Pale of Settlement (see the chapter "Around the Russian Empire, 1801–1861") and could live and work, be lawyers and physicians, and be elected to zemstvo office anywhere (with the notable exception of St. Petersburg). In general, the slogan of the period—for other ethnic groups as well as Jews—was participation and inclusion in the "mainstream": an 1856 decree advised investigation into the possibility of merging Jews with the majority population. Members of ethnic groups, if they were willing to accept the standards of Russian society, had the opportunity to move up within it. Thus this period witnessed, for example, the flowering of the Russianized Armenian city Nakhichevan and education in both languages for Armenian children at the same time as radical nationalists rejected this assimilationist spirit and fomented revolution.

The Conquest of Central Asia

A campaign of conquest reaching beyond the Kazakh steppes augmented Russia's borderlands with deserts and mountains. Statistics for this period are unreliable, but it brought perhaps 5 million Muslims into the empire as the reforms were taking hold throughout European Russia, the western borderlands, and Siberia. Alexander II's foreign minister, Alexander Gorchakov (1798–1883), in 1864 conceptualized the process of Russia's Central Asian expansion in the following terms: When Russia, as a civilized state, sought to protect its boundaries and its security, it had to suppress the banditry and incursions of the wild tribes on its borderlands. Inevitably, as the state subdued one group, it came into contact with the next, thus pushing its own borders farther and farther into the Asian wilds. Gorchakov's principle was quite close to an ideology of imperialism, and its author saw analogies between Russian expansion and that of the United States, France, Holland, and England.

In the middle of the nineteenth century, Central Asia's great deserts (Kara-Kum, Kyzyl-Kum), oases (watered by the Amu-Darya and Syr-Darya Rivers, flowing into the Aral Sea), and mountains (Tienshan, Pamir)—roughly, the territory between the Kazakh steppes on the north, Persia and Afghanistan in the south, the Caspian Sea to the west, and China to the east—were inhabited by a variety of settled and nomadic peoples, predominantly of Muslim religion and Turkic, or sometimes Iranian, language. Once the focus of a rich caravan trade in silk and spices, the Central Asian cities—Tashkent, Khiva, Merv, Samarkand, Bukhara—had, in the medieval period, formed a link between East and West. Islamic, Iranian, and Arabic cultures and traditions intersected and flourished; Bukhara in particular became a center of Muslim learning, while the reign of the conqueror Tamerlane made Samarkand into an architectural jewel in the early fifteenth century. At mid nineteenth century the territory was dominated by three kingdoms, all ruled by Uzbek (Turkic) dynasties—the emirate of Bukhara and the khanates of Khiva and Kokand. A more fluid area to their southeast—the Turkmen steppes—remained under the looser control of Khiva, Bukhara, and Iran.

In the seventeenth and eighteenth centuries, expanding maritime routes shifted trade away from the overland roads, causing a steady decline in the international status of the Central Asian kingdoms. Yet they maintained an elaborate political structure and taxation system and a rich culture, dominated by the Islamic clergy and the traditional Muslim educational institutions of *maktab* (primary school) and *madrasa* (college).

Russian eyes had roved over Central Asia for a century, making Great Britain, whose Indian possessions were nearby, nervous. The actual conquest began the same year that Gorchakov made his pronouncement. General Mikhail Chernyaev, with twenty-six hundred troops, made his way south in May 1864, taking Tashkent in 1865. By 1867, the conquered territories, which included the whole of the kingdom of Kokand and parts of Khiva and Bukhara, were consolidated into the province of Turkistan, with General Konstantin Kaufmann appointed governor general. The emirate of Bukhara and the kingdom of Khiva remained Russian protectorates, and were not actually incorporated into the empire, in part as a result of British apprehensions. A Russo-British agreement was hammered out making the northern border of Afghanistan the limit of Russian influence. At first, and up to

Shir-Dar madrasa, Samarkand. Constructed 1648. Photo by N.V. Bogaevsky, 1872. *Library of Congress.*

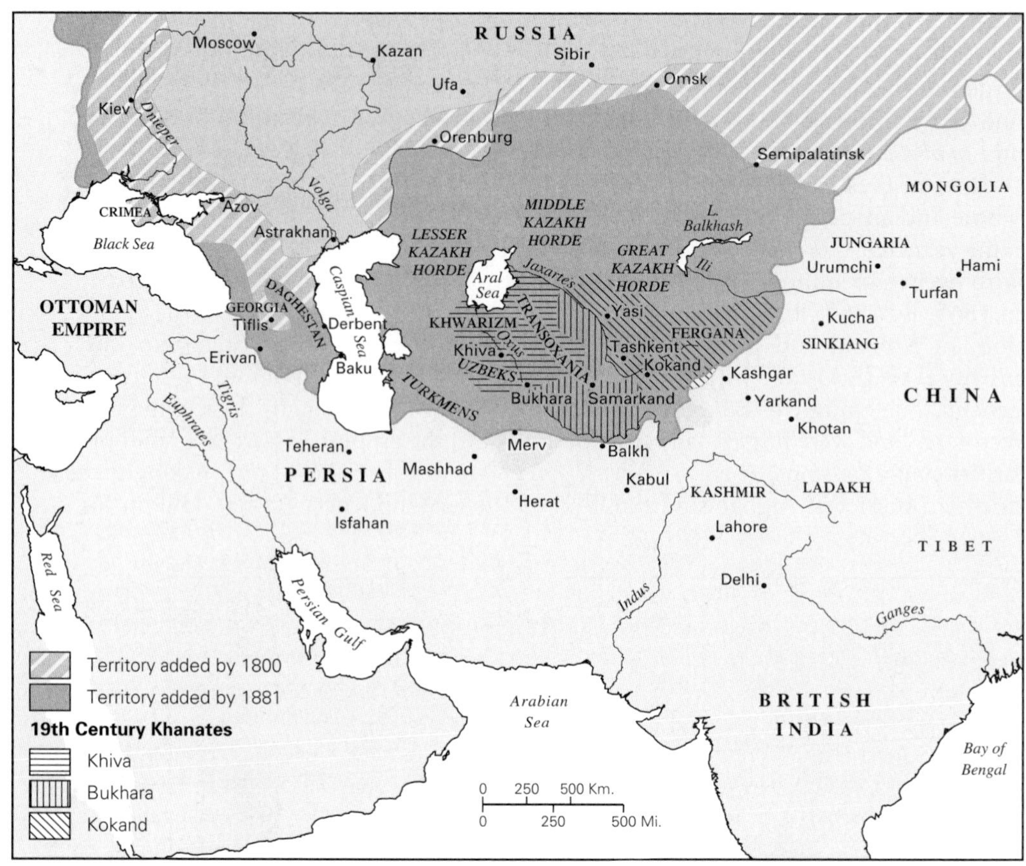

Russian expansion in Muslim Central Asia.

the 1880s, Russia adopted a conscious policy of maintaining local judicial and political institutions and practices, establishing only a loose administrative jurisdiction over the new territories.

GOING TO THE PEOPLE, 1873–1874

Russia's colonial expansion won the attention of the public in the "metropole" at sensational moments: the capture of Shamyl (see the chapter "Around the Russian Empire, 1801–1861"), for example, stimulated an entire literary genre of Caucasian stories and popular novels that captivated European audiences as well. Travel stories and tales of the exotic formed a staple of illustrated journals like *Niva* and even daily newspapers. But the imagination of educated society never strayed far from a theme that was closer to home: the plight of the peasantry.

The Populist Movement

Since Alexander Radishchev's first "discovery" of peasant life as his carriage traveled from St. Petersburg to Moscow, the Russian educated public had become increasingly fascinated by the mores and ways of life of "the people," so far removed from the bureaucratic ladder climbing and social pageantry of urban existence. "Simple folk" and provincial scenes had become the staple of "realism" in literature in the 1840s. After the reforms, fascination turned into obsession. Educated men and women, many of whom knew little or nothing about peasants or about farming, were alternately captivated by the richness of peasant folklore and rituals and horrified by the poverty and persisting lack of sanitation or medical care they observed on their excursions into the countryside.

In the summer of 1873, and with renewed energy in 1874, a wave of enthusiastic students and young people flooded the Russian countryside, armed with leaflets, primers, medical expertise, and an urgent desire to help "the people"—whom, despite the latter's formal emancipation, they saw as enslaved by poverty, lack of education, and judicial discrimination. Their aim was to immerse themselves in peasant and village life, to teach the people, and to persuade them to rise up against the injustices of their existence. Behind the collective crisis of conscience lay an acute awareness of an enormous gap between the "intelligentsia" and the *narod*—Russia's vast peasant population. The activists' perception of the gulf between well-off and poor, the educated and uneducated, prompted many to dedicate their lives to education or public service through the zemstvos, the new municipal institutions, the church, or science. But others looked to a more radical and sometimes a revolutionary solution.

The movement "to the people" originated in a variety of circles of young men and women that formed in the late 1860s and early 1870s, all of which were concerned with ways to reach the *narod*. The Chaikovsky Circle in St. Petersburg was one of the earliest; they published socialist literature (including the works of the German radical philosopher Karl Marx, as well as Chernyshevsky and Dobrolyubov) and distributed propaganda among urban workers. The Fritschi Circle, another example, was formed by émigrés and joined forces with a group of Georgian radicals. Many of the radicals of the 1870s became known as *narodniki,* or populists.

The mass movement in the spring of 1874 was inspired largely by the writings of two influential figures—Pëtr Lavrov (1823–1900) and Mikhail Bakunin (1824–1876), who stood for the two basic branches of the movement. Lavrov, in his enormously popular *Historical Letters* (1869), argued that the injustices of historical development had created an ever-widening gap between the intelligentsia and the people. The highly educated "critically thinking individuals" who had unjustly won superior status at the expense of the rest of the population had a debt to pay and a mission before them. It was only with their participation, their elaboration of a theory of social action, that revolution could take place. Russia's young people, therefore, had a responsibility to complete their education and then take what they had learned to the masses. The anarchist (i.e., advocate of a stateless society) Bakunin, in contrast, writing from abroad, had a much more direct and spontaneous vision: he encouraged students to abandon their useless studies at the university and go immediately to live and work among the people, igniting a peasant revolution.

The enthusiastic response of "Lavrovists" and "Bakuninists," as students left the universities in droves to "serve the people," prompted the German sociologist Max Weber to describe Russian populism as "the last major religious movement in modern history." The heady days of 1874, however, ended in disaster. In many cases, the peasants were not at all receptive to the mass invasion by alien young people. They could not understand the activists' arguments and were suspicious of efforts to rouse their enmity to the tsar, who for many of them was a figure beyond questioning or debate. Partly, the lack of response was the fault of the populists themselves: frequently, they were not the least bit clear what they actually wanted the peasants to do. More dramatically, however, it was the government that put an end to this first wave of enthusiasm. Some leaflets captured in the Middle Volga town of Saratov put police forces on the trail of circles in Kursk, then populist circles in thirty-seven provinces. Seven hundred and seventy arrests were made (158 of them women) and 265 people imprisoned. Any nonpeasant wearing peasant clothes—the mark of a Bakuninist, but also of some innocent investigators of peasant culture—was likely to end up in the local jail.

The failure of populism as a social movement did not end its influence as a way of thinking and a code of behavior. "The people" and the need to help them continued to dominate the social consciousness for at least the next two decades. In this sense, populism was a phenomenon that transcended by far the narrow boundaries of a revolutionary movement, though some of the radical fringe were revolutionaries. Populism found its most sophisticated philosophical expression in the writings of Nikolai Mikhailovsky (1842–1904), who in the late 1860s became editor of the journal *Notes of the Fatherland*. Articulating the belief in progress and science of his day, Mikhailovsky argued that, although Russia was lagging behind other European countries in industrial and social development, it could "skip a stage." On the basis of indigenous Russian institutions like the peasant commune, Russia could find an equal place among European nations. Mikhailovsky's theory of "subjective sociology" sought to introduce an element of free will into the objective laws of progress and historical development, so that although progress was both inevitable and desirable, Russians could mold their development in a manner more suited to the conditions of their country.

Wanderers and Civic Poets

The theme of "going to the people" dominated or even monopolized the cultural consciousness of the late 1860s and 1870s as well. Writers like Gleb Uspensky, Vladimir Korolenko, and the poet Nikolai Nekrasov created a new "civic" poetry and literature that depicted the harsh aspects of peasant life. At the same time, an active and iconoclastic group of young artists revolted against the official codes of painting and sculpture of the Academy of Arts (just about simultaneously with the rebellious formation of the Salon des Refusés in Paris). These artists, calling themselves the Wanderers, staged their own exhibits in various Russian cities; instead of the classical subjects favored by the academy, they painted scenes of peasants at work and rural landscapes and tried to capture on canvas the rhythms of life in the countryside. Ilya Repin (1844–1930) was himself a serf whose freedom his fellow artists purchased by selling a canvas by the academic painter Alexander Briullov; Repin's *Barge-Haulers on the Volga* (1870), among other paintings, won him lasting fame. Ivan Shishkin's bears and forest scenes have become familiar to art lovers; Vasily Surikov's *Boyarina Morozova* (from the 1880s) captured a scene from the life of the Old Believers. The desire to depict "real life," including social problems, gave the name *realism* to this movement that developed in both literature and art. Russian realism, in turn, was part of a general European trend in art that had begun around the time of the 1848 revolutions: the aims and style of Repin and Nekrasov echoed, though in their own way, the art of Millet and Corot and the novels of Flaubert, Zola, and George Eliot.

Ultimately, the populist movement brought about indelible changes in Russian society. For educated people themselves, choosing to live and work in the countryside or in the provincial towns gradually became an accepted and even prestigious decision. Once the crucial step had been made, the *narod* irreversibly became a part of their lives, and the following decades witnessed an unceasing immersion in

The propagandist's arrest, by Ilya Repin (1878). *Tretyakov Gallery, Moscow, Russia/Scala/Art Resource, NY.*

popular culture and the astoundingly detailed, enthusiastic, and dedicated study of peasant life and economy. On the other hand, as provincial life flourished, the peasants slowly gained increasing opportunities to change their status, to enter into urban life as tavern keepers, factory workers, or merchants. Perhaps the most important legacy of populism was the obsession with literacy and education: as Russia learned to read, the first step was taken to overcoming the infamous gap between the intelligentsia and the people. The lasting effects of the populist movement, despite its radical origins, came in the milder form of literacy and the flowering of life in Russia's provinces.

CULTURAL LIFE IN THE CAPITALS

The capital cities—St. Petersburg and Moscow—flourished in the reform era. Industrialization in their respective regions and the heavy volume of trade resulting from a newly active merchantry and low customs duties contributed to an unprecedented growth in population. Inhabitants of Moscow, according to a contemporary local census, numbered 364,148 in 1864, and 753,469 by 1882. The figures for St. Petersburg are 667,963 in 1869, and 861,303 in 1881. The two cities were, at last, linked by railroad in1851. St. Petersburg's broad boulevards—the three radial lines of Nevsky and Voznesensky Prospects and Gorokhovaia Street—became lined with bourgeois-style buildings, shopfronts, and restaurants. The festive city had an "underbelly," too: much of Petersburg's new population consisted of poor laborers in the factories, and improvements in sanitation and municipal institutions did not keep pace. Dark courtyards and dank passageways, taverns, brothels, and street beggars provided Dostoevsky and others with ample material for their grim portrayals of the city.

Both St. Petersburg and Moscow provided the backdrop for a lively cultural scene that included music, ballet, painting, history, and science, as well as literature and journalism.

Music and Ballet

Secular musical life in Russia took wing in the 1860s. The foundations had been laid in the first half of the century with the "romance"—or art song—of Alexander Gurilëv, Alexander Varlamov, and Nikolai Titov (nicknamed the "grandfather of Russian song"). The romance, incorporating the poetry of Alexander Pushkin (1799–1837) and others, provided melodic material on which later composers of operas and symphonies could draw. In addition, Mikhail Glinka's operas, *Life for the Tsar* (1836) and *Ruslan and Lyudmila* (1842), and his songs and orchestral pieces, became the inspiration for a generation of young composers.

In the 1860s, music became a passion for these young men. A necessary stimulus was provided by the brothers Nikolai and Anton Rubinstein, who in 1859 founded a Russian Musical Society, with courses in both St. Petersburg and

Moscow. Not long afterward, the society became the basis for a conservatory at St. Petersburg (1862), and then at Moscow (1866). Almost immediately, the Russian musical world split in two. The conservatories, with their rigorous academic training in harmony, orchestration, and counterpoint and grounding in European musical tradition, raised the professional level of Russian music. Pëtr Ilich Tchaikovsky (1840–1893) was their first illustrious product: having studied under Anton Rubinstein, he became a professor at the Moscow Conservatory from its inception. In the meantime, a group of five youthful composers, disciples of Alexander Dargomyzhsky and enthusiasts of a distinctively "Russian" music, poured disdain on the conservatories' foreignness and academism. Soon to be known as "The Five," or "The Mighty Bunch," Mily Balakirev, Cesar Cui, Alexander Borodin, Modest Mussorgsky, and Nikolai Rimsky-Korsakov gathered informally to study scores and discuss techniques of composition, relying on innate talent instead of rigorous training. At one point, Mussorgsky and Rimsky-Korsakov, inspired by Chernyshevsky, decided to form a "commune," living together and writing operas; the experiment fizzled in short order. This group of immensely talented musicians formed the nucleus of the alternative Free Music School, established in St. Petersburg in 1862, partly at Balakirev's initiative.

The music of "The Mighty Bunch" relied for its distinctive flavor on folk songs and religious culture, with which all were well acquainted from childhood. Their "Russianness" was not merely an ideological position: instead of the Western system of harmony, which privileges the tonic, dominant, and subdominant, they used the harmonic system of Orthodox choral music, in which all degrees of the scale have equal weight. The most consistent practitioner of this Russian harmony was Modest Mussorgsky (1839–1881). His major works were the historical operas *Boris Godunov* (1869)—which used Pushkin's drama as a libretto—and *Khovanshchina* (1886). Mussorgsky was inspired by the populist enthusiasm of the day: in both operas, the people (*narod*) plays a dominant role, indeed became the "hero" of *Khovanshchina;* to achieve the desired effect, Mussorgsky made innovative, unusual use of the opera chorus. Like Mussorgsky's two works, the exotic *Prince Igor,* by Borodin (1833–1887), replete with Oriental princesses and horsemen of the steppe, remains part of the standard opera repertoire. Rimsky-Korsakov (1844–1908) was the most independent of the Five, accepting a position at the St. Petersburg Conservatory and achieving, though late, a solid grounding in musical theory. Rimsky's symphonic poem *Sadko* (1867), together with his First Symphony, won him early fame; he went on to compose the now forgotten opera *The Maid of Pskov* (1888) and the well-remembered Oriental symphonic poem *Scheherazade* (also 1888.) Rimsky's most important works belong to a later era: the operas *Sadko, The Legend of the City of Kitezh, The Golden Cockerel,* and *The Tale of the Tsar-Saltan* all made a splash in the Silver Age (1890s and 1900s).

Despite his contemporary reputation as "cosmopolitan" and "academic," Tchaikovsky, too, was not immune to the national and folk themes of the Five; in his music, however, such themes were made to fit purely Western harmonizations. He wrote six symphonies, of which the Sixth (1893) is the most frequently performed. The finale of the Fourth Symphony (1877) uses the folk song "A Birchtree

Stood in the Field" as its main motif. Tchaikovsky commented that its message was "Go to the people!" His operas *Evgeny Onegin* and *The Queen of Spades* brought to life the culture of Pushkin's time for the audiences of the 1870s; Tchaikovsky himself wrote romances and drew heavily on their style in his operatic writing. Arguably, Tchaikovsky's true vocation was ballet music—a genre he discovered in 1877 with the "flair and brilliance" and "brooding fatalism" of *Swan Lake*. This success was followed, in the early 1890s, by *Sleeping Beauty* and *The Nutcracker.* Tchaikovsky's personal life was tinged with sadness, as we know from his correspondence with his patroness, Nadezhda von Meck; his melancholy was most likely related to his homosexuality. He died in 1893.

Tchaikovsky's turn to ballet music coincided with the beginning of the age of glory of the Russian Imperial Ballet. The choreographer Marius Petipa (1818–1910), the Frenchman whose name is practically synonymous with so-called classical ballet, had come to St. Petersburg in 1847. Over the ensuing half century he created forty-six original ballets. The Mariinsky Theater in St. Petersburg and the Bolshoi Theater in Moscow became the scene of many triumphant performances as Russian dancers became internationally renowned.

Academies, Museums, and Universities

Despite the disdain of the Wanderers for the world of academic art, and of the Five for that of academic music, official institutions of culture prospered in the 1860s and 1870s. The Academy of Arts was granted a new statute, creating separate divisions for painting and sculpture on the one hand, and architecture on the other. The 1860s signaled a new era in the consumption of culture. The Hermitage collection of fine arts, begun in the late eighteenth century as Catherine II's private refuge inside the Winter Palace, for the first time opened its doors to the general public in 1866. The rules of Nicholas I's era—visitors could enter only in a frock coat, top hat, and gloves, having first obtained a ticket at the office of the imperial court—were replaced with the simpler requirement of generally neat dress, even if it was that of a peasant. In the meantime, private art galleries were established as merchants used their wealth to become patrons of the arts; the Moscow merchant Pavel Tretyakov's lavish collection of Russian art, transferred to the city of Moscow in 1892, was the most remarkable, and the nucleus of an eventually world-famous museum. The Rumyantsev Museum (later to become the basis for the Lenin Library) was transferred to Moscow in 1861, where it continued to build up its fine collections of manuscripts—particularly relating to history and to church law—coins, and ethnographic objects. An Imperial Russian Historical Museum was initiated in Moscow in the 1870s and opened a decade later. Both capitals by the 1870s boasted dozens of cultural, ethnographic, scientific, and professional organizations; many of them had their own public reading rooms and exhibits. In this respect, the capital cities functioned as magnified copies of their provincial counterparts.

In the wake of the university reform of 1863, universities broadened their admissions, so that by the 1870s only 25 percent of students were enrolled without a full fellowship. Dostoevsky's impoverished, garret-bound students had a very real prototype in contemporary "undergraduates," some of them sons of clergy or even peasants. Among the professoriate, major scholars emerged. Sergei Soloviëv (1820–1879) established a vision of Russian history, laid out in twenty-nine heavy volumes (1851–1879), that has influenced historians throughout the nineteenth and twentieth centuries. Russian history, for Soloviëv as for other adherents of the "state" school of historiography, was the story of the continuous, triumphant unfolding of the Russian state as it incorporated and ordered the vast lands of Eurasia. For the first time, Russian scholars made significant contributions to the natural sciences: the most remarkable achievement was that of the chemist Dmitry Mendeleev (1834–1907), who created the periodic table of elements in 1869. The mathematician Sophia Kovalevskaya (1850–1891) became a professor in Sweden.

Russian women, who in the 1860s flocked to foreign universities (particularly in Switzerland) because they could not enter Russian ones, were admitted to separate university courses in the 1870s. The government, embarrassed by the conspicuous flow of women students abroad, gave its support, and courses were established at St. Petersburg, Moscow, Kazan, and Kiev Universities, on the same level as for men. Women could concentrate in humanities or in natural sciences. In 1872, the Guerrier Higher Courses for Women, emphasizing mathematics and the natural sciences, were initiated at Moscow University. With the approval of Dmitry Tolstoy, minister of education, the prestigious Bestuzhev courses, sponsored by some of the country's most prominent scholars, were triumphantly opened at St. Petersburg in 1878. Soon growing into a full four-year program, the courses offered specialization in history and philology, physics and mathematics, or advanced mathematics alone, and began to train students for university-level teaching and research. The exodus of women students abroad ceased almost completely.

The Age of the Novel

It would be a venial sin to forget all of Russian history; what would remain, though, would be the great novels of the nineteenth century. The work of Lev Tolstoy (1828–1910) and Fëdor Dostoevsky (1821–1881) reached its apogee in the late 1860s and 1870s. Tolstoy, immensely popular in Russia and abroad and the dominant figure of Russian literature during his lifetime, published *War and Peace* in 1869 and *Anna Karenina* in 1877. Dostoevsky's *Crime and Punishment* (1866), *The Idiot* (1868), *The Possessed* (1871–1872), and *The Brothers Karamazov* (1880) all appeared within the same fifteen-year period. The two great writers represent two poles of human sensibility. It is hard to know whether one is reading Tolstoy or living his narrative. He creates a world that is historical, personal, familial, and ultimately sane. Dostoevsky's demonic genius, in contrast, ingests the reader and spits him back out. Scandal, conspiracy, sexual humiliation, murder, and alienation form the stuff of his work, all inscribed in an atmosphere of fragmentation (in part due to poor editing) and ever-mounting hysteria. Curiously, Dostoevsky was relatively little read and little respected in his lifetime. He would be "discovered" and rediscovered several times throughout the twentieth century. The works of both are perhaps most productively discussed in relation to the great European novelists of the nineteenth century: Dickens, Eliot, Flaubert, Stendhal, Balzac.

Tolstoy and Dostoevsky were the brightest stars in the literary firmament. Still, many different kinds of people, from different regions and social backgrounds, participated in the new art and literature. The aging poet Pëtr Vyazemsky (1792–1878), one of the few living relics of the Golden Age (the Pushkin era), surveyed the new cultural scene with horror: to him, the new era was an "Age of Animals," vulgar and insensitive, and made by men who had no business in the refined world of literature and art. Among those he might have had in mind were the satirical novelist Mikhail Saltykov-Shchedrin (1826–1889), who abandoned his aristocratic roots to take up the banner of the radical intelligentsia. He was appointed a provincial vice-governor in 1858, and his *Provincial Sketches* (1856–1857) and *History of a Town* (1869–1870) caricatured provincial life while transparently alluding to Russian sovereigns and ministers. His major novel, *The Golovlëv Family* (1872–1876), painted a bleak picture of the history of a provincial gentry family, intended to show the brutality and inhumanity of the serf-owning class. Nikolai Leskov (1831–1895) also became a great social novelist; he has recently experienced a new surge of popularity as readers turn, in particular, to his detailed and informative portrayals of the life of the clergy—for example, in the chronicle *Cathedral Folk* (1872). In the 1870s, Pavel Melnikov-Pechersky (1819–1883) drew on his experience, almost thirty years earlier, as a government bureaucrat responsible for reporting on the Old Belief, to create a brilliant and quite sympathetic picture of the religious and mercantile culture of Old Believers in *In the Forests* (1871–1874) and *On the Hills* (1875–1881).

PAN-SLAVISM AND THE BALKANS, 1870–1878

While many artists and writers were inspired by populism, broadly conceived as empathy for "the people," another kind of radical ideology emerged at about the same time, that of the radical right. The early 1870s gave birth to some truly racist theories, which appealed to science, particularly biology, to justify the superiority and world historical role of Russian and Slavic civilization.

Pan-Slavism

Pan-Slavism, in simplest terms, was an imperial ideology that pronounced the brotherhood of all Slavic peoples and claimed a mission for Russia, as an "elder brother," to come to the aid of Slavs in the Balkan territories who were suffering from Ottoman misrule. In short, the acquisition of territories for Russia in Eastern Europe was a matter not of imperial aggrandizement but of historical fate and Slavic solidarity. Thinkers like Konstantin Leontyev, Mikhail Katkov, and Nikolai Danilevsky constructed theories justifying and encouraging Russian imperial expansion. Danilevsky, who, like the left intelligentsia, shared a fascination with science, and biology in particular, drew radically different conclusions. Drawing on evolutionary theory, Danilevsky, in the book *Russia and Europe* (1870), postulated the existence of "historical-cultural types" or organisms. There were, in other words, no universals in human history; instead, each nation had its own clearly defined biological and typological characteristics and its own corresponding role and mission in history. Russia's day was dawning: its time had come to replace the old and corrupt West in the struggle of nations for survival. On Danilevsky's model, each territory of the Russian Empire was such by historical inevitability: Finns, Poles, Armenians, Ukrainians, as inferior peoples, were fulfilling their proper fate by being subject to the great Russian Empire.

Curiously, the call for solidarity with the brother Slavs who shared Russia's mission had as broad a resonance in Russian educated society as the left intelligentsia's exhortations to go to the people or to construct a new, socialist person. Dostoevsky joined his voice to the chorus, writing enraged and graphic articles about Turkish atrocities in Bulgaria. Doubtless, although other factors were more important in the outbreak of a new war with Turkey in 1877, pan-Slav sentiment played a significant role in the enthusiasm with which Russian troops went to the rescue of the Balkan Slavs.

The Russo-Turkish War

In the first half of Alexander II's reign, Russia withdrew almost completely from European diplomacy, as government and gentry directed their attention to internal reform. The earth-shattering—and balance-of-power transforming—events of international politics in the 1860s, most notably the unification of Germany through three short, victorious wars, transpired with virtually no Russian participation. Prussian Chancellor Bismarck's wars of unification, followed by his brilliant diplomacy, resolved the issue of unity by asserting Prussian dominance, and decisively reshaped the European balance of power by implanting a strong and highly militarized German state in the very middle of the continent.

In the 1870s, however, European attention began to shift toward the Balkan peninsula: the Ottoman Empire's continued instability and intensifying nationalist movements in Bulgaria and Serbia created an explosive situation. Europe's Great Powers watched each other nervously: with Austria's loss of north Italy (the result of Italian unification) and its exclusion from Germany (following war of 1866), the Balkan territories, tantalizingly located near the center of Europe, could hold the key to the new power balance, depending on who might absorb them if they broke off from the Ottoman Empire. In an age of powerful foreign ministers, Russian policy in this context was shaped by the remarkable Alexander Gorchakov (1798–1883). A one-time classmate of Pushkin at the Lyceum and a participant in the major international congresses of the post-1815 era, Gorchakov became minister in time to lead the negotiations at Paris in 1856, following the Crimean War. The cornerstone of his program subsequently became the abrogation of the humiliating terms of that treaty—in particular, the restoration of Russian power in the Black Sea. And, in 1871, Gorchakov used the occasion of the London Conference that followed the German victory over France at Sedan to obtain international endorsement of a Russian fleet in the Black Sea. In 1873, Bismarck was able to engineer a Three Emperors' League of Germany, Austria, and Russia that, under the guise of imperial friendship, actually tied Russia's hands in the Balkans by linking its policy to that of its main competitor, Austria.

In 1875, rebellion erupted among the Ottoman sultan's Christian subjects in Bosnia and Herzegovina. All the European powers, and particularly Russia and Austria, felt that this was their business and spent the next two years developing plans for reforming the governance of the Ottoman territories. The crisis, which was merely one in a series of rebellions in the Balkans, thus had time to ripen slowly; during this period, rebellion spread to Bulgaria and involved Serbia and Montenegro as well. Ottomans and Europeans could reach no agreement in two years of negotiations, and, following the Budapest Convention of January 1877, in which Austria promised Russia benevolent neutrality in return for Austria's claim to the provinces of Bosnia and Herzegovina, the powers left Russia free to declare war on Turkey.

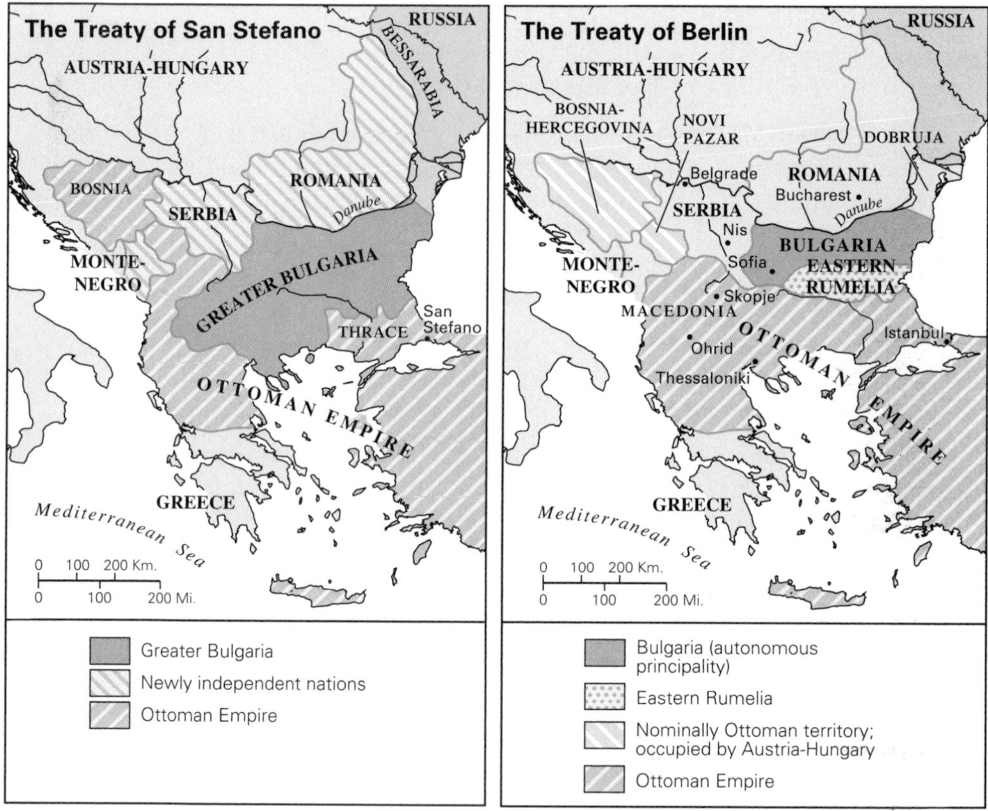

Outcome of the Russo-Turkish War, 1877–78. *From Barbara Jelavich,* History of the Balkans: Eighteenth and Nineteenth Centuries, *Volume II. Copyright © 1983. Reprinted with the permission of Cambridge University Press.*

In the meantime, Russian popular sentiment in favor of the "brother Slavs" was growing, fomented by the writings of Danilevsky, Dostoevsky, the Slavophile Ivan Aksakov, and others. The Russo-Turkish War of 1877–1878 was the first military endeavor that, taking place in the dynamic postreform society, genuinely involved popular participation and relied on popular patriotism. The Russian army occupied the Shipka Pass in Bulgaria on July 19 in a spectacular advance. The European powers, and particularly Britain, watched from the sidelines, waiting to take action if the Russians showed signs of taking Istanbul. Meanwhile the Turkish general, Osman Pasha, occupied the fortress of Plevna, checking the Russian advance. Military maneuvers remained at an impasse for months, until a bloody Russian attack in September led to a full-fledged siege. Plevna capitulated on December 10, while Russian armies took Sofia and poured over the Balkan Mountains, wisely stopping just short of invading Istanbul.

This relatively uneventful, if bloody, war was of decisive importance for the contours of Balkan political geography and was a crucial turning point in the evolution of the Balkan states. The Treaty of San Stefano, signed by Russia and Turkey in March of 1878, created a large Bulgarian state—which, it was assumed, would be subservient to Russia—from the Black Sea to the Aegean, and in a position to dominate the Straits. It also enlarged and confirmed the independence of Montenegro; created a completely independent Serbian state and gave it some territory toward the southeast; and recognized Romanian independence based on a union of Moldavia and Wallachia. Russia took Bessarabia for itself.

The European powers had, in contrast to Crimea, played no military role in the war, leaving Russia free rein so long as it did not touch Istanbul. But they were determined, under Bismarck's leadership as "honest broker," to have a say in the outcome. An international congress was called at Berlin in 1878 whose mission it was to revise the Treaty of San Stefano. The result was a considerable reduction of Russia's gains: Bulgaria's frontiers were whittled away, Bosnia and Herzegovina were occupied (not annexed) by Austria, and Turkey was maintained as a power when Macedonia was returned. The problem of the Straits, so far as Russia was concerned, remained in limbo. The most important consequences of the postwar power politics were for the Balkan states themselves: Serbia, Bulgaria, and Romania were independent; the specific configuration of alignments and boundaries on the Balkan peninsula remained a dominant concern of international politics and was eventually to form the focal point of World War I.

TERRORISTS AND REVOLUTIONARIES

In the two or three years following Karakozov's attempt on the life of Alexander II in 1866, severe government repression made open radical circles, characteristic of the early 1860s, impossible. However, this repression, instead of suppressing all revolutionary activity as the government intended, merely forced radical circles underground. Revolutionary and terrorist organizations in the late 1860s and 1870s were more organized, more sophisticated, and more violent than their precursors. Revolutionaries formed a growing community in emigration, where they gained support from European socialists and anarchists. These hard-boiled revolutionaries were distinguished from the milder populists *(narodniki)* by their single-mindedness of purpose: all goals, including enlightening "the people," took second place to the aim of overthrowing the existing order.

The Revolutionary as Cultural Type: Nechaev

Sergei Nechaev was born in 1847, in Ivanovo, a textile center not far from Moscow; his father was a house painter, and his mother a former serf. Determined to improve his lot in life, he eventually became an extension student at Moscow University, where he met Pëtr Tkachëv (1844–1886) and other radicals. Nechaev became consumed by the idea that, nine years after the emancipation, on February 19, 1870, when the peasants' "temporary obligation" status was to cease, revolution would erupt. He threw himself into fomenting this revolt, amazing his fellow revolutionaries with his zeal and the single-minded glint in his eyes. Bakunin, until he himself became frightened by Nechaev's extremism, honored him with the title of "revolutionary prototype": "They are magnificent, these young fanatics, believers without God, heroes without rhetoric." Nechaev, aided by Bakunin, was the author of a booklet called the *Revolutionary Catechism;* it imparts, better than any other document, the flavor of Russian revolutionary circles of the day.

> The revolutionary is a lost man; he has no interests of his own, no cause of his own, no feelings, no habits, no belonging; he does not even have a name. Everything in him is absorbed by a single, exclusive interest, a single thought, a single passion—the revolution. . . . Hard with himself, he must be hard toward others. All the tender feelings of family life, of friendship, love, gratitude, and even honor must be stifled in him by a single cold passion for the revolutionary cause. For him there is only one pleasure, one consolation, one reward, and one satisfaction—the success of the revolution. Day and night he must have one single thought, one single purpose: merciless destruction. With this aim in view, tirelessly and in cold blood, he must always be prepared to die and to kill with his own hands anyone who stands in the way of achieving it.

Revolution, for the young people inspired by the *Catechism,* was to become not just a political aim, but an entire way of life, a mode of behavior, and the single purpose of individual existence.

Nechaev's clandestine organization, People's Retribution, was composed of groups of five, in which each participant knew only the two others to whom he or she immediately reported. On November 21, 1869, Nechaev and three others murdered their fellow conspirator, the student Ivan Ivanov, in the garden of the Moscow School of Agriculture, apparently on suspicion that he would denounce them. The police discovered the body after Nechaev had gone abroad, and the incident caused the downfall of some eighty revolutionaries unearthed in the course of the investigation. Dostoevsky's novel *The Possessed* is constructed around a fictionalized version of Ivanov's murder and captures the demonic, conspiratorial atmosphere of the revolutionary circles. Nechaev was extradited to Russia by the Swiss in 1872 and imprisoned in the Peter and Paul Fortress; he died of scurvy in 1882.

Land and Freedom

The Bosnian revolt in 1875, and the Russo-Turkish War that followed, gave a fresh stimulus to Russian revolutionaries. Several radicals traipsed off to Herzegovina to take part in the revolt. In the meantime, a nucleus of men nicknamed "the Troglodytes"—Mark Natanson, Alexei Oboleshev, and Alexander Mikhailov—formed a new revolutionary organization in St. Petersburg. Fed by similar societies in southern Russia, it eventually grew into the powerful and well-organized group called Land and Freedom. The name, adopted in 1876, referred to the organization's primary goals: the transfer of all land into the hands of the peasant communes and "the substitution of the existing state by a structure determined by the will of the people." In addition, they wished to see the Russian Empire broken up "according to local desires." These aims were to be achieved by violent revolution. The men were joined by a number of equally dedicated women—Maria Kovalevskaya, Vera Zasulich (1851–1919), Anna Makarevich, and Vera Figner (1852–1942).

Like those who had gone "to the people" in the summer of 1874, the members of Land and Freedom went off into the countryside. Their goals, however, were less ambiguous: they included the formation of revolutionary peasant "colonies," agitation among religious sectarians, and "agrarian terrorism." Their conflict with the government came to a head at the height of the Balkan war. Huge trials—50 defendants in one, 193 in another—were held in St. Petersburg; it was the government's effort to put an end to terrorism once and for all. Although only 58 of the 193 received sentences of hard labor or exile (the rest were freed), the lengthy and highly publicized trials served only to exacerbate tensions.

The trials were followed by a rash of assassination attempts, starting with one by Vera Zasulich. General F. F. Trepov, governor of St. Petersburg, had aroused general public indignation by ordering the flogging of the prisoner Bogolyubov following a disturbance in the prison courtyard. In January 1878, Vera Zasulich entered the governor's office and fired at him at point-blank range. Zasulich's trial was the sensation of the decade: despite her obvious guilt, the jury pronounced her innocent. What opponents of trial by jury feared most had happened: jury members had voted according to their emotions (and, possibly, their sense of social justice) rather than according to the letter of the law. Most Petersburg newspapers supported the verdict.

In 1878–1879, Valerian Osinsky, a member of the "Executive Committee of the Social Revolutionary Party," shot the vice-prosecutor of the Kiev court; Grigory Popko, of the same organization, stabbed the adjutant of the Kiev police; the returned emigré Sergei Kravchinsky stabbed General Mezentsov, head of the Third

Section, to death; Grigory Goldenberg shot the governor of Kharkov; and Leonid Mirsky and Alexander Soloviëv, on separate occasions, tried to kill Alexander II. Terrorism was not unique to Russia; the same year bore witness to attempts on the lives of the German Kaiser and the king of Italy.

Along with tighter organization and greater intransigence, the revolutionaries of the 1870s developed closer links with a growing international revolutionary movement, mostly through the emigré community. The various socialist doctrines of Ferdinand Lasalle, Pierre Proudhon, and Marx were introduced to the Russians by figures like Georgy Plekhanov (1856–1918) and Pavel Axelrod (1850–1928). Reversing the flow, Bakunin and Pëtr Kropotkin (1842–1921) became the founders of an international anarchist movement that, by the close of the nineteenth century, had greater success abroad than in Russia.

At the end of the 1870s, Land and Freedom split into two separate groups. The Black Repartition, the less successful of the two, threw its energies into the fight to redistribute the land. The Will of the People became obsessed with pure terrorism. Andrei Zhelyabov, Sofia Perovskaya, and others perfected the art of obtaining dynamite and building bombs. The express aim was the assassination of Alexander II: three unsuccessful attempts to blow up his train were made in 1880. The cabinet maker Stepan Khalturin, who had a private desire to kill the tsar with an ax, was persuaded by Zhelyabov to try dynamite instead; he blew up a room in the Winter Palace. Perovskaya and cohorts made another try in Odessa, dynamiting a tunnel through which the tsar should have passed. Remarkably, the emperor survived all these attempts on his life. A series of trials of revolutionaries, including that of a founder of Land and Freedom, ensued in the fall of 1880; they were variously sentenced to death, hard labor, or imprisonment.

MURDER OF AN EMPEROR, 1881

The numerous assassination attempts of the 1870s yielded a hardened, seasoned core of experts in terrorism. In early 1881, the Executive Committee of the People's Will, including Zhelyabov, Vera Figner, and Perovskaya, began to construct a foolproof plan for the assassination of Alexander II. The plot included renting a cheese shop at an appropriate distance from the Winter Palace, from which the conspirators constructed a tunnel. In the event that the tsar passed along a different route, four assassins were appointed: if the first bomb failed to kill the tsar, the second assassin would go into action, and so forth. Indeed, on March 1,1881, as the tsar passed along the Catherine Canal, Nikolai Rysakov exploded the first bomb, which injured some members of the entourage. The second—launched by the student Ignaty Grinevitsky—hit the tsar, injuring some twenty others. Alexander II was taken to the Winter Palace, where he died an hour later. On April 3, 1881, Rysakov, Mikhailov, N. I. Kibalchich, Zhelyabov, and Perovskaya were hanged.

The latter part of Alexander II's reign, which had begun with such uplift and enthusiasm, was not happy. Russian society was in ferment, unleashed by the reforms, in both a positive and a negative sense: at the same time that the society became more open and local and provincial life expanded, ideological tensions grew, and the hold of the autocracy on an increasingly sophisticated population became more and more untenable. In 1880 Alexander had a new minister of the interior: Mikhail Loris-Melikov (1825–1888) was a remarkable and much beloved administrator who came from a wealthy Armenian family in Tiflis and, after serving in various posts in the Caucasus, had been ennobled for taking Kars in the Russo-Turkish War. A man who had the sympathies of the zemstvo activists behind him, Loris-Melikov introduced projects for improving peasant farming, for shifting the tax base toward the wealthy, and for worker insurance. In 1881 he drafted a proposal to convene a national commission, which would include zemstvo and municipal representatives, to debate administrative, economic, and financial measures proposed by the government. This project—an effort to create an adequate political framework for the new society—came to be known as the Loris-Melikov constitution. In 1881, however, it was the revolutionaries who had the final say: Alexander II was assassinated on the day he was scheduled to discuss the new proposals with his ministers.

Alexander II's assassination was emblematic of the contradictions of his reign. In the end, Alexander II's "new monarchy" represented an uneasy compromise of absolute monarchy with limited representative government and local participation; far-reaching reform coexisted with a culture of uncompromising terrorism. Alexander's turbulent quarter century in power witnessed a remarkable experiment in social engineering; a revolt in Poland and Russian expansion in Central Asia; the emergence of an energetic, enthusiastic movement, populism, that also inspired literature, art, and music; a growing civic consciousness and local political activism in the zemstvos and provinces; a Balkan war; and the articulation of highly polarized ideologies both left and right. Ironically, it was the man who presided over these dramatic changes, and not one of the more conservative autocrats before and after him, who fell prey to the assassins' bomb. Loris-Melikov's "constitution" was filed away as Alexander II's less sympathetic successor took power.

CHAPTER 23

Orthodoxy, Autocracy, Nationality Reaffirmed, 1881–1905

Among the falsest of political principles is the principle of the sovereignty of the people, the principle that all power issues from the people, and is based upon the national will—a principle which has unhappily become more firmly established since the time of the French Revolution.

—Konstantin Pobedonostsev, "The Great Falsehood of Our Time" (1896)

To the British historian Eric Hobsbawm, the end of the nineteenth century was the "age of empire," when a handful of powerful states systematically sought to translate their dominance into "formal conquest, annexation, and administration." The Russian Empire under the last two tsars, Alexander III (r. 1881–1894) and Nicholas II (r. 1894–1917) might be seen as a variant of this general scenario. The two reigns, up to 1905, were characterized by an increasing urge to uniformity and bureaucratic control over the vast contiguous space of the empire. The growth of the administrative machinery ensured the importance, in the daily process of governance, of not only the monarchs but their ministers, governors, and administrators as well. In a departure from the European pattern, the institutional church acquired new visibility and political power in this period, in cooperation with the state. On the empire's peripheries, the desire for administrative uniformity had an ugly face: the Russian government abandoned the traditional practice of reliance on local elites and use of local languages and, like Britain in India or France in North Africa, imposed the Russian language, educational system, and Orthodox religion.

Within European Russia as well, Alexander III in particular sought to limit local autonomy, instituting between 1885 and 1890 a series of measures that curbed and cut back the reforms of the previous reign. The Ministry of Finance launched an ambitious program of industrialization and economic modernization, perhaps best symbolized by the Trans-Siberian Railroad, which ultimately stretched across the entire continent. As 1900 approached, tensions between the conservative monarchy and a growing educated public mounted: Nicholas II premised his reign on the defense of autocracy and rejection of participatory government. It makes sense to posit a fundamental continuity between the reigns of Alexander III and Nicholas

II, at least up to 1905. Many of the essential policies of this period were initiated under Alexander III and inherited and continued by Nicholas II: Russification, church-state cooperation, the economic push and construction of the Trans-Siberian Railroad, and, in foreign policy, alliance with France.

THE EUROPEAN EMPIRES

As the nineteenth century drew to a close, the great European empires seemed on the verge of dominating the entire globe. Britain's vast maritime United Kingdom incorporated lands from Australia to India to Africa; French domination in North Africa was secure; Germany, a latecomer to the colonial race, acquired lands in East Africa in the 1880s. The land-based empire of Austria-Hungary presented a complicated but colorful case: the many nationalities, languages, and religions united under the rule of the Emperor Franz-Joseph (1848–1916) proved difficult to govern yet at the same time produced a culture of remarkable wealth and diversity. The older powers, Spain and the Ottoman Empire, fared less well: Spain's colonies in Latin America broke away in a series of revolutions, while the other Great Powers chipped away steadily at Turkey's holdings in the Balkan peninsula. There were newcomers, once colonies themselves, to the imperial club: the United States under the presidency of Theodore Roosevelt staked a claim in Central America and the Caribbean, after a war with Spain in 1898. European dominance was cultural as well: countries like Mexico and Argentina were proud to share a common culture and consciousness with the European world. By 1900, however, challenges to the prevailing colonial order became increasingly tangible: Britain became embroiled in the Boer War in South Africa, while the Boxer Rebellion in China and Japan's war with Russia in 1904–1905 sent signals indicating the weak foundations of European faith in the eventual conquest of Asia.

A combination of an intricate system of alliances, treaties, and diplomatic alignments, with some amount of good luck, kept the international scene in a delicate balance: the European world was at peace from the Congress of Berlin (1878) up to the turn of the century. Rulers, from Porfirio Díaz in Mexico to Nicholas II in Russia, made haste to attribute the peaceful interlude to their own judicious policies. Indeed, more generally, the regimes of the 1880s and 1890s were characterized by a certain complacency and prosperous self-satisfaction, a faith that the world could be ruled rationally by the right people—namely, middle-aged men in Victorian black suits with a good education, the proper moral principles, and gently swelling bellies. At the same time, other groups in society grew increasingly confident in their claims to a share of wealth and civic rights: workers' movements, women's movements, socialist movements, as well as liberal and centrist political parties, attracted ever greater numbers to causes ranging from equal participation and suffrage to violent revolution. It was in the Russian Empire that revolution would in fact erupt in 1905; its shadow became increasingly tangible over the preceding two decades.

RULING RUSSIA: PERSONALITIES

Konstantin Pobedonostsev, over-procurator of the Holy Synod from 1881 to 1905, echoed the thinking of many of his contemporaries when he spoke of government in terms of "the best individuals, the true representatives of the land, who know their people *(narod).*" One recent scholar called the emphasis on individuals, rather than on institutions or legal norms, a "central tenet of Russian governmental conservatism" since the times of the historian Nikolai Karamzin (1766–1826), who told Alexander I, "Men, not documents, govern." At the end of the nineteenth century, only Russia, Turkey, and Montenegro, in all of Europe, lacked a parliament. Instead, the government and administration of the Russian Empire relied on an extensive and growing bureaucracy—and, by the same token, on those "best" individuals, Pobedonostsev among them, that one hoped filled its administrative posts. Not just the monarchs and their families, but ministers and administrators became the brightest figures of Russian governance; the noble elite, in the meantime, faded from the public stage except as position holders in the governmental machine.

Alexander III (1845–1894)

Alexander III, physically large and corpulent, became heir to throne with the death of his older brother Nicholas at age twenty-two. He was a strong personality—a man of honor and principle, with deep faith in Russia and a belief that his role, as tsar, was to defend its honor and to be as one with his people. In politics, this attitude translated into a paramount concern with foreign policy, in which Alexander III was indeed successful: his thirteen-year reign saw almost no military action (the exception was a conflict with Britain on the border of Afghanistan) and Russia's reassertion of its position among the Great Powers following the disappointment of Crimea. A Russian alliance with France against Russia's traditional ally Germany crowned the edifice of Alexander's policy. International status was bought back at considerable expense: internally, the regime of Alexander III constituted virtually a complete reversal of his father's policies. The new ruler did what he could to stymie the growth of local participatory institutions and to reinstitute control from the center. This consistent policy earned Alexander III's reign the rubric of "counter-reform," of an attempt to minimize the "damage" done by the great reforms of the 1860s. Apart from foreign policy, Alexander III's reign was successful in the related matter of finance. Under the leadership of his finance minister, Ivan Vyshnegradsky (1831–1895), the ruble was stabilized and the industrialization drive begun.

Nicholas II (1868–1918)

It is difficult to imagine a more unfortunate ruler of Russia in dangerous and critical times than Alexander III's son, Nicholas II, who ascended the throne in 1894. Nicholas II combined softness in manner and weakness of character with an exaggerated sense of his own mission as ruler of the Russian Empire and an unalloyed faith in the institution of autocracy. His reign began inauspiciously, when over a thousand people were trampled to death at the coronation ceremonies at Khodynka, outside Moscow. Nicholas's single great passion was for Princess Alix (1872–1918) of Hesse-Darmstadt, granddaughter of England's Queen Victoria; he met her when they were sixteen and twelve, respectively. He married her ten years later, just before Alexander III's death. The couple kept up a passionate correspondence (in English) in a lifelong romance, and Alexandra bore four beautiful daughters between 1895 and 1901. The highlight of court life in Nicholas's first decade was a great costume ball in 1903, for which Nicholas and Alexandra donned ornate gowns evocative of seventeenth-century Muscovy, posing as Tsar Alexei Mikhailovich and his consort. Nicholas's dedication to his wife and family only grew when his son and heir to the throne, Alexis (born in 1904), turned out to be a hemophiliac. But it became a liability when it caused him to neglect the country as he became increasingly drawn into the decadence and mysticism of court life.

Alexander III and his family. Nicholas II stands behind his father. *Sovfoto/Eastfoto.*

Konstantin Pobedonostsev (1827–1907)

The tone of Alexander III's reign was set less by the tsar himself than by his mentor—and from 1881, over-procurator of the Holy Synod—Konstantin Pobedonostsev. Previously a relatively obscure position, occupied by a series of relatively obscure men, the over-procuratorship became, in Pobedonostsev's firm grasp, the guiding light of the new regime. Apart from reasserting the political power of the church, Pobedonostsev sought, as well, to influence the course of the Russian Empire as a whole. His *Moscow Essays* (1896) sum up the philosophy of the last two Russian autocrats, whose tutor he was in their youth, better than anything they themselves ever wrote; he kept up a steady stream of correspondence with Alexander III on subjects from ministerial appointments to parishioners' complaints.

Trained as a lawyer, and later a senator (in other words, a visible secular public figure), Pobedonostsev was not simply an unthinking reactionary, as he has often been portrayed. Rather, he developed a sophisticated vision of an organic, harmonious society guided by the principles of Orthodoxy, autocracy, and nationality. Although this formula sounds familiar from the days of Nicholas I, Pobedonostsev gave its terms an innovative interpretation: Orthodoxy now meant that no other religions were to be tolerated; autocracy meant an utter rejection of popular participation on any level; and nationality meant the imposition of the Russian language and a complete suppression of national consciousness for other ethnic groups. Above all else, Pobedonostsev hated parliaments and liberal ideas of any kind. At a time when the principle of monarchy was becoming increasingly discredited, Pobedonostsev launched a concerted campaign to reaffirm its sway. He was reacting, in part, to Pope Leo XII's 1870 encyclical the *Rerum novarum* ("Of New Matters"), in which the Catholic Church acknowledged the workers' movement and proclaimed a role for the church in promoting social welfare. Pobedonostsev had a sense of mission: in the face of liberalism, nationalism, and even socialism, it was Orthodox Russia's duty to uphold, with the autocrat's firm hand, the social harmony that such movements were steadily destroying.

Pobedonostsev, whom the poet Alexander Blok saw as an owl, with his "wings unfurled over Russia," became the symbol of a new period in Russian history. His time in office, 1881–1905, delineates this period, and the change of monarch in 1894 did not constitute a significant break.

Sergei Witte (1849–1915)

The other man who brought new importance to his post, and set the tone for the period, had a style that could not have been more different from Pobedonostsev's. Appointed minister of finance in 1893, Sergei Witte came from a family that included characters ranging from the flamboyant and talented Madame Blavatskaya—a leader of the spiritist movement in the 1860s and 1870s and Sergei's first cousin—to entirely ordinary middling servitors like his brother Boris, a judge in the Odessa court. Witte was born in Tiflis, Georgia, a son of the director of the Department of State Properties for the Caucasus (his Lutheran grandfather came from the Baltic region). His modest successes in mathematics at the New Russia University in Odessa led him to a twenty-year career in the southwest railway conglomerate; by 1886 he had become director of all railways under their jurisdiction. Thus when Witte came to work at the Ministry of Finance, then under Ivan Vyshnegradsky, he had plenty of solid hands-on experience in industrial management. Under his guidance, the ministry began to define the entire course of Russian economic development. In his memoirs, written when he still hoped to regain his position (from which he was fired in 1906), Witte comes across as a tremendously energetic, able, and practical, if also a spiteful and less than straightforward, man.

Ministers and Administrators

A number of lesser personalities also imprinted their stamp on the administrations of the last two monarchs. Among them one might name Dmitry Tolstoy (1823–1889), a lifetime bureaucrat who simultaneously (1866–1880) occupied the posts of over-procurator of the Holy Synod and minister of education before heading the Ministry of the Interior (1882–1889). Tolstoy was also a historian who wrote about non-Orthodox confessions in the empire. He became identified with policies of counterreform and strengthening of the state. Another example would be Vyacheslav Plehve (1846–1904), who in his tenure as minister of the interior (1902–1904) came to epitomize the police state and bureaucratic control through his harsh suppression of peasant uprisings in Kharkov and Poltava and his support for Russification policies. Nikolai Giers (1820–1895), who had risen in the ranks of the foreign service, beginning in the Asian department, pursued a careful line in foreign policy as minister of foreign affairs (1882–1895), finally concluding an alliance with France in 1894. Sometimes, appointees to less prominent posts could also shape imperial policy: such for example was Nikolai Bobrikov (1839–1904), a military man who became governor general of Finland in 1898 and who was partly responsible for the gradual abrogation of Finnish autonomy; Bobrikov was killed by the son of a Finnish senator.

RULING RUSSIA: BUREAUCRACY AND COUNTERREFORM

A hallmark of the reigns of Alexander III and Nicholas II was the departure from traditional policies of maintaining regional diversity in favor of a bureaucratic uniformity throughout the empire. In part, this tendency was made possible by increasing technological capacity for control. It would be interesting to trace the specific consequences of the new attitude toward the borderlands for the structure of the central government itself. Until more such research has been accomplished, however, it remains safe to say that, in a renewal of the bureaucratization that had taken place under Nicholas I, policy under Alexander III and Nicholas II was directed toward a systematization, tightening, and expansion of the administrative system. The government was propelled by a desire for order in the immense spaces

The State Council, by Ilya Repin (1901–03). *Superstock.*

of the empire and a longing for centralized control. The imperial Russian state in this period evolved into a bulky administrative machine with its center in St. Petersburg and tentacles reaching not only throughout European Russia but into the distant reaches of the imperial territories.

The Central Administration

At the summit of Russian government stood the Senate, the State Council, the Committee of Ministers, the ministers themselves, and various ad hoc special commissions. The once powerful Senate had diminished in influence over two centuries, and by 1900 its real functions were limited to overseeing the work of the judicial chambers (to which the district courts, in turn, were responsible); publishing laws and overseeing their execution; and ensuring the legality of local administration. The State Council, with sixty appointed members in 1890, reported to the emperor on matters concerning civil legislation, administration, budget, and finance. The State Council remained up to 1914 a haven for Russia's ancient ruling families, counting Obolenskys, Dolgorukys, Volkonskys, Patrikeevs, Vyazemskys, and others among its members. Of 215 appointees between 1894 and 1914, 60 percent came from well-established noble families. They were predominantly Russian or Russianized, and most were landowners. The councilors generally also served in the bureaucracy, particularly in the Ministry of the Interior, but also in the Ministries of Justice and Finance or the State Chancellery.

Bureaucratization and professionalization were the order of the day; these trends equally affected the central ministries, the military, and the police. Within the central government, powerful ministries and their appointed heads began to play an active and critical role in the actual process of decision making, and interministerial rivalries and strong personalities in the government became as crucial to the direction of policy as unilateral decisions by the autocrat. The most prominent and influential posts, apart from over-procurator of the Holy Synod, became minister of the interior (responsible for everything from police, passports, and postal services to medicine, military recruit levies, and peasant resettlement) and minister of finance, with education and war following close behind. Held by a succession of forceful men with clear visions, these positions proved important in shaping the course of Russian development. Thus Loris-Melikov's inability, as minister of the interior, to coexist with Pobedonostsev, and his replacement by Count Ignatiev, was decisive in shaping the general tone of Alexander III's reign. A constellation of Dmitry Tolstoy (a conservative bureaucrat) at the Ministry of the Interior, Nikolai Bunge (1881–1887) and Ivan Vyshnegradsky (1887–1892) at the Ministry of Finance, and Nikolai Giers in the Foreign Ministry assured consistently firm and conservative policies throughout the 1880s, including efforts to curb zemstvo rights and limit university autonomy. Tolstoy's successors at Interior—I. N. Durnovo (1889–1895), then I. L. Goremykin (1895–1899), D. S. Sipyagin (1899–1902), and V. K. Plehve (1902–1904)—were considered, whether justly or not, emblematic of bureaucratic repression; the last two met their deaths by assassination.

In the 1890s, the Ministry of Finance became arguably more important than Interior: Sergei Witte, building on the policies of his predecessors Bunge and Vyshnegradsky, was single-handedly responsible for much of the tremendous push to industrialize (discussed in the next chapter). Ministers were, naturally, dismissed if their views came in direct conflict with those of the tsar—Ignatiev, for example, resigned in 1882, after only a year, when his ideas of convening a national Council of the Land *(zemsky sobor)* became known. But there was still considerable room for autonomy and policymaking within the province of each ministry. Indeed, the Council of Ministers, established in 1857, was not convened between 1882 and 1905, and many members of the bureaucracy complained about lack of policy coordination and a tendency among ministries to go off on their own tracks, sometimes pursuing conflicting goals.

The War Ministry under P. S. Vannovsky tended to lose out in its battles with powerful Interior and Finance. Nonetheless, the period from 1881 to 1905 witnessed some fruits of the Milyutin reforms of the 1860s and 1870s (see the chapter "Alexander II and the Era of the Great Reforms, 1855–1870"): graduates of the reformed academies came to dominate the chancellery, the general staff, and important district posts, creating a professional elite within the military. The Russian army in 1893 numbered 992,000, maintained at a cost of 267 million rubles, or 25 percent of total state expenditures. At the turn of the century, the army was an important instrument in quelling domestic unrest.

On the Ground: Regional and Local Bureaucracy

One symptom of the expansion of the administrative network was a dramatic increase in the sheer numbers of officials and bureaucrats. Estimates have ranged from 62 to 336 for every 10,000 inhabitants; parallel figures for France were 176, for Germany 126, and for England 73. Nikolai Gogol's short stories in the 1840s sometimes took as their theme the unexpected and calamitous occasional incursions of the central authorities into the sleepy life of provincial Russia. But by the 1880s and 1890s, the petty government official became a permanent fixture in the provincial towns of Anton Chekhov's stories or Fëdor Dostoevsky's novels. Although the basic units of administration remained the same—the province and, below it, the district—the local population experienced the hand of the government in a fairly tangible manner. The central government had a direct hand in local affairs only down to the provincial level—primarily, in the appointment of the governor but also in the usual offices of the post and telegraph, customs, army, navy, education ministry, and clergy. For a resident of Lukoyanov District in Nizhny Novgorod Province, for example, the government was represented by an eclectic mixture of state and local institutions—the local tax bureau, the local division of the state alcohol monopoly, the provincial budget committee, the office of state property, the zemstvo assembly and board, the provincial factory supervisory board, the forest conservation committee, the local temperance committee (in the 1890s), the committee on public health, and even a smallpox committee. The capital town of each province boasted, too, the office of the provincial governor, the provincial direction, the provincial statistical committee, and so on. These institutions all only peripherally affected the peasant population, who were subject to the decisions of their particular communes.

The powers of the provincial governor, representative of the central authorities, were considerable but limited if his province had its own courts, over which he had no control, or if it had a zemstvo, which he could supervise but not direct. An 1881 law gave him increased control over the local police; although 1890 rules regulating civil-military relations granted greater authority to the army division commander. One of the major problems of local government was overlapping jurisdictions. Institutions responsible to the central bureaucracy sometimes duplicated functions of institutions of local self-government, such as the provincial zemstvo. In addition, the spheres of self-governing institutions themselves frequently conflicted: cities fell within the jurisdiction of provincial zemstvos, so that the municipal *duma* (town council), for example, might assert control over finances that the zemstvo considered its domain; a tug of war between the district and provincial zemstvos was a constant feature of local politics throughout European Russia.

Policies: the Counterreforms

The general tenor of the administrations of Alexander III and Nicholas II—of control, order, central regulation—was epitomized in the "Temporary Regulations," issued immediately after the assassination of Alexander II and, belying their title, in effect up to the revolution of 1905. These rules—originally meant as an action against the People's Will movement specifically, and terrorism generally—amounted nearly to martial law that permitted the government to go about its business without interference from revolutionary or even liberal elements. A major instrument of their execution became the so-called Okhrana—the twenty-six security detachments formed within the Department of Police; they replaced the infamous Third Section, abolished in 1880. Russian society in the last twenty years of the nineteenth century functioned under strict censorship and constant police surveillance, so that anyone engaged in virtually any public activity—from writers and professors to organizers and political activists—had a file in the archives of the secret police.

Within European Russia, the major symptom of the new, bureaucratizing trend was the local government reform of 1889, which instituted the office of the so-called *zemsky nachalnik,* or land captain. Although the simple creation of a new administrative position may seem a trivial detail, the land captain immediately became the emblem of reaction and "counterreform": he represented a retraction of the hard-won zemstvo independence and a renewed interference of the state in local affairs. The land captain was supposed to oversee peasant self-government and had the authority to direct the agendas and veto the decisions of the peasant assemblies. To make matters worse, he was necessarily to be chosen by the governor from the lists of the local nobility, with certain property qualifications. This choice, in turn, was subject to review by the minister of the interior. The simultaneous abolition, in the zemstvo provinces, of the office of communal judge meant that the government-appointed land captain often became responsible for the distribution of justice: this erased the carefully instituted division of judicial and administrative powers intended by the great reforms. The office of *zemsky nachalnik* represented a remarkable penetration by central government authority into the very fabric of local life.

This measure was accompanied by a series of other efforts to reverse the autonomy that had been granted to zemstvo and municipal government. Regressive election laws for zemstvo and town assemblies augmented the power of the gentry while curbing local initiative; the zemstvo's rights to collect taxes were limited, depriving them of the necessary funds fully to carry out their many medical, sanitary, educational, charitable and other functions.

CHURCH AND STATE: A CONSERVATIVE SYMPHONY

On a balance sheet of the Russian Empire's successes and failures in the last decades of the nineteenth century, high on both lists would be a cooperation of church and state unprecedented in the modern period. At the end of the century, the Catholic and Protestant Churches in Europe were forced to adapt to increasingly secular social practices, but the Russian Church under Pobedonostsev's firm guidance and the protection of the autocratic state responded to the challenges of the workers' movement, changing sexual mores, and liberal ideas with a rigid and adamant reassertion of tradition. And if the church as an institution had played a relatively passive role in politics and government over the preceding two centuries, its continuing hold on matters of piety and personal conduct began significantly to shape official policy in the last years of the century, particularly with respect to such traditional preserves of the church as education and family policy.

The main battleground in defining the spheres of civil versus ecclesiastical control during the period of "counterreforms" was education: who would be responsible for teaching the barely literate peasant population the elements of reading, writing, and mathematics: the church, through the parish schools, or the secular primary schools? In general, education was undoubtedly one of the central issues in the postreform world, in which literacy and knowledge could hold the key to social mobility. The church's traditional responsibility for education had been eroded by secularization in the eighteenth and nineteenth centuries, and the great reforms placed the supervision of primary schools under the secular aegis of the Ministry of National Enlightenment. At the same time, the 1860s and 1870s had seen a spontaneous flowering of parish schools, often started on the independent initiative of poor but dedicated parish priests, sometimes beginning with only two or three students and no resources.

In the 1880s, Pobedonostsev took the parish school movement under his wing: in one of the major counterreforms, which he saw as his most important project, a large proportion of schools were removed from the auspices of the secular ministry and placed under the control of the Holy Synod. The result was an explosion in the number of parish schools. On the positive side, the reform meant that more pupils were receiving primary education, and with what its creator felt was the proper orientation; on the negative, many objected that religious instruction interfered with more basic educational needs, and that educational methods were unimaginative and boring. Moreover, many among the clergy were disappointed by the homogenized rigidity of the new schools—a sharp contrast to the inspired if penurious efforts of the immediate postreform period. Placing the schools under church control was a way to ensure their immunity from the radical teaching methods of the young populist teachers who had flooded the countryside in the 1870s.

The church was also responsible for regulating another fundamental part of people's lives: the family. From medieval times, it was church law—not civil law—that set the rules for how marriages were to be made and broken. In most European countries, marriage and divorce legally became a matter of civil procedure by the late nineteenth century, as the spheres of church and state became increasingly separated; the Russian Church would manage to retain its exclusive prerogative in this area up to the February Revolution in 1917. In practice, this meant that obtaining a divorce actually became increasingly difficult over the course of the nineteenth century; the church statutes contained, for example, the peculiar provision that divorce was admissible in the case of adultery by one spouse, but not if both were guilty.

The church also tightened control, in this period, over its clergy. In the relative freedom of the emancipation period, many priests became directly involved in the life of society, through social activism, education, or charity. Now, the new administration made the seminary curriculum more rigorous, discouraged independent initiative, and forbade political activity. In some cases, it actually tried to use priests as a nationwide network of informants, encouraging them to inform on their parishioners. This policy, not surprisingly, lowered morale among the clergy and was at least partly responsible for their children's abandoning the seminaries in droves in the 1880s and 1890s.

On the borders of European Russia, the newly active policy of the church expressed itself in a continuing campaign of conversion, directed toward major religious groups like the Old Belief and Muslims. The local diocesan journals reported, each month, the number of successful conversions. There are no traces of a major effort to justify the faith to others; conversion seems to have been a fairly external matter, not exactly forced but highly encouraged.

This peculiar power of the church had two significant, and unintended, consequences. First, a strong movement for reform began to gather force, particularly from the 1890s onward, which advocated everything from parish reform to convening a national church council to reinstituting the patriarchate, which Peter the Great (Peter I) had abolished in 1721; this movement had adherents both within the church itself and among the secular intelligentsia. Second, the strength of the church in the government led some intellectuals, who were disillusioned with the autocracy, to seek answers to social problems through reform in the church: a corrupt and poorly educated clergy, regressive policies with respect to personal morality, and unwillingness to accommodate the concerns of modernity seemed to them as much responsible for Russia's ills as problems with government or society proper.

ADMINISTERING EMPIRE: RUSSIFYING THE BORDERLANDS

The Russian Empire in 1881 was near the high point of territorial expansion. Although Alaska had been sold to the United States in 1867, the continental empire extended from Finland in the north to Poland and Ukraine in the west and Armenia and Georgia in the south. It stretched over the Kazakh steppes, Central Asia, and Siberia and ended at the Pacific island of Sakhalin in the east. By the end of the century, the Russian sphere of influence extended into Manchuria.

The unusual cooperation of church and state produced a shift in patterns of control of the many non-Russian nationalities that made up the empire. Poland had been the first to test, in the reign of Alexander II, the liberal intentions of the autocracy; the result was the strict limitation of local autonomy. After 1863, Alexander II's government introduced mandatory instruction in the Russian language in Polish schools, restricted local participation in government, and replaced Polish with Russian officials. These measures included, ironically, the dispossession of the gentry and the transfer of their lands to the peasants. This policy of "Russification"—in which Russian became the official language, Orthodoxy the official religion, and Russians a privileged group—became the rule rather than the exception in the reigns of the last two monarchs. Whereas, under Nicholas I, ethnic and linguistic minorities had always been able to carve out a niche or subculture within whose limits they could have relative autonomy, even such limited participation became very difficult with the new drive toward uniformity and central control.

In practice, administrative integration produced a considerable variety of arrangements. The region most profoundly affected was the northwest: Poland, the "western provinces," and Finland. Here the imperial legacy had bequeathed the distinct political systems of Poland and Finland; several languages; the Catholic, Uniate, Lutheran, and Orthodox Churches; and a significant Jewish and Baltic German population (see the chapter "Around the Russian Empire, 1801–1861"). In Poland and Ukraine, Russification was nothing new. The suppression of nationalism, the use of Russian language in the schools, and an ongoing effort to install Russian officials (by means of quotas) to administer these areas continued with full force.

In Alexander III's reign, the Baltic region became another focus of Russification policies. Alexander III concentrated on education, substituting Russian for German as the primary language of instruction, appointing Russian officials to the education offices and Russian scholars to university rectorships—most notably, of the venerable University of Dorpat in Estonia (renamed Yuriev). The governors of Livland and Estland,—A. M. Zinoviev and S. V. Shakhovskoy, appointed in the 1880s—proved loyal executors. Pobedonostsev also had a hand in Russification policy, standing behind the construction of an Orthodox cathedral in Riga as well as the campaign to limit Protestant churches. Sometimes, paradoxical situations arose. On one occasion, for example, Pobedonostsev was forced grudgingly to submit to the enthusiasm of local authorities who arranged a mass conversion of Estonians to celebrate Alexander III's coronation in 1883. Such displays, he grumbled, were counterproductive and would only end in apostasy.

The group most strongly and adversely affected by the shift in the psychology of rule was, doubtless, the Jews. The empire's Jewish population was concentrated in the western borderlands, having been absorbed largely during the partitions of Poland, and then restricted to the Pale of Settlement (see the chapter "Around the Russian Empire, 1801–1861")—a restriction that became more rigid in the 1830s. Movement had become easier in the period of reforms, and some Jewish families began to settle in Moscow and St. Petersburg and became integrated into Russian society. The era of counterreform witnessed not only a reversal of this trend but, for the first time, an actual codification of anti-Semitism as state policy. Jews now residing within Russia proper could not very well be deported back to the Pale; but laws were passed to keep them within the towns and to restrict their rights to property ownership. Most importantly, quotas were set to regulate their admission to universities as well as to certain professions—for example, medicine and law; their voting rights in zemstvo elections were curtailed.

This policy of systematic discrimination coincided with an outbreak of intense anti-Semitic feeling among certain elements of the population. Soon after the assassination of Alexander II, the first pogroms broke out in the Ukrainian territories. On the pretext that the Jews were responsible for the assassination, people in Elizavetgrad, Kiev, Odessa, Warsaw, and other areas, inflamed with hatred, destroyed Jewish property and attacked Jews. These spontaneous, bloody, and destructive uprisings terrorized the Jewish population over the years leading up to the revolution of 1905. It was in this period, when life for Jews became close to unbearable, that the first mass emigration of Jews to America occurred; and it was the policies of this particular tsarist government that were etched indelibly on the memories of East European Jews and their descendants.

Nicholas II distinguished himself by extending Russification to the traditionally friendly territories of Finland and Armenia. Finland had benefited from a special status in the empire: since its annexation in 1809, it had been granted its own constitution, a Finnish Diet (parliament), and virtual autonomy within the boundaries of the empire. For this reason, Finland was the happiest and least problematic of Russian-dominated areas. Nicholas II seemed determined to change this: apparently unaware of the advantages of the existing arrangement, and animated by a desire to protect Russian commercial interests, he appointed a Russian governor general, Nikolai Bobrikov, to Finland in 1898. Under Bobrikov's leadership, the imperial government proceeded to implement mandatory military service in the Russian army, shut down the diet, and amend the Finnish constitution to make Finland essentially into a Russian province. Russian became the official language in the administration and in the schools.

With regard to Finland, Nicholas II seems to have been following—blindly and having lost sight of the basic goal of administrative efficiency that animated his father—the sorts of policies Alexander III had instituted, some fifteen years earlier, in the Baltic provinces of Estonia, Latvia, and Lithuania. The result of these policies, especially those of Nicholas, not surprisingly was the arousal of an intense hatred of the imperial government, and even of Russians generally, on the part of people who previously had been relatively well disposed and willing to cooperate with the government. If anything, the end of the century was characterized by the emergence of active, if illegal, nationalist movements.

Roughly the same was true of Armenia, where the Russification policies of the last two tsars shut down the independent school system administered by the Armenian Church and replaced it with schools of the central Ministry of Education. The state then confiscated the holdings of the church itself and, finally, encouraged pogroms, most notably in Baku in 1905, of the Armenian population by Azerbaijani Muslims.

In general, it is fair to say that the Russification policies of the tsarist government from the 1880s to 1905 were not only its most repressive but also the most shortsighted and ultimately self-destructive. Repressive policies naturally inspired hatred by the population. Moreover, the government's efforts to exploit ethnic antagonisms and turn a blind eye to pogroms gave license to unruly mobs and fomented radical and violent sentiments and ideologies—all dangerous elements that, if properly manipulated, could as easily turn against the regime as with it and erupt in violent revolution.

Russification was a religious, as well as a political, ethnic, and linguistic policy. As such, it also affected religious minorities like Old Believers, Protestants (Volga Germans), Uniates, Muslims (Tatars), and sectarians. Although many Old Believer religious communities had been destroyed in a campaign of the 1850s, efforts now intensified to convert Old Believers to Orthodoxy.

Russification was limited primarily to the western parts of the empire. There was no such systematic policy in Central Asia, which remained basically under the control of a colonial administration. There was some settlement of cities like Tashkent (the capital of Russian Turkistan) and Orenburg (the old outpost bordering the Kazakh steppes), and Russian schools were introduced for the benefit of Russian colonists. Mainly, however, interest in Central Asia was centered on economic development—cotton production was introduced on a large scale, and although some missionary work was conducted, the local population was basically left to its own devices. Russian settlers lived in their own, fairly segregated and Europeanized, parts of town and did not blend with the local population as they did in the Baltic provinces or the Caucasus.

FROM BERLIN TO PARIS

After his death, Alexander III received the title "Peacemaker"; his son and successor, Nicholas II, called an international peace conference—the first of its kind—at The Hague in 1899. Indeed, Russia was involved in absolutely no wars during the quarter century following the Congress of Berlin in 1878. This surface tranquility, however, was belied by the gradual ripening of a number of serious crises in international politics. At the same time, a storm of diplomatic activity changed the century-old terms of the European balance of power and set the stage for growing international conflict in the years leading up to World War I.

It is also true that much of the initiative in international diplomacy had passed out of Russian hands. The successful containment of the Russian Empire, at least along its western and southern frontiers, had begun with the 1856 Treaty of Paris following the Crimean War and been confirmed with the abrogation of the Treaty of San Stefano. It turned into an outright offensive by the 1890s, as a powerful Germany gained increasing influence in the Ottoman Empire, the Balkans, and the Black Sea. Russian foreign policy in the European arena was largely reactive; up to his dismissal in 1890, it was Bismarck who called the shots, constructing an unlikely system of alliances to protect Germany's hard-won position in the center of Europe.

Initiative also came from the inhabitants of the Balkans, which the Treaty of Berlin, ignoring nationalist sentiment, had carved up and divided between Austria-Hungary and Russia. Ironically, each of these powers managed utterly to alienate the Balkan state assigned to its control. Serbia, supposed to be in Austria's sphere of influence, instead became friendly to its "older brother," Russia, while Russia completely lost Bulgarian sympathies through the ineptness of its efforts to govern that country and guide its economic development. The antagonism was sealed in a Bulgarian crisis of 1885: Russian opposition to an incorporation of Eastern Rumelia (Plovdiv) into Bulgaria included an arranged kidnapping of the Bulgarian ruler, Prince Battenberg. In defiance, Bulgarian liberals elected a new ruler, Prince Ferdinand of Coburg, and proceeded to establish the diplomatically mandated governor generalship of Eastern Rumelia. Diplomatic relations between Russia and Bulgaria were broken off in November 1886. Another source of tension between Russia and Austria-Hungary during this period, although here no open conflict occurred at all, was Poland: Austria's comparative tolerance of Polish and Ukrainian nationalism, and the relative looseness of Austrian domination, was a constant irritation to the Russian government.

The closest Russia actually came to war during this period was in 1885, but in another area: Afghanistan. This was essentially a colonial conflict: Russian expansion beyond the Caspian Sea had brought it dangerously close—from Britain's perspective—to British territories in India. Border skirmishes between Russian and Afghan forces worried the British and brought international diplomatic efforts into play. Lack of Great Power support for Britain, and Russia's lack of real colonial interests in that region, brought the crisis to a peaceful conclusion. A lasting result, however, was a basic antagonism between Britain and Russia—an antagonism that was to grow, and which would be crowned by British support for Japan in the Russo-Japanese War of 1904–1905.

Although the politics of these "crisis areas" significantly shaped relations among the Great Powers, these relations also followed their own internal logic. They unfolded through the diplomatic efforts of Russia's foreign ministers—Giers and then V. N. Lamsdorff—and their colleagues. Bismarck's dismissal in 1890 resulted in the collapse of his carefully constructed politics of alliance with Russia (reaffirmed, for the last time, in the Reinsurance Treaty of 1887). In the meantime, growing French investment in the Russian economy and Russian fear of a potential British-Austrian-German coalition against Russia brought a gradual warming of relations between autocratic Russia and republican France. In a reversal of long-standing diplomacy, the two powers finally drafted a military convention in 1892. Russia hoped the German response would be a renewal of friendly relations, but when that did not come, Russia and France signed a full military alliance in 1894. The terms stipulated that each of the allies would come to the other's aid, using all available forces, if it were attacked by Germany. The main consequence of this alliance seems to have been a cultural and economic rapprochement between France and Russia, rather than any immediate and dramatic effect on foreign policy. This, it has been argued, was because the major conflicts of the 1890s took place in East Asia and in Africa—both regions where opposition to Russian and French aims was British rather than German, and where neither had as immediate interests in coming to the other's defense as they would have if conflicts had erupted in the Balkans.

The consistent policies of Alexander III, Nicholas II, and their ministers had by 1900 homogenized the administration of the Russian Empire. Russia's international position had strengthened and changed as the Franco-Russian alliance shifted the focus from Berlin to Paris. The status of the empire, however, depended on two factors yet to be examined—the spurt in economic growth in the 1890s, largely Sergei Witte's creation, and Russia's gradual emergence as a Eurasian, as well as a European, power. Policies of Russification and lack of representative institutions, furthermore, met challenges from an increasingly sophisticated and numerous educated society.

CHAPTER 24

Economic Structures and Visions, 1881–1905

For the supremacy of the metropole over the colonies is in our day established less through weapons than through trade, and Your Majesty's servant does not rejoice in the thought that, perhaps, the slow growth of our industry will hamper the monarch's great political tasks, that the continuing industrial subservience of the Russian people might weaken its political strength, or that insufficient economic development may result in political and cultural backwardness, as well.

—*Sergei Witte (1900)*

Russia's transformation into a modern industrial state involved not only growth in military power but the evolution of an infrastructure of urban life, from the penetration and consolidation of powerful industrial firms, to newspaper publishing and advertising, to restaurants, cafés, and concert halls. Russian modernization took place some half century after industrialization took off in England, and perhaps a quarter century after industrialization in Germany. State support, however, and the so-called technological advantages of backwardness, ensured the remarkable rapidity of Russian industrialization, particularly in the 1890s. In addition, geographical location gave Russia certain innate advantages over its European neighbors: Russia's possession of iron, coal, ammunition, and manufacturing capabilities, not to mention European culture, foreshadowed Russia's potential emergence as the supreme "modern" and "European" power on the Eurasian continent. The Russian Empire occupied a unique position in the world economy. If, on one hand, it was one of the European Great Powers, on the other it displayed many of the features of what we now call developing countries: the empire experienced difficulties in sustaining an exploding population (from 70 million in 1860 to 130 million in 1900) and in stimulating industrial development.

THE DRAMA OF INDUSTRIALIZATION

In his novel *The Idiot* (1868) Dostoevsky called the nineteenth century an "iron age" and painted an apocalyptic image of railways and their steadily expanding network as gradually encircling and ultimately suffocating the globe in their iron grip. Though we may or may not share Dostoevsky's pessimism, it was, indeed, the Industrial Revolution of his age that began creating the world of steel and concrete that surrounds the inhabitant of any modern city. The twentieth century tended to take dramatic economic change and rapid industrial expansion for granted, incessantly calculating growth rates and expecting constant technological advances. Wherever and whenever it happens, a country's industrialization can be like a pact with the devil, inevitably producing unexpected results: a higher and more generalized level of material comfort can be accompanied by greater consciousness of a gap between rich and poor, by new kinds of aspirations and social tensions, and by pollution and ecological disaster. Russia's concerted spurt of industrial growth in the second half of the nineteenth century converted the Russian economy from one based largely on internal trade and agriculture to that of one of the top industrial powers in the world, increasingly ready to take on the military machines of the other Great Powers. The process was painful and uneven, creating new kinds of poverty as well as unheard-of levels of prosperity.

Why Industrialize?

In the eighteenth century, industrialization had undoubtedly presented certain advantages: Peter the Great (Peter I) had developed mining and metallurgical enterprises in European Russia and in the Urals, and the continuation of his policies by his successors, Anna and Elizabeth, was indispensable for strengthening the Russian military and also helped to improve agricultural techniques and raise the quality of urban life. By the middle of the nineteenth century, however, the terms of the game had changed dramatically. The Industrial Revolution—beginning in England and spreading rapidly to America, France, then Germany, Austria, Russia, Japan, and Italy—involved the rapid and fundamental transformation of technology—from railways, steamships, and cotton mills in the 1800s to electricity, telephones, automobiles, and airplanes at the turn of the twentieth century—accompanied by an increase in the sheer volume of production of material goods of all kinds. Being industrialized, following this revolution in technology and industrial production, no longer meant simply minor technical advantages but a transformation in a country's entire way of life, from international status to social structure. Industrial countries, by definition, had strong military machines; they were urbanized and had a broad and prosperous middle class, as well as a new growing and significant social group—the working class. The Industrial Revolution definitively set off those countries that had experienced it from those that had not.

In the case of Russia in particular, the urge to industrialize seems to have been based less on a mystical need to "catch up with the West" than on the more tangible exigencies of Great Power politics. Industrialization, of course, was intimately related to the kinds of weapons a nation could produce, the sorts of goods it could export, and, last but not least, its population's general level of prosperity. In the balance of power game, all three were essential to remaining a member of the elite club of European nations—a club that, following German and Italian unification, included England, France, Germany, Austria-Hungary, Italy, and Russia. Although voices of doom like Dostoevsky's could be found in all of these countries, in general the imperative to industrialize was taken for granted and, indeed, inspired joy and enthusiasm among many who sensed limitless possibilities for technological, scientific, industrial, and thus human progress.

By the last third of the nineteenth century, Russia was poised to industrialize. With its broad expanses and predominantly agricultural orientation, it had experienced relatively slow industrial growth until this time. Russia had a mere 1,626 kilometers (1,008 miles) of railways in 1860 (to Germany's 11,000 kilometers [6,820 miles]) and an urban population of only 5.68 million in 1856 (which would balloon to 26.3 million by 1914). Russian agriculture itself did not keep up with the modern agricultural revolution, missing the improvements in breeding stock, varieties of crops, use of mineral fertilizers, and other innovations. Industries like textiles and metals production (together employing two-thirds of the work force) lagged behind those of France and Britain, although Russian pig iron production had been first in Europe in 1800. These purely economic indicators were accompanied by even more dramatic social characteristics peculiar to Russia: the recent liquidation of serfdom, despite the reformers' best efforts, had left masses of the peasant population without the means to make a decent life for themselves; and the legacy of serfdom and the continuation of a predominantly rural way of life combined to keep literacy at levels that were shockingly low by European standards.

Still, the empire was generously endowed with both human and natural resources. While trade and industry were a tradition for Old Believer "thousanders" in the Volga region and in Moscow, the dislocations of the postemancipation period made business an attractive possibility for newcomers as well—both for gentry setting up factories on their estates and for peasants coming to the cities to set up shops or taverns. The breakdown of the old social order, often associated with industrialization, was in Russia already taking place as a result of agrarian change. Statesmen and entrepreneurs, moreover, were well aware that the Russian Empire was extraordinarily rich in natural resources, from the grain fields and coal deposits of Ukraine and Poland to iron ore in the Urals, oil in the Caucasus, and gold, diamonds, and furs in Siberia. The empire was much richer, in fact, than most of the European states that were rapidly on their way to becoming industrial giants.

The Push to Industrialize

One of the great economies at the close of the eighteenth century—for example, the largest producer of iron ore—Russia had allowed industrial production to stagnate in the first half of the nineteenth century as the industries of England, France, and Germany accelerated. The rude shock of the Crimean War served as a reminder of the importance of industrial development. Even so, growth proceeded at a relatively leisurely pace for some twenty years after the great reforms (indeed, it was temporarily, and briefly, hampered by emancipation as serf laborers deserted factories in the Urals and the central manufacturing regions around Moscow). The first harbinger of change, true to Dostoevsky's image, was the railroad, which added an artificial artery to the network of rivers that crisscrossed the country and had traditionally carried trade. From the first tiny railroad line linking St. Petersburg to Pavlovsk, opened with much pomp and ceremony in 1837, and the first major railway, connecting St. Petersburg and Moscow, begun in 1842, Russia's railway system increased from a mere 2,372 kilometers (1,471 miles) in 1861 to 29,734 kilometers (18,435 miles) in 1887. The railways radiated out from Moscow and St. Petersburg to Warsaw, Kursk, Nizhny Novgorod, Voronezh, Yaroslavl, and other provincial cities and, eventually, into the Caucasus and Central Asia.

Railway construction, apart from providing the transportation network necessary for the development of industry, also created a need for capital and materials: as railways were built, Russia imported huge quantities of iron, while much of the investment in the network came from abroad, including from the French Crédit Mobilier. In the meantime, domestic growth, though unremarkable in itself, laid the foundations for the rapid industrial spurt to come in the 1890s. It was in the postreform period that coal mining began in Ukraine, extraction of oil began in the Caucasus, and large-scale industry—from metals and coalmining to textiles, manufactures and sugar refineries—developed in Poland.

Industrial growth began in earnest midway through the reign of Alexander III, aided immensely by the aggressively industrial policies of the two ministers of finance: Ivan Vyshnegradsky (1886–1892) and, particularly, Sergei Witte (1892–1903). Industry was concentrated in a number of clearly defined areas, each with particular products; one might count five or six major industrial regions, limited largely to European Russia and the western territories. The vast eastward expansion was of limited relevance to industrial growth, with the exception of Siberian gold and silver mines and some raw materials (cotton from Central Asia). In the 1890s, industrialists began intensive exploitation of the tremendously rich coal and iron resources of Ukraine; by 1901, three great companies in the Donets basin and Krivoi Rog and expanding as far as Kharkov and Ekaterinoslav, had far outstripped the Urals—the old eighteenth-century industrial center—in pig iron and steel production. In 1897 one of these companies, the Bryansk Company, produced 160,000 tons of pig iron, 111,000 tons of steel, and 93,000 tons of sheet iron and employed more than four thousand workers. Production stimulated further expansion: A half-dozen new companies entered the region in the 1890s, and seventeen metals production and refining factories sprang up in Ukraine, most of them in Ekaterinoslav Province.

Ukraine, in short, flourished: long a center of agricultural production, it now became the progenitor of industrial wealth as well. In the meantime, exploitation of the coal and iron resources in the Urals continued, though less productively than in Ukraine; state-owned enterprises were more common there, continuing an old tradition, although foreign firms began to penetrate by the end of the century. Not

TABLE 1 INDUSTRIAL PRODUCTION, 1881–1905

Distribution of Metallurgical Production in Russia (in million poods*)

	Ukraine		Urals		Moscow region		Baltic region		Poland		Total	
	I	IS	I	IS	I	IS	I	IS	I	IS	I	IS
1887	4.2	3.2	23.8	15.7	4.4	4.1	—	5.5	3.7	6.8	36.1	35.5
1897	46.3	3.2	41.2	26.2	10.9	12.1	0.1	14.5	13.7	16.4	112.2	103.3
1901	92	75	49.2	33.6	11	17.6	1.1	6.4**	19.6	23	172.9	157.9

I: Pig-iron. IS: Iron and Steel.

*One million poods is 36.11 million pounds.
**The crisis began earlier. Maximum production in 1899: 15.9 (11.3 in 1900).

The Development of Production (in million poods)

	1887	1890	1900
Pig-iron	36.1	54.8	176.8
Coal	276.2	366.5	986.4
Iron and steel	35.5	48.3	163
Oil	155	226	631.1
Cotton (requirements)	11.5	8.3	16
Sugar	25.9	24.6	48.5

Source: From Roger Portal, *The Industrialization of Russia,* in H. J. Habakkuk and M. Postan, eds., *The Cambridge Economic History of Europe,* Volume VI. Copyright © 1965. Reprinted with the permission of Cambridge University Press.

surprisingly, development brought with it an alteration in the entire landscape and a new culture in which workers relied on factories for housing, education, and medicine.

While mining and metals centered in Ukraine and the Urals (there were smaller plants in the St. Petersburg area and elsewhere), light industry also experienced a tremendous push in this period. In the central industrial region, etching a wide circle around Moscow (Moscow, Vladimir, Kaluga, Nizhny Novgorod, Ryazan, Tver, Tula, Kostroma, and Yaroslavl Provinces) and long famous for artisanal production of textiles, craft turned into industry. Centers like Ivanovo imported cotton from Turkistan and other areas and produced cotton, flax, and wool cloths. Miscellaneous other industries, like food and perfume manufacture, also centered in this region, while some metals plants and heavy industry also provided railways with necessary equipment. European Russia's other major urban area, around Petersburg and in the Baltic lands, faced competition from the new industries and began increasingly to specialize: light industry—manufactures, leather, food, tobacco—de-

veloped alongside the older metal production enterprises, which also expanded. The famous Putilov factory in St. Petersburg employed more than seven thousand workers in 1895.

Poland presented a special case: once obstacles to development—most notably serfdom and unfavorable tariffs—were lifted, industry had grown tremendously in the 1870s and 1880s and slowed down in the 1890s. Production was particularly diversified: enormously rich in coal and iron, Poland also produced textiles and manufactured chemicals. Nevertheless, however much Poland was incorporated into the empire, Russian industrialists continued to see it as a foreign country, and customs duties were imposed to limit competition from Polish goods (some two-thirds of production was exported to Russia), although cooperation increased as the century drew to a close.

Finally, oil production—less important in the nineteenth century than in the twentieth—grew rapidly at its only source: Baku, on the Caspian Sea, where the Swedish Nobel brothers founded a petroleum plant—the first continuous cracking plant in the world, producing kerosene. Crude oil production, mostly for export, increased from 8,912 tons in 1865 to 27,200 in 1870 and 244,000 in 1887.

In short, industrial production—most of it needed for domestic consumption—grew at an astonishing rate until halted, temporarily, by depression at the turn of the century. Total growth indices have been calculated at an extraordinary 7 or 8 percent yearly (5.72 for 1885–1914, including all downswings), compared with 5.26 for America, 4.49 for Germany, and 2.11 for Britain.

The Role of the State

What made this industrial explosion possible? First, of course, it could not have happened without the Great Reforms. The emancipation of the serfs created a wage-labor force whose mobility was essential to a factory economy; at the same time, the peasants helped to create a market for consumer goods. Other consequences of the reforms that benefited industry were legal guarantees, possibilities for local political participation, and a general dynamism—in which individuals might change their profession or line of business. Second, the industrial spurt of the 1890s would not have been possible without the proindustrial slant of state policy. "Infant industry," as the eighteenth-century British example illustrates, generally requires the protection of the state: this principle had been the basis of mercantilism. This was even more the case for a country that, like Russia, was industrializing toward the end of the nineteenth century, when relatively powerful technology and equipment were available and necessary. The postreform ministers of finance had taken a cautious approach to industry; it took the sweeping vision of Witte to create the conditions in which growth could take off at an astronomical rate.

The need to endorse industrial growth was felt by Alexander III's ministers of finance from the outset: the first, N. K. Bunge (1881–1887), sought to encourage industry by active state intervention in railway construction and by protectionist import duties while at the same time trying to minimize negative effects on agriculture. It was on Bunge's initiative that a Peasant Land Bank was set up in 1883, the head tax and salt tax were abolished, and certain initial laws were passed to

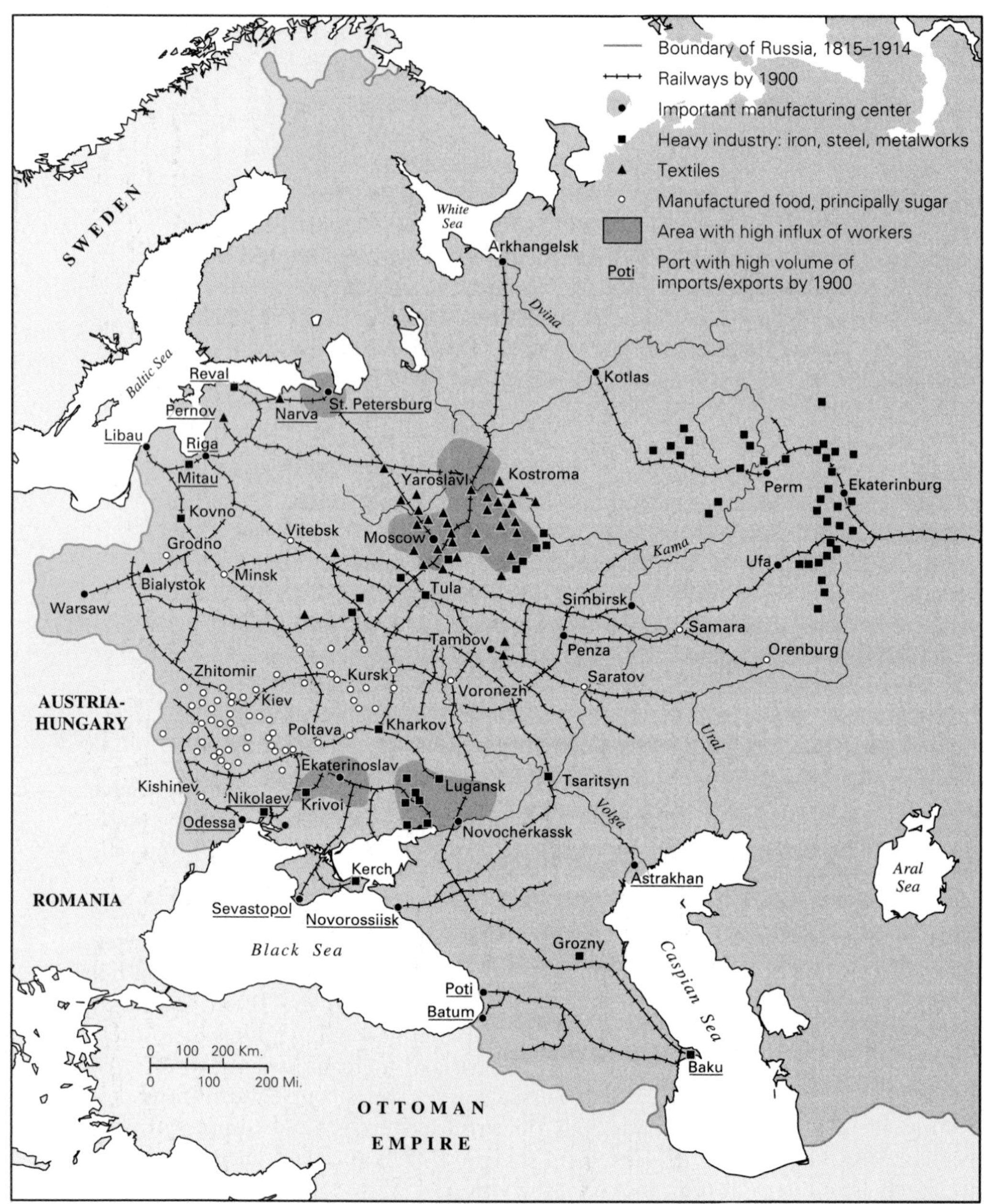

Main industrial regions to 1900. Atlas of Russian History *by Martin Gilbert (New Edition published by Routledge in 2002) 0415281199 PB & 0415281180 HB. Please visit our website for further details on the new edition: www.taylorandfrancis.com.*

protect workers. The first minister of finance to advocate a concerted industrial push was Ivan Vyshnegradsky (1887–1892), whose program involved soliciting French loans, raising import duties to stymie consumption of foreign goods, and an aggressive export policy that both stimulated industry and caused many to blame him for advancing industrial development at the expense of the agricultural sphere. Radicals, particularly, held Vyshnegradsky responsible for the severe famine of 1891: his insistence on increasing grain exports, they argued, had emiserated the peasantry and left them with no supplies in case of a poor harvest.

Sergei Witte succeeded Vyshnegradsky as minister of finance in 1892. A strong sense of national pride was not the least factor in Witte's determined push to make Russia into not just a prosperous country but one that could justly take its place among the elite of nations. Witte's program was even more aggressive than the policies of his predecessors. Its ingredients were heavy foreign investment, high import duties, increased exports, and currency stabilization—the latter a crucial step that Witte achieved by putting the ruble on the gold standard in 1897. Railroad construction, in which Witte had made his career, was the cornerstone of the entire system. The "Witte system" took its inspiration in part from the theories of the German economist Friedrich List (1789–1846), who advocated intensive industrial development, including protectionist tariffs, as a national economic policy. Thus Witte finally initiated the construction of the Trans-Siberian Railway, whose precise route had been under debate for decades, followed by massive railway construction throughout the country as a whole. Construction was accompanied by freight rate adjustments to stimulate traffic. Witte next directed his attention to shipping and the development of a commercial fleet. Interestingly, the percentage of the budget allocated to the army and navy declined slightly during this period of intensive industrialization.

Part of the revenue necessary for industrialization came from a rise in indirect taxes and, the most innovative measure, the creation of a state liquor monopoly. The Ministry of Finance under Witte's direction sought to increase the value of Russia's cereal exports and created a sugar cartel while imposing high tariffs on imported goods, from Germany in particular. Finally, the implementation of the gold standard became the key to attracting increased foreign investment, building up industry, thus eventually coming full circle and enabling the government to pay off its foreign debts: Witte's emphasis on foreign loans, exports, restricted imports, and domestic gold production built up gold reserves sufficiently (about 50 million rubles a year) to permit conversion to the gold standard in 1897. These specific and consistent measures were crucial to the success of investment and industry, as was the energy and spirit with which they were implemented.

Influential American historians in the 1960s—most notably, Alexander Gerschenkron and Theodore von Laue—had a tendency to exaggerate the importance of state intervention for the creation of Russian industry. In part, this was the result of a false analogy between imperial Russian and Soviet industrial development. The imperial Russian state did not, as the Soviet state did in the 1930s, build its own factories; instead, by fiscal and monetary policies, it created conditions in which industry could flourish. Currently, economic historians generally see the state, with its encouragement of foreign investment, manipulation of tariffs, and institution of the gold standard, as only one among many factors contributing to industrial development, albeit a crucial one. Without the active intervention of the Russian imperial state, the industrial spurt would have been impossible; yet Russian industrialists and entrepreneurs, the associations they formed, foreign investors, and the workers and managers who ran the factories deserve ultimate credit for the rapid industrial expansion of the 1890s.

Industrialization: Change and Instability

Industrialization usually brings a generally higher level of prosperity, but it brings extremes of wealth and poverty as well; and extremes of economic inequality bring social instability. Many of the 2 million workers of St. Petersburg, Moscow, Warsaw, and other urban and provincial centers of industry lived poorly, and few had apartments of their own, while the streets of Moscow and the river embankments of some provincial cities were graced by the ornate private houses of wealthy industrialists and merchants. Labor legislation and social insurance were slow to develop, and in the 1890s government officials continued to deny the existence of a "workers' issue" in Russia. The absence of basic rights and protection explains the appeal, in primarily industrial areas like the Donbass, of radical ideologies. The financial status of the nobility fluctuated after the end of serfdom: many landowners were forced by the new economic conditions to sell off much of their property, which found its way into the hands sometimes of peasant communes and sometimes of enterprising merchants consolidating their financial gains. Yet extremes of poverty were not only the result of industrial growth but also the legacy of centuries of serfdom.

MONEY AND MARKETS

Healthy economic expansion requires an extensive apparatus of commercial and monetary mechanisms and institutions, such as banks and stock exchanges, to facilitate investment, capital formation, and profit. Although industrialization altered the Russian economic landscape most visibly, even more fundamental transformations occurred in less spectacular but equally important areas like banking and retail trade. Without an adequate commercial infrastructure, the spurt in industrial production, too, would have been impossible. Creating this infrastructure, despite the energy with which it was undertaken, meant overcoming a number of obstacles: the state's reluctance to relinquish control over the economy, continued *soslovie*-oriented policies, and a complicated taxation system hampered enterprise, while protective tariffs and an easing of restrictions on private commercial activities made a positive contribution. The postemancipation period gave birth to a series of new institutions, from private banks to joint stock and insurance companies, while the older trade fairs and informal credit associations flourished as well.

Capital

Political scientists sometimes refer to intensive development financed by foreign capital as dependent development. Though coined a century later to describe developing economies in various parts of the globe, the term fits the process of Russian economic development at the close of the nineteenth century. In the initial stages of economic expansion, in agreement with Witte's policies, much of the necessary capital came from abroad. Total foreign investments amounted to about 2 billion rubles (when, using the economist Paul Gregory's figures, national income was about 11 billion), with the bulk going to heavy industry (mining, metals, textiles) and some to credit and commercial enterprises and real estate. Investment took the form of government bonds, and railway bonds with a government guarantee, in addition to direct investment. The Franco-Russian alliance signaled an abrupt shift in investment patterns, from German predominance in the 1870s and 1880s to French in the 1890s and 1900s, with almost two-thirds of Russian government bonds held in France by 1914. The French, the Crédit Mobilier in particular, invested heavily in Russian railways and industry. Together, France and Germany accounted for about one-third of total new investment, reaching an all-time high of 81 percent in the difficult 1903–1905 period. One factor stimulating such high rates was the implementation of the gold standard in 1897; in addition, a higher rate of return on investment in Russia than in France succeeded in making Russia more attractive. Not only foreign money, but French and German firms and also individuals (such as managers and engineers) formed a crucial part of the developing Russian economy. Some of the more prominent foreign firms included Hughes's New Russia Steel Company, Bell Telephone, Singer Sewing Machines, and International Harvester; the German Ludwig Knoop was one of the first big financiers and managers.

The elements of a modern banking system, both state and private, took shape in Russia beginning in the 1860s, although the first banks date to the reign of Anna in the eighteenth century. Here there is almost no point in European comparisons, since sophisticated banking systems had formed the backbone of, for example, the Italian or British financial empires in the sixteenth century and earlier. The Russian State Bank was established in 1860, in part to facilitate the reforms. While playing the role of a central government institution—minting and regulating currency, regulating the money supply and lending rates, and issuing bonds and securities (like the Federal Reserve Bank in the United States)—the state bank also functioned as a commercial bank, extending credit to borrowers. The government bank system was supplemented by two specialized, *soslovie*-oriented banks whose main business was land mortgages: The Gentry Bank extended discount rate loans to the gentry and landowners, while the Peasant Land Bank (1883) performed the same functions—provided credit, resold land—for the peasants, at a higher rate. In addition, the government operated savings institutions where urban and, by the 1880s, rural dwellers could deposit their money and receive interest payments.

Private banks—of which three or four became extremely powerful—first appeared in the 1860s and multiplied in the period up to the World War I in 1914. Beginning on a modest scale, by the end of the century they were operating with credits from foreign banks and the state bank and contributed particularly to both urban and rural land sales. In the meantime, many merchants relied on cooperative banks and mutual assistance institutions for credit. Partly taking a hint from companies in France and Germany, Russian entrepreneurs began to develop more sophisticated financial arrangements in conducting their business. No longer content to do business by intuition or to make deals in smoky taverns on the waterfront, younger businessmen sought to enter into new kinds of partnerships, and to keep accounts according to rational methods. This led to the formation of not only mutual credit agencies but also joint stock companies, as well as some peculiar institutions like exchange counters where money could be exchanged but not stored, bills of credit, and so forth.

Insurance was a flourishing business in this period, as well, and one that contributed to the infrastructure of economic expansion. Fire insurance companies, such as Salamandra or the Moscow Insurance Company, were particularly important given the frequency of rural fires (some of them intentionally set by peasants to collect the premiums). In the mid-1870s private insurance companies, threatened by increased government intervention, successfully formed the first syndicate in Russia.

Beginning in the reign of Peter I, stocks and bonds could be bought and sold on the Petersburg stock exchange. However, the stock market as a financial mechanism was less developed than in other European countries or the United States because of the dominance of the local and national trade fairs: thus trade in real goods in general prevailed over the sale and purchase of stocks. Still, Moscow had its own stock market in the first half of the nineteenth century, while regional exchanges sprang up in the 1860s, 1870s, and 1880s, from Irkutsk (Siberia) and Kiev (Ukraine) to Baku and Taganrog (South Russia).

Trade and Commerce

Traditionally, Russia's broad expanses and richness in raw materials had meant that nonagricultural economic activity focused on trade and commerce. Internal trade—that is, within the empire itself—was an important part of Russia's economy. Relying on the natural arteries of the Volga, Don, and Dnieper Rivers, Old Believer merchants—based primarily in Moscow or Nizhny Novgorod—piled their boats high with salted fish from Astrakhan at the Volga's mouth and honey from the Russian forests; Tatar traders brought spices and exotic goods from Central Asia and Turkey; Armenians traded carpets and gold; hardy adventurers brought back furs from Siberia. In a colorful pageant of bright clothes and Turkic, Slavic, Caucasian and Baltic languages, these entrepreneurs converged each year at the immense and tumultuous All-Russian Trade Fair at Nizhny Novgorod—strategically located not only at the confluence of the Volga and Oka Rivers but also at the geographical point of convergence of the many cultures and ethnicities that made up the Russian Empire. The yearly fair was the crowning event of an entire network of smaller markets and trade fairs where most of the country's commerce was transacted; the most successful and prosperous merchants sometimes made their entire year's income through a clever sale of their boatloads.

Retail sales at the Nizhny Novgorod fair. Photo by M.P. Dmitriev, 1890s. *Private collection.*

The terms of this sort of commerce and petty industry began to change dramatically in the second half of the nineteenth century. The advent of steamships had already significantly improved traffic on the Volga and eliminated the need for human mules—the *burlaki,* or barge haulers (the subject of a painting by Ilya Repin). Railway construction, of course, created steady ties, not only from north to south but also from west to east, and linked Moscow and Petersburg to other provincial cities off the river routes.

At the same time, the new health of the cities following the municipal reforms of 1870 (see the chapter "Alexander II and the Era of the Great Reforms, 1855–1870") permitted rapid growth in retail trade not only in Moscow and St. Petersburg but also in provincial centers like Kazan, Smolensk, Orël, even Irkutsk. Many goods, in other words, could now be directly bought by consumers in a store on the town's main street. Correspondingly, the hotel, restaurant, and bar businesses mushroomed by 1900.

Foreign trade was also an integral part of the Russian economy. Russia was a net exporter of agricultural products in the last third of the nineteenth century. The main export was grain, which defined Russia's role in the international economy. After a major growth in grain exports in the 1870s and into the 1880s, the level remained steady up to about 1903, mostly because of new competition from North and South America. The Black Sea ports of Odessa and Nikolaev flourished, becoming the main outlet for Russian grain and overtaking by far the Baltic ports. Livestock products (eggs and butter), forestry products, and raw materials from the mining sector (oil and manganese ore) became increasingly important. Imports, in the meantime, were primarily cotton, fine wool, and machinery—that is, materials needed for manufacture and the production of consumer goods. During this period, the commodity trade balance was in surplus, though not the balance of payments. The government had a consistently very active tariff policy to encourage exports and resorted to all possible means to this end, including export subsidies, assignment of export quotas, low freight rates in the ports, low interest loans to exporters, and efforts to include a tariff clause in international treaties.

A satisfactory assessment of both "internal" and "external" trade would include trade relations among different regions of the empire. Poland (one of the most highly industrialized regions) and Central Asia would be the most important of these regions. After all, tariffs and customs persisted within the empire. Were "internal" markets really internal, or were they colonial? Were manufactured goods "exported" to non-European parts of the empire? Unfortunately, almost no research exists on these questions.

The emergence of a capitalist economy meant that Russia was subject to the same international business cycles as the rest of the world. A fairly severe depression hit in 1900, ending the more or less uninterrupted growth rates of the 1890s. Industry experienced a significant fall in production, and it was not until after the 1905 revolution that the economy resumed its dramatic expansion—this time building on past achievements and with a much smaller contribution from foreign capital.

THE AGRICULTURAL SECTOR

When famine swept the Russian countryside in 1891, public opinion, quiescent in the 1880s, erupted in a storm of protest. Writers like Tolstoy, Gleb Uspensky, and Vladimir Korolenko traveled to the provinces and returned with tales of starvation and goosefoot-flour bread, while radicals blamed the government's—that is, Vyshnegradsky's—attention to industry, to the detriment of agriculture, for the disaster. There was another serious famine in 1897, and yet another followed in 1901. Ironically, during this same period, 1880–1905, Russia became one of the world's largest grain exporters; in fifty districts of European Russia, average grain production rose from 29.6 million tons in 1861–1865 to 57.5 million in 1901–1905 (it reached 65.6 million tons by 1910–1913).

Crisis or Growth?

Agriculture at the end of the nineteenth century, like other aspects of the changing Russian economy, was full of contradictions and painful paradoxes. Oceans of ink were expended by politicians, radicals, and, later, historians on arguably the most acutely troubling social and economic issue of the age—the "agrarian question."

Generalizations about the state of Russian agriculture are difficult to make; nonetheless, on some points there is more or less general agreement. First, the finance ministers were clearly less interested in agriculture than in industrial development. Eventually Witte did turn his attention to the agricultural sector. However, during the massive industrial push of the 1890s, agriculture was primarily the domain of the zemstvo, which tried to implement technical changes, improve the level of agricultural education, and regulate land distribution. Unfortunately, as the counterreforms gained in force, the central government interfered increasingly with zemstvo affairs, limiting their financial resources and powers of taxation and thus hampering their ability to bring about improvement. Second, agriculture bore a significant part of the burden of capital formation for industrialization. Although the horrors of collectivization in the 1930s and the Soviet policy of squeezing nonexistent grain out of the peasants make nineteenth-century problems pale in comparison, a policy of using grain exports to finance industrialization was in evidence in the 1890s. A gap in industrial and agricultural prices was the result. It was, however, potentially resolvable in the framework of capitalist, as opposed to socialist, economics.

Third, there was widespread poverty and hunger among peasants, made all the more shocking by the expectations of prosperity that accompanied industrialization. Contemporaries cited statistics of decline in livestock holdings in peasant households, and the peasant diet rarely included milk, butter, and eggs, not to speak of meat. But the most serious problem was the lack of sufficient land for cultivation—a legacy of the compromise solution at emancipation. The peasant economy was caught in a vicious circle: with insufficient funds and education for more intensive cultivation of existing land, peasants also lacked enough resources (once taxation and redemption payments were made) to expand their acreage. This difficulty was related to a fourth characteristic of late-nineteenth-century agriculture: although improvements in techniques of cultivation did take place—for example, minor changes in the three-field rotation system, better fertilizers, and soil improvement—they were slower than they should have been, so that peasants could not compensate for quantity by quality. Though contemporaries had a tendency to attribute such slow improvement exclusively to peasant backwardness, irrationality, and general "darkness," it is more accurate to ascribe this difficulty to the impossibility of breaking out of the self-perpetuating cycle of poverty.

Finally, on a more optimistic note, it is also true that modernization of agriculture definitely did occur over the half century following the reforms. However severe its problems, agriculture did provide food to the growing urban population while still maintaining its own rocky existence. Economic historians have recently noted that the overall outlook appears better once regions outside the central black-earth area—the northwest, southwest, and Siberia—are included in calculations.

Changing Landlord and Peasant Economies

On a microeconomic scale, neither the households of landlords, nor of peasants, provided a happy picture in the years preceding the 1905 revolution. Many gentry estates ceased to be profitable with the end of serfdom, while the division of land into strips, poor resources for cultivation, and the demands of taxation and redemption payments made peasant farming an unrewarding business. The major constants in postreform agriculture were continued government assistance (generally misguided) for its traditional pillar of support, the gentry, and the preservation of the commune as the basic unit of peasant agriculture. The decline of the gentry, both economic and political, was a major feature of the end of the nineteenth century.

The primary change in the agricultural economy was the status of the peasantry, who now largely lived by sharecropping or tenant farming, although opportunities for the purchase of land also increased. On gentry estates in the black-earth provinces, the percentage of land cultivated by the proprietors declined from 33 percent in 1886–1890 to 22 percent in 1896–1900; the percentage leased went up from 32 to 44 percent, while mixed arrangements remained constant at 35 and 34 percent. Analogous figures for gentry estates in non-black-earth provinces during the same periods are a decline from 31 to 20 percent for the percentage of land cultivated by the proprietors; an increase from 30 to 54 percent in the percentage of lands leased; and a decline from 39 to 26 percent in mixed arrangements. With the aid of the Peasant Land Bank, peasants expanded their property ownership. In Kursk Province, for example, the total area purchased by peasant associations (not village communes or individuals) was 17,444 hectares (43,0887 acres) in 1884–1895, and 100,072 hectares (247,178 acres) in 1896–1906. Most of this land was sold by the gentry estates.

Changes, however, were haphazard and uneven, and the prevailing sense in the countryside was of decline and depression. Neither landlords nor peasants could make ends meet. The agrarian question was a burning issue in the political world of the end of the century and would finally come to a head in the revolution of 1905, the debates of the revolutionary Dumas, and the reforms that were finally implemented in the revolution's wake by Prime Minister Stolypin.

Handicrafts *(Kustar)*

Those individuals in the agrarian world, whether gentry or peasants, who did best in the late nineteenth century were those who could adapt to the increasingly commercialized economy. Paradoxically, this meant, above all, those in provinces with poorer soil and harsher climatic conditions, who had always supplemented income from the land with cottage industry and handicrafts, known as *kustar* industry. Much larger-scale trade was carried out by men who had made trade their profession (most of the successful Old Believer merchants were peasants by origin and had bought their way into the merchant guilds). But a large proportion of Russia's rural population significantly supplemented their agricultural income by engaging in cottage industry or the production of various handicrafts—wooden spoons, bast shoes, pottery, lace, and even icons. This brought them into the growing exchange network and plugged them into the new commercial economy.

For many peasant families, especially in the non-black-soil areas, less than 50 percent of their real income came from the land—which, in any case, could be farmed only a few months in the year. They made up the deficit in agricultural production by sales of such handicrafts, which were generally of fairly low quality and meant for use by the peasant population. (Going to a factory to earn a supplementary living was therefore not much of a departure from traditional norms, in which one might go to work for the local major wooden spoon maker.) Gentry, struggling to keep solvent or wealthy in the postemancipation period, began to engage in petty manufacture on their estates—from glassware and textiles to carriages—and to employ the local peasantry in these industries.

A curious feature of government policy in this period is that, while pushing forward large-scale industrialization, unusual legislation (paralleled nowhere in Europe) was passed to protect *kustar* from the inroads of heavy industry. Thus small-scale handicrafts flourished alongside metals production and coal mining.

OTHER VISIONS: MARXISTS AND POPULISTS

Witte's vision of Russia as a modern, industrial nation was by no means universally accepted and was challenged by several equally sophisticated and well-developed views of where the Russian economy should be headed. In the wake of the 1891 famine, the Russian intelligentsia and educated society mobilized to implement alternative strategies of development. Every economic issue, from capitalism in general to grain prices in a particular province, stimulated intense debate and extreme emotion, not unlike the atmosphere of the "Marvelous Decade" of the 1840s (see the chapter "Nicholas I: Monarchy, Society, Empire, 1825–1855"); young girls were said to faint from excitement at the university lectures of Marxist professor Pëtr Struve (1870–1944) on grain prices. The two most vocal groups to emerge from this discussion, whose polemics dominated the intellectual scene in the capitals, were the Marxists and the populists (see the chapter "The Turbulent Seventies")—the latter being the heirs of their namesakes a generation earlier.

The theories of Karl Marx (1818–1883) took hold seriously among Russian intellectuals for the first time in the 1890s, when orthodoxies had not yet been established and to be a Marxist could mean holding a variety of convictions and shades of belief. Russian Marxists, accordingly, were a diverse assortment of individuals, preaching various degrees of revolutionary involvement and more or less willing to work within existing legal frameworks. In terms of economic theory, however, they shared a belief that capitalism was a necessary stage in the historical development of any nation, including Russia, and that only following a period of full-fledged capitalist industry could a proletarian revolution and the ensuing socialist society occur. Thus Russia would eventually experience the transition from "feudalism" to "capitalism" already undergone by England, France, and Germany. In his first major work, *The Development of Capitalism in Russia* (1900), Vladimir Lenin (1870–1924) argued that Russia had entered the stage of capitalism in 1861. (Eventually, this was to become the "party line" for Marxist historians in the Soviet Union.) Less rigid Marxist thinkers, who came to be known as legal Marxists—Pëtr

Struve, Mikhail Tugan-Baranovsky, Sergei Bulgakov—also tended to look favorably on Russian industrial development, since it was historically inevitable and brought the country closer to the next stage—socialism.

The Marxists were opposed by the populists, who, in contrast, continued to propound a "special path" for Russia. Unlike Marxists, the populists were above all oriented toward rural Russia and, like their predecessors, saw a unique good in the peasant commune that they sought to preserve. Whereas Marxists tended to concentrate in the capitals and to be either academics or professional revolutionaries, populists and their followers fanned out through the countryside, doing a good deal to raise literacy levels and trying to improve farming techniques among peasants. They were horrified by the traumas induced by industrialization, and many among them felt that Russia should find its place among modern nations as an agrarian country—as the "world's breadbasket." The peasant commune remained at the center of their vision. Although their position seems, in hindsight, utterly impractical, the populists succeeded at least in giving some voice to agrarian concerns.

Not all thinkers fit neatly into the two categories. For example, throughout the Russian provinces, as well as in the central universities, many educated people who thought of themselves as emphatically apolitical shared the belief that science, as applied to Russian agriculture, could ultimately resolve Russia's economic problems. Though they were not necessarily anti-industrial, their focus was on agricultural concerns. These people, united more by common cultural assumptions than by any group organization, included meteorologists, chemists (of whom Dmitry Mendeleev was one), soil scientists (a new discipline headed by Vasily Dokuchaev), and statisticians, as well as rural clergy, teachers, doctors, and zemstvo intelligentsia. They sought to harness the elements to improve the soil and peasant agricultural techniques and believed, above all, that knowledge and serious scientific study held the key to social transformation. Once peasant farming was completely understood, it could be changed. And, indeed, the achievements of Russian statistics, meteorology, and chemistry in this period were astounding: probably no country has ever been described down to the last detail of every peasant household as Russia was in the independent (sometimes zemstvo-commissioned) statistical studies of the 1890s, which drew on the observations of rural priests and teachers. These efforts, against all sorts of bureaucratic odds, contributed to the preservation and growth of Russian agriculture at a time when the government was primarily concerned with industrial development.

These intellectual perspectives proved remarkably long-lived. The general worldview of legal Marxism, for example, in which a nation must experience particular stages of economic development, still underlay the influential picture of "Russian backwardness" propounded by the economic historian Alexander Gerschenkron (1904–1978) in the 1960s. According to this vision, the states of Europe were arranged on a descending scale from West to East, with England and France industrializing earlier while Germany, Italy, and Russia lagged behind; the later a country industrialized, the larger the role played by the state and by ideology in pushing this inevitable process through. To follow this argument further, the revolution of 1917 and the forced industrialization by the powerful Soviet state under Stalin were "necessary" stages in Russia's belated but inevitable "modernization." Russia's economic development (or lack thereof) in the second half of the nineteenth century, in other words, carried the burden of accounting for the entire course of its history in the twentieth.

A EURASIAN POWER

After the debacle of the Russo-Japanese War (1904–1905), both the memoir and historiographical literature tended to portray Russian expansion in the East as a haphazard enterprise and the result of the harebrained schemes of a group of "adventurers," in particular the Yalu timber firm, with Alexander Bezobrazov at its head. Subsequent research has taken the Russian eastward push a good deal more seriously, as the result of a confluence of conscious decisions, policy directives, and imperialist competition that ultimately involved Russia in a disastrous war with Japan. Industrial and technological progress opened up new possibilities in the

The Great Path: views of Siberia and its railways. Cover of a book by that title, 1899. (Velikii put: vidy Sibiri i eia zheheznykh dorog, *Krasnoyarsk, 1899.*) *Courtesy Stephen Marks.*

continuous process of Russian expansion and colonization, and the close of the nineteenth century saw Russia's emergence as a Eurasian power. If railroads were the symbol of economic expansion generally, the immense transcontinental Trans-Siberian Railroad was a specific central symbol of Witte's economic policy. Whatever the defects of its actual operation, the Trans-Siberian reached over 8,000 kilometers (4,960 miles) from Moscow to East Asia, ending at the new warm-water port of Vladivostok. The eastward push took its impulse in the reign of Alexander III, who not only initiated the railroad but sent his twenty-year-old son and heir Nicholas on a grand tour, not of Europe, but of Asia, beginning in Egypt and India and ending in China and Japan. Still, Russia—whose traditional orientation had been toward Europe for at least two centuries—turned decisively eastward only with the accession to the throne of its last monarch—the same Nicholas II. A significant constellation of individuals, including the autocrat, looked to Asia as Russia's colonial equivalent of India or perhaps Africa. One was Witte himself, known for his ideology of "peaceful penetration" (which could include military means) and naturally concerned with the economic implications of Asian expansion. Another was Prince Esper Ukhtomsky, who accompanied the tsarevich on his travels and saw Russia's future in an Asia whose civilization was in no way inferior to Europe's. A firm foothold in East Asia could make the Russian Empire competitive with Britain as the latter practically took over China in the second half of the nineteenth century.

Expansion into East Asia involved Russia in an entirely new foreign policy configuration. The eighteenth and nineteenth centuries had been dominated by the game of the European Great Powers (and, to go further back, the seventeenth by the neighbor competitors: Poland, Turkey, and Sweden). But now the Russian Empire found its interests immediately connected with those of Japan and China. The stakes in the game were the territories of Manchuria and Korea, where Russia sought, beginning in the 1880s, to obtain an ice-free port. The construction of the Trans-Siberian Railway itself directly affected relations with China, as the most direct route would cut through Manchuria. Russia built the outpost of Harbin in Manchuria, and good relations with China became a prerequisite for the railway's functioning. Russian penetration into Asia deepened following a war between China and Japan in 1895, when Russia pledged support to China in its loss against the unsuspected strength of its island neighbor. In the meantime, the European powers, as well, were developing growing interests in the region: Germany's lease of land on the Liaodong peninsula (1897) set off a flurry of colonial competition, in the course of which Russia acquired a stake in ice-free Port Arthur (1898), while Britain and the United States also sought influence. Witte, aware of the difficulties of control over distant territories, was anxious to avoid conflict in East Asia and wished to pursue a conciliatory policy while extracting maximum economic benefit from expansion. The Boxer Rebellion in 1900—a widespread and violent revolt against foreign economic and political control—pushed the European powers (Britain in particular) out of China.

Thus East Asia became, like Africa, one of the primary zones of international imperial competition among the Great Powers. With its penetration into Manchuria,

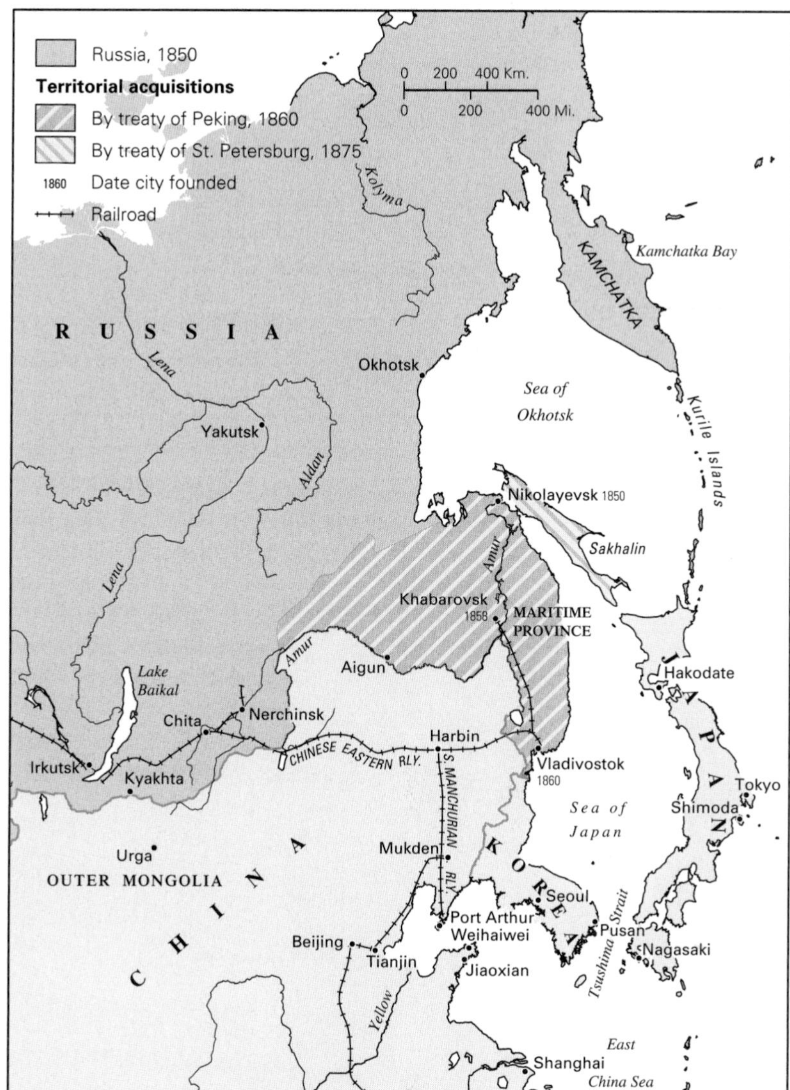

The Russian Far East, 1895–1901.

as well as into Central Asia, Russia was a major player, confronting Britain and Germany. Witte, and others, saw immense potential for Russia's emergence as a great Eurasian power if its policies in the region were successful. Asian themes began to seep into Russian literature, becoming, for example, the subject of important poems by Vladimir Soloviëv ("Pan-Mongolism," 1894) and Alexander Blok ("The Scythians," 1918).

Expansion was accompanied by a process of colonization of the sparsely populated Siberian territories that lay between European Russia and its Manchurian interests. The government, represented by the manager of the Committee of the Siberian Railroad, Anatoly Kulomzin, sought to manage the flow of Russian peasants to Siberia by distributing land plots, providing free food and medical care, and overseeing a mixed system of individual and communal farming. In the two decades preceding World War I, Siberia counted some 5 million migrants, and agricultural, livestock, and butter production were thriving. The natural resources that made Siberia attractive to the Russians included gold and silver. The government program also included efforts to settle and organize the native Kazakhs, Buryats, Mari, Komi, Chuvash, and other peoples. As elsewhere in the world, Russian colonization brought both prosperity and new problems, including disease and displacement and even the extinction of some of the smaller northern peoples.

CHAPTER 25

Society, Culture, Politics, 1881–1905

The business of worldly self-improvement was now so attractive to me that I secretly began to search for books on these matters. 'Indeed,' I thought, 'why shouldn't there be books like that? Why, there are even books on how to write letters!' I had bought just such a book on letter writing, one that I used with some success and that rendered great service to me.

—*Worker and writer Semën Kanatchikov,* Story of My Life *(1929)*

The profound yet remarkably peaceful transformations of the second half of the nineteenth century—the agrarian reforms of the 1860s, followed by the push to industrialize in the 1890s—went hand in hand with equally fundamental changes in the fabric of Russian society itself. The flux in Russian society defies any neat categorization in terms of class or estate; certainly, the rigid *soslovie* (estate) headings—gentry, clergy, merchantry, *meshchantsvo,* and peasantry—which continued to be used in official censuses and revisions of the population, were no longer adequate to describe a society in which professionals, workers, intellectuals, industrialists, and politicians, among others, played a visible and arguably even a dominant role. One thing was certain: it was no longer by any means clear that children would comfortably follow the vocation and status of their parents; a new generation had its own way to find, and a school or university education could be the key to a different path in life.

Russian society, it seemed, developed in a world apart from the harmonious and organic, constitutionless state that the government sought to preserve—or, sometimes, by the 1890s, in active opposition to it. Political discourse was rife with references to the "building without a cupola," meaning the absence of a national legislature; social activists, however, did what they could to perfect the structure of the building itself to the smallest details, and by 1900 the infrastructure of local societies, press, and national groupings throughout Russia provided a powerful organizational base for an opposition movement. Tentacles of the European revolutionary, socialist, and feminist movements reached into Russia while, moving in the other direction, Russian radicalism and anarchism decisively shaped those currents internationally. Moreover, real national movements began to emerge in various regions of the empire; to varying degrees they intersected, on one hand, with religious consciousness and, on the other, with incipient socialist and revolutionary organizations.

CLASS, STATUS, PROFESSION, HOUSEHOLD

In 1897, the first comprehensive, "scientific" census of the entire Russian Empire (in contrast to the earlier, rougher revisions for tax-collecting purposes) painted a detailed, colorful portrait of a land of many geographical regions, languages, ethnicities, religions, social groups, and occupations. As a whole, although the same demographic growth was in evidence as in the rest of Europe, including some flow toward the cities, the total population of 128.2 million (double the 1850 figure) still meant quite sparse settlement, and more so if one considers that most of the 17 million urban dwellers were concentrated in the western provinces and in European Russia. Thus European Russia and Poland contained 130 cities with over 20,000 residents, whereas the Caucasus, Siberia, and Central Asia together had only 37,000. Around 83.9 million people counted Russian as their native language; the next largest groups were Polish, 7.9 million; Tatar, 3.7 million; and Mordvinian, 1.0 million. Some of the many different languages (and the ethnic groups who spoke them) in the Caucasus Mountains counted no more than 226,496—the figure for the Chechens. The empire included about 5 million Jews. The census counted 69.4 percent Orthodox for the empire as a whole; next were Muslims, with 11.1 percent (90.3 percent in Central Asia); Roman Catholics, 9.1 percent; Jews, 4.2 percent (14.1 percent in Poland); then Lutherans, Old Believers, Armenian Gregorians, Buddhists, and a residue of animists and others.

Ambitiously, the census also sought to account for the social status of the overall population; not including Finland, the breakdown by *soslovie* is shown in Table 1.

A full 75 percent of the population were shown as engaging in agricultural pursuits; 9.4 percent worked in industry; 4.6 percent in the service sector; 4 percent in trade; and smaller numbers in transport, government service, the military, mining, and public service.

TABLE 1 Population, by *Soslovie*

Hereditary gentry	1.0%
Nonhereditary gentry and civil servants	0.5%
Clergy	0.5%
Honorary citizens	0.3%
Merchants	0.2%
Meshchane	10.6%
Peasants	77.1%
Cossack troops	2.3%
Ethnic minorities *(inorodtsy)*	6.6%
Others	0.4%
Foreigners	0.5%

Source: 1897 census

Middle and Working Classes

Behind these numbers, however, lay some major trends that the statistical methods of the census were not geared to reflect. First were the growing numbers and growing importance of the middle classes. From European history, we have become accustomed to think of "the bourgeoisie" as an urban phenomenon whose emergence is intimately related to the beginnings of industrialization and the expansion of towns. In Russia, it was the agrarian reforms of the 1860s, preceding industrialization, that created a space for new kinds of "middle people"; some of them, indeed, lived in the larger cities, but others found a home in institutions like the zemstvo, the provincial courts, hospitals, schools, and churches that occupied a niche between city and countryside. They were mainly professionals: teachers, engineers, doctors, journalists, lawyers, professors, veterinarians, statisticians, agronomists, meteorologists, and architects. They could also belong to the commercial world—merchants, bankers, industrialists, hotel keepers, and tavern owners—or to the state or local bureaucracy—provincial governors, military officers, foresters, and postmasters. The same phenomenon occurred in the borderlands as well, where a class of fully integrated professionals, retaining their native language but also fluent

Family Portrait in a Suite of Rooms. By the provincial photographer A.O. Karelin (1880s). *Private collection.*

in Russian, took shape. Thus individuals whom the census counted merely as "gentry," "ethnic minority," or even "peasant" might, by occupation, actually belong to this amorphous but essential middle segment of the population. Exactly how many of them there were is, thanks to the same data-gathering inadequacies, harder to say. One estimate (for 1916, later than the other data here) counts 36,019 members of the "professional middle class" in the Middle Volga town of Saratov, and 22,870 for the "commercial middle class," or a total of about 25 percent of the local urban population.

The professional, commercial, and bureaucratic middle classes made their weight felt through clubs, societies, and professional organizations, which flourished in the 1880s and 1890s; these groups were also heavily represented in the provincial zemstvos. On the local level, the primary organizations in which they convened were scientific, commercial, educational, charitable, or medical clubs. On the national level, several powerful collective bodies played a key role, most notably the Free Economic Society (founded under Catherine II in the interests of agricultural improvement), the Russian Technical Society, the Imperial Geographic Society, and the Union of Physicians and Naturalists, among others. Many of these organizations had links with the zemstvos, and there was a growing clamor, unheeded by the government despite the recommendations of some of its ministers, to crown the edifice of state with a *zemsky sobor,* or national body inspired by the Muscovite institution with the same name.

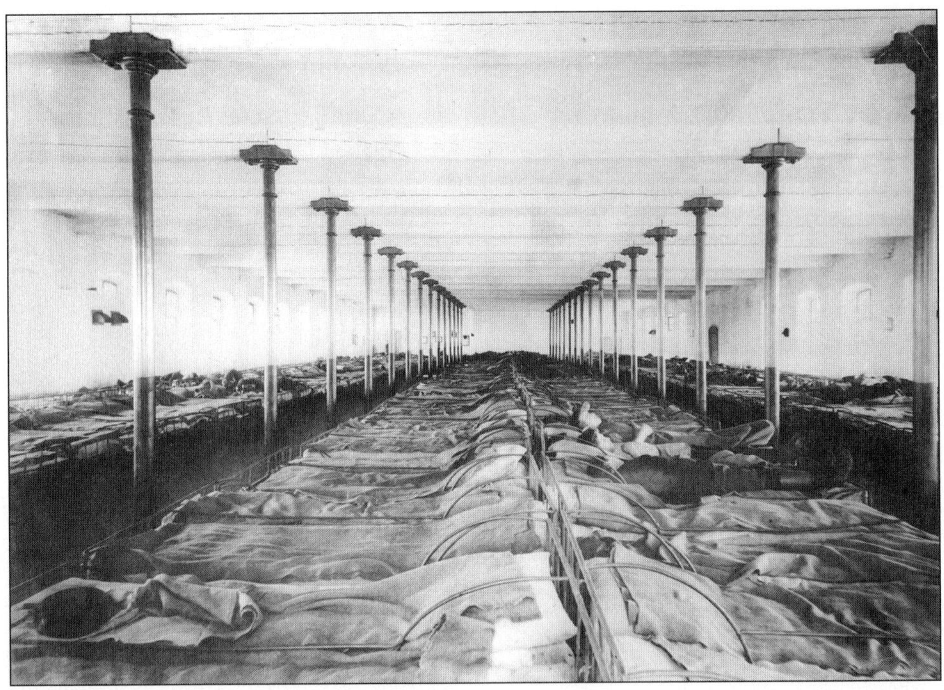

Workers' dormitory at a textile factory in Ivanovo in the 1890s. *Sovfoto/Eastfoto.*

The second major trend that completely eluded the census takers was the formation of a working class: workers in the factories, mines, and refining plants numbered over 2 million by 1900. Although industrial workers accounted for a relatively small percentage of the total population, they were an important social force in the cities and a tangible presence in late-nineteenth-century life. In older industrial cities, real working-class suburbs existed as in Paris or London; for example, Sormovo, outside Nizhny Novgorod—a setting used by Maxim Gorky (1868–1936) in many of his novels—had been a working-class region since the 1840s. Large numbers of workers were concentrated in heavy industrial centers like the Donbass region. Here, as in industrial Manchester in England or the Ruhr Valley in Germany, workers' lives followed the imperatives of factory whistle and late-night tavern. Many Russian workers retained close ties to their home peasant villages: often they still had families in the village, and they owed dues to the village commune. Workers' dormitories were standard in many factories. Year-round labor was supplemented by the seasonal labor of peasants from poor agricultural regions. This peculiar status has prompted historians to coin the term peasant-workers: although they earned their livelihood in the factories, their identity remained linked to their peasant past (see the chapter "The Turbulent Seventies"). In hierarchical societies, numerically small groups can be highly influential. By the late nineteenth century, Russian workers—with an extremely high literacy rate (97 percent) and often an avid interest in the theatrical and literary offerings of the city, a deep religious sense, and a growing culture of their own—were becoming such a group. The state, in the meantime, largely ignored them: social legislation was still virtually nonexistent on the eve of 1905, and radical groups fought for such gains as limits on the working day, a minimum wage, accident insurance, and the right to organize. Laws passed in 1886 regulated relations between factory owners and workers, requiring, for example, the payment of wages in cash rather than goods, and prohibiting the lowering of contractually set wages; but they did not introduce any substantive changes in the basic rights of workers in relation to their employers. A wave of strikes broke out in 1896 and 1897 as factory cotton spinners and weavers in St. Petersburg demanded a reduction in work hours from thirteen to ten and a half hours per day. The passports of most workers still designated them as peasants, which accounts for the absence of this growing and important social group from the census data.

The emergence of these two important groups—bourgeoisie and workers—amply demonstrates the porousness of the old social categories, and the richness and variety of social life behind the façade of the "old regime" *soslovie* (estate) system. In the new world, some gentry landowners set up factories on their land (sometimes from an inability to subsist on diminished income from the land, about half of which they had collectively lost since the reforms). Others began professional careers. "Peasant," in the meantime, could now mean almost anything: Old Believer millionaires, workers, small shopkeepers, actors, and musicians were often still classified as peasants, together with those who remained tied to the village commune. The *meshchanstvo* and merchant guilds often functioned as a corporative organization, effective for professional advancement, more than as a designation of status or occupation. The clerical estate lost its hold on a new generation as seminarians broke away to attend secular universities.

City and Countryside

Indeed, although the image created by the census statistics appeared to confirm the classic stereotype of Russia as a primarily agrarian country, the relation between city and countryside had changed in fundamental ways. In rural Russia, the ties of dependence that had bound landlords to the state, and peasants to landlords, were all but completely eroded. Urbanization itself was further along than the census could count: according to government categories, only district centers could be classified as towns; yet many villages, as well as Cossack settlements, had populations well over those of small towns in Germany. The difference was that villages lacked the bureaucratic administration of a city and were run instead by peasant elders and assemblies and, after 1889, the land captain. Marketplaces and fairs were held regularly throughout the empire, with only the largest and most famous at Nizhny Novgorod; they contributed to making Russian villages, at least for several months

Peasants in a non-black-soil village. Photo by B.W. Kilburn (c.1896). *California Museum of Photography/ Keystone-Mast Coll. UC Riverside.*

of the year, remarkably like towns elsewhere. At other times, traveling salesmen helped to maintain ties with other towns and regions.

The urban landscape itself, moreover, became peopled by a variety of types that sharply distinguished the atmosphere of the cities and towns from the slow, semi-rural character of towns in the first half of the nineteenth century. Apart from industrialists and workers, these people included students in the universities and technical schools. Their numbers had increased to fifteen thousand in 1897, from five thousand in 1859. And, although university or technical studies can always be a path to a career or vocation, in nineteenth-century Europe, including Russia, "studenthood" was also an identity and an organization. Russian students, by definition equipped with education and free time, though generally very poor, gathered in regionally based student associations and organized meetings. Together they discussed or questioned university regulations (notably, the 1884 statute limiting university autonomy), the quality of professors, and, eventually, politics. Students had their songs and poems, and their ritual celebrations—most notably St. Tatyana's feast day in mid-January, which became a traditional student holiday with much drinking, eating, and singing. Russia was also by no means immune to the phenomenon of urban poverty, and urbanization also produced an underclass of beggars, hooligans, holy fools, and others that tended to congregate in particular parts of the city (for example, the Haymarket Square in St. Petersburg, the equivalent of London's Whitechapel). In response, charitable organizations or wealthy industrialists sometimes set up soup kitchens, dormitories, and homeless shelters. Prostitution flourished in St. Petersburg, Moscow, Kiev, Odessa, and Kazan—regulated starting in 1843 by the "yellow ticket," the official license that required regular medical inspection. Somewhere between extreme poverty and comfortable existence were the people who made the nineteenth-century city run—from coachmen and lamplighters to cesspool cleaners (known as the Golden Platoon) to petty shopkeepers.

Family and Household

In many ways, the culture of the Russian middle classes replicated the patterns of "bourgeois" culture throughout Europe; an ethic of hard work, family, and concern for "the people" characterized their lifestyle. Even in the far provincial reaches of the empire, their households subscribed to two or three national illustrated weeklies as well as to the local newspapers and magazines. The success of historical journals that had begun in the 1870s, like *The Russian Archive* and *Russia's Past,* rested on their popularity among the "bourgeois" reading public. Tales of exotic travel adventures, mildly risqué scenes from theater life, and, of course, romance were also favorite subjects. Women had a particularly important cultural role in the household: they cultivated literature, art, and music (a piano became a standard fixture in the living room), and they played the primary part in the upbringing of children. In general, upbringing was a highly valued aspect of family and social life: whereas the early-nineteenth-century aristocracy had been content to leave children to serf nannies and foreign tutors, now mothers, fathers, psychologists, and pedagogues focused their attention on children's care and education. An expanding literature especially for children produced eventual classics like Lydia Charskaya's *Princess Dzhavakha*—the story of a tomboyish Georgian princess sent to boarding school at the Pavlovsky Institute in St. Petersburg for young girls of noble birth. The importance of class distinctions and proper consciousness of one's social status was one theme that ran through children's books of the late nineteenth century. Outside the middle classes, the family as an institution was less sacrosanct; military recruitment and seasonal labor continued to disrupt the running of peasant households, though less drastically than in the old times of twenty-five-year—or, before that, lifetime—military service.

One might say that the final decades of the nineteenth century witnessed the gradual "emancipation" of society from the control of the state despite the latter's ideal of social harmony; historians have spoken of this period in terms of the emergence of civil society, as well as the breakdown of the landlord-serf relationship. But persistent problems included the difficulty of creating a central crowning edifice to local participation, and the government's insistence on making policy on the basis of *soslovie* politics, including, for example, the retention of separate peasant and gentry land banks. Perhaps most importantly, in 1900 the agrarian question still remained unresolved.

THE 1880s: UNIVERSITIES AND INTELLECTUAL LIFE IN A POSITIVIST AGE

As Russian society evolved, despite government reliance on its traditional ally—the gentry—as an increasingly fragile pillar of support, so did cultural life in capitals and provinces. Traditionally, the decade of the 1880s has been depicted as a period of cultural stagnation, when the single-minded intensity and excitement of the 1870s movement "to the people" faded in response to the atmosphere of counterreform. Dostoevsky died in 1881 and Ivan Turgenev in 1883; Tolstoy, who lived until 1910, dramatically if falsely announced his withdrawal from literature. Yet the thirteen years of Alexander III's reign witnessed some remarkable developments: first, the emergence and affirmation of a quieter "mainstream" cultural life; second, the marketing and commercialization of culture, attracting new and wider audiences for literature, theater, ballet, opera, and museums. The 1880s became a period of the formation of deep and broad roots for Russian culture. The two major loci of cultural and intellectual development in this staid, self-confident, and positivist age became the universities and the press. University professors transmitted new ideas to an unprecedented number of students. And the press reached far beyond the elite of the two capitals. Literature, particularly poetry, was very much alive, and the 1880s and 1890s were the productive years for the brilliant philosopher and creator of an independent modern Russian philosophical tradition, Vladimir Soloviëv.

Universities and the Press

Moscow University experienced a flowering in the 1880s. Student enrollments, stable in the 1870s, shot up over the ensuing decade, from sixteen hundred in 1880 to almost thirty-five hundred in 1890. A generation of humanities students was captivated by the calm, precisely worded, and insightful lectures on Russian history of Vasily Osipovich Klyuchevsky (1841–1911), who according to one listener, brought the world of medieval Muscovy alive for his audience. Klyuchevsky's course on Russian history, inspired partly by the end of serfdom, was one of the earliest and most successful works of social history and anticipated the further development of this approach by twentieth-century researchers. Klyuchevsky's charisma was matched by the scholarship of other Moscow professors, such as Kliment Timiryazev, a plant physiologist and a proponent of interaction of science and society; the physicist A. G. Stoletov, director of a major physics laboratory in Moscow; I. M. Sechenov, who pioneered the study of the eye and had links with the nihilist movement; and the neurophysiologist Ivan Pavlov, whose name is a household term because of his work with reflexes.. The comparative pathologist Ilya Mechnikov, while recognized internationally for his work in embryology, along with that of his colleague Alexander Kovalevsky, did not receive a post in Petersburg and taught at Odessa University. The horticulturalist and self-taught biologist I. V. Michurin's experiments in applying Lamarck's theories of acquired traits bore (dubious) fruit in the Soviet period, when scientists sought to base Soviet agriculture on a denial of Mendelian genetics. The final decades of the nineteenth century were, in short, extremely productive in virtually all fields of scientific endeavor.

Many scholars in the social and natural sciences were as engaged in Russian social and political life as their populist predecessors, if in a more unobtrusive way. Alexander Chuprov (1842–1908), for example, a very influential political economist whose research centered on such issues as the economy of railroads and the relation of grain prices to available markets, became the intellectual founder of the discipline of local (zemstvo) statistics. An expedition by soil scientist Vasily Dokuchaev (1846–1903) to Nizhny Novgorod Province in 1883–1884 produced a detailed map of all the soils in the region, thus aiding in the land redistribution that was in continuous process since the reforms of the 1860s. Dokuchaev also became the founder of the first regional natural history museum—intended to be an instrument in the education of the local population. The work of Dmitry Mendeleev (1834–1907) at the end of the 1880s included studies of import and export tariffs in addition to his scientific research. In the meantime, scientific societies and congresses flourished, gaining new organizations such as the Congress of Natural Scientists and the Congress of Physicians, among others.

Both the national press—including the thick journals, daily newspapers, and illustrated weeklies—and provincial newspapers increased in volume and expanded their circulation. The once popular *Contemporary* was replaced by more conservative journals like *Russian Thought,* while *Niva (Plowlands)* experienced its heyday, and local *Provincial Messengers* acquired the trappings of sophisticated urban newspapers, complete with advertising pages selling everything from pianos and books to birchbark facial lotions (containing what are now known as alpha-hydroxy acids) and remedies for impotence. Opera, ballet, and theater became objects of consumption in the emerging commercial culture. Cheap brochures for the broad public proliferated, and readers were treated to tales of adventure, history, or folklore.

Literature and Philosophy

Despite the laments of "progressive" writers who saw a void in literature in these years, the 1880s were particularly productive for poetry. Afanasy Fet (1820–1892) wrote metaphysical and love poetry in the seclusion of his estate, perfecting the school of "art for art's sake" in response to the "civic poetry" of the 1860s and 1870s. But in terms of popular appeal, few could rival Semën Yakovlevich Nadson (1862–1887). Mocked by literary scholars as "the low-water mark of Russian poetical technique," Nadson won the hearts of, and brought many a tear to, virtually every young girl in Russia's educated classes—and he affected the worldview of many women and men of the succeeding generation. Nadson's sentimental poetry, reproduced on the pages of the illustrated journals, appeared alongside poems by minor figures like A. Apukhtin (1841–1893), Konstantin Fofanov (1862–1911), and Myrrha Lokhvitskaya (1869–1905).

Two figures, however, each completely different from the other, left perhaps the brightest mark on the cultural landscape. Vladimir Soloviëv (1853–1900), the first real Russian philosopher of the modern period and eventually the founder of an entire tradition in Russian thought, came entirely from within the Moscow University environment: his father was the historian Sergei Soloviëv, and Vladimir grew up in university circles, achieving erudition at an early age. Soloviëv's first treatise, *The Crisis of Western Philosophy* (1875), was directed as much against his undereducated and ignorant fellow students—as he perceived them—and their nihilist fantasies as against the doctrine of positivism. Soon afterward, while doing research in the British Museum, he had a vision of Sophia, the Divine Wisdom, that told him to travel to Egypt, where he indeed experienced revelation. By the end of the 1880s he had completed a book entitled *Russia and the Universal Church,* which leaned toward Catholicism; finally in the 1890s, *The Justification of the Good* established his reputation as a completely original and independent moral philosopher. Soloviëv was also a poet with a sense of humor and an essayist. In "The Meaning of Love," he argued that sexual love was the supreme fulfillment of a human being's worth and that love should recognize the worth of the other rather than being exclusively directed toward some other purpose, such as bearing children. This and other essays were enormously influential for a later generation of poets and writers.

Anton Chekhov (1860–1904), whose world could not have been more different from that of Soloviëv, was by profession a physician. A master of drama and short stories in particular, Chekhov recreated the world of the Russian provincial intelligentsia and the profound psychological experiences that underlie a superficially quiet and uneventful life. His plays—in particular, *Uncle Vanya* (1900), *The Three Sisters* (1901), and *The Cherry Orchard* (1904)—remain a staple of repertory theaters to this day. They capture the world of the rural gentry as their social position eroded in the postemancipation era and have contributed a good deal to a lasting image of "Russians" as passive characters unable, through inner weakness, to execute their hopes and dreams through work and entrepreneurship.

THE 1890s: POSTFAMINE POLITICS

The famine that struck throughout the Russian countryside on 1891 etched a distinct line on the political landscape as well. Intelligentsia activists, and especially students, descended on the villages en masse, setting up soup kitchens, organizing produce distribution centers, and bringing whatever medical knowledge they could; one local zemstvo bought up grain to distribute to the peasants. Beginning as a purely humanitarian effort, aid to the famine victims mobilized zemstvo agronomists, physicians, teachers, and particularly statisticians—who, together, came to be known as the Third Element—in a revival of the dormant spirit of 1870s populism. Despite government expenditures of some half-billion rubles on famine relief, many held state grain export policies responsible for the disaster. The 1891 famine became a landmark on the scale of the Irish potato famine of 1848: as the journals erupted in a storm of protest, the famine became the symbol of a sharp rift between the government and the intelligentsia.

Radicalization

Politics in the 1890s took the form of a powerful social movement based on already existing institutions such as the universities, technical and scientific societies (especially the Free Economic Society), and local institutions like the zemstvo and local clubs and organizations. The first half of the decade witnessed a growth and consolidation of societies and organizations, mostly under the rubrics of self-help, mutual aid, and moral and intellectual improvement. In the universities, the student associations were transformed from clubs of students with a common regional origin into quasi-political organizations that disseminated literature among workers or became a forum for political discussion; at Moscow University, these associations numbered forty-three in 1894, up from twenty in 1892, with a total of seventeen hundred members, and they united in a single organization, the Union Council. Peaceful in its aims, the council sought to further student self-education, distribute books and literature, and create a network for material aid. The Moscow council was paralleled by St. Petersburg's Mutual Aid Fund, a more radical organization, numbering some three hundred to four hundred members and growing out of student circles that also created a link among the student associations. A similar process of consolidation took place among various professional associations—technical, medical, and scientific. A landmark was the Ninth Congress of Russian Natural Scientists and Physicians in 1894, which created a forum not only for scientific discussions but also for the expression of Third Element political concerns; statisticians were overrepresented at this congress. The Free Economic Society provided a natural meeting place for disparate members of the zemstvo intelligentsia; many of the most important statistical surveys and agricultural and meteorological data were published in their papers, and they took up the cause of education as well, organizing a committee on literacy.

Tsar and Intelligentsia

A speech by Nicholas II on January 17, 1895—in which he responded to zemstvo petitions concerning national representative institutions with the epithet of "senseless dreams"—marked the initiation of a cat-and-mouse game, characteristic of his reign, between government and the "progressive" elements of society. The calm of university life was punctuated by several dramatic incidents: when the Moscow University Union Council requested that the new tsar repeal the 1884 University Statute, police raided student leaders' apartments; Professor Klyuchevsky's panegyric lecture to the memory of Alexander III set off catcalls, protests, and eventually a demonstration among students; and student meetings were greeted by police arrests. A progressive radicalization of the key student organizations followed, and mutual provocations became characteristic of relations between students and government starting about 1896, when ninety-two students were expelled for the coronation ceremonies; a half year later student commemorations of the Khodynka disaster (where people were trampled at the coronation) led to more arrests. At the same time, Marxism caught on with a vengeance among the student population in the second half of the decade; Sergei Bulgakov's *On Markets in Capitalist Conditions of Production,* Pëtr Struve's work on prices, and Mikhail Tugan-Baranovsky's major work *The Russian Factory in Past and Present* were composed on a wave of Marxist enthusiasm that placed an indelible mark on the thinking of a generation of young economists, historians, social scientists, and philosophers.

A parallel radicalization took place within associations such as the Free Economic Society, which, in Count P. A. Geiden's presidency, beginning in 1895, became increasingly a gathering place for radical statisticians and zemstvo intelligentsia. This shift did not escape the attention of the authorities, who increasingly sought, with limited success, to confine the sphere of activities of the society to purely agricultural questions. A similar shift affected local zemstvo politics: the main feature of the latter part of the 1890s became the domination of the more left-wing provincial zemstvos over the more moderate district zemstvos: their determined intelligentsia representatives, who had already been filtered through the sieve of the districts, found increasingly greater means for self-assertion. National congresses burgeoned in these years, including those of physicians and natural scientists, technical instructors, representatives of *kustar* industry (handicrafts), teachers, and so forth. Here again the government response was a careful curb on their activities, including legislation once again (as in the 1880s) limiting the taxation rights of the zemstvos and circumscribing their power over local management. An All-Russian Fair of Trade and Industry at Nizhny Novgorod in 1896 was meant to bring together the government (represented, in person, by Witte), representatives of merchant guilds and industrialists, zemstvo activists, and agriculturalists. Though the pavilions were lavish and Russian industrial successes were much in evidence, a lack of popular entertainments and a generally heavy, didactic tone kept attendance figures much lower than expected, and participants from different branches of trade and industry had difficulty in finding common ground.

The mid-decade shift in politics—radicalization and mutual "irritation" of government and society—had one more significant consequence: for the first time, intelligentsia radicals and discontented workers began to form real links with one another. Thus the Donbass-Dnieper region, for example, experienced a sharp upturn in labor unrest in 1895–1899. A riot at the Bryansk mill in Ekaterinoslav in May 1898 was among the first in which active mass Social Democratic agitation played a significant role, though it ultimately erupted in the violent and elemental traditional style rather than the quieter walkout advocated by the Social Democratic agitators. Strike movements in St. Petersburg, Moscow, and heavily industrialized Poland intensified in 1895–1898, greeted by severe repressions by factory management but also resulting in some worker gains, including limitations on the adult workday (set at eleven and a half hours by an 1897 law). Jewish worker and artisan organizations first took shape and developed an independent political strategy in the 1890s.

On the opposite side of the political spectrum, a radical right movement was slow to emerge. The earliest organizations, which would not take on concrete shape until revolution erupted in 1904–1905, included a Holy Brotherhood in the 1880s, a failed patriotic society later in that same decade that was denied police permission, and a grouping around the journal *The Russian Review,* founded in 1897. In 1900, however, forty individuals, many of them high up in the government bureaucracy and cultural circles, formed an organization called the Russian Assembly. This nationalist organization and defender of autocracy eventually numbered future influential right-wing radicals like V. M. Purishkevich (1870–1920) among its members; its aim was to defend against "the spreading cosmopolitanism of the upper strata of Russian society"—a battle fought through dissemination of brochures, lectures, meetings, and readings. Still, right-wing sentiments found more violent and less organized expression in anti-Semitism and pogroms, which broke out in the Donbass and elsewhere between the wave that followed 1881 (see the chapter "Orthodoxy, Autocracy, Nationality Reaffirmed, 1881–1905") and a massive pogrom in Kishinëv in Bessarabia in 1903.

Russia and the International Left

In contrast to the populism of the 1870s, which was an indigenous Russian movement, Social Democratic agitation among the workers in the Donbass was part of a larger phenomenon. The close of the nineteenth century was the heyday of the international socialist movement, and the high point of what the philosopher Leszek Kolakowski has called Marxism's golden age. In July 1889, representatives of socialist parties and trade unions from twenty countries convened at an inaugural congress in Paris; over the ensuing quarter century (up to 1914), they met eight more times. This series of congresses was the Second International—the implementation of Marxism's promise to be a revolutionary movement that crossed national boundaries and united the workers of the world. Dominated by German social democracy, with the French socialist parties and syndicalists (trade unionists) in a close second, the Second International brought ideology and practical politics together, fusing socialist theory and the workers' movement. The groups that made up the International accepted, in general terms, the premises of Marxism: that history unfolded as a succession of different systems or modes of production; that feudalism had been succeeded by capitalism; and that the latter would be overcome from within by the class struggle, in which an international proletariat would rise up against capitalism's inherent contradictions and establish its own dictatorship, ultimately leading to an egalitarian socialist society. But, in 1900, the basic doctrine was subject to a wide variety of interpretations, and Marxism could mean different things in different countries and have varying implications for a political program.

In Russia, the first leading theoretician of Marxism was Georgy Plekhanov (1856–1918), as important in the international movement as the German theoretician Karl Kautsky (1845–1938). Plekhanov developed his ideas largely as an émigré in Geneva, where a group of exiles gathered around him and in 1883 formed the Labor Emancipation Group, which counted Vera Zasulich (who shot at the Petersburg chief of police in 1878) and the future prominent Menshevik Pavel Axelrod (1850–1928) among its members. His main innovation was the application of Marxism to Russian conditions—no small task, given Russia's relatively undeveloped urban/industrial society and the unsophisticated (because illegal) framework of workers' organizations. Plekhanov argued that a liberal democratic revolution must precede a socialist revolution; that Russia needed to develop capitalism before it was ready for socialist transformation; and specifically that an industrial proletariat needed to carry through that transformation, rather than the peasantry.

Vladimir Ulyanov (1870–1924), who took the pseudonym Lenin in 1901, began as a relatively obscure participant in the theoretical debates of the populists and "legal Marxists" (see the chapter "Economic Structures and Visions, 1881–1905") in the 1890s. The son of a school inspector in provincial Simbirsk, Ulyanov came from precisely the stratum of "middle people" that emerged in the postreform period. His older brother, Alexander, was involved in a plot by the radical People's Freedom organization to assassinate Alexander III. The conspiracy was discovered, and fifteen of the perpetrators, including the brother, were executed in 1887. Lenin's biographers agree that the incident had a decisive influence on him. When he entered Kazan University to study law, he was soon recognized as the brother of a terrorist and drawn into revolutionary activity. Expelled from the university following a student demonstration in 1887, he earned his law degree through independent reading; but his interests shifted to political economy, and his mood grew increasingly radical. He found his own voice by 1900, with the publication of *The Development of Capitalism in Russia* (which saw the emancipation of the serfs as the line dividing feudalism from capitalism) and the founding of the newspaper *Iskra (Spark).* Some of the elements original to Lenin's interpretation of Marxism were his advocacy of an alliance of workers and peasants in the revolutionary movement;

his willingness to use national movements as a tool in the service of socialist revolution; and a peculiar notion of party organization, taking its inspiration from Russian populism, in which an elite revolutionary vanguard directed the political actions of a mass party. This last issue, in particular, would itself come out at the Second Congress of the Russian Social Democratic Party in London in July 1903, where it split the party into Bolsheviks and Mensheviks (as discussed in the chapter "Russia on the Barricades: The Revolution of 1904–1907"). Many elements of the future structure of the Communist Party were evident in Lenin's theoretical formulations before 1910 (made, like Plekhanov's, in Swiss exile). Both Lenin's and Plekhanov's ideas developed in close interaction with European Marxism; German and Austrian Marxists were gurus for Russian socialists; and the ideas of European materialist philosophers (Ernst Mach and Richard Avenarius in particular) became assimilated into Russian Marxist doctrine.

A special role in the international socialist movement belongs to Poland, where several powerful socialist parties formed in the 1890s. Two of them—the first initiated by Julian Marchlewski (1866–1925) and Rosa Luxemburg (1871–1919) and the second, the Social Democratic Party of Lithuania, founded by Felix Dzerzhinsky (Dzierzyński) (1877–1926)—fused in 1900 to form the Social Democratic Party of the Kingdom of Poland and Lithuania. Thus Polish Social Democrats definitively set themselves off from their socialist compatriots, whose line was rather nationalist and patriotic, and from adherents of conciliation such as Roman Dmowski (1864–1939) and the novelist Boleslaw Prus (1847–1912). A significant social democratic movement took shape in Georgia as well, although Marxism tended to become an instrument of the national cause. The early political education of Iosif Jugashvili (1879–1953; later Stalin) took place in the Bolshevik minority of Georgia's Social Democratic Party.

The international left was not only about Marxism. Two Russians, Mikhail Bakunin (1814–1876) and Prince Pëtr Kropotkin (1842–1921), became the main theoretical inspiration behind an international anarchist movement, premised on the abolition of the state. Like Marx, Bakunin, whose fascinating intellectual trajectory had included Romanticism and then Populism, had the most influence after his own lifetime: the First Socialist International split between anarchists and Marxists, and Bakunin's ideas gave birth to an anarchist movement in Europe and the United States. Anarchist thought played a powerful role in left-wing politics in France and England and throughout Europe and continues to have adherents more than a century later. Prince Kropotkin, a well-known geographer and naturalist, founded his ideas of social organization on his own researches on the structure of animal societies, introducing the notion of mutual aid as the foundation of social interaction. His autobiography, *Memoirs of a Revolutionist* (1898–1899), is a fascinating and wonderfully written text that evokes Alexander Herzen's earlier memoirs (1852–1867) in its pervasive sense of freedom.

ORTHODOXY AND RELIGIOUS REFORM

The daily, weekly, and yearly cycles of prayer, the Orthodox liturgy, and religious fasts and holidays retained their place at the center of the lives of Russian people of all social backgrounds. Diocesan reports from many regions of the country noted high attendance at church services, though church officials sometimes expressed dissatisfaction with the numbers actually going to confession and hence preparing themselves for the central sacrament of the Eucharist. Russia's provincial libraries contain a number of tracts written by laypeople seeking to reconcile the equally powerful claims of religion and science. Parish members had a limited opportunity for self-regulation, particularly through election of the *blagochinnye,* or parish superintendents—an office that Konstantin Pobedonostsev eventually abolished. The church school movement, though coopted by the official church establishment under Pobedonostsev's direction, attracted ever greater numbers of grassroots activists, and the 1896 All-Russian Exhibition included a "Church School" pavilion constructed quite literally as a two-story wooden house with a schoolroom on the bottom floor and a church on the upper. The 1880s in particular witnessed a Synod-sponsored flowering of religious brotherhoods, modeled on the Ukrainian brotherhoods of the Reformation period, and with the aim of encouraging lay piety and particularly of converting the non-Orthodox.

The proportion of the Russian population that lived in cities was still relatively low, and it is difficult to say to what degree urban existence and the break with rural tradition affected their religious beliefs. Certainly the preaching of radicals and Social Democrats encouraged secularization, as might have the new rhythms of factory life. But the bells tolling from a plethora of churches, daily prayers and church services, and the "beautiful corner" for icons in workers' dormitories and middle-class households alike were equally a part of life in the city.

Within the institutional church itself not all was well. Parish clergy reacted to the Pobedonostsev administration's strict controls—and its efforts sometimes even to use the clergy as government informers—by deserting the church in droves. The clerical liberals and local enthusiasts of the 1860s and 1870s found it difficult to find a place in an increasingly rigid and regimented church. Dropping out of the seminaries became a widespread new pattern in the 1880s and 1890s, following the example of such individual rebels as Nikolai Chernyshevsky or Nikolai Dobrolyubov in the prereform period. Among those who remained, some began to voice protest and call for reform. One of the most important documents of this type was Moscow priest A. M. Ivantsov-Platonov's text *On Russian Church Governance* (1882), which, for the first time, presented a coherent argument advocating the abolition of the Petrine Holy Synod with its civilian over-procurator and a restoration of the Russian patriarchate, abolished in 1721, to head the Orthodox Church.

MOVEMENTS OF NATIONAL LIBERATION

The government's nostalgia for social harmony in Russia included, as an essential element, the full integration and administrative uniformity of the empire's multitude of regions and peoples. In a letter to Alexander III, Pobedonostsev once acknowledged that a major reason for his distrust of constitutional government was the fear that a national legislature would be dominated by, and quickly come under the control of, the Poles. As with society in general, the vision of hierarchical harmony for the empire proved more than elusive: the empire looked more multiform and diverse than ever at century's end. At the same time, however, Orthodoxy did function as a cohesive force, counting—to return to the 1897 census—70 percent of the population among its adherents. In addition, the same processes of industrialization and urbanization as in the "metropole" affected some regions, most notably Poland, the Baltic region, and parts of the Caucasus. On the other hand, intellectuals in Poland, Finland, and Ukraine, as well as among the peasant populations of Lithuania, Estonia, and Latvia, won adherents to rapidly expanding national movements. In Turkic Central Asia, national consciousness was not a factor, but a cultural and religious awakening among the empire's 11 percent Muslim population did take place.

Social Change in the Borderlands

Many of the same processes of social change occurred in parts of the empire as in the zemstvo provinces of Russia. Warsaw, Odessa, Lodz, Riga, Kiev, Kharkov, Tiflis, Tashkent, Vilna, Saratov, Kazan, Rostov-on-Don, Tula, Astrakhan, Ekaterinoslav, Baku, and Kishinëv all had populations of over 100,000 by 1897. All of these cities counted significant Russian-speaking (often as a second language) professional and commercial middle classes. Characteristically, the urban population was ethnically quite mixed: Almost 50 percent of Jews lived in cities; Germans (23.4 percent), Armenians (23.25 percent), Greeks (18 percent), and, to a lesser degree, Tatars were a visible presence in cities everywhere from St. Petersburg to Kazan and tended to dominate industry and trade. A working class naturally took shape in those regions with the greatest concentration of industry. Literacy rates went up significantly, reaching over 90 percent in parts of the Baltic region (98 percent in Finland) and over 40 percent for the Catholic Lithuanians and Poles. However, literacy hovered around 25 percent among Muslims; 20 percent among Orthodox Belorussians, Ukrainians, and Russians; around 10 percent for the peoples of the Middle Volga region; and even less for the nomadic peoples of Central Asia and mountain peoples of the Caucasus. Conversion was an important factor as well: adopting Orthodoxy was a key to success in a commercial or bureaucratic career. A special place belongs to Nikolai Ilminsky (1822–1891) at Kazan, who developed a system for winning Tatar children over to Orthodoxy by teaching them the catechism in their native language but written in Cyrillic script; the Orthodox liturgy was performed in some Kazan churches entirely in Tatar. The absorption of people for whom Russian was not a native language and Orthodoxy not an inherited creed into the social "mainstream" applied to elites as well as middle classes: Mikhail Loris-Melikov (author of the abortive constitution under Alexander II) was a Russified and Orthodox Armenian, while Russified Orthodox Baltic Germans regularly filled high administrative posts (hence such German-sounding names as Reutern, Bunge, Giers, and Lamsdorff).

Despite certain common trends, the social composition of different regions varied widely: Poland and Georgia remained societies with a heavy concentration of nobles: the remarkable figures of 5 and 6 percent, respectively, are recorded in the census. Both, however, were also among the most urbanized societies, with a significant middle class; the twist in the case of Georgia was that most of the urban inhabitants were Armenians (there were more in the capital, Tiflis, than either Russians or Georgians). A full 7 percent of Baltic Germans belonged to the nobility. Among the largely peasant populations of Lithuania and Belorussia, the local nobility was Polish or Russian; Latvians, Estonians, and peoples of the Middle Volga and Urals, in contrast, had virtually no nobles. Armenians, Jews, and Germans dominated the trading and urban classes; almost 30 percent of Tajiks, too, lived in cities. Most of Central Asia, in the meantime, began to look like a true colony as the traditional Uzbek elite were replaced by Russian officials. Very small percentages of the inhabitants of Finland (0.2 percent), Poland, Belorussia-Lithuania, the Baltic states, Transcaucasia, southern Central Asia, and northern and eastern Siberia (11.4 percent) considered Russian their native language by 1897. In the oldest parts of the empire, such as the Middle Volga region, the figure was up to 73 percent, while Russian and Ukrainian settlers made significant inroads in New Russia (the southern steppes, Bessarabia, the Crimea, and the Don region), the Urals, and Siberia.

National Consciousness and Liberation Movements

Nationalism among the "young" peoples of Central Europe moved to the forefront of international politics in the last third of the nineteenth century as some Serbs, Czechs, Hungarians, Galicians, and Jews sought to establish their independence from the Austro-Hungarian and Ottoman Empires, even as other groups—among them Sorbs, Wends, Polabians, and other Slavic peoples in Prussia—became absorbed into their environment and gradually disappeared. The Czech historian Miroslav Hroch postulated three basic phases characterizing the development of various European nationalisms among "young" nations: Phase A involved a cultural awakening among a small, highly educated elite who discovered a national tradition of folklore, recorded the grammar of the language and were able to discern a national history. In phase B, a group of patriots, again a small elite, began a campaign of national agitation. The final phase, C, witnessed an expansion of this awakened national consciousness to a broader public and sometimes resulted in the formation of a nation or nation-state. This schema has some application to the nineteenth-century Russian Empire, particularly to its western parts, which, after all, were part of Central Europe as well.

Nationalism was nothing new in Poland, where dreams of independence and even the restoration of the old Polish-Lithuanian Commonwealth (1569–1795) had attained only very partial realization with the Napoleonic Grand Duchy of Warsaw (1807–1815). Finland was also unquestionably a nation within the confines of the Russian Empire, at least until Russification policies undermined separate institutions and self-government. What was new at the close of the nineteenth century was the emergence of national consciousness among the peasant populations of the Baltic and western borderlands as the ideas of nationalist intellectuals began to find a response. In Finland, nationalism was intimately tied up with the language question: into the 1880s, the Fennoman movement—with the tacit support of Russian authorities and following in the footsteps of earlier literary figures like J. V. Snellman (1806–1881)—challenged the authority of the Swedish-speaking minority and sought to introduce Finnish as the official language. Finnish nationalism entered the domain of real politics with Governor General Nikolai Bobrikov's extreme Russification policies, leading to a mass protest in 1899 against the February manifesto, in which some 500,000 Finns took part. Among Latvians and Estonians, parallel nationalist movements directed against the German nobility, rather than against Russia, gathered strength around 1900 as liberal and social democratic parties gained adherents. Among these three mostly Lutheran nations, teachers and pastors were leaders of nationalisms that, on one hand, were oriented around principles of education (teaching native languages in the schools) and, on the other, constituted a social protest of lower classes against elites and therefore coincided with larger socialist and populist movements.

Ukrainian nationalism had by 1900 been long in the making. Its roots stretched back to the cultural and linguistic awakening of the 1840s and the Romantic-era dialogue between Taras Shevchenko's vision of a Ukrainian nation versus Nikolai Gogol's depiction of the spirit of Malorossiya, or Little Russia (see the chapter "Nicholas I: Monarchy, Society, Empire, 1825–1855"). In the reform era, nationalism gained adherents among the intelligentsia, acquiring an organ in the press—the Petersburg–based *Osnova (Foundation)*—while nationalist societies called *hromady* were formed in Kiev as well as in the Russian capital. The Ukrainian *khlopomany* were a specifically Ukrainian-language version of the populists. A network of Sunday schools was one of the main means of spreading literacy and national consciousness among the peasantry. Ukrainian consciousness figured in the work of important cultural figures like the historian Nikolai Kostomarov (1817–1885). Links with Galicia (western Ukraine) in the Austro-Hungarian Empire remained essential to Ukrainian nationalism; Mykhailo Drahomanov (1841–1895), one of the founders of Ukrainian socialism, continued his work in Galicia after his exile from the Russian Empire. Russian policy toward Ukraine was unique in its categorical refusal to acknowledge the existence of the Ukrainian language altogether: the use of the Ukrainian language in print and on the stage was explicitly prohibited in what has become known as the Ems Ukaz (Edict) of 1876. Throughout the nineteenth century, proponents of the "Ukrainian idea" had differed with respect to issues of separatism, integration, and cooperation with the imperial authorities. The national movement acquired a revolutionary edge and a broader constituency in the 1890s, mostly among students. The movement culminated in

1897 in the General Ukrainian Organization, which sought to unite all Ukrainian activists in the empire while also emancipating this specifically Ukrainian organization from its radical counterparts in Russia itself.

The general pattern of politicization of national consciousness and its conversion into real political movements in the 1890s holds for other peoples of the empire as well. Sympathy for Turkish Armenians in the 1870s developed in 1887 into an Armenian socialist organization based in Geneva and, more significantly, in 1890, into the Revolutionary Armenian Federation, or Dashnaks, in Tiflis; both of these groups sought liberation for Armenians in the Ottoman Empire. A special case was that of the Jews: the impulse of cultural enlightenment known as the Haskalah (enlightenment) was replaced at century's end by Zionism. Originally associated with the name of Theodor Herzl (1860–1904) in Austria-Hungary, Zionism—or the movement to found a Jewish national state in Palestine—acquired many adherents in Russia beginning in the 1880s. A branch of Zionism advocated national and cultural consolidation of Jews in the diaspora as well. Many Russian Jews took part in the first international Zionist congress in 1897 and in those that followed. Also in the 1890s, a Jewish workers' party spanning Lithuania, Poland, and Russia and known as the Bund (union) gained enough strength to organize massive strike actions; by 1903 it counted some twenty-five thousand members. National movements, in contrast, were almost nonexistent in the far reaches of Siberia, although incipient traces were present among Zyryans, Yakuts, and Chuvash.

Self-definition along national lines is alien to the culture of Turkic Eurasia. The presently existing states of Uzbekistan, Turkmenia, Tajikistan, and Kyrgyzstan were entirely a creation of twentieth-century Soviet bureaucracy. It was their religion, Islam, that gave the Turkic peoples of the Russian Empire a sense of unity and cohesion. In 1883, Ismail Bey Gasprali, who was from an impoverished noble Crimean Tatar family and had studied in Moscow, Paris, and Istanbul, founded a journal in the Crimean Tatar capital, Bahçesaray, called *Tercuman, (The Interpreter).* For thirty years it was the organ of Jadidism, a philosophy of reformed Muslim culture and education that sought to unite Islamic culture with Western science and technology; Gasprali also wished to instruct Muslim children in a common Ottoman Turkish–based language in school. Gasprali's movement was entirely cultural and religious in its thrust, with no anti-imperial political aims. In the last third of the nineteenth century it was Kazan, home of the Volga Tatars, that became the main focal point for Tatar and more generally Islamic culture. Kazan University (founded in 1804) had become a center of Oriental studies and Turkic language publications. As nationalisms were becoming politicized elsewhere in the empire, Islamic circles formed among students and intellectuals beginning in the mid-1880s. All of these developments eventually became the basis for a pan-Islamic movement.

Cultural richness and growing social tensions existed side by side in the empire as the nineteenth century came to an end. Both would explode in the first years of the new century, in a remarkable flowering of cultural life and, simultaneously, in the outbreak of a violent revolution.

CHAPTER 26

Cultural Explosion, 1900–1920

So we lived in two worlds. But, incapable of discerning the laws that governed events in the second—which seemed to us more real than simple reality—we merely languished in vague and obscure forebodings. We experienced everything that happened around us as an omen. But of what?

—Vladislav Khodasevich, Necropolis *(1926)*

The end of a century and the beginning of a new one can be a moment of self-consciousness when people pause in their usual activities to reflect on the direction of their civilization and to wonder what the future might hold. The cities of Europe—from Paris to St. Petersburg, from Berlin and Vienna to Moscow and Kiev—became consumed in the final years of the nineteenth century by a passion for introspection and experimentation, by a rejection of old moral norms and a taste for the good life, and by a joyful creative energy and a worldly decadence. The ideas of Nietzsche, Schopenhauer, Kierkegaard, and Dostoevsky tore through the complacent fabric of bourgeois life, urging resentment and revolt and focusing attention on the darker sides of human nature. Artists like Klimt, Cézanne, Matisse, and Picasso created new aesthetic sensibilities, making a travesty of the nineteenth-century academic codes of line, perspective, color, and composition. Symbolist poets experimented with new types of verse and enveloped their readers in webs of correspondences, while composers—Satie, Debussy, Scriabin, Medtner—invented harmonies and played with unusual integrations of word, music, and image. Their less talented contemporaries, in the meantime, flocked with them to restaurants, cafés, and cabarets to enjoy the art of song and dance, as well as good food, drink, and the possibility of sexual adventure.

If throughout most of the nineteenth century the Russian intelligentsia had been obsessed with a sense of inferiority toward Western Europe, many people ceased to think in these terms at the beginning of the twentieth. One striking emblem of the cultural richness of the new age was the extravagant illustrated literary journal *The World of Art,* which first appeared in 1898 and whose gilded pages contained the best of the new poetry, essays, and art from Russia, France, and elsewhere; it also began the tradition of bilingual (Russian and French) publication. The images of the fin de siècle and the constant interaction of cultures serve as a powerful reminder that the cultural world of the Russian Empire in its final years was a part of a larger cultural unity comprising, at the time, France, Germany, Britain, Austro-Hungary, Italy, and America. An educated person traveling from, say, New York to St. Petersburg in 1900 would have felt less of a gulf of cultural difference than that person's descendant in the year 2000.

NEW BEGINNINGS: MOSCOW, ST. PETERSBURG, KIEV

Russia's cities were full-fledged participants in the heady atmosphere of the fin de siècle—the end of the century. Modernist architecture began to transform the streets not only of Moscow and Petersburg but also of Helsinki, Warsaw, and Kiev, and even provincial centers like Nizhny Novgorod. Sophisticated Petersburgians gathered in cabarets such as the Bat and the Wandering Dog, and literary and philosophical salons convened to discuss the latest in modern art and poetry. Sensational art exhibits with inventive names like the Blue Rose, the Knave of Diamonds, and the Donkey's Tail proliferated, shocking the bourgeois public with their disrespect for artistic convention. This whirlwind of creative activity arrived on the European scene in a burst of color and exoticism with Sergei Diaghilev's Ballets Russes; the dancers' sheer energy, the exquisite stage sets and costume designs, and the innovations in choreography were greeted as a "revelation."

Nymph's costume for Stravinsky's ballet *L'Après-midi d'un faune* for the Ballets Russes. By Leon Bakst (1912). *Private Collection Paris/Dagli Orti/The Art Archive.*

The period of intense creative activity—indeed, cultural explosion—that gripped urban Russia in the early years of the twentieth century has come to be called, following the nomenclature of the ages of ancient Rome, the Silver Age. Why did this explosion, this burst of creative energy, take place? What happened between 1894, when one of the most influential figures of the Silver Age, Dmitry Merezhkovsky (1865–1941), lamented the absence of a nurturing literary and artistic environment and, say, 1910, when the Russian public, in the national and provincial capitals, was enmeshed in a network of journals, exhibitions, theaters, literary salons, and philosophical meetings, overwhelming by their sheer number and vitality? The creative impulse can never be fully explained by external factors. Nonetheless, the cultural explosion was not a mere borrowing of European trends and ideas and was profoundly related to developments in postemancipation Russian society and culture. If these developments cannot, ultimately, explain why the explosion in culture happened, they can give us a sense of its context, and of the environment that helped it to take shape.

Cities and Provinces

First, the Silver Age was an urban phenomenon. Russia's cities blossomed in the postemancipation period, as they were granted municipal self-government and as people from the countryside became drawn to the greater possibilities of urban life. By 1900, the urban infrastructure—with its factories, shops, trams, trolleys, hotels, taverns, and restaurants and a social structure that included workers and beggars—had come to resemble more closely the profile of any European city. As Russian society became less defined by state service, urban diversity increased along with the rapidly expanding population. The urban theme, in fact, fascinated turn-of-the-century writers: Valery Bryusov (1873–1924) and Alexander Blok (1880–1921) made Petersburg, with its broad perspectives, bustling crowds, and vaporous canals a constant theme of their poetry. The city had its apotheosis in Andrei Bely's fantastic novel *Petersburg* (1913), written in a powerful mixture of poetry and prose and exalting the straight lines and unhealthy, mysterious vapors of the empire's capital.

At the same time, the expansion of the capital cities was accompanied by a flowering of, and a change in the general level of, provincial life. Whereas we know the artists, poets, and philosophers of the Silver Age as a sophisticated urban elite, they came, in fact, from a variety of social backgrounds. Valery Briusov came from a merchant family; the poet and essayist Zinaïda Gippius (1869–1945) was the daughter of a petty bureaucrat; the philosopher and economist Sergei Bulgakov was the son of a provincial priest; Andrei Bely's father was a prominent mathematician; and Nikolai Berdyaev came from an aristocratic family in Kiev. This diversity of origin would have been unthinkable in an earlier age: the Slavophiles, for example, were uniformly of Moscow gentry background, while the mentality of *raznochintsy* like Nikolai Chernyshevsky or Vissarion Belinsky was utterly alien to their gentry contemporaries. By the close of the nineteenth century, diverse social groups were united by a shared culture that penetrated cities and provinces alike in the widely read illustrated journals and newspapers that flourished starting in the 1870s. Even as they became part of a sophisticated urban elite, most of the participants in the cultural explosion of the turn of the century continued to feel a connection with the broader, popular culture on which they had grown up; popular sentimental poetry and conventional attitudes about art and religion remained a part of their sensibility. This shared national culture was an essential precondition of the Silver Age.

The "Revolt Against Positivism"

While these changes in specifically Russian life were important in the emergence of the Silver Age, no less crucial was a general intellectual trend, common to all of

Europe. In all European countries, the beginning of the new century brought a challenge to the reigning philosophy of positivism, the fervent belief that science could resolve not only physical, biological, and technological problems but social and human questions as well. The "crisis of positivism" at the conclusion of the nineteenth century and the formulation of new methods and philosophies of science and research took place in various fields, perhaps most notably in physics, psychology, and linguistics. Dissatisfaction with empirical scientific methods that, it had seemed only recently, were on the verge of explaining all existing phenomena developed either because existing theories could not account for new experimental results (as occurred in physics) or because the unmanageable quantity of results generated by positivistic methods demanded a better organizing principle (linguistics). In each case the formulation of new approaches and methodologies involved a reevaluation of underlying philosophical principles as well; positivism gave way to idealism, mysticism, or pragmatism—or, in the case of England, a still more extreme positivism. The names associated with the late-nineteenth- and early-twentieth-century scientific and philosophical revolution include Einstein, Freud, Saussure, and Henri Bergson. The ferment also affected the social sciences: Max Weber's sociology developed largely as a part of this general movement. This disillusionment and search for new answers inspired Russian thinkers as much as their European contemporaries.

The search for new forms in Russia had, as well, a particular dimension that set it apart from the general European movement. The Russian Orthodox Church, under Pobedonostsev's leadership, had dealt singularly badly with the advent of modern society. Its response to the emergence of the workers' movement, urban problems, and broad social change was to reaffirm the value of traditional hierarchy. As a result, not only did priests' sons desert the seminaries in droves, but thinking people found it impossible to accommodate the values of modern life within the established church. A strong movement for church reform, for a reevaluation of Orthodox dogma, thus became an important undercurrent in the literary, artistic, and philosophical production of the Silver Age. Most importantly, the tone for this religious rethinking was established by the immensely powerful ideas of four great nineteenth-century writers and philosophers who both stimulated and provided material for the flowering of the Silver Age.

FORERUNNERS: FOUR GIANTS

A major intellectual impulse for the silver age came from Vladimir Soloviëv (1853–1900), Lev Tolstoy (1828–1910), Fëdor Dostoevsky (1821–1881), and Nikolai Fëdorov (1829–1903). In the 1870s and 1880s, Russia, like the rest of Europe, was in the iron grip of positivism, thoroughly immersed in the cult of progress and the belief in scientific laws of historical necessity. Yet each of these extraordinary thinkers independently shook free of the reigning philosophy. In various ways, they had the audacity to pose the ultimate questions of human existence—summed up best, perhaps, in the query with which Vladimir Soloviëv (the only academic philosopher among them) prefaced his *Justification of the Good:* "Does our life ultimately have any kind of meaning?"

The ideas of these men defy classification into the tidy categories of nineteenth-century intellectual history. As writers, Tolstoy and Dostoevsky had license to ignore the positivist mentality that dominated philosophy; standing outside the philosophical mainstream, they tore through the constricting fabric of the "iron age" with extraordinary energy. Although the best, and most famous, of Tolstoy's literary works are *War and Peace* (1869) and *Anna Karenina* (1877), those aspects of his thought that had most influence on the Silver Age belong to the later stage of his life, when he became consumed by religious passion and a sense of social mission. Tolstoy's contempt for the official church, coupled with an intense, individualistic religiosity—both of which are particularly apparent in works like the novel *Resurrection* (1899)—led, ultimately, to the rare phenomenon of his excommunication by the Orthodox Church. Tolstoy's inner struggle, his fascination with the idea of relinquishing noble property and distributing it among the peasants, and his projects to bring education to the peasantry had a broad appeal among a nobility suffering from a severe guilty conscience and an inner compulsion to repay the damage done by centuries of serfdom. Giving away one's property with philanthropic intentions became, indeed, a fashion in the last years of the century; Tolstoy's pamphlets describing his conversion and faith became the basis for a broad social movement known as Tolstoyism.

In the early 1900s, the Russian intelligentsia also "discovered" Dostoevsky, who had been little read until that time. Although it is difficult to pinpoint the demonic genius that animates all of his works, if one had to choose a single most influential text it would probably be the "Legend of the Grand Inquisitor," from *The Brothers Karamazov*. In a movement of total revolt, Ivan Karamazov, in this passage, offers to return his ticket to the Kingdom of Heaven for the sake of the tears of a single suffering child. The unresolvable moral questions posed with ineluctable force in this and other novels encapsulated the intellectual restlessness and ferment that became essential characteristics of the Silver Age.

Nikolai Fëdorov, in the meantime, eccentric recluse and intellectually insatiable librarian of the Rumyantsev Museum, captured the attention of the educated public with his philosophy, which he expounded in a book titled *The Philosophy of the Common Task.* Taking nineteenth-century positivism's belief in science to its extreme logical conclusion, Fëdorov proposed that humanity, working together, should "regulate" nature, and the cosmos, to finally conquer them and to assert complete control. His schemes included the production of artificial rain, space flight, and finally, a religious vision of universal resurrection—in which, instead of procreating, people would go about resurrecting their ancestors.

Last but perhaps most important, Vladimir Soloviëv (see the chapter "Society, Culture, Politics, 1881–1905") was the only one who took on positivism, head on. Drawing on the somewhat vague, Romantically based anti-rationalism of his predecessors, the Slavophiles, he launched a full-scale assault on Western positivism and rationalism, constructing a philosophical system whose cornerstones were wholeness, organicism, morality, and metaphysics. More than any single thinker, Soloviëv was responsible for the creation of a fully viable and original Russian philosophical tradition, within whose framework all subsequent thinkers inevitably found themselves. His introduction of the gnostic concept of Sophia, which combined elements of the romantic Eternal Feminine with the biblical Divine Wisdom—the feminine principle that was with God at the Creation—proved immensely productive for a generation of poets and philosophers. Perhaps most significantly, Soloviëv managed to articulate a fusion of materialism and idealism that was an essential characteristic of a Russian philosophical tradition: finding harmony between these two approaches proved a worthy task for pursuit by Silver Age philosophers. In post-Soviet Russia, some scholars see Soloviëv's thought as a "philosophy of all-unity."

What all four thinkers—Soloviëv, Tolstoy, Dostoevsky, and Fëdorov—had in common was that they posed the problems of morality, metaphysics, and religion. Once their works had been discovered in the early 1900s, the succeeding generation had no choice but to pay attention; and, indeed, the thought of the Silver Age constitutes in a sense a working out and development of the powerful ideas of the four giants of the 1870s and 1880s.

Main stairway in the Ryabushinsky mansion in Moscow. Fëdor Shekhtel, architect (1900–02). *Photograph by William Brumfield.*

THE SILVER AGE

The Silver Age transformed every field of cultural creativity—literature, art, architecture, music, theater, philosophy, and literary theory. Naturally, given the large number of artists and thinkers involved, one is first of all struck by the variety and diversity of their products. Yet the creators of the Silver Age were quite self-conscious of the culture they were building and of its significance for Russia. They were all participants in a common cultural milieu, taking their stimulus from the same network of journals and salons and engaging in frequent polemics with each other about everything from the use of iambic tetrameter to the role of the Russian intelligentsia. This common environment makes it possible to delineate a number of themes that, however loosely, were shared by the participants in the cultural movement of the turn of the century.

The Old and the New

The artists, poets, and thinkers of the Silver Age thought of themselves as making a radical break with the past and beginning anew. Although historians sometimes date the beginning of the Silver Age to 1898, with the appearance of *The World of Art,* perhaps a more significant date is 1901. Andrei Bely called this year the "year of dawns," while the poet Alexander Blok referred to this moment as a "nodal point" when vague anticipations began to crystallize into a new poetry and the "new people" began to seek out and find each other. They shared a rejection of the civic art and poetry, the aesthetic realism, that had dominated the cultural scene since the 1860s and turned instead to more abstract themes, symbolic representations, and a concern with form, color, and meter—in short, the internal workings of the work of art.

The "newness" of their artistic endeavor meant more than a change in aesthetic style; it was also a credo. It was with a tremendous sense of discovery and innovation that, in 1902, a group of prominent intellectuals published an extremely influential collection of articles called *Problems of Idealism,* in which they, like their artistic counterparts, rejected the fundamental beliefs of preceding generations and proclaimed a new concern with ethics, metaphysics, and religion. Appealing to Dostoevsky and Soloviëv, these thinkers—among them Nikolai Berdyaev, Sergei Bulgakov, Semën Frank, and Pëtr Struve—denounced the nineteenth century's essential faith in progress and the powers of science. It was time, they argued, for the Russian intelligentsia to cease their preoccupation with Russian backwardness and need to "catch up" with Western Europe. Instead, the very depth of the intelligentsia's moral consciousness, its guilt before the people—encapsulated in the figure of Ivan Karamazov—constituted a signal strength, and one from which other nations had much to learn. Likewise, Vladimir Soloviëv's articulation of a philosophy of wholeness and organicity provided a new and original way of thinking. Many participants in this collection had, only recently, been Marxists: to them, this turn toward ethics, metaphysics, and religion was a fundamental rift with their past and a rejection of the notion of the forward march of history and Russia's backwardness that Marxists and populists had shared.

Princess-Swan, by Mikhail Vrubel (1900). *Tretyakov Gallery, Moscow, Russia/Scala/Art Resource, NY.*

This proclamation of novelty, this challenge to established codes and beliefs—in itself an emblem of the "modern" sensibility—was picked up and taken to a much greater extreme by a still younger generation. The claims of Symbolists and idealists would seem mild in comparison with the ravings and manifestoes of the avant-garde. With an energy surpassing even that of their collaborators in France and Italy, the futurist poets and artists in the 1910s went about happily delivering "a slap in the face of public taste" (the title of one of their manifestoes) and declaring all old forms, from language to representational art, to be defunct and useless.

Interestingly, in their search for new forms, many of the participants in the Silver Age turned to the past, to tradition, and to their cultural roots. This meant, on one hand, a turning inward, into the history of Russian culture. Whereas the dominant tendency in the nineteenth century had been to reject things Russian (with the possible exception of the village commune) as inferior and culturally inadequate, the Silver Age suddenly rediscovered the pre-Petrine past, the deep roots of Orthodoxy, and the conciliar tradition of Russian governance. The councils—councils of the land *(zemsky sobor),* and church councils—of old Muscovy began to seem like a tradition on which institutions of representative government could be

Madonna and Child, by Natalia Goncharova (1905–07). *Superstock.*

built. Perhaps most remarkably, the Silver Age discovered icons as works of art: new processes of restoration revealed the brilliant colors and sophisticated, if "unrealistic," uses of perspective in medieval Russian art. This discovery proved immensely productive, as modern painters—perhaps most notably, Mikhail Vrubel (1856–1910) and Natalia Goncharova (1881–1962), but even Malevich and others—incorporated elements from the tradition of icon painting into their art.

The Silver Age conceived of itself as not only Russian—building on a deep Russian cultural tradition—but also as universal. In this spirit, which the poet Osip Mandelstam (1891–1938) called a "nostalgia for world culture," many artists and thinkers appealed to even more profound roots in the pagan and Christian worlds of antiquity. The makers of the Silver Age, in other words, tried to build on the most basic elements of world culture, which they sought in history, and, by doing so, to place their own creative enterprise firmly in this universal tradition. Dmitry Merezhkovsky, for example, tried to trace Russian culture to a synthesis of classical paganism and Christianity in his long and rather badly written trilogy *Christ and Antichrist.* Mandelstam, in a different fashion, claimed that the Russian language was the "Greek" of his time—that no other language could so accurately and eloquently capture the Hellenic spirit. In this vein, one of the most fundamental concepts of the Silver Age, which expressed this thirst for universality, was that of the Logos—which could be interpreted, at once, as Christ and as the Word. Stimulated by the philosopher S. N. Trubetskoy's 1902 theory of the Logos in Hellenic philosophy and in early Christianity, poets and thinkers made the question of Christ's nature central to their art. In the Silver Age mentality, the Logos became inseparably linked to the Sophia of Soloviëv's writings—again, as present with God at the Creation, a concept that reached back to origins, fundamentals, the beginnings of history.

Other Worlds

In Dostoevsky's *Brothers Karamazov,* the monk Zosima speaks of "other worlds" beyond everyday reality, of deeper truths and realities hiding behind the surface of daily life, of mystical, transcendent realms beyond consciousness. In contrast to the mentality of nineteenth-century positivism, firmly anchored in this world with its belief in science and progress, the notion of transcendence, of daily experience as a mere cloak for higher truth, became a central category of turn-of-the-century consciousness. This fascination with essences beyond appearances could take a variety of forms. For some, it meant a penchant for mystical experience or even spiritism—the occult and spiritistic séances were a great fad; for others, it meant taking a philosophical stance that emphasized metaphysics. Perhaps most fundamentally, it meant a renewed concern with religion—which could be anything from a vague pantheism to a rejuvenation of Orthodoxy to an impassioned but antiecclesiastical Christianity like Tolstoy's.

Eventually the Silver Age gave birth to a plethora of literary schools and movements. In its initial creative stage, however, the main driving force of the cultural outburst was the school known as Symbolism; Symbolist poets and the Symbolist aesthetic dominated the cultural landscape of the first decade of the century—from about 1900 to 1910. Its main figures were Blok, Bely, Viacheslav Ivanov, Briusov, Konstantin Balmont, and Gippius. Russian Symbolism shared much with its more prominent French counterpart: Charles Baudelaire's poem "Correspondances" became, in a sense, its manifesto. Central to the Symbolist aesthetic were several key characteristics. First, as the name implies, and Baudelaire's poem confirms, Symbolism held that no object, no word could be taken at face value: behind every appearance lay a transcendental essence, and the words of a poem or an object encountered in daily life functioned as a key to unlock this deeper, truer reality. Every minor experience was capable of triggering the poet's, or the reader's, entry into this mystical realm, where everything connected with everything else and where true meanings became revealed. Second, the Symbolists, although they invented no new literary forms and, indeed, took pleasure in the conventionality of verse, enveloped themselves in a foggy haze of ornamental language in their quest for meaning—forests of symbols, azure skies, and golden sunsets. The colors of Symbolism—caught up and replicated by Vrubel and Borisov-Musatov—were muted blue, gray, and green, daubed on canvas in impressionistic strokes, constantly in motion. Third, the Symbolists were neoromantics. Like their predecessors at the beginning of the nineteenth century, Symbolists rejected the calm rationalism of the Enlightenment or positivism, with its faith in the human intellect, and willingly lost themselves in a sea of mystical associations and divine powers. The Symbolists were obsessed by the Romantic notion of the Eternal Feminine—an elusive, attractive feminine essence that appeared to them, "breathing perfumes and fogs," in their visions and entered into their poetry. Finally, a peculiar characteristic of Russian Symbolism, not shared with the European schools, was a powerful religious element. Briusov, Ivanov, and Blok in particular experienced their mystical, romantic visions as a correspondence not with just any "other worlds" but as a means of achieving a fleeting union with Christ.

The mood of Symbolism intersected with a similar orientation in philosophy. In 1901, Sergei Bulgakov coined the slogan "From Marxism to idealism"—a phrase that summed up the intellectual evolution of a small but important part of the Russian intelligentsia. Apart from rejecting the beliefs of a previous generation, the new idealists turned to Immanuel Kant's transcendental philosophy, also asserting the primacy of "other worlds" and arguing that a glance beyond empirical reality would reveal the poverty of the nineteenth-century theory of progress. Their assertion of the existence of a transcendental ideal, of a world beyond the one we see before us, helped them to see history no longer as unfolding inexorably toward a predetermined goal, but as open-ended and contingent, admitting of free will and human action. From idealism, it was but one step further to religion. By the second decade of the century, Bulgakov *(Philosophy of Economy, The Unfading Light),* Nikolai Berdyaev, Semën Frank *(Man's Soul, The Spiritual Foundations of Society),* Lev Shestov *(Apotheosis of the Void),* Pavel Florensky *(The Pillar and Affirmation of Truth),* and others had established an entire original philosophical genre known as religious philosophy. This discipline was conceived as a philosophical reflection on received Christian truths. Idealists, religious thinkers, and Symbolists had ample opportunity for cross-fertilization and exchange of ideas. The most fertile forum for interaction became the Religious-Philosophical Societies, originally founded by Zinaïda Gippius and Dmitry Merezhkovsky in Petersburg in 1898, but eventually with independent branches in both Moscow and Kiev.

In the western areas of the empire, particularly Poland and Ukraine, the "other-worldly" impulse received particularly strong expression in religious architecture. The extraordinary, modernist St. Vladimir's Cathedral in Kiev (ca. 1900) was adorned with frescoes by Nesterov, and Vrubel's icons are in evidence in many Kiev churches. The religious, mystical spirit penetrated other areas of the arts, as well. Nikolai Medtner brought a symbolist aesthetic to music with his dreamy "fairy tales" for the piano, evoking the same mysterious depths with his bass line as did the poets with their rich imagery. In a sense, the emblematic figure of the Silver Age is the composer Alexander Scriabin (1872–1915), who seized on the ideas of the symbolist poet and theorist Vyacheslav Ivanov. Ivanov, strongly influenced by the German philosopher Friedrich Nietzsche, proposed that art was based on an interplay of "Apollonian" and "Dionysian" principles: Apollo, the Western hellenic god, represented harmony and order; Dionysus, the god of wine, was the "Slavic" god, representing the demonic instinct. Scriabin invented something he called the "mystic" or "Promethean" chord, based not on classical harmony but on the demonic Dionysian tritone—dissonant and jarring to the ear—but which was supposed to form the basis of a new kind of music. Writing a composition called "Le divin poème" as a prologue, Scriabin set himself the task of creating a "mystery"—an art form based on a total synthesis of music, color, and theater—which he intended to have performed on the banks of the Ganges River in India. This notion of a mystical synthesis of all the arts became broadly popular during this period and influenced the productions of the Ballets Russes as well as the theater.

Kullervo Cursing, by Finnish artist Akseli Gallen-Kallela (1899). Kullervo is a character from the Finnish national epic, the Kalevala. *Atheneum Art Museum, Helsinki, Finland.*

Art and Life

However sincere their sense of breaking with the past and however genuine their turn to idealism, metaphysics, and religion, the creators of the Silver Age remained very much the heirs of their intelligentsia predecessors: Nikolai Chernyshevsky's dictum of the 1860s that art must reflect and transform reality was transmitted to the new poets and thinkers through Soloviëv, who saw art as "theurgy," or the transformation of life. Symbolists, religious thinkers, composers, and painters all saw their enterprise as a creation not only of art but of life itself. One's life path, relations with other people, and intellectual interests were something to be carefully constructed, as if one were writing a poem or a novel. The culture of the Silver Age, in other words, was intimately connected to the structure of daily life and even to politics.

A fruitful field of experimentation at the close of the Victorian era was sexuality. Never explicitly discussed even in works in which sex was a central theme—as in Chernyshevsky's *What Is to Be Done?* (1863) (see the chapter "Alexander II and the Era of the Great Reforms, 1855–1870")—sex now entered the realm of public discourse. Vasily Rozanov made sex his literary specialty, and ménages à trois and homosexuality became fashionable in the elite intelligentsia salons of Petersburg and Moscow. Thus the triplet of Zinaïda Gippius, her husband Dmitry Merezhkovsky (with whom she was reputed to have a "white" (sexless) marriage), and (her/his?) lover Dmitry Filosofov became a famous Petersburg institution. Lyubov Dmitrievna Blok formed the focus of a love triangle involving her husband, Alexander, and his friend Andrei Bely, while the unfortunate Nina Petrovskaya (famous for no other reason) fell victim to a similar triangle between Bryusov and Bely. Gippius endowed these arrangements with an exalted religious meaning in which the "mystery of the three" was a revelation of an apocalyptic "Third Testament." Mikhail Kuzmin, in the meantime, wrote extremely beautiful, sensuous love poems that for the first time made explicit their homosexual content. Indeed, the joys of sexuality, even promiscuity, intertwined with a deep religious feeling became a dominant theme of the literature and life of the age as people sought to create their lives in new ways.

Portrait of Zinaïda Gippius, by Leon Bakst (1906). The Hermitage, St. Petersburg, Russia. *Photograph from the personal archives of Professor Temira Pachmuss.*

Not surprisingly, the effort to restructure life intersected, as well, with the sphere of politics. Before the Revolution of 1905, most among the intelligentsia sympathized or even took an active role in various liberal and revolutionary movements. Merezhkovsky made hatred for the autocracy a key message in his novels, and he and Gippius patronized and encouraged the Socialist Revolutionary terrorist Boris Savinkov. Under their guidance, Savinkov, using the pseudonym Ropshin, published two Symbolist novels about terrorism. Bulgakov, Berdyaev, and Struve became founding members of the Union of Liberation and were later active in Duma politics (see next chapter). Although the poets Blok and Bely had a more distant relation to politics (and were better poets than Merezhkovsky or Gippius), the atmosphere of revolution permeates works like Bely's *Petersburg,* and the performance of Blok's *Fairground Booth (Balaganchik)* would be one of the important events of the 1905 revolution. The mood changed after Prime Minister Pëtr Stolypin closed the Second Duma in 1907 (see next chapter), and in 1909 a group of prominent intelligentsia—Berdyaev, Bulgakov, Frank, Struve, and Gershenzon, among others—gathered to produce an explosive and seminal collection of articles called *Vekhi,* or *Landmarks,* in which they lamented the intelligentsia's arrogance, self-obsession, and unthinking commitment to radical politics. They collectively suggested that they should turn, instead, to the religious culture of the people and try to understand and work with it for social change. The publication of this collection set off a barrage of public debate in which the authors were accused by their former left allies of betraying the revolutionary cause and retreating into mysticism and by Duma politicians of being impractical.

The Silver Age intelligentsia were also a crucial element of a powerful, though ultimately unsuccessful, movement to reform the Orthodox Church that began with the new century. Over-procurator Pobedonostsev's tight reign over the governance of the country was a thorn in the side not only of the clergy but of the liberal-minded intelligentsia. The Religious-Philosophical Societies were originally conceived in this period as a forum in which the secular but religiously inclined intelligentsia could work with priests and bishops to influence the course of church reform. As it turned out, they did not understand each other well, and Pobedonostsev shut the first society down in 1904. Nonetheless, one of the important results of 1905 was, with Pobedonostsev's dismissal, the convening of a body to implement reform in the church. Although it bore no immediate fruit, the efforts of the intelligentsia and reform-minded clergy would ultimately culminate in a momentous Church Council of 1917–1918—the first since the seventeenth century—which, in the face of the revolutionary battles that were already raging in Moscow, achieved the feat of restoring the patriarchate. At one time, the council's head would be a former president of the Religious-Philosophical Societies, Anton Kartashëv.

Offshoots: The 1910s

The creative impulse of the turn of the century created a milieu in which new literary and artistic movements could thrive. The year 1910 marked a transition in the cultural currents of the age: Blok, in his poem "Retribution," listed the landmarks of that year—the end of Symbolism and the deaths of Tolstoy, Vrubel, and the actress Vera Komissarzhevskaya. The ensuing decade saw a burgeoning of rich and varied literary, artistic, and philosophical activity, drawing in not only a new generation but new kinds of people and branching out in completely different directions. The "offshoot" movements of the 1910s, however, while constructing themselves as a revolt against symbolists, idealists, or God seekers, inherited the fundamental characteristics of the turn-of-the-century "core" of the Silver Age—an infatuation with the new, a yearning for transcendence, and a fundamental belief that art could shape life.

The earliest rebellion against the mood of the 1900s came to a head in about 1908 and was spearheaded by a group of thinkers who called themselves God-builders. Alexander Bogdanov (1873–1928) and Anatoly Lunacharsky (1875–1933), whose ideas were eventually to play a determining role in the culture of the early Soviet period (1920s), fulminated against the religious fantasies of their contemporaries. Arguing against idealism, they explicitly called themselves "positivists"

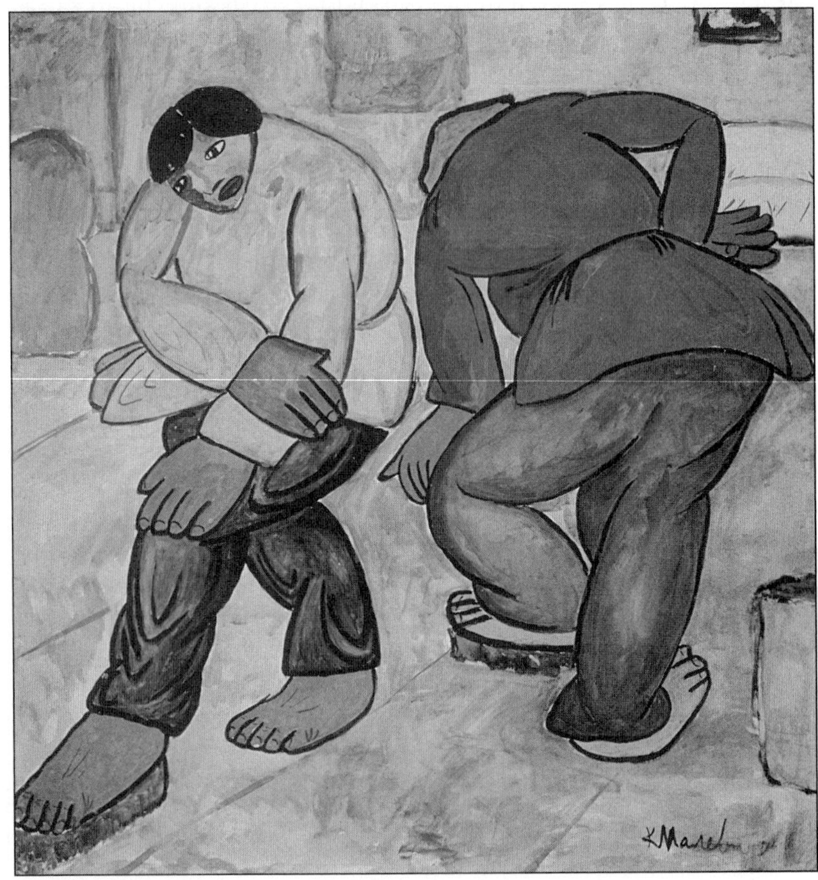

Floor Polishers, by Kasimir Malevich (1911–12). *Stedelijk Museum, Amsterdam, The Netherlands.*

and took to an extreme their nineteenth-century predecessors' belief in science. Bogdanov's science fiction novel *The Red Star* (1908) described a utopian society on Mars, where socialist principles were fully implemented and even mortality had been overcome. Socialism, in the writings of Lunacharsky, Bogdanov, and their followers, took the form of literary utopia. Bogdanov later headed the Proletkult movement, and Lunacharsky became commissar of enlightenment in the 1920s; socialist experiments of this early Soviet period were colored by the utopian dreams of the God-builders.

The cultural explosion branched out in the 1910s into a variety of other directions as well. A plethora of literary schools emerged, with a variety of inventive names like Imagism, Clarism, Rayonnism, and so on; but the most important were Acmeism and Futurism. Acmeism was a direction created by the poets Mandelstam, Anna Akhmatova (1889–1966), and Nikolai Gumilëv (1886–1921) that rejected the flowery language of Symbolism and sought to return to the Word as a carrier of world culture. The Futurist poets—Vladimir Mayakovsky, Velimir Khlebnikov, and Alexei Kruchënykh (1886–1970)—experimented with language in an unprecedented way, trying to annihilate standard connections of sound and meaning and breaking down poetic form. Futurism erupted on the scene with a tremendous destructive energy, shocking even the by now aging decadent poets. This movement in literature, coupled with a parallel movement in art, was the avant-garde. The emblem of the 1910s was the 1915 *Black Square,* by Kasimir Malevich. Hung, in the original exhibition, in the corner usually occupied by an icon, Malevich's Red and Black Squares epitomized the avant-garde's notion of the spiritual.

While idealists-turned-religious-philosophers like Bulgakov, Frank, and Berdiaev remained relatively untouched by the avant-garde, which they abhorred, it was nonetheless during this decade of the 1910s that they produced their key religious-philosophical works. In the same decade (1915), a group of young linguists and futurist poets formed a distinctive school of linguistics and literary criticism that came to be known as Russian Formalism and that would have its heyday in Prague in the 1920s. They were pioneers of the structuralist method, which has decisively shaped cultural studies in Europe and the United States, from linguistics to anthropology, throughout the twentieth century.

ART GOES TO THE PEOPLE

The Silver Age intelligentsia were so emphatic in proclaiming their break with the traditions of civic poetry and social consciousness that, to this day, many have remained convinced that they were doing something utterly new, that they were engaged in "art for art's sake," and that their movement has had little or no relation to the social history of their country. While a certain emancipation of the aesthetic consciousness did, indeed, take place, the artists and poets of the Silver Age actually continued the tradition of their populist predecessors in more ways than they admitted. Most of them remained extremely conscious of the situation of the Russian people—as, for example, the *Vekhi* volume confirms—although they sought to achieve the long-sought union of intelligentsia and people in new ways.

This desire to fuse with the people took the form of a sort of aesthetic "going to the people." Gippius and Merezhkovsky, for example, and Kuzmin as well, spent long months among the Old Believers and made a pilgrimage to holy Lake Svetloyar, deep in the forests beyond the Volga, in their quest for oneness with the popular consciousness. Producers and playwrights created a whole genre of theater "for the people." Most symptomatic of this trend were the artists' colonies of Abramtsevo, outside Moscow, and Talashkino, outside Smolensk. Here Vrubel, Nesterov, and Vasnetsov immersed themselves in old Russian folk art, making ceramic tile and objects for daily use as well as painting icons and building churches. Talashkino in particular, a creation of the Princess Maria Tenisheva, was conceived in a socially conscious vein: an integral part of the colony was a school for peasants, where they could resurrect the crafts of old Muscovy and receive an education. Tenisheva conceived her colony as a microcosm of a new Russia, building on tradition, art, and peasant culture.

Ironically, apart from such conscious efforts, Silver Age culture was actually connected with genuine popular culture in a more natural manner than ever before possible. Throughout Europe and America, the turn of the twentieth century witnessed the emergence of urban popular culture as a dominant genre. In Russia, the first feature movie, *Stenka Razin,* based on the story of the seventeenth-century brigand, was made in 1908. Symbolist and avant-garde aesthetics made their way immediately into film and, perhaps even more importantly, into popular journals with a broad circulation throughout all of Russia. Merezhkovsky's decadent poetry, however much a provincial schoolteacher in, say, Kharkov might shake his head with dismay, became a part of the teacher's universe in a way that was never true for the writings of the populists Pëtr Lavrov or Nikolai Mikhailovsky. The Silver Age erupted at a moment when potentials for diffusion and interaction—a natural narrowing of the long-lamented gap between intelligentsia and people—were unprecedented.

CHAPTER 27

Russia on the Barricades: The Revolution of 1904–1907

This is the inhabitant of the island—the stranger with the black mustache, elusive, invisible, he has vanished; there he is in the provinces; and before you know it the provincial depths are muttering and whispering out there in space; and—out in those provincial depths—it is Russia that will soon be thundering and hooting.

—*Andrei Bely,* Petersburg *(1913)*

The events we know as the Revolution of 1905 have been among the most reflected-on and self-conscious in modern European history. People thought about the revolution before it happened—liberals in anxious anticipation of the revolution that would serve as proof of Russia's "Europeanness," conservatives in fear that the evil "principles of 1789" would at last penetrate into Russia, undermining the harmony and stability of the monarchy. They thought about it while it was happening: events like "Bloody Sunday" or the mutiny on the battleship *Potëmkin* on the Black Sea became instantly mythologized, feeding into strikes and rebellions. Observers from abroad kept up a running commentary, and the revolution in Russia had immediate consequences for debates within, for example, the German Social Democratic movement. In the century since the revolution, there has been plenty of time for postfactum evaluations, which have also proliferated. Commentators have managed to see in 1905 everything from an 1848-style "bourgeois revolution" that finally reached Russia to the first of the great agrarian revolutions of the twentieth century, an example for China, Mexico, or India.

The present account brings out the following elements, some familiar from other revolutions and others not. In conditions of rapid industrial growth, widespread discontent—with grievances ranging from economic to political—led to an intellectually coherent protest movement, with adherents in the universities and among urban workers. A painful and disastrous war triggered urban strikes and agrarian uprisings as the term of redemption payments came to an unsuccessful conclusion. The revolution became progressively radicalized until by October 1905 it passed out of the hands of the liberals and turned into a conflagration on a scale not seen for a century (not since the violent mass uprising led by the rebel Emelyan Pugachëv under Catherine II). The granting of a constitutional regime was followed

October Idyll, by the Petersburg artist Mstislav Dobuzhinsky (1905). *David King Collection, London.*

by a flailing government's resort to brutal suppression of revolution as the only way it could regain control (which it should have relinquished).

THE PALE HORSEMAN

Valery Bryusov's 1902 poem "The Pale Horse" captured an imaginary moment of horror in an urban crowd when an unknown horseman—one of the four horsemen of the Apocalypse—appears suddenly, scattering people in every direction. Bryusov's vision seemed to resonate in life two years later, when the horse-drawn carriage of Nicholas II's minister of the interior, Vyacheslav Plehve, was rocked by a powerful explosion as it wended its way through the streets and canals of St. Petersburg. As in the poem, Petersburgians soon continued about their business, paying little attention to the gruesomely scattered carriage and body parts on the pavement. Terrorism had quietly become an almost accepted, or at least habitual, part of the political landscape.

When did the revolution begin? Tradition starts the tale on January 9, 1905. Yet the implicit tension that marked Nicholas II's reign from the 1895 "senseless dreams" speech began to acquire a violent twist much earlier. Perhaps it was in February 1899, when St. Petersburg University students responded to the government's nervous disruption of their celebrations of the founding of the university—including alleged police beatings of students on Rumyantsev Square—by declaring a strike. Student organizers helped spread the strike movement to Moscow, Kiev, and Kharkov Universities, where it found the support of sympathetic professors as well. A government-appointed commission's issuance of "Temporary Rules" (July 29, 1899) threatening military conscription for disruptive students resulted only in temporary calm; the student movement came to a head in street demonstrations two years later. The 1901 demonstrations demanded—and gained—the rescinding of the July 29 rules and won, as well, the promise of a reconsideration of the 1884 statute limiting university autonomy.

One might be tempted to see the beginnings of revolution in peasant uprisings that erupted in Kharkov and Poltava Provinces in 1902 and 1903, intensifying in the summer months and echoing in Saratov, Tambov, Chernigov, Kovno, Pskov, Vyatka, Perm, and Ufa. Rural poverty, inadequate land distribution, a disproportionate share of the burdens of industrialization, and peasants' inferior financial and juridical status were, after all, acute social problems, acknowledged by government and radicals alike. Even radical activists wishing passionately to discern a revolutionary peasant movement, however, were forced to admit the general passivity of the countryside; the peasants still had little means to express their discontent save by what Pushkin once called the "Russian revolt, senseless and merciless" that had been the basis for the great mass uprisings of Razin and Pugachëv in the seventeenth and eighteenth centuries. A possible exception was the Georgian province of Guria, where by 1902 peasants, under social democratic tutelage, formulated concrete demands (one-tenth of the harvest to landowners instead of one-half or one-third), staged a boycott, and gained control of a significant part of Kutaïsi Province under the auspices of a "Gurian republic."

The search for revolutionary beginnings is slightly more productive if we turn our attention to the smaller but more cohesive milieu of urban workers. Both turn-of-the-century politics and subsequent historiography have revolved significantly around the struggle for the hearts and minds of the 2 million workers of St. Petersburg, Moscow, Warsaw, the Don basin, Baku, and the Urals. In the absence of legal labor unions, workers continued to rely on artisanal guilds and mutual aid societies for institutional and material support. The earliest and most advanced societies were formed by printers (Warsaw, 1814; Riga and Odessa, 1816) and salesclerks; the latter held a series of three national congresses in 1896 and 1898. Strikes, too, remained illegal, which means neither that they didn't happen nor that they could not be successful (historians have, not very meaningfully, counted an average of 176 strikes per year between 1895 and 1904). A 1901 strike in the Petersburg metalworking industry, for example, demanded and won worker representation in factory administration. Having attracted the attention of the Ministry of Finance, it also led eventually to a 1903 law on the "Establishment of Elders in Industrial

Enterprises," which, though limited and narrowly implemented, gave official sanction to the participation of elders in factory management.

The government's concessions were rare and grudging, and workers lacked any means to impose demands on employers; the workday still ran eleven and a half hours, and wages were chronically low. These circumstances should have made the factory floor a fruitful arena for socialist and Marxist propaganda. Indeed, radical political activists managed to penetrate virtually every branch of industry, beginning with discussion circles and reading groups and culminating in illegal unions. Nonetheless, their numbers and their influence remained small. Contemporary labor historians have suggested that workers in general continued to believe, with the Petersburg metalworker Alexei Buzinov, that "the tsar would provide justice and defend us against [our] enemies." Again, possible exceptions come from the Kingdom of Poland and the Transcaucasus, where major strikes in Warsaw and Baku (1903) followed more closely the more conflictual "European" pattern.

Ironically, the most successful effort at labor organization was initiated by the government itself. Instead of legalizing unions and strikes (though Witte claimed in his memoirs that he wished to do so in 1902), the Ministry of the Interior launched a peculiar scheme to coopt and control the labor movement through a network of "police unions." The general idea here was not without precedent: Pope Leo IX's *Rerum novarum* (see the chapter "Orthodoxy, Autocracy, Nationality Reaffirmed, 1881–1905") and a social insurance scheme instituted by German chancellor Otto von Bismarck in the 1870s had sought to take the wind out of social democracy's sails by adopting parts of its program. The police unions of Moscow and St. Petersburg, however, were a particularly dangerous and entirely original version of this game. The initiator was the chief of the Moscow police, Sergei Zubatov, who was in turn inspired by an ideal of "social monarchy." The ten police-sponsored unions that operated in Moscow between 1901 and 1905 organized lectures and meetings and provided information about European labor organization. They even organized work stoppages (notably of fifteen hundred weavers at two Moscow silk mills in 1902). All this took place under close official surveillance. Zubatov himself was dismissed after his unions actually became a major force behind a 1903 general strike in Odessa—the largest strike to that date; but his idea lived on in a new set of police unions organized by his protégé, Father Georgy Gapon (1870–1906), in St. Petersburg in 1903, with the sanction of the new minister of the interior, Vyacheslav Plehve. By January 1905, Gapon's assembly, which had begun with a tearoom for workers, counted some nine thousand members, among them one thousand women.

Given such tactics by the government, it was often not easy to tell who was a revolutionary and who was a government agent. Some people were both—most notably the extraordinary Evno Azef (1869–1918), a double agent who became a leader of the battle organization of one of the major revolutionary parties while simultaneously reporting its activities to the police. Revolutionary expectations and government fear fed on each other in a cycle with no beginning and no end. Spies and terrorists became habitual characters in the urban landscape, contributing to an atmosphere of vague foreboding and mutual suspicion—brilliantly painted in

Andrei Bely's novel *Petersburg.* The elimination of two ministers of the interior in succession—Dmitry Sipyagin (1902) and Vyacheslav Plehve (July 1904)—provoked little public reaction; their names joined a list that included Minister of Education Bogolepov and others. If it is difficult to point to any precise moment, person, or social group as the initial impulse of revolution, it is fair to speak of anticipation as well as of a general politicization that affected, as Witte chose to put it, "everyone in all regions and all strata of society."

POLITICAL PARTIES AND MOVEMENTS

Workers' movements, with an increasingly strong leadership and sophisticated demands, were characteristic of all industrialized societies at the close of the nineteenth century—Germany; France, where the movement was called syndicalism; Britain, with trade unions and the Labor Party; and the United States, with the American Federation of Labor (AFL). However, the Russian case was peculiar in that the discontents of workers and peasants were paralleled by an equally powerful and probably more vocal dissatisfaction among those groups that, in Europe and the United States, formed the bulwark of the existing regimes. Such people—the "progressive intelligentsia" broadly defined—formed the nucleus of the political parties that took shape at the turn of the century, some thirty years after national political parties had become an accepted mode of political activity in France, Germany, and Austria-Hungary.

Can illegal political parties be called parties at all? The three major political groups—Social Democrats, Socialist Revolutionaries, and the Union of Liberation—that emerged between 1898 and 1905 were all clandestine revolutionary organizations, heavily dependent on émigré congresses and publications. This had a determining effect on their structure—which continued, in many ways, to replicate the populist model of a "progressive" intelligentsia elite on one hand and, presumably, a mass following on the other. It also affected their ability to reach broad strata of the Russian population.

Farthest to the left were the Social Democrats (SDs), who held their first, aborted founding congress in Minsk in 1898; many of the participants were arrested. Under the leadership of Georgy Plekhanov (1856–1918), Yuly Martov (1873–1923), and Lenin, the RSDWP (Russian Social Democratic Workers' Party—the party's full name) mounted a coherent and dogmatically Marxist platform that placed the problem of the working class and the proletarian revolution at the heart of their demands. The Social Democratic Party met at its Second Congress in London in 1903, where it split into two powerful rival factions over an issue of party organization. The Bolsheviks, headed by Lenin and taking their name from the Russian word for "majority," wished the party to remain a small but efficient band of professional revolutionaries, whereas the Mensheviks (from "minority") stood for a broader organization. Lenin spelled this out in a 1902 pamphlet with its title borrowed from Chernyshevsky, *What Is to Be Done?*

One of the most interesting and original parties was the Socialist Revolutionaries (SRs)—more or less conscious heirs to the populists. Unlike the urban-oriented SDs, the SRs were an agrarian party whose program focused on peasant interests. Several aspects of their program—most notably its emphasis on the small peasant proprietor—were extremely powerful in their appeal and were eventually coopted by the Bolsheviks as they sought to gain power. The SRs included gentry land expropriation in their program as one of the necessary measures in agrarian reform. They also organized workers. The SRs relied, more than others, on terrorism as a tactic; they counted Boris Savinkov, who wrote two novels about terrorists (see the chapter "Cultural Explosion, 1900–1920"), as well as the double-agent Azef and assassins such as Ivan Kalyaev and Maria Spiridonova among their members.

The Union of Liberation was an umbrella organization that grouped together primarily zemstvo activists and members of the liberal intelligentsia. It was founded in Switzerland in 1903, and its organ, *Liberation,* edited by Pëtr Struve, was published there, following the tradition of émigré publications set by Herzen's *The Bell.* The union was the mouthpiece of the broad-based movement that called itself the Liberation movement. Its diverse members found common ground in their hatred for the autocracy that, they felt, limited the possibilities for action in every field of endeavor—business, the university, the theater, politics, or anywhere else. Some, following Struve's example, adopted a classic Western-style liberal agenda focused on civil rights, freedom of speech and press, a constitution, and a parliament. The slogan of the day in Russia, the "four-tail suffrage"—referring to voting rights that would be equal, direct, universal, and secret, with no distinction of gender, religion, or nationality—belongs to the liberationists. Other members focused on solutions to the agrarian or workers' problems as the key agenda; some had a religious, transformative vision of society. The philosophy of the Union of Liberation was brilliantly represented in the 1902 collection of articles *Problems of Idealism.* Its authors, who included ex-Marxists Nikolai Berdyaev, Sergei Bulgakov, Semën Frank, and Pëtr Struve, expressed a peculiarly Russian variant of liberalism based not on external claims of voting rights and institutions but on an understanding of the ultimate primacy of the individual and the inviolability of the human soul. *Liberation* proved a powerful journal, smuggled regularly into Russia, and provided a forum for many of the "progressive" groups in society to vent their discontents and propose plans for change and renewal.

The Union of Liberation overlapped with the zemstvo movement, which provided a legal outlet for political activism. By 1900, the zemstvos had cultivated a numerous, active, and purposeful stratum of politicians who felt hampered by the absence of a national forum and the ever-present limitations on their power and finances. Tension turned into confrontation in Russia's major associations: the government periodically closed down even such respectable institutions as the Free Economic Society (whose minutes in 1904 and 1905 read like the proceedings of a radical-left political party), while national congresses of *kustar* (handicrafts) industry (1902), animal husbandry (1903), and two 1904 congresses—a technical education congress and the Pirogov medical congress—became the forum for impassioned political speeches.

The radical right was no less active as a participant in the tensions of the new century. A rabidly anti-Semitic group known as the Black Hundreds expanded its membership and influence, staging pogroms throughout the western provinces in the 1900s. They were joined by such dubious organizations as the Union of Russian People, for whom xenophobia, anti-Semitism and reactionary sentiments masqueraded as patriotism.

A women's movement that had already made significant gains, winning the crucial access to higher education, now sought to make further progress, including the right to vote. The women's movement was particularly powerful in Finland, which in 1906 became the first European country to give women the vote.

WAR AND REVOLUTION I: FROM LIAODONG TO THE ZEMSTVO CONGRESS

On January 27, 1904, the Japanese admiral Togo launched a surprise attack on the Russian fleet harbored in Port Arthur on the Liaodong peninsula. This single attack, while leaving its perpetrators virtually undamaged, incapacitated more than half the Russian naval force in the Yellow Sea. Even so, Russian officials tried to dismiss Japanese aggression as a mere "incident," much as they had dismissed months of diplomacy that had preceded it. The Russian government knew little about Japan; still less was the government capable of taking this "backward Asian island" seriously. To the extent that it did, its attitude was shaped by contradictory impulses: while the Ministry of Foreign Affairs urged the preservation of peace at all costs, an influential timber speculator, Alexander Bezobrazov, seconded by Admiral A. M. Abaza, wished to maintain and expand Russian influence in Manchuria even if this antagonized Japan.

If the Russo-Japanese war that ensued represented another stage in a generally ill-formulated and unreflective Far Eastern policy for Russia, the same was not the case for Japan. Now at the height of the industrializing and expansionist spurt of the Meiji period (1868–1912), Japan had acquired the southern island of Formosa in 1895 and had set its sights on Sakhalin (an 1875 Russian acquisition) and, especially, Korea. The Japanese grudgingly tolerated the Russian presence on the Liaodong peninsula and viewed Bezobrazov's expansionist timber schemes in Manchuria with suspicion. Their diplomatic overtures and subsequent attack were a conscious and well-planned strategy. Japan's economy had grown rapidly over the preceding two decades, and its military presence included 180,000 troops (with an additional 670,000 reserves), modern military and naval equipment, and first-rate training. All of this surpassed by far the forces Russia could deploy in what was, from the perspective of St. Petersburg, a distant military outpost. In gross numbers, of course, Russian strength was greater: the Trans-Siberian Railroad was nearly complete, the navy had grown by 680,000 tons since 1894, and the state-run arms industry was flourishing, picking up yet more speed in 1904. But the railway was missing a crucial section around Lake Baikal (which therefore could be traversed

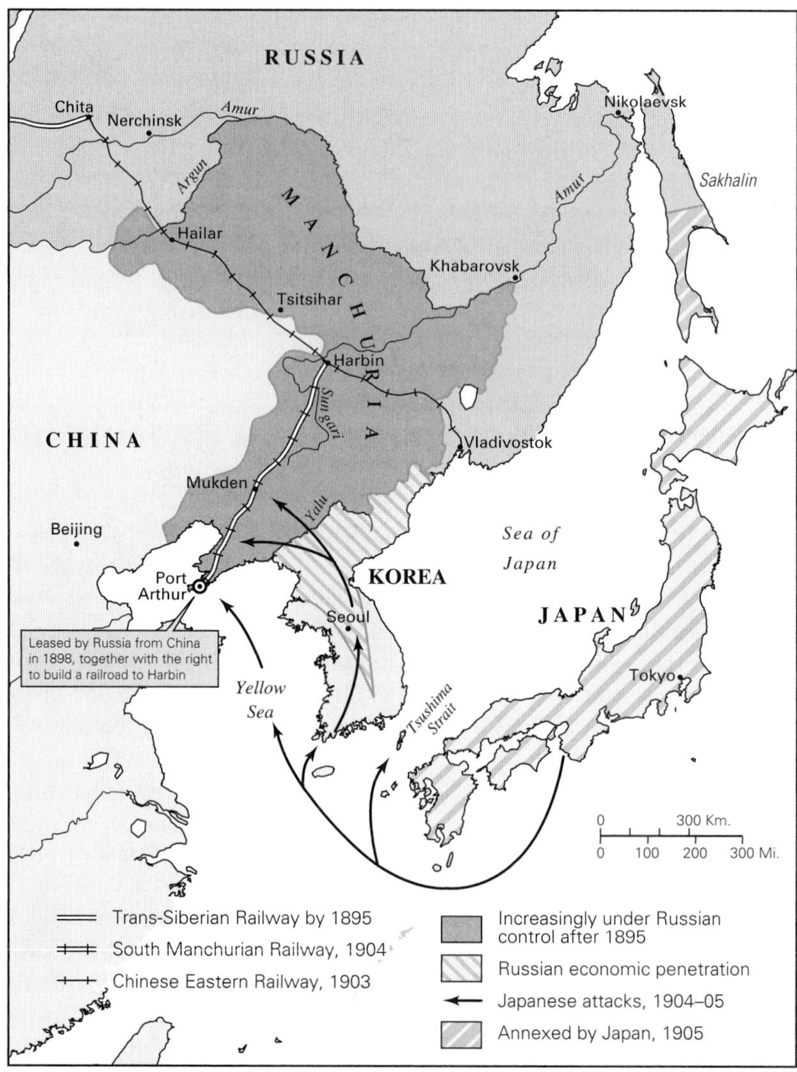

The Russo-Japanese War, 1904–1905. Atlas of Russian History *by Martin Gilbert (New Edition published by Routledge in 2002) 0415281199 PB & 0415281180 HB. Please visit our website for further details on the new edition: www.taylorandfrancis.com*

only in winter, when the lake was frozen, but not in summer), the ships were almost all in the Baltic or Black Seas, and military training and preparation remained inadequate and ineffective.

What was expected to be a minor incident turned quickly into a string of humiliating Russian defeats. The first real battle, at Tyurenchensk in April 1904, pitted 60,000 Japanese troops against 23,000 Russians and ended in retreat with 2,000 casualties for the Russians. The initial outbreak of war was greeted by everyone except the extreme left with general expressions of solidarity, but the public mood began to sour with the news of every new defeat. A renewed terrorist campaign gathered strength in the spring, culminating in the bomb, orchestrated by Azef, that blew Plehve's carriage to pieces in July. Plehve's replacement as minister of the interior by the liberal Prince P. D. Svyatopolk-Mirsky (1857–1914) (despite Witte's hopes of winning the post) was followed by a new military disaster in August. In the battle of Liaoyang, 125,000 Japanese troops with 485 guns defeated 160,000 Russians with 592 guns—primarily, as subsequent researches assert, because of poor training, inferior equipment, and low morale. Tales reached the capitals of the army commander General A. N. Kuropatkin's essentially defensive strategy: he avoided engagement until he was sure of superior numbers yet kept large numbers of troops in reserve; as a result he was generally forced into battle by the Japanese.

The Paris Conference and the Zemstvo Congress

Defeat and disillusionment created the right opening for revolutionaries, who saw the war as their cue for revolt. By the fall of 1904, eight different parties (including Polish, Finnish, Latvian, Georgian, and Armenian socialists, but not the Russian Social Democrats) responded to the call by Finnish nationalist and socialist Konni Zilliacus (1855–1924) to convene in Paris (September 30–October 9). The Conference of Oppositional and Revolutionary Organizations of the Russian State chose this symbolic location to proclaim their own tennis court oath (mimicking French constitutionalists in June 1789): they vowed to destroy the autocracy, restore the Finnish constitution, establish democratic government based on universal suffrage, and grant self-determination to national minorities.

Within Russia itself, in the meantime, the standoff between "progressive" society and the government came to a head. Taking advantage of Mirsky's ministership, zemstvo leaders convened a congress in St. Petersburg November 6–9. The results were ambiguous. Mirsky, who found the tsar agreeing with him in his zemstvo sympathies—only to change his mind depending on the next delegation to visit him—approved only a meeting for "tea" in a private apartment—the screen behind which the congress was actually held. The 103 people attending the congress had not been elected and were not therefore technically representatives of their zemstvos. Despite some disagreement among the delegates themselves, they in the end adopted a resolution calling for a popular representative body that would have legislative, financial, and administrative rights.

The real action in the months of November and December 1904 was outside the congress itself: concurrently, organizers launched a banquet campaign (modeled on the banquets of the 1848 revolution in France) throughout most of the zemstvo provinces but also in the Baltic, western, southern, and Caucasus provinces. Of the thirty-eight banquets, twenty endorsed the resolutions of the Zemstvo Congress, while eleven went further and called for a constituent assembly. The empirewide banquets proved a forum for political organization and formed the basis for broader congresses, called unions, which were to proliferate in the following year. The Zemstvo Congress, in addition, received some five thousand telegrams from around the country openly criticizing the "unbearable" political situation.

A small delegation from the congress submitted its resolutions to Mirsky, who used them as the basis for a decree by the tsar of December 12, 1904. This resolution stipulated what to the government seemed great concessions, proposing to legislate equal rights for the peasantry, elimination of arbitrariness in the law and in the courts, more powers to the zemstvos, insurance for workers, religious toleration, fewer restrictions on non-Russians in the empire, and greater freedom of the press. The decree, however, was met with disappointment. For one thing, promises of legislation were not deemed sufficient from a sovereign by now notorious for changing his mind. But, more importantly, the sticking point was once again the same: after consulting with Mirsky and Witte, Nicholas decided to omit the crucial measure promising the election of national representatives to help in the process of legislation.

The dramatic capitulation, eight days later, of Port Arthur to the Japanese, following a siege of 156 days and the death of twenty-eight thousand Russians and twice as many Japanese, found the monarch and the progressive intelligentsia once more at a complete impasse.

WAR AND REVOLUTION II: THE BLOODY YEAR 1905

The fall of Port Arthur disrupted the entire Russian strategy (such as it was) for the conduct of the war with Japan. The news reached the Russian fleet, dispatched all the way from the Baltic Sea to reinforce the defense of Port Arthur, just as it was rounding the southern tip of Africa at the Cape of Good Hope. The new year ushered in an increasingly violent and chaotic phase both of the war and of revolution, beginning with the first blood in St. Petersburg in January and concluding with the brutal suppression of revolution throughout the countryside in December and into 1906.

From Bloody Sunday to the Polish General Strike

Russian factories had stepped up military production in 1904 in response to pressing demand from the front. The percentage of total production accounted for by arms manufacture at, for example, the major Petersburg Putilov factory increased from 15 percent in 1900 to 27 percent in 1905. Shipbuilding reached a feverish pace at the Obukhov and Baltic shipyards, from 264,000 tons per year in 1895–1899, to 340,000 in 1900–1904, and 416,000 tons in 1905 alone. It was in the context of the state's particular dependence on the arms industry that workers at the Putilov plant, under the auspices of Gapon's assembly, began in the early days of January 1905 to organize a strike to protest the dismissal of four workers. The strikers were soon joined by workers from other major factories—the Franco-Russian works, the Nevsky shipbuilding plant, the Shtiglits factory, and—by January 7—100,000 workers at 382 enterprises.

The experiment with "police socialism" came to an ignominious end on Sunday,

January 9, when a crowd of some 50,000 to 100,000 workers wended its way through the streets of Petersburg toward the Winter Palace. Father Gapon led the procession, bearing a petition protesting the impoverishment, voicelessness, and lack of rights of the workers; among other measures, they asked for freedom of speech and equality before the law, abolition of land redemption payments, allocation of military orders to Russian and not foreign factories, an eight-hour day, "normal" wage rates, social insurance, and worker representation on factory committees. As they broached the vast, awkward expanse of the Palace Square, the demonstrators were confronted by a regiment of Cossack horse guards facing them in formation, rifles poised. The troops had been given orders not to allow the procession onto the square itself; the soldiers opened fire, killing perhaps two hundred people and wounding many more as the procession dissolved in a chaos of screams and blood. Gapon managed to escape and eventually found his way to Switzerland. The massacre struck a nerve throughout the empire and in Europe as well; newspapers picked it up immediately, and the event, immediately christened "Bloody Sunday," was taken by many as symbolic proof that the regime stood in fatal opposition to its own people.

The wave of strikes that followed through January and February—not only in Petersburg and Moscow but also in previously quiet provinces like Novgorod, Smolensk, Tauride, Samara, Saratov, Kaluga, and Tula—formulated demands that ranged from shorter working hours and increased pay to worker representation in factory administration. A Menshevik scholar estimated that 35 percent of these strikes were "purely economic," and the rest involved some sort of "political" demands. Labor unrest seriously disrupted military production at this critical moment. At the end of 1905 the Putilov factory had to ask for eight months' grace in filling its orders; in addition, some troops were diverted from the front to deal with striking workers. Railway and dock workers' strikes interrupted the flow of supplies to the east until a government decree militarized the railways. Mirsky was dismissed on January 18 and replaced with the more conservative A. G. Bulygin (1851–1919).

Perhaps the most important protests, however, came from the Kingdom of Poland, where the structure of industry and politics gave workers their own set of grievances. In heavily industrialized Warsaw, Bloody Sunday triggered a general strike, declared on January 14 by the Polish Socialist Party and the Social Democratic Party; the strike led to armed conflict and perhaps ninety deaths in the city itself and was echoed in other western provinces of the empire. The strike movement reverberated in Poland's other major industrial centers, Lodz and the Dabrowski basin, mobilizing hundreds of thousands of Polish and Jewish workers for a month. A nationwide boycott of Russian-language high schools lasted for nearly three years. As violence intensified over 1905, more troops were diverted from the Japanese front to supplement the 250,000 already permanently stationed in Poland. Another major center of strikes and demonstrations following Bloody Sunday was the Latvian city of Riga, where the social democratic movement was particularly powerful.

Mukden, Tsushima, and the Descent into Chaos

The land war in Manchuria came to an end in the enormous Battle of Mukden in March 1905, when General Kuropatkin planned an offensive that failed to materialize in time to prevent a Japanese attack. The three-week conflict drove Russian forces back along the Manchurian railway tracks at the cost of 72,008 Japanese casualties; but Japanese inability to cut off the retreating armies made the defeat less than decisive. The Japanese War Ministry entertained thoughts of peace negotiations. In Russia, Mukden looked like another in a ceaseless chain of humiliations; to make matters worse, stories of drunken carousing by officers on the eve of battle circulated in the capitals.

The decisive catastrophe came in May, when the Russian fleet of thirty-four ships, among them four ultramodern battleships, finally reached the Yellow Sea after diplomatic conflicts and delays on its lengthy route around Africa. Completely unprepared for battle and intending to proceed up to Vladivostok, the fleet was intercepted at the Tsushima Straits by an equally large Japanese fleet led by Admiral Togo; within one day (May 14) all the major Russian battleships except the *Orël* were sunk, as were several cruisers and destroyers. The cruiser *Aurora* and two others turned tail and fled toward Manila; only four ships made it to Vladivostok. By the following day much of the Russian fleet lay at the bottom of the Pacific Ocean. The government was left with little recourse but to agree to peace negotiations. In the first serious entry of the United States, the recent victor in the Spanish-American War (1898), into international diplomacy outside the Western Hemisphere, the peace treaty was signed under Theodore Roosevelt's mediation at Portsmouth, New Hampshire, on September 5. Japan, whose resources were exhausted, was unable to convert its victories into negotiating capital: although the treaty (negotiated by Witte on the Russian side) stipulated the retrocession of Port Arthur and Liaodong to Japan, the latter did not gain the financial indemnity it sought and won only part of Sakhalin. The peace treaty set off antipeace and antigovernment riots in Tokyo.

In Russia, the organization of the liberation movement had made considerable gains since the Zemstvo Congress in December 1904. On May 8–9, 1905, the eve of Tsushima, delegates from fourteen newly founded professional unions convened in Moscow to create an umbrella organization, the Union of Unions. It brought together the Unions of Lawyers, Medical Personnel, Engineers and Technicians, Pharmacists, Academicians, Office Workers and Accountants, Railway Employees, Agronomists and Statisticians, Writers, Veterinarians, Teachers, and Zemstvo Activists, as well as those for Jewish equality and for the equality of women. Despite its rather tame title, the Union had explicitly revolutionary aims, above all the abolition of autocracy, and declared its support for the idea of a general strike.

Newspapers throughout Russia during the spring of 1905 reported an atmosphere of increasing domestic chaos, ranging from attacks by hooligans to pogroms (Zhitomir in April, for example, where twenty-nine Jews were killed and much property destroyed). Although many of these reports may have been the result of an increasing willingness to ignore censorship, they still reflected a trend. Disorder and discontent seem to have been particularly acute in Poland, where police generally looked the other way; in May, crowds launched an attack on the city brothels, prompted by the abduction of a Jewish woman and by her forced employment in one of them.

Vague disorder crystallized into open mutiny and revolt in the summer months. On June 14, sailors on one of Russia's few remaining battleships, the *Potëmkin,* stationed in the Black Sea, shot several of their officers, including the captain, and threw others overboard. The full-scale mutiny was triggered by the execution of a sailor who had protested maggot-infested rations; it was the product of months of agitation by incognito socialists among the crew. Coming after a strike-filled April and May in the port city of Odessa, where the ship had dropped anchor to wait for support from the rest of the fleet, the mutiny on the *Potëmkin* set off a rampage of plunder and looting by marauding crowds on the wharves. Trapped in the port area by a police cordon, hundreds of people (many drunk on the vodka that was stored in the warehouses) perished either in fires, when the wooden warehouses were ignited, or when police fired volleys into the crowd, following orders to restore peace. From the perspective of revolutionaries (Lenin, for example, watching from abroad, saw in the mutiny the beginning of insurrection), the mutiny was a relative failure: the *Potëmkin* sailors did not shell the city as expected in support of demonstrations on land, and the incident failed to win the backing of other vessels in the fleet.

Demobilization on the Far Eastern front brought thousands of troops (over 1 million were in Manchuria by the war's end) trailing back to European Russia, humiliated by their losses and, perhaps more importantly, exhausted by chronic supply shortages. Briefly, rebellious troops, supported by sympathetic railway workers, controlled the Trans-Siberian Railroad and hence Siberian territory.

In the summer months a wave of agrarian uprisings—long feared by the government and anticipated by radicals—swept the central and southern provinces, signaling the spread of the revolutionary impulse to the peasants. The unrest, which affected sixty-two districts (14 percent of European Russia) in early summer, often took the form of organized looting, particularly the theft of lumber from landlords' estates. In the Middle Volga region and the central black-earth provinces in particular, though, the peasants burned and trashed estates in a paroxysm of rural violence. A detailed investigation by the Free Economic Society (which of course had its own radical agenda) in 1908 pinpointed outsiders as instigators of specific uprisings—usually workers coming back from the capitals, Rostov, Kharkov, Baku, or elsewhere, or "Manchurian" soldiers, and much less frequently socialist and revolutionary agitators. The study also found a relatively high level of political consciousness: peasant demands in Moscow Province, for example, included "equality," the restoration of "excised" lands, equalization of taxes, the abolition of land captains, "amnesty," abolition of capital punishment, equal education, and so forth. Investigators proudly noted the formation of such organizations as a Bobrovsk "Peasant Union" and stressed (perhaps in a display of wishful thinking) the hopes that peasants placed on representative government.

On August 6, 1905, amidst continuing urban and rural violence, in the course of peace negotiations at Portsmouth and following a sustained campaign among his ministers and advisers, Nicholas II signed a document authorizing a consultative assembly. This Bulygin Constitution, named for the prime minister who headed the committee that drafted it, created an elected Duma that could recommend legislation to the monarch via the State Council but could not address any changes in the structure of governance. The monarch remained free to make legislation without the Duma's approval. Limitations on suffrage were such that, according to contemporary newspaper calculations, 7,130 people out of a total of 1,400,000 in St. Petersburg would have the right to vote (542 out of 85,000 in Tsaritsyn, as another example). The Duma, seen as too little too late by liberals, was never convened on the terms specified in the Bulygin project, which thus existed on paper only, joining Loris-Melikov's unrealized project from 1881.

Radicalization: General Strike, October Manifesto, Days of Liberty, Moscow Uprising

Neither the apparent constitutional concessions nor the peace treaty with Japan halted the revolution, which by now had taken on a dynamic of its own. Agrarian uprisings continued through the fall, while printers, bakers, tobacco workers, metal workers, among others, struck in Moscow in September. In early October the All-Russian Union of Railroad Workers and Employees, founded the previous April with help from socialist organizers, declared a strike on the Moscow-Kazan railroad. The strikers' demands included everything from an eight-hour workday and higher wages to freedom of speech and assembly; the movement spread to factories, and by the second week of October Moscow was in the grip of a general strike. The October strike became the occasion for the formation of a Council of Workers' Deputies ("soviet") in St. Petersburg—a meeting of some forty deputies under the tense co-sponsorship of Mensheviks, Bolsheviks, and SRs, who took upon themselves the direction of the strike movement. The St. Petersburg soviet, led initially by the lawyer G. S. Khrustalëv-Nosar (1879–1918) and then, after his arrest in November, by Lev Bronstein (Trotsky) (1879–1940), was reproduced in about eighty such councils of workers, peasants, and soldiers in forty to fifty cities throughout Russia. The spirit of the strike was taken up by university students, who staged meetings and street demonstrations in support.

Though the general strike seems to have been waning by the middle of the month, it nonetheless served as the final straw by which Nicholas's advisers convinced him to issue a new constitutional decree. The manifesto of October 17 provided the essential corrective to the feeble Bulygin project: its brief text clearly and unambiguously declared (1) civic freedom, (2) a Duma based on universal suffrage, and (3) the granting of legislative powers to the Duma. The manifesto undermined the principle of autocracy and signified a capitulation by the monarch who had begun his reign with an indictment of liberalism and constitutionalism as "senseless dreams." Symbolically, Pobedonostsev was dismissed as over-procurator of the Holy Synod, and Witte was made prime minister.

The celebrations throughout Russia that marked the promulgation of the long-awaited constitution presaged the general mood of the "Days of Liberty" (October 18 through early December) that ensued. In Odessa, for example, joyful street demonstrations turned sour when, in one of the city's Jewish districts, Russian workers were offended by a group of Jews celebrating by displaying desecrated portraits of the tsar and red flags. By the next morning, confrontation had turned into a full-scale pogrom: for three days mobs stormed Jewish property and attacked the Jewish population, killing over five hundred people. Pogroms erupted in Poltava, Kiev, Rostov-on-Don, and Minsk, and Armenians were attacked in Baku. The disorders resonated in Moscow and St. Petersburg, where Black Hundreds and gangs roamed the streets, destroying some storefronts and terrorizing the population. The spontaneous wave of pogroms was echoed by renewed agrarian uprisings in October and by a series of mutinies in the navy and army, at Kronstadt in the Gulf of Finland, in Sevastopol in the Crimea, and later among army officers in the Far East (Chita and Harbin).

At the same time, the "Days of Liberty" created a space in which political activity could flourish. The days of the general strike coincided with the founding congresses of three new parties, in anticipation of impending elections. The Union of Liberation split into fragments, in part as a result of the manifesto: the new Union of October 17 (Octobrists) was a conservative party that fully accepted the tsar's

Barricades on Kropotkinskaya Street in Moscow after uprising on October 27, 1905. *Sovfoto.*

proposals; another offshoot, the Constitutional Democratic (Kadet) Party, was disappointed with the manifesto, which neglected the crucial land question and said nothing explicitly of the workers' complaints. The ultraconservative Union of Russian People stood for the defense of the old order. SRs and SDs remained on the margins of the political process, operating rather through the soviets, which in late October and November began to gain considerable power in some cities such as Chita, as well as in St. Petersburg.

The end of 1905 and early 1906 brought a spate of national and religious congresses and publications. On April 17, 1905, Nicholas II signed an act guaranteeing full toleration of all religious groups. Old Believers began to hold open conferences that would continue up to 1917. A first, conspiratorial Muslim conference gathered on a boat on the Oka River in August 1905. Two more convened in January (under the name Ittifak, or Muslim Union) and April 1906 and provided a base for Muslim participation in elections to the new legislative body. Between 1905 and 1907 more than fifty Arabic-script newspapers and journals were published in Russia, thirty-one of these in Tatar; they dealt with questions of culture and political reform. Ukrainian scientific and educational societies with their newspapers emerged, followed by a Belorussian newspaper. The German colonists in the Volga region experienced a political awakening; and Chuvash, Yakuts, and Buryats published newspapers and held congresses, including a four-hundred-delegate Yakut congress in 1906 and Lamaist gatherings in Chita and Irkutsk.

Perhaps the most tangible expression of the spirit of the last months of 1905 was the cultural scene in St. Petersburg and Moscow. The removal of censorship transformed the world of journalism, theater, and literature. Theaters—once called the "Russian parliament"—staged controversial and almost overtly political plays and operas. Theatergoers could see composer Nikolai Rimsky-Korsakov's blatantly antimonarchical *Story of the Tsar Saltan* (1900) and Blok's *Balaganshchik*—one of the key political events of 1905. The fall season of 1905 erupted, in provincial cities as well as in the capitals, in a thrilling panorama of charged theatrical art.

For Bolsheviks and Mensheviks alike, the month that followed the October manifesto was their opportunity to further the revolutionary cause; Lenin arrived from Switzerland in November. The events of December 1905 in Moscow were the only part of the revolution that was primarily orchestrated by the Social Democrats. A mutiny by soldiers in the Rostov Grenadier Regiment in early December encouraged the Bolsheviks' Moscow Committee to declare a strike that was intended from the beginning to expand into a full-scale street insurrection. What followed was the most violent episode of the year—the Moscow uprising. As barricades went up throughout the city, Moscow became the site of raging street battles, buildings were consumed in flames, and the conflict of strikers and government turned into an all-out war. The workers' soviet gained remarkable political authority, instructing shopkeepers when to open and close, and giving bakers the order to stop baking white bread since the proletariat needed only black. The focal point of the conflict became the Presnya District—a center of textile industry, and a militant neighborhood—where the local soviet took full control of the government, a revolutionary militia controlled the streets, and tribunals dispensed revolutionary justice. On December 15 government troops bombarded Presnya, breaking the insurrection two days later. What followed was a brutal government suppression of the uprising—possible in part because the revolutionaries failed to win the expected support of sympathizers in other cities and regions.

The December uprising marked a clear break. It ended cooperation between liberals and revolutionaries, for the former were as horrified by the brutality of the latter's tactics as by the ensuing government suppression. The gains of the October manifesto, in the meantime, seemed to evaporate as the government, with Witte's clear approval, launched a pacification campaign throughout the empire. Troops fanned out to the Baltic provinces, Siberia, Ukraine, the Caucasus, and elsewhere in a total of about ten "punitive expeditions." The soldiers had orders not only to reassert control of railways and telegraph posts (in Siberia in particular) but to punish or make examples of participants in the uprisings; the result was a rampage of beatings, executions, and the burning of entire villages. In the Baltic region, over a thousand people were killed by troops between December and the following spring; tales of particular sadism accompanied the Siberian expedition. The promised rule of law faded as "exceptional laws" for security were instituted for two-thirds of the empire.

THE REVOLUTIONARY DUMAS

The first elections to Russia's new Duma were called in this atmosphere of unresolved conflict and open antagonism. On the eve of elections, a new government was in place: both guiding lights of the 1881–1905 period, Pobedonostsev and Witte, had resigned—the first immediately following the October manifesto, the second in April 1906; P. A. Stolypin (1862–1911), known at that moment for his firm suppression of rebellion in Saratov Province, where he was governor, was appointed minister of the interior the day before the Duma opened. In July he was also appointed prime minister.

To accommodate a representative institution like the Duma, the Fundamental Laws of the empire, in place since 1832, had to be changed; thus, on April 23, 1906 (four days before the Duma opened), a new version gave the representatives significant legislative and budgetary powers. At the same time, the monarch retained the title of autocrat, though the adjective "unlimited" was removed over Nicholas's protests. The monarch had the initiative in all legislative matters and was the only one who could change the Fundamental Laws themselves. The Duma's rights over the budget did not include military, naval, and court expenditures—one-third of the total; and the possibilities for actual introduction of legislation by the Duma were limited. The Duma could be dissolved at the monarch's prerogative; in addition, the subsequently infamous Article 87 allowed the monarch to issue emergency decrees when the legislature was not in session. There was no universal, equal, and direct suffrage in any European country in 1905; nor, despite liberal demands, was it instituted in Russia, though the extended franchise came close.

Landowners, urban dwellers, peasants, and—an innovation—workers voted according to a curial system, adapted from the one already in use in zemstvo elections.

Another essential change in the government structure was the conversion of the State Council, previously a noble and entirely appointive advisory body, into the upper house of the legislature, with an expanded membership, some of which was elected by the "corporations"—nobility, Orthodox Church, zemstvos, universities, stock exchange committees.

Political Parties and Leaders

Scrambling to attract votes, Russian political parties had to transform themselves overnight from revolutionary organizations into campaign machines. Dominating the election campaign were the Constitutional Democrats (Kadets) under the leadership of liberal politician and historian Pavel Milyukov (1849–1943), and the Union of October 17 (Octobrists). Only these two parties had extensive organizational networks throughout European Russia: the Kadets may have had as many as two hundred provincial, town, and district committees, with slightly fewer for the Octobrists. Kadet membership has been estimated at 120,000; Octobrists probably counted somewhere between 10,000 and 25,000. They were followed by the Trade Industry Party (TIP) and the Party of Legal Order (PLO), both of which had at least some representation in various provinces.

In addition to these basically center or center-left organizations, some parties of the radical right, such as the Union of Russian People (URP), which had branches in fourteen provinces, also distributed political pamphlets, while the Peasant Union, the SRs, and the SDs (in what they later acknowledged was a tactical error) encouraged voters to boycott the elections. Other visible competitors included the Group for Peaceful Renewal (between the Kadets and Octobrists), the Trudoviks (mainly peasants, organized in May 1906), and a tiny Christian Socialist Party. The western provinces erupted in a flurry of political activity: Jews and Poles proved most active, in particular the Union for Equal Rights for Jews, many of whose members were affiliated with the Union of Liberation; and the Polish Constitutionalist-Catholic Party. The National Democrats dominated the political landscape in the Kingdom of Poland.

Elections and the First Duma

Between February and April 1906, representatives of the Kadets, SR, and Octobrist parties scoured the towns and countryside, seeking to win the population over to their cause. The campaigners—reminiscent of the "going to the people" some thirty years earlier—were viewed with suspicion by local police, who did their best to hamper the vote seekers. The Kadets' and Octobrists' tactics involved mainly distributing party literature and holding meetings; lecturers, some trained at "agitational courses" in the capitals, traveled to the provinces, using the forum of local reading groups or, in university towns, the resources of the local professoriate. Some forty or fifty newspapers popped up in the course of the campaign, most of them lasting only until censorship closed them again. Some villages—most notably in Vladimir, Kostroma, and Tver—began to think of the Kadets as "their" party, while perhaps thirty provincial newspapers gave their support to the Octobrists.

The curial, three-stage system gave the vote to some 20–25 million citizens, electing 524 deputies. Historians have calculated that the representation was about one elector for 2,000 landowners, 4,000 urban dwellers, 30,000 peasants, and 90,000 workers. Nonetheless victory went clearly to the center and left parties. The Kadets won about 40 percent of the seats, and the Trudoviks had 20 percent. Nonpartisans gained 112 seats, while the progressive and socialist parties, the Octobrists, and Polish National Democrats were visible quantities. Peasants sat in 231 seats and the nobility in 180. Behind them were Cossacks with 14; merchants, 16; and lower middle classes, 24.

Ethnicity was not a principle in the elections; nonetheless, the makeup reflected the general composition of the empire. The First Duma counted 270 Russians (about 55 percent, though closer to 44 percent of the population); from the western parts of the empire, 63 Ukrainians, 50–60 Poles, 12 Jews, 12 Belorussians, 7 Lithuanians, 6 Latvians, 5 Estonians, 4–6 Germans; from the Caucasus, 8 Azerbaijanis, 7 Georgians, 4 Armenians and 1 Chechen; from the Volga-Urals region, 8 Tatars, 4 Bashkirs, 2 Mordvinians and Votyaks, and 1 Chuvash; and from Central Asia, following a strict quota, 4 Kazakhs and 6 Muslims from Turkistan (of whom

Nicholas II addresses the first Duma. From the illustrated weekly *Niva,* 1906. *Itar-Tass/Sovfoto/Eastfoto.*

only one actually made it to St. Petersburg); finally, 1 each Moldavian, Bulgarian, and Kalmyk.

The convocation of the First Duma on April 27, 1906, signified the transference of the revolutionary process from the plane of violence and armed struggle to that of rostrum and chamber; by no means did it signal the end of revolution. The opening ceremony itself was emblematic of the chasm dividing the emperor and the delegates. In an elaborate display of ritual reminiscent of the imperial coronation ceremonies, Nicholas proceeded to the head of the Duma to read a lukewarm address that completely ignored the ongoing unrest in the country and reaffirmed the principles of autocracy. No one, it appeared, knew exactly what a Duma was: to Nicholas, it was to be a consultative body like the boyar dumas that had advised Ivan IV in Muscovite times; many of the delegates, in the meantime, perceived the Duma as merely a new and better platform—an enhanced Free Economic Society or Zemstvo Congress—from which to carry on the revolutionary struggle for agrarian reform and against the autocracy.

The Duma lasted only two months. Nicholas made use of the prerogative afforded him by the Fundamental Laws to dissolve it on July 6. During this short time in session, it became clear that the most pressing social question confronting Russia was the agrarian question. The government and the delegates came into a head-on and utterly unresolvable confrontation over the question of the expropriation of gentry land. Even the "moderates" and "liberals" in the Kadet Party included in their agrarian programs the redistribution of land from gentry to peasants—a radical position untenable for the government, which continued to throw in its lot with the gentry. This was the ultimate reason for the First Duma's dissolution. Arguably, it was dissolved, as well, because the government saw the Duma as a hindrance to the imposition of order throughout the country—something it could better accomplish using the prerogative of Article 87 of the Fundamental Laws, which gave the government the right to make all key decisions in between Duma sessions.

The Second Duma and the June 3 Coup

A Second Duma was convened in 1907, in accordance with the Fundamental Laws. In the intervening months, Nicholas's new minister, P. A. Stolypin, had taken advantage of Article 87 to institute courts martial throughout the countryside and, even more importantly, to pass agrarian legislation (see the chapter "The 'Duma Monarchy,' 1907–1914") of his own creation, thus usurping the prerogative of the Duma. Members of the First Duma, too, had sought, rather less successfully, to continue their struggle by extraparliamentary means: a group of them, meeting in Finland, issued the Vyborg Manifesto, urging the population not to participate in voting for the next Duma or to pay taxes. The unfortunate result was merely the arrest of most of the participants, resulting in a smaller representation of moderate parties in the next Duma.

The new elections produced a body with slightly fewer non-Russian representatives, counting only forty-seven Ukrainians and Poles and four to six Jews; there

were six Muslims from Turkistan and one Buryat. The Second Duma was significantly more radical than its predecessor. It began inauspiciously: the first several days were dedicated to complaints about the hall in which the government had deemed fit to house the sessions—it had a decaying ceiling that, indeed, caved in just days after the Duma had managed to remove to a more convenient gathering place. This the delegates took as symbolic of the government's disrespect for their proceedings. The session of the Second Duma was even briefer than that of the first. Very soon, discussions turned once more to the fatal sticking point—the agrarian question. After a month of futile debate, Stolypin's patience wore thin. On June 3, 1907, in what has been called a coup d'état, Stolypin dissolved the Duma once more.

Stolypin's June 3 coup finished much more than the session of the Second Duma. Together with his "pacification" campaign in the countryside, the disillusionment of radicals and liberals alike, and the institution of new electoral laws guaranteeing a moderate-to-right majority in future Dumas, the closing of the Second Duma effectively terminated the revolution. In the head-on confrontation with the autocracy, it was the latter—after all, the institution with the monopoly on the tools of power—that triumphed. The victory itself is undoubted; how meaningful it was, however, is open to question. In the revolutionary process new styles of behavior; new freedom of speech, press, and theater; a heightened political consciousness; and political participation had been tried out. The experience of revolution during three years from 1904 to 1907 was one that could not be erased, and it became an integral part of Russian life.

CHAPTER 28

The "Duma Monarchy," 1907–1914

. . . the land of infinite possibilities
—National Geographic Magazine *(November 1914)*

In 1914, *National Geographic* magazine published a special issue on the Russian Empire. Its pages gushed with enthusiasm, detailing the rich diversity of the many regions and peoples, marveling at their sudden prosperity, and predicting a great future for this burgeoning land over the course of the twentieth century. Instead, from that very moment, Russia plunged into a seven-year Armageddon of war and revolution, followed by decades of terror and even demographic annihilation; at the same time, the new Soviet state that emerged by the 1920s provided workers' and socialist movements throughout the world with the tempting (though, unfortunately, imaginary) example of true social equality incarnate, here and now.

The catastrophic failure of expectations—or, alternatively, the determination to vindicate the revolution—has made a dispassionate glance at the years immediately preceding the outbreak of world war in 1914 virtually impossible. Was Russia headed for disaster, was revolution imminent and "necessary," or, in contrast, were the new society and economy that followed the 1904–1907 revolution flourishing, only to be dashed by the misfortune of war in 1914? Each policy, event, and personality of the seven years between 1907 and 1914 has been painstakingly interpreted and reinterpreted to support one or the other position. The monarchist émigré historian Sergei Oldenburg praised the apparently paradoxical coexistence of autocracy with a constitutional regime and saw the signs of Russia's completed Europeanization in this period. Official Soviet historiography telescoped 1907–1914 into a broader vision of structural flaws in the tsarist social system, while Soviet dissident Alexander Solzhenitsyn perceived the key to Russia's renewal in the agrarian reforms implemented by P. A. Stolypin, and consequently the key to its demise in his assassination in 1911. The Gorbachëv-era intellectual Stanislav Govorukhin cast a nostalgic glance in his film *The Russia We Have Lost.* In America, Leopold Haimson argued that social fragmentation—a disconnect among governing elites, educated society, and workers and peasants—led to increasing discontent and eventually revolution.

Recently, however, a wealth of studies has begun to sketch a multidimensional picture that emphasizes the step-by-step workings of agrarian reform, the role of industrialists and entrepreneurs, the mechanisms of representational politics, the flourishing of print culture, and the burning questions of empire, nationality, regionalism, and nationalism. In some ways, the Russian Empire was not so different in 1914 from what it had been in 1881: the monarchy remained in place, if somewhat shaken; loopholes in the Fundamental Laws meant that reform would still be implemented from above, fully in the tradition of Peter the Great (Peter I) and Alexander II; and imperial policy continued to strive for the ideal of administrative uniformity. In other ways, a combination of long-term trends and results of revolution had changed the terms of Russian life: political parties and organizations, however circumscribed, were legal and could openly meet and campaign; the removal of censorship meant a burgeoning press and theatrical and artistic life; economic growth picked up after a slump, bringing industrialists and merchants to the forefront of urban life; and the most radical of the revolutionaries went into exile. Russia shared these features with contemporary Germany, Austria-Hungary, France, or the Ottoman Empire—that is, Europe, broadly defined. Between 1907 and 1914, newspaper readers in these countries were kept informed of a shadow that hung over all of them: sharp conflicts in Bosnia and Morocco, an increasingly self-propelling system of alliances, an intense arms race, and imperial rivalries soon involved them in a war that would transform Europe, Russia, and the world.

GOVERNMENT AND SOCIETY: A NEW DIALOGUE?

In the years leading up to 1905, the monarchy and the "progressive" intelligentsia had been locked in a cycle of mutual irritation and occasional open conflict; social problems remained irresolvable while unions, parties, and political organizations were illegal. Under the "Duma Monarchy," some of these tensions were defused, and the state and some among the intelligentsia found areas of common ground. By 1911, however, discontent in factories and universities resurfaced; new issues also emerged as industrial politics became increasingly important. Questions of the state's relation to national and religious questions were revitalized.

A New Institution: The Duma

Stolypin's June 3 "coup" did not change the bases of the Russian political order, which continued to be defined by the 1906 Fundamental Laws: the Third (1907–1911) and Fourth (1912–1917) Dumas formed a part of the state administrative apparatus rather than an independent branch of the government. What did change dramatically was the electoral law. If, in other European countries and the United States, the last third of the nineteenth century and the early twentieth century were a time of the gradual extension of the franchise, culminating in universal manhood suffrage and the vote for women by 1920, the process zigzagged in the Russian Empire. The sudden granting of a nearly universal male franchise in 1906 was abruptly rescinded a year later. The new electoral law of June 3, 1907, increased the relative weight of the landowners' curia in the provincial electoral assemblies and cut workers' and, more generally, urban representation. Probably the most significant provision was the limitation of participation from Poland, Siberia, and the Caucasus; Central Asian representation was eliminated altogether. The elections of 1907 for the Third Duma, and of 1912 for the Fourth, produced a majority of Octobrists and moderate Kadets; representatives of non-Russian regions retained only thirty-nine seats.

The Duma, recrafted in this fashion, added another institutional layer to the already top-heavy mechanism of state administration. Elections according to the new law justified the government's intention "to tear the State Duma from the hands of the revolutionaries, to assimilate it to the historical institutions, to bring it into the state system." The aim of the government, in other words, was to integrate the legislative function into the existing state administrative apparatus. To Nicholas, the parliament merely furnished an additional source for the mutually conflicting recommendations that bombarded him from State Council, Senate, and ministries. On issues such as the introduction of a naval general staff, for example, or of the zemstvo in the western provinces (discussed in the next section), the Duma vote broke differently from the decisions of the State Council and ministries of the navy and interior, respectively.

At the same time, the introduction of what was, after all, a representative institution, could not fail to transform the image of the monarchy. The new political system was something less than a constitutional monarchy, because of the state's tendency to absorb everything into itself; but it certainly looked like one. One Western historian, in fact, proposed that it was one, though damaged by the June 3 electoral law. More modestly, another has spoken of a "constitutional experiment," while Sergei Oldenburg, as mentioned above, marveled at the combination of autocracy with representative government. Like parliaments everywhere, the Duma functioned as theater, and party leaders like Pavel Milyukov (Kadets), V. A. Maklakov (Kadets), A. I. Guchkov (Octobrists), and the notorious extreme-right V. M. Purishkevich (Union of Russian People) became household names as the reading public pored over and discussed their speeches. As reconstituted in 1907, the parliamentary body represented a victory for the zemstvo world—for the intelligentsia who had clamored for a "crown" to the edifice of local institutions and organizations since their creation in the 1860s and 1870s. The short-lived attempt to create a more open, broader-based franchise had failed. The Duma created a bridge between the highly developed infrastructure of public organizations and local zemstvos—venerable quasi-political institutions in which members had had a long experience of parliamentary-style debate and discussion—and the central government, which until 1905 had remained largely oblivious to the sophisticated networks formed by these various societies.

The parliaments of 1907–1914 represented a grudging synthesis of the monarchy's ideal of an administratively controlled advisory body with the zemstvo progressive vision. At any rate, the cat-and-mouse game of the 1890s and early 1900s was broken.

Managers and Entrepreneurs: Industrial Russia

The long-term economic trends that had been interrupted by depression in 1902–1903, and then by revolution, picked up again by 1908–1909. The total growth rate between 1908 and 1913 was an extraordinary 8 percent, higher than that of any country in the industrializing world. Much of the stimulus for industrial expansion came from the resumption of state projects like railway building, production of transport equipment, and arms manufacture; some of the fastest-growing products were thus iron ore, coal, pig iron, and rolled steel. Economic historians have yet to reach any decisive conclusions regarding the role that consumer demand might have played, although Alexander Gerschenkron, for example, thought that it was a major driving force. A Soviet historian calculated a growth of 12.9 percent per annum for industrial goods and 4.7 percent for consumer goods (though the latter began from a less depressed base).

At any rate, engineering firms like Putilov, Kolomna Engineering, and Bryansk Ironworks (the three largest) flourished, while Phoenix Engineering, for example, recovered from the slump and diversified to manufacture machine tools. Iron- and steelworks tended toward consolidation, and twelve firms owned more than thirty iron ore mines by 1913. The three largest names in steel were Bryansk, South Russian Dnieper, and the Russo-Belgian Company; all three had their foot in coal as well, as did Makeevka Steel and New Russia Ironworks. Manufacture of electrotechnical equipment, sewing machines, internal combustion engines, and boilers grew with particular speed; 64 percent of the rapidly growing market for sewing machines, for example, could be satisfied by domestic production by 1913. In some branches of industry, foreign, and particularly French, investment remained significant, though the economy no longer depended on it; German firms—AEG in Kharkov and Riga, Siemens-Schuckert in St. Petersburg, Westinghouse in Moscow—accounted for half the capital invested in electrical engineering by 1913. The major banks underpinning investment became the Russo-Asiatic Bank (13 percent),

TABLE 1 Evolution of Production from 1900 to 1913

	1900	1908	1913
Population (millions)	132.9	152.5	170.9
	million poods		
Pig-iron	176.8	171.1	283
Coal	986.4	1,608.5	2,215.5
Iron and steel	163	147.5	246.5
Oil	631.1	528.6	561.3
Cotton (requirements)	16	21.2	25.9
Sugar	48.5	76.7	75.4 (1912: 112.8)

*one million poods = 36.11 million pounds

Source: From Roger Portal, *The Industrialization of Russia*, in H. J. Habakkuk and M. Postan, eds., *The Cambridge Economic History of Europe*, Volume VI. Copyright © 1965. Reprinted with the permission of Cambridge University Press.

the International Bank (10 percent), and the Foreign Trade, Azov-Don, and Trade Industry Banks (8 percent apiece). Industry in the Donets basin grew rapidly, and Poland, St. Petersburg, and the central industrial region remained key centers. By 1913 industry employed almost 3 million workers, up from 2 million in 1900.

At the same time, retail trade and the service sector (restaurants, hotels) expanded in cities throughout the empire, supplementing the traditional trade fairs. Unfortunately, this fascinating development remains completely unstudied. What has recently attracted attention, particularly among post-Soviet Russian historians, is the individuals and families who were responsible for trade and industry. The Gintsburg (banking and gold), Polyakov (banking, railroads), Brodsky (sugar), Knopp (cotton), and Ryabushinsky (banking) families were among the oldest and wealthiest, tracing their roots back to the middle of the nineteenth century. Some of the capitalists became famous for their patronage of the arts—most notably S. I. Mamontov, supporter of the painter Mikhail Vrubel and the sensational opera tenor Fëdor Shalyapin (1873–1938); P. M. and S. M. Tretyakov, whose art collection formed the kernel of the future Tretyakov Gallery in Moscow; and S. T. Morozov, supporter of the Moscow Art Theater. G. G. Solodovnikov, owner of a shopping arcade and a theater, willed more than 20 million rubles for the construction of affordable housing in Moscow; the two apartment buildings that were erected before 1917 are still in use. On a more modest level, mine and factory directors, shop managers, and chief engineers like Nikolai Avdakov, F. E. Enakiev, or A. I. Fenin made careers in the industrial enterprises of Ukraine, Poland, and the capital cities. Some of the new industrialists came from Germany, France, or Austria, as well as Poland or Russia.

Industrialists formed organizations to further their political aims. In 1901 steel producers, on the initiative of the French investment firm Société Générale, had united to form the Company for the Sale of Goods Produced by Russian Metallurgical Plants, or Prodamet; by 1904 coal producers had followed suit with the formation of Produgol. Similar syndicates were formed in other branches—for example, Prodvagon (*vagon* = railway car) and Prodparovoz (*parovoz* = steam engine). The most powerful group was the Association of Southern Coal and Steel Producers. A Confederation of the Northern and Baltic Engineering Industry was formed in 1902, and a Confederation of Agricultural Machine Building in 1906. The most important new national organization was the Association of Industry and Trade (AIT), formed in 1905 and chaired by the former president of the Association of Southern Coal and Steel Producers, Nikolai Avdakov. The government took some steps to meet the needs of Russian industry by establishing a new Ministry of Trade and Industry in 1905. A major, though ultimately unsuccessful, business-government conference convened in May 1908, bringing together Duma members, business experts, representatives of banks, the AIT, and the major iron, steel, and engineering firms. A commission to regulate the domestic iron market in 1913 also represented an effort at state-business cooperation. On the whole, though, the structure of government was inadequate to lend support to industrial Russia. The post-1907 Duma, to industrialists and managers, had become a sort of super-zemstvo, overrepresenting the countryside and failing to provide channels for the became *khoziain* (the independent proprietor), *khutor* (the independent farm), and, a couple of years later, *zemleustroistvo* (land organization). It is to overemphasize the magnitude of this planned transformation: it was to e real private property, to put the Russian peasant on his own feet for the e in many centuries, and to transform the countryside into a patchwork of dent fields.

rst promulgated by imperial decree, the 1906 laws were approved by both rs of the Duma on June 14, 1910. In addition to earlier provisions abolish- commune, the later legislation introduced a program of resettlement to rel- npopulated regions of the empire like Kazakhstan and Siberia. This was 's answer to the problem of gentry expropriation, so loudly debated in the Dumas: instead of taking away any gentry land—a possibility that he dis- categorically—Stolypin proposed that the "virgin lands" of the east be to peasants from European Russia who might wish to move there. It was, , a program of colonization supposed to bring the lands of the Kazakh, and Mongolian steppes under cultivation.

retely, so far as individual peasants were concerned, the reforms were sup- work as follows: The peasant who already regularly farmed a unified plot simply received it as his household's private property. If he belonged to a e in which repartition was practiced, he could petition for a particular land to become his own. If, as frequently happened, the commune did not ufficient land, resettlement to the east was encouraged.

eral meaningful ways, the agrarian reform was a consequence of the 1904– olution. Stolypin's legislation "solved" the agrarian question as it had crys- n the debates of the first two Dumas. Posed initially by the great reforms 860s, the key sticking points for improving Russia's agrarian structure re- the division of land into strips insufficient for a single peasant's livelihood; tion of gentry expropriation; and the problem of making agricultural im- nts where much of the peasantry remained illiterate and uneducated. addressed each of these issues: his plan for exit from the commune in- rovisions for the consolidation of land; gentry expropriation was settled by itution of his colonial program; and further legislation promoted the use ced farming methods, encouraging peasants to engage in intensive rather ensive cultivation, improving the soil through planting of nitrous crops peas or beans) and so on. In addition, much to the initial resentment of the n the left, Stolypin's reforms actually coopted much of their own agrarian , with a significant difference: whereas they had wished a spontaneous im- tion from below, he had legislated much-needed agrarian change in the al imperial manner—as a revolution from above. The abolition of the e, land improvement, and other measures had all been discussed and ngly worked out by radical statisticians, agronomists, soil scientists, and icultural specialists working in the Free Economic Society and elsewhere. s legislation was a master stroke in the purely political sense: by coopting l program yet conserving the monarchy's insistence on the integrity of nd, Stolypin made opposition to his plan extremely difficult.

industrial lobby; managers were forced to rely on older and less effective methods of ministerial influence. Industrial managers never became a part of Russia's inner elite, confronting frequent antipathy from monarchy and public alike.

Social Problems and the Revolutionary Movement

The resumption of industrial growth was accompanied by a renewed strike movement. After a five-year hiatus, eight mine strikes involving three thousand workers broke out in the Donbass in 1911, affecting among others the Golubov, Seleznevsky, and New Russian mines. Steelworkers followed the next year. In early 1912 several thousand workers at the Lena Goldfields in Siberia struck to protest low wages and harsh conditions. In the absence of a local police force, they virtually took over running their settlement until the government called in an army division. The conflict exploded in April, when troops confronted a crowd of five thousand, killing two hundred people and wounding at least two hundred more. Gold mining, in Siberia as in California, was a peculiar business involving heightened greed, exploitation, and vigilantism. Nevertheless, the events at Lena, reminiscent of the chaos in Siberia that accompanied the defeated troops returning from war with Japan, touched off a wave of sympathy strikes throughout industrial Russia. In 1911 and 1912, twenty-five thousand workers struck in the Donbass and as many again from 1913 to mid-1914; many of the strikes were prompted by wage and shop control issues. Employer responses varied, ranging from pay increases—for example, at the Uspensky Coal and Iron Company in 1913—to suppression with the aid of Cossack forces—for example, at the Rykovsky mine in December 1913, when miners and employees asked for higher pay, a school, and baths. Strikes became fewer but larger in the first half of 1914.

The strike movement, together with lobbying by industrialists' organizations, was not without results on a national scale. In June 1912 the Duma passed, and the tsar approved, a sickness and accident insurance law that was more extensive than any in the Western world. Among its provisions were the establishment of workers' sick funds based on joint employer-employee contributions and a reaffirmation of 1903 legislation requiring employers to cover medical care.

As in the early 1900s, the labor movement coincided with a radicalization of the universities. A student strike in 1908 attracted little public support. In 1910, however, the death of Lev Tolstoy prompted student memorial services that turned into mass student demonstrations. Crisis came in 1911, when students protested the ensuing police crackdown, as well as government suppression of campus politics in general, with a national strike. At Moscow University, three professors resigned their administrative (but not teaching) posts as a protest against police intervention; when the Ministry of Education, with the tsar's and Stolypin's approval, dismissed the three, the faculty responded with a mass resignation that ultimately involved a third of all professors. They were reinstated only under the Provisional Government in 1917 (by A. A. Manuilov, the new minister of education—one of the three professors who resigned originally).

The year 1908 found the leaders of the major revolutionary parties—Bolsheviks,

Mensheviks, Socialist Revolutionaries, anarchists—once more in exile, in Geneva, London, or Paris. The Bolsheviks were split by factional struggles. Maxim Gorky hosted a "school" for the discussion of Marxist philosophy at his villa on the island of Capri, off the southern Italian coast, where Alexander Bogdanov and Anatoly Lunacharsky discussed the empiriocriticism of Mach and Avenarius—the philosophical basis for their notion of "God-building," by which they meant that socialists could create God by constructing a socialist society. Lenin, impatient with such theorizing, formed an alternate discussion circle at Longjumeau, outside Paris, that focused on more practical questions of party organization and revolutionary politics. The Menshevik leader Yuly Martov, in London, counseled a temporary alliance with the liberals; while Viktor Chernov (1876–1952) and the Socialist Revolutionaries—discredited, in addition, by the 1909 revelation that Azef was a double agent—abandoned their defense of the peasant commune. Inside Russia, the revolutionary parties continued to be represented in the Duma, but with dwindling popular support: by 1910 Social Democratic Party membership had fallen to 10,000 from 150,000 in 1907; only five or six Bolshevik committees remained active.

Following 1907, the liberal intelligentsia went through a phase of helpless depression, not knowing which was worse—the fury of the *narod* (people) or the brute force used by the regime to subdue it. By 1909, a group that included the Marxists-turned-idealists Struve, Berdyaev, Bulgakov, and Frank published the sensational volume *Vekhi (Landmarks),* in which they questioned the traditional oppositional role of the intelligentsia and proposed a return to the religious values of the *narod. Vekhi* signaled the fragmentation of the intelligentsia as a unified political force, and in the 1910s individual members became absorbed in the broader patterns of cultural activity or political organization.

Nationality and Religion

A recent historian of the Russian Empire has commented that, insofar as there was any policy at all toward non-Russians in the post-1907 period, it was a tendency to slip back into older patterns of imperial rule: a reliance on national elites and a looser structure of empire, with considerable administrative diversity. Non-Russians did not participate significantly in any emerging dialogue between government and society: the Third Duma counted 24 percent non-Russians, and the Fourth included 19 percent. The only exception was the Baltic German elite. The Polish Club's representation was abruptly cut, and the National Democratic leader Roman Dmowski resigned in 1909. Muslims now counted only nine delegates instead of thirty-three; the twenty Ukrainians no longer constituted an independent fraction. In Duma debates, almost all the non-Russian delegates supported education in the native language in the borderlands. Russian nationalism in the parliament, represented by the Nationalist Party, which the Union of Russian People sponsored, sharpened and became openly directed against Jews, Poles, Germans, Finns, and foreigners in general. At the same time, the imperial borderlands and

particularly Poland, Finland, Ukraine, and south Rus
industrial upswing.

The fall of Pobedonostsev in 1905 removed a signifi
form. The 1906 law on religious toleration was echo
the Orthodox Church itself. In 1911–1912 negotiatio
reopened, though they bore no fruit until after the Fel

REFORM FROM ABOVE: ST

Whatever innovations had been introduced into Rus
sues confronting Russia immediately following the
question of agrarian reform and the issue of imperial
tion—were addressed in the traditional fashion of t
The new minister of the interior, P. A. Stolypin (186
resort to Article 87 of the Fundamental Laws (see the
cades: The Revolution of 1904–1907") to bypass the
legislation; only afterward did he bother to garner sup
style and the magnitude of Stolypin's reform progra
modern Russia's great reformers—Peter I, Alexander

A brilliant and ruthless administrator, Stolypin h
ranks of the central government but in the provincial
from Petersburg University in natural sciences Stoly
shal of the nobility in Kovno, in Lithuania, and
Province. He had dealt summarily and mercilessly
his region and, later, with others on a national sca
hands-on experience of the greatest problem plaguin
"agrarian question." Stolypin was appointed ministe

Land Reform

Immediately upon the closing of the First Duma in
sive program of agrarian reform. The initial agraria
proposed the following radical measures: the comm
any member would be permitted to obtain the title
consolidate strips of land into a single plot. These co
part of a much larger conceptual schema that was in
ture of Russian agriculture and peasant life. The thr
break apart the peasant commune once and for all.
a new type of person and a new type of agricultu
countryside. The independent peasant proprietor,
ual farm were to become the basic unit of agricultur
ditional commune, much exalted by Slavophiles a

The real genius of Stolypin's reforms was that it took the peasant—at least the male head of the household—seriously as a person and an economic actor. Working toward the acquisition of an independent farm was clearly something that made sense for an ambitious peasant, or even one who wanted to ensure a reasonable livelihood. The reforms might be seen as a sort of "agrarian capitalism," for they favored peasants who were willing and able to make a profit from their labor, removing the burden of the poorer peasants in the commune who had hampered their progress. In a direct dismissal of the communal daydreams of Slavophiles and populists, this very unsocialistic policy basically left poor peasants to their own devices; presumably, they would move to the cities to work in factories or shops as the countryside prospered. This is what became known as Stolypin's "wager on the strong"—a policy that favored the formation of a sort of peasant "middle class."

Stolypin's independent proprietor became in a sense the symbol of the new age. Whether a peasant farmer making his risky way to the Kazakh steppes, a worker buying his own shop, an Old Believer industrialist, or a landlord turning his hand to manufacturing, the new proprietor personified the bourgeois ethic and the spirit of entrepreneurship that pervaded the Russian town, city, and countryside in the prosperous postrevolutionary years.

Indeed, as the various parts of the legislation were implemented, peasants reacted immediately to the new possibilities unfolding before them. In the eight years between the first laws and the outbreak of World War I in 1914, some 24 percent of the peasant population took advantage of the laws to establish their own farms. More participated in the eastward move, boarding trains to Tashkent or Bukhara to start a new life in the Asian steppes. The agricultural "specialists" and liberals who had initially resented or opposed the reforms were drawn, as time went on, into the fold: from about 1909, indeed, it was the specialists who, once again, took the program back into their own hands and were responsible (rather than government agencies) for the actual process of implementing of the reforms.

The Western Zemstvo and Finland

Stolypin's position in the Duma was based on an alliance with both Octobrists and nationalists. Though an imperial administrator first, he has often been seen as an instrument of specifically Russian national aims. Russian nationalism was a new phenomenon that only became an identifiable political force in this period, though elements were clearly in evidence in pre-1905 movements like the Black Hundreds.

Discussions about extending zemstvo institutions to the nine western provinces (essentially the territory of Poland, Lithuania, and Belorussia) originated in the region itself in the late 1890s—about the time Stolypin was serving in Kovno. The Polish uprising had prevented the establishment of zemstvos there in the 1860s (see the chapter "Alexander II and the Era of the Great Reforms, 1855–1870"); their introduction now would institute administrative uniformity with the central provinces, as well as some measure of self-government. A 1903 law set up so-called margarine (i.e., imitation) zemstvos, to be entirely appointed by the local governor and the Ministry of Internal Affairs. In 1906 Stolypin, thwarted by the State Council when he tried to circumvent the Duma by once more resorting to Article 87, proposed legislation introducing an elective zemstvo for the western provinces, with provisions for protecting the Russian minority. The measure reached the floor in 1910, passing 165 votes to 139 after violent debate, only to be rejected by the State Council. Turning to more reliable methods, Stolypin took advantage of a brief recess of both legislative chambers to promulgate the zemstvo law administratively (again, Article 87). In its new form, the zemstvo was introduced in only six provinces (excluding Vilna, Grodno, and Kovno—the Lithuanian provinces); elections were based on a system of national curiae, establishing priority for Russians and excluding Jews altogether; executive boards were to be staffed by a majority from the first curia—that is, Russians. Traditional administrative methods had resolved another crucial issue—this time of imperial uniformity versus local nationalism.

Stolypin reaffirmed and extended Nicholas II's already unfortunate Finnish policy. In 1910, both Duma and State Council passed a law abrogating the legislative powers of the Finnish Diet, essentially bringing the autonomy of Finland to an end and inspiring the rightist Purishkevich's exclamation "*Finis Finlandiae!*"

THE NEW POLITICAL CULTURE: PRESS AND PUBLIC OPINION

The least ambiguous result of 1905 was the easing of censorship. Between 1905 and 1917, many writings of the political thinkers Herzen and Chaadaev, and even the early-nineteenth-century dramatist Griboedov, saw the light for the first time. Literary publishing houses proliferated. Under the direction of Mikhail Gershenzon, Valery Bryusov, Lyubov Gurevich, and Maxim Gorky, they released the works of Russian philosophers and poets of the nineteenth century, while also creating an infrastructure for the prolific production of Blok, Bely, Berdyaev, Ivanov, and others. *Among Books*, by N. A. Rubakin (1862–1946), chronicled literary output—the equivalent of *Books in Print*—and went through several editions. Newspaper publishers V. M. Doroshevich and N. I. Pastukhov followed an earlier example set by Suvorin *(New Times)* and S. M. Propper in creating their journalistic empires. Sytin's liberal *The Russian Word* recovered from a momentary drop in circulation to reach a readership of 1 million in 1917. "Thick journals" like the *Messenger of Europe* and *Russian Thought* flourished. New titles appeared every year, though not as many as the record 608 in 1906. Among them was *Gazeta kopeika*—literally, *Penny Paper*—a paper clearly intended for working and other lower classes, which reached a phenomenal circulation of 250,000 in only its second year, 1909. The boulevard press exploded, entertaining and shocking readers with tales of crime, hooliganism, and suicide as well as coverage of events like the Lena Goldfields massacre and the sinking of the *Titanic.*

Public opinion had played some role in Russian politics since the Russo-Turkish War of 1877–1878 (see the chapter "The Turbulent Seventies"). The expansion of print culture and the accessibility of news to a broad public increased the potential of writers and readers to influence events. Tolstoy's death, the en masse professorial resignations of 1911, and the Lena events were drawn into the vortex of public opinion, provoking floods of articles, arguments, and commentaries. The publication of *Vekhi (Landmarks)* produced just such a journalistic storm in 1909. So, in 1912, did the affair of Bishop Hermogen—a member of the Holy Synod who was banished to his diocese, provoking speculation on the influence at court of Grigory Rasputin (see below), whom he opposed and with whom he had even had a fistfight. Perhaps the most dramatic scandal was the Beilis affair, reminiscent of the sensational Dreyfus case in France twenty years earlier, in which a Jewish army officer had been accused of spying for Germany. In 1913, a Jewish clerk, Mendel Beilis, was put on trial in Kiev for the murder of a child, allegedly committed to obtain blood for purposes of Jewish ritual. Although it was soon established that the child had been killed by thieves, the trial dragged on for two years, allowing ample time for an extraordinary demonstration of anti-Semitism by prosecutors and police authorities. In the end the jury acquitted Beilis, though insisting that a ritual murder of some sort had occurred.

The publishing explosion took a different pattern for subcultures in the empire. The Old Believers published scores of new journals and liturgical texts. The Islamic and Ukrainian presses fared less well: after a brief period of openness in 1905–1907, censorship was reinstituted, and many new journals were shut down. In 1912, however, a Persian-language paper, *Bukhara-i Sharif (Noble Bukhara),* and an Uzbek paper, *Turan,* came out for about a year. The Russian Academy of Sciences acknowledged Ukrainian as a legitimate language for the first time in 1905. A Russian-language Armenian press flourished in the diaspora, particularly in south Russia, directed by figures like Grigor Artsruni, who published the journal *Mshak (The Cultivator).*

As significant as the loosening of censorship was the 1905 law on religious toleration. As a result, Old Believers built churches, held open religious processions, produced and sold icons—in short, became a visible and vibrant part of urban life. The Muslim congresses of the revolutionary period were followed by an era of secret societies, mostly in the guise of organizations "for the dissemination of knowledge." The Jadid (Muslim reformist) movement gained considerable adherents in 1910–1914, influenced in part by the Young Turk revolution (1908), which led to constitutional government in the Ottoman Empire, and by revolution in Persia. In the meantime, reformist clergy and laity in the Orthodox Church itself clamored for a law that would give them freedom equal to that promised to other religious groups. In 1911–1912, a second serious attempt was made to convene an Orthodox Church council, but it also came to naught.

Societies and organizations flourished in the freer atmosphere that followed the harsh repressions of the revolutionary period. The four years from 1909 to 1913 constitute an unusual and happy episode in modern Russian history, when, recovering from their initial resentment at Stolypin's policies, the zemstvos, local and imperial economic societies, meteorological and agricultural associations, and professional organizations met regularly and on a national scale.

The "Duma Monarchy" was a golden age of theater and opera. Producers and playwrights took full advantage of the right to portray monarchs on stage or screen. Nikolai Rimsky-Korsakov's *Tale of the Invisible City of Kitezh* (first performed in 1907 in St. Petersburg) and *The Golden Cockerel* (1909 in Moscow) captivated audiences. Stolypin was attending a performance of Rimsky's *Tale of the Tsar Saltan* in Kiev, on September 14, 1911, when he was assassinated by a police agent who was also a member of a revolutionary organization.

In 1915, a remarkable art exhibit opened in Petrograd: called "0.10," it displayed canvases of a type never before seen in the European art world. Paintings of geometric objects and other "nonobjective"—that is, "nonrealistic"—subjects densely covered the walls of the gallery. In a corner, precisely in the spot where icons usually hung in Russian houses and huts, was the new creation of the artist Kasimir Malevich (1878–1935)—a slightly irregular black square, luminous on its white field. The "0.10" exhibit was a dramatic opening sally in a battle proclaimed by the artists, poets, and writers of the Russian avant-garde against all "old" and traditional forms of art—including, this time, the golden sunsets and azure skies of the Symbolists as well as the earlier civic art and poetry.

The Russian avant-garde, the most radical of any such movement in Europe, took shape from a variety of artistic currents. They called themselves Futurists, Imagists, Clarists, and Suprematists (the name Malevich gave his art). If the artistic movements of the 1910s constituted an offshoot of the rich culture of the Silver

Malevich's Black Square in the icon's place at the "0.10" exhibit, 1915. *Andre Nakov.*

Age, they also represented a real departure from its artistic canons and the creation of a new culture. The 1915 exhibit followed the visit of the Italian Futurist Tommaso Marinetti in January 1914, and also the founding manifesto of Russian Futurism, composed by the poets Alexei Kruchënykh, Vladimir Mayakovsky, and Velimir Khlebnikov and the painter David Burlyuk in 1912: "Throw Pushkin, Dostoevsky, Tolstoy, et al., overboard from the Ship of Modernity." One theme of the Russian avant-garde was the struggle against nature; as one statement put it, "the deep forest is disgusting and so are uncultivated steppes and unutilized waterfalls . . . what is beautiful is what bears the marks of man's organizing hand." Others were the glorification of technology, human immortality, rejection of the past, and transformation of life, language, and ultimately the world to create a new reality. The 1910s were an extraordinarily creative period for these artists. But they had yet to say their final word in the 1920s, when the art of the avant-garde became, for a time, the art of revolution and of the new regime, officially endorsed by the Soviet Commissariat of Enlightenment under the leadership of Anatoly Lunacharsky.

CELEBRATING RUSSIA: THE ROMANOV TERCENTENARY

On February 21, 1913, a triumphal religious procession, carrying the holy icons of the Virgin of Vladimir, Iversk, and Kazan, wound its way through the Petersburg streets toward Kazan Cathedral. In the months surrounding the lavish celebrations, newspapers and provincial journals were filled with talk of the three-hundred-year anniversary of Russia's second ruling dynasty. The historian Sergei Platonov (1860–1933)—known to most Russians as the author of their school textbook on Russian history—spoke before large crowds, extolling the achievements of the Romanov dynasty in the three hundred years since the *zemsky sobor* of 1613 had installed Mikhail Romanov as tsar and thereby ended the dynastic crisis known as the Time of Troubles. Historians published special popular volumes dedicated to the history of Romanov rule from Mikhail and Alexei Mikhailovich to Alexander III. It was a time to celebrate, and to reflect on, the achievements, and problems, of one of the few remaining powerful ruling houses of Europe.

The celebrations of the Romanov tercentenary included, as well, a voyage by the tsar to the central provinces of Russia. On May 15 he and his family set out for Vladimir, then Suzdal, and along the Volga to Nizhny Novgorod, Kostroma, Yaroslavl, and Rostov, finishing in Moscow. Everywhere he was greeted by manifestations—with varying degrees of orchestration by the authorities—of popular enthusiasm, including well-rehearsed displays of gymnastics and dance by proud and excited schoolchildren. The ceremonies in Kostroma were particularly magnificent and, apparently, sincere; even the most skeptical observers acknowledged the real sentiment with which the huge crowds welcomed the monarch. The voyage—a traditional element of the monarchy's image since Alexander II's journey through Russia in the 1860s—had a simultaneously encouraging and sobering effect on

The Imperial family leaving the Trinity Cathedral in Kostroma—part of the tercentenary celebrations, May 1913. From the illustrated weekly, *Niva,* June 1913. *Library of Congress. Courtesy Richard Wortman.*

Nicholas II. Subsequently, he wrote that he had been impressed by the creative potential and power of labor that he had witnessed, yet sobered by the poverty and injustice he saw as well among the people. Nicholas cut an imposing figure in his ceremonial role, as did his family: a dignified and handsome man in his uniform and epaulets, he traveled surrounded by his lovely daughters and the frail and delicate heir to the throne—the Tsarevich Alexis.

The court of Nicholas II continued and elaborated on the ceremonial tradition of his Romanov forebears—such an important contribution to the effectiveness of the monarchy's rule over the centuries. In the years after the 1905 revolution in particular, an appellation to history and tradition became the fashion in the life of the court. Muscovite dress became the style of many court balls, and Nicholas had a village in the style of old Muscovy built at Tsarskoe Selo, where he spent much of his time. The new fashion doubtless resonated among the Russian bourgeois public, for whom national history—often appearing on the pages of popular journals like *Niva (Plowlands),* or even in special publications like *Russia's Past* or *The*

Russian Archive—had great appeal and helped to form their own sense of national identity.

The relatively successful ceremonial aspects of Nicholas's role as monarch concealed increasing rifts and tensions in the conception of the monarchy itself. Nicholas, until the bitter end, proved unable to abandon his cherished and ill-founded vision of the glory and self-sufficiency of the principle of autocracy. He was disappointed, for example, by a salute to him by the generally cooperative Third Duma, because it (quite consciously and after much venomous debate) left out his title of Autocrat. He tried to have as little to do with the proceedings of the representative body as possible, leaving the task to Stolypin. Failing to exploit the potential loyalty of the middle classes, who demonstrated their willingness to support the monarchy in the tercentenary ceremonies, Nicholas consistently fell back on the support of the autocracy's traditional yet no longer powerful bulwark—the gentry and aristocracy.

Worse, Nicholas, always a good family man, withdrew into the crisis of his son's hemophilia precisely at the moment when his guidance—given his own insistence on holding the reins of government in his hands—was most desperately needed. In 1910, a new figure appeared on the scene of court life in the person of Grigory Rasputin (1871–1918). A peasant who claimed to be a holy man, Rasputin (whose name means "dissipated") seems to have cast a sort of spell over the Empress Alexandra, whom he convinced of his abilities to make blood coagulate. Managing to keep his behavior within the bounds of relative decency while he was at court, Rasputin gave full rein to his impulse toward drunkenness and debauchery in less prestigious surroundings. In any case, within the next few years, Rasputin's religious persona managed to draw the empress, and through her a number of her retinue and the tsar as well, into his circle of influence; by 1913 or so, Rasputin had a powerful hold over the spiritual being of the imperial family. Rasputin's influence hardly went unnoticed in government circles; increasingly, Duma deputies, zemstvo representatives, and members of the aristocracy alike began to speak out against this embarrassing phenomenon.

There was a clear disjuncture between Nicholas's exalted vision of the monarchy and his own ability to fulfill a role that, had he himself defined it more modestly, might have steadily diminished to everyone's satisfaction.

ON THE EVE: WAR AND DIPLOMACY IN THE BALKANS

The Ottoman Empire had been decisively pushed out of Europe in 1878. By 1887, Bulgarian autonomy and the independence of Greece, Montenegro, Romania, and Serbia set the terms for a new power game in the Balkans. In an era that followed Italian and German unification (1861 and 1871, respectively), the Balkan states had unifying ambitions of their own; Serbian nationalists in particular nurtured dreams of a Greater Serbia that would include the linguistically and ethnically South Slavic territories of Bosnia-Herzegovina and Macedonia. Thus when Austria annexed Bosnia-Herzegovina outright in 1908, thumbing its nose at both Turkey and Russia, the biggest losers were Serbia and Montenegro, for whom the path to the Adriatic was now closed. The Austrian annexation also provoked Nicholas II to abandon for good the traditional links with Germany and Austria and to throw Russia's lot in with Britain and France. As Turkey became successively embroiled in the Young Turk Revolution (1908), an Albanian revolt (1910–1912), and a war with Italy over Tripoli (1911), the Balkan Slavs turned their sights southward, seeking compensation for the loss of Bosnia-Herzegovina. Bulgaria, Greece, and Montenegro had overcome their differences (mostly hinging on the status of Macedonia) to form an alliance against the Ottomans.

The First Balkan War that followed (the four Balkan countries against Turkey) was a disaster for Turkey: the 1913 Treaty of London codified its loss of all remaining European territories, as well as of Crete and the Aegean Islands, and created an independent Albania. Military defeat in the meantime provoked civil unrest in Istanbul. The Balkan victors, predictably, quarreled over the spoils: a Second Balkan War (roughly following the pattern of the Prussian-Austrian conflict of 1866) essentially pitted Serbia (eventually joined by Greece, Rumania, and Montenegro) against Bulgaria. The creation of an independent Albania upset Serbian designs on Albanian territories, so Serbia turned, instead, to carve parts of Macedonia away from Bulgaria. Bulgaria lost, and the Treaty of Bucharest (August 1913) divided Macedonia among three nations, doubling Serbian territory, enabling Greece to stretch north beyond Salonica, and leaving a small piece of eastern Macedonia to Bulgaria. Throughout these conflicts, Russian diplomacy consistently backed the Serbs, the Slav brothers of the last Russo-Turkish War (1877–1878), though never going far enough to risk direct confrontation with Austria.

The struggle for power and territory in the Balkans unfolded against a dense network of imperial rivalries and diplomatic alliances among the Great Powers. Conflicts and encounters in Morocco, South Africa, or Manchuria could be as crucial to European politics as events on the continent itself. Russia, as we have seen, was a major imperial player not only in eastern Europe but also in Central and East Asia, although it had no overseas colonies in Africa or the Caribbean. England, France, Germany, and Russia backed their stakes abroad with a significant military and naval buildup. By the time a second international peace conference convened at The Hague in 1907, this time at the initiative of Theodore Roosevelt, the European powers were in fact embarking on an all-out arms race. The Anglo-German naval rivalry, in particular, accelerated beginning in 1906 as the two countries strove to outdo each other in the construction of bigger and more modern battleships. In the meantime, the European alliance system underwent adjustments and realignments. The Franco-Russian alliance of 1894 laid the groundwork for a further rapprochement between those two countries. In 1904, Britain and France signed an Entente Cordiale, promising diplomatic cooperation; Russia joined in 1907, thus forming the Triple Entente. Austria-Hungary remained allied with Germany, and also with Italy, since the three had signed a Triple Alliance in 1881. The combination of Balkan troubles, the intensity of armament (or in the Russian case, rearmament after the Japanese fiasco) and imperial rivalry, and an excessively

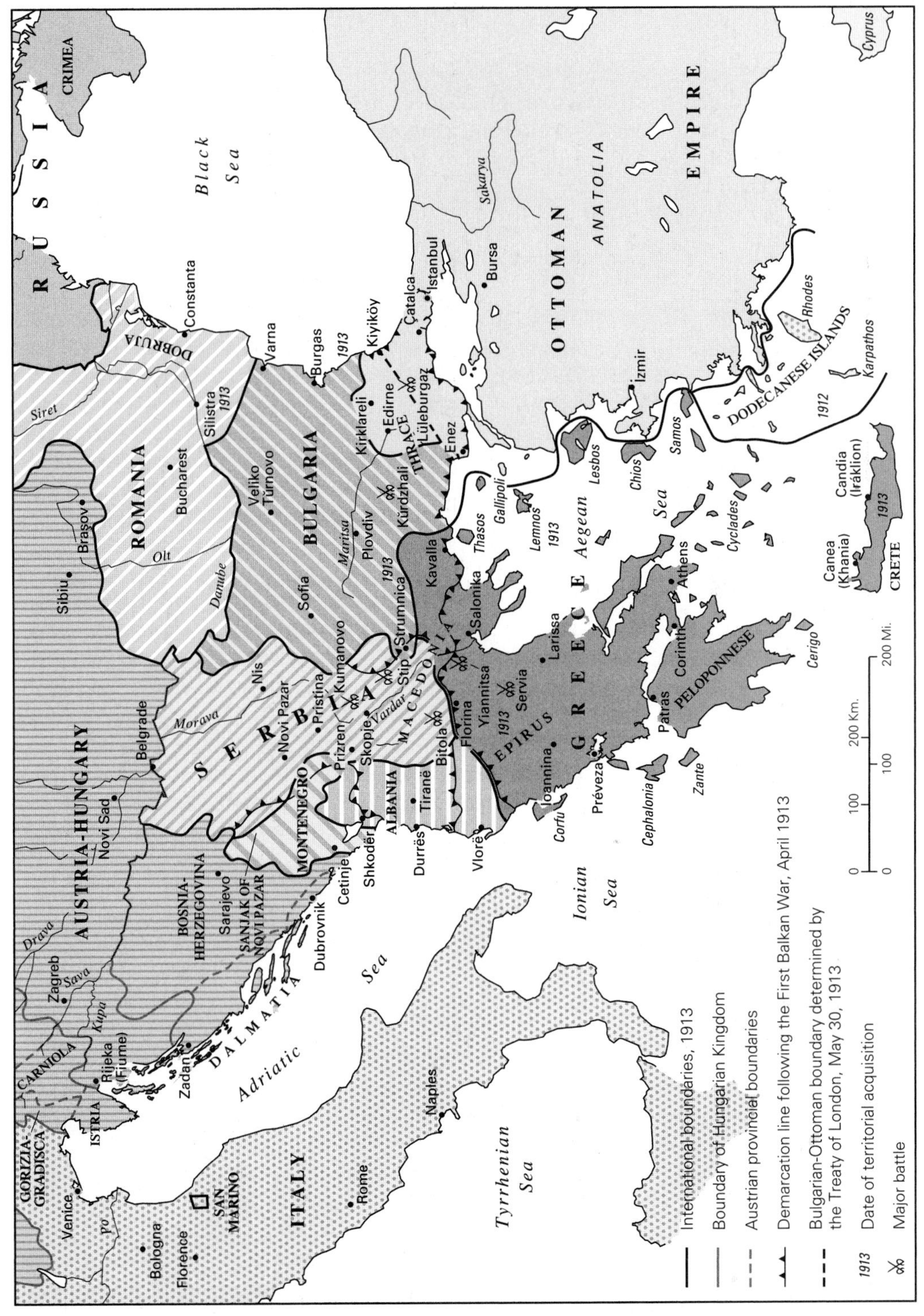

The Balkan peninsula, 1912–1913. *From Paul Magocsi,* Historical Atlas of East Central Europe. *Copyright © 1933. Reprinted by permission of the University of Washington Press.*

perfect and automatized system of alliances meant that, when in June 1914 the Bosnian Serb nationalist Gavrilo Princip assassinated Austrian archduke Franz Ferdinand in Sarajevo and Austria responded with an ultimatum to Serbia, the countries of Europe were, one by one, drawn into war. Russia came to Serbia's defense; Germany backed Austria; and Russia's ally, France, backed Russia. On August 4, 1914, the German army invaded Belgium on its way to Paris, bringing Britain, bound by treaty to defend a neutral Belgium, into the war.

PART IV

Russia's Turbulent Twentieth Century and After, Since 1914

In contrast to Russia's "long nineteenth century" (1796–1914), the Soviet period (1917–1991) represented a major retreat from Europe. The blockades and battlegrounds of the War of 1914–1918 cut Russia off physically from France and Britain, its allies. That war led to the fall of the monarchy in 1917 and a short-lived attempt to introduce democracy and other Western institutions onto Russian soil. The attempt failed, and the ensuing Bolshevik Revolution of October 1917 ushered in the seventy-four-year rule of a Soviet (Communist) regime set on remaking itself and the world into a socialist paradise. After a bloody civil war between 1918 and 1921, the death of the Soviet founder Vladimir Lenin in 1924, and a decade or so of experiment and power struggle, new rulers emerged, led by Iosif Stalin. These leaders established in the 1930s one of the most brutal regimes in modern history, sending hundreds of thousands of people to their deaths. That regime abolished capitalism, imposed collectivization of farming and rapid industrialization, arrested oppositionists—real or imagined—and fixed rigid controls over society and culture.

In spite of the social trauma, Russian and other Soviet nationalities fought and defeated the Nazi invaders in World War II, and the Soviet regime survived until 1991. In the decades after Stalin's death in 1953, his successors softened some of the harsher aspects of Soviet rule, but the system remained in place through the eras of Nikita Khrushchëv and Leonid Brezhnev. Mikhail Gorbachëv, who came to power in 1985 as leader of the Communist Party, launched radical reforms that proved inadequate to meet the rising demands of key portions of the population. The system came to an end in 1991, the Soviet Union lost most of its former empire in the form of national republics, and a new leadership attempted to create a modern pluralistic society in what became the Russian Republic.

Throughout the years of Soviet power, a Russian emigration living all over the world sought to nourish some of the family, cultural, and religious values and traditions that the leaders of their former homeland had destroyed. Since 1991, many Russians inside the country have rediscovered and exalted these once reviled traditions in the search for a new set of values and identities.

CHAPTER 29

Russia in World War I, 1914–1917

In the event of [Russia's military] defeat, the possibility of which in a struggle with a foe like Germany cannot be overlooked, social revolution in its most extreme form is inevitable.

—*P. N. Durnovo, tsarist official, in a memorandum to Tsar Nicholas II, February 1914*

The above-quoted words, written by a devoted servant of the monarchy a little more than half a year before the outbreak of World War I, turned out to be all too prophetic. World War I, or the Great War—as it was once called—proved destructive enough to pull down four empires, including the Russian. Russia entered a war that affected not only Europe but eventually parts of East Asia, India, the Middle East, Africa, North America, and Australasia. One by one—catapulted by prior agreements, imperial ambition, and opportunism, among other reasons—the nations marched to war: Austria and Serbia, followed by Germany, Russia, Belgium, France, and England. In their wake came the Ottoman Empire and Bulgaria on the side of the Central Powers (Germany and Austria), and Italy, Greece, Romania, China, Japan, and the United States on the side of the Allies (Russia, France, and Britain). The geopolitics of empire pulled in people of color from the colonies of the Great Powers. This war and its aftermath flung Oxford dons into the Arabian desert; pious Sikhs of India against armored trains operating in Turkmenia; Viennese and Budapest journalists and Bohemian peasants into the whirlwind of Siberia; Senegalese porters and Vietnamese cooks into northern France; Bavarian farmers into the Kenya bushland; and cattlemen from the deep interior of Australia into Palestine and Baku.

Communism, fascism, Nazism, the Holocaust, World War II, the Cold War, and the Arab-Israeli conflict can all be traced to the forces unleashed in the Great War of 1914. New weapons—machine guns, tanks, warplanes, and poison gas—raised the death toll exponentially. Media technologies heightened communications among people and also increased their power to persuade. The public mind in all belligerent states was shaped by wartime propaganda that left a residue of hate for decades. When the historian reaches the rocketing events set off in 1914, it becomes tempting—if not mandatory—to pose "what if" questions that force us to confront issues of causation and moral judgment. Might Russia have survived in something of its former state had there been no war? Should Russia have avoided entering the conflict? Could Tsar Nicholas II have saved his country from revolution had he allowed educated society more participation in wartime governance? When pondering these matters, it is prudent to remember that the people who made the fatal decisions at the time did not have the wisdom that sometimes comes with hindsight. Wars almost never turn out the way they are envisioned at their beginning.

THE CLASH OF ARMS

The European alliance system, built up since 1870, was put to the test in 1914. The assassination in June of Austrian Archduke Franz Ferdinand triggered a crisis that pitted Serbia against the Habsburg monarchy like a bothersome gnat on a big ox. When Germany backed Habsburg Austria's decision to humiliate and punish Serbia, the Russian government had to decide whether and how it would back its ally Serbia. One way would be to mobilize Russian troops on the Austrian border. However, the prewar general mobilization plan envisioned only a war against both Germany and Austria, and there was no plan for separate or partial mobilization against either power. The tsar had not known this because—even more astonishingly—the chief of staff, General N. N. Yanushkevich (1868–1918), did not inquire about it until months after he took up his duties. The decision to order general mobilization in preparation for war was the tsar's: if war did come, a delay in Russian mobilization could mean rapid defeat by a more efficiently geared Germany, whereas the very act of mobilizing could provoke an attack by Germany. Hesitant at first, in the days July 15–19, the tsar ordered, canceled, and reordered mobilization. Six days after the Austro-Serbian war began, his troops were massing from the Baltic to the Black Sea.

The Setting

Russia's army was immense, a "steamroller" that some thought might roll into Berlin through exposed and thinly defended East Prussia. Russia's patriotic officers and obedient soldiers probably would have won had they been fighting only Austria or Turkey. But Russia was no match for Germany either in command structure or industrial backup. The tsarist army's talented commanders and modernizing reformers had to coexist with High Command generals whose reactionary politics were paralleled by military conservatism. Aristocratic servants of autocracy, the latter were accustomed to unthinking obedience, aloof to modern battlefield technology, and contemptuous of civilian authorities. Though the tall commander in chief, Grand Duke Nikolai Nikolaevich (1856–1929), the tsar's cousin, cut an imposing figure, he left most decision making to his arrogant and incompetent chief of staff, General Yanushkevich, who owed his advancement to high ranks from his right-wing connections. Central coordination of command and control was among the first casualties. Separate branches—such as the artillery—acted independently, impervious to the needs of other branches. When the tsar went to the front and took supreme command after a year of fighting, he allowed professionals to run the war, but his absence from the capital was a disaster. A politically wise monarch would have stayed in the capital to work with domestic parties and interests and lead a concerted effort.

Though many officers treated their men decently, social antagonism often eroded mutual trust between the ranks. The arrogance of some officers fueled the resentment that began to pile up in the wake of horrendous defeats, ineptitude, and mounting casualties. As the war went on, fresh reserves and ill-trained recruits showed less readiness for the suicidal charges than the old army had.

Russia's technological lag damaged its fighting ability. Russia trailed Germany in railroad speed and capacity, production of uniforms and shell, weaponry, troop training, communications, and the industrial might on the home front that supported armies in the field. Although ammunition was often in short supply at the front, fortress commanders refused to release their enormous stores, which finally fell to the enemy with the forts. Hundreds of thousands of soldiers—mostly peasants—perished under gas, machine-gun, and artillery assaults. The number of shell shock victims who suffered mental illness; paralysis; and memory, hearing, and speech loss was so great that psychiatric hospitals could not take them all in. Some survivors of the numerous bloodbaths deserted, surrendered, or resorted to self-mutilation to escape frontline duty. A batch of Russian prisoners of war resisted being rescued since it meant renewed frontline combat. As early as 1914 desertion began to plague the army.

The Fighting

The eastern front was more mobile than that in France and Belgium, where static trench warfare prevailed. Troops, horses, guns, and wagons moved constantly through the fields and villages of East Prussia, Poland, and Galicia, the Polish-Ukrainian region of the Austrian Empire. Initial Russian plans called for deployment from Poland into Galicia, partly to secure future annexation. But at the request of their French ally, whose capital, Paris, was menaced by German armies, two Russian armies, one under General Rennenkampf from the east and the other under General Samsonov from the south, rolled into the forests and lakelands of German East Prussia. The Russian clash with the Germans there is known as the Battle of Tannenberg and the Masurian Lakes. Separated by the lakes, the Russian armies were badly coordinated, and their uncoded radio signals were picked up by the Germans. In the meantime, the German High Command rushed thousands of troops eastward by rail from the French front—thus saving Paris. When these troops smashed the Russian invaders near where Slavic armies had defeated German knights in 1410, much was made of this second Battle of Tannenberg. Russian losses ran to 250,000–300,000, and Samsonov committed suicide. Commander in Chief Nikolai Nikolaevich, commenting on the losses, had this to say: "We are happy to make such sacrifices for our allies."

The defeat was temporarily offset by Russian victories in Galicia. Although Russian casualties were heavy there also, Austria's defeat was symptomatic of that empire's weakness, particularly in its high surrender and desertion rate. The Russian army took key towns, scaled the Carpathians, and even darted for a while onto the Hungarian plain. But in April 1915, the Germans and Austrians counterattacked. At a moment of acute shortage of shell on the Russian side, enemy forces lined up their cannons along a broad front and laid down an unending screen of artillery fire against the Russian emplacements. A British observer on this front reported in April 1915 that "of some regiments the news was that they were practically all gone; in one case the answer was that 'the Regiment does not exist. . . .' Of forty officers and four thousand men, in the end two hundred and fifty were left." As the tsar's armies staggered back in the Great Retreat of 1915, Germans and Austrians pushed steadily into the interior of Russian Poland and took all of it by the end of the year, in addition to large swaths of Russia's western provinces. The enemy lines at year's end ran roughly from near Riga in the north to the Romanian border in the south.

Although the drainage on manpower and matériel was immense, the Russian war effort was nowhere near collapse in 1916. The decimated upper-class junior officers were replaced by those from a lower social stratum. Despite the attrition, the draft continued to pump more men into the frontlines, which stabilized around a trench system. By 1916 arms and ammunition were flowing, although the Russians were still outgunned. But once again the Allies implored Russia to renew pressure on the enemy, this time to relieve the German assault on the French fortress of Verdun—one of the bloodiest engagements of the entire war. In June the Russians mounted a major offensive—the last in the tsarist era under General A. A. Brusilov (1853–1926), a meticulous commander whose elaborate preparations included rehearsals for occupying enemy positions. Success crowned his feint-and-surprise tactics during the first phase of the attack on Austrian positions. But Russian headquarters failed to mount a coordinated follow-up against the Germans, who brought in reinforcements. Brusilov's triumph became a retreat. Inspired by Brusilov's initial victories, Romania entered the war on the side of the Allies. This proved to be a disadvantage for Russia, whose forces were no longer shielded on the flank by neutral territory. German armies crashed through the soft resistance of the Romanians and outflanked the Russians from the south, halting the Russian offensive. The immense number of Russian men and officers lost in this campaign made it necessary to call up a fresh batch of recruits, an ominous development for the morale of the army and the civilian population alike.

TRAGEDY BEHIND THE LINES

It is common in Western memory of the Great War to see it as one in which civilian casualties were rather low. In comparison with World War II, this is true, but in fact civilian deaths were very high, particularly in Eastern Europe. Recent scholarship on this long-neglected tragedy has thrown light on some of the greatest acts of

The Main Front and Occupied Lands: The Eastern Front in 1916.

inhumanity toward noncombatants that took place in and on the edge of the Russian Empire: the displacements in the western borderlands of 1914–1915; the genocidal Armenian massacres of 1915; and the suppression of a revolt in Central Asia during 1916. Each had a powerful impact on the mutual antagonism between national and ethnic groups that would burst forth during and after the revolution of 1917.

The Great Retreat

The civilians of occupied Poland and adjacent territories suffered more than most others in Europe. Aside from the death and destruction that rained down from the shelling and the firing, they endured the heavy-handed actions of the Russian military authorities. Following directives from headquarters, local commanders who controlled frontline provinces and those immediately to the rear treated them as occupied enemy territory. They viewed Poles, Germans, Jews, and others in the Polish lands as disloyal and during the great retreat of 1915, the High Command even temporarily ordered a policy of "devastated space," or scorched earth, as Russian forces withdrew.

The zenith of military administrative harshness was the policy of forced removal of populations seen to be "enemy aliens" from Poland and the Baltic and western provinces. From spring to autumn 1915, hordes of these people, rousted from their homes and driven back from the advancing front, swelled the stream of refugees fleeing combat areas or frightened by tales of alleged German bestiality. A recent historian has called the outcome "a whole empire walking." Tragedy erupted in the death marches of an uprooted population and in villages laid waste by Russian soldiery. Even landowners who refused to leave were rooted out and sometimes killed in punitive raids. Soldiers burned buildings and destroyed crops. Instances were reported of Cossacks "evacuating" women into their own units as sexual playthings.

Peasants armed themselves against the raids. This war within a war brought death from cold, hunger, disease, and mistreatment to hundreds of thousands of Polish, Ukrainian, German, Jewish, Lithuanian, and Latvian civilians of all classes—men, women, and children. A Russian recalled seeing how "Polish peasants who had fled from their villages sat or lay on the ground near their covered wagons. Babies howled, turning blue in the arms of their exhausted and disheveled mothers." An estimated 1 million people were driven into the interior and another 5 to 10 million more or less voluntarily left their homes to rear area evacuation centers located as far away as the Lower Volga and the Orenburg steppe.

Death stalked the roads, and the refugee mass burst the already meager welfare capacities of the cities in Russia's interior where they were sent, aggravated food shortages, and spread disease. Evacuees were not always welcome in towns whose people were facing their own problems. The unavoidable disruption of families swelled the war orphan population, and armies of homeless children formed into the street gangs that would later become notorious under the Bolshevik regime. The great evacuation harmed rather than helped the war effort: the ragged crowds

Uprooted refugees on the Eastern front. *Hulton/Archive/Getty Images.*

congested the roads and the rail lines, blocking the movement of precious matériel to the front. One of the tsar's ministers likened the epic march of the refugees in Poland to the great "migration of peoples" across Europe in the early Middle Ages.

The enormous Jewish population of Galicia, Poland, and the legal region of Jewish residence known as the Pale of Settlement was the target of special attention by the military authorities, particularly the anti-Semitic chief of staff General Yanushkevich. Declaring the Jewish community along the front to be espionage agents responsible for the defeats of the Russian army, he ordered their unceremonious removal: expulsion from their homes with no place to go or deportation by train to the interior. From cities and shtetls (market towns) where they had resided for centuries, Jews were herded out of their homes by Cossack whips: old people, women, children, and expectant mothers, thrown into the street with a few belongings, were occasionally killed or raped. The removal process degenerated into pogroms in dozens of places. Jewish towns and villages were looted, and thousands were cast onto the flood of refugees or packed into boxcars, which raging typhus converted into coffins for many. Those unable to travel were sometimes shot. From a half million to a million Jewish civilians were affected by the army's policies.

In rear areas, anti-Semitism increased with the mass exodus eastward from the Pale, which was abolished in August 1915, since it had effectively ceased to exist. Many Jews who experienced the terrors of World War I became radicalized by what they saw as the brutality of the tsarist government. For East European Jews, until the advent of Nazism, the Russian Cossack was a familiar specter of evil, often invoked by mothers to frighten their children. Forced displacement during the Great Retreat was another in a series of ordeals undergone by the East European Jews that would culminate in the Holocaust twenty-five years later.

Poles who remained in their homeland suffered some of these hazards as well and had their own grievances. About 3 million were drafted into the armies of the three powers that had ruled Polish territory—Germany, Austria, and Russia—thus pitting brother against brother. Towns crumbled under shelling from all sides. The Russians imprisoned Polish patriots in Warsaw on the eve of abandoning the city. After a time, Russians softened their measures, and high officials, including the tsar, made vague and watery promises about a "unified" and autonomous Poland at the conclusion of hostilities. Similar promises by Germany and Austria were hardly more encouraging. But since the Central Powers were in occupation as of 1915 and Polish was being taught in schools for the first time since the 1860s, their side seemed to offer more. The Polish revolutionary Jozef Pilsudski, operating on Austrian soil, organized legions to fight against Russia. His hope that both Russia and the Central Powers would be defeated was actually realized.

The Ukrainians of Galicia also suffered the ravages of war and occupation. The Russian occupiers brought with them to Austrian Galicia in 1914 long-standing hostility to Uniate Ukrainians (see the chapters "Orthodoxy, Autocracy, Nationality Reaffirmed, 1881–1905" and "Society, Culture, Politics, 1881–1905") and cultural warfare carried out by a reactionary military governor. The state sent Russian Orthodox priests to the eastern part of Galicia to help Russianize it. Military officials interned Ukrainian Uniate priests and intellectuals, suppressed the Ukrainian language, and even changed street signs into Russian. When Hungarian troops of the Habsburg Empire, long trained in contempt for Slavic peoples, retook Galicia, they committed atrocities on the Ukrainian peasants.

Genocide at the Border

One of the great acts of collective slaughter of the twentieth century, the massacre of Armenians in 1915, was directly tied to the war on the Russo-Turkish front and just as surely to wartime geopolitics. German war strategy included "revolution politics"—the defeat of their enemies by uprisings from within. This involved the use of radicals (including Bolsheviks) and nationalists of every sort who would help them weaken or overthrow the Russian and British Empires. The Kaiser's agents persuaded the sultan-caliph of the Ottoman Empire and the chief religious leader, the Sheik-ul-Islam, to announce a jihad, or holy war of Islam, directed against Petersburg, London, and Delhi. This was a familiar political extension of battlefield war and a preview of the coming Soviet efforts to undermine the British Empire in the 1920s. Though an ultimate failure, the German-sponsored jihad was more elaborate and effective than the feeble German efforts to finance revolution within Russia. The main Turkish leader, Enver Pasha, saw jihad as a vehicle to carry Turkish power into the Caucasus and Central Asia in pursuit of a Pan-Turkic empire.

Knowing this, the British and Russians opened another chapter of the Great Game, or struggle for Asia—this time as allies—on the well-worn espionage fields of Persia and Afghanistan. The main center of violence in this game was the Russo-Turkish front; and its chief victims the unsuspecting Ottoman Armenians.

When the Ottoman Turks entered on the side of Germany, Russian Transcaucasia adjacent to Turkish Anatolia became a war zone, with Armenians on both sides of the frontier. The Georgians exhibited no war fever. Many in Azerbaijan actually looked forward to liberation by Turks, who shared their Muslim faith. Owing to this, the Russian authorities treated Azeris as disloyal elements in the way that they treated Jews in Poland. Only the Armenians fully supported the Russians, out of animosity for the Ottoman government, which had allowed the slaughter by Turks in 1894–1896 of some 300,000 Armenians. Armenians formed fighting units for duty at the front, with the aim of liberating their fellow Armenians across the border from Ottoman rule. In this lay part of the reason for the terrible killings of 1915. The other lay in the Turkish military's claim that the Turkish Armenians were working with the Russians to defeat the Turks. The inflammatory propaganda war of the Turkish and German leaders fueled this belief.

In the winter of 1915, Enver's Army of Islam suffered losses near Erzerum, the biggest Turkish stronghold in eastern Anatolia, where the presence of Armenian volunteer units on the Russian side added bitter gall to the defeat. Shortly after the fighting began, the Turkish government issued deportation orders for the Armenian population of selected locales. The forced removals quickly turned into a massacre, and in the summer of 1915 massacre escalated to genocide by Turkish troops and Kurds, a Muslim people of the region. They began to exterminate the Armenian civilian population all over eastern Anatolia, murdering, raping, and burning. Mothers went insane after seeing Turkish or Kurdish soldiers smash their children's heads against a wall. Troops forced the survivors of the carnage into the bleak wilderness to die. Over 1 million Armenians perished. Only a pitiful remnant managed to drag themselves in agony to Damascus and other temporary shelters. The tragedy also flooded Russian Armenia with refugees who brought with them an unforgiving hatred for the Turks and their Azeri coreligionists, a hatred that would cause further bloodshed in the Caucasus during the Russian Revolution and civil war.

Massacre on the Steppe

The revolt in Central Asia of 1916 was rooted in the long-term imperial process of displacing nomadic societies on the Eurasian steppe with Russian agricultural settlements—a process accelerated by Stolypin's agrarian reforms in the immediate prewar years. The simmering resentment over this intrusion turned into violence as a result of wartime policies of labor conscription. Although the Turkic-speaking population on the steppe was exempt from military service, the tsarist government imitated its allies and mobilized about half a million of its "colonials" for labor behind the lines. A rumor that the men were to be sent into combat triggered a riot in the city of Samarkand, where angered locals beat or killed native draft officials.

The Russian governor declared martial law, and the rebels cut telegraph lines and tore up railroad tracks. Cossacks, whom the tsarist regime regularly used to repress disorders, retaliated savagely. Punitive detachments armed with machine guns rode into the native settlements with orders to "destroy them completely." By September a procession of three dozen trains was carrying Central Asian conscripts to help build a new rail line to Murmansk.

Events were repeated on a wider scale across the broad stretches of Kazakhstan. Russian homesteaders sided with the government troops to settle their own scores and to take more land from the grazing natives; the latter responded with terror against Russian settlements. It was a classic prairie war of armed horsemen and lightning hit-and-run raids. During an autumn bloodbath three thousand to four thousand Russian civilians and a much larger number of Kazakhs and Kirgiz were killed—estimates run into the tens of thousands. Refugees fled across the mountains to Chinese Turkestan. Back home, hundreds were tried, about fifty were hanged, and the conscription proceeded. The Kazakh revolt was the largest of any internal disturbance among the warring powers in World War I. The six months of killing in Central Asia in 1916 shed more blood than did the entire Russian conquest in the nineteenth century, and the memory of it was a major cause of the extreme violence that would attend the coming revolution and civil war in Central Asia.

THE WAR BUSINESS

Every war tests the participating states' capacity to produce, deliver, and use technology and to harness bodies, minds, and hearts for the struggle. A key ingredient in twentieth-century warfare was the involvement of the population, or at least its most energetic members, in the war effort. The tsarist regime scored very low in wartime leadership because its supreme leader for the most part refused to accept the spontaneous cooperation of "society"—that is, the civic and political party leaders. For that reason, Nicholas II must bear a great deal of the blame for losing the war and bringing on the revolution.

The Economic Front

Russia's most serious economic problems were arming the soldiers, keeping the civilians fed, and paying for the war. The tsar's army relied initially on the supply of arms from its more industrialized allies. But, owing to the German fleet's blockade of the Baltic Sea and the Turkish blockade of the Black Sea straits, arms shipments had to travel the perilous route of the White Sea to Arkhangelsk or across the Pacific to Vladivostok and thence along the single-track Trans-Siberian Railroad. Many of the cargoes that got through sat rusting on the ground in port cities because of Russia's poor internal transport system. It took until 1916 for Russian industry to manufacture enough shells to ease the shell shortage. Even then, the mismanagement of the railroads held up delivery of arms to the front and of food to the cities. The government had given virtual control of the railways to the military, who hoarded rolling stock and drove the equipment beyond capacity in their understandable need to fling reserves into the frontlines with all possible speed. By the end of 1916, the flow of imports rose owing to the double-tracking of some lines and the completion of a new rail line connecting St. Petersburg (now Petrograd) to the port of Murmansk, which, though above the Arctic Circle, was made ice-free by the Gulf Stream.

The loss of grain-producing territories to the enemy worsened the food situation. In addition to this and the problems in transport, two other difficulties contributed. One was the swelling of cities in the interior by refugees who had to be fed. The other was the decline in grain output in the Russian agricultural lands. The large landowners' estates that produced for the market with hired labor were hurt most by the loss of labor to the army. Peasant villages were relatively unaffected since many male peasant draftees had been surplus labor. Women and children managed the farm work and consumed most of the produce. But the peasant farms would not produce marketable surpluses because food prices stayed low, whereas those of consumer goods were inflationary. These were also in short supply owing to the shift to armaments production. So the peasants held their grain in storage or consumed more than usual. This combination of low grain prices and high consumer goods prices would be repeated during the revolution of 1917 and again in the 1920s. In the winter of 1916–1917 the announcement of rationing in the cities led to panic, hoarding, and long bread lines—a grim prelude to the uprising in Petrograd that would bring down the monarchy.

The enormous expense of arming, feeding, and clothing millions of soldiers squeezed the treasury, which lost its largest source of income, the vodka monopoly revenue, in 1914. The tsar, bowing to decades of temperance activity in the empire, and fearing the impact of drink on the fighting forces, introduced prohibition by stages. Although this measure was popular among the lower classes on the home front for a time, illegal moonshine soon replaced the state-taxed liquor. Officers and patrons of expensive restaurants were exempt from the ban. Income and war profits taxes came only in 1916, and the regime resorted to printing money and deficit spending, which caused inflation. Prices shot upward, whereas wages remained stable.

The Political Front

Participating in war management were the royal court, the army, the royally appointed Council of Ministers, the Duma, organized industry, and the voluntary organizations and societies. Had these bodies been able to work together in harmony, the final collapse of the regime might have been averted. But the tsar consistently ignored his ministers' warnings and imprecations, the military despised civilian interlopers, and the ministers were wary of the Duma and the voluntary organizations. Political conflict dogged other wartime regimes, but in Russia mistrust and incompetence at the top turned out to be lethal.

In the first year of the war, Nicholas II—flushed with the apparent patriotic backing of his subjects—enjoyed moderate respect as a leader in the face of tremendous military losses, the supply problem, and the occasional scandal—including the dismissal of a war minister for corruption and incompetence and the hanging of his associate for alleged espionage. Prompted by the crisis of 1915 at the front, the tsar replaced reactionaries in the cabinet in June. The war cabinet of 1915, among the best that tsarism had ever assembled, ardently desired to serve the monarchy and win the war. They were appalled at the actions of the military, which denied entry into their zones to Russian volunteers, medical personnel, and hospital trains in the early stages of the war. The shortage of such trains on some sectors of the front meant that Russian wounded were loaded onto boxcars under frightful conditions or left on station platforms in the rain and mud. Sensitive to the suffering caused by military mismanagement and the evacuations, members of the cabinet desired to curb it.

In the summer of 1915, the cabinet suggested cooperation with the Duma, whose leaders shared its views. Led by liberals, moderates, and conservatives, the Duma was more reform minded than the cabinet, but just as interested in prosecuting the war successfully and, except for a few deputies, was patriotic in the usual sense of the term: progovernment, prowar, proarmy. The defeats of 1915 convinced many in the Duma that the government did not know how to run a war properly. In the summer a broad coalition of Duma deputies calling itself the Progressive Bloc demanded that the government put an end to the arbitrary military regime over civilians behind the lines. To this they added further demands: amnesty for certain noncriminal religious and political offenders, greater rights for the nationalities and non-Orthodox religions, and respect for labor unions. To implement these demands, the bloc also asked for a ministry enjoying the "confidence of the country," though some in the bloc really wanted a cabinet responsible to the Duma—in other words, a true parliamentary government. To the politicians of the Progressive Bloc, reform in the midst of war seemed essential to engage the whole population.

To the tsar, this looked like usurpation of power. He did not trust the Duma and turned a deaf ear to its offers of assisting in the war effort, which was in his view solely the business of the dynasty and the army. His appointed prime minister, the aged Ivan Goremykin (1839–1917), simply echoed these sentiments, and the Empress Alexandra, under the influence of the healer Grigory Rasputin, reinforced them. The empress warned her husband in June 1915 that the Duma leaders "will try to mix in & speak about things that do not concern them. Never forget that *you are & must* remain autocratic Emperor." In August, Tsar Nicholas made a fateful decision to replace Grand Duke Nikolai Nikolaevich as commander in chief of his army. His ministers realized this meant assuming responsibility for further losses of territory and lives. But the Empress Alexandra feared the alleged ambitions of Nikolai Nikolaevich and persuaded her husband to take up command. Through Goremykin, the tsar informed the ministers of his departure to the front and adjourned the Duma. On August 21, the ministers protested to the tsar that his decision to leave the capital to take up command "threatens Russia, yourself, and your dynasty with serious consequences." Tsar Nicholas soon replaced most of them, in some cases with the advice of Rasputin. Installed at staff headquarters in Mogilëv in distant Belorussia, the tsar was isolated from the capital, Petrograd. Alexandra sometimes interfered in affairs of state, and she was in turn influenced by the advice of Rasputin. The tsar, enveloped in a mystique of war and dynastic honor, found it more and more natural to ignore advisers and politicians.

A more successful initiative to harness the efforts of public leaders in the war effort was the organization of town and country self-government bodies. A wave of civic voluntarism took up army supply and care of the wounded, who were subjected to dreadful medical conditions. Zemstvo leaders called for a permanent body to coordinate the expertise of public figures, physicians, and specialists. In August 1915, the government approved the Union of Zemstvos, headed by a prominent liberal, Prince Georgy Lvov (1861–1925). Town governments followed suit and eventually joined the zemstvos in the Zemgor—Union of Zemstvos and Towns—a huge network of hundreds of provincial and town bodies coordinated from the center. Under the slogan, "organizing victory in the rear," the Zemgor released a tremendous spurt of civic energy. Volunteers dramatically increased the production of food, boots, blankets, and medicines. Simultaneously, the Association of Industry and Trade—the chief organ of private entrepreneurs—set up a Central War Industries Committee to coordinate defense industry. Hundreds of local branches sprang up all over Russia. The moderate conservative Octobrist Duma deputy and industrialist Alexander Guchkov headed the committee, added a Labor Section, and worked with the Zemgor.

This burst of public spontaneity aimed at saving the nation was not without self-interest. The War Industries Committee then and later greatly inflated its role in fighting heroically against a selfish and stupid government. In fact, much of the economy was in the hands of very large industrialists and monopolists who worked with the government, reaping huge profits, to achieve an enormous growth in production. Bypassing the Duma politicians and the volunteer structure, they brought together responsible officials and zealous organizational talent from the private sector—an effective way to harness human energy and one used by many warring nations in the twentieth century. The various volunteer civic and industrial organizations made a positive contribution to the war effort but also showed themselves open to greed and corruption. The tsarist government was not always wrong when it feared that opening up direction of the war economy to zemstvo, urban, and business groups would lead them to advance their own interests. The greatest significance of the volunteer groups was that they gained organizational experience. Government response to their efforts ranged from gratitude to suspicion. The empress despised Guchkov, and Rasputin had enemies throughout the voluntary associations. The police put them under surveillance as potential sources of danger to the monarchy precisely because of their dynamism and general popularity. Reactionaries in the government, including the royal couple, were prey to the imprudent habit of identifying public spontaneity with subversive activity and of seeing liberal and moderate reform aspirations as radicalism.

In 1916, the forces of public action and those of ostrichlike inaction faced off.

The royal couple as puppets of Rasputin.
Stock Montage.

The ancient Goremykin was finally retired, but his replacement, Boris Stürmer (Shtyurmer in Russian) (1848–1917), was—if anything—worse. Bearing a German name, the new prime minister aroused anger and disdain from Duma leaders and volunteers, who saw him as a man without energy or talent. Since his chief attribute seems to have been that he was the choice of Rasputin, the internal war between educated society and government whirled around the issue of Rasputin's alleged power. False rumors flew accusing him and the German-born empress of consorting with the enemy and of a love affair between them. Gossip told of Rasputin's sexual escapades with society ladies and his corrupt dealings with shady figures. Those bold enough to inform the tsar or the empress of Rasputin's reputation were fired. The imperial couple, especially the empress, could not bear the thought of parting with the one man who actually had the power to assuage the sufferings of their hemophiliac son.

Of much greater impact on politics and the war was Rasputin's influence on appointments to high government posts and even his occasional attempts to interfere in military matters, though both of these were exaggerated by gossip. The appointment of Stürmer was followed by a whole chapter of firing and hiring—called "ministerial leapfrog" by a Duma member and "musical chairs" by a foreign observer—a major public relations failure even though the ministries continued to function pretty much as usual. With each new appointment and scandal, the temper of the Duma rose. Zemgor leaders were also being pressed by the rank and file—the Third Element—to implement "radical" measures: more votes for urban residents, wider popular participation, better welfare and labor laws. But Duma moderates in the Progressive Bloc—particularly the influential Kadet Party leader, Pavel Milyukov (1859–1943)—still frightened by the remembrance of 1905 and its popular unrest, were averse to whipping up popular opinion against the regime. Though angry and critical of the government, Duma leaders called for restraint. They saw educated society as the barrier between the government they detested and the masses they dreaded, and they hoped to keep the nation intact against the threat of a German conquest of Russia.

ON THE HOME FRONT

Thousands of upper- and middle-class officers died at the front. But members of these classes who stayed home lived pretty well. Town life changed surprisingly little except where evacuees crowded in. Moscow and Petrograd were hundreds of miles from the front, and strategic bombing by planes lay in the future. Luxury and high life remained in place for the affluent. Ministerial chambers echoed with complaints about all-night restaurants and illegal consumption of alcohol. Although motor cars were needed for war, they careened around the streets of the capitals carrying top-hatted dandies and fur-clad ladies. Newspapers lampooned speculators, war profiteers, and draft dodgers. The latter included both the newly pious, who entered monasteries to escape service, and the public volunteers—the "Zemgor Hussars"—who wore gaudy uniforms but saw no action outside their valiant nocturnal assaults on restaurants and cabarets. The less fortunate resented the conspicuous consumption in the midst of a war that supposedly required common sacrifice. The lower classes, faced with inflation and rationing, came to believe that they bore the brunt of the war at home and at the front. They did indeed suffer immensely, though a proportionately large number of young noblemen were wiped out in battle as well.

Workers and Women

The status of the urban working class was complicated. After an initial mass conscription, skilled workers in key industries were exempted from army service—a virtual lease on life. At first, workers greeted the war patriotically. But labor policies were harsher than in most other belligerent countries, where unions and even socialists collaborated in the war effort. Industrial peace ended in the summer of 1915, although even then strikes numbered only half those of the prewar peak. Some of the unrest was funded by German money funneled in by the Kaiser's agents, but most of it stemmed from economic issues. The wartime inflation, which in a few places raised prices at ten times the rate of wages, had worsened the lot of industrial workers by 1916, especially in the capital, and by then the rise in strike activity was ominous and dramatic.

War is one of the most gendered of all collective human activities. Russian women felt its impact in various ways. The biggest loss fell on war wives and widows. Over 1 million men per month on average were mobilized in 1914; altogether over 14 million men went to war. At one point as many as 36 percent of working-age men were in service. To the estimated 7 to 8.5 million military casualties—killed, wounded, and missing—must be added those who perished from disease and all the civilian losses. Aside from causing unspeakable grief to the loved ones of those killed or maimed, the war also brought economic change in women's lives. They were pulled into new kinds of work in field and factory. Although those employed in the light industries lost jobs to downsizing or conversion to war industry, more jobs opened up than closed down. Women made up 35 percent of all railroad employees. In 1916, 18 percent of the metallurgical workers in Moscow region alone were women. As a whole, their percentage in industry jumped from 27 percent in 1914 to 43 percent 1917. They remained poorly paid and subject to factory floor abuse and were also resented by some male workers, who could lose their livelihoods (and lives) if replaced by females and then sent to the front.

Upper- and middle-class women rushed into nursing and work in the volunteer organizations, even the "spoilt beauties of the Smart Set," as a foreign resident put it. One volunteer nurse declared that "the feminine in me decreased more and more, and I did not know whether to be sad or glad about this." The prominence of women nurses made the female figure the allegory for an innocent and kindly Russia being violated by German brutality. Great mobility in the work force, including office work, led to sexual freedom for women, which in turn affected marriage and birth rates. One of the most startling episodes was the enlistment of women into the fighting forces. One, a princess, became a military pilot. Several hundred women of all classes and widely divergent motivations joined the infantry ranks and, after the fall of the monarchy, were formed into all-female combat units.

Wartime Culture

The cultural scene roughly reflected what went on in wartime society—more so perhaps than did the political ballets staged at the top. The arts—high and popular—were drawn into the national struggle, though with greatly divergent themes and effects. Modernist posters, popular cartoons, and postcards served up pictures of the Kaiser as the main evil force, rather than the German people, and of Austria as a mere puppet of Germany. The same media ridiculed the Ottoman sultan by references to his harem. Circus acts and cabarets put on satirical shows, while concerts and drama offered more serious patriotic material. Popular film, song, and folk performers all made a contribution. Artists engaged strenuously in lifting wartime morale through benefit performances for hospitals. Even the stately imperial ballet gave a few performances at the front.

Among the cultural intelligentsia, some writers fell mute before the tragic spectacle of war, while others agonized and philosophized. Some Symbolist poets tended to see the war as an apocalyptic premonition of cosmic spiritual upheaval. An extreme case of literary war fever was that of the poet Nikolai Gumilëv (1886–1921), who experienced a kind of euphoria through danger, a masculine thrill at risking death in the "cleansing fire" of battle. One of those who helped in the scorched earth operations, he exulted—"burning everything that would burn"—and viewed killing as a supreme work of art, a "festival of the spirit," a religious experience in which man communes with God.

Russia accused German troops of the utmost bestiality, particularly in their treatment of Belgium, where they shot civilians and vandalized churches. Propaganda reserved special venom for the alleged perfidy of German residents and Russians of German ancestry. Adventure fiction and film featured them as traitors who stabbed Russians in the back at the outbreak of war. Some anti-German gestures were harmless: changing the name of St. Petersburg to Petrograd, banning the

German language in public places, and boycotting the music of Wagner and Beethoven. But long-held resentment toward those of German stock fed more violent reactions. Dachshund dogs were killed on the street. In 1914, students stormed the German embassy and then painted over German street and shop names. Police expelled Austrian and German nationals but often rounded up the wrong nationality. In 1915 anti-German anger erupted in a three-day pogrom against persons, property, and businesses of "Germans" in Moscow. Most of the victims were Russians with foreign names or citizens of allied countries. People with German, Jewish, or Scandinavian names changed them to Russian ones.

The greatness of Russia and the rightness of its cause were rarely embodied in the image of the tsar but more often in symbols—the flag, the double-headed eagle, the anthem. Slogans invoked the Russian victory over Napoleon in 1812 and Lev Tolstoy's novel about it, *War and Peace.* Heroic leaders of the past who had vanquished foreign invaders stood in for the missing ones in this war. For combat heroes, readers and viewers had only a few air aces and the colorful young Cossack Kuzma Kryuchkov, who allegedly impaled eleven Germans on his lance. Although the censors endeavored to play down losses and defeats, the press revealed and criticized them and also attacked speculators and the bumbling of the government itself, which readers knew was so great that they were ready to believe the worst. After the first flush of patriotism in 1914, the cultural contribution to the effort declined visibly, marking the diminution of war spirit among large segments of the population. The most popular of film genres, for example—the high-society sexual melodrama—said nothing about the war but much about the cruelty of upper-class people toward the humble and the poor.

WAR AND PEACE

The Russian liberal, Pavel Milyukov, at the outbreak of war commented on the "eternal silence [that] reigned in the depths of rural Russia." He noted no spontaneous wave of patriotism or popular protest. In fact, both erupted in towns all over the country, as did a rush of volunteers on the one hand and draft riots that claimed a few hundred lives on the other. In widespread "vodka pogroms," people smashed liquor stores, either to get the alcohol or to destroy it. In educated society, the spectrum of views on war and peace was wide: the tsar and his supporters stood for victory and autocracy, liberals for victory and democracy, pacifists for peace at any price, "defensists" for peace without defeat, and Bolsheviks for defeat and revolution in both Russia and Germany.

Leading the "prowar" forces was the tsar himself, backed by family and court, though the empress and Rasputin voiced their hopes to end the fighting. Motives for supporting a war to victory included national honor and alliance obligations, obedience to the state, nationalism, Pan-Slavism, hatred of Germans, and territorial ambitions. Among the territorial war aims, one was to weaken Austria by annexing Galicia and adding it to a reconstructed and dependent Poland. Another was to annex Istanbul and nearby lands as well as stretches of northern and eastern Anatolia. Possessing these lands would enhance security and "solve" at last the Eastern Question by making the Black Sea a Russian lake, controlling the straits into the Mediterranean, and realizing an old dream of a Russian Tsargrad (Constantinople) at Istanbul. Russian diplomats, suspecting the activities of the British and the Greeks in the region, in March 1915 extracted the straits agreement from France and Britain, compensating them then and in subsequent treaties with other Ottoman territories. These agreements were later supplemented by contradictory British and French promises to Arab leaders and Jewish Zionists. Most of the Duma liberals were happy with Russia's war aims and differed from the official party only in their view of how to prosecute the war and in pushing more democratic reforms.

Straight-out traitors working for a German victory were widely suspected but few in number. Some pro-German elements at court and in society thought Russia was fighting on the wrong side, but they played no significant role. The pacifist banner was held aloft sporadically in urban demonstrations by Tolstoyans, followers of the great novelist's teachings about nonviolent behavior. Some Social Democratic leaders spoke of opposing the "tsar's" or the "imperialist" war, though workers and the party rank and file evinced a patriotic stand in the early period of the war. The prewar international socialist movement had vociferously promised to oppose their governments if they went to war. But in 1914, nationalism won out and the majority of European Social Democrats (SDs) stood behind their countries' war efforts. A minority of European Marxist SDs, however, convened in Switzerland on two occasions, declared the present conflict to be an immoral "capitalist war" that was slaughtering the working class, and resolved to work for a peace "without indemnities or annexations." In Russia, moderate SDs (mostly Mensheviks) and Socialist Revolutionaries (SRs) adopted a "defensist" line: to work for a democratic peace but in the meantime defend their country against German aggression.

A much more radical position was advanced by the Bolshevik leader, Vladimir Lenin, one of many Russian revolutionaries then living abroad to elude the clutches of the tsarist secret police. At the first of the SD conferences, in Zimmerwald, he unveiled and later developed a revolutionary line. Defeat of Russia, argued Lenin, was a "lesser evil." Socialists should convert the international war, fought by peasants and workers on behalf of the propertied classes, into a series of civil wars in which the soldiers would turn their rifles against their officers and the workers would overthrow their governments. Lenin remained abroad until 1917. He also wrote one of his most influential works, *Imperialism, the Highest Stage of Capitalism* (1915), elaborating his reactions to the war. But in Petrograd, the defensists predominated, their Duma deputies abstaining on the war credits but refraining from open antiwar activism.

In the complex debate on the war, organized women came out loudly on several sides. Feminist leaders, mostly upper- and middle-class women, backed the war effort in the hope that the government would reward their loyalty by giving them the vote. Serving the country, said one feminist leader, "will give us the right to participate as the equals of men in the new life of a victorious Russia." Socialist women divided more or less along party lines into defensists and Leninists. The Menshevik Alexandra Kollontai (1872–1952) was so appalled by the bloodletting that she converted to Bolshevism and opposed the war. Much of the war's horror was masked in the early stages by censorship and patriotic euphoria. The repressive machinery of the state restricted unions, curbed the press, and exiled the Bolshevik Duma deputies. Because of a lack of sources, we can never know what all or even most of the broad masses were feeling at various stages of the war—only that many at the outset and for a long time fought in and otherwise supported the war effort; and that a portion of them toward the end could bear it no longer. Their insurrection proved enough to destroy the monarchy.

MIDNIGHT OF EMPIRE, 1916–1917

After the initially successful but ultimately costly Brusilov offensive, the line stabilized, and the losses of 1916 were fewer than those of 1915, but the continuing accumulation of the dead and wounded deepened the war weariness of the population. In the autumn and winter of 1916, political deterioration set in. To the key post of minister of interior, with sweeping police powers, Stürmer appointed A. D. Protopopov (1866–1918). Though once a liberal Duma member, Protopopov had lost credibility with his colleagues—and to some, even his mind—by his association with Rasputin. Government misrule led the moderate liberal Milyukov to make a famous Duma speech in which he wondered aloud whether the behavior of the government was "stupidity or treason." Rasputin's escapades—when contrasted with the frontline world of troop trains and mountains of corpses—sickened onlookers on all sides. From among his many enemies, three men from the right end of the political spectrum—Vladimir Purishkevich, Prince Felix Yusupov, and Grand Duke Dmitry Pavlovich, the last two related to the tsar—took the final step of murdering Rasputin in December 1916. After poisoning, kicking, and shooting failed to kill Rasputin, whom they had lured to the sumptuous Yusupov palace, the conspirators finally threw him into a river, where he drowned.

The grotesque story of his assassination blended with the whispers and gossip that had long transformed Rasputin into an evil genius. After the revolution, a flood of garish stories and movies portrayed him as an oversexed, corrupt, and treasonous seducer of the empress. Absent from the picture was his genuine concern for the royal family. Not all Rasputin's actions were negative, but his interference in state matters, and especially how that interference was perceived, harmed the monarchy immensely. Although Rasputin did not—as myth would have it—cause the revolution, the tsar's tolerance of his sins eroded waning support for the monarchy. The significance of the murder of Rasputin is that nothing essential changed after his death. The romanticization of the royal couple, lasting right up to our time, has obscured the fact that Rasputin was a mere symptom of the tragic incapacity of the tsar to rule a great empire at war. War losses, hunger, and poor judgment at the top had increased widespread disillusionment with the royal family as much as Rasputin had.

By early 1917, generals, diplomats, and even the emperor's relatives sought ways to replace Tsar Nicholas II with a stronger monarch whose regime might wage the war successfully and avoid a revolution. The shadowy plots hatched in salons, officers' mess halls, and diplomatic receptions pointed more toward a possible palace coup by generals and grand dukes than to a full-scale revolution. But the tsar remained almost to the end oblivious of the ominous murmuring, and he stubbornly ignored the political clamor and growing mass disenchantment with the war.

How great was that disenchantment? At the outbreak of war, a kneeling patriotic crowd at the Winter Palace Square in Petrograd persuaded Nicholas that the entire people supported the war. But the adoring crowd that cheered the tsar on the opening day of war represented a minute fraction of Petrograd and not necessarily the masses. Even the war fever among some in the upper classes and intelligentsia had by 1917 faded or had turned into a belief that the monarch himself was the main obstacle to social mobilization for victory. There was some grumbling in the army. "They've put out an order that there will be no peace until full victory," wrote a soldier in a letter from the front in January 1917. "And now you know how badly they feed us—only beans for dinner and supper. Tell your comrades that we all ought to stage an uprising against the war." This mood, which caught hold a few months later, was still untypical, and the lines held firm. Peasant views by then ranged from indifferent to sullen, and they darkened as the hardships and human losses piled up. More crucial was the plummeting morale in the cities. By early January 1917, more than 600,000 workers were on strike, and the police regularly reported on the general public's constant talk of war weariness. In January 1917, the commander of the Petrograd military district was in readiness for an uprising, but no one knew how or if it would break out.

CHAPTER 30

The Revolutions of 1917

"Long live free Russia."
The joyous cry floods my soul—
"Long live our freedom."
The red flag stills my heart.
A leaden weight has fallen,
The world dreams a shining dream.
—Mikhail Serafimovich, soldier, March 1917

In February 1917, a revolt, triggered by a women's food protest, began in a poor industrial quarter of wintry Petrograd, the Vyborg District, named after a city in Finland to the north. It took only a week—from Thursday, February 23, to the following Thursday, March 2—to run its course.* Thereafter, crises proliferated, and the tempo of historical change accelerated dizzyingly. Within eight months the monarchy fell, a moderate caretaker government tried to survive, and the Bolsheviks overthrew it in October. How an uprising ended in a revolution that shook the world has divided historians along bitter political lines ever since. Theories of a Jewish plot, German espionage, or a conspiracy of the secret society of Freemasons have stalked the history of the February Revolution. Conversely, the Bolsheviks long held that they led that revolution. Most historians, while admitting the impact of socialist propaganda, rightly stress the spontaneous nature of the Petrograd events. That most of the nation followed suit after the overthrow in the capital suggests that the hatred of war, economic hardship, and scandal at the center probably could not have been subdued by a mere palace coup replacing one tsar for another. The monarchy itself had become so brittle and unresponsive during the war that any major crisis might have toppled it.

*For the Russian calendar, see Preface.

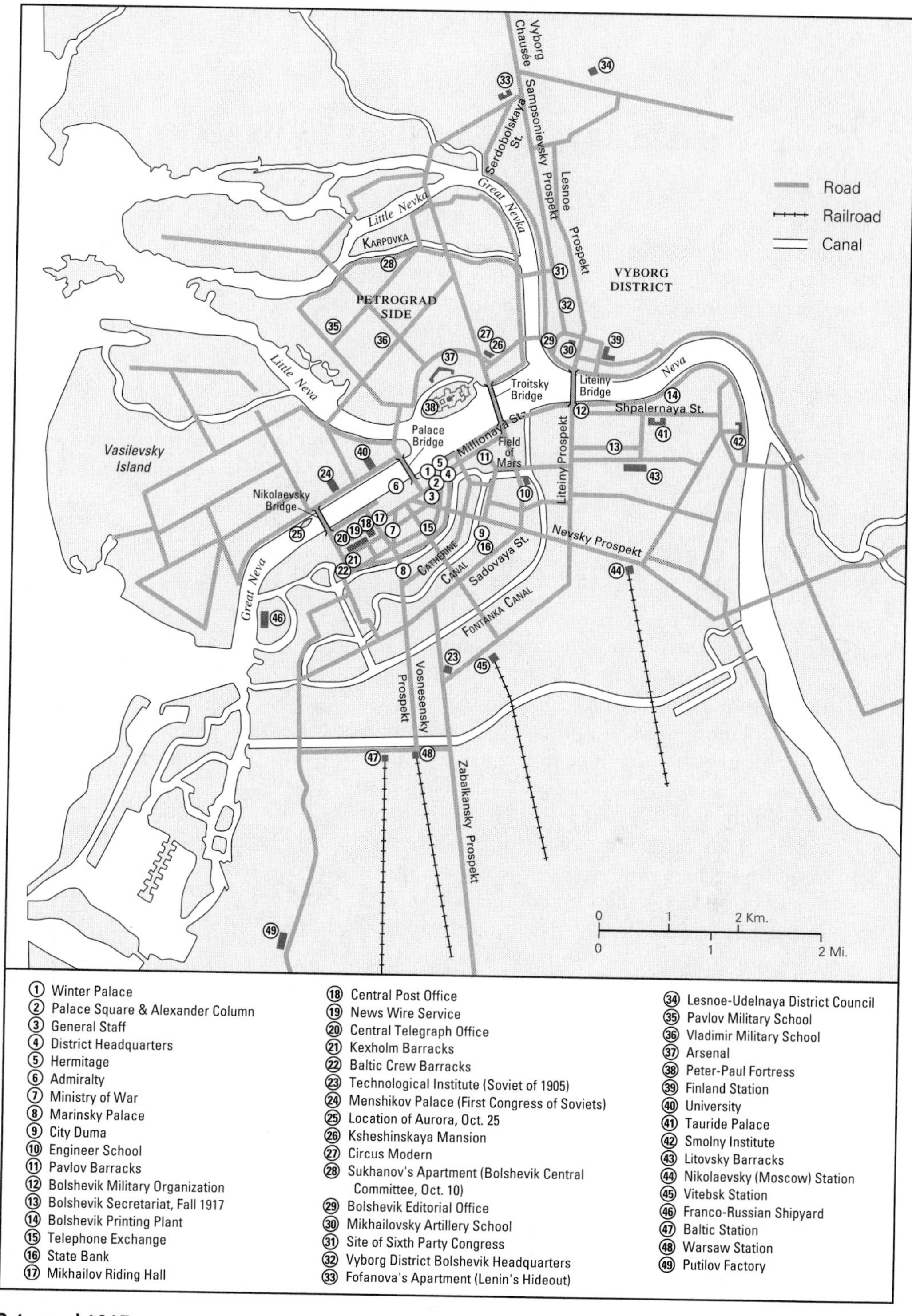

Vyborg Chausée
Sampsonievsky Prospekt
Serdobolskaya St.
Lesnoe Prospekt
Road
Railroad
Canal
VYBORG DISTRICT
Little Nevka
Great Nevka
Karpovka
PETROGRAD SIDE
Little Neva
Neva
Troitsky Bridge
Liteiny Bridge
Shpalernaya St.
Palace Bridge
Millionaya St.
Field of Mars
Liteiny Prospekt
Vasilevsky Island
Nikolaevsky Bridge
Nevsky Prospekt
Catherine Canal
Sadovaya St.
Fontanka Canal
Great Neva
Vosnesensky Prospekt
Zabalkansky Prospekt
0 1 2 Km.
0 1 2 Mi.
① Winter Palace
② Palace Square & Alexander Column
③ General Staff
④ District Headquarters
⑤ Hermitage
⑥ Admiralty
⑦ Ministry of War
⑧ Marinsky Palace
⑨ City Duma
⑩ Engineer School
⑪ Pavlov Barracks
⑫ Bolshevik Military Organization
⑬ Bolshevik Secretariat, Fall 1917
⑭ Bolshevik Printing Plant
⑮ Telephone Exchange
⑯ State Bank
⑰ Mikhailov Riding Hall
⑱ Central Post Office
⑲ News Wire Service
⑳ Central Telegraph Office
㉑ Kexholm Barracks
㉒ Baltic Crew Barracks
㉓ Technological Institute (Soviet of 1905)
㉔ Menshikov Palace (First Congress of Soviets)
㉕ Location of Aurora, Oct. 25
㉖ Ksheshinskaya Mansion
㉗ Circus Modern
㉘ Sukhanov's Apartment (Bolshevik Central Committee, Oct. 10)
㉙ Bolshevik Editorial Office
㉚ Mikhailovsky Artillery School
㉛ Site of Sixth Party Congress
㉜ Vyborg District Bolshevik Headquarters
㉝ Fofanova's Apartment (Lenin's Hideout)
㉞ Lesnoe-Udelnaya District Council
㉟ Pavlov Military School
㊱ Vladimir Military School
㊲ Arsenal
㊳ Peter-Paul Fortress
㊴ Finland Station
㊵ University
㊶ Tauride Palace
㊷ Smolny Institute
㊸ Litovsky Barracks
㊹ Nikolaevsky (Moscow) Station
㊺ Vitebsk Station
㊻ Franco-Russian Shipyard
㊼ Baltic Station
㊽ Warsaw Station
㊾ Putilov Factory

Petrograd 1917. *From Rex Wade,* The Russian Revolution, *1917. Copyright © 2000. Reprinted with the permission of Cambridge University Press.*

FEBRUARY: THE FALL OF THE MONARCHY

By 1917, the rising inflation rate was causing strikes whose leaders tied their economic grievances to the war and the autocratic government. It was that segment of the working class that socialists considered "backward"—proletarian women—who escalated the fray. Food distribution problems created long lines where hungry women needing to feed hungry families waited in the biting cold. On February 23 (March 8 in the West), International Women's Day, Petrograd Social Democrats issued a leaflet declaring that "the government is guilty; it started the war and cannot end it. It is destroying the country and your starving is their fault. The capitalists are guilty; for their profit the war goes on. It's about time to tell them loud: Enough! Down with the criminal government and all its gang of thieves and murderers. Long live peace!" On the same day, throngs of women workers, housewives, and war wives protested the bread shortage. The unrest energized factory workers in the Vyborg District and the giant Putilov Factory workers at the opposite end of town, who had been locked out after a strike. The movement was spurred on by activists who had been working and waiting decades for a manifestation of popular fury. Once the demonstrators crossed the frozen Neva River to center city, they clashed with the police. The revolution had begun.

On day two, the number of protesters rose dramatically all over the city. To the bread protest slogans, a few now added demands to end the war and abolish the autocracy. These voices brought the first serious clashes with the police; but, to the joy of the insurgents, the once dreaded Cossacks, known for their brutal repression of workers' demonstrations, refused to charge into the crowds.

On February 25, Tsar Nicholas at headquarters awoke to the danger of the rebellion in his capital and ordered the garrison commander to put it down. By then some troops had gone over to the crowds in the streets. Later whole units defected; some expelled, and a few killed, their officers. On the ships of the nearby Baltic fleet anchored at Helsinki and Kronstadt, sailors dumped their officers overboard or threw them alive down smokestacks into the furnaces. Shocked by the violence, Duma leaders tried to contact the tsar and urge immediate political measures that they thought might save his throne. But the tsar dismissed the Duma and offered no response to the unrest except police repression. As fast as the forces of order made arrests, the mob stormed prisons and released their inmates. "Civil war has started and is spreading rapidly," telegraphed the president of the Duma to the tsar.

On February 27, two shadow governments appeared to help control what was seen to be a genuine revolution: At the Tauride Palace, seat of the Duma, senior members, instead of disbanding as ordered, formed a committee that a few days later created a temporary, or "provisional," government, self-appointed and not elected. In another wing of the palace, the Petrograd soviet was recreated in the image of its 1905 predecessor, the Council of Workers' Deputies, as a body representing the working class. On that day one of the tsar's crack units, the Volynian Regiment, mutinied, magnifying the crisis. The next day, the Provisional

Government arrested some of the tsar's ministers, mostly to protect them. The stunned Nicholas ordered armed units into Petrograd, departed headquarters, and headed to the capital himself. Blocked by railwaymen, his train was diverted to Pskov, boxing him in physically, geographically, and politically.

A Duma delegation to Pskov tried to persuade the tsar to step down, and his own generals finally convinced him. After anguished hours during which Nicholas considered abdicating in favor of his ailing son, he named his brother successor on March 2. "In agreement with the State Duma, we have thought it best to abdicate the throne of the Russian state and to lay down the supreme power. Not wishing to part with our beloved son, we hand down our inheritance to our brother, Grand Duke Michael Alexandrovich." When Duma members next day urged Michael (1878–1918), king for a day, to give up the honor, conscience, good sense, or fear induced him to decline the throne for the moment, a moment that would never return. Thus on March 3—though no one was yet sure of it—the thousand-year old monarchy, the four-hundred-year-old tsardom, and the three-hundred-year-old Romanov dynasty came crashing down.

Similar revolts occurred in other belligerent states, and some of those—the German, Austro-Hungarian, and Ottoman Empires—later collapsed as well. The fall of the Romanov dynasty is therefore not astonishing. World War I toppled regimes and unleashed terrifying forces that darkened the landscape of Europe between the world wars. The obtuse policies of Tsar Nicholas, whose vaunted love for Russia was mystical and self-defined, made him one of the most unwittingly destructive figures in Russian history. It is unwise to speak confidently of a single cause of revolution. Contributing factors were the uneven development of Russian society; incompetence at the center; war-related turbulence of every sort; and the immediate events on the snowclad streets of the capital. One thing is certain: the forces released by the tsar's fall gave the twentieth century much of its shape.

DUAL POWERLESSNESS: GOVERNMENT AND SOVIETS

The history of the Provisional Government in 1917 unfolded in four roughly two-month segments: the first Provisional Government, March–April; the First Coalition (two or more parties in the cabinet), late May–July; the Second Coalition, late July–August; and the Third (and final) Coalition, September–October. The main Russian parties on the new political landscape were, roughly right to left: the nonsocialist Octobrists (moderate conservative, led by Alexander Guchkov [1862–1936]), and the Kadets (liberal), led by Pavel Milyukov (1859–1943); then came the three leftist parties—the Marxist Social Democrats (SDs), with two branches—Mensheviks (moderate), with several new leaders, and Bolsheviks (radical), led by Vladimir Lenin. The peasant-oriented Socialist Revolutionaries (SRs) had a contested leadership. The anarchists, obeying their creed, confined themselves to disruption and havoc. Further adding to the political complexity and fluidity was the fact that several of these parties split into factions. The main arenas of their struggle were the Provisional Government and the soviets, both of which had to face the masses who burst upon the political scene.

The Provisional Government

To fill the power vacuum, the Provisional Government declared itself the legitimate temporary power in Russia. It resided first in the Tauride Palace and in its last weeks in the Winter Palace, the former tsar's official residence and today the Hermitage Museum. The new prime minister, Prince Georgy Lvov (1861–1925), was a revered public figure rather than a dynamic leader. The foreign minister, Pavel Milyukov (1859–1943), a history professor and leader of the Kadet Party, became the backbone of the first Provisional Government. The war minister, Guchkov, a prominent industrialist, headed the moderate conservative Octobrist Party. Other ministers included businessmen, professionals, and liberal nobles—mostly Kadets and Octobrists, except for one lone socialist lawyer, the justice minister, Alexander Kerensky (1881–1970).

The government believed in law and order, not just to protect property interests, but to preserve lives and a normal flow of life behind the military lines. Appalled at the chaos, violence, and crime that had broken out in the streets in the wake of the February days, its leaders had few means to fight the disorder since they had dismissed most of the hated police and officials of the old regime. As admirers of European and American democracy, they began with sweeping liberal reforms, including "an immediate and complete amnesty in all cases of a political and religious nature, including terrorists acts, military revolts, and agrarian offenses." They also established freedom of speech and the press and other civil liberties and ended discrimination on the basis of class, ethnicity, religion, and—later—gender. For the first time, labor unions were given full freedom to strike. Russia had become a democracy almost overnight. The government made no claim to permanent power. Russia's new system of government was to be decided by a democratically elected constitutional congress, or Constituent Assembly. Leaders of the Provisional Government assumed that the outcome would be either a constitutional monarchy as in England or a republic as in France or the United States. Since continuing the war required national purpose, discipline, and mobilization of energies, they argued that no major changes in land, property rights, and labor legislation—precisely the areas of interest to the lower classes—could be made until the Provisional Government ended and a Constituent Assembly was in place. Though these arguments were presented with great juridical clarity, to their opponents on the left, they reeked of class politics.

In March 1917, a Moscow worker and army deserter wrote: "You (I am addressing the Provisional Government) have the audacity to say that freedom has come. But isn't your current power over the people a power that the bourgeoisie delivered to you, based on coercion?" "The bourgeoisie," he continued, "is striving for democratic forms of governance because in them it sees the most convenient method of oppression and exploitation."

The most divisive issue of 1917 was the war. The government opposed making peace with the Central Powers. Russia's allies, France, Britain, and—from April onward—the United States, applied continuous pressure to stay in the war. If the Allies won, the argument went, Russia would sit at the peace table as an equal in a victorious democratic community of nations. And it would be strengthened by its possession of Istanbul and Galicia and its sway over the Black Sea, in accordance with the secret treaties. The foreign minister Milyukov, a liberal nationalist and a disciple of Russia's historical "destiny," clung to a belief that only victory in league with the Allies would ensure Russia's greatness and potential to build a democracy; and he also felt that staying in the war was the only way to keep society together. He thus identified battlefield discipline with order and obedience at home. Enmeshed in wishful thinking about the stoic endurance of the Russian masses and their desire for new lands to conquer, Milyukov insisted on a war to victory and the retention of the war aims reflected in the secret treaties. On April 20 his views were made public, though couched in cautious terms. A few days later, thousands of outraged citizens and soldiers demonstrated in protest, pummeled his car, and demanded his ouster, which came on May 3. The war minister, Guchkov, appalled at the decline of discipline inside the army, also resigned. Thus ended the first stage of the Provisional Government's agony.

The Soviets

Sharing the Tauride Palace with the Provisional Government, the Petrograd soviet quickly went beyond the 1905 soviet's function as a strike committee or insurrectional base. Established first in February 1917 as a soviet (council) of workers' deputies elected from the factories, it was soon flooded by soldiers sent by their units. Its mission was to keep an eye on the Provisional Government in defense of lower-class interests. The extraordinary juxtaposition of the soviet and the Provisional Government temporarily housed in the same building gave rise to the phrase "dual power," though in fact the situation turned out to be dual powerlessness.

One could hardly imagine an assemblage more different in appearance and manners from the government down the hall. Mass participation came into play as about three thousand deputies—roughly dressed factory hands, recruits, and frontline veterans—shouted out of turn at meetings and voiced their emotions in speeches flowery and crude. The apparent chaos of the soviet meetings, resembling those of a village commune, was misleading: positions were advanced, votes held, measures taken. Bespectacled socialist intellectuals stumbled over sleeping sergeants with rifles in hand and were choked by the smell of the soldiers' cheap tobacco. Most of them were thrilled to be rubbing shoulders with "the people."

An Executive Committee guided the work of the huge and heaving Petrograd soviet. Until late summer, the executive bodies of the larger soviets were dominated by moderate socialists—Mensheviks and SRs. Hundreds of local soviets, each with its own executive committee, sprouted up in towns and garrisons, forming a national network of lower-class politics as counterweight to the town *dumas* and other organs beholden to the Provisional Government. A national congress of

Soldiers and other deputies in the Petrograd Soviet. *Sovfoto.*

soviets gathered in Petrograd in June and in October. The June congress elected a Central Executive Committee and published its *News (Izvestiya),* ancestor of what would be the second most important newspaper of the Soviet Union. Although the Bolshevik Party was marginal in these bodies at first, they were the nucleus of the future Soviet Union's legislative system.

The moderate socialists who guided soviet politics in the eight months after the February Revolution have been dismissed by Soviet historians as "bourgeois conciliators," scolded by liberals for impeding the Provisional Government, condemned as traitors by conservatives, and taxed by some Western historians for making all the wrong moves. They believed they represented the thoughts and feelings of the people and acted on this belief. The Georgian Menshevik Irakli Tsereteli emerged as the main figure in the Petrograd soviet. His Marxist interpretation of events told him that the socialists in the soviets should control the revolutionary energies of the masses, protect and advance their class interests, monitor the "bourgeois" government, and support a war of defense. He and most Mensheviks believed they should not take power because, historically speaking, it was not their turn. In the Marxist scheme (see the chapters "Economic Structures and Visions, 1881–1905" and "Russia on the Barricades: The Revolution of 1904–1907"), the Provisional Government was the bourgeois stage of the revolution. Socialists would have to wait an indefinite period for the growth and crises of Russian capitalism and the upsurge in the size and consciousness of the Russian proletariat. Moderate SRs generally shared the view, if not the theory. Soviet leaders also feared a counterrevolution from the right if they sought to take power.

The soviet leaders opposed chaos from below: "A breakdown of discipline and anarchy will ruin the revolution and the freedom of the people," they warned in their first public statement. Although they distrusted the bourgeoisie, they grudgingly agreed to work with it, but "only in so far as the emergent government acts in the direction of . . . struggling against the old regime." This guarded phrasing indicated that the soviet was the real protector of what it called "the revolutionary democracy," or lower classes, and that the "bourgeois Provisional Government" needed monitoring. Relations between the soviets and the government were thus marked by ambivalence and distrust. The former angered the latter by supporting demands of soldiers, workers, and peasants in the very first days of the revolution. Against the Provisional Government's continuing policy of war to victory and conquest of territory, the socialists proclaimed "revolutionary defensism:" defend the revolution against the Kaiser's army and simultaneously seek a general peace without the territorial and financial spoils of war. But neither the Allies nor the Central Powers were interested in such a peace. Probably no moderate democratic government could have solved the issue of the war. To end it by surrendering could invite a military coup by right-wing nationalists and generals or bring the occupation of Russia by the Germans and the end of democracy. Some who had no love for the war itself feared exactly that.

At first the soviet leaders held aloof from the government. Only Alexander Kerensky, a radical lawyer from Lenin's home town, a nominal SR, and vice-chairman of the Petrograd soviet, decided on his own to join the first Provisional Government as justice minister. When the first cabinet fell in early May, a new one, the First Coalition, retained Lvov as prime minister and brought in socialist ministers: Kerensky moving over to war, the SR Viktor Chernov (1876–1953) coming in for agriculture, Tsereteli for post and telegraph, and a few others. In the summer several more socialists joined, and by the end of the Provisional Government they practically dominated it. These moves, designed to bridge the gap between government and soviet, weakened them both. The very presence of socialists in the government scandalized rightists, as well as some conservatives, nationalists, and military figures, and yet was seen by the far left as betrayal of the revolution. Thus an internal fault line and the flailing pressures from without rendered all the coalition governments unstable. The moderate socialists, precariously straddling the divide between the soviet and the Provisional Government, were further weakened by division within their own ranks and the growing distance between them and the soldiers, sailors, and workers comprising the main body of the soviets.

The Far Left and Lenin

In the Russian revolutionary tradition, there had always been a "far left" that sought radical political and economic solutions to the nation's problems. Such a force reemerged rapidly in the wake of the February Revolution among Bolsheviks and anarchists and the more extreme SRs who came to suspect and oppose not only the Provisional Government but the Petrograd soviet as well of betraying the class interests of the proletariat and of other lower-class people. In a major upheaval such as the Russian Revolution, political figures who had once seemed progressive or even leftist were left behind by the flow of events. To those on the extreme left, the liberals who dominated the Provisional Government now seemed conservative, and the soviet leaders—each and every one a socialist—now seemed bourgeois.

Lenin's Bolshevik Party, which grew into the best-organized element of the far left, was in disarray right after the February Revolution. In Petrograd, Vyacheslav Molotov (a pseudonym derived from the word for hammer) (1890–1986) was a young Bolshevik in charge of *Pravda (Truth),* the Bolshevik newspaper. He was replaced by Iosif Jugashvili ("man of steel") (1889–1953) and Lev Kamenev ("man of stone") (1883–1936), who arrived in Petrograd from Siberia, where they had been exiled by the tsarist authorities for revolutionary activity. They adopted a conciliatory line in *Pravda* toward the Provisional Government. This contradicted the thinking of Bolshevik leader Vladimir Lenin, who was anxious to return to Russia from Switzerland. The Allied powers, seeing all Russian radicals in exile as disruptive of the war effort, hindered their passage; the Germans for the opposite reason had financed Bolshevik revolutionary activity and now let Lenin pass through Germany in a visa-free railroad car. Those who later accused him of treason had a different notion of loyalty from that of Lenin, who was happy to use German money to overthrow the Russian government and to foment revolt in Germany against the very people who had paid him. With a small entourage, Lenin traveled through Germany, Sweden, and Finland and arrived at the Petrograd Finland Station on April 3, 1917.

As a revolutionary Marxist, Lenin wanted to destroy what he saw as an imperialist conspiracy of European capitalists to keep the workers in chains. Since Russia, the weakest member of this club, was now in turmoil, Lenin pushed for radical change. In his "April Theses," delivered orally on April 3 and published a few days later, Lenin assaulted the Provisional Government and the soviet leadership's cooperation with it and its policy of revolutionary defensism. A democratic peace was impossible under the present capitalist government, he said, since capitalism was by nature imperialist. "We preach the need to transfer all state power to the Soviet of Workers' Deputies." To Lenin, "soviet power" meant that the soviets—shorn of their present compromising leaders—would rule Russia without a partnership with the Provisional Government. Such a republic of soviets would have the support of workers and poor peasants because it would confiscate the land and give it to the peasants, and would control—not yet abolish—capitalism to the advantage of the proletariat. Lenin broke definitively with the moderate socialists, whom he considered class traitors. The "April Theses" was a time bomb that did not explode right away because the soviet leaders were shocked at its extremism. Lenin's own party was not yet ready for his line, and the popular mood had yet to reach his level of radicalism.

The Masses

Historians have argued for decades about how radical the population really was in 1917. It is crucial to make distinctions within and among those who pressured the government for more change than was immediately occurring: workers, peasants, nationalities, and the armed forces. The industrial work force, though streaked with radicalism, was stratified in terms of wages and skills, and its explosiveness varied from place to place. Some entire mill towns turned radical and pro-Bolshevik; elsewhere workers were relatively inert. In Petrograd most workers aspired in the early months to an end to the war and an eight-hour day. The latter was so central to workers' demands that many of them simply stopped work at the conclusion of eight hours in the mill. Workers also wanted better conditions, respectful treatment, and higher wages, since rampant inflation was eating away their earnings. Their aspirations included a more egalitarian society and something like a welfare state. Labor unions pressed their demands, which were sometimes met by lockouts.

More radical than the unions were the factory committees of workers formed in various industrial plants for direct action. On their own or in response to owners' lockouts, they began exercising "workers' control"—not direct management but the dismissal of unpopular foremen and checking on profits. When bosses shut down in protest to this unheard-of breach of business etiquette, workers carted bosses out of the plant on wheelbarrows and took over the factory. Mispronouncing the Russian word for bourgeois, workers flung out the abusive term *burzhui* to indicate bosses and rich people. The SRs and Bolsheviks organized factory cells and conducted propaganda among men and women of every occupation—including laundresses, prostitutes, waitresses, and servants. Strikes embraced oil, mining, transport, industrial, catering, and even white-collar employees. Some 2.4 million workers struck from March to October and added political demands to bread-and-butter issues like hours and wages. Radical class consciousness increased among workers, and class hatred heated up on both sides. The strike wave rose to a peak by October.

Peasant demands were couched in the elementary vocabulary of sustenance, peace, and land. Although noble landowning had been declining for decades and peasants had been buying up land, most village people considered themselves land poor and deemed state, gentry, or absentee landowning unjust. After February peasants sent thousands of letters and telegrams to the capitals. One, addressed in May 1917 to the Petrograd soviet and the Provisional Government from peasants in Petrograd Province, stated that "the land in its entirety must belong to whoever cultivates it, since the land was taken away from us by forcible authority and so the land should transfer into the hands of the working people." Village delegations arrived in Petrograd and asked that "the Revolution" grant them all the land. Political parties divided over how or whether to do this, and the Provisional Government turned a legalistic face to them, created Land Committees, and talked of land laws to come. Even when the SR leader Chernov became minister of agriculture, political squabbling hindered any real settlement. Once a radical, Chernov had become a moderate, and although his party, the SRs, called for the transfer of all land without compensation to the peasantry, the SR leaders insisted on slow legal procedures. Peasants waited for a time, and then in May, with the aid of the local committees and returning soldiers, many seized private cropland, meadows, pastures, forests, buildings, horses, and equipment to be divided among the families in the peasant commune. Most illegal agrarian actions in 1917—with estimates ranging from five thousand to over sixteen thousand—were nonviolent. The days of large-scale pillage and arson were yet to come.

In the midst of war and political unrest, the non-Russian nationalities saw a chance to pull out of the imperial orbit and one by one voiced demands, ranging from autonomy to full independence. Finnish patriots argued that since the Grand Duke of Finland (the tsar) was no more, Finland was free. Since Poland was in the hands of the German army, the Provisional Government had no trouble granting it independence. The Baltic lands, Ukraine, and some of the Transcaucasian nations were also straining for national freedom. Only Armenia remained solidly loyal, owing to its fear of the Turks. Ukraine, the Russian Empire's largest non-Russian land, posed the greatest threat. When in March Ukrainian nationalists in Kiev proclaimed the Rada (council or soviet) as the new government and began campaigning for autonomy, the Russian government grew alarmed for the integrity of the state. Separatist demands continued to plague the Provisional Government, though without resolution, until its collapse.

The most volatile force on the revolutionary landscape turned out to be the armed forces. As the tsar was abdicating in February, the Petrograd soviet, induced by soldiers' and sailors' deputies, issued a subsequently famous decree called Order No. 1, a stunning intervention into traditional military life. It required the election of committees in all units of the armed forces, land and sea, and of deputies to the local soviet. The units were to obey the military orders of their commanders but were to be subordinate in political—as opposed to military—matters to the Petrograd soviet. This in effect placed the armed forces under dual control. Soldiers and sailors, though subject to discipline while on duty, were to be treated as citizens while off duty and at all times with respect by officers, who could no longer address them with the familiar form of "you"—an important social distinction in Russian. The elected committees soon went well beyond Order No. 1 by holding elections of officers and voting to refuse to go into combat.

Officers of the old school were scandalized by Order No. 1, but contrary to beliefs held then and now, Order No. 1 was not designed to disrupt the army, though the intellectuals and garrison soldiers who drafted it did not understand the impact that democracy would have. The effect was at first far from uniform. Some soldiers' committees were dominated by the government or the general staff rather than by the soviets. Also, up until June, most frontline units kept to military discipline as Order No. 1 demanded. Like the soviet leaders, many of the troops also believed in revolutionary defensism, which to them meant exactly that: passive defense against German attacks while the politicians worked out a peace. Yet regardless of intention, the order further radicalized the garrisons and infected the front by giving soldiers a voice in a culture where the officers' word had been law. Troop deputies elected to the soviets received further training in suspicion of officers and the upper classes. Bolshevik and SR agitators visited units to preach frontline democracy.

Key figures among the educated and privileged public loathed the chaos and the unheard-of entry into politics and foreign policy of what some called "the rabble" and "those lunatics and dreamers" of the left, as one ex-Duma member called them. The radicals believed that the high and mighty were shedding the people's blood in a war for profits and imperialist land grabs and that the Provisional Government was "a brake on the revolutionary cause." Black hatred of the war and of capitalism and a vigorous surge toward deeper social revolution did not engulf the masses immediately, was never complete, and alternated with moods of caution—with great diversity among locales and social groups. However, the inflammatory mixture of war and social stress ultimately burst traditional constraints. Society was divided over whether to continue a war or deepen the revolution. A political culture of moderation might have reached a compromise.

THE LID COMES OFF: SPECTACLES OF FREEDOM

Revolutions, like wars, are often remembered as panoramas of violence and suffering. What noble feelings could possibly arise in the midst of human wreckage? And yet, hard as it is to credit, there is often romance in revolution as there is sometimes whimsy, adventure, and even lyricism in war. The springtime of the Russian Revolution was euphoric, in spite of the continuing anxiety and tension about the war. The early months actually coincided with spring. Popular moods warmed up like the weather, and poetic minds began flinging out metaphors of nature—thaw, melting the ice of autocracy, the cruel winter of tsarism giving way to torrents of creative renewal and the sprouting of freedom. Political bloodshed was surprisingly low at first. Only about four hundred were killed in Petrograd during the February fighting. Increased urban violence stemmed mostly from everyday crime. Vandalism was directed against tsarist double-headed eagles and hated police stations, insurrection against prisons—which were raided by crowds who liberated prisoners and displayed them in triumphant parades.

In Petrograd, the "Victims Who Fell for Freedom" in the February days were interred in a common grave on the Field of Mars—the old drill ground of the tsar's military—with thousands of citizens in attendance. A metal worker of Smolensk Province fashioned his own tribute to the martyrs:

To the Fallen Freedom Fighters
Memory eternal to all who have fought.
For freedom through great tribulation!
The blood they sacrificed has bought
This sacred freedom for our nation.

The demise of the monarchy ushered in a temporary era of good feelings, and people of all ranks began calling each other "citizen," to the dismay of certain aristocrats. Soldiers and sailors, formerly barred as potential unruly elements, now strolled in public gardens and rode inside the trams. Working-class public life became highly politicized. Revolutionary orators harangued the multitudes in huge halls and circus arenas.

After February 1917, women entered political life on an unprecedented scale. Organized socialists and feminists divided over the great issues. Feminists confronted the government with suffrage demands, which, after some stalling, were met on July 20, 1917, when all citizens of both sexes aged twenty and over got the right to vote. Russia thus became the first major country in Europe to grant women the vote (Finland had done so in 1906). Most feminists supported the government's war effort and eagerly blessed the women's volunteer combat units, which were drawn from all classes. Socialist women, particularly the Bolsheviks, organized working-class women and struggled against feminist bids to win them over to "bourgeois" politics.

In the lavish imperial theaters, the traditions of high culture persisted: the large

Long Live Equal Rights for Women. *Tass/Sovfoto.*

stages continued to offer foreign and Russian classic plays; the concert hall presented Beethoven and Tchaikovsky. But the management became democratic, actors gained more rights, and free tickets were issued to workers. The great stages of the capital were also opened up to gala productions commemorating the fall of the autocracy, at which audiences of all classes roared out the French revolutionary anthem "The Marseillaise"—a bow to the French ally. Conservative cultural leaders hoped to expose the lower classes to the beauties of high culture, while the socialists wished to promote political art. But when socialists organized their own workers' theaters, audiences sometimes spoiled the offerings through rowdiness. The lower classes, while enjoying revolutionary spectacles, delighted even more in vulgar farces and melodrama and a rash of explicit plays and movies about Rasputin and Satanism, now liberated from the censor. Though the intelligentsia was dismayed by this, the government largely refrained from interference.

Religious and ethnic discrimination was officially ended. The Russian Orthodox Church took the opportunity to revivify itself by calling a church council in August and restoring the patriarchate, which had been in abeyance since the eighteenth century. Now free of its fetters, the church had no desire to lose its privileges as the state religion—or its property and schools. It also voiced some fears about anarchy and collapse. This huge and diverse council, comprising both laity and clergy, represented real hope for religious revival in Russia in the context of order, harmony, and rejuvenation of the living faith, as well as a linkup of the church to civil society and private lives.

One ethnic minority that stood out in the thick of events in the capitals was the Jews. Although they could be found in all the parties except those of the far right, Jews were most visible on the left, in the SR, Bolshevik, Menshevik, and anarchist parties. Even though those parties were numerically more Russian than anything else, the presence of Jews gave rise to the poisonous belief that the revolution was somehow a Jewish conspiracy—a notion that would inspire frightful atrocities later, when civil war erupted.

THE SUMMER OF 1917

By summer, the civic solidarity of the first months had eroded. In the second phase of the Provisional Government's history, the First Coalition, socialists sat alongside liberals and conservatives in the cabinet, which fell under the blows of a failed offensive in Galicia and the so-called July Days. The late summer, July and August, was the time of the Second Coalition, under Prime Minister Kerensky, and of a threat to his power by a military strong man. In the heat of the summer, moderate leaders—liberals, conservatives, and socialists—were menaced from both the left and the right.

Danger from the Left: The Days of June and July

Trouble erupted when soviets from all over the land sent over eight hundred delegates to the first national Congress of Soviets in Petrograd, June 3–24. The congress elected mostly moderate Mensheviks and SRs to a Central Executive Committee, which confirmed their support for the Provisional Government. Although the Bolsheviks held only 15 percent of the seats, Lenin stated publicly that his party stood ready to assume power. The "street"—workers, soldiers, and sailors—angrily pressed the Bolsheviks to mount an antiwar and antigovernment "demonstration," or protest march, on June 10. When the march was forbidden by the congress, the Bolsheviks, fearing a political backlash, called it off. A week later the congress mounted its own demonstration, designed to uphold its moderate policies. But an unprecedented mass of more than a third of a million people strode through the city with posters bearing radical slogans, some—like "Down with the Ten Capitalist Ministers"—aimed directly against the Provisional Government. These incidents, known as the June Days, revealed the growing gulf between the militant Petrograd masses and the soviet leaders.

The replacement in May of War Minister Guchkov by Kerensky and of Foreign Minister Milyukov by Mikhail Tereshchenko, a Kadet sugar manufacturer, had not fundamentally changed the First Coalition's conduct of the war. Kerensky, pressured by Allied ambassadors to relieve the Western front, gambled that a successful offensive would bring peace and, on June 16, launched an attack against Austrian Galicia, one of the territorial prizes promised by the secret treaties. The action began with a flourish as the minister himself harangued the troops at the front and volunteer units were formed: Czech deserters from the Austro-Hungarian army, shock brigades, decorated heroes, and a volunteer women's combat unit. Radical agitators saw the offensive as opposite of the stated policy of defensive war, and they suspected imperialist war aims were involved. As the enemy pushed back and overran Russian lines, thousands of troops deserted, and the campaign sputtered to a halt on July 2.

At that point, as a direct result of Kerensky's offensive, occurred a major uprising, known as the July Days. Demonstrators took to the streets, calling irately for an immediate peace and the transfer of government to the soviets—basic slogans from Lenin's arsenal. Lenin wavered on the decision to join forces with this largely spontaneous street action and then followed the tide. Whipped up by agitators, tens of thousands joined the march, carrying the slogans "Bread, Land, Peace" and "All Power to the Soviets" on their banners. A machine-gun regiment, reinforced by workers and sailors from the nearby Kronstadt Island naval base, on July 3–5 engaged in skirmishes with police and Provisional Government troops and in random shootings that took hundreds of lives. "Enough hesitations!" went the Bolshevik-inspired resolution of a workers' meeting at a gunpowder factory on July 4, 1917, which urged the soviet leaders to seize power "in the name of freedom, in the name of peace, in the name of the worldwide proletarian revolution." At the Tauride Palace, armed demonstrators terrorized the soviet leaders and ordered them to take power. The SR leader Chernov was almost lynched by sailors, one of whom screamed

at him, "Take power, you son-of-a-bitch, when it is offered to you." Cossacks and regular regiments put down the demonstrators.

These violent events raised the stakes in the power struggle and almost destroyed the Provisional Government. The uprising failed because the soviet leaders refused to take power and because Bolshevik leadership of the crowds was belated and poorly organized. In the aftermath, the government mounted a military and ecclesiastical public funeral for its loyal Cossack defenders killed in the fray, a symbolic celebration of the counterrevolutionary mood that deepened among public figures. The authorities closed *Pravda,* arrested some Bolshevik leaders (Lenin fled), and unleashed a campaign to discredit the Bolsheviks as traitors in the pay of the German general staff. Some of the accusations were based on forged documents.

Danger from the Right: General Kornilov

There were eight socialist and ten Kadet ministers in the First Coalition. In early July, five Kadets, including Prince Lvov, resigned over issues of rural, labor, and army unrest and the rising demands of the Ukrainian Rada. After two weeks, a Second Coalition was formed, with Kerensky now as prime minister and with the socialists outnumbering Kadet ministers. Kerensky, a Russian patriot with socialist leanings, was a far more colorful leader than the gentle Prince Lvov. But neither flamboyant and emotional speechmaking nor the dashing energy of the new prime minister could hold together what was moving rapidly beyond the control of his well-meaning government. The month of July brought nightmares to Kerensky: strident demands by Ukrainian and other nationalist leaders for autonomy or independence; a trebling of strikes by industrial workers; and a spiraling of class war in the villages and estates. After the disastrous failure of the Galicia offensive, hordes of peasant soldiers deserted to save their lives and to return to the village and share in land settlements. Officials reported that about 200,000 soldiers had deserted before the February Revolution, and more than 365,000 from March to August 1917. On top of all this, Kerensky had to send troops to suppress a so-called Tsaritsyn Republic, declared by Bolsheviks and radicalized soldiers stationed in that Volga town.

While beleaguered by these problems stirred up on the left, Kerensky at the same time had to face a shadow looming up on the right. It was cast by Lavr Kornilov, a brave Cossack general of humble birth appointed commander in chief after the dismissal of General Brusilov, who had led the recent offensive. Kornilov became a rallying point for the forces of law and order in August at a special Moscow State Conference summoned by Kerensky. The old capital deep inside Russia was more conservative than Petrograd and less encumbered by disaffected troops, though even here arriving delegates were greeted by a transport strike organized by Bolsheviks. Kerensky invited former Duma members and other public figures to lend weight and stability to its proceedings. His sincere effort to build consensus among social strata failed, because the will was not there. With each speech the audience polarized into booing and applauding sides. Kerensky won adoring response from some and hateful sneers from others. When Kornilov spoke in straightforward patriotic tones, he evoked the enthusiastic adulation of those who saw in him the strong man—a new Bonaparte who could unite Russia, curb the revolutionary fever, and restore Russia's greatness. Kornilov's iron bearing, his undiluted patriotism, and even his colorful escort of Turkmenian warriors bespoke the values of empire and old-fashioned military obedience. He easily won the support of professional officers' associations and nationalist groups; among industrialists and conservative party leaders he met both success and resistance.

After the Moscow State Conference, in an atmosphere of mutual hostility between Kerensky and the forces on the right, occurred the famous "Kornilov Affair," which brought about a reassortment of revolutionary forces. Although the episode is still wrapped in controversy, it is clear that some Kornilov supporters wished to overthrow the government, demote Kerensky, and install Kornilov as a military dictator. The general himself did not hatch such a plot. He did want a strong hand in Petrograd that would restore army discipline, prosecute the war, and repress the Bolsheviks. According to a colleague, Kornilov appointed as one of his commanders a man who would not, if need be, hesitate to hang every member in the soviet. This suggests that Kornilov had a blurred view of the distinctions among socialists. There is no doubt that he and his backers wanted to reverse much of what the Russian Revolution stood for up to that time. In the early stages of the episode, Kornilov's and Kerensky's wishes seemed to coincide. In a telegraph conversation marked by gross misunderstanding and in messages suspiciously garbled by intermediaries, the general claimed to believe that Kerensky needed troops to stave off a Bolshevik coup; Kerensky claimed to believe that Kornilov was planning a coup, and he dismissed him as commander in chief. At that point Kornilov sent troops toward the capital, who were stopped by railway workers and soldiers. Kornilov was arrested.

Summer ended with a new balance of forces and an upsurge of disorder. To fend off forces supporting Kornilov, Kerensky released Bolsheviks from prison and sought help from the Red Guard, paramilitary detachments that had grown out of workers' militias of earlier months. The swing to the left caused by the Kornilov threat won votes for the Bolsheviks in the soviets of the capitals. Strikes brought industrial production almost to a halt. During this last summer and autumn of the Russian gentry, the specter of agrarian mutiny that had been lurking in the landlords' consciousness since 1905 rose again as peasants occupied ancient nests of gentlefolk, cut down orchards, gutted manor houses, and forced noble families to flee. A landowner's daughter described what happened on her estate in October: "The whole village assembled and once again the axes began to strike. . . . They chopped out the windows, doors and floors, smashed the mirrors and divided up the pieces, and so on. At three o'clock in the afternoon they set light to the house from all sides, using for the purpose . . . kerosene." Stolypin's grand plan of "privatizing" the peasantry (see the chapter "The 'Duma Monarchy,' 1907–1914") was reversed as peasants took land collectively and even forced individual farmers back into the commune. Neither landlords nor the Stolypin individual farmers stood by passively: they sued trespassers and petitioned the Provisional Government for punitive military action along the lines of the 1905 suppression of peasant unrest.

Soldiers' hatred of the "Kornilovites" deepened distrust of and violence toward officers at the front and in the rear. A passionate desire for peace exacerbated popular dissatisfaction with the Provisional Government, which was accused by Kornilovites of catering to socialism and tarred by radical socialists for its alleged "Kornilovism." Both government and soviet leaders misjudged the temper of the masses. It is a mark of the titanic social divisions accelerated by the revolution that the well-meaning and largely moderate figures who ran government affairs in Petrograd in the autumn probably had no chance to bridge the gap. The whole situation invited extreme solutions. The liberal Milyukov believed that the only real alternatives were a Kornilov or a Lenin—in other words, a dictatorship of the right or of the left.

OCTOBER IN PETROGRAD

In September, Kerensky formed a five-man directory, a term from the French Revolution that suggested stabilization of the revolution—and declared Russia a republic. To shore up legitimacy for his frazzled government, Kerensky agreed to a soviet proposal for a Democratic Conference, which in turn created yet another consultative assembly. With almost five hundred people and a moderate socialist majority, this gathering bore the cumbersome name Provisional Council of the Russian Republic, or Pre-Parliament. On September 25, Kerensky formed his last cabinet—the Third Coalition, mostly moderate socialists. The latter seemed to be inching toward national power but would not make the leap by expelling the nonsocialists from the Provisional Government. The Bolsheviks cast acrimonious insults at the government for continuing to work with the "bourgeoisie" and demonstratively walked out of the Democratic Conference and later the Pre-Parliament.

Lenin Prepares an Uprising

As strike activity peaked toward September, labor support in the cities had shifted to the best-organized party on the left, the Bolsheviks. After the disarray following the July Days, Bolshevik strength grew in industrial centers and military units. One estimate puts the leap in membership from about twenty-three thousand in early 1917 to about seventy-nine thousand in May, and then—after a dip in July—to about two hundred thousand in August. In reaction to the Kornilov scare, voters had elected Bolshevik majorities in the Petrograd, Moscow, and many local soviets. The Bolshevik appeal to soldiers and workers was enhanced by the party's loose alliance with the left SRs. The Socialist Revolutionary Party, the largest political organization in Russia, was buffeted by personal and ideological differences and was driven by the events of 1917. Prime Minister Kerensky, a nominal SR, and the Petrograd SR leadership would not countenance fundamental land reform for the time being, and they feared the radicalism of the rank and file and of local agitators who promoted agrarian disorders. So the more radical wing of the SR Party began calling themselves Left SRs, and they joined the Bolshevik assaults on the Provisional Government. The most important individual crossover came in August, when Lev Trotsky (1879–1940) joined the Bolsheviks. Born Lev Davidovich Bronstein of a prosperous Jewish family, Trotsky had been an independent Menshevik since 1903 and then joined the Bolshevik Central Committee at the party's Sixth Congress. A man of remarkable oratorical power and adorned with the halo of the 1905 days, Trotsky became once again the chairman of the Petrograd soviet.

After fleeing following the July Days, Lenin had hidden in various places until October, mostly in adjacent Finnish territory, where Kerensky's police had no jurisdiction. Lenin's attitude to the soviets had always depended on who held sway in them. From September on, he called for an armed uprising against the Provisional Government in the name of soviet power. After sending letters urging his comrades to prepare the uprising, Lenin returned to Petrograd for a secret meeting of a dozen members of the Central Committee on October 10 in a conspiratorial flat of a friend. The debate over an armed uprising revealed deep rifts still lingering in Lenin's party. Two of his closest comrades, Grigory Zinoviev (1883–1936) and Lev Kamenev (1883–1936), like the moderate Mensheviks and SRs, feared both losing and winning: history, they maintained, would ensure the first or avenge the second. It was a position drawn from the moderate Russian Marxist claim that Russia was not ripe for a proletarian revolution and from Friedrich Engels's famous warning about the inevitability of a harsh dictatorship if a premature seizure took place. Lenin's position that the rising was both possible and mandatory was backed by the majority. Zinoviev and Kamenev leaked this information to the press and drew Lenin's wrath. In spite of their grievous breach of revolutionary etiquette—tantamount to treason in Bolshevik politics—the pair remained in the party and reentered Lenin's orbit. Another fight broke out over the timing of the uprising. Lenin wanted to strike for power independently of other socialist parties, who would soon assemble for the second national Congress of Soviets. Trotsky and others persuaded him to coordinate the uprising with that congress to ensure it some legitimacy and socialist support. In the chaotic conditions of the time, the congress was postponed until October 25; the insurrection came about partly by chance and partly by planning.

The Seizure of Power

In mid-October a Military Revolutionary Committee of the Petrograd soviet was set up, originally to stop Petrograd troops from being sent to the front, then to defend the city against possible German or Provisional Government attack. Eventually it was used by the Bolsheviks to organize the takeover. Under Trotsky's effective guidance, the Military Revolutionary Committee won support in the garrisons. Trotsky ordered arms from weapons plants for the Red Guard units and planned the infiltration of key tactical points in the city. With two decades of underground experience, Bolshevik leaders had no trouble deploying their agents. They also spread false rumors that Kerensky was planning to hand over Petrograd to the Germans and thus bury the revolution, though some on the right would have welcomed this. Just as the right was unwilling to distinguish between Kerensky, moderate socialists, and Bolsheviks, so the Bolsheviks put all their foes into the box of counterrevolution. The Bolshevik leaders looked on the insurrection as a war and were happy to use all means, fair or foul.

On October 23, Trotsky won over the garrison of the Peter and Paul Fortress. Kerensky seized the Bolshevik press, which was soon recaptured. On the night of October 25, while Trotsky spoke to the soviet congress about defensive measures against Kerensky, Bolshevik forces fanned out over the city. They occupied military strongholds, the railroad station to interdict the movement of troops, and the post and telegraph office to deny its use to the Provisional Government and to broadcast news of the coup. Next morning the Military Revolutionary Committee proclaimed the Provisional Government overthrown. Kerensky fled the capital in an unsuccessful bid to rally troops to his side. He later left the country and eventually became an American professor, defending himself for decades from vilification by left and right.

The capture of the Winter Palace, headquarters of the Provisional Government, on the night of October 26 was later mythologized in Sergei Eisenstein's film masterpiece *October* (1927) as a mighty epic with hundreds of workers and soldiers storming the palace and overcoming stiff resistance. In fact, the event was a modest affair and relatively bloodless compared with the street fighting in Moscow and other cities that soon followed. From early evening till two o'clock in the morning, workers and soldiers waited around for reinforcements from Kronstadt. Red Guards disarmed officer cadets and a unit of the Women's Battalion defending the Winter Palace after some exchange of fire and a handful of casualties. A blank shell fired from the ship *Aurora,* anchored in the Neva River, and some live rounds from the Peter and Paul Fortress simply added embellishments to the struggle. The last members of the Provisional Government, seated in the Circular Dining Room, were arrested and taken to the fortress. For decades, Soviet museum guides would show tourists this room in the Hermitage (the former Winter Palace) as the setting for the culmination of a heroic exploit.

Across town, in Bolshevik headquarters at the Smolny Institute—recently a finishing school for aristocratic girls—the soviet congress was informed that the coup d'état had succeeded. Tempestuous protests rose from the moderate socialists, who then indignantly walked out. In doing so, they left the congress in the hands of the Bolsheviks. Trotsky, in one of the most famous of all revolutionary utterances, contemptuously told them to "go into the trash can of history."

The seizure of power on October 23–26,* known as the Bolshevik or October Revolution—or in Communist poetics as Red October—was of course an urban coup d'état reflecting local circumstances. But its success and aftermath were made

*The official date was October 25, which in the modern calendar is November 7.

possible by much broader developments, most particularly the radicalization of the masses, who, while often influenced by political slogans, were driven by spontaneous passions about class justice. The Bolshevik takeover, once accomplished, triggered an even larger chain of events across Russia that plunged the country into a bloody civil war. The Bolsheviks, renamed Communists, established Soviet power and would keep it for almost seventy-four years, but only by abandoning the democratic elements of socialism and erecting a revolutionary dictatorship.

CHAPTER 31

Civil War: Reds, Whites, and Greens, 1917–1921

1. United, Great, Indivisible Russia. Defense of the faith. Establishment of order. Reconstruction of the productive forces of the country and of the national economy. Raising labor productivity. 2. Struggle with bolshevism to the end. 3. Military dictatorship.
—Points 1–3 of the program of General Anton Denikin, leader of the Anticommunist White Armies, 1920

It is necessary to protect the Soviet Republic from class enemies by isolating them in concentration camps. All those involved in White Guard organizations, plots, and revolts are to be shot.
—Soviet Commissar of Justice D. I. Kursky, September 5, 1918

The crises that had faced Kerensky paled beside those of the Bolsheviks, who had no experience administering a country. Among their first tasks were forming a government, issuing revolutionary decrees, ending the war, and consolidating power in scores of cities where the Bolsheviks had come to power. The new regime moved the capital to Moscow, fleeing a possible German occupation of Petrograd. From the very beginning, the Bolsheviks were confronted with opposition among a wide range of forces—conservatives, liberals, democratic socialists, and sometimes even elements of the working class who had helped them into power. The most active of the anti-Bolshevik forces conspired to foment uprisings in the towns or began gathering military forces on the edges of the empire.

SOVIET RUSSIA

One of the first questions to emerge after the Bolshevik seizure of power in October 1917 was, Who would rule? An all-Bolshevik cabinet headed by Lenin was formed. But the majority of workers, soldiers, rank-and-file socialists, and the Congress of Soviets and its Central Executive Committee, as well as several Bolshevik leaders championed an all-socialist coalition of Bolsheviks, Mensheviks, and SRs that would exclude the Kadets and all parties to their right. Though undemocratic, this program was more inclusive than the one-party dictatorship that Lenin wanted. He feared the irresolution that had made the Provisional Government and the soviets impotent. Given the stubbornness of the moderate Mensheviks and SRs and their demonstrative walkout from the Congress of Soviets, Lenin was not completely wrong. Lenin also doubted the political wisdom of the masses and believed that only he and his party were fit to rule. This led him to resist forming a coalition government and later to close down the Constituent Assembly and persecute opposition. After weeks of squabbling, Lenin, pressured by his own people and by railway workers, relented. Left SRs were brought into the cabinet in December.

The new government was based on the national network of soviets and their elected congress, whose Central Executive Committee was now chaired by an energetic Bolshevik, Yakov Sverdlov (1885–1919), the first head of state, or president. That body nominally chose the cabinet, or Council of People's Commissars (Sovnarkom, the Russian acronym), the term *commissar* being considered more revolutionary than *minister.* Lenin was the Sovnarkom chairman (equivalent to prime minister and the real chief executive). Trotsky was named foreign commissar and Stalin commissar of nationalities. The Left SR Isaak Steinberg headed the Justice Commissariat. After Left SR cabinet resignations in 1918 and the gradual disappearance of non-Bolsheviks everywhere in government, the soviet state became a one-party dictatorship in which the party made its presence felt in every institution created or inherited by the new regime—police, courts, press, the economy. In 1918 the Bolsheviks took the name Russian Communist Party, a sign of the transition from revolutionary movement to ruling machine. The party chose a Central Committee and held congresses yearly until Stalin's time. But power lay in the half-dozen-member Political Bureau, or Politburo—first named in 1917 but in continuous operation only from 1919—and in the Secretariat and Orgburo, which handled internal party matters.

Revolutionary Politics

The regime's decrees of the first few weeks alternated between moderation and startling radicalism. The moderate ones (some inherited from the Provisional Government) decreed secular education, separation of church and state, abolition of class distinctions and titles, and equality of nationalities. Calendar reform aligned Russian chronology with the West, starting in February 1918, and the Russian alphabet was simplified. Much more novel, but still within a reformist tradition, was the declaration of sexual equality: legal divorce (and abortion in 1920) and gender equality in the law, the family, the economy, and politics—an equal rights amendment before the term was invented.

The more radical measures that shocked conservatives and liberals cut straight to economic and social foreign policies. Lenin fashioned the slogan of "Bread, Peace, Land" into decrees. For the countryside, Lenin's Decree on Land, issued October 27, 1917, was adapted from the SR program and recent peasant resolutions. It recognized what had already been accomplished in part by peasant actions: the transfer of all private land into the tillers' hands. Since Lenin thought that full socialism would have to await the dawn of revolution in Europe, for the first eight months he limited economic revolution in the cities to partial nationalizing—of the banks and some major industries—but left most enterprises in private hands, under the watchful eye from above of a Supreme Economic Council, and from below of legalized workers' control. The new government, in an act of social reversal, appointed residence committees, who expelled the wealthy or forced them to share their apartments with working-class families; servants sometimes took vengeful glee in relocating former masters. Lenin's new regime was well received by important sections of the lower-class population, though some of it would soon erode.

Lenin grudgingly approved elections to the Constituent Assembly, that long-promised body that the Provisional Government believed would reorder Russia on a democratic basis. For the major parties, the voting produced roughly the results found in Table 1. The clear SR victory indicated the popularity of that party, especially in the countryside, where its vote was heaviest. The splitoff of the Left SRs, whose program resembled that of the Bolsheviks, came after the election and was not reflected in the tally. This and the strong Bolshevik showing in towns, railroad centers, and the army strengthened the party's belief that it should govern—though the evidence shows that it could not do so democratically.

On January 5, 1918, the long-awaited body met in the Tauride Palace. The Bolshevik-controlled secret police spied on the delegates and allowed only anti–Constituent Assembly demonstrations. Clothed in frock coats, peasant blouses, and Central Asian and Tatar costumes, delegates brought candles and food to the palace in fear of a blackout or siege. In an atmosphere of solemn piety, they sang revolutionary songs and elected the SR Viktor Chernov as chair. But the regime packed the hall with armed men who threatened him with such remarks as, "This guy should get a bayonet between his ribs." When the assembly refused to endorse soviet power, the Bolsheviks walked out. After hours of debate among remaining delegates, a sailor told the "granddads" to go home because the guard was tired.

TABLE 1 Selected Data on the Election to the Constituent Assembly, 1917

Parties	Votes
SRs	16,535,680
Bolsheviks	10,536,768
Kadets	2,072,258
Mensheviks	1,433,909
Total	44,218,555

Source: From Oliver Radkey, *Russia Goes to the Polls: The Election to the All-Russian Constituent Assembly, 1917* (Ithaca, 1990), pp. 150–151.

With this crude utterance of class and generational contempt, Russia's only democratically elected parliament until the late twentieth century was dismissed. Next day, the palace was locked.

The March 10, 1918, relocation of the government to Moscow positioned it in Russia's heartland and its transportation and communications hub. On May Day 1918, the commissar of enlightenment, the Bolshevik intellectual and literary dilettante Anatoly Lunacharsky (1875–1933), organized parades and street theater and had pro-Communist artists of the avant-garde adorn the squares with revolutionary motifs. A contest for a new national emblem yielded the crossed hammer and sickle, designating the alleged social bases of soviet Communism, and this emblem was set on the new red flag. The European socialist hymn "The Internationale" became the national anthem.

On July 10, the Bolsheviks published the first constitution of the new state, called the RSFSR, or Russian Soviet Federated Socialist Republic, which laid out the structure of ascending soviets and committees but omitted mentioning the fact of a one-party state. It gave city voters, considered more reliable by Lenin, more voting power than rural ones. Nothing in this document offered the remotest hint of the inexperience of the rulers and the chaos among the ruled. Various shorthand names used—"Soviet" and "Bolshevik" (or "Communist")—reveal the regime's dual nature as state apparatus and ruling party. From the outset, the Communist Party used the "soviet," or state, framework as its apparatus. "Federated" pointed to a desired solution of the nationality question. The term *socialist* indicated a belief in the eventual elimination of capitalism and the market—though what this meant in terms of actual economic policy was subject to wide interpretation in the coming years. On one thing the Bolshevik leaders agreed: the party's monopolistic role and its determination to use violence to retain it.

Revolutionary Diplomacy

For the outside world, the most important of the new decrees was the one on peace. Lev Trotsky, the man in charge, cheerfully published the Allies' secret treaties, which showed in a flash the predatory nature of war aims. He also announced the confiscation of foreign capital and the renunciation of tsarist debts. For good measure, he called on the masses in the states at war to take peacemaking into their own hands. In terms of European diplomatic etiquette these acts were utterly "ungentlemanly," though they reflected some of the ideas of the American president, Woodrow Wilson, who deplored "secret diplomacy" and colonialism. British and French statesmen and business investors were scandalized by the "Bolshies," and the Western press circulated slanderous tales about barbaric decrees on the "nationalization" of women for the free sexual enjoyment of all males.

The peace decree of October 27, 1917, called for an immediate armistice, and in December Soviet envoys entrained to the border town of Brest-Litovsk for negotiations with German and Austro-Hungarian diplomatists and generals. These high-ranking personages, "black-coated or much beribboned and bestarred, exquisitely polite," were startled to meet a delegation of rather shabbily dressed figures: intellectuals, Jews, ex-terrorists, men in the ranks, a peasant picked up along the way, and a woman who was famous for having assassinated a general in the 1905 revolution. The Central Powers presented their territorial peace terms—the detachment of the Baltic lands and Poland from the Russian state—a not unreasonable demand from victors in that they occupied most of those lands and in that the Bolsheviks had endorsed independence for non-Russian nationalities. Trotsky in January 1918 replaced the earlier head of the peace parlays. His stalling tactics and disagreements among the Central Powers stretched the talks through the winter of 1917–1918.

In Moscow, the Soviet debate over the peace terms was tempestuous. The brilliant young speaker Nikolai Bukharin (1888–1938), a party leader close to Lenin, offered the most original solution: a revolutionary partisan war of defense that would pull the German army deep into Russia and destroy it. Others sought cooperation with the Allies. Trotsky insisted on a meaningless but time-gaining formula of "Neither war nor peace." But the Germans advanced their armies and upped their demands, which now included Russia's loss of Ukraine. Lenin, hoping a proletarian revolution in Germany would eventually restore the land ceded in the treaty, stubbornly held out for capitulation as the only realistic policy for saving the revolution. On March 3 he prevailed, and the harsh Treaty of Brest-Litovsk was signed, surrendering over 60 million people, about half of Russia's industrial might, and several hundred years of tsarist acquisitions: Finland, the Baltic lands, Poland, Belorussia, Ukraine, and—by another treaty—Bessarabia. Though some of these lands had already declared independence before the treaty, the losses incurred by it were staggering.

Angered by the surrender, the Left SRs withdrew from the government and went into active opposition. Bukharin was also appalled, but, contrary to later charges, he joined no alleged Left SR plan to kidnap Lenin and resume the war. Trotsky resigned as foreign commissar and became commissar of war. The treaty was nullified in November with Germany's defeat in World War I.

Opposition

At home the repressive face of the revolution showed itself even before the dispersal of the Constituent Assembly. In late 1917 the press was silenced, key political figures were arrested, and revolutionary tribunals were set up, though without the power to issue death sentences. Most ominous of all was the creation in December of the secret police, Cheka (from the first two Russian initials of Extraordinary Commission to Fight Counterrevolution and Sabotage). From the very beginning, the Cheka operated above the law under the supervision of Felix Dzerzhinsky (1877–1926), a Polish ex-Catholic turned revolutionary fanatic who had endured prison and torture himself and was now prepared to inflict punishment on others in the name of defending the Soviet Republic. Justice Commissar Steinberg for months fought a losing battle to maintain decency and mercy based on law.

Active opposition to the new regime began almost at once. Anarchists and Kadets organized surreptitiously. Menshevik-influenced workers launched antiregime demonstrations in the spring of 1918. The Communists managed to win back some worker support and repressed the Menshevik opposition, but armed socialists of all stripes continued in many locales to battle against the new regime. Under the shock of Brest-Litovsk and draconian Communist food policies, the Left SRs struck at them in the summer of 1918 by assassinating the German ambassador to Moscow and Soviet officials in Petrograd. An anticommunist conspiracy rose up in the Volga town of Yaroslavl but failed to seize power there. An unaffiliated terrorist, Fanya Kaplan, shot Lenin at a Moscow factory in the summer of 1918 and almost killed him. The Communists falsely identified her as an SR. These flashpoints of resistance were crushed by Cheka firing squads. Though Lenin spouted class war from day one, few people were shot by the regime until the mass terror in the summer of 1918. Cheka terror became institutionalized with executions and detainment camps, the nucleus of what later became the Gulag (network of forced labor camps in the Soviet Union). Victims included not only oppositionists but whole groups whom Lenin personally ordered killed as a symbolic expression of class hatred. Lenin was heartlessly committed to state terror, as were his comrades, including Trotsky, who wrote a 1920 pamphlet in its defense.

Communist authorities had inherited the former tsar, who had been unable to negotiate his departure from Russia. Shuttled around the backcountry by the Provisional Government and the Bolsheviks, Nicholas and his family ended up in the Urals town of Ekaterinburg, where local authorities executed him and his entire family on the night of July 16–17, 1918. New archival research offers no definitive clue as to who gave the final order in Moscow, only that Lenin and Trotsky were closely involved. Communists also executed other members of the Romanov family, including Nicholas's brother Michael.

CIVIL WAR, FRONT AND REAR

After the Communists took power, the street actions of Petrograd and Moscow in the fall of 1917 were replicated in scores of towns and cities all over the empire. Urban revolts, peasant uprisings, national liberation struggles, Communist and anticommunist violence flowed together in a war with hundreds of physical and mental fronts, framed by military operations and known as the Russian Civil War.

The Whites

After Kerensky's failure to dislodge the Communists from Petrograd, the anticommunist initiative fell to the generals, who were politically, socially, and psychologically alien to a radical government that made peace with the Germans. The unguarded General Kornilov walked out of confinement, headed south, and rallied anticommunist forces. These were called *kontras* (counterrevolutionaries) by the Communists, but they called themselves Whites, a word with monarchist overtones, in contrast to the hated Reds, or Communists. In fact, few White leaders were monarchists, though most were conservative officers; and, since the military possessed the battlefield skills, they came to dominate the movement, which included liberals, moderate socialists, and even some left-wing terrorists. This broad spectrum was a source of political weakness. White officers were not above overthrowing local anticommunist Menshevik and SR governments and executing the leaders.

Though not committed to restoring a tsar, White generals were weakened by their attitude to the population for whom they were allegedly fighting. Their motto of "One, Great, and Indivisible Russia" had little resonance among the common people and nationalists in the borderlands. The sympathy of the property-owning classes and most churchmen was with the Whites (hundreds of priests and dozens of bishops paid for this allegiance with their lives). White forces reversed social revolution almost everywhere they went and waged class war as savage as that of their foes. Peasants feared that White victory meant a restoration of landlord ownership. Some people were actually shot on the spot by the Whites for having calloused hands (and others by the Reds for wearing a tie).

The Whites created bases on the fringes of the former empire—the Baltic, Ukraine, Crimea, the Caucasus, Central Asia, Siberia, and the far north of Russia. Such geographical dispersion impeded unity of military action but allowed the intervention of the Allied powers on their side. British, French, Japanese, American, and a dozen other foreign flags fluttered in Russian harbors and towns and railyards between 1918 and 1920. The Allied powers made their first landings in spring 1918 at Murmansk and Arkhangelsk in the far north and Vladivostok on the Pacific, to protect wartime supplies that had been sent to the Provisional Government and keep them from being funneled through Red Russia to the Germans. In June the Allies escalated intervention to assist the Czech legions, composed of Czech and Slovak residents of Russia and prisoners taken by the Russians during World War I. With the Soviet government's permission and the Allies' blessing, the legions headed through Siberia on the Trans-Siberian Railroad to the Pacific coast in the hope of shipping out to Europe. Once there, they could fight on the side of the Allies and thus gain a Czechoslovak state at war's end. But the Czechs, harassed by Communist troops on the way, took over lengthy sections of the track and sided with the Whites. After the armistice with Germany in November 1918, the Allies lost their war-related purpose for intervention but stayed on nevertheless.

The interventionists' motives were a mix of anticommunism, imperial ambition, desire to help the legions, and sometimes even Great Power rivalry over influence in Russia. The foreigners were initially impressed with the White officers and saw the "Bolshies" as riffraff. However, some of the interventionists grew disillusioned with the discord and corruption among the Whites and disgusted at atrocities that occurred on both sides. In a few cases, interventionist troops mutinied at the prospect of dying in a faraway land after the Central Powers had been defeated. Except for the more expansionist Japanese in Siberia, the interventionists withdrew in 1919 and 1920, leaving the Whites in the lurch. Although at several points, the intervention had offered crucial aid in the form of supplies, tanks, and railroad personnel, this was never sufficient for a White victory. And the Communists used the presence of foreign troops on Russian soil to label the Whites traitors and puppets of imperialist powers.

Armored train of the Czech Legion in Siberia: June 1918. *Imperial War Museum, London.*

The Reds

Although the Whites seemed more threatening to most working the land and factories, the Communists, or Reds, barely stronger than the Whites, also faced resistance, especially from peasants who evaded the draft, deserted, and sometimes revolted. In the towns, Communists won the loyalty of most workers in the mills, mines, and railroads. They welcomed groups traditionally excluded from military life. Jews, Latvians, Poles, and other non-Russians, held suspect in the White camp, were prominent on the Red side. Some eighty thousand women served in combat on the Red side in the civil war in every kind of fighting and support capacity. Artists and actors took the message of revolution across the land on decorated agitation trains and boats equipped with printing presses, musical bands, and movies. Whites also used some of these devices, but the Communists were much better at propaganda, and they enjoyed interior lines of communication, enabling Moscow to dispatch troop trains in every direction.

The Red Army initially suffered from a lack of seasoned officers, so War

Commissar Trotsky recruited or coerced ex-tsarist officers. This caused some envy and suspicion in the ranks, but it also delivered important skills. Political commissars appointed to each unit monitored commanders and saw to the ideological education of the troops. Though flawed by a high desertion rate and lack of discipline, conscript units sometimes got molded into crack fighting forces, especially if workers dominated the ranks. Frontline comradeship lasted well beyond the war. Among the Whites, prominent names were associated with certain territories, armies, and governments. In the Red Army, command was more flexible, and some legendary figures played a key role in strategy and battlefield leadership, such as Mikhail Tukhachevsky, or in partisan-like raids, such as Vasily Chapaev.

Trotsky presented a spectacular figure of command, an intellectual turned warrior, hastening to every front on his extravagant armored train, haranguing the troops, restoring discipline, ordering deserters executed and hostile villages burned. His was an image of stern and romantic heroism wedded to a steel-like intellect. For many radicals in the following decades—especially Jews—the icon of Trotsky was irresistible. For Stalin, however, who resented his eminence and brilliance,

Lev Trotsky as Red Army leader.
Hulton/Archive/Getty Images.

Trotsky was a detested newcomer who had become a Bolshevik only in 1917. Many who shared the aversion for Trotsky and served together at various fronts became Stalin's political allies in the 1920s. When Stalin came to power, Trotsky's name was expunged from Soviet history for decades; and this in turn led his admirers to exaggerate somewhat his martial virtues.

On the Battlefield

The earliest military operations took place in the winter of 1917–1918 in Ukraine, the Don, and the North Caucasus. Cavalry battles and forced marches under horrendous conditions alternated with fiery duels between armored trains, a weapon that symbolized the vast spaces and sweeping movements of these campaigns. After Kornilov was killed by a stray shell in the Kuban region of South Russia, his newly formed Volunteer Army was commanded by General Anton Denikin (1872–1947). But friction arose when it joined up with Cossacks. The poorer Cossacks supported the Reds, inflaming the Don region with class war and weakening the White cause there. In August 1918, the Czechs and the troops of a short-lived SR government on the Volga took the city of Kazan, a gateway to Moscow. Trotsky retook the city and stopped further advance in that direction. When the White Army tried to link up with the Don Cossacks on the Lower Volga, in late 1918, Stalin got credit for stopping them. The episode worsened relations with Trotsky, whose orders Stalin constantly ignored. At one point Trotsky wrote to Sverdlov from the front: "I categorically insist on Stalin's recall."

In Siberia, where long-submerged impulses of regionalism now exploded, a whole array of *dumas,* soviets, and provisional governments came and went. The most important of them, a five-man directory of SRs and liberals at Omsk, was beset by hateful disputes between the civilian leaders and the army officers nominally under their command. When the former commander of the Black Sea fleet, Admiral Alexander Kolchak (1873–1920), appeared on the scene, he offered the perfect symbol of unity. Though not a land warrior, the generals admired him for having cast his sword into the Black Sea and resigned when sailors' committees began organizing in the summer of 1918. The White military overthrew the directory and installed Kolchak as supreme commander, a title eventually recognized by the other White generals.

In 1919, the Whites launched a combined but badly coordinated offensive against both Petrograd and Moscow. Broken on nearly all fronts, they were pushed back by the Red Army. Kolchak began a steady retreat to the east. He eventually fell into the hands of the Communists when they took Irkutsk, and they executed him in February 1920. The Reds repelled the Whites on the Ukrainian front with the help of an independent peasant army under Nestor Makhno (1889–1934). Only Denikin, in some of the fiercest battles of the war, broke through and almost got to Moscow. His army was halted in October, and he turned over his command in March to Baron Pëtr Wrangel (1878–1928). Known for his summary executions of Red officers, Wrangel was dubbed the Black Baron. Cruel, but no crueler than most, Wrangel had 370 enemy officers and noncommissioned officers shot after

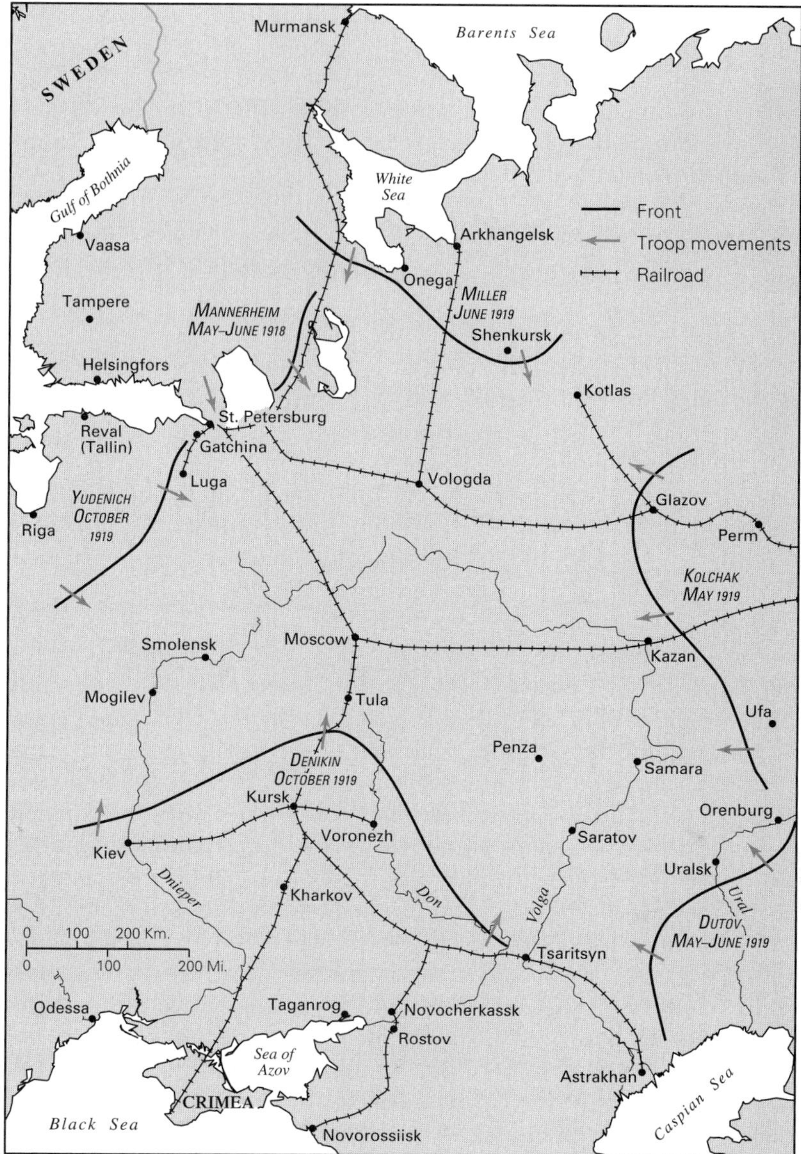

The Russian Civil War, European fronts. *From Richard Luckett, The White Generals. Copyright © 1971 by Richard Luckett. Reprinted by permission of the author.*

they surrendered in a battle near Stavropol in 1918. He was among the best administrators on the White side. Boxed up in the Crimea, he even attempted to launch progressive social policies designed by his cabinet, which included as foreign minister the ex-Marxist and ex-liberal Pëtr Struve.

As fighting on the western fronts was winding down, the Soviets suffered another attack from Polish forces, which invaded Ukraine. Poland had emerged at the end of the world war in 1918 as an independent state led by Jozef Pilsudski (1867–1935), a seasoned patriot and revolutionary who had spent time in tsarist prisons. Pilsudski yearned to regain the eastern territories of Poland and weaken Soviet Russia. Ignoring offers of White collaboration, he struck in April 1920 and by May had taken Kiev. The invasion, marked by untold havoc and more atrocities, was short-lived. In June the Red Army expelled Pilsudski's forces from Soviet soil, and Lenin, against the advice of colleagues, ordered the army forward into Poland. A recently uncovered speech suggests that he did so primarily to deter invasion of Russia by Western powers through their client state Poland. Lenin also hoped that the incursion would spark a proletarian revolution in Poland, which would then spread to Germany and Europe. His hope proved a delusion, and the Soviet thrust was stopped in front of Warsaw in August by Polish troops. This pivotal event was known in the West as the Miracle on the Vistula, reflecting Europe's fear that revolution could indeed be exported. The defeat before Warsaw put another nail in the coffin of the European proletarian revolution. The failed Polish campaign also excited serious recriminations among Soviet commanders and between them and Commissar of War Trotsky—with Stalin, as always, opposing the commissar. The Treaty of Riga in 1921 transferred considerable Belorussian and Ukrainian areas to the new Poland—lands that would be reclaimed with a vengeance eighteen years later.

The last act of the civil war was played out in the vast expanse of the Russian Far East lying between Lake Baikal, Mongolia, Manchuria, and the northern taiga, a classic borderland guarded by Cossack hosts. The Far Eastern Cossacks were more ferociously anticommunist than any other White force in the civil war. Two of them achieved notoriety for their sadistic treatment of the local population: Grigory Semënov, ataman, or chief, of the Transbaikal Cossacks, and his colleague, the Ussuri River Cossack ataman Ivan Kalmykov. They collaborated with the Japanese interventionists and maintained trains equipped with torture chambers. Another associate, based on the Mongolian frontier, was the ex-tsarist officer Roman von Ungern-Sternberg, the "Bloody Baron," who planned to construct a new empire in Asia and restore the monarchy in Russia. He also preached and practiced a policy of killing disabled and "unfit" people and slaughtering enemies by the most fiendish methods. "Commissars, Communists, and Jews, together with their families," he declared, "shall be destroyed." Kolchak had shared neither the views nor the gruesome practices of these butchers, but he was never able to control them. Against the White atamans and their Japanese cohorts were arrayed a motley force of Reds, who also engaged in pogroms. When the Japanese withdrew in 1922, foreign intervention in the Russian Civil War came to an end.

WAR COMMUNISM AND POPULAR ANTICOMMUNISM

The ravaged economy and the surge of violence devastated life in town and country. Both sides arrested, conscripted, looted, and killed with boundless fury. Ragged legions roamed the forests and occupied the cities, some of which changed flags (and victims) a dozen times. Fearful urban residents fled to the country in search of food and safety, among them the vaunted proletariat, which virtually melted away or was drafted. In such conditions no orderly economy could function. Inspired by their understanding of Marxism and responding to anarchic conditions, economists in Moscow tried to replace the semicapitalist system of the early months with a state-run economy. In retrospect, it was called war communism, reflecting the wishful thinking of those who wanted to make the jump to communism at once—though much of it consisted of measures adopted piecemeal in response to the disintegrating production and circulation of goods. The harsh enforcement of these measures, combined with other unpopular practices of the Communists, led to large-scale popular armed resistance.

War Communism

In summer 1918, the state nationalized banks, private trade, and large industries. Within two years all industry was in state hands, and normal retailing and private enterprise had almost ceased to exist. Industry was a shambles. With civil war, the loss of workers and management skills, a shortfall of raw materials, and the takeover of the railroads by the armies combined to plunge production well below prewar levels. Travel was perilous: "Practically every train from Odessa to Kiev, except the one I traveled in, was held up, looted, and robbed," wrote an American journalist in 1920. Factory discipline suffered when the factory committees born of revolution interpreted workers' control to mean higher wages, shorter hours, and division of the product among themselves. They were unable to comprehend the abstract concept that the whole economy "belonged to them" as proletarians and that their duty was to maximize production. In desperation, the Communist government dissolved the factory committees, abolished workers' control, and reduced the power of unions. One-man rule by appointed managers became the norm.

Even when goods were made or grown, it was hard to get them because the market mechanism was closed down. By the end of the civil war, private trade and money were almost completely replaced by barter; by unequal rationing, whereby workers and party chiefs were privileged over other classes; and by the black market, which—though its practitioners were often put to death—flourished wildly. Depots and train stations became swirling bazaars. Black-marketeers with bags went into the country and returned with foodstuffs. Ruined aristocrats sold their jewels one by one for a piece of bread.

One of the noted features of war communism was compulsory labor, which came in many forms. Soviet officials—often poor tenants—ordered former landlords and affluent apartment dwellers to clean corridors and sweep courtyards. Once mighty magnates had their very first encounter with manual labor—all in the name of compensatory justice. But many more peasants and workers were dragooned into labor battalions and forced to make roads, cut trees, or lay tracks. Trotsky deployed entire army units in the same kind of work. A Menshevik critic compared Trotsky's "militarization of labor" to the forced labor of ancient Egypt and to the military colonies of Arakcheev under Tsar Alexander I.

Procuring food for the cities was the most vexing problem. Lenin's government went well beyond previous efforts of the tsarist regime and the Provisional Government to take food from the countryside by creating a "food dictatorship." From June to December 1918, Committees of Poor Peasants, consisting mostly of landless laborers, were established in the villages to wage class war against allegedly prosperous peasants, called *kulaks.* They were joined in August by Food Requisition Detachments, which sometimes took provisions by force. Armed bands of workers and Communists rode into a village, searched homes, and stripped the area of food supplies—grain reserves, potatoes, a cow—sometimes leaving the inhabitants bereft of anything to eat. Peasants retaliated with the passion that they had often exhibited when their livelihood was threatened by city folks. They killed thousands of the requisitioners. In some places, peasants disemboweled food requisitioners and stuffed some grain into their guts with a sign "Here Is Your Food!" In some places, peasants fought both the Reds, who took their food, and the Whites, who, they believed, would take away their land.

Popular Resistance: The Greens

Economic breakdown and the means used by the new state to curb it piled untold misery on top of the suffering incurred by the fighting and the terror launched from every side. Peasants all over the republic formed themselves into rural partisan armies, called Greens because of their forest hideouts, to fight the Reds and the Whites. As the Whites receded, Green armies tried to take power and expel the Communists in Ukraine, the Volga, the Urals, Siberia, and some central Russian provinces. Their atrocities sometimes matched those of Reds and Whites in savagery. The peasant rebel Makhno and his spectacular Insurgent Army, called a republic on wheels, rolled across the Ukrainian steppe on rustic carts mounted with machine guns dealing death to the Whites. Under the black banner of anarchism, Makhno sought to create a peasant utopia on the land and was the only partisan leader to punish anti-Jewish pogroms. After an unsteady two-year alliance with the Communists in the civil war, the latter suppressed Makhno's army in November 1920.

The winding down of war enabled simmering rebellion to erupt in full force. One of the bloodiest episodes broke out in 1920 in the central Russian province of Tambov, a densely populated, heavily rural region that fiercely resisted grain requisition. Red Army detachments moved into Tambov and smashed the uprising with a ferocity surpassing that of the rebels. Meanwhile, up and down the Volga, the "Tunics" and the "Black Eagle" peasant armies struck terror into the Bolshevik ranks, as did thousands of rebels throughout the western Siberian provinces. Eventually they were all brutally repressed.

The irony of revolutionaries killing rebels was fully illuminated in the most famous anticommunist insurrection: the Kronstadt Rebellion. From this island naval base in the Gulf of Finland, radical sailors had crossed over to Petrograd and vigorously fought in street battles throughout 1917. Filled with utopian ideals taught them by anarchists, the Kronstadt seamen distributed land, food, and housing equally and exalted a socialist way of life. Originally stalwart supporters of the Bolsheviks, the Kronstadters by 1921 were inspired by a wave of antigovernment strikes by Petrograd workers, and they excoriated the Communists for betraying the goals of revolution, terrorizing dissenters, and robbing the peasantry of food. Declaring independence for their miniature republic in the sea, they demanded a "third revolution" for the common people—a new Soviet regime without landowners, capitalists, or bloodthirsty Communists. Without hesitation, the Communist leaders struck at this outpost of lower-class opposition and falsely accused Kronstadt of being the puppet of émigré Whites and foreign capital. Organized by Trotsky, Red Army units, the Cheka, and party volunteers stormed the island across the ice in March 1921 and mounted cold-blooded mass executions. This episode of a "leftist" government suppressing the left brewed a crisis of conscience among many in and out of Russia who felt intuitive sympathies for the Communist regime.

But, while Kronstadt remained a symbol of Bolshevik ruthlessness for decades, the provinces experienced their own "Kronstadts": in Saratov on the Volga, Communists requisitioned food, and the Cheka suppressed ordinary civil liberties. When these measures generated mass uprisings that continued even after the civil war officially ended, the local regime responded with martial law and executions.

RETAKING THE EMPIRE

As self-defined liberators of colonized people—the non-Russian nationalities—the Communists advanced a doctrine of national equality and the right to secede embedded in a Declaration of the Rights of Peoples. But they were ambivalent from the very outset. As Marxists, they opposed nationalism, viewing it as a spur to bourgeois domination and chauvinism—a delusion, like religion, that made the masses forget class interests. As rulers of a large multinational state, they feared dismemberment and the formation of potentially anti-Soviet border states that could become anticommunist bastions and staging areas for a new wave of intervention. Communists themselves had helped create the anticommunist fear and hatred by supporting local insurrections in neighboring states such as Finland and the Baltic.

Breakaway Neighbors

The states that got away formed an anticommunist corridor from Finland to Romania for the next twenty years. No sooner had Finland's declaration of independence in December 1917 been recognized by the Soviet regime than radical Finnish workers and Red Guards, aided by thousands of Russian garrison troops, seized power in Helsinki, the capital. This triggered a White countermovement and a bloody four-month civil war. In early 1918, the Whites, under General Gustaf Mannerheim, crushed the Reds and subjected them to wholesale executions. The Finns then settled into a parliamentary republic. In the 1920s, chauvinist movements clamored for a surge eastward to claim Finnic inhabitants of Russia.

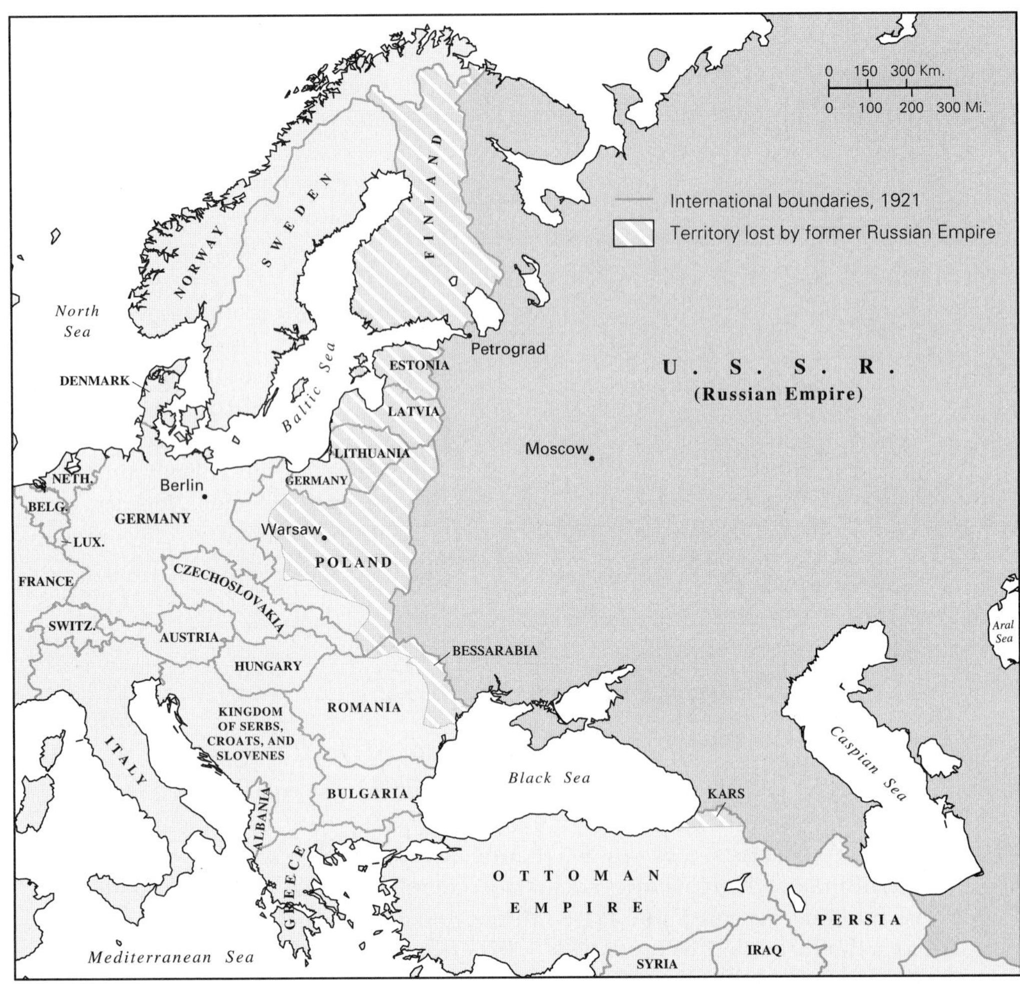

Border States, 1919–1920. Atlas of Russian History *by Martin Gilbert (New Edition published by Routledge in 2002) 0415281199 PB & 0415281180 HB. Please visit our website for further details on the new edition: www.taylorandfrancis.com.*

Hostility to Soviet Russia remained a feature of Finnish foreign policy in the 1920s and 1930s. A similar mood prevailed in the tiny independent Baltic republics of Estonia, Latvia, and Lithuania, which had also been the scene of revolutionary bloodshed. In each, a rocky period of democracy in the 1920s, assaulted by fascists on the far right, ended in a conservative nationalist dictatorship and a mild police state in the 1930s. Polish democracy succumbed in 1926 to Pilsudski's constitutional dictatorship, followed after his death in 1935 by a military government hostile to its eastern neighbor. Romania was beset by authoritarian politics and anticommunist fascist groups, most prominently the green-shirted Iron Guard.

Regained Borderlands: West

Belorussia had a very small corps of nationalist intellectuals. In 1917, a National Committee there requested autonomy. The Hramada, a socialist party, opposed the Bolshevik takeover in Russia and summoned a national congress to declare Belorussian independence in December. When the Germans retreated in 1918, Communists moved in and established a short-lived Lithuanian-Belorussian Soviet Republic. Most of it fell to Polish occupation after a few months. Lithuania went its own way, and the Belorussian land was divided between Poland and the Soviet state after the Soviet-Polish War.

In Ukraine, the Rada (council) government was led by nationalist intellectuals, the most energetic of whom was Symon Petlyura (1879–1926), a leftist nationalist anticommunist with military ambitions. The Rada resisted a Communist attempt to seize Kiev in late 1917, declared a republic, and made a separate peace with Germany. The Communists set up a Soviet government in Kharkov in eastern Ukraine, where both the working class and ethnic Russians were more prominent. From there an army marched into Kiev, the first of many Communist occupations of that unlucky city, but was forced out by the Brest-Litovsk treaty and German occupation. The Germans took grain from the peasantry, unseated the Rada, and installed as a puppet the monarchist general Pavlo Skoropadsky, who lasted until the Germans were expelled at the end of World War I.

No sooner had the Rada assumed power again in Kiev than another Red force entered the country in 1919. The Rada, finding no mass support, left Kiev and went into an almost continuous state of transit, a "government in a railway carriage." The Communist regime in Ukraine, on the other hand, while initially popular, lost good will by attempting to collectivize the peasants. This and other acts stirred the Greens to opposition. Countergovernments and private armies popped up everywhere, an enormous peasant uprising engulfed the land, and cities changed hands, with each new occupier bringing a bloodbath. The biggest victims were the Jews: in over thirteen hundred recorded pogroms in 1919 alone, some fifty thousand to sixty thousand Jews (the most conservative tally) were brutally put to death. The poorly controlled troops of the Ukrainian regime and the White armies carried out most of the outrages, though Reds, Greens, and local warlords were guilty as well. This made 1919 the most horrifying year in Jewish history from the great Cossack massacres of the seventeenth century up until the Holocaust. Once they repulsed the Polish menace in 1920–1921, the Communists consolidated power in Ukraine.

Regained Borderlands: South

The Soviet incorporation of the Caucasus was by no means inevitable. Breakaway regimes were set up during the Russian disorders of 1917–1918: in Georgia by the Mensheviks; in Armenia by the revolutionary nationalists, or Dashnaks; and in Azerbaijan by the reformist Muslim Musavat Party. For a while, these governments enjoyed popular support and potential foreign sponsorship, but their attempts at federalism came to naught. Disunity resulted from the intervention of Turks, Germans, and British, all with differing motives, and from sharp class and ethnic tensions.

The first Musavat regime, set up in 1917, was overthrown by an urban-based uprising in 1918, led by the Armenian Bolshevik Stepan Shaumian (real name, Shahumian) (1878–1918), who formed a leftist government called the Baku Commune, seated in the Azerbaijan capital. After several months of radical policies, it was also ousted, and its leaders—legendary as the Twenty-Six Commissars—were executed. For the next two years a new Musavat parliamentary regime under the lawyer Feth Ali of Khoja sent vain appeals to the Allies for help and recognition. It welcomed the Ottoman Turkish army. That army held Baku for a few months and spun dreams of a Pan-Turkic empire, to include the Azeris, but then had to leave owing to their country's military defeat in World War I. In their wake came Australian, New Zealand, and Canadian battalions, who stayed until August 1919. In spring 1920, after defeating Denikin, Red Army units under Tukhachevsky and Orjonikidze turned south, took Baku with the help of the underground, reduced the remainder of the country, and executed Feth Ali and many others. The whole episode was marked by ethnic strife between Azeris and Armenians inside Azerbaijan.

In Armenia itself, a popular Dashnak government declared an independent republic in May 1918. Anxiety about an Ottoman invasion led it by turns to seek aid from Denikin, Georgia, and Azerbaijan. Between 1918 and 1920, the Armenian regime sought a League of Nations mandate (protectorship) status, to be managed by the United States. Nothing came of this because the United States declined to join the league. When Soviet forces arrived in December 1920, many welcomed them because of the persisting fear of another Turkish massacre. The invading Communists arrested and repressed the Dashnak leaders who did resist, and Armenia fell under Soviet sway.

The Georgian Menshevik Republic, founded in 1917, also rejected the October Revolution, and Georgian workers repulsed a Bolshevik putsch in the capital, Tiflis, in November. Headed after 1918 by Noi Zhordania (1869–1953), the republic sought aid from both sides in the civil war, nationalized industry, and redistributed land. A 1920 treaty with Russia recognized Georgian independence. But, early in 1921, in conjunction with a Bolshevik-engineered non-Georgian ethnic uprising, Soviet troops arrived from Azerbaijan and ended the popularly based regime.

In the mountain regions, militant religious leaders, rugged terrain, and guerilla traditions helped against outsiders. But the crushing weight of the Red Army eventually prevailed. Attempts in 1917 to unite the Muslim populations there into one mountain nation came to naught. A dozen uprisings exploded, and phantom "people's republics" came and went during the civil war. In Dagestan, wealthy and pious scholars, religious militants, and descendants of the nineteenth-century resistance leader Shamyl and his commanders launched revolts against the Communists and all the appurtenances of Western civilization. The two chief Communist organizers of the conquest of the Caucasus—the Georgians Stalin and Orjonikidze—wove diplomatic missions and military actions together to choke off these and other independence movements in the mountains. The Red Army passed through to subdue Azerbaijan and then returned to mop up continued resistance to incorporation into the RSFSR. By 1922, except for small pockets of partisan or guerilla warfare, the Caucasus was retaken.

Regained Borderlands: East

The Muslims of Central Asia and elsewhere attempted concerted action in their relations with Moscow. In 1917, gatherings of Muslim delegates in Moscow, Kazan, and elsewhere had offered a whole panorama of positions and parties that crisscrossed the Russian Islamic world with great complexity. Plans for the future varied from autonomy to regional arrangements of two or more Muslim peoples (such as Bashkirs and Tatars) to federalism and full independence. The last increased in popularity in the further reaches of empire, as events unfolded and as civil war reduced the possibility of pan-Islamic cooperation. When the Reds retook the Urals-Volga region, they began setting up autonomous regions and republics for the minorities in that vast tract but had to face a major revolt of the Bashkirs.

Out on the Central Asian steppe, fresh memories of the 1916 revolt (see the chapter "Russia in World War I, 1914–1917") fed anti-Russian violence that the civil war only inflamed. Clashes between Russian settlers and nomads had led to martial law under the Provisional Government. A Muslim party called Alash-Orda at a 1917 conference in Orenburg called for a Kirgiz Steppe State. For a time, an anticommunist alliance was forged between Orenburg Cossacks, Bashkirs, Kazakhs, and Kirgiz. The circumstances of battle and geography eroded this bond, and by 1919–1920 Red victory by military force was won.

Of the major cities, Tashkent was the first to feel the blows of social revolution. Although few in numbers, Bolsheviks and radical-Left SRs had influence among prisoners of war and Russian soldiers, railway workers, and settlers there. The Muslims divided into religious, liberal, and socialist camps. In October 1917, a Bolshevik-Left SR soviet assumed power and proclaimed a Soviet Turkistan. Early in 1918, its troops traveled over a hundred miles to suppress a liberal Muslim regime in the city of Kokand, which they sacked. The bloodletting there and elsewhere was colored by ethnic animosity having little to do with the Russian Revolution, and the locals went well beyond the orders of Moscow. Similar turmoil erupted elsewhere. In Turkmenia, a moderate socialist government installed itself in the capital, Ashkhabad, and invited British forces to enter. Although this intervention was short-lived, it took a decade for the Communists to subdue the Turkmenian horsemen. Some thousands of Turkmens perished or fled to Afghanistan. In Central Asia, as in the Caucasus, many old scores were settled between Russians and locals, and among the locals themselves. When in 1920 the Red Army arrived, some order was established. The old khans and amirs were gone, but resistance movements flared up for years.

BOLSHEVISM IN EUROPE

In November 1918, as Germany was leaving the war, the more radical socialists tried to emulate the Bolsheviks by creating a German Soviet republic in Berlin but were crushed by a government run by moderate socialists. Another attempt, launched in 1919 by the revolutionary Spartacus League and led by Rosa Luxemburg (1871–1919), an eminent figure of European socialism, was also suppressed, and Luxemburg was murdered. Catholic peasant Bavaria, for one week, and Hungary, for three months, were scenes of Soviet Republics, the latter marked by a Red terror, though their power hardly extended beyond Munich and Budapest. These complex revolts arose as much from the impact of the war and the collapse of empires as from the beacon light of the Russian Revolution. In none could be found the circumstances that prevailed in Petrograd. European economies and societies were too resilient to collapse under a Red assault. But the radical wave engendered fear and anger among counterrevolutionary forces, whose victories were often accompanied by bloodshed. Rightists looked to men in uniform—military or paramilitary—to rescue the nation from dishonor and from democrats, socialists, and intellectuals—including in some places, Jews. The overflow of the Russian Revolution into Europe did not create fascist formations, but it fed their successes.

The legends and martyrs accumulated in the street fighting of these urban wars continued to fuel hopes for a Marxist revolution in Europe, especially Germany, right up to 1923. Lenin, possessed by the vision of a European proletarian revolution that had gripped him during World War I, hoped that the Communist parties now being formed in Europe would find in its war-battered capitals the human materials to destroy capitalism. Acting on this hope, in 1919 he invited European radicals to Moscow to found the Comintern—the Communist, or Third, International—the would-be successor of the prewar Socialist, or Second, International, founded in 1889. At the conclusion of the Comintern's first congress, Lenin, with considerable optimism, said that "the victory of the proletarian revolution around the entire world is guaranteed. At hand is the foundation of an international Soviet republic." The Comintern soon became wholly subordinated to the Soviet Communist Party, which would control it for the next two decades, finance it, and organize its splits, purges, and failed bids for power.

LOOKING BACK

The Russian Revolution and civil war forced festering social pathologies to the surface in the Russian Empire and demolished the fragile political order. For decades, people have glorified, vilified, or analyzed the Communist seizure of power in various ways. Soviet historians, party leaders, and millions of citizens right up to the collapse of the Soviet Union saw it as the Great October Revolution, organized by Lenin, drawing the masses behind it, majestically marching across the vastness of

Russia, and creating a system designed to bring freedom and justice to humanity. This idealized vision was adopted by leftists around the world and mythologized in political art. In contrast, some commentators lamented the revolution precisely because they viewed it as a genuine social upheaval. Other anticommunist historians argued that the February Revolution was the true revolution and that the Bolshevik ascension to power was a mere coup d'état supported only by riffraff and those tricked by propaganda. Although the Bolsheviks certainly capitalized on the discontent of hundreds of thousands among the lower classes, they did not invent class hatred and clothe the masses in it. It was created by the circumstances of tsarist society locked in the worst war of modern times up to that moment. The Bolsheviks' propaganda slogans and their apparent intentions appealed to large segments of the population in 1917.

Once in power, the Communists—like revolutionaries elsewhere—alienated not only the privileged and the propertied but some people from every class and ethnic group by their dogmatic intolerance, authoritarianism, and organized state violence. In spite of these opposition currents, the Bolsheviks managed to win enough popular support to defeat the Whites, crush the Greens, and neutralize the rest. They accomplished this by superior organization, energy, imaginative social slogans, and terror. When appeal and persuasion failed, the new regime employed the discipline, repression, mentalities, and even language of war. The militarization of public life during the civil war, partly traceable to the World War, laid the foundations of subsequent Soviet authoritarianism, which reached into the very fabric of society. It was during the peacetime 1920s that the new regime was consolidated—in the era known as NEP, the New Economic Policy.

CHAPTER 32

The Years of New Economic Policy: Power, Society, and Culture, 1921–1928

Up—
flag!
Riff-raff—
rise!
Foe—
fall!
The day—
trash!
For bread!
For peace!
For freedom!

—*Vladimir Mayakovsky,* It's Good! An October Poem, *1927*

Some historians see the period of New Economic Policy, or NEP (1921–1928), as a brief interlude between the bloody horrors of the civil war and the even bloodier reign of Stalin. Much misery and social pathology, poverty, and turmoil continued. Yet the 1920s were also alive with political acrobatics, open debate in the ruling party, revolutionary adventurism abroad, and a whole array of novel experiments in the arts, gender relations, nationality policy, and daily life. As the decade progressed, acute social tensions and economic problems—both inherited and created by the Soviet regime—asserted themselves. Major political debates among Lenin's successors ended in the late 1920s with the emergence of Stalin as the supreme leader of party and nation.

THE NEW REGIME: PARTY AND STATE

As the Communists bloodily suppressed Kronstadt, the party assembled in March 1921 for its Tenth Congress, where numerous oppositional factions *within the party* noisily demanded a voice. Called by one historian "the conscience of the revolution," they were not democrats and did not protest when non-Communist parties were eliminated from public life by fiat, arrest, trial, and expulsion from the country. They did insist that leaders respond to the demands of those below: party rank and file, workers, or soldiers. The Military Opposition within the party had objected to inequality and the use of ex-tsarist officers in the civil war but was already neutralized by 1921. Democratic Centralists, mostly party intellectuals, wanted more democracy and less centralism in the party. Of the groups clustered around labor—the Workers' Opposition, the Workers' Truth, and the Workers' Group—only the last had a real proletarian makeup. The Workers' Opposition, led by Alexandra Kollontai (1872–1952), demanded a major role for workers in running the state. As to whether labor unions should be independent or subjected to the state, the Soviet leaders squabbled but finally chose the latter. Oppositionists who lobbied for their programs even after being defeated in party bodies, were defying Lenin's doctrine of "democratic centralism" within the party: free debate of issues and then unconditional adherence to the majority decision. The Tenth Congress' endorsement of Lenin's prohibition of "factionalism" tightened up the new autocracy and laid the ground for Stalin's later punishment of personal enemies. Henceforth, no faction was to enter a debate with its own agenda—in other words, no parties within the party. But factions continued, and the party was not yet a monolith.

The failure of war communism and the fierce peasant opposition to grain requisition led Lenin in 1921 to introduce the New Economic Policy, his last major political act, as a compromise with capitalism and the market. Laid low by a stroke in 1922, he died early in 1924. Though Lenin's widow, Nadezhda Krupskaya, cited Lenin's hostility to superstitious rituals, a quasi-religious "Lenin cult," begun after the assassination attempt of 1918, now blossomed. Lenin's mummified corpse was interred in a glass-covered coffin in a mausoleum on Red Square in front of the Kremlin, where it remains for public viewing until this day. With Stalin's blessing, the Lenin cult cleverly drew on popular monarchy (undiluted belief in the leader), saint cults, and folkloric reverence toward legendary rebels.

What kind of a state did Lenin leave behind? The new constitution of 1922, ratified in 1924, established the Union of Soviet Socialist Republics (USSR), which incorporated the hierarchy of elected soviets from local levels, an All-Union Congress. The congress elected a Central Executive Committee—whose chair was the head of state, or president, a ceremonial office—and a cabinet, or Sovnarkom, whose chair was prime minister, or head of government. Although the new regime often invoked Marx's phrase "the dictatorship of the proletariat," it was really an oligarchy—that is, a state run by a few self-appointed people, in this case the Bolshevik leaders who had made the revolution and those whom they coopted into the leadership.

Two irrepressible forces impeded democratic procedure: party control of state organs at all levels, especially at the top; and the authoritarian mentality of officials who appointed and coopted instead of holding elections and who squelched criticism and barked out commands to the lower levels. Various oversight bodies, such as the Workers' and Peasants' Inspection, were too weak to provide checks and

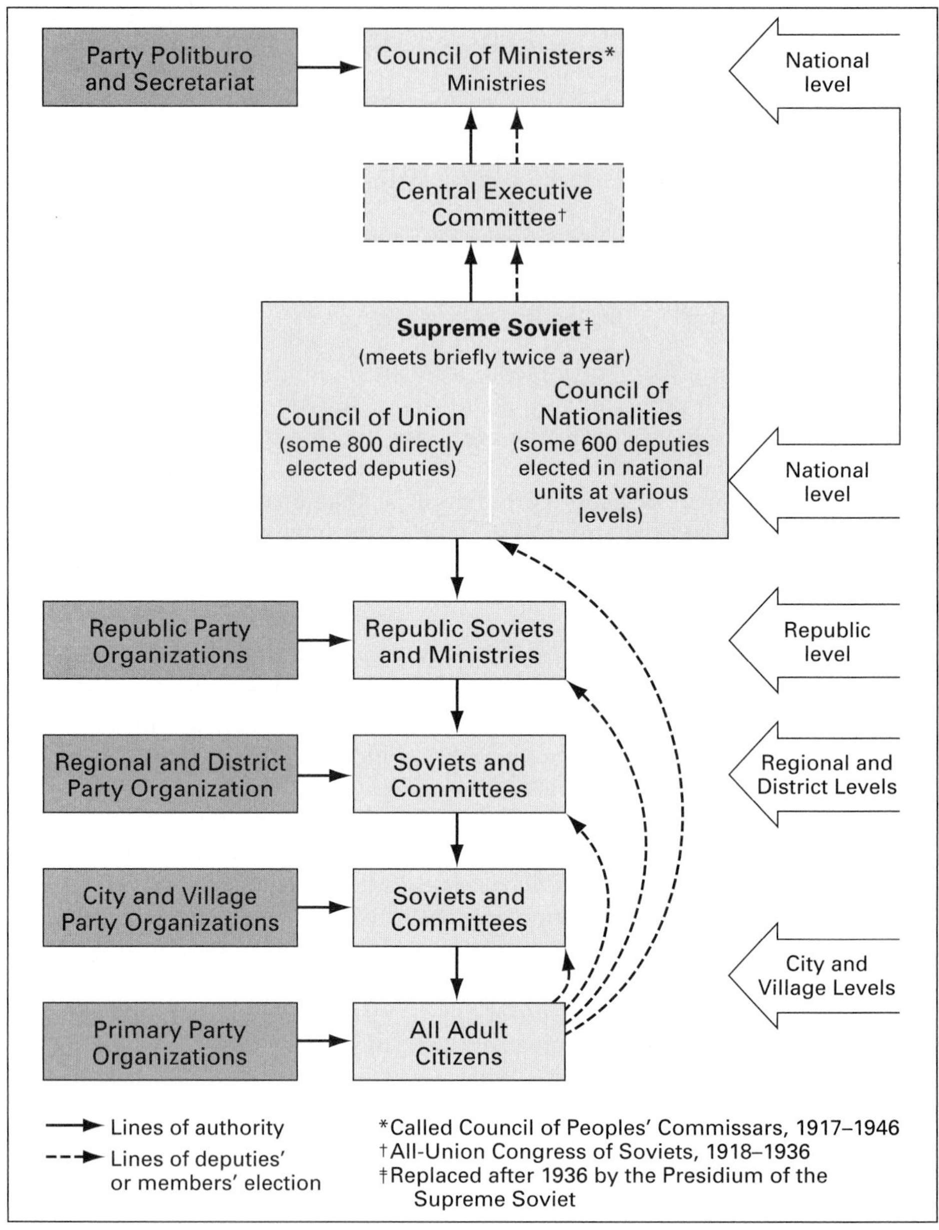

The organization of the Communist Party and the Soviet State. *From John M. Thompson,* A Vision Unfulfilled: Russia and the Soviet Union in the Twentieth Century. *Copyright © 1996 by D.C. Heath. Reprinted with permission of Houghton Mifflin Publishing.*

balances. Power flowed outward from Moscow and downward from the leaders. The *apparat,* or permanent corps of Communist officials, expanded and stiffened into a bureaucracy resembling its tsarist predecessor in many ways, but infinitely larger, which neither voters nor party rank and file could control. Officials still sat behind closed doors attending to "state work" while petitioners waited for hours. Self-importance, aloofness, and arrogance caught on among full-time party and state officials at all levels.

Although the war-era terror had cooled down, citizens who spoke out against the regime fell victim to police harassment and arrest. The Cheka was reorganized as the GPU, or State Political Administration, then as the OGPU, or Unified State Political Administration. When Felix Dzerzhinsky died in 1926, he was followed by less colorful but no less ruthless bosses. A show trial of the SRs in 1922 was both a judicial perversion and a medium of propaganda—to win mass support against alleged traitors and to deter organized disaffection. Though hardly unique to Soviet Russia, this brand of twisted justice became dominant there.

The army, the biggest organized bastion of popular support for the regime, survived some shakeups and disorders at the end of the civil war. Heavily peasant (and male: fighting women were demobilized), soldiers were privileged in Soviet society by favoritism in party membership, greater social mobility than in the old caste-ridden army, and school and family welfare benefits. In the 1920s, some Communists worried about the specter of a Russian Bonaparte who might engineer a military coup. Trotsky was replaced as war commissar in 1925 partly out of this fear. His successor, the war hero Mikhail Frunze (1885–1925), warned in 1925 of Russia's vulnerability to long-range enemy bombers, and he floated a doctrine of peacetime militarization of society. His death under surgery is rumored to have been ordered from above, and he was succeeded by a Stalin supporter, Kliment Voroshilov.

By 1921, the Communist Party had a membership of about 730,000. Workers and Red Army veterans were regularly welcomed into its ranks by means of recruitment campaigns. Those with organization and agitational talents and a clean political record could rise in the apparatus. Wherever three Communists worked or operated, they formed a party cell. From these rose an edifice of local, district, provincial and national meetings, executive bodies, and secretaries. The highest leadership in the 1920s consisted of men—there were no women at the top—who had been professional revolutionaries: ideologists, intellectuals, journalists, and a few workers. They occupied the leading bodies of the Communist Party. The Politburo made policy; the Orgburo appointed key officials. The Secretariat, which coordinated management of the party, kept records and set congress and Central Committee agendas. The function of the Secretariat, originally located in Krupskaya's briefcases and desks, was taken over in 1917 by the energetic Yakov Sverdlov (1885–1919), who had created a staff of about two hundred by 1919, when he died. In 1920 the office was placed in the hands of a troika (three persons), which was then superseded in 1921–1922 by Vyacheslav Molotov (1890–1986) and Lazar Kaganovich (1893–1991)—later to be the most loyal of Stalin's men.

Stalin was born Iosif Vissarionovich Jugashvili in 1879 in the Georgian village of Gori, the son of a cobbler. Expelled from the theological seminary in Tbilisi for his radical ideas, he entered a career of professional revolutionary, joined the Bolsheviks, and became a favorite of Lenin for his energy and his special knowledge of the nationality question. Though a shadowy figure in 1917, the renamed Stalin won prominence in the civil war, in which he was frequently at odds with Trotsky, and quietly built up a large base of disciples in the party apparatus. In 1922, Stalin was assigned to the new post of General Secretary, which he held until his death. The Orgburo, which Stalin also controlled, had become a virtual adjunct of the Secretariat. During the first year of Stalin's tenure, some ten thousand positions in party, government, and economy were at the disposal of this office, which most Communists considered a dull cog of the bureaucracy. In 1923, Stalin relocated his staff of about six hundred people into the Central Committee building on Old Square. In its offices and crannies, a permanent apparatus of great power and secrecy was assembled. At the end of the 1920s, Stalin moved into the nearby Kremlin.

THE NEW ECONOMIC POLICY: SOCIALISM AND CAPITALISM

The economic ruin caused by seven years of war and revolution brought Russia to the edge of collapse by 1921, a year of continued scattered resistance and famine. The decision to allow a mixed economy that was partly socialist and partly capitalist, taken at the Tenth Party Congress, ended food requisitioning and levied a new and lower tax on agricultural produce. Surplus grain could now be sold legally on the free market. The policy originated in the regime's fear of continuing rural anticommunist revolts. The NEP triggered the hidden forces and invisible hands of the market. Keeping one's surplus meant incentive; market meant legal free trade and implied a flow of finished goods from the towns. Lenin recognized that privatizing a sector of industry was the only way to unleash a flood of products since the state was not yet prepared to do so, owing to the party's lack of economic expertise and experience.

The Socialist Sector

The NEP allowed two competing and conflicting economic universes: private business and the much larger state sector—publicly owned and operated enterprises and utilities. The state sector, "the commanding heights of the economy" run by the Supreme Economic Council, included foreign trade, banking, railroads, and all major industries. Before the revolution, these had been the preserve of the "big bourgeoisie," which disappeared from Russian history until the 1990s. Huge state complexes arose to administer particular industries. Foreign trade and currency exchange were closely controlled. Soviet big business was a morass of ambition, idealism, shrewdness, and incompetence run by politicians, revolutionaries, economists, and ideologists devoted to a Marxist vision of harmonious production. They were assisted by old-style entrepreneurs and engineers taken on as advisers.

Central planning, inaugurated on a partial scale by the founding in 1921 of the

Gosplan, or State Planning Committee, was the ultimate goal. Referring to part of the vision, Lenin once uttered the resonant slogan "Communism equals Soviet power plus the electrification of the entire country." But these grandiose dreams were hard to realize given the weaknesses in labor, the market, and technology. Schemes for universal electrification and giant industrial complexes could not answer everyday needs. To some Communists, reliance on foreign technical assistance or investment—widely practiced in the 1920s—seemed like an acknowledgment of defeat. To the chagrin of Soviet leaders, the recovery in the private sector—both field and shop—far outstripped the sluggish pace of industrial recovery.

The Capitalist Sector

The Communists needed to come to terms with a land-owning peasantry, rendered nearly independent by the NEP, who preferred to grow and sell surpluses only when city goods were available and affordable. In 1923, farm output was so good that grain prices fell as the price of industrial goods rose owing to inefficient management, unproductive labor, and a poor distribution system. The two price curves met like blades of a scissors and opened up into a wide gap between agrarian and industrial production. Though resolved by the end of the year, the "scissors crisis" and subsequent problems set the stage for the continuing debate over the peasant question. For those at the center, the rural *muzhik* (male) and the *baba* (female) seemed to embody "backwardness." Wishing women to be more like men, peasants more like workers, and all more like city dwellers, Communists lauded punctuality and efficiency and tried to turn peasants from God to science, from drunken wedding feasts to bright revolutionary songs. Trotsky, in an insulting metaphor, called the village a hotbed of "icons and cockroaches," by which he meant irrational thinking, poor sanitary habits, and lack of modern medicine. Populists of an earlier age had idealized the peasants, but irate Communists saw *kulaks,* or tight-fisted rich peasants, as agents of a capitalist countryside. Communist ideology transformed the realities of the village, socially divided into rich and poor, into a class war. The antirural and the anti-*kulak* seeds of Communist thinking about the country eventually matured into an outright war in the late 1920s. Conversely, the peasants themselves resented attempts to change their way of life and scorned the feminist and atheist activists who came to agitate in their villages.

The NEP businessmen or nepmen, new characters on the historical stage, were legally permitted by a decree of 1921 to move products on the free market. They responded with well-stocked shops and assertive salespeople. The legalized nepmen first appeared on street markets, and about 70 percent of them remained on the stalls as the lowest category of private traders. Nepmen of a slightly higher status were shopowners who employed labor. In collusion with officials, they often purloined state goods for private sale. These small businessmen were not old-regime big industrialists or merchants but came from a variety of classes. The relatively large percentage of Jewish nepmen, especially in the former Pale of Settlement, arose from the fact that trade had been a major occupation earlier, in some places the only one open to them. This was ignored by anti-Semites who wanted to link the Jews to capitalism. As capitalists in a mixed economy, nepmen were tolerated but satirized in cartoon, movie, and novel as wild spenders, companions of fancy women, devotees of jazz and gypsy music, and frequenters of hotel restaurants, where they mixed with foreigners. Soviet journals talked of "Dirty Dealers of the NEP World" and compared NEP to gangrene. Such animosities set the strategic debates about the economic future and helped fuel the desire of some people to "finish" the revolution by collectivizing the villages and abolishing capitalism forever.

SOCIETY TURNED UPSIDE DOWN

Social revolutions by definition claim to reverse the old order by taking the power, land, property, and status of the "ruling class" and giving it to the formerly despised poor and weak. Although Soviet decrees of 1917–1918 had weakened the church's power and abolished the gentry as a class of nobles, priests and former nobles survived into the 1920s and beyond. Seen as holdovers from a hated order, they were contemptuously labeled "former people." Conversely, workers were exalted as the agents of a victorious revolution and the foundation of a new society.

Former People

Social envy and old grudges fueled the common people's hostility to surviving ex-aristocrats, who were mocked as "people of a bygone age," those who had once counted and now counted for naught. A few noblemen were able to change their stripes and join the new regime; but most, dispossessed and suspect, were reduced to poverty, crowded into corners of their own homes, and forced to give piano or language lessons. Priests were persecuted because the Bolsheviks, as Marxists, rejected religion as the "opium of the people" and saw the churches as reactionary upholders of the old order. Churches were closed, and thousands of priests were arrested or shot during a 1922 campaign to strip churches of their valuables. Social identity in the new state became politicized. Since the rulers used crude and insulting terms for the bourgeoisie, the nobles, and the clergy, some people sought new identities by changing their documents, clothes, and even manners in order to pass for proletarians and escape persecution.

The Proletariat

At the other end of the social hierarchy stood the "workers in a worker state," whose lot was replete with paradoxes. They wore a badge of pride fashioned by the regime and embedded in the mythology of the revolution. Poster art conveyed their sinuous strength, choirs sang their songs, proletarian poets exalted their workplace and its industrial rhythms, and films exalted their collective energies and noble martyrdom. The working class was also privileged in terms of party recruitment, housing, and the new educational system of literacy programs, Workers' Faculties, founded in 1919 to prepare poorly schooled workers for higher education, and preferential university admission. With all their shortcomings, these programs laid the foundations for the education of an entire population. But behind the heroization of proletarian "dictators" stood a "dictatorship without the proletariat" run largely by middle- and lower-middle-class elements. An underground workers' journal put it bluntly in 1923: "We vigorously reject the notion that there is a dictatorship of the proletariat. There is not and has never been a dictatorship of the proletariat." The civil war flight from the cities for food and security had also brought about "deproletarianization"—a decline in the number of real workers and of their percentage in the party.

Soviet blacksmith and peasant at the altar of learning, presided over by Karl Marx. *Rabfakoverts, no. 1 (1923) front page.*

Divided as they were by gender, skill, age, experience, and occupation, some workers found it hard to feel proletarian unity. The skilled cried out for higher wages and the unskilled for equality; bosses' use of "scientific management" and piecework raised the specter of capitalism's faceless assembly lines and speedups. Many factories offered low wages, poor conditions, and managers all too reminiscent of former owners. Unions, the struggle for which had caused much blood to flow under the old regime, now seemed to be instruments of the state. Unemployment, fueled by peasant migration to the towns, remained a chronic problem; and women proletarians were the first to be laid off. From the very onset of Soviet history, many workers deserted the workbench, enrolled in the party, and, if able, rose within it as functionaries. Many more, particularly younger ones, depleted their proletarian consciousness—if any—in the bottle, sexual misbehavior, and fighting.

The Peasantry

A combination of climatic conditions, years of economic disruption since 1914, and Bolshevik civil war grain policies led to the outbreak of a horrendous famine and typhus epidemic in 1921–1922 that killed off millions of peasants. Soviet leaders accepted the aid of Herbert Hoover's American Relief Administration, which saved millions of lives, though they later accused it of spying. Still, with the NEP's end of grain requisition came relative peace and a scaling down of direct intervention in the countryside. Where uprisings continued, as in Saratov Province, the raging famine actually weakened resistance. Overall, the peasants had kept their land, gained a bit by confiscation, and restored the *mir,* or village commune. Poverty and backwardness enmeshed the world of farming, but peasants could grow and sell crops from their own plots. An immense variety prevailed in occupation—fieldwork, livestock tending, migrant labor, and crafts—and also in gender and generation, and in urban versus rural experience and values. Inequalities in landholding and income also remained.

The new village looked strikingly like the old one in buildings, inhabitants, clothing, diet, religion, revelry, banditry, and hooliganism. Rumors and miracle tales abounded in the countryside about a coming war, the collapse of Soviet power, and the restoration of a tsar. A few antiurban intellectuals, such as the "*muzhik* poet" Sergei Esenin (1895–1925) or the economist Alexander Chayanov (1888–1939), hoped that peasants would preserve their ancient lifeways. Although squads of young urban party activists streamed into the countryside to challenge old habits and mentalities, such alien forces, almost "colonial" in behavior and motivation, remained extremely weak, and the Soviet state wielded little power in the countryside. To revolutionaries with a modernizing vision, such weakness of the state was intolerable.

Women and the Family

The Communist program of women's emancipation, which Western anticommunists often mocked as nothing more than "free love," would take a prominent place in most leftist movements of the twentieth century. An unprecedented combination of laws granted women the right of retaining their own names after marriage, secular weddings, unimpeded divorce, abortion, maternity protection, paid family leave, and equal opportunities in all walks of life—including education and equal pay for equal work. The Zhenotdel, or the Women's Department of the Communist Party, tried to enforce them. And although the hard social realities of the time made it a difficult and painful process, the Zhenotdel and other organs made a notable advance in the status of women—especially in education. Alexandra Kollontai, the most radical Communist proponent of female equality, glorified women's work.

Kollontai longed to unleash "Eros with wings" and encourage both sexes to experience true physical ecstasy in a bond of mutual affection under socialism. She rejected coarse sex, prostitution, rape, and even irresponsible abortion. But her theories were opposed and misunderstood. Lenin condemned what he called her "glass of water" interpretation of sex as a sheer physiological desire that required satisfaction on demand. A gender-conservative male Communist physician opposed the new sexuality by proposing revolutionary sublimation and erotic self-control. Influential Communist women seemed to prefer legal safeguards, sex education, the reform of men, full employment, and empowerment to Kollontai's sometimes ethereal teachings of sublime mutual respect. In any case, the new freedoms led to increased misbehavior of men, who now felt licensed by revolution to practice promiscuity more openly. Marriage became as easy as signing a civil register, and the Soviet family law of 1926 recognized common law marriages as equal to registered ones. Divorce by either partner could be obtained by simply declaring it so in a postcard to the spouse. Abandonment, instant divorce, and female unemployment helped revive prostitution and took away some of what the revolution had bestowed on women. Wide was the gulf in gender practices and family values between village, where patriarchal notions reigned, and city, where experimental concepts floated freely.

Wretched of the Earth

"Arise, ye wretched of the earth," the opening words of the Soviet anthem, had evoked images of deliverance through social revolution. But in Soviet cities, the wretched still swarmed in their misery. Beyond the power centers, cafés frequented by nepmen, and the workers' clubs lay the back alleys and slums of the disinherited. Beneath the chatter of Marxist theory and the clamor of liberation rumbled the drunken howl of the tavern and the lament of the poor. Criminal communities abounded in great capitals and small towns despite efforts of the police. Odessa was legendary for romanticized Jewish hoods such as Mishka the Gangster and marvelous fictional counterparts immortalized by the writer Isaac Babel (1894–1941): Benya Krik and Lyubka the Cossack. Alcoholism and prostitution remained moving and growing targets of the new regime. Pitifully blending all the vices were the 7 million homeless children who roamed the streets and the railroads in armed gangs, begging, thieving, and selling their bodies for sex. Intellectuals agonized over these "vestiges of the past," campaigned against them, and founded colonies for their victims. Utopians, scorning the charitable approach, dreamed of the model homes, futuristic cities, and communal life described in science fiction.

CULTURE AND REVOLUTION

The Commissariat of Enlightenment, headed by Anatoly Lunacharsky (1875–1933), sought to elevate the masses through education and the arts. A communist with literary pretensions, Lunacharsky, "an intellectual among the Bolsheviks and a Bolshevik among the intellectuals," tried to bridge the gulf between the party and the creative artists, to encourage innovation, and to preserve the cultural treasures of the past.

Reaching the People

A Soviet campaign to eliminate illiteracy had notable success; by 1939 percentages of literacy for those up to age fifty had reached the nineties in the towns, and the eighties in the villages. Church and private schools were abolished. Soviet schools of the 1920s, often experimental, incorporated classes on the industrial production process, technical subjects, and socialist values. Universities and academies were staffed mostly by the old intelligentsia, who still had scope for teaching the canons of traditional culture and science, balancing the stiffer orthodoxies taught in various party academies.

Outside the system of formal education, a Young Communist League was formed as a gateway into the regular party. Its members and other activist organizations took to the road with their propaganda campaigns. The most dramatic of these was that of the Godless League, from 1925, which periodically ridiculed religion and promoted science. The league's militant atheism was especially offensive to peasants, who used traditional and novel ways to resist it. Paradoxically, organized atheists, who fought admirably in these years against anti-Semitism and other forms of religious and ethnic prejudice, did not curb their own intolerance toward organized faith. To further weaken the Orthodox Church, the regime backed the Living Church (1922–1927), which reflected grievances of the priests against the monastic clergy. Together, the antireligious and anticlerical measures did much to weaken organized religion in Russia.

The Art of Revolution

To cultural radicals, "high" culture meant elitist, privileged, "old," and thus negative. Early in the revolution they tried to demolish all artifacts of established culture in an iconoclastic sweep. But what was to replace it? Proletarian culture, or Proletcult, was a first attempt, inaugurated by the maverick Bolshevik Alexander Bogdanov (1873–1928). For three or four years, this movement of more than a half-million workers and intellectuals exalted the workplace, technology, and the romance of revolution. Bureaucratic feuds and financial problems brought the dissolution of Proletcult after the civil war. The more elitist avant-garde culture, Proletcult's main rival, promoted "revolutionary" innovation in modernist forms often confusing to the masses. More cautious Communist leaders frowned on the avant-garde for its brash novelty, though it flourished through the 1920s.

Poetry of the era ranged from the radically experimental work of Velimir Khlebnikov (1885–1922), who attempted to annihilate established versification and spelling, to that of Vladimir Mayakovsky (1893–1930), whose verses clapped like thunder as they announced a coming world of machinery and an antibourgeois order. The words of his poem cited at the head of this chapter seemed to shout. In Soviet novels, the more open the celebration of politics was, the lower the literary quality tended to be. *Chapaev* (1923) by Dmitry Furmanov, though weak as art, captured the imagination of millions and the approval of the regime for its straightforward archetypical hero—Vasily Chapaev (1887–1919), unlettered peasant and Red civil war commander. The better prose authors displayed more ambivalence to the revolution. For serious works of literature that mounted or implied a critique of communism, great trouble was in store. Evgeny Zamyatin's frightening science fiction antiutopia of a Communist nightmare, *We* (1920), was not published in Russia until the 1980s; the author whose book depicted a coming order of robotic slaves was silenced, and he emigrated in 1931. The satirical and truthful tongue of Mikhail Zoshchenko wagged freely in the 1920s but was partly tied in the 1930s. Isaac Babel wrote of Jewish life in the revolution and portrayed the hideous realities of the civil war in his *Red Cavalry.*

Soviet theater exploded with political melodramas and "agit-trials"—mock court dramas in which actors prosecuted social ills such as prostitution or enemies such as White generals. The great avant-garde director Vsevolod Meyerhold put on stylized works that aspired to capture the inner spirit of the revolution, though common folks could not always catch their meanings. They were more comfortable with easily grasped dramas of love and revolution like *Lyubov Yarovaya* (1925), by Konstantin Trenev. The Theater of Working Class Youth (TRAM), Blue Blouse, and other groups combined ideology and audience appeal with plays about everyday dilemmas of love, work, and building socialism.

Variance in tastes was equally present in the graphic arts—poster, stage set, costume design, sculpture, pottery, and all manner of visual materials executed by some of the greatest artists of the twentieth century: Vladimir Tatlin, Lyubov Popova, Kazimir Malevich, and a dozen others. Constructivism, a daring prewar artistic ideology that glorified geometric patterns and machinery, was now applied to revolutionary regeneration. Music was vigorously enlisted to emulate the sounds of industry: by means of the orchestra in Alexander Mosolov's *The Factory* (1928); by means of factory whistles and dynamos in compositions of the Engineerists. A Moscow symphony orchestra announced its radicalism by abolishing the conductor. Proletarian choirs sang anthems of production and hymns of the civil war.

The Soviet art that captured world renown at the time was the cinema of Sergei Eisenstein (1898–1948) and a handful of other directors who sanctified the class struggle in monumental film sagas. No other cinema culture of the era, except that of Germany in the 1920s, produced so many experimental masterpieces. Eisenstein's *Battleship Potemkin* remains one of the classic films of all time. Inspired by a 1905 naval mutiny in the Black Sea (see the chapter "Russia on the Barricades: The Revolution of 1904–1907"), it invented a massacre of citizens by tsarist troops on the Odessa staircase, using camera techniques that have been taught in cinema classes the world over for decades.

Popular Taste

Although the regime heartily sponsored revolutionary culture, the masses preferred light entertainment. Under the rickety roof of the NEP, commercial culture reentered as urbanites packed the cinemas to watch old-time film stars and Hollywood silents. Pulp fiction, though hated by the government, continued to find avid readers. Pro-Communist writers tried to slake the popular thirst for adventure by concocting "red detective stories" where proletarian agents foiled capitalist spies, and revolutionary science fiction which projected a bright new communist future. On the cinema front, elitist cultural leaders wanted the masses to consume great art and radical politics and were shocked to find that workers would rather thrill to American swashbuckler Douglas Fairbanks in *The Thief of Baghdad* than to the exploits of proletarian throngs.

Ignoring popular tastes, the new cultural guardians sought to impose "good" culture on allegedly benighted workers drugged by the decadent commercial output of the West. They had little success in enforcing their views until the Russian Association of Proletarian Writers (RAPP) replaced smaller groups in 1928 and launched its campaigns. Government repression and control of popular culture was sporadic. Though pluralism was not a conscious policy, cultural diversity was greater in the 1920s than at any time in Soviet history until the years after 1986.

WORLD COMMUNISM AND WORLD RELATIONS

The red tide of radicalism in Central and Eastern Europe had receded by the early 1920s, and Communists did not attain power there until after World War II. A promising Chinese Communist movement in the 1920s was brutally repressed. Communist parties founded in the United States, Latin America, and Africa fared no better in the years between the world wars. Faced with the failure of a worldwide proletarian revolution to materialize, in the early 1920s the Soviet Union sought more conventional means to enter world politics through ordinary diplomacy.

The Quest for Revolution

The failure of social revolution in Europe from 1918 to the early 1920s did not mean failure of communism as a magnet. Artistic sympathizers were drawn by the belief, nourished as they watched the genius of Eisenstein flicker on screens in Berlin or New York, that communism meant the triumph of experimental culture over conventional bourgeois art. Although some leftists who admired the Soviet experiment from afar or as pilgrims to Moscow were foolish dupes or naive cranks, communism also attracted a large number of serious, morally motivated intellectuals and writers. The Hungarian journalist and novelist Arthur Koestler (1905–1983) was repelled by the injustice and hypocrisy of his capitalist governments and ruling classes, sins he wrongly believed the Communists were above. Foreign journalists and visitors to Russia, except the few who knew the language, usually saw very little of Soviet life. Intourist, the agency for handling foreign excursions, was already perfecting skills at masking realities and showing off the best. Professional revolutionaries, Comintern agents, romantic adventurers, antifascists, and "progressives" were variously possessed by hope, idealism, self-delusion, or desperation. Many would perish in fascist dungeons or, ironically, in Stalinist labor camps.

Communist success seemed possible in many parts of Asia that were engulfed in poverty, colonial rule, and internal strife. Comintern agents held aloft the banner of liberation to the intellectuals, dockworkers, and peasants of the sprawling continent. Unfurled at the 1920 Congress of Toilers of the East in the Azerbaijani

capital of Baku, revolutionary anti-imperialist slogans were taken to the foreign-dominated ports of China and to British India and Malaya, French Indochina, and the Dutch East Indies. Only China experienced a major upheaval. The Nationalist Kuomintang Party, under Dr. Sun Yat-sen, joined forces with a tiny new Chinese Communist Party founded in 1921 to free the country of warlords and imperialists; Comintern agents assisted him. But Sun's successor, Chiang K'ai-shek, fearful of the Communists, slaughtered them in the streets of Shanghai in 1927. Unwise directives from Stalin to try to maintain the Kuomintang-Communist alliance resulted in further risings, followed by Kuomintang massacres of workers and peasants. Rural-based survivors under the firm direction of the young Mao Zedong made their way in epic marches to the mountain fastnesses, their bases for a later reemergence.

Soviet Diplomacy

Diplomatic relations between Soviet Russia and the outer world ceased in the years of foreign intervention. As the specter of European revolution faded in the early 1920s, the Soviet state sought recognition and trade with a world it both admired and despised. Ambivalence reigned on the other side too. The Comintern's embarrassing activities weakened the position of foreign commissar Georgy Chicherin (1872–1936), who pushed for diplomatic recognition. He tried to dissociate his policies from revolutionary adventurism. Against recognition were arrayed anti-Soviet European and American conservatives and religious believers, as well as liberals and democratic socialists who loathed communism. Still, many Western businessmen, backed by their governments, wanted to trade with and invest in the new Soviet Russia. Some Western statesmen believed that diplomatic relations would have a civilizing effect on the Soviet regime. Most European states by the end of the decade had established embassies in Moscow. The United States withheld recognition until 1933, but American trade missions, investment, and technicians poured into Russia.

Turbulence marked relations with Britain in the 1920s, owing to the unceasing Communist propaganda in Britain and her colonies. Unpleasant incidents plagued Anglo-Soviet relations as the Comintern replayed the nineteenth-century imperial Great Game in Turkey, Persia, Afghanistan, India, and China—all traditional areas of British interest. This led to a minor panic in 1923, when the British foreign secretary Lord Curzon sent a threatening ultimatum demanding cessation of revolutionary agitation. But in 1924 a new Labour Party government in London recognized the Soviet Union, in spite of Communist thrusts at the Labourites as servants of the bourgeoisie. Fresh incidents of Comintern meddling brought down that government and escalated Soviet-British hostility to the point that a new Conservative government in Britain broke off relations for two years (1927–1929). Around the same time the Chinese Communist Party suffered failure, an assassin murdered a Soviet envoy in Warsaw, and the French broke off economic relations with the USSR. To Communists fearful of the "capitalist encirclement" of the USSR by hostile powers, this constituted a real danger. Stalin inflated the resulting "war scare" of the summer of 1927 and cleverly used it to discredit oppositionists who were criticizing the party leadership at a moment of national danger.

During its Weimar period (1919–1933), a name taken from the birthplace of its postwar constitution, Germany, though democratic and capitalist, was a defeated and outcast nation like Russia. The Germans wanted a partner to balance off the victors. Communist radical activity since 1919, coupled with Soviet repudiation of tsarist debts, were obstacles to these and most other negotiations over recognition. The two nations reached a trade agreement in 1921. During a 1922 international conference on debts in Genoa, Italy, Soviet and German negotiators met secretly in nearby Rapallo to establish diplomatic relations and a secret pact on military and technical cooperation. In 1923, during some friction between Germans and French forces occupying former German territory, a Bolshevik and Comintern leader, Karl Radek, floated the idea of "national Bolshevism"—an alliance of German Communists and patriots with Soviet support against the victorious Versailles powers. Shocked, England and France proceeded to woo the defeated enemy Germany away from a romance with Russia. But the German-Soviet tie, capped by a 1926 neutrality treaty, held firm until Hitler came to power in the 1930s. German officers and weapons technicians, severely limited by the Versailles Treaty, secretly went to Russia in the years 1922–1934 to train their own and Soviet personnel in tank and aerial warfare and to assist in rebuilding the Soviet armaments industry.

WHO WILL RULE?

Through the 1920s the ruling party oligarchy tussled over power and policies in the midst of nagging problems. It faced a peasantry that seemed to possess too much economic power. Among workers grew a conviction that NEP could never solve their problems, and among party and "proletarian" ideologists a belief that the present order was a counterrevolutionary seedbed of bourgeois decadence. Sharpening these discontents was the perceived menace from capitalist warmongers in the West.

The Heirs of Lenin

The struggle for leadership that began in 1922 as Lenin lay incapacitated was rooted partly in personal animosities going back to the revolution and civil war. Lenin's will offered a balanced assessment of the strengths and weaknesses of Stalin, Trotsky, Grigory Zinoviev (1883–1936), Lev Kamenev (1883–1936), Nikolai Bukharin, and Grigory Pyatakov. But in his last days of consciousness Lenin broke with the once admired Stalin. The General Secretary's harshness in some actions and his impudent treatment of Krupskaya, Lenin's wife and a respected revolutionary, induced Lenin to write to the Central Committee: "Stalin is too rude, and this defect, though quite tolerable in our midst and in dealings among us Communists, becomes intolerable in a General Secretary. That is why I suggest that the comrades think about a way to remove Stalin from that post." Lenin's plan to attack Stalin personally was never realized because of his incapacitation. Fear, loyalty, indifference, and misunderstanding caused the leadership to retain Stalin and suppress Lenin's comments.

After Lenin's death, the Politburo—Stalin, Trotsky, Zinoviev, Kamenev, Premier Alexei Rykov (1881–1938), and head of the labor unions Mikhail Tomsky (1880–1936)—pretended to rule collectively. But three of Lenin's longstanding comrades had formed a loose alliance, or troika, already in 1922: Zinoviev, head of the Comintern and the Petrograd (renamed Leningrad in 1924) party organization; Kamenev, party chief in Moscow; and Stalin. The troika was designed to offset the brilliant and talented Trotsky, who was popular among youth and in the army. The duel between the troika and Trotsky, largely over who was the best "Leninist," was conducted in public bodies and on the printed page, with Trotsky and his supporters dubbed the Left Opposition. Trotsky's previous disagreements with Lenin were held against him; and his arrogance and choice to remain aloof from power building inside the party weakened his position. By the time of the party's Fourteenth

Lenin, Bukharin, and Zinoviev at a Communist International congress, July 1920.
Sovfoto.

Congress in 1925, Kamenev and Zinoviev had come to distrust Stalin and publicly challenged his leadership, thus dissolving the troika. In 1926 they joined Trotsky in a United Opposition against Stalin. Although anti-Semitism was officially outlawed, many party members resented these three men as Jews. The trio were heads without bodies: high party bodies removed Trotsky from his post as war commissar in 1925, and Zinoviev from his at the Comintern. Stalin's chief allies in the Politburo in 1925–1927 were Rykov and the new member, Bukharin. Interwoven with personal hostility and ambition were the issues of bureaucratization of the party, the tempo of industrialization, and world revolution.

Trotsky and his allies attacked Stalin's party machine and his growing personal power. Stalin was by no means assured of victory. His conflict with Lenin had almost cost him his main post. To a party nurtured on the intellectual acrobatics of Lenin, Trotsky, and Bukharin, Stalin seemed somewhat pedestrian. But he was a gifted political leader, and he projected an image of both solidity and renewable revolutionary energy. Time and again Stalin defeated his rivals on organizational and policy issues by outnumbering them in the Central Committee and other bodies that he was able to pack with his own people by virtue of his post as General Secretary. Stalin's foes, in attacking bureaucracy, were really attacking him.

Economic Revolution?

Another divisive issue was the tempo of industrialization. The party, fearing that the economy was vulnerable to the forces of world capitalism or a passive peasantry, saw further industrialization under socialism as the key to unlock the doors leading to national security and economic success. The "superindustrializers," led by Trotsky, pushed for a rapid surge at once in the belief that the mere reconstruction of a damaged economy would not even guarantee survival, much less the building of socialism. They aimed to escape backwardness by using socialism as a development mechanism to industrialize the nation. This reversal of Marxism, which, referring to Europe in the nineteenth century, had taught that the capitalists were the agents of full industrialization, has been called the "easternization" of Marxism. Its chief theorist, Evgeny Preobrazhensky (1886–1937), adapting a Marxist term for capitalism, called for a "primitive socialist accumulation" under which the peasants would pay—and suffer—for the massive industrial buildup. Preobrazhensky promoted a plan that would depress grain prices, raise industrial ones, feed the cities cheaply, and export grain for the world market. Profits from this would allow purchase of machinery for the takeoff into economic modernization. This "leftist" position appealed to the urban-oriented heroic notion of revolutionary willpower armed with technology.

Ranged against the superindustrializers was Bukharin (1888–1938), one of Lenin's favorite younger disciples, who believed in the long road at slow tempo. A political ally of Stalin in 1925–1927, Bukharin enlarged on Lenin's comments on the continuance of NEP and a worker-peasant alliance, and he advocated a gradual "growing into socialism" by retaining the NEP mixed economy and the peasant land system for decades. In contrast to Preobrazhensky's fiscal exploitation of the peasantry, Bukharin proposed to unblock the cash channel between town and country, hurl industrial goods into rural markets, and pump food products into the town from a willing, entrepreneurial private peasantry to whom he addressed the poorly chosen words, "Enrich yourselves." By this he meant: work hard, produce, and make the country prosper; but to some Communists it sounded like an emblem of capitalist greed. Bukharin also argued that state industry would gradually (and peacefully) swallow up private production and pave the way for a planned socialist society. A believer in party dictatorship, Bukharin was no democrat; but his political concern for the peasantry, his advocacy of persuasion, and his deemphasis on class conflict set him off first from the superindustrializers and later from Stalin.

World Revolution?

Divisions over the issue of spreading communism had taken on clarity in 1924, when Stalin launched the slogan "socialism in one country" against Trotsky's "permanent revolution." Stalin argued that the USSR could build socialism without waiting for revolution elsewhere; and he made it look as though Trotsky put the workers of Europe first. Zinoviev and Trotsky angrily assaulted Stalin's thesis, but their constant appeal for international revolution sounded hollow and to some comrades reeked of a cosmopolitan unconcern for Russia itself. A 1923 failed German Communist rising was attributed to Zinoviev, and his Comintern chairmanship was transferred to Stalin's ally Bukharin in 1926. On the other hand, the blundering Stalin line of continued alliance with the Kuomintang in the Chinese tragedy of 1927 cost him nothing. He blamed the outcome on local scapegoats and, in response to Trotsky's constant criticism, used the partly fabricated war scare of 1927 to accuse him of sabotaging the leadership in its hour of peril.

Stalin Victorious

Efforts by the United Opposition of Trotsky, Zinoviev, and Kamenev to enlist popular support met little popular response and were stampeded by gangster-style harassment, breakup of meetings, and police interference. The United Opposition lacked a power base among the workers. In 1927 Trotsky, though his supporters demonstrated in public, was defeated, expelled first from the Central Committee and then from the party at the Fifteenth Party Congress. In 1928 he was exiled to Kazakhstan and soon afterward expelled from the Soviet Union altogether. Trotsky did poorly as a political infighter: he chose not to win popularity by attending Lenin's funeral, accepted his dismissals from key posts, and—most important—declined to build an organizational machine around himself. Zinoviev and Kamenev ceased open opposition to Stalin and recanted their errors. But no sooner had Trotsky suffered defeat than Stalin and Bukharin fell out. They agreed on "socialism in one country" but not on the means of economic transformation, and Stalin favored a higher scale of political repression. Stalin, always ambivalent about Bukharin's program, pushed the party into a decision for a rapid surge to industrialization that went beyond that of the superindustrializers in scale and tempo.

A grain crisis in the late 1920s was a major turning point. The harvest of 1927 was good, but the peasants withheld grain from the market partly because of the war scare and also because of the low prices offered by the state. Without cheap grain to feed cities and sell for imported machinery the new Five-Year Plan of rapid industrial growth stalled. Stalin's observations of peasant hoarding during a visit to Siberian villages in January 1928 convinced him to prevent hoarding by means of rigorous searches and blockades and then to launch collectivization. Bukharin, Rykov, and labor union head Tomsky—known as the Right Opposition—resented Stalin's change of course and advocated social peace with the villages and downscaling the plan. Although Bukharin unwisely contacted the former oppositionists he did not try to create a movement in the party at large or on the streets as Trotsky had done. Stalin and his supporters in the Politburo defeated the leaders of the Right Opposition and dismissed them from key posts. Stalin's organizing power also removed their bases of support in the party. Bukharin's defeat in 1929 was momentous for Soviet history because he showed more sympathy than either Stalin or Trotsky for moderate policies and pluralistic elements within a one-party state.

By 1929, when Stalin's fiftieth birthday was celebrated as a national holiday, he had become the supreme and almost unchallengeable leader of the Soviet Union. He triumphed for both organizational and programmatic reasons. Factions had arisen at the summit all through the 1920s, and Stalin had been outvoted on occasion in the Central Committee. Positioned at the very center of the circle, Stalin applied the same rules to his opponents as they had applied to theirs about criticism of the party leadership. By decade's end, platforms opposing the bureaucracy were seen as something akin to treason. Stalin carefully used his position as General Secretary of the Communist Party to dismiss the adherents of his rivals and to appoint his own people. Backed by this core of loyalists in police, party, and state organizations, Stalin could make policy, win votes, and force issues. His enemies were constantly outflanked by Stalin's political machine.

On the ideological front, Stalin's adversaries argued that "socialism in one country" violated Marx's international vision and Lenin's call for world revolution as necessary for Soviet survival. Yet many Communists saw virtue in Stalin's position. Active commitment to revolution abroad meant facing ever-rising waves of defeat and the subsequent flourishing of anticommunist movements such as fascism. Some in the party came to distrust foreign Communists after their failures. Stalin's tortured theory about the victory (though not the final victory) of socialism being possible in Russia alone appealed especially to newer party recruits. On the other hand, simply giving up world revolution and committing the nation to slow economic growth à la Bukharin might lead to bowing before a hostile capitalist world.

The brief interlude of the NEP, in spite of contradictions and what came before and after it, remained a legendary epoch for Russians who remembered it and for outsiders who mythologized it. In terms of cultural flowering, nationality policies, and intensity of debate, there was a notable divergence between the NEP and the following two and a half decades of blood-soaked, repressive Stalinism, the subject of the chapters "Stalinism Established, 1928–1939" and "Stalinism: Life Inside the System, 1928–1941." For this reason, some historians have attempted to visualize a different scenario, one with a longer-lived Lenin, a Trotsky, or a Bukharin in charge. And yet, some of the horrors to come—show trials, camps, and executions of innocent people—were in place already. The structure of the Soviet system with its rule by party and ideology was well established before Stalin achieved full power, and that ideology looked forward to collectivization and the full realization of socialism and communism. Because of this, other scholars have heatedly argued that the hand had already been dealt and that NEP with its relative pluralism was doomed from the start.

CHAPTER 33

Revolution in the Life of Peoples, 1921–1928

The Soviet Union was the world's first Affirmative Action Empire. Russia's new revolutionary government was the first of the old European multiethnic states to confront the rising tide of nationalism and respond by systematically promoting the national consciousness of its ethnic minorities.

—*Terry Martin,* The Affirmative Action Empire

The eruptions of the revolution were magnified in the outlying non-Russian borderlands by ethnic and religious diversity. On paper, the imperial and nationality problem was sewn up by the establishment between 1922 and 1924 of the Union of Soviet Socialist Republics, whose very name proclaimed unity in an equal association. Some of the lands were "gathered in" by conquest masked as free affiliation to the center. By destroying the noncommunist nationalist regimes of the civil war period, the Communists claimed that they were enacting the wishes of the toiling masses. But this was true only in certain places. Spreading Soviet power to the outer reaches brought much more than military mastery and political dominance. In some remote corners, it meant exposing local people whose inner lives had been relatively untouched by the tsars to a completely new worldview largely alien to them. And everywhere it entailed an unprecedented program of preferential treatment for non-Russian nationalities on a vast scale, resulting in what the author of the most comprehensive study of the issue has called "the affirmative action empire."

USSR: A MULTINATIONAL STATE

Soviet nationality policy proceeded along several lines: drawing and redrawing the internal boundaries of the multinational state, establishing Soviet institutions and Communist Party power, suppressing opposition where present, promoting local national cultures, and bringing local people into the administration.

Peoples and Boundaries

Between sojourns at the civil war front, Commissar of Nationalities Stalin presided over these affairs from 1917 to 1924. His commissariat grew from a desk in Smolny Institute in Petrograd to a Moscow organization containing subcommissariats for the numerous peoples of the Russian Soviet Federated Socialist Republic (RSFSR). At Stalin's behest, the 1918 constitution of the RSFSR allowed for autonomous republics and regions for its non-Russian nationalities. As a result of central or local Soviet initiative, a patchwork of national territories appeared in the first half-dozen years of Soviet power. Table 1, by no means exhaustive, may give an idea of the ethnic complexity facing the commissariat. As of 1921, the technically independent Soviet Socialist Republics of Ukraine, Belorussia, Azerbaijan, Armenia, and Georgia—as well as ephemeral People's Republics established in the Far East and in Khwarezm (Khiva) and Bukhara in Central Asia—had treaty relations with the RSFSR. But in practice, Moscow's intrusion into administration, food policy, military affairs, and other matters brought about Communist political control.

Stalin, the commissar of nationalities, proposed that the RSFSR incorporate the above-named republics as merely units with limited autonomy. Lenin desired a union of equal republics, including the RSFSR as one of them. By December 1922, Lenin had rejected Stalin's Greater RSFSR project in favor of a Union of Soviet

TABLE 1 National Territories Appearing on the Former Russian Empire, 1917–1924

1917	RSFSR, Ukrainian SSR (temporary)
1918	Turkistan ASSR, Toilers' Commune of the Volga Germans, Tatar-Bashkir Republic (1918–1919)
1919	Bashkir ASSR, Belorussian SSR
1920	Azerbaijan SSR, Armenian SSR; Far Eastern Republic; People's Republic of Khwarezm (Khiva); People's Republic of Bukhara; South Ossetian AR, Tatar ASSR, Karelian Toilers' Commune, Chuvash AR, Kirgiz ASSR, Votinsk AR, Kalmyk AR, Mari AR
1921	Georgian SSR, Mountain ASSR, Nakhichevan ASSR, Abkhazian ASSR, Far Eastern Buryat AR, Ajarian ASSR, Komi (Zyryan) AR, Kabardinian AR, Crimean ASSR, Dagestan ASSR
1922	East Siberian Buryat AR, Karachai-Cherkess AR, Yakut ASSR, Oirot AR, Cherkess-Adyg AR, Chechen AR
1924	Uzbek SSR, Turkmen SSR, Tajik ASSR, and Kara-Kirgiz AR

Not included are various short-lived White, Green, and regional "republics." Variant and conflicting designations in use at the time account for the difference in nomenclature. Many of the ephemeral units existed largely on paper.
AR: Autonomous Region.
ASSR: Autonomous Soviet Socialist Republic
SSR: Soviet Socialist Republic

Socialist Republics, approved by an ad hoc body at the end of the year. The new constitution of the USSR was ratified early in 1924. The commissariat was replaced by an elected Chamber of Nationalities—the second house of the All-Union Central Executive Committee, itself a body of the All-Union Congress of Soviets (the Soviet "parliament"). The other house was called the Chamber of the Union. The USSR granted some local autonomy but no independent political power. The original Union Republics of the USSR were the RSFSR, the Belorussian and Ukrainian Soviet Socialist Republics, and the Transcaucasian Federation, itself a conglomerate of three nations—Georgia, Armenia, and Azerbaijan. In 1924, Turkmenia and Uzbekistan, previously autonomous republics, were elevated to union republics, as was Tajikistan in 1929 and Kazakhstan in 1936. Within most of the republics were created smaller autonomous Soviet socialist republics and autonomous provinces *(oblasts)* and regions with defined linguistic and cultural identities.

The constituent republics possessed, following Lenin's concept, the theoretical right to secede. In practice, once a republic was absorbed into the USSR, no republic leader ever dreamed of applying for secession from the Soviet Union. Lenin insisted on a unified Communist Party ruling the entire Soviet Union, with only local branches in the republics. But he denounced roughshod treatment of the nationalities and urged a respectful attitude toward local concerns and sensibilities. Lenin's sympathy for non-Russian nationalities and his hatred of crude Russian nationalism was also driven by a concern about the Soviet image in the eyes of its neighbors and of colonial and semicolonial peoples of the East. When Stalin acted arrogantly toward his fellow Georgian Communists, and his comrade Sergo Orjonikidze struck one of them in the face, Lenin became furious and angrily denounced "Great Russian chauvinism," the Russian-centered bias shared by the Russian Communists Vyacheslav Molotov and Sergei Kirov and by Russianized ones such as Felix Dzerzhinsky (a Pole) and Lazar Kaganovich (a Jew). The resulting feud between Lenin and Stalin finally convinced the former to attempt to remove the latter as General Secretary. Stalin was more complex than Lenin's charges implied. Stalin was, in fact, coarchitect with Lenin of the overall nationalities program as well as its major theorist. Furthermore, he enforced territorial, promotional, and cultural policies that favored non-Russians over Russians right up into the 1930s.

What did this enormous variegated new empire look like on the charts and tables drawn up in the cluttered offices of the Commissariat of Nationalities? Between 1917 and 1924, while scores of "republics" rose and fell, almost forty territorial units designated by nationality appeared on the Soviet map. One can get a vivid sense of the fluidity and complexity of nationality histories and of the discrepancy between cartography and reality by reviewing Table 1 and Map 1 while recalling the turbulent history of those years in which ghost republics of all shades came and went, sometimes proclaimed for a day simply by raising a flag of one's political coloring: Red, White, Green, Black (for anarchists), or national. As Soviet power advanced and prevailed, map makers carved out all kinds of autonomous republics and regions, right down to "national soviets" and villages to accommodate ethnic enclaves. National territories-within-republics appeared as tiny mountainous areas of Armenia and in the inner Asian ranges of the Altai and the Hindu

USSR, December, 1922. *Reprinted from Terry Martin,* The Affirmative Action Empire: Nations and Nationalism in the Soviet Union, 1923–1939. *Copyright © 2001 by Cornell University. Used by permission of the publisher, Cornell University Press.*

Kush. These would be juggled through the decades, and the smallest units would be dissolved in the 1930s, but the basic structure in place by 1924 would remain until the late 1980s, when activists began redrawing the map once again and places such as High Karabagh and Chechnya—virtually unknown to outsiders—splashed across the world's headlines.

Indigenization

One historian has accurately characterized Soviet nationality policies in these years as modernization and renationalization. This formula can be put in a larger context. For example, the new and revived independent nations of postwar Eastern Europe—though much freer than any of the Soviet nations—also faced the task of state building, economic recovery, education, land reform, and other social policies, while simultaneously building a new identity through self-conscious and assertive cultural nationalism—much of it in reaction to the epochs of dominion by Romanovs, Habsburgs, or Ottomans. The result there was often persecution of minority nationalities. In the USSR, modernization of the nationalities meant industry, literacy, schools, science and public health, women's emancipation, and the assault on organized religion. But both Lenin and Stalin insisted on differentiating Soviet from tsarist policies by favoring non-Russian nationalities. In 1923, the government introduced "indigenization" *(korenizatsiya),* a compensatory program of affirmative action for nationalities by way of preferential hiring, enforced promotion of local languages, and revival or creation of national cultures. During the 1920s, these measures often resulted in "reverse discrimination" against Russians living in the non-Russian areas.

Linguistic indigenization was a striking reversal of tsarist practices (and of those almost everywhere in the world). In every national unit, the local language would be the language of instruction in schools and in the public sphere—government and economy; nonspeakers were expected to learn that language. National sensitivities were to be observed, and selected aspects of culture—whether Turkmen, Belorussian, or Abkhazian—were to be nurtured by local leaders in the form of a native language press and the publication and performance of works in their languages. These cultural forms were to enwrap a "socialist" content—a concept still in flux during the 1920s.

In some of the republics and autonomous lands, indigenization during the 1920s amounted to a cultural renaissance. For smaller nationalities who had never had literary languages or alphabets, new ones were actually created. To avoid any charge of Russification, "eastern" alphabets such as Arabic were replaced by Latin rather than Cyrillic. Concrete measures were taken to hire first, fire last, and promote persons from the local nationality in government and economy to establish native elites. Reversing the tsarist practice of excluding or limiting the admission of certain ethnic groups into university (such as Jews), Soviet policy established preferential quotas for non-Russians. The indigenization program went beyond the carving out of autonomous republics, provinces, and regions. Eventually, wherever national clusters existed, however small, enclaves at district, village soviet, and even

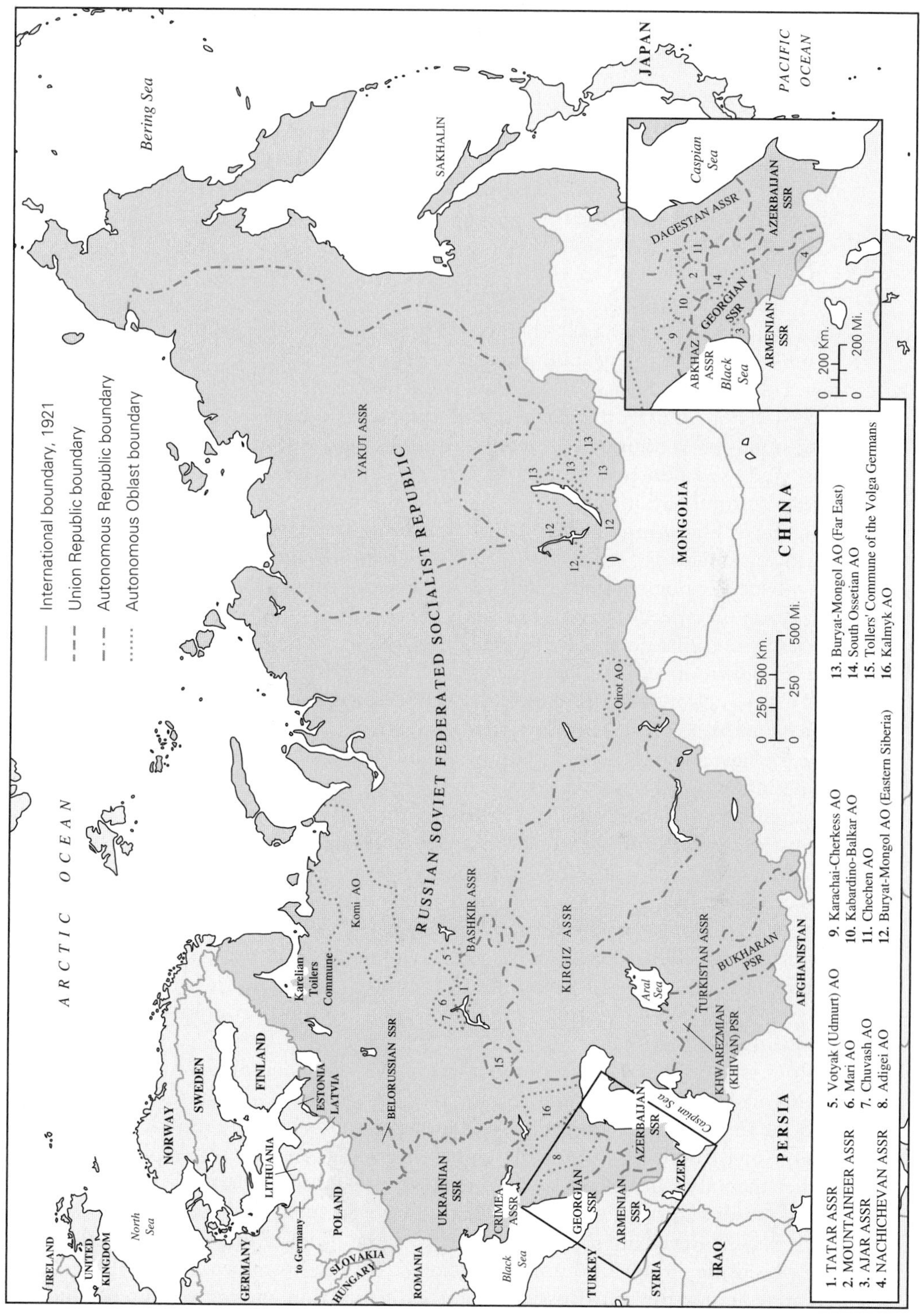

USSR, December, 1922. *Reprinted from Terry Martin,* The Affirmative Action Empire: Nations and Nationalism in the Soviet Union, 1923–1939. *Copyright © 2001 by Cornell University. Used by permission of the publisher, Cornell University Press.*

Kush. These would be juggled through the decades, and the smallest units would be dissolved in the 1930s, but the basic structure in place by 1924 would remain until the late 1980s, when activists began redrawing the map once again and places such as High Karabagh and Chechnya—virtually unknown to outsiders—splashed across the world's headlines.

Indigenization

One historian has accurately characterized Soviet nationality policies in these years as modernization and renationalization. This formula can be put in a larger context. For example, the new and revived independent nations of postwar Eastern Europe—though much freer than any of the Soviet nations—also faced the task of state building, economic recovery, education, land reform, and other social policies, while simultaneously building a new identity through self-conscious and assertive cultural nationalism—much of it in reaction to the epochs of dominion by Romanovs, Habsburgs, or Ottomans. The result there was often persecution of minority nationalities. In the USSR, modernization of the nationalities meant industry, literacy, schools, science and public health, women's emancipation, and the assault on organized religion. But both Lenin and Stalin insisted on differentiating Soviet from tsarist policies by favoring non-Russian nationalities. In 1923, the government introduced "indigenization" *(korenizatsiya),* a compensatory program of affirmative action for nationalities by way of preferential hiring, enforced promotion of local languages, and revival or creation of national cultures. During the 1920s, these measures often resulted in "reverse discrimination" against Russians living in the non-Russian areas.

Linguistic indigenization was a striking reversal of tsarist practices (and of those almost everywhere in the world). In every national unit, the local language would be the language of instruction in schools and in the public sphere—government and economy; nonspeakers were expected to learn that language. National sensitivities were to be observed, and selected aspects of culture—whether Turkmen, Belorussian, or Abkhazian—were to be nurtured by local leaders in the form of a native language press and the publication and performance of works in their languages. These cultural forms were to enwrap a "socialist" content—a concept still in flux during the 1920s.

In some of the republics and autonomous lands, indigenization during the 1920s amounted to a cultural renaissance. For smaller nationalities who had never had literary languages or alphabets, new ones were actually created. To avoid any charge of Russification, "eastern" alphabets such as Arabic were replaced by Latin rather than Cyrillic. Concrete measures were taken to hire first, fire last, and promote persons from the local nationality in government and economy to establish native elites. Reversing the tsarist practice of excluding or limiting the admission of certain ethnic groups into university (such as Jews), Soviet policy established preferential quotas for non-Russians. The indigenization program went beyond the carving out of autonomous republics, provinces, and regions. Eventually, wherever national clusters existed, however small, enclaves at district, village soviet, and even collective farm levels were formed as miniature ethnic communities with their own official language and schools. This developed into an immense mosaic and a babble of tongues, comprising tens of thousands of ghettoized national soviets surrounded, so to speak, by linguistic fences. Until the mid-1930s, linguistic assimilation was officially prohibited.

This extraordinary system of "payback" to once submerged nationalities and the advancement of "ethnic pride" also had its instrumental purpose: to deflect Soviet peoples from harmful brands of nationalism such as separatism, political contact with diasporas of national or ethnic groups living abroad, and foreign-inspired movements such as Pan-Finnism or Pan-Turkism. Soviet leaders believed that national consciousness had to flourish for a time until class consciousness was able to develop. Russian domination or "Great Power chauvinism," a vestige of tsarist colonialism, was seen as a greater danger than local nationalism.

Indigenization did not of course include the encouragement of religions or customs considered "backward" but rather stressed "symbolic markers of national identity" in folklore, music, literature, and dance. No mere window dressing, indigenization was taken seriously and administered comprehensively with great enthusiasm both at the center and at the local level. Yet in spite of its progressive aims, in practice indigenization generated a great deal of resentment among Russians who were now forced to learn a new language and made to witness the advancement of people previously disempowered. Many party members vocally opposed it, and many others offered passive resistance. Still others remained ambivalent. In the late 1920s, certain features and individuals associated with this national policy came under attack.

SLAVIC RENAISSANCE: UKRAINE AND BELORUSSIA

Ukraine emerged from the torments of civil war as a virtual civilization in the making, exercising a fierce cultural rebuff of Russianness and a frenzied renaissance that has been called a golden age of Ukrainian cultural nationalism. Lacerated by revolution, economic breakdown, and famine, the Ukrainian masses at the outset of the 1920s had little love for the Ukrainian Soviet regime. With its capital in the heavily Russian city of Kharkov in eastern Ukraine, and its big cities and its government still dominated by non-Ukrainians, this state looked like an arm of Moscow. But the NEP economic recovery, the lessening of repression, and the active policies of Ukrainization, the local version of indigenization, reduced the hostility of the population and brought hope of national revival to many Ukrainian intellectuals.

Some Russian Communists in Ukraine resisted the idea of Ukrainization. The Russian Communist Dmitry Lebed viewed Ukrainian culture as inferior. The Russian language, he argued, dominated the cities, the outposts of progress, while Ukrainian was the language of backward peasants. This view was officially rejected, and the new party head, Lazar Kaganovich, a Russianized Ukrainian Jew close to Stalin, and the state leader, Vlas Chubar, tried to enforce indigenization. Hard-line

Russianists were removed. Two leaders of the indigenization project in the 1920s—Oleksandr Shumsky (1890–1946), a former Ukrainian Socialist Revolutionary (SR), and Mykola Skrypnyk (1872–1933), a Bolshevik—combined Marxism with Ukrainian cultural nationalism. Since almost all local party members spoke Russian as their first tongue, a drive was launched to recruit Ukrainian speakers into state and party. Russians were required to learn Ukrainian—an unprecedented act in Russian history. National schools blossomed, and literacy in the 1920s grew from 40 to 70 percent in the towns and from 15 to 50 percent in country. This and a flood of books and newspapers in Ukrainian spurred the growth of the Ukrainian-speaking population in the cities, the state machine, and the party organization.

The cultural scene was marked by returning émigrés, the revival of nineteenth-century figures, the emergence of a Ukrainian avant-garde, and great diversity in literature, theater, music, and film. Peasant and proletarian authors, folklorists, symbolists, and modernists jostled each other in a dynamic arena. In its vortex stood Russian-born Mykola Khvylovy (real name, Nikolai Fitilov) (1893–1933) and his avant-garde literary movement of the 1920s. A gifted writer, Khvylovy fused Marxist internationalism, revolutionary romanticism, modernism, and Ukrainian nationalism into a countercultural force. Rejecting Russian influence, he envisioned Ukraine as a bridge between a renewed Europe and an emerging Asia, with Kharkov as a new world cultural center. Les Kurbas (1887–1942), a modernist theater director, mounted the first Ukrainian play staged after the revolution, *The Haidamaks* (1841), based on an epic poem about an eighteenth-century Ukrainian revolt against the Poles written by Ukraine's national poet, Taras Shevchenko (1814–1861) (see the chapter "Around the Russian Empire, 1801–1861"). Oleksandr Dovzhenko (1894–1956) ranked with the great cinematographers of the 1920s in his experimental and poetic films about the Ukrainian land. The historian and ex-leader of the Ukrainian Rada (council government), Mihajlo Hrushevsky, and other luminaries of science and learning returned from abroad. The combination of traditional and modern was in a way Ukraine's belated version of the Russian Silver Age of culture (see the chapter "Cultural Explosion, 1900–1920").

Belorussia, which had never been a nation, presented a more difficult picture: a vast illiterate Belorussian peasantry surrounding cities dominated by Russians, Poles, Ukrainians, and Jews. Indigenization was aggressively pursued, and cultural assertiveness surged through Belorussian literature, the academy, press, and theater. Literary figures such as Janka Kupala (real name Ivan Lutsevich) (1882–1942) led a revival. Even Polish, Belorussian, and Ukrainian anticommunists have conceded that the two Soviet republics in the 1920s showed a much better record of cultural and national development than did neighboring Poland in regard to its Belorussian and Ukrainian populations. Language revival, mass education, and cultural awakening were all part of incipient nation building —though well short of independence—that initially aroused optimism in Ukrainian and Belorussian leaders and intellectuals of the era. In both republics, however, linguistic Ukrainization failed in the face of local Russian resistance, and several key figures, including Commissar of Education Shumsky fell from grace, foreshadowing a shift in national policy that was to come.

THE JEWS OF SOCIALISM

The Jewish proletariat and many intellectuals had imbibed socialist teachings before the revolution—and indeed had contributed radical ideas to Russian Marxism. Leaders of the indigenization departments—a Jewish Commissariat within the government, and a Jewish section of the party—attempted to build a socialist community with a distinct Jewish ethnic (but not religious) identity based on Yiddish, the language of the former Jewish Pale. The government officially fought against anti-Semitism because it was linked to the hated tsarist past. Soviet policies, combined with negative propaganda and repression, worked to reduce the influence of the biblical language Hebrew, Judaism, and Zionism. The last was a movement born in the late nineteenth century to foster the settlement of all the world's Jews in the Holy Land (Palestine).

The cultural campaign sponsored Yiddish literature, song, cinema, and theater. As late as 1933, twelve Yiddish theaters, as opposed to only nine Russian, operated in Ukraine. The Moscow State Yiddish Theater mounted sparkling and original plays that reflected the values of great prerevolutionary Jewish writers like Sholom Aleichem (Rabinovich) (1859–1916). Traditional Jewish festivity music, called klezmer, enlivened productions that attracted Jewish and non-Jewish audiences. New and old works were put to the service of antireligious working-class values, though clever directors sometimes inserted coded references to Judaic themes in the scripts. The success of the cultural program was limited by the difficulty in

Scene from L. Mizandrontsev's The Wailing Wall at the Moscow Yiddish Theater.
Sovfoto/Eastfoto.

reaching out to the scattered Jewish towns and in communicating with ordinary Jews, who did not respond to the subtle symbolism of Yiddish-Bolshevik culture when it was presented in avant-garde forms. Needless to say, those who remained Orthodox Jewish believers and detested Communist atheism were left out of the picture and periodically persecuted.

In another innovation, Communists who had always exalted the proletariat now promoted rural settlement for Jews. Influential Jewish and non-Jewish Communists believed that to be a nation a people needed both a peasantry and a territory. "Ruralizing" the Jews offered a chance to eradicate the popular stereotype of the Jew as an urbanite, a pallid and devout weakling with no roots on the land. As hardworking, robust, suntanned farmers living in rural communes as Zionists were doing in Palestine, Jews could engage in truly productive labor, build socialism, and reverse the harmful images that had haunted them through the ages. In pursuit of this goal, Soviet Jews, often joined by American Jews who came to settle in the USSR, moved onto Jewish communes or voluntary collective farms, mostly in Ukraine, and began working the soil.

In spite of campaigns against it, anti-Semitism reared its head among those peasants who resented land being set off for Jews. A geographical territory was also sought for a Jewish national homeland, not in Palestine, as the Zionists were teaching, but inside the USSR. Possible sites canvassed in the 1920s included Crimea, parts of Ukraine and Belorussia, and the shores of the Caspian Sea. The bizarre locale chosen by the government for a Jewish Autonomous Region was the distant region of Birobijan in the Soviet Far East. It was meant to be a refuge where Jews could abandon their allegedly unproductive mercantile habits in favor of communal agriculture. Through Yiddish culture and language, they would remain "Jews," but of a different order from those misguided by the God of Abraham, Isaac, and Jacob or by "imperialist" Zionism. The first wave of settlers departed in 1928.

TRANSCAUCASIA

From 1922 until the 1930s, the power in Transcaucasia lay in the hands of a Transcaucasus Regional Committee of the Communist Party, situated first in Azerbaijan's capital, Baku, and then in Tbilisi, formerly Tiflis, capital of Georgia. Run by Stalin's cohort Orjonikidze in the early years, it tried to treat the region as a single economic and political unit called the Transcaucasian Federation (1922–1937). One of its more positive achievements during the NEP was partially to recreate the interregional economic life of the tsarist period that had been shattered by the emergence of the three independent republics during the civil war. On the negative side, the Communists had destroyed by force the last vestiges of independent regimes in Georgia, Armenia, and Azerbaijan. Resistance and resentment of Soviet power could be found everywhere, but acceptance of the new order was highest in Armenia and lowest in Georgia, owing to the fact that the latter's popular Menshevik regime had been overthrown by the Communists. Indigenization, however, met few obstacles in these two republics because of the preponderance there of local elites over Russians.

As in the nineteenth century, the establishment of Russian state power over Armenia was made easier by fear of the Turks. But a territorial decision irked Armenian nationalists: the awarding of the mostly Armenian enclave of High Karabagh to neighboring Azerbaijan as part of territorial indigenization. In spite of this perceived insult, a minor revolt in 1921, and the repression of the Dashnak national movement, Soviet power offered latitude for growth of national culture and political stability until the 1930s. Economic recovery was the first order of the day. In spite of Armenia's mercantile traditions, the bulk of the population was still rural. The Communist regime mounted the usual campaigns to promote literacy, advance women, and fight religion—although the head of the Armenian Church remained, and religious persecution was relatively mild. Much of the indigenization activity was carried out by diaspora Armenians, cut off during the civil war, who returned to build up their ravaged homeland in response to the genocide of 1915. A university was founded in the capital, Erevan, as well as an opera and a movie studio.

Russian-Georgian relations began on two bitter notes: the Bolshevik takeover of power from a popular Menshevik regime in 1921, and the attempt by Stalin and Orjonikidze to lord it over the Georgian Communist Party and the republic. A faction in the party headed by Budu Mdivani (1877–1937) opposed Georgia's being merely a part of the Transcaucasian Federation and demanded a slow pace of sovietization and economic gradualism. Orjonikidze's hard line, backed by Stalin, won out. They weakened or dispersed the opposition, which was calling for mild treatment of Mensheviks and other intellectuals. At a melodramatic and confrontational conference in 1923, attended by some European socialists, the Georgian Menshevik Party disbanded, curtly terminating a brief but brilliant period of Georgian history. The Menshevik leaders emigrated, and some of them organized along with other socialists a 1924 anticommunist uprising from abroad. This aroused only a half-dozen provincial centers, and it collapsed within a few days. About four thousand people were killed, and the Bolsheviks executed the leaders.

Land reform began with the nationalization of state, church, and some private estates. But the holdings of many distinguished noble families went untouched until 1923, when all lands were taken, and the role of the nobility as a force in Georgian life came to an end, though some of its former members later became prominent in Soviet academic and scientific life. The introduction of NEP softened peasant resentment for the remainder of the decade.

Although an antireligious drive occurred, and the highest Georgian prelate was arrested for a short time, a certain mix of accommodation and tension in general prevailed among the common people. The intelligentsia remained mostly hostile. Even so, indigenization proceeded apace. Much of it—including cultural institutions and a university—had been initiated under the Menshevik Republic. As in Ukraine and elsewhere, some Communists opposed affirmative action. Orjonikidze complained that qualified non-Georgians were being passed over to hire less-than-qualified native Georgians. A literary ferment in Georgia paralleled those of Russia and Ukraine, with a panorama of proletarian writers and avant-garde poets—some of whom would be shot in the 1930s. The best-known writer of the decade, Konstantine Gamsakhurdia (1891–1944), whose son would be Georgian dictator of the 1990s, wrote *The Smile of Dionysius* (1925), a novel decadent by Soviet standards, showing that European and Silver Age influences were still alive in some parts of the Soviet Union.

RED FLAG OVER OASIS AND STEPPE

The Muslim "east" included Azerbaijan in Transcaucasia, Crimea and Tatarstan in the RSFSR, and other regions, in addition to the republics of Central Asia. Soviet leaders saw Muslim lands as a backward "east" compared with the Soviet "west," inhabited by Slavs, Jews, Georgians, Armenians, and a few others. The largest conglomeration of Muslims lived in Central Asia. Soviet rule there was framed by two violent upheavals: the Basmachi Revolt of the early 1920s, and the Islamic backlash against Soviet attempts to liberate Muslim women in the late 1920s. Both illustrated grimly and vividly the great difficulty Communists had with the people in this region, who displayed much more ethnic friction, both toward Russians and among themselves, than in other republics. During and between these episodes, the Soviet authorities, native and Russian, established institutions and launched programs of modernization and indigenization.

The Basmachi

The most serious regional upheaval, the Basmachi Revolt, lasted from 1918 to 1924, followed by several more years of sporadic unrest and a final outburst in 1934. "Basmachi" (from *basmak,* a raider or bandit who attacked Russians and their collaborators) were small, largely unconnected clan- and family-based units, never a single movement. Though some rebels called themselves Freedom Fighters or the Army of Islam, the Basmachi lacked a unifying leader, program, and ideology, and they were unresponsive to those who wished to turn them into a Pan-Islamic or Pan-Turkic force. They constituted a rural resistance movement by those who wished to preserve, or get back, their land and way of life.

The immediate impetus for the uprising was the violence of the revolution, particularly the Kokand massacres carried out by the Tashkent Soviet in February 1918 (see the chapter "Civil War: Reds, Whites, and Greens, 1917–1921"). It was fed by old resentments of Russian land grabs and the memory of the 1916 revolts and massacres (see the chapter "Russia in World War I, 1914–1917"), and it was reinforced by Communist assaults on Muslim religion and customs. By 1919, about fifty thousand armed fighters held sway over much of the countryside and smaller towns. A so-called Muslim People's Army collaborated for a time with an anticommunist Russian Peasant Army, belying Communist charges that the Basmachi Revolt was merely a racist anti-Russian movement. In 1921, Enver Pasha (b. 1881), one of the former rulers of Turkey who had left his defeated country and fled to

Moscow, was sent by Lenin to Central Asia to help subdue the Basmachi. On arrival, however, Enver joined them and set out to defeat the Soviets and realize his dream of a pan-Turkic empire to include Chinese Sinkiang, Afghanistan, Turkey, and all of Central Asia. Before his death in battle in 1922, Enver had stiffened the back of some Basmachi groups by his personal charisma and the German organizational methods he had learned as a young officer.

The Basmachi were strongest in the Uzbek lands, but similar bands appeared in Turkmen and Tajik areas. In spite of their sometimes harsh measures of forced recruitment, taxation, and punishment of deserters and traitors, the Basmachi won broad support from the population. Their strength lay in familiarity with the terrain, tribal fighting traditions, guerrilla warfare, and limited night raids. But the movement that peaked in 1922 was also beset by constant internal squabbles and rivalry. A combination of Red Army might and Communist concessions, including amnesty and land grants to rebels, brought the movement largely to a halt in the mid-1920s.

Islamic Women Under Siege

Next to the Basmachi Revolt, the most spectacular political event of the 1920s was the Communist-sponsored mass unveiling of women. Women of Central Asia were besieged on two sides: Communist organizers tried to force the issue of women's equality by assaulting Muslim traditions of female servility; and Muslim men fought the assault with great ferocity. The struggle was most intense in Uzbekistan, where centuries of interpretation and practice had sanctioned bride purchase, kidnapping, child marriages, polygyny, female illiteracy, and the seclusion of women. The last was symbolized and enforced by the *paranji,* a cotton veil covered over with a body-length horsehair garment that women were expected to wear in public. According to prevailing sensibilities, showing the female face in public was an erotic provocation equivalent to showing other intimate parts of the body. Patterns of nomadic life and female labor made face and body covering less important in the steppe regions. The Communists did not invent unveiling or women's equality in the region, for it was advocated in Jadid writings before the revolution and by a congress of Muslims held in Moscow in May 1917. But the reforming models in neighboring Turkey and Afghanistan spurred Soviet authorities to action.

Soviet laws on women's equality were even more difficult to apply in Central Asia than in Russia proper. Alexandra Kollontai and other Communist feminist leaders sent activists from Zhenotdel, the party's women's organization, to bring education, family enlightenment, and gestures of symbolic defiance to Muslim women. Teachers, physicians, and atheist agitators visited gendered spaces such as wells, markets, and bathhouses and set up clubs in towns and in Red yurts (tents) in the steppe. They taught literacy and counseled women on sanitation, land and water rights, and divorce procedures. Utilizing the idiom of the missionary and the colonialist, Zhenotdel used plays, mock trials, and films to denounce sexual slavery and seclusion. A 1927 motion picture, *The Veil,* featured a Muslim heroine who escapes the sexual advances of an older man and becomes an educated woman garbed in shirt and tie. Since a crucial element of all "consciousness raising" is personal involvement, Zhenotdel recruited activists among the Muslim women and sent them as delegates to women's congresses in Moscow. Out of this milieu came a number of well-known Uzbek women writers and public figures.

Zhenotdel's biggest success was with the divorced, abandoned, or abused among wives, orphan girls, child brides, and those engaged in family property suits. The more assertive converts among Muslim women in the towns became actresses, dancers, and singers; divorced their husbands; and marched into public male-dominated places and even religious quarters. The attendant scandal and risk was so great that most women resisted joining this struggle. Here as elsewhere in the Soviet Union, rumors circulated in the bazaars that the Communists were planning to boil women into soap or force them to sleep under a communal blanket with men. In folk language, Zhenotdel was dubbed *jinotdel* ("demon's section"), and its activists were said to be men in disguise.

Muslim men blocked emancipatory efforts by threatening women or taking evasive measures such as keeping multiple marriages secret. The poor progress in improving women's status led the party to launch a *hujum,* the name later given to an administrative assault on old customs. The veil became the main symbolic target in Uzbekistan. On International Women's Day, March 8, 1927—exactly ten years after the beginning of the February Revolution—thousands of women gathered on selected Uzbekistan town squares, demonstratively tore off their *paranjis,* and threw them into bonfires. Thousands more did so in the summer, to the accompaniment of passionate speeches. The antiveil speakers stressed the practice's crippling effects on mind and body as an implement and emblem of social inequality, economic immobility, and cultural isolation.

Bolshevik women's activity in Central Asia. *Tass/Sovfoto/Eastfoto.*

The male backlash against this politically theatrical act and its aftermath was fueled by anxiety, impotence, fear, and anger. Soviet power was said to "take away women" by schooling them to ignore custom by talking to men in public. Most resistance—by men and women—took the form of harassing and shaming, which led the majority of unveiled women to reveil. Violence erupted as well. Killing a "sinful" wife or relative was justified by a distorted reading of traditional jurisprudence. The mass unveiling transformed rage into cruel acts that targeted actresses, Zhenotdel workers, party members of both sexes, and unveiled women. An earthquake in 1927 was interpreted as divine punishment for the unveiling, and rumors of the end of the world attended an escalating terror campaign that included beating, rape, and barbarous murder. According to official figures, eight hundred women were killed in 1927–1928 alone, though other estimates reach into the thousands.

The regime responded with show trials and executions, which further escalated the savagery. In 1929 the party backed off, realizing that the population had not been sufficiently prepared for the *hujum.* It reverted to a more gradual pace. The counterproductive campaign caused further loss of party influence in the region, entrenchment of tradition, and even the spread of veiling. Lacking a real proletariat as a base for social transformation in largely rural Central Asia, the authorities had used women as what one scholar called a "surrogate proletariat" whose liberation was meant to subvert the old order. Its failure to do so led to partial accommodation with local social and gender customs and to a stability that was favored over social revolution and transformation. The veil remained a commonplace in Uzbekistan for three more decades.

Soviet Power

The Soviet Union's initial national boundary designations in Central Asia differed from the old tsarist ones. Gone were the Steppe Province, Turkistan, and the khanates of Khiva and Bukhara. The People's Republics were submerged into the Uzbek and Turkmen Soviet Socialist Republics, set up in 1924. Further upgrading and renaming took place in the late 1920s and 1930s.

The new boundaries cut through ethnic entities and flung people from one political community to another. They sometimes exacerbated old enmities among national groups and were frequently redrawn. The main power center in the region was the Communist Party's Central Asian Bureau in Tashkent, the town that later replaced Samarkand as capital of Uzbekistan. Led by Russians, Jews, and Latvians, with Central Asians in secondary positions, the bureau reported regularly to Moscow and attempted to carry out the central party's economic and social policies. As in all the borderlands, war and social turmoil had brought virtual economic collapse. With the NEP came a rough economic coordination of the region as a whole, famine relief via grain shipments from Russia, restoration of irrigation works, and a development of cotton at the expense of other crops. In addition to upgrading of women's status, modernization, as elsewhere, revolved around issues of health and education.

Soviet Central Asia, c. 1922. *Reprinted with permission of Duke University Press from Edward Allworth,* Central Asia. *Copyright © 1989.*

As the Islamic backlash of the late 1920s suggests, the thorniest issue facing the Communists in the Muslim lands was Islam. Its pious obligations—pillars of Islam such as alms, prayer, fasting, and hajj (pilgrimage to Mecca)—were not all easy to observe in a god-hostile state. In the 1920s, Communists waged sporadic campaigns to undermine the social bases of Islam by nationalizing the property of the waqf—that is, clergy-owned lands and charitable institutions, and outlawing Quran schools and Islamic courts. These policies had a limited impact because of Russian official ignorance of local conditions, Muslims' skill at evasion, lack of substitutes for abolished institutions, and poor coordination between Moscow and the Communists on the ground. The Allahsizlar, or Godless Organization, in Uzbekistan, headed by the Communist leader Akmal Ikramov (1898–1938), fought an uphill battle against Islam. Local Communist activists often ignored the regime's orders not to attack religious believers or clergy. An Uzbek education official in

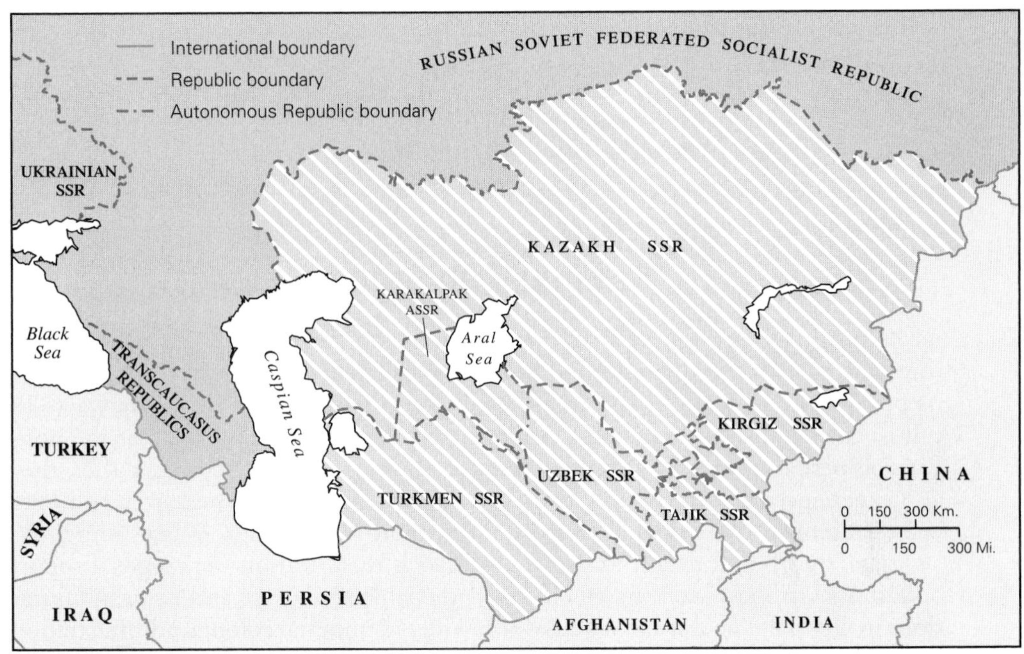

Soviet Central Asia, 1936. *Reprinted with permission of Duke University Press from Edward Allworth,* Central Asia. *Copyright © 1989.*

1927 cautioned against coercion: "When starting agitation among the peasants do not begin directly by saying 'there is no god' or 'the prophets are liars,' rather you must explain the foundations of Marxism to the peasants easily, understandably, with simple words." To offset the Basmachi appeal and win some support from the people, the Communists reversed or softened these policies through the mid-1920s.

The Soviet system deeply affected other aspects of Central Asian culture. The Latinization of the Arabic alphabet from the 1920s to the late 1930s, when it was changed to Cyrillic, hindered scholarly communication. Poets and singers and devout liberal Muslims lamented the dashed hopes for independence or pan-Turkism. Writers produced a fiction of gloom, and one poet called the Russian dominance a "black winter." On the other hand, proletarian and women writers took up revolutionary themes and transformed traditional tales about suicide, broken love, age and youth, and purchased brides into struggles for justice with happy endings. One of these writers, Mairy Shamsudinova, a fighter for women's rights, was killed in the Islamic backlash.

In spite of local Russian resistance to it, indigenization in these lands continued. Although linguistic programs made little headway, affirmative action was pushed. Lands taken by Russians from 1916 onward were given to the locals, helping to defuse the Basmachi Revolt but causing Russian resentment and even pogroms against the natives. Ironically, some of the dispossessed Russian settlers hoped to emigrate to China just as the Kazakhs had done in 1916. Most important, favored hiring and promotion of locals were pursued vigorously and even escalated, reaching a zenith at the end of the 1920s and early 1930s.

EMPIRE AND UNION

As political stability set in after the civil war, the Communist Party held sway through the 1920s and allowed no political challenge, nationalist or otherwise, to its power. The new Soviet empire differed from its predecessor in many ways. To call its rule simply an imperialist despotism would fail to recognize that the non-Russian peoples were not merely objects of Soviet policy and power; rather, they also experienced the revolution in their own lives. Tsarist administrators had long been content to rule regional peoples and exploit their wealth. When, under the last tsars, they began to intrude, it was to launch Russification campaigns, support occasional Orthodox conversion efforts, and enable land grabs and labor mobilizations in Central Asia during World War I. The old imperial colonial administration harbored no ambition to remake civilizations, though many private organizations and individuals did. The Communists, ever with an eye on the tsarist past, pushed much more deeply into the lives of the nationalities. Soviet power assaulted all religions, rather than trying to replace one with another, and tried to turn some social traditions upside down. The nationalities project, directed from above and carried out below, confounded and even angered many party members, who could understand affirmative action for the proletariat and, to a lesser degree, even for women, but not for national groups. But indigenization was no anomaly. It drew from Bolshevik interpretations of Marxism and from other utopian egalitarian strands in the Russian revolutionary past. A sense of mission invested the rulers sitting in Moscow to civilize the imperial backland through science and literacy; and in the application of indigenization they were engaged in nation building, not merely in the maintenance of empire.

CHAPTER 34

Stalinism Established, 1928–1939

They took you away at dawn,
I followed you, as if to a funeral,
Children wept in the dark room,
The candle guttered in the icon case.
The cold of the icon was on your lips,
The sweat of death on your brow . . . Not to be forgotten!
*I shall, like the wives of the Streltsy,**
Howl beneath the Kremlin towers.

—*Anna Akhmatova, "Requiem," 1935*

By 1929, Stalin possessed sufficient power in the nation and support in the party to launch the greatest economic transformation of its kind up to that time, named by Stalin himself the Great Breakthrough. In that year, a "socialist offensive" ended the mixed economy of the New Economic Policy (NEP), outlawed private capital, introduced centralized economic planning, launched a furious drive to heavy industrialization, and collectivized agriculture. Some historians have attached the label "revolution from above" to the following turbulent decade of Stalin's leadership. Not merely an economic revolution, Stalin's involved a war on the peasants, a cultural revolution, the shutdown of the remnants of intellectual freedom and of open debate within the party, a tyrannical personal dictatorship, and a hideous reign of terror. Society was shaken to its foundations.

IRON AND STEEL: INDUSTRIALIZATION

By 1929–1930, private ownership of factories, shops, and other enterprises had been abolished, as well as the consumer market and the remnants of NEP. The key to the new economic system was central planning. The state agency Gosplan had authority to organize the production of the entire nation. A committee of economists

*The *streltsy,* or musketeers, rebelled against Peter the Great (Peter I) and were beheaded on Red Square in 1698.

and political bosses would decide how many dresses or tractors to produce and how much would be invested in heavy industry. Output was sliced like a pie in advance and not according to popular demands or needs, although limited forms of trade continued in rural markets and in illegal exchanges. The concept of a directed economy appealed to many intellectuals and others around the world at the time of the Great Depression, when capitalism seemed to promise only the "anarchy of production," as Marx had put it: cycles of prosperity and economic woe. Rational planning seemed the right antidote to chaotic capitalism. As one of the main Stalinist planners put it as early as 1927, "We will never draw back from targets simply because their realization is not a 1,000 percent certainty, since it is the will of the proletariat and our plans, concentrating that will on the struggle to achieve the task at hand, that themselves can and must be the decisive factor needed for their successful fulfillment."

For Soviet leaders, planning was the very essence of Marxism, a belief that would grip their imagination for the next six decades. In the backward conditions of the USSR, planning meant rapid industrialization as well as controlled distribution. In human terms, this was a political economy of sacrifice rather than of consumption, because the planners who had the power always decided that a base of heavy industry took precedence over dresses. Dresses could not defend a state encircled by enemies or make it a Great Power; and the manufacture of dresses required a modern heavy-industry infrastructure. Recent war scares fueled the leadership's fear of an attack on Russia by foreign powers. In 1931, a decade before Hitler's invasion of Russia, Stalin told a group of Soviet managers that unless it overtook the "advanced countries" in industrial and military might in the next ten years, the USSR would be crushed by them. Recent oral testimony suggests that some people accepted harsh industrial discipline. Said one about the 1930s, "If you stole a spike from the field you would go to jail. The most brutal conditions, you see, but if it weren't for them, we would not have made it, we would not have won the war."

An Industrial Revolution

Planning in a mature economy is what Marx had predicted would happen after a proletarian revolution in a society with highly developed machinery and an efficient, well-trained work force. The USSR had neither, and its leaders tried to compensate for backwardness through willpower and discipline. Planners were constantly ordered from the top to revise their initial projections and ratchet up goals to fantasy levels. The saga of industrialization brought spontaneous bursts of enthusiasm among young Communist workers, continuous pressure on managers to meet quotas and deadlines, and managerial harassment of workers who did not keep pace. Given the relative inexperience with machines of the new unskilled labor force of peasants, youth, and women, chaos ensued: workers misused equipment, and industrial accidents abounded. Work force inefficiency was aggravated by an internalized fear of innovation, risk, or personal responsibility and by a high job turnover. The response from on high was verbal abuse, new quotas, and charges of sabotage, leveled especially against managers and alleged oppositionists within the party. In show trials beginning in 1927, Russian and foreign technicians were accused of wrecking Soviet industry at the behest of White émigrés, famed European firms such as Nobel, and even the British adventurer Lawrence of Arabia. Some of the accused were shot on the flimsiest of evidence.

The First Five-Year Plan (1928–1932) is one of the great epics of twentieth-century history and was so presented by the authorities. Put underway in October 1928 and officially announced in April 1929, it was designed to increase Soviet industrial production by an extraordinary 20 percent a year. Fulfillment would require good harvests, increased foreign trade, and much greater efficiency in the work force and management. Early into the plan, Stalin, allegedly responding to workers' demands, called for its completion in four years instead of five, a wish instantly translated into national slogans. Production targets were plotted for the number of trucks and tractors and tons of iron and coal. The economic geography of the country shifted eastward, and new "Chicagos"—a Russian nickname for huge industrial centers—appeared in the Urals and Siberia. Giant projects and new construction sites for heavy industry, machine tools, coal mining and steel founding, hydroelectric power, rail lines, and armaments mushroomed up out of steppe, riverbed, forest, and desert. Old plants expanded output. Cities rose amid the plains and forests of Siberia and Soviet Asia. Names of canals and power stations were used as brand names for cigarettes and candy. Like an army, the builders assembled. The commanders were party activists, freshly trained engineers, a new wave of foreign experts on a lark to make money or build new civilizations. The soldiers were uprooted and bewildered peasants, natives of the outer reaches, and young city boys and girls who sought a surrogate for the revolutionary adventure of 1917–1921 that they had missed. The romance of production appealed also to many American workers and engineers, who made their way to join the "great experiment."

Tent city at Magnitogorsk. *Sovfoto/Eastfoto.*

Magnitogorsk (Magnetic Mountain), a brand new Soviet city built from scratch, whose creation caused an agony of accidents and wasted labor, was also a bivouac of creative celebration. "Magnitka [Magnitogorsk] taught us how to work. Magnitka taught us how to live," wrote a Young Communist woman. A view of Soviet industrialization that sees it as wholly repressive and manipulative cannot accommodate the genuine sense of adventure that young people felt as they rode out to the mammoth construction works and toiled night and day. But tragedy and deprivation stalked the great plans as well. The leading symbol of hardship was the White Sea (Belomor) Canal building project in the far north, which became a forced labor camp where death from overwork was routine.

The visible result of the first plan as it wound down at the end of 1932 was a chain of industrial edifices in Ukraine, the Urals, the Donets River basin (Donbass), the Volga, and Siberia. Official figures (see Table 1) for 1932, even when corrected for inflation, revealed spectacular results in some sectors where the targets were reached or surpassed: a huge machine-building industry (then a central feature

TABLE 1 Achievements of the First Five-year Plan Official Figures

	1927–8 (actual)	1932–3 (plan)	1932 (actual)
National income (milliard 1926–7 roubles	24.4	49.7	45.5
Gross industrial production (milliard 1926–7 roubles)	18.3	43.2	43.3
Producers' goods (millard 1926–7 roubles)	6.0	18.1	23.1
Consumers' goods (millard 1926–7 roubles)	12.3	25.1	20.2
Gross agricultural production (milliard 1926–7 roubles)	13.1	25.8	16.6
Electricity (milliard kWhs)	5.05	22.0	13.4
Hard coal (million tons)	35.4	75	64.3
Oil (million tons)	11.7	22	21.4
Iron ore (million tons)	5.7	19	12.1
Pig iron (million tons)	3.3	10	6.2
Steel (million tons)	4.0	10.4	5.9
Machinery (million 1926–7 roubles)	1,822	4,688	7,362
Superphosphates (million tons)	0.15	3.4	0.61
Wool cloth (million metres)	97	270	93.3
Total employed labour force millions)	11.3	15.8	22.8

Source: From *An Economic History of the USSR, 1917–1991* by Alex Nove/Penguin Books, 1996, Third Revised Edition 1992).

of modern industrial life), an explosion of hydroelectric power, and new railway lines. Breakthroughs occurred in virtually every sector of production, but often at the cost of product quality. Coal, iron, steel, chemicals, and consumer goods production fell short of the goals.

No sooner had the drive ended in 1932, than the Second Five-Year Plan began (1933–1937). It continued to stress heavy industry and put greater emphasis on military hardware. Magnitogorsk produced 10 percent of the nation's steel by 1939 and in World War II would produce half the steel used in Soviet tanks. The railroads in 1939 carried freight and passenger weight that was 91.8 percent higher than in 1932. The Soviet regime claimed for the decade 1929–1939 a growth rate of 16 to 20 percent per year. Recent estimates by Russian and Western economists have reduced this to 3.4 to 5 percent. Some economists believe that Stalin's industrialization, despite costs in human lives and flagrant wastefulness, helped immensely in the USSR's war against Nazi Germany. Others disagree and argue forcefully that the entire economic system was built on "faulty foundations."

The Impact of Rapid Industrialization

The results for society were mixed. Officially, unemployment virtually ended, though many laborers were inefficient. Women were drawn into the wage-labor economy in large numbers. Social benefits expanded to serve the new soldiers of labor: paid vacations (only recently won by labor forces in advanced countries); free clinical care from a medical profession dominated by women; education; and subsidized housing and transport. A side effect and a stated goal of the revolution was affirmative action and social mobility for workers through crash courses and technical education. A whole generation of engineers, agronomists, and industrial managers emerged from the peasantry and the working class during the late 1920s to the mid-1930s. Poetically called by one scholar the Class of 1931, they would work their way upward through the party ranks and one day rule the country. Members included party and state leaders Leonid Brezhnev, Alexei Kosygin, and many other figures of Soviet political history.

The negative results, aside from loss of life and limb to accidents and overwork, were overcrowded communal apartments; shortages of consumer goods, resulting in long lines; and a severe drop in living standards for workers and peasants from that of the 1920s. To the workplace came regimentation, fines, and the further emasculation of unions. Women now bore a double burden, laboring at home and in the mill or office. From 1926 to 1939, some 30 million people, mostly peasants, migrated to the cities. Newcomers brought along rural habits of mind and work that had the effect of rusticating the cities and, in a way, peasantizing much of Soviet life. The industrialization led to decades of disastrous environmental policies and to a swollen state apparatus required to oversee the economy.

TRACTORS AND CORPSES: COLLECTIVIZATION

In the late 1920s, the countryside contained millions of rural households with peasants who owned their tools, homes, and livestock. The land was still at the disposal of the village commune, which allotted to each family a collection of scattered strips for cultivation. The free market and most churches still functioned. The Communist propaganda campaigns of the 1920s had hardly scratched the surface of rural habits and mental sets. Collectivization of the countryside—shared land, cooperative labor, and state control—had long been a key feature of the Communist vision for the future. Stalin and his supporters had come to believe that the old village structure could not or would not provide food for the fast-growing cities and would cramp continuing efforts to change society. The decision to collectivize rapidly and by force, therefore, was directly related to forced industrialization. The planners believed that pooling land and labor would allow large-scale mechanization and thus increase the output of grain. This in turn would feed the towns and enable the state to sell surplus grain to finance its ambitious industrial projects. Collectivization was also meant to siphon off unproductive rural labor into industry. The resultant state control of the countryside would also allow the destruction of the perceived harmful elements of traditional peasant culture and society, such as religion. Since the peasantry was not likely to enroll in collective farms voluntarily, the state unleashed a bitter war. The agrarian revolution was unlike any previous one in history, an attempt at the total reordering of a rural civilization from the top down.

A Rural War

The question of how and when to begin collectivization was answered for Stalin in 1928, when peasants withheld grain from the market (see the chapter "The Years of New Economic Policy: Power, Society, and Culture, 1921–1928"). At that point, Stalin reverted to civil war methods of forced grain requisitions, or "procurements." Until late in 1929 emergency measures prevailed. In the summer and fall of 1929, Stalin ordered teams to collectivize selected regions. At some moment, still undocumented, Stalin decided on full-scale collectivization of the peasantry, probably because continued requisitions would only result in peasants reducing sown acreage. Stalin announced the program in his "Great Breakthrough" article of November 7, 1929, and proclaimed a "revolution from above." Though hindered by poor preparation, lack of clarity about goals, and a shortage of activists, a frightful campaign of large-scale collectivization was launched in the winter of 1929–1930. The goal was to pool all land and animals and to organize labor on consolidated farms. Peasants spread rumors of doomsday and resisted by evasion and arson, by destroying property and livestock, and by killing Soviet officials. They mounted thousands of "mass disturbances"—over thirteen thousand in 1930 alone—including those staged by women. Stalin warned that the more prosperous villagers, or *kulaks,* would sabotage the new farms. Such villagers were therefore excluded and "dekulakized," or eliminated as a class. As the definition of *kulak* widened, the war escalated, with shootings and the deportation in 1930–1931 alone of about 1.8 million *"kulaks,"* mostly simple peasants. Appealing for help to Soviet president Mikhail Kalinin (1875–1945), a deported *kulak* wrote in 1930: "We were driven into exile in [Siberia]. . . . We are perishing here from hunger, the children will die, there is no bread and food." No response is recorded.

By February 1930, 50 percent of the peasantry were collectivized, in conditions producing utter chaos. Stalin, unable to ignore the fiasco or admit blame, intervened with an article, "Dizziness with Success," accusing local collectivizers of taking his strategies too far. The tempo was temporarily reduced, and peasants fled the collective farms in droves. But the campaign resumed: by 1933, two-thirds of the peasants were collectivized, and by 1939 virtually all. Some horrors of this war were hidden from the Soviet people and from foreign eyes as well. Trucks bursting with volunteer agents of forced collectivization stormed into the countryside: civil war veterans with shaven skulls and leather jackets, factory workers, militant atheists, Young Communist agitators of both sexes, Russians and non-Russians, backed up by army troops and security forces. They occupied villages as in wartime, organized houses into blocks, forced villagers into the new order, shot resisters, confiscated animals, and burned churches. More than half the dekulakized peasants, thrown off the land, migrated to factory towns. Others ended in forced labor camps or settlements far from home in the bleak wildernesses of northern Russia, Siberia, and Central Asia. Still others perished miserably on the way. These unfortunates were crammed into cattle cars that dragged them through days and nights of torment by hunger and thirst and overcrowding. When the excruciatingly slow trains stopped to unload, corpses tumbled out of the excrement-filled boxcars.

Equal in horror was the famine of 1932–1933, resulting partly from climatic conditions and partly from Soviet policies of requisition and forced collectivization. Sections of Central Russia, the Volga, and the northern Caucasus suffered immensely, and the death toll fell most heavily on the Central Asian Kazakhs and Ukrainians. When the Ukrainian harvest failed, authorities, instead of setting up famine relief as in 1921, hauled away seed, blocked roads from starving villages to cities, and diverted food shipments elsewhere. The famine in Ukraine, though not planned as deliberate mass murder, was seen by many Ukrainians as attempted genocide because it coincided with a terror campaign against Ukrainian nationalists, who were allegedly attempting to detach Ukraine from the USSR (see the chapter "Stalinism: Life Inside the System, 1928–1941"). The agony of slow starvation, episodes of cannibalism, and the decimation of the population have been meticulously documented. This atrocity poisoned relations between the two ancient Slavic peoples more than anything else in previous history. Estimates of deaths caused by the famine in the USSR as a whole range from 5 to 7 million.

Apologists for collectivization argued that it was a precondition for industrialization. But prominent Communists such as Nikolai Bukharin had argued in the 1920s that a continuation of NEP would allow a gradual spread of socialism into the countryside (see the chapter "The Years of New Economic Policy: Power, Society, and Culture, 1921–1928"). Professional economists in the West believed that

Russian wealth and power could have been achieved without forced collectivization. Others rightly observed that the ruthlessness could certainly have been avoided and that the political culture of Stalinism itself allowed and indeed encouraged the bloodbath. Soviet people who dared raise such issues in the early thirties were a few years later accused of treason and executed. From any humane perspective, the terrible costs were far greater than the rewards, costs not only in lives lost but in the way the violence in the villages helped shape the Stalinist regime. Collectivization, conceived to extract the optimum of grain and promote productivity in the villages, had an almost opposite effect.

The Collective Farm

Under collectivism, the physical contours of the village remained, but the peasant commune, or *mir,* was dissolved—and with it a long, rich, and fiercely debated institution of Russian history. Replacing it were implanted Soviet institutions: local soviets, party organizations, security organs, propaganda bases, and districtwide Machine Tractor Stations (MTS), which were to service the district collective farms at ploughing and harvesting time. The MTS became outposts of Moscow's power, magnets for letters of denunciation, and staging areas for political intervention in rural life. Through the 1920s, Soviet economists had suggested a number of forms that collective farming should take. The two settled on were the state farm and the collective farm. The first was an agrarian state enterprise worked by landless waged laborers. The collective farm, the dominant type, joined the lands of a village together, left intact families and households with a small half-acre private plot of land on which to grow crops for free sale in the market (a belated concession), and reimbursed joint work by labor teams according to days worked and harvest gleaned.

Stalin's war on the countryside left many pitiful legacies—the death of millions, decimation of livestock, an artificial social and cultural wall between town and country, and collaboration with German invaders in 1941. Agricultural performance would remain sluggish for seven decades. However, two outcomes assumed immediate significance. First, the collectivized countryside finally fell under the control of the state. No mechanism in the past—tax collectors, military tribute takers, private landowners, rural officials, or food requisitioners—had ever managed to achieve this end. With it came the parching language of bureaucracy, the ponderous politicization of life, the loss of the traditional village commune, and the intensified persecution of religion. The second was a rumble of discontent in the party and the state.

PURGE AND TERROR: THE ROAD TO DEATH

Violent political repression was nothing new for the Soviet regime. Opposition party members, industrialists accused of sabotage, and various other offenders had been arrested and executed in the 1920s. But in the 1930s under Stalin the slaughter rose to unprecedented heights and took in party members at every level, even Stalin's closest associates. With the help of the political police, now called NKVD (Narodnyi Kommissariat Vnutrennykh Del—People's Commissariat of Internal Affairs), and other organs, Stalin was able to strike out against his opponents, real or imagined. An exceptionally vindictive leader, he could not abide the slightest criticism of his policies and saw any kind of opposition to them as treason. Those who harbored doubts about Stalin as a leader were for the most part cowed into submission and remained silent.

Yet there is evidence that, in the division of opinion in the Politburo during the forced industrialization and collectivization of the early 1930s, the economic administrator Sergo Orjonikidze and the Leningrad party chief Sergei Kirov favored moderation in industrial tempo and levels of violence in the countryside. Dismay over the brutality of the recent years was brewing in diverse quarters. Stalinist collectivization was assailed not only by peasants and émigré commentators such as Lev Trotsky, who, from his places of exile—first in Europe, then in Mexico—was thundering anti-Stalin diatribes. Prominent Soviet writers and veterans of civil war food requisition raids protested to Stalin. In this time of escalating economic offensives and peasant persecution, opposition currents flowed.

The first sign of overt opposition came in 1932, when a Moscow Communist and ex-Bukharin supporter, M. I. Ryutin, circulated an appeal to the party Central Committee openly attacking Stalin's assault on the peasantry and his personal dictatorship. Calling Stalin an "evil genius," Ryutin demanded an end to forced collectivization, a slowdown of the industrial gallop, and greater democracy in the party—without Stalin as its leader. Stalin demanded Ryutin's execution, but Kirov and other Politburo members objected. Ryutin was then banished from Moscow, later imprisoned, and in 1937 executed. Ryutin's sons were also killed and his wife sent to a prison camp. Old rivals of Stalin from the 1920s, Grigory Zinoviev (1883–1936) and Lev Kamenev (1883–1936), were implicated in the Ryutin affair and temporarily exiled, though not to prison camps. Even in his own home, Stalin faced criticism: late in 1932 his second wife, Nadezhda Allilueva (b. 1901), became bitterly disillusioned with him personally and politically. According to one account, her angry husband rudely insulted Allilueva at a dinner party, and she was found dead the next day, probably a suicide. Stalin was deeply shaken, and his government partially lightened up the repressive rural policies for a year or so. Stalin was now put to a painful test of will and power.

Thus, as the First Five-Year Plan and the worst years of collectivization ended, the leaders pulled back slightly on the economic front, though arrests occurred in the national republics, as discussed in the next chapter. In January 1934, the mood was buoyant as delegates assembled for the Seventeenth Party Congress to celebrate economic achievements. As they sang the state hymn, "The Internationale," amid red bunting and fresh flowers in Moscow's most luxurious theater, the Bolshoi, the 1,966 party men and women could not have known that over 1,000 of them would disappear before the next congress assembled in 1939. In Stalin's Politburo sat Stanislaw Kosior, Jan Rudzutak, Lazar Kaganovich, Sergo Orjonikidze, Vyacheslav Molotov, Kliment Voroshilov, Sergei Kirov, Mikhail Kalinin, and Valerian

Kuibyshev—a Pole, a Latvian, a Jew, two Georgians, and five Russians, all ruthless men. The presence of ethnic representatives at the top had no necessary influence on the treatment of their countrymen. Five of these ten men would soon be dead.

A major turning point in the turn toward mass terror was the "Kirov affair," one of the fateful murder cases of the century. According to a widely believed account, in 1934 some party members beseeched the popular Kirov to replace Stalin. Dissatisfaction with Stalin was recorded in some of the voting of the 1934 congress. A persistent theory argues that Stalin, fearing Kirov, sent to Leningrad a new security chief, who then hired Leonid Nikolaev to assassinate Kirov—which, in fact, he did, in the Smolny Institute on December 1, 1934. The evidence of Stalin's guilt, though strong, remains circumstantial even after a dozen investigation commissions and numerous books on the subject. In any case, attributing the murder to "enemies of the people," Stalin used it as a means to turn on his real and supposed enemies. The Kirov murder was followed by the jailing of Stalin's old comrades Zinoviev and Kamenev, whom he had expelled from the party and readmitted several times and whom he no longer trusted. Nikolai Ezhov, a trusted associate of Stalin, conducted mass inquiries and purges of the Communist Party that resulted in thousands of expulsions and executions. The recently reorganized security empire, the NKVD, was placed in the hands of Genrikh Yagoda (in Polish, Henryk Jagoda), who sharpened judicial and police procedures and built a monstrous apparatus of state murder and incarceration.

First row, from left: Politburo members Molotov, Stalin, Voroshilov, and Kaganovich at a meeting of the Supreme Soviet, 1938. *Sovfoto/Eastfoto.*

The Moscow Trials

By 1936, Stalin was ready to strike against enemies at the highest level, including those "Old Bolsheviks" who had made the revolution. The assault on the party leadership with the first of three Moscow "Show Trials" of 1936–1938 made world headlines. Trial and theater had been blended from the very beginning of Soviet power, both in mock trials and in the legal proceedings against SRs, Mensheviks, and industrial saboteurs. Some of the indictment narratives resembled the lurid plots of the era's popular detective fiction, with clandestine meetings in foreign towns and carpets soaked in poison and designed to kill the Soviet leaders. The trials were meant to make acute political points to masses of people unsophisticated in the ways of printed propaganda and to provide a dramatic emotional impact. They served the organizers' desire not only for assent to a program, but for passionate commitment fueled by hatred and fear of opponents. In the 1936 trial, sixteen Old Bolsheviks, including Kamenev and Zinoviev, were falsely accused of treason, the Kirov murder, and a plot to kill Stalin. The defendants were forced to confess. Said Zinoviev: "Through Trotskyism I arrived at fascism. Trotskyism is a variety of fascism. Zinovievism is a variety of Trotskyism." They also had to implicate others before they themselves were convicted and shot. Later in the year, Ezhov replaced Yagoda as NKVD chief and stepped up the inquiries. In January 1937, members of a so-called Anti-Soviet Trotskyite Center comprising the Comintern luminary Karl Radek (b. 1885) and other Old Bolsheviks were indicted as fascist agents hired by foreign powers to wreck and spy, murder Soviet leaders, and restore capitalism. Thirteen were shot; Radek got ten years but was murdered in a prison camp in 1939. All of this activity was alleged to have been led by the exiled Trotsky, though he was well known to the rest of the world as a principled foe of capitalism and fascism.

Summertime brought the unexpected massacre of the Soviet officer corps. Stalin feared the top military brass on personal and political grounds. He was spurred on by the false testimony of previous arrestees and perhaps by documents either forged in German Gestapo headquarters to demoralize the Red Army or by Ezhov to buttress his own position (though these were not used in the trial). At Stalin's behest, Ezhov arrested the civil war hero Marshal Tukhachevsky (1893–1937), whom Stalin had hated ever since that war (see the chapter "Civil War: Reds, Whites, and Greens, 1917–1921"). Tukhachevsky and other high-ranking officers were accused of conspiring with Trotsky and the German High Command, convicted by a special military tribunal, and immediately executed. Perishing in their wake were thirty-five thousand to forty-one thousand men, including 60 percent of the marshals, about 90 percent of the highest army commanders, all the admirals, about 90 percent of corps commanders, and alarmingly high percentages of divisional and brigadier generals. Like nothing before it, this act displayed Stalin's ruthlessness, for it endangered the security of the nation for the sake of the leader's vengefulness or peace of mind. Though many talented commanders died in the purges, the armed forces were also harmed by structural and psychological weaknesses before and after the purges.

The last show trial of Old Bolsheviks, held in the ballroom of the former Moscow Nobles' Club in March 1938, put in the dock former members of the Right Opposition of the 1920s (see the chapter "The Years of New Economic Policy: Power, Society, and Culture, 1921–1928"): Bukharin and the former prime minister Alexei Rykov (the labor union leader Mikhail Tomsky had committed suicide in 1936). Joining them was the demoted security chief Yagoda (his successor, Ezhov, would be shot in 1939). The abusive ex-Menshevik prosecutor Andrei Vyshinsky (1883–1954) called the defendants agents of foreign powers, fascists, and imperialists enmeshed in a plot to kill Soviet leaders and establish capitalism—all charges based on fraudulent evidence or forced confessions. They were even accused of having murdered Kirov and the famed proletarian writer Maxim Gorky (1868–1936), who had returned from abroad to Russia in the late 1920s and had died in 1936 (see the chapter "The 'Duma Monarchy,' 1907–1914"). Vyshinsky in his closing speech shouted: "These mad dogs of capitalism . . . they killed Kirov, they wounded our hearts . . . I demand that these dogs gone mad be shot—every one of them!" And they were. Arrested and executed also were friends, relatives, and associates of the convicted; revolutionary heroes; and most members of Lenin's Politburo.

Thus fell before the executioner's bullet an entire revolutionary generation, Lenin's former comrades. Three books of the time show how differently the Moscow trials were perceived. The American philosopher John Dewey issued a report on charges against the defendants and Trotsky (tried in absentia), entitled *Not Guilty.* The U.S. ambassador in Moscow, Joseph Davies, however, in his naive book *Mission to Moscow,* fully credited the guilt of the accused. Based on that book, an even more notorious 1943 Hollywood film starred Walter Huston as the ambassador and justified Stalin, then a wartime ally of the United States. The Hungarian-born ex-Communist Arthur Koestler produced the most moving document of that moment in the novel *Darkness at Noon,* whose hero, a composite of Old Bolsheviks, fell victim to the purges.

The question of why the falsely accused confessed to the fantastic crimes is not really an intellectual puzzle: Some feared for the lives of loved ones (Bukharin had a young wife and baby). Others were subjected to unbearable torture. A few may have been convinced of the rightness of false confession for a higher good: the future of communism.

Massive Liquidation

The Moscow trials, shocking and spectacular as they were, affected a relatively small number of former Bolshevik leaders and army brass. However, the trials were paralleled by a purge of the party and mass repression of large segments of society that rose to a crescendo in 1937–1938. In the early and mid-1930s, widespread but bloodless cleansing or purging of the party went on to weed out dissident, corrupt, inept, and undesirable elements. The party purges of these years were not planned preparations for the terror that later ensued, but the result of political rivalry at the top, center-periphery tensions, and economic disorder. Even when this process converged in the great bloodletting of 1937, much confusion and unanticipated chaos ensued. Stalin struck at new party members and state appointees. Among those who perished were 70 percent of the Central Committee of 1934 and many members of the security police, unions (almost 90 percent of the leaders), diplomatic corps, and Comintern. One local official, before being purged himself, arrested all 110 district party secretaries in his province. The entire leadership of the Polish Communist Party fell victim, as did the many other foreign Communists and those who had served in Spain and China. Comintern activists were recalled to Moscow from all over the world and shot. Non-Russian nationalities were assailed; a large segment of the party leadership in Ukraine was annihilated. Foes who could not be reached directly were assassinated by Soviet agents—as was the most famous of them all, Trotsky, who was murdered with an alpine pickax in Mexico in 1940. The bloodbath inside the USSR came to be known as the Ezhov terror, though Stalin and his associates as well as local leaders drew up death lists.

Outside the ranks of the party, the terror was fueled by various factors unrelated to the Moscow purge trials. The repressive process unrolled in provincial party meetings, Moscow artists' congresses, collective farms, labor union sessions, national republics—anywhere and everywhere. Denouncers were driven by angry demands from all quarters for vigilance and by their own fears. In the Stalinist witch-hunt, speakers would not only accuse a colleague of Trotskyism, sabotage, or some other imagined crime but implicate all the associates of the accused for not having denounced the person earlier. That charge was often followed by a countercharge indicting the accuser. Motives included fear for one's own life, revenge on a rival, anti-intellectualism, class hatred, ethnic animosity, party rivalry, generational revolt, envy and resentment, designs on a neighbor's wife or spare room—or almost anything else. In May 1937, workers in a Donbass town denounced their enemies, who were engaged in orgies and binges, as "a nest of Trotskyites."

Victims, if not shot outright, were processed through the barbarous passages of the NKVD, which combined the functions of security police, intelligence agency, and penal administration. For many, arrest came by night, and solitary confinement followed in the dread cellars of Lubyanka Prison. Interrogators employed inhuman modes of physical and psychic torment: urine baths, broken limbs, sweat boxes, screams of loved ones in an adjoining cell. Then came the cattle cars and death ships that conveyed prisoners to years of hard labor, if they survived, in the new prison camps that enlarged the original nucleus of the system on the Solovetsky Islands in the Arctic Circle. What came to be known as the Gulag (*Glavnoye upravlenie lagerei,* State Camp Administration) was a vast network of slave stations presided over by Matvei Berman (until he was executed in 1938), where inmates toiled, starved, and died cutting timber, building railroads, constructing works, or digging canals. The very names of camp locations came to possess a frightening sound: Vorkuta, Kolyma, and its capital, Magadan.

Local units of the NKVD set competitive arrest quotas and constantly enlarged the net to ensnare huge numbers from the middle and upper ranks of Soviet society: former nobles, priests, teachers, intellectuals, ethnic leaders, and scientists (often spared to continue research inside the camps). An infamous document from the archives signed by Ezhov on July 30, 1937, reveals the scope of the inhumanity: a numerical quota singled out over seventy-two thousand people for "immediate arrest and, after consideration of their case by the troikas [three-person tribunals], to be shot." Among the many famous cultural figures who perished were the writer Isaac Babel and the experimental theater director of the 1920s, Vsevolod Meyerhold (see the chapter "The Years of New Economic Policy: Power, Society, and Culture, 1921–1928"). Millions perished, millions survived, and millions of loved ones eked out their shattered lives. Although the numbers are still contested, the most cautious and fully documented estimate for 1937–1938, the peak of the terror, gives at least a million and half persons arrested, a half million sent to camps, and hundreds of thousands shot. The human costs cannot be counted in numbers. Anna Akhmatova's "Requiem," Nadezhda Mandelshtam's memoirs, and Lidiya Chukovskaya's novel *Sofya Petrovna* remain eloquent monuments by and to "those left behind." By late 1938, the worst was over.

Why the Terror?

The magnitude of the terror confounds human reason. Members of opposition parties, former leaders of the ruling party, local officials, ex-chiefs of security, former cabinet ministers, and the intellectual cream of a hundred towns and cities were liquidated physically; the diplomatic and officer corps were decimated; and millions of ordinary citizens fell victim to arrest. Why? The word was uttered countless times and scratched on prison walls by bewildered convicts, particularly by those who had made the revolution, fought in the civil war, and served the state faithfully. Why, indeed? It remains the unsolved puzzle of modern times. No simple invocation of ideological fanaticism or totalitarian evil can offer a convincing explanation. Nor can comparisons of Stalin with the bloody sixteenth-century Russian tyrant Tsar Ivan IV, or the terror with the witch-hunts of early modern Europe; each is of its own time. The victims were made to confess to Stalin's satisfaction, and to admit to much more heinous crimes for public consumption. Stalin's own vengeful—some have said even pathological—character certainly accounts for some of the great bloodletting. He had the families of some of the accused liquidated, an act of vengeance that was also meant to avoid the revenge of the enemies' "clan." Stalin was fond of the phrase attributed to Chinggis Khan, the thirteenth-century Mongol conqueror: "The deaths of the conquered are necessary for the conqueror's peace of mind." It seems certain that Stalin really believed that his victims were guilty of opposing him, and he was ready to cast the net wide to catch them, even if the net pulled in the guiltless. As his chief henchman Molotov recalled years later without apology, "Stalin insisted on making doubly sure: Spare no one. . . . Let innocent heads roll."

To Stalin's motivations must be added the impossible economic goals, the legacy of Leninist repression and civil war violence, the weakly rooted principles of fair play and due process in Russia, and the traditions of repression—though Soviet methods far exceeded the tsarist order in cruelty and number of victims. International tension caused by the remilitarization of Germany under Adolph Hitler, the spread of fascism, and the fear of an invasion let loose rumors of war and of espionage and treason. The colossal scope of the scourge must be partially explained also by the mass participation of the population, including many common people who denounced their colleagues and coworkers. One of the motives in what seems such a heinous crime was certainly "true belief": faith in a socialist remaking of humanity, emotional commitment to the regime, and uncomprehending horror at the alleged atrocities committed by "saboteurs" and "enemies of the people." Although some may be loathe to credit such mass hatred, it has been common throughout history, including modern times—as is shown by the various preposterous popular beliefs promoted and held about Jews, Muslims, Germans, Japanese, Americans, Chinese, and Russians by various populations in our own century. The result of collective hatred and fear was mass support of the terror.

To this unpleasant reality, we must add a psychosocial momentum that turns certain patterns of political behavior in unexpected directions. It is hard to believe that the Kremlin leaders lost any sleep over the acceleration of atrocities; but they probably did not plan it that way. The fact that many likely victims—such as the former oppositionist Alexandra Kollontai—escaped arrest also attests to the lack of a master plan or logical pattern. Rifts within the party—independent of Stalin's planning—were at the root of some of the mass arrests. Historians, on the basis of growing but as yet unsure evidence, are still debating motivations and Stalin's role.

Aspects of the Stalinism have led some to equate it to Adolph Hitler's dictatorship, with its Gestapo (Geheime Staatspolizei—Secret State Police) tormentors and its concentration camps. Hitler's personality cult, Joseph Goebbels's propaganda machine, and Heinrich Himmler's SS (Shutzstaffel—Defense Corps) police state all suggest similarity. But the differences are equally striking. Stalinism was more pervasive and made deeper inroads into traditional society, with church closings, prohibition of private enterprise and farms, and the abolition of noble titles and class designations. Stalinism differed from Nazism and fascism in other fundamental and symbolic ways: its peacetime promotion of women in the economy and the professions; the upgrading of nationalities; and its lavish use of Jews and other minorities in the high ranks of state power, the economy, and culture—practices that were totally alien to Nazi Germany's patriarchalism and racism. Thus the USSR, while crueler to its own people than was Hitler's regime to Germans, was also more "progressive" in its official façade and in some of its actual practices. This blinded many Western sympathizers to the horrors that lay behind it.

STATE MACHINE AND POLITICAL CULTURE

The official blueprint for Soviet political life in the 1930s was the "Stalin Constitution" of 1936. As show trials were being prepared, a national debate over the constitution was generating millions of words. The entire litany of Western civil rights—except for those of private property—was incorporated into the new constitution. Former members of exploiting classes were now given full citizenship rights. Called "the most democratic constitution in the world," it was touted in Stalinist lore as the charter of a unique society: "I know no other land where a person can breathe so freely," went the most popular song of the decade.

The 1936 constitution replaced the All-Union Congress of Soviets and its

Central Executive Committee with a Supreme Soviet. Like its predecessor, the new body comprised two chambers, the Soviet of the Union and the Soviet of Nationalities, as well as a small "presidium," whose chair was the official president of the USSR, a ceremonial office. The chair of the cabinet, or Sovnarkom, was the equivalent in form to a Western prime minister—a post held in the 1930s by Vyacheslav Molotov, a survivor and major figure in Stalin's government. Unmentioned in the previous constitutions of 1918 and 1924, the Communist Party's role as the vanguard of society was barely noted in the new document. By this time a system known as *nomenklatura* had been established: a secret "list of names" of those eligible for employment, transfer, or removal in hundreds of key party, state, and economic positions as well ranks within those jobs. Beside the Communist Party, and now often above it, stood the organs of repression—border guards, security police, and army—and Stalin's inner circle, with himself at the center. The raw might of this machine rendered the official blueprint of the constitution fictitious.

Behind the official façade lay a world of political competition. Leaders squabbled among themselves and lobbied with the Great Leader for influence as at some eighteenth-century European court. Conflict and rivalry continued all through the years of the dictatorship. The foundations of Soviet power—party, bureaucracy, armed forces, and police—remained in place, but they were weakened in the terror, and Stalin's personal power towered above them. The party especially suffered decline: after 1934, no congress met until 1939, and none again until 1952. Though never a democratic instrument, the party congress had at least echoed with debate and clashing policies in the heady days of revolution and the 1920s. Now, to dissent publicly was almost suicidal. Policy was made inside the Kremlin by Stalin, assisted by his party General Secretariat and his personal chancery. Nearby—only blocks away—stood Central Committee headquarters on Old Square and the Lubyanka, center of the NKVD. Government agencies were savaged by the purges, and the military was so mutilated that Soviet defense capacity was severely damaged. The NKVD ranged far and wide in its hunt for suspects and slave laborers—but it too was vulnerable to the whims of the dictator.

One of the keystones of Stalinism was an economy in which one could own personal property (books, furniture), but not a hotel, a ship, a shop, or a business of any kind; no stocks, no bonds, no corporations, no free market, no commercial law codes. This simple and comprehensive economic fact required that the economy and much of society had to be run by a huge bureaucracy that dealt with things that democratic market states left to private activity: production and distribution of goods and cultural and social life. Whereas parliamentary states could manage with a few cabinet posts, the Soviet state needed dozens—eventually scores—to plan and oversee all the branches of industry, mining, transport, and agriculture. The very nature of state ownership and management, the frantic tempo of the Five-Year Plans, and the authoritarian background of Communist administrators—many of them veterans of revolution and civil war—reinforced a military style in all walks of life. Official paranoia at home and the genuine international tensions—from the war scare of 1927, to the rise of Nazism, to the real war of 1939—led willy-nilly to grotesque efforts to control tightly the lives of the population.

CHAPTER 35

Stalinism: Life Inside the System, 1928–1939

Past lakes, through hills and woods and fields
Along the road [Stalin] rides
In his gray trenchcoat with his pipe.
Straight on his horse he guides
He stops and speaks
To peasantfolk
Throughout the countryside
And making necessary notes,
Goes on about his ride.

—*Alexander Tvardovsky,* The Land of Muravia,
folkloric epic poem about collectivization, 1936

Stalinist culture in the 1930s, an integral element of the industrial and agrarian revolutions and even of the terror, exalted the achievements and denied the suffering. The cultural managers sought the public's internalization of Stalinism—the system, values, and dictator cult—through dual representation: first in the fine arts and popular culture, second in the actual workings of society itself—that is to say, through living, breathing, working citizens of the Soviet state. The Soviet nation took on the features of a colossal theater in which each person was to play a role. Art both presented models and drew them from the social order. This complicated social drama comprised myths and practices that were laid down after much heated discussion in the middle of the 1930s and that would last in attenuated form until the end of the Soviet regime.

CULTURAL REVOLUTION, 1928–1932

During the 1920s, modernist or avant-garde forms, though future oriented, were occasionally assaulted for their inaccessibility to the masses. The great figures in graphic art, architecture, and design had produced genuinely inspired works that art lovers now adore. But the creators wanted the masses to use art in their daily lives—to sit in chairs, live in homes, wear clothes, and eat from pottery designed in avant-garde studios. These artists were puzzled when housewives spurned dresses with a tractor design in favor of floral prints. With the onset of industrialization, self-styled cultural "proletarians," mostly minor intellectuals and journalists, launched a cultural revolution and accused the avant-garde of ignoring the true tastes of the masses. They also assaulted old high culture as a rotting product of the exploitative past; folk culture as an expression of backwardness and religion; and urban mass entertainment as vulgar and counterrevolutionary. Claiming to speak on behalf of the proletariat, they demanded a liquidation of the NEP cultural system and a monopoly on proletarian culture.

In the frenzied campaign to remake the Russian landscape, Soviet authorities backed the cultural revolution until 1932. The proletarians used their power to censor plays and to ban truly original writers, as well as light adventure, science fiction, and detective stories. The Russian Association of Proletarian Writers (RAPP) persecuted rivals and promoted stories of production, in which the pouring of cement into a new construction site attained the poetic status of a medieval knightly exploit. RAPP abused the peasant culture of fairy tales and folk music. Proletarian musicians called Western popular music "the song and dance of the period of the catastrophe of capitalism," foxtrot a "dance of slaves," and tango "the music of impotents." Jazz was especially hard hit: the great prerevolutionary writer Maxim Gorky (1868–1936) had recently returned from abroad to become the prophet of a new Soviet culture. He linked jazz with homosexuality, drug use, and "bourgeois eroticism." Promoters of proletarian choirs were outraged to hear classical music played in public. Yet the music produced by the "proletarians" was often unsingable. Critics attacked both imported Hollywood movies and the innovative films of Sergei Eisenstein (see the chapter "The Years of New Economic Policy: Power, Society, and Culture, 1921–1928").

A particular feature of the cultural revolution was "specialist baiting," the persecution of professionals, academics, and industrial managers by young hotheads who saw them as privileged and "unproletarian." This antielitist movement was reinforced by the show trials of foreigners and specialists accused of sabotage. Indeed, a whole utopian surge sought to abolish not only capitalism and social classes but everything connected with the "old world"—law, the state, family, school discipline. In regard to nationality, utopian visions clashed: while some preached the imminent disappearance of nations, others worked furiously to proliferate national units all over the USSR.

SOCIALIST REALISM AND MASS CULTURE, 1932–1941

In 1932, the men in the Kremlin, prompted by a fear of artistic anarchy, ended the cultural revolution. In what is sometimes called the Great Retreat, they halted specialist baiting and dissolved the "proletarian" groups. Of humble birth and limited formal education, the leaders could no more stomach the "proletarian culture" of RAPP and other groups than they could the boldness of the avant-garde. Like many newly successful people, they looked on established high culture as a status symbol, so they canonized classical music, ballet, and architecture; realistic theater; and traditional painting. However, they recognized that only a fraction of Soviet people could or would enjoy ballet or opera at the Bolshoi Theater; for the rest they sponsored a culture that was free of decadence, accessible to the masses, and filled with proper socialist values.

Socialist Realism

In a series of stormy meetings, literary figures, including the influential Gorky, worked out a formula known as "socialist realism," designed to reflect the real world (realism) and to inspire a better world to come (socialist). In fact, the treatment of "reality" was highly romanticized. Although taking on everyday subjects, socialist realist works ignored or mystified much of Soviet reality and promoted optimism and exuberance rather than introspection, comradeship rather than erotic love.

In its aspiration to change people and the world, socialist realism echoed some of the principles of avant-garde culture, but unlike the avant-garde, it gained wide readership through simplified styles, naturalistic representation, strongly etched characters, highlighted messages, a clear narrative with a formulaic closure, and the dense detail of everyday life. The masses consumed the new literature partly because of these features and partly because no competition was permitted. Selected foreign classics were widely distributed in translation. Victor Hugo's *Les Misérables* (1862) was exceptionally popular because it dealt with a virtuous poor man unjustly treated by the system. However, key elements of foreign and Russian modernism and of some traditional literature were disallowed: psychological complexity, religiophilosophical questioning, and eroticism. Presented instead were the values of reason, technology, and socialism. Idealized political personalities marched through a master plot in which the hero, tutored by a wise mentor, reaches moral triumph by doing battle with political foes, or simply fumbling bureaucrats who are holding up socialist production. Nikolai Ostrovsky's *How the Steel Was Tempered* (1932–1934) became the classic novel of socialist realism; its protagonist, Pavel Korchagin—the quintessential positive hero—as a Young Communist fought the White armies in the civil war, became a model worker and then, disabled, inspired other youth with his autobiographical novel. Writers, designated "engineers of the human soul," were organized into a union in 1934. Other "cultural workers" followed suit.

Paintings and posters, novels and children's tales, songs and movies braided romance and adventure into the motifs of economic achievement and national security. The construction of cities, giant steel plants, and hydroelectric dams was likened to a titanic struggle against nature and the builders to mythic heroes and heroines. The machine itself supplanted the old gods. Mechanization and technology were glamorized in town and country—as were engineers. In a series of rustic film comedies, the tractor became the emblem not only of progress but of courtship and romance. Organized sports and physical education promoted a cult of the body as a human machine. Taming the wilderness, prospecting uncut frontiers, and guarding the state were linked in adventure tales and films. Historical fiction glorified the revolution and selected episodes of the tsarist past, such as the Russian victory over Napoleon.

The new cultural codes shaped not only political and historical writing but also real life, as citizens learned new modes of speech and behavior: equating capitalism with fascism, publicly demanding the death penalty for show trial defendants, and shouting slogans on parade days. They also absorbed a way of seeing the world as something unfolding and not yet here—the "radiant future" awaiting at the dawn of communism. Scholars now write of "everyday Stalinism" and Stalinism as a "civilization" and as a "way of life" in their attempt to uncover the inner experience of the individual personality or "subject" in these extraordinary times. For no simple dichotomy between rulers and oppressed can account for life in the 1930s. Newly discovered diaries suggest that Soviet citizens could fuse personal success with their country's achievement, suffer self-doubt, and seek moral correction on their own but within the parameters and using the language of the system they lived in.

Art for the Masses

Except for Eisenstein's 1938 film *Alexander Nevsky,* few great works of Russian cinema were produced in the 1930s. The most popular film of this and many decades was *Chapaev* (1934), based on the semifictionalized account by Dmitry Furmanov of Chapaev's military adventures in the civil war (see the chapter "The Years of New Economic Policy: Power, Society, and Culture, 1921–1928"). Other well-liked movies dealt with aviation, polar expeditions, and mammoth construction. Stunningly successful and long-remembered was a string of musical comedies directed by Grigory Alexandrov that offered a winning recipe of patriotism, cornball sentiment, spectacular cinematic effects, and singable tunes done up with Hollywood effects. They celebrated the then current slogan of a "happy life," social mobility, and economic achievements. Not one hint of the harsh conditions of life or the murderous purges could be found in these films. Although modernist cubes and squares of the twenties were gone, Stalinist poster art possessed its own brand of fantasy, combining photography, airbrush technique, bright primary colors, and dramatic diagonals to extol production and depict the happy life. Cartoonists, who had previously satirized White generals and interventionists, in the late 1930s demonized Hitler, Trotsky, and Bukharin.

Stalinist architecture and city planning shunned the bold experimentation of the 1920s, when modernism had flourished. In creating a new Soviet Moscow, Politburo member and city boss Lazar Kaganovich (1893–1991) ordered churches razed, old quarters demolished, and boulevards widened to make room for the great parades. But "architecture of socialist realism" remained an elusive concept. In practice, the huge buildings of the 1930s were meant to match not the world of Soviet workers, but the grandeur, power, and hierarchy of the political edifice by the use of façade ornament, large square entrances, and small windows. Kaganovich's most famous legacy was the Moscow Metro, then known as the Subway of Revolution, built under harsh conditions. Its main lines were completed under his young

assistant, Nikita Khrushchëv (1894–1971). The mosaics, sculptures, and friezes of the lavish Metro stations replicated all the thematic symbols of Stalinism beneath the streets. In 1939 a huge Agricultural Exhibition was built in Moscow, displaying domes, gothic buildings, fountains, broad walkways, and a giant statue of Stalin.

With the demise of the proletarian composers, the music of the past reasserted itself. On the great stages of the Moscow and Leningrad theaters, tradition held sway. Russia's celebrated classical composer Tchaikovsky, and the other Russian and European masters dominated the concert hall repertoires. Soviet composers of serious music wrote in a more modern idiom but attempted to balance innovation with melodious passages pleasing to their public. Those who could not were expelled from the profession. The leading figures, Dmitry Shostakovich (1906–1975) and Sergei Prokofiev (1891–1953), were occasionally at odds with their political masters for ignoring the rules and producing music that was allegedly "difficult." The former got into trouble temporarily with his 1934 opera *Lady Macbeth of Mtsensk,* based on a nineteenth century novel by Nikolai Leskov about rural adultery and murder. Shostakovich's sin was both moral (a double bed dominated the set) and musical ("noise rather than music," said a hostile review). *Pravda* described the opera in 1936 as "un-Soviet, unwholesome, cheap, eccentric, tuneless, and leftist." Shostakovich and others went on to produce a great corpus of music that was artistic, acceptable to the authorities, and often both. But in no way could the best serious music produced under Stalin be called socialist, although composers often lied to their bosses and said it was.

Jazz was subjected to periodic persecution as decadent but was eventually legalized in a sanitized and sweetened form, complete with violins and accordions. Songs of seduction and illicit passion were banished in a perfect illustration of the mentality of the parental state, which shielded its children from harmful influences. To make the nation sing, the state had professionals compose "mass songs" that celebrated Soviet achievements. Catchy tunes and uplifting themes acted as concise socialist realist bulletins from the state to the people that all was well in the land of Stalinism.

Stalin eventually became, metaphorically speaking, chief literary, drama, film, art, and music critic. He personally intervened in all the arts, screening new movies in the Kremlin and inspecting architectural blueprints. Socialist realism became, as one scholar put it, "the compulsory style sheet for all the arts."

Soviet mass culture, because of the artists' and writers' skills, was and remained for decades genuinely appealing to the people, however much scorned by intellectuals and foreign critics. We know from survivors of the Stalinist era that mass enthusiasm did exist. This does not mean that audiences necessarily believed or internalized all of the political meanings embedded in film, picture, and story. Recent studies of popular opinion and public celebrations indicate that citizens processed official propaganda in their own way: accepting it, rejecting it, criticizing the regime for not keeping its promises, or all of these. People screened out what bored them, and sometimes the negative depictions of prerevolutionary or foreign "decadence"—sex, religion, amusements—appealed to the public when they were not supposed to.

CITIZENS: FROM THE KREMLIN TO THE GULAG

With the promulgation of the Stalin constitution of 1936 and the announcement that the USSR had achieved "socialism," society was officially divided into workers, collective farmers, and intelligentsia (almost everybody else), though this was a highly oversimplified schema. After the tumult of industrialization and collectivization, people who escaped the terror continued to work, talk, live, and love—and did not become the faceless robots marching in unison and living in "total loneliness, total fear" as depicted in Evgeny Zamyatin's novel *We* (see the chapter "The Years of New Economic Policy: Power, Society, and Culture, 1921–1928") or in some versions of totalitarian theory.

Although extremely varied and complex, and still subjected to shakeups from above, Stalinist society possessed one persistent characteristic that seemed a betrayal of socialism: inequality. Although Marx had maintained that under socialism, people would be rewarded according to their work and not in equal shares, many who fought in the revolution had done so in the cause of equality. In the early 1930s, Stalin denounced as "petty bourgeois" the leveling and egalitarianism that had driven the revolution, and Soviet society hardened into a hierarchical pattern.

Ordinary People

The proletariat, divested of union power, became more stratified than ever. Differentiated wages and skills magnified the diversity among older workers, new peasant recruits, and young superworkers. As a class, the industrial work force had lost much of its revolutionary spark, although youth of both sexes were still propelled by idealism to the great construction sites. The main body of workers, whose living standard had fallen, often resented the explosion of youthful energy and its orchestration by the state. In the mills and on the sites, most workers toiled for modest rewards under hard conditions and strict discipline—though the government could never fully tame the work force or stop it from changing jobs. The massive rural influx into the cities hindered the molding of a skilled proletariat as peasants brought their slower work habits to the factory floor. Rural civilization was in a sense replicated in Moscow and in the barracks and shanty towns of industrial sites. Although the party continued to fight against village "backwardness," it tacitly allowed features of peasant life that made for stability: conservative tastes in culture and patriarchalism in the home. To the surprise of many outsiders, a huge segment of the lower classes never saw the inside of a mill but earned a living as servants of the new political and economic elite—as drivers, cooks, and domestics of every description, mostly women. Their faces and those of white collar employees, called the hidden class by a historian, never appeared on posters, and their "stories" never made print.

For the peasantry, whether displaced or on collective farms, the indescribable famines and deportations left a permanent scar on the land and in memory. The Stalin regime tried to heal the wounds more through imagination than practice. While not abandoning the Marxist urbanist vision, ideologists set up a counterimage of

Soviet rusticity, representing the countryside as an idyll combining traditional values of hard work and strong family with those of modern technology. Folk dance ensembles, paintings, operettas, novels, and films romanticized the collective farm as a blend of new and old: tractors and collective farm feasts, work brigades and peasant fertility. A heroine of the Soviet farmland, champion tractor driver Pasha Angelina, became the most famous young woman in Russia of the early 1930s when she was presented to Stalin in the Kremlin. But most tractor drivers were men; and it was Angelina's marriage plans that inspired "tractor novels" and movies. In the film *A Wealthy Bride* (1938), a champion tractor driver, after some harmless intrigue, wins the hand of a female superfarmer.

Real life was grim, though certainly more tranquil than during collectivization. Remnants of the old life remained; the collective farm was roughly coterminous with the village. But the *kulaks* were gone—killed, deported, or banished to the margins outside the collective farm. Two great losses to the peasantry were horses, which were taken into the common herd, and churches, about half of which were closed in the early and late 1930s. Religion, the binding force of peasant culture for centuries, did not disappear (perhaps half the rural population or more remained believers), but its observance lay under the shadow of persecution.

No technologized countryside, as promised, arose in place of the "backward" village. Tractors remained few, usually far away at the Machine Tractor Station (MTS), badly maintained, and generally unappealing to peasants, who had to pay for their use. The standard of living had dropped, and amenities such as electrification and indoor toilets were decades away. In many ways, the peasantry had become more isolated from town and nation than in the 1920s.

Life inside the peasant hut had not altered drastically, and the father still ruled, even though women were officially equals to men in the collective farm. Women, some of whom had led anticollectivization mutinies a few years earlier, worked the fields with men but also performed traditional tasks of homemaking and livestock tending. Male collective farm and MTS directors ran things. In the later 1930s, locals replaced the tough city folk of the collectivization period as collective farm heads. The old pattern of family cultivated strips gave way to supervised brigades of field workers paid on the basis of "labor days," calculated by the amount and nature of work performed in the year. State labor requirements (resembling the *barshchina,* or unpaid labor, of serfdom), high crop contributions to the state (resembling *obrok,* or quitrent), and low pay reminded many of the serfdom of old (see the chapter "Russian Society and Daily Life in the Twilight of Serfdom, 1800–1861"). Although the private plot and the right to take up off-farm work were concessions that lightened the burden somewhat, the terms *second serfdom, slavery,* and *barshchina* were actually used by some Soviet peasants to describe their lot. Most resented the system and their status as second-class citizens. Feeling little or no veneration for Stalin or deep loyalty to the regime, peasants silently resisted state exactions whenever possible, avoiding work on the common lands in favor of tending their private plots. Amid rumors of a possible war in 1937, a collective farmer angrily shouted, "To hell with this kind of life! Let there be war! The sooner the better! I'll be the first to go!"

Amidst the transformation, some things—such as periodic feasts, with carousing and missed work days—never vanished. Vestiges of the turbulent micropolitics of the old peasant commune lived on: feuding and settling scores. Peasants even engaged in political resistance. Anti-Stalinist underground folklore circulated surreptitiously. During a brief interval of multicandidate elections in 1937, some peasants nominated priests. And some even ventured to pray for the souls of the top leaders killed in the purges. In 1937 rural district show trials, collective farmers testified against officials in the dock who had recently plagued them. In the constant buzz of the rural rumor mill, speculation arose that if a war came, the invaders would abolish the collective farm system.

Women belonged to all social categories, including that of victim and widow, but their particular roles as a gender and as sexual beings were also affected by the Stalin revolution. The medical profession became feminized in the 1930s. The public image Stalinist culture advanced was designed both to mask reality and to change it. Posters depicting women as pilots, steelworkers, and Metro tunnel diggers stressed the positive value of such occupations and a place for women in them. But films such as *Member of the Government* (1940) suggested that women, even peasant women, now shared state power with men, when in fact they had almost none even in matters dealing with women's lives. Zhenotdel, the women's section of the Communist Party, was abolished in 1930 and voices of Communist feminists silenced. Women peasants and workers were glorified as superproducers in field and factory but not in the home, though housekeeping was clearly their province. Administrators' wives usually remained out of the wage-labor force and were expected to fulfill their civic duty by decorating the homes and offices of their husbands.

Women in Soviet industry. *Sovfoto/Eastfoto.*

To stabilize the family and increase the birth rate for military reasons, the Stalin regime enacted laws in 1936 restricting divorce and abortion. These laws were well received by many Soviet women after the marital instability of the 1920s (see the chapter "The Years of New Economic Policy: Power, Society, and Culture, 1921–1928"). But they also engendered hardship for those unhappily married or burdened with a host of children; and they propelled many into the underworld of illegal abortion. Maternity was subsidized as a national duty, with medals and cash rewards for those Heroines of Motherhood who bore multiple children for the state. On posters, matronly mother-workers superseded the tough female revolutionaries as the symbol of Soviet womanhood. The subliminal identification of women with the countryside, an old Russian cultural image, and thus with subordination to the masculine city, was emblazoned on Vera Mukhina's renowned statue *The Worker and the Collective Farmer,* in which the male holds an industrial hammer and the woman a sickle.

An extraordinary collection of archival documents about "Stalinism as a way of life" reveals both the complexity and the ordinariness of life amidst the horrors of the terror: people got married, committed adultery, had abortions, cheated and stole from the state, defended one another, denounced one another, and deluged Stalin and Kalinin with warnings about the infiltration into the NKVD (secret police) of fascists, Trotskyites, and *kulaks.* Life went on. A by no means unusual letter to a newspaper gave the following report. The seventy-year-old collective farmer Matvei Rusinov "made up his mind to take what is already his third wife. In the first few days of December 1938 he performed a modest Soviet-style wedding, he trimmed his beard, trimmed his hair, and that made him seem just about right for his third wife, who is forty-two years old."

Heroes and Slaves

On the production front, it was not the plant manager who stood in the aureole of heroism but the superworker. At the giant new industrial site of Magnitogorsk, workers couched their identity as heroes not only in production achievements but also in their "proletarian" pedigrees, proudly referring to the great factories where their forebears had labored. In 1935, Donbass coal miner Alexei Stakhanov set a record by producing fourteen times the norm. The regime immediately initiated a movement—partly faked—in which selected "stakhanovite" workers emulated his achievements and were mythologized for doing so in the mass media. Men, women, steelworkers, farmers—all provided stakhanovite idols for public esteem. Such synthetic folklore glorified factory life and a proletarian ethic of hard work and sobriety.

In the armed forces, whose officer corps was shredded in the 1937 purges, no commanders were glorified except those of the past. Instead, publicity glared on particular branches of the defense system that appealed to the imagination. Pilots, tank drivers, NKVD spy catchers, and border guards on motorcycles embodied the virtues of bravery, technical know-how, and total loyalty to country and leader. The seriousness of the last virtue was gruesomely illustrated in the partly invented story of the little boy Pavlik Morozov, who denounced his father for allegedly helping *kulaks* in the early 1930s, was then murdered by relatives, and thus became a cult figure in Soviet martyrology.

The pantheon of heroic types rarely included a professor. But although the intelligentsia suffered persecution in the cultural revolution and the purges, surviving members regained security, prestige, and material benefits by the decade's end, and some of their values came to dominate academia and culture. The political intelligentsia, constantly purged, was rapidly supplanted by engineers and managers of a lower-middle-class or working-class background with technical schooling. The "promoted," as they were called, received perquisites along with awesome responsibilities, to say nothing of risks. Turning its back on sturdy proletarian values, this backbone of the Soviet elite assumed tastes, apparel, and status symbols formerly considered capitalist.

The "bourgeoisified" managers and engineers joined the approved artistic and academic intelligentsia, surviving officer corps, and party hierarchy in the new Soviet elite, partaking of special housing, restaurants, shops, and clinics. Above them stood a new aristocracy of wealthy and prestigious figures who had risen to the top of their professions: ballerinas, eminent conductors, "court" painters, favorite writers of Stalin. The "millionaire" novelist Alexei Tolstoy (1883–1945), whose brilliant *Road to Calvary* won a Stalin prize, was notorious for devouring mountains of black caviar at state dinners. Mikhail Sholokhov (1905–1984), a 1965 Nobel Prize winner in literature, owned a large Moscow flat, an airplane, and a Don River estate filled with imported cattle. Party leaders enjoyed relative luxury but never risked displaying it in conspicuous consumption. At the pinnacle lived Stalin, moving between his Kremlin apartment and his heavily guarded dachas. He and his cronies indulged themselves night after night, in between issuing commands and execution orders, feasting and toasting in the manner of gangland chiefs.

Far from Moscow's banquet halls, the ruling elite's victims toiled, languished, and perished in the vast archipelago of labor camps. To take but one example, the construction of the Moscow-Volga Canal by slave labor under NKVD chief Genrikh Yagoda from 1932 to 1937 resulted in mass deaths from overwork, undernourishment, and execution. Not only was this ghastly episode hidden from the world, but the delightful musical comedy film *Volga, Volga* (1938) featured the waterway as a glorious Soviet achievement linking loyal Russian provincials to the sacred center of Moscow. The atrocities committed in these camps did not begin with Stalin, but they escalated in scope during his reign. The day-to-day existence of the average Soviet person was a paradise compared with life and death in the Gulag. Roused at dawn, the convicts labored in subzero temperatures on a minimal diet and were beaten and abused and sometimes slain at the whim of a guard. Political prisoners, mostly intellectuals, were at the mercy of hardened criminals, who added their own brand of torment to that of the guards. "Politicals" were immune to this only if they, in the words of one, "could tell stories or give a verbal rendition of some adventurous novel." In Stalin's time, millions starved or were worked to death. "You are nothing," said one guard to an inmate. "You will die here. You are dust."

NATIONS OF THE UNION

The general structure of the republics and nationalities remained in place (see the chapter "Revolution in the Life of Peoples, 1921–1928"). New union republics were added by abolishing the overarching body in Transcaucasia and adding some in Central Asia. The USSR now contained three Slavic (Russian, Ukrainian, Belorussian); three Transcaucasian (Georgian, Armenian, Azerbaijani); and five Central Asian (Kazakh, Kirgiz, Tajik, Uzbek, Turkmen) members. Each had its own collection of national units; within the eleven Soviet Socialist Republics altogether were twenty-two autonomous republics, nine autonomous provinces, and ten national regions. The surge of building new national units and national languages during the cultural revolution ceased in the mid-1930s, and the "national soviets" and other smaller ethnic units were abolished. Officially and partly in practice, indigenization policies remained in force. But the socialist offensive, the tightening of dictatorship, the violent resistance to collectivization in the borderlands, and the fear of foreign influences and "bourgeois nationalism" reduced some of the non-Russians to "enemy nations" whose people were repressed in the tens of thousands. Slowly there emerged an ideology that Russians were the preeminent members of the Soviet community of nations.

Stalin's Empire

Through the 1930s, the terror spread to remote reaches of the country and struck local party cadres at a very high rate. Envoys of darkness from Moscow—Prime Minister Vyacheslav Molotov, city bosses Kaganovich and Khrushchёv, and Ezhov—appeared in the non-Russian republics to purge party, government, military, cultural, and educational establishments. The secret police concocted "nationalist plots" and brutally repressed their alleged instigators, accused of being fifth-column agents of hostile nations, such as Poland, Finland, or Nazi Germany. About eight hundred thousand non-Russians were arrested, deported, or executed in 1935–1938.

The NKVD launched the so-called National Operations to ferret out real or suspected "bourgeois nationalists." An early 1930s law making unauthorized crossing of the Soviet border in either direction a capital offense cut many remaining ties with the West and reduced those of Azeris, Tatars, and Central Asians with the rest of the Muslim world. The borders, once porous, if dangerous to traverse, were sealed, though mountainous regions near China still allowed escape. Only a few daring westerners ventured to the deep interior to describe life under the Soviets. Army and NKVD frontier guards posted along the vast confines of the USSR interdicted the passage of unwanted visitors and spies. Whole communities along the reinforced security borders with China were uprooted and replaced by military personnel during the 1930s. Eastern regions became especially sensitive in response to Japanese aggression in Manchuria and China.

Across the empire, collectivization varied in pace and kind. In the grasslands, the compulsory herding of cattle into the common fold caused dreadful famine in Kazakhstan and bloody revolts in Buryat Mongolia and Turkmenia. The enforced settlement of steppe nomads sent thousands in flight through unguarded passes into China. In the far north, reindeer herders—and in the far east, fishermen—felt the sting of the state as it forced them into collectives. Resistance to collectivization was especially fierce in non-Russian areas. Everywhere, Soviet authorities terminated or severely limited private enterprise, sometimes rooted in ancient practices. They nationalized the great bazaars along the ancient Silk Road from China to Europe, the caravansaries, and the caravans themselves. The conquering Armenian merchant of the Caucasus vanished from sight. During renewed godless assaults of the First Five-Year Plan of the early 1930s, Communists universally persecuted Orthodoxy and other Christian faiths, Judaism, Islam, Buddhism, shamanism, and animism; they demolished venerable cathedrals, synagogues, mosques, and shrines or turned them into storehouses and clubs.

The Soviet Communist habit of ascribing to everyone an official identity led the regime to a quasi-racist notion that ethnicities were unchangeable. No melting pot was created in the USSR; instead, nationality was stamped in a citizen's documents as a permanent mark. Mass culture invented traditions, rituals, and art forms for each nationality, along with patronizing stereotypes: in the film *The Tractor Drivers* (1940), a Georgian gesticulates gaily and sings the praises of the wine and fruits of his sunny homeland. Any sign of authentic, as opposed to fabricated and folkloric, national assertion became punishable. By the end of the decade, what Lenin had called the sin of Great Power chauvinism—that is Russian arrogance toward the minorities—was overshadowed by the crime of "bourgeois nationalism." The Cyrillic alphabet replaced the Latin, which had been introduced for many tongues. Cultures were refashioned and their histories rewritten to make Russians appear as liberators. Russian settlement in the borderlands increased. If the policy of the 1920s had been modernization and renationalization, that of the 1930s was modernization and folklorization.

Modernization?

But what kind of "modernization"? New industries cropped up in lands that had never seen a factory. Railroad tracks appeared in desolate wastes that had known only the winds and the hooves of nomad herds. The Turkistan-Siberian Railroad (Turksib), completed in the early 1930s, linked Central Asia to Siberia and gave birth to new towns and the expansion of old fort settlements like Alma Ata in Kazakhstan, whose population grew to a quarter million.

Soviet social policy raised levels of health care, literacy, and education, and broadened the horizons of many women—particularly, despite male resistance, in the Muslim regions. Linguistic indigenization was largely abandoned, and national regions became bilingual, meaning that every citizen had to learn Russian alongside the native tongue, which remained the language of instruction in all schools. However, affirmative action promotional and educational programs continued. The constant propaganda bombardment about ethnic equality, though it never matched practice, certainly had an effect on Russians and non-Russians alike.

But if industrialization's rapid pace and giant scale brought massive disruption, the resulting modernization, for all its headlong tempo and ambitious designs, was superficial. For every boxcar, hundreds of camel and donkey teams still provided transport. Women were wearing horsehair veils in Bukhara in 1937. Men in turbans, skull caps, and robes sat on rugs in the *chai-khana,* or tea room, or gathered for prayer in those mosques still allowed to function.

One leading scholar of Soviet nationalities has compared the USSR to "a multicolored Soviet quilt sewn tightly by the Communist Party," and another has likened it to a "communal apartment" where nations dwelt in their separate rooms. The regime did not attempt to Russify the other nationalities; but, in contrast to the 1920s, it required Russian as the working language in the armed forces and promoted linguistic assimilation to the now exalted Russian culture, even though nationality was stamped in every passport. The officially inspired notion of nationality from the Stalin period onward was "Friendship of the Peoples"—not "brotherhood," which implies equality—with Russians as the first among equals. Yet compared with governments who scorned "minority" languages and who herded native peoples onto reservations, the Soviet Union turned out to be an impressive preserver and even builder of nations.

From Kiev to Bukhara

The Stalinist revolution from above also had varying effects from region to region. In Ukraine, economic advances were dramatic: its industrial capacity rose by 1940 to seven times that of 1913. Cities became Ukrainized. Kiev again became the capital in 1934. But purges and show trials from 1930 onward brought repression long before the Great Terror. The main cause was the size of Ukraine as the second largest republic, its proximity to Europe, and the vigorous nationalism of its leaders, which was perceived in Moscow as going well beyond indigenization. In 1932, the Politburo in Moscow linked the withholding of grain to Ukrainization activists who were arrested for treasonous separatism. In 1933, high Soviet officials, including Politburo member Stanislaw Kosior (b. 1889, liquidated 1939), were assigned to curb the cultural renaissance. Ukrainian nativizers Mykola Skrypnyk and Mykola Khvylovy committed suicide in 1933 at the height of the famine; former education minister Oleksandr Shumsky and theater director Les Kurbas were arrested and died in prison. Collectivization and famine engendered national despair, as did mass deportations and executions: the corpses of tens of thousands of executed people were unearthed fifty years later. Similar terror was applied to Belorussia, though the writer Janka Kupala somehow managed to survive.

In 1930 the party abolished its Jewish section, a sign that autonomous activity would now be curbed. By renouncing anti-Semitism and allowing Jews into the highest positions in culture, the economy, and even government, the Soviet system had provided a model diametrically opposed to Nazism. Soviet Jews were not singled out as "enemy nations" as were Soviet Finns, Baltic peoples, Germans, and Poles in the western regions; Kurds, Iranians, and a few others in the south; and Chinese and Koreans in the east. But the "Jewish homeland" that had been established in Birobijan in the late 1920s proved a great disappointment. In spite of some Yiddish cultural institutions there and much propaganda, by the time of World War II Jewish settlers numbered only a bit more than one hundred thousand, a small percentage of the local population of mostly Buryat Mongols. Most Jews remained in the European USSR, ultimately to face the Holocaust, followed by postwar Soviet anti-Semitism.

The Georgian Lavrenty Beria (1899–1953) had succeeded the executed Nikolai Ezhov as chief of the NKVD in 1939. He also headed the Transcaucasian Federation until 1936, when Georgia, Armenia, and Azerbaijan became full-fledged republics. As party leader in Georgia he carried out a frenzied vendetta against former rivals. His terror campaign liquidated Mensheviks in Tbilisi, Dashnaks in Erevan, and Musavats in Baku, as well as the Old Bolsheviks, who had shaped Caucasian revolutionary history in the early twentieth century. Beria oversaw the introduction of a specialized economy—tobacco, wine, petroleum—but also introduced industries, such as a giant steel mill, that were not always useful or functional. As elsewhere, the cultural ax descended. In Georgia, Konstantine Gamsakhurdia abandoned his cosmopolitan modernist style (see the chapter "Revolution in the Life of Peoples, 1921–1928") and wrote historical epic novels.

The Islamic world also felt the shakeups. Evgeniya Ginzburg (1896–1980), an editor at the paper *Red Tartary,* described how in Kazan Russians, Tatars, Jews, and Latvians denounced the locals and each other. In Central Asia, party officials mounted show trials for "oppositionists" and crushed resistance ruthlessly. Show trials of the last Basmachi (see the chapter "Revolution in the Life of Peoples, 1921–1928"), finally subdued with the aid of machine guns and airplanes, were staged in Bukhara's Registan Square. At the very top, Akmal Ikramov and other high party figures were brought to Moscow, tried beside Bukharin, and shot in 1938, allegedly for planning to turn Central Asia over to British imperialists. Although terror hung in the air, some citizens talked openly to a British diplomat traveling incognito, Fitzroy Maclean, about the horrors of collectivization. Yet newly promoted party functionaries, seemingly aloof to the attendant hazards of political life, spoke to him glowingly of their budding careers. Soviet workers built useful power stations and textile factories, but planners extended the exploitative system of planting cotton and neglecting other crops. Thousands of Russians and World War I prisoners, who had been shipped there and never returned, mingled in the Central Asian cities with the new native working class and intelligentsia.

Symbolic changes abounded in Islamic regions. The city of Dushanbe in Tajikistan became Stalinabad. The Bukhara Citadel was converted into the headquarters of the City Soviet. The law code shariat and the charities of waqf were officially abolished. Hajj, or pilgrimage to Mecca, became unthinkable. Still, many local collaborators adapted to Soviet rule. The Tajik poet Sadridin Aini helped the Russians purge Arab and Islamic influences from literature. The most famous of the Islamic bards, Jambil Jabaz-uli (Jambul) (1846–1945), wrote folkloric odes to Stalin. Soviet investment provided opera houses, conservatories, theaters, and orchestras playing European and local traditional music. Some of the latter, however, was subjected to "reform" by those who claimed that its sobbing figures reflected the remnants of feudal exploitation. Although, despite ceaseless affirmative action, the region remained short on technically trained personnel, Stalinist edifices rose above the steppe, and ponderous city grids were imported to oasis towns. And yet elements of the Islamic way of life, social customs, and family structure survived into our own times.

STALIN'S PARADE

In the 1930s, the Stalin cult made the dictator an object of national veneration as hero and father-protector. Historians rewrote the story of the revolution so that Stalin's rivals were deleted, their photos erased, and they became, in George Orwell's term, "nonpersons." One-time rivals such as Trotsky, Zinoviev, and Bukharin simply disappeared from books for sixty years. Children's tales and academic history portrayed Stalin as a poor man from a backwater of the Russian Empire, a friend of Lenin. His role as a commander in the civil war was magnified in art and literature, and the heroic image was enhanced by representing great historical figures as his predecessors. In the 1920s, history writing had been dominated by the school of Mikhail Pokrovsky (1868–1932), which ignored individuals and reduced the rich and colorful flow of bygone days to grand economic and social forces. Stalin rejected this approach and revived the glorious exploits of Russia's great rulers and commanders. Eisenstein's 1938 film on Russian Orthodox Prince Alexander Nevsky's thirteenth-century struggle with the German Catholic Teutonic Knights underlined the urgency of strong leadership, the courage of the Russian people, and the purported sadistic impulses of the German invader. The fusion of heroism and nationalism in academic and popularized history tended to deemphasize the once vaunted internationalism of the Communist movement.

Stalin became the ultimate arbiter of intellectual life. Genuine debate and academic discourse were curtailed and punished in the name of a churchlike Soviet orthodoxy. Economics fell hostage to the Soviet version of Marxism, and sociology as an independent discipline disappeared. History departed from its traditional mode of interpreting sources in various ways and entered the misty climes of ideology. Philosophical problems of ethics and aesthetics, ontology and epistemology were resolved in tormented formulas claiming their source in Marx and Engels. Even biology fell under the spell when the charlatan Trofim Lysenko (1898–1976) promised to bypass Darwinian laws of heredity in plants and produce new breeds. His main accomplishment in the 1930s was, with Stalin's blessing, to purge the biology establishment.

The main reason for the enforcement of Stalinist "truth" was his and the party's desire for a unitary system of thought that would instill the mental habit of obedience. The new dogma filtered down into the vastly expanded school system, in which the educational experiments of the 1920s and the cultural revolution were renounced and traditional methods restored: uniforms, textbooks, homework, examinations, discipline, and, in a few years, separate schools for the sexes.

The Stalin cult was meant to engender reverence for the wise leader and arbitrator of revolutionary truth. Wearing a plain tunic among bemedalled marshals and dignitaries, Stalin hobnobbed with working-class and peasant achievers, who were invited to the Kremlin in a kind of political theater that flattered the guests and made the host seem humble and approachable. Stakhanovite superworkers and gifted pilots marveled at the simplicity of the great leader and admired his small gestures of politeness to "ordinary" people. His disdain for melodramatic oratory made the Great Leader *(veliky vozhd)* seem more a man of the people than were his fascist contemporaries Mussolini of Italy and Hitler of Germany—Il Duce and Der Führer. An entire industry arose for the mass production of Stalin portraits and busts to hang or stand alongside those of Lenin in every office and factory in the land. The Lenin cult was manipulated to present Stalin as his friend and pupil—the crown prince of communism, now fulfilling his inherited duty. Stalin's favorite painter, Alexander Gerasimov (1881–1963), in the 1938 canvas *Stalin and Voroshilov in the Kremlin,* was careful to make the shorter Stalin look taller than Kliment Voroshilov (1881–1969), his war minister since 1925, as they strolled and conferred on the welfare and defense of the Soviet people. Gerasimov and others employed the kind of contrastive lighting used by the great masters to dramatize the scene and deify the leader. In poems, songs, posters, and statues, Stalin was made accessible to the masses, and not only the Russians. Folksingers and tale tellers from all the republics were enlisted to invent "folklore" crediting him with their happiness.

A recent historian has called Stalin's public culture a "magic theater." Another has written of "parading the nation." The Stalin parade reversed the original anti-tsarist show of protest and evolved into a carefully orchestrated public demonstration of support for the regime and its leaders, especially Stalin. In a mobile

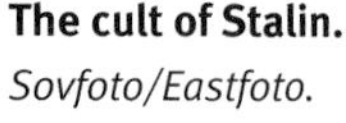

The cult of Stalin.
Sovfoto/Eastfoto.

assembly of popular "types" deployed in reverential formations, thousands marched past the Kremlin reviewing stand on holidays. Factory workers held graphs of production exploits, while peasants performed folk dances on truckbeds. Women in sport costumes bent their bodies in choreographed calisthenics like dancers in a Hollywood film. Children in red scarves and citizens of the far-flung republics in their national costumes marched in unison. In the hands of marchers, on floats, on motorcycles were the portraits of the dead Lenin and the living Stalin. The party newspaper *Pravda* in 1937 described one such parade: "It was as if the whole country unfolded in front of the spectators, and they felt that in every corner of the county, no matter how far away, creative work was boiling."

Inside every citizen marching on Red Square, outwardly glorifying the Stalinist state, lay a personal story—of success, ambition, puzzlement, grief, fear, numbness, euphoria. On parade day, May 1 or November 7, only the outward persona was shown, though sometimes in fact it matched the inner person completely. How far these marchers and the huge population they were said to represent would stand loyal to the system or to Stalin in time of stress would soon be demonstrated by the outbreak of war.

CHAPTER 36

The Soviet Homeland Defended: World War II, 1939–1945

Sister, we vow to avenge ourselves for your death, for the burned villages and cities, for the earth trampled by German boots, for our tears and grief . . . for everything! We swear on your death to scorn death and to show no mercy in battle. We swear to destroy pity in ourselves and to hate the enemy as fervently as we love life and our fatherland. Blood for blood, and death for death; our vengeance will be terrible. We swear it!

—On the Eve, *a play by Alexander Afinogenov, 1941*

In 1941, two years into World War II, the Soviet regime faced the most dangerous moment in its history when the armed forces of Adolf Hitler's Third Reich, assisted by his allies in the so-called Axis, invaded the USSR with the intention of destroying the regime, executing all Communists, exterminating the Jews, and turning the land into a colony. The old Russian Empire had been defeated in World War I, its regime reduced to dust. Soviet Russia survived the vastly stronger German assault of 1941 and emerged victorious beside its British and American allies. Both the conflict and its resolution were rooted in the ideological and international history of Europe in the 1930s.

FACING FASCISM, 1933–1939

Between the world wars, Europe witnessed a struggle between Communists and fascists, which became a key factor leading to the German invasion of the USSR in World War II. Fascism, a social and political movement of the right with populist elements, grew out of nineteenth-century racism and extreme nationalism. It differed in each setting but was often based on national, ethnic, or economic insecurity. The Italian fascists who invented the name came to power under Benito Mussolini (1883–1945) in 1922 through legal means combined with political extortion and violence. Their style—the straight-armed salute, uniforms, and paramilitary units—was mimicked. Fascist bands roved across the political terrain of the new or reshaped states in Central and Eastern Europe, wearing colored shirts and bearing picturesque names such as Iron Wolf (Lithuania), Arrow Cross (Hungary), Iron Guard (Romania), and Ustasha (Croatia, in Yugoslavia). Fascists also assisted in the victory of General Francisco Franco's Nationalists in the Spanish Civil War of 1936–1939. During and after the Great Depression, even relatively stable democracies that withstood fascism had their assortments of fascist groups: Silver Shirts (United States), Blue Shirts (Ireland), Fiery Cross (France), and the Union of British Fascists. As right-wing radicals and nationalists, fascists everywhere hated any kind of international socialism but reserved their bitterest venom for Soviet Russia and the Communists of their own counties. The reality of the "red menace" in the West declined in the 1920s, but not the fear of it.

The most dynamic fascist movement was German National Socialism, or Nazism, which came to power, also legally, in 1933 under Adolf Hitler (1889–1945). Although early Nazis were often working-class oriented and spouted anticapitalist slogans, the Comintern and the German Communists who fought Nazis on the city streets in the 1920s saw them as little more that the palace guard of capitalism and a sign of its coming demise. The Bolshevik hatred of their democratic socialist Menshevik rivals caused them to identify German Social Democrats as the other ally of capitalism along with the Nazis. This false notion led in 1928 to the Comintern doctrine of "social fascism," the twinning of fascism and social democracy as common enemies, and thus prevented an alliance with moderate democratic socialists against the Nazis. Hitler and his secret police, the Gestapo, on achieving power exhibited their own version of this simplistic doctrine as they hanged, shot, and beheaded Communist and socialist leaders indiscriminately in their prisons and concentration camps. Hitler's anticommunism was fortified by a contempt for Slavs and, since he identified Bolshevism with Jews, by a profoundly racist anti-Semitism.

Stalin Versus Hitler

Soon after Hitler came to power, the Soviet-German military cooperation fashioned in the 1920s (see the chapter "The Years of New Economic Policy: Power, Society, and Culture, 1921–1928") was abandoned; the Nazis began to rearm, and their territorial ambitions became manifest. Hitler believed it was Germany's destiny to expand into the broad lands of the Slavic peoples—Russians, Belorussians, Ukrainians, Poles, Czechs, Slovaks, and South Slavs—whom he considered racially inferior. Nazi authoritarianism, nationalism, and anticommunism fit well with Italian fascism and Japanese militarism and led the three states to sign an Anti-Comintern Pact in 1936–1937, by which time they were known as the Axis. The Axis powers suppressed domestic Communists and displayed hostility to the Western democracies, the League of Nations, and the USSR. They sallied forth in expansive actions: the Japanese in China in 1931, the Italians in Ethiopia in 1935, the Germans in Central Europe in 1938.

Opposition to Axis aggression by the other powers was slow in building. But the clear hostility to fascism and Nazism shared by democrats, liberals, socialists—and Communists—almost everywhere led Stalin to reverse his line of "social fascism" and to support a "Popular Front": political alliances of left and center parties against fascism. This alignment began in France in 1934, in the face of an upsurge of right-wing forces there, and was made a general policy in 1935 by the Seventh, and last, Comintern Congress. Popular Front coalition governments emerged in France and Spain in 1936, and in a few other countries. Trotsky, commenting from exile on Moscow's complete control of the Comintern, remarked that Stalin had transformed the vanguard of revolution into the border guard of the Soviet state.

Stalin's manipulative international policy came into full play in the Spanish Civil War. When the rebel Nationalist armies of General Franco moved on Madrid to destroy a democratic republic elected in 1931, liberals, leftists, and renowned writers such as America's Ernest Hemingway, Britain's George Orwell, and France's André Malraux went to Spain to defend the republic. So did Soviet military advisers, who were helpful in the early stages of this war. But Stalin feared his leftist rivals in Spain more than he did Franco. NKVD (Russian secret police) agents there ruthlessly exterminated Spanish and international socialists, Trotskyists, and anarchists. In the meantime, Franco was assisted by Italian volunteers and by Hitler's vaunted Condor Legion of the Luftwaffe, the German air force. The Western democracies denounced the fascist intervention but did virtually nothing. Franco emerged victorious in 1939.

Japan in the 1930s had become a militaristic and aggressive power in Asia. The invasion by Japanese forces of Manchuria in 1931 led the Soviet Union to sell Japan the Chinese Eastern Railway and to beef up defenses in the east. Then, starting in 1937, Japan's crack fighting forces occupied Chinese cities and inflicted appalling atrocities on the population as they pushed into the interior. The war enabled a temporary alliance, akin to the Popular Front, between Chiang K'ai-shek's Nationalists and Mao Zedong's Communists to fight the Japanese. In 1938–1939, danger of a two-front war seemed very real to Stalin as Japanese attacked Soviet forces in full-scale battles in an undeclared war along the Soviet-Manchurian border. But Japan focused on its Chinese campaigns and on a later drive to Southeast Asia in 1940 and against the U.S. base at Pearl Harbor in late 1941, all of which deflected Japanese expansion away from the USSR.

In Europe, fear of Germany turned Stalin toward Britain and France. No altruism attended Stalin's switches in foreign policy. He pursued self-interest and remained flexible, though often blind to danger. Foreign Commissar Maxim Litvinov (1876–1951), a strong antifascist and a Jew, pursued a policy of collective security against fascist aggression. He turned to the Western democracies and to the League of Nations, an international body created after World War I, on behalf of peace, disarmament, and treaty guarantees. The initiative won his country recognition by the United States in 1933, membership in the League in 1934, and a series of treaties with neighboring states. The most important of these, a 1935 pact that committed France and the Soviet Union to defend Czechoslovakia against German expansion, was weakened by a clause that required both France and the USSR to aid Czechoslovakia for it to have effect.

The quest for collective security was hindered in the late 1930s by Soviet military purges. Western fear of Hitler was insufficient to counteract a widespread re-

pugnance at Soviet communism and its terror campaigns. Neither the Comintern Popular Front nor Soviet diplomacy was taken very seriously as a sure deterrent against fascist aggression. By 1937—after Hitler had rearmed Germany and intervened in Spain—diplomacy was befogged by conflicting political perceptions in the triangle of fascism, communism, and democracy: Hitler, Stalin, and many Western statesmen were engulfed in mutual suspicion, though for a while Hitler hoped for an understanding with Britain. As the Popular Front and collective security dimmed in 1938–1939, a defensive pact with Germany arose as an alternative in Soviet policy.

In March 1938 Hitler annexed German-speaking Austria. Fired by the lack of serious deterrence to his actions from Western nations, he then arranged a partition of Czechoslovakia to annex its German-speaking region, the Sudetenland. France, Britain, and Italy agreed to this partition in the famous Munich settlement of September 1938, often cited as the classic example of appeasing aggressors. German forces marched into the Sudetenland and then, violating the Munich pact, occupied the remaining Czech half of the lands in 1939. Hungary, an ally of Hitler, seized a piece of the Slovak half, and the rest seceded as Slovakia, a semifascist dictatorship friendly to Hitler. Early in 1939, Hitler annexed the German-populated town of Memel in Lithuania. Mussolini joined the land grab by invading Albania, across the Adriatic Sea.

Stalin, who opposed these moves vehemently, had not even been invited to the Munich conference. He had offered to defend Czechoslovakia, and recently published sources show that he launched active military preparations to stop Hitler there, but France declined to act. Neither then nor later could Stalin reach agreement with the Western powers on how to curb German aggression. Many Western leaders in 1939, who poorly understood Hitler's aims and ardently desired to avoid another war, believed that Hitler could be sated by a few annexations.

Stalin Allied with Hitler, 1939–1941

By spring 1939, it had become clear that Hitler's next victim would be Poland, the USSR's neighbor. Stalin, in response to an obvious danger, played two hands at once. He distrusted and hated both the democracies and Nazi Germany. His main concern was national security, and his method was realpolitik. Stalin's Eighteenth Party Congress speech in March 1939 hinted at his waning confidence in Britain and France as security partners and warned against the USSR being "drawn into conflicts by warmongers who are used to having others pull chestnuts out of the fire for them." This was not, as sometimes claimed, a reorientation toward Germany. Though rankled by the Munich settlement, Stalin continued talks with Britain and France about countering Hitler. A Stalin proposal to send Red Army troops into Poland to protect it from Hitler raised alarms in Poland and in the democracies. On a parallel track, Stalin replaced Foreign Commissar Litvinov, a Jew, whose policy of collective security was vigorously opposed by isolationists in the Kremlin, and allowed new trade talks with Hitler. This cleared the way for, but did not require, a possible rapprochement with the Third Reich. Hitler, not yet ready to face off in armed struggle with the Soviet Union, sought an arrangement that would allow him to conquer Poland unhindered by a German-Soviet war. All through the summer of 1939 Stalin kept his options open as he listened to German offers of a reconciliation while receiving little encouragement from the West.

Mutual probing between Russia and Germany in the summer resulted in a Nazi-Soviet Pact. On August 23, the German foreign minister, Joachim von Ribbentrop, arrived in Moscow to sign a ten-year nonaggression pact with the USSR. A secret protocol called for Soviet spheres of influence in eastern Poland, Finland, the Baltic, and Bessarabia and a Soviet pledge to supply Hitler with key materials. A line drawn through Eastern Europe, slightly revised a month later, effectively set up its division between Nazis and Soviets in the event of a war. Though the secret terms of the pact were not immediately known, it sent political shock waves around the world. The agreement stunned leftist intellectuals and workers, who had believed that Moscow was the vital center of international revolution and anti-Nazism. As Arthur Koestler recalled, the sight of the swastika flying at the Moscow Airport destroyed his allegiance to communism.

Stalin's desire for buffer areas to protect the Russian heartland led him to territorial aggression. On September 1, 1939, Hitler's armed forces plunged into Poland from the west to defeat and despoil that nation and usher in World War II. A few weeks later, the Red Army occupied and then annexed the Belorussian and Ukrainian lands ceded to Poland in the War of 1920 (see the chapter "Civil War: Reds, Whites, and Greens, 1917–1921"). The border of hostile Finland was dangerously close to Leningrad. When Stalin demanded territorial and other concessions from the Finns, they refused, and the Winter War of 1939–1940 began. After months of stubborn and competent Finnish resistance in the snowy forests, the USSR emerged victorious, though it squandered any remaining international goodwill as the world cheered the heroic little nation in the north. In response to Nazi victories in Western Europe in the spring of 1940, and to ensure security on his flank, Stalin next menaced Estonia, Latvia, and Lithuania, first with political blackmail, then with military occupation as the three tiny states were transformed for the first time into Soviet republics. Two chunks of Romanian land were also seized, extending Soviet power now to the Carpathian Mountains.

Hitler, responding to British and French declarations of war, chalked up stunning victories in the west: Denmark, Norway, the Low Countries, and France fell by the summer of 1940. Hitler occupied northern France and created a fascist puppet state, Vichy France, in the south. Stalin hoped that Hitler would soon be either sated or defeated by Britain. But Hitler had no intention of letting the Soviet Union alone. His utterances, writings, and military plans left no doubt that the USSR was the ultimate target. Put simply, Hitler wished to turn Slavic lands into slave states and colonies. Mutual suspicions nursed by years of antagonism between Germany and Russia, Nazis and Communists, were inflamed by Hitler's successes in the west and Soviet expansion in the east. A visit to Berlin by the new Soviet foreign minister, Vyacheslav Molotov, in November 1940 merely exacerbated relations. Recent theories that Stalin planned a war against Hitler, and not the other way around, have been thoroughly discredited. Hitler's formal plan to invade the

Eastern Europe, 1939–1940. *From* The People's War: Popular Responses to World War II in the Soviet Union. *Copyright 2000 by the Board of Trustees of the University of Illinois. Used with permission of the University of Illinois Press.*

USSR by May 1941 was first shown to his officers on July 29, 1940, almost a year before he struck. Failing to win the Battle of Britain, a terror bombing assault, Hitler turned his eyes eastward again. But he was temporarily diverted by unexpected operations in the south to bail out the Italians, who had got bogged down during their campaigns of expansion into Egypt and Greece. Hitler's assistance in Greece resulted in the occupation of Yugoslavia and the creation of yet another Axis fascist satellite, Croatia. Only in the summer of 1941 was Hitler's Operation Barbarossa ready to launch. Master of most of continental Europe, flushed with a chain of victories, and allied with Vichy France, Italy, Slovakia, Hungary, Romania, Bulgaria, Croatia, and Finland, he struck.

During the period of the pact, 1939–1941, Stalin had adhered to its terms. He forbade Comintern anti-Nazi activities and even arranged an NKVD-Gestapo exchange of political prisoners, most of whom were put to death. He sent wheat and war-related supplies to Germany, broke with anti-Nazi governments in exile from German-occupied lands, and publicly praised Hitler's victories. In private, Stalin was far from happy about those victories. Khrushchëv recalled that when Hitler defeated France in June 1940, Stalin "let fly with some choice Russian curses and said that now Hitler was sure to beat our brains in." To prevent this, Stalin signed a treaty with Japan in April 1941 to fend off an attack in the east. He began a military upgrade by firing the incompetent war commissar Kliment Voroshilov (1881–1969), though Voroshilov's successor in 1940–1941, Semën Timoshenko (1895–1970), turned out to be almost as backward in military thinking. Stalin made himself commissar of defense, pulled some of the purged generals out of the camps, reorganized the army and enlarged its mechanized components, and beefed up the defense industries.

But a wrong-headed military doctrine based on a strict scenario of constant offensive hurt the Soviet defense posture and allowed no plans for withdrawal or provision for surprise attack. Stalin was informed of the imminent German onslaught by foreign statesmen, whom he distrusted, and by a German double agent in Tokyo, Richard Sorge (1895–1944), whom he ignored. His own military intelligence told of enemy invasion preparations. Yet thin troop lines strung along the border with Nazi-occupied Poland made easy targets for rapid destruction and encirclement. Fortified positions remained incomplete, and armor and aircraft lay in formations vulnerable to aerial bombing. Stalin neglected to bring frontline units up to full strength or to ensure adequate communications and command-and-control structures. Stories conflict about Stalin's refusal to heed the eighty-four intelligence warnings he received. He is variously reported to have feared that Hitler was pressuring or "provoking" the USSR; or that the German army was doing so behind Hitler's back.

INVASION AND OCCUPATION

At 3:30 A.M. on June 22, 1941, without a declaration of war, more than 3 million German and satellite troops, the greatest invasion force in military history, poured across the Soviet border at points from the top of Finland to the shores of the Black Sea. Hitler was confidant that his forces would bring the Soviet Union to its knees.

Operation Barbarossa

Army Group North, under General Wilhelm von Leeb, headed toward Leningrad, the city of Peter the Great, as the Finnish armies of Marshal Gustaf Mannerheim (1867–1951) invaded from the North. Army Group South—including units of Slovak, Italian, Hungarian, and Romanian troops and commanded by General Gerd von Rundstedt—sped southward through Ukrainian lands and the center of ancient Rus. Army Group Center, under General Fedor von Bock and spearheaded by the battle-proven tanks of Heinz Guderian, headed straight for Moscow, the Soviet capital and the original seat of the tsars. Within weeks, dozens of ancient Russian towns were occupied or almost totally destroyed. By September Leningrad was besieged, Moscow threatened with capture, and Kiev taken. Hitler's Blitzkrieg, or "lightning warfare," the rapid movement of massive mechanized forces, triumphed, as it had all over Europe.

Stalin, shaken by this sudden attack that threatened to bring Soviet history to a violent conclusion, disappeared from the public scene for a few weeks and then, revived, came back to speak on the radio to his people on July 3, addressing them as comrades, citizens, brothers, and sisters. "The enemy is cruel and implacable," he said. "He is out to seize our lands watered with our sweat, to seize our grain and soil secured by our labor. He is out to restore the rule of landlords, to restore tsarism, to destroy national culture . . . to Germanize [our peoples], to turn them into slaves of German princes and barons." The speech ended on a note of optimistic rallying. But for the present, the picture was utterly black: airfields and planes torn up, huge armies devoured in German pincer movements, and hundreds of thousands of casualties and prisoners destined to a terrible end in German camps. Citizens shivered in terror of the bombers that hovered over cities with their dreadful cargo. In Moscow, hundreds of thousands of women dug trenches. When Kiev fell to the invader, its huge Jewish population was rounded up and machine-gunned—over thirty-three thousand men, women, and children in two days—in the suburban ravine of Babi Yar. Leningrad was subjected to a hideous three-year blockade unprecedented in the annals of modern war: a million or more of its citizens perished of cold, hunger, and enemy shells. The phrases "900 Days" and "Road to Life" (an ice route across Lake Ladoga used to supply the city) entered the vocabulary of wartime suffering and endurance. A Russian historian of our time recalled: "I was one of the children. Nine years old at the time, I well remember the sound of the motors of the German planes, the whistles of the bombs, and the bright traces of machine-gun fire in the night sky."

The early onset of winter and Hitler's diversion of Guderian's armor southward slowed the German attack. Meanwhile the Red Army was reinforced by ten divisions called in from Soviet Asia, a move made possible by intelligence from Sorge about Japan's intentions elsewhere. They rolled out in December from behind Moscow and pressed the line back away from the city, the first time the German juggernaut had been stopped and reversed anywhere. The Battle of Moscow, which caused jubilation in the Allied world, entailed huge losses of life on both sides. Germans began to experience casualty levels unheard of in their Blitzkriegs of 1939–1941.

Old-time civil war commanders—with their ideas of cavalry charge, individual heroism, and lax discipline—were replaced by innovators in the use of air power and armored mechanized units. New tanks rolled off assembly lines of factories in the Urals, far from German lines. The T-34, a heavily armed and highly mobile medium tank, soon to be massed into large units, emerged as a major weapon. But

Burying the dead in besieged Leningrad. *Sovfoto/Eastfoto.*

the victory near Moscow was temporary, and the Germans continued to forge ahead in the south and to renew other assaults in 1942. The farthest line of enemy advance cut off all of Belorussia, Ukraine, and a large segment of European Russia, altogether about 40 percent of the population.

Axis Rule in Occupied Areas

After absorbing the initial jolt of invasion, the unconquered populace gradually began to hear news of the huge losses at the front and of the German occupation: massacres, execution of hostages, peasants dragged off as slave laborers to German factories. The occupation was a genuinely horrifying experience. No recitation of numbers slaughtered, tortured, or enslaved can elicit a suitable emotional response. Entire villages were burned alive in a barn. Captive partisans were shot in the belly on army orders so that they would be buried alive in the greatest torment. Whenever the Soviet forces began moving back into the formerly occupied areas, they found the grisly evidence: villagers hanged; young girls raped; men, women, children, old folks cut down by machine-gun fire. Soviet war prisoners starved and died of thirst as German movie cameras recorded their unbearable agonies; about 3 mil-

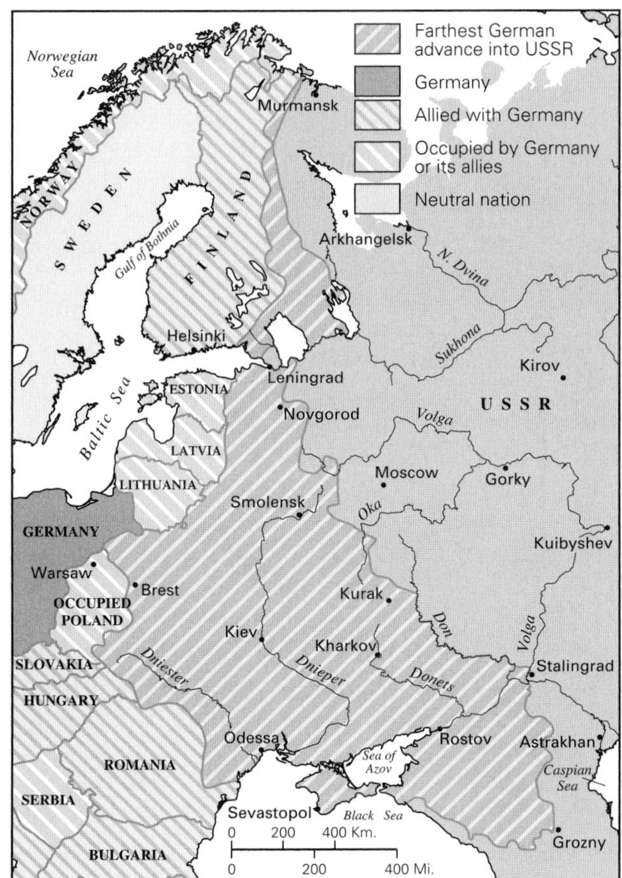

Furthest lines of German Advance, 1942–1943.

lion perished in German captivity. The Soviet peoples, along with Poles, Yugoslavs, and Jews, perished in numbers so large and in ways so barbarous as to defy the imagination. The Soviet dead probably reached close to 27 million, including 1.5 million of the 6 million Jews exterminated in the Holocaust. Said Hitler in March 1941, "We do not wage war to preserve the enemy"; and in October: "This enemy consists not of soldiers but to a large extent only of beasts."

The brutal German administration was racked by rivalry among military, political, and economic interests, all inhumane. On the fate of the Jews there was no division. Nazi special forces used firing squads and gas vans at first to liquidate whole villages; now wiped out forever were the little Jewish market towns that had suffered so many pogroms in the past. Mechanized death camps appeared, mostly on Polish territory. Fascist volunteers from Spain, Portugal, and Scandinavia later joined the original Axis troops in an anticommunist crusade of vengeance. The two-decade-long battle between fascism and communism was now magnified into a war of conquest and extermination waged in the marshes, plains, and forests of the eastern Slavic lands. Belorussians and Ukrainians, by the mere fact of geography, suffered more than any other non-Russian nationality except the Jews. Some Ukrainians in the western regions that had been conquered from Poland in 1939 welcomed the invaders as liberators from oppression. Those in the rest of Ukraine who collaborated did so partly because of their immense suffering in the collectivization, the famine, and the purges of the 1930s, and partly because of their mistaken belief that the Germans, who had been relatively well behaved during the occupation of World War I, would privatize farms and open churches.

FRONT AND REAR

How did the bulk of the Soviet population respond to catastrophic invasion? High-school students of both sexes and women of all ages enlisted. "What was there to talk about?" recalled a female veteran. "We had graduated, they had given us our diplomas. Naturally it was our duty to go to the front." A million women served in the armed forces as nurses, doctors, antiaircraft gunners, pilots, snipers, and tankers. German troops came to fear the raids of female aviators, whom they called Night Witches.

Villagers melted into the forests as partisans to harry the occupiers. The story of the partisan high-school girl Zoya Kosmodemyanskaya, who was tortured and hanged by the Germans early in the war, was widely publicized. In another cele-

Soviet women combat pilots in World War II. *Sovfoto/Eastfoto.*

brated incident, a women resistance fighter masquerading as a housemaid blew to bits a German commander, known locally as the Butcher of Belorussia. Elsewhere, the Young Guard of the Donbass—teenagers and students—wreaked sabotage on the German garrisons until they were captured, tortured, and buried alive in a coal mine. The partisan movement inspired courage, but the military, who often distrusted spontaneous armed locals, did not heavily support it.

The regime successfully mobilized civilians, moved whole segments of the population from the danger zones, relocated government offices and cultural establishments, and oversaw the manufacture of weapons, troop transport, and recruitment of ever fresh levees. An Evacuation Council under future premier Alexei Kosygin (1904–1980) and the armaments tsar, future defense minister Dmitry Ustinov (1908–1984), moved or converted factories for wartime production. Within six months of the invasion, over fifteen hundred large-scale enterprises, including over one hundred aircraft factories, were evacuated. About one-eighth of the nation's industrial assets were dismantled, relocated, and reassembled in the Urals, Central Asia, and Siberia. War industries operating day and night turned out guns, planes, and tanks by the thousands. Whole armies of women worked in the defense industry under a stringent labor discipline. Endless reserves of troops seemed to flow out of the eastern regions, many of them Asian recruits.

The military response saw its share of corruption, cowardice, and incompetence as well as superhuman physical effort and martial valor. Stalin assumed the posts of commander in chief and war commissar as well as the title of marshal. He maintained iron confidence through most of the war, but his portrayal in the Soviet film *The Fall of Berlin* (1949) as a wartime leader endowed with strategic brilliance is a distortion; his blunders were legion in the first year of the war. But so is the version of Stalin as a military illiterate and criminal incompetent floated in the 1950s by his successor Nikita Khrushchëv (1894–1971). Stalin learned to behave with cool and intelligent competence in the Kremlin war room. A British strategist in 1944 was "more than ever impressed by the dictator's military ability." Assisting him was a staff of senior commanders and a State Defense Committee composed of the prewar civilian party and state leaders closest to Stalin, plus a few new faces. Future leaders such as Khrushchëv and Leonid Brezhnev (1906–1982) were sent to the front commands as political troubleshooters. The interference of political commissars in military units, abolished and reinstated several times since 1918, remained for about a year and was then repudiated. The younger well-trained generals, such as Georgy Zhukov (1896–1974) and some released from Stalin's prison camps, performed admirably under the dual pressure of battle and their forbidding master, Stalin.

Personal heroism was perhaps no greater in the Soviet army than in others, but morale was stiffened by the national mission of ridding the country of a murderous occupier. Mythic cults of human exploits arose around such heroes as the pilot who plunged his burning plane into an enemy column and the soldier who allegedly threw his body across a German machine-gun nest to block its fire. Although some of these episodes, such as that of the partisan Zoya, were embellished and even manufactured, the compelling myths became a significant element of wartime psychology.

An important factor of the Soviet war effort was American economic aid, known as Lend-Lease. Britain after June 22, and the United States after Pearl Harbor, became Soviet allies. U.S. president Franklin D. Roosevelt (1882–1945) authorized shipment of crucial war supplies into Murmansk and Arkhangelsk, across the Pacific, or up through Persia (jointly occupied against its will by the Allies). Tons of food and thousands of aircraft, fuel, Studebaker trucks, and railroad tracks and cars flowed into the country. In the Cold War years, Soviets would discount and Americans would inflate the decisiveness of this aid. New research suggests that Lend-Lease was crucial to the Soviet victory, but only after the Germans were stopped and the Red Army was on the offensive.

TURN OF THE TIDE

Stalin hoped for a second front in 1942—that is, an Allied invasion of Europe that would force Hitler to pull troops away from the eastern front. But since it did not come until 1944, the Soviet army faced the Nazi behemoth alone and suffered withering losses. During the "Black Summer" of 1942, the Germans took Rostov-on-Don, the Crimea, and other key points in the south. But Hitler overextended himself late in the year in Operation Blue: to protect the left flank of a long strike force penetrating the Caucasus on the way to oil-rich Baku, he threw a huge force into the Don River bend toward Stalingrad, on the Volga. This throbbing industrial base possessed strategic as well as symbolic significance in the name of the Soviet ruler. The battle that raged there for almost six months, from August 1942 to January 1943, was titanic. Ferocious street-by-street, house-by-house, room-by-room engagements as well as aerial dogfights, massive bombing, and shelling reduced the city to rubble. "Trenches ran through the factory yards and through the workshops themselves," a British journalist observed; "and now at the bottom of the trenches there still lay frozen green Germans and frozen grey Russians and frozen fragments of human shapes." The Red Army on November 19 launched a massive counteroffensive. Soviet pincer movements and Volga crossings produced enormous casualties on both sides. The outcome was a great circle of large newly formed Soviet armored units that surrounded the inner "ring" of Germans around the city. The entire German Sixth Army and twenty-four of its generals, including the commander, Field Marshal Friedrich Paulus, surrendered. Only about ninety thousand of his three hundred thousand troops had survived. Stalingrad, immortalized in many a novel and film, was a major turning point in World War II, equivalent at least to key victories that year of the British in Africa and the Americans in the Pacific.

The Battle of Kursk (July 5 to August 23, 1943) was the largest battle in history and another decisive victory for Soviet arms. Hitler, reeling from his defeat at Stalingrad, sought a new victory in the summer of 1943 and ordered an offensive against a huge Soviet salient near the south Russian town of Kursk. The German attack was met by a huge Soviet counteroffensive, both sides employing entire armored armies, with thousands of tanks lined up against each other—2,700 German armored vehicles to 3,598 Soviet ones. The Germans, though equipped with Tigers and Ferdinands (the latter named after its designer, Ferdinand Porsche) were no match for the Soviet forces and their KV heavy and T-34 medium tanks. The Soviet army crushed the enemy—on one day alone, destroying over 500 German tanks. Both sides suffered: on another day, "over 700 tanks lay battered and broken, caught in death in grotesque shapes, their hulls pierced, their guns askew, turrets blown off. . . . Beside them lay thousands of burned and burning corpses." But improved use of concentrated air power and artillery had transformed the Soviet military, and the Kursk triumph opened the road for the liberation of Ukraine.

Although no one knew it then, Kursk was the last major German offensive on the eastern front. Yet the Soviet "march to victory" would take almost two more years of fierce combat. Kiev was liberated late in 1943, Leningrad in early 1944. In the summer, colossal Soviet pounding drove the Germans out of Belorussia. As the enemy retreated westward, Soviet troops stormed into Finland, the Baltic, eastern Poland, Romania, Bulgaria, and Hungary. The puppet state of Slovakia, racked by rebellion, was occupied by the Germans and eventually cleared by the Soviet army. Hitler's European imperial system had virtually disintegrated.

But the Red Army ground down in front of Warsaw and was held up for almost half a year before mounting the final assault on Germany. As the Russians approached Warsaw in July 1944, the underground anti-German and anti-Soviet Polish resistance movement, the Home Army, launched a doomed uprising to try to take the city from the Germans. They did so without informing the Russian military. The Red Army paused across the Vistula as the Germans massacred the Poles. Did they do so on purpose, as has often been claimed? Stalin had no love for the anticommunist as well as ant-Nazi Warsaw underground, which had close ties to the Polish government in exile in London. But there seems little doubt that the Soviet army, which made a thrust and was repelled, would have taken Warsaw much sooner if it could have. On the other hand, Stalin dropped only meager supplies to the insurgents and refused facilities for Allied planes to do so until it was too late. The Germans were able to reduce the great city to ruins and to exterminate the Home Army with the Soviet armed forces near by. The episode left bad blood between the two peoples and added to recriminations during the Cold War.

The Allies knocked Mussolini out of the war in 1943 by invading Italy but had to fight bloody engagements against the Germans in the north until 1945. The second front that Stalin wanted finally materialized when the Allies landed on the French coast at Normandy on D-Day, June 6, 1944. But by winter the Allied push toward Germany had bogged down. At Allied request, in January 1945 General Zhukov launched an offensive that reached the Oder River in the eastern part of Germany. By April, American and Russian forces had linked up farther west on the Elbe River in an orgy of joyous celebration. In Berlin, which the Red Army entered on April 21, Hitler committed suicide on April 30. On May 7, Germany surrendered to the Western Allies—and two days later more fully and formally to all the Allies in Berlin. The red flag, planted by Soviet soldiers, was flying over the Reichstag.

Why did the Soviets prevail? No amount of analysis can single out the main cause of this or any other military triumph. German generals liked to blame Hitler's or each other's mistakes. Cold warriors on both sides argued about the impact of Lend-Lease. Stalin's official patriotic line attributed everything to the leader and the party. Later Soviet rulers discounted Stalin and even blamed him for almost fatal errors. High on the list of factors contributing to the Soviet victory were the reform of the military command system and demotion of the old commissars, the quasi-military nature of the political system, and the technological base built by force in the 1930s. In spite of distortions and wastage, and of the argument by some scholars that a different system would have done better, Stalin's economy performed extraordinarily during the war and in the second half of 1942 was outproducing Nazi Germany in armaments. The terror apparatus frightened certain elements into battle, but it also stupidly arrested competent warriors for minor infractions. Soviet soldiers fought well: it was rapid German maneuvering that caught so many prisoners of war, not cowardice. Other factors contributing to the Soviet victory included the massive participation of women and the nationalities, and the cultural propaganda machines that fostered the widely shared belief that the war was a holy cause. "At that time we all felt closer to our government than at any other time in our lives," wrote a participant years later. "It was not their war, but our war." Virtually none of these conditions had been present when Russia fought in World War I.

THE HIDDEN WARS

The final Soviet campaigns of the war were couched in triumphalism and rhetoric about the Red Army as heroic liberators of enslaved peoples and saviors to inmates of the Nazi death camps of Poland. This was truth, but not the whole truth. Between 1939 and 1941, while allied with Hitler, the Soviet government had forcibly deported about a million and a half Poles, Ukrainians, Belorussians, Jews, Estonians, Latvians, Lithuanians, and others to the Arctic north, Siberia, and Central Asia. In the nightmare of nocturnal arrests and searches, cattle cars, resettlements, and executions, almost three hundred thousand people perished. About seventeen thousand captured Polish officers, young and old, were shot by Soviet security forces. Some were buried in Katyn Forest in 1940. Others were taken to Russian towns and, night after night, taken to soundproof execution chambers, their bodies then loaded into dump trucks and buried with the aid of heavy equipment. When German forces unearthed some of the corpses in 1943, the Soviet government angrily denied the atrocity and continued to do so right up to its last years. The principal motive in the deportations and murders was the Soviet fear of disloyalty and retaliation from untrustworthy conquered peoples.

Distrust also applied to certain Soviet non-Russians. Among the most inhumane of Soviet acts was the wholesale punishment in 1944 of entire nations accused of, or suspected of, working for the Germans—such as the Volga Germans, Crimean

Tatars, and some of the mountain peoples of the Caucasus. Non-Tatar residents of the Crimea, motivated by greed or envy, spread rumors about Tatar espionage during the German occupation, a repeat of the false charges made during the Crimean War (1853–1856) (see the chapter "Around the Russian Empire, 1801–1861"). Populations marked for deportations were uprooted and relocated under ghastly conditions—Chechen and Ingush victims were packed forty-five to a boxcar. The vast majority among these nationalities did not collaborate, and many of their compatriots served and died at the front. These events were, in many ways, a wartime revival of the national deportations of the 1930s (see the chapter "Stalinism: Life Inside the System, 1928–1941"). Imperial Russia's forced relocations, even those of World War I, could not compare with the 1944 atrocities in terms of human devastation.

By the time of the Eastern European campaigns of 1944–1945, Red Army soldiers were filled with hate for the Germans. The sight of mountains of corpses and living skeletons in the liberated Nazi death camps, plain military rage, and the effect of the propaganda poured forth throughout the war increased the hatred. Soviet troops entering German territory unleashed an orgy of vengeance and sickening cruelty. They raped thousands of females of all ages, ran over civilians with tanks, and ignited kerosene-soaked prisoners. At war's end Stalin insisted on the repatriation of Soviet prisoners of war, who were then jailed and sometimes shot for alleged desertion when they returned. Old émigrés—Cossacks, Russians, Ukrainians, White Army veterans of the civil war, and others—were routinely taken back to Moscow by force and shot or sent to suffer the horrors of Gulag life. Over 5 million people were thus repatriated.

The vaunted unity of the Soviet people in the war effort was partially belied by the defection of some captured military personnel to the Germans. War prisoner General Andrei Vlasov (1900–1946) organized them as the Russian Liberation Army to fight on the side of Hitler for a Russia without Stalinism. But they were deployed only late in the war. Vlasov and some of his men were brought home at war's end and executed. Nor did harmony reign universal inside the Soviet heartland. Drunkenness, looting, food riots, arson, and panic erupted in the early days of the invasion. So did collaboration with German occupiers in the Baltic states and in western Ukraine, where religious and political passions turned many against the Soviet authorities. Some collaborators took their hate out on Jews and Communists in vile atrocities. Surviving film footage shows local collaborators hacking and beating Jews to death.

The Soviet authorities, for their part, persecuted those it thought guilty of disloyalty, cowardice, desertion, or shirking, and in some cases ineptitude. Executions were unleashed inside the camps, and punishment units composed of prisoners were formed for suicidal missions. A unit called SMERSH (Death to Spies) dealt with real or suspected collaborators. Both sides used death units to kill their own soldiers who fled the enemy onslaught. In July 1942, Stalin issued Order No. 227 ("Not One Step Back"), which resulted in the execution of thousands of retreating Soviet soldiers: it was not made public until 1988.

SACRED WAR AND MODERN MEMORY

Most of the dark story of Soviet wartime atrocities remained unknown to the general population, though some of the vengeful acts would have found popular acceptance. The official view of the war was that of a struggle against "fascism" and a defense of the homeland, a "patriotic war" and a "sacred war." The notion of a sacred or holy war is a contradiction in terms, given war's essence and purpose. But almost all nations, particularly those attacked and invaded, try to sanctify the struggle. The USSR was no exception. The ideology of communism, though not abandoned, was downplayed, the Comintern was abolished, and patriotic slogans replaced international proletarian ones. The official name of the war, the Great Patriotic War, did not contain the words *world, Communist,* or *Soviet.* The cult of the war became the legitimizing cement of the regime. Tapping the emotions of his people, Stalin abolished the Godless League, which had been fighting religion since the 1920s, and arranged a truce with the Orthodox Church. In return, the metropolitan of Moscow publicly announced in 1942 that Stalin was "the divinely anointed leader of our armed and cultural forces leading us to victory over the barbarian invasion." In 1943, the patriarchate was restored. Church reopenings, begun unofficially in 1941–1942, were legalized and attended by multitudes of devout believers.

The Russian land—its rivers, steppes, meadows, and birch forests—provided apt metaphors for wartime culture. "Germans lusted after Russian earth," went the slogan. "Let them each have six feet of it." Popular poems and songs evoked images of a rustic cabin or a hometown street. Women were often represented as defenseless, menaced, or victimized by a German. There was nothing false about this: women and children were being slaughtered by the thousands in cold blood, a fact graphically shown in newsreels and in feature films such as *Rainbow* (1944). Stalin enlisted culture and history in the war effort in a November 6 radio address during the Battle of Moscow, in which he summoned up the image of "the great Russian nation, the nation of Plekhanov and of Lenin, of Belinsky and of Chernyshevsky, of Pushkin and of Tolstoy, of Glinka and of Tchaikovsky, of Gorky and of Chekhov," as well as of the marshals who had fought Napoleon: Suvorov and Kutuzov. Eisenstein's heroic historical film about the Russian repulsion of German knights in the thirteenth century, *Alexander Nevsky,* shelved during the Nazi-Soviet Pact, was rereleased after the invasion. Propagandists refurbished military heroes of the past. Parallels with the French invasion under Napoleon in 1812 were heavily underlined. Dmitry Moor's poster *Then and Now, 1812–1941* showed Hitler with a Napoleonic silhouette lurking behind him. Readers devoured Tolstoy's *War and Peace,* the great saga of 1812.

In war-racked cities, the most mournful late-nineteenth-century strains of Tchaikovsky filled the concert halls and airwaves. Soviet composers turned their talents to war-related subjects—Dmitry Shostakovich's 1942 Leningrad Symphony being the most famous of these. A semiofficial culture expressing the feelings of a people at war unleashed a certain authenticity and creative freedom. Shostakovich and the poet Boris Pasternak (1890–1960) later recalled that the war brought a sense of release and solidarity. A community of shared grief helped to reshape national consciousness. The regime's writers and journalists fomented hatred of the enemy. Ilya Ehrenburg (1891–1967) reduced them to inhuman beasts, and the poet Konstantin Simonov (1915–1979) urged readers to "Kill a German, kill him soon / And every time you see one—kill him."

The popular memory of the war persisted down the decades alongside its ponderous memorialization in state celebrations. The Soviet Union's human losses in this war were forty times greater than those of Britain and seventy times those of the United States, greater indeed than those of all other belligerents combined. Soviet people knew that their collective suffering was colossal. And yet they took pride in being able to endure the unendurable and bring their nation to victory. "Those were our finest hours, the most brilliant time of our lives," some female veterans reported many years afterward. For such people still living decades later, the horrors, recalled with equal vividness, did not blot out the golden glow of that memory.

CHAPTER 37

At the Dawn of the Cold War, 1945–1953

Everybody expected that once victory had been won, people would know real happiness. We realized, of course, that the country had been devastated, impoverished, that we would have to work hard, and we did not have fantasies about mountains of gold. But we believed that victory would bring justice, that human dignity would triumph.
—*Ilya Ehrenburg, Soviet writer, 1964*

Although the roots of the Cold War, a term coined in 1947 by the American journalist Walter Lippman, go back to the revolution itself, the immediate cause was the emergence after the war of two ideologically antagonistic Great Powers. The falling out of victorious allies after a titanic war has many historical precedents. The breach between the USSR on the one hand, and Britain and the United States on the other, had numerous causes. One was the division of liberated Europe into rival zones and their hardening into blocs dominated by the victors. The Soviet physical presence in Eastern Europe, a major theater of recent war, and the Soviet leaders' determination to retain influence there, provoked a negative reaction from the USSR's recent allies. At a deeper level lay mutual suspicion and the incompatibility of the conflicting systems: democratic market societies versus a one-party dictatorship and command economy.

The postwar rivalry over Europe burgeoned into a prolonged global contest involving weaponry, economics, and ideas. Scholars still argue over who bore the main responsibility for the Cold War's onset. There is less controversy over its effects on the USSR. It deepened the conviction of an East-West dichotomy, the fear of foreign aggression, and the talk of Western "decadence" that had informed so much of Russian discourse in the past. The Soviet postwar regime sponsored a vaulting and understandable sense of national greatness and a smugness about Russia's victory over the dark forces of fascism. Upgrading a theme of the 1930s, Stalin invoked the doctrine of Russia as "first among equals" in the Soviet Union to single out the Russian people for special commendation on their mammoth wartime heroism. To Russian chauvinism he joined a retightening of ideological orthodoxy, an austerity program, official optimism, and the magnification of the Stalin cult.

THE BIG THREE: WARTIME ALLIANCE, 1941–1945

When the Germans attacked Russia in 1941, British prime minister Winston Churchill (1874–1965) welcomed Stalin as an ally, and American president Franklin D. Roosevelt (1882–1945) offered Lend-Lease in August 1941. After the Japanese attack on the United States at Pearl Harbor in December 1941, the three powers fashioned the Grand Alliance. Stalin hoped that his allies would mount a cross-channel assault on Hitler's Fortress Europe to deflect some of Hitler's troops from Russia and was unhappy when they chose North Africa instead in 1942. From this point onward he was periodically angered at the lack of a second front, which did not come until D-Day—June 6, 1944. But few other major disagreements among the Allies arose until the spring of 1945.

Allied Diplomacy

Serious interallied diplomacy got underway in 1943, a year of Axis defeats. Conferring at Casablanca in Morocco, Roosevelt and Churchill agreed on an Allied invasion of Europe to relieve the Red Army, which was still taking the brunt of the German war effort. But the Western leaders chose to attack Europe from the bottom first, in Italy, which surrendered in the summer of 1943, although German troops still occupied northern Italy. This choice of operations also angered Stalin, though he readily agreed that Italy was a Western preserve, and he surely expected a quid pro quo in his own future sphere of influence. Before seeing Stalin in person, the Anglo-American leaders convened twice again—at Quebec and at Cairo. Stalin, though invited, did not attend.

The Big Three finally met for a few days in late November 1943 in Tehran, the capital of Allied-occupied Persia, where the utter defeat and unconditional surrender of Japan and Germany took precedence over all other considerations, including those of small nations in East Central Europe. The British and Americans unfolded the second-front plan to invade France and asked Stalin to make war on Japan to speed up victory in the Pacific. He agreed, but at the price of taking former tsarist possessions held by the Japanese: north of Japan, the Kurile Islands and the southern half of the Island of Sakhalin; and on mainland Asia, Port Arthur in Manchuria (see the chapter "Russia on the Barricades: The Revolution of 1904–1907"). The Allies drew up tentative occupation lines for U.S., British, French, and Soviet zones in Germany, with Berlin in the Soviet zone. The future borders sketched out for East Central Europe and Poland largely confirmed Stalin's 1939 conquests in eastern Poland. Although the United States and Britain refused to countenance the Soviet takeover of the Baltic states, these would remain part of the USSR until 1991. Stalin accepted a relatively small share of German territory to occupy, considering the weight of his country's suffering and fighting and the fact that his troops were nearing the gates of German-occupied Poland.

The unstated principle of negotiations was that liberated territories would come under the immediate command of the liberators. This was a crucial issue for

Churchill during his visit to Moscow in October 1944. In view of the Red Army's continuing advances toward the Balkans, he endeavored to ensure some Western presence there by having Stalin sign a "percentages" agreement that assigned various degrees of Soviet and Western influence respectively: in Hungary and Yugoslavia (50-50); Romania (90-10), Bulgaria (75-25), and Greece (10-90). For the Balkans, Churchill's figures corresponded roughly to the proximity of the nations concerned to the eastern Mediterranean, still Britain's lifeline to empire. Within five years, the Soviets would have full control of Hungary, Romania, and Bulgaria and a zero presence in Yugoslavia and Greece.

Endgame at Yalta

The Big Three's Yalta Conference of February 1945, held in the Crimea and hosted by Stalin, has been the subject of acrid controversy, arising particularly from those American and East European statesmen and scholars who saw it as a "sellout" of Eastern Europe to communism. It was hardly that. In many ways, the Yalta Conference was a detailed footnote to Tehran, where the future of Eastern Europe had been roughly outlined. Of enormous importance is what happened between the two conferences. Out of the morass of complicated events, two stand out. The first was the sheer military presence of the Red Army in East Central Europe and now approaching Germany's heartland. The second was the hardening of Stalin's determination to create at the very least a Poland friendly to the USSR, or at best to have a Communist satellite there, and to have friendly regimes elsewhere in East Central Europe, which the Soviets perceived as a geopolitical security belt. These regions had in the recent war been either allies of Hitler or corridors for his invasion of the USSR. The Western Allies, the regimes in exile, and the local political forces could not modify either the presence of the Red Army or Stalin's design in any significant way—short of a war against the USSR, which few people wanted. The trick was to limit the expansionist juggernaut through diplomacy. On the Polish issues, Stalin had remained stubborn. He had brazenly denied the massacre of Polish offices at Katyn in 1940, broken relations with the Polish government in exile in London, and promoted his own coterie of Polish Communists as a provisional government in the recently liberated town of Lublin.

The mood was heady in the opulent Livadia Palace at Yalta, where the meetings were held. Victory was no longer in doubt, and the Soviet position was much stronger than it had been at Tehran. Stalin was more assertive, Churchill more wary than ever of Stalin, and Roosevelt acted the careful mediator, suspecting Churchill's ambitions to reconstruct the broken British Empire as much or more than he feared Stalin's clearly discernable expansive aspirations in East Central Europe. Stalin's main concession on Poland was to accept members of the exiled government and to hold free elections—later—of anti-Nazi and democratic elements. The key to this was: Who would ratify "democratic" credentials? In other major agreements, the final lines of partition in Germany placed Berlin in the Soviet zone though the powers jointly occupied it. The participation of the Soviets in the war against Japan was codified, and Stalin agreed to join the American-sponsored United

Nations with three seats: for the USSR, Belorussia, and Ukraine. A few months later, in April, Roosevelt died, and a month later the war in Europe ended.

LOWERING THE IRON CURTAIN

The Allies met again in July 1945 at Potsdam, outside Berlin, to settle matters pertaining to the defeated Germany. The American administration had become incensed at Soviet-sponsored political repressions in Poland and the Balkans. The new president, Harry Truman, had cut off Lend-Lease the day after victory in Europe. At Potsdam, informed that the Americans' powerful new atom bomb was ready to deploy, Truman showed a tough face. The USSR entered the war against Japan on August 9, as previously agreed, and after the first U.S. atom bomb attack on the city of Hiroshima on August 6. Japan surrendered on September 2, and World War II came to an end. The Soviets played no role in the occupation of Japan, which was a completely American affair. Now that the war was over, the wartime cordiality, sometimes forced, sometimes sincere, all but disappeared. Truman stated publicly that there "isn't any difference in totalitarian states. I don't care what you call them, Nazi, Communist, or Fascist." Speeches, correspondence, and diplomatic meetings widened the gap between the two Great Powers—or as Stalin put it, "the two camps."

Churchill, Truman, and Stalin at Potsdam, July, 1945. *Sovfoto/Eastfoto.*

Communist Takeover in Eastern Europe

In the postwar settlement, the USSR took back the part of Poland granted to it at Tehran and pushed Polish frontiers into the old Germany; sliced off a piece of Finland but allowed the Finns independence under a treaty of friendship; reannexed the Baltic countries and a piece of Romania; and took over the ancient Prussian city of Königsberg (renamed Kaliningrad) and its environs. Aside from the German problem, the Communist takeover in East Central Europe was the most important source of friction between the two sides in the Cold War. Winston Churchill, in a celebrated 1946 speech in Fulton, Missouri, described an "iron curtain" that had divided Europe into free and oppressed peoples. Stalin, whose country had suffered the most in the war, replied that much of the area he sought to dominate had formed a staging area for invasion of Russia and called Churchill's speech "a dangerous act calculated to sow the seed of discord among the Allied governments."

As East-West hostilities hardened, so did Soviet intentions. The takeover of East Central Europe was unevenly planned and executed, and the timing and motivation of some decisions are still unclear. To the cities of Poland, Czechoslovakia, Hungary, Romania, and Bulgaria, the Red Army brought with it Liberation Committees made up of East European Communists who had survived the purges in Moscow. Soviet repression of foes (often falsely labeled fascists) began at once. Communists did well in free elections in Hungary and Czechoslovakia, and multiparty systems and coalition governments functioned at first, though Communists or their appointees held key security and communications posts. Later, the peasant, democratic, socialist, and other noncommunist (but emphatically antifascist) parties were purged or dissolved. A well-oiled machine of intimidation, propaganda, and arrest brought Communist-dominated coalitions to power by 1948. In Czechoslovakia, where the USSR and the Czech Communist Party were very popular, internal political rivalry brought a cabinet crisis in early 1948. By the end of the year, a coalition dominated by the Communists gave way to a near Soviet-style regime. Thus the one real democracy of interwar Eastern Europe and the original victim of Nazi aggression fell into the Soviet orbit. The East European satellite nations, self-styled as "people's democracies," remained in that orbit until the revolutions of 1989.

The Sovietization of East Central Europe was the second of three waves of Communist revolution in the twentieth century, the first being the Russian Revolution and its European aftermath and the third the revolutionary liberation movements that would arise in China and the Third World. The East European "revolution" came mostly from the top down, imported and backed by Soviet power. It amplified practices developed in the areas occupied in 1939–1941 during the Nazi-Soviet alliance. An exception was Yugoslavia, where partisans freed the country from German occupation mostly on their own. Their leader, Tito (Josip Broz) (1892–1980), was a staunch Communist but resented Soviet interference in his country. When he asserted independence from Moscow, Soviet propagandists accused him of "Turkish terrorism," and the two regimes broke relations in 1948.

Elsewhere, although tempo and style varied greatly from place to place, the local

NORWAY
SWEDEN
FINLAND
Vyborg
Leningrad
Tallin
(Reval)
North
Sea
DENMARK
Baltic Sea
Riga
Klaypeda
(Memel)
Kaliningrad
Gdansk
Rostock
SOVIET UNION
(USSR)
NETHERLANDS
East
Berlin
EAST
GERMANY
POLAND
Posnan
Warsaw
WEST
GERMANY
BELGIUM
LUXEMBOURG
Halle
Dresden
Lodz
Wroclaw
Lublin
Kiev
Prague
CZECHOSLOVAKIA
Cracow
Przemysl
Brno
Lvov
FRANCE
Kosice
0 100 200 Km.
0 100 200 Mi.
Bratislava
SWITZERLAND
AUSTRIA
Debrecen
Budapest
HUNGARY
Jassy
Cluj
Pursues an independent foreign policy after 1968
Odessa
Zagreb
Pécs
Arad
Rijeka
ROMANIA
ITALY
Adriatic Sea
YUGOSLAVIA
Belgrade
Not aligned with USSR
Bucharest
Constanza
Split
Nish
Black
Sea
Varna
Kotor
BULGARIA
Sofia
Burgas
Closely aligned with Soviet policy
Tirana
Durres
ALBANIA
Vlone
TURKEY
GREECE
Soviet satellites
Communist regime outside the Soviet Bloc from 1948
Aligned with China; no contact with USSR after 1961

Postwar Europe.

Communist parties nationalized industry, planned the economy, dispossessed landowners, collectivized the peasants, neglected the consumer, persecuted clergy, and controlled information and culture. In the late 1940s and early 1950s, they arrested alleged nationalists, or "Titoists," and tried and executed them in a grisly replay of Moscow in the 1930s. The heavy Soviet influence was organized through its embassies, local Communist parties, police forces, and the 1949 Council of Mutual Economic Assistance, centered in Moscow. A Communist Information Bureau, or Cominform, was established to coordinate the ruling Communist parties in power and others around the world.

Land reform brought a long-overdue economic adjustment to the countryside, especially in Poland and Hungary, where church and rural elites had held sway. But the collectivization of agriculture was so unpopular that some of the regimes had to roll it back. The Communist struggle with the churches was especially harsh, particularly in Catholic countries. Stalinism was doubly galling to the those people in the satellites who had known a good deal of personal, intellectual, and economic freedom, if not much democracy. Repression and periodic acts of state violence were not wholly new to some of these regions but were now institutionalized under a foreign yoke. Intellectuals and creative spirits were persecuted and subjected to the petty tyrannies of intolerant regimes in Warsaw, Prague, Budapest, Bucharest, and Sofia. As a Hungarian Politburo member put it in the late Stalinist period: "We have to struggle against capitalist ideology in people's consciousness, in morals and habits. . . . We have to use all possible means to reeducate our people in a socialist spirit: schools, propaganda, arts, literature, movies, and all of forms of popular cultural activities have to serve this aim." Post-Stalin defections and revolts would provide commanding evidence of mass disaffection with the satellite system.

East-West Confrontations

Other episodes aggravated Soviet-Western friction. In Persia (Iran), Soviet troops overstayed the end of the war and tried to set up a Communist enclave in the corner adjacent to Soviet Azerbaijan and populated by Iranian Azeris. Moscow, in the tsarist tradition, also pressured Turkey for territory and special rights in the Black Sea straits. Both moves were geopolitical probes made partly to offset British hegemony in the Middle East; the first also related to a desire for Iranian oil. In both cases, the United States forced the USSR to back down in 1946. The resumption of civil war in Greece between Communist and anticommunist forces in 1946 and an upsurge of Communist electoral strength in Western Europe, neither with much Soviet support, brought swift responses from the United States in 1947: in March, the Truman Doctrine, promising military aid to governments endangered by outside pressure or armed minorities (read Communists); in June, the Marshall Plan of economic aid to Europe to hasten recovery and thus weaken Communist party appeals; and in July, the doctrine of "containment" publicly outlined in an article by George Kennan, diplomat and expert on Soviet affairs. Containment was a policy of stopping the spread of communism to any part of the globe.

In 1948, responding to what they considered Soviet breaches of economic agreements in the eastern occupation zone of Germany, the Western Allies began combining their zones. In spring and summer 1948, they issued a common currency and prepared for a West German state as a potential rearmed security partner separate from the Soviet zone. Alarmed, Stalin ordered a blockade of supplies into the Western Allies' zones of jointly occupied Berlin. The Americans and British answered with the massive Berlin Airlift of 1948–1949, which delivered adequate provisions. Stalin lifted the blockade, and the Western victors went on in 1949 to form a North Atlantic Treaty Organization (NATO) and a Federal Republic of Germany. In that year, Soviet policy responded by transforming the Soviet zone into a German Democratic Republic (or East Germany), run by German Communists. In response to NATO's efforts to rearm West Germany, Stalin's successors in 1955 created the Warsaw Pact, which bound all the satellites together in a military alliance. For four decades there would be two Berlins, two Germanies, two Europes, two global powers.

Communism in Asia

Events in East Asia underlined the widening global polarity between East and West. China "fell" to the Communists in 1949, and few Americans were willing to see this as anything but a Stalinist plot and Beijing as an advanced outpost of aggressive Soviet Communism. In fact, Stalin played a double role almost to the end, officially backing Chiang K'ai-shek and the Kuomintang Nationalists while unofficially aiding the Chinese Communists led by Mao Zedong. Mao had been in the wilderness for twenty years, building his bases and fighting both the Japanese and the Kuomintang. When civil war broke out anew between Communists and the Nationalists in 1946, Mao received little help from Stalin, a fact noted by Mao then and later. The Communists took power in China in October 1949, and the Kuomintang set up a regime on the island of Taiwan. Soon afterward, Mao and Stalin signed a treaty of friendship and alliance in Moscow, which set off a tremendous fear in the West.

Anticommunist fear intensified at the outbreak of war in Korea in 1950. The origins of this war lay in the postwar division of the peninsula between two mutually hostile regimes: a pro-Soviet Communist one in the north and a pro-Western capitalist one in the south. When the North Korean regime made plans to invade the south, Stalin, after several vetoes, approved. The North Koreans invaded South Korea in June 1950, the Americans responded under United Nations auspices, and Communist China sent troops in to push back UN forces. A 1953 truce ended the hostilities, and Korea has remained divided ever since.

Cold War and the Superpowers

Militarily, the Soviet Union was inferior to the combined Western powers in the first few years of the Cold War, partly because the Americans possessed the atomic bomb, whose frightful destructiveness had been displayed in the 1945 bombing of Hiroshima and Nagasaki. The Soviet effort to develop an atomic bomb flowed from the work of prewar nuclear scientists assigned to the project during the war when Stalin learned through espionage about the British and American projects. After Hiroshima, Soviet research accelerated. Soviet physicists, assisted by captured German scientists and aided by crucial information supplied by secret agents working in American laboratories, were set up in secure labs far in the interior. At Chelyabinsk-40 in Siberia, tests were conducted and the first atomic explosion set off in August 1949. The creation of a hydrogen bomb followed in 1953. These events marked the USSR's rise to superpower status in weaponry. They also reinforced the habit of pouring investment into megaweapons at the expense of the rest of the economy and to neglecting health, safety, and environmental concerns. In terms of global power, the presence of atomic weapons of mass destruction in the hands of both superpowers created what came to be called the Balance of Terror.

The mental patterns established on both sides of the Cold War in the years 1945–1950, institutionalized and perpetuated by "threat inflation" (the tendency to exaggerate the enemy's forces), persisted for decades, even through periods of relaxation of tension. Some historians have blamed the United States for not cooperating with the USSR in the postwar era. Others have placed the blame wholly on the Russians and have lamented American failure to stop the Soviet Union by military force. One-sided arguments over guilt do little justice to the complexity of Soviet and American intentions and to political and psychological realties. Despite claims of recent scholars, following the breakup of the Soviet Union and the opening of Soviet historical sources, that "we now know" the full story of the origins of the Cold War, much remains obscure. Russians and their sympathizers found themselves greatly isolated from the West and genuinely abhorred by most of its peoples, a fact that puzzled the Soviet people but was answered in full by the hate campaign sponsored by their government. In 1948–1952, a Soviet-sponsored international peace movement to ban nuclear weapons, assisted by a gigantic propaganda campaign, sought to persuade world opinion of the USSR's peaceful intentions. At home, Cold War passions were translated into harsh domestic policies.

THE CULTURAL POGROM

The Soviet Union's civilians and returning soldiers in 1945 expected from the government gratitude for their wartime efforts and some improvement in their lives. But the official mood turned icy after the exuberant celebrations, and an aura of vigilance and suspicion prevailed. Security agents and the tourist guides they appointed kept track of foreign diplomats and journalists. With rare exceptions, intimate association and marriage with foreigners were punished. For Westerners, the frosty and exotic air of Moscow, replicated in the satellite capitals, gave life to one of the most popular of all Western fictional genres, the Cold War spy novel, which depicted life behind the Iron Curtain as one of intrigue, provocation, entrapment, and sexual seduction by police agents.

The slight wartime relaxation in cultural oversight continued for a while after the war but was blasted away by triumphalism and xenophobia, or antiforeignism. A backlash against "unpatriotic" or "rootless" culture took shape as the *zhdanovshchina,* named after its principal witch hunter, Andrei Zhdanov (1896–1948), Politburo member, Leningrad party boss, and the nation's ideological watchdog. He reinforced the rule of party over art and of "mass interest" over individual artistic expression. To Zhdanov, "incorrect art" or imitation of the West was sabotage.

In 1946 the party attacked the popular writer Mikhail Zoshchenko (1895–1958) for a satirical piece that was seen as mocking Russian fairy tales, Soviet life, and Communist values and assaulted the poetry of Anna Akhmatova (1889–1966), held by victims of the terror as the recorder of its agonies. Eisenstein had to apologize for a film about Ivan IV that offended Stalin and secret police chief Lavrenty Beria (1889–1953). The party newspaper, *Pravda,* escalated attacks on theaters and children's literature and warned of "attempts by literary riffraff to poison our youth." Zhdanov found subversion even in music. He assailed Shostakovich and Sergei Prokofiev (1891–1953) in public for "formalism," here meaning abstraction, atonalism, and excessive complexity traceable to the modernism of the West. Music, said Zhdanov in 1948, must be melodious, national in content, rooted in the people, and accessible to them. Jazz bandleaders were arrested, their groups dissolved or toned down, and saxophones were confiscated as the emblem of a decadent civilization.

Writers concocted novels lacking any conflict. Composers turned out cheerful operettas, film musicals, and songs of patriotic optimism. Nostalgia, vividly represented by fabricated folk music, became the handmaiden of Soviet stability. Some hard sciences also felt the chauvinistic barrage. Trofim Lysenko (1898–1976), trumpeting his "Marxist" theory of plant genetics, continued to assault competent scientists (some of whom died in camps) for their "enslavement" to Western theories. He would dominate Soviet biology for two more decades. His theories of acquired characteristics rested on a few successes in plant breeding, weak references to old and discredited biology, and a failure to understand genetic structure. Politics defeated empirical research, and the science of genetics suffered along with the jailed geneticists.

The revival of anti-Semitism, another byproduct of the Cold War, was fueled by official nationalism and the desire of non-Jews for more upward mobility. The relevant catch phrase of the cultural pogrom was "rootless cosmopolitanism," the sin of persons devoid of mystical attachment to the land, "un-Russian" though bearing a Russian name, and inclined to exalt foreign culture. Many Jews were replaced in jobs by "real" Russians, especially in the high ranks of state service. After the creation of Israel in 1948, which the Soviet government endorsed to reduce British power in the Middle East, crowds of Moscow Jews enthusiastically greeted the new Israeli envoy Golda Meyerson (later Meir), an act officials regarded as disloyal. The anti-Jewish campaign turned ugly: the wartime Antifascist Jewish Committee was disbanded in 1948, its members arrested as Zionist spies and almost all executed, as were a number of Jewish writers. Shlomo Mikhoels (b. 1890), star of the Yiddish stage, was murdered in January 1948 in an arranged accident, and his theater and other Jewish cultural establishments were closed. Many feared a repeat of the

Holocaust. The Soviet authorities, unlike the Nazis, never launched a racial doctrine or even admitted anti-Semitic policies, which directly contradicted Marxist ideology. Because of this, some Western admirers of the Soviet system could not bring themselves to believe in its crimes.

TOWN AND COUNTRY, MEN AND WOMEN

The physical wartime devastation of the western Soviet Union, equal to that in all the rest of Europe, left a staggering vista. Some two thousand towns and cities, seventy thousand villages, one hundred thousand collective farms, two thousand state farms, thirty-two thousand industrial enterprises, and half of the nation's railroad net had been burned, dynamited, bombed, flooded, or razed to the ground. Much of the destruction had been culturally rather than tactically motivated: the Germans plundered cultural treasures and vandalized art museums, palaces, and the nineteenth-century homes of novelist Tolstoy and composer Tchaikovsky, among others. Twenty-five million homeless people lived in dugouts or skeletal ruins, waiting for new housing. Food rationing until 1947 and overcrowding made life dreadful by any standard.

Rebuilding of homes, farms, and factories began as soon as an area was liberated. Industrial reconstruction was assisted partly through the transfer of German facto-

Soviet citizens living in dugouts during and after World War II. *Sovfoto/Eastfoto.*

ries to Russia and Ukraine, where they were reassembled. The Third Five-Year Plan (1938–1942) had been curtailed by the war; the Fourth (1946–1950) aimed at recovering prewar levels of growth and output and surpassing all previous plans. The Soviet Union chalked up some impressive achievements, however doctored were the official figures. While the depleted male work force toiled in the factories, millions of women and war prisoners labored at rebuilding homes and other edifices. Labor discipline was firmly reestablished. Weapons production was upgraded, and production was again tilted toward iron and steel, machine building and mining. Consumer goods and agriculture remained neglected orphans. A currency devaluation in 1947 reduced or wiped out the savings of those who hoarded cash. On the credit side, people long remembered the policy of lower food prices in the last years of Stalin.

In 1946 a drought in the countryside caused an immense grain shortfall. In response, the government raised food prices, extracted grain from the collective farms, and reduced the quality of bread. Hunger stalked the war-ravaged land: an estimated 2 million starved to death, and millions more suffered from malnutrition. Peasants who stole food were arrested. The government, whose official culture lauded the sainted bread thief of Victor Hugo's *Les Misérables* (1862), sent thousands of men, women, and children Jean Valjeans into exile. Yet novels, operettas, and films released at the time mythologized the economic life of rural Russia. During the lax period of the wartime and the immediate postwar period, collective farmers had pushed the fences of their private plots into the common plowland. Starting in 1946, the state sent out demobilized soldiers to chair collective farms and assigned a special agency to restore work norms and recover state lands.

In 1950, Nikita Khrushchëv, the central figure of midcentury Soviet agriculture, promoted the cumbersome and unpopular brigade system of large, unwieldy work gangs. He also consolidated a quarter-million collective farms into about 125,000 much larger ones within two years. Khrushchëv's idea of building agro-cities, rural conglomerates of five thousand farmers quartered in apartment buildings, was rejected. Though peasants produced efficiently on their private plots, the regime sought solutions to a drooping rural economy in gimmicks, avoiding central problems of lagging investment and individual incentive.

In factory towns—behind the idealized reports in Soviet journalism and fiction—overcrowding, drunkenness, crime, and unrest abounded. Heavy industrial investment meant a continued low standard of living. The wartime ruination of apartment houses, in short supply ever since the 1930s, brought barracks or dorm living and tiny residential spaces for most families and virtually all single people. For married couples squeezed into a small room with a child and a parent, this meant little privacy for conversational or sexual intimacy; for dating or courting couples it brought a continuous quest for private space.

Soviet women suffered grievously in the postwar decade. Those in uniform were demobilized, and many in industry were demoted to make way for returning male veterans, a familiar story in other states as well. Women in the work force were also saddled with housekeeping and child care—a virtual double shift. The greatest emotional burden for women was the loss in the war of the men they loved—husbands, sons, fathers, brothers, lovers, and fiancés. In 1939, there were 7 million more women than men in the Soviet Union; in 1959, about 20 million more. The unremitting facts of demography sentenced millions of widows and single women to a life without marriage, and for many, without sexual and romantic partnership. The suffering was passed on to children, legitimate or otherwise, who had to grow up without a father. A whole new wave of orphans and homeless children threatened to replicate the terrible problems of the 1920s. And a new generation of one-parent children enlarged the pool of alienated youth too young to have fought in the war, but victims of it nonetheless.

POSTWAR BLUES: MALAISE AND COUNTERCULTURE

Postwar police documents published since the collapse of the Soviet empire indicate that most Soviet citizens in the aftermath of the war worked hard and greeted with relief the end of the ghastly fighting. Disappointed at the lack of a better life after victory, they also grumbled bitterly, though this rarely amounted to political dissidence. Muscovites above the age of twenty-five or so focused on earning a living, finding a better job, getting into a bathhouse once a week (for example, only three serviced the heavily populated Taganka District), buying a new five-tube Salute radio set, and putting some form and substance to a life. Provincials could hope for much less and were mostly denied residence in the capital. At a 1946 "film festival," rural club members were treated to such riveting films as *Socialist Animal Husbandry* and *For a Big Potato Harvest.* Official culture encouraged a return to normality and celebrated comforts and consumer goods even though these were in short supply. The regime continued to provide goods and status symbols to the Soviet middle class in return for political loyalty, which one scholar described as "the big deal" of Stalinist society. When one considers the immense suffering that Soviet people endured in the war and the titanic rebuilding efforts they expended afterward, it is hardly surprising that they longed for some comfort and respite from great struggles and heroic deeds.

Among youth in the big cities and provincial towns, a handful turned to outright opposition, were caught, and were executed or interned. Others formed illegal intellectual circles. Future sculptor Ernst Neizvestny recalled: "We did not pose any political questions, we did not in any event have political conceptions. . . . We all intended, however, to educate ourselves well, and the reading of, say, Trotsky, or Saint Augustine, or Orwell, or Berdyaev was punishable. Therefore we needed a conspiracy." For the vast majority of young people, however, a kind of cultural malaise developed that led them to embrace foreign goods and styles, a harmless gesture of resisting the state's ideological purity. Though the counterculture's models were the gilded youth of the Soviet elite, its troops were the kids of missing parents and tiny flats and its outposts the streets and apartment house yards. Cramped housing led youths into the courtyards and sometimes into gangs, where informal subcultures arose from a need for identity and assertion. The official culture of collective farm feasts, wartime exploits, industrial melodramas, and reworked folk songs did not connect with the new generation of youngsters, who instead sought adventure, escape, and entertainment. The long-time cultivation of American jazz among many and recent exposure to it during the war made it the prime commodity for youth, the more so after the regime forbade it.

U.S. films confiscated by Soviet troops in Europe, in spite of censors' editing, led Soviet boys to emulate lions of American cinema—John Wayne as cowboy, James Cagney as gangster, and Johnny Weismuller as Tarzan—while their sisters swooned over the romantic Hollywood singing star Deanna Durbin. Those who copied Western dances, manners, and dress codes were dubbed *stilyagi* (from the word *style*). Party activists harassed them sporadically, without much success in changing their habits. The symbolic flirting with the national enemy was not directly political, but it did begin a long process of alienation that culminated in the rock revolution of later decades. The state had managed to engage large sections of the population in a revolution, socialist construction, and a war of survival. That power of engagement began to diminish as a new generation came of age in the postwar years.

EXIT STALIN

After the war, the Stalin cult reached a climax. In the late 1940s, Stalin's utterances on science, history, and culture became more oracular, and monuments to him proliferated in the USSR and in the public squares of Warsaw, Sofia, and Prague. "Court" painters portrayed him as a wise and sainted ruler of the socialist peoples radiating benevolence and love, and Stalinist films, employing monumental settings, mythologized his role as a wartime leader of genius. Stalin glorified the army in the abstract but out of fear and spite obscured the exploits of the star commanders and restored to the party the political powers in the army that had been withdrawn during the war. The Communist Party itself was not restored to its pre-1936 eminence until after Stalin's death. In the semiprivate round of life at the Kremlin court, Stalin's revelries were marked by greater self-indulgence, social sadism, and personal despotism. Party, state, military, and secret police leaders vied for his favor.

Political Struggles

Kremlin politics in this period remain shrouded in mystery, owing partly to lack of archival evidence, partly to the secrecy of the participants, and partly to Stalin's often puzzling behavior. His capriciousness grew in his last years. A key figure then and later related that the supreme leader was not always fully aware of what went on around him, and this situation played into the machinations of his underlings, who savagely plotted against each other.

Andrei Zhdanov, successor of the murdered Kirov in 1934 as Leningrad party chief and the main postwar ideological and cultural enforcer, was a major figure in Soviet politics until his death in 1948. One theory about Zhdanov speculates that he was a force for moderation, though the evidence is sparse. A rival force in the party emerged around two men who had risen to political prominence after the war: Lavrenty Beria, the minister of internal affairs (MVD, successor of the NKVD, the secret police), and Georgy Malenkov (1902–1988), deputy premier. Scholars claim that a clanlike rivalry arose between the Zhdanov and the Malenkov-Beria party factions. When Zhdanov died in 1948, his party organization was decimated by blood purge in the so-called Leningrad Affair, in which over two thousand of the city's officials lost their posts between 1949 and 1952. Six of Leningrad's nine leading functionaries were shot, and three were sent to the Gulag. They were followed by dozens of lesser figures. The Leningrad Affair was apparently another fabricated conspiracy. Its most notable victim was the Soviet planning tsar since 1938, Nikolai Voznesensky (1903–1950). His views on development differed from Stalin's, but his execution was probably a result of political intrigues. Similar purges occurred in other locales as well.

In 1952, the Nineteenth Party Congress assembled. It was the first since 1939, reflecting the party's decline in power vis-à-vis General Secretary Stalin. The party changed its name from the All-Russian Communist Party (of Bolsheviks) to the Communist Party of the Soviet Union (commissariats had been renamed ministries after the war). The Politburo, renamed Presidium, more than doubled its size—from eleven to twenty-five members, plus eleven alternates—thus weakening it. For greater personal control, Stalin also insisted on a small bureau of nine within it, and a yet smaller group of five or so within that, whose composition he changed at each meeting. Among the members of the new Presidium were the prewar Politburo incumbents Stalin, Molotov, Voroshilov, Kaganovich, Khrushchëv, and the resilient Armenian Anastas Mikoyan (1895–1978), minister of foreign trade from 1926 to 1949 and a high official in every regime from Stalin's onward. The postwar promotees were Beria and future prime ministers Malenkov, Nikolai Bulganin, and Alexei Kosygin.

At various points in his reign, Stalin had placed certain men in prominent positions—Kaganovich, Molotov, Voroshilov in the 1930s; Zhdanov, Beria, and Malenkov in the 1940s—but had never named an heir apparent. Malenkov, from his rank as second secretary of the party and the prominent public role that Stalin gave him during the congress, seemed to be the current favorite. Stalin retained his old posts as General Secretary of the party, assumed in 1922, and prime minister, assumed in 1941. The congress changed nothing of substance in the Soviet political and social system except to allow new party leaders to rise and to frighten some of them. Some of Stalin's actions were so bizarre as to be inexplicable. He kept Molotov, Malenkov, and Mikoyan on the Presidium, and yet from time to time would announce to party assemblies that they were spies in the service of foreign powers. Also characteristic of Stalin's arbitrary and seemingly irrational behavior was his arrest of Molotov's wife and Lazar Kaganovich's brother (who was shot) while those men sat at the pinnacle of power.

On the eve of Stalin's death, a new wave of repression seemed about to break: in

December 1952, in a grotesque scenario resembling a Renaissance poisoning melodrama, nine Kremlin physicians, most of them Jews, were arrested and accused of murdering Zhdanov and other figures with the aim of overthrowing Soviet power at the orders of a Zionist organization. Some citizens were ready to believe in a "Jewish plot." But Stalin died before this contemptible case could unfold into a wider terror, which many feared. On March 1–2, 1953, Stalin suffered a massive brain hemorrhage, passing away on March 5. In a solemn ceremony, he was buried in the mausoleum beside the mummy of Lenin. Ironically, the sense of relief on the part of those who had helped create the cult of Stalin contrasted with the genuine mourning of the masses who had come to believe in it. The grief of millions of Soviet citizens at the loss of their leader is well attested. A recent interviewee recalled the spontaneous sorrow of a provincial town. "By the central parade stand there were piles and wreaths and flowers, portraits of Stalin . . . and tears, tears, tears." All through the subsequent regimes, people taught for years to say "Thank you, Comrade Stalin" would look back on Stalinism as a golden age, much to the puzzlement of outsiders.

Stalinism and Totalitarianism

The Soviet system under Stalin was a murderous dictatorship crowned by an elaborate cult of personality, a concentration of Stalin's power, periodic terror, and an authoritarian and patriarchal political culture that, because of the state's intrusion into so much of life, pervaded social relations. The state wrought dogmatic control over science, learning, education, and culture and spawned chauvinistic outbreaks of Great Russian arrogance and anti-Semitism even though it verbally repudiated them. Stalinism was a deeply conservative structure of privilege for a ruling class that rejected many of the utopian ideals of the revolution. But that same system industrialized the country on an unprecedented scale and defeated the greatest invasion force ever assembled in history. Not a limitless despot, Stalin could never control everything in the vastness of the Soviet Union and its imperial hinterland. All kinds of power struggles, debates, intrigues, and even disobedience ran rampant. But Stalin did have the power to end struggle, silence debate, and punish dissent on an immense scale, and he used that power awesomely and unlike any other ruler of modern times.

Is there any possible alternative to an exclusively harsh historical verdict on the bloodthirsty, power-hungry, vindictive potentate Stalin and on the system over which he presided? In an oft-cited moral cost analysis posed in Dostoevsky's 1880 novel *Brothers Karamazov,* no program, "progressive" or otherwise, can justify the death of even one child, and Stalinism caused the death of hundreds of thousands of children. Yet people of widely divergent political persuasions have credited Stalin and his regime with the forced rapid industrialization of the country that was tested successfully in the crucible of war; with cultural growth and social mobility among the old lower classes of Russia and some nonliterate traditionalist nationalities; with economic security for the bulk of the population plus opportunity within the system; and with rhetorical promotion of peace and social justice. These achievements help explain communism's long-lasting appeal to intellectuals in the West and insurgent movements elsewhere. Against them must be set two things. First, the question, unanswerable but impossible to ignore: Could not some of the above have been reached by a Russian government organized along different lines? Second, the Soviet Union, among other abominations during Stalin's quarter century of governance, harbored an immense penal complex in which literally millions of innocent people suffered the agony of a living death or met a horrible premature one. By the most recent tabulations, the camp population grew from about 1.5 to 2.5 million from 1945 to 1950.

A theory of totalitarianism, first aired in the 1930s and achieving prominence in the 1940s, equated Hitlerism and Stalinism because of a structural similarity between them that overshadowed the economic, social, and cultural differences. Put simply, totalitarian regimes aspired to and partly succeeded in deploying power, controlling resources, and regimenting the lives of their people through indoctrination, mobilization, and terror—all beneath the umbrella of a one-party state. In this view, the "total state" resembled an army in terms of rank and discipline but intruded more deeply into minds and personal lives. Extreme and sometimes fictionalized forms of the totalitarian theory portrayed Soviet citizens as mindless slaves paralyzed by terror. In 1948, the British socialist and anticommunist novelist George Orwell drew a nightmarish picture of a communist slave society of mobilized "proles" (proletarians) in the antiutopian novel *1984.* Both the sophisticated theories and the fictional versions led outsiders to see the Soviet state and party as the only units worth studying, to see society as a mere extension of the state, and to see culture as its propaganda arm. Though useful in approaching the political machinery of the USSR under Stalin and in making some justifiable comparisons, the totalitarian model is much less useful—and often counterproductive—in studying the inner experience and values of the mass of the population.

CHAPTER 38

Khrushchëv and the Decline of Stalinism, 1953–1964

Here we'd overthrown the monarchy and the bourgeoisie, we'd won our freedom, but people were living worse than before. No wonder some asked, "What kind of freedom is this? You promised us paradise; maybe we'll reach paradise after death, but we'd like to have at least a taste of it here on earth. We're not making any extravagant demands. Just give us a corner to live in."

—*Nikita Khrushchëv, on his efforts to improve housing*

Stalin's successor made a dramatic effort to vilify the deceased dictator and to erase some of the more brutal aspects of the Stalin era. In doing so, he opened up floodgates that he would have preferred to leave closed. The successor was Nikita Sergeevich Khrushchëv, born in 1894 of a Russian peasant family living near Kursk. Having worked as a boy in Ukrainian mines, he later boasted that when he read Emile Zola's nineteenth-century novel *Germinal,* about industrial violence in a French mining town, he could empathize with the miners from personal experience. In 1918 Khrushchëv fought as a Bolshevik in the civil war; in later years he claimed to have stopped an anti-Jewish pogrom. After attending workers' school, he came under the patronage of Moscow party boss Lazar Kaganovich and in the 1930s headed the city's party organization and oversaw the harrowing construction of the Moscow Metro. During the war he coordinated partisan activity and grew disillusioned with Stalin's bungling and refusal to evacuate Kiev as the Germans approached. In 1938–1949, with a gap in 1947, he headed the Communist Party in Ukraine and was prime minister there after 1944. Khrushchëv carried out a savage purge against the Ukrainian party and state leadership and the intelligentsia. Though his rule in postwar Ukraine was threatened in 1947, when Kaganovich took over leadership to conduct a hard policy line, the more popular Khrushchëv regained his leadership the same year. A Politburo member since 1939, Khrushchëv was recalled to Moscow in 1949, became a Central Committee secretary in 1950, and was designated a specialist in agriculture.

COLLECTIVE LEADERSHIP: DESTALINIZATION OF THE DEED

After Stalin's death on March 5, 1953, Georgy Malenkov, allied with Lavrenty Beria and Vyacheslav Molotov, became both prime minister and party leader. Then on March 14 the top party echelons, fearing the rise of a new personal dictatorship, divided power by making Khrushchëv party chief, later first secretary, and declared a policy of "collective leadership," or rule by committee, a dramatic reversal of Stalin's one-man rule. Beria was arrested in June and put to death before the year was out. This and the shooting of about two dozen other security forces figures were the last known high-level political executions of the Soviet period. Beria's alleged crime was having been a British secret agent since the revolution. His real offense was the potential to create a new secret police dictatorship. The fact that Beria had released the surviving Kremlin doctors and some camp prisoners and had eased up on nationalities did not save him.

Two striking developments occurred during the period of shared power between Malenkov and Khrushchëv. One was a verbal duel that began in December 1954, clearly reflecting competition, in the nation's leading newspapers: *Izvestiya* (*The News,* organ of the Soviet state since 1917 and thus under Malenkov's control) and *Pravda* (*The Truth,* organ of the party since 1912 and under Khrushchëv's control). The papers had rarely diverged before, and some citizens joked privately that there was no truth in *The News* and no news in *The Truth.* Differences erupted when Malenkov charted a "new course" of increased consumer investment and détente—that is, the relaxation of tension with the West—while Khrushchëv was taking a harder line. After a few months of political dancing, the Central Committee, beholden to Khrushchëv, forced Malenkov to relinquish his post as prime minister. The novel thing about Malenkov's 1955 defeat was that he was not shot and was allowed to retain high posts, an outcome unimaginable under Stalin. In fact, Khrushchëv went on to adopt many of Malenkov's reformist policies. Khrushchëv made rapid and numerous appointments of his loyal followers to key party posts. Together with the relatively modest new prime minister, Nikolai Bulganin (1895–1975), Khrushchëv began to travel abroad on diplomatic missions, another departure from Stalin's ways. The Western press, ever ready to caricature and save print space, called this duo of heavy-set men K and B, icons of the new Soviet leadership.

The other striking development was an amnesty and release of a mass of political prisoners from the camps, which in 1952 had a population estimated at 2.5 million, about a third of whom were political prisoners. An amnesty of 1953 began the release of prisoners, sending judicial troikas—teams of three investigators—into the camps to conduct inquiries about alleged crimes and to "rehabilitate" the innocent. As a result, two-thirds of the prison camps were closed, and hundreds of thousands of inmates were liberated. Though many of the "rehabilitated" were already dead, this act caused great joy among releasees and loved ones. It also brought bewilderment, even fear, to some. "I became two-faced," recounted a released political prisoner. "Inside I was still afraid. But on the outside I was just like everyone else." The pain of coming home to friends and enemies was captured in Vasily

Grossman's moving novel *Forever Flowing.* The regime curbed but did not end the power of the political police (now called KGB, Committee of State Security) and gave more attention to "socialist legality." Dissidents were no longer shot. But the release process fizzled out in 1962, the KGB and police continued to arrest political offenders, and the reduced Gulag remained in place.

REVELATIONS AND ECHOES: DESTALINIZATION OF THE WORD

Destalinization was the buzzword for the Khrushchëv era in the West, though Soviet people rarely uttered it, even after great revelations about the Stalin era. Destalinization took place on two levels: the political aftermath of Khrushchëv's famous "destalinization" speech of 1956 and a literary-cultural melting of the subarctic ice of the recent past.

The Secret Speech

Khrushchëv, who was given to sensations and shakeups, exploded a bombshell in a speech at the Twentieth Party Congress in February 1956. In the weeks prior to the meeting, Stalin's birthday was not publicly noted, and articles by Presidium member Anastas Mikoyan were less than flattering to his former boss. After the formal deliberations of the congress, Khrushchëv removed visitors, locked the doors, and delivered a four-hour speech unlike any previous party congress address. He riveted the audience with many revelations, including the contents of Lenin's will and his request that the leadership remove Stalin as General Secretary. Next came a selective description of Stalin's crimes: "Stalin," charged Khrushchëv, "organized the concept 'enemy of the people.' The term automatically rendered it unnecessary that the ideological errors of a person or persons engaged in a controversy be proven; this term made possible the use of the cruelest repression." The indictment against Stalin went on: innocent party members jailed and shot, police bestiality, mass terror, economic ignorance, wartime bungling, foreign policy blunders, and an overweening "cult of personality." The inner circle had known about these things, but many of the more than fourteen hundred listeners had heard about them only through innuendo and never officially. The dismay of the newly informed was genuine, as was the anger of some of the old Stalinists.

Khrushchëv knew that eventually some of the truth of the Stalin era would come out, especially with the mass release of prisoners from the Gulag. The destalinization speech gave him the chance to establish his own political image and to differentiate himself from his older colleagues who had played a greater role in the purges. But there were limits: he did not rehabilitate the reputations of Stalin's major purge victims, such as Tukhachevsky, Bukharin, or the murdered Trotsky, who had to wait until near the end of Soviet history. Khrushchëv stressed the Lenin legacy and collective leadership. The speech, though not published at home, was leaked to the foreign press and published abroad, shocking many who had refused to believe in the crimes of the Stalin period, though these were well known in the West. Although it maintained many half-truths and cover-ups, Khrushchëv's speech alienated key members of the Stalinist old guard, who hated seeing so much history revealed. Most immediately, it sent convulsions through the Soviet bloc, which Khrushchëv survived. The good harvest of 1956 helped him stabilize his still shaky tenure. He even softened his attack on Stalin early in 1957. Nevertheless, his enemies in the Presidium hatched a plot to overthrow him.

In June 1957, in the most electrifying political event in years, seven of the eleven Presidium members—led by Malenkov, his ally Molotov, and Khrushchëv's former mentor Kaganovich—voted to remove the first secretary. Their motives were largely defensive, to avoid further demotion or worse. Khrushchëv countered by calling a Central Committee meeting, which rapidly assembled with the help of military transport arranged by World War II hero Marshal Zhukov (1896–1974), who had carried out the arrest of Beria in 1953 and had been named minister of defense in 1955. The Central Committee, packed with Khrushchëv supporters, upheld him and reversed the Presidium decision, which Khrushchëv called an antiparty plot, though in fact it was an intraparty affair. He punished the plotters in a very un-Stalinist manner by appointing Molotov ambassador to Mongolia, posting Malenkov as minister of electric power in the Kazakh Republic, and making Kaganovich manager of a Urals cement factory—hardly kind treatment, but a far cry from the cellars of the Lubyanka Prison or the Gulag. Khrushchëv replaced Bulganin, who had joined them, as prime minister and fired Marshal Zhukov, even though he had given crucial support to Khrushchëv. The war hero was a possible threat, and he also challenged Khrushchëv's polices on political control of the military.

The Twenty-Second Party Congress in 1961 brought further destalinization. The fabled city of Stalingrad was given the new name of Volgograd. And, following the account of a congress deputy of her dream vision of Lenin lamenting Stalin's presence, the latter's body was removed from the mausoleum on Red Square. Molotov was expelled from the party (not to be reinstated until 1984, two years before his death and long after Khrushchëv's). This was one of the most important demotions in Soviet history, considering Molotov's role in the rise of Stalin and the persecution of his enemies, as prime minister, and as a molder of foreign policy. Khrushchëv, at the peak of his power, put through a new party program that predicted in twenty years a prosperity exceeding that of capitalism and the virtual dawn in the USSR of communism, at which time, in Marx's formula, each would work according to his or her ability and be rewarded according to his or her need.

The Thaw

A cultural thaw commenced almost immediately after Stalin's death. The falseness of socialist realist literature (see the chapter "Stalinism: Life Inside the System, 1928–1941") created a wave of revulsion among writers. Nobel Prize–winning novelist Mikhail Sholokhov (1905–1984) characterized it as "gray trash," and wartime poet and journalist Konstantin Simonov (1915–1979) labeled it "bakers' confections." Ilya Ehrenburg (1891–1967) gave a name to the post-Stalin era with his 1954 novel *The Thaw.* Vladimir Dudintsev's *Not By Bread Alone* (1956) shone garish light on the dark sides of the Soviet scientific-industrial bureaucracy. Evgeny Evtushenko's poem "Babi Yar" (1961), a moving elegy to the Jews murdered by the Germans in Kiev in 1941, condemned anti-Semitism in any form, and his "Heirs of Stalin" (1962) warned against a resurgence of Stalinism. Public poetry readings in huge stadiums thrilled audiences. Citizens were now permitted to read, again or for the first time, the works of the once proscribed Soviet writer Isaac Babel and the American Ernest Hemingway (but not modernists such as France's Marcel Proust or Ireland's James Joyce). Alexander Solzhenitsyn's *One Day in the Life of Ivan Denisovich,* published in 1962 with the approval of Khrushchëv, offered a searing portrait of everyday life and death inside a Gulag slave labor camp, going well beyond the selective revelations of the destalinization speech.

By the time of the Second Congress of Writers in 1959, the first since the group's founding in 1934, literature had started to probe long-neglected themes of spiritual life, the bleakness of the countryside, Stalin's victims, and problems of sex, abortion, illegitimacy, divorce, and alcoholism. Other arts followed suit. Theater offered unvarnished truths about bureaucratic arrogance, inequality, corruption, and the hard life of ordinary people. The film world could pay tribute to foreign masters such as Shakespeare and the seventeenth-century Spanish novelist Miguel Cervantes, and war movies presented gritty and realistic pictures of suffering. Jazz was also allowed after years of persecution, and its revival was soon followed by the first wave of American rock-and-roll. Popular songs took on new life in the guitar poetry performances of Bulat Okudzhava (1924–1997), who became an idol for the younger generation. Destalinization entered university and academy. Historians after 1956 produced a spurt of research on the purges. Sociology resurfaced, as did some innovations in political theory. Real debates about policy issues surfaced in a somewhat freer press.

Toward the end of the Khrushchëv period, some of this limited freedom was curbed. Soviet leaders never believed in complete intellectual or artistic freedom. In 1957 Boris Pasternak (1890–1960) produced in his novel *Doctor Zhivago* a moral perspective on the revolution that seemed to make personal life, lyrical poetry, and individual passion as important as class struggle. The protagonist, a poet and physician, sought cures for the soul as well as the body. Published abroad and awarded the Nobel Prize in literature, the novel was roundly condemned by the Soviet authorities. The episode clearly indicated the limits of the thaw. Khrushchëv sent out additional warning signals. At a Moscow art show in 1962, he called the creators of modernist canvases homosexuals and their work excrement. "Are you a pederast or a normal man?" he said to one painter. "We aren't going to spend a kopeck on this dog shit." Khrushchëv's own taste—shaped by ignorance, arrogance, and paternalism—molded state policy. But the undercurrents of cultural change continued to flow strongly in and out of official places. The hunger for Western music and movies in the 1950s proved that many people desired something more than officially sponsored culture. Increased Soviet travel abroad, a tourist inflow, and annual arrivals of serious, Russian-speaking foreign exchange scholars all added to the pace of change, in spite of the persisting apparatus that harassed travelers with surveillance, bugging, and sexual entrapment used to blackmail foreigners into becoming Soviet informants.

REACHING OUT: RELIGION AND ROCKETRY

On the spiritual level, the Soviet regime in the 1950s faced two daunting challenges: social unraveling and religious revival. The first was associated with the postwar generation of hip youth known as *stilyagi,* who continued to display short skirts for girls, zoot-suits for the boys, and a "cool" foreign style for both. The growth of religious activity among believers stemmed from the end of the Stalin cult, the need for solace after the loss of so many in the war, and the work of priests released from the camps. Social and religious concerns, together with the loosening of the repressive apparatus of fear and terror, led the regime to seek new social cement. The cultural mobilization campaigns of the Khrushchëv years, modeled on those of the thirties, were partly designed to recapture the energies and the faith of the masses.

Persecution of religious belief and practice, the harshest measure adopted by Khrushchëv, resembled the periodic campaigns of many major world religions in history to extirpate heresy and enforce an orthodox belief. Soviet antireligious campaigns had been muted during and after the war, and church reopenings had continued. Although antireligious propaganda had never ceased, it escalated in 1959 into an ugly physical assault on churches, two-thirds of which were closed or demolished. In Uzbekistan, 3,567 known mosques were closed. Some clerics were arrested, and a scurrilous press campaign insulted and demeaned religion.

Civic rituals were crafted to divert the young from religious ceremonies. The most popular of them was a new and formal marriage ceremony enacted in ornamental "wedding palaces," the first of which appeared in 1959, designed to endow the wedding with proper Soviet solemnity. Mobilized "volunteer" campaigns also provided the possibility of roping in the young by putting them to work on grand tasks. In the Virgin Lands project, launched in 1954, Khrushchëv set out to increase agricultural production by cultivating previously nonarable land in Central Asia and nearby areas. The project harnessed the energies of young people, portraying them as patriotic pioneers. Over 640,000 volunteers went out in the first three years, over half of them youth recruited by the Young Communist League and sent off with ceremonies and parades. Kazakhstan was deluged by the Virgin Landers, who developed a kind of frontier subculture and unleashed a flood of poems and songs. Young women, facing gender imbalance, were pulled in by marriage hopes as well as genuine enthusiasm.

More consequential in the long run was the Scientific Technical Revolution (STR). The media were enlisted to win over the new generation from religion to science. Cosmonaut Yuri Gagarin (1934–1968), on his return from a space flight, spoke of the heavens he had seen as devoid of any gods. His flights made him a cult

Nikita Khrushchëv in the Virgin Lands, 1964.
Sovfoto/Eastfoto.

figure of STR in the 1960s. Science fiction endowed STR with special appeal. Amid real advances in aerospace technology, youths were enraptured by the 1957 science-fiction novel, *The Andromeda Nebula* by academician Ivan Efremov, who projected a cosmic victory of communism over capitalism and the merger of all races into a humanity living free of conflict or conquest.

STR was no mere state-fashioned myth. The USSR began a rapid climb to scientific and technological eminence. If the metaphors of technical achievements in the 1930s had been automobile, tractor, and electric power, in the 1960s they were rocket, spaceship, and nuclear power. Achievements under Khrushchëv were undeniable and resulted not only in large-scale technologies that functioned impressively but also in global prestige, a scientific elite at home, and popular science awareness fueled by the fantasy-inducing exploits of the cosmonauts. Professional world-class research, subsidized by the state and aided by German scientists taken to the USSR after World War II, could function without the heavy-handed interventions of the Stalin years. I. V. Kurchatov, one of the pioneers of the nuclear bomb, was even invited to speak at the Twentieth Party Congress. Rocket science gradually made Khrushchëv aware of the looming obsolescence of surface warships and long-range bombers. He downsized these branches of the military and in 1957 made intercontinental ballistic missiles (ICBMs) the core of the Soviet strategic arsenal.

A heated "space race" with the United States brought out that old Soviet ambivalence toward American scientific attainments: admiration mixed with envy and a desire to catch up with and surpass the rival. With the release of rocket scientist Sergei Korolëv (1906–1966), who had been sent to the Gulag by Stalin, the Soviet program got fully underway, paralleling the development of ICBMs. The Soviet launch in 1957 of the first space satellite, *Sputnik,* wrought panic in the United States about American science education. *Sputnik* was followed in 1961 by the first man in space, Gagarin; in 1963 by the first woman in space, Valentina Tereshkova (b. 1937); and by a variety of moon shots and animal flights. These achievements—made possible by heavy investment, Russian traditions of excellence in research, and some foreign know-how—challenged America's self-image of its primacy in virtually everything material and technical. Space also afforded Soviet propaganda a victory: Radio Moscow announced that a Soviet satellite would pass over the American town of Little Rock, Arkansas, where local authorities had just barred a young black girl from attending an all-white school.

STR functioned as a badge of modernity, a foe of religion, a legitimizer of Soviet

Khrushchëv with cosmonauts Valentina Tereshkova and Valery Bykovsky, 1963.
Sovfoto/Eastfoto.

power, and a beacon for bored youth. But the massive investment required fed a fiscal policy that neglected consumer industry in favor of militarily related technologies. Overall, in spite of STR, the Soviet Union remained behind the West in scientific and technical development.

IMPERIAL ARENA: THE BLOC

After Stalin's death, Communist regimes in East Central Europe played copycat with Moscow: party reshuffling, collective leadership, amnesties, and cultural thaw. Collectivization, late in coming even where it existed, was slowed down in places. In East Berlin, a workers' strike in June 1953 had to be repressed by Soviet forces, an event that revealed in a flash the unpopularity of the East German Communist government. In 1955, Khrushchëv made peace with Tito and the breakaway Yugoslav leadership, which had been demonized by Stalin. In response to NATO and Germany's 1955 entry into the organization, Khrushchëv organized the Warsaw Pact, a military alliance of the USSR and its satellites.

Khrushchëv's destalinization speech almost immediately sent paroxysms up and down the Vistula and the Danube, where Stalinist leaders were replaced by more reform-minded Communists. The impact was greatest in Poland and Hungary. The Polish Communists were embarrassed by strikes in July 1956 that escalated into an urban uprising in the industrial town of Poznan. The Polish Diet unanimously condemned the rebels and turned on the repressive machinery. But an alarm had rung for the Polish Communist leadership. To stave off further unrest, they turned in the autumn of 1956 to the reformist and nationalist-minded Wladyslaw Gomulka (1905–1982), who had been an anti-Nazi street fighter and had sat in a Polish jail in the Stalin years. Khrushchëv, Molotov, Kaganovich, and Mikoyan flew to Warsaw and sensibly allowed Poland to initiate a few reforms. The compromise, known as the Polish Way to Socialism, allowed for symbolic changes and two major ones: the cessation of collectivization and an independent status for the Catholic Church—the only such one in Eastern Europe.

The Hungarian Communist regime had been harsher than the Polish, and reaction against it was more vigorous. In the summer of 1956, Soviet leaders intervened to depose Hungarian party hard-liners and appointed a moderate, Ernö Gerö (1918–1980) as Communist Party leader. This gesture was insufficient for those Hungarians who wanted changes in the system and not just a new leadership. Heartened by events in Poland, students and other restless forces took to the streets on October 22, 1956, and were fired on by the police. A more radical regime, headed by Imre Nagy (1896–1958), then took power, declared Hungary neutral, withdrew from the Warsaw Pact, and enacted democratic reforms ending the power of police, party, and censors. "We have had enough," proclaimed a workers' council. "We too want socialism, but according to our own special Hungarian conditions." Ruthless intervention ensued: Russian tanks rolled through the streets of Budapest and other towns, ripping up bodies as well as the aspirations of Hungarian anticommunists, who were falsely accused by Moscow of being fascist hirelings. Almost three thousand Hungarians were killed in the fighting. Nagy and other leaders were executed. The resultant anger and revulsion in the West was shared by many leftist intellectuals, the French philosopher Jean-Paul Sartre among them, who resigned in disgust from their parties. Communism survived in East Central Europe, and Khrushchëv laid down an ominous formula, later codified by Brezhnev, that Soviet authorities would not suffer the overturn of "socialism" in that part of the world.

GLOBAL ARENA: VICTORIES AND DEFEATS

Although he had taken a hard line in the duel with Malenkov, Khrushchëv by 1956 was offering innovations in the theory and conduct of Soviet foreign policy. Lenin, while envisioning a final victory of world socialism, had allowed for its peaceful coexistence with capitalism, in the belief that capitalism would be undermined by revolution. Stalin had postulated the inevitability of war between socialism and capitalism and, in a later gloss, of war among capitalist nations. Khrushchëv claimed that the age of peaceful coexistence was indefinite, war was not inevitable, and nuclear war was mutually destructive. "We hold," he said in 1959, "that the struggle must be economic, political, and ideological, but not military." But he also asserted that socialism would ultimately prevail; his oft-quoted informal comment of 1956 at a diplomatic reception, "We will bury capitalism," meant that socialism would inevitably replace moribund capitalism, but it was understood otherwise in the West. Far from ending, the Cold War continued as a global contest marked by a permanent undercurrent of mutual suspicion and a veering between diplomatic relaxation and icy hostility.

The Socialist Rival

Both superpowers, the United States and the USSR, sought influence in the Third World for reasons of strategy, ideology, prestige, and, in some cases, markets and raw goods. Khrushchëv's policy, though often seen as aggressive and duplicitous by the West, hardly differed except in technique and rhetoric from the imperial activity of other powers. All wished to win minds, buy politicians, draft advantageous treaties, and fish in or stir up troubled waters. Complicating matters in this turbulent, poverty-ridden belt of humanity were the immense cultural and historical variation among regions, a postcolonial surge of nation building fed by national pride, lingering regional and tribal conflict, political inexperience, and in some cases a natural instinct to promote neutralism and play off global rivals against each other. These factors practically guaranteed that the superpowers would stumble into embarrassing situations.

Ever since the Baku Congress of Toilers of the East in 1920, Communists had couched their appeal to the non-Western world in terms of the solidarity of underdogs against imperialists, of social justice and racial equality, and of a model for economic development unfettered by the coils of local landlords and capitalists, foreign bankers, and colonial masters. Under Stalin, very little had been done about this. In the postwar world the United States had replaced Great Britain as the imperialist villain in Soviet eyes. Partly in response to this, the USSR began to flex its muscle over far-flung crumbling empires. On his visit to the United Nations in New York in 1960, after some critical remarks on Soviet policy by the British representative, Khrushchëv said: "If the colonialists now rail at me, I am proud of the fact; it means that I am loyally serving the peoples who are fighting for their freedom."

By 1960, Africa churned with political intrigue and violence. The Congo, much abused by Belgian colonial exploiters, tore itself free and almost immediately descended into internal warfare. In a complex scenario of United Nations intervention, the West and the USSR took opposite positions. The latter sided with one of the protagonists, Patrice Lumumba, after whom it later named a university in Moscow. The outcome of the Congo episode was ambiguous, but the Soviet role and its courting of other African nationalist and anticolonial leaders such as Sékou Touré of Guinea and Kwame Nkruma of Ghana allowed Moscow to claim with some justice to be the champions of African peoples against European colonialists. African students appeared in Moscow and Leningrad halls of learning. Some returned home, bolstered by the belief that only revolution and socialism could bring their new nations success. Others, ironically, were disillusioned by the racism they encountered in Russia, and hundreds of African students protested on Red Square in December 1963. The irony was especially heavy in that Soviet propaganda insistently focused on American racism.

The Middle East was more crucial in Russian foreign policy than Africa because of French, British, and American economic and security interests there and the inflammatory nature of relations between Israel and the Arabs. Gamal Abdel Nasser of Egypt (1918–1970), a major figure of Third World nationalism, responded well to the courting of Soviet diplomats. The Soviets financed an important dam project on the Nile River in Egypt, which some Western powers had declined to do, arranged an arms deal, and nourished Nasser's belligerent posturing. When Israel, France, and Britain attacked Egypt in 1956 after it nationalized the Suez Canal, both the USSR and the United States condemned the attack.

India, a leader of neutralism and one of the largest countries in the world, became a major target of Soviet diplomacy soon after Khrushchëv came to power. Highly visible visits of Soviet leaders were supplemented by gifts of steel mills and trade agreements. This friendship and the neutral Soviet policy during India-China border clashes from 1959 to 1962 enraged Communist China and helped fuel a decline in Sino-Russian relations that had begun under Khrushchëv. Soviet influence had some limited successes in Burma, Indonesia, and other Southeast Asian countries, although most of these diminished or later backfired. Indonesia's leader, Sukarno (1901–1970), was courted by Khrushchëv, but its powerful Communist Party was beholden to China. In 1965, a year after Khrushchëv's ouster, an anticommunist Indonesian military regime succeeded Sukarno and, with unofficial American approval, massacred hundreds of thousands of Indonesian Communists, leftists, and nonpolitical ethnic minorities—a tragedy that actually served both the United States and the new Soviet leadership.

The Sino-Soviet conflict was rooted in the arrogant attitudes of the leaders of two enormous countries, whose national interests and recent history tore the feeble bonds of a common ideology. Both regimes adhered to "Marxism-Leninism," a self-serving hyphenation invented by the Communists and adopted by some Western Kremlinologists in the erroneous belief that all Communists had to be alike. But the Stalin–Mao Zedong alliance of 1950 began eroding slowly in the early 1950s in spite of some Soviet foreign aid to the People's Republic of China. At issue was Mao's insistence on a greater share of command and prestige in the international Communist arena and on broader technical and military assistance. Mao, China's leader, also desired strong Soviet backing of China's ambitions to seize a chunk of territory belonging to the Nationalist Chinese government, which had moved to the island of Taiwan in 1945.

Such cooperation did not come to pass. Mao's verbal interference in the European bloc events of 1956, Khrushchëv's destalinization, and personal difficulties between the two men exacerbated the standing concerns, and the mild feud escalated into acrid recriminations. Mao at one point called Khrushchëv a "buffoon." China's spokesmen pointed to the periodic thaws in Soviet-American relations and to Khrushchëv's doctrine of peaceful coexistence as evidence of Soviet betrayal of the revolutionary tradition and its cowardly retreat from the prospect of a just nuclear war against capitalism. Moscow in turn heaped contempt on China's Great Leap Forward of 1957, a frenzied, poorly planned, and badly managed spurt from an agrarian economy to industrialization that failed. Mao excoriated the Soviet leadership when Khrushchëv visited the United States in 1959 and made other accommodating gestures toward the West. After a 1960 withdrawal of Soviet specialists from China and the Sino-Indian border conflict, the insults became ludicrous in their references to historical villainy: according to the Chinese leaders, the Moscow regime was a horde of bandits and a Hitlerite dictatorship. At international Communist conferences, animosity erupted openly between Soviet and Chinese representatives. The two nations were bitter enemies by the time Khrushchëv departed.

The Capitalist Rival

The relatively warm aura of the Soviet thaw produced a few words of goodwill in Khrushchëv's early years, such as the "spirit of Geneva," so called after a friendly diplomatic exchange between the superpowers in that Swiss city in 1955, the first summit meeting since Potsdam in 1945. Khrushchëv signed a treaty in 1955 with the wartime allies that made tiny Austria, a defeated power, politically neutral but placed it socially, economically, and ideologically in the Western sphere. In the same years, the USSR also recognized the Federal Republic of Germany (West Germany) and released batches of war prisoners.

But arctic blasts of enmity regularly pierced the balmy moods. A menacing pall overhung Berlin, Moscow, Washington, and Havana in Khrushchëv's last years, when he faced the American presidents Eisenhower and Kennedy. Phrases such "Sword of Damocles" and "nuclear blackmail" were used on both sides. Fearing that West Germany was about to be armed with nuclear weapons, from 1958 onward Khrushchëv began hurling ultimatums about unifying Germany, ending the Western presence in Berlin, and getting the American army out of Europe.

A "spirit of Camp David" (the summer White House) kept tempers cool during Khrushchëv's American visit in 1959. But before the next summit with Eisenhower, in Paris in 1960, Khrushchëv unveiled the news that an American U-2 intelligence-gathering plane had been shot down in Soviet territory. Its pilot, Francis Gary Powers, survived and was later freed in an exchange for a Soviet agent, but his ruined plane was displayed in a Moscow park as a demonstration of Western perfidy. When Eisenhower, belatedly admitting the flight, refused to apologize, the Paris meeting ended, and relations froze up again.

The most provocative gesture in an almost continuous harangue over the Berlin issue occurred in 1961. Khrushchëv approved East Germany's Communist leader Walter Ulbricht's order to build a wall through Berlin to stop the flow of escapees from the eastern into the western sector of the city. East German flight had publicized the fierce desire of many Germans to bite the apple of good life and freedom in the dynamic city of West Berlin. John F. Kennedy, who was elected United States president in 1960, went to Berlin in 1963 to assure the inhabitants, in a melodramatic speech, that he stood firmly against Soviet plans to incorporate them into the German Democratic Republic: "All free men, wherever they may live, are citizens of Berlin, and, therefore, as a free man, I take pride in the words *Ich bin ein Berliner.*"

Following the Berlin crisis came the Cuban missile crisis of 1962. The United States had long considered Central America and the Caribbean its security preserve. In 1954, it had organized the overthrow of a Guatemalan regime it considered too radical. Thus the United States took alarm when the young radical Cuban lawyer Fidel Castro (b. 1926) led a band of bearded guerrillas through the mountains into Havana in 1959 to evict the corrupt and brutal government of dictator Fulgencio Batista. Ideologically fuzzy at first, Castro quickly turned Cuba into a Communist one-party state, complete with his own brand of repression. Soviet aid poured in, and the break with Washington was complete. Under Eisenhower, a special force of counterrevolutionaries was assembled under Central Intelligence Agency (CIA) auspices in Florida. In April 1961, after Kennedy was in power, the force landed at Cuba's Bay of Pigs, where it met defeat.

In the summer of 1962, Cuban Communist Che Guevara (1928–1967) and Castro's brother Raúl went to Moscow and were promised Soviet protection against future U.S.-sponsored aggression. Khrushchëv, on a visit to the Black Sea, was vividly reminded that U.S. missiles were siloed in Turkey, across a short stretch of water. Soon after, in early September, Khrushchëv secretly delivered nuclear missiles to Cuba designed to protect this island against invasion and to counterbalance the U.S. nuclear ring around the USSR.

In October 1962, after learning of this act, Kennedy issued the USSR an ultimatum to cease further delivery and remove the missiles. Khrushchëv refused to recall a missile-laden flotilla steaming down the Atlantic to Cuba. The American president then threw a "quarantine" of warships around the island and thus confronted both sides with the probability of war. Because of the "balance of terror" and the rigid war plans of both powers, this blockade could have led to a mutual nuclear assault. Khrushchëv backed off, however, the ships returned to Leningrad, and the missiles were removed in return for Kennedy's promise not to launch another Bay of Pigs. Though kept secret at the time, Kennedy also agreed to remove the missiles from Turkey. Military leaders on both sides considered the whole deal a treasonous humiliation. A brief détente ensued, which led to a telephone hot line for emergency communications between the two leaders and a limited nuclear test ban agreement. Some commentators then and later claimed that Khrushchëv launched the Cuban adventure to blackmail the Americans over the Berlin issue; others saw it as a result of pressure from Communist China. But modern scholarship suggests that neither of these factors played a role.

With the many diplomatic crises and freezes, Khrushchëv presented a new kind of Soviet image, if a split image, to the outer world. But his regime also witnessed a gradual opening outward, especially to the mistrusted West. The thaws, cultural exchanges, and meetings of the leaders provided a limited number of people with an equally limited vista into "the enemy's" way of life. Khrushchëv's sojourn in the United States in 1959 embodied the contradictions of the new relationship. His down-to-earth manners appealed to many; his judgmentalism and occasional rudeness repelled many as well (a year later he would remove a shoe and bang it on his desk at the United Nations in New York). At home his motto "Catch up and overtake America" was taken by many to mean "Let's start living like Americans." The most famous icebreaker was the young Texas pianist Van Cliburn, who won the Tchaikovsky Competition in Moscow in 1958. Rave reviews appeared in the staid journal *Soviet Music,* which had always kept its distance from politics and whose foreign coverage had naturally focused on Europe. Van Cliburn was the hero of the hour to millions of Soviet citizens—with the blessing of the regime.

THE PLOT THAT WORKED

Khrushchëv, at the zenith of his power in 1958–1964, was glorified by birthday celebrations, ubiquitous portraits, and the mass publication and ritual citation of his speeches. His rustic style, amusing to some, occasionally embarrassed younger party cadres; 40 percent of the delegates to the Twenty-Second Congress of 1961 had joined after the war. Jokes about leaders were now more freely told than under Stalin. But it was Khrushchëv's actions and policies and not his image that did him in.

Khrushchëv's Reforms

Reforms generally accepted by the population and the other leaders were relegalization of abortion, easing up on divorce, a reduced work week, a more egalitarian school system, and the amplification of welfare benefits. With these came a rise in the standard of living and increased social mobility. Efforts were made to solve the housing crunch through prefabricated buildings, with a stress on quantity, not quality. Even though, when façades began crumbling, people joked about Khrushchëv's five-story buildings as *khrushchoby,* a play on the word *trushchoby* (slums), they were glad to live in them. Some citizens welcomed looser laws on contact with foreigners: marriage with a non-Soviet was now permitted, visas easier to get, traffic in and out less clogged by red tape. The least popular measure, though backed by Khrushchëv's colleagues, was the antireligious campaign.

On other issues, Khrushchëv fell down badly. Foremost among them was agriculture. Recognizing its poor performance, he was unable to better it. He lightened fiscal burdens for peasants but upset them with constant changes; saw a good harvest in 1956 but faced climatic disasters in 1960; promised to surpass the United States in milk and meat output in 1957 but had to renege on it; abolished the Machine Tractor Stations (MTS) but further consolidated farms into unwieldy units. All of it had little discernible effect on farm production. The hastily planned Virgin Lands campaign, though initially successful, was plagued by misuse of resources, soils, and labor, resulting in crop failures. Khrushchëv's 1955 scheme to turn vast areas of arable earth into Iowa-like cornfields to feed both livestock and humans turned sour because of unsuitable soil and climate and popular resistance to eating corn. A hopeful experiment in meat production begun in Ryazan Province turned into a major fiasco, with officials frantically buying, confiscating, and rustling cattle to fulfill inflated quotas. Ryazan's agriculture was ravaged, and the organizer committed suicide, but not before this device of robbing Pëtr to pay Pavel spread elsewhere with disastrous results. Khrushchëv, a tireless visitor to farmlands and a fountain of lectures about crop management, convened mammoth meetings of party leaders and agronomists to brainstorm the persistent production problem. They did not help: agriculture remained the weakest link in the system right up to the end. The USSR had to endure the humiliation, as some saw it, of harnessing American farm advisers and in 1963 importing American wheat to feed their people for the first time in Soviet history.

Industrial life, once the central arena of revolutionary remaking, sagged under the weight of the system, choked by an inordinate web of regulations and state demands that made managers resort to corrupt informal "family" deals among suppliers and local party bosses. In the distribution network, pilfering was endemic. The labor force was aging, and it lacked the enthusiasm of the 1930s. Khrushchëv tried to make industry more efficient and introduced the death penalty for economic crimes such as embezzlement. The Sixth Five-Year Plan of 1956 brought impressive results in steel production, but iron and steel were no longer the crucial products they had been in earlier times. The most successful sectors of the economy were the military and space science industries, based on heavy investment and the use of highly trained and well-paid experts. Consumers, as always, were relatively neglected. Khrushchëv tried to satisfy Moscow shoppers by opening the famous GUM (State Department Store) across from the Kremlin. But goods and services remained inferior or unavailable.

Unlike Stalin, Khrushchëv traveled the country, was well aware of the real economic life of ordinary people, and genuinely wished to alleviate their lot. But his remedies were ineffective, given the nonmarket command economy that he and his colleagues believed in. He also allowed only his own brand of reform. When workers took even moderate measures to challenge the system, they were rebuffed. Food and price riots broke out in a number of places. Things turned violent in 1962 in the southern town of Novocherkassk. In response to wage cuts and a price rise on meat and dairy products—irony of ironies—workers confronted their manager. In the spirit of Marie Antoinette, the eighteenth-century queen of France, he told them to eat jam instead of meat. Demonstrators were shot at by the police, just as in tsarist days, and seventy to eighty people were killed. News about the event was suppressed.

Khrushchëv's most radical economic reform was the 1957 abolition of dozens of the almost 40 central economic ministries and the division of the country into 105 economic regions run by newly formed local Economic Councils. This was an attempt to decentralize the massive command economy. Designed to provide real coordination in a system originally built for total coordination from the center, it was disconcerting for many. Instead of yielding its intended result, the scheme further complicated coordination of the economy and alienated ministry officials, who had to move from Moscow to small towns. In another rash move, Khrushchëv divided the Communist Party into industrial and agrarian halves in an effort to get members out onto the ground of production. But none of these devices, called "harebrained" by his successors, could break the gridlock inherent in the command economy and swollen bureaucracy. Also generating anger was Khrushchëv's decision to rotate membership in high party bodies by having one-third replaced periodically by fresh blood. The generals were outraged by his attempts to retire hundreds of officers, lower pensions, and cut military budgets by as much as a third in favor of missile development.

Khrushchëv's Fall

Khrushchëv did not try to abandon the Soviet system but to make it work better. Nevertheless, he was overthrown. On October 13–14, 1964, while Khrushchëv was on vacation, his opponents, much better prepared than the plotters of 1957, made their move. They summoned him back to Moscow, verbally abused and demoted him, but permitted him to live out his days in peace as a private citizen until his death in 1971. The new government announced that the former leader had retired for reasons of health. This was the first and only successful coup in Soviet history.

Policies relating to China, the East European bloc, Cuba, and Berlin played some role in Khrushchëv's downfall. But the main trigger was the fear of further domestic flights of administrative fancy, reorganizations, relocations, and redefinitions of a party that had, its members thought, successfully made a revolution and won a war and was now at the mercy of whim. Some near the top felt it was time for different (if not new) blood. Khrushchëv's colleagues resented his arrogance and

his appointment of outsiders and even relatives to key positions. Personal and political concerns coalesced to overthrow him.

The USSR was a safer and better place to live in 1964 than it was in 1953, and certainly part of the credit for this belongs to the ousted leader. But the historic decade of Khrushchëv's leadership had shown that Stalinism had declined without wholly disappearing. It also indicated how difficult it was to serve the interests of the population while retaining the main features of the Soviet system: party monopoly and state socialism. Khrushchëv's successors would cling tightly to both of these.

CHAPTER 39

The Brezhnev Years: Order and Stability, 1964–1982

Man thinks he is master of life, but he lost that mastery lo-o-ong ago. . . . Life has got the better of him, has climbed onto his back and demands what she wants of him. He ought to take the time to turn around, hold her back, slow down a bit and take stock of what's still there and what's been carried away by the winds. But no, no, he makes it worse, he tries to drive her on and on! That way he'll overstrain himself, he can't last out. In fact he's overstrained himself already.

—*Valentin Rasputin, Siberian writer,* Farewell to Matëra, *1976*

The years of Brezhnev and of his short-termed successors (1983–1985) witnessed an apparent rise of Soviet power and influence in the world and an atmosphere of domestic stability that many former Soviet citizens still fondly remember. Yet education and continuing urbanization created new demands from the population: the majority wanted material betterment; a minority sought spiritual or intellectual freedom. The bloated economic system and the budgetary raids by the military impeded the former, and the party leadership fought the latter.

THE POLITICS OF HOLDING ON

The man who held the Soviet Union together was perfectly suited for the job. Leonid Brezhnev (1906–1982) was no ideological theoretician but a conservative Communist proud of Soviet achievements. Son of a Russian worker and a metal worker himself, he was born in 1906 in the Ukrainian town of Kamenskoe, a few miles up the Dnieper River from Ekaterinoslav. As was the man himself, these towns were remade during his Soviet youth: the first into Dneprodzerzhinsk and the second into Dnepropetrovsk. After attending agricultural and technical institutes, Brezhnev became an engineer while making his way up through the party, which he joined in 1931. The marriage of technical education and party work was a hallmark of the generation that took full power in the last third of the twentieth century. Wearing general's epaulets, Brezhnev served as a wartime political troubleshooter and helped rebuild the heavily symbolic Dnepropetrovsk power site (built in Stalin's time and dynamited during the war to deny it to the invader). In the 1950s, he made political capital in Kazakhstan as a manager of Khrushchëv's Virgin Lands project. Skillful at organization and forging a network of friends and connections dubbed "the Dnepropetrovsk mafia," Brezhnev had risen by 1957 to a high rank. After the coup of 1964 he replaced Khrushchëv as party first secretary.

The Power Structure

The leaders of this mature stage of Soviet history were lower-class males, most born in the provinces before 1917. They had surged into middle-level leadership in the 1930s on Stalin's ladder of success for the offspring of peasants and workers. Of the two who flanked Brezhnev on ceremonial days, Alexei Kosygin (1904–1980), son of a St. Petersburg worker, rose through the pathways of industrial technology and economic management to become Brezhnev's prime minister until a few months before the former's death. Few in the inner circle could match him in brains. But brains, in Russia as elsewhere, do not guarantee power—in Kosygin's case, the power to implement his reformist impulses. Nikolai Podgorny (1903–1983), a peasant from Ukraine, was also a product of Soviet technical education and served as president from 1965 to 1977. The two highest military figures in the nation offer another contrast. Andrei Grechko (1903–1976) was a professional officer who had fought in the civil war. He held important combat commands during World War II and civilian posts in postwar Ukraine and East Germany. By 1960 he had become supreme commander of the Warsaw Pact forces and then Soviet minister of defense (1967–1976). Five years his junior, his successor Dmitry Ustinov (1908–1984) came from a working-class family in Samara and joined the party a decade after the revolution. An engineer by training, he became the "armament tsar" at the age of thirty-two, on the eve of the war. A hard-liner, moving steadily up in party ranks, in 1976 he was made a Politburo member, marshal, and defense minister.

To those outside the Soviet Union, the most prominent figure near the top was foreign minister Andrei Gromyko (1909–1989). Born a peasant in the Belorussian village of Stare Gromiki from which his name derives, he became a Communist in 1931, an economist in 1932, and a diplomat in 1939. Gromyko, Soviet ambassador to the United Nations from 1946 to1948, achieved notoriety as the stone-faced Mr. Net ("no") for his many vetoes. After ambassadorial and other assignments, he became foreign minister (1957–1985). Ideological watchdog Mikhail Suslov (1902–1982), another son of the peasantry, gained infamy abroad for his persecution of dissident thinkers and independent scholarship. A Communist since 1921 and an enthusiastic purger, policeman, and deporter, he was once called the last Stalinist, though in fact he was only one among many. The man who succeeded Brezhnev, Yuri Andropov (1914–1984), chief of the KGB (secret police) from 1967 and Politburo member from 1969, perfectly blended foreign affairs with political repression. Unlike Khrushchëv's inner circle, Brezhnev's included the nation's top soldier and the top policeman.

The Central Committee had swollen to almost three hundred members by the 1970s, compared with the dozen who had voted to seize power in October 1917. This and other bodies were filled with Brezhnev's cronies from his Dnepropetrovsk days; the country was ruled by old men. Party leadership interlocked with the military, the KGB, and the industrial order. The party congresses and the Supreme Soviet were largely echo chambers. Local politics operated in a continuous tension between orders from the center and the interests of localities, from republic down to collective farm village and local soviet. Key power centers were the republics that formed the Soviet Union and their *oblasts*, or provinces. Their secretaries were the Soviet equivalents of tsarist governors or Roman prefects. Some, like Grigory Romanov of Leningrad Oblast and Dinmukhamed Kunaev of the Kazakh Republic, gained legendary status for their extravagant corruption. Both sat on the Politburo and were close to Brezhnev. But the "iron ties" that linked the Kremlin offices to the outlying regions could never fully bind the center and the periphery. Entrenched local party organizations were ultimately an obstacle to political reform in the Gorbachëv years.

The Communist Party, the backbone of the state, in 1976 had about 15.7 million members, 41 percent of them workers, 61 percent of them Russian, about 25 percent of them women, and a high proportion of them technically educated people. By the end of Brezhnev's time, the party had more than 19 million members. The party's *nomenklatura,* an appointment system, disposed of some 2 million jobs for loyal activists, who were fattened with privileges.

The new regime abolished Khrushchëv's division of the party into two halves and ended his rotation system. At the Twenty-Third Party Congress of 1966, the Presidium became the Politburo again, and Brezhnev assumed the old title of General Secretary. Avoiding Khrushchëv's proposed leap to "communism," at the next congress, Brezhnev characterized the current stage of Soviet history as "mature socialism." The Ninth Five-Year Plan (1971–1975) offered modest projections. A new constitution of 1977 upgraded the role of the party as "the leading and guiding force of Soviet society." Despite the fanfare, it brought no significant changes in major policies, though it did represent the peak of Brezhnev's power and glory. He replaced Podgorny as president or head of state, a honorific post, but did not become prime minister or head of government, as had Stalin and Khrushchëv. Prime Minister Kosygin resigned in 1980 because of illness and was replaced by Brezhnev's old friend Nikolai Tikhonov (b. 1905).

The Leader

The eighteen-year rule of Brezhnev was marked by a cult of personality more bloated than Khrushchëv's but less fearful than Stalin's. Propagandists called him "a tireless champion of peace and real social justice" and "a generous contributor to the treasure house of Marxism-Leninism." Though not a martial man, he acquired marshal's epaulets, sat for busts and portraits, and basked in the warmth of organized adulation. Thirsting for intellectual recognition, he commissioned the ghostwriting of his wartime memoirs, *Little Land.* Its title referred to a 1943 campaign at Malaya Zemlya (Little Land) on the Black Sea, in which Brezhnev had played a role. For this book Brezhnev received the USSR's highest literary prize. The pettiness of his vision was illustrated by an inordinate fondness for expensive foreign cars and other luxury items.

Fully aware of what drastic measures had cost his predecessor, the cautious Brezhnev undertook no major reforms, ruled by collective leadership, took care of his own, and closed his eyes to their corruption. His rule brought more contact with the West, public participation in policy, and improved social welfare. Old Stalinists opposed further destalinization, vast rehabilitations, and a proposed monument to the victims of the terror. Some would have enjoyed a reversion to Stalinism. Brezhnev, harsh enough on occasions, neither reinstituted the full apparatus of Stalinist terror nor lorded it over his colleagues in the Politburo.

PRODUCTION AND CONSUMPTION

The Soviet economy, molded into shape by Stalin in the 1930s, had survived the greatest war in history and the tinkering of Khrushchëv in the 1950s and 1960s. At its base remained the state or public ownership of the means of production and

Leonid Brezhnev and his colleagues at a Kremlin reception for Fidel Castro, 1972.
Sovfoto/Eastfoto.

distribution—land, factories, and all wholesale and retail outlets. After some impressive initial successes, the Soviet economy slowed down in the mid-1970s.

The View from the Top

In agriculture, the state paid higher procurement prices to farmers than before and sold the produce, especially meat, to consumers at subsidized prices. Meat was fairly cheap in the Brezhnev days, but also hard to get. Collective farmers were given a regular wage and were no longer at the mercy of a bad harvest. The private plots, left in peace by the state, were remarkably productive. The state invested more in agriculture, but the lack of attention to rural roads, silos, and refrigerated storage space often led to rotted grain. Some of the chemical fertilizers poured onto the countryside later produced environmental nightmares. The collective farm system remained enmeshed in inefficient centralized planning. Despite official efforts, output began again to plod downward, marked by disastrous harvests in 1972 and 1975. When American grain was purchased in 1975, the Soviet press was silent.

The industrial growth rate declined from the late 1970s to its lowest point in fifty years, except for the war period. Income and productivity figures rose by a tiny notch, and agricultural output fell. Although planning called for increases in the production of consumer goods, flaws in the system kept overall output low. The economy, which became more complex with every passing year and every new product, was too massive for any kind of office-managed system to handle. Bureaucrats in the over seventy elephantine ministries of Moscow had to decide on the worth and price of almost every item produced. A cumbersome machine of targets, plans, norms, and top-down orders left little room for lateral communication or input from below. Factory managers declined to overfulfill their quotas for fear that quotas would then be raised by the central planners. Underfulfilling could mean dismissal. Since norms were set according to mind-numbingly irrational categories (such as bulk or weight), a factory theoretically could win laurels by producing a single multi-ton spike rather than a million ordinary nails.

Inspired by ideas of the economist Evsei Liberman, which had first been discussed under Khrushchëv, Prime Minister Kosygin in 1965 sponsored reforms to promote efficiency and rationalism, to allow enterprise managers more leeway in decision making, and to privilege profitability over gross output—a vision close to the "market socialism" much loved in some Soviet bloc countries. But the leaders had no desire to tamper with the command economy, to bow to market forces and profit seeking, or to weaken the guiding hand of the party in favor of the "invisible hand" of capitalism. After the 1968 liberalization experiment in Czechoslovakia, to be discussed in the next chapter, this concern was joined by a fear of the slide from economic reform to political reform. Antireform impulses ranged from conservative self-interest, authoritarianism, and fear of "liberalism" to moral revulsion against "profitability." Brezhnev reversed some of Khrushchëv's schemes by abolishing the Economic Councils, but his "mature socialism" did not bring much more to the problems of the economy than cosmetic reorganization.

Economic Life at the Grassroots

The social benefits of the Brezhnev era, established in the 1930s under Stalin, included full employment, free services, and state subsidies. Full employment was Soviet socialism's answer to what Marxists saw as a dreaded feature of capitalism: periodic unemployment resulting from depression. Soviet planners guaranteed a job for everyone and made it almost impossible to be fired. This meant hiring and retaining people who were not really needed, the underutilization of labor, and thus gross inefficiency. Soviet people in the Brezhnev era certainly favored the state's policy, which gave everyone the dignity of gainful employment, even at the expense of efficient national economic performance. Free health care, free education right up to the graduate level, and subsidized housing, food items, transportation, and certain durables added to the picture.

Furthermore, in Brezhnev's time, the standard of living rose for the poorest people—the workers and the peasants. People could buy televisions, Yugoslav washing machines, and refrigerators. The communal apartment, in which each family had one room in a flat and shared the kitchen and bath, had been the standard in urban living for decades. In the words of a prominent scholar who grew up in one, the communal flat was "a place where many battles for reconstruction of daily life were launched and most of them were lost. Here neighbors engaged in quite un-Marxist class struggles; 'domestic trash' triumphed, and privacy was prohibited only to be reinvented against all odds." Now young folks began to live in the once unthinkable separate one-family apartments—with a telephone. Only 15 to 18 percent of the urban population lived in communal or shared apartments at the end of the 1980s, compared with about 40 percent in the late 1960s. Cars were no longer exclusive possessions of the privileged few. In a survey of émigrés generally hostile to the government who left the country in the late Brezhnev years, only 14 percent were distressed with the standard of living there and fewer still with housing. Many expressed satisfaction with free health care, education, police protection, and job security.

But the minus side was immense. Inefficiency was contagious: people's nonperformance rippled out to those they were supposed to serve or supply. If shops closed early or took long lunches, consumers had to come back, thus losing time and energy in their own jobs. A poor work ethic partially paralyzed an already lumbering system. Productivity was a hostage to low incentive, low wages, a shortage of things to buy, and no place to invest. The drinking habits of urban working-class males in particular added to lateness and absences at work. The eternal norms and production quotas encouraged sluggish rhythms until a few days before a deadline, when "storming"—a huge burst of energy—was employed to catch up, resulting in hasty, low-quality work. A second economy of illegal black and semilegal gray markets arose to parallel the creaky distribution network. Black-marketeers produced illegal consumer items, stole state property, dealt in antiques, and ran gambling and vice rings. They in turn had to pay criminal extortionists, such as the Gang of the Mongol, which in the early 1970s terrorized shady entrepreneurs by threatening to bury them alive (which they sometimes did). Managers bypassed the red tape and surreptitiously exchanged needed parts or raw materials. Big-time embezzlement could be, and was, punished by death, but petty and not-so-petty theft was almost universal. Like old-regime peasants, people believed that stealing from each other was a crime but stealing from the master was not. Such an un-Soviet ethos and view of the state boded ill for socialism.

A prime example of how the second economy worked was found in restaurants, whose employees often refused ordinary customers in favor of well-known tippers or people with connections, worked as little as possible, and divided the unserved food among themselves. A familiar mechanism at many enterprises was the family circle—a network of friendship, patronage, influence, and favor swapping—which enabled its members to acquire needed goods and services. Moonlighting became a national pastime. Adding color to the black and gray markets were the traders from the southern republics, who, since air travel was cheap, flew parcels of privately grown fruits and vegetables to sell in Russian cities. This enriched some Georgian merchants and reinforced a legend that all people from that region were affluent. Corruption and bribery blossomed, and the government and the state economy could be rightly compared to a huge mafia. Some flourished while others, such as mineworkers, sweated out short lives down in the black holes. Too often, instead of answers and solutions to problems, the regime offered slogans.

Communism's Victory is Inevitable! *Dagli Orti/The Art Archive.*

TECHNOLOGY AND THE ENVIRONMENT

The USSR was richly endowed with natural resources. Its geological map glowed with deposits of gold, precious and industrial minerals, and the "black gold" of our century: oil. Soviet rulers put gold and petroleum on the world markets for economic gain but did not fully harness the nation's natural wealth. Moscow and other cities boasted a bright constellation of mathematicians, scientists, and research establishments. Leaders trumpeted the Scientific Technical Revolution but did not readily translate lofty theoretical achievements into everyday benefits for society. Rather, they pumped lavish subsidies and talent into the space program and the military-industrial complex—that is, the intermeshing of defense needs and industrial investment. The hefty revenues from oil exports were diverted from social programs into the war industry, which was pampered with new hardware and electronic devices. Precision, efficiency, and productivity marked the defense-related research havens that were justified by a national ethos of military might and the official memory of World War II. The Soviet military, like its Pentagon counterparts, inflated threats and budgets to buy the best scientists and machines. Unlike the Pentagon, it did this without the interference of an inquisitive press or Congress. Technological breakthroughs were applied to weaponry and cosmic exploration.

Consumers suffered from the giant defense budgets, and industrial advancement caused environmental degradation. Ecological catastrophes accelerated in the Brezhnev years. Regulation of industrial fumes was almost nonexistent. In Magnitogorsk, Zaporozhe, and Volgograd—the pride of Stalinist gigantomanic construction—factory smokestacks, the emblem of progress, belched dirty air into residential areas, turning the bright dreams of earlier town planners into blackened cityscapes. Scores of rust-belt towns produced children retarded at birth, old folks who could not breathe, and unfit army recruits. In rural areas, indiscriminate use of fertilizer and pesticides such as DDT poisoned 25 million acres of farmland. Negligence ruined nearly half the plowland in the Virgin Lands in Central Asia, Khrushchëv's vaunted symbol of material progress.

Lakes, rivers, and seas fell victim to ignorance, twisted ambition, and thoughtless planning. Negligent waste disposal practices turned the Volga, Don, and Dnieper—the great arteries of Russian and Ukrainian history—into open sewers. In Central Asia, the Aral Sea, around which legions of invaders had ridden, was devastated. Planners diverted its river sources, Syr Darya and Amu Darya, to irrigation, eliminating two-thirds of the sea's water supply. Pesticides and defoliants poisoned the waters, and the winds blew the resulting toxic salts thousands of miles to do their harm elsewhere. The water of the region became unpotable, and the chemicals created a noxious rain that sickened local mothers and increased infant mortality. The catastrophe was allowed in the name of agricultural progress: increasing cotton production, a monoculture that pushed food crops out of cultivation. Accidents in nuclear plants and the scattering of radioactive wastes in Kazakhstan led one environmental activist later to call his republic "the junk heap where Russia threw its garbage." Cleanups were derailed and the more notable disasters hidden.

As to human ecology, health care may have been free, but its quality plummeted to unprecedented depths. The second economy enabled unqualified students to buy admission to medical school; sick people bribed underpaid medical workers for medicine or a hospital bed. Poor training and technology and unsanitary conditions resulted in needless deaths. The worst cases occurred in the Muslim republics. There were no sewer connections in almost half the medical facilities in Turkmenia. Crowded hospitals and a shortage of drugs and hot water blighted health care everywhere. Male life expectancy in the mid-1960s, 66.1 years, dropped to 63.3 years by the mid-1980s. An average of 4 million workers a day missed work because of illness, although it was often feigned or alcohol related. The authorities knew about a rise in infant mortality but suppressed the data. An American demographer documented the Soviet health and environmental disaster year after year, but it was only after Brezhnev that the public awakened to the ecocide being committed in their country.

PEOPLE: PROGRESS AND PASSIVITY

Of a population of about 260 million at the end of the Brezhnev period, roughly three-fourths lived in cities and towns. Amenities obviously varied from the capitals to the small towns, but general styles of urban life were apparent in the final decades of Soviet history. The Soviet "worker" in the 1970s was still envisaged as the brawny proletarian in a blue shirt, taut muscles applied to a throbbing machine: such was the imagery of the Stalin years. Soviet plants and mills could still boast of such work forces—male and female. But a huge proportion of urbanites were white-collar office workers, cashiers and salespersons, micromanagers, doormen and waiters and cooks, drivers, and petty officials. Women were at least as visible as men in the public workplace, though almost always in secondary positions.

Offices and shops lacked the smooth intensity of those in the West, reflecting a more passive Soviet attitude to the job. Most employees were underutilized in a relatively slow-motion communal atmosphere. Salesclerks, who got paid no matter who bought what, often saw customers as intruders. Surliness at the counter was often interpreted by foreigners as a Russian personality trait, yet those same Russians in their leisure time could blossom into vivacious friends and hosts. Reading, movie going, and club attendance declined with the growth of television. The private sphere meant visiting, entertaining, or "hanging out," with endless talking over a cup of tea or a bottle. The restaurants, reproducing domestic forms of conviviality on a bigger scale—food, drink, music, dance, and companions—was a place were where genders and generations could mix without the state to inhibit them. For men, another favored meeting place was the stadium, where spectator sports, especially hockey and soccer, pulled in millions.

The rural percentage of the population declined continuously. Farmers made less money than city workers and enjoyed fewer cultural and material amenities, even though schooling was getting better and electricity finally arrived. Many sought better lives in town, though this was denied to most peasants until they got internal passports in the 1970s, which allowed them to move legally. Many sought greater opportunity in the big city. The most famous movie treatment of this theme, *Moscow Does Not Believe in Tears* (1980), told of the perils and joys of rural females coming to Moscow to find a life. The state launched campaigns to draw young women from the city back to the village to marry farm boys and preserve the countryside, but most women moved in the other direction.

The Soviet regime continued the policies established by Stalin in the 1930s to encourage a high birth rate and kept condoms in low supply. Working women, who in spite of improved housing lived in cramped flats, had few means of family planning except abortion, which reached an enormous rate. Aside from the physical and mental toll this took on women, the constant visits to abortion clinics, legal since 1955, caused family tensions and often divorce. Women of the 1960s and 1970s lived better than their mothers had. Laws on illegitimacy, paternity suits, and divorce afforded them some protection. While the rising divorce rate seemed to some a symptom of social weakness, it offered an exit from difficult marriages for many wives. The regime continued to voice a doctrine of sexual equality, but the official system, embedded in early education, was antifeminist: boys learned to build cities and railroads, girls to fashion houses with furniture. In textbooks, the male child was endowed with reason and strength, the female with passion and weakness. Yet in their "weakness," women were pillars who propped up the home while bearing the enduring second burden of work force participation.

Behind Soviet propaganda's glossy pictures of happy-faced and successful women rose an ugly sore: prostitution. "Intergirls," recruited from poor city women and part-time students, plied their trade in hotels catering to foreigners. They were enmeshed in a system of police corruption and organized crime. Authorities alternately winked at the trade or cracked down, as during the 1980 Olympics, held in Moscow, when busloads of prostitutes were transported out of the city.

Young people of both sexes had long since lost a revolutionary spirit. The Brezhnev leadership tried again to capture the enthusiasm of the 1930s by recruiting the youth to a new construction epic: BAM, the Baikal-Amur Mainline, a highway and rail complex laid out as a second link to the Pacific. Its economic utility is still in doubt, but its harmful ecological effect on Lake Baikal is well established. BAM generated little idealism. A post-Brezhnev film exposé showed mismanagement and lack of facilities for workers rather than the touted "great eastern adventure."

Western Cold War commentary often depicted Soviet society as a withered arm of the state with no life or purpose of its own; a herd of mobilized "neoserfs" or Orwellian "proles" in the thrall of higher power, bored and unhappy. This fuzzy image arose from ignorance, hatred, wishful thinking, and the clinging notion of a Stalinist monolith—all fed by the often exaggerated comments of disaffected insiders. But life and love, adventure and romance went on, the quotient of "happiness" depending on generation and gender, geography and class, talent, spirit, or even sense of humor. "Society," no abstract entity, was conditioned by family, state policy, economy, ethnicity, and ideology. To take one example: The low birth level among Russians brought a labor shortage and an imbalance between Slavic birth rates and those of the Muslim population, for whom big families were a source of pride. This imbalance in turn contributed to a large and growing proportion of non-Russians in the army, which further fueled the fear and hatred of Muslims by ultranationalist and racist Russians of the right wing and Muslims' resentment at the brutal treatment they received as recruits.

THE CULTURAL LANDSCAPE

As in the case of Soviet society, Western commentators often simplified the picture of the Brezhnev cultural scene as a simple dichotomy of official and unofficial cultures: the one false, bombastic, and unpopular; the other dissident, heroic, and reflecting a popular spirit. In fact, official culture varied greatly and much of it was genuinely popular. Alongside patriotic war films, placards of healthy productive workers, cantatas about Soviet exploits, and socialist realist novels, the modern crime novel came into its own. Science fiction continued to flourish in the Brezhnev era, feeding readers who looked to technology, the city, and the future. Other trends that blossomed within the bounds of permitted expression reflected social currents that went beyond official culture. By far the most important of these was Russian nationalism. Both the terrible losses and the pride of victory in the world war had deepened this sentiment among the population. The leaders, themselves steeped in nostalgia, came to see Russian nationalism as a positive emotional force that helped legitimize the regime in the face of waning Marxist ideological enthusiasm. They permitted and encouraged cultural forms that fed love of country, even when those forms exalted in a distinctly un-Marxist way the alleged symbols of Russianness—rural life, religion, and the tsarist past. New nationalists, called Russophiles, in their hostility to the West and their belief in Russia's spiritual superiority came to share many of the values of their nineteenth-century forebears, the Slavophiles (see the chapter "Nicholas I: Monarchy, Society, Empire, 1825–1855").

A school of literature called village prose, which reached maturity in this era, depicted the countryside as the authentic repository of a "radiant past" of honesty, simplicity, family values, and even belief in God, in contrast to the "radiant future" promised each generation by the regime. Valentin Rasputin (b. 1937), author of the passage quoted at the opening of this chapter, became the voice of those who resented the destruction of old traditions by headlong economic development. This un-Bolshevik literature was inspired in part by a perception of vanishing rural mentalities and the spiritual erosion of the soul. Some authors were bold enough to comment on the visible effects of environmental wreckage. Those excited by the national past turned to the hundreds of war novels that rolled off the presses and to stories dealing with aristocratic life in tsarist times. The historical novelist Valentin Pikul (1928–1990) became the most popular author of his time for his romanticized treatments of imperial Russia. His fervent nationalism and xenophobia were sometimes expressed in anti-Semitism. Russian nationalism was also reflected in popular religious observance, icon collecting, and preservation societies. Much of it was an expression of disenchantment with official ideology and a nostalgic longing for traditional "Russian" values, seen to be threatened by urbanization, machines, and heartless bureaucrats.

Soviet music came in many different forms. The state-favored classical, "mass song," and folk music, allowed a "neutral zone" of Soviet pop and jazz, and forbade most forms of rock. Moscow and Leningrad held the best conservatories, opera houses, ballet companies, and symphony orchestras, world renowned through tours and recordings. Performances of the Bolshoi and the Kirov Theaters—havens for the elite of all persuasions, from Kremlin bigwigs to pure lovers of art—were widely available on radio and television. "Mass songs" and war songs, still beloved by the older generation, continued to drench the airwaves and bore youngsters to tears as did the ubiquitous folk ensembles. The pop singer Alla Pugachëva (born ca. 1940?) was the biggest celebrity of the Brezhnev years, far better known to ordinary people than the classical soloists David Oistrakh or Emil Gilels. Youth reveled in imported Western music, but its inflow was controlled by record producers and repertory committees, who policed dance clubs and restaurants.

Theater tastes also varied. Elite theaters in the capitals alternated the classics of Pushkin, Gogol, Ostrovsky, Chekhov, Shakespeare, France's Racine, and Germany's Schiller with those of Soviet playwrights who explored the margins of everyday life. Bold directors, such as Georgy Tovstonogov at the Great Drama Theater in Leningrad and Yuri Lyubimov (b. 1917) of the Taganka in Moscow, thrilled audiences with drama poised on the edge of political criticism. Brezhnev even called Lyubimov in for artistic counseling, but the Taganka persisted until Lyubimov defected in 1983. The masses preferred television, pop concerts, circuses, and variety shows. Russian standup comedians, mostly Jewish, danced on the edge of dissidence with critical barbs about Soviet social mores.

A flourishing cinema industry gave scant attention to revolution, the proletariat, or the communist future. War films functioned as part of a campaign, including huge commemorative rituals, to keep alive the official memory of World War II as proof of Soviet superiority, its role in obliterating fascism, and the manly virtues of soldiering. The public liked films and TV dramas for their pure entertainment value: comedies, crime stories, and musicals. "Daily life" films seen by millions conveyed something of what life was like and what Soviet people would have liked it to be. But those that showed too much reality were shelved by a keen-eyed censorship: showing the rumpled bed of a married couple was prohibited. Some clever directors managed to get real-life problems on the screen, particularly those dealing with woman's lot, juvenile crime, and the degraded conditions of country life—alien themes in the old Stalin cosmology. Even popular comedies poked fun at faceless officials and drab city life. A few artistic filmmakers appeared, such as Andrei Tarkovsky (1932–1986), who made the masterpiece *Andrei Rublëv* (1966). The most effective voice of nostalgic "Russianism" was that of Nikita Mikhalkov in films such as *Slave of Love* (1975) and *Oblomov* (1980), which idealized the pastoral qualities of the old regime.

On the surface of things, the USSR looked like a going concern. By means of stick (control and repression) and carrot (a rising living standard), the Soviet old regime maintained the loyalty of the bulk of the population. Yet its inner tensions and strains were formidable. To dissidents, East European reformers, to anyone who believed in real freedom—to be discussed in the next chapter—Brezhnev's reign was a scourge.

CHAPTER 40

The Brezhnev Years: Change and Ferment, 1964–1982

What ought to be done? The ideological monism of our society should be liquidated. It's an ideological structure which is essentially anti-democratic and it is a tragedy for the state. Our isolation from the outside world, for example, the absence of the right to leave the country and return to it, is having an extremely pernicious effect on domestic life.

—*Andrei Sakharov, Russian dissident, 1973*

In its last years, the USSR became a "shadowland," casting distorted images that doubled socialism with a second economy, society with subcultures, patriotism with rising ethnic identities, official with unofficial art, and government with a dissident underground chorus. Erosion set in, and currents of change flowed at many different levels, under and above ground. The long slide away from active commitment to the Soviet ethos by key elements in the population exacerbated the structural weakness of the Brezhnev regime and its successors.

COUNTERPOLITICS: THE DISSIDENTS

The major challenges to Khrushchëv's power had come from within the party itself in 1957 and 1964. For his successors, it took the form of a moral critique issuing from a corner of the intelligentsia, mostly Muscovites, Kievans, and Leningraders. They were known as dissidents or "nonconformists," bold men and women who challenged various aspects of the system or fought to hold it to its own laws and principles. The movement emerged when the new "hard men" who replaced Khrushchëv quickly ended lingering dreams of genuinely free political, moral, and artistic expression.

The Trial Begins

A little over a year after coming to power, the regime tried two writers, Andrei Sinyavsky and Yuly Daniel, who, under the names Abram Terts and Nikolai

Arzhak, had allegedly slandered the Soviet system in satirical fiction published abroad. The hero of Terts's satire, Lyubimov, promised his people water that tastes like champagne. Arzhak's "Public Murder Day" had the leaders allowing citizens to kill one another, but not them. The authors were at first jailed and later allowed to emigrate. Conservative writers thought the jail sentences too lenient. But other writers, scientists, and artists defended the condemned writers, and their outcry prompted a cycle of demonstrations and arrests. In 1968, after the Soviet intervention in Czechoslovakia (see below), demonstrators on Red Square bitingly compared the Soviet crackdown on Czech democratic reforms to the tsarist crushing of Poland in 1863 and to American aggression in the Vietnam War (ca. 1964–1975). The demonstration organizer, Pasha Litvinov, was the grandson of Stalin's foreign minister. Since he and others in the crowd were Jewish, the demonstration sharpened the anti-Semitism of the party and government leaders. A recent quickening of Jewish emigration deepened official beliefs in disloyalty among Jews.

Dissidents spread illegal *samizdat* (self-published) manuscripts at home and abroad, a practice dating from the Khrushchëv period. They mingled with foreign diplomats, journalists, and students and told them some of the hidden truths of repression. Notable figures, such as author Alexander Solzhenitsyn (b. 1918) and

The 1966 trial of Sinyavsky and Daniel. *Sovfoto/Eastfoto.*

cellist Mstislav Rostropovich (b. 1927), were forcibly expatriated or denied reentry. The opposite happened, too: famous artistic performers defected to Europe or America in embarrassing numbers. As the joke went: "Question: What is a Soviet string quartet? Answer: A Soviet orchestra that has been traveling in the West." The KGB spied on, harassed, and arrested disaffected elements. People were dismissed from jobs and then charged with vagrancy for being unemployed. The least fortunate ended up in labor camps, prisons, or psychiatric wards, where they were injected with mind-altering drugs. The loosely defined socialist legality ended as far as political offenses were concerned. If the state did not exactly return to Stalinism, it certainly seemed so to those incarcerated and dehumanized. The chief architect of repression was KGB chairman Yuri Andropov, who would be Brezhnev's successor.

Dissident Visions

Two early dissidents were the twin Medvedev brothers (b. 1925), historian Roy and biologist Zhores, who in 1970 was consigned to a mental hospital. Roy Medvedev, simultaneously harassed by the KGB and protected by high-ranking connections, believed that Lenin's socialism had been a humane system that was perverted by Stalin and his successors. He pleaded for détente with the West and a mixed economy, freedom, and decentralization. "Without a free exchange of ideas and opinions, it is absolutely impossible to create any satisfactory spiritual values," he wrote in 1973. Andrei Amalrik (1938–1980) added an apocalyptic edge in his 1969 book *Will the Soviet Union Survive Until 1984?*—a clear reference to British writer George Orwell's famous antiutopian novel *1984.* The USSR did survive until 1984, but in the very next year it began the slide to dissolution.

Andrei Sakharov (1921–1989), a noted physicist who had helped develop the hydrogen bomb, emerged as an important liberal dissident in the 1960s. As he moved into open dissent, his program evolved from socialism to capitalism and from mere détente to a call for Western pressure for human rights in Russia. In *Thoughts on Progress, Peaceful Coexistence, and Intellectual Freedom* (1968), Sakharov deployed his intelligence and argumentative skill to assault Marxism, party dictatorship, nuclear terror, and the suppression of the free flow of scientific information, and in 1970 he formed a Human Rights Committee. For a time he hoped for some kind of convergence between a liberalized USSR and the Western capitalist democracies but warned in 1973 that "détente without democratization, détente in which the West in effect accepts the Soviet rules of the game, would be dangerous." For his courage Sakharov was awarded the Nobel Peace Prize in 1975. But five years later the authorities banished him to Gorky (formerly Nizhny Novgorod), a city on the Middle Volga.

The neo-Slavophile Alexander Solzhenitsyn (b. 1918) collided with the authorities over his novels *The Cancer Ward* and *The First Circle* (both 1968), which went much deeper in condemning Stalinism than had his *One Day in the Life of Ivan Denisovich,* legally published in 1962. His designation as a Nobel Prize laureate for these works in 1970 further angered the party's ideological watchdogs. Solzhenitsyn's religious, patriarchal, conservative, and anti-industrial vista rejected not only

Marx and Lenin but also much of capitalism. He spoke of "the ruinous path of Western civilization" and dreamed of a deindustrialized Russian state in Siberia based on old Muscovite values and Orthodox Christianity. In a 1973 letter to Soviet leaders, Solzhenitsyn urged them to scrap communism but to keep authoritarian power to prevent anarchy. "Authoritarian regimes as such are not frightening," he told them, "only those which are answerable to no one and nothing." Solzhenitsyn's chronicle of the camp system, *The Gulag Archipelago* (1973–1976), published in the West, was so horrifying that authorities expelled him in 1974.

Other dissident currents expressed religious messages, Jewish, Muslim, and Christian. Followers of the Orthodox theologians and philosophers of the pre-1917 Silver Age appeared in the illegal *samizdat* literature. The struggle between church and state was complicated by the fact that the police had infiltrated the clergy. The most spectacular of the resisters was Father Gleb Yakunin (b. 1934), a heroic figure who suffered prison and exile in his fight for an independent church.

Underground presses also published right-wing nationalist and even fascist writings. The group known as Rossit (from the word *Rossiya,* or Russia) proclaimed a demographic menace posed by the Jews and by the "yellowing" of the Soviet armed forces—that is, the numerical growth of Asian soldiers. The dissidents of the Brezhnev years, hopelessly divided and lacking wide support, did not constitute anything like a shadow government. Many ordinary citizens saw them as no better than traitors; and that Jews and other non-Russians were among them was proof enough to unreflective minds that the whole movement was a subversive arm of foreign powers. Yet these dissidents not only constituted countercommunities but also generated a "shadow politics"—a whole spectrum of political ideas, from reasonable to outrageous—destined to surface publicly in the future.

UNDERLIFE: INTERNAL EMIGRATION

Long before Brezhnev's exit, sizable segments of society disengaged from grand designs and personality cults. Helpless to effect major changes, those members of the intelligentsia unwilling to step into the hazardous terrain of dissidence withdrew into private life, cultural work, nostalgia, and religion—what one scholar called a "third space." They skirted the edge of disaffection by telling political jokes or listening to the underground tapes of semilegal guitar poets. The most famous of these was Vladimir Vysotsky (1938–1980), who appealed to all classes and generations with his raucous songs mocking Soviet heroes and evoking the world of liquor, sex, and street life. Unofficial creative artists exhibited surrealistic paintings in their flats for the cognoscenti and foreign buyers. Actors performed absurdist plays on suburban train cars or in tiny apartments. Though submerged and occasionally raided, this art community provided the vocabulary of cultural rebellion that would erupt later.

Lack of real commitment to regime values was not always so self-conscious. Russian workingmen in particular were prone to scorn career or public activity in favor of conviviality and the bottle. To many of them, drinking meant quickly consumed volumes of vodka rather than the sociable cocktail or casual glass of wine. It was a serious business requiring time, effort, and money to procure the stuff and consume it in the right company. Absenteeism, poor work, accidents, illness, hooliganism, and wife beating often ensued. Drunk tanks did not even touch the surface of a problem that took on mammoth, life-threatening proportions.

Soviet youth, like young people elsewhere, varied greatly in their aspirations. A sampling of young Soviet urbanites in the 1970s recorded theirs as material well-being, a good job, education, foreign travel, a decent place to live, and family life and friends—more or less in that order. But authorities perceived a disturbing phenomenon among some youth: the love of things foreign. Détente boosted the influx of Western visitors and goods—jeans, T-shirts, and imported artifacts. For the young, rock-and-roll became a means of self-expression. Since the 1950s, rock music had held a semilegal to illegal status, and in the early 1980s it exploded in festivals, rock clubs, and hundreds of thousands of unofficial groups. Communist conservatives, like those elsewhere, hated rockers for the music, greasy long hair, in-your-face performance style, and alleged lack of patriotism. Periodic crackdowns could not crush rock music because of its massive support among young people. As one singer put it, "Rock is our thing; rock can never die." Countercultures of hippies, rockers, bikers, pacifists, and punks created identities and folkways alien to the norms of the Young Communist League. Further complicating the urban landscape, gangs of shaved-headed toughs from the poor suburbs of Moscow and other towns hunted out rockers and beat them up. Before this tapestry of subcultures, authorities and elders stood bewildered. The dropping out of so many intellectuals, artists, and youths formed another of the many strains emerging in a now urbanized society ruled by the fading red banner of ideological orthodoxy.

THE OTHER HALF: SOVIET REPUBLICS

The lands taken during and after the war were ruthlessly Sovietized. A sixteenth union republic, set up in Karelia in 1940 with a mixed Russian, Karelian, and Finnish population, had been reduced in 1956 to the lesser status of an autonomous republic within the Russian Soviet Federated Socialist Republic (RSFSR). The Baltic states had been forcefully turned from independent states outside the USSR into union republics in 1940. Poland's eastern Slavic populations were added to Belorussia and Ukraine, which also received the Carpathian tip of Czechoslovakia. Romanian Bessarabia became the Moldavian SSR. The "punished peoples" deported during the war from the Volga, Crimea, and Caucasus were living in Siberia and Central Asia in cultures vastly different from their own. Homecoming had begun in 1956 for the Kalmyks and for the Chechen, Ingush, and Balkar people of the Caucasus, the Muslims expelled from Georgia in 1948, and the Volga Germans. The Crimean Tatars had to wait until 1967 for partial, and much later for full, return. (See Table 1.)

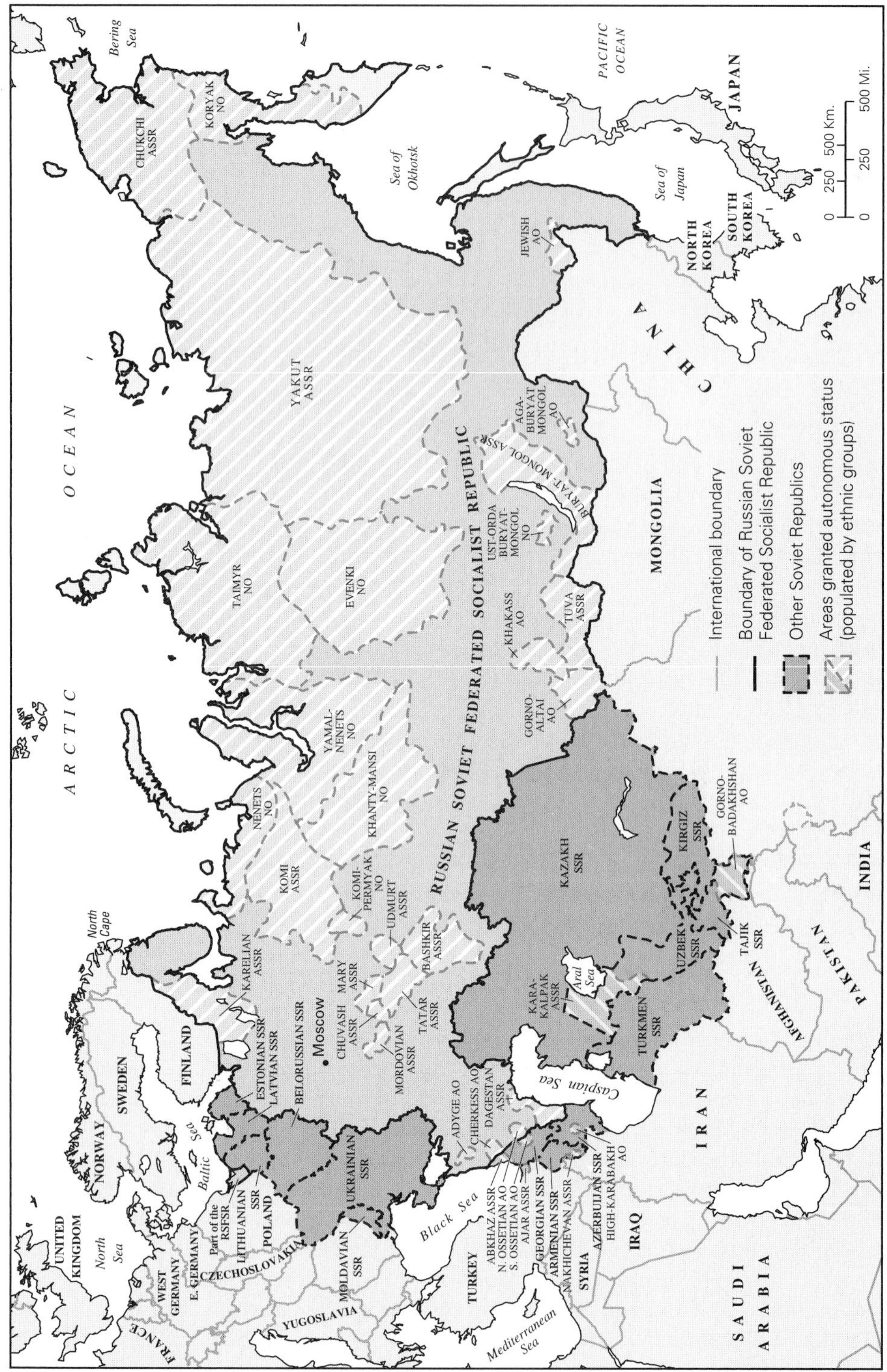

The national republics. Atlas of Russian History, *by Martin Gilbert (New Edition published by Routledge in 2002) 0415281199 PB & 0415281180 HB. Please visit our website for further details on the new edition: www.taylorandfrancis.com.*

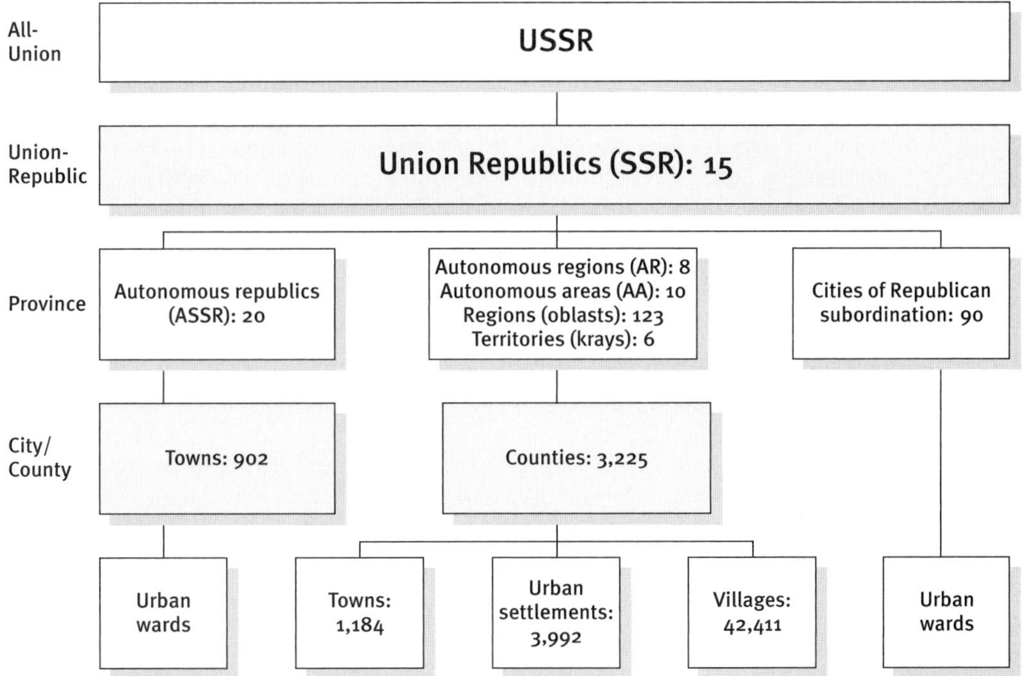

TABLE 1 Titular and Non-Titular Populations, 1989

Republic	Population (thousands	Nationality, of which: Titular (%)	Russian (%)	Titular population living outside this territory (%)
Russia	147,022	81.5	na	17.4
Ukraine	51,452	72.7	22.1	15.3
Belarus	10,152	77.9	13.2	21.2
Uzbekistan	19,810	71.4	8.4	15.3
Kazakhstan	16,464	39.7	37.8	19.7
Georgia	5,401	70.1	6.3	4.9
Azerbaijan	7,021	82.7	5.6	14.3
Lithuania	3,675	79.6	9.4	4.7
Moldova	4,335	64.5	13.0	16.6
Latvia	2,667	52.0	34.0	4.9
Kyrgyzstan	4,258	52.4	21.5	11.8
Tajikistan	5,093	62.3	7.6	24.7
Armenia	3,305	93.3	1.6	33.3
Turkmenistan	3,523	72.0	9.5	7.1
Estonia	1,565	61.5	30.3	6.2

Source: From Archie Brown, Michael Kaser, and Gerald S. Smith, eds., *The Cambridge Encyclopedia of Russia and the Former Soviet Union* Second Edition, p. 349. Copyright © 1994. Reprinted by permission of Cambridge University Press.

Friendship of the Peoples

Half the USSR's population were non–Great Russians, most of them living outside the RSFSR. Anti-Soviet writers saw the Soviet Union, even after Stalin, as nothing more than an exploitative empire. Yet otherwise hostile émigrés recalled the teaching of ethnic equality, rarely found in old colonial empires, as a positive aspect of Soviet rule. Stalin's slogan "Friendship of the Peoples" remained in force, as did indigenization policies (see the chapter "Stalinism: Life Inside the System, 1928–1941"). Added to them was the practice of planting a local figure as head of the republic's party, state, or both, with a Russian as second in command. The largely symbolic constitution of 1977 reaffirmed the republics' fictitious right to secede, but they could not form armies or have foreign relations (even though Ukraine and Belorussia had been given foreign ministers and seats in the United Nations at the end of World War II).

If all Soviet nationalities were equal in the friendship formula, Russians were the first among equals. Language practices and the presence of Russian and Ukrainian officials and settlers everywhere in the non-Russian lands, often in high places, remained sources of discontent. In most republics the study of the native language was mandatory in all schools, though the language of instruction varied from place to place. Russians, unable to conduct business in 150 languages, reasonably wanted a lingua franca. The state needed bilingual citizens, but even Russians long resident in republics rarely learned the local language. This practice smacked of colonialism. Those sensitive to the issue had also been alarmed when Khrushchëv in 1961 had spoken of the flourishing of national cultures followed by gradual "mutual assimilation" among all cultures and then their eventual merger. He offered no explanation of how this would occur.

Brezhnev dropped the goal of merger and stressed spontaneous and natural forces. But mutual assimilation implied the decline of specific national sentiments in history, literature, and legends that could deepen feelings of "otherness" and produce reveries of bygone greatness instead of a Russia-centered understanding of the past. Ideologists in the Kremlin frowned on local historians who heroized certain aspects of their past, especially resistance against the Russians. Those historians found it rankling to rewrite books and be persecuted for "bourgeois nationalism." They had to downplay tsarist Russia's historical cruelty or maladministration and highlight its progressive role. The founding of academies of science in most republics during and after World War II had been a gesture of cultural advance, but it also served to integrate intellectuals into the larger Soviet sphere. In the realm of expressive culture, the republics had become more "Soviet" as they gradually adopted local and stylized versions of socialist realism. And yet with all the pressures from the center, local identity and power had grown enormously since World War II. Its extent would startle the leaders in the late 1980s.

The Western Republics

In the Baltic lands, the legacy of killings and deportations was bitter, even though conditions had bettered markedly after Stalin's death and the quality of life in places like Tallinn in Estonia or Riga in Latvia was superior to that in Moscow or Leningrad. Postwar Estonia led the USSR in standard of living and productivity. Deportees had started returning to the Baltic republics in 1956, but Russian immigration was much heavier: by 1989, Latvia was only half Latvian. Baltic citizens suffered the humiliation of having their Lutheran and Catholic cathedrals turned into concert halls and museums of atheism.

In Ukraine the pain of wartime occupation had been followed by a bloody civil war between Soviet troops and a Ukrainian Insurgent Army. The rebels, particularly strong in western Ukraine, had killed thousands of officials and fought against Soviet power until about 1950, with considerable popular support and extensive clandestine American aid. The insurgents focused on two hated Soviet policies: collectivization, which they deplored in principle and which had threatened their food supplies; and the banning of the Uniate or Greek Catholic Church, under the pretext that some clergy had collaborated with the Nazis. Both sides had used terror, and Soviet authorities resorted to public executions. After Stalin's death, Khrushchëv had made conciliatory gestures, such as awarding the Crimea to Ukraine in 1954, in connection with the tricentennial of the 1654 "unification" of Ukraine with Muscovy. More substantial had been a softer style of leadership and a limited respect for Ukrainian national sensibilities. Many Ukrainian state and party figures, including Soviet president Nikolai Podgorny (Mykola Pidhorny) (1905–1983), promoted Russian-Ukrainian amity. This did not prevent the emergence, arrest, and trial of Ukrainian nationalist dissidents in the 1950s and 1960s, including groups of workers, peasants, students, and intellectuals, the most prominent of whom was Vyacheslav Chornovil (b. 1938).

In the Brezhnev period, from the mid-1960s, the Ukrainian literary community was divided into Stalinists, who wished for the good old days of socialist realism, party control, and subservience to Moscow; destalinizers, who, like the Ukrainizers of the 1920s, wanted more national expression and artistic freedom; and younger radical modernists, who wished to break all restraints. The last group, known as "the Sixtiers," adopted the slogan "Back to the Truth!" and created a ferment in university halls and clubs. Although more than 80 percent of Ukraine's twenty-nine thousand or so schools in the 1950s had taught all subjects in Ukrainian and the study of Ukrainian was mandatory in all schools, complaints still arose on the language issue. Many Russians were insensitive to Ukrainian cultural aspirations, and the millions of Ukrainians who lived in other republics noted that they were replete with Russian libraries, newspapers, and theaters but not Ukrainian ones. Suspicious Russian officials, on the other hand, launched a campaign against Oles Honchar's national novel *The Cathedral* (1968), which symbolically pitted the ancient church—and thus traditional Ukrainian values—against the nearby modern metallurgical combine.

Georgia and Armenia

The urbanization of half the Georgian population did little to weaken such traditions as elaborate feasting and restrictions on women's sphere. Ancient mentalities exalting hospitality, display of wealth, manliness, shame in the face of failure (especially in front of women), and the honor of expert horsemanship and swordplay were transmuted into notions about success in business and politics, nepotism and patronage, and defiance of outsiders. Three-quarters of the population were not fluent in Russian. Soviet officials in Moscow viewed the Georgians with ambivalence: some admired their flamboyance, generosity, and independence and envied their wealth; others, whose idea of desirable "Georgianness" was embodied in state-sponsored dance ensembles and other quaint cultural expressions, looked askance at a culture that in many ways was so obviously un-Soviet.

With little interference from Moscow, Vasily Mzhavanadze (1902-1988), party first secretary from 1953 to 1972, allowed local elites to share power among themselves, the state economy to falter, private enrichment to flourish, and corrupt practices to spread. The Georgian authorities took care of their own in the sharing of political appointments and wealth. The Soviet central government could turn a blind eye to local corruption; the open expression of chauvinism was another matter. One of these had occurred in Georgia's capital, Tbilisi, on March 9, 1956 (Stalin's birthday). When Georgian citizens who had admired the dead Stalin as a Georgian hero and who contested Khrushchëv's destalinization speech assembled in public to honor Stalin's memory, the police shot at and killed dozens of them for alleged disorder. This episode had further determined Georgians to pursue their own path. In defiance of the principle of "Friendship of the Peoples," Georgian nationalist scholars began attacking the historical record of their Transcaucasian neighbors and were answered in kind. Within the Georgian Republic, the government discriminated against national minorities in university admissions and other matters. The two main minorities, the Abkhazians and the Ossetians, protested in favor of their own cultural and linguistic rights.

In 1972, Eduard Shevardnadze (b. 1928) replaced Mzhavanadze, fired his supporters, and launched campaigns against bribery and against chauvinism in the arts, academia, and the church. A dissident current appeared at this time that opposed both corruption and Soviet interference. One of its leaders, Zviad Gamsakhurdia (1939–1993)—son of a leading literary figure in the Georgian literary ferment of the 1920s, Konstantine Gamsakhurdia—focused at first on preserving historical and cultural monuments. When he moved to human rights agitation, he was arrested and spent a few years in jail. His name, his religious anti-Russian and anti-Armenian ideas, and his imprisonment later helped win his election as the first president of independent Georgia. Further trouble broke out in 1978, when a clause was omitted from the new Georgian constitution naming Georgian as the sole official state language. Shevardnadze weathered these events, and his moderate rule brought him to the attention of future reform-minded leaders in Moscow.

Armenian patriots, who had fought loyally in the Soviet armed forces, had emerged from the war with dreams of their nation enlarged by the Soviet incorporation of territory in Turkish Anatolia and a population amplified by the diaspora, including survivors and descendants of the 1915 genocide. But Turkey was not a belligerent in World War II, and Stalin, though he tried to pressure the Turks for lands in eastern Anatolia in 1945–1947, backed off after U.S. president Harry Truman had supported Turkey in the dispute. Thus the numerous returnees from the diaspora squeezed into the same old small Armenian Republic.

Armenia enjoyed a relatively stable party and state leadership and had passed through destalinization under Khrushchëv, including changes in leadership, an easing of the repressive machinery, and a cultural thaw. Armenia's national revival, permitted by Khrushchëv's thaw, was less subject to censorship than in places such as Georgia, Ukraine, the Baltic, and the Muslim regions, where historical memory was connected to struggle against Russia. Writers of the distant and more recent past could now be exalted. But nationalist ferment did emerge among dissidents, who in 1967 demanded the return to Armenia of the Autonomous Region of High Karabagh, an ethnic enclave with a largely Armenian population inside Azerbaijan. The dissidents were suppressed, but not the aspiration. Eventually this simmering issue would explode in violence.

The Muslim Regions

The massive programs of development and education that continued in the postwar years put Soviet Muslims impressively ahead of many former Asian and African colonies. In spite of persisting patriarchal values, a high birth rate, and resistance to the expansion of women's roles, those roles did expand. In the political arena, no such progress was made. Some regimes combined party privilege and power with the clan traditions of enrichment and vengeance in a variant of Soviet power at the center. Azerbaijan's Heidar Aliev (b. 1923) emerged as a local KGB chief and crusader against corruption and then as party boss (1969–1989). This regional strongman appointed relatives to political posts and earned himself the nickname "Ceausescu of the Caspian" after the corrupt Communist dictator of Romania. He eventually gained appointment to the Politburo.

In Kazakhstan, Politburo member Dinmukhammed Kunaev (b. 1912) ruled as party boss from 1964 to 1986. His counterpart in Uzbekistan was Shafar Rashidov (1917–1983), a writer whose novel *Mighty Wave* (1964), combining a socialist realist style with local colors, told the story of an Uzbek war veteran's travails as he returned to his home town. In 1949, Rashidov had become chair of the Uzbek Writers' Union, and in 1959 party chief. His record of scandal and corruption became so noxious that he lost all his posts and died in 1983, possibly a suicide. At the local level, Akhmajan Adylov, boss of Uzbekistan's Fergana Valley region for two decades, employed slave labor, filled jails with his enemies, and maintained a bevy of concubines.

Soviet rulers in Moscow for the most part closed their eyes to local corruption and misrule in these regions and were more concerned about nationalist currents among the intelligentsia. Since history, legend, and art were blended in the great heroic epics of steppe and mountain warriors, the constant purge of national themes from the historical record constituted an assault on hallowed traditions. Historical figures such as Shamyl (1797–1871) and Kenisary Qasimov (1837–1846), leaders of anticolonial wars against the tsar in the early nineteenth century, were ignored or thoroughly varnished to fit Soviet standards, as were folk heroes of nomadic epics (see the chapter "Around the Russian Empire, 1801–1861").

More galling still was Russian migration into the region. From the postwar years onward, the capitals Alma Ata, Frunze, Leninabad, Ashkhabad, and Tashkent had Russian pluralities. Wartime evacuation, deportations, and postwar immigration had brought war prisoners and other populations of many nationalities. Japanese World War II prisoners had actually built the Alma Ata opera house. In some of the larger towns, one heard not only eastern Slavic tongues but Yiddish, Lithuanian, Polish, German, and Caucasian and East Asian languages. Everyone seemed welcome in Central Asian cities except the natives themselves. The flood of Russian settlers to Kazakhstan during Khrushchëv's Virgin Lands agricultural program had made Kazakhs a minority in their own republic. Less than 1 percent of the Russian dwellers spoke Kazakh: at the center of Russianized Alma Ata lay Brezhnev Square. Russians also got the skilled jobs, largely because of superior training; the locals tended to work in light industry, farming, or service—often as policemen or menials.

The Heartland

The huge Russian Soviet Federated Socialist Republic dwarfed all others combined. In a 1946 speech at a Kremlin reception, Stalin singled out the Great Russian people for a toast: "the most outstanding nation of all the nations entering into the Soviet Union . . . the leading force among all the peoples of our country." This was a clear bow to Russian nationalism, which had grown during the war in direct proportion to the suffering and to the victory. In its benign form, Russian nationalism was an elegiac, sometimes idealized appreciation of a glorious past and of the country's natural beauty and its people's alleged virtues. But it could also take the shape of an ultranationalist xenophobia harbored not only by dissident extremists of the right but also by ordinary people of all classes, including Communists. Nationalism fed the delusion that Russians had suffered and built while others were enjoying life.

One result of this attitude was friction between Russians and Jews. Jews fared worse and better than the average Russian. Although Jews were highly assimilated, unofficial anti-Semitism operated at work and school. There were no pogroms, but daily indignities—insults or anti-Semitic jokes—inflicted quieter forms of violence. There was always the fear that things could get worse. Jews often did better than Russians in a career sense because they worked hard and generally drank less. In spite of the Soviet revival of limiting quotas for Jews in university and other restrictions, they were as a whole better educated, and many held high-ranking jobs. Though intermarriage was common, so was hatred and scapegoating, sometimes fed by resentment at Jewish emigration privileges. Jews responded in a variety of ways. Some became dissidents; a few were pulled toward new religious consciousness. When Israel defeated its Arab enemies in the 1967 Six-Day War, many Soviet Jews were filled with pride and a recaptured feeling of "Jewishness." Recalled a physicist: "Until then I had always thought of Jews as people of the mind—Christ,

Marx, Einstein, Freud. I never thought of Jews as fighting men, capable of carrying out brilliant operations. I had no image of the brave and daring Jew." Many more, lacking the new consciousness, simply wished to emigrate to Europe or America for a better and freer life. The way was thorny: After they applied to leave, Jews were delayed, harassed, and fired from their jobs. Others, the "refuseniks," were denied exit visas. One, Anatoly (now Natan) Shcharansky (b. 1958), later an Israeli politician, was sentenced in 1978 to thirteen years in prison for agitating for emigration to Israel. With the help of U.S. diplomatic pressure, emigration rose and peaked in 1979, with fifty-one thousand leaving that year. But the onset of the Afghan War reduced Jewish emigration to a low point in 1985 of only about one thousand.

EMPIRE: CUBA TO HIGH ASIA

During the Brezhnev years, the external problems facing and created by Moscow became truly immense: erosion in the East European bloc and rivalry with China escalated, as did distant entanglements in the Third World and the perilous power duel with the United States. In dealing with these challenges, party leaders, strategists, the military, and sometimes ideological guardians possessed far more weight than area specialists or diplomatically experienced foreign ministers and ambassadors. At its end, the Brezhnev regime, despite its awesome military strength, was less globally secure than at the outset.

Military Posture

The armed forces became especially influential after the Cuban missile crisis. The military lobbied for large, well-armed, well-paid forces and got from Brezhnev lavish defense budgets that rose from 13 to 20 billion rubles, some 20 to 25 percent of the gross national product. Under Andrei Grechko (1903-1976), defense minister from 1967 to 1976, the "correlation of forces" had shifted, and Soviet power had reached near parity with that of the United States in armaments and global reach. Grechko's successor, Dmitry Ustinov (1908–1984), the first civilian defense minister (1976–1984) since the revolution, also headed the military-industrial complex.

The USSR possessed the largest standing army in the world. Like that of its rival, it was staffed with well-trained officers and rugged soldiers and backed by a huge missile park. Most land forces abroad were positioned in the East European bloc countries. How to deploy the hardware and the troops was the subject of endless debates over strategy and doctrine. Said Marshal N. V. Ogarkov in 1979: "Soviet military strategy views a future war, if the imperialists [meaning the North Atlantic Treaty Organization (NATO)] manage to unleash it, as a decisive clash between two opposed world socioeconomic systems—socialist and capitalist." At issue were how, and how forcefully, to advance Soviet strength and influence around the world without squandering forces on risky wars.

The Soviet navy, restored by Brezhnev after Khrushchëv's cuts in favor of missiles, was the second largest, after that of the United States, in the world. It became an arm of diplomacy, as had the British navy a hundred years earlier. Naval chief Admiral Sergei Gorshkov (1910-1988) announced in 1968 that "we now have forces capable not only of checking imperialist aggression, but also, if needed, of delivering a blow from which the aggressor could not recover." When he codified some of his geostrategic ideas in a 1972 book, there was much gnashing of teeth in the West about Soviet force projection and maritime aggression. Most Soviet naval operations were conducted by anticarrier forces designed to stalk and offset the powerful U.S. carrier-based units that roamed the seven seas unhindered. But the Soviets went beyond defensive operations when they sent reconnaissance submarines into Swedish waters, thus violating sea law and also unsettling a neutral state. Soviet warships sailing strategic waterways such as the Red Sea, the Gulf of Aden, and the Indian Ocean raised further alarms. Yet the Soviet blue-water fleet never matched that of the United States in scope or power.

Cracks in the Communist Bloc

One of the many dilemmas facing Soviet power in East Central Europe was that since some of these countries—notably East Germany, Czechoslovakia, Hungary, and Poland—were more advanced in many ways than Russia itself, Soviet domination was all the more resented. Hungary had tried to free itself in 1956 and since then had settled for mild economic reforms known as the New Economic Mechanism, or "market socialism." Poland and Czechoslovakia, in different ways, tried to push much further.

In Czechoslovakia, reformers, aching under the heavy hand of the old Czech Stalinist Antonin Novotny (1904–1975), removed him with Soviet approval in 1967 and in 1968 began to democratize the party, abolish censorship, rehabilitate victims of the previous regime, and curb the police—all without rebelling against or defying the USSR. Alexander Dubcek, the new party leader, called for "socialism with a human face" but retained a modified central planning and party leadership of the state. This burst of reform, the Prague Spring of 1968, was a heady time, full of bright promise because its leaders really believed that Moscow would not intervene. A reformist literary journal editor later recalled that "for the first time in our lives we were producing a paper with no censorship and no outside dictation of ideas: nothing but our own conscience and sense of responsibility." But high party officials in the bloc feared that Czechoslovak reforms would spread to their lands and jeopardize security. After tortuous negotiations among Soviet, Czechoslovak, and other bloc leaders in the summer, USSR-led Warsaw Pact nations invaded the country and ended the experiment. Tanks on the streets of Prague crushed popular protest. The reform leaders were arrested and taken in chains to Moscow. They were not executed but were brought back to Prague, eventually replaced by those accommodating to Moscow, and given demeaning jobs. Brezhnev enunciated what came to be called the Brezhnev Doctrine: any threat to socialism in a bloc country would be met by combined force of the Warsaw Pact. The 1968 events helped gird Soviet leaders against significant reform at home.

Riots in Warsaw against the Czechoslovak invasion went unpunished. But in 1970 Edward Gierek (b. 1913) replaced the aging Wladyslaw Gomulka (1905–1982), the moderate who had negotiated a "Polish road to socialism" in 1956. Gierek, although an ex-coalminer, did little to satisfy workers' demands in a sagging economy. Discontent led intellectuals and workers to form a Committee for the Defense of Workers (KOR), which was supported by the Catholic Church. The prestige of the church skyrocketed when a Pole, Cardinal Karol Wojtyla (b. 1920) became Pope John Paul II. In the summer of 1980, a strike wave in the port cities of Gdansk and Gdynia inspired the formation of a free trade union, Solidarity, headed by the shipyard worker Lech Walesa (b. 1943). He made the union into a major political force, fashioned a moral alliance with the Catholic Church, and won the state's recognition of Solidarity as an independent movement—unprecedented in a Communist country. Fearing intervention, the Warsaw party chiefs flew to Moscow to reassure the Soviet leaders that Poland was still under their control. The distractions of a war in Afghanistan convinced Kremlin leaders to keep their hands off, though they feared the very idea of a free trade union. General Wojtech Jaruzelski (b. 1923), prime minister and party leader, to stem the continuing unrest, erected a military dictatorship in the middle of a December night in 1981 and declared martial law. He arrested thousands of oppositionists, drove Solidarity underground, and launched subsidies to ease the nation's economic plight. But this apparent victory was hollow: Polish society had virtually withdrawn from all but nominal obedience to a state it loathed.

The People's Republic of China had long since left the Soviet bloc, and the Sino-Soviet feud continued along their mutual frontier, as well as in global politics. In 1966, China accused the USSR of arming the Mongolian People's Republic on China's border, a Soviet satellite since the 1920s. In 1967, Chinese citizens staged a government-sponsored protest demonstration in front of the Soviet embassy in Beijing. War scares and armed clashes erupted periodically in the borderlands. The USSR directly supported North Vietnam in its war with the United States and South Vietnam, but the Chinese would not allow Soviet use of their airfields to ferry supplies to the North Vietnamese. A kind of proxy war broke out when Soviet-backed North Vietnam fought against China-backed Cambodia. The most fearful development hit Moscow in 1972, when U.S. president Richard Nixon established détente with China.

The Sino-Soviet split also affected East European bloc nations. The Communist regime in Albania had already aligned itself with Maoist China under Khrushchëv and gotten away with it. Romania, under Nicolae Ceausescu (1918–1989), in the 1960s achieved economic independence from the USSR by means of an implied promise not to join a "China bloc." Both of these Balkan countries retained brutal neo-Stalinist regimes until the end.

Global Reach

Though poised between potentially menacing China and America, Kremlin policymakers succumbed—as did the United States—to the lure of adventures in the

Third World, whose regions seemed ripe for revolution because of their political volatility, grueling poverty, and colonial past. Policy in the Middle East yielded mixed results. Three years after Brezhnev came to power, in 1967, the Soviet Union suffered defeat there when, in the Six-Day War, Israel for the third time trounced its Arab foes—this time Iraq, Syria, and Egypt, all armed with Soviet weaponry. Pro-Soviet president Gamal Abdel Nasser of Egypt died in 1970, and his successor, Anwar Sadat, turning to the West, expelled twenty-one thousand Soviet advisers in 1972, when the USSR refused to supply his country with the latest military hardware. Moscow drew closer to Syria, Iraq, Libya, and the Palestine Liberation Organization.

When Soviet neighbor Iran overthrew its shah and its U.S.-oriented regime in 1979, it established a revolutionary state with a Muslim fundamentalist, the Ayatolla Khomeini, at its head. Soviet policymakers saw Khomeini as a new Kerensky, a straw man who would soon fall to more radical forces. Communists had a hard time believing that any anticommunist regime could win the genuine loyalty of the Iranian people. But the USSR kept peace with Iran and stayed neutral in the Iran-Iraq war that began in 1980.

Soviet interest in South Asia was mostly interdictive: to keep India from joining either the Chinese or American security systems. In this the Russians were successful, much to the anger and chagrin of American statesmen, some of whom equated India's neutralism with procommunism. Soviet envoys learned the languages of the subcontinent, arranged cultural exchanges, and showed some respect for Indian life. Premier Alexei Kosygin made world headlines at Tashkent in 1966 by brokering a peace between India and Pakistan after their 1965 war. The USSR sided with India against Pakistan in their 1971 war.

Africa and Latin America, remote from the Soviet landmass, seemed to have little importance for national security. But in the scheme of geopolitics and long-distance nuclear weapons, contiguity no longer had the same force as in the days when armies simply stepped across frontiers. The Soviet foothold in Latin America had come with Fidel Castro's revolution, which survived the Bay of Pigs and the missile crisis. Latin American unrest seemed to be on the rise in the 1960s and 1970s. Nagging destitution, immense social inequality, and oppressive military juntas and elites enjoying U.S. backing fueled hatred for the Yanqui colossus to the north. A rebel movement, the Sandinistas, came to power in Nicaragua in 1979 with Soviet support. Aside from aid to a few other "national liberation movements," Soviet influence in Latin America was extremely weak. But in the United States, the conviction grew that any communist rebel or leftist victory to the south was a prelude to a Communist surge into Mexico and even onto U.S. territory. In the 1980s, President Ronald Reagan financed powerful "contra" forces to fight the Sandinista government. This added to the bitterness between the two superpowers. A joint Soviet-Nicaraguan communiqué of 1982 condemned "the growing aggressiveness of the forces of imperialism and reaction, headed by the United States of America."

In the 1970s the USSR parlayed Cuba's great interest in Third World revolution into a series of African adventures that won considerable victories. When the Portuguese abandoned their African colony in Angola in 1974, the Marxist-oriented

Popular Movement for the Liberation of Angola was assisted by over fifteen thousand Cuban volunteers sent by Castro to extend world revolution. Soviet forces carried in the Cubans and bolstered them in 1975–1976. Similar interventions took place in other former Portuguese colonies, known for their misrule, especially Mozambique, where the Soviet Union championed a liberation movement. At another corner of the great continent, the Horn of Africa comprises Ethiopia, Eritrea, Somalia, and parts of neighboring lands. Washing the Horn are the Red Sea, the Gulf of Aden, the Arabian Sea, and the Indian Ocean, all strategic waterways. When the Soviet navy was expelled from its docks in Egypt, it found temporary refuge in Somalia, where port facilities were made available. But Moscow lost influence there and among Eritrean separatists when it turned face and helped their foe, the Ethiopian Marxist government of Mengistu Haile Marian. Soviet ships moved to the harbors of the revolutionary state of South Yemen on the nearby Arabian Peninsula. Soviet-Cuban sorties in Africa, though alarming to Cold War adversaries, were ephemeral and left a bitter taste.

Dangerous Relations

Superpower diplomacy swung between freeze, thaw, and refreeze. Early in the Brezhnev years, the freeze was connected to the arms race, Moscow's crackdown on dissidents, and Vietnam. The ice melted a bit in 1972–1973 when U.S. president Richard Nixon went to Moscow and Brezhnev visited the United States. Brezhnev wanted peace, trade, and technology transfer to help solve domestic failings. In a 1972 agreement, America provided credits and technology to the USSR and gave it a most-favored-nation status in trade and tariffs, making it equal to all trading partners of the United States. The Soviets paid off some of the Lend Lease debts remaining from World War II. In the same year, the superpowers signed a Strategic Arms Limitation Treaty (SALT I), which reduced the rate at which strategic nuclear missiles were built. Three U.S. presidents—Nixon, Gerald Ford, and Jimmy Carter—met Brezhnev at a total of five summits in the 1970s.

German chancellor Willy Brandt's *Ostpolitik,* a more open policy toward the Communist states, normalized relations between Germany, Poland, and the USSR and ended Germany's place as epicenter of Great Power rivalry. The Helsinki Conference of 1975, at the peak of détente, brought together European and North American delegates, who ratified postwar frontiers, declared human rights a part of the international order, and provided for groups to monitor them. When the Soviets failed to live up to the agreements and continued to hinder Jewish emigration, U.S. lawmakers made Soviet most-favored-nation status and trade between the two countries contingent on the observance of the Helsinki accords. This and continued bickering over arms control ended the short-lived harmony.

Through the late 1970s Soviet leaders refused to renounce Third World alliances and arms buildups as U.S. administrations desired. The freeze deepened with the Soviet invasion of Afghanistan in 1979, followed by the election in 1980 of Ronald Reagan. The colder Cold War of the 1980s was due partly to Soviet moves in the world arena and partly to Reagan's crusading—and often insulting—zeal against communism in any form. "Let us pray," he said in 1983, "for the salvation of all those who live in totalitarian darkness, pray that they will discover the joy of knowing God." He called his adversary an "evil empire" and whipped up fears of fatigue-clad Nicaraguan guerrillas storming into Texas. Reagan pushed for a U.S. Strategic Defense Initiative (Star Wars) that could be easily interpreted as a menacing escalation in the arms race. In Europe, "rocket politics" intensified. In the 1970s, Soviet intermediate-range SS-20 missiles had been deployed in bloc countries. In the 1980s, the Americans, at the request of their Western European allies, emplaced Pershing and Cruise missiles, which with lightning speed could knock out Soviet cities, including the capital. Each superpower called the other a warmonger. The last ugly episode in the standoff came in 1983, when the Soviets shot down a South Korean passenger plane that had strayed into its air space, killing all aboard.

At War in Asia

In 1979, the Soviet regime stepped in to try to stabilize a turbulent neighbor bordering its southern republics. The Soviet intervention in Afghanistan was hideous and violent in the extreme. This wretchedly poor country of 20 million people, mostly Muslims, was organized in tribal alliances, some of whom were locked in deep-seated hatred. Mild competition for influence there between the United States and the more entrenched USSR ended when a bloody revolution in 1978 installed a leftist regime, which received Moscow's support. The new government aroused loathing and opposition among Afghans and was plagued by inner struggles. In 1979, a more radical leader, Hafizullah Amin, seized power and killed his predecessor. At this point, the Soviet Politburo acted on the Brezhnev Doctrine. Only this time it was to "save" a socialist regime, not from Prague Spring–type reformers, but from extremist leaders who threatened to invite destruction from increased opposition. In late December 1979, Soviet troops airlifted into the capital, Kabul, deposed Amin, had him killed, and installed Babrak Karmal. These actions escalated the resistance, and to meet it, more Soviet troops moved in. Thousands of Afghan tribesmen rose in the valleys and mountain fastnesses and attacked the occupying troops. Moscow leaders could not understand the force and nature of the resistance; they believed that the tribal divisiveness of their enemies would undo them, as had happened to the Basmachi decades ago in Soviet Central Asia (see the chapter "Revolution in the Life of Peoples, 1921–1928").

The fallout of this ten-year war was tremendous. Soviet soldiers inflicted torments on the local population with flamethrowers and mines: Afghan rebels sometimes subjected their prisoners to agonizing tortures and dismemberment. About 15,000 Soviet solders died, and 35,000 were wounded in this war. The flow of American arms and money across the Khyber Pass to the rebels, including the later infamous Osama Bin Laden, further exacerbated the superpower rivalry. Communist China and parts of the Third World expressed anti-Soviet outrage. Tensions increased with Muslims inside and outside of the USSR. The drain of manpower and the reaction at home to the casualties made this one of the most unpopular wars in Russian history. In this sense, even if in no other, it resembled Vietnam.

A Soviet tank rolls through a town during the Afghan war. *Hulton/Archive/Getty Images.*

THE OLD MEN DEPART, 1982–1985

Brezhnev's seventy-fifth birthday in 1981 was celebrated with grandiose pomp, but behind the solemn festivities rose the odor of decay. Corruption erupted in Brezhnev's own family when his daughter Galina was caught speculating in diamonds with a criminal ring whose web extended even into the KGB. The scandal was suppressed until his death, but Brezhnev's ailing health could not be so well hidden. The frail old man made a pitiful spectacle at public occasions, where he sometimes forgot where he was. Merciless jokes were told about his senility, intellectual pretensions, and cultural primitivism. He died in November 1982 and was succeeded, after some hesitation, by Yuri Andropov, the first police chief in Soviet history to assume power.

Born in 1914 near Stavropol in a family of railway employees, Andropov entered party work via a successful career with the Young Communist League. He had been ambassador to Hungary in 1954–1957, where he acted both in the repression and in the transition afterward. Andropov headed the KGB in 1967–1982 and became a Politburo member in 1973. On succeeding Brezhnev, he instantly launched a vigorous campaign against shirking, drink, and corruption, but his cosmetic measures were largely unenforceable. A few heads rolled during his brief tenure, including some of Brezhnev's relatives by marriage. None of this touched the structures of authority, privilege, and inefficiency. The KGB, under Andropov's deputy, Viktor Chebrikov, became more intrusive in surveilling citizens and foreigners. Its harassments and dirty tricks increased, and the Cold War froze up again. Andropov, ill and virtually incapacitated since August 1983, died early in 1984.

When Andropov died, hesitation and ambivalence set in. The younger generation of party leaders, the "fifty-year-olds," were ready to move into top spots but were thwarted in favor of an old-timer, Konstantin Chernenko, who reigned from February 1984 to March 1985. The son of a Siberian peasant and the last Soviet leader to have been born (1911) before the revolution, his only symbolic resonance was that as a youngster he had been one of the Border Guards, a force vaunted in Stalinist propaganda. When he expired on March 10, 1985, leaving the posts of General Secretary and president vacant once again, no one dreamed that his successor would help usher in the collapse of the Soviet system.

In the eyes of millions of loyalists and true believers, that system possessed certain strengths: stability, peace until 1979, Great Power prestige, and an array of social guarantees. But the weaknesses were formidable. The black market revealed the reality of a rotting economy. Countercultures and dissidence promoted creative and human rights denied by the state. The bloated and ornate political system with its leader cults and propaganda barrages could not obscure the realities of mismanagement, corruption, ineptitude, and callousness. Glaring contradictions steadily diminished the regime's power to persuade, as did ever-increasing exposure to foreign ways and thought. The regime's alienation of one of society's most productive elements, the Jews, was both harmful and immoral—as was the even more devastating bloodletting in Afghanistan. The fabric hiding all these flaws would be ripped off by the new man who took up residence in the Kremlin: Mikhail Gorbachëv.

CHAPTER 41

The Gorbachëv Revolution, 1985–1991

People are tired of tension and confrontation. They prefer a search for a more secure and reliable world, a world in which everyone would preserve their own philosophic, political, and ideological views and their way of life.

—*Mikhail Gorbachev,* Perestroika and New Thinking for Russia and for the Entire World, *1987*

Beginning in 1985, the dramatic element of Soviet history—long acted out in foreign adventures, persecution of dissidents, or cultural scandals—found a spectacular performance space inside the Kremlin itself. The Brezhnev era, like a Tolstoy novel, had rolled along and ended without a sense of closure or resolution. The enthralling stories in those years were at the margin. With the advent of Mikhail Gorbachëv, political life at the top became the subject of worldwide attention. The nation seemed to revive, and Moscow became the vortex of suspense and innovation.

PERESTROIKA: CONTROLLED REFORM

By the 1980s, the party that had made a revolution, mobilized a nation, and won a world war had become fat, old, and infirm at the top. Gerontocracy—rule by the old—accounted for weaknesses in later years. The party itself and the central planning system were no longer capable of "learning" fast enough; self-correcting mechanisms were rusted or broken. Through its master list, the *nomenklatura,* the party gave out jobs and fed and cared for itself but did not earn its keep. By lavishly investing in the armed forces to maintain superpower status, it squandered resources. The party apparatus did shelter some vigorous shadow reformers, but they were outnumbered, and their aspirations to better the system were mostly blocked by conservatives. When Mikhail Gorbachëv came along, reformers from academic think tanks and the Central Committee moved to the forefront. Gorbachëv saw through the reassuring façade of the Soviet edifice into the shambles of the interior. When he began the move to repair it, he was able to draw on his fellow reformers' brains and energies. The big question would be: Did he or they see deeply enough into the structural faults of that edifice?

Mikhail Sergeevich Gorbachëv was born in 1931 in a village in the Stavropol region of the northern Caucasus. The son of a tractor operator, the young Mikhail worked in the fields before going in 1950 to study law at Moscow University, a magnet for ambitious people. One of his best friends there, Anatoly Lukyanov (b. 1930), in August 1991 would become his Judas. Another friend was a Czech exchange student, Zdenek Mlynar (b. 1930), who in 1967, on the eve of becoming a key figure in the Prague Spring of 1968, visited Gorbachëv and probably planted some of his reform notions. Starting a steady upward path in the Young Communist League and Communist Party, after graduating in 1956, Gorbachëv returned to his home region. After eight years as party secretary there, he moved up to the Central Committee in 1978 and, with Andropov's help, to the Politburo in 1980. Passed over at the death of Andropov, Gorbachëv was chosen General Secretary after the demise of Chernenko in 1985. A man of the "younger generation," Gorbachëv was seen as a vigorous pilot who in difficult times could navigate without sinking the ship of state.

Gorbachëv wanted to reform, not abolish, socialism, party rule, and the Soviet Union. Typical of many who lost family in the Stalinist purges (both his grandfathers had been arrested), he remained committed to the system that his father had fought for in the war. But he believed he could humanize it. Like others who served as local party men and who would join his team—Eduard Shevardnadze in Georgia and Boris Yeltsin in the Urals—Gorbachëv had already shown the signs of a would-be reformer. No populist, he nevertheless exhibited a responsive "democratic" style with crowds and colleagues, a refreshing change of manner from that of the old guard. He realized that centralized control inevitably generated underground

Mikhail Gorbachëv makes a point.
Novosti/Sovfoto.

countersystems. Spontaneity, responsibility, and the right to organize and advance a particular interest were alien to the system Gorbachëv inherited. But he believed they could flourish within a framework of limited reform, including cultural expression, political participation, economic flexibility, and détente, an agenda he described as *perestroika,* or "restructuring." He envisioned something like Western civil society inside a party state. He had to steer carefully between supporters of root-and-branch change and the "dinosaurs" who yearned to stand pat out of self-interest, sincerely held beliefs, habit, or fear of the unknown.

Gorbachëv drew sustenance from a remarkable network of men and women in and out of government, a group radically different from those who had surrounded Brezhnev. Politburo member Alexander Yakovlev (b. 1923), once an ambassador to Canada and a convinced Communist, became Gorbachëv's principal Western-oriented adviser, offering ideas that would have sent Brezhnev's ideologists into shock. The new foreign minister, Shevardnadze, had made a career as reforming party boss of Georgia. Yeltsin was brought in to clean up the city of Moscow, and he soon became an outspoken critic of the Soviet system. Outside of the top party ranks, Gorbachëv reached out to a liberal group, the Moscow Tribune, which included ethnosociologist Galina Starovoitova (assassinated in the late 1990s), journalist Len Karpinsky, economist Nikolai Shmelev, and historian Yuri Afanasev. Gorbachëv drew on the ideas of economist and sociologist Tatyana Zaslavskaya (b. 1927), who had been stressing "the human factor" in society. She and her team of 150 researchers produced in 1983 the *Novosibirsk Report,* which charted the negative impact of central planning and urged drastic reform.

GLASNOST: THE RAISED VOICE

In tsarist times, *glasnost* (from *golos,* "voice") had meant limited discussion of government-sponsored reforms; for Gorbachëv it meant publicity, openness, and freedom of expression in support of his programs. In practice, *glasnost* went beyond Gorbachëv's definition and enabled citizens to speak, assemble, and act in ways almost unknown in Soviet history. From 1987 onward, at a remarkable tempo, came a burst of writing on every conceivable subject in all the media and across the spectrum of opinion—evoking some notions not welcomed by the government. As an early gesture of goodwill, Gorbachëv released dissident scientist Andrei Sakharov from exile and invited him to Moscow.

Once-forbidden books rolled off the press: Evgeny Zamyatin's antiutopian *We* from the 1920s; George Orwell's *1984;* poems of Anna Akhmatova, who had been silenced in the postwar years; Boris Pasternak's *Doctor Zhivago;* and Alexander Solzhenitsyn's *Gulag Archipelago.* Texts whispered about for decades in the kitchens of dissidents went public. New and daring journals and newspapers sprouted up to make Moscow the most interesting journalistic town in the world. Historians excavated data from once-closed archives on the atrocities of the past. Others exhumed bones and skulls, hideous remnants of Stalinist mass executions. Documentaries and talk shows exposed the sores of environmental devastation, crime, youth gangs, corruption, and religious persecution.

Movie directors outdid themselves in the labors of *glasnost.* After a 1986 revolt in the Union of Soviet Filmmakers, sanctioned by Gorbachëv, a batch of prohibited films was released, the most important of which was Tengis Abuladze's Georgian masterpiece *Repentance* (made in 1984, released in 1987), which presented a terrifying allegory of cruel dictatorship in the person of its lead character, a composite of Stalin, Beria, Hitler, and Mussolini. A whole new genre of popular and sensational films appeared. The factory smoke of a southern industrial town was vividly depicted in the movie *Little Vera* (1989), whose theme was degradation of urban bodies and souls. *Intergirl* (1989) put the reality of Soviet prostitution on screen for the first time. The liberal intelligentsia were less happy with some side effects of *glasnost:* pulp fiction, pornography, tabloids, and reactionary papers enraged by Gorbachëv's programs and the new cultural freedom. A writer for the conservative *Young Guard* in 1990 believed that a combination of public pornography, Israeli and NATO influences, and Elvis Presley was responsible for the "destruction of the soul and the mind."

Glasnost encouraged a sense of civil identity outside a state that had usurped the roles of teacher, parent, and preacher. Within a few years, thousands of groups called "informals," with millions of members, were focusing on the environment, historical preservation, or social issues. Newly independent women's organizations vigorously addressed the problems of females of every age. Memorial, a group created by liberal intellectuals, helped rehabilitate Stalin's victims and agitate for democratic reform.

The Orthodox Church, submerged for decades by persecution and police infiltration, was released from its bonds. Religion flourished openly, priests spoke up in political bodies, and chaplains were appointed to the army. Catholics, Protestants, Muslims, Buddhists, and other believers followed suit. A Jewish religious center opened in Moscow. Local populations restored old tsarist names to cities, towns, and streets—reversing what had happened in the Russian Revolution. Leningrad became St. Petersburg again by vote of its inhabitants in 1991. Those former leaders previously considered traitors—among them Nikolai Bukharin, the gifted Lenin disciple and mixed-economy advocate who fell to Stalin's terror—were rehabilitated, and almost all political prisoners were released. Muckraking exposed Soviet legends as fraudulent stories, bringing joy to those who thirsted for truth but exciting wrath among those who saw it as spitting on their heritage.

NEW THINKING AND GLOBAL DÉTENTE

Although Gorbachëv's main focus was domestic reform, his achievement on the international scene was remarkably positive for all except dyed-in-the-wool Russian nationalists, Third World allies left in the lurch, and Fidel Castro (eleven thousand Soviet troops were withdrawn from Cuba). The dynamic Gorbachëv quickly won friends among old enemy powers with a style that some skeptics called a "charm offensive." His book *Perestroika and New Thinking for Russia and for the Entire World* (1987) advocated peace and international security as the requirement for Soviet economic advance. It offered a vista of future cooperation in tones of mutual dependence and even humility hardly ever heard in Soviet diplomatic language. The familiar Cold War bluster and rhetoric of class struggle gave way to talk of "universal human values" in world relations. Tying global interdependence to the Scientific Technical Revolution, Gorbachëv echoed Sakharov and other scientists and dissidents of the preceding era when he spoke urgently of international scientific cooperation, control of nuclear weapons, and protection of the environment. Gorbachëv visited Beijing to restore friendly relations, reestablished diplomatic relations with Israel, ended the paternalistic treaty with Finland signed under Stalin, and even exchanged envoys with the Vatican. Most restrictions on foreign travel for Soviet citizens were lifted.

A comic incident with serious repercussions occurred in 1987 when an adventurous young German flew a small plane through the vaunted Soviet air security ring and landed on Red Square. This allowed Gorbachëv to take a crack at the military and replace defense minister Sergei Sokolov (b. 1911), an aging hard-liner, with General Dmitry Yazov (b. 1923), who would betray his promoter in a few years. Soviet support for revolutionaries in Africa and Central America was wound down. The most momentous of Gorbachëv's initiatives was to end the war in Afghanistan; by early 1989, the last Soviet troops had withdrawn. This and his foreign policies won him world respect and in 1990 the Nobel Peace Prize.

In reacting to events closer to home, Gorbachëv also exhibited wise statesmanship. In the late 1980s, the East Central European satellite states once again echoed the reform impulses of Moscow; and in the spring and summer of 1989, forces of change gathered momentum. In Poland, the free trade union Solidarity was legalized, and a Catholic intellectual became prime minister, the first noncommunist to do so in forty years. In Hungary, Janos Kadar (1912–1989), in power since 1956, was removed, paving the way for more drastic change. Soon after a Gorbachëv visit to Berlin, East Germans held mass demonstrations that culminated in November 1989 with the opening and later destruction of the Berlin Wall. The Communist regime was toppled, and the Germanies were fused again into one state, which Gorbachëv recognized after a year. In autumn 1989 also, Bulgaria witnessed the fall of another long-term Stalinist, Todor Zhivkov. Czechoslovak events took the form of a bloodless "velvet revolution" that brought Alexander Dubcek out of obscurity as a national hero and installed the dissident playwright Vaclav Havel in Prague's ancient Hradcany Castle as president. Among Havel's announcements, one rang out like a clarion: "The Czechoslovak Republic must be a legal, democratic state in the spirit and traditions of Czechoslovak statehood and of internationally valid principles." Only in Romania was the velvet spattered with blood: street fighting took many lives before the regime was overthrown. The Communist dictator Nicolae Ceausescu and his wife were executed.

Gorbachëv did not expect such sudden and dramatic transformations, and some of his signals were overinterpreted. But he was unwilling to keep the burden of a satellite empire and, in the midst of these turbulent events, indicated that the Brezhnev Doctrine was no more and that the Soviets would not intervene, even against the reunification of Germany. The effective end of Soviet dominance in East Central Europe after more than four decades signaled the disappearance of the bloc and two years later of the Warsaw Pact. With the Iron Curtain torn down, Gorbachëv's idea of a "common European home" became a possibility.

Gorbachëv publicly recognized the burdens and perils of excessive military buildup. His demilitarization measures included the reduction of missiles and conventional forces in Europe, a policy dictated by his program of maintaining only a defensive posture, accommodation with the West, and economic health. Though negotiations were stalled by President Reagan's Star Wars plan, a mutual cutback of Intermediate Range Nuclear Forces was agreed to in 1987. A spectacular instance of U.S.-Soviet cooperation in global politics was Gorbachëv's endorsement of President Bush's attack on Iraq in the Gulf War of 1991, the first time the two powers had been on the same side in a major conflict since 1945. Gorbachëv's policies won him effulgent praise in the West, praise that some contemptuously called "Gorbomania." The Cold War was declared over by the superpower leaders. But in the USSR, some considered Gorbachëv's pro-Western, noninterventionist pacifism tantamount to treason. Not a few officers were more sympathetic to Saddam Hussein than to the United States in the 1991 Gulf War.

ECONOMIC WOES

On the economic front, Gorbachëv enjoyed little success. He had inherited the problems of the Brezhnev period, themselves anchored in the Stalinist command economy. The sluggish growth rate of recent years was now named "stagnation." Far too much of the state's revenue had been drawn from petroleum export and vodka sales, the first subject to world prices and the second harmful to health and productivity. Gorbachëv added new state expenditures to alleviate environmental and natural disasters. He remained committed to state ownership of the bulk of the means of production, full (if under) employment, affordable housing, free health care and education, and the subsidy of foodstuffs and transport. Within this framework, Gorbachëv sought to reform the economy by technological modernization, more incentives for enterprise managers, increased productivity of the work force, and agricultural diversity. In 1986 he announced a policy of "acceleration," or rapid economic growth to end stagnation. His scheme was projected in the Twelfth (and last) Five-Year Plan (1986–1990), with later refinements and additions.

Economic Acceleration

Early proposals by economic advisers Abel Aganbegyan (b. 1932) and Zaslavskaya envisioned a planned economy without party interference and went only a little beyond those of previous regimes. Capitalism's free market based on supply and demand, private enterprise, and a stock market were not even considered in the first few years. A few bold reformers around Gorbachëv believed that an economy based on planning rather than consumer choice had to go. But party officials smelled a threat to their self-interest, which was tied to the command economy. Fear and reluctance at the lower levels of party and management brought sabotage of even minor changes.

Industrial reform converted rigid central planning into a long-term coordinating mechanism. A 1988 law gave state enterprises freedom to set prices and wages and formulate their own plan based on sales to the state and to other enterprises or organizations. Workers were to elect managers. But these reforms resulted in higher-priced goods and wages with no increase in labor productivity.

Like Andropov, Gorbachëv tried to create a disciplined and sober work force with a renewed campaign against alcohol. Vodka rationing cause a marked improvement in life expectancy in 1987–1988. Yet home distilling rose massively, and sugar, a key ingredient, vanished from the shops. The policy hurt state revenue and fueled popular rancor against the General Secretary, or GenSek, who was now nicknamed GenSok, or General Juice. In a popular anecdote, a worker leaves a long vodka queue to go and shoot Gorbachëv but finds the line waiting at the Kremlin to shoot him even longer.

Between 1986 and 1990, Gorbachëv took cautious moves toward a partial market economy by legalizing small urban private businesses designed to give work to the nonemployed—students, the elderly, and others. The 1988 Cooperative Law projected a quasi-market network of retailers and producers who would serve the public on demand. Legally operating outside the planned economy and setting their own prices and wages, these small firms began to sprout up, averaging about twenty-five employees. By 1990, some 260,000 co-ops with 6.2 million employees were politely selling the public meals, computers, and appliances. Co-ops charged high prices, which some buyers resented. Though they answered the real needs of some people, some party officials saw their "unearned incomes" as illegal, and the KGB harassed, taxed, and occasionally closed them. A policeman was quoted as saying "Why should we care about these cooperators if they only care about their own pockets." The public, imbued for decades with anticapitalist values, despised them as their parents had despised the nepmen in the 1920s. Thriving co-ops also invited "protection" rackets, whereby crooks threatened violence to owners unless they paid up. One of the racketeers recalled proudly: "Those who did not agree [to pay] were subjected to our pressure. After all, we had good manuals, those Mafia movies. The soldering iron was pretty popular and so were handcuffs, which we attached to the radiator."

Gorbachëv's policies gave the agricultural sector some needed investment, and groups of farmers or families could lease state land and tools outside the collective farm and produce independently for the market. Gorbachëv wanted these peasants to be "masters of the land they tilled" in a mixed agrarian system of state, collective, and private or semiprivate holdings that went well beyond the private plots. This plan was also beset by old obstacles and unforeseen consequences: the lack of a financial infrastructure, of a legal framework, and of a surrounding capitalist culture;

the overwork and stresses of a small family business; and the hostility of collective farm managers, neighbors, and the aged and infirm toward new successful farms. Neither Gorbachëv nor his successors solved the age-old agrarian problem.

Economic Confusion

Many of Gorbachëv's reforms remained on paper and were fiercely resisted down below. Despite all efforts, ministries continued to swell in personnel, float wasteful new construction, and interfere in enterprises. Shortages and inflation worsened, and economic crime ran rampant. Contrary to plan projections, industrial and agricultural production, labor productivity, and real income, instead of rising, fell, weighed down by the gridlock of old practices and the confusion caused by new and often conflicting decrees. The bulk of the economy remained state owned, and it groaned with inefficiency.

Ironically, the reforms, designed to retain the "social guarantees" as the economy moved ahead, spread misery among the poorest and allowed a new class of tycoons to emerge. When enterprises were given more choice in what to produce and charge for their products, prices shot up. Retired people and others living on fixed income were made poor by the changing prices. Thousands of illegal millionaires flourished in the shadows of the huge black market, and hundreds of new legal ones appeared as well through co-ops, joint ventures, and creative interpretations or distortions of the law. These vigorous men, some from the top echelons of party and government, often used party funds and property as startup capital. The most visible of them tended to be adventurous, gaudy, and fond of conspicuous consumption. Lack of legal clarity made new businesses seem shady (as indeed many were) and thus vulnerable to blackmailing squeeze by officials. Organized crime cartels forced new tycoons to hand over a chunk of their profits. Working-class strongmen and Afghan War veterans were hired as extortionists, kidnappers, or assassins.

A frightening growth of crime and violence and the growing gap between rich and poor generated anxiety that had been unknown to the general population for decades. Particularly vulnerable to inflation and the erosion of services were millions of World War II veterans, the handicapped, and elderly pensioners. Certain sectors of the labor force were also hard hit. The summer of 1989 brought a wave of strikes in the mining centers of Donbass, the Kuzbass, Karaganda, Vorkuta, and Sakhalin over substandard conditions—a lifetime in the dark holes, lung infections, overwork, and miserable housing. Aimed at mine directors, local party chiefs, the government, and Gorbachëv, the strikes intensified and became political. Though the authorities did precious little to accommodate the strikers, they were shaken.

A brewing crisis faced the leaders by 1990. Prime Minister N. I. Ryzhkov (b. 1929) suggested a conservative course: a five-year transition to a regulated market with controlled price rises. Much more radical was the "shock therapy" program, called the Five Hundred Days plan, proposed by Gorbachëv's economic adviser Stanislav Shatalin (b. 1934) and Yeltsin's free-market specialist, Grigory Yavlinsky (b. 1952). They got their bosses to agree on this rapid path to a free market. Though the five-hundred-day timetable was largely rhetorical, the plan would have shut down defense industries, reduced military budgets, and sold off of state property (privatization). But Gorbachëv bent to influential figures in government and the economy who opposed this dramatic reversal of sixty years of Soviet economic history. In October he shelved the Five Hundred Days plan in favor of a more cautious approach, much to the dismay of his market-oriented advisers. Various alternatives were fashioned into a compromise plan that included some military cuts and a new mixture of freedom and regulation.

Despite wide publicity about economic reforms, Soviet citizens remained puzzled, suspicious, and divided. The shortages and other economic woes led to a sharp increase in emigration, made possible by another Gorbachëv reform. The increasing popular opposition to the General Secretary in 1989–1991 was largely the result of economic hardship.

POLITICAL EXPERIMENTS

Gorbachëv proceeded slowly with "democratization"—by which he meant reform within a party-ruled state. This was more than the old Soviet meaning of that word, but certainly less than its meaning to the West. Though little was accomplished in his first three years, once begun, democratization took on unexpected momentum.

Starting at the Top

With what Brezhnev's foreign minister Andrei Gromyko had called the "iron teeth" lurking behind Gorbachëv's smile, the General Secretary bit into the tough fabric of the establishment. He ousted troublesome old guard figures such as KGB chief Viktor Chebrikov (b. 1923) and the obnoxious party bosses of Leningrad, Ukraine, and Azerbaijan and replaced the Brezhnevite Nikolai Tikhonov (b. 1905) with the moderate N. I. Ryzhkov as prime minister and Gromyko with Shevardnadze as foreign minister. A conservative, Egor Ligachëv (b. 1920), strong in the Politburo and the Secretariat, and other party faithful resisted these measures and were dismayed at the "blackening" of Soviet history, rehabilitation of purge victims, release of more arrestees, and attack on the *nomenklatura.*

Into this volatile arena stepped Boris Yeltsin, who had won a reputation for efficiency and honesty in Sverdlovsk, a major industry and defense center in the Urals. In 1985 he was appointed candidate—that is, not quite full member—to the Politburo and the new party chief of Moscow. A gruff populist, Yeltsin fired incompetent and corrupt subordinates, cracked down on state thievery, abolished do-nothing organizations, and wrested privileges from the *nomenklatura,* such as cars, drivers, special stores, and admissions to higher learning. Yeltsin walked the streets of the city, visiting shops incognito, searching out the rot. These gestures endeared him to many Muscovites and fueled hatred among those who had lived for decades on party privilege. In the fall of 1987, Yeltsin complained in a letter to Gorbachëv that in the party there still prevailed "the same old approach: time-serving, petty, bureaucratic, loud without substance." He warned the Central Committee of a gathering cult of personality around Gorbachëv and blasted Ligachëv for opposing reform. This scandalous truth telling and name calling in a high-level party forum won Yeltsin a harsh reprimand, and Gorbachëv fired him from his Moscow post.

Gorbachëv, feeling heat from both the forces for change and those for order, muscled opponents on both sides. He pushed the Central Committee to weaken the party stranglehold on Soviet life, abolish secret nominations and elections, give greater power to Soviets, and reform the justice system. With his 1988 reorganization of the party Secretariat, a key organ in supervising national republic affairs, Gorbachëv unwittingly loosened party control over those republics and paved the way for burgeoning independence movements.

Grassroots

Political reform from above was outstripped by the emergence below of new parties with roots in the pre-Gorbachëv schools of thought, think tanks, reform lobbies, private groups, and the shadow world of dissidence. Supporting Gorbachëv's center position were a diffuse group of moderate outsiders who formed a link between state and society. To Gorbachëv's left—ironic as it must sound—were the anticommunists: liberals, democrats, socialists, anarchists, and populists, all of whom shared a common view of the party-dominated state as an "old regime" that needed overthrowing or reforms more radical than those envisioned by Gorbachëv.

The right, united only in its hatred of Gorbachëv's path to the future, included nationalists, anti-Semites, and even monarchists. Neo-Stalinists longed for the strong arm of the state and a freezing of reforms. The group Pamyat (Memory) reheated a brew of nineteenth-century Official Nationalism and Slavophilism and launched demonstrations calling for "law and order," patriotism, military education, patriarchal households, and rural culture. Anti-Semites among them falsely claimed that Lenin, Bukharin, and Kerensky were Jews. The ultranationalist Vladimir Zhirinovsky (b. 1946) turned his following into the ill-named Liberal Democratic Party. Neo-Nazi gangs, who had made their first appearance in the Brezhnev years, mostly young males of working-class families, marched around in Hitlerite costumes. Eventually some of the extreme neo-Stalinists and nostalgic nationalists fused into a "Red-Brown" alliance (brown from the early Nazi Brownshirts, or Storm Troopers)—in other words, a union of Stalinism and fascism. Thus the long-standing but discreet romance between Russian nationalism and communism now became an open liaison.

Less noticed at the time was the steady growth of a more pragmatic movement based on the national identity of the Russian Soviet Federated Socialist Republic (RSFSR), the original Bolshevik state and the largest of the union republics. Among the many complaints issuing from Russian Republic nationalists was the lack of a specifically Russian Communist Party as such, since, although the party was a unified structure, all the other republics had their own chapters: the Lithuanian CP, the Kazakh CP, and so on. Another issue was the absence of various Russian institutions, as opposed to all-Soviet ones headquartered in the RSFSR. Eventually these sentiments fed into a coalition of democratic forces in the Russian Republic led by Yeltsin.

Politics with a New Face

The June 1988 Nineteenth Special Party Conference, a type of meeting that had fallen into disuse under Stalin, provided the greatest scene of political debate in Russia since the 1920s. Partial TV coverage aired antigovernment speeches to millions of viewers. Renewed verbal bouts between Yeltsin and hard-liner Ligachëv, refereed by Gorbachëv, offered unprecedented political theater. Yeltsin demanded an end to special stores for the party elite, whom he sarcastically called "the starving *nomenklatura.*" Gorbachëv delivered a withering exposé of the ills of Soviet society and called for a rejuvenated democratic and humane one-party socialist system. By means of free elections and debates on issues in a setting of checks and balances, he aimed at substituting real politics for mere policymaking. A democratized party would rule, with a reduced role in the economy. Like Moses, Gorbachëv took his people to the edge of a new promised land, a true multiparty democratic order and a market economy, but he would not cross the frontier.

In 1989 a new parliament was established. The USSR Supreme Soviet created in 1936 had 1,500 deputies, who met only a few days a year and had practically no oversight over government organs. This was now replaced by a Congress of People's Deputies, whose 2,250 members were to meet twice annually for two weeks; and a new Supreme Soviet of over 500 representatives, chosen by the congress, that would sit most of the year. A third of the deputies to the new congress were chosen by public bodies, such as the Communist Party, trade unions, and the Academy of Sciences; the other two-thirds were elected in the first real political contest in the country since the election of the Constituent Assembly in 1917. Since then, voters had had no real choice: the candidates were selected by, and usually from, the party. One could vote yes on the entire slate or publicly retire to a booth to cross out names, a right that few citizens were willing to exercise. In 1989, though not all voters had a choice of candidates, they had a secret ballot and could mark "none of the candidates" to defeat some Communists who ran unopposed.

The country became a school for democracy. People from every walk of life began talking about slates, programs, candidates; some voters were mystified, some cynical, but many were pulled into the fascinating web of politics. Mass meetings and freewheeling debates brought out new grievances. Some voters expected too many immediate results. When the congress convened in May 1989, the Communists had won the great bulk of the seats, but many "safe" candidates of party and government were knocked out of the race by angry voters. The deputies—including priests, poets, and ex-dissidents—represented a rough cross-section of society. Yeltsin won 90 percent of the votes in Moscow. Sakharov and historian and Gorbachëv adviser Yuri Afanasev were elected, as was the Estonian Marju Lauristin, who would soon help lead her country to freedom.

The first congress formed, in the words of a Yeltsin biographer, a scene of "disorderly brilliance and plain proto-democratic tumult in which some of the nation's best minds, liveliest tongues and largest egos, suddenly liberated, competed for national attention." Gorbachëv opened the new body and gave the first word to the venerable Andrei Sakharov. For two weeks in May, and again in December, a considerable portion of the population was engrossed by the televised debates. The angry exchanges gave legislative politics a vitality unknown in Soviet history. Yeltsin pounded the party leadership again; a female deputy publicly challenged the government to make good on its promises to women; speakers unleashed floods of invective about the brutalities of the Soviet past, the poor state of housing and health, the crime rate, and a dozen other issues. Here a Central Asian novelist took the floor, there an Orthodox prelate. A national hero, the champion weightlifter Yuri Vlasov, denounced the KGB on screen as "a veritable underground empire" and a threat to democracy. On the closing day, Sakharov openly challenged Gorbachëv to transfer power completely from the Communist Party to elected deputies. Gorbachëv, angered that Sakharov had gone too far in his critique, turned off his microphone.

The congress elected a Supreme Soviet with Gorbachëv as chair, thus head of state. Yeltsin, with many enemies in the establishment, was not elected, but one of the deputies yielded his seat to him. The new body, though dominated by unreconstructed communists, displayed unheard-of vigor in committee work and in the questioning of appointed ministers. Even more radical was the emergence of the democratically oriented Interregional Group, led by Sakharov and Afanasev, which announced itself as a faction within the Supreme Soviet. Other political formations followed suit. In contrast to the Interregional Group, Soyuz, headed by the ultranationalist Colonel Viktor Alksnis (b. 1950), dedicated itself to preserving the Soviet Union intact, topped by an authoritarian state that would introduce the free market from above. The intelligentsia were stricken by the death in December of Sakharov, whose funeral turned into a solemn demonstration of the nation's conscience. In the winter of 1989–1990, people wearied of endless debate and polarized political activists showed ominous signs of wrath in their meetings and public marches.

Gorbachëv Challenged

In February 1990, the Central Committee abolished the party's "leading role" in the state, in place since the civil war. Henceforth it would have to try to win that role through elections. Gorbachëv desired a competitive, democratic, "updated" party that would "guide" society but have no monopoly on power. Communists continued to win elections and play a major role in society, but they were divided into old guard and reformists who opposed each other in elections, joined other blocs, and fought openly. Communists in the republics divided into nationalists and Muscovites—virtually creating two Communist Parties everywhere. In July, the Twenty-Eighth Congress of the Communist Party of the Soviet Union (CPSU), its last, assembled in Moscow. By year's end embryonic competing parties were in place—about twenty nationwide and hundreds of local ones—bearing a profusion of names, such as Democratic Party, Democratic Union, and Democratic Russia.

To buttress his own power, in March 1990 Gorbachëv had himself elected by the Third Congress of People's Deputies, rather than by popular vote, to a newly strengthened executive presidency. His power was no longer based on the party that he himself had helped to weaken, but on the state. A cartoon of the time showed him trying on a tsar's crown. Opposition forces took to the streets in antigovernment demonstrations. On May 1, 1990, during the traditional May Day parade, reviewed by government leaders on Red Square, a crowd untraditionally waved their fists at the reviewing stand and screamed, "Down with Gorbachëv." Although he had ascended to great heights, as the year 1990 ended, Gorbachëv was challenged from all quarters. As one political scientist observed, the new system "lent itself to the articulation of grievances rather than solutions." *Glasnost,* the critical voice of reform, was more successful than political restructuring. National unity, Gorbachëv's greatest aspiration, was further from the horizon than ever, and his personal popularity had plummeted to a new low.

In the meantime, major opposition took shape in the form of Boris Yeltsin and a Democratic Russia bloc, with its base in the Russian Republic. In May 1990, Russia's own Congress of People's Deputies elected Yeltsin head of the Russian Supreme Soviet and thus leader of the Russian Republic; two other antagonists of Gorbachëv, Gavriil Popov (b. 1936) and Anatoly Sobchak (1937–2000) were elected mayors of Moscow and Leningrad respectively. Yeltsin's platform of democracy without a Communist Party, federalism without an empire, and private property (still vaguely defined) was far to the "left" of Gorbachëv. The deputies declared Russian sovereignty on June 12, now celebrated as Russia's day of independence from the USSR. Yeltsin endowed his republic with the trappings of a full-scale state, signed treaties with other republics, offered sovereignty to the ethnic minority regions within the RSFSR, and appointed a Moscow Chechen, Ruslan Khasbulatov (b. 1942), as his first deputy chairman. In a farewell to the Soviet past, Yeltsin resigned from the Communist Party. He had chosen "nation building" inside Russia over Gorbachëv's "empire saving" of the USSR.

"AND NATIONS WAKEN IN THE NIGHT"?

The above heading, a line from a Pushkin poem, expresses what one historian has criticized as the erroneous "sleeping beauty" view of nationalism, that of historic nations slumbering beneath alien rule and then suddenly awakening. In fact, throughout the Soviet period, national identities were steadily being reshaped by affirmative action, social mobility, intermarriage, the Russian presence, and territorial boundaries. Nevertheless, the ferment in the non-Russian republics under Gorbachëv was greater than anything seen there since the 1920s. National movements were driven by revelations about history, environmental concerns, and the climate of free publicity. In the republics, "national fronts" transcending narrower political interests held seminars on independence tactics. Former dissidents emerged as possible leaders. Voters used the new electoral machinery to put nationalists in their own parliaments. The nationality issue turned out to be insoluble under the continued existence of the USSR.

A bright politician who could comprehend competing interests and conflicts, Gorbachëv was practically blind to the power of national feelings and the degree to which they had grown in the last thirty years or so. Gorbachëv could readily sympathize with the ardent desire of the Crimean Tatars to return to their homeland after a half century of exile imposed during World War II, especially when hundreds demonstrated on Red Square in 1987. But he flew into a rage at the pretensions of independence movements in the republics. In regard to the Baltic peoples, who certainly lived better than Russians, he could not understand what many Estonians, Latvians, and Lithuanians remembered—that in the years between the world wars, they had lived even better and had enjoyed certain freedoms as well.

Baltic activists were among the earliest to organize. They mounted religious and cultural revivals in public and on television and demanded that the USSR renounce the illegal Nazi-Soviet protocol of 1939 that had led to the savaging of the Baltic lands. To do so would be to admit the illegitimacy of Soviet power in those three small countries. This demand formed the basis for the 1988 declarations of sovereignty and a "war of laws" against decrees issued in Moscow. Behind the legal niceties, of course, lay the heavy resentment of the Russian population growth in these tiny states. Local Communist Parties split into nationalists and Soviet loyalists, and the National Front leaders began speaking out for independence. In Lithuania, Sajudis (the Movement), a party headed by Professor Vytautas Landsbergis, challenged the monopoly of the Lithuanian Communist Party, and the Communist party leader, Algirdas Brazauskas (1932), also kept his distance from Moscow. Landsbergis took a moral stance for the sanctity of Lithuania's language, Catholic faith, and native culture—a case made all the more difficult because the rest of the world knew next to nothing about Lithuania's history and its era of greatness and power. Both Landsbergis's grandfathers had been nationalist activists under the tsars, and he himself taught and promoted the music of Lithuania's great composer and painter Mikolajus Ciurlionis (1875–1910). When, in 1990, Sajudis won a majority in its own parliament and declared independence, the Soviet government refused recognition. To Gorbachëv, scandalized at the uppity behavior of these little nations, Landsbergis was a stubborn old professor; to his people he was a revered father. The independence issue would not go away.

Environment, health, and economic issues helped shape the nationalist movement in Ukraine. In 1986, the worst nuclear disaster in history occurred when a reactor at the Chernobyl nuclear plant exploded through negligence and spread death-dealing radioactive contamination. This event and the criminal attempts to cover it up spurred a quest for new decision-making mechanisms in this vast republic. Ukrainian independence sentiments grew rapidly, grounded in historical memory, from medieval Kievan Rus to the famine and purges of the 1930s. Ex-dissidents Vyacheslav Chornovil and others now became respected public figures. The Ukrainian Popular Front for Perestroika (Rukh) was founded in 1989 with a program of economic and cultural autonomy, environmental protection, and human rights. By May Day 1990, Chornovil was Mayor of Lviv—once the capital of

Galicia in the Austrian Habsburg Empire, and always a stronghold of Ukrainian nationalism and the Uniate Church. As citizens reveled in a Uniate festival, he applied to the USSR an 1848 slogan that had called Austria a "prison house of nations."

Unfortunately, national independence movements were marred in some places by interethnic hostility. In the Caucasus, old resentments boiled over into bloody wars. In February 1988, the Armenian majority in High Karabagh, a mountainous enclave of 190,000 people inside Azerbaijan, declared High Karabagh part of the Armenian Republic. A fury of killing erupted on both sides. A three-day reign of terror broke loose in the dingy Caspian Sea industrial Azerbaijani town of Sumgait as Azeris hacked or beat to death dozens of Armenians. More bloodshed followed in the next two years, and armies of refugees wound their way in both directions. A terrible earthquake in 1988 inside Armenia piled on another tragedy. Azerbaijan, though still retaining the disputed region of High Karabagh, turned against Moscow as well after Soviet troops fired on crowds in Baku early in 1990 to suppress a nationalist movement there.

The Georgians, inspired by the weakening of Soviet power, referred back with fondness to the years 1917–1921, when Georgia was an independent republic before being invaded by the Red Army (see the chapter "Civil War: Reds, Whites, and Greens, 1917–1921"). Tempers were frazzled by the desire of the Abkhazian minority in Georgia for its own independence. In April 1989, strikes and demonstrations in Tbilisi, the capital, called for Georgian independence and the incorporation of Abkhazia. Security forces broke them up with great brutality. In 1990 the once jailed dissident Zviad Gamsakhurdia (1940–1993) headed a new government demanding full independence.

In Central Asia, trouble arose when Gorbachëv, determined to end corruption in the republics, pressured the resignation of long-time Kazakhstan party chief Dinmukhamed Kunaev in 1986 and replaced him with a Russian, G. V. Kobin—a move he later regretted. Resulting riots forced Gorbachëv to supplant Kobin with Nursultan Nazarbaev. But the damage was done, and incidents of ethnic violence spread to other Islamic republics. In 1989, Uzbek gangs brutally killed Meshkhetian Turks of Georgia, who had been deported to Uzbekistan in 1944. In 1990 a massacre of Uzbeks by Kirgiz occurred in and near Osh, the second city of Kirgizia. In Turkmenia, disorder took a milder form. In 1989 the young writer Mukhamed Velsapar organized a group of intellectuals who were driven by anticolonial concerns about the economy and the environment. Party bosses in the Turkmen capital, Ashkhabad, were enraged when independence activists from the Baltic states arrived there to give training to Turkmens in methods of struggle for national self-determination.

Gorbachëv, appalled at the prospect of the dissolution of the Soviet Union, attempted to avert it by fashioning a new and looser bond. Before he could accomplish this, the forces of political reaction in Russia struck.

FROM PUTSCH TO COLLAPSE, 1990–1991

By the fall of 1990, right-wing figures around Gorbachëv were gaining strength and pushing him to the right. Army generals made menacing noises. On October 16, the day after he received the Nobel Peace Prize, Gorbachëv made a sharp turn by postponing the Shatalin plan for economic reforms and taking a hard line on the Baltic states. He appointed Boris Pugo, a tough policeman of the old school, as minister of interior, and several conservatives to high posts. Gorbachëv lost the support of some of his early Western-oriented supporters. Shevardnadze predicted a coming dictatorship and resigned as foreign minister. Hard-line media executives began to curb *glasnost.* Many wondered if *perestroika* had reached a dead end or if Gorbachëv had become the hostage to a right-wing military-police junta. The right became more openly audacious. Valentin Rasputin, a prominent writer of village prose, which exalted rural traditions, shared the podium at the Red Army Theater with Orthodox priests and generals in a show of patriotic hatred. The most charismatic hero of the right was the Black Colonel, the leather-clad Viktor Alksnis, who sounded the tones of counterrevolution in the name of the army's "honor" and hinted none too subtly that democratic blood would flow.

The Putschists

Gorbachëv's new associates were incensed at breakaway movements in the national republics. In January 1991, Pugo and defense minister General Yazov took steps to terminate the drive toward independence in the Baltic. Soviet special troops, the Black Berets, stormed government buildings in Riga, Latvia, and four people were killed. In Vilnius, capital of Lithuania, on January 13, after numerous arrests and provocations, Soviet troops assaulted and captured the radio and television installation, killing a dozen people in the action. Lithuanian resistance grew more determined. For many liberals and reformers in Moscow the action was the moment of disillusionment with Gorbachëv. Boris Yeltsin supported Baltic aspirations and called for Gorbachëv's resignation. The streets of Moscow again came alive with antigovernment demonstrators.

Those on the right, disenchanted with Gorbachëv for his alleged softness toward national movements, became alarmed over a March 1991 referendum endorsing Gorbachëv's scheme for a new and looser federation of the USSR. This was to be based on a negotiated Union Treaty with all the republics except the Baltic, Moldovan, Georgian, and Armenian ones. Gorbachëv, Yeltsin, and eight other republic leaders discussed Gorbachëv's plan in a dacha near Moscow between April and August. Gorbachëv hoped that this treaty, replacing the previous constitutions of the USSR, would hold the conglomeration of peoples together. On the same referendum, the Russian Republic placed the question of electing its own president, a step that was endorsed by the popular vote. To the disgust of the antireform forces, Yeltsin defeated Ryzhkov and Zhirinovsky on June 12 in an extraordinary electoral victory. Yeltsin, unlike Gorbachëv, faced the voters and became the most popular political figure in the nation.

Enraged and determined to sabotage the new Union Treaty, conservative elements began plotting Gorbachëv's overthrow. Their intent was virtually advertised in a long article, "A Word to the People," published in the right-wing paper *Soviet Russia* and signed by writers of village prose and war novels, military men, and defense industry leaders who warned against the swing to reform under Western influence. "How is it that we have let people come to power who do not love their country, who kowtow to foreign patrons and seek advice and blessings abroad?" In paranoid tones, the article spoke of looming danger and emergency.

March on Moscow

Gorbachëv's overthrow was planned by members of the regular police, KGB, and armed forces, headed respectively by Pugo; Vladimir Kryuchkov (b. 1924), a veteran of the Hungarian and Czechoslovakian repressions; and Yazov. These were joined by Gorbachëv's old friend and speaker of parliament Lukyanov, Vice President Yanaev, Prime Minister Pavlov, and Gorbachëv's military adviser, Sergei Akhromeev. High-ranking officers in the plot, accustomed to enormous power and to deference from politicians, could not stomach the sight of intellectuals appropriating policy under *perestroika.* They were alarmed by the retreat from Afghanistan, the loss of the bloc, budget cuts, draft evasions, and the specter of imperial dissolution and loss of superpower status. Driven by a blend of patriotic fervor and self-interest, the plotters believed that when the chips were down, the other commanders would follow their lead. To his credit, Yazov ordered that there be no bloodshed. But the conspirators neglected to arrest possible resistance leaders, such as Yeltsin, and to secure the cooperation of all military and KGB forces. In some of the outlying towns and republics, commanders either defied the junta or sat tight.

On August 18, a few days before the Union Treaty was to be signed, the conspirators placed the Gorbachëv family, who were vacationing in the Crimea, under house arrest. Asked either to resign or to endorse martial law, Gorbachëv refused. The conspirators, calling themselves the State Committee for the Emergency, had the media declare next morning that Gorbachëv had resigned because of health problems and that the country was threatened by an unspecified coup. They had no real agenda except to stop further reform and punish those responsible for the unraveling of the status quo. For this, they had ready hundreds of thousands of handcuffs and arrest orders—for Yeltsin, Yakovlev, Shevardnadze, and the St. Peterburg mayor, Sobchak, among others.

On the morning of August 19, classical music filled the airwaves, a familiar sign of trouble at the top. But that soothing sound was accompanied by the racket of tanks rolling down Moscow boulevards, deployed to prevent resistance to the emergency government. As troops occupied the city, censors invaded the media centers to control information. The ultranationalist Soyuz Party, the Liberal Democrats under Zhirinovsky, and the bulk of the Communist Party accepted the coup. But

Sobchak in Petersburg rebuffed it, and Yeltsin took measures to reverse it. He and his followers drove to the Russian White House, seat of the parliament, and set up headquarters. Outside the building, Yeltsin climbed atop an armored vehicle and appealed to the people to resist. His main assistants at that moment—Ruslan Khasbulatov, speaker of parliament, and Colonel Alexander Rutskoi, vice president of the Russian Republic—were ironically the men who would revolt against him in 1993. The parliament supported him.

Although the bulk of the Moscow populace remained passive, thousands of Muscovites from all walks of life gathered near the parliament building and defied the putschists' tanks. Women defenders of the White House held up a placard: "Soviet Soldiers: Don't Shoot Your Mothers." The tankers themselves were not sure what they were supposed to be doing. That evening Gorbachëv's vice president, Yanaev, hands trembling, made a pitiful TV appearance explaining the events with barefaced lies. Black Monday, August 19, ended in a stalemate. The world was electrified. American and European leaders telephoned their support to Yeltsin. Celebrities and poets harangued the crowds, which by Tuesday had reached about twenty-five thousand. The besieging troops broke ranks: some joined the resisters; others balked at firing on civilians. Many unit commanders refused to deploy. The crack Alpha Group, seasoned by combat in Afghanistan and Lithuania, never appeared. Conversely, the air force chief promised to strike against the putschist forces. By August 21, after two and a half days, the putschists released Gorbachëv, who flew to Moscow.

A Moscow crowd with the new Russian flag confronts tankers at the Soviet White House during the 1991 putsch. *Sovfoto/Eastfoto.*

The Anticommunist Revolution

At the moment of Gorbachëv's apparent victory, his power slipped away. Yeltsin, chief of the Russian Republic and moral leader of the antiputsch forces, arrested the conspirators. Pugo and Akhromeev committed suicide. Yeltsin virtually outlawed the Communist Party in Russia, dismissed real or suspected organizers and supporters of the plot, and cracked down temporarily on the press. In Moscow, rage against the KGB led citizens to pull down the statue of Felix Dzerzhinsky, founder of the secret police in 1917. Mikhail Gorbachëv was left behind by the rapid sweep of history. He resigned as General Secretary of the party, dissolved the Central Committee, and set up new state bodies in an attempt to hold together what nature now seemed bent on sundering. The Baltic states declared full independence, and no one moved against them. Other republics drifted in that direction. In December, Ukraine followed suit. A week later, in the Minsk agreement, Russia, Ukraine, and Belorussia formed the Commonwealth of Independent States (CIS), thus effectively terminating the USSR, whose formal dissolution (and Gorbachëv's resignation) came on December 25.

The Gorbachëv experiment was a failure in some eyes, a welcome transition in others. To explain certain events, historians often invoke images of Pandora's box, the genie in the bottle, the sorcerer's apprentice, or the Frankenstein monster: by releasing, inviting, or creating unknown forces, the would-be reformer unleashes unforeseen and uncontrollable energies. Like all radical reformers, Gorbachëv was caught between pressures of the past and present, slammed both by the old guard for tampering with established order and by those wanting rapid change for moving too slowly. He tried to bridge conflicting forces for a while. But when the gulf widened, he fell into it. What Gorbachëv accomplished, intended and unintended, was astonishing to those who witnessed it. But as a transitional figure, he was castigated from almost every side and eventually cast out.

History will probably be kinder to Gorbachëv than have been his own people. He made history by opening up the public voice, weakening the Communist Party, implanting parliamentary life, allowing the liberation of East Central Europe, ending a war, and seeking security and friendship with the West and with China. His passage was marked by the end of seventy-four years of Soviet power and the onset of a new era of Russian history.

CHAPTER 42

The Parting of the Ways: After 1991

Russia is one of history's great survivors. In one form or another it has existed for more than a thousand years, and for part of that time it has been the largest territorial power on our planet. Today it is one of the most formidable powers in Eurasia, and it will remain so.

— *Geoffrey Hosking,* Russia and the Russians: A History *(2001)*

Boris Yeltsin, in his eight years as president of the new Russia, endured some severe shocks. One, stemming from his economic policies and aggravated by personal and political animosities, eventuated in the violent and bloody storming of the Russian White House in October 1993. The others, much bloodier, were the two Chechen wars, 1994–1996, and 1999–. Aside from those events, Yeltsin's course was far from smooth, and yet he managed to launch a genuine revolution in Russian life that went beyond Gorbachëv's shakeups. At the end of the century, Yeltsin—exhausted from the struggle, his country still facing enormous problems—relinquished power to a younger man.

BORIS YELTSIN: BLOODSHED IN MOSCOW AND CHECHNYA

Yeltsin faced the problems endemic in any new state, and his, aggravated by the radical rejection of the Soviet past, were quick in coming. He inherited the tension between those who wanted to speed up or slow down the march to democracy and a free market. In a Russian parliament elected before the shattering events of 1991, nationalists and Communists fought Yeltsin's plans to move fast and far. Some who had stood with him in the crisis of 1991 came to oppose him. Political discourse was inflamed all through the decade by the confrontational styles of the parliamentarians and the sometimes stubborn and authoritarian postures of the president.

President and Parliament

In trying for political balance, Yeltsin's vice president, Alexander Rutskoi—air force general, Afghan war hero, and head of Communists for Democracy—had supported him and had run together with him in the 1991 Russian Republic election. But the president's main advisers were squarely in the reform camp: top aid Gennady Burbulis (b. 1945); Andrei Kozyrev (b. 1951), who became foreign minister of the new Russian Republic in 1990; and Egor Gaidar (b. 1956). The last, grandson of well-known writer Arkady Gaidar, had been a student of economics at Moscow University with future mayor Gavriil Popov (b. 1936) and Stanislav Shatalin, architect of the ill-fated Five Hundred Days plan. Gaidar became chief economic adviser and then acting prime minister. His circle of young enthusiastic reformers in October 1991 hammered out a radical economic reform proposal for Yeltsin that was initially approved by the Russian Republic Congress of People's Deputies.

The uneasy concord was short-lived. Gaidar and Ruslan Khasbulatov were old rivals. Khasbulatov turned on Yeltsin and in 1992 led bitter parliamentary clashes with the government over the new economic reforms. The National Salvation Front—a bloc in the congress that included village prose writers Fëdor Belov and Valentin Rasputin, Communist Gennady Zyuganov (b. 1944), a few neo-Nazis, and elements of the right-wing Pamyat organization—resisted Yeltsin's economic reforms as well as his pro-Western policies. When in December 1992 Yeltsin proposed a new constitution, to be approved by a popular referendum, the opposition threatened to impeach him. As a compromise, Yeltsin replaced Gaidar with Viktor Chernomyrdin (b. 1938) as prime minister, and the opposition agreed to Yeltsin's referendum. Khasbulatov's followers reneged on the December agreement and renewed the fight. But their attempt to impeach the president in March 1993 failed. In April, the referendum gave Yeltsin support and endorsed the drafting of a new constitution, to be worked out by a Constitutional Assembly. Summertime brought increased turbulent verbal battles in that body over the division of power. At issue was the legitimate concern of the opposition that too much power was being vested in the president's hands. Although the assembly survived the tumult, the gulf between president and parliament had by then so deepened that there remained little chance of bridging it.

Revolt in the White House

The prolonged war between president and parliament led Yeltsin in September 1993 to dissolve the parliament and hold new elections. It was an illegal coup, as even some of Yeltsin's supporters conceded. But before the elections could proceed, a few hundred deputies and their supporters, led by Khasbulatov and Rutskoi, defiantly occupied the White House and sat out a ten-day siege by government troops. In late September, those deputies impeached Yeltsin, designated Rutskoi as acting president, and hoisted the Communist red flag. The occupiers, dressed in camouflage fatigues, were joined by some of the 1991 putsch supporters and a number of armed extremist groups, which included admirers of Iraqi dictator Saddam Hussein and admirers of Adolf Hitler. Truce talks at the Danilov Monastery in the presence of the mayor of Moscow and the Orthodox patriarch of Russia bore no fruit. White House forces took the battle to the streets and tried to capture the nearby mayor's office and the Ostankino television center in northern Moscow. In an ironic reversal, Yeltsin, recently the champion of a beleaguered assembly based in that same White House, now led the siege, cut off the electricity, initiated talks with the rebels, and when they faltered used force. On October 4, with the military on his side, he called in the tanks, and the building was stormed.

The plotters were defeated and arrested, though eventually amnestied, and censorship of some opposition organs was imposed but also soon lifted. During this episode, 150 to 175 people were killed. As the biggest civil crisis to that point in post-Soviet politics, the 1993 bloodletting shocked the nation. Yeltsin had beaten the opposition, but at a terrible price. "The hangover in Moscow was deadening," wrote an American correspondent. "Everywhere I went . . . there was a sense of hopelessness about political life. No more heroes, no great expectations." The uprising at the White House has been seen by some as a legitimate gesture on the part of parliamentarians, determined to defend their lawful prerogatives to oppose the executive and to protect the suffering Russian people from the pain inflicted by the radical economic reform. Others called it a brazen attempt to reinstate some of the uglier aspects of the old Soviet order. Similarly, Yeltsin's bloody quelling of the insurrection has been seen both as a brave defense of democracy and rational economic life and as an unwise resort to violence for the sake of personal power. The verdict is by no means final. A new referendum endorsed Yeltsin's strong-president constitution in December 1993.

The time between the blood on Moscow streets and the blood on the streets of Grozny in Chechnya brought no solution to Russia's political problems. The new constitution replaced the Supreme Soviet and the Congress of People's Deputies with a bicameral Federal Assembly. The lower house, the Duma, consisted of 450 members; the upper house, the Council of the Federation, had 178—two delegates from each of the republic's eighty-nine units (Chechnya boycotted the election for reasons that will become clear). Although the president had more power now, the results of the low turnout for the election in December 1993 indicated trouble ahead. A conservative parliament again faced Yeltsin, who declined to endorse any of the parties. Those closest to him—Gaidar's party, Russia's Choice; and Yabloko, a liberal party formed in 1991 by Grigory Yavlinsky (b. 1952)—together won ninety-three seats in the Duma. The parties most strongly opposed to the Yeltsin regime were the now relegalized Communists, who together with the Agrarians won eighty-one seats, and Vladimir Zhirinovsky's Liberal Democratic Party (LDP), with sixty-four.

Zhirinovsky (b. 1946), with army service and law school behind him, in 1991 had founded his party and, with 6.2 million votes, had come in third in the Russian Republic presidential race of that year, losing to Yeltsin. After the 1991 putsch, which he supported, and his 1993 electoral success, Zhirinovsky became ever blunter in his views, which were promarket but angrily nationalist, imperialist, anticommunist, antidemocratic, and anti-Semitic. He wanted Russia to reclaim Alaska, Finland, the Baltic lands, Ukraine, Moldova, and half of Poland and to launch a colonial surge toward Turkey, Iran, and Afghanistan. "How I dream," he wrote in his book *The Last Surge to the South,* "of our Russian soldiers washing their boots in the warm waters of the Indian Ocean [and of] the pealing of bells from a

Russian Orthodox church on the shores of the Indian Ocean or Mediterranean." Zhirinovsky purveyed these views with clowning and macho talk as he appealed to the army, the unemployed, and various right-wing or nationalist constituencies.

The Communists reemerged under Gennady Zyuganov (b. 1944), who had worked in the Central Committee. Seeing Gorbachëv's *perestroika* as an American plot, Zyuganov had helped form the Russian (as opposed to the Soviet) Communist Party, and though he did not join the 1991 putsch, he had helped draft the ominous "Word to the People" that advertised its coming. His ideas blended Slavophilism and anti-Western chauvinism with a Soviet-style economic vision. In 1993, he organized the Communist Party of the Russian Federation, the largest of many parties bearing the Communist tag. With a membership of 560,000 in the mid-1990s, compared with the 20 million of the old Communist Party of the Soviet Union, it attracted various rightist and leftist politicians, including 1991 putschist Anatol Lukyanov, ultranationalist Viktor Alksnis, and village prose writer Fëdor Belov. At mass meetings, the Communists drew on the old imagery of red flags, Lenin posters, and the party hymn, "The Internationale." This party's greatest appeal was to people on pension, poor workers, and residents of the provinces and small towns, especially in the agricultural regions of central and south Russia.

Arrayed against Reds like Zyuganov and Browns like Zhirinovsky stood those wedded to the free market and democracy. Prominent among them were Grigory Yavlinsky and his party, Yabloko, a word that means "apple" in Russian but which was derived from the names of its founders. Yavlinsky, like many reform-minded politicians, trained as an economist and entered the political scene as a free-market democrat deeply opposed to corruption, oligarchy, and regional despotism. Though supported by many urban, educated professionals, he was distrusted by the military and many rural voters and detested by the extreme left and right for his ideas. Yabloko and other moderate, reformist parties were weakened not only by the forces opposing them but by their own refusal or inability to form strong coalitions.

War in Chechnya

The tiny Autonomous Republic of Chechnya-Ingushetia, formed in 1934, by the 1990s had a population of about nine hundred thousand indigenous peoples and about three hundred thousand Russians. Many Chechens could not forget or forgive the cruelties inflicted on them by the Soviet state during World War II and its failure to compensate them fully for their suffering (see the chapter "The Soviet Homeland Defended: World War II, 1939–1945"). When the chance came in 1990, Jokhar Dudaev (1944–1996), an air force general, asserted Chechen independence from the USSR; in 1991–1992 he declared separation from the new Russia and from Ingushetia. The memory of Shamyl's heroic struggle against the tsar's army in the early nineteenth century and of the World War II deportations helped fuel support for Dudaev. Yeltsin had allowed the union republics to fall away from the USSR but feared the dangerous precedent of a secession from the Russian Republic. He sent in airborne units to quell separatism in 1991 and, when this failed, negotiated for a few years until December 1994, when hostilities flared up into a real war (1994–1996). Moscow was also aggrieved by Chechen crime rings in Russia proper, though in fact Russian gangs predominated (see below). At a moment of cooling toward NATO and the United States, Yeltsin turned to his inner circle of advisers and the "force" ministries—security, police, and army—which had backed him in the 1993 putsch. The president heeded the views of Defense Minister Pavel Grachëv (b. 1948), who thought an easy victory in Chechnya would steal thunder from the ultranationalists.

The forty thousand Russian troops, entering Chechnya through Ingushetia, battered towns and villages and took the capital, Grozny, in January 1995, but they could not quell the "uprising." Though their land was roughly the size of Connecticut and only ten miles across in one place, Chechens relied heavily on terrain and warrior spirit. Two daring exploits frightened and angered Russians: the 1995 kidnapping of about one hundred hostages in the south Russian town of Budënovsk and a raid on Russian-held Kizlyar in 1996. Armistices came and went as casualties mounted on both sides, though Chechen combatants and civilians suffered the most. The Duma passed a no-confidence vote on the president, and by 1995 public opinion was turning against the war. Some of Yeltsin's former supporters had opposed intervention. Gaidar even darkly hinted that the war was a right-wing plot to provoke border risings, after the suppression of which civil liberties would be suspended throughout the nation. A few military leaders joined the antiwar chorus as Yeltsin wavered.

Dudaev was killed in April 1996 in a Russian missile attack, but fighting continued until August, when General Alexander Lebed (1950–2002) signed a treaty that postponed the question of Chechen independence for five years. Some eighty

A Chechen rebel points his rifle at a Russian prisoner. *Mindaugas Kulbis/AP Photo.*

thousand to one hundred thousand lives were lost in the first Chechnya war, four times those of the Afghan war. Grozny, the largest city in the Caucasus Mountains, was reduced to rubble, and its population fell from about four hundred thousand to about one hundred thousand. Through the two-year struggle, atrocities were committed on both sides, including village massacres by Russian soldiers of women, children, and old people. The legacy of hatred and suspicion lingered on, exploding anew when the next war broke out in 1999.

BORIS YELTSIN: POLITICAL AND ECONOMIC ACHIEVEMENTS

In October 1995 Yeltsin had a heart attack, the first of many health crises during his tenure. The December Duma elections gave the Communists 22.3 percent of the vote and 157 seats; Zhirinovksy's LDP, 11.2 percent of the vote and 51 seats; Chernomyrdin's Our Home Is Russia, 10.5 percent of the vote and 55 seats; and Yabloko 6.9 percent of the vote and 45 seats. Though no clear majority prevailed, Communists and nationalists dominated the body as it again defied a strong president. By 1996,Yeltsin had become increasingly cut off from the public and former advisers. Given to autocratic gestures and occasional drunken spells, he relied on an inner circle dominated by his personal bodyguard, Alexander Korzhakov (b. 1950).

Election Day, 1996

As the presidential election of 1996 approached, the opposition to Yeltsin went beyond parliamentary squabbles and was rooted in the popular reaction to his economic reforms (see below). Yeltsin's rating in the opinion polls fell as that of Zyuganov and his well-organized Communists rose. They were supported now by Egor Ligachëv, Lukyanov, and veterans of the 1991 and 1993 putsches. Yeltsin headed no party, and his allies were sharply divided. When the Korzhakov circle urged some kind of deal with the Communists, Yeltsin wisely ignored this advice. He recently revealed that he considered outlawing the Communist Party, dismissing parliament, and postponing the election—emphatically undemocratic moves—but was dissuaded from this by his family and advisers. Then—like Ilya Muromets of Russian legend, who rose from a long slumber—the president awoke from a period of lethargy with renewed vigor to face the opposition with the simple program of retaining the free market and democracy and stopping the Communists. Adviser Anatoly Chubais (b. 1955) organized a brilliant electoral campaign for Yeltsin, financed by business magnates close to government (called oligarchs) and supported by foreign contributions, popular entertainers, and the media, which refused to run Communist party ads.

Yeltsin ran well in large urban areas, whereas Zyuganov did better in rural districts and small towns. In round one, Yeltsin got 35.3 percent of the vote, Zyuganov 32 percent. Lebed, Yavlinksy, and Zhirinovsky trailed well behind them. Yeltsin fired Korzhakov and made General Lebed, in return for support, chair of the

National Security Council, a body that coordinated the military, police, and security forces. With Lebed out of the race, round two brought victory to the president in July: 53.8 percent of the vote to Zyuganov's 40.3 percent. Defense Minister Grachëv lost his post for alleged mishandling of the Chechen war. Boris Berezovsky (b. 1946), a media tycoon and Yeltsin supporter, became deputy chief of the National Security Council, helped negotiate the peace in Chechnya in 1996, and was appointed executive secretary of the Commonwealth of Independent States. Chubais was made chief of staff, and Chernomyrdin was kept on as prime minister. At the end of the year, Yeltsin suffered another heart attack. To add new faces to his regime, he brought in Boris Nemtsov (b. 1959) from Nizhny Novgorod, the third largest city in Russia, where Nemtsov had racked up a good record as a progressive and dynamic administrator. The electoral victory and the truce in Chechnya brought Yeltsin to the peak of his power in 1997.

To Market, to Market

Even more than the wars in Chechnya, Yeltsin's severest problems throughout his presidency were the economy and related issues of corruption and crime. The transition to a free market proved predictably difficult, since it required a firm structure of contract, property, tax, and bankruptcy laws and involved not only the legal transfer of capital to private hands but decisions as to which hands would get it at what price. Two general approaches, with many intermediate variants, were "shock therapy" and slow motion. Gaidar and other advocates of shock want rapid unlocking of prices, privatization, high taxes, low government spending, and the liquidation of the extraordinarily large number of inefficient enterprises. They asserted that the resulting pain of unemployment would gradually give way to prosperity after the initial blows. Gradualists, no less convinced that capitalism would have to come, advised a slower and longer route. This meant maintaining wasteful firms and retaining welfare and subsidy.

Starting in 1992, Yeltsin vigorously pushed through Gaidar's shock therapy measures by executive decrees. The quick release of goods onto the market and the lifting of price controls meant that the poor could not afford the goods. These measures were among the chief sources of antagonism between president and parliament that led to the White House episode. The privatization scheme, drafted by Chubais and his team, was a remarkable reversal of the Stalinist economic revolution of the 1930s, when the state had confiscated all private industry. The state now sold off its property to private buyers in a very complex scheme allowing enterprises, individuals, or groups of private citizens to buy shares at set prices or at auctions. In practice, given the confusion and the unfamiliarity of the population with finance, powerful insiders acquired the lion's share of the new privately owned economy. Massive swindles accompanied the whole process, and the wealth, instead of being spread among the millions, as Yeltsin envisioned, got concentrated in relatively few hands—clever financiers, former party *nomenklatura,* and even criminal syndicates. By the end of the 1990s, most of the economy was capitalist. For those with big disposable incomes, the result seemed like a bonanza. In Moscow and Petersburg, Western-style hotels, restaurants, clubs, and upscale shops sprang up with gleaming interiors and the friendly and efficient service long associated with foreign enterprise. Many liberal reformers and Western observers saw the privatization as a monumental step into the modern world for Russians, in spite of the abuses that accompanied it.

The privatization process created instant millionaires, the New Russians, and a cohort of oligarchs with connections to the government. They managed to purchase on favorable terms some of Russia's most lucrative businesses, including natural resources and media conglomerates. Of the better-known figures, Rem Vyakhirev got his hands on the Gazprom cartel, which produced a third of the world's gas reserves, held a million acres of land, and employed 365,000 people. Vladimir Gusinsky, a former theater manager, became a media mogul as controlling owner of Media-Most, including newspapers, radio stations, and Russia's only independent television company, NTV—now no longer independent. Boris Berezovsky, mathematician and political guru, acquired interests in lucrative auto and petroleum enterprises and 49 percent of ORT (Russian Public Television), the remainder of which was owned by the state. Several of the oligarchs later fell out with Yeltsin and were hounded by his successor.

The new millionaires—all male—lived high, with dachas, Mediterranean or Caribbean homes, and Swiss private schools for their children. The more flamboyant displayed flashy cars and clothes and glamorous sexual partners. Tax evasion and the transfer of billions of rubles into foreign bank accounts meant that the state acquired little revenue from its richest citizens. But the rich had to pay as well. Organized crime rings sprang up in the wake of privatization and peaked in 1995 at a figure of more than fourteen thousand gangs, organized into "authorities" (leaders), brigadiers, and soldiers. These "violent entrepreneurs" comprised members of sports clubs, Afghan veterans, former security service people, and ex-convicts or "Thieves-in-the-Law"—cons who upheld a rigid code of honor among themselves, rejected state authority, and exalted violence. Short-haired muscle men bristling with tattoos (thus called "dark blues") used extortion, blackmail, and physical violence to force business men to accept their services as a "roof" and take them on as "partners," sharing 20 to 30 percent of the revenue. Their services included collecting debts—hard to do in a weak legal system—and assassinating creditors. In the late 1990s, most of these gangs went legal in the face of increasing law enforcement actions and the growth of thousands of legal private protection agencies.

With over a million new businesses in existence, large segments of the population entered the exhilarating, if sometimes unstable, universe of the middle class—self-supporting and self-managing business men and women vying actively in a market society, an extraordinary novelty not seen in Russia for most of the century. For the rest of the population, things were not so rosy. The poor watched as limousines rolled by, filled with New Russians and their bodyguards and escorts. The wrenching economic reforms and freeing up of prices fell heavily on women, the elderly, children, and retired people on fixed incomes.

In 1998, a major economic crisis, resulting partly from a sharp drop in oil prices and an economic downturn in Asia, threatened Russia's stability once again. Yeltsin fired Chubais and replaced Chernomyrdin with a dizzying array of short-term prime ministers: Sergei Kirienko, Evgeny Primakov, and Sergei Stepashin.

Finale

Things seemed to fall apart for Yeltsin in late 1999. In September a Moscow apartment house bomb killed 292 people, and the Russian government pointed the finger at Chechen terrorists. This and similar incidents in other cities led to a renewal of hostilities. The federation's leaders and many of its citizens viewed Aslan Maskhadov—the elected president of Chechnya and Dudaev's successor as military chief—as a standing threat to Russian national security. Chechnya also formed the hub of the oil pipeline that ran from the Caspian Sea to the Black Sea. These concerns and the sturdy Chechen resistance kept the war alive into the new century. Yeltsin also faced environmental degradation, a national health crisis, alcoholism, and unemployment caused by the shutdown of unproductive factories. On top of this, Yeltsin's health was deteriorating, and he was often absent from his duties. At the end of December 1999, he resigned from office and appointed Vladimir Putin as acting president.

What was Boris Yeltsin's legacy? A fair-minded biographer recorded Yeltsin's weaknesses and lapses of judgment and noted that Yeltsin built on many of the foundations laid by Gorbachëv. On the minus side stood the bloodletting at the White House in 1993, the Chechen wars, corruption, authoritarian rule, loose affiliation with business oligarchs, and the continuing intrusiveness of the successors to the KGB, the Federal Security Service (FSB) and the Foreign Intelligence Service—to say nothing of the fractious relations between executive and legislative branches of government. But the biographer also credited Yeltsin with ending empire and freeing the republics without the bloodbaths that attended the end of empire in our century, from Ireland and India to Africa and Yugoslavia. Yeltsin slashed the military budget, amnestied his foes, promoted the growth of independent courts, and weakened the secret police. Though his reign was accompanied by incessant grumbling from many quarters, he had won support in one referendum and two elections. In short, Yeltsin was "a friend of democracy," if not a democrat himself in the full sense. His regime had brought decentralization to the huge state, along with the free market and privatization, and had sustained a governable public while containing those who would introduce extremism and polarization.

VLADIMIR PUTIN

Vladimir Putin's childhood was in many respects typical of postwar Soviet children in the big city. Born in 1952, he was a Leningrad "courtyard kid"—though neither an orphan or a gang member—whose father survived combat in World War II and whose mother survived the German blockade that decimated the city; he showed fairly common signs of mild schoolboy hooliganism but gradually developed seri-

Vladimir Putin and Boris Yeltsin: The torch is passed. *Sovfoto/Eastfoto.*

ous interest in the German language, martial arts, and the law. As a boy, he was riveted by spy movies; as a young man he felt the pull of genuine Soviet patriotism but also had a taste for the sometimes shady and off-color songs of the semidissident Vladimir Vysotsky. After law school, Putin was recruited by the KGB, thus fulfilling the boyhood fantasy. "I was a pure and utterly successful product of Soviet patriotic education," he said proudly in a 2000 interview. After serving in intelligence for the KGB in the East German Democratic Republic during the *perestroika* years and witnessing the collapse of that regime, Putin returned to Leningrad (soon to be St. Petersburg) and served for several years in the office of the liberal mayor, Anatoly Sobchak. Putin resigned from the KGB in 1990 and, in the final years of Yeltsin's regime, was brought to Moscow, where he rose rapidly through a series of top offices of the central government, including civilian head of the FSB. In August 1999 he was appointed prime minister. After Yeltsin made him acting president on December 31, Putin's tough line on Chechnya and his law-and-order program won him a five-year term as president in March 2000.

In terms of style and image, Putin, in vivid contrast with his predecessor, was slim, athletic, cool, understated, businesslike, a light drinker, and a can-do manager. A recent biographer of P. A. Stolypin, tsarist prime minister in 1906–1911 (see the chapter "The 'Duma Monarchy,' 1907–1914"), pointed out some similarities between the two men. In fact Putin cited Stolypin in a July 2000 speech and called for private land ownership and a strong state. Unlike Stolypin, Putin stressed democracy and the need for legal consciousness among the Russian population, indeed a "dictatorship of the law." But he also believed in a strong army and regretted the too rapid collapse of the Soviet Union.

Putin's no-nonsense approach to policy, his energy, and his oft-noted tendency to authoritarianism won him both praise and blame in his native land. His policies on the economic front quickly became popular. An ardent foe of the oligarchs and what he took to be undue big-business influence in government, Putin fired Yeltsin's daughter, a behind-the-scenes operator in this shadow world, and harassed others. More important was the turnaround of the Russian economy from one of near disaster to apparent stability. On the one hand, Putin made it clear that the old ideas of state ownership of the means of production were no longer viable. On the other, he cracked down on large private enterprises with hard-line tax collection supplemented by raids on business offices and by stanching the illegal outflow of money, which had run into billions of rubles. Nevertheless, the Russian economy remained fragile, without a firm national banking system and with national incomes somewhere between those of Brazil and Mexico.

Russian liberals were not very happy with Putin's leadership, which they saw as autocratic. The president did not suffer criticism easily; he engaged in a war with the media and closed down or took over TV networks, arrested and otherwise harassed their owners, and allowed the use of dirty tricks and coercion. Although Putin evinced no sign of personal animus toward Jews, some of his underlings made anti-Semitic remarks in their campaigns against the Jewish media moguls Boris Berezovsky and Vladimir Gusinsky. Alarming to some also were the various deals Putin made with the largest party in the Duma, the Communists, including the symbolically resonant restoration of the honor guard at Lenin's tomb. Anti-Western mentalities were very much alive in the Communist party, among some in the military, and in splinter groups such as the National Bolsheviks, whose symbolism embodied the blend contained in their name: the salute of an outstretched right arm (as opposed to the old Comintern left-arm salute) ending in a fist and hammer-and-sickle armbands that resembled the swastika.

Yet Putin's occasional flirtation with the Communists and rightists did not tie his hands in a foreign policy often friendly to NATO and the United States. He also reduced the power of the Russian Federal Assembly's upper house, the Federation Council, and tightened up Moscow's control of the periphery by sending out federal overseers to monitor the administrations of the country's eighty-nine regions. Local strongholds such as Great Novgorod, Nizhny Novgorod, and Tatarstan were to be bent to the will of the central government. But for the general public, Putin's approval rate remained very high—around 73 to 75 percent. In August 2000, when the Russian submarine *Kursk* went down in the Barents Seas with 118 dead, Putin incurred some of the blame for the mishandling of the rescue operation. But in the following year, he fired some navy chiefs for mismanagement.

The Chechen insurrection that had plagued his predecessor was both a bane and a boost to Putin. Although Russian troops captured the Chechen capital, Grozny, in February 2000, they were unable to subdue the country. At first, Western criticism of Putin's prosecution of the war and of the undeniable Russian atrocities committed there was balanced by Russian public support, though this slipped fairly quickly. In 2000, a good 24 percent of those polled named Putin's Chechnya policy as an aspect of his popularity; but in 2001 only 7 percent did so. Putin saw the breakaway movement in Chechnya as a mortal danger to Russia, a precedent for the explosion of the country into tiny republics. He feared what he called the "Yugoslavization of Russia." His worst-case scenario was the complete loss of the Caucasus, with the flame of Muslim independence ignited up the Volga to Tatarstan. Putin was adamant that the bombing of Russian apartment houses in 1999 was the work of Chechen terrorists and not, as some Russians alleged, a provocation by the Russian security forces to inflame hatred for Chechens and justify a new war.

Putin's experience with terror at the hands of Muslim insurgents was a major factor in his vigorous support of U.S. president George W. Bush's war on terrorism following the events of September 11, 2001. Putin was the first world leader to call Bush after September 11. On September 22 he met on the Black Sea with his military and won their support for U.S. efforts. He opened Russian air space to U.S. warplanes, lobbied the Central Asian republics for American use of Russian facilities convenient to Afghanistan, and saw to the sharing of intelligence.

MEMORIES OF EMPIRE

Inside the Russian Federation, Russians accounted for over 80 percent of the population. The 1992 Federation Treaty (which Chechnya and Tatarstan did not sign) bound together the eighty-nine territorial units: fifty-seven largely Russian provinces and other units and thirty-two autonomous republics and regions. Among the former, economic levels and political cultures varied immensely, with towns like Novgorod and Nizhny Novgorod developing special identities and a safe legal environment for foreign investors. Some regions inside the federation made side agreements with the Russian government in Moscow. Tatarstan was given control of its natural resources and the right to conduct foreign policy—an enormous leap from Soviet practices. Unrest broke out in a few of the borderlands—Ingushetia, Ossetia, and the Cossack regions—but nothing comparable to the bloody conflict in Chechnya.

The collapse of the USSR and the creation of its successor, the Commonwealth of Independent States (CIS), formed at the end of 1991, was not accompanied by the large-scale interrepublic war that some had predicted. The CIS expanded and contracted for several years. In December 1991 it had contained eleven units, which did not include the Baltic states and Georgia. Azerbaijan also withdrew for a while and then rejoined. Georgia joined in 1993. All members of CIS separately joined the United Nations in 1992, and the states that did not belong to the CIS remained outside the direct control, if not always outside the sphere, of Russia. Relations between the old Russian "center" and what was now termed the Near

Abroad—the fourteen former Soviet republics—were plagued with problems of the ownership of economic resources, status of Russians living in the Near Abroad, and passage through corridors.

In Ukraine, a volatile President Leonid Kravchuk (b. 1934), who had some right-wing support, was defeated in 1994 by Leonid Kuchma (b. 1938), a Russian-speaking Ukrainian former prime minister. Since independence, the Black Sea fleet was divided, with a provision for Russian repurchase of most of Ukraine's allotment; Russia leased Sevastopol, on the Crimean Peninsula, as a naval base; and Crimea itself remained in Ukraine, even though a Russian secession group had wanted Crimea to be a part of Russia. Of Ukraine's population of 52 million, 11 to 12 million were Russians, living mostly in the eastern industrial areas. In 1994, U.S. president Bill Clinton, Kravchuk, and Yeltsin agreed that Ukraine would return its missiles to Russia, which would guarantee its security. The 1990s also witnessed a renaissance of Ukrainian language and cultural flowering. However,

Russia and its former republics.

president Kuchma's program of marketization had a slow and rocky development. Kuchma himself generated widespread opposition in Ukraine to corruption, authoritarianism, and persecution of the press. In 2002, he was accused of ordering the murder of a journalist, and by the fall of that year, tens of thousands of citizens were demonstrating in Ukraine's capital for his overthrow. Kuchma also faced accusations of delivering radar equipment to Iraq in violation of international agreements.

Belorussia, now officially called Belarus, with its 11 million people remained a poor and badly run nation. In 1994, A. I. Lukashenka (b. 1954) became the first president. His dismal political record of Stalin-style military parades, repression of dissidents, and cult of personality won him notoriety as one of the CIS leaders most abusive of human rights. The economy was plagued by inefficient subsidies to industry and an absence of privatization. Belarus came closest to rejoining the Russian state, an idea with strong popular support, given Belarus's dependence on Russia for economic livelihood and cheap energy sources. In the fall of 2001, Lukashenka emerged victorious again in a shady election and continued to harass the free press.

Moldova, independent since 1991, had a population of about 4.4 million, which was 64 percent Romanian. The government made Romanian the official language. But in the region known as Trans-Dniestria, east of the Dniester River, the plurality of Russians and Ukrainians set up a secessionist self-styled republic in 1990, supported by the Fourteenth Army, stationed there under General Alexander Lebed. The clash was settled, though the issue still smoldered. Moldova remained independent, if very weak, since most of its inhabitants did not wish to join a neighboring Romania that was beset by its own problems.

Georgia, a country of 5 to 5.5 million, elected ex-political prisoner Zviad Gamsakhurdia (1939–1993) its first president and proclaimed complete independence from Russia in 1991. An authoritarian admirer of the Spanish dictator Francisco Franco (1892–1975), Gamsakhurdia soon alienated large portions of the electorate and the prodemocracy forces. Armed conflict erupted with South Ossetia in 1991, and with Abkhazia in 1992, over their wish to secede from Georgia. Georgians were driven out of Abkhazia with the help of Russian forces. Gamsakhurdia was replaced in 1992 by Eduard Shevardnadze, who had left Gorbachëv's government and returned home. After Russia reversed its stance and supported Georgia against the armies of Abkhazia, Shevardnadze made his country a member of the CIS in 1993.

Armenia's roughly 3.5 million people were outnumbered (and assisted) by the diaspora of Armenians living outside the region. President Levon Ter-Petrosian (b. 1945), head of state since 1990, served as president from 1996 to 1998, when he was succeeded by Robert Kocharian. The Armenian-Azerbaijan war over High Karabagh ended in 1994, the Azeris losing about 16 percent of their territory. In Azerbaijan (population 7 million, 70 percent Azeri), ex-Communists came to power in 1991 but were overthrown in 1992 by a Popular Front. Heidar Aliev, who had been removed by Gorbachëv, returned to power in 1993, rejoined the CIS, and was reelected president in 1998.

The newly independent nations of Central Asia, with a total population of about 50 million, inherited severe economic problems, particularly the cotton monoculture begun in tsarist times and extended by the Soviets, ecological disaster areas, and insufficient economic and environmental cooperation in land, water, transport, and markets. Cooperative efforts were inhibited by short-sighted programs of self-sufficiency. Politically, a kind of three-way division emerged in most of the five republics: former Communists, fundamentalist Muslims, and "liberals" or human rights activists, crosscut in some places by interethnic tensions. Communist parties dissolved or changed their names but retained the power, jobs, property, and buildings once assigned to the party. Some leaders turned to the free market and quickly enriched themselves. New Muslim parties often emerged as militant, especially in Uzbekistan. Secular liberals remained weak and were usually persecuted. Assassinations and civil war among various political factions plagued Tajikistan from 1992 to the end of the decade.

Despite the eminently familiar spectacle of democratic forms masking old habits, the new Islamic revival turned Central Asians back to the past and outward to the world. Saudi Arabians came to build mosques and Muslim schools, Turks to offer technical assistance. Newly admitted foreign archaeologists and scholars and native Islamic enthusiasts sought to recover a lost history. Reversing decades of experience, some nations began writing their languages in the Latin instead of the Cyrillic alphabet. Islam tied Central Asia to the Muslims of the Volga, Crimea, and the Urals. Their Sunni Islam linked the majority of Central Asian believers to the Muslim world majority. Tajiks, as Shiites, had their own ties to Azerbaijan, Iran, Afghanistan, and Pakistan. As a whole, Central Asia enjoyed unprecedented connections among the republics and with the outer world. An irony in all this was that the ancient Silk Road linking China to Europe and other caravan routes became the arteries that bore inner Asia's illegal drug traffic. Many Russians remained in the region, in spite of an exodus of Russian skilled personnel, and Moscow remained concerned over economic ties, border security, and brush wars.

Given the impetus among the non-Russian members of the CIS for assertive independence and a natural concern about renewed Russian influence, the commonwealth became an extremely loose entity. Early blueprints for a single-currency (ruble) bloc and other forms of economic cooperation faded rather soon, and the commonwealth's future remained suspended in uncertainty.

The Baltic states—by culture, external connections, and bitter memory of the 1940s Soviet outrages—decisively faced west and rejected membership in the CIS. The last Russian troops had withdrawn by 1994, and the three small countries put themselves up for membership in the once enemy alliance NATO. Estonia had a population of only 1.6 million, almost one-third of it Russian, in a tiny land roughly the size of West Virginia. Its close ties to neighboring prosperous and democratic Finland helped to bring stability. Latvia, with 2.7 million, had an even greater percentage of Russians left behind. The largest of the Baltic states, Lithuania, with 3.8 million (10 percent Russians) experienced a slower pace in economic reform. In 1992, the Democratic Labor Party, a body of ex-Communists, beat the Sajudis Party, which had ushered in independence. Lithuanians, with a relatively small number of Russians in their country, demonstrated generally less anti-Russianism on citizenship policies.

THE OUTER WORLD

From 1990 to 1996, Russian foreign minister Andrei Kozyrev conducted a cautiously friendly policy toward the West born of a certain desire for membership in the club of powerful nations, anxiety about the West's intentions, and fear of a nationalist backlash at home. Russia joined the International Monetary Fund in 1992 and was given a voice in the political discussions of the Big Seven (G-7) of advanced industrial nations of Western Europe, North America, and Japan. On the matter of Western financial support, the Russian government was not always happy. In 1993, a new and stronger Strategic Arms Limitation Treaty was worked out with the United States but was not ratified by the Duma. Nuclear weapons remaining in Russia, Belarus, Ukraine, and Kazakhstan were the subject of negotiation.

Vexing differences remained on several fronts. One was the Balkan crisis. The Communist and multinational Yugoslavia, like the USSR, fell to pieces in 1991. As its components seceded, fighting erupted among Orthodox Serbs, Muslim Bosnians, and Catholic Croats that soon turned into genocidal ethnic cleansing. The Bosnian region of Yugoslavia became the chief battleground. The war there evoked an old Russian response rooted in the memories of the nineteenth-century Balkan wars of liberation, Pan-Slavism, and the two world wars. In contrast to most governments in the West, Russia favored the Serbs over the Bosnians and Croats and gave only cautious support to NATO. Russians later joined peacekeeping forces in Bosnia, and the issue softened for a while after the peace accords of 1996. The ambivalence continued in a crisis at the end of the decade that pitted Serbs against ethnic Albanians in the Yugoslav district of Kosovo. The Kremlin also sought a sphere of influence over the Near Abroad, with the right to intervene in cases involving Russia's national security and the protection of Russians, a right it exercised in Georgia, Azerbaijan, and Tajikistan. Despite East-West differences in the 1990s, no fewer than fourteen Yeltsin-Clinton summits took place to iron them out.

The renewal of the Chechen war in 1999 once again chilled Russian-Western relations. Yeltsin had replaced Kozyrev as foreign minister in 1996 with Evgeny Primakov, whose KGB background made him far less accommodating to the West. Nationalism, the border wars, fear of NATO, and the Balkan crises served to turn Yeltsin to a tougher stance. Episodes of mutual espionage recalled the bad old days of the Cold War. Russians became incensed at U.S. unilateral actions in the Balkans and Iraq in the mid-1990s, taken without consultation with Russia or even the United Nations. The biggest bone of contention was the expansion of NATO into East Central Europe—the former Soviet bloc. Yeltsin and his ministers adopted a number of different stances on this issue, including an all-European security system that would supersede NATO and include Russia and an agreement for the Partnership for Peace (a security bloc with less than full membership in NATO for the nations concerned). Moscow opposed haste in incorporating Poland, Czechoslovakia, and Hungary into NATO and was avidly against pulling in the Baltic states. Many in the government and the population saw NATO's penetration of the East as an insult and even as a threat to Russian dignity and Great Power status.

Putin, though not a flashy speaker, was exceptionally well informed about world politics. He impressed the Germans with his fluency in their language and reassured most Western statesmen with his statements "We are Europeans" and "The Cold War is over." Problems and suspicions remained over issues of Russia's relatively cordial relations with opponents of the West—Iran, Iraq, and North Korea. At home, Putin was successful in convincing his own people that he was not giving away Russia's security interests. Late in 2001, he met with the power ministries—police, security, and military—to give the military more money, but also to announce the closing of a Russian base at Cam Ranh Bay in Vietnam and of an electronic spy center in Cuba. He thus often stayed ahead of his military and of much of public opinion in his pro-Western moves. His cooperation with NATO and the United States in the anti-Taliban war in Afghanistan included sending a small unit of Russian troops. As a quid pro quo, NATO planned to form a new body that would give Russia more input into certain security issues. In 2002, Putin withdrew Russia's opposition to the admission of the Baltic states into NATO.

RUSSIA IN A NEW MILLENNIUM

A notable change in the last years of the century occurred in Russians' self-image. Many city dwellers had developed a novel sense of self-sufficiency, a belief in their ability to solve problems, work with dedication, and shape their own lives. This new self was still tempered, though, by a traditional reliance on close friends and "useful" people and by the nagging problems of Russian society. Another novelty in post-Soviet life was the presence of a large diaspora that—unlike the émigrés in the Soviet period, who were considered traitors or spies—was engaged in Russian life and politics, traveling back and forth and spreading ideas about their experience in many countries. Certainly other Russians did not enjoy these processes and contacts, continuing a passive or an extremist attitude to politics and a suspicion of foreigners and of Russians who lived abroad. Almost all Russians went through a multiple crisis of identity bred by deep changes in the national, economic, social, gender, cultural, and religious environments.

For ordinary people, the specter of wholesale innovation brought disorientation. Polling data indicated that most people favored a market economy, but within limits and at a slow pace. The burst of capitalism, unemployment, a new work ethic, a weakened state, an apparent oligarchy, corruption, and crime made it seem as though the state had been captured by heartless and wild private interests. Classes had not disappeared under the Soviet system, but the stark visibility of the New Russians made people ask themselves where they belonged in the scheme of things. Nostalgia surfaced for older, simpler, but feasible ambitions: car, flat, TV, pensions, and price subsidies. Said one recent interviewee: "I was not an important person under Soviet power, I was an ordinary worker, I did not have any special privileges, yet I can still say that they treated the Russian people better. And now—we are neglected." Life expectancy for males and the quality of health service continued to decline. Poverty breeds discontent that is often expressed in nationalist and racist forms. Said a labor union leader in 1999, "We are seeing a dramatic increase in nationalist outbursts and wide popular support for the ultranationalist Vladimir Zhirinovsky."

The former superpower had been master of half of Europe and center of world communism. Those who might have felt pride as a people who held sway (which they considered benevolent) over more than a dozen non-Russian republics felt it no longer. Russia remained a huge country, but was only three-fourths its previous size, minus lands accrued over centuries of expansion. Damaged self-esteem at losing the empire could still be whipped into aggression by chauvinist demagogues. People with racist mentalities wondered whether Jews and people from the Caucasus living in Moscow could be trusted. Patriots bemoaned the diminished strength of their once vaunted army, whose morale had dropped when it was used against civilians and whose status had declined when the empire fell. Budget cuts also meant increasingly miserable garrison conditions. The state made efforts to instill a new national identity for the Russian people. Yeltsin proclaimed a new anthem (from Mikhail Glinka's 1836 patriotic opera *Life for the Tsar,* abandoned by Putin in 2000), a new flag with the old tsarist colors, and a new state emblem with a modified double-headed eagle. But such gestures could not allay the anxieties and disorientation brought on by the dizzying changes in the post-Soviet world. Yet those who would restore a Soviet empire—mostly older and less educated people—remained few in number.

"I do not believe that Russia needs a unifying ideology, nor do I think that Orthodoxy should try to assume such a role. But I do believe that Russia needs a clear vision of its path and its role in the world," said a young priest, Hilarion Alfeev, in a 1999 interview. The striking revival of the Orthodox Church, begun under Gorbachëv, promised to fill the ideological vacuum left by the defeat of Soviet Marxism. The picture at the dawn of this century was one of flux. Mass baptisms into the Orthodox Church and a vigorous growth of faith among the young were signs of renewed vitality. Couples wed in civic ceremonies were remarrying in church. Many Orthodox believers saw the faith as part of their heritage and identity. Among the many restorations of church buildings, the total rebuilding of the famous Church of Christ the Savior in Moscow (1994–1997) was the most spectacular. Church leaders such as the Patriarch Alexi II and Metropolitan Ioann of Moscow (d. 1995) displayed a relatively enlightened toleration of other faiths and of social changes, although some clergy were part of an authoritarian stream of monarchists, quasi-fascists, and anti-Semites. The more rigid priests and prelates banned (and even burned) books by liberal or controversial Orthodox theologians. Side by side with the Orthodox Church, other religions and their followers were flourishing as well: Roman Catholics, Protestants, Muslims, Buddhists, animists, and Jews. Imported evangelical Christianity won a considerable following in Russia through television appearances, Bible societies, and popular preachers, though a new Law on Religion seemed designed to stifle precisely those imported evangelists.

The lid that flew off Russian culture when Gorbachëv introduced *glasnost* was not put back on. The relative weakening of high, native, and Soviet cultural forms escalated all during the 1990s. Retro movie houses opened to serve both those alienated by imported culture and the trendy who liked to combine nostalgia with knowing condescension toward the "old." Strip clubs, all-night discos, and sexually explicit TV coverage boomed. Fiction bestsellers included the Moscow crime novels of Alexandra Marinina and instant pop hits like Vasily Staroi's *Pierre and Natasha* (1996), a "sequel" to Tolstoy's 1869 epic *War and Peace.* Postmodernists had entered the scene with such works as Evgeny Popov's *On the Eve of the Eve,* a parody of the nineteenth-century Turgenev novel *On the Eve.* Madonna, Harry Potter, and Eminem were better known to young people than the masters and entertainers of the past. Except among the old and hardened, the October Revolution, Lenin, and World War II belonged to ancient history. Universities, publishers, and movie studios were strapped for funds. The intelligentsia, who had feasted on ideas and had been fed by the state, felt irrelevant in a new cultural marketplace that seemed to spurn spiritual values and ideas. Caught between loss of subsidies and the flood of global imports, high-minded people raised on a diet of Shakespeare, Anna Akhmatova, and Alexander Pushkin languished in their own special identity crisis.

Even the gender system was rocked. New waves of feminist ideas and mobilization campaigns sought to undermine the deep notions of division of labor and Soviet "femininity" fostered by previous regimes. Watching nude females at a circus performance was much less puzzling to older Russian women than the entry of women into high politics and business. Not that women had much success in breaking old codes, but their very effort to do so launched a quest for new gender identities. For men, the search for gender identity took different forms. Acts of criminal male violence against women doubled from 1994 to 1996. Symbolic male chauvinism was on full display among New Russian males and certain criminal types. An interview-based study of "the man question" has described "anxious masculinization"—stress and insecurity about gender roles.

Given all these real and perceived problems, it was no surprise that commentators put on a pessimistic face about the prospects for the Russian people. Some invoked the analogy of the doomed Weimar Republic of Germany in the 1920s, the prelude to Adolf Hitler, marked by wiped-out savings, unemployment and inflation, rightist and leftist extremists, fear and shame, and a loosening of morals and culture. Against this, other accounts of the new order used words like *awakening, reawakening,* or *resurrection* to suggest that, in spite of all the obvious flaws and setbacks of the last ten or fifteen years, Russia had entered a new age. Observers noticed that this transition, or rebirth, was slow and bumpy, deliberate and cautious, and not accompanied by the kind of euphoric catharsis or jubilation that all too often in the past had given way to agonizing disillusionment. Russians tended to be much better in complaining than in expressing gratitude when big changes occurred. That there was no national euphoria was, in fact, a healthy sign. People set out on their own journeys of discovery, engaged in political reform, profit, religious piety, a yearning for monarchy, genealogical searches, restoration of manor houses, and hundreds of what used to be called in the nineteenth century "small deeds." In the midst of these quests, Russia entered the twenty-first century. Looking ahead, the widely admired scholar of early Russian culture and history Dmitry Likhachëv (1906-1999) stated: "Our future lies in openness to the entire world and in enlightenment."

CHAPTER 43

Another Russia: Emigration in the Twentieth Century

In an alien land, with parched tongue, walking naked and barefoot, feet torn by thorns, answering each other in tears, some saying: "I am from this town," and others—"And I from that village." So they speak to each other tearfully, sighing as they recognize their kin, raising their eyes to the Lord in heaven, keeper of secret wisdom.

—*Russian Primary Chronicle (1093)*

Displacement and migration have become fundamental categories of human life in the twentieth century. Two world wars, revolutions, and a basic economic disparity between industrialized and "less developed" countries have sent millions of people searching for a better life, political asylum, or just survival in places other than where they were born. It has become "normal" for children to grow up, or adults to live, surrounded by more than one culture, each of which they may identify with in only fragmentary fashion. The tumultuous history of Russia in the twentieth century is not complete unless it includes the story of those who found themselves, whether by choice or necessity, beyond its borders. The nature of the Soviet state was such that emigration was a permanent and virtually irreversible phenomenon: to leave meant to cut all ties; there could be no looking back. This finality—except for a brief window in the 1920s—formed the backdrop to the adaptation and creative life of the Russian emigration. The importance of the emigration lies not only in its numbers, which by themselves make it a significant demographic phenomenon, but in the individuals involved, who, at various points, included the cream of the country's literary, musical, scientific, and artistic talent.

THREE WAVES

Oral tradition constructs the history of the emigration through the apt metaphor of "waves," emanating from Russian territory at moments of crisis and dispersing over several continents, from Europe to North and South America to Australia. The events precipitating the first two waves were indeed watersheds in world history:

the October Revolution of 1917 (followed by the Civil War) and World War II. Although these events have already been examined in depth in this textbook, each has an underside in terms of the millions of people it displaced, made homeless, or forced into exile. Neither war nor revolution can be understood without taking into account, on the one hand, the repercussions for the individuals making up the civilian population and, on the other, their perspectives on these events. In each case, the numbers ending up abroad were sufficient, or the individuals involved prominent enough, to make their experience an integral part of the history of Russia in the twentieth century. The "third wave" did not have any such specific stimulus: the term is used to refer to a peacetime emigration, focused in the 1970s, primarily of Jews who, with the help of international organizations, were able to leave the closed Soviet Union. Historically, the antecedent to the story told here is the Jewish emigration from the Russian Empire and Eastern Europe at the end of the nineteenth century, when, in the wake of the post-1881 pogroms and general poverty and persecution, about 2.5 million Jews left the region, mostly for the United States (see the chapter "Orthodoxy, Autocracy, Nationality Reaffirmed, 1881–1905").

These twentieth-century migrations were distinguished from the phenomenon of exile in the nineteenth century by the sheer numbers involved. These were not individuals motivated primarily by an intellectual opposition to the regime, like Alexander Herzen—the nineteenth-century émigré par excellence—or the radical Marxists, socialists, and anarchists who found refuge in Switzerland, France, or England at the turn of the century. Rather, they fit the description of *diaspora:* the dispersion of a whole people when the place of origin becomes uninhabitable for them. In this, the Russian emigration has analogies with the expulsion of the people of Israel from Jerusalem, or the dispersion of Armenians from their historical homeland. That said, it is interesting to note that the three waves had little indeed in common with each other: they differed not only in social composition and culture but also in the country they had left behind. The first emigration preserved intact the memory of old-regime Russia; the second came out of the "high Stalinism" of the 1930s, followed by the total destruction of World War II; the third abandoned the functioning, if decrepit and oppressive, society of Brezhnev's "real socialism." Not only material conditions and regimes but language, culture, and fundamental social habits and attitudes were radically different in each wave.

"RUSSIA ABROAD": BETWEEN TWO WARS

The revolution and civil war were about movement and migration as much as about armed conflict and political struggle. Displaced families, homeless children, and roving bands of marauders became a customary feature of the landscape, whether in Petrograd, Ukraine, or Siberia. Like the French Revolution over a century earlier, the Russian Revolution created a sizeable emigration. The first wave included not only convinced monarchists and supporters of the old regime but also political figures from the Provisional Government, intellectuals, artists, "bourgeois" escaping from persecution or death, and people simply caught up in the maelstrom of civil war and fleeing for survival. A significant proportion of the emigration consisted of officers and soldiers in the White Army. It is reasonably safe to estimate the number of emigrants at about 1 million, although the fact that some counts have put the number as high as 3 million indicates the difficulty of even this basic calculation.

Trajectories

It has been remarked that the first Russian emigration has no "history" as such, for it is merely the composite of a plethora of individual histories. Still, with almost a century's hindsight, certain patterns become discernible. There were two major escape routes from the war-torn Russian continent. The first led west: directly, to Poland, eastern Germany, or the Baltic states; or indirectly, via Istanbul and thence to Belgrade, Prague, or Sofia, often continuing on to Berlin, until Weimar Germany's economic collapse in 1923 forced a renewed flight, usually onward to Paris. The southern detour was typical for Wrangel's and Denikin's retreating officers and soldiers as the southern flank of the White Army was squeezed out of European Russia. Wrangel sought to preserve the military organization of his soldiers. Russian encampments on the Gallipoli peninsula sometimes outnumbered the local population. The second, longer route went east, all the way to Manchuria and sometimes Shanghai, and from there across the ocean to San Francisco.

The 1920s witnessed the remarkable phenomenon of a Russian city on Chinese territory: Harbin, in Manchuria, once a Russian railway town, became a focal point of émigré life and culture. There were other offshoots from the emigration routes as well, including a Russian community in Finland, which took shape in part from Russians living in Karelia who simply stayed put after Finland secured its independence from the empire in 1918. Perhaps the oddest incident was the boatload of some two hundred intellectuals and artists who, on an explicit order from Lenin in the summer of 1922, were literally shipped out of the new Soviet Union so they could do no harm, across the Black Sea to Istanbul. Most then made their way to Prague, Berlin, and Paris, becoming the founders of an entire institutional infrastructure of émigré universities and organizations and forming the kernel of a new epoch in Russian intellectual history.

Sociology of Exile: Statelessness and Assimilation

Who were the émigrés? In comparison with prerevolutionary Russian society, they included a disproportionately large educated elite, and a disproportionately small number of peasants. For the most part, they were urban bourgeoisie, small landowners, and agriculturalists (mostly Cossacks). They also included Jews, Ukrainians, Armenians, Georgians, and some Kalmyks. In Europe, they came under the jurisdiction of a newly established League of Nations High Commission on Refugees, headed by the Norwegian Fridtjof Nansen. In a highly regimented postwar society, where passports and visas became a necessity of international travel, the Russians (like some other groups, most notably Armenians fleeing the defunct Ottoman Empire) were stateless and without papers. A new invention, the "Nansen passport" (1922), provided them with such documentation while sealing their officially stateless status; many retained this status for the rest of their lives. As countries gradually granted recognition to the Soviet government (Britain, Italy, and France in 1924; the United States in 1933) the refugees' homelessness was confirmed: until then, in France for example, Vasily Maklakov had continued to represent them through the old Russian Embassy.

Émigrés remained poised between the construction of separate and isolated communities, and gradual integration into the social fabric of their adopted countries. Not until 1924 or 1926—or sometimes much later—did the realization begin to sink in that the Bolshevik "occupation" of Russia was not temporary. Between the wars, the main centers of separate émigré communities became Prague, Paris, and Harbin, with echoes in Riga, Belgrade, Berlin, and San Francisco. Paris was the undisputed "capital" of this shadow nation. A rich infrastructure of émigré institutions, mimicking those of prerevolutionary St. Petersburg and Moscow, sprang up almost immediately. Perhaps the most important was the Zemgor—the Union of Zemstvos and Towns—which had done so much to promote production and assist civilians behind the front lines in the Great War. It was reconstituted in Paris in 1918, with branches in Prague and elsewhere; funded by Russian embassies abroad, the Zemgor took over administration of refugee needs, medical care, and children's welfare.

In Paris, the Orthodox Church on the rue Daru, dating from the nineteenth century; the St. Sergius Theological Seminary; the Tourguéneff Library; the Renaissance and YMCA Press publishing houses; the newspaper *La Pensée russe (Russian Thought);* and the Orthodox cemetery at Ste-Geneviève-des-Bois became focal points of the Russian community. Prague, in the meantime, became the site of a Russian university, a law school, numerous clubs and organizations, and youth groups like *Sokol*—a sports and socially oriented organization much like the Girl and Boy Scouts. Harbin boasted literary clubs, schools, and newspapers. Participants in this vibrant cultural life lived in the constant expectation of eventual return to Russia, where their efforts would be channeled into re-creating post-Soviet society.

Yet at the same time, the exigencies of simple survival—the need to find paid employment in particular—demanded assimilation into the society of the host country. Sir John Hope Simpson's survey of the European refugee problem found, in 1937, Russian colonies at steel plants in the eastern industrial region of France (Mosel, Alsace) and at Nice, Lyons, and Marseilles. In 1930, one-third of the twenty-four thousand workers employed at the Renault automobile works on the outskirts of Paris were Russians. Émigrés found work as taxi drivers (at one point there were four thousand in Paris), domestic servants, or farmers. Conditions were especially propitious in Yugoslavia, where the predominantly urban and professional émigrés could find employment in government agencies and universities on an equal footing with Yugoslav citizens; émigrés in government service included judges, military officers, statisticians, and physicians. Economic conditions were far

Russian Law Faculty in Prague, 1922–1927. *St. Vladimir's Seminary, Mt. Vernon, NY.*

more difficult in the Far East: in Xinjiang, Manchukuo, and Shanghai, Russians worked as agriculturalists, artisans, and shopkeepers but found themselves increasingly displaced by Chinese or Japanese.

Still, employment is only one index of assimilation. The rate of mixed marriages in France was not high, and generally involved Russian men with French women (for demographic reasons—there were significantly more men than women among the émigrés). Observers reported a strong tendency to preserve the Russian language and Russian traditions and to do everything possible to pass them on to the next generation. In Paris, the Russians congregated in the fifteen and sixteenth arrondissements, near the Orthodox cathedral on the rue Daru. In Yugoslavia, mixed marriages were frequent, while in the Far East, Russian women often married European men. The adaptation strategies of émigré children varied widely: some achieved renown in the idiom of their adopted country—for example, the writers Henri Troyat and Zoë Oldenbourg, the intellectual historian Isaiah Berlin, or the revolutionary Victor Serge; others identified mainly with the culture of their insular émigré communities; still others simply became swallowed up in the mainstream of the societies in which they lived.

Politics in Exile

The political life of the emigration was concentrated in Paris. Throughout the interwar years, the touchstone for émigré politics remained, first and foremost, the Soviet Union and its evolution; events in France or internationally entered in only secondarily. The full spectrum of pre–civil war political parties was represented in emigration, and usually by their leaders. Thus the liberals Pavel Milyukov and Vasily Maklakov, the moderate socialist Alexander Kerensky, and the Socialist Revolutionary (SR) terrorist Boris Savinkov were all figures on the Parisian scene. The Mensheviks, banished from the Soviet Union in 1922, remained in Berlin until Hitler's seizure of power in 1933; they were grouped around the journal *Socialist Courier.*

The early years witnessed a number of efforts at political cohesion: in January 1921, thirty-two members of the dispersed Constituent Assembly (fifty-six were in exile) convened in Paris at the initiative of an SR–Left Kadet alliance that included Milyukov, and published proposals for the organization of post-Bolshevik Russia; some months later a Right Kadet–dominated "National Congress" followed suit. In 1924, Grand Duke Cyril Vladimirovich (1876–1938) proclaimed himself successor to the Russian throne, causing little more than additional rifts and dissensions in the émigré community. A 1926 "Congress of Russia Abroad" constituted the most ambitious effort to rally supporters of the anti-Bolshevik cause, headed by the moderate right. But most of this activity resulted merely in a good deal of spilled ink and internecine rivalries among the "democratic sector" under Milyukov's leadership, the moderate right, and the restorationist far right. Mensheviks, in the meantime, remained more tightly linked to their fellow Social Democrats in the Soviet Union and sought to enlist the aid of European Social Democracy in influencing a softening of the Bolshevik regime. All of these political debates and conflicts worked themselves out in a sophisticated journalistic milieu that continued the tradition of the imperial Russian press: Paris, Berlin, Riga, and Belgrade had daily Russian-language newspapers, while periodicals like the *New Review* (New York) replicated the prerevolutionary thick journals.

The emigration only rarely extruded on the political consciousness of its French milieu. When it did, the news took the form of spy scandals, abductions, and even an assassination. In 1924, General Wrangel had formed a successor organization to the White Army, the Russian General Military Union (ROVS). On January 26, 1930, the organization's next leader, General Alexander Kutëpov, was kidnapped on a Paris street in broad daylight. Kutëpov disappeared, apparently into the bowels of a Soviet freighter, to the accompaniment of a storm of articles in the French press, ranging from accusations of similar vile deeds by the Soviet secret police (the GPU) on the premises of the Soviet embassy, to the French Communist Party newspaper *l'Humanité*'s indictment of a supposed White plot to poison Franco-Soviet relations. The next eruption occurred two years later when a Russian émigré (a Kuban Cossack), Paul Gorgulov, apparently overwhelmed by the loneliness and frustrations of rootless existence to the point of mental instability, fired point-blank and killed the president of the republic, Paul Doumer, on May 6, 1932. ROVS, in the meantime, could not be permitted to exist in peace, and in 1937 Kutëpov's successor, General E. K. Miller, vanished in similar fashion.

The political energies of the emigration were most creative in the realm of ideology. The 1920s gave birth to an original political doctrine called Eurasianism: its proponents, grouped around the journal *Eurasian Courier,* proposed what was then a radically new perspective on Russian identity and history. If, throughout the nineteenth century, Russian intellectuals had been primarily concerned with Russia's relation to Europe, the Eurasians now saw its nature as essentially poised between East and West. The linguist Nikolai Trubetskoy (1890–1938), for example, suggested that the contemporary Russian/Soviet state represented above all the legacy of the Mongol ruler Chinggis Khan. Politically, the Eurasians hovered between acceptance of aspects of the new Soviet state, with its historic capital in Moscow, and the wish to preserve the current geographical (but not political) structure while infusing it with Orthodoxy. Curiously, although it was developed in emigration, the Eurasian perspective eventually fitted quite well with that of the Soviet Union, and with post-Soviet Russia's definition of its own identity.

A more radical ideology was *"smenovekhovstvo,"* or "changing landmarks"; this was a strategy adopted by intellectuals in the emigration who came to an acceptance, pure and simple, of the Soviet regime. A number of them moved back to the Soviet Union in the late 1920s. As the entire European continent became increasingly polarized after Hitler's rise to power in Germany, some Russian émigrés participated in the political redefinition: a number fought on the republican side in the Spanish Civil War, while others joined a Russian fascist movement in Germany.

It is hard to say whether one more major figure belongs to the history of the emigration or not. But it bears mentioning in this context that the drama of Leon Trotsky's demise played itself out, as well, beyond the borders of the Soviet Union. Exiled from the Soviet Union in 1929, Stalin's archrival came to Mexico in 1937 with the help of the painter Diego Rivera; he was assassinated by Soviet agents in August 1940.

The Church: A Special Role

Political parties fall flat in the absence of a government, and ideologies ring hollow in the absence of the resonance provided by a "normal" society. In the world of the emigration, suspended in its own peculiar space, there was one institution that could provide an anchor, a link with tradition, and a focus for spiritual and even political energies: this was the Orthodox Church, to which the vast majority of émigrés fervently belonged. The October Revolution had caught the church at a moment of renewal: the All-Russian Church Council appointed Patriarch Tikhon in Moscow in the very days that the Bolsheviks took over Smolny in Petersburg (see the chapter "The Revolutions of 1917"). Among the émigrés were the last overprocurator of the Holy Synod, Anton Kartashëv (1875–1961), and many council members, including such prominent ones as the Silver-Age philosopher and economist Sergei Bulgakov. Russian Orthodox cathedrals had been constructed in Paris, Helsinki, and Revel (Tallinn) in the nineteenth century, some as part of Alexander

III's campaign to cover the empire, and beyond, with golden cupolas. Where they did not already exist, they were built, or improvised, sometimes in converted private houses. The Sunday liturgy, the church choir, and church schools that instructed children in Russian grammar and the basics of Orthodox catechism, were an integral part of émigré existence; the opulent midnight service at Easter attracted as many curious onlookers as Russians.

From the outset, authority in the church was split. During the civil war, a Temporary Ecclesiastical Administration, under White jurisdiction, had emerged in the south. This body relocated to Sremski Karlovci in Serbia, forming the basis of the Bishops' Synod (Church in Exile) under the leadership of Metropolitan Antony (Alexei Khrapovitsky, 1864–1934), former metropolitan of Kiev. Soon afterward, the Moscow patriarchate appointed another churchman, Evlogy (Vasily Georgievsky, 1868–1948), metropolitan of the Russian Church in Western Europe. His seat was in Berlin and, after 1923, Paris. Thus the church became divided between the Karlovci Synod, which did not recognize the Soviet-controlled Moscow patriarchate, and Evlogy's metropolitanate, which did, and which accepted the Soviet demand that it remain uninvolved in politics. Variants on this split emerged in different countries. In the United States, for example, authority remains divided between the Church in Exile and the Orthodox Church of America (OCA).

Divisions notwithstanding, within a remarkably short time the church, as a social institution, had evolved a complete infrastructure, and one that could provide for its flock for the full cycle of life. Essential to the functioning of a church without state support, as the Old Believers had once found out, are mechanisms of self-perpetuation. The St. Sergius Theological Institute, founded in Paris in 1925, ensured the production of priests and the flourishing of theological studies. The church became the base for the most important youth movement in emigration—the Russian Student Christian Association (RSKhD). Supported, materially, by the YMCA and the World Christian Student Movement, the organization's program called for the mutual penetration of secular and religious life, or the "Christianization of life." To this end, the RSKhD organized lectures, classes, sports activities, festivities, and international conferences. This was a degree of social activism reminiscent of the Christian brotherhoods in seventeenth-century Ukraine. Both the RSKhD and the professors at the St. Sergius Theological Institute, Sergei Bulgakov and Georges Florovsky in particular, did much to shape the interwar ecumenical movement, involving Catholic and Protestant churches. The Brotherhood of St. Alban and St. Sergius brought Anglicans and Orthodox together in dialogue. The Orthodox Work, headed by Elizaveta Skobtsova (Mother Maria, 1891–1945) was a charitable institution that revived the tradition of voluntary lay communities that cared for the poor. Finally, many found their resting place at the Russian cemetery of Ste-Geneviève-des-Bois, whose tombstones read like a telephone book of the emigration; an old-age home was also founded on the premises.

Encounters: Mutual Images

Joseph Kessel's novel *Nuits de princes* (*Nights of Princes,* 1928) painted the Russian émigré as nobleman-turned-taxi-driver. Fashion-model princesses and rich landowners-turned-peanut-salesmen joined the Russian cabaret, the exoticism of Russian women, and the mysteries of the "Russian soul" in the popular imagination. Destitute counts played themselves as extras in Hollywood B-movies. The Russian old regime became a fashion in the 1920s. Like most sensationalized images, this one took off from a grain of truth. Alexander Vertinsky's nostalgic and melancholy songs—traveling with him from the Black Rose cabaret he opened in Istanbul in 1919 and throughout Europe, before he settled in Shanghai—evoked a lost and distant aristocratic past. Still, the interactions between émigrés and their hosts were in daily life less felicitous. Parisians ignored the Russians at best, and despised them at worst: not least among the contributing factors was a leftward shift in French politics, especially as the Popular Front came into being in 1934 and the Soviet Union became fashionable. Left-leaning intellectuals, in particular, had no use for a population they perceived as uniformly monarchist. The Russians, in the meantime, continued to regard the host populations as "other," singing songs of loneliness and isolation (Marina Tsvetaeva, for example) or, more productively, simply going about their business with the minimum interaction necessary for material subsistence.

DISPLACED PERSONS: WORLD WAR II

How many people were displaced from their homes in World War II? One estimate puts the overall number (that is, from all countries) at 30 million. In mid-1941, the Inter-Allied Committee on Post-War Requirements counted 21 million in Europe, of whom 8 million had been imported as forced laborers to Germany, and another 8 million displaced within their own countries. At the close of the war, 11 million Europeans were counted as requiring repatriation. The largest group of refugees were Soviet citizens—more than 7.2 million individuals, including forced laborers, prisoners of war, and former residents of German-occupied territories fleeing the return of Soviet power.

German Occupation and Soviet Advance

At its height, the German occupation of the Soviet Union covered all of Belorussia, Moldavia, and Ukraine and extended into south Russia and the north Caucasus. The cities of Kharkov and Rostov had changed hands three times by 1943 as Soviet troops seized territories only to be pushed back, once again, by the occupying forces. The retreating Soviet armies did their best to leave nothing behind for the Germans: the massive evacuation of industry, including factory personnel, from the Donbass to the Urals in 1941, was followed by a scorched-earth policy that left cities, including Kiev, burned to the ground, collective farms destroyed, and factories ravaged. Still, the population of a large region, including the parts of Poland and Belorussia that had been annexed following the Nazi-Soviet pact in 1939, found themselves under German administration—the Ostministerium—divided up into four sections: Ostland (the Baltic region), Ukraine, Muscovy, and the north Caucasus. In an area that had experienced the worst of both collectivization and the purges of the technical intelligentsia, many were ready to greet Hitler's armies as liberators from the scourge they already knew. In the 1957 book that remains the most thorough investigation of the subject, Alexander Dallin suggested that, had the Germans capitalized on this sentiment instead of proceeding to implement the Nazi philosophy of Slavs as *Untermenschen* (subhumans), they might easily have won the support of the population, in turn perhaps affecting the outcome of the war. Instead, and perhaps inevitably, the conquerors, in these early stages of a projected German colonization of their "India," rounded up the Jews to be shipped to concentration camps; staged raids on markets, churches, and movie houses to collect a work force to export to Germany; summarily executed individuals taken into custody by police for arbitrary reasons; failed to disperse the hated collective farms; and so on. At the same time they sought, with limited success, to keep agriculture and industry operating to supply the homeland with desperately needed products.

The story of the emigration begins with the advance of the Soviet armies following the Battles of Stalingrad and Kursk. In 1943 there were already two significant groups of Russians outside the boundaries of the Soviet Union: Soviet soldiers taken prisoner by the Germans, and the forced laborers *(Ostarbeiter)* the latter had begun to export in 1942. The Germans took the astounding number of 5.7 million Soviet prisoners of war (3.8 million already in December 1941). That more than 2 million of them died in captivity is an index of their treatment, occurring in part because the Soviet Union had refused to sign the Geneva Convention in 1929. The *Ostarbeiter* numbered 2.8 million: they were civilians recruited to work, in Germany, as cheap laborers. The first shipment, from Ukraine in February 1942, was 80 percent volunteers—a percentage that dwindled to zero when news of conditions in the freight cars that transported laborers, and in the camps in which they were subsequently housed, reached those left behind. "Labor" included forced prostitution, and Russian and Ukrainian women were captured for that purpose. These two groups were joined by a third as the Soviet armies reclaimed the territory of south Russia and Ukraine: these were civilians (among them, for example, engineers who had managed to fall through the cracks during Stalin's evacuation of industry) who followed the retreating German armies out of the Soviet Union in a ragtag tail, taking advantage of this last chance to escape the encroaching return of Soviet power. What all three groups of refugees had in common was, on the one hand, a precarious and unknown future and, on the other, a certain fate should they fall into the hands of their "legitimate" government: the Soviets regarded anyone who had been on enemy territory or in enemy hands as ipso facto a traitor, and hence subject to execution or imprisonment in a labor camp.

On July 12, 1942, along the front between Novgorod and Leningrad, the German army captured the Soviet general Andrei Vlasov (1900–1946). His story subsequently became emblematic of the situation of the "second emigration." Vlasov's

Second Shock Army became caught in a pocket protruding out westward from the front, which the Germans easily cut off at its narrow bottleneck at Myasnoi Bor; General Headquarters had chosen to concentrate its forces on the defense of Leningrad, liquidating the Volkhov front, of which Vlasov was deputy commander, at a critical moment and subordinating its command to the Leningrad front. Soon after his capture, Vlasov, with a fellow prisoner, wrote a letter to the German authorities suggesting that their *Ostpolitik*—the term for German policy toward the Soviet Union and the occupied territories—was misguided. Vlasov suggested that, were the Germans to take advantage of existing anti-Soviet sentiment, they would find a good deal of support among the population of the occupied territories and also among prisoners of war; they advocated the formation of a Russian National Army. Over the next year, the Germans used Vlasov for propaganda in prisoner-of-war camps and among the civilian population in the occupied territories; but it was not until the fall of 1944 that Vlasov received permission from SS commander Heinrich Himmler to form the KONR (Committee for the Liberation of the Peoples of Russia). In the last stages of the war, Vlasov was given two divisions to fight against the Soviet army. The divisions were sent essentially to their own destruction, being deployed to places where the German army had previously failed; coordination was disastrous, and the divisions were never sure to whom they answered. On May 12, 1945 Vlasov was once again captured, this time by the Soviets; he and his entourage were hanged on August 2, 1946—according to rumor, on piano wire with the hook inserted at the base of the skull.

Active military collaboration took other forms, as well. The Germans made use of volunteers in nonmilitary positions (*Hilfswillige,* or *Hiwis*); *Osttruppen* ("east troops," battalions made up of Russians); and the larger *Ostlegionen*, recruited from non-Russian Soviet nationalities and comprising the Turkestan, Armenian, north Caucasian, Georgian, Azerbaijan, and Volga Tatar legions. In Ukraine, where partisan warfare eventually became most violent, the two factions of the Organization of Ukrainian Nationalists—the Banderites and the Melnykites—initially tried to work with the occupying forces to promote their own goals of liberation and independence. In 1941, two Ukrainian military units directed by the Bandera faction, known by the code names Nachtigall and Roland, marched with the German armies into Galicia and Bessarabia; but the goal of Ukrainian independence had little appeal for the Germans, and the Ukrainian officers eventually ended up in German prisons and concentration camps.

Cultural Microcosm: The DP Camps, 1945–1950

The last two years of the war found several million Soviet citizens on German soil, whether employed in Silesian coal mines and metallurgical plants or surviving in prisoner-of-war camps. "Stalin's ten blows"—the march through Eastern Europe in 1944—sent many of them scurrying farther westward. The refugees were so numerous that the U.S. Army consciously blew up bridges to dampen their flow. When the war ended in May 1945, an organization called UNRRA (United Nations Relief and Rehabilitation Administration), established in late 1943, took over the administration of refugee problems in the Allied zones from the military. Camps for the displaced persons (DPs) dotted the map of Germany, particularly Bavaria, at Füssen, Kempten, and Schleissheim. The initial aim of the Allied administration was to return such persons to their homes. Still, by 1947, when UNRRA ceased its operations, nearly 650,000 refugees, virtually all Eastern Europeans—Poles, Balts, Ukrainians, Jews, and Russians—remained in the camps. Their administration was charged to the International Refugee Organization (IRO), created at the end of 1946, also under the auspices of the United Nations.

In comparison with the population of the Soviet Union as a whole, the numbers of people in the DP camps were, of course, not large. Still, relatively small numbers can create entire movements and intellectual orientations in the history of ideas and culture. A glance inside the camps—where, like refugees the world over, people lived several families to a barrack and in primitive sanitary conditions—reveals a remarkable cultural microcosm that is essential to an understanding of twentieth-century Russia. In 1949, the largest DP camp at Schleissheim, near Munich, counted 5,066 residents—a colorful intersection not only of the Baltic, Ukrainian, Belorussian, Cossack, Polish, and Russian ethnicities but also of the two emigrations: representatives of the first wave who had lived, between the wars, in Yugoslavia or Czechoslovakia found themselves mingling with their Soviet compatriots in the camps. Residents had constructed five houses of worship—two Russian Orthodox churches, one Ukrainian Orthodox, one Protestant, and a Buddhist temple. The infrastructure resembled that of a small provincial town, with schools, a theater and cinema, clubs and offices, craftsmen's workshops, kitchens, a hospital, a laundry, a bathhouse, storehouses, and even a home for the aged. The library—the donation of an émigré prince—contained 2,632 books with a high circulation rate. A Russian and a Ukrainian elementary school, a Russian high school, a music school, and English language courses (provided by a Quaker organization) ensured the proper education of young people. There were more than thirty political, professional and civic organizations, from sports clubs to political parties to associations of engineers, artists, or physicians. After four years, residents had organized their own administrative structure—a Camp Committee, whose five-member Presidium counted two Russians, a Ukrainian, a Cossack, and a Kalmyk; elections were likewise conducted by national curia. The Kuban Cossacks organized an independent settlement *(stanitsa)* within the camp. Particularly remarkable was the proportion of young people—some 30 percent of the total population—who received, in this context, a unique and intense exposure to varieties of Russian culture. Some of their high school teachers were old-regime professors from the first emigration, and immersion in Russian history and literature and Orthodox religion, as well as math and science, created a generation of European Russians with a completely original and quite strong culture, resembling neither their Soviet counterparts nor their forebears in imperial Russia.

German military barrack converted into a Russian Orthodox church in the DP camp at Schleissheim. Photo ca. 1948. *Courtesy Viktor Evtuhov.*

Repatriation

The Yalta accords signed by the Allies in February 1945 included a secret agreement on the exchange of prisoners of war. The agreement, in which Stalin insisted on the repatriation of all Soviet citizens, continued an informal arrangement between British foreign secretary Anthony Eden and Stalin a year earlier in Moscow, known as the "Tolstoy conference"; it became the basis for the return, by Allied and particularly British forces, of Russians in Germany to the Soviet Union. The repatriation issue was the single dominant political question—one of life and death—for the millions of Russians (2 million in the Allied zone in Germany) in Europe after the Nazi defeat. A "Soviet citizen" was considered to be anyone born within the pre-1939 boundaries of the Soviet Union, and the Soviets insisted, in negotiations with the Allies, that individual choice should not play a role. Thus, although the Yalta agreement did not specify forcible repatriation, Russians were—in England, Germany, France, Italy, and Norway—rounded up, herded onto trucks, and shipped eastward, often to the ironic accompaniment of marching bands and festive party decorations. Once in the Soviet Union, they were mercifully shot, or less mercifully dispatched to labor camps at Kolyma or Magadan.

One of the most dramatic cases of forced repatriation was that of a large Cossack settlement in the north of Italy, whose leaders were taken to a fictitious "conference" in May 1945, only to be handed over, by the British, to the Soviet authorities. Among the Cossacks were the seventy-six-year-old General Pëtr Krasnov, who had emigrated after the civil war and thus was not a Soviet citizen, and others like him. Another example is the case of the refugee camp at Kempten. Here, on August 12, 1945, American troops, with a list of 410 individuals to be repatriated (some of them soldiers from Vlasov's army), dragged those who had not managed to escape out of the church where they were huddling and loaded them onto waiting trucks with the aid of blows and rifle butts. Apart from physical resistance, those subject to repatriation responded in a number of ways: one was suicide; another was the creation of a burgeoning industry, inside the DP camps, of falsified documents, usually certifying that their holders had been born in the post-1939 Soviet-occupied parts of Poland, Ukraine, or the Baltic states. The incident at Kempten, augmented by numerous tales of the resistance to repatriation, was crucial in changing particularly American policy on this issue; by 1946 repatriations dwindled, but over 2 million transfers had already taken place.

Dissemination

Unlike the first emigration, which remained concentrated in Prague, then Berlin and Paris, or Harbin and then San Francisco, the second wave dispersed to a plethora of points on the globe. As the camps closed in 1950, ex-residents wrote letters back to the camp newspaper describing their experiences in Venezuela, Colombia, Brazil, Norway, Belgium, Holland, England, France, Australia, New Zealand, New York, and California. At this point their history becomes a part of the drama of the international refugee issue. The IRO, with its own fleet of forty vessels for the transport of refugees, worked with sixty volunteer relief agencies in different countries and spent an impressive $450 million in the process of resettlement. The 1948 Displaced Persons Act in the United States made possible the admission of 329,000 individuals, through cooperation with such organizations as the World Council of Churches; refugees needed a sponsor in the United States who would vouch for their employment and solvency. The other three countries receiving the largest number of refugees were Australia (thanks to a compulsory labor scheme in 1948), Israel, and Canada. Other possibilities included employment in Belgian coal mines, hospitals in Holland, or agriculture and industry in Venezuela.

The issue of their origins remained with the ex-DPs for a lifetime, giving rise to a phenomenon called the "Berëzov illness," after the writer and theatrical performer Rodion Berëzov, who in 1954 was nearly deported from the United States when he revealed that he was Russian rather than Polish, as his camp-manufactured documents stated. A congressional bill sponsored by Senator John F. Kennedy in 1957 reversed the decision and ensured the legitimacy of the immigrants' presence.

THE THIRD WAVE AND BEYOND

The Soviet Union in the era of "real socialism" (the Brezhnev years) was a closed society. It was not possible to leave, and travel abroad and contact with foreigners were both a luxury and a risky business. Paradoxically, this period witnessed the third major wave of emigration from Soviet territory in the twentieth century. The nature of this emigration was highly specific and affected almost exclusively the Jewish population. The exodus of Jews from the Soviet Union, peaking in the years, 1971–1974, and again in 1978–1980, is inscribed in the context of the international politics of the Cold War. Soviet emigration policy became a standard item of international diplomacy, in particular the Helsinki accords of 1975 promising freer movement of Soviet citizens across national borders; human rights groups in the West urged a linkage of emigration policy with arms control and other issues.

In 1966 (one year after the Sinyavsky-Daniel trial—see the chapter "The Brezhnev Years: Change and Ferment, 1964–1982"), Premier Alexei Kosygin declared an open door for individuals wishing to meet with or even rejoin their families abroad. Over the next years a minute trickle grew to a flood: by 1989, more than 250,000 people had left. Many came from peripheral regions—Georgia, Moldavia, Lithuania, Latvia. The complexities of the process gave rise to an entire subculture of emigration within the Soviet Union. In principle, being Jewish was a sufficient criterion to apply for an exit visa. In practice, however, this qualification was frequently limited by other factors—for example, the employment of anyone in the family, at any time, in scientific research institutes in which classified information was available. Once the application was made, the potential emigrant became a pariah within Soviet society, losing his or her job, apartment, and other benefits. Over 60 percent of applicants were refused permission. Theoretically, the émigrés were all destined for Israel. In fact, however, the standard train route through Vienna and thence to Rome led to a processing center where individuals could declare their preference for the United States: in 1981 this "dropout rate" peaked at 81 percent. Thus two societies became the main recipients for the "third wave": Israel and the United States.

The second group affected by Soviet policies toward emigration in this period were the ethnic Germans, of whom 70,500 left in 1971–1983. Otherwise, exit could be achieved through defection, a path followed by athletes, musicians, dancers, and sailors; or through close family ties—resulting in the institution of the fictitious marriage with a foreigner, contracted for the purpose of leaving the country.

Dissidence and Exile

The Brezhnev era witnessed a renaissance of the phenomenon of exile proper, generally associated more with the nineteenth century. The most notable case is that of Alexander Solzhenitsyn, whom the Soviet authorities chose to force into exile instead of sending him to prison. The author of the *Gulag Archipelago* remained in Vermont until the collapse of the Soviet Union, writing and rewriting his ambitious chronicle of World War I and chastising the West for its decadence. The poet Joseph Brodsky (1940–1996), tried in 1964 for "parasitism," was exiled in 1972. He lived in the United States and in Italy, winning the Nobel Prize in literature in 1987. The writer Andrei Sinyavsky (1925–1997) emigrated in 1973 after seven years in a hard-labor camp and continued to write both literature and political essays from abroad. Their counterparts who remained in the Soviet Union—Jewish human rights activist Natan Shcharansky (1948–) and the physicist Andrei Sakharov (1921–1989)—were, respectively, sentenced to hard labor and exiled to the provincial city of Gorky.

Émigrés, Expatriates, and the "Near Abroad" (the 1990s)

The "real" Jewish emigration, in terms of numbers, in fact took place as the Soviet Union collapsed. Whether we are to classify them as part of the "third wave" or as a new phenomenon, over 1 million Jews left the Soviet Union following the liberalization of emigration laws in 1987, the gradual easing of restrictions on exit visas, and finally the opening of the borders in 1991. The new outflow, concentrated in 1989–1994, had serious consequences for Israeli demographics: ex-Soviet Jews ultimately constituted 11 percent of the total population. The numbers put a strain even on the sophisticated Israeli mechanisms for assimilation, prompting a "direct absorption" policy that included everything from instruction in Hebrew to the provision of fully furnished apartments complete with pots and pans, light bulbs, and toilet paper. A disproportionate number of physicians, scientists, and musicians led to significant downward shifts in professional employment. Former Soviet émigrés sometimes furnished willing settlers for Israeli-occupied territories. As in the United States (Brighton Beach in New York, or the Fairfax neighborhood in Los Angeles), the émigrés formed tight-knit communities where they could work, shop, socialize, and receive medical care without speaking any language but Russian; in Israel they acquired their own television stations, and much programming was subtitled in Russian. In terms of religion and culture, the ex-Soviet Jews proved a good deal less "Jewish" than the receiving communities might have expected, but sometimes compensated with patriotism. Whereas in the 1980s ex-Soviet Jews in Israel tended to be extremely conservative, anti-Soviet, and supportive of right-wing policies in their new country, the profile in the 1990s became more complex, in part because of the new émigrés' high educational level. Their political organizations, headed among others by Natan Shcharansky (who was finally allowed to emigrate in 1986), have the capacity to swing elections to the Israeli parliament.

The Soviet Union's collapse also gave rise to two new phenomena: first, an explosion of expatriates, or Russian citizens who leave their country for extended periods to work or study without relinquishing their Russian passports; second, significant numbers—more than 25 million—of ethnic Russians who found themselves living "abroad" when the fifteen Soviet republics parted ways. As one study put it, Russians in the republics were transformed, overnight, from an "imperial minority" to a minority pure and simple. The dimensions of this situation varied with the geography. In Kazakhstan, for example, ethnic Russians made up more than 50 percent of the population, partly as a result of Khrushchëv's "virgin lands" campaign in the 1950s (see the chapter "Khrushchëv and the Decline of Stalinism, 1953–1964"); significant numbers left in the 1990s. In the Baltic states, with the exception of Lithuania, which was 90 percent Lithuanian, discrimination quickly became an issue: it became difficult for the Russian minority, many of whom did not know the Estonian or Latvian languages, to meet new citizenship requirements. The key issue here is that the new Russian state did not acknowledge its former colonists, either.

INTERCONNECTIONS AND DISLOCATIONS: ÉMIGRÉ THOUGHT AND CULTURE

Homelessness brings loneliness and despair; it can also bring creative liberation. The intellectual and cultural history of the twentieth century would have taken a different course without the contributions of Russia Abroad. Virtually every sphere of creative endeavor—literature, philosophy, linguistics, theology, music and the arts, history—was represented in the emigration. Thinkers, writers, artists, and scholars oscillated around the poles of integration and international renown, on the one hand, and the continuation of specifically Russian culture on the other.

Lenin's remarkable decision to load unlike-minded thinkers and writers onto a boat and deport them resulted in the transplantation of the Russian Silver Age to European soil. The emigration, though fragmented, isolated, and often melancholy, provided a fertile milieu: Berlin and Paris counted dozens of Russian poets and novelists grouped around several important journals and publishing houses. *Sovremennye zapiski (Contemporary Annals),* published in Paris from 1920 to 1940, was the most influential journal; curiously, the entire editorial board were SRs, though they published materials of a wide ideological spectrum. Although Berlin, in the early years, counted some 188 émigré publishing enterprises, these were eventually overshadowed by the YMCA Press in Paris, initially set up to publish textbooks in Russian but then expanding its operations to literature, philosophy, and history, including the reprinting of nineteenth-century classics. This was the milieu that allowed such already well known writers and poets as Merezhkovsky, Gippius, Ivanov, Balmont, and Khodasevich to keep publishing, and a younger generation to begin its literary career. (To review the prerevolutionary Silver Age and its leading cultural figures, see the chapter "Cultural Explosion, 1900–1920.")

Though it is not possible to discuss everyone here, it might be valuable to single out several major figures representative of different tendencies in the emigration. Vladimir Nabokov (1899–1977), the cosmopolitan par excellence who, as his biographer puts it, was "in a category of his own," wrote with equal ornate fluidity in Russian and English; his entire career took shape outside Russia. The novel *The Gift* (1937) actually took the emigration as its main subject, while *Pnin* (1957) acidly recreated the type of an émigré professor at a small American college. Other works, such as *Ada* (1969), continued the nineteenth-century tradition of the Russian novel, while *Lolita* (1955) gained its succès de scandale by recounting the tale of the aging Humbert Humbert's passion for a prepubescent "nymphet." Ivan Bunin (1870–1953) stands in stark contrast to Nabokov's international persona. Bunin won the Nobel Prize in 1933—in part for his realist short stories in the tradition of Turgenev and Chekhov, but also as a political recognition of the existence of a Russia outside the Soviet Union—but remained little translated or read outside émigré circles. The modernist poet Marina Tsvetaeva (1892–1941) presents yet a third type. Her remarkably concrete poetry, suffused with incurable pain and melancholy, found echoes in the work of the German poet Rainer Maria Rilke and the Russian poet and novelist Boris Pasternak. She returned to the Soviet Union in

1939, where her husband (who had in Paris been implicated in the Miller affair) and daughter were arrested; she killed herself while in evacuation in the Tatar Republic. A special place in the world of letters belongs to memoir literature, because it brought to life the extraordinary experiences of its authors: two cases in point are Nabokov's *Speak, Memory* (1966) and Nina Berberova's *The Italics Are Mine* (1973).

Some writers of émigré origin merged completely with their adopted cultures. Such, for example, are the historical novelist Henri Troyat (1911–) in France and the American writer Ayn Rand (1905–1982), author of *The Fountainhead* (1943) and *Atlas Shrugged* (1957). Rand, a theorist of capitalism writing in a style that remarkably resembles socialist realism, finished university in Petrograd before leaving in 1926. This pattern is perhaps even more evident in the visual arts: one does not particularly think, for example, of the painters Vasily Kandinsky or Marc Chagall or, later, Mark Rothko, as "Russian," although they shared this origin.

Virtually all of the important philosophers of the Silver Age (Shestov, Frank, Rozanov, etc.) continued their work in Russia Abroad. Without question, however, the most influential in his own time was Nicholas Berdyaev (1874–1948). A core member of the Marxists-turned-idealists and then a key contributor to *Vekhi* (*Landmarks,* 1909), Berdiaev blossomed in emigration: his philosophical paean to freedom captured the imagination of his Western public; his *Origin of Russian Communism* (1937) conveyed much about the Soviet atheist state to a broad audience, while his essay on the Silver Age re-created and conserved the culture of that age as it receded. Perhaps more than any Russian writer except Dostoevsky, Berdiaev was responsible for igniting passionate interest in Russian history and culture in other parts of the world.

The Silver Age was obsessed by the problem of the word—its structure, meaning, uses, and philosophical implications. These discussions, ranging from the linguistic to the theological, had their culmination in the emigration. In 1926, Nikolai Trubetskoy (1890–1938) and Roman Jakobson (1896–1982) founded the Prague Linguistics Circle, where they continued to develop the highly influential doctrine of Russian Formalism. Jakobson had been close to the Futurist poets before the revolution. The Formalist method of literary criticism sought to elevate the study of texts to a science, concentrating on their intrinsic structure rather than on the cultural or historical context in which they were written. This approach proved immensely productive, opening up new dimensions of analysis. Both Trubetskoy and Jakobson also built on linguist Ferdinand de Saussure's turn-of-the-century structural approach to language itself; Trubetskoy developed the theory of the phoneme (the smallest unit of language with an immediate link to meaning). The work of the Prague school paralleled the research of colleagues in the Soviet Union, among them Yuri Tynianov, Viktor Shklovsky, and Boris Eikhenbaum. But it was the émigrés—and Jakobson in particular, who eventually became much revered in his position at Harvard University—who brought Formalism into circulation internationally, and helped shape the evolution of structuralism not only in linguistics but in cultural studies more generally: anthropology, sociology, psychology, and film studies, as well as the New Literary Criticism.

One might wonder whether, without the crisis of revolution and civil war, the diffuse, quasi-theological discussions of Sophia and the natures of Christ so fashionable in the Silver Age would ever have led anywhere. As it happened, they ultimately made their return, albeit transformed, back into the realm of theology proper. Sergei Bulgakov, the Marxist-turned-idealist and then religious philosopher, took a further step in emigration, becoming the century's most significant Orthodox theologian. His two trilogies, the "major" and the "minor," constructed a comprehensive theological system that mimicked the structure of the Orthodox liturgy. The doctrine of Sophia the Divine Wisdom, or sophiology, became a cornerstone of Bulgakov's interpretation. In a sensational controversy in 1937, both the Moscow church authorities and the Karlovci Synod condemned the concept of Sophia as heretical. Bulgakov's final work, on the eve of his death in 1944, was an exegesis of the Apocalypse of St. John the Divine. Two other major thinkers were instrumental in shaping Orthodox theology in this period. The first is Georges Florovsky (1893–1979), whose main theme (and departure from Bulgakov) was a return to patristics—that is, the texts of the Eastern Church Fathers of the fourth and fifth centuries. Florovsky was very active in the ecumenical movement and wrote many articles and a book elucidating the central dogma of Orthodoxy in its relation to Catholicism and Protestantism. Georgy Fedotov (1886–1952), like Florovsky a historian as well as a thinker, captured the spiritual world of Orthodox Christianity in *The Russian Religious Mind* (1946) and in his investigations of Orthodox hagiography (lives of the saints).

The twentieth century, whether in the Soviet Union or abroad, was an era of transcendence for Russian music. Although Sergei Prokofiev (1891–1953) did not technically emigrate, much of his music was composed abroad. Among the true émigrés, Igor Stravinsky (1882–1971) created the musical avant-garde along with contemporaries like Arnold Schoenberg. Sergei Rachmaninoff (1873–1943) both composed and performed throughout Europe and the United States, while Fëdor Shaliapin, Serge Koussevitzky, Jascha Heifetz, Arthur Rubinstein, and Nadia Boulanger are a few of the pianists, violinists, singers, conductors, and teachers who helped shape the world of contemporary music performance. Diaghilev's Ballets Russes (1909–1929) lived on in Monte Carlo, while Serge Lifar and George Balanchine placed their indelible stamp on the dance troupes of Paris and New York. The ballet's turn-of-the-century collaborators from the *World of Art* group were there as well: Alexander Benois (1870–1960), Mstislav Dobuzhinsky (1875–1957), Leon Bakst (1866–1924), Natalia Goncharova (1881–1962), and others continued to create their magnificent costumes and stage sets for the world at large. Even theater, though ostensibly more limited by language, found its path into contemporary performance: although the Moscow Art Theater in emigration performed largely for Russian speakers, the methods and techniques of Konstantin Stanislavsky (1863–1938), Vladimir Nemirovich-Danchenko (1848–1936), and Vsevolod Meyerhold (1874–1940) profoundly affected drama in Europe and particularly in the United States. The Stanislavsky method's insistence on real-life experience as a necessary preparation for acting has shaped the style of Broadway and Hollywood actors such as Dustin Hoffman.

This survey of culture and ideas would not be complete without mention of one more field of endeavor, namely, history. Here one must go further back than the early twentieth century to find intellectual origins. Paul Milyukov (1859–1943) was, after all, a historian, and student of V. O. Klyuchevsky (see the chapter "Society, Culture, Politics, 1881–1905"), as much as a politician; a new edition of his *Outlines of Russian Culture* and a coauthored history of Russia, sponsored by the French historian Charles Seignobos, were products of the émigré period. George Vernadsky elaborated a Eurasianist perspective on Russian history, downplaying the links between Kiev and Muscovy and emphasizing the influence of the Mongols. The brilliant historian of classical antiquity, Michael Rostovtzeff (1870–1952), worked in a tradition of social and economic history with parallels to the Annales school in France. The historian of Byzantium George Ostrogorsky (1902–1976) received part of his training at the émigré research institute, the Seminarium Kondakovianum. One of the most original works of cultural history is Georges Florovsky's *Paths of Russian Theology* (1937), a brilliant and idiosyncratic re-creation of Russian thought through the ages in its relation to Orthodox theology; the chapter on Silver-Age culture, which Florovsky experienced as a young man, remains the best synthesis of that period. In the United States, Michael Karpovich (1888–1959) brought the historiography of S. M. Soloviëv and V. O. Klyuchevsky (see the chapter "Society, Culture, Politics, 1881–1905") to the newly founded field of Slavic studies. These prerevolutionary historians maintained an extraordinarily long influence through the continued effort of Karpovich's students, among them Nicholas Riasanovsky, Martin Malia, and Richard Pipes. What is fascinating here is the transmission and preservation of ideas and methods across more than a century. The serious student of Russian history in an American university today soon learns that the methods and approaches are quite different from those in European or other historical fields: this is because the tradition of the great historical schools of the nineteenth century remains uninterrupted.

The second emigration stands in stark contrast to the first: it boasts no "big names." Its history belongs to the realm of sociology rather than ideas. It is more valuable to see its representatives as part of a post–World War II European displacement to various parts of the world, and contributing to the export of European bourgeois values and culture. Some of the journals of the second emigration, most notably the German-based *Posev (Germination),* as well as this wave's contribution to religious and cultural life, helped sustain the infrastructure of Russian life in the West and came alive once again after 1991. Curiously, the most prominent figures in the realm of culture and ideas in the "third wave" were not necessarily Jewish. The creativity of the third wave falls primarily in the fields of literature, semiotics, and music. It counts such figures as the writers Vasily Aksenov and Edward Limonov, pop artists Komar and Melamid, émigré representatives of the Moscow-Tartu school of semiotics, and the Estonian and Orthodox composer Arvo Pärt. One of the dominant third-wave journals was the Paris-based *Kontinent,* established in 1974.

The history of the emigration forms a fascinating postscript to a dramatic century on the territory of Russia and the Soviet Union. Yet it is also more than that: the stories of the people who were forced or wished to leave the country where they were born provides a unique glimpse into the historical events—the Revolution of 1917, World War II—and social conditions that prompted their departure. The extent of opposition to the Soviet regime, for example, makes untenable an account of World War II as a tale of the unalloyed heroism of the Soviet army and puts into question a simple view of the Soviet Union as the liberator of Europe in 1945. But the history of the emigration is also a chapter in world history. Large-scale migrations and displacements have resulted from revolutions in China and Iran, wars in Ethiopia and Rwanda, and difficult economic conditions in Guatemala, Italy, or Turkey—to name just a few examples. The experience of the Russian emigration provides a useful point of comparison with these other situations.

In 1880, Fëdor Dostoevsky asserted in a speech on Pushkin: "Yes, the destiny of the Russian is unquestionably pan-European and universal. To become a true Russian, completely Russian, might mean nothing (in the long run, note this) but to become the brother of all people, to become the *universal human being*, if you wish." Dostoevsky's messianic prophecy has perhaps had a very modest realization. Russian émigrés decisively shaped European and American culture and intellectual life over the course of the twentieth century. For contemporary Russia, the emigration represents at once a link with history and tradition, and a window on worlds outside Russia's geographical borders. Surely, this "other Russia"—a land located in the imagination rather than anchored in space—will become one of the many elements in the journeys of discovery undertaken by Russians in the new century.

SUGGESTED READINGS

General Works, Covering Russian History

Billington, James. *The Icon and the Axe*. New York, 1966.

Brumfield, William Craft. *A History of Russian Architecture*. New York, 1993.

Cherniavsky, Michael. *Tsar and People: Studies in Russian Myths*. New York, 1961.

Chew, Allen F. *An Atlas of Russian History. Eleven Centuries of Changing Borders*. 2d ed. New Haven/London, 1970.

Davies, Norman. *God's Playground, a History of Poland*. 2 vols. New York, 1982.

Gilbert, Martin. *Atlas of Russian History*. New York, 1993.

Kaiser, Daniel H., and Gary Marker, eds. *Reinterpreting Russian History, 860–1860*. New York/Oxford, 1994.

Magosci, Paul. *A History of Ukraine*. Seattle, 1966.

Moon, David. *The Russian Peasantry 1600–1930. The World the Peasants Made*. London, 1999.

Pintner, Walter, and Daniel K. Rowney, eds. *Russian Officialdom. The Bureaucratization of Russian Society from the Seventeenth to the Twentieth Century*. Chapel Hill, 1980.

Pushkareva, Natalia. *Women in Russian History: From the Tenth to the Twentieth Century*. Translated and edited by Eve Levin. Armonk, N.Y., 1997.

Vernadsky, George, Sergei Pushkarev, Ralph T. Fisher, Andrew Lossky, and Alan D. Ferguson, trans. and eds. *A Source Book for Russian History from Early Times to 1917*. 3 vols. New Haven, 1972.

Wieczynski, Joseph L., ed. *Modern Encyclopedia of Russian and Soviet History*. Gulf Breeze, Fla., 1976–.

General Works, Covering Russian History to 1800

Dmytryshyn, Basil. *Medieval Russia. A Source Book, 850–1700*. 3d ed. Orlando, Fla., 1990.

Kliuchevskii, Vasilii (Klyuchevsky, Vasily). *A History of Russia*. 5 vols. Translated by J. C. Hogarth. London/New York, 1911–1931/1960.

Langer, Lawrence N. *Historical Dictionary of Medieval Russia*. Lanham, Md./London, 2002.

Smith, R. E. F., and David Christian. *Bread and Salt. A Social and Economic History of Food in Russia*. Cambridge, U.K./New York, 1984.

Solovev, Sergei. *History of Russia*. 48 vols. projected. Various translators. Gulf Breeze, Fla., 1976–.

Works Covering Russian History to 1613

Fedotov, George B. *The Russian Religious Mind*. 2 vols. Cambridge, Mass. 1946–1966/Belmont, Mass., 1975.

Golden, Peter. *An Introduction to the Study of the Turkic Peoples*. Wiesbaden, 1992.

Grousset, René. *Empire of the Steppes: a History of Central Asia*. New Brunswick, N.J., 1970.

Lazarev, Viktor. *Old Russian Murals and Mosaics from the XI to the XVI Century*. London, 1966.

Levin, Eve. *Sex and Society in the World of the Orthodox Slavs, 900–1700*. Ithaca, 1989.

Martin, Janet. *Medieval Russia 980–1584*. Cambridge, U.K./New York/Melbourne, 1995.

Mitchell, Robert, and Nevill Forbes, trans. *The Chronicle of Novgorod, 1016–1471*. London, 1914.

Obolensky, Dmitri. *The Byzantine Commonwealth: Eastern Europe, 500–1453*. London, 1974/Crestwood, N.Y., 1982.

Sinor, Denis, ed. *The Cambridge History of Early Inner Asia*. Cambridge, U.K., 1990.

Spassky, I. G. *The Russian Monetary System: A Historico-Numismatic Survey*. Amsterdam, Neth., 1967.

Vernadsky, George, trans. and ed. *Medieval Russian Laws.* New York, 1947–1969.

Zenkovsky, Serge N. *Medieval Russia's Epics, Chronicles, and Tales.* New York, 1974.

Zenkovsky, Serge N., trans. and ed. Betty Jean Zenkovsky, trans. *The Nikonian Chronicle.* 5 vols. Princeton, 1984–1989.

Zguta, Russell. *Russian Minstrels: A History of the Skomorokhi.* Oxford, U.K., 1978.

Works Covering Russian History to 1455

Birnbaum, Henryk. *Lord Novgorod the Great. Essays in the History and Culture of a Medieval City-State.* Columbus, Ohio, 1981.

Christian, David. *A History of Russia, Central Asia and Mongolia.* Vol. I, *Inner Eurasia from Prehistory to the Mongol Empire.* London/Malden, Mass., 1998.

Fennell, John. *The Crisis of Medieval Russia, 1200–1304.* London/New York, 1983.

_____. *A History of the Russian Church to 1448.* London/New York, 1995.

Franklin, Simon. *Writing, Society, and Culture in Early Rus, c. 950–1300.* Cambridge, U.K., 2002.

Kaiser, Daniel. *The Growth of Law in Medieval Russia.* Princeton, 1980.

Kaiser, Daniel, trans. and ed. *The Laws of Rus'—Tenth to Fifteenth Centuries.* Salt Lake City, 1992.

Martin, Janet. *Treasure in the Land of Darkness: The Fur Trade and Its Significance for Medieval Russia.* London, 1986.

Perfecky, George. *The Galician-Volynian Chronicle. An Annotated Translation.* Munich, 1973.

Senyk, Sophia. *A History of the Church in Ukraine.* Vol. 1, *To the End of the Thirteenth Century* (*Orientalia Christiana Analecta,* No. 243). Rome, 1993.

Thompson, M. W. *Novgorod the Great. Excavations of a Medieval City.* New York, 1967.

Works Covering Russian History to 1240

Cross, Samuel Hazzard, and Olgerd P. Sherbowitz-Wetzor, trans. and eds. *The Russian Primary Chronicle.* Cambridge, Mass., 1953.

Franklin, Simon, and Jonathan Shepherd. *The Emergence of Rus, 750–1200.* London/New York, 1996.

Grekov, Boris D. *Kiev Rus.* Moscow, 1959.

Smith, R. E. F. *The Origins of Farming in Russia.* The Hague/Paris, 1959.

Vernadsky, George. *Kievan Russia. A History of Russia.* Vol. 2. New Haven/London, 1948.

Chapter 1

Barford, P. M. *The Early Slavs. Culture and Society in Early Medieval Eastern Europe*. Ithaca, 2001.

Dolukhanov, P. M. *The Early Slavs: Eastern Europe from the Initial Settlement to Kievan Rus'.* London, 1996.

Dunlop, John. *The History of the Jewish Khazars.* Princeton, 1954.

Dvornik, Francis. *The Slavs: Their Early History and Civilization*. Boston/London, 1956.

Golden, Peter. *Khazar Studies.* 2 vols. Budapest, 1980.

Melnikova, Elena A., ed. *The Eastern World of the Vikings*. Gothenburg, Swed., 1996.

Pritsak, Omeljan. *The Origin of Rus'.* Vol. 1, *Old Scandinavian Sources Other Than the Sagas* Cambridge, Mass., 1981.

_____. *Studies in Medieval Eurasian History.* London, 1981.

Urbanczyk, Premyslaw, ed. *Origins of Central Europe*. Warsaw, 1977.

Vernadsky, George. *Ancient Russia. A History of Russia.* Vol. 1. New Haven/London, 1943.

Chapter 2

Dimnik, Martin. *The Dynasty of Chernigov, 1054–1146.* Toronto, 1994.

_____. *Mikhail, Prince of Chernigov and Grand Prince of Kiev, 1224–1246.* Toronto, 1981.

Hurwitz, Ellen. *Andrej Bogoljubskij: The Man and the Myth*. Florence, 1980.

Tikhomirov, M. N. *The Towns of Ancient Russia*. Moscow, 1959.

Chapter 3

Franklin, Simon, trans. and ed. *Sermons and Rhetoric of Kievan Rus'.* Cambridge, Mass., 1991.

Heppell, Muriel, trans. and ed. *The "Paterik" of the Kievan Caves Monastery.* Cambridge, Mass., 1989.

Hollingsworth, Paul, trans. and ed. *The Hagiography of Kievan Rus'.* Cambridge, Mass., 1992.

Lennhof, Gale. *The Martyred Princes Boris and Gleb: A Socio-Cultural Study of the Cult and the Texts.* Columbus, Ohio, 1989.

Poppe, Andrzej. *The Rise of Christian Russia.* London, 1982.

Rappoport, P.A. *Building the Churches of Kievan Russia.* Aldershot, U.K., 1995.

Shchapov, Ia. N. *State and Church in Early Russia, 10th–13th Centuries.* New Rochelle, N.Y./Athens/Moscow, 1993.

Works Covering Russian History, 1240–1455

Fennell, John. *The Emergence of Moscow, 1304–1359.* Berkeley/Los Angeles, 1968.

Halperin, Charles. *Russia and the Golden Horde: The Mongol Impact on Medieval Russian History.* Bloomington, Ind., 1985.

_____. *The Tatar Yoke.* Columbus, Ohio, 1986.

Meyendorff, John. *Byzantium and the Rise of Russia: A Study of Byzantino-Russian Relations in the Fourteenth Century.* Cambridge, U.K., 1981.

Morgan, David. *The Mongols.* Oxford, U.K., 1986.

Vernadsky, George. *The Mongols and Russia. A History of Russia.* Vol. 3. New Haven/London, 1953.

Chapter 4

Allsen, T. T. *Mongol Imperialism: The Policies of the Grand Qan Möngke in China, Russia, and the Islamic Lands, 1251–1259.* Berkeley, 1987.

Beazley, C. Raymond, ed. *The Texts and Versions of John de Plano Carpini and William de Rubuquis.* London, 1903/Liechtenstein, 1967.

Cleaves, Francis Woodman, trans. and ed. *The Secret History of the Mongols.* Cambridge, Mass., 1982.

Juvaini. *The History of the World-Conqueror by 'Ala-al-Dion Ara-Mali.* 2 vols. Translated from the text of Mirza Muhammed Qazvini by John Andrew Boyle. Manchester, U.K., 1958.

Lenhoff, Gail. *Early Russian Hagiography: The Lives of Prince Fedor the Black.* Berlin, 1995.

Rashid al-Din Tabib. *The Successors of Genghis Khan.* Translated by J. A. Boyle. New York, 1971.

Rowell, Stephen C. *Lithuania Ascending: A Pagan Empire in East-Central Europe, 1293–1345.* Cambridge, U.K., 1994.

Works Covering Russian History, 1300–1613

Alef, Gustave. *Rulers and Nobles in Fifteenth-Century Muscovy.* London, 1983.

Berry, Lloyd E., and Robert O. Crummey, eds. *Rude and Barbarous Kingdom.* Madison, Wis., 1968.

Crummey, Robert O. *The Formation of Muscovy, 1304–1613.* London/New York, 1987.

Dewey, Horace W., trans. and ed. *Muscovite Judicial Texts, 1488–1556.* Ann Arbor, 1966.

Howes, Robert Craig, ed. *The Testaments of the Grand Princes of Moscow.* Ithaca, 1967.

Kollmann, Nancy Shields. *Kinship and Politics: The Making of the Muscovite Political System, 1345–1547.* Stanford, 1987.

Ostrowski, Donald. *Muscovy and the Mongols. Cross-Cultural Influences on the Steppe Frontier, 1304–1589.* Cambridge, U.K., 1998.

Pelenski, Jaroslaw. *Russia and Kazan: Conquest and Imperial Ideology. 1438–1560s.* The Hague/Paris, 1974.

Presniakov, A. E. *The Formation of the Great Russian State.* Translated by A. E. Moorhouse and introduced by Alfred Rieber. Chicago, 1970.

Works Covering Russian History, 1450–1800

Baron, Samuel, and Nancy Kollmann. *Religion and Culture in Early Modern Russia and Ukraine.* Dekalb, 1997.

Bushkovitch, Paul. *The Merchants of Moscow, 1580–1650.* Cambridge, U.K., 1980.

_____. *Religion and Society in Russia. Sixteenth and Seventeenth Centuries.* New York/Oxford, U.K., 1992.

Frost, Robert I. *The Northern Wars, 1558–1721.* Harlow, U.K., 2000.

Hellie, Richard. *Enserfment and Military Change in Muscovy.* Chicago, 1971.

_____. *Slavery in Russia, 1450–1725.* Chicago, 1982.

_____. *The Economy and Material Culture of Russia, 1600–1715.* Chicago/London, 1999.

Kirchner, Walter. *Commercial Relations Between Russia and Europe, 1400–1800. Collected Essays.* Bloomington, Ind., 1966.

Kliuchevsky, Vasily. *A Course in Russian History. The Seventeenth Century* (vol. 4 of the five-volume *History*). Translated by Natalie Duddington and introduced by Alfred J. Rieber. Chicago, 1968/Armonk, 1994.

Poe, Marshall T. *"A People Born to Slavery." Russia in Early Modern European Ethnography, 1476–1748.* Ithaca/London, 2000.

R. E. F. Smith. *Peasant Farming in Muscovy.* Cambridge, U.K., 1977.

Thyret, Isolde. *Between God and Tsar. Religious Symbolism and the Royal Women of Muscovite Russia.* DeKalb, 2001.

Vernadsky, George. *The Tsardom of Moscow, 1547–1682,* 2 parts. Vol. 5, *A History of Russia.* New Haven/London, 1969.

Chapter 6

Alef, Gustave. *The Origins of Muscovite Autocracy: The Age of Ivan III.* Forschungen zur Osteuropäischen Geschichte 39, 1986.

Crosky, Robert M. *Muscovite Diplomatic Practice in the Reign of Ivan III.* New York/London, 1987.

Fennell, John. *Ivan the Great of Moscow.* London/New York, 1961.

Goldfrank, David, trans. and ed. *The Monastic Rule of Iosif Volotsky.* Rev. ed. Kalamazoo, Mich., 2000.

Herberstein, Sigismund von. *Notes upon Russia.* London, 1851/New York, n.d.

Vernadsky, George. *Russia at the Dawn of the Modern Age. A History of Russia.* Vol. 4. New Haven/London, 1959.

Chapter 7

Fennell, John, trans. and ed. *The Correspondence Between Prince A. M. Kurbsky and Tsar Ivan IV of Russia, 1564–1579.* Cambridge, U.K., 1955.

_____. *Prince A. M. Kurbsky's History of Ivan IV.* Cambridge, U.K., 1965.

Grobovsky, Antony. *The "Chosen Council" of Ivan IV: A Reinterpretation.* Brooklyn, 1969.

Hellie, Richard, ed. "Ivan the Terrible: A Quarcentenary Celebration of His Death." *Russian History/Histoire russe* 14 (1987): 1–4.

Keenan, Edward L. *The Kurbsky-Groznyi Apocrypha: The Seventeenth Century Genesis of the "Correspondence" Attributed to Prince A. M. Kurbsky and Tsar Ivan IV.* Cambridge, Mass., 1971.

Platonov, Sergei F. *Ivan the Terrible.* Gulf Breeze, Fla., 1974.

Pouncy, Carolyn Johnston, trans. and ed. *The Domostroi. Rules for Russian Households in the Time of Ivan the Terrible.* Ithaca/London, 1994.

Skrynnikov, Ruslan G. *Ivan the Terrible.* Translated and edited by Hugh F. Graham. Gulf Breeze, Fla., 1981.

Staden, Heinrich von. *The Land and Government of Muscovy.* Translated and edited by Thomas Esper. Stanford, 1967.

Works, Covering Russian History, ca. 1600–1800

Avrich, Paul. *Russian Rebels 1600–1800.* New York, 1972.

Dixon, Simon. *The Modernisation of Russia 1676–1825.* Cambridge, U.K., 1999.

Dukes, Paul. *The Making of Russian Absolutism. 1613–1801.* London, 1990.

Hartley, Janet. *A Social History of the Russian Empire 1650–1825.* London, 1999.

Hittle, J. Michael. *The Service City. State and Townsmen in Russia 1600–1800.* Cambridge, Mass., 1979.

Hughes, Lindsey. "The Courts of Moscow and St Petersburg." In *The Princely Courts of Europe 1500–1750,* edited by John Adamson. London, 1999.

Karlinsky, Simon. *Russian Drama from Its Beginnings to the Age of Pushkin.* Berkeley, 1985.

Chapter 8

Bussow, Conrad. *The Disturbed State of the Russian Realm.* Translated by G. Edward Orchard. Montreal, 1994.

Dunning, Chester. *Russia's First Civil War: The Time of Troubles and the Founding of the Romanov Dynasty.* University Park, Pa., 2001.

Margaret, Jacques. *The Russian Empire and the Grand Duchy of Muscovy. A Seventeenth-Century French Account.* Translated and edited by Chester Dunning. Pittsburgh, 1983.

Massa, Isaac. *A Short History of the Beginnings and Origins of These Present Wars in Moscow Under the Reigns of Various Sovereigns Down to the Year 1610.* Translated and edited by G. Edward Orchard. Toronto, 1982.

Perrie, Maureen. *Pretenders and Popular Monarchism in Early Modern Russia: The False Tsars in the Time of Troubles.* New York/Cambridge, 1995.

Platonov, Sergei F. *Boris Godunov, Tsar of Russia.* Translated by L. Rex Pyles. Gulf Breeze, Fla., 1973.

______. *The Time of Troubles.* Lawrence, Kans., 1970.

Skrynnikov, Ruslan G. *Boris Godunov.* Translated and edited by Hugh F. Graham. Gulf Breeze, Fla., 1982.

______. *The Time of Troubles: Russia in Crisis, 1604–1618.* Translated by John T. Alexander. Gulf Breeze, Fla., 1988.

Zolkiewski, Stanislas. *Expedition to Moscow.* Translated and edited by J. Giertych. London, 1959.

Chapter 9

Crummey, Robert O. *Aristocrats and Servitors: The Boyar Elite in Russia, 1613–1689.* Princeton, 1983.

Jansson, Maija, N. Rogozhin, P. Bushkovitch, V. I. Buganov, and M. P. Lukichev, eds., *England and the North: The Russian Embassy of 1613–1614.* Translated and edited by Paul Bushkovitch et al. Philadelphia, 1994.

Fuhrmann, Joseph. *Tsar Alexis, His Reign and His Russia.* Gulf Breeze, Fla., 1981.

Keep, John. "The Regime of Filaret." *Slavonic Review* 38 (1959–1960): 334–360.

Kivelson, Valerie. *Autocracy in the Provinces. The Muscovite Gentry and Political Culture in the Seventeenth Century.* Stanford, 1997.

Kollmann, Nancy S. *By Honor Bound. State and Society in Early Modern Russia.* Ithaca, 1999.

Longworth, Philip. *Alexis Tsar of All the Russias.* London, 1984.

Hellie, Richard *The Muscovite Law Code (Ulozhenie) of 1649.* Part I: *Text and Translation.* Translated and edited by Richard Hellie. Irvine, 1988.

Olearius, Adam. *The Travels of Olearius in Seventeenth-Century Russia.* Translated and edited by Samuel Baron. Stanford, 1967.

Stevens, Carol. *Soldiers on the Steppe. Army Reform and Social Change in Early Modern Russia.* DeKalb, 1995.

Chapter 10

Cherniavsky, Michael. "The Old Believers and the New Religion." *Slavic Review* 25 (1966): 1–39.

Crummey, Robert O. "Court Spectacles in Seventeenth-Century Russia: Illusion and Reality." In *Essays in Honor of A. A. Zimin,* edited by D. C. Waugh. Columbus, Ohio, 1985.

Hughes, Lindsey. "Attitudes Towards Foreigners in Early Modern Russia." In *Russia and the Wider World in Historical Perspective,* edited by C. Brennan and M. Frame. Basingstoke, U.K., 1999.

_____. *Russia and the West. The Life of a Seventeenth-Century Westernizer, Prince Vasily VasilEvich Golitsyn (1643–1714).* Newtonville, Mass., 1984.

_____. *Sophia Regent of Russia, 1657–1704.* New Haven, 1990.

Kollmann, Nancy S. "The Seclusion of Elite Muscovite Women." *Russian History/Histoire russe* 10 (1983): 170–187.

Michels, Georg B. *At War with the Church. Religious Dissent in Seventeenth-Century Russia.* Stanford, 1999.

Neuville, Foy de la. *A Curious and New Account of Muscovy in the Year 1689.* Edited by Lindsey Hughes. London, 1994.

Works, Covering Russian History, 1700–1917

Kohut, Zenon. *Russian Centralism and Ukrainian Autonomy. The Absorption of the Hetmanate, 1760s–1830s.* Cambridge, Mass., 1988.

Marrese, Michelle. *A Woman's Kingdom: Noblewomen and the Control of Property in Russia, 1700–1861.* Ithaca, 2002.

Roosevelt, Priscilla. *Life on the Russian Country Estate. A Social and Cultural History*. New Haven, 1995.

Wirtschafter, Elise Kimerling. *Social Identity in Imperial Russia.* DeKalb, 1997.

_____. *Structures of Society. Imperial Russia's "People of Various Ranks."* DeKalb, 1994.

Works, Covering Russian History, ca. 1700–1800

Baehr, Steven. *The Paradise Myth in Eighteenth-Century Russia*. Stanford, 1991.

Bartlett, Roger, ed. *Russia and the World of the Eighteenth Century*. Columbus, Ohio, 1988.

Black, J. L. *Citizens for the Fatherland. Education, Educators and Pedagogical Ideals in Eighteenth-Century Russia.* Boulder, Colo., 1979.

Brown, William. *A History of Eighteenth-Century Russian Literature.* Ann Arbor, 1978.

Cross, Anthony G. "By the Banks of the Neva": *Chapters from the Lives and Careers of the British in Eighteenth-Century Russia.* Cambridge, U.K., 1996.

Duffy, Christopher. *Russia's Military Way to the West: The Origins and Nature of Russian Military Power, 1700–1800.* London, 1981.

Freeze, Gregory. *The Russian Levites. The Parish Clergy in the Eighteenth Century*. Cambridge, Mass., 1977.

Garrard, John, ed. *The Eighteenth Century in Russia*. Oxford, U.K., 1973.

Givens, R. D. *Servitors or Seigneurs: The Nobility and the Eighteenth-Century Russian State.* Ann Arbor, 1984.

Kahan, Aracadius. *The Plow, the Hammer and the Knout*. Chicago, 1985.

Kamenskii, Aleksandr B. *The Russian Empire in the Eighteenth Century*. Translated by David Griffiths. New York, 1997.

LeDonne, John P. *Absolutism and Ruling Class. The Formation of the Russian Political Order 1700–1825.* Oxford, U.K., 1991.

Marker, Gary. *Publishing, Printing, and the Origins of Intellectual Life in Russia, 1700–1800.* Princeton, 1985.

Raeff, Marc. *Origins of the Russian Intelligentsia. The Eighteenth-Century Nobility.* New York, 1966.

Rogger, Hans. *National Consciousness in Eighteenth-Century Russia*. Cambridge, Mass., 1960.

Chapters 11 and 12

Anderson, Matthew S. *Peter the Great.* London, 1995.

Anisimov, Evgeny. *Progress through Coercion. The Reforms of Peter the Great.* Translated and introduced by John T. Alexander. New York, 1993.

Bushkovitch, Paul. *Peter the Great. The Struggle for Power, 1671–1725.* Cambridge, U.K., 2001.

Canadian American Slavic Studies 8 (1974). Special issue on Peter I's reign.

Cracraft, James. *The Church Reform of Peter the Great.* Oxford, U.K., 1971.

_____. *The Petrine Revolution in Russian Architecture.* Chicago, 1990.

_____. *The Petrine Revolution in Russian Imagery.* Chicago, 1997.

Englund, Peter. *The Battle of Poltava. The Birth of the Russian Empire.* London, 1992.

Hughes, Lindsey. *Peter the Great. A Biography.* New Haven, 2002.

_____. *Russia in the Age of Peter the Great.* New Haven, 1998.

Kliuchevsky, Vasily. *Peter the Great.* (The first ten chapters of vol. 4 of the five-volume *History*). Translated by L. Archibald. New York, 1958.

Lentin, Antony. *Peter the Great: His Law on the Imperial Succession. The Official Commentary.* Oxford, U.K., 1996.

Massie, Robert. K. *Peter the Great His Life and World.* London, 1981.

Muller, Alexander, trans. and ed. *The Spiritual Regulation of Peter the Great.* Seattle, 1972.

Peterson, Claus. *Peter the Great's Administrative and Judicial Reforms.* Stockholm, 1979.

Phillips, E. J. *The Founding of Russia's Navy. Peter the Great and the Azov Fleet 1688–1714.* Westport, Conn., 1995.

Pososhkov, Ivan. *The Book of Poverty and Wealth.* Translated and edited by A. P. Vlasto and L. R. Lewitter. London, 1987.

Raeff, Marc, ed. *Peter the Great Changes Russia.* Lexington, Mass., 1972.

Riasanovsky, Nicholas. *The Image of Peter the Great in Russian History and Thought.* Oxford, U.K., 1984.

Sumner, B. H. *Peter the Great and the Ottoman Empire.* Oxford, U.K., 1949/Hamden, Conn., 1965.

Chapter 13

Anisimov, Evgeny. "Anna Ivanovna," and Naumov, V. P. "Elizaveta Petrovna," in *Russian Studies in History* 32, no. 4 (1994): 8–36, 37–72.

_____. *Empress Elizabeth: Her Reign and Her Russia.* Translated and edited by John T. Alexander. Gulf Breeze, Fla., 1995.

Canadian-American Slavic Studies 12 (1978), no. 1. Special Issue: "'The Doldrums?' Russian History, 1725–1762."

Curtis, Minna. *A Forgotten Empress. Anna Ivanovna and Her Era 1730–1740.* New York, 1974.

Leonard, Carol. *Reform and Regicide: The Reign of Peter III of Russia.* Bloomington, Ind., 1993.

Lipski, A. "Some Aspects of Russia's Westernization During the Reign of Anna Ioannovna." *American Slavic and East European Review* 18 (1959): 1–11.

Longworth, Philip. *The Three Empresses: Catherine I, Anne and Elizabeth of Russia.* New York: 1972.

Meehan Waters, Brenda. *Autocracy and Aristocracy. The Russian Service Elite of 1730.* New Brunswick, N.J., 1984.

Raeff, Marc. "The Domestic Policies of Peter III and His Overthrow." *American Historical Review* 75 (1970): 1289–1310.

Chapters 14 and 15

Alexander, John T. *Catherine the Great. Life and Legend.* Oxford, U.K., 1989.

Bartlett, Roger, and Janet Hartley, eds. *Russia in the Age of Enlightenment.* London, 1990.

Canadian-American Slavic Studies 4, no. 3 (1970) and 23, no. 1 (1989). Special issues on Catherine II.

Dixon, Simon. *Catherine the Great.* (Profiles in Power Series). London, 2001.

Griffiths, David. "Catherine II: The Republican Empress." *Jahrbücher für Geschichte Osteuropas* 21 (1973): 323–344.

Jones, Robert E. *Provincial Development in Russia. Catherine II and Jacob Sievers.* New Brunswick, N.J., 1984.

_____. *The Emancipation of the Russian Nobility, 1782–1785.* Princeton, 1973.

Madariaga, Isabel de. *Catherine the Great. A Short History.* New Haven, 1990.

_____. *Russia in the Age of Catherine the Great.* London, 1981.

Meehan-Waters, Brenda. "Catherine the Great and the Problem of Female Rule." *Russian Review* 34 (1975): 293–307.

Oliver, L. Jay, ed. *Catherine the Great. Great Lives Observed.* Englewood Cliffs, N.J., 1971.

Ransel, David. *The Politics of Catherinian Russia. The Panin Party.* New Haven, 1975.

Shcherbatov, Mikhail. *On the Corruption of Morals in Russia.* Translated and edited by A. Lentin. Cambridge, U.K., 1969.

General Works, Covering Russian History from 1800

Allworth, Edward. *Central Asia, 130 Years of Russian Dominance: A Historical Overview.* Durham, 1994.

Christian, David. *Imperial and Soviet Russia: Power, Privilege and the Challenge of Modernity.* New York, 1997.

Kappeler, Andreas. *The Russian Empire: A Multiethnic History,* Harlow, U.K., 2001.

Lieven, Dominic. *Empire: The Russian Empire and its Rivals.* London, 2000.

Westwood, J. *Endurance and Endeavor: Russian History, 1812–1992.* Oxford, U.K., 1993.

General Works, Covering Russian History from 1796 to 1917

Kornilov, A.A. *Modern Russian History.* New York, 1924.

Mironov, Boris, with Ben Eklof. *The Social History of Imperial Russia,* 1700–1917. 2 vols. Boulder, 2000.

Pipes, Richard. *Russia under the Old Regime.* London, 1974.

Seton-Watson, Hugh. *The Russian Empire, 1801–1917.* Oxford, 1967.

Walicki, Andrzej. *A History of Russian Thought from the Enlightenment to Marxism.* Translated from the Polish by Hilda Andrews-Rusiecka. Stanford, 1979.

Wortman, Richard. *Scenarios of Power: Myth and Ceremony in Russian Monarchy.* 2 vols. Princeton, 1995–2000.

Chapter 16

Caulaincourt, Armand de. *With Napoleon in Russia.* New York, 1959.

Flynn, James. *The University Reform of Tsar Alexander I, 1802–1835.* Washington, D.C., 1988.

Hartley, Janet. *Alexander I.* London, 1994.

Karamzin, N. M. *Memoir on Ancient and Modern Russia.* Translated and edited by Richard Pipes. Cambridge, Mass., 1959.

Markham, Felix. *Napoleon.* London, 1963.

McConnell, Allen. *Tsar Alexander I: Paternalistic Reformer.* Northbrook, Ill., 1970.

McGrew, Roderick. *Paul I of Russia, 1754–1801.* Oxford, U.K., 1992.

Raeff, Marc. *Michael Speransky: Statesman of Imperial Russia.* The Hague, 1957.

Ragsdale, Hugh, ed. *Paul I: A Reassessment of his Life and Reign.* Pittsburgh, 1979.

Tarle, E. V. *Napoleon's Invasion of Russia, 1812.* New York, 1942.

Tolstoy, Leo. *War and Peace.* 1869. Edited by George Gibian. New York, 1966.

Chapter 17

Hinsley, F. H. *Power and the Pursuit of Peace: Theory and Practice in the History of Relations Between States.* London, 1967.

Jenkins, Michael. *Arakcheev: Grand Vizier of the Russian Empire.* New York, 1969.
Kissinger, Henry. *A World Restored: Metternich, Castlereagh and the Problems of Peace, 1812–1822.* Boston, 1973.
Lotman, Iurii. "The Decembrist in Daily Life." In *The Semiotics of Russian Culture,* edited by Alexander D. Nakhimovsky and Alice Stone Nakhimovsky. Ithaca, 1985.
Martin, Alexander. *Romantics, Reformers, Reactionaries: Russian Conservative Thought and Politics in the Reign of Alexander I.* DeKalb, Ill., 1997.
Prousis, Theophilus C. *Russian Society and the Greek Revolution.* DeKalb, Ill., 1994.
Pushkin, Alexander. *Eugene Onegin: A Novel in Verse.* 1833. Translated by James Falen. Carbondale, Ill. 1990.
Raeff, Marc. *The Decembrist Movement.* Englewood Cliffs, N.J., 1966.

Chapter 18

Annenkov, Pavel. *The Extraordinary Decade: Literary Memoirs by P. V. Annenkov.* Edited by A. P. Mendel. Ann Arbor, 1968.
Bassin, Mark. *Nationalist Imagination and Geographical Expansion in the Russian Far East, 1840–1865.* Cambridge, 1999.
Berlin, Isaiah. *Russian Thinkers.* New York, 1978.
Curtiss, J. S. *The Russian Army Under Nicholas I, 1825–1855.* Durham, N.C., 1965.
Goldfrank, David. *The Origins of the Crimean War.* London, 1994.
Herzen, Alexander. *My Past and Thoughts.* Translated by C. Garnett and edited by Dwight McDonald. Berkeley, 1982.
Lincoln, W. Bruce. *In the Vanguard of Reform: Russia's Enlightened Bureaucrats, 1825–1861.* DeKalb, Ill., 1982.
_____. *Nicholas I: Emperor and Autocrat of All the Russias.* Bloomington, Ind., 1978.
Malia, Martin. *Alexander Herzen and the Birth of Russian Socialism, 1812–1855.* Cambridge, Mass., 1961.
Raeff, Marc. *Russian Intellectual History: An Anthology.* New York, 1999.
Riasanovsky, Nicholas V. *Russia and the West in the Teachings of the Slavophiles.* Cambridge, Mass., 1952.
Shaw, Stanford J., and Ezel Kural Shaw. *History of the Ottoman Empire and Modern Turkey.* Vol. 2, *Reform Revolution, and Republic: The Rise of Modern Turkey, 1808–1975.* New York, 1977.
Walicki, Andrzej. *The Slavophile Controversy: History of a Conservative Utopia in Nineteenth-Century Russian Thought.* Translated by Hilda Andrews-Rusiecka. Oxford, U.K., 1975.
Whittaker, Cynthia. *The Origins of Modern Russian Education: An Intellectual Biography of Count Sergei Uvarov, 1786–1855.* DeKalb, Ill., 1984.

Chapter 19

Belliustin, I. S. *Description of the Clergy in Rural Russia* 1858. Translated by Gregory Freeze. Ithaca, 1985.
Bernstein, Laurie. *Sonia's Daughters: Prostitutes and Their Regulation in Imperial Russia.* Berkeley, 1995.
Custine, Astolphe, Marquis de. *Letters from Russia.* London, 1991.
Haxthausen, August. *Studies on the Interior of Russia.* Chicago, 1972.
Hilton, Alison. *Russian Folk Culture.* Bloomington, Ind., 1995.
Hoch, Steven. *Serfdom and Social Control: Petrovskoe, a Village in Tambov.* Chicago, 1986.
Kelly, Catriona. *Refining Russia: From Catherine to Yeltsin.* Oxford, U.K., 2000.
Lincoln, W. Bruce. *Sunlight at Midnight: St. Petersburg and the Rise of Modern Russia.* New York, 2001.
Worobec, Christine. *Possessed: Women, Witches, and Demons in Imperial Russia.* DeKalb, Ill., 2001.

Chapter 20

Barrett, Thomas. *At the Edge of Empire: The Terek Cossacks and the North Caucasus Frontier, 1700–1860.* Boulder, 1999.
Bennigsen-Broxup, Marie. *The North Caucasus Barrier: The Russian Advance towards the Muslim World.* New York, 1992.
Brower, Daniel, and Edward Lazzerini, eds. *Russia's Orient: Imperial Borderlands and Peoples, 1700–1917.* Bloomington, Ind., 1997.
Fisher, Alan. *The Crimean Tatars.* Stanford, 1978.
Hamm, Michael. *Kiev: A Portrait, 1800–1917.* Princeton, 1993.
Layton, Susan. *Russian Literature and Empire: Conquest of the Caucasus from Pushkin to Tolstoy.* New York, 1994.
Martin, Virginia. *Law and Custom in the Steppe: The Kazakhs of the Middle Horde and Russian Colonialism in the Nineteenth Century.* Richmond, U.K., 2001.
Stanislawski, Michael. *Tsar Nicholas and the Jews: The Transformation of Jewish Society in Russia, 1825–1855.* Philadelphia, 1983.
Suny, Ronald. *Looking Toward Ararat: Armenia in Modern History.* Bloomington, Ind., 1993.
______. *The Making of the Georgian Nation.* 2d ed. Bloomington, Ind., 1994.
Thaden, Edward. *Russia's Western Borderlands, 1710–1870.* Princeton, 1984.
Wandycz, Piotr. *The Lands of Partitioned Poland, 1795–1918.* Seattle, 1974.
Wood, Alan. *History of Siberia from Russian Conquest to Revolution.* London, 1991.

Chapter 21

Eklof, Ben; John Bushnell; and Larissa Zakharova, eds. *Russia's Great Reforms, 1855–1881.* Bloomington, Ind., 1994.
Emmons, Terence. *The Russian Landed Gentry and the Peasant Emancipation of 1861.* Cambridge, 1967.
Emmons, Terence, and Wayne S. Vucinich, eds. *The Zemstvo in Russia: An Experiment in Local Self-Government.* New York, 1982.
Field, Daniel. *The End of Serfdom: Nobility and Bureaucracy in Russia, 1855–1861.* Cambridge, Mass., 1976.
Kolchin, Peter. *Unfree Labor: American Slavery and Russian Serfdom.* Cambridge, Mass., 1987.
Lincoln, W. Bruce. *The Great Reforms: Autocracy, Bureaucracy, and the Politics of Change in Imperial Russia.* DeKalb, Ill., 1990.
Paperno, Irina. *Chernyshevsky and the Age of Realism: A Study in the Semiotics of Behavior.* Stanford, 1988.
Rieber, Alfred. "The Politics of Autocracy." Excerpted in *Emancipation of the Russian Serfs,* edited by Terence Emmons. New York, 1970.
Starr, S. Frederick. *Decentralization and Self-Government in Russia, 1830–1870.* Princeton, 1972.
Turgenev, Ivan. *Fathers and Sons.* 1861. Translated by Michael Katz. New York. 1996.
Zaionchkovsky, Peter A. *The Abolition of Serfdom in Russia.* Gulf Breeze, Fla., 1978.
Zelnik, Reginald. *Labor and Society in Tsarist Russia: The Factory Workers of St. Petersburg, 1855–1870.* Stanford, 1971.

Chapter 22

Dostoevsky, Fëdor. *The Diary of a Writer.* Translated and annotated by Boris Brasol. New York, 1949.
Engel, Barbara. *Mothers and Daughters: Women of the Intelligentsia in Nineteenth-Century Russia.* Evanston, Ill., 2000.
Field, Daniel. *Rebels in the Name of the Tsar.* Boston, 1989.
Gleason, Abbott. *Young Russia: The Genesis of Russian Radicalism in the 1860s.* New York, 1980.
Jelavich, Barbara. *History of the Balkans.* 2 vols. New York, 1983.

Lavrov, Pëtr. *Historical Letters.* Translated and introduced by James P. Scanlan. Berkeley, 1967.
McReynolds, Louise. *The News Under Russia's Old Regime: The Development of a Mass-Circulation Press.* Princeton, 1991.
Nathans, Benjamin. *Beyond the Pale: The Jewish Encounter with Late Imperial Russia.* Berkeley, 2002.
Stavrou, Theofanis George, ed. *Art and Culture in Nineteenth-Century Russia.* Bloomington, Ind., 1983.
Stites, Richard. *The Women's Liberation Movement in Russia: Feminism, Nihilism, and Bolshevism, 1860–1930.* Princeton, 1978.
Venturi, Franco. *Roots of Revolution: A History of the Populist and Socialist Movements in Nineteenth Century Russia.* New York, 1960.
Walicki, Andrzej. *The Controversy over Capitalism: Studies in the Social Philosophy of the Russian Populists.* Oxford, 1969.
Wortman, Richard. *The Crisis of Russian Populism.* London, 1967.
______. *The Development of a Russian Legal Consciousness.* Chicago, 1976.

Chapter 23

Byrnes, Robert. *Pobedonostsev: His Life and Thought.* Bloomington, Ind., 1968.
Fuller, William. *Civil-Military Conflict in Imperial Russia, 1881–1914.* Princeton, 1985.
Lieven, Dominic. *Nicholas II: Twilight of the Empire.* New York, 1993.
______. *Russia's Rulers Under the Old Regime.* New Haven, 1989.
Orlovsky, Daniel. *The Limits of Reform: The Ministry of Internal Affairs in Imperial Russia, 1802–1881.* Cambridge, Mass., 1981.
Pobedonostsev, Konstantin. *Reflections of a Russian Statesman.* Ann Arbor, 1968.
Robbins, Richard G. *The Tsar's Viceroys: Russian Provincial Governors in the Last Years of the Empire.* Ithaca, 1987.
Rogger, Hans. *Jewish Policies and Right-Wing Politics in Imperial Russia.* Berkeley, 1986.
______. *Russia in the Age of Modernization and Revolution, 1881–1917.* London, 1983.
Thaden, Edward, ed. *Russification in the Baltic Provinces and Finland, 1855–1914.* Princeton, 1981.
Weeks, Theodore. *Nation and State in Late Imperial Russia: Nationalism and Russification on the Western Frontier, 1863–1914.* DeKalb, Ill., 1996.
Yaney, George. *The Systematization of Russian Government: Social Evolution in the Domestic Administration of Imperial Russia, 1711–1905.* Urbana, Ill., 1973.

Chapter 24

Crisp, Olga. *Studies in the Russian Economy Before 1914.* New York, 1976.
Gatrell, Peter. *The Tsarist Economy, 1850–1917.* New York, 1986.
Gerschenkron, Alexander. *Economic Backwardness in Historical Perspective.* Cambridge, Mass., 1962.
Gregory, Paul R.. *Russian National Income, 1885–1913.* New York, 1982.
Kahan, Arcadius. *Russian Economic History: The Nineteenth Century.* Chicago, 1989.
Marks, Steven. *The Road to Power: The Trans-Siberian Railroad and the Colonization of Asian Russia, 1850–1917.* Ithaca, 1991.
McCaffray, Susan. *The Politics of Industrialization in Tsarist Russia: The Association of Southern Coal and Steel Producers, 1874–1914.* DeKalb, Ill., 1996.
Portal, Roger. "The Industrialization of Russia." In *New Cambridge Economic History.* Vol. 6, bk. 2, *The Industrial Revolutions and After.* Cambridge, U.K., 1965.
Schimmelpenninck van der Oye, David. *Toward the Rising Sun: Russian Ideologies of Empire and the Path to War with Japan.* DeKalb, Ill., 2001.
Stephan, John. *The Russian Far East: A History.* Stanford, 1994.
Volin, Lazar. *A Century of Russian Agriculture: From Alexander II to Khrushchev.* Cambridge, Mass., 1970.
Von Laue, Theodore. *Sergei Witte and the Industrialization of Russia.* New York, 1963.

Walicki, Andrzej. *The Controversy Over Capitalism: Studies in the Social Philosophy of the Russian Populists.* Oxford, U.K., 1969.

Witte, Sergei. *The Memoirs of Count Witte.* Edited and translated by Sidney Harcave. Armonk, N.Y., 1990.

Wolff, David. *To the Harbin Station: The Liberal Alternative in Russian Manchuria, 1898–1914.* Stanford, 1999.

Chapter 25

Balzer, Harley. *Russia's Missing Middle Class: The Professions in Russian History.* Armonk, N.Y., 1996.

Becker, Seymour. *Nobility and Privilege in Late Imperial Russia.* DeKalb, Ill., 1985.

Bradley, Joseph. *Muzhik and Muscovite: Urbanization in Late Imperial Russia.* Berkeley, 1985.

Brooks, Jeffrey. *When Russia Learned to Read: Literacy and Popular Literature, 1861–1917.* Princeton, 1985.

Brower, Daniel. *The Russian City between Tradition and Modernity, 1850–1900.* Berkeley, 1990.

Clowes, Edith; Samuel Kassow; and James West, eds. *Between Tsar and People: Educated Society and the Quest for Public Identity in Late Imperial Russia.* Princeton, 1991.

Eklof, Ben. *Russian Peasant Schools: Officialdom, Village Culture, and Popular Pedagogy, 1861–1914.* Berkeley, 1986.

Freeze, Gregory. *The Parish Clergy in Nineteenth-Century Russia: Crisis, Reform, Counter-Reform* Princeton, 1983.

______. "The Soslovie Estate Paradigm in Russian Social History." *American Historical Review* 21, no.1 (February 1986): 11–36.

Frieden, Nancy. *Russian Physicians in an Era of Reform and Revolution, 1856–1905.* Princeton, 1981.

Herlihy, Patricia. *The Alcoholic Empire: Vodka and Politics in Late Imperial Russia.* New York, 2002.

Kassow, Samuel. *Students, Professors, and the State in Tsarist Russia.* Berkeley, 1989.

Kingston-Mann, Esther, and Timothy Mixter, eds. *Peasant Economy, Culture, and Politics of European Russia, 1800–1921.* Princeton, 1991.

Lindenmeyr, Adele. *Poverty Is Not a Vice: Charity, Society, and the State in Imperial Russia.* Princeton, 1996.

Manning, Roberta. *The Crisis of the Old Order in Russia: Gentry and Government.* Princeton, 1982.

Rieber, Alfred. *Merchants and Entrepreneurs in Imperial Russia.* Chapel Hill, 1982.

West, James, and Iurii Petrov. *Merchant Moscow: Images of Russia's Vanished Bourgeoisie.* Princeton, 1998.

Wirtschafter, Elise Kimerling. *Structures of Society: Imperial Russia's "People of Various Ranks."* DeKalb, Ill., 1994.

Worobec, Christine. *Peasant Russia: Family and Community in the Post-Emancipation Period.* Princeton, 1991.

Wynn, Charters. *Workers, Strikes, and Pogroms: The Donbass-Dnepr Bend in Late Imperial Russia, 1870–1905.* Princeton, 1992.

Zelnik, Reginald, ed. and trans. *A Radical Worker in Tsarist Russia: The Autobiography of Semën Ivanovich Kanatchikov.* Stanford, 1986.

Chapter 26

Berdiaev, Nikolai. *The Russian Idea.* New York, 1948.

Bowlt, John. *The Silver Age: Russian Art of the Early Twentieth Century and the "World of Art" Group.* Newtonville, Mass., 1979.

Engelstein, Laura. *The Keys to Happiness: Sex and the Search for Modernity in Fin-de-Siècle Russia.* Ithaca, 1992.

Evtuhov, Catherine. *The Cross and the Sickle: Sergei Bulgakov and the Fate of Russian Religious Philosophy, 1890–1920.* Ithaca, 1997.

Florovsky, Georges. "On the Eve." In *The Ways of Russian Theology.* Belmont, Mass., 1979.
Gray, Camilla. *The Russian Experiment in Art, 1863–1922.* New York, 1986.
Gustafson, Richard, and Judith Kornblatt, eds. *Russian Religious Thought.* Madison, 1996.
Hughes, H. Stuart. *Consciousness and Society: The Reorientation of European Social Thought, 1890–1930.* New York, 1977.
Matich, Olga, and John Bowlt, eds. *Laboratory of Dreams: The Russian Avant-Garde and Cultural Experiment.* Stanford, 1996.
Paperno, Irina, and Joan Delaney Grossman, eds. *Creating Life: The Aesthetic Utopia of Russian Modernism.* Stanford, 1994.
Pipes, Richard. *Struve, Liberal on the Left, 1870–1905.* Cambridge, Mass., 1970.
Rosenthal, Bernice, ed. *Nietzsche in Russia.* Princeton, 1986.
Rosenthal, Bernice, and Martha Bohachevsky-Chomiak, eds. *A Revolution of the Spirit: Crisis of Value in Russia, 1890–1924.* New York, 1990.
Shatz, Marshall, and Judith Zimmerman, eds. and trans. *Vekhi = Landmarks: A Collection of Articles About the Russian Intelligentsia.* Armonk, N.Y., 1994.
Weiss, Peg. *Kandinsky and Old Russia: The Artist as Ethnographer and Shaman.* New Haven, 1995.
Zernov, Nicolas. *The Russian Religious Renaissance of the Twentieth Century.* London, 1963.

Chapter 27

Ascher, Abraham. *The Revolution of 1905.* 2 vols. Stanford, 1988.
Bely, Andrei. *Petersburg.* 1913. Translated, edited and introduced by Robert Maguire and John Malmstad, Bloomington, Ind., 1978.
Bonnell, Victoria. *Roots of Rebellion: Workers' Politics and Organizations in St. Petersburg and Moscow, 1900–1914.* Berkeley, 1983.
Eisenstein, Sergei. *Potemkin.* 1925. (Film.)
Emmons, Terence. *The Formation of Political Parties and the First National Elections in Russia.* Cambridge, Mass., 1983.
Engelstein, Laura. *Moscow, 1905: Working-Class Organization and Political Conflict.* Stanford, 1982.
Galai, Shmuel. *The Liberation Movement in Russia, 1900–1905.* Cambridge, 1973.
Morrissey, Susan. *Heralds of Revolution: Russian Students and the Mythologies of Radicalism.* Oxford, 1998.
Nish, Ian. *The Origins of the Russo-Japanese War.* London, 1985.
Perrie, Maureen. *The Agrarian Policy of the Russian Socialist-Revolutionary Party from its Origins through the Revolution of 1905–1907.* Cambridge, 1975.
Shanin, Teodor. *Russia, 1905–1907: Revolution as a Moment of Truth.* New Haven, 1986.
Surh, Gerald. *1905 in St. Petersburg: Labor, Society, and Revolution.* Stanford, 1989.
Swift, E. Anthony. *Popular Theater and Society in Tsarist Russia.* Berkeley, 2002.
Weinberg, Robert. *The Revolution of 1905 in Odessa: Blood on the Steps.* Bloomington, Ind., 1993.

Chapter 28

Ascher, Abraham. *P. A. Stolypin: The Search for Stability in Late Imperial Russia.* Stanford, 2001.
Gatrell, Peter. *Government, Industry, and Rearmament in Russia, 1900–1914: The Last Argument of Tsarism.* New York, 1994.
The Great Utopia: The Russian and Soviet Avant-Garde, 1915–1982. New York, 1992.
Haimson, Leopold. "The Problem of Social Stability in Urban Russia, 1905–1917." In *The Structure of Russian History,* edited by Michael Cherniavsky. New York, 1970.
Hosking, Geoffrey. *The Russian Constitutional Experiment: Government and Duma, 1907–1914.* Cambridge, U.K., 1973.

Macey, David. *Government and Peasant in Russia, 1860–1906: The Prehistory of the Stolypin Reforms.* DeKalb, Ill., 1987.

Neuberger, Joan. *Hooliganism: Crime, Culture, and Power in St. Petersburg, 1900–1914.* Berkeley, 1993.

Oldenburg, Sergei. *The Last Tsar: Nicholas II, His Reign and His Russia.* Edited by Patrick Rollins and translated by Leonid Mihalap. Gulf Breeze, Fla., 1975–1978.

Von Geldern, James, and Louise McReynolds. *Entertaining Tsarist Russia: Tales, Songs, Plays, Movies, Jokes, Ads, and Images from Russia Urban Life, 1779–1917.* Bloomington, Ind., 1998.

Wortman, Richard. "'Invisible Threads': The Historical Imagery of the Romanov Tercentenary." *Russian History* 16, nos. 2–4 (1989): 389–408.

Yaney, George. *The Urge to Mobilize: Agrarian Reform in Russia, 1861–1930.* Urbana, Ill., 1982.

Chapter 29

Ferro, Marc. *The Great War, 1914–1918.* London, 1973.

Florinsky, Michael. *The End of the Russian Empire: A Study in the Economic and Social History of the War.* New Haven, 1931.

Gatrell, Peter. *A Whole Empire Walking: Refugees in Russia During World War I.* Bloomington, Ind., 1999.

Holquist, Peter. *Making War, Forging Revolution: Russia's Continuum of Crisis, 1914–1921.* Cambridge, Mass., 2002.

Jahn, Hubertus. *Patriotic Culture in Russia During World War I.* Ithaca, 1995.

Lohr, Eric. *Nationalizing the Russian Empire: The Campaign Against Enemy Minorities During World War I.* Cambridge, Mass., 2003.

Pares, Bernard. *The Fall of the Russian Empire.* London, 1939.

Sanborn, Joshua. *Drafting the Russian Nation: Military Conscription, Total War, and Mass Politics, 1905–1925.* DeKalb, Ill., 2003.

Siegelbaum, Lewis. *The Politics of Industrial Mobilization: A Study of the War-Industries Committees in Russia, 1914–1917.* New York, 1983.

Steinberg, Mark, and Vladimir Khrustalev. *The Fall of the Romanovs: Political Dreams and Personal Struggles in a Time of Revolution.* New Haven, 1995.

Stone, Norman. *The Eastern Front, 1914–1917.* London, 1975.

Wildman, Alan. *The End of the Russian Imperial Army.* 2 vols. Princeton, 1980–1987.

General Works, Covering the Period from 1917 Onward

Engel, Barbara, and Anastasia Posadskaya-Vanderbeck, eds. *A Revolution of Their Own: Voices of Women in Soviet History.* Boulder, 1998.

Heller, Mikhail, and Aleksandr Nekrich. *Utopia in Power.* New York, 1986.

Hosking, Geoffrey. *A History of the Soviet Union, 1917–1991.* London, 1992.

Kenez, Peter. *A History of the Soviet Union from the Beginning to the End.* New York, 1999.

Malia, Martin. *The Soviet Tragedy.* New York, 1994.

Nove, Alec. *An Economic History of the USSR, 1917–1991.* London, 1992.

Raleigh, Donald. *Provincial Landscapes: Local Dimensions of Soviet Power.* Pittsburgh, 2001.

Service, Robert. *A History of Twentieth-Century Russia.* Cambridge, Mass., 1998.

Suny, Ronald. *The Soviet Experiment.* New York, 1998.

Chapter 30

Acton, Edward, et al. *Critical Companion to the Russian Revolution, 1917–1921.* Bloomington, Ind., 1997.

Burbank, Jane. *Intelligentsia and Revolution: Russian Views of Bolshevism, 1917–1922.* New York, 1986.

Carr, E. H. *The Bolshevik Revolution.* 3 vols. London, 1950–1953.

Figes, Orlando. *A People's Tragedy: The Russian Revolution, 1891–1924.* London, 1996.
Fitzpatrick, Sheila. *The Russian Revolution.* 2d ed. Oxford, U.K., 1994.
Hasegawa, T. *The February Revolution: Petrograd, 1917.* Seattle, 1981.
Keep, John. *The Russian Revolution: A Study in Mass Mobilization.* London, 1976.
Kerensky, Alexander. *Russia and History's Turning Point.* New York, 1965.
Koenker, Diane. *Moscow Workers and the 1917 Revolution.* Princeton, 1981.
Milyukov, Paul. *The Russian Revolution.* 3 vols. Gulf Breeze, Fla., 1978–1987.
Pipes, Richard. *The Russian Revolution.* London, 1995.
Rabinowitch, Alexander. *The Bolsheviks Come to Power.* New York, 1976.
Radkey, Oliver. *Russia Goes to the Polls: The Election to the All-Russian Constituent Assembly, 1917.* Ithaca, 1990.
Raleigh, Donald. *Revolution on the Volga: 1917 in Saratov.* Ithaca, 1986.
Smith, Steve A. *Red Petrograd: Revolution in the Factories, 1917–1918.* New York, 1983.
Steinberg, Mark, ed. *Voices of Revolution, 1917.* New Haven, 2001. Documents.
Trotsky, L. D. *The History of the Russian Revolution.* Ann Arbor, 1957.
Wade, Rex A. *The Bolshevik Revolution and Russian Civil War.* Westport, Conn., 2001.
_____. *The Russian Revolution, 1917.* New York, 2000.

Chapter 31

Abramson, Henry. *A Prayer for the Government: Ukrainians and Jews in Revolutionary Times, 1917–1920.* Cambridge, Mass., 1999.
Avrich, Paul. *Kronstadt, 1921.* Princeton, 1970.
_____. *The Russian Anarchists.* Princeton, 1967.
Borkenau, Franz. *World Communism: A History of the Communist International.* Ann Arbor, 1962.
Brovkin, Vladimir. *Behind the Front Lines of the Civil War: Political Parties and Social Movements in Russia, 1918–1922.* Princeton, 1994.
Denikin, Anton. *The Russian Turmoil: Memoirs—Military, Social, and Political.* London, 1922.
Got'e, Iurii. *Time of Troubles: The Diary.* Princeton, 1988.
Hunczak, Taras, ed. *The Ukraine, 1917–1921: A Study in Revolution.* Cambridge, Mass., 1977.
Kenez, Peter. *Civil War in South Russia.* 2 vols. Berkeley, 1971–1977.
Koenker, Diane; William Rosenberg; and Ronald Suny, eds. *Party, State, and Society in the Russian Civil War: Explorations in Social History.* Bloomington, Ind., 1989.
Mally, Lynn. *Culture of the Future: The Proletkult Movement in Revolutionary Russia.* Berkeley, 1990.
Mawdsley, Evan. *The Russian Civil War.* Boston, 1987.
Radkey, Oliver. *The Unknown Civil War in Soviet Russia: A Study of the Green Movement in the Tambov Region, 1920–1921.* Stanford, 1976.
Raleigh, Donald. *Experiencing Civil War: Politics, Society, and Revolutionary Culture in Saratov, 1917–1922.* Princeton, 2002.
Suny, Ronald. *The Baku Commune.* Princeton, 1972.
Tucker, Robert, ed. *The Lenin Anthology.* New York, 1975.
Von Hagen, Mark. *Soldiers in the Proletarian Dictatorship: The Red Army and the Soviet Socialist State, 1917–1930.* Ithaca, 1990.

Chapter 32

Ball, Alan. *Russia's Last Capitalists: The Nepmen, 1921–1929.* Berkeley, 1987.
Banerji, Arup. *Merchants and Markets in Revolutionary Russia, 1917–30.* Birmingham, 1997.
Brovkin, Vladimir. *Russia After Lenin: Politics, Culture, and Society, 1921–1929.* New York, 1998.
Clark, Katerina. *Petersburg, Crucible of Cultural Revolution.* Cambridge, Mass., 1995.
Clements, Barbara. *Bolshevik Feminist: The Life of Alexandra Kollontai.* Bloomington, Ind., 1979.

Cohen, Stephen F. *Bukharin and the Bolshevik Revolution: A Political Biography.* 2d ed. Oxford, U.K., 1980.

Danilov, V. P. *Rural Russia Under the New Regime.* London, 1988.

David-Fox, Michael. *Revolution of the Mind: Higher Learning Among the Bolsheviks, 1918–1929.* Ithaca, 1997.

Gleason, Abbott; Peter Kenez; and Richard Stites, eds. *Bolshevik Culture: Experiment and Order in the Russian Revolution.* Bloomington, Ind., 1985.

Goldman, Wendy. *Women, the State, and Revolution: Soviet Family Policy and Social Life, 1917–1936.* New York, 1993.

Holmes, Larry. *The Kremlin and the Schoolhouse: Reforming Education in Soviet Russia, 1917–1931.* Bloomington, Ind., 1991.

Husband, William. *Godless Communists: Atheism and Society in Soviet Russia, 1917–1932.* DeKalb, Ill., 2000.

Kenez, Peter. *The Birth of the Propaganda State.* New York, 1985.

Lewin, Moshe. *Russian Peasants and Soviet Power: A Study of Collectivization.* Evanston, Ill., 1968.

Luukkanen, Arto. *The Party of Unbelief.* Helsinki, 1994.

Service, Robert. *Lenin: A Political Life.* 3 vols. Bloomington, Ind., 1985.

Siegelbaum, Lewis. *Soviet State and Society Between Revolutions, 1918–1929.* New York, 1992.

Stites, Richard. *Revolutionary Dreams: Utopian Vision and Experimental Life in the Russian Revolution.* New York, 1989.

Trotsky, L. D. *My Life.* New York, 1930.

Tucker, Robert. *Stalin as Revolutionary: A Study in History and Personality.* New York, 1974.

Tumarkin, Nina. *Lenin Lives! The Lenin Cult in Soviet Russia.* Cambridge, Mass., 1983.

Weiner, Douglas. *Models of Nature: Ecology, Conservation, and Cultural Revolution in Soviet Russia.* Bloomington, Ind., 1988.

Wood, Elizabeth. *The Baba and the Comrade: Gender and Politics in Revolutionary Russia.* Bloomington, Ind., 1997.

Young, Glennys. *Power and the Sacred in Revolutionary Russia: Religious Activists in the Village.* University Park, Pa., 1997.

Chapter 33

Gitelman, Zvi. *Jewish Nationality and Soviet Politics: The Jewish Sections of the CPSU, 1917–1930.* Princeton, 1972.

Keller, Shoshana. *To Moscow, Not Mecca: The Soviet Campaign Against Islam in Central Asia, 1917–1941.* Westport, Conn., 2001.

Liber, George. *Soviet Nationality Policy, Urban Growth, and Identity Change in the Ukrainian SSR, 1923–1934.* New York, 1992.

Martin, Terry. *The Affirmative Action Empire: Nations and Nationalism in the Soviet Union, 1923–1939.* Ithaca, 2001.

Massell, Gregory. *The Surrogate Proletariat: Moslem Women and Revolutionary Strategies in Soviet Central Asia, 1919–1929.* Princeton, 1974.

Olcott, Martha. *The Kazakhs.* 2d ed. Stanford, 1995.

Pipes, Richard. *The Formation of the Soviet Union: Communism and Nationalism, 1917–1923.* Rev. ed. Cambridge, Mass., 1964.

Said, Kurban. *Ali and Nino.* London, 1971. A novel of revolution in Azerbaijan.

Smith, Jeremy. *The Bolsheviks and the National Question, 1917–23.* Basingstoke, U.K., 1999.

Smith, Michael. *Language and Power in the Creation of the USSR, 1917–1953.* Berlin, 1998.

Suny, Ronald, ed. *Transcaucasia, Nationalism, and Social Change.* Ann Arbor, 1983.

Suny, Ronald, and Terry Martin, eds. *A State of Nations: Empire and Nation-Making in the Age of Lenin and Stalin.* New York, 2001.

Vakar, Nicholas. *Belorussia: The Making of a Nation.* Cambridge, Mass., 1956.

Veidlinger, Jeffrey. *The Moscow State Yiddish Theater: Jewish Culture on the Soviet Stage.* Bloomington, Ind., 2000.

Chapter 34

Conquest, Robert. *The Great Terror: A Reassessment.* London, 1990.

_____. *Harvest of Sorrow: Soviet Collectivization and the Terror-Famine.* New York, 1986.

Davies, Robert. *The Industrialization of Soviet Russia.* 3 vols. London, 1980–1989.

Garros, V., et al., eds. *Intimacy and Terror.* New York, 1995.

Getty, J. Arch, and Roberta Manning, eds. *Stalinist Terror: New Perspectives.* New York, 1993.

Getty, J. Arch, and Oleg Naumov, eds. *The Road to Terror: Stalin and the Self-Destruction of the Bolsheviks, 1932–1939.* New Haven, 1999.

Graziosi, Andrea. *The Great Soviet Peasant War: Bolsheviks and Peasants, 1917–1933.* Cambridge, Mass., 1996.

Knight, Amy. *Who Killed Kirov? The Kremlin's Greatest Mystery.* New York, 1999.

Kotkin, Stephen. *Magnetic Mountain: Stalinism as a Civilization.* Berkeley, 1997.

Kuromiya, Hiroaki. *Freedom and Terror in the Donbas: A Ukrainian-Russian Borderland, 1870s–1990s.* New York, 1998.

Luukkanen, Arto. *The Religious Policy of the Stalinist State.* Helsinki, 1997.

Merridale, Catherine. *Night of Stone: Death and Memory in Russia.* London, 2000.

Molotov, Vyacheslav. *Molotov Remembers: Inside Kremlin Politics.* Chicago, 1993.

Siegelbaum, Lewis. *Stakhanovism and the Politics of Productivity in the USSR, 1935–1941.* New York, 1988.

Toker, Leona. *Return from the Archipelago: Narratives of Gulag Survivors.* Bloomington, Ind., 2000.

Tucker, Robert. *Stalin in Power: The Revolution from Above.* New York, 1990.

Vilensky, Simon, et al., eds. *Till My Tale Is Told: Women's Memoirs of the Gulag.* London, 1999.

Viola, Lynne. *Peasant Rebels Under Stalin: Collectivization and the Culture of Peasant Resistance.* New York, 1996.

Ward, Chris. *Stalin's Russia.* 2d ed. London, 1999.

Chapter 35

Bacon, Elizabeth. *Central Asians Under Russian Rule: A Study in Cultural Change.* Ithaca, 1966. Based on a 1933–1934 visit.

Bown, Matthew C. *Art under Stalin.* New York, 1991.

Brooks, Jeffrey. *Thank You, Comrade Stalin: Soviet Public Culture from Revolution to Cold War.* Princeton, 2000.

Clark, Katerina. *The Soviet Novel: History as Ritual.* Chicago, 1981.

Fitzpatrick, Sheila. *The Cultural Front: Power and Culture in Revolutionary Russia.* Ithaca, 1992.

_____. *Education and Social Mobility in the Soviet Union, 1921–1934.* New York, 1979.

_____. *Everyday Stalinism: Ordinary Life in Extraordinary Times—Soviet Russia in the 1930s.* New York, 1999.

Fitzpatrick, Sheila, ed. *Stalinism: New Directions.* London, 2000.

_____. *Stalin's Peasants: Resistance and Survival in the Russian Village After Collectivization.* New York, 1996.

Fitzpatrick, Sheila, and Yuri Slezkine, eds. *In the Shadow of Revolution: Life Stories of Russian Women from 1917 to the Second World War.* Princeton, 2000.

Goldman, Wendy. *Women at the Gates: Gender and Industry in Stalin's Russia.* New York, 2002.

Groys, Boris. *The Total Art of Stalinism.* Princeton, 1992.
Günther, Hans, ed. *The Culture of the Stalin Period.* Basingstoke, U.K., 1990.
Hoffman, David. *Peasant Metropolis: Social Identities in Moscow, 1929–1941.* Ithaca, 1994.
Kharkhordin, Oleg. *The Collective and the Individual in Russia: A Study of Practices.* Berkeley, 1999.
Petrone, Karen. *Life Has Become More Joyous, Comrades: Celebrations in the Time of Stalin.* Bloomington, Ind., 2000.
Siegelbaum, Lewis, and Ronald Suny, eds. *Making Workers Soviet: Power, Class, and Identity.* Ithaca, 1994.
Siegelbaum, Lewis; Andrei Sokolov; and Sergei Zhuravlev, eds. *Stalinism as a Way of Life: A Narrative in Documents.* New Haven, 2000.
Taylor, Richard, and Derek Spring, eds. *Stalinism and Soviet Cinema.* New York, 1993.
Thurston, Robert. *Life and Terror in Stalin's Russia, 1934–1941.* New Haven, 1996.
Von Geldern, James, and Richard Stites, eds. *Mass Culture in Soviet Russia.* Bloomington, Ind., 1995.

Chapter 36

Barber, John, and Mark Harrison. *The Soviet Home Front, 1941–1945: A Social and Economic History.* London, 1991.
Beevor, Anthony. *Stalingrad.* New York, 1998.
Carr, E. H. *The Twilight of Comintern, 1930–1935.* London, 1982.
Conquest, Robert. *The Nation Killers: The Soviet Deportation of Nationalities.* New York, 1970.
Duffy, Christopher. *Red Storm on the Reich.* New York, 1991.
Erickson, John. *The Road to Berlin.* Boulder, 1983.
______. *The Road to Stalingrad.* New York, 1975.
Gorodetsky, Gabriel. *Grand Delusion: Stalin and the German Invasion of Russia.* New Haven, 1999.
Gross, Jan. *Revolution from Abroad: The Soviet Conquest of Poland's Western Ukraine and Western Belorussia.* Princeton, 1988.
Nekrich, Alexander. *The Punished Peoples.* New York, 1978.
Overy, Richard. *Russia's War.* London, 1997.
Rich, Norman. *Hitler's War Aims.* 2 vols. New York, 1973–1974.
Seaton, Albert. *Stalin as Military Commander.* New York, 1976.
Smirnova-Medvedeva, Zoya. *On the Road to Stalingrad: Memoirs of a Soviet Woman Machine Gunner.* New York, 1996.
Stites, Richard, ed. *Culture and Entertainment in Wartime Russia.* Bloomington, Ind., 1995.
Thurston, Robert, ed. *A People's War: Popular Responses to World War II in the Soviet Union.* Champaign-Urbana, Ill., 2000.
Weiner, Amir. *Making Sense of War: The Second World War and the Fate of the Bolshevik Revolution.* Princeton, 2001.

Chapter 37

Boeterbloem, Kees. *Life and Death Under Stalin: Kalinin Province, 1945–1953.* Montreal, 1999.
Dunham, Vera. *In Stalin's Time: Middleclass Values in Soviet Fiction.* New York, 1979.
Duskin, J. Eric. *Stalinist Reconstruction and the Confirmation of a New Elite, 1945–1953.* Basingstoke, U.K., 2001.
Gaddis, John. *We Now Know: Rethinking Cold War History.* Oxford, U.K., 1997.
Gleason, Abbott. *Totalitarianism: The Inner History of the Cold War.* New York, 1995.
Hahn, Werner. *Postwar Soviet Politics: The Fall of Zhdanov and the Defeat of Moderation, 1946–1953.* Ithaca, 1982.
Holloway, David. *Stalin and the Bomb: The Soviet Union and Atomic Energy, 1939–1956.* New Haven, 1994.
Joravsky, David. *The Lysenko Affair.* Cambridge, Mass., 1979.

Knight, Amy. *Beria: Stalin's First Lieutenant.* Princeton, 1993.
Linz, Susan, ed. *The Impact of World War II on the Soviet Union.* Totowa, N.J., 1985.
Mastny, Vojtech. *Russia's Road to the Cold War: Diplomacy, Warfare, and the Politics of Communism, 1942–1945.* New York, 1979.
Seton-Watson, Hugh. *The East European Revolution.* Boulder, 1985.
Starr, S. Frederick. *Red and Hot: The Fate of Jazz in the Soviet Union.* New York, 1983.
Tumarkin, Nina. *The Living and the Dead: The Rise and Fall of the Cult of World War II in Russia.* New York, 1994.
Vaksberg, A. *Stalin Against the Jews.* New York, 1994.
Volkogonov, Dmitry. *Stalin: Triumph and Tragedy.* London, 2000.
Zubkova, Elena. *Russia After the War: Hopes, Illusions, and Disappointments, 1945–1957.* Armonk, N.Y., 1998.
Zubok, Vladislav. *Inside the Kremlin's Cold War: From Stalin to Khrushchev.* Cambridge, Mass., 1996.

Chapter 38

Blight, James, and David Welch. *On the Brink: Americans and Soviets Reexamine the Cuban Missile Crisis.* New York, 1990.
Breslauer, George. *Khrushchev and Brezhnev as Leaders.* Boston, 1983.
Brumberg, Abraham, ed. *Russia Under Khrushchev.* New York, 1962.
Graham, Loren. *Science in Russia and the Soviet Union: A Short History.* New York, 1993.
Khrushchev, Nikita. *Khrushchev Remembers.* 3 vols. Boston, 1970–1990.
McMillan, Priscilla. *Khrushchev and the Arts.* Cambridge, Mass., 1965.
Medvedev, Roy. *Khrushchev.* New York, 1982.
Oberg, James. *Red Star in Orbit.* New York, 1981.
Taubman, William; Sergei Khrushchev; and Abbott Gleason, eds. *Nikita Khrushchev.* New Haven, 2000.
Tompson, William. *Khrushchev: A Political Life.* London, 1995.
Woll, Josephine. *Real Images: Soviet Cinema and the Thaw.* New York, 2000.

Chapter 39

Atkinson, Dorothy; Alexander Dallin; and Gail Lapidus, eds. *Women in Russia.* Stanford, 1978.
Azreal, Jeremy. *Managerial Power and Soviet Politics.* Cambridge, Mass., 1966.
Berliner, Joseph. *Soviet Industry from Stalin to Gorbachev.* Ithaca, 1988.
Boym, Svetlana. *Common Places: Mythologies of Everyday Life in Russia.* Cambridge, Mass., 1994.
Byrnes, Robert, ed. *After Brezhnev.* Washington, 1983.
Dornberg, John. *Brezhnev: The Masks of Power.* New York, 1974.
Edelman, Robert. *Serious Fun: A History of Spectator Sports in the USSR.* New York, 1993.
Feshbach, Murray, and Alfred Friendly Jr. *Ecocide in the USSR: Health and Nature Under Siege.* New York, 1992.
Hough, Jerry. *The Soviet Prefects: The Local Party Organs in Industrial Decision-making.* Cambridge, Mass., 1969.
Lewin, Moshe. *Political Undercurrents in Soviet Economic Debates.* Princeton, 1974.
Millar, James R. *Politics, Work, and Daily Life: A Survey of Former Soviet Citizens.* New York, 1987.

Chapter 40

Bradsher, Henry. *Afghan Communism and Soviet Intervention.* New York, 1999.
Medvedev, Roy. *On Socialist Democracy.* London, 1972.
Medvedev, Zhores. *Andropov.* London, 1984.
Reddaway, Peter. *Uncensored Russia: Protest and Dissent in the Soviet Union.* New York, 1972.
Sakharov, Andrei. *Progress, Coexistence, and Intellectual Freedom.* New York, 1970.

Smith, Gerald Stanton. *Songs to Seven Strings: Russian Guitar Poetry and Soviet Mass Song.* Bloomington, Ind., 1984.
Smith, Hedrick. *The Russians.* New York, 1976.
Solzhenitsyn, Alexander. *From Under the Rubble.* Boston, 1979.
Ulam, Adam. *Dangerous Relations: The Soviet Union in World Affairs, 1970–1982.* New York, 1984.

Chapter 41

Ash, Timothy Garton. *We the People: The Revolution of '89: Witnesses in Warsaw, Budapest, Berlin, and Prague.* New York, 1990.
Åslund, Anders. *Gorbachev's Struggle for Economic Reform.* London, 1990.
Brown, Archie. *The Gorbachev Factor.* Oxford, U.K., 1996.
Gorbachev, Mikhail. *Perestroika: New Thinking for Our Country and the World.* New York, 1987.
Hosking, Geoffrey, et al., eds. *The Road to Post-Communism: Independent Political Movements in the Soviet Union, 1985–1991.* London, 1992.
Lawton, Anna. *Kinoglasnost: Soviet Cinema of Our Time.* New York, 1992.
Lewin, Moshe. *The Gorbachev Phenomenon.* 2d ed. Berkeley, 1991.
Nove, Alec. *Glasnost in Action: Cultural Renaissance in Russia.* Boston, 1989.
Remnick, David. *Lenin's Tomb: The Last Days of the Soviet Empire.* New York, 1993.
Sperling, Valerie. *Organizing Women in Contemporary Russia: Engendering Transition.* New York, 1999.
Stites, Richard. *Russian Popular Culture.* New York, 1992.
Suny, Ronald. *The Revenge of the Past: Nationalism, Revolution, and the Collapse of the Soviet Union.* Stanford, 1993.
White, Stephen. *Gorbachev and After.* 3d ed. New York, 1991.
Zaslavskaya, Tatyana. *The Second Socialist Revolution.* London, 1991.

Chapter 42

Aron, Leon. *Yeltsin: A Revolutionary Life.* New York, 2000.
Åslund, Anders. *How Russia Became a Market Economy.* Washington, 1995.
Blasi, Joseph, et al. *Kremlin Capitalism: The Privatization of the Russian Economy.* Ithaca, 1997.
Gleason, Gregory. *The Central Asian States: Discovering Independence.* Boulder, 1997.
Isham, Heyward, ed. *Russia's Fate Through Russian Eyes: Voices of the New Generation.* Boulder, 2001.
Kotkin, Stephen. *Armageddon Averted: The Soviet Collapse, 1970–2000.* Oxford, U.K., 2001.
Lieven, Anatole. *Chechnya: Tombstone of Russian Power.* New Haven, 1999.
Pilkington, Hilary. *Migration, Displacement, and Identity in Post-Soviet Russia.* London, 1998.
Putin, Vladimir. *First Person.* London, 2000.
Remnick, David. *Resurrection: The Struggle for a New Russia.* New York, 1997.
Rotkirch, Anna. *The Man Question: Loves and Lives in the Late 20th Century Russia.* Helsinki, 2000.
Shaw, Denis. *Russia in the Modern World: A New Geography.* Oxford, U.K., 1999.
Sutela, Pekka. *The Road to the Russian Market Economy.* Helsinki, 1998.
Volkov, Vadim. *Violent Entrepreneurs: The Use of Force in the Making of Russian Capitalism.* Ithaca, 2002.
White, Stephen. *Russia's New Politics.* New York, 2000.
Yeltsin, Boris. *Against the Grain: An Autobiography.* London, 1990.
______. *Midnight Diaries.* New York, 2000.

Chapter 43

Andreyev, Catherine. *Vlasov and the Russian Liberation Movement: Soviet Reality and Émigré Theories.* New York, 1987.
Dallin, Alexander. *German Rule in Russia, 1941–1945: A Study of Occupation Policies.* Boulder, 1981.

Johnson, Robert H. *"New Mecca, New Babylon": Paris and the Russian Exiles, 1920–1945.* Kingston/Montreal, 1988.

Karlinsky, Simon, and Alfred Appel Jr., eds. *The Bitter Air of Exile: Russian Writers in the West, 1922–1972.* Berkeley, 1977.

Lewin-Epstein, Noah; Yaacov Ro'i; and Paul Ritterband, eds. *Russian Jews on Three Continents: Migration and Resettlement.* London, 1997.

Liebich, André. *From the Other Shore: Russian Social Democracy After 1921.* Cambridge, Mass., 1997.

Marrus, Michael. *Unwanted: European Refugees in the Twentieth Century.* Oxford, U.K., 1985.

Raeff, Marc. *Russia Abroad: A Cultural History of the Russian Emigration, 1919–1939.* New York, 1990.

Shlapentokh, Vladimir; Munir Sendich; and Emil Payin, eds. *The New Russian Diaspora: Russian Minorities in the Former Soviet Republics.* Armonk, N.Y., 1994.

Tolstoy, Nikolai. *The Secret Betrayal.* New York, 1977.

RULERS OF VARIOUS RUSSIAN STATES

By tradition, Founder of the Dynasty, in Novgorod

Ryurik, possibly of Denmark

Reigns of the Princes and Grand Princes of Kiev, 900s–1240

Igor, by tradition, Ryurikovich, ?–945
Svyatoslav Igorevich, 945–972
Yaropolk (I) Svyatoslavich, 972–980
Vladimir (I) Svyatoslavich, Saint, 980–1015
Svyatopolk (I) Vladimirovich, 1015–1019
Yaroslav (I) and Mstislav (I) Vladmirovich, 1019–1036
Yaroslav (I) Vladimirovich, the Wise (sole ruler), 1037–1054
Izyaslav (I) Yaroslavich, 1054–1076, 1078
Svyatoslav (II) Yaroslavich, 1076–1078
Vsevolod (I) Yaroslavich, 1078–1094
Svyatopolk (II) Izyaslavich, 1094–1113
Vladimir (II) Vsevolodich *Monomakh*, 1113–1125
Mstislav (II) Vladimirovich, the Great, 1125–1132
Yaropolk (II) Vladimirovich, 1132–1139
Vsevolod (II) Olgovich of Chernigov, 1138–1146
Izyaslav (II) Mstislavich of Volynia, 1146–1154
Yuri Vladimirovich, *Dolgoruky*, of Rostov-Suzdal, 1155–1157
Rostislav Mstislavich of Smolensk, 1158–1167
Izyaslav (III) Mstislavich of Volynia, 1167–1169
Gleb Yurevich of (Southern) Pereyaslavl, 1169–1171
Yaroslav Izyaslavich of Volynia, 1172–1174
Svyatoslav Vsevolodich of Chernigov, 1174–1194
Ryurik Rostislavich of Smolensk, 1194–1203, 1205–1211
Roman Mstislavich of Volynia, 1203–1205
Vsevolod Svyatoslavich, *Chermny*, of Chernigov, 1211–1212
Mstislav Romanovich of Smolensk, 1212–1223
Vladimir Ryurikovich of Smolensk, 1223–1236, 1236–1238
Yaroslav Vsevolodich of (Northern) Pereyaslavl, 1236
Mikhail Vsevolodich of Chernigov, Saint, 1236–1239
Danilo Romanovich of Halych-Volynia, 1239–1240

Reigns of the Grand Princes of Vladimir, 1155–1327

Andrey Yurevich, *Bogolyubsky*, 1155–1174
Vsevolod Yurevich, *Big Nest*, 1176–1212
Yuri Vsevolodich, 1212–1216, 1218–1238

Konstantin Vsevolodich, 1216–1218
Yaroslav Vsevolodich, 1238–1246
Svyatoslav Vsevolodich, 1246–1247
Andrey Yaroslavich, 1247–1252
Alexander Yaroslavich, *Nevsky*, 1252–1263
Yaroslav Yaroslavich, 1264–1272
Vasily Yaroslavich, 1272–1276
Dmitry Alexandrovich, 1277–1294
Andrey Alexandrovich, 1294–1304
Mikhail Yaroslavich, of Tver, Saint, 1304–1318
Yuri Danilovich of Moscow, 1318–1322
Dmitry Mikhailovich of Tver, 1322–1326
Alexander Mikhailovich of Tver, 1326–1327

Reigns of the Grand Princes of Vladimir and Moscow, 1328–1547

Ivan (I) Danilovich, *Kalita*, 1328–1341
Symeon Ivanovich, the Proud, 1341–1353
Ivan (II) Ivanovich, 1353–1359
Dmitry Ivanovich, *Donskoy*, 1359–1389
Vasily (I) Dmitrevich, 1389–1425
Vasily (II) Vasilevich, 1425–1433, 1434, 1434–1445, 1447–1462
Yuri Dmitrevich, 1433, 1434
Dmitry Yurevich, *Shemyaka*, 1445–1447
Ivan (III) Vasilevich, the Great, 1462–1505
Vasily (III) Ivanovich, 1505–1533
Ivan (IV) Vasilevich, 1533–1547(–1584)

Reigns of the Russian Tsars (as of 1721, Emperors, Empresses), 1547–1917

Ivan (IV) Vasilevich, *Groznyi*, (1533–)1547–1584
Fëdor (I) Ivanovich, 1584–1598
Boris Godunov, 1598–1605
(False) Dmitry, 1605–1606
Vasily Shuisky, 1606–1610
Interregnum, 1611–1612
Michael, 1613–1645
Alexis, 1645–1676
Fëdor (II), 1676–1682
Peter I and Ivan V, 1682–1696
Peter I, the Great (sole ruler), 1696–1725
Catherine I, 1725–1727
Peter III, 1727–1730
Anna, 1730–1740
Ivan VI, 1740–1741
Elizabeth, 1741–1761
Peter III, 1761–1762
Catherine II, the Great, 1762–1796
Paul I, 1796–1801

Reigns of the Russian Tsars, 1796–1917

Paul I, 1796–1801
Alexander I, 1801–25
Nicholas I, 1825–55
Alexander II, 1855–81
Alexander III, 1881–94
Nicholas II, 1894–1917

Leaders of the Russian Provisional Government, 1917

Prince Georgy Lvov
Alexander Kerensky

Soviet Leaders, 1917–91

Vladimir Lenin, 1917–24
Iosif Stalin, 1928–53
Nikita Khrushchev, 1953–64
Leonid Brezhnev, 1964–82
Yury Andropov, 1982–84
Konstantin Chernenko, 1984–85
Mikhail Gorbachev, 1985–91

Leaders of the Russian Republic, 1991–

Boris Yeltsin, 1991–99
Vladimir Putin, 2000–

INDEX